Detroit Studies in Music Bibliography, No. 65

Editor
J. Bunker Clark
University of Kansas

Selected Musical Terms of Non-Western Cultures: A Notebook-Glossary

Walter Kaufmann

HARMONIE PARK PRESS MICHIGAN 1990

Printed and bound in the United States of America
Published by
Harmonie Park Press
23630 Pinewood
Warren, Michigan 48091

Editing, J. Bunker Clark
Book design, Elaine J. Gorzelski
Music typesetting, Randall P. Wilkens
Text typesetting, Colleen Osborne
Proofreading, Austin B. Caswell

Library of Congress Cataloging-in-Publication Data

Kaufmann, Walter, 1907-
Selected musical terms of non-Western cultures : a notebook -glossary / Walter Kaufmann.
p. cm. — (Detroit studies in music bibliography ; no. 65)
Includes bibliographical references and index.
ISBN 0-89990-039-9
1. Ethnomusicology—Terminology. I. Title. II. Series.
ML108.K37 1990
780'.89—dc20 90-40670

Contents

Prologue

This volume represents the last completed research of the musicologist, composer, and conductor Walter Kaufmann, who spent the last 27 years of his distinguished, multi-faceted, and world-circling career on the musicology faculty of the School of Music of Indiana University, a colleague and teacher beloved by all who had the privilege of working with him.

Walter Kaufmann was born on 1 April 1907 in Karlsbad, Bohemia (now Czechoslovakia). After attending public schools there, he enrolled at the Staatliche Hochschule für Musik in Berlin and later at the German University in Prague. His teachers included Franz Schreker in composition, and Curt Sachs, Georg Schünemann, and Paul Nettl in musicology. He wrote his doctoral dissertation, a study of the symphonies of Gustav Mahler, in 1933. While still a student, Kaufmann was appointed conductor at the Stadttheater in Karlsbad, beginning a career that he pursued world-wide.

Rather than defend his thesis before a faculty increasingly influenced by Nazism, Kaufmann chose to leave his native country in 1934. Settling in Bombay, he became Director of European Music for All-India Radio and dove eagerly into the study of the musics and cultures of his new home. His interest took many forms. He composed scores incorporating Indian musical material, wrote music for Indian films, became familiar with many Indian musical traditions, and began the career for which he is most famous, that of scholarship in Asian art-musics. His research first resulted in a 1944 study entitled *The Art-Music of Hindusthan*, which, though unpublished, is held in manuscript at the New York Public Library. This initial study was to be followed by many publications that earned him world-wide recognition. His interests were not limited to India, but extended to Tibet, Nepal, China, and Indo-China, and developed a breadth and depth that flabbergasted experts of both East and West.

During World War II Kaufmann served in the British Navy, and shortly after the war settled in England, where he continued and amplified his multiple careers as a guest conductor for the British Broadcasting Corporation, a composer of stage, concert, and film music, and an active scholar. His studies of Indian musics began to appear in scholarly journals and his conducting came to the attention of audiences in England, the U.S., and Canada. In 1947 he left England to chair the piano and theory departments at the Conservatory of Music in Halifax, Nova Scotia, and the following year was appointed conductor of the newly-established Winnipeg Symphony Orchestra. During his eight-year tenure at Winnipeg, he shaped the orchestra into one of the finest in Canada, bringing it international recognition. His compositional activity flourished, and he produced symphonies, concertos, sonatas, ballets, cantatas, scores for the Canadian Broadcasting Corporation, and six of his fifteen operas. There he met the young Canadian pianist Freda Trepel, who played the première of his first Piano Concerto in 1949. They were married in 1951.

In 1957 Kaufmann took the position of Professor of Musicology at Indiana University, but that field was not the only one he benefitted. He continued to conduct for a decade, bringing his international experience to bear in the training of orchestral performers, and to compose at the same pace he had established in England and Canada. His opera *The Scarlet Letter* was premièred in 1961 (and revived in 1977). The Indiana Historical Society commissioned an opera celebrating the sesquicentennial of the state, resulting in *A Hoosier Tale*, which was premièred at Indiana University in 1965. His scholarly impact began to increase as well. Most of his studies on Indian music date from his Indiana tenure, and he began writing the books that were to reach publication in the sixties and seventies: *Musical Notations of the Orient* (1967), *The Ragas of North India* (1968), *Tibetan Buddhist Chant* (1975), *Musical References in the Chinese Classics* (this publisher, 1976), *The Ragas of South India* (1976), and the volume *Altindien* (1981) in the series *Musikgeschichte in Bildern.* His reputation as a teacher grew as well. He knew the western classical repertory thoroughly and could play keyboard reductions of orchestral works on command—without score. But rather than flaunt this expertise, he preferred to serve students as their guide to the music of the Far East, insisting that a knowledge of its structure and aesthetics was every bit as important as was that of the West. His courses in that area preceded those at other schools by decades, and were always over-filled with students from many different cultures. He was appointed Distinguished Professor of Music in 1975 and was honored in 1981 with a Festschrift, *Music East and West*, contributed by students and colleagues from around the world.

Even more significant than his encyclopedic knowledge of many diverse musics was his deep conviction that the arts were meant to serve life, rather than the other way around. An important part of his daily schedule was spent not in his study, the library, or the archives, but in administrative offices engaged in animated and extended conversation with his many close friends on the secretarial and clerical staff of the University. He knew that good music sustained life, but do did good food, good drink, and good friends.

Walter Kaufmann completed this dictionary and placed it in the hands of the publisher before his death in the fall of 1984. Thus, we who have helped it come to fruition have facilitated the work of this great scholar and friend, but the intellect and scholarship is all his.

AUSTIN B. CASWELL

Indiana University
July 1989

Preface

The drafting of this book dealing with musical terms of the non-Western world (Asia, Africa, and Oceania) reaches back about fifty years. My aim was to set up a modest notebook into which I jotted down at random musical terms I had come across in various places. By no means does this notebook claim to be a complete dictionary of musical terms, but as it proved useful to me during the past years, I hope that as a "Notizbuch" and Glossary it may be of some use to scholars interested in non-Western terms if they wish to obtain quickly brief information by consulting a one-volume work.

The terms listed are often those used by performing musicians. Dialectal and other distorted forms have in my book the same importance as correctly spelled terms and have been listed irrespective of the fact that they appear spelled differently in scholastic dictionaries or in some theoretical treatises.

As the writing of this book began a long time ago, sources (Lit.) referred to are not always recent publications. Furthermore in numerous instances terms presented in this notebook have been given to me orally and, as far as I know, have not appeared in print at all; hence no sources are cited.

I have used a variety of current spelling of terms such as *adan*, *adhan*, *adhdhan*, or *tai-keum*, *tae-kum*, *tae-gum*, and others. For clarification of Chinese terms which could become confusing in Romanized script, reference numbers of the easily obtainable *Mathew's Chinese-English Dictionary* (Cambridge, Mass., 1960) are given whenever it seemed to be helpful (e.g., M 4129). In a few instances reference had to be made to the *Chinese-English Dictionary* by Herbert A. Giles (New York, 1964). Musical notes are generally referred to in Romanized form. A note of a lower octave range (e.g., below middle C) is shown by an italic letter such as *B*♭ (low B♭). Geographic, tribal, or linguistic information is placed in brackets next to each term. Diacritical markings are avoided whenever there is no risk of misunderstanding.

The long erratic past of this book and its uneven expansion obstructed in some ways the application of exacting standards as they occur in scholastic dictionaries, standards that would only impede the basic idea of my Notebook that freely includes dialectal and various other semi-literary features.

I am grateful to the many musicians of the East who advised me during my fifteen years sojourn in India; to my wife Freda and to my friends Drs. Austin B. Caswell, Ralph T. Daniel, Harold Briggs, and Terry Miller. I am also obliged to Indiana University for the support that enabled me to complete this manuscript.

WALTER KAUFMANN

Indiana University
January 1984

EDITOR'S NOTE concerning tambourin/tambourine. The *tambourin* (tambourin de Provence, tambour provençal), a diminutive of the medieval generic term for drum, *tambour*, is a long double-headed drum. The term, however, is also used in German and Italian for "tambourine." The *tambourine* is the familiar shallow single-headed frame drum, usually with jingles on the frame, originating in the Near East. In this book, Walter Kaufmann used both spellings. Even though it is likely that some references to "tambourin" should instead have been to "tambourine," it was decided to retain his original spelling.

Selected Musical Terms of Non-Western Cultures

A

A (Korea). A long, slim bamboo stick, in which the middle is slightly thicker where it is held horizontally by the player. When moved up and down the slim ends swing and touch the ground with a clicking sound.
Lit.: no. 52.

Aak (Korea). See *Ah-ak.*

Aamamata (Solomon Isl. – Malkaita). Funeral laments sung by women.
Lit.: no. 318.

'Aaunga (Solomon Isl. – Bellona Isl.). Several conventional hand and arm gestures of the dancers.
Lit.: no. 246.

Aba (Java). Military signal; musical indication of a beat.

Abā (Egypt). A popular bulky oboe of recent times. The name is derived from the French hautbois. Cf. *Mizmār; Sibs.*
Lit.: no. 250.

Ab'ad (Arabia). Term for "intervals," consonant and dissonant (as specified by Al-Kindī [d. 870] in his *Kitāab al-musīqī al-Kabīr*).
Lit.: no. 76.

Ab-a'-fü (Philippines – Bontoc Igorot). Jew's harp made of bamboo, copper, or brass. Used by courting young men.
Lit.: nos. 126, 255.

Ābāli (South India). A rare and obscure *rāga* allegedly used by Tāllapākam musicians.
Lit.: no. 261.

Abam (New Guinea). Drum.
Lit: no. 255.

Abanangbweli (Abivadongbwali) (Congo – Azande). A bell made of thin metal. It is struck when the chief arrives, when a meeting is called or when guests are being entertained.
Lit.: nos. 184, 190.

Abaran (Nigeria). See *Dundun.*

Abare (Japan). Drum pattern of Kabuki music played in a hurried manner. If, e.g., the preceding drum beats were spaced and appeared only at accented beats, the *abare* pattern would produce fast moving strokes that divide the basic beats into halves. This pattern extends for approximately a dozen measures.
Lit.: no. 187.

Abbuba (Ancient Syria). Cf. *Abobas*; *Abuba.*

Abdhi (South India). Synonym for the *chatusra jāti* of *eka tāla.* Cf. *Tāla* (South India).
Lit.: nos. 136, 261.

Abendaīr (Algeria—Kabylia). Large tambourin. Cf. *Bandaīr.*
Lit.: no. 255.

Abeng (*Abeṅ*) (Gabon Republic—Twi). Term for various wind instruments made of animal horns.
Lit.: 255.

Abeng (Cameroon—Fang). A tiny tube of cane, closed at one end with a thin membrane, is inserted into one nostril. Into the second nostril is placed an *efam.* Both inserted tubes are called *abeng* and serve to produce a nasal timbre of the performer's voice.
Lit.: no. 255.

Abhanga (South India). Sacred songs with Mahrathi text, appearing in religious songs such as *bhajanas* and *kālaksepas.*
Lit.: no. 261.

Abhāva (South India). The "not-*bhāva*"; the wiping out of the *bhāva* (the mood or individuality of a *rāga*) by repeating and stressing certain notes and phrases that normally should be used only sparingly.
Lit.: no. 261.

Ābhēri (South India). *Janya rāga* of the 20th *mēḷa* (*Naṭabhairavī*).
Tone material:
C E♭ F G B♭ c
c B♭ A♭ G F E♭ D C
Lit.: no. 139.

Ābhēri (South India). *Janya rāga* of the 22nd *mēḷa* (*Kharaharapriyā*).
Tone material:
C E♭ F G B♭ c
c B♭ A G F E♭ D C
Lit.: no. 139.

Abhigīta (Vedic India). Notational sāmavedic chant symbol of the Kauthuma school expressed by the numeral 7 or (in South India) by the letter "a." These symbols indicate a sequence consisting of half a *mātra* being followed by one and a half *mātras.*
Lit.: no. 119.

Abhigīta-kṛṣṭa (Vedic India). Sāmavedic notational term of the Kauthuma school that indicates a prolongation of the *abhigīta.* The lengthening of the generally brief notes is shown by an additional numeral (*vikṛti*). Cf. *Abhigīta.*
Lit.: 119.

Abhimānini (South India). *Janya rāga* of the 5th *mēḷa* (*Mānavātī*).
Tone material:
C D♭ E♭♭ F A B c
c B A F E♭♭ D♭ C
Lit.: no. 139.

Abhinandana (South India). *Tāla* consisting of: 2 *laghus* (♩ ♩), 2 *drutas* (♫), and 1 *guru* (𝅗𝅥), amounting to five metrical units (e.g., ♩ ♩ ♫ 𝅗𝅥).
Lit.: nos. 139, 261.

Abhinaya (India). Sanskrit term for action, movements, gestures that express sentiment and mood of the dance (cf. *Bharata nāṭyam*). Four types are distinguished:

1. *Angika abhinaya*, gestures of body and limbs.
2. *Vachika abhinaya*, speech expressing mood and sentiment.
3. *Aharya abhinaya*, costume, jewelry that help in the expression of mood.
4. *Satvika abhinaya*, illustration of emotional states (trembling, signs of horror, etc.). Cf. *Nṛtta*; *Nṛtya* (*Nritta, Nritaya*).

Lit.: no. 261.

Abhir (North India). Obscure *rāga.*
Tone material:
B♭ C E♭ F G B♭ c
c B♭ A G F E♭ D C; *Vādis*: G, c
Lit.: no. 138.

Ābhiru (South India). *Janya rāga* of the 47th *mēḷa* (*Suvarṇāṅgī*).
Tone material:
C D♭ E♭ D♭ F♯ G B c
c A G F♯ E♭ C
Lit.: no. 139.

Abhirudgatā (Ancient India). The name of the seventh of the seven *Mūrchhanās* derived from the *Sa-grāma*.
Lit.: no. 261.

Ābhōg (North India). Concluding section of the ancient *dhrūpad*; *prabhanda*.
Lit.: nos. 138, 231.

Abhogari (*Tabuh gari*) (Bali). Coda of a composition and closing section of an entire musical performance. Cf. *Ābhōg*.
Lit.: no. 197.

Ābhōgi (*Ābhōgi-kanada*) (North India). Subordinated *rāga* to *Kafi thāta*.
Tone material:
C D E♭ F A c
c B♭ A F E♭ D C; *Vādis*: C (F)
Lit.: no. 138.

Ābhōgi (South India). *Janya rāga* of the 22nd *mēḷa* (*Kharaharapriyā*).
Tone material:
C D E♭ F A c
c A F E♭ D C
Lit.: no. 139.

Abhyāsa (Ancient India). (1) Repetition; musically or textually. The latter signifies the repetition or adjustment of an original text to a given melody. (2) A section in which the *bahutva* ("profusion"), the frequent occurrence of characteristic (mood-producing) notes or passages is stressed.
Lit.: nos. 119, 261.

Abhyāsa gāna (South India). A piece of music used as a study, an exercise, and not as a part of a musical performance. The opposite of *abhyāsa gāna*, a concertized and publicly performed piece is called *sabhā gāna*.
Lit.: no. 261.

Abhyuchchaya (India). Ascending scale forms in which every second note is deleted (e.g., C E G B).
Lit: no 261.

Abi (Sudan). Term for *ibi* (drum).
Lit.: no. 190.

Abida deni (Congo – Walengola). Drum.
Lit.: no. 26.

Abigolo (Nigeria – Igbo). Xylophone.

Abita (Congo – Bapopoie). Conical drum with two heads.
Lit: no. 21.

A-bitin (Sierra Leone – Temne). Drum.
Lit.: no. 255.

Abivadongbwali (Congo). See *Abanangbweli*.

Abobas (Ancient Syria). Reed pipe. Cf. *Abuba*; *Abbuba*; *Imbubu*.
Lit.: no. 255.

Abole (Uganda – Labwor). Vertical flute without any finger holes.
Lit.: no. 302.

Abombo (Congo – Bangelima). Small drum.
Lit.: no. 26.

Abowa mokindja (Congo – Walengola). Drum.
Lit.: no. 26.

Ābradēsi (South India). *Janya rāga* of the 62nd *mēḷa* (*Riṣabhapriyā*).
Tone material:
C E F♯ G A♭ B♭ A♭ c
c B♭ A♭ G F♯ E D E C
Lit.: no. 139.

Abu (Kenya – Luo). Trumpet made of a gourd.

Abu atā (*Āwāz*) (Iran). See *Dastgāh*.

Abūb(a) (Ancient Israel). Term for a reed instrument. Cf. *Abobas*.
Lit.: nos. 89, 250.

Abu qurun (Arabia). "Father of horns." Old, large horn.
Lit.: no. 65.

Aburukuwa (Ghana). Royal drum, small and high-pitched.
Lit.: no. 218.

Abuteni (Ghana). See *Agbadza*.

Abyāt (North Africa; Near East). (1) Lines of a strophe. (2) See *Al-Abyāt* (Tunisia).
Lit.: no. 171.

Achaeng (*Achaing*; *Ajaeng*) (Korea). A seven-string bowed zither. The instrument consists of a long rectangular board placed in an oblique position in front of the player. The left end of the board is placed higher resting on a small wooden stand; the right end rests on the floor. Each string runs across its own high bridge. The variable tunings of the *achaeng* can be A♭ B♭ c e♭ f a♭ b♭, or D E F# (or G) A B d e, or similar anhemitonic pentatonic forms. A short bow without hair, is a slim stick of resined wood. The instrument is of Chinese origin and is used in classical music. Cf. *Habak*; *Ya-cheng*.
Lit.: nos. 52, 186.

Achaing (Korea). See *Achaeng*.

Achala Nāta (South India). *Janya rāga* of the 36th *mēḷa* (*Chalanāṭa*).
Tone material:
C D# E F A# B c
c B A# F E D# C
Lit.: no. 139.

Achala svara (India). Two notes, *sa* (C) and *pa* (G), which have to stay unaltered in North and South Indian art music. Another term for these two fixed notes is *avikṛta svaras*.
Lit.: no. 261.

Achang (*Acheng*) (Korea). See *Achaeng*.

Acheng (Korea). See *Achaeng*.

Acholi (Uganda). See *Achorr*.

Achrauṭī (North India). A little used Hindustani name used for *sītar*.
Lit.: no. 254.

Ache-lhamo (Tibet). Religious theater performed outside the monastery building. The performers wear masks and present animated dances. Long songs are chanted with recitatives and prose sections interspersed. The performances represent serious, often frightening episodes of religious legends, but are frequently interrupted by comic situations.
Lit.: no. 62.

Achorr (*Acholi*) (Upper Nile region – Uganda). The king's drum.
Lit.: no. 255.

Achyuta madhyama (India). Theoretical term for *śuddha ma* (F).
Lit.: no. 261.

Achyuta shadja (India). Theoretical term for *sa* (C).
Lit.: no. 261.

Aḍ (India). A rhythmic alteration in the closing section of a *khyāl*. The *aḍ* can follow the end of the *dugan* when the durational value of every note of the melody is shortened to one (occasionally two) thirds of its original duration. For details see Lit. no. 136, p. 263.

Ada-ada (Java). Recitations sung by the *dalang* characterizing specific violent passions shown by the *wayang* figures. Each of the numerous *ada-ada* formulas consists of its own note-sequence that represents specific emotion. Cf. *Suluk*; *Greget saut*.
Lit.: no. 163.

Adab (Sumeria). Confusing term; probably a song of praise, a hymn or prayer.
Lit.: no. 94.

Adaban (Ghana). Drumming and dancing.
Lit.: no. 218.

Aḍabatram (Ghana—Ewe). War drum.
Lit.: nos. 190, 255.

Adabo (Malagasy Republic). Short barrel drum with two heads.
Lit.: no. 251.

Ādachautāl (North India). Popular *tāla* with 14 beats:

1 2 3 4 5 6 7 8 9 10 11 12 13 14
x 2 0 3 0 4 0

Cf. *Tāla.*
Lit.: no. 136.

Aḍaivu (*Adavu*) (South India). Beginner's simple exercises in dancing and singing.
Lit.: no. 261.

Adaka (Ghana). A box used as a drum. Cf. *Adakam.*
Lit.: no. 218.

Adakam (Ghana). Recreational music; the main instrument is the *adaka.*
Lit.: no. 218.

Adāl (Sudan). Rattle.
Lit.: nos. 107-08.

Adama (*Apala*) (Nigeria—Yoruba). See *Gangan.*
Lit.: no. 293.

Ādamādalā (Bengal). Barrel drum.
Lit.: nos. 190, 255.

Adamo bata (Nigeria—Yoruba). Cf. *Bata.*

'Aḏān (*'Adhdhān*) (Arabia). Call to prayer. Cf. *Mu'adhdhin.*
Lit.: nos. 65, 76.

Adan (Celebes—Southern Toradja District). Cf. *Pellē*; *Serubay.*
Lit.: no. 166.

Adana Bahar (North India). Obscure *rāga.*
Tone material:

C E♭ F G B c
c B♭ G (F) D C

Lit.: no. 138.

Adana-Kanada (North India). *Rāga* subordinated to the *Kafi thāta.*
Tone material:

C D (E♭) F G A♭ B♭ c
c B♭ (A♭) G F (E♭) D C; *Vādis*: C (c) G

Lit.: no. 138.

A-da-pa (Mesopotamia; Ancient Babylon). A rectangular or square frame drum.
Lit.: no. 87.

Adapu (Mesopotamia; Akkad). See *A-da-pa.*

Āḍarkūttiyar (South India—Tamil). Girl dancer.

Aḍavu (South India). Basic movements and musical passages which are taught to the beginner of classical dance.
Lit.: no. 261.

Adavu (Ghana—Ewe). One of the seven dances for Yeve, the god of thunder. (The names of the other six dances are listed under the heading of *Husago.*)
Lit.: no. 218.

Ad Bānsari (North India). Long, deep sounding flute.
Lit.: no. 261.

Adbhodam (South India). *Janya rāga* of the 8th *mēḷa* (*Hanumattōḍi*).
Tone material:

C E♭ F A♭ B♭ c
c B♭ A♭ F E♭ C

Lit.: no. 139.

Adbhuta (India). "Surprise," "wonder." One of the nine *rasas* (emotions) expressed in music. Cf. *Navarsas*; *Rasa*.
Lit.: no. 140.

Ad-darābukka (Egypt). Drum with a pot-shaped clay body. Cf. *Darābukkeh*.
Lit.: no. 100.

Ad-dor (Egypt). Song.
Lit.: no. 100.

Addu (North India). Cf. *Tabla*.

Adenden (Uganda – Teso). Harpists (generally female players).
Lit.: no. 29.

Adeng (Bali). See *Gending lambat*.

Adenkum (Ghana). (1) Long gourd used as stamping tube. (2) Piece of music accompanied by the *adenkum*.
Lit.: no. 218.

Adesan (Nigeria). See *Dundun*.

Adeudeu (Nigeria – Teso). Slim long harp with six strings.
Lit.: nos. 218, 302.

Adewu (Ghana – Ewe). Hunting drum.
Lit.: no. 95.

Adhān (*'Aḏan*) (Arabia). The call to prayer sung by the *mu'adhdhin* (muezzin). It can be executed either in a simple melodic or in a complex coloratura manner.
Lit.: no. 65.

Adhuna prasiddha rāgas (Medieval North India). Frequently performed *rāgas*. Well known *rāgas* of former ages were called *Prakprasiddha* (according to no. 263).

Adhyarda (North India). The term implies the durational note value of one *mātra* plus one *ardhamātrā* (♩ + ♪). (Other terms for durational note values of North Indian music are listed under the heading of *Anumātrā*.)
Lit.: no. 136.

Aḍi (South India). (1) Part (strophe) of a hymn (*khaṇḍika*). (2) Gesture; step in dancing.
Lit.: no. 261.

Ādī (South India). (1) Term for the *chatusra jāti* of *triputa tāla* (4+2+2). See *Tāla*. (2) Term occasionally used to denote the first *mēḷa*.
Lit.: nos. 86, 136.

Ādi Bhairavī (South India). *Janya rāga* of the 20th *mēḷa* (*Naṭabhairavī*).
Tone material:
C E♭ D E♭ F G A♭ c
c A♭ G F G E♭ D C
Lit.: no. 139.

Ādi Dēśya (South India). *Janya rāga* of the 39th *mēḷa* (*Jhālavarāḷi*).
Tone material:
C D♭ E♭♭ F♯ G B c
c B A♭ G F♯ E♭♭ D♭ C
Lit.: no. 139.

Adil (Assam, Burma). A bamboo trumpet with a buffalo horn as bell.
Lit.: no. 252.

Adingili (Uganda). A musical bow played by women. See *Adungu*.
Lit.: no. 302.

Ādi pañchama (South India). *Janya rāga* of the 48th *mēḷa* (*Divyamaṇī*).
Tone material:
C D♭ G A♯ B c
c B A♯ B G F♯ E♭ D♭ C
Lit.: no. 139.

Āditya (South India). Name of the 12th *chakra* in the system of the 72 *mēḷas*. Cf. *Rāga* (South India, IXb).
Lit.: no. 136.

Ādi Varāḷi (South India). *Janya rāga* of the 57th *mēḷa* (*Siṃhendramadhyama*).
Tone material:
C D F♯ G A♭ c
c B A♭ G F♯ D F♯ E♭ C
Lit.: no. 139.

Ādi Vasu (South India). *Janya rāga* of the 41st *mēḷa* (*Pāvani*).
Tone material:
C D♭ E♭♭ F♯ G F♯ A B c
c B A F♯ E♭♭ C
Lit.: no. 139.

Adiyāzh (South India). According to Lit. no. 261: I, 8, the term indicates a legendary ancient harp allegedly "with a thousand strings." See *Yāzh*.

Adok (Sunda Isl.). Tambourine identical with the *rebana* (of Sumatra).
Lit.: no. 255.

Adok (Arabia; Middle East; North Africa). Turn; time. In a suite performed by a group of musicians (singers and players), each member presents a section individually. Whenever the sequence of singing or playing by an individual is due, the saying is that his *ador*, his turn (time), has come. See *Nauba*; *Nuba*.

Adowa (Ghana – Akan). Ceremonial, formerly funeral, music.
Lit.: no. 218.

Adungu (*Adingili*) (Uganda – Alur). A musical bow or a harp with a triangular body and seven strings.
Lit.: nos. 190, 218, 302.

Adwār (singular: *Daur*) (Arabia). Term for compositions in combined modes; e.g., a family of melodies of which each is made of notes of the lower tetrachord of one particular melodic mode (*aṣba'*), while the notes of the upper tetrachord of the same melody are taken from another (different) melodic mode. Cf. *Shudūd*.
Lit.: no. 65.

Adya oro (Nigeria – Ibo). Bull roarer.
Lit.: no. 223.

Adzida (Ghana). See *Agbadza*.

Adzobo (Dahomey). Drum music and dance.
Lit.: no. 218.

Adzra (Ghana). See *Agbadza*.

Aeo lao (Northeast Thailand). Traditional singing.
Lit.: no. 203.

Afa (Ghana – Ewe). See *Hatsiasia*.

Afonpe (Nigeria – Yoruba). A horn or trumpet player.

Afosangu (Sudan). A *sansa* held between the feet of the player. Cf. *Sangu*; *Tresangu*.
Lit.: nos. 95, 190.

Afovu (Ghana – Ewe). One of seven dances for Yeve, the god of thunder. (The names of the other six dances are listed under heading of *Husago*.)
Lit.: no. 128.

Afrāsiyāb būrūsī (Turkey). Afrāsiyāb's trumpet (a 17th-century instrument) used as the courts of the Khans of the Crimea. Cf. *'Ajamī būrū*.
Lit.: no. 81.

Afsāne (Iran). Song that relates a story.

Afshārī (*Awaz*) (Persia). See *Dastgāh*.
Lit.: no. 146.

Agada (Ethiopia). Vertical flute with 7-8 finger holes in front and one in the back. Cf. *Zagu*; *Zaguf*.
Lit.: no. 255.

Agada (Kashmir; Turkestan). Transverse flute with five finger holes.

Agadhapala (India). Ancient, obscure percussion instrument, according to Lit. no. 289.
Lit.: no. 255.

Agaita (North Cameroon). Wooden trumpet.
Lit.: nos. 157, 190.

'Ağām (Arabia). See *'Ajām.*

Agama (Akama) (Nigeria). Drum with one head.

Agama (Vedic India). "Augmentation." The term indicates the altering of textual syllables in order to adjust them to an already existing melody.
Lit.: no. 119.

Aganga (Central and Southern Sahara). Cf. *Ganga*. Barrel drum.
Lit.: nos. 95, 255.

Agappaikkinnari (South India). Tamil term for a primitive fiddle with one, occasionally two, strings. It is supposed to be the same instrument as the obscure *Rāvaṇa hasta(m)*, the "hand of the giant Ravana."
Lit.: nos. 254-55, 261.

Agaramut (Bismarck Archipelago; Gazelle Peninsula). Wooden slit-drum. See *Garamut.*
Lit.: no. 255.

Agari (Japan). Term in *koto* music that indicates the upward moving of the bridge and thus changing the pitch of the string.
Lit.: nos. 187, 225.

A-gātṛi (India; Sanskrit). A bad singer.

Agau (Indonesia, Mentawei Kepulauan). Small, fanciful lobster-claw bells, usually used as ornaments.
Lit.: no. 254.

Agba (Nigeria—Yoruba). Drum; rattle. Cf. *Gbedu.*

Agbadza (Ghana). Social club dances: Abuteni, Adzida, Adzro, Atsia, Britannia, English, Kedzangi, Kete, Kpete, Kpomeghe, Man of War, Takara, Woleke.
Lit.: no. 128.

Agblo (Ghana). Wooden drum beaten with heavy sticks. The body of the drum is made from a tree trunk.
Lit.: no. 128.

Agbuda (Nigeria—Yoruba). Probably an older name of the *kerikeri.*
Lit.: no. 303.

Ageng (Bali). Large, deep sounding. E.g., *gong ageng*, the largest metallophone in the *gamelan gong.*
Lit.: no. 197.

Agere (Nigeria). A drum with a cylindrical corpus with one skin. The instrument rests on a pedestal and is used at religious occasions and at funerals of hunters.
Lit.: no. 293.

Age-uta (Japan). A type of *michiyuki*, a song longer and higher in range than the *sage-uta.* It appears in the *ha* section of the *noh* play. Cf. *Sage-uta.*
Lit.: no. 185.

Aghakand (Persia). General term for percussion instruments.
Lit.: no. 255.

Aghanim (Morocco). Heterophonic double reed instrument.
Lit.: nos. 34, 190.

Āghāṭa (Āghāṭi) (Vedic India). The Sanskrit term of an obscure instrument that appears in the *Rig Veda*, 10, 146, 2 (transl. K. F. Geldner, Leipzig, 1951) and is described as a certain musical instrument, a "Zimbel oder Laute. . . ." The term appears also in the *Atharvaveda*, 4,37,4. Lit. no. 205 translates *āghāṭa* as a "cymbal or rattle. . . ."

Aghiz tanbūrasī (Turkey). Obscure jew's harp.
Lit.: nos. 81, 255.

Agidigbo (Nigeria—Yoruba). Plucked idiophone (*sansa*). Cf. *Molo.*
Lit.: no. 293.

Agīht (Indonesia; Wetar Isl.; Moluccas). Bamboo tube zither. Cf. *Tabuan*; *Lakado.* Lit.: nos. 156, 254.

Ağit (Turkey). Specific rhythm type of *uzun hava.* Generally combined with a mourning lament.
Lit.: no. 243.

Agni (South India). Name of the third *chakra* in the system of the 72 *mēḷas*. Cf. *Rāga* (South India, IXb).

Agnikōpam (South India). *Janya rāga* of the 20th *mēḷa* (*Naṭabhairavī*);
Tone material:
C E♭ F G B♭ c
c B♭ G F E♭ D C
Lit.: no. 139.

Agogo (Nigeria). Iron gong. Bell-shaped, single or double, percussion kettles.
Lit.: no. 190.

Agoṅ (Philippines). See *Agong.*

Agong (Philippines). A bamboo tube psaltery with two strings which are slightly detached from the tube surface and are plucked or drummed. Across the strings is placed a small piece of bark which is beaten with two small bamboo sticks. Cf. *Valiha* (Madagascar); *Tuban iotta* (Sula-Besi); *Krumba* (Nias); *Gandaṅ bavoi* (Borneo).
Lit.: no. 254.

Agonga (Sahara, Sudan–Tuareg). Barrel drum. Cf. *Ganga.*
Lit.: no. 95.

Agongo (Togo). Cylindrical drum. Drumming.
Lit.: no. 255.

Agovu (Ghana–Ewe). One of the seven dances of Yeve, the god of thunder. Cf. *Husago.*
Lit.: no. 218.

Agrembi (Algeria–Kabylia). See *Agurembi.*
Lit.: no. 255.

Agrumbi (Algeria–Kabylia). See *Agurembi.*

Aguma (Nigeria–Igbo). Drum with one head.

Agun (Agung) (Philippines, South Mindanao–Bagobo). Gong imported from China (Cf. *Yin, Ch'ing*). The *agun* is beaten with a padded wooden stick.
Lit.: no. 255.

Agung (Philippines). See *Agun.*

Agurembi (Algeria–Kabylia). String instrument.

Agwāl (Morocco). See *Agwel.*

Agwara (Uganda–Alur). Long trumpets, used in groups for dance music. Cf. *Kanga.*

Agwel (Morocco). Drum made of a goblet-shaped clay jar covered with a painted skin which is beaten with the hands. See *Darābukkeh.*
Lit.: no. 255.

Aha (Nigeria–Igbo). Half a gourd, beaten at its outside by iron rings which the player wears on his fingers.
Lit.: no. 293.

Ah-ak (Korea). "Pure, elegant music" (M 7222.13). Ritual music of the Confucian temple, imported from China about the 12th-century. It is a dignified music performed in slow tempo by (theoretically) all the "Eight Sounds" (see *Pa-kua*). The music is either purely instrumental or instrumental and vocal and, at certain occasions, noble, stately dances are added.

Ah-ak was performed in the Confucian temple by two orchestras, one on the terrace (*tungga*), the other on the ground (*hon'ga*). The instruments, representing the Eight Sounds were made of stone, metal, silk, gourd, bamboo, skin, wood, and earth (clay).

Ah-ak embraced six types of Korean sacred and court music. They were:

1. *Un-mun-ak*, "cloud gate music," in honor of the spirits of heaven.
2. *Ham-chi-ak*, "entire influence of king's virtual music," in honor of the spirits of earth.
3. *Tae-kwun-ak*, "big turn music," dance music honoring the spirits of the four directions.
4. *Tae-ha-ak*, "big summer music," in honor of the mountain and river spirits.
5. *Tae-ho-ak*, "great protection music," in honor of the (female) ancestors.
6. *Tae-mu-ak*, "great Mu (military) music," in honor of the rulers Mun and Mu.

Cf. *Tang-ak*; *Hyang-ak*; *Tae-so-ak*.
Lit.: nos. 52, 136, 145, 179.

Āhari (South India). See *Āhiri* (*rāga*).
Lit.: no. 139.

Āhata (India). See *Gamak(a).*

Ahellil (Tunisia—Gurara Region). Prelude to a festive song, a *taqsīm*, played on a flute accompanied by several percussion instruments. If performed by a solo singer, the song is accompanied by a chorus that produces the bourdon sound. Cf. *Tagerrabt.*

Ahenk (Iran). Plucked lute.
Lit.: no. 255.

Ahiãvui (Ghana). Social club dances performed by men and women, accompanied by drums. Cf. *Agbadza*; *Sovu.*
Lit.: no. 128.

Āhir-bhairav (North India). *Rāga* subordinated to the *Bhairav thāta.*
Tone material:
C D♭ E F G A B♭ (c)
c B♭ A G F E D♭ C; *Vādis*: F C
Lit.: no. 138.

Āhiri (South India). 8th *mēḷa*. See *Āhiri-Todi.*

Āhiri (South India). *Janya rāga* of the 14th *mēḷa* (*Vakulābharaṇam*).
Tone material:
C D♭ C E F G A♭ B♭ c
c B♭ A♭ G F E D♭ C
(Not to be confused with *āhiri* of the 8th *mēḷa*.)
Lit.: no. 139.

Āhirinaṭa (South India). *Janya rāga* of the 29th *mēḷa* (*Dhīraśaṅkarābharaṇam*).
Tone material:
C F E F G A B c
c B G A B G E F E C
Lit.: no. 139.

Āhiri-Tōḍi (North India). *Rāga* ascribed to the *Tōḍi thāta.*
Tone material:
C (*B*) $\overset{\flat}{D}$♭ $\overset{\flat}{E}$♭ F♯ A♭ B c
c B A♭ G F♯ E♭ D♭ C (*B*) (*D*♭) (C)
Lit.: no. 138.

Āhiri Tōḍi (South India). *Janya rāga* of the 8th *mēḷa* (*Hanumattōḍi*). A popular *rāga*; several versions are in use. It appears frequently in religious songs sung at night.
Tone material:
C D♭ C E♭ F G A♭ B♭ c
c B♭ A♭ G F E♭ D♭ C
Lit.: no. 139.

Aho (Ghana—Akan). Introductory song in free rhythm.
Lit.: no. 218.

Āhōri (South India). *Janya rāga* of the 20th *mēḷa* (*Naṭabhairavī*).
Tone material:
C D E♭ F G A♭ c
c B♭ A♭ G F E♭ D C
Lit.: no. 139.

Ah-tu (China). Probably a Shantung dialectal term for *hao* (M 2064), *t'ou* (M 6489). A small *la-pa* with a flat mouthpiece. Cf. *Dokaku.*
Lit.: nos. 255, 306.

Ahuri'au (Solomon Isl.). Simple bamboo trumpet.
Lit.: no. 84.

Ai (*Aikata*) (Japan). Interludes performed by the *shamisen* and *ō-daiko* in *odoriji.*
Lit.: no. 187.

Aidsam duun (Mongolia). Songs originating in the time of Genghis Khan which have historical value. Their texts relate heroic deeds or praise the greathearted times of the past. According to tradition there are still 34 songs.
Lit.: no. 61.

Aikata (Japan). See *Ai.*

'Ain (Arabia). Sound hole (of *'ūd*). Cf. *Shemsha.*
Lit.: no. 255.

Ai-no-te (Japan). *Shamisen* passages interpolated in long vocal pieces.
Lit.: no. 185.

Ainu-tonkori (*Tonkori*) (Japan—Hokkaido). Zither consisting of a slim, long body with five strings. The open strings are plucked with both hands.
Lit.: no. 185.

Aiole (Flores). Songs sung by a precentor whose melody is (in parts) repeated over and over again by the chorus.
Lit.: no. 166.

Aipan (India). Paste made of Indian saffron, boiled rice and other ingredients, that is smeared in form of a circular patch upon drumheads of *tablas* and *mridangas* for tuning purposes. Cf. *Āṭa.*
Lit.: no. 136.

Airāvati (South India). *Janya rāga* of the 44th *mēḷa* (*Ṡubhapantuvarālī*).
Tone material:
C D♭ E♭ F♯ G B c
c B G F♯ E♭ D♭ C
Lit.: no. 139.

Airāvati (South India). *Janya rāga* of the 64th *mēḷa* (*Vachaspati*).
Tone material:
C D E F♯ G A c
c A G F♯ E D C
(Not to be mistaken for *airāvati* of the 44th *mēḷa.*)
Lit.: no. 139.

Ai-take (Japan). (Complete) chord produced on the *shō*.

Aja (Nigeria). Iron bell with clapper.
Lit.: no. 293.

Ajaeng (Korea). See *Achaeng.*

Ajak-ajakan (*Ayak-ayakan*) (Java). Characteristic accompaniment of irregular gong beats. They indicate the mood when *wayang* figures and a *wayang* dancer appear on the stage.
Lit.: no. 163.

'Ajam (Iran). Vocal modus. The scale is the same as that of *sasgar*. In Persia the modus was called *nev ruuz* ("the new day").
Lit.: no. 121.

'Ajām (Arabia). See *Maqām.* The Arabs call Persia *'Ajam* ("abroad").
Lit.: no. 121.

'Ajām (Modern Tunisia). *Maqām.*
Tone material:
D $\overset{+}{\text{E}}$♭ F G A B♭ c d
Lit.: no. 64.

'Ajām-'Ashirān (*'Ajām-'ushayrān*) (Arabia). A tone name of a note a semitone higher than *'ashirān* (*'ushayrān*). (A list of all tone names and tones through two octaves can be seen under the heading of *Jagā* [*Yagā*].)
Lit.: no. 64.

'Ajām-Ḥusaynī (Arabia). Tone name of a note one half tone higher than *huseni.* (A list of all tone names and notes through two octaves can be seen under the heading of *Jagā* [*Yagā*].)
Lit.: no. 64.

'Ajamī Būrū (Turkey). A 17th-century Persian trumpet. Cf. *Afrāsiyāb būrūsī*.
Lit.: no. 81.

'Ajām-Muraṣṣa (Middle East). *Maqām*.
Tone material:
D $\overset{+}{\text{E}\flat}$ F G $\overset{(\text{A}\flat)}{\text{A}}$ $\overset{(\text{B})}{\text{B}\flat}$ c d
Lit.: no. 64.

'Ajām-'Ushayrān (Arabia). Tone name. See *'Ajam-'Ashirān*.

'Ajām-'Ushayrān (Arabia; Egypt). *Maqām*.
Tone material:
B♭ C D E♭ F G A B♭
Lit.: no. 64.

'Ajām-'Ushayrān (Modern Tunisia). *Maqām*.
Tone material:
A $\overset{+}{\textit{B}\flat}$ C D E F G A B♭ c d
Lit.: no. 64.

'Ajamī Zūrnā (Turkey). "Persian oboe." A large heterophonic double reed instrument, popular during the 17th century.
Lit.: no. 81.

Aje (Central Pacific, Marshall Isl.). Wooden drum.
Lit.: nos. 190, 278.

Ajeng (Java). See *Surupan Ajeng*.

Ajit (Turkey). Mourning lament.
Lit.: no. 243.

Ajjub Būrūsī (Turkey). "Turkish horn."
Lit.: no. 243.

Ajnās (Arabia). Characteristic melody features. Each *maqām* scale is divided into *ajnās* which consist of fixed intervals, similar to tetrachord or pentachord structures.
Lit.: no. 64.

Ajogan (Dahomey). Music performed by the wives of the king accompanied by drums and bells.
Lit.: no. 218.

Ājya (Vedic India). Name of four ritual song groups (**stotras*) chanted at the soma sacrifice.
Lit.: no. 119.

'Ajz (Islamic North Africa). See *Misrā*.

Akacence (*Ensegu*) (Uganda—Kiga). See *Akakyenke*.

Akache (North Rhodesia—Lala; Ghana—Ewe). "The little one"; small drum.
Lit.: nos. 128, 190.

Akadankama (Cameroon—Fan). See *Ndöna*.
Lit.: no. 255.

Akadinda (Uganda). Xylophone with 17 slabs.
Lit.: nos. 190, 218.

Akadingidi (Uganda—Ganda). Toy stick zither with one string.
Lit.: nos. 190, 302.

Akadongo K'abaluru (Uganda—Alur; South Africa—Bantu). Term for *sansa*.
Lit.: no. 302.

Akadu (Malaysia). See *Susunu*.
Lit.: no. 255.

Akakyenkye (*Akacence*; *Ruganira*) (Uganda—Nkole). Rattle. Cf. *Ensegu*.
Lit.: nos. 190, 302.

A-kalumbe (Sierre Leone—Temne). Term for harp.
Lit.: no. 255.

Akam (*Akadankama*) (Cameroon). Cf. *Ndöna*.
Lit.: no. 255.

Akando (Former Belgian Congo—Bantu). Wooden whistle.
Lit.: nos. 28, 29.

Akanḡ (Armenia). Tuning peg.
Lit.: no. 255.

Akarana (*Akora*; *Ankarana*) (Madagascar). See *Antsiva*.
Lit.: no. 255.

Akāra Sādhakam (South India). Vocal exercise using as text simply vowels and the consonant "m" in developing the singer's ability to produce ornaments and clearly intoned phrases in fast tempo.
Lit.: no. 261.

Akasaa (Ghana). Metal rattle suspended from the top of a drum.
Lit.: no. 218.

Akatuba K'abakuru (Uganda; Congo–Konjo). Trough-shaped zither. Cf. *Enanga*.
Lit.: no. 302.

Akayamba (Uganda–Toro). Rattle. See also *Ensegu*.
Lit.: no. 302.

Akbele (Nigeria–Igbo). (1) Long flute made of a calabash. (2) Ivory horn.
Lit.: no. 95.

Akebono (Japan). See *Koto* tuning.
Lit.: no. 225.

Akene (Ghana–Twi). Drum. See *Akyene*.
Lit.: no. 95.

Akhang (Burma). Mouthpiece.
Lit.: no. 255.

Akhilarāga mēḷa vīṇa (*Sarva rāga mēḷa vīṇa*) (South India). The modern *vīṇa* of South India; the frets are fixed on the fingerboard. In contrast to this type of instrument is the *eka rāga mēḷa vīṇa* with movable (adjustable) frets.
Lit.: no. 261.

Akidi (Congo–Momvu). Board zither.
Lit.: no. 176.

Akika (Nigeria). A small *iya'lu* drum beaten at festivals linked with masquerading. Cf. *Bembe*.
Lit.: no. 293.

Akikiri Koto (Japan). "The autumn mist *koto*." A *koto* made of special hardwood.
Lit.: no. 255.

Akimbi (Congo–Budu). Board zither with resonator.
Lit.: nos. 176, 190.

Akofe (Ghana–Ewe; Dahomey). Animal horn. Cf. *Kofen*.
Lit.: no. 218.

Akofin (West Africa; Dahomey). Trumpets played at the royal court.
Lit.: no. 218.

A-konde (West Africa–Susu; Sierra Leone–Temne). Fiddle. Cf. *Ekende*.
Lit.: no. 255.

Akōra (*Akārana*; *Ankārana*) (Madagascar). Cf. *Antsiva*.
Lit.: no. 255.

Ākoṭparai (South India). A Tamil term for a war drum that is beaten when the cattle of the enemy is captured.
Lit.: no. 261.

Akpaluvu (Ghana). See *Nyayito*.
Lit.: no. 128.

Akpatare (Nigeria–Yoruba). See *Pagugu*.

Akpossi (Dahomey–Nago). Drum.
Lit.: no. 303.

Aksak (India). Mixed rhythm, not divisible by 2, 3, or 5. The *aksak* appear in extended periods which occur repeatedly.

Aksak (Turkey). "Limping rhythm":
$$\frac{2+2+2+3}{8}$$

Akṣara (Ancient India). Syllable; letter.
Lit.: no. 292.

Akshara (*Akṣara*). Cf. *Parvan*.
Lit.: no. 119.

Aksharakalā (South India). The duration of lines measured by the number of *aksharas.* Lit.: no. 119.

Ak-shi-cho (Korea). See *Ak-shijo.*

Ak-shijo (Korea). Recited music.
Lit.: no. 136.

Ākshīptīka (*Āyittam*) (South India). Opening section of the *ālāp* in which the characteristic features of the *rāga* are presented.
Lit.: no. 261.

Akum (Southeast India, Abujhmar Mountains — Hill Maria Gond tribe). The Hill Maria name of the *tori.* The name *akum* may be related to the *akora* of Madagascar, a shell or copper trumpet. Cf. *Tori.*
Lit.: no. 135.

Akunde (Nilotic Sudan; Congo — Bari). Drum. Cf. *Maroto.*
Lit.: no. 184.

Akwasidae (Ghana). Music in honor of ancestor-chiefs, performed on Memorial Sundays.
Lit.: no. 218.

Akyene (Ghana). See *Akene.*

Ala (Mesopotamia; Sumeria). Term for large drum.
Lit.: no. 94.

Ālābu-Sāraṅgī (India). A gourd fiddle (*sārangī* type) with four gut strings. Below these strings are strung 7-9 resonance strings.
Lit.: nos, 198, 255.

Al-Abyāt (Tunisia). (1) "The Verses." The third movement of the *Nauba.* A song performed by a group of singers in a slow and dignified manner. The short instrumental prelude of *al-abyāt* is called *dukhūl.* Cf. *Dukhūl al-btāyhī.*
(2) Rhythmic modes used in *al-abyāt*:

Adagio 

Adagio 

Final allegro 

Cf. Lit. no. 171.

Alagu (South India). Term for *śruti.*

Alahiya Bilaval (North India). *Rāga.* See *Bilaval.*

Alakavarāli (South India). *Janya rāga* of the 28th *mēḷa* (*Harikāmbhōji*).
Tone material:
C D F G A c
c B♭ A G F E D E C
Lit.: no. 139.

Alakōja (South India). Simple double clarinet consisting of one melody pipe and one for the drone. The melody pipe is called *svara nāḍi*, the drone pipe *ṣruti nāḍi.* The instrument is played at village festivals. Cf. *Pambunagasuram.*
Lit.: no. 261.

Alal (West Java — Toba District). See *Oli-Oli*; *Ra'us Woja.*

Alal (Mesopotamia; Sumeria). Ancient frame drum or cymbal. Cf. *Alū.*
Lit.: nos. 94, 190, 250.

Alamoru (Uganda). (1) Vertical flute of the Karamojong. (2) Bamboo flute with four finger holes of the Acholi. The instrument is vertically blown. (3) Flutes with four finger holes of various sizes, transversely blown. The large flute has a gourd as bell.
Lit.: no. 302.

Alankāra (India). Musical exercises and vocalises illustrating seven principal *tālas.* The term was also used for "beauty," "ornament," "embellishment."
Lit.: no. 261.

Alankārapriya (South India). *Janya rāga* of the 10th *mēḷa* (*Nāṭakapriya*).
Tone material:
C D♭ E♭ F A B♭ c
c B♭ A F E♭ D♭ C
Lit.: no. 139.

Ālāp (*Ālāpa*; *Ālāpana*) (India). The prelude, introduction to a concertized piece in a distinct *rāga*. The *ālāp* is performed without any ornamentation and drum accompaniment. In strict clarity it shows the essential characteristics of the *rāga*, its mood and atmosphere and prepares the performers and audience for the *rāga* that is to follow. The *ālāp* is performed only by the soloist (e.g., a singer) and by the drone sounds of the *tanbura*. Rhythmically it is entirely free and instead of a text the singer uses the syllables *ta*, *da*, *ri*, *nom*, *tom*, or, if he wishes, the name of a deity.
Theorists of the 17th-century divided the *ālāp* into several sections: *ākshīptīka* (beginning); *rāgavardhani* (*eduppu*; *karana*, the body of the *ālāp*); *sthayi* (conclusion) and *nyāsa* or *muktayi* (end).
Lit.: nos. 138, 261.

Ālāpa (*Ālāp*) (India). The name of the *ma mūrchhanā* of the *Gāndhāragrāma*. Cf. *Mūrchhanā*; *Grāma*; *Ma*; *Ga*.
Lit.: no. 231.

Ālāpana (India). See *Ālāp*.

Ālāpi (South India). *Janya rāga* of the 37th *mēḷa* (*Sālaga*). This *rāga* is identical with its primary *rāga Sālaga*.
Tone material:
C D♭ E♭♭ F♯ G A♭ B♭♭ c
c B♭♭ A♭ G F♯ E♭♭ D♭ C
Lit.: no. 139.

Ālāpinī (India). Theoretical name of the 17th *śruti*. The corresponding note name is *catuśśruti dha* (*Śuddha Ni*). Cf. *Śruti*.

Ālāpinī Vīṇā (India). See *Surbāhār*.
Lit.: no. 255.

Ālāp proper (India). See *Khyāl*.

Ālāpti (India). The general term for *ālāp* or *ālāpana* without the use of a (specific) theme, while *rūpaka ālāpti* is the *ālāpana* performed on the basis of a (specific) theme.
Lit.: no. 261.

Ālāpu Sāraṅgī (India). See *Ālābu Sāraṅgī*.

Al-arghūl (Egypt). See *Arghūl*.

Al-'arif (Egypt – Copts). Coptic church singer.
Lit.: no. 102.

Alarippu (South India). The opening dance of the *bharata nāṭyam* performance. It shows the fine technical ability of the dancer but does not present any symbolism in her gestures and postures. This prelude is meant to be a special gift offered to the gods and audience in the hope to gain the approval of the female dancer.
Lit.: no. 46.

Alaru (South India). *Janya rāga* of the 37th *mēḷa* (*Sālaga*).
Tone material:
C E♭♭ F♯ A♭ B♭♭ c
c B♭♭ A♭ F♯ E♭♭ C
Lit.: no. 139.

Alāt (Arabia). Musical instruments.
Lit.: no. 255.

Ālātī (Arabia). Instrumentalists.

Alaunut (South Pacific; New Hebrides). See *Nunut*.
Lit.: no. 84.

Alava (South India). *Janya rāga* of the 42nd *mēḷa* (*Raghupriyā*).
Tone material:
C E♭♭ F♯ A♯ B c
c B A♯ F♯ E♭♭ C
Lit.: no. 139.

Al-Barbet (Persia; Arabia; Turkey). See *Barbat.*
Lit.: no. 255.

Al-Barwal (Tunisia). The 7th movement of the *nauba*, the closing piece of the first part of the suite performed by a singer and accompanied by various instruments in double meter. The piece begins slowly and gradually accelerates throughout the movement.
Lit.: no. 171.

Al-Beshraf (Egypt). Instrumental music generally in rondo form.
Lit.: no. 100.

Al-Btāyhī (Tunisia). The 4th movement of the *nauba.* A slow, solemn chant in common meter. The movement can consist of two or more songs. Its instrumental introduction is called *dukhūl al-btāhyī.*
Lit.: no. 171.

Al-Darwal (Tunisia). Rhythmic mode in double meter:

Lit.: no. 171.

Al-Draj (Tunisia). The 8th movement of the *Nauba*, a song in slow $\frac{6}{4}$. The mode is:

(Adagio)

A brief introduction to the movement is in the same meter and tempo. It is called *Dukhūl al-draj.*
Lit.: no. 171.

Āle (Arabia). Instrument.
Lit.: no. 255.

Aleane (New Pomerania). See *Angremut.*
Lit.: no. 255.

Alema (Congo—Bantu). Dance performed by women.
Lit.: no. 29.

Alende (Uganda—Kibira). Drum. Cf. *Ngoma.*
Lit.: no. 255.

Alenga (Cameroon—Fan). Cattle bell.
Lit.: no. 255.

Al-fkitaī (Arabia). Rhythmic mode of Persian origin:

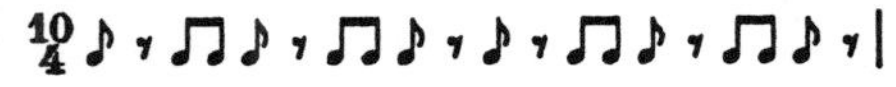

Lit.: no. 65.

Algāiṭa (Africa—Hausa). Conical oboe with five or six finger holes and a bell. It is related to the Arabian *zamr.* In Morocco and Algeria the instrument is known as *ḡaiṭa* (*ghaiṭa*). The Tuareg make it of bamboo and place a metal bell in front of the tube. The reed of this instrument is called *semara.* Cf. *Ḡaiṭa.*
Lit.: no. 255.

Al-gaiṭaru (Sudan). Name of the *alḡaiṭa.*
Lit.: no. 95.

Algaiṭasu (Sudan—Fulbe). Name of the *Alḡaiṭa.*

Al-gar (Mesopotamia—Ancient Babylon). (1) Lyre. (2) Sumerian instrument; probably a hand drum or sistrum; perhaps lyra.
Lit.: nos. 87, 94.

Algeta (Nigeria—Nupe). Name of the Arabia *ghaiṭa.*
Lit.: no. 95.

Ālghōza (North India). Urdu term for bamboo beak flute (occasionally also wooden) with 5-8 finger holes and one at the back. The instrument has a very gentle sound.
Lit.: nos. 190, 255.

Ālgōsa (North India). See *Ālghōza.*
Lit.: no. 261.

Ālgōya (North India). See *Ālghōza.*

Alḥān (Arabia). Melody used in the recitation of the Koran.
Lit.: no. 70.

Alḥān mauzūna (Old Arabian). "Measured melodies."
Lit.: no. 70.

Al-Ḥazaj (Arabia). Rhythmic mode (according to Al Farabi, d. 950):

Later form:

Cf. *Īqā'āt.*
Lit.: no. 70.

Al-Iftitaḥ (Egypt). Instrumental prelude; prelude. Cf. *At-Taḥmīla.*
Lit.: no. 100.

Aligeta (Sahara, Togo—Hausa). Name for the Arabic *ghaiṭa* used by the Hausa in North Togo.
Lit.: no. 95.

Alii la iti (Samoa). See *O le polotu.*
Lit.: no. 84.

Alindi (Congo). A wooden drum played for dances. Cf. *Lukumbi.*
Lit.: no. 26.

Al-Istiftākh (Tunisia). The first movement of the *nauba.* It is an instrumental prelude performed by the entire ensemble without drum and rattles. Cf. *Al-Iftitaḥ.*
Lit.: no. 171.

Alit (Bali). High pitched; small. The term indicates the upper octave, e.g., *ben alit.* In the Sunda District the term is *leutik.* Other terms used for indication of the higher octave are: *chilik*; *chenik.* Cf. *Gedē.*
Lit.: no. 163.

Alivardhani (South India). *Janya rāga* of the 17th *mēḷa* (*Sūryakānta*).
Tone material:
C D♭ E F B c
c B A G F E D♭ C
Lit.: no. 139.

Al-Kahin (Egypt). The Coptic priest who leads the sacred service.
Lit.: no. 102.

Al-Khafīf (Tunisia). The ninth movement of the *nauba*, a song in triple meter in slow tempo.
Lit.: no. 171.

Al-Khatm (Tunisia). The tenth and final movement of the *nauba* is sung in a fast and accelerating triple meter.
Lit.: no. 171.

Al-Mafrūḍa (Arabia). Tone name used by Al-Kindī (10th century). Notated with the Arabic letter *alif.*
Lit.: no. 69.

Al-Mākhūri (Arabia). According to Al-Kindī *Al-Mākhūri* is the following rhythmic mode:

See *Iqa'at.*
Lit.: no. 65.

Al-Mauwal (Egypt). See *Mauwal.*

Al-Mizmār (Egypt). Heterophonic double reed instrument. Cf. *Zamr.*
Lit.: nos. 100, 255.

Al-Mshad (Tunisia). The sixth movement of the *nauba.* It is linked to the preceding movement by an interlude played on the lute accompanied by percussion instruments.
Lit.: no. 171.

Al-Mshad (Tunisia). Rhythmic mode:

Lit.: no. 171.

Al-Mshaddar (*Al-Muṣaddar*) (Tunisia). (1) The second movement of the *nauba*. An introductory piece, slowly played by the instrumental ensemble together with drum and rattle. (2) Rhythmic mode of the 2nd movement of the *nauba*:

(3) Rhythmic modes of the closing section:

Lit.: no. 171.

Al Muṣaddar (Tunisia). See *Al Mshaddar.*

Al nafir (Arabia). See *Anafil.*

Al-Oud (Arabia; Persia; Afghanistan). See *'Ud.*

Alpa (India). See *Alpatva svara.*

Alptva svara (Ancient India). A note of a *rāga* that is used rarely and treated weakly.
Lit.: no. 292.

Al-qānūn (Egypt). Board zither played with a plectrum. Cf. *Qānūn.*
Lit.: no. 100.

Al-qaṣāba (Arabia – Maghrib). See *Qaṣāba.*

Al-Ramal (Arabia). See *Ramal.*
Lit.: no. 70.

Al-samā (Old Middle East). Listening to music.
Lit.: no. 76.

Al-thaqīl al-awwal (Arabia). See *Īqā'āt.*
Lit.: no. 70.

Al-thaqīl al-thānī (Arabia). See *Īqā'āt.*
Lit.: no. 70.

Al-thaqīl al-tarjī (Arabia). Slow refrain.
Lit.: no. 73.

Al-tubel (North Africa – Tuareg). See *Gangatan.*

Al-Tūshiyah (Tunisia). (1) The fifth movement of the *nauba*; an interlude played on a solo fiddle presenting richly ornamented passages. (2) Rhythmic mode (larghetto):

Lit.: no. 171.

Alū (Mesopotamia – Akkadia). See *Alal.*

Alu (Flores). Rice stamping sticks used to accompany jumping dances. These dances are called *rangku alu* in Todo, and *paking alu* in Radjong.
Lit.: no. 166.

Al-'Ud (Arabia). See *'Ud.*

Alugoji (South India). Term for *Alghōza.*

Alu gurung (Flores). Rattling stamping stick in the southern Manggaray District.
Lit.: no. 166.

Alungu (Congo; Uganda). Board zither.
Lit.: no. 302.

Alus (Bali). Soft; gentle; refined.
Lit.: no. 197.

Alus (Java). Soft; gentle; manner of *gamelan* playing; a style appropriate for puppet performance. The term refers also to an actor in *wayang wong* performances.
Lit.: no. 163.

Alus impur (Java). See *Alus.*
Lit.: no. 163.

Alus kalang kinantang (Java). Refined and proud character of an actor in *wayang wong.*
Lit.: no. 163.

Al-uṭāyḥī (Tunisia). Rhythmic mode:

Lit.: no. 171.

Aluut (Uganda – Karamojong). Side-blown animal horn.
Lit.: nos. 190, 302.

Āmad (Afghanistan; North India). "Coming," "arriving"; melodic drive toward the basic note (*sa*) and the rhythmic down beat (*sam*).
Lit.: no. 276.

Amadinda (Uganda – Baganda). Xylophone with 12-19 keys played by three players.
Lit.: nos. 155, 218.

Amafohlwane (*Amahahlazo*) (South Africa – Zulu). Small containers made of palm leaf or cocoons filled with small rattling pebbles. The containers are tied with cords around the ankles of dancers. Cf. *Umfece.*
Lit.: nos. 150-51.

Amagala (Uganda – Amba; Congo – Madi). Several wooden sticks used at circumcision rites: one stick, held under the arm, is beaten with a piece of wood by the initiate.
Lit.: no. 302.

Amahahlazo (South Africa – Pondo). Dancing rattles. Cf. *Amafohlwane.*
Lit.: no. 151.

Amahoto (Congo – Bantu). From the skin of a bottomless drum is stretched a string that is rubbed by the player.
Lit.: no. 29.

Amakonezi (Uganda – Baganda). Xylophone (*amadinda*) style where the melodic line is embellished in the upper octave.
Lit.: no. 304.

'Amal (Arabia; Persia). Old, popular instrumental piece with a prelude. Other, similar pieces were the *naqsh*, *ṣaut*, *hawā'ī*, and *muraṣṣa'*, all of considerable popularity. Cf. *Dastgāh.*
Lit.: no. 76.

Amālāt (Arabia). Long held notes sung to vowels. Cf. *Dastgāh.*
Lit.: no. 76.

Amang (Malay Peninsula – Semang). Bamboo tube zither.
Lit.: nos. 156, 190.

Aman-khuur (Mongolia). See *Temur.*
Lit.: nos. 60-61.

Ama-no-iwabue (Japan). See *Ama-no-toribue.*

Ama-no-toribue (*Ama-no-iwabue*) (Japan). Ancient flute, the forerunner of the *yamatobue* and, later, the *kagurabue.* The latter is a cross-flute with six finger holes.
Lit.: no. 53.

Amanqashele (South Africa – Xhosa). Ankle rattles worn by dancers.
Lit.: nos. 151, 190.

Ama Pañchamam (South India). *Janya rāga* of the 48th *mēḷa* (*Divyamaṇī*).
Tone material:

C D♭ E♭ F♯ G A♯ B c
c B A♯ F♯ E♭ C

Lit.: no. 139.

Amarāvali (South India). *Janya rāga* of the 28th *mēḷa* (*Harikāmbhōji*).
Tone material:

C D E F A c
c B♭ A G F E D C

Lit.: no. 139.

Amatambo (South Africa – Zulu). Clappers made of bones. Cf. *Marapo.*
Lit.: no. 151.

Ambah (*Ampah*) (Bali). Performing within a particular mode.
Lit.: no. 197.

Ambāmanōharī (South India). *Janya rāga* of the 23rd *mēḷa* (*Gaurīmanōharī*).
Tone material:
C D E♭ F A B c
c B A F E♭ D C
Lit.: no. 139.

Amban (New Guinea—Bismarck Archipelago). Drum of hourglass shape. Cf. *Oñ*.
Lit.: no. 25.

Amben (West Java). See *Ketuk tilu*.

Ambhaṇa (Vedic India). Resonator of the *vīṇā*.

Ambhōgini (South India). *Janya rāga* of the 28th *mēḷa* (*Harikāmbhōji*).
Tone material:
C D E F A B c
c A F E D C
Lit.: no. 139.

Ambhōruham (South India). *Janya rāga* of the 44th *mēḷa* (*Bhāvapriyā*).
Tone material:
C D♭ E♭ G A♭ B♭ c
c B♭ G A♭ F♯ E D C
Lit.: no. 139.

Ambilta (Ethiopia). Huge vertically-blown bamboo flutes played in sets of five. Each flute produces only one note.
Lit.: no. 190.

Ambira (Mozambique). *Sansa* with nine keys.
Lit.: no. 149.

Ambira (Ethiopia). Xylophone with gourd resonators. Cf. *Mbira* (*Mbila*).
Lit.: nos. 151, 218.

Ambrang (*Banbrang*) (West Java). Cf. *Ḍogḍog*.
Lit.: no. 163.

Ambruk (Sunda District). See *Indung*.
Lit.: no. 163.

Amejoni (West Africa; Togo). Slit-drum.
Lit.: no. 33.

Amg'ad (Sahara; Sudan—Tuareg). Spike fiddle with one horsehair string.
Lit.: nos. 190, 255.

Amhara (Ethiopia). End blown flute without finger holes.

Amita (Central and South Africa—Bantu). Percussion sticks.
Lit.: no. 29.

Amizad (Algeria—Tuareg). Name for *Rebāb*.
Lit.: no. 64.

Amma-no-fuye (Japan). Double pipe consisting of two vertically-blown bamboo tubes fastened together side by side. The instrument with its long held notes was used by blind masseurs in order to create attention.
Lit.: no. 255.

Amokoderi (Tanganyika). Groups of side-blown antelope horns.
Lit.: no. 190.

Amor (Uganda—Alur). A two-headed drum representing the ruler.
Lit.: no. 26.

Ampah (Bali). See *Ambah*.

Ampondokaka (Malagasy Republic). Horn.
Lit.: no. 251.

Amponga (Malagasy Republic). Drum; ground zither.
Lit.: nos. 250-51.

Ampongabē (Malagasy Republic). An imitation of the European big drum. Cf. *Langoro*.
Lit.: no. 255.

Ampongakēly (Malagasy Republic). Small drum.
Lit.: nos. 190, 255.

Ampongalava (Malagasy Republic). Long, slim kettledrum. When played the kettle is inserted into a spacious resonating clay vessel.
Lit.: no. 255.

Ampongavilany (Malagasy Republic). Kettle-drum with clay corpus. The oxhide head is beaten with both hands.
Lit.: no. 255.

Āmradēśi (South India). *Janya rāga* of the 62nd *mēḷa* (*Riṣabhapriyā*).
Tone material:
C E F# G Ab Bb Ab c
c Bb Ab F# E C
Lit.: no. 139.

Āmra Pañchamam (South India). *Janya rāga* of the 48th *mēḷa* (*Divyamaṇī*).
Tone material:
C Db Eb F# A# B c
c B A# F# Eb C Db C
Lit.: no. 139.

Amrita (South India). Ancient fiddle resembling the *rebāb*.
Lit.: nos. 190, 255.

Amrita Dhanyāsi (South India). *Janya rāga* of the 8th *mēḷa* (*Hanumattōḍi*).
Tone material:
C Db Eb F G Bb c
c Bb G F Eb Db C
Lit.: no. 139.

Amritalaharī (South India). *Janya rāga* of the 29th *mēḷa* (*Dhīraśaṅkarābharaṇam*).
Tone material:
C E D F G B c
c B A G F E D C
Lit.: no. 139.

Amritalaharī (*Amrutalaharī*) (South India). *Janya rāga* of the 46th *mēḷa* (*Ṣaḍvidhamārgiṇī*).
Tone material:
C Db Eb F# G A c
c A G F# Eb Db C
Lit.: no. 139.

Amrita Pañchamam (South India). *Janya rāga* of the 48th *mēḷa* (*Divyamaṇī*). The scale of this *rāga* is identical with that of *Āmra Pañchamam.* The reason why this *rāga* is mentioned here is because South Indian theoretical works list *Amrita-* and *Āmra Pañchamam.* Tonally there is no difference, but allegedly there exists a subtle difference in interpretation between the two *rāgas.*
Lit.: no. 139.

Amrita Rañjaṇi (South India). See *Amrita Taraṅgiṇī.*

Amrita Svarūpiṇi (South India). *Janya rāga* of the 72nd *mēḷa* (*Rasikapriyā*).
Tone material:
C D# E F# G A# c
c A# G F# E D# C
Lit.: no. 139.

Amrita Taraṅgiṇī (*Amrita Rañjaṇī*) (South India). *Janya rāga* of the 19th *mēḷa* (*Jhaṅkāradhvani*).
Tone material:
C D Eb F Ab Bbb c
c Ab Bbb Ab G F Eb D C
Lit.: no. 139.

Amritavāhini (South India). *Janya rāga* of the 20th *mēḷa* (*Naṭabhairavī*).
Tone material:
C D F G Ab Bb c
c Bb Ab F Eb D C
Lit.: no. 139.

Amrita Varśaṇi (South India). See *Amrita Varśiṇi.*

Amrita Varśiṇi (*Amrita Varśaṇi*) (South India). *Janya rāga* of the 39th *mēḷa* (*Jhālavarāḷi*).
Tone material:
C Db Ebb F# G Ab B G c
c B G Ab F# Ebb Db C
Lit.: no. 139.

Amrita Varśiṇi (South India). *Janya rāga* of the 66th *mēḷa* (*Chitrāmbarī*).
Tone material:
C E F# G B c
c B G F# E C
Lit.: no. 139.

Amrita Vasantam (South India). *Janya rāga* of the 57th *mēḷa* (*Siṃhendramadhyama*).
Tone material:
C D Eb G Ab B c
c B Ab F# Eb C
Lit.: no. 139.

Amrutalaharī (South India). See *Amritalaharī.*

Aṃśa (India). *Aṃśa* is the predominant note of lesser importance in the music of the South than the *vādī* in the North.
Lit.: no. 138.

A'mūd (Arabia). "Pillar." The neck of the *kemanjah.*
Lit.: no. 255.

Amukta (South India). "Closed." The term refers to finger holes on wind instruments. It may be added that *mukta* means "open" (finger hole), and *ardhamukta* "partly closed."

Amz'ad (Sahara—Tuareg). Music bow with a large gourd as corpus. A strand of horsehair serves the string. The string is usually plucked, rarely bowed. The almost obsolete instrument was played by women of the ruler's court.
Lit.: no. 255.

Ana-batching (Celebes). Iron percussion sticks beaten or stamped, used as magic against evil spirits.
Lit.: no. 132.

Ana-bettjing (Celebes). See *Ana-Batching*; *Tjuriga.*
Lit.: no. 162.

Ānaddha-yantra (India; Benga). Drums.
Lit.: no. 255.

Ānāgata eḍuppu (South India). Cf. *Eḍuppu* (*Ālāp*).

Ānāgata graha (South India). A piece of music in which the *āvarta* of the drummer begins several "upbeats" earlier than the melody. Cf. *Atīta graha.*
Lit.: no. 261.

Anāhata nāda (India). The music of nature (as perceived by the yogis), in contrast to *āhata*, music created by man.

Aṇaisu (South India). The metallic head piece (bell) of a wind instrument.
Lit.: no. 261.

Anak (West Java). Term used either for a small drum (low pitched in sound) such as *chikibung*, *indung* (*blung*), or for the biggest (low-pitched) kettle of a single-row *bonang* (also called *indung*).
Lit.: no. 163.

Ānaka (India). An ancient large kettledrum with a clay body.
Lit.: no. 255.

Ānaka dundubhi (India). Ancient war drum.
Lit.: no. 261.

Anakidory (Madagascar). A small ivory *dory.*
Lit.: no. 251.

Ānandabhairavī (South India). *Janya rāga* of the 20th *mēḷa* (*Naṭabhairavī*).
Tone material:
C Eb D Eb F G Ab G (Bb) c
(. . . G A Bb A Bb c)
c Bb A Bb c Bb Ab G
(c Bb Ab G F . . .) (Ab G F) Eb D C
Lit.: no. 139.

Ānandabhōgi (South India). See *Ānandhabhōgi.*

Ānanda laharī (India). A plucked string instrument used by beggars, never by professional musicians. It consists of one gut string which runs from the membrane bottom of a barrel (which is open at the top) to a small cup (or button). The string is attached to the upper closed end of the cup which is held in the player's left hand, while the barrel is held in the left arm. The player's right hand plucks the tightly stretched string which produces a nasal vibrating sound. Cf. *Gopi yantra*; *Yektar*.
Lit.: no. 254.

Ānanda Laharī (South India). *Janya rāga* of the 29th *mēḷa* (*Dhīraśaṅkarābharaṇam*).
Tone material:
C D E F G A B G c
c B G F E D C
Lit.: no. 139.

Ānanda Līlā (South India). *Janya rāga* of the 23rd *mēḷa* (*Gāṅgeyabhushanī*).
Tone material:
C D# E F G B c
c B Ab G F E D# C
Lit.: no. 139.

Ānandamukhi (South India). *Janya rāga* of the 29th *mēḷa* (*Dhīraśaṅkarābharaṇam*).
Tone material:
C F E F G A B G c
c B A G F E D C
Lit.: no. 139.

Ānanda Nāṭani (South India). *Janya rāga* of the 2nd *mēḷa* (*Ratnangi*).
Tone material:
C Db Ebb F G Bb c
c Bb G F Ebb Db C
Lit.: no. 139.

Ānanda Vāridhi (South India). *Janya rāga* of the 22nd *mēḷa* (*Karaharapriyā*).
Tone material:
C D F G Bb A G c
c Bb A G F Eb D C
Lit.: no. 139.

Ānand-bhairav (North India). *Rāga* related to the *Bhairav thāta*.
Tone material (ambiguous):
C Db E F G A G B G c
db c A Bb G F E F Db C
Lit.: no. 138.

Ānandabhōgi (*Ānandabhōgi*) (South India). *Janya rāga* of the 42nd *mēḷa* (*Raghupriyā*).
Tone material:
C Db Ebb F# G B A# B
B A# G F# Ebb Db C *B*
The scale of this *rāga* has *niṣādāntya* character.
Lit.: no. 139.

Ānandlaharī (South India). See *Ānanda laharī.*

Anaṅgādhari (South India). *Janya rāga* of the 39th *mēḷa* (*Jhālavarāḷi*).
Tone material:
C Db Ebb Db F# G B Ab B c
c B G Ab F# Ebb F# Db C
Lit.: no. 139.

Anānīz (*Unnaīz*) (Arabia). Bagpipe.
Lit.: no. 255.

Ananta (South India). *Janya rāga* of the 17th *mēḷa* (*Sūryakānta*).
Tone material:
C Db F G A B c
c G F E Db C
Lit.: no. 139.

Ananta vijaya (Ancient India). Sanskrit "boundless victory." Legendary shell horn (mentioned in the *Mahābhārata*).
Lit.: no. 255.

An-ch'aebi sori (Korea). "Song of inside musicians." Very simple Buddhist chants sung by monks of all classes, persons not always trained in chanting. The texts of *an-cha'ebi sori* (cf. *Yombul*) are Chinese prayers for the dead.
Lit.: no. 287.

Andat (Kampuchea). Reed; tongue.
Lit.: no. 255.

Āndhāli (South India). Old and well-known *janya rāga* of the 28th *mēḷa* (*Harikāmbhōji*).
Tone material:
C D F G B♭ c
c B♭ G F D E F D C
Lit.: no. 139.

Āndhōliki (South India). *Janya rāga* of the 28th *mēḷa* (*Harikāmbhōji*).
Tone material:
C D F G (A) B♭ c
c B♭ A F D C
Lit.: no. 139.

Āndhra Dēśika (South India). *Janya rāga* of the 15th *mēḷa* (*Māyāmāḷavagauḷa*).
Tone material:
C D♭ E F G A♭ B c
c B G A♭ G F E D♭ C
Lit.: no. 139.

Andhri (Ancient India). See *Jāti.*

Andobu (Congo—Bakongo Pygmies). Musical bow.
Lit.: no. 176.

Āndōlika (South India). *Janya rāga* of the 22nd *mēḷa* (*Kharaharapriyā*).
Tone material:
C D F G B♭ c
c B♭ A F D C
Lit.: no. 139.

Āndōlita (India). Musical ornament performed on the *vīṇā.* After a note has been sounded, its vibrating string is raised toward a higher pitch by either pulling it or by gliding the stopping finger along the string upward. Cf. *Gamak(a).*
Lit.: no. 261.

Anfār (plural of *nafīr*) (Arabia). Trumpet.

Aṅgalata (South India). *Janya rāga* of the 28th *mēḷa* (*Harikāmbhōji*).
Tone material:
C E D E F G A B♭ A c
c A F E D F E C
Lit.: no. 139.

Angang-angang (Java). See *Gong anggang-anggang.*

Angangvena (New Guinea—Finschhafen). "Female" transverse flute.
Lit.: no. 255.

Ang en tsuma (Micronesia, Ponape). Nose flute. Cf. *Chup en parri.*
Lit.: nos. 190, 313.

Angguk (Java—Chilachup District). A play that has its musical accompaniment performed by three drums: *kendang, terbang, jidor.*
Lit.: no. 163.

Angkat-angkatan (Bali). A sequence of musical pieces performed in *wayang kulit* and *wayang wong.* They are used during scenes with lively actions, hurried departures or flights.
Lit.: no. 197.

Angklung (*Aṅkluṅ*; *Haṅkluṅ*) (Java; Bali; Borneo). A rattle made of two or three bamboo tubes suspended vertically in a wooden or bamboo frame. At the lower end of the frame the vertical tubes are fitted into slits cut into a thick, horizontal bamboo tube. By shaking the frame the vertical tubes rattle against the slits. The tubes are tuned in octaves. The *angklungs* are made in several sizes usually in such a way that each *angklung* of a group produces one note (and its octave) of a pentatonic scale (e.g., G A B d). The instruments are used at funeral ceremonies and at dignified processions. Recently, *angklung* ensembles play also *gong kebyar* pieces. The *angklung* of Banjuwangi (Java) is a xylophone with 12 to 15 bamboo tubes, fixed in a frame by tying a string through holes in the tubes. It is played with two small wooden hammers. Cf. *Kechuk*; *Grantang.*
Lit.: nos. 215, 265.

Angklung ubrug (Sunda District). The large sized *angklung.*
Lit.: no. 163.

Angkring (*Trachak*) (Java). See *Sanggan*.
Lit.: no. 163.

Angra okwena (Uganda—Waganda). Lute made of a solid wooden box in the shape of a throne with a high back. To its back are fixed five rods with five fiber strings. Cf. *Wambi*.
Lit.: no. 255.

Angremut (Oceania—New Pomerania). A primitive xylophone consisting of two large slabs of burned wood placed across a narrow slit-shaped hole dug into the ground. The instrument may only be played by men. Women are not permitted to see it. Cf. *Garamut*.
Lit.: no. 255.

Angrim tancha (Burma). "Gently sounding instruments."
Lit.: no. 255.

Angsel (Bali). Measured interruption in music and dance.
Lit.: no. 197.

Angtalung (*Nangtalung*) (Thailand). Bamboo rattle music that is used to take part in the accompaniment of popular shadow plays. Cf. *Angklung* (Java).
Lit.: no. 163.

Angulistata (India). Instruments with plucked strings.
Lit.: no. 255.

Angulisthan (India). Fingerboard.
Lit.: no. 255.

Angun (Caroline Isl.). "Cane." A cane flute, generally nose-blown, occasionally also mouth-blown, with none or three finger holes. Cf. *Anim*.
Lit.: no. 313.

Aṅguru (South India). *Janya rāga* of the 7th *mēḷa* (*Senāpāti*).
Tone material:
C E♭ F A♭ B♭♭ c
c B♭♭ A♭ F E♭ C
Lit.: no. 139.

Aṇi (South India). Musical ornaments.

Āṇi (India). Screw that holds the corpus to the *daṇḍi* (stem) of the *vīṇā*.
Lit.: no. 261.

Anibaddha (India). Rhythmically free music. The opposite, strictly rhythmical music, is termed *nibaddha*.
Lit.: no. 261.

Anikini (South India). *Janya rāga* of the 7th *mēḷa* (*Senāpāti*).
Tone material:
C D♭ E♭ F A♭ B♭♭ c
c B♭♭ A♭ F E♭ D♭ C
Lit.: no. 139.

Anilāvaḷi (South India). *Janya rāga* of the 22nd *mēḷa* (*Kharaharapriyā*).
Tone material:
C D E♭ F G B♭ A B♭ c
c B♭ G F D C
Lit.: no. 139.

Anilamadhya (South India). *Janya rāga* of the 53rd *mēḷa* (*Gamanaśrama*).
Tone material:
C D♭ F♯ G A c
c B A G F♯ E D♭ C
Lit.: no. 139.

Anim (East Caroline Isl.; Truk). Nose flute with or without finger holes. Cf. *Angun*.
Lit.: nos. 190, 313.

Añjanāvati (South India). *Janya rāga* of the 43rd *mēḷa* (*Gavāmbōdhi*).
Tone material:
C D♭ E♭ F♯ G A♭ c
c A♭ G F♯ E♭ D♭ C
Lit.: no. 139.

Anjani-tōḍi (North India). *Rāga* ascribed to the *Tōḍi thāta*.
Obscure tone material:
C D F G A♭ B♭ (B) c
c B♭ A (A♭) G F E♭ D C; *Vādis*: G, C
Lit.: no. 138.

Anjomara (Malagasy Republic). Oboe type. Cf. *Zomari*; *Zamr*.

Anjomary varahina (Malagasy Republic). A wind instrument, described as a "trumpet."
Lit.: no. 251.

Anjombo (Malagasy Republic). Horn.
Lit.: no. 251.

Anjombona (Malagasy Republic). Shell horn, side-blown.
Lit.: no. 251.

Ankarana (Malagasy Republic). Shell trumpet blown by the retinue of the ruler. See *Antsiva*.
Lit.: no. 255.

Ankī (India). Small drum. Cf. *Ankya*.
Lit.: no. 261.

Aṅkluṅ (Java). See *Angklung*.

Ankora (Malagasy Republic). See *Antsiva*.

An kuo (China). Music imported from Bukhara. One of the 10 orchestral ensembles directed by the *yüeh-fu*. See *Shih-pu-chi*.
Lit.: no. 137.

Ankya (India). Drum.
Lit.: no. 261.

Anlung (Kampuchea). Wooden clapper.
Lit.: no. 255.

An Nafīr (Egypt). Trumpet without ventils.
Lit.: no. 100.

An-nay (Egypt). Long flute, held obliquely. Cf. *Nāy*.
Lit.: no. 100.

An-nungsü (Northeast Thailand). Chanting a sacred text. One of two anhemitonic pentatonic scales is in use; the other scale is called *lum*. *An-nungsü* is used in two forms:
(a) A C D E G (called *lai yai*)
(b) D F G A c (called *lai noi*)
Lit.: no. 203.

An-oin (Malaysia, Malacca). Wooden jew's harp in form of a bottle.
Lit.: no. 254.

Antanatra (Southwest Malagasy Republic). Slit-drum.
Lit.: no. 251.

Antarā (North India). "Interval." The second section of the *khyāl* and *dhrūpad*, usually employing the notes of the upper tetrachord within the octave.
Lit.: no. 138.

Antara dundubhi (India). Celestial drum.
Lit.: no. 261.

Antara Ga (*Antara Gāndhāra*) (India). The note name corresponding to the 8th *śruti* (*Raudrī*). Cf. *Śruti*.
Lit.: no. 261.

Antara mārga (India). The occasional insertion of a note foreign to the fixed tone material of the *rāga*. This can be done in a few *rāgas* with good and acceptable effect.
Lit.: no. 261.

Antara Vāhini (South India). See *Antar Vāhini*.

Antari (India). End phrase of linking pasage between two sections of a song.
Lit.: no. 261.

Antar Vāhini (*Antara Vāhini*) (South India). *Janya rāga* of the 29th *mēḷa* (*Dhīraśaṅkarābharaṇam*).
Tone material:
C D E F G B A B c
c B A G F E D C
Lit.: no. 139.

Antawis (Java). "Interval."

Antchak (Korea). "Inside half." The first two lines of a quatrain of the *hossari*. Lines three and four of the quatrain are called *pattchak*.
Lit.: no. 287.

Anthuot (Cambodia). Bamboo zither.
Lit.: no. 215.

Antsiva (Madagascar). Shell trumpet employed at royal processions. Cf. *Akarana*; *Akora*; *Ankora*; *Ankarana*.
Lit.: no. 255.

Antsivambazaha (Madagascar). Trumpet of the white man. A long and simple instrument.
Lit.: no. 190.

Antsiva-varahina (Madagascar). Copper or shell trumpet.
Lit.: no. 255.

Antya (Vedic India). See *Atisvarya*.

Anubandha (India). One of the ancient 10 basic ways of touching *vina* strings (*dhatu*); separating and combining of two or more of *puṣpa*, *kala*, *tala*, *niṣkoṭita*, *unmṛṣṭa*, *repha*, *anusvanita*, *bindu*, and *avamṛṣṭa*.
Lit.: no. 292.

Anubandham (South India). Coda section, often elaborately performed.
Lit.: no. 261.

Anudātta (Vedic India). The not-raised note in Vedic chant; the note that stands below the *udātta* and *svarita*.
Lit.: nos. 136, 141.

Anudrutam (South India). "Under-quick." Durational note value. If the *laghu* is assumed to be the metrical unit of one western quarter note (♩), the *Anudrutam* represents one 16th (𝅘𝅥𝅯). The other note values of South Indian music are: *drutam* (♪), *laghu* (♩), *laghu drutam* (♩ ♪), *guru* (𝅗𝅥), *guru drutam* (𝅗𝅥 ♪), *pluta(m)* (𝅗𝅥.), *Kākapādam* (𝅝). Cf. *Akshara*.
Lit.: no. 261.

Anughaṇta (South India). *Janya rāga* of the 47th *mēḷa* (*Suvarṇāṅgī*).
Tone material:

C D♭ F♯ E D♭ A B c
c B A G F♯ E♭ D♭ C

Lit.: no. 139.

Anuhāti (India). A method of plucking the *vīṇā* string as mentioned by Sōmanātha (17th-century) in his *Rāgavibōdha*.
Lit.: no. 261.

Anulōma (South India). The rendering of a melody in three different speeds, always maintaining the same rhythm. The first tempo is doubled in the second rendering, and quadrupled in the third.
Lit.: no. 261.

Anuman (Ivory Coast Republic—Baule). Wooden whistle.
Lit.: nos. 190, 303.

Anumandaram (South India). Term for the 4th string of the *vīṇā*, tuned to the low note *pa* (*G*). Cf. *Anumandra sthāyi*.
Lit.: no. 261.

Anumandra sthāyi (South India). An octave range below the *mandra sthāyi* (generally the lowest of the three octave ranges). Usually Indian art music moves only within the range of three octaves: *mandra*, the lowest; *madhya*, the middle; and *tara*, the highest range. In rare instances an *anumandra* octave range can be observed that is one octave below the *mandra* range. Cf. *Anumandaram*.
Lit.: no. 261.

Anumātrā (North India). A durational note value. If the *matra* is assumed to have the metrical value of one quarter note (♩), the *anumatra* represents one 16th (𝅘𝅥𝅯). All other durational note values of North Indian music are: *ardhamātrā* (♪); *mātrā* (or *hrasva* = "short") (♩), *adhyardha* (1½ *matras* ♩ ♪), *dirgha* ("long," 𝅗𝅥), *ardhatisra* (𝅗𝅥 ♪), *pluta* (or vrddha—"augmented," 𝅗𝅥.).
Lit.: no. 136.

Anunāsika nadam (India). A faulty nasal voice production.
Lit.: no. 261.

Anupallavi (South India). The second part of an art song that follows the first part, the

pallavi. In North India the *pallavi* has its counterpart in the *sthāyi* (*asthāyi*), and the southern *anupallavi* corresponds to the northern *antara*.
Lit.: no. 261.

Anusvanita (India). One of the ancient 10 basic ways of touching *vīṇā* strings (*dhātu*): a *tala* performed in the lower part of the string.
Lit.: no. 292.

Anusvaram (South India). Lightly touched ornamental note foreign to the fixed tone material of the *rāga*. This foreign note is used before or after the sounding of a regular note of the *rāga*.
Lit.: no. 261.

Anuvādī (India). In a *rāga* appear stressed notes (*vādī*, *saṃvādī*, *vishrantisthan*), not-stressed notes (*anuvādī*) and dissonant notes (*vivādī*). Any not-stressed note (but being a proper note of the fixed tone material) is called *anuvādī*.
Lit.: no. 138.

Anya svara (South India). A foreign note used in a *rāga*; a note that does not belong to the basic tone material of its parent scale (*mēḷa*).
Lit.: no. 261.

Anyomara (*Anjomara*) (Madagascar). Oboe type.
Lit.: no. 255.

Anyomary (*Anjomara*) (Madagascar). Simple trumpet. See *Anjomara*.
Lit.: no. 255.

Anzaṅ (Congo; Gabon Republic). Xylophone. Cf. *Menzaṅ*.
Lit.: no. 33.

Anzel (French Congo). Iron bell.
Lit.: no. 255.

Aopoh (Flores, Ngada). Fast and violent dance.
Lit.: no. 166.

Ao-yü (China—M66, 7668). A large *mu-yü* often used by Taoists. Cf. *Moko*; *Moku-gyo*.
Lit.: no. 209.

Apada (Bali). Strophe; stanza.
Lit.: no. 197.

Apakura (New Zealand—Maori). Chanted lament performed at funeral ceremonies.
Lit.: no. 298.

Apala (Nigeria—Yoruba). See *Adama*; *Gangan*.
Lit.: no. 293.

A-pankal (Sierra Leone—Temne). Harp.
Lit.: no. 255.

Apanyāsa (Ancient India). Secondary final note. (The term for the primary final was *nyāsa*.)
Lit.: no. 23.

Apaśruti (South India). Also called *apasvaram*; wrong note; wrong pitch.
Lit.: no. 261.

Apasvaram (South India). See *Apaśruti*.

Apesin (Nigeria—Yoruba). Drum; small group of drums. The *apesin* is handbeaten. It has one skin and a cylindrical corpus carved of a block of wood. The drum ensemble consists of an *iya'lu* (leading drum) and two or three *apesin*. Cf. *Omolu*.
Lit.: no. 293.

Apik (Java, Cheribon). See *Laras*.

Apik (West Java). Name of the sixth note in *pelog*. See also *Laras*; *Nem*; *Surupan*. The term signifies also "beautiful melodies."
Lit.: no. 163.

Aping (Borneo). Bamboo jew's harp.
Lit.: nos. 190, 255.

Aporo (Congo—Azande; Uganda—Labwor). (1) Double bell. Two clapperless bells linked by a curved handle. They are beaten with a stick.

(2) A large flute with cylindrical bore blown from either side. Played only by women.
Lit.: nos. 184, 303.

Appo (South Celebes). Bamboo percussion stick, split at one end. Used only in ritual ceremonies. The term is also applied to the *tjuriga*.
Lit.: nos. 132, 162.

Āpradēśi (South India). *Janya rāga* of the 62nd *mēḷa* (*Riṣabhapriyā*).
Tone material:
C E F♯ G A B♭ A♭ c
c B♭ A♭ G F♯ E C
Lit.: no. 139.

Apramēyam (South India). *Janya rāga* of the 65th *mēḷa* (*Mechakalyāṇī*).
Tone material:
C D F♯ G A c
c B A F♯ E F♯ D C
Lit.: no. 139.

Aprati Madhyama (South India). A *śruti* that can appear between *śuddha ma* (F natural) and *prati ma* (F♯). This note occurs, e.g., in *rāga Bēgaḍa*.
Lit.: no. 261.

Apsarā(s) (India). The lovely musician-wives of the celestial Gāndharvas, nymphs who are able to change their bodies at will.
Lit.: no. 205.

Apunga (Angola). Ivory horn blown from the side. Cf. *Ponga*.
Lit.: no. 255.

Apūrṇa (India). Term meaning the same as *asampūrna*: a scale consisting of less than seven degrees within the octave.
Lit.: no. 261.

'Aqd (North Africa; Middle East). Lowest tetrachord (on string instruments).

Arabābu (Moluccas, Halmahera). *Rebāb* with a coconut body, one fiber string that can be plucked or bowed.
Lit.: nos. 162, 254.

Arabābu (Talaud Isl.; Pulau-Pulau Isl.). Long-necked bowed lute with one string.
Lit.: no. 162.

Arabana (Kai Isl.). Round, occasionally octagonal, frame drum, with or without jingles. Cf. *Rabana*; *Rēbana*.
Lit.: no. 156.

Arabhi (South India). *Janya rāga* of the 29th *mēḷa* (*Dhiraśaṅkarābharaṇam*).
Tone material:
C D F G A c
c B A G F E D C
Lit.: no. 139.

Arabi (*Arabhi*) (North India). An obscure *rāga* that can be ascribed to the *Bilaval thāta*. It is similar to *rāga Durga* of the *Bilaval thāta* but uses the note *ga* (E) in descent.
Tone material:
C D F G A c
c A G F E D C
Lit.: no. 138.

'Arabī dūdūk (Turkey). Arabian vertical flute, probably the same as the Arabian *saffāra*.
Lit.: nos. 76, 81.

'Arabī zūrnā (Turkey). Arabian oboe.
Lit.: no. 81.

Aragoto (Japan). The term signifies violent fighting scenes in *kabuki* plays. Their musical accompaniment is provided by a wooden rattle (clapper) *hyoshigi*.
Lit.: no. 185.

Araiyar (South India). Temple dancers.

Aran (North Borneo). A wooden plate that covers the body of a *busoi*.
Lit.: no. 254.

Arang (*Awis*; *Hawis*) (Java). "Far apart" (rhythmically), such as the *keṭuk* beats in relation to those of the *kenongan*. See also *Hawis*.
Lit.: no. 163.

Arāray (Ethiopia). One of three liturgical modes. Cf. *Gheez*.
Lit.: no. 102.

Arbāb (Sumatra). *Rebāb* with a heart-shaped body and two silk strings. Cf. *Arabābu*.
Lit.: no. 163.

Arbu (New Guinea; Christmas Isl.). Rattle of snail shells in form of a bracelet worn by dancers.
Lit.: no. 184.

Ārchika (Vedic India). Chanting on one note.
Lit.: no. 261.

Ardablis (Ancient Israel). Hebrew term for *hydraulos* (Greek) organ.
Lit.: no. 250.

'Ardāwī (Modern Tunisia). *Maqām*.
Tone material:

F G A♭(+) B♭(+) c d e♭

Lit.: no. 64.

Ardhamātrā (North India). Durational note value. If the *mātrā* is assumed to be the metrical unit of one quarter note, the *ardhamātrā* ("half matra") represents an 8th note. Other durational note values are listed under the heading of *Anumātrā*.
Lit.: no. 136.

Ardhamukta (South India). See *Amukta*.

Ardhasthāyi Vādya (India). An obscure musical instrument with a limited compass of half an octave.
Lit.: no. 261.

Ardhatisra (North India). The durational note value of two *mātrās* plus one *ardhamātrā*. In western notation this signifies the duration of two quarter notes plus an 8th. All other durational note values of North India are given under the heading of *Anumātrā*.
Lit.: no. 136.

'Ardibār (Middle East). *Maqām*.
Tone material:

D E♭ F G A(♭) B♭ c d

Lit.: no. 64.

Ardja (*Arja*) (Bali). Opera; musical comedy.
Lit.: no. 265.

Ārdradēśi (*Ārdradēśika*) (South India). *Janya rāga* of the 15th *mēḷa* (*Māyāmāḷavagauḷa*).
Tone material:

C D♭ E F G A♭ c B c (C D♭ F G A♭ [B] c)
c A♭ G F E D♭ C

Lit.: no. 139.

Ārdradēśika (South India). See *Ārdradēśi*.

Arebane (Arabia). Tambourin. See *Rēbana*.

Arelu (Nigeria – Yoruba). The chief drummers.
Lit.: no. 29.

Areng'as (Southwest Transvaal – Hottentots). Tube vertically blown, made of the shinbone of a springbok.
Lit.: nos. 151, 190.

Argham (Tibet). At the word *argham* in Buddhist service the cymbals are held horizontally and the striking hand has to hold its mid-finger erect.
Lit.: nos. 143, 305.

Arghanūn (Arabia). "Byzantine organ"; bagpipe. Cf. *Arghun*.
Lit.: no. 67.

Arghūl (*Argūl*) (Turkey; Egypt; Middle East). Ancient double clarinet of the Fellahin. The two pipes are linked side by side; the right one, the melody pipe, has six finger holes, the left one usually without any finger holes is used for the bourdon accompaniment. The instrument has a single reed which is partly detached from the tube. The bourdon tube can be lengthened by adding one, two, or three extension tubes. The names of the three extended forms of the *arghūl* are:

1. *Arghūl el-asghar*, the small *arghūl* with one additional tube.
2. *Arghūl el-soghaīr*, an instrument of medium size, uses two extension tubes.
3. *Arghūl el-kebīr*, the big *arghūl*, with three extensions.

Lit.: nos. 243, 255.

Arghūl el-asghar (Arabia; Middle East). See *Arghūl.*

Arghūl el-kebīr (Arabia; Middle East). See *Arghūl.*

Arghūl el-soghaīr (Arabia; Middle East). See *Arghūl.*

Arghun (Arabia). Organ; bagpipe. Cf. *Arghanūn*.
Lit.: no. 255.

Argūl (Arabia). See *Arghūl.*

Ari (Uganda—Lugbwara). Drum.
Lit.: no. 255.

Ari (New Guinea). Bamboo slit tube; the slit is lengthwise and the player causes it to vibrate by blowing against it and creating a rattling sound.
Lit.: nos. 84, 190.

Äris (written: *arisun*) (Mongolia). "Hide"; the hide that covers both sides of the *tologhä.*
Lit.: no. 61.

Arisun (Mongolia). See *Äris.*

Arja (Bali). (1) Pentatonic tone material, not always distinct whether *pelog* or *slendro*: C♯ D E G♯ A or C♯ D♯ E♯ G♯ A. (2) The term is applied also to several scales (*saih angklung*). (3) *Arja* can also refer to a popular musical comedy of considerable variety.
Lit.: no. 197.

Arkavardhanī (South India). *Janya rāga* of the 28th *mēḷa* (*Harikāmbhōji*).
Tone material:

C D E F G c
c B♭ A G F E C

Lit.: no. 139.

Arnaba (Egypt). The spike fiddle (*kamānjah*) of modern Egypt.
Lit.: no. 68.

Aro (Nigeria—Yoruba). Ring-formed iron rattles or cymbals.
Lit.: no. 255.

Aroba (East New Guinea—Roro). Song performed without the accompaniment of the drum.

Ārōha (*Ārōhaṇa*) (India). (1) The ascending form of the scale. (2) See *Gamaka.*
Lit.: no. 138.

Ārōhaṇa (India). See *Ārōha.*

A-rōko (plural: *ma-rōko*) (Sierra Leone—Temne). Drumstick.
Lit.: no. 255.

Ar-req (Egypt). Frame drum. See *Req.*
Lit.: no. 100.

Ārshabhī (*ārṣabhī*) (India). Old name of the second degree of a heptatonic scale. The present name is *rishabha* (*ṛṣabha*).
Lit.: no. 261.

Arub (South Africa—Bergdama). Wooden pot-shaped drum beaten with the thumbs when the village medicine man is called to come and cure sickness.
Lit.: nos. 151, 190.

'Arūḍ (Arabia). Poetic, textual meter.
Lit.: no. 70.

Arudi (South India). A note that usually appears at the end (rarely at the beginning) of a *pallavi* and *anupallavi.*
Lit.: no. 261.

Aruḷ Taṇḍavam (South India). Benediction dance performed by devotees of Shiva.
Lit.: no. 261.

Arum-aruman (Bali). Several musical items of quiet character used in *gender wayang* performances. These items, allegedly derived from the *kekawin* songs, were used in serious religious services.
Lit.: no. 197.

Aruṇa Chandrikā (South India). *Janya rāga* of the 22nd *mēḷa* (*Kharaharapriyā*).
Tone materials:
(a) C E♭ F G B♭ c
c B♭ G A G F E♭ D C
(b) C D E♭ G B♭ c
c B♭ G F E♭ C
Lit.: no. 139.

Aruṇagiri (South India). *Janya rāga* of the 64th *mēḷa* (*Vāchaspati*).
Tone material:
C D E F♯ A c
c A F♯ E D C
Lit.: no. 139.

Aruṇajvalita (South India). *Janya rāga* of the 59th *mēḷa* (*Dharmavatī*).
Tone material:
C D E♭ F♯ A B c
c B A G F♯ E♭ D C
Lit.: no. 139.

Aruṇakāntam (South India). *Janya rāga* of the 28th *mēḷa* (*Harikāmbhōji*).
Tone material:
C D F G F A B♭ c
c B♭ A G F A F E D C
Lit.: no. 139.

Aruṇakriya (South India). *Janya rāga* of the 57th *mēḷa* (*Siṃhendramadhyama*).
Tone material:
C D F♯ G B c
c B A♭ G F♯ E♭ D C
Lit.: no. 139.

Aruṇāmbari (South India). *Janya rāga* of the 38th *mēḷa* (*Jalārṇava*).
Tone material:
C D♭ E♭♭ F♯ G A♭ B♭ c
c A♭ B♭ G A♭ F♯ E♭♭ D♭ C
Lit.: no. 139.

A-runu (Sierra Leone – Temne). Drum.
Lit.: no. 255.

Arupepe (Uganda – Karamojong). Side-blown straight or conical wooden trumpet.
Lit.: no. 190.

Arusaram (South India). An instrument with six strings (according to Lit. no. 261).

Aṣāb' (*Aṣabi'*) (Old Arabia). "Fingers." The old eight finger modes in *'ud* playing. They were referred to in music theoretical works before the 11th century. The following are the finger modes of Ibn Misjah (ca. 715):

1. *Muṭlaq fī majrā al-wuṣtā*:
   G A B♭ C D E F G
2. *Muṭlaq fī majrā al-binṣir*:
   G A B C D E F G
3. *Sabbāba fī majrā al-wuṣtā*:
   A B♭ C D E F G A
4. *Sabbāba fī majrā al-binṣir*:
   A B C D E F G A
5. *Wuṣtā fī majrāhā*:
   B♭ C D E F G A B♭
6. *Binṣir fī majrāhā*:
   B C D E F G A B
7. *Khinṣir fī majrā al-wuṣtā*:
   C D E♭ F G A B c
8. *Khinṣir fī majrā al-binṣir*:
   C D E F G A B c

Lit.: nos. 66, 76.

Aṣābi' (Arabia). See *Aṣāb'*.

Asafo (Ghana – Ewe). Royal dancing and drumming performed by men only.
Lit.: no. 128.

Aṣafi zūrnā (Turkey). "Asaph's shawm," an obscure wind instrument. Cf. *Wazīrlī zūrnā.* Lit.: no. 81.

Asakasaka (Nigeria—Ibo). Rattles. Cf. *Shaq-shaq.*
Lit.: nos. 95, 190.

Asambāda (South India). *Janya rāga* of the 29th *mēḷa (Dhīraśaṅkarāṇam).*
Tone material:
C D C F G A B A c
c B A G F E C D C
Lit.: no. 139.

A-sámbori (Sierra Leone—Temne). Drum.
Lit.: no. 255.

Asampūrṇa (India). Scale forms that are not *sampūrṇa* (heptatonic) and consist either of less than seven tones within the octave, and/or have one or more *vakra* (zig-zag) features that distort the straight step-by-step basic scale character. Cf. *Apūrṇa.*
Lit.: no. 261.

Asampūrṇa mēḷarāgas (with *kaṭapayādi* prefixes) (South India). See South Indian *Rāgas*; list of *Mēḷas.*

Asampūrṇa mēḷaragas (without *kaṭapayādi* prefixes) (India). See South Indian *Rāgas*; list of *Mēḷas.*

Asa-ori (Japan—Tendai sect.). A *kyōkusetzu.* The feature consists of a sequence of four rising notes followed by a sharp drop of the interval of a sixth, concluded with another rise of (about) four notes. Cf. *Kyōkusetzu.*

Asati (South India). *Janya rāga* of the 59th *mēḷa (Dharmavatī).*
Tone material:
C E♭ F♯ A B c
c B A F♯ E♭ C
Lit.: no. 139.

Āsāvari (*Rāga*) (North India). *Rāga* derived from the *Āsāvari thāta.* Two types of this *rāga* are in use: one with D♭ and the other with D-natural.
Tone material:
(a) C D♭ F G A♭ c
c B♭ A♭ G F E♭ D♭ C
(b) C D F G A♭ c
c B♭ A♭ G F E♭ D C; *Vādis*: A♭, E♭
Lit.: no. 138.

Āsāvari-bhairav (North India). See *Jivan-bhairav.*

Āsāvari thāta (North India). Cf. *Thāta.*

Āsāvēri (South India). *Janya rāga* of the 8th *mēḷa (Hanumattoḍi).*
Tone material:
C D♭ F G A♭ c
c B♭ A♭ G F E♭ D♭ C
(or: c B♭ c G A♭ G E♭ D♭ C)
A second form of this *rāga*, called *Āsāvēri tōḍi*, is:
C D♭ F G A♭ B♭ c
c B♭ A♭ G F E♭ D♭ C
Lit.: no. 139.

Āsāvēri Tōḍi (South India). See *Āsāvēri.*

Aṣba' (Arabia). Melodic mode. Cf. *Aṣab'.*
Lit.: no. 70.

Aṣbu'ayn (Modern Tunisia). *Maqām.*
Tone material:
D E♭ F♯ G A B♭ c♯ d e f
Lit.: no. 64.

A'sfūr (Arabia). Peg with a disk-shaped handle, ornamented with buttons.
Lit.: no. 255.

Ash (Bengal). See *Mīnd.*

Ashirai (Japan). A number of motives, brief tunes used by the *noh* flute. These short features are traditional and serve to demonstrate to the chorus the required pitch.
Lit.: no. 185.

'Ashirān (*'Ushayrān*) (Arabia). Tone name of the second main note of the basic scale. (A list of all tone names can be seen under the heading of *Jagā* [*Yagā*].)

'Ashirān (Arabia). "The one with ten notes." An art-*maqām* little known in Syria and almost unknown in Egypt. Its scale is the same as that of *Ḥusēni*, but is used an octave lower. The range is a tenth.
   Maqām 'Ashirān can begin with the first, fourth, eighth, and eleventh notes of its scale. If it ends with the fourth or eighth notes it is called *'Ashirān ka-duga* or *'Ashirān kar-husēni*.
The scale is:
   A B♭ C D E♭ F G A B♭ c d
Lit.: no. 121.

'Ashirān kar-duga (Arabia). *Maqām.* See *'Ashirān.*

'Ashirān kar-Ḥusēni (Arabia). *Maqām.* See *'Ashirān.*

Ashta daśāṅguḷa (India). Flute with seven finger holes.
Lit.: no. 263.

Ashta Gaṇas (South India). Theoretically there are eight *gaṇas* (groups) of syllables employed in the metrical structures of verses. Each *gaṇa* consists of three *angas* (limbs). Each *anga* represents either a long or a short syllable shown below as a L or S.
The eight *gaṇas*:

ma gaṇa	L L L	*na gaṇa*	S S S
bha gaṇa	L S S	*ya gaṇa*	S L L
ja gaṇa	S L S	*ra gaṇa*	L S L
sa gaṇa	S S L	*ta gaṇa*	L L S

Lit.: no. 261.

Ashṭakam (South India). Song consisting of eight strophes.
Lit.: no. 261.

Ashṭamurti (*Aṣṭamurti*) (South India). *Janya rāga* of the 36th *mēḷa* (*Chalanāṭa*).
Tone material:
   C E D♯ F G B A♯ c
   c B A♯ F B F E D♯ C
Lit.: no. 139.

Ashṭavādam (*Aṣṭavādam*) (South India). *Janya rāga* of the 20th *mēḷa* (*Naṭabhairavī*).
Tone material:
   C F G A♭ B♭ c
   c B♭ A♭ G F C
Lit.: no. 139.

Ashṭi (*Aṣṭi*) (South India). *Janya rāga* of the 24th *mēḷa* (*Varuṇapriyā*).
Tone material:
   C E♭ F A♯ B c
   c B A♯ F E♭ C
Lit.: no. 139.

Ashṭōttaraśata tālas (South India). A system of 108 rhythmic modes (*tālas*). Cf. *Ashṭa gaṇas.*
Lit.: no. 261.

Ashyk (Turkey). Cf. *Sha'er.*

Asiko (Nigeria — Yoruba). Large rectangular frame drum with one head. Two smaller drums, called *samba*, accompany the *asiko*.
Lit.: no. 190.

Asik Saz (Turkey). Lute with nine strings which are plucked with a plectrum.
Lit.: no. 32.

As-it (Ancient Egypt). Double flute (or clarinet).
Lit.: no. 190.

Asmarandana (Java). One of the poetic meters of *tembang machapat* generally occurring in love songs. See *Machapat.*
Lit.: no. 163.

Asmari (Ethiopia – Shoa Province). Spike fiddle with one horsehair-string. See *Cherewata*.
Lit.: no. 38.

Asobi-daiko (Japan). Childrens' tambourin with one head and a handle.
Lit.: no. 255.

Asok (Congo; Cameroun – Pangwa). Tube rattle used as a toy.
Lit.: no. 255.

Asokoben (Ghana – Ashanti). Ivory horn.
Lit.: no. 95.

Asopi (Sumatra). See *Hapetan*.
Lit.: no. 255.

'Asor (Ancient Israel). "Ten." Obscure zither with ten strings (mentioned in Psalm 92).
Lit.: no. 250.

Āśrita Rañjani (South India). *Janya rāga* of the 67th *mēḷa* (*Sucharitra*).
Tone material:
C D♯ E F♯ G B𝄫 c
c B𝄫 A♭ G F♯ E D♯ C
Lit.: no. 139.

Aṣ-sāgat (Egypt). Pairs of little metal castanets.
Lit.: no. 100.

Assa muta'chatī (Algeria). Rattle that accompanies dances. It has a long, saber-shaped wooden handle with shells attached to it.
Lit.: no. 255.

Assogui (Gabon Republic; Congo – Ndasa; Mbamba). Basketwork work rattle used for accompanying dances during the circumcision rites.
Lit.: no. 280.

Astai (India). See *Asthāyī*; *Sthāyī*.

Aṣṭamūrti (South India). See *Ashṭamūrti*.

Aṣṭavādam (South India). See *Ashṭavādam*.

Asthāyī (*Asati*) (North India). See *Sthāyī*.

Aṣṭi (South India). See *Ashṭi*.

Aṣṭūkhūsiyya (Arabia). A music theorist.
Lit.: no. 70.

Astuti (Nepal). Hindu prayer song.
Lit.: no. 133.

Asukusuk (Uganda – Teso). Wooden trumpet.
Lit.: no. 302.

Asure gīt (Nepal). Song sung during Ashar, the months of June and July.
Lit.: no. 133.

Aśvakrāntā (India). The sixth of the seven ancient *murchhanās* of the *sa grāma*.
Lit.: no. 261.

Asvār (plural of *sūr*) (Iran). See *Sūr*.
Lit.: no. 255.

Aśva tāna (South India). A *tāna* form in which sequences of seven notes are frequented.
Lit.: no. 261.

Aṣwat (singular: *ṣaut*) (Arabia). Ancient term for verses set to music and accompanied by a single instrument.
Lit.: no. 70.

Āṭa (*Yakshagāna*). Dance drama.
Lit.: no. 261.

Āṭa (India). A paste consisting of flour and water applied to the tuned heads of *mṛdangas* and *tablas* for tuning purposes. Cf. *Tabla* (see *Gila āṭa*; *Aipan*).
Lit.: no. 136.

A-tābale (Sierra Leone – Temne). Cf. *Atabule*; *Atbal*.
Lit.: no. 255.

Atabule (Sierra Leone – Yela). An hourglass-shaped drum assigned to one of the rulers.
Lit.: no. 255.

Atāget (Uganda—Elgumi). Drum.
Lit.: no. 255.

Ata Lepa (Flores). Working song sung by the leader and followed or joined by a chorus of workers when new covering is placed on the roof of a house.
Lit.: no. 166.

A-tama (Sierra Leone—Temne). Small hour-glass shaped drum.
Lit.: no. 255.

Atāmo (Ethiopia). Popular tambourin with jingles in various sizes, used to accompany dances. The drum is also used to keep persons awake who had to drink human urine as medicine against the bite of the snake ebab.
Lit.: nos. 102, 218, 255.

Atari-gane (Japan). Small brass gong, beaten with a mallet and used in folk performances and *kabuki.*
Lit.: no. 185.

At asi (Ghana—Ewe). See *Atupani.*

Atasi (India). Wandering beggar.

Āṭa tāla (India). See *Tāla* (South India).
Lit.: no. 136.

Ātata-tsaṅ (Burma). Drum; closed on one end.
Lit.: no. 255.

Ātata-witata (Burma). Drum, with both ends closed.
Lit.: no. 255.

Āt atsu (Ghana). See *Atupani.*

Aṭbal (plural of *ṭabil*) (Arabia). Drum with two heads.
Lit.: no. 255.

Ateba (*tauwi*) (Bismarck Arch.; New Mecklenburg—St. Mathias). Shell horn.
Lit.: no. 255.

Ategawa (Japan). Deerskin protection that covers the hand of the *ōtsuzumi* player. Cf. *Yubikawa.*
Lit.: no. 185.

Atele (Nigeria). See *Dundun*; *Bembe.*

Aṭhāṇa (South India). *Janya rāga* of the 29th *mēḷa* (*Dhīraśaṅkarābharaṇam*).
Tone material:
C D F G B c
c B A G F G E D C (c B A G F E D C)
Variants:
F G E♭ F G
G A A B♭ B♭ c
G A B♭ G
Lit.: no. 139.

Ati- (India). "Very" (e.g., *atitīvra*, "very sharp"). See *Tīvra.*

Ati kōmal (India). "Very flat" (e.g., *dha kōmaḷ* [A♭] and *dha ati kōmaḷ* [A♭̣]). Neither North nor South Indian notations use any symbols for *ati tīvra* and *ati kōmaḷ*. In South Indian notation there are no indications for semitonal and microtonal alterations. The performing musician is expected to know these features. See *Tīvra.*
Lit.: no. 136.

Atisvārya (*Ṣaṣṭha*; *Antya*) (Vedic India). In the notation of the Vedic chant (*sāma*) the lowest note is notated with "6." Cf. Lit. nos. 141, 261.

Atīta eḍuppu (South India). See *Eḍuppu.*
Lit.: no. 261.

Atīta graha (South India). A piece of music in which the melody begins earlier than the *avarta* of the drummer; similar to a western upbeat feature.
Lit.: no. 261.

Atnach (Ancient Israel). A notational symbol used in biblical chant. It indicates a strong disjunctive function.
Lit.: no. 309.

Atodya (Ancient India). Musical instruments.

Atoke (Ghana – Ewe). Iron gongs (high or low in pitch) in the shape of small boats, played with nails.
Lit.: no. 174.

Atoros (Uganda – Toro). Wooden trumpet. Cf. *Asukusuk*.
Lit.: no. 302.

Atouta (Japan). The closing song of a *jiuta* (*kumiuta*) cycle. The opening song is the *maeuta*, the interlude played on the *koto* is the *tegoto*, and the closing song the *atouta*.
Lit.: no. 185.

Atsia (Ghana). See *Agbadza*.

Atsiagbekor (Ghana – Ewe). Social dance (originally a war dance). It is accompanied by five drums, gongs, and 3-6 rattles. The drums are: *wuga*, *kroboto*, *totogi*, *kidi*, *kaganu*, *ganhogui* (double gong), *axatse* (rattle).
Lit.: no. 215.

Atsimevu (Ghana – Ewe). Long barrel drum beaten with two sticks. Cf. *Soga*; *Kidi*; *Kaganu*.
Lit.: no. 218.

Atsuma asobi (Japan). See *Azuma asobi*.

Atsuma fue (*Azuma fuye*) (Japan). Cf. *Yamato bue* (*fue*); *Koma bue*.
Lit.: no. 255.

Atsuma koto (Japan). See *Azuma koto*.
Lit.: no. 255.

At-taḥmīla (*Al-iftitaḥ*) (Egypt). Musical prelude; overture.
Lit.: no. 100.

Āṭṭakatha (South India; Kerala). Dance play. Synonym for *kathakali*.
Lit.: no. 123.

Āṭṭam (South India). Dance.

At-Taqsīm (Egypt). Composition in free form.
Lit.: no. 100.

Atuamba (Congo – Bapere). Bull roarer used at the circumcision rite.
Lit.: no. 29.

Atukpani (Ghana – Ewe). Drum. Cf. *Atupani*.

Atumpan (Ghana – Ashanti). See *Atupani*.

Atungblan (*Atumpan*) (Ivory Coast – Baule). Pair of drums (talking drums).

Atupani (Ghana – Ewe). The big speaking drums, used in pairs. The two drums are called:
1. *At atsu*, the male drum.
2. *At asi*, the female drum.

The Ashanti people call these drums *ntumpani*.
Lit.: no. 255.

A-turma (Sierra Leone – Temne). Small horn.
Lit.: no. 255.

Atvur (Indonesia – Kai Isl.). Shell trumpet. Also called *tewur*.
Lit.: nos. 156, 162.

A-tyang (Korea). See *A-chaeng*.

'Au (Solomon Isl.; Malaita). "Bamboo." Musical instrument made of bamboo.
Lit.: no. 318.

Auḍava (*Oḍava*) (India; Sanskrit). A set of five; pentatonic scale. *Auḍava-sampurna* (India). *Rāga* with five tones in ascent (*aroha*) and seven tones in descent (*avaroha*). *Auḍava-shadava*; *rāga* with five tones in ascent and six tones in descent.

Audd (Morocco – Rif Pirates). An *'ud* (lute) instrument. Cf. *Gnbrī*.
Lit.: no. 255.

Aufeda (Celebes – Sulawesi Prov.). Rattle; a bamboo stick split at its end.
Lit.: no. 254.

Auǧ (Arabia; Middle East). See *'Auj.*

A-ugāgueng (New Guinea). Flute.
Lit.: no. 255.

'Auj (Arabia). Name of a main tone an octave higher than *'irāq*, hence the tone is also named *'auj 'irāq* (in Persian the name *auk* means "the higher one"). (A list of all tone names and notes through two octaves can be seen under the heading of *Jagā* [*Yagā*].)
Lit.: no. 121.

'Auj (Arabia; Egypt). *Maqām.* The note *'auj* is the same as the note *'iraq*, but when intoned an octave higher, it is interpreted as an (upper) e flat while the lower note e (*'auj*) is flat only microtonally: (♭)E.

Idelssohn (Lit. no. 121, pp. 38-39) reports that Darwish Muhammed does not mention this *maqām*, but quotes a [similar] *maqām Ḥizam-a-Siga* instead; its scale is:

♭E F G A♭ ♭B c d e♭

Sub-modes of *'auj* are:

1. *'Auj-ara*
2. *Faraḥnak*
3. *Bosta-nagar.*

'Auj-'ara (*'Awj-'ara*) (Arabia). "The highest splendor"; Sub-*maqām* of *'auj*:

♭*B* C D♯ ♭E F♯ G A♯ ♭B c♯ d (c d♯)

Lit.: nos. 64, 121.

Auk (Persia). See *'Auj* (*Auǧ*).

Auk-pyan (Burma). Cf. *Chauk-pauk auk-pyan.*

Auravasheyapriya (South India). *Janya rāga* of the 1st *mēḷa* (*Kanakangi*).
Tone material:

C D♭ G A♭ B♭♭ c

c B♭♭ A♭ G D♭ C

Lit.: no. 139.

Autār (*Awtār*) (Arabia). Seven double strings of the *'ud.*
Lit.: no. 255.

Auwi Kakueng (New Mecklenburg). "The ripe woman"; a long flute used at circumcision ceremonies. Its pitch can be changed by moving a stopper inside the flute, but no melody can be played. Only the sounds of a "howling monster" are produced that are supposed to frighten the women.
Lit.: no. 255.

Avagraha (India). "Separation." A notational symbol placed within the textual line indicating sung notes usually held across beats where no specific textual syllables are required.
Lit.: no. 136.

Avamṛṣta (Ancient India). One of the old 10 basic ways of touching *vīṇā* strings (*dhatu*).
Lit.: no. 292.

Avanaddha (India). General term for drums.
Lit.: no. 261.

Avanaddha kutapa (Ancient India). See *Kutapa.*

Avanaddha vādya (South India). Drum with one head.
Lit.: no. 261.

Avanji (South India). Drum; its head covered with cowskin.
Lit.: no. 261.

Āvarōha(ṇa) (India). Descending motion; descending scale.

Āvarta (India). Fixed group of measures (*vibhāga*) which is repeated throughout the composition. Cf. *Tāla.*
Lit.: no. 136.

Avāzat (Arabia). Term of Persian origin denoting secondary modes (sub-*maqām* forms).
Lit.: no. 76.

Avelevu (Ghana—Ewe). One of the seven dances of Yeve, the god of thunder. (The names of the other six dances are listed under the heading of *Husago.*)

Avikruta svara (India). See *Achala svara.*
Lit.: no. 261.

Avodah (Ancient Israel). Vocal interpolation to the Report concerning the Temple Service.
Lit.: no. 12.

Awaseru (Japan). "To put together," "to harmonize." The term is used in *koto* music if the player performs an additional note to the melody note, thus creating an effect of harmony. Several intervals may occur: octaves, sevenths and sixths. When octaves are used, the upper note is called *kan*, the lower *ryo.*
Lit.: no. 225.

Āwāz (Persia). (1) Song; also general term for art music of Iran. At present *āwāz* is the vocal part that follows the first (instrumental) section, the *pīshdarāmad* of the *dastgāh.* (2) *Āwāz* (*naghmeh*). Derived, subordinated, and related melody types. Cf. *Dastgāh.*
Lit.: no. 146.

Awe (Sudan). Horn.
Lit.: no. 95.

Awi; awi-awi (Bali). To create music, text, and dance.
Lit.: no. 197.

Awis (*Hawis*) (Java). Cf. *Arang.*
Lit.: no. 163.

'Awj (Arabia). See *'Auj.*

'Awj-'ārā (Middle East; Modern Egypt). See *'Auj-'ārā.*

Awtār (Arabia). See *Autār.*

Awunene (Uganda – Teso). Ground bow; used as a toy.
Lit.: no. 190.

'Awwāda (North Africa – Berber). Flute; used in performing magic.

Awzan (Arabia). Measures; bars.

Axatse (Ghana – Ewe). Calabash rattle.
Lit.: no. 128.

A-yābi (Sierra Leone – Temne). Horn; pipe.
Lit.: no. 255.

Ayak-ayakan (Java). A *gending lampeh* form. The word indicates the regular shaking of a sieve to and fro. There are two types:
1. *Ayak-ayakan tamban*, the slow one.
2. *Ayak-ayakan seseg*, the faster one.

Both rhythmical patterns accompany (e.g.) the beginning and end of a *wayang* performance.
Lit.: no. 163.

Ayak-ayakan seseg (Java). See *Ayak-ayakan.*

Ayak-ayakan tamban (Java). See *Ayak-ayakan.*

Ayam sepenan(g) (Java). "The isolated chicken." See *Gending koḍok ngorek ayam sepenan(g).*
Lit.: no. 163.

Ayāqlī kemām (Turkey). "Foot-fiddle"; identical with the *kemanje a' jūz.*
Lit.: no. 255.

Ayasse (South New Guinea – Marind Anim). Song of the headhunters.

Ayasugi (Japan). Herringbone carvings carved into the inside of *koto* and *shamisen* in order to enhance the tone.
Lit.: no. 185.

Ayatsuri-ningyo (Japan). Puppets used in common (simple) shows.
Lit.: no. 185.

Ayi (Ghana – West Ewe). Term for small drum.
Lit.: no. 190.

Āyin (Turkey). Religious vocal and instrumental piece (cf. *Ezan*) that presents four times the *selām* (greeting). It is preceded by the *ezan*, *mevlid*, *nait*, and *peşrev*. The *āyin* is followed by *yürüksemai*, a short concluding *peşrev*.

Āyittam (*Ākshīptīka*) (South India). Introductory part of the *ālāp*.
Lit.: no. 261.

'Āyyār (Somali Republic). Dance song (performed by women).
Lit.: no. 98.

Ayyūb būrūsī (Turkey). "Job's cornet." A wind instrument of the 17th century, made of reed. According to Lit. no. 81 it may have been the *nāy-i chādūr*, a favorite wind instrument of the Turks.

Azān (Afghanistan). Koran cantillation.

Aẕān (Iraq). See *Adhān* (Arabia).

Azē broshim (Ancient Israel). Probably wooden rattles.
Lit.: no. 12.

'Azf (Arabia). Ancient string instruments.

Azibwasi (Congo—Azande). Rattle made of fruitshells, worn by dancers tied around their ankles.
Lit.: no. 184.

Azoe (Dahomey Republic). Flute.
Lit.: no. 255.

Azu lahe (Madagascar). Drum.
Lit.: no. 255.

Azuma asobi (*Atsuma asobi*) (Japan). Ancient, very sacred dance in Shinto music, dating back to the 8th century. It was performed at the spring and autumn equinoxes. Its instrumental ensemble consisted of *wagon* (*yamato goto*), *kagura bue*, *hichiriki*, and *shakubyoshi*. It was the ambition of every temple musician to play in the *azuma asobi*. Another important (female) dance in Shinto music was the *shirabyoshi*, performed to the singing of *imayo*.
Lit.: no. 185.

Azuma-fuye (Japan). See *Yamato bue*.

Azuma koto (Japan). "Eastern *koto*" with three strings. Inside the flat corpus were strung loosely three wires which produced light vibrations when the instrument was played.
Lit.: no. 225.

Az-zummārah (Egypt). Clarinet type.
Lit.: no. 100.

B

Baaseree (Java). Beak flute. See *Bānsulī*.

Baba (East Flores). A one-string tubular bamboo zither called *go weto* (*go beto*) in Nagé of Ngada and *bemu nggri-nggo* (*tinding*) in the Manggaray. The zither is made by loosening a part of the outer layer of the bamboo stick (closed at both ends) and by inserting a bridge below the loosened layer section.
Lit.: no. 163.

Baba (Sierra Leone). Metal clappers.

Babad (Bali). Skin used to cover the belly of the *rebāb* (of Java).
Lit.: no. 197.

Babakungbu (Congo). Ground bow.
Lit.: no. 176.

Babakungu (Congo). See *Babakungbu*.

Babaling (Malaysia). See *Berbaling*.

Babandi (*Pahawang*) (Southeast Borneo—Dayak). Gong.
Lit.: no. 176.

Babarangan (Bali; Lombok; Madura). *Bonang*-shaped instrument consisting of a range of small bronze gong kettles placed horizontally and tuned one octave higher than the *trompong*.
Lit.: no. 163.

Babhu (Nepal). A pair of small thin cymbals.

Babon (Nepal). See *Babhu*.
Lit.: no. 46.

Babon (Indonesia; South Borneo; Banjermasin). The first note of the *slendro* system (of Banjermasin). Cf. *Slendro*, Table C.
Lit.: no. 163.

Babon ing laras (Java). The tone that stands a fifth below the *dasar*.
Lit.: no. 163.

Bac (South Vietnam). "North." Modal system (*dieu*); representing various moods by shifting the names of scale degrees: *hoi bac* (joyful mood); *hoi quang* (fantastic mood); *hoi nhac* (solemn mood); *hoi xuan* (serene mood); *hoi ai* (melancholy mood); *hoi dao* (solemn mood; appears also in the *nam* system); *hoi oan* (*dieu oan*; sad mood).

The Vietnamese word *dieu* has the same significance as the Chinese *tiao* ("to harmonize"). The following list illustrates some of the Vietnamese scales. The ringed-in notes are stressed:

Bac
Ⓒ D . Ⓕ Ⓖ A . c
Nhac
C Ⓓ F G Ⓐ c
Sap (cheo)
C Ⓓ F Ⓖ A c
Nam (Hue)
Ⓒ D Ⓕ Ⓖ B♭ c
Nam (South Vietnam)
Ⓒ E♭ Ⓕ Ⓖ B♭ c
Oan (South Vietnam)
Ⓒ E♭ Ⓕ Ⓖ B♭ c
Vong co (South Vietnam)
Ⓒ E Ⓕ Ⓖ A♭ c
Nam ai (Hue)
Ⓒ D♭ Ⓕ Ⓖ A♭ c
Ho ai day (Hue)
Ⓒ D♭ Ⓕ Ⓖ A♭ c
Sa mac (North Vietnam)
Ⓒ Ⓔ♭ F Ⓖ B♭ c

For tone syllables see *Ho*. Cf. *Nam*.
Lit.: no. 297.

Bachi (Japan). Plectrum used in playing *koto*, *biwa*, and *shamisen*. The term is also used for drumsticks.
Lit.: no. 185.

Bachigawa (Japan). A protective patch placed on the *shamisen* in order to avoid scratches caused by the *bachi*.
Lit.: no. 185.

Badaga Koḍu (India). Kotar term for the *Rāṇaśṛṅga*.

Badalik (East Turkestan). Cf. *Sochiba*.

Badaniyah (*Dawr*) (Arabia). See *Muwashaḥ*.

Badari (South India). *Janya rāga* of the 26th *mēḷa* (*Chārukeśī*).
Tone material:
C D E G A♭ c
c A♭ G B♭ G F E D C
Lit.: no. 139.

Badarika (South India). *Janya rāga* of the 51st *mēḷa* (*Kāmavardhanī*).
Tone material:
C D♭ E F♯ G F♯ B A♭ B c
c B A♭ E D♭ C
Lit.: no. 139.

Badh (North India). Cf. *Tabla*.

Badhauns-sarang (North India). Subordinate *rāga* to the *Kafi thāta* (some theorists ascribe this raga to the *Khamaj* or *Bilaval thātas*).
Tone material:
C D F A B♭ (B) c
c B♭ (A) G F D C
Lit.: no. 138.

Badut (Indonesia; Sunda District). An orchestra with nine *angklungs*, one to four *ḍogḍogs* and one *tarompet*. During the performance the musicians perform the most whimsical dances.
Lit.: no. 163.

Bagah (*Bajah*) (North India). Monochord (stick zither). See *tuila*.
Lit.: no. 254.

Baganā (*Beg*) (Ethiopia). A large, rectangular, only occasionally round, kithara with 10 strings tuned in pairs in octaves. It is played with a plectrum. Cf. *Bangia*; *Begana*.
Lit.: no. 255.

Bagannā (Egypt; Ethiopia; Coptic). See *Baganā*

Bagazege (Congo – Ababua). Rattle consisting of two gourds.
Lit.: no. 255.

Bagele (Congo). Bell with handle.
Lit.: no. 255.

Bāgēsari-Bahar (South India). *Janya rāga* of the 9th *mēḷa* (*Dhēnuka*).
Tone material:
C D♭ E♭ F G B c
c d♭ c B G F E♭ D♭ C
Lit.: no. 139.

Bageshri (*Vageshvari*) (North India). Subordinate *rāga* of the *Kafi thāta*.
Tone material:
C E♭ F (G) A B♭ c
c B♭ A (G) F E♭ D C; *Vādis*: F, C
Lit.: no. 138.

Bageshri-Kanada (North India). Subordinate *rāga* of the *Kafi thāta*. The *rāga* is rare. Its tone material shows combinations of scales of *Darbari-Kanada* and *Bageshri*.
For instance:
C D E♭ F G B♭ c
c B♭ A F D C; *Vādis*: F, C
Lit.: no. 138.

Bāgēśvari (South India). *Janya rāga* of the 28th *mēḷa* (*Harikāmbhōji*).
Tone material:
C E F G A B♭ c
c B (B♭) A G F E D C
Lit.: no. 139.

Baggay (West Pakistan; Baluchistan). Solo improvisation on the *saroz* (*sarod*).

Bagha dewkhe (written: *baga tebke*) (Mongolia). "The little bridge" of the *khil khuur*. This little bridge is placed on the neck rather close and below the *Darabch* (written: *darubchi*). From there the strings are strung to the *yikhe dewkhe*, the "big bridge."
Lit.: no. 61.

Baghdadi (Syria). *Maqām*. See *Raḥat-il-arawaḥ* (of Egypt).

Baghlama (*Bağlama*) (Arabia; Turkey). *Tanbur* with four to six wire strings and 16 frets. The instrument with four strings is tuned E D A G.
Lit.: no. 255.

Bagili (Nilotic Sudan—Congo; Basiri). Musical bow. A small *nzolo* is attached to its upper end.
Lit.: no. 184.

Baglama (*Bajlama*) (Turkey—Anatolia, Caucasus). A medium-sized *saz* with six strings tuned in pairs and played with a plectrum. Cf. *Tanbur baglama*.
Lit.: no. 255.

Bagur (Flores). Dance.
Lit.: no. 166.

Bagyendanwa (Uganda—Ankole). Sacred drum.
Lit.: no. 218.

Bah (Java). Drum word. Cf. *Deng*; *Bem*.

Bahaduri-tōḍi (North India). Rare *rāga* subordinated to the *Tōḍi thāta*.
Tone material:
C *B* D♭ C D♭ E♭ F♯ G A♭ B c
c B A♭ G F♯ (E♭) D♭ C; *Vādis*: A♭, E♭
Several variants are possible such as one with B, the other with *tōḍi* material and deleting the note G.
Lit.: no. 138.

Bahar (North India). Subordinated *rāga* to the *Kafi thāta*.
Tone material:
C E♭ F G (A) B c
c B♭ A G F E♭ (d C); *Vādis*: F, C
Rāga Bahar is frequently employed in combination with other *rāgas*. North Indian musicians create combined features, *hindol-bahar*, *adana-bahar*, *vasant-bahar*, *bhairav-bahar*, and others illustrate this method.
Lit.: no. 138.

Bahiri (India; Hindu-Javanese). (1) Gong. (2) Ancient, obscure drum type.
Lit.: no. 166.

Bahortsañ (Burma). Big palace-drum, beaten every three hours.
Lit.: no. 255.

Bahudāmani (South India). *Janya rāga* of the 51st *mēḷa* (*Kāmavardhanī*).
Tone material:
C E D♭ E F♯ G A♭ B c
c B A♭ F♯ E D♭ C
Lit.: no. 139.

Bahudāri (South India). *Janya rāga* of the 28th *mēḷa* (*Harikāmbhōji*).
Tone material:
C E F G A B♭ c
c B♭ G F E C
Lit.: no. 139.

Bahula (South India). *Janya rāga* of the 71st *mēḷa* (*Kōsala*).
Tone material:
C D♯ F♯ B A B c
c B A G F♯ D♯ C
Lit.: no. 139.

Bahula prayōga (India). A phrase frequently used in a *rāga*. Its opposite, a phrase rarely used, is *kvachit prayōga*.
Lit.: no. 261.

Bahumāriṇi (South India). *Janya rāga* of the 46th *mēḷa* (*Śaḍvidhamārgiṇī*).
Tone material:
C D♭ E♭ F♯ A B♭ c
c B♭ A F♯ E♭ D♭ C
Lit.: no. 139.

Bahutva (India). "Muchness." One or more notes (and passages) that have to be used frequently in a *rāga* in order to establish its characteristic mood.
Lit.: no. 261.

Bāhyā (North India). A small drum; related to *banya*.
Lit.: no. 261.

Bai (*Bombai*) (Japan). (1) Buddhist chant with Sanskrit (or Pali) texts. See *Kansan*. Cf. *Shōmyō*. (2) Reciters; chanters of *Shōmyō*. At the "Great Buddha's Opening of Eyes" Festival at the Todai temple in A.D. 752, there were 10 *Bai* who recited, 200 who danced, and 200 who waved sticks.
Lit.: no. 185.

Bairāgā (India). An iron stick rattle, of which one end is bent into a fork. The other end has the traditional endplate that prevents the rattling rings from falling off. Similar rattles (all sistrum types) are the *dara* of Kashmir and the ancient *khakkara* of Central Asia.
Lit.: no. 254.

Bai-so (Korea). See *So*. Cf. *P'ai hsiao* (of China).

Bait (Arabia). Stanza; verse of a song.
Lit.: no. 76.

Bajah (Orissa; Chhota Nagpur). Primitive stick zither with a single string. Cf. *Bagah*. Cf. also *Tuila*; *Tohila*.

Bajānā-śruti (South India). Bagpipe made of goatskin. The pipe has a heterophonic beating reed mouthpiece. The instrument is favored by snake charmers.
Lit.: no. 254.

Bajang (*Kerek*) (Java). A very small *sundaren* is held in the mouth. Its string is made to vibrate by breathing against it. The instrument is used in secret ceremonies and services.
Lit.: no. 163.

Bajiḍor (Java; Sunda District). Name of the Javanese *jiḍor* (*jeḍor*), a one-headed drum the body of which has a truncated conical shape. The instrument resembles the Sundanese *ḍogḍog*. Cf. *Reog* (East Java).
Lit.: no. 163.

Bajlama (*Bağlama*) (Turkey). Long-necked lute with a variable number of strings and frets. The lowest string serves as bourdon. The smallest type of this instrument is called *cura* or *saz*.
Lit.: no. 243.

Baka-baka (Moluccas—Ternate). A bamboo instrument in the shape of a tuning fork. It correlates to the *genggong sakai* and *buncacan.* See *Druri dana.*
Lit.: no. 167.

Bakāshīya (Arabia). See *Dhikr.*

Bake (West Africa, Gabon—Tsogho). Wooden percussion beam.

Bakilo (Southwest Malagasy Republic). Slit-drum.
Lit.: no. 190.

Bakora (Malagasy Republic). Snail horn.
Lit.: nos. 251, 255.

Bakōra varāhina (Malagasy Republic). "Big copper." Trumpet.
Lit.: trumpet.

Baksa (West Java). Part of the circumcision celebration. The music for the dance is provided by a small, ancient *gamelan.*

Bakshi (Turkestan). Musician (an honorific title).

Bākura (Vedic India). Ancient horn or shell trumpet. The original meaning is bagpipe. Cf. *Śankha*; *Bakora.*
Lit.: no. 250.

Bal (*Lal*) (Nilotic Sudan—Ingassana). Gourd trumpet, played in sets of six; tuned to *C C F G B♭* C.
Lit.: no. 111.

Bala (West Africa; Mali; Guinea). Xylophone. Cf. *Balofo.*
Lit.: no. 33.

Bala (Liberia—Kpelle). Three *feli* tied together.
Lit.: no. 284.

Balābān (Turkey; Iran). (1) Turkoman (17th-century) reed pipe with a cylindrical tube and single reed. It has no bell. It was allegedly invented in Shiraz. Also called *Nāy-i-balābān.* (2) Kettledrum.
Lit.: no. 255.

Balabi (South India). *Janya rāga* of the 54th *mēḷa* (*Viśvambharī*).
Tone material:
C F♯ E F♯ A♯ B G B c
c B A♯ G F♯ E D♭ C
Lit.: no. 139.

Bālachandrikā (South India). *Janya rāga* of the 22nd *mēḷa* (*Kharaharapriyā*).
Tone material:
C E♭ F G A B♭ c
c B♭ A F E♭ D C
Lit.: no. 139.

Bālacharitra (South India). *Janya rāga* of the 60th *mēḷa* (*Nītimatī*).
Tone material:
C D E♭ D F♯ G A♯ B A♯ c
c B A♯ B G F♯ E♭ D C
Lit.: no. 139.

Balafo (Burma). Xylophone with 22 slabs placed across a wooden trough. Cf. *Pattala.*
Lit.: no. 255.

Balafo (West Sudan; Congo—Banda, Nduka). Xylophone with gourd resonators.
Lit.: nos. 21, 33.

Balag (Sumeria). Harp, lyra, or drum. According to Lit. no. 87, an hourglass-shaped drum (Babylonia).
Lit.: no. 94.

Bāla Gambhīrya (South India). *Janya rāga* of the 59th *mēḷa* (*Dharmavatī*).
Tone material:
C E♭ D E♭ F♯ A G A B c
c B A G F♯ E♭ D C
Lit.: no. 139.

Balag-di (Sumeria). Small frame drum.
Lit.: no. 281.

Balaggu (Babylonia). Cf. *Balag* (Sumer).
Lit.: no. 94.

Bālaghōshi (*Bālaghōshiṇi*; *Bālaghōṣi*; *Bālaghōṣiṇi*) (South India). *Janya rāga* of the 22nd *mēḷa* (*Kharaharapriyā*).
Tone material:
C D E♭ G F B♭ A c
c B♭ A G F E♭ D C
Lit.: no. 139.

Balaḥ (West Africa; Guinea – Sarakole). A slit-drum made of a hollowed tree stump, beaten with padded sticks. Cf. *Kiringi.*
Lit.: no. 255.

Balahaṃsa (South India). *Janya rāga* of the 28th *mēḷa* (*Harikāmbhōji*).
Tone material:
C D F G A c
c B♭ A G F D F E C
Lit.: no. 139.

Balaharī (South India). See *Bilaharī.*

Balak (West Africa – Mandingo; Sarakole). See *Marimba.*

Balangi (Sierra Leone). *Marimba* with 15-16 keys.
Lit.: no. 255.

Balanyi (West Africa; Dahomey). Raft zither with 10 bamboo sticks. Each stick has one string.
Lit.: no. 206.

Bālasarasvati (North India). "Peacock-sitar"; also called *mayuri*, *taus* or *tayus*; a fiddle with three strings, movable frets, and a varying number of sympathetic strings.
Lit.: no. 261.

Balbal (North Philippines). Cf. *Topayya.*

Balban (Persia). Ancient double-reed instrument.
Lit.: no. 255.

Balè Bandung (West Java – Cheribon). A *gamelan renteng.*
Lit.: no. 163.

Bali balen (*Balibalian*) (Java). "À la Bali." A small ensemble, very rare in Java, routinely used in Bali, consisting of one *saron* (with seven keys), two *slentem* (iron keys placed above resonance tubes inside a trough), and two *angklung.* Added to this group can be a *chontang.* Cf. *Tabuhan Bali*; *Genḍing charabalen.*
Lit.: no. 163.

Balikavasantam (South India). *Janya rāga* of the 15th *mēḷa* (*Māyāmaḷavagauḷa*).
Tone material:
C D♭ E F G A♭ B c
c B A♭ B G F E D♭ C
Lit.: no. 139.

Balimbo (Guinea-Bissau). Jew's harp.
Lit.: no. 190.

Baling (Malaysia). See also *Berbaling.* Bull roarer.
Lit.: no. 19.

Balingi (Congo – Balika). Xylophone with 8 wooden slabs placed across two banana tree trunks.
Lit.: nos. 27, 190.

Balivalam (South India). *Janya rāga* of the 53rd *mēḷa* (*Gamanaśrama*).
Tone material:
C D♭ E F♯ A C
c B G F♯ D♭ C
Lit.: no. 139.

Ballāti (*Bhallādi*) (South India). *Janya rāga* of the 16th *mēḷa* (*Chakravāka*).
Tone material:
C D♭ E F G A B♭ c
c B♭ G F D♭ E F D♭ C
Lit.: no. 139.

Balling-balling (Malaysia). See *Baling*; *Berbaling.*

Balofo (West Sudan). Xylophone.

Baltār (India). Rattle. A basket or clay pot containing little stones.
Lit.: no. 254.

Balu (Congo). Musical bow.
Lit.: no. 176.

Baluh (Malaysia). See *Rebāna Ibu.*

Balungan (Java). The nuclear theme, the skeleton, of a *gamelan* melody.
Lit.: no. 163.

Balunganing genḍing (Sumatra). The frame work of the basic theme in *gamelan* music. Also called *mlampah.*

Balung genḍing (Bali). Nuclear theme of a *genḍing*.
Lit.: no. 197.

Balun gīt (Nepal). Religious songs sung by men only; their texts are derived from the *Mahābhārata* or *Rāmāyāna.*
Lit.: no. 133.

Balut-dü (Northeast Thailand). The comic main servant figure of the puppet theater.
Lit.: no. 203.

Bam (South Borneo; Bandjermasin). Tone name of the fourth note of the *slendro* scale (*bandjermasin*). See *Nam*; *Slendro.*

Bam (Borneo – Dayak). See *Gendang mara.*

Bam (Arabia). A term of Persian origin that denotes the lowest pitched (bass) string of the *'ud.* Although the literal meaning of *bam* (similar to that of the Greek *hypate*) is "the highest," "the light of the morning," and "the cupola," *bam* has also been called "the black string" or "the melancholic one." Originally the string was made of 64 silken threads; later a single gut string was employed. Cf. *'Ud.*
Lit.: no. 64.

Bamboli (Congo – Momvu). Term for *sansa.*
Lit.: no. 21.

Bamboo mese (Flores; Manggaray). Term for *bomberdom.*
Lit.: no. 166.

Bambur (Congo; Cameroon – Fang). Five-stringed harp with a wooden corpus. The instrument is probably identical with the *ombi.*
Lit.: no. 255.

Bamm (Arabia). See *Bam.*

Bāṃśī (India). See *Vāṃśi.*

Bamtal (Nepal). A small tambourine used for beating time.

Bāṃyā (India). See *Banya* (*bayan*); *tabla.*

Ban (Japan). Stereotyped melodies played on the *Chikuzen biwa*, *Satsuma biwa*, and in *gidayu bushi.* For identification the *ban* tunes are numbered (*ichi-ban*, *ni-ban*, etc.).
Lit.: no. 185.

Bana (South India). Name of the fifth *chakra* in the system of 72 *mēḷas.* See *Rāga* (South India, IXb).
Lit.: no. 139.

Bana (Liberia – Vai). Harp with seven strings.
Lit.: no. 255.

Banbhajan (Southeast India). Forest song. See *Dadaria.*

Bañchi (India; Bengal). Flute.

Banchi (Borneo – Dayak). Bamboo beak flute. Cf. *Suling nyawa.*
Lit.: no. 255.

Banchi-banchi (Borneo; Celebes). Cf. *Lolowe.*
Lit.: no. 132.

Banchik (Java). The wooden frame that supports the *kendang*. See *Bantyik*.
Lit.: no. 163.

Band (India). "Closed." The term is used in *tabla* playing. The *band bayan* ("closed *bayan*") denotes a particular manner of the player striking the head of the *bayan* (the drum word [*bol*] is *ge*). The stroke obstructs the vibration of the head that would follow an "open bayan" (*khola bayan*). The sound of the *band bayan* is muted and dull, while the sound of the *khola bayan* is open and reverberating. Cf. *Tabla*.
Lit.: no. 136.

Bandaīr (Arabia). Large frame drum with snares. Cf. *Abendair*.
Lit.: no. 250.

Bandar (Algeria – Sidi Aisa). Tambourine with snare strings strung in its inside. The instrument is also called *bender* or *bandir*.
Lit.: no. 255.

Bandi (Lower Congo; Kenya – Kamba). A flat cylindrical drum, an imitation of the European drum used in bands. It is beaten with a stick.
Lit.: no. 190.

Bandingba (Congo). Musical bow.
Lit.: no. 176.

Bandīr (Algeria; Biskra). See *Bandar*; *Bendeyr*.

mBandju (*mBandyu*) (North Congo). Rectangular primitive board zither.
Lit.: no. 255.

Baṇdolan (Java). A drumming pattern, frisky, full of fun, without any strict rhythmical rules. The word *bandol* implies a mischievous, playful attitude that is welcome after listeners have been subjected to serious performances and some *ladrangan*. *Baṇdolan* occurs during the *Nguyu-uyu*, creating a lively relief.
Lit.: no. 163.

Baṇdulan (Java). Small bamboo "markers" fixed about the middle of the strings (e.g., at the *kowangan*). The function of these markers is to produce interpunctuating sounds.
Lit.: no. 163.

mBandyu (Congo). See *mBandju*.

Banengbeng (Philippines). Cf. *Itundak*.

Banga (Sahara; Sudan). Drum.
Lit.: no. 112.

Baṅgāḷa (South India). *Janya rāga*, usually ascribed to the 29th *mēḷa*. The tone material shown below shows its occasional affinity to the 28th *mēḷa* (*Harikāmbhōji*), because the note B♭ is used:

C D E F D G
c B♭ G F D E D C

Lit.: no. 139.

Baṅgāḷa (South India). *Janya rāga* of the 29th *mēḷa* (*Dhīraśaṅkarābharaṇam*).
Tone material:

C D E F G F D G c
c B G F D E D C

Lit.: no. 139.

Baṅgāḷa Gauḷa (South India). *Janya rāga* of the 5th *mēḷa* (*Śyāmalāṅgi*).
Tone material:

C D F♯ G F♯ A♭ B♭♭ c
c A♭ G F♯ E♭ D C

Lit.: no. 139.

Baṅgāl-bhairav (*Bengal-bhairav*; *Bangala*; *Bangali*) (North India). Rare *rāga* subordinate to the *Bhairav thāta*.
Tone material:

C D♭ E F G A♭ c
c A♭ G F E D♭ C

Lit.: no. 138.

Bangal-bilaval (North India). See *Patmanjri*.

Bangbrang (*Ambrang*) (West Java). See *Ḍogḍog*.

Bang bung (Java). Bamboo trumpet.
Lit.: nos. 163, 215.

Bang-dze (*Bang tse*) (China). Cf. *Pang-tzu.*

Banggi (Flores). Cf. *Gong tondu.*

Bangi (Congo – Azande). See *Kweningba.*

Bangia (Eastern Sudan). Lyre with five strings tuned pentatonically. Its Ethiopian name is *kerar.* Cf. *Kissar*; *Baganā*; *Brimbiri.*

Bangkula (Celebes). See *Bankula.*

Bangsi (India). See *Bañsi* (cf. *Bañsarī*).

Bangsi (West Borneo). The second (thin) tube of the *bikut* (Borneo).

Bangsi (South Sumatra). Bamboo whistle flute with six finger holes in the front and one in the back. Cf. *Salung.*
Lit.: no. 162.

Bangsi (Java). See *Wangsi.*
Lit.: no. 163.

Bangsil (*Gala*) (North Moluccas – Halmahera). See *Gambus.*

Bangsing (Sunda Isl.). (1) Term for *bangsi* (Java, Sumatra). (2) Long flute with six or seven holes (Sumatra).
Lit.: no. 163.

Bang-tse (*Bang-dze*) (China). See *Pang-tzu.*

Bania (Senegal). Lute.
Lit.: no. 255.

Banjanga (Congo – Bwaka). See *Manja.*

Banjet (West Java). See *Ketuk tilu.*

Banju (Congo – Azande). Board zither.
Lit.: no. 21.

Bānkā (South India). A conically-shaped brass tube used as horn during religious rites (*pavitra utsavam*) in Hindu temples.
Lit.: no. 261.

Bankiya (Congo). Drum played with bare hands. When used as a war drum, it is played with sticks.
Lit.: no. 26.

Banku (*Buruga*) (South India). Name of the *karnā.*
Lit.: no. 255.

Bānkula (*Bāngkula*) (Celebes). Metal jingles worn by warriors after successful headhunting.
Lit.: no. 254.

Bañsarī (India). Bamboo beak flute with 4-6 finger holes. Also called *bañsrī* or *bansurī.*
Lit.: no. 255.

Banshī (*Vanshī*) (North India). General term for flute, vertical and cross, double, even triple forms. Derived from the Sanskrit *vāṃsha*, "bamboo."
Lit.: no. 46.

Bañshi (Assam; Burma). Bamboo cross flute with three finger holes. Cf. *Bāṃśī*; *Vāṃśī.*
Lit.: no. 252.

Banshiki (Japan). One of the 12 pitches of traditional music. Cf. *Banshikichō.*
Lit.: no. 185.

Banshiki (Japan). Cf. *Sō-no-koto* tunings.

Banshiki(chō) (Japan). The *gagaku* and *shōmyō* scale based on the note *banshiki* (B, if *ichikotsu*, the first note of the Japanese 12 tones, is transcribed as D):
B C# (d) E F# G# (a) b

Bañsi (India). Ancient transverse flute, already mentioned in the *Rig Veda*, with 3-4 finger holes. Cf. *Vāṃsī.*
Lit.: no. 254.

Bansi (Flores). Bamboo clarinet with 6-7 finger holes. Cf. *Pupui* (Sumatra).
Lit.: nos. 166, 254.

Bansi (Java). Common term for *suling.*
Lit.: no. 163.

Banskanada (North India). An obscure *rāga* using various features of *rāga Kafi.* Tone material and *vādis* are indistinct.
Lit.: no. 138.

Bāṅslī (India). Cross flute with 3-4 finger holes.
Lit.: no. 254.

Bānsrī (Nepal). See *Bānsarī.*

Bānsulī (*Vānsalī*). (1) Bamboo beak flute of Indian origin with seven holes in front and one at the back. Cf. *Bānsurī.* (The instrument can also be called *baugsin.*) (2) *Bānsulī* or *basuli*, a bamboo cross flute of Nepal.
Lit.: no. 163.

Bānsurī (India; Punjab). A gently sounding beak flute with 4-6 finger holes. In Nepal the term *bānsurī* is also applied to a transverse flute. Cf. *Bansarī.*
Lit.: no. 254.

Bant (Ancient Egypt). See *Bin't.*

Bantyik (*Banchik*) (Java). Wooden stand upon which the *ketipung* is placed.
Lit.: no. 163.

Bānyā (*Bayan*) (North India). Cf. *Tablas.*

Banzie (Congo – Azande). Stick zither. .
Lit.: no. 176.

Banzu (Congo – Mangbetu). Board zither.
Lit.: no. 176.

Bapang (Bali). Repeated tone sequences that announce the arrival of an official of high position. The same feature represents the central section of the *baris gede* (war dance). See also *Batel.*
Lit.: no. 197.

Bapang (*Bapang dengklik*) (Java). Demonic character of an actor in the *wayang wong.*
Lit.: no. 163.

Bapili (Congo). Board zither.
Lit.: no. 303.

Baqiya (and *Infiṣāl*) (Arabia). Cf. *Faḍla.*

Bara (Korea). See *Ja-bara* (*Chabara*).

Baradundu (West Africa; Senegal – Dioula). Calabash drum.
Lit.: no. 95.

Baragumu, Mbiu, Siwa, Kigunda (East Africa – Swahili). Horn.

Bara mase git (Nepal). Lament sung by women whose husbands are away.
Lit.: no. 133.

Barang (Java). Literally, "matter," "starting point." Tone name:

1. In Central Java, Cheribon, Majakerta, Prabalingga, the term indicates the seventh note of the *pelog* system.
2. In Jombang and Prabalingga it indicates (as *barang alit*) the first note of the *slendro* system.
3. In the Sunda District it represents the 6th note of the *pelog* system (*laras, mamanis*) and also the 6th note of *surupan melog.*
4. In the Sunda District it can also indicate the 5th note of the *slendro* system.
5. In modern Java it is the 2nd note of *pelog*, sounding 165 cents higher than *nem*, and the term indicates also the 2nd note of *Slendro*, sounding 240 cents higher than *nem.*

Lit.: no. 163.

Barang alit (Indonesia; Jombang; Prabalingga). The upper octave of *barang* (the first note of *slendro* of Jombang and Prabalingga. Cf. *Slendro.*
Lit.: no. 163.

Barangan (Bali). Small gongs (*trompong*), tuned an octave higher than the melody instruments; they accompany (follow) the melody.
Lit.: no. 197.

Barari (North India). *Raga*. See *Varati.*

Barassi (Flores). A special working song of the people who live "behind the mountain."
Lit.: no. 166.

Barāṭaka (East India; Bengal). Horn made of a cowrie shell.
Lit.: nos. 184, 255.

Barbarā (*Bharbarā*) (South India). *Janya rāga* of the 64th *mēḷa* (*Vāchaspatī*).
Tone material:

C E F♯ D E F♯ A B♭ c
(C E F♯ D E F♯ A B♭ A c)
c B♭ A F♯ E D C

Lit.: no. 139.

Barbat (Iran; Arabia). Ancient lute with four strings.
Lit.: no. 255.

Bardzrasing (Armenia). Oboe.
Lit.: no. 255.

Bare (Japan). Rattle used by dancers.
Lit.: no. 258.

Barghoumi (East Africa—Zanzibar; Swahili). See *Barugumu.*
Lit.: no. 255.

Barhidhvaja (South India). *Janya rāga* of the 30th *mēḷa* (*Nāgānandī*).
Tone material:

C D E A♭ B c
c B A♯ E D C

Lit.: no. 139.

Bāri (South India). A large oboe form (cf. *Nāgasuram*). The same instrument, slightly smaller, is called *idaibāri*, and the smallest type is called *timiri.*
Lit.: no. 260.

Barikendikendi (Congo—Amadi). Musical bow.
Lit.: no. 176.

Barimbo (*Kulang*) (Philippines). Large bamboo jew's harp.
Lit.: no. 255.

Barinung (Vietnam). Large frame drum with one head.

Baris (Bali). A number of ceremonial dances performed by men. Some of these dances are: *baris gede*, the Great Baris (warriors' dance); *baris goak*, the crow dance; *baris irengan*, the black ape dance; *baris kupukupu*, the butterfly dance; *baris china*, the China dance; *baris pendet*, ritual dance. According to Lit. no. 197, there were 30 variants of *baris* listed.

Baris china (Bali). See *Baris.*

Baris gede (Bali). See *Baris.*

Baris goak (Bali). See *Baris.*

Baris irengan (Bali). See *Baris.*

Baris kupukupu (Bali). See *Baris.*

Baris pendet (Bali). See *Baris.*

Barlum (New Guinea—Finschhafen). Bull roarer.
Lit.: no. 255.

Baro (Bali). Scale used in *gambuh-semar-pegulingan.* It consists of the notes *ding*, *dong*, *deng*, *dung*, *dang* (e.g., D E♭ F♭ A B♭).

Barong (Bali). A theatrical masked dragon performed by two dancers dressed in horsehair and feathers. In various moods, fierce, gentle, playful, whimsical, it fights battles against the sorceress Rangda.
Lit.: no. 197.

Barongan-kuda kepang (Malaysia). Cf. *Gamelan* (Malaysia).

Barrakah (Libya). Battle songs.

Barugumu (East Africa—Swahili). Side-blown antelope horn. Cf. *Barghoumi.*
Lit.: no. 255.

Barum (Melanesia; Kaiser Wilhelm Land). Wooden drum.
Lit.: no. 255.

Barung (Java). Medium sized metal slabs that produce tones of the middle octave of the *gender.* (The low octave of the instrument is called *gender panembung* and the high octave range *gender panerus.*) Cf. *Gender barung.*
Lit.: no. 163.

Barva (North India). *Rāga* subordinate to the *Kafi thāta.*
Tone material:
C D E F G (B♭) B c
c B♭ A G F E♭ D C
The *rāga* can be treated either seriously or light and flirtatiously. In the latter *rasa* both natural (*shuddha*) and flat (*komal*) forms of the notes D, A, and B can be used (an unusual feature).
Lit.: no. 138.

Barwal (Tunisia). See *Al-Barwal.*

Basamāna (South India). *Janya rāga* of the 15th *mēḷa* (*Māyāmāḷavagauḷa*).
Tone material:
C D♭ E F G A♭ B c
c B A♭ B G F D♭ E F E C
Lit.: no. 139.

Bāsāmkūb (South Sudan). Ancient lyre.
Lit.: no. 108.

Basandīdah (Middle East). *Maqām.*
Tone material:
C D E♭ (E) F♯ G A B♭ c
Lit.: no. 64.

Basant (North India). Bengali term for *vasant.*

Basare (India). Cf. *Bansarī.*

Bashingili (North Rhodesia). Drum.
Lit.: no. 26.

Bashraf (*Peshref*) (Middle East; North Africa). An overture used as second movement of the Tunisian *nauba* suite (the first movement is the *taqsīm*).
The *bashraf*, which can also appear at the end of art songs, usually consists of 4-6 sections. These sections, performed by an instrumental ensemble, frequently use tonally related *maqāmāt* in the following order: *rast*, *siga*, *sasgar* and, as closing, *rast* again. Cf. *Al-Mshaddar*; *Taqsīm.*
Lit.: no. 171.

Basing-basing (*Basing-basing apembeng*, *Basing bugisi*) (South Celebes). Cf. *Serubay*; *Suling.*
Lit.: no. 162.

Basīt (Arabia). A light vocal piece with an instrumental prelude.
Lit.: no. 76.

Basītah (Islamic culture; North Africa; Near East). Grace note. Cf. *Murakkabah.*

Bastaḥ Iṣfahān (Iran; Arabia). *Maqām.*
Tone material:
+B♭ C D E +F G A +B♭
Lit.: no. 64.

Bastaḥ-nakar (Egypt). See *Bastaḥ-nigār.*

Bastaḥ-nigār (*Bastaḥ-nakar*) (Modern Egypt). *Maqām.*
Tone material:
+B♭ C D +E♭ F G♭ A B♭ c d
Lit.: no. 64.

Bastran (Burma). Xylophone with boat-shaped resonator. It has 21 bamboo slabs struck with wooden sticks.

Basulī (*Basurī*) (Nepal). Cross flute played at weddings and festivals. Cf. *Bañsi*; *vāṃśī.*

Basurī (*Basuli*) (India). Poetic term for cross flute. Cf. also *Bañsī.*

Bata (Nigeria—Yoruba). Drum; drum family. The *bata* drum has a body in the shape of a truncated cone with two skins. The *bata* ensemble is: *iya'lu bata*, the leading drum; *omele abu iyu'lu*, a shorter drum than the *iya'lu bata*; *omele ako*, drum with a sharp sound; *omele abo* (*kudi*), drum with a dull sound; *adamo bata*, short drum standing upright, the broader end at the top.
Lit.: no. 293.

Bat âm (Annam). The eight sounds (and materials) of musical instruments. Cf. *Pa-yin* (China).

Batang (Malaysia). Term for the tube of the *serunai*.

Batang (West Borneo). The first tube of the *bikut*.
Lit.: no. 254.

Batangan (*Chiblon*) (Java). Small drum used in dances; drumming. See *Kenḍang batangan*.
Lit.: no. 163.

Batar (East Africa—Somali Republic). Dance song.
Lit.: no. 96.

Batē (Sierra Leone—Temne). Wooden kettle-drum.
Lit.: no. 255.

Batēl (Bali). Percussive music for lively, excited battle scenes in *wayang* performances. The music consists of repeated brief rhythmical motives.
Lit.: no. 265.

Batel maya (Bali). A noisy piece of music performed by the entire ensemble of *gambangs*, using as characteristic feature the repetition of a single note. It marks the beginning of the *legong* dance. Cf. *Penarik*.
Lit.: nos. 197, 265.

Batiwtiw (Philippines—Hanunoo). A bamboo bull roarer.
Lit.: no. 303.

Batok (Java). "Cover." The upper front board of the body of a string instrument. The term extends also to the complete (usually heart-shaped), flat corpus of the *rebāb*.
Lit.: no. 163.

Batok (Bali). The corpus of a *rebāb* if it is made of half a coconut shell.
Lit.: no. 197.

Batsi (Japan). Cf. *Bachi*.

Batsu (*Hatsu*) (Japan). Cymbals with large central bosses.
Lit.: no. 255.

Batta (Sudan; Nigeria—Hausa). Calabash drum.
Lit.: no. 95.

Baṭṭa bīn (India). Term occasionally used for *rudra vīṇā* (without frets); also called *vichitra vīṇā*. In the South the instrument is called *hindusthani gōṭuvādyam*.
Lit.: no. 261.

Battal (Turkey). Very large *nāy*, now obsolete.

Baṭṭāl-i dāwudī (Turkey). Cf. *Nay*.
Lit.: no. 81.

Batzi (Japan). See *Batsi*; *Bachi*.

Bau (Java). The outer edge of a gong turned inward.
Lit.: no. 163.

Baugsin (Java). See *Bānsulī*.

Baul (India; Bengal). Religious, mystical songs sung by travelling monks and beggars. The songs are often accompanied on the *dotāra*.
Lit.: nos. 46, 261.

Bauḷamukhi (South India). *Janya rāga* of the 45th *mēḷa* (*Śubhapantuvarālī*).
Tone material:
C D♭ E♭ F♯ G B c
c B A♭ G F♯ E♭ D♭ C
Lit.: no. 139.

Bauḷi (South India). *Janya rāga* of the 15th *mēḷa* (*Māyāmāḷavagauḷa*).
Tone material:
C D♭ E G A♭ c
c B A♭ G E D♭ C
Lit.: no. 139.

Bava (Indonesia; Alor Isl.). Barrel drum.
Lit.: no. 254.

Bawa (Congo). Musical bow.
Lit.: no. 176.

Bawa (Java). Vocal introduction.
Lit.: no. 163.

Bawa sekar (Java). See *Bebuka*.

Bawāwīq (Arabia). See *Bawwāqe*.

Bawle (Burma). Lamenting songs.

Bawwāqe (*Bawāwīq*) (Arabia). Trumpet.
Lit.: no. 255.

Baya (Nepal). Bamboo flute.

Baya (Congo—Teke). Stick zither.
Lit.: no. 280.

Bayan (Arabia). Piano.

Bāyan (*Bānya*) (North India). Cf. *Tabla*.
Lit.: no. 136.

Bayāt (Arabia). See *Bayātī*.

Bayātī (Middle East). *Maqām*.
Tone material:
D $\overset{+}{\text{E}}$♭ F G A B♭ c d
Bayāti is a typically Arabic *maqām*, frequently used in folk music. The name *bayāt* means "indigenous," "home-bred." It is little known in Iran, favored in Syria and modern Egypt.
Lit.: nos. 64, 121.

Bayātī 'Arabān (Middle East). *Maqām*.
Tone material:
D $\overset{+}{\text{E}}$♭ F G A♭ B c d
Lit.: no. 64.

Bayāt-shuri (Arabia; Middle East). *Maqām*.
Tone material:
D $\overset{+}{\text{E}}$♭ F G A $\overset{+}{\text{B}}$♭ c d
A popular *maqām*, particularly in Egypt. *Bayāt-shuri* (*shuri*, "clever") is a mixture of *mahur* and *bayātī*. Melodies in this *maqām* start with the note *nawā* and end with *duga* or *kardan*. (For tone names see list placed under the heading of *Jagā* [*Yagā*].)
Lit.: no. 121.

Bayātī-sulṭānī (Arabia; Middle East). *Maqām*.
Tone material:
D $\overset{+}{\text{E}}$♭ F G A $\overset{(+)}{\text{B}}$♭ c d
Lit.: no. 64.

Bayātī 'Uśayrān (Middle East). *Maqām*.
Tone material:
A $\overset{+}{B}$♭ C D $\overset{+}{\text{E}}$♭ F G A $\overset{+}{\text{B}}$♭ c d /
d c $\overset{+}{\text{B}}$♭ A G F E D C $\overset{+}{B}$♭ *A*
Lit.: no. 64.

Bayote Tork (*Āwāz*) (Persia). See *Dastgāh*.

Bayt (Tunisia). See *Abyāt*.

Bāz (Turkey; Arabia; Egypt). A small kettledrum held in the left hand. It is beaten with a leather strap held in the right. The instrument is used by beggars and by the *musaḥḥir*, a chanter who wakes the people during the nights of the month of Ramadan and reminds them to eat. Cf. *Ṭabl-i bāz*.
Lit.: nos. 81, 175, 255.

Baza (Congo—Gobu). Xylophone resembling the *kalanba*.
Lit.: no. 27.

Bazara (Tanganyika; Kenya—Washambala). Stamping bamboo tube used to accompany dances.
Lit.: no. 130.

Bazombe (Congo). Musical bow.
Lit.: no. 220.

Bazruq (Arabia). Tone name. (All tone names within the range of two octaves are listed under the heading of *Jagā* [*Yagā*].) See *Jwab-sigā*.

Bdung-pa (Tibet). Beating a drum.

Beabobo (*Maromena*) (Malagasy Republic—Tullar District). Ritual shell trumpet.
Lit.: no. 251.

Bebaling (Malaysia). See *Berbaling*.

Bebende (*Bende*) (Bali). Large gong with a hollowed boss. It appears in the *gamelan gong* and *bonang* ensembles.
Lit.: no. 197.

Bebuka (*Buka*; *Bukaning genḍing*; *Wiwitan*) (Java). The instrumental introduction to the beginning of a *genḍing*. One of these introductions, the *bebuka swara* (*bawa sekar*), is vocal. The terms for *bebuka* in the Sunda Districts are *pangkat* and *pamangkat*. Each *bebuka* term is combined with the name of the instrument that dominates the *bebuka*. Some of these terms are: *bebuka bonang*, *bebuka (saron) barung*, *bebuka kendang*, *bebuka bedug*, *bebuka ketipung*, *bebuka rebab*, *bebuka genḍer*. The following introduce loudly played compositions (*genḍing sabetan*): *bebuka bonang*, *bebuka kenḍang*, *bebuka (saron) barung*. The following introduce gently played compositions (*genḍing alus*): *bebuka rebab*, *bebuka genḍer*. *Bebuka swara* (*bawa sekar*), the vocal introduction, is performed in free rhythm (*tembang*, *sekar ageng*, *sekar tengahan*) or in *machapat* meters.
Lit.: no. 163.

Bebuka barung (*Bebuka bonang*) (Java). See *Bebuka*.

Bebuka beḍug (Java). See *Bebuka*.

Bebuka bonang (*Bebuka barung*) (Java). See *Bebuka*.

Bebuka genḍer (Java). See *Bebuka*.

Bebuka kenḍang (Java). See *Bebuka*.

Bebuka ketipung (Java). See *Bebuka*.

Bebuka rebāb (Java). See *Bebuka*.

Bebuka swara (Java). Vocal introduction. See *Bebuka*.

Beda (*Ral-pa*) (Tibet). Wandering beggar musicians who accompany their songs on the *sgra-snyan* (or *k'opong*), a fiddle with three, four, or six strings.
Lit.: no. 62.

Beḍaya (dance) (Java). The female court dancers (*beḍayas*, *serimpis*) are accompanied by a small instrumental ensemble that consists of two drums: *kenḍang genḍing*, *ketipung*, and three phrase indicators: *gong ageng*, *kenong*, and *ketuk*. The melody is sung by a choir (cf. *Pasinden*). Occasionally a pair of *kemanak* is added: small bronze cymbals in the size of carved-out bananas.
Lit.: nos. 158, 163.

Bedoyo (Bali; Java). Popular dance performed by nine girls.
Lit.: no. 197.

B̠ee bai dawng glui (Northeast Thailand). A cone-chaped kazoo made from a banana leaf.
Lit.: no. 203.

B̠ee chawa (*Pi java*) (Northeast Thailand). An oboe type.
Lit.: no. 203.

B̠ee tae (Northeast Thailand). Signalling shawm, blown at night to indicate the time and procedure of the *yam tae*.
Lit.: no. 203.

Bedug (*Teteg*) (Java). A large barrel drum with two heads. The drum is suspended in a wooden frame and is beaten with a *tabuh*. It is used in *gamelan sekati*, also in the toilet dance (*kiprah* or *nglana*), in the *wayang wong*, and to call people to prayer.
Lit.: no. 215.

Been (India). See *Bīn*.

B̲eepat (Thailand). Cf. *Pi-phat*.

B̲ee sanai (Northeast Thailand). Water buffalo horn with open ends and a metal reed.

B̲ee saw (Northeast Thailand). A reed pipe.
Lit.: no. 203.

Beg (Ethiopia). Cf. *Baganā*.
Lit.: no. 255.

Bēgaḍa (South India). *Janya rāga* of the 29th *mēḷa* (*Dhīraśaṅkarābharaṇam*).
Tone material:
C E D E F G A G c
(C E D E F G A B A G c)
c B A G F E D C
Cf. *Aprati madhyama*.
Lit.: no. 139.

Begagra (North India). See *Bihagda*.

Begana (*Begena*) (Ethiopia). A rare large lyre with a box-shaped body and 8-12 strings, considered to be a sacred instrument. It is used during Lent and other religious festivals of the Ethiopian church. Cf. *Baganā*; *Krar*.
Lit.: nos. 144, 218.

Beguri (South Africa). Synonym for *gedzo*.

Beh (*Krishna-beh*) (Nepal). A vertically-blown shepherd's flute with seven finger holes and a beak mouthpiece.
Lit.: no. 255.

Behāg (North India). *Rāga*. Cf. also *Bihāg*.

Behāg (South India). Also called *byāg*, *byāgu*, *hindusthāni behāg*. *Janya rāga* of the 29th *mēḷa* (*Dhīraśaṅkarābharaṇam*).
Tone material:
C E F G B A B c
c B A G F E D C
Lit.: no. 139.

Behālā (*Beyāla*) (India; Bengal). A crude spike fiddle with two strings in the form of a lute with a small corpus. The neck is a thick piece of bamboo.
Lit.: no. 255.

Bei (Japan). See *Bi*.

Beit el-melāwī (Arabia). Peg stick of the *qanun*.

Beko-beko (*Beko-fui*) (Flores—Ngada). Tubular bamboo zither with two, five, or six strings. Cf. *Gong tondu*.
Lit.: no. 166.

Beko-fui (Flores). See *Beko-beko*.

Beksan (Java). Dance performance. The accompaniment is performed by the *karawitan*.

Bela (*mbila*) (South Africa—Venda). Term for *sansa*.
Lit.: no. 151.

Belangy (Sierra Leone). See *Balangi*.

Belebān (Kurdistan). Trumpet.
Lit.: no. 255.

Belek (Java). Term for a *genḍing*. See *Genḍing Mianggong*.
Lit.: no. 163.

Belemban-batchot (Micronesia). Jew's harp.

Belikan (Malaysia; Sarawak—Iban). Lute with two strings and a box-shaped body.

Beluk (West Java). A type of *tembang buhun*, a style of singing in which the leader does not sing. First he recites clearly each line of the text, then the singers who surround him sing the text he had recited.
Lit.: no. 163.

Beluwan (Sumatra). See *Beluwat*.

Beluwat (*Beluwan*) (Sumatra—Batak). Long bamboo flute (*suling* type).
Lit.: no. 255.

Bem (*Bah*) (Java—Jogya). A drum word indicating a stroke performed with the middle, ring, and little fingers on the large drumhead. The sound produced is called *deng*.
Lit.: no. 163.

Bem (Java; Sunda District). (1) First degree of the *pelog* system (Central Java, Cheribon). (2) The second degree of *pelog* and *slendro* systems in the Sunda Districts. (3) *Bem* can become *galimer* in both systems (*pelog* or *slendro*) in the Sunda District. The name *bem* was probably derived from the Persian-Arabic *bam*, "low note." Cf. *Penunggul*.
Lit.: no. 163.

Bem alit (Java). "Little *bem*." Term for a tone that indicates a note an octave higher than *bem* (also *penunggul*) of *pelog* in Central Java and Cheribon. Cf. *Pelog*.
Lit.: no. 163.

Bembe (Nigeria—Yoruba). Drum; drum ensemble consisting of: *iya'lu bembe*, the leading drum, stick beaten, with two skins and snare; *atele*, smaller drum; *kerikeri*, drum with an hourglass-shaped corpus and two skins; *issaju*, drum of the same form as the *kerikeri*; *gudugudu*, a small *iya'lu bembe* with two skins but no snare.
Lit.: no. 293.

Bemunggri-nggo (*Tinding*) (Flores). Cf. *Baba*.

Bende (Bali). See *Bebende*.

Beṇḍe (Java). Two small gongs in *gamelan pelog* tuned to the tones *lima* and *nem*. Cf. *Beri* (*gong Beri*).
Lit.: no. 163.

Bendere (Islamic Africa). Calabash drum. Cf. *Bandaīr*.
Lit.: no. 95.

Bendeyr (Algeria). Cf. *Bandar* (*Bandaīr*).

Bendīr (Morocco). Term for *Bandaīr*.
Lit.: no. 95.

Bendi rojo muku (Central Flores). Papaya clapper; instrument for children. In West Java the clapper is called *paralak*; *perelek*.
Lit.: no. 166.

Bendo (West Africa; Upper Volta; Mali; northern Ivory Coast). Calabash drum. Cf. *Bandaīr*.
Lit.: no. 95.

Bendrong (*Genḍong*; *Gejongan*; *Koṭekan*; *Gondang*) (Java). Riceblock stamping music performed by women during moonlit nights and at times of solar and lunar eclipses.
Lit.: no. 163.

mBendu (Angola—Mbundu). Flute. (Described as "hell for the ear.")
Lit.: no. 255.

Benduku (Congo). Musical bow with a gourd resonator (not attached to the bow).
Lit.: no. 176.

Beng (Java). Drum word. Cf. *Ḍeng*.

Benğak (Arabia). Peg box.

Bengãla (Sudan). Lute with an egg-shaped corpus covered with skin. It has a broad, flat neck, four pegs, and two double strings.
Lit.: no. 255.

Bengalu (Former French Equatorial Africa—Nzakara). Cross flute with two finger holes.
Lit.: no. 33.

Bengsi (Flores—Gayo District). Ring flute. Cf. *Nuren.*
Lit.: no. 166.

Bent (Egypt). See *Bint.*

Benta (West India). Primitive musical bow.
Lit.: no. 18.

Bentere (Ghana). Drum made of a gourd (*Pentre*).

Bentwa (Ghana—Twi, Ashanti). Musical bow with one or two strings.
Lit.: no. 95.

Benu (India; Orissa, Bengal). Bamboo flute. Cf. *Veṇu.*

Be-oh (Burma). See *Byo.*
Lit.: no. 255.

Be-orla (E. Timor). Tube zither. Cf. *Tabuan*; *Dakado.*
Lit.: no. 156.

Berari (North India). See *Varati.*

Beraya (Sinhalese). Kettledrum.
Lit.: no. 254.

Berbaling (*Bebaling*; *Baling*; *Balling-balling*) (Malaysia). Obscure bull roarer used to drive away wild elephants from plantations. Cf. *Jata* (Flores).
Lit.: no. 255.

Berbat (Arabia). See *Barbat.*

Beri (Java). Two small flat gongs placed on a wooden stand. The gongs are tuned to *lima* and *nem.* They are used in *gamelan slendro.* Cf. *Beṇḍe.*
Lit.: no. 254.

Berni vin (Armenia). Jew's harp.
Lit.: no. 255.

Berri (Sri Lanka). Small two-headed barrel drum struck with the hands.
Lit.: no. 255.

Berulung-ulung (Bali). See *Ulung.*

Beta (West Africa—Ewe). See *Bentwa.*

Berrigodea (Sri Lanka). Long drum, beaten with the hands.
Lit.: no. 255.

Beulit (Sunda District). Term for octave.
Lit.: no. 163.

Beure hevehe (Papua—Elema). See *Hevehe.*
Lit.: no. 311.

Beyālā (India). See *Behālā.*

Bhadra (South India). *Janya rāga* of the 25th *mēḷa* (*Mārarañjanī*).
Tone material:
C D E D F A G A♭ G AB B♭♭ c
c B♭♭ A♭ F E D C
Lit.: no. 139.

Bhadragāndhāri (South India). *Janya rāga* of the 29th *mēḷa* (*Dhīraśaṅkarābharaṇam*).
Tone material:
C D F G B c
c B A F D E C
Lit.: no. 139.

Bhadrakāḷipaṭṭu (India). Sacred songs for the deity Bhadrakāḷi sung in the Hindu temples of the Malabar district.

Bhadrakara (South India). *Janya rāga* of the 33rd *mēḷa* (*Gāṅgeyabhushanī*).
Tone material:
C D♯ E D♯ F G A♭ B c
c B A♭ B G F D♯ E C
Lit.: no. 139.

Bhadra Sāraṅga Līla (South India). *Janya rāga* of the 22nd *mēḷa* (*Kharaharapriyā*).
Tone material:
C D E♭ F G A G B♭ c
c A G F D C
Lit.: no. 139.

Bhadraśrī (South India). *Janya rāga* of the 17th *mēḷa* (*Suryakānta*).
Tone material:
C D♭ E A B c
c B A E D♭ C
Lit.: no. 139.

Bha-gaṇa (South India). See *Ashṭa gaṇas.*

Bhāgavat gōhṭhi (India). An assembly of devotees who chant sacred hymns and songs.
Lit.: no. 261.

Bhāgavata naṭanam (South India). Sacred dance of the devotees (*bhāgavatars*).
Lit.: no. 261.

Bhāgavatapriya (South India). *Janya rāga* of the 22nd *mēḷa* (*Kharaharapriyā*).
Tone material:
C D E♭ F D F G A B♭ c
c B♭ A G F D C
Lit.: no. 139.

Bhāgavatar (South India; Tamil). Reciters of *kathā kālakshēpam* (religious discourses), with musical accompaniment. In the Malabar region music teachers and professional musicians are called *bhāgavatars* (singing storytellers). Cf. *Bhāgavata gōshṭi*; *Bhāgavata naṭanam.* See also *Yakshagana.*
Lit.: no. 261.

Bhāgavata sampradāyam (South India). Term for *herikathā kālakshepam* (religious discourse with musical accompaniment).
Lit.: no. 261.

Bhāgavati (South India). *Janya rāga* of the 26th *mēḷa* (*chārukeśī*).
Tone material:
C D E F B♭ c
c B♭ F E D C
Lit.: no. 139.

Bhāgavatulu (South India). Telugu term for *bhāgavatar* (Tamil).

Bhāgīrati (South India). *Janya rāga* of the 20th *mēḷa* (*Naṭabhairavī*).
Tone material:
C D E♭ A♭ B♭ c
c B♭ A♭ E♭ D C
Lit.: no. 139.

Bhāgya Rañjaṇi (South India). *Janya rāga* of the 22nd *mēḷa* (*Kharaharapriyā*).
Tone material:
C D E♭ F A B♭ c
c G F E♭ D C
Lit.: no. 139.

Bhailo-, (*Densi-git*) (Nepal). Songs sung on holidays by children who go from house to house begging for sweets.
Lit.: no. 133.

Bhairaon (North India). See *Bhairav.*

Bhairau (North India). See *Bhairav.*

Bhairav (*Bhairava*; *Bhairau*; *Bhairaon*; *Bhairo*) (North India). *Thāta* and *rāga.*
Tone material:
C D♭ E F G A♭ B c
c B A♭ G F E D♭ C; *Vādis*: A♭, D♭
Lit.: no. 138.

Bhairava (South India). *Janya rāga* of the 17th *mēḷa* (*Suryakānta*).
Tone material:
C D♭ E F G A B c
c A G F E D♭ C
Lit.: no. 139.

Bhairavadhvani (South India). *Janya rāga* of the 52nd *mēḷa* (*Rāmapriyā*).
Tone material:
C D♭ E F♯ G F♯ B♭ A c
c A G F♯ E D♭ C
Lit.: no. 139.

Bhairav-bahar (North India). *Rāga.* A combination of *Bhairav* and *Bahar* elements. As the sequence of elements varies, a fixed tone material cannot be shown. For instance, one version of *Bhairav-bahar* could show the following order:
Bhairav
C D♭ E F
Bahar
G E♭ F B A B♭ c B c
Bhairav
B A♭ G F E D♭ C
Lit.: no. 138.

Bhairavī (*Bhairvī*) (North India). *Thāṭa* and *rāga*.
Tone material:
C D♭ E♭ F G A♭ B c
c B♭ A♭ G F E♭ D♭ C
Lit.: no. 138.

Bhairavī (South India). *Janya rāga* of the 20th *mēḷa* (*Naṭabhairavī*).
Tone material:
C D E♭ F G A B♭ c (appr. A in ascent)
c B♭ A♭ G F E♭ D C (A♭ in descent)
Lit.: no. 139.

Bhairo (North India). See *Bhairav*.

Bhairvī (North India). See *Bhairavī*.

Bhajana (Bengal). Religious song. Its melody always obeys the rules of an appropriate *rāga*, sung in alternation by a chorus and a solo singer. The texts can be in Sanskrit or, more often, in Hindi, and are shaped in strophic form. All strophes are sung to the same melody. The instrumental accompaniment is variable. Often one hears a *tanbura*, cymbals, fiddle, harmonium, and others. *Bhajana* singing generally lasts through the better part of the night.
Lit.: no. 46.

Bhaka Mañjari (South India). *Janya rāga* of the 47th *mēḷa* (*Suvarṇāṅgī*).
Tone material:
C E♭ F♯ B G A B c
c B G F♯ E♭ D♭ C
Lit.: no. 139.

Bhakāra rathaṃtara (Vedic India). In order to conceal the powerful magic of the textual syllables of the *Sāmaveda* from uninitiated persons, the syllables were purposefully distorted in such a manner that the chanters appeared to perform meaningless syllables which began with the letter *bh* and utilized the vowel of the proper syllable.

Bhakkar (North India). See *Bhankar*.

Bhaktapriya (South India). *Janya rāga* of the 16th *mēḷa* (*Chakravāka*).
Tone material:
C E F G A B♭ c
c B♭ A G F D♭ E F F C
Lit.: no. 139.

Bhakti (India). "Devotion." One of the emotions (*rasas*) expressed in music.
Lit.: no. 140.

Bhallādi (South India). See *Ballāti*.

Bhāmāmaṇi (South India). *Janya rāga* of the 15th *mēḷa* (*Māyāmāḷavagauḷa*).
Tone material:
C F D♭ E F A♭ B c
c A♭ G E D♭ C
Lit.: no. 139.

Bhāmāmaṇi (South India). *Janya rāga* of the 61st *mēḷa* (*Kāntāmaṇi*).
Tone material:
C F♯ D E F♯ A♭ B♭♭ c
c A♭ G E D C
Lit.: no. 139.

Bhambhā (South India). Barrel drum.

Bhāṇḍa (*Bhāṇḍavādā*) (India). Sanskrit term for "instrument."
Lit.: nos. 205, 255.

Bhāṇḍavādā (India). See *Bhāṇḍa*.

Bhangra (North India). Popular dance (harvest dance) in form of a circle accompanied by Pahari music. *Bhangra* is prevalent in Jammu, Kashmir (Bhadarwah, Kishtwar). Cf. *Dhris*.
Lit.: nos. 46, 234.

Bhankar (*Bhakar*; *Bhikkar*) (North India). A rare *rāga* ascribed to the *Marva thāta*.
Tone material:
C D♭ E (F) (F♯) G A B c
c B A G (F♯) (F) E D♭ C
Vādis vague (cf. with *Gauri rāga* of *Purvi thāta*).
Lit.: no. 138.

Bhansli (India). See *Bansuli*.

Bhānu Chandrika (South India). *Janya rāga* of the 8th *mēḷa* (*Hanumattōḍi*).
Tone material:
C F A♭ B♭ c
c B♭ A♭ F E♭ C
Lit.: no. 139.

Bhānu Chūḍāmaṇī (*Bhānu Cūḍāmaṇī*) (South India). *Janya rāga* of the 18th *mēḷa* (*Hāṭakāmbarī*).
Tone material:
C D♭ E F G c
c B A♯ B G F E D♭ C
Lit.: no. 139.

Bhānu Cūḍāmaṇī (South India). See *Bhānu Chūḍāmaṇī*.

Bhānu Dhanyāsi (South India). *Janya rāga* of the 45th *mēḷa* (*Śubhapantuvarālī*).
Tone material:
C D♭ E♭ F♯ B A♭ B
A♭ G F♯ E♭ D♭ C *B* C
This *rāga* has a *niṣādāntya* scale.
Lit.: no. 139.

Bhānu Dīpakam (South India). *Janya rāga* of the 24th *mēḷa* (*Varuṇapriyā*).
Tone material:
C D E♭ F G A♯ B c
c B G F D C
Lit.: no. 139.

Bhānu Dīparam (South India). *Janya rāga* of the 34th *mēḷa* (*Vāgadhīśvarī*).
Tone material:
C F D♯ E F G c
c A G F E F D♯ C
Lit.: no. 139.

Bhānu Gauḷa (South India). *Janya rāga* of the 7th *mēḷa* (*Senāpāti*).
Tone material:
A♭ C D♭ E♭ F G A♭ B♭♭
A♭ G F E♭ D♭ C *B♭♭ A♭ G*
Lit.: no. 139.

Bhānu Gīrvāṇi (South India). *Janya rāga* of the 45th *mēḷa* (*Śubhapantuvarālī*).
Tone material:
C D♭ E♭ F♯ G A♭ B c
c B A♭ F♯ E♭ D♭ C
Lit.: no. 139.

Bhānu Jyōtiṣmati (South India). *Janya rāga* (*Sucharitra*).
Tone material:
C D♯ E F♯ G A♭ B♭♭ A♭ c
c B♭♭ A♭ G E F♯ D♯ C
Lit.: no. 139.

Bhānukānti (South India). *Janya rāga* of the 25th *mēḷa* (*Māraranjanī*).
Tone material:
C D F G A♭ B♭♭ c
c B♭♭ A♭ G F D C
Lit.: no. 139.

Bhānukatayan (South India). *Janya rāga* of the 44th *mēḷa* (*Bhāvapriyā*).
Tone material:
C E♭ F♯ G A♭ B♭ c
c B♭ A♭ G F♯ E♭ C
Lit.: no. 139.

Bhānukiraṇi (South India). *Janya rāga* of the 27th *mēḷa* (*Sarasāṅgī*).
Tone material:
C E F A♭ B c
c B A♭ G F E D C
Lit.: no. 139.

Bhānukōkila (South India). *Janya rāga* of the 12th *mēḷa* (*Rūpāvatī*).
Tone material:
C F G A♯ B c
c A♯ B G F E♭ C
Lit.: no. 139.

Bhānukriya (South India). *Janya rāga* of the 30th *mēḷa* (*Nāgānandī*).
Tone material:
C F E F G A♯ B c
c B A♯ G F E D C
Lit.: no. 139.

Bhānumañjari (South India). *Janya rāga* of the 34th *mēḷa* (*Vāgadhīśvarī*).
Tone material:
C D♯ E F G B♭ c
c B♭ G F D♯ E D♯ C
Lit.: no. 139.

Bhānumatī (South India). *Janya rāga* of the 4th *mēḷa* (*Vanaspāti*).
Tone material:
C D♭ E♭♭ D♭ F G c
c B♭ A G F E♭♭ D♭ C
Lit.: no. 139.

Bhānumātī (South India). (1) Name of the 4th *asampūrṇa mēḷa-rāga* without the *kaṭapayādi* prefix:
C D♭ E♭♭ F G A B♭ c
Cf. *Vanaspāti.* (2) The name of the 4th *asampūrṇa mēḷa-rāga* with the *kaṭapayādi* prefix:
C D♭ E♭♭ D♭ F G c / c B♭ A G F E♭♭ D♭ C
See *Rāgas* (South India).
Lit.: no. 139.

Bhānupratā pam (South India). *Janya rāga* of the 25th *mēḷa* (*Māraranjanī*).
Tone material:
C D E F G A♭ c
c A♭ G F E D C
Lit.: no. 139.

Bhānupriya (South India). *Janya rāga* of the 1st *mēḷa* (*Kanakangi*).
Tone material:
C D♭ E♭♭ F G c
c G F E♭♭ D♭ C
Lit.: no. 139.

Bhānupriya (South India). *Janya rāga* of the 21st *mēḷa* (*Kiravāṇi*).
Tone material:
C D E♭ A♭ B c
c B A♭ E♭ D C
Lit.: no. 139.

Bhānuta (South India). *Janya rāga* of the 29th *mēḷa* (*Dhīraśaṅkarābharaṇam*).
Tone material:
C F E F G A B c
c A G F E D C
Lit.: no. 139.

Bhānu Tivra (South India). *Janya rāga* of the 34th *mēḷa* (*Vāgadhīśvarī*).
C F D♯ E F G c
c B♭ A G F D♯ E F E C
Lit.: no. 139.

Bharang (Indonesia; Madura). The fourth note of the *slendro* system of Madura. Cf. *Slendro* (Java).
Lit.: no. 163.

Bhāratā (India). Ornament performed in *vīṇa* playing. The open string *sa* (C) is struck and the player's hand quickly and briefly touches the tone *ri* (D).
Lit.: no. 255.

Bharata Nāṭyam (South India). The pure classical dance that does not represent a story. The original significance of *bharata nāṭya* is "dance drama." The *bharata-nāṭyam* consists of seven parts: *alarippu*, *jātisvaram*, *śabda*, *varṇam*, *padam*, *tillānā*, and a concluding brief verse in Sanskrit.

The dancing is performed only by female dancers. The music is provided by a small ensemble consisting of a transverse flute, a *mridanga*, a reed box (*śruti*) and a jew's harp. Several songs are sung by a man, one by a man (master) and a youth (disciple), one by a girl and a man, and one by a woman.
Lit.: no. 261.

Bhāratā Vīṇā (India). A *sitar* type similar to the *kacha vīṇā*.The appearance of the instrument is that of a long-necked lute. The neck is covered with parchment. The wide neck shows 17 frets and five strings (two made of steel, three made of brass). The tuning is: F C C F *C*.
Lit.: no. 254.

Bhārati (South India). *Janya rāga* of the 44th *mēḷa* (*Bhāvapriyā*).
Tone material:
C D♭ F♯ G A♭ B♭ c
c B♭ A♭ G F♯ D♭ C
Lit.: no. 139.

Bharbarā (South India). See *Barbarā*.

Bhargapriya (South India). *Janya rāga* of the 25th *mēḷa* (*Mārarañjanī*).
Tone material:
C D E A♭ B♭♭ c
c B♭♭ A♭ E D C
Lit.: no. 139.

Bhārgavī (South India). *Janya rāga* of the 9th *mēḷa* (*Dhēnuka*).
Tone material:
C E♭ F G A♭ B c
c B A♭ G F E♭ C
Lit.: no. 139.

Bhārgavī (South India). *Janya rāga* of the 37th *mēḷa* (*Sālaga*).
Tone material:
C E♭♭ F♯ G A♭ B♭♭ c
c B♭♭ A♭ G F♯ E♭♭ C
Lit.: no. 139.

Bharmāmbari (South India). *Janya rāga* of the 30th *mēḷa* (*Nāgānandī*).
Tone material:
C D F A♯ B c
c B A♯ F D C
Lit.: no. 139.

Bharmāṅgi (South India). *Janya rāga* of the 33rd *mēḷa* (*Gāṅgeyabhushanī*).
Tone material:
C D♯ E A♭ B c
c B A♭ E D♯ C
Lit.: no. 139.

Bhāshānga (India). At the present time the term signifies a *janya rāga* that employs 1-3 notes foreign to its primary *mēḷa*. Cf. *Upāṅga rāga*.
Lit.: no. 261.

Bhāshini (*Bhāṣiṇi*) (South India). *Janya rāga* of the 56th *mēḷa* (*Śaṇmukhapriyā*).
Tone material:
C E♭ D E♭ F♯ G A♭ B♭ c
c B♭ A♭ G F♯ E♭ D C
Lit.: no. 139.

Bhāṣiṇi (South India). See *Bhāshiṇi*.

Bhāskarapriya (South India). *Janya rāga* of the 36th *mēḷa* (*Chalanāṭa*).
Tone material:
C D♯ F G A♯ B c
c B A♯ G F D♭ C
Lit.: no. 139.

Bhatiyar (*Bhatyar*; *Bhatihar*). *Rāga* ascribed to the *Marva thāta.*
Tone material:
C D♭ E (F) (F♯) G A B c
c B A G (F♯) F E D♭ C
For other types of *Bhatiyar*, cf. Lit. no. 138.

Bhāva (India). The soul, the individual emotional essence of a *rāga*. This becomes manifest when the performer applies all rules of the *rāga*, when he presents the correct passages, the stressed and weak notes, the required intonations, and the prescribed ornaments. Cf. *Rasa.*
Lit.: nos. 138, 140.

Bhavā Bharaṇam (South India). *Janya rāga* of the 29th *mēḷa* (*Dhīraśaṅkarabharaṇam*).
Tone material:
C D E F A B c
c B A F E D C
Lit.: no. 139.

Bhāva Hamsa (South India). *Janya rāga* of the 15th *mēḷa* (*Māyāmāḷavagauḷa*).
Tone material:
C E G A♭ B c
c B A♭ G F E C
Lit.: no. 139.

Bhavai (India). Gujarati folk operatic performance. The actors stand or move about the stage in a circle.

Bhāvajapriya (South India). *Janya rāga* of the 3rd *mēḷa* (*Gānamūrti*).
Tone material:
C E♭♭ F G A♭ B c
c B A♭ G F E♭♭ C
Lit.: no. 139.

Bhavāḷi (South India). *Janya rāga* of the 46th *mēḷa* (*Śaḍvidhamārgiṇī*).
Tone material
C D♭ F♯ G A c
c B♭ A B♭ A G F♯ E♭ D♭ C
Lit.: no. 139.

Bhavamanōharī (South India). *Janya rāga* of the 53rd *mēḷa* (*Gamanaśrama*).
Tone material:
C D♭ E F♯ A G B c
c B A B G F♯ E F♯ D♭ C
Lit.: no. 139.

Bhavāni (South India). *Janya rāga* of the 44th *mēḷa* (*Bhāvapriyā*).
Tone material:
C D♭ E♭ F♯ A♭ B♭ c
c B♭ A♭ F♯ E♭ D♭ C
Lit.: no. 139.

Bhavāni (South India). See *Bhāvapriyā* (44th *asampūrṇa mēḷa rāga*).

Bhāvapriyā (South India). The 44th *mēḷa*:
C D♭ E♭ F♯ G A♭ B♭ c
As a *rāga* it can be performed at any time.
Lit.: no. 139.

Bhāvapriyā (South India). (1) The 44th *asampūrṇa mēḷa-rāga* without *kaṭapayādi* prefix:
C D♭ E♭ F♯ G A♭ B♭ c
(2) The 44th *mēḷa-rāga* with *kaṭapayādi* prefix. It was called *Bhavāni*:
C D♭ E♭ F♯ A♭ B♭ c / c B♭ A♭ F♯ E♭ D♭ C
Cf. *Rāga* (South India).
Lit.: no. 139.

Bhavarkatū (India). Drum beaten at funerals.
Lit.: no. 255.

Bhavasindhu (South India). *Janya rāga* of the 28th *mēḷa* (*Harikambhōji*).
Tone material:
C D E G A B♭ c
c B♭ G F E F D C
Lit.: no. 139.

Bhavgit (North India). Light, popular song which does not observe a specific *rāga*. Its text is mostly in Marathi.

Bhāvini (South India). *Janya rāga* of the 15th *mēḷa* (*Māyāmāḷavagauḷa*).
Tone material:
C E F G A♭ B c
c B A♭ G F E C
Lit.: no. 139.

Bhavsak (North India). Obscure *rāga*.
Tone material approximately:
C F G A c
c B A G F E D (*B♭* D) C
The *vādis* can be F and C.
Lit.: no. 138.

Bhāvukadāyini (South India). *Janya rāga* of the 44th *mēḷa* (*Bhāvapriyā*).
Tone material:
C E♭ F♯ G A♭ B♭ c
c B♭ A♭ G F♯ E♭ C
Lit.: no. 139.

Bhavyalīla (South India). *Janya rāga* of the 16th *mēḷa* (*Chakravāka*).
Tone material:
C E F A B♭ c
c B♭ A G F E C
Lit.: no. 139.

Bhayadindima (India). Sanskrit term for battle drum.
Lit.: no. 255.

Bhayānaka (India). "Fear." One of the nine emotions (*rasas*) expressed in music. Cf. *Navarasa*; *Rasa.*

Bhazana-śruti (India). Synonym for *nagabaddha.*
Lit.: no. 255.

Bhed (India). See *Bherī.*

Bhēndrūla (South India). *Janya rāga* of the 20th *mēḷa* (*Naṭabhairavī*).
Tone material:
C D E♭ F G A♭ B♭ c
c G F E♭ D C
Lit.: no. 139.

Bheng (Java; Madura). The first note of the *slendro* system of Madura.

Bhēri (Bali). Formerly a kettledrum, now a small gong; also called *benḍē.*
Lit.: no. 197.

Bherī (India; Bengal). Kettledrum. See *Nāgara.*
Lit.: no. 254.

Bheri (*Bheḍ*) (India). Sanskrit term for long brass or copper trumpet. Cf. *Tūrya.*
Lit.: no. 254.

Bhēri karṇīka (South India). *Janya rāga* of the 3rd *mēḷa* (*Gānamūrti*).
Tone material:
C D♭ E♭♭ F G A♭ B A♭ c
c B A♭ G F E♭♭ D♭ C
Lit.: no. 139.

Bhīkara Ghōshiṇi (*Bhīkara Ghōṣiṇi*) (South India). *Janya rāga* of the 44th *mēḷa* (*Bhāvapriyā*).
Tone material:
C D♭ E♭ F♯ G A♭ B♭ c
c B♭ A♭ F♯ G F♯ E♭ D♭ C
Lit.: no. 139.

Bhīkara Ghōṣiṇi (South India). See *Bhīkara Ghōshiṇi.*

Bhikkar (North India). See *Bhankar.*

Bhim (North India). Rare *rāga* ascribed to the *Kafi thāta.*
Tone material:
B♭ (C F G) B♭ c
B♭ A G E D C (*B♭*); *Vādis*: G, C
Lit.: no. 138.

Bhimpalashri (North India). See *Bhimpalasi.*

Bhimpalasi (*Bhimpalashri*) (North India). *Rāga* ascribed to the *Kafi thāta.*
Tone material:
(*B*♭) C E♭ F G B♭ c
c B♭ A G F E♭ D C; *Vādis:* F, C
The note is *vishrantisthan.*
Lit.: no. 138.

Bhinna Gāndhāri (South India). *Janya rāga* of the 27th *mēḷa* (*Sarasāṅgī*).
Tone material:
C D E F G A♭ B c
c A♭ G F E F D C
Lit.: no. 139.

Bhinna Hērāḷi (South India). *Janya rāga* of the 49th *mēḷa* (*Dhavalāmbarī*).
Tone material:
C F♯ G A♭ B♭♭ A♭ c
c B♭♭ A♭ G F♯ E C
Lit.: no. 139.

Bhinnaniṣāda (South India). *Janya rāga* of the 6th *mēḷa* (*Tānarūpi*).
Tone material:
C D♭ E♭♭ F A♯ c
c A♯ F E♭♭ D♭ C
Lit.: no. 139.

Bhinnaniṣāda (South India). *Janya rāga* of the 63rd *mēḷa* (*Latangi*).
Tone material:
C D E F♯ G A♭ B
B A♭ G F♯ E D C *B*
The scale of this *rāga* has *niṣādāntya* character.
Lit.: no. 139.

Bhinnapaurāḷi (South India). *Janya rāga* of the 49th *mēḷa* (*Dhavalambarī*).
Tone material:
C F♯ G A♭ B♭♭ c
c B♭♭ A♭ G F♯ E C
Lit.: no. 139.

Bhinnaṣaḍja(m) (South India). *Janya rāga* of the 9th *mēḷa* (*Dhēnuka*).
Tone material:
C D♭ E♭ D♭ G F G B c (C D♭ E♭ D♭ F G B b)
c A♭ G F E♭ D♭ C
Lit.: no. 139.

Bhinnaṣaḍja (South India). (1) The 9th *asampūrṇa mēḷa-rāga* without the *kaṭapayādi* prefix:
C D♭ E♭ D♭ G F (F G) G B c
c A♭ G F E♭ D♭ C
(2) The 9th *asampūrṇa mēḷa-rāga* with the *kaṭapayādi* prefix was called *Dhunibhinnaṣaḍja.* Cf. *Dhēnuka.* See *Rāgas* (South India).
Lit.: no. 139.

Bhinna Varaḷi (South India). *Janya rāga* of the 49th *mēḷa* (*Dhavalāmbarī*).
Tone material:
C F♯ G A♭ B♭♭ A♭ c
c B♭♭ A♭ G F♯ C
Lit.: no. 139.

Bhinna Vikrama (South India). *Janya rāga* of the 29th *mēḷa* (*Dhīraśaṅkarābharaṇam*).
Tone material:
C D E F A c
c B A G D C
Lit.: no. 139.

Bhinna Vikriya (South India). *Janya rāga* of the 28th *mēḷa* (*Harikambhōji*).
Tone material:
C D E F G A c
c A G F D C
Lit.: no. 139.

Bhinnapañcama (South India). *Janya rāga* of the 3rd *mēḷa* (*Gānamūrti*).

Tone material:

C E♭♭ F G A♭ B c

c B A♭ G F E♭♭ D♭ C

Lit.: no. 139.

Bhīshmāvaḷi (South India). *Janya rāga* of the 8th *mēḷa* (*Hanumattōḍi*).

Tone material:

C E♭ D♭ E♭ F A♭ G B♭ A♭ c

c B♭ A♭ F E♭ D♭ C

Lit.: no. 139.

Bhōgachhāyānāta (South India). (1) See *Vāgadhīśvarī*. (2) See *Chhāyānāṭa* (34th *asampūrṇa mēḷa-rāga*).

Bhōga Chintāmaṇi (South India). See *Bhōga Cintāmaṇi* (or *Chintāmaṇi*).

Bhōga Cintāmaṇi (South India). *Janya rāga* of the 1st *mēḷa* (*Kanakangi*).

Tone material:

C D♭ G F G A♭ B♭♭ c

c A♭ G F E♭♭ D♭ E♭♭ D♭ C

Lit.: no. 139.

Bhōga Dhanyāsi (South India). *Janya rāga* of the 48th *mēḷa* (*Divyamaṇī*).

Tone material:

C E♭ F♯ G B c

c B G A♯ B G F♯ E♭ D♭ C

Lit.: no. 139.

Bhōga Dhvajā (South India). *Janya rāga* of the 39th *mēḷa* (*Jhālavarāḷi*).

Tone material:

C D♭ E♭♭ F♯ G A♭ B c

c A♭ G F♯ D♭ C

Lit.: no. 139

Bhōga Dhvaji (South India). *Janya rāga* of the 47th *mēḷa* (*Suvarṇāṅgī*).

Tone material:

C D♭ E♭ F♯ G A B c

c A G F♯ D♭ C

Lit.: no. 139.

Bhōga Kannada (South India). *Janya rāga* of the 22nd *mēḷa* (*Kharaharapriyā*).

Tone material:

C D F G A G B♭ c

c A B♭ G A F E♭ D E♭ C

Lit.: no. 139.

Bhōga Līlā (South India). *Janya rāga* of the 27th *mēḷa* (*Sarasaṅgī*).

Tone material:

C D E G A♭ B c

c B A♭ F E D C

Lit.: no. 139.

Bhōga Rañjani (South India). *Janya rāga* of the 7th *mēḷa* (*Senāpāti*).

Tone material:

C D♭ F G A♭ c

c B♭♭ A♭ G F E♭ D♭ C

Lit.: no. 139.

Bhōga Rasāḷig (South India). *Janya rāga* of the 38th *mēḷa* (*Jalārṇava*).

Tone material:

C D♭ E♭♭ F♯ A♭ G B♭ c

c B♭ A♭ B♭ G F♯ E♭♭ D♭ C

Lit.: no. 139.

Bhōga Rasāvaḷi (South India). See *Bhōga Rasāḷi*.

Bhōga Sāmantam (South India). *Janya rāga* of the 51st *mēḷa* (*Kāmavardhanī*).

Tone material:

C E F♯ G A♭ G c

c A♭ B G F♯ E D♭ C

Lit.: no. 139.

Bhōga Sāvēri (South India). *Janya rāga* of the 37th *mēḷa* (*Sālaga*).
Tone material:

C Db (F#) G Ab Bbb
Ab G F# Ebb Db C Bbb

This *rāga* is a *niṣādāntya* type.
Lit.: no. 139.

Bhōga Śikhāmaṇi (South India). *Janya rāga* of the 7th *mēḷa* (*Senāpāti*).
Tone material:

C F Eb F Ab Bbb c
c Bbb Ab G F Eb Db C

Lit.: no. 139.

Bhōga Varāḷi (South India). *Janya rāga* of the 37th *mēḷa* (*Sālaga*).
Tone material:

C Db Ebb F# G Bbb Ab Bbb c
c Bbb Ab F# Ebb Db C
(c Bbb G Ab F# Ebb Db C)

Lit.: no. 139.

Bhōga Vardhani (South India). *Janya rāga* of the 37th *mēḷa* (*Sālaga*).
Tone material:

C Db Ebb F# Ab c
c Ab F# Ebb Db C

Lit.: no. 139.

Bhōga Vasantam (South India). *Janya rāga* of the 51st *mēḷa* (*Kāmavardhanī*).
Tone material:

C Db E F# Ab B c
c B Ab F# E Db C

Lit.: no. 139.

Bhōgavati (South India). *Janya rāga* of the 12th *mēḷa* (*Rūpāvatī*).
Tone material:

C Db Eb F A# c
c A# F Eb Db C

Lit.: no. 139.

Bhōgavati (South India). *Janya rāga* of the 22nd *mēḷa* (*Kharaharapriyā*).
Tone material:

C D Eb F Bb c
c Bb F Eb D C

Lit.: no. 139.

Bhōgi (South India). *Janya rāga* of the 12th *mēḷa* (*Senāpāti*).
Tone material:

C Eb F G Ab Bbb Ab c
c Bbb Ab G F Eb C

Lit.: no. 139.

Bhōgi Bhairavī (South India). *Janya rāga* of the 28th *mēḷa* (*Harikāmbhōji*).
Tone material:

C D E F G Bb A Bb c
c A G F D E D C

Lit.: no. 139.

Bhōgi Sindhu (South India). *Janya rāga* of the 48th *mēḷa* (*Divyamaṇī*).
Tone material:

C G F# G A# B c
c B A# B G F# C

Lit.: no. 139.

Bhōgīśvari (South India). *Janya rāga* of the 64th *mēḷa* (*Vāchaspati*).
Tone material:

C D E G A Bb A c
c Bb A G F# E D C

Lit.: no. 139.

Bhoushya (Nepal). A single brass cymbal.
Lit.: no. 46.

Bhramara (South India). *Janya rāga* of the 19th *mēḷa* (*Jhaṅkaradhvani*).
Tone material:

C D Eb F Ab Bbb c
c Bbb Ab F Eb D C

Lit.: no. 139.

Bhramarabhōgi (South India). *Janya rāga* of the 44th *mēḷa* (*Bhāvapriyā*).
Tone material:
F♯ G A♭ B♭ C D♭ E♭
F♯ E♭ D♭ *B♭ A♭ G*
Lit.: no. 139.

Bhramara Dhvani (South India). *Janya rāga* of the 54th *mēḷa* (*Viśvambharī*).
Tone material:
C D F♯ A♯ B c
c A♯ B G F♯ E D♭ C
Lit.: no. 139.

Bhramara Haṃsi (South India). *Janya rāga* of the 57th *mēḷa* (*Siṃhendramadhyama*).
Tone material:
C D E♭ F♯ G B c
c B A♭ G F♯ E♭ C
Lit.: no. 139.

Bhramara Kētanam (South India). *Janya rāga* of the 8th *mēḷa* (*Hanumattōḍi*).
Tone material:
C D♭ E♭ F G B♭ A♭ B♭ c
c B♭ A♭ G F E♭ C
Lit.: no. 139.

Bhramara Kōkilam (South India). *Janya rāga* of the 57th *mēḷa* (*Siṃhendramadhyama*).
Tone material:
C D F♯ G B A♭ B c
c B A♭ G F♯ D C
Lit.: no. 139.

Bhramara Kusuman (South India). *Janya rāga* of the 56th *mēḷa* (*Śaṇmukhapriyā*).
Tone material:
C E♭ F♯ G B♭ c
c B♭ A♭ G F♯ E♭ D C
Lit.: no. 139.

Bhramara Nārāyaṇi (South India). *Janya rāga* of the 54th *mēḷa* (*Viśvambharī*).
Tone material:
C D♭ E F♯ G B A♯ B c
c B F♯ E D♭ C
Lit.: no. 139.

Bhramara Puttari (South India). *Janya rāga* of the 58th *mēḷa* (*Hemāvatī*).
Tone material:
C D E♭ F♯ G F♯ A B♭ c
c A G F♯ E♭ D C
Lit.: no. 139.

Bhramara Sāraṅga (South India). *Janya rāga* of the 56th *mēḷa* (*Śaṇmukhapriyā*).
Tone material:
C D E♭ F♯ G F♯ A♭ B♭ c
c A♭ G F♯ E♭ D C
Lit.: no. 139.

Bhramara Sukhi (South India). *Janya rāga* of the 57th *mēḷa* (*Siṃhendramadhyama*).
Tone material:
C D E♭ F♯ G A♭ B c
c G F♯ E♭ D C
Lit.: no. 139.

Bhramara Vardhani (South India). *Janya rāga* of the 10th *mēḷa* (*Nāṭakapriya*).
Tone material:
C D♭ F G A B♭ c
c B♭ A G F D♭ C
Lit.: no. 139.

Bhramarika Mañjari (South India). *Janya rāga* of the 28th *mēḷa* (*Kharaharapriyā*).
Tone material:
C E♭ F A G B♭ c
c B♭ A G A F E♭ D C
Lit.: no. 139.

Bhṛṅgadhvani (South India). *Janya rāga* of the 62nd *mēḷa* (*Riṣabhapriyā*).
Tone material:
C E F♯ G A♭ B♭ c
c B♭ A♭ G F♯ E C
Lit.: no. 139.

Bhṛṅgamōhi (South India). *Janya rāga* of the 47th *mēḷa* (*Suvarṇaṅgī*).
Tone material:

C D♭ F♯ G A B c
c B A G F♯ D♭ C

Lit.: no. 139.

Bhṛṅga Vilasita (South India). *Janya rāga* of the 20th *mēḷa* (*Naṭabhairavī*).
Tone material:

C D F A♭ B♭ c
c A♭ G F D C

Lit.: no. 139.

Bhṛṅgu Kuṅga (South India). *Janya rāga* of the 24th *mēḷa* (*Varunapriyā*).
Tone material:

C D F G B A♯ c
c B A♯ G F D C

Lit.: no. 139.

Bhū (South India). One of the six mnenonics applied to the system of the 72 *mēḷas*. *Bhu* indicates the fourth *mēḷa* of each of the 12 *chakras*.

The six mnemonics are: *pa* representing the 1st *mēḷa* of each *chakra*, *śrī* standing for the 2nd, *go* for the 3rd, *bhū* for the 4th, *mā* for the 5th, and *shā* for the 6th. Cf. *Rāga* (South India).
Lit.: no. 139.

Bhujaga Chintāmaṇi (South India). *Janya rāga* of the 13th *mēḷa* (*Gāyakapriya*).
Tone material:

C G F G A♭ B♭♭ A♭ c
c B♭♭ A♭ G F E D♭ C

Lit.: no. 139.

Bhūjagamiṇi (South India). *Janya rāga* of the 16th *mēḷa* (*Chakravāka*).
Tone material:

C D♭ F A B♭ E G c
c B♭ A G F E D♭ C

Lit.: no. 139.

Bhujaṅga Svaram (South India). A snake charmer's pipe made of a gourd and a slim bamboo tube with (occasionally without) finger holes and an inserted reed that serves as a mouthpiece. The Tamil term of this instrument is *maguḍi*.
Lit.: no. 261.

Bhujaṅga vādyam (South India). See *Bhujaṅga Svaram*.

Bhujangi (South India). *Janya rāga* of the 3rd *mēḷa* (*Gānamūrti*).
Tone material:

C D♭ E♭♭ F B c
c B F E♭♭ D♭ C

Lit.: no. 139.

Bhūjangini (South India). *Janya rāga* of the 16th *mēḷa* (*Chakravāka*).
Tone material:

C D♭ C F E F B♭ A B♭ c
c B♭ A F E D♭ C (D♭ C)

Lit.: no. 139.

Bhūmi dundubhi (Ancient India). A big drum. A pit in the ground was covered with the skin of a bull which was beaten with the bull's tail at sacred (Mahavrata) services.

Bhūpu Kalyāṇī (South India). *Janya rāga* of the 64th *mēḷa* (*Mechakalyāṇī*).
Tone material:

C D F♯ G A c
c B A G F♯ E D C

Lit.: no. 139.

Bhūpaḷa(m) (South India). *Janya rāga* of the 8th *mēḷa* (*Hanumattōḍi*).
Tone material:

C D♭ E♭ G A♭ c
c A♭ G E♭ D♭ C

Lit.: no. 139.

Bhūpaḷa Cintāmaṇi (South India). *Janya rāga* of the 2nd *mēḷa* (*Ratnangī*).
Tone material:
C D♭ E♭♭ F G A♭ B♭ A♭ c
c A♭ B♭ A♭ G F D♭ C
Lit.: no. 139.

Bhūpāḷam (*Revagupti*; *Bibāsu*) (South India). *Janya rāga* of the 15th *mēḷa* (*Māyāmāḷavagauḷa*).
Tone material:
C D♭ E G A♭ c
c AB G E D♭ C
This *rāga* is also listed under the heading of the 8th *mēḷa* where the note *ga* is E♭. (Cf. also *Revagupti* and *Bibasu*.) For further details see Lit. no. 139.

Bhūpāḷa Manōhari (South India). *Janya rāga* of the 5th *mēḷa* (*Mānavātī*).
Tone material:
C E♭♭ F G A B c
c B A G F E♭♭ C
Lit.: no. 139.

Bhūpāḷa Pañchama (South India). *Janya rāga* of the 39th *mēḷa* (*Jhālavarāḷi*).
Tone material:
C E♭♭ D♭ E♭♭ G F♯ A♭ c
c G A♭ F♯ C D♭ C (C E♭♭ D♭ C)
Lit.: no. 139.

Bhūpāḷa Rañjani (South India). *Janya rāga* of the 33rd *mēḷa* (*Gāṅgeyabhushanī*).
Tone material:
C D♯ F G A♭ B c
c B A♭ G F D♯ C
Lit.: no. 139.

Bhūpāḷa Taraṅgiṇi (South India). *Janya rāga* of the 18th *mēḷa* (*Hāṭakāmbarī*).
Tone material:
C D♭ F G B c
c B A♯ B G F E F D♭ C
Lit.: no. 139.

Bhūpāli (North India). An important *rāga* ascribed to the *Kalyan thāta*.
Tone material:
C D E G A c
c A G E D C; *Vādis*: E, A
Lit.: no. 138.

Bhūpāḷika (South India). *Janya rāga* of the 16th *mēḷa* (*Chakravāka*).
Tone material:
C E F G B♭ c
c B♭ A G F E C
Lit.: no. 139.

Bhūpal-tōḍi (North India). *Rāga* ascribed to the *Bhairavi thāta*.
Tone material:
C D♭ E♭ G A♭ c
c A♭ G E♭ D♭ C; *Vādis*: A♭, E♭
Lit.: no. 138.

Bhūpāvaḷi (South India). *Janya rāga* of the 59th *mēḷa* (*Dharmavatī*).
Tone material:
C D E♭ D F♯ G B c
c B A G F♯ E♭ D C
Lit.: no. 139.

Bhūpkalyāṇ (South India). *Janya rāga* of the 29th *mēḷa* (*Dhīraśaṅkarābharaṇam*).
Tone material:
C D E G A c
c A G F E D C
Lit.: no. 139.

Bhūrañjani (South India). *Janya rāga* of the 64th *mēḷa* (*Mechakalyāṇi*).

Tone material:

C D E G A B c

c B A F# E D C

Lit.: no. 139.

Bhūṛi (South India). Telugu term for a curved brass horn used in religious ceremonies. Cf. *Tūrya*; *Bheṛī*.
Lit.: no. 254.

Bhūṣaṇa Dhāriṇi (South India). See *Bhūshana Dhāriṇi.*

Bhūṣaṇi (South India). See *Bhūshaṇi.*

Bhūshaṇa Dhāriṇi (*Bhūṣaṇa Dhāriṇi*) (South India). *Janya rāga* of the 35th *mēḷa* (*Śūlinī*).
Tone material:

C D# E F G A B c

c B A G F D# C

Lit.: no. 139.

Bhūshaṇi (South India). *Janya rāga* of the 28th *mēḷa* (*Harikāmbhōji*).
Tone material:

C E D E F G A Bb c

c Bb A G F E D C

Lit.: no. 139.

Bhūṣāvaḷi (South India). *Janya rāga* of the 64th *mēḷa* (*Vāchaspati*).
Tone material:

C D E F# G A c

c Bb A G F# E D C

Lit.: no. 139.

Bhūshā Kalyāṇi (South India). *Janya rāga* of the 54th *mēḷa* (*Viśvambharī*).
Tone material

C Db E F# G A# B c

c B G F# E Db C

Lit.: no. 139

Bhusya (Nepal). A pair of cymbals.

Bhūta sankhya (South India). System of musical mnemonics linked with the *kāṭapayādī sankhya.* In the *bhūta sankhya* the *chakra* names used in the *mēḷa* system (*indu chakra*, *netra chakra*, etc.; see *Chakra*) are combined with the syllables representing the six *mēḷas* in each of the 12 *chakras* (*pa*, *śrī*, *go*, *bhū*, *mā*, *shā*; cf. *Bhū*). E.g., *diśī bhū* indicates the 4th *mēḷa* (*bhū*) of the 10th *chakra* (*Diśī*).
Lit.: no. 261.

Bhūteśapriya (South India). *Janya rāga* of the 39th *mēḷa* (*Jhālavarāḷi*).
Tone material:

C Ebb F# G Ab B c

c B Ab G F# Ebb C

Lit.: no. 139.

Bhūvana Gāndhāri (South India). *Janya rāga* of the 20th *mēḷa* (*Naṭabhairavī*).
Tone material:

C D F G Bb c

c Bb Ab G F Eb C

Lit.: no. 139.

Bhūvana Kuntali (South India). *Janya rāga* of the 68th *mēḷa* (*Jyōtisvarūpiṇī*).
Tone material:

C D# E F# G Ab c

c Ab G F# E C

Lit.: no. 139.

Bhūvana Mōhiṇi (South India). *Janya rāga* of the 16th *mēḷa* (*Chakravāka*).
Tone material:

C E F Bb A c

c Bb G A F E Db C

Lit.: no. 139.

Bhūvana Rañjani (South India). *Janya rāga* of the 14th *mēḷa* (*Vakuḷābharaṇam*).
Tone material:
C E F G A♭ B♭ c
c B♭ A♭ G F E C
Lit.: no. 139.

Bhuvana Sundari (South India). *Janya rāga* of the 29th *mēḷa* (*Dhīraśaṅkarābharaṇam*).
Tone material:
C D E F B c
c B A G F E D C
Lit.: no. 139.

Bhūvanēśvari (South India). *Janya rāga* of the 4th *mēḷa* (*Vanaspāti*).
Tone material:
C D♭ E♭♭ F G A c
c A G F E♭♭ D♭ C
Lit.: no. 139.

Bhūyōmani (South India). *Janya rāga* of the 22nd *mēḷa* (*Kharaharapriyā*).
Tone material:
C E♭ F G A B♭ c
c B♭ G F E♭ D C
Lit.: no. 139.

Bi (*Bei*) (Japan). Name of the twelfth pipe of the *shō*.
Lit.: no. 226.

Bia (Congo – Bwaka). Long cylindrical drum.
Lit.: no. 226.

Biasa (Java). See *Jawar*.

Bibāsu (South India). *Janya rāga* of the 15th *mēḷa* (*Māyāmāḷavagauḷa*). See *Rēvagupti* and *Bhūpāḷam*, both of the 15th *mēḷa*.
Lit.: no. 139.

Bibhas (*Vibhasa*; *Vibhas*) (North India). *Rāga* ascribed to the *Bhairav thāta*.
Tone material:
C D♭ E G A♭ c
c A♭ G E D♭ C; *Vādis*: A♭, E or D♭
Lit.: no. 138.

Bibhas (North India). *Rāga* ascribed to the *Marva thāta*.
Tone material:
C D♭ E (F♯) (G) A B c
c B A G F♯ E D♭ C; *Vādis*: A, E
Lit.: no. 138.

Bibhas (North India). *Rāga* ascribed to the *Purvi thāta*.
Tone material:
C (D♭) E (F♯) G A♭ c
c B A♭ G F♯ E D♭ C; *Vādis*: A♭, D♭
Lit.: no. 138.

Bībhatsa (India). "Disgust." One of the nine emotions (*rasas*) expressed in music. Cf. *Navarasa*.
Lit.: no. 140.

Bibih (Bali). The rim of the *kenḍang* (drum).

Bibiliku (Timor). See *Tihar*.

Bibita (Congo). Long slim drum.
Lit.: no. 26.

Bibo (New Guinea). Bamboo jew's harp.
Lit.: no. 255.

Bichitrabīṇ (India). Cf. *Vichitra vīṇā*.

Biḍājapriya (South India). *Janya rāga* of the 31st *mēḷa* (*Yāgapriyā*).

Tone material:
C D♯ E A♭ B♭♭ c
c B♭♭ A♭ E D♯ C
Lit.: no. 139.

Bideru (Ethiopia). Signal drum made of a hollowed tree trunk.
Lit.: no. 255.

Biderū (Kenya—Galla). Slit-drum.
Lit.: no. 255.

Bifam (Cameroon—Fang). Cf. *Efam.*

Biglo (Ghana). Term for "bugle" in the *Gā* language.
Lit.: no. 95.

Bigu (Torres Strait). Bull roarer.
Lit.: no. 255.

Bihag (*Bihaga*; *Behag*) (North India). *Rāga* ascribed to the *Bilaval thāta.*
Tone material:
B C E F G B c
c B A G F♯ E F E D C; *Vādis*: E, B
Lit.: no. 138.

Bihagda (*Bihagada*; *Begagra*) (North India). *Rāga* ascribed to the *Bilaval thāta.* Two types are in use.
Tone material:
(a) *C E F G A B♭* (B) c
c A G F E D A
(b) C (D) E F G (A) B c
c B♭ A G F E D A; *Vādis*: (a) E, B
(b) E, B, or G, C
Lit.: no. 138.

Biki (Solomon Isl.). Songs of praise.
Lit.: no. 246.

Bikife (Congo). Musical bow.
Lit.: no. 176.

Bikuara (Congo). Cf. *Ekuara.*
Lit.: no. 255.

Bikut (North Borneo—Sarawak). A complex bird-call flute without finger holes. A large tube (*batang*) rests on the ground. The air from the player's mouth comes through a second, slimmer tube (*bangsi*) which connects with the larger tube at a sharp angle. The Sea Dayak term for *bikut* is *bum-bun.* Cf. *Dikoot* (*Dikut*).
Lit.: no. 254.

Bilaharī (*Bilahurī*; *Balaharī*) (South India). *Janya rāga* of the 29th *mēḷa* (*Dhīraśaṅkarābharaṇam*).
Tone material:
C D E G A c
c B A G F E D C
For the several variants of this *rāga*, see Lit. no. 139.

Bilahurī (South India). See *Bilaharī.*

Bilampet (North India). Slow tempo. Cf. *Vilamba Kāla* (South India).

Bilan (India). Oboe type.
Lit.: no. 255.

Bilap (*Vilap*) (Nepal). Lament; song of mourning.
Lit.: no. 133.

Bilaskhani-tōḍi (*Vilaskhani-tōḍi*) (North India). *Rāga* ascribed to the *Bhairavi thāta.*
Tone material:
C D♭ E♭ (F) G A♭ B♭ c
c B♭ A♭ G F E♭ D♭ C; *Vādis*: A♭, E♭
Lit.: no. 138.

Bilaval thāta (North India). See *Thāta.*

Bilaval (*Alahiya-bilaval*) (North India). *Rāga* and *Thāta*.
Tone material:
C D E (F) G A B c
c B A G F E D C; *Vādis*: A, E
Lit.: no. 138.

Bilbilla (Ethiopia – Galla). Bell used as signal instrument.
Lit.: nos. 102, 255.

Bili (Congo – Logo). Drum. It is the same instrument as the *bia* and is played together with the *larimva*, a drum of slightly smaller size.
Lit.: no. 26.

Biludi (Congo – Kikongo – Bwende). Side-blown wooden trumpet. Cf. *Ludi.*
Lit.: no. 280.

Bilūr (Kurdistan). Flute. Cf. *Bilyūr.*
Lit.: no. 255.

Bilyūr (Kurdistan). Flute; also oboe type.
Lit.: no. 255.

Bima (Indonesia; Sumbawa). Clarinet type. Cf. *Bima-gumuyu.*
Lit.: no. 163.

Bima-gumuyu (Java; Sunda District). The deep slow laugh of the *wayang* hero Bima. Cf. *Ombak* (*Ombak banyu*).
Lit.: no. 163.

Bima kurda (Java). The angry Bima. A violent "stretta" of the "gangsaran."
Lit.: no. 163.

Bima ngguguk (Java). Bima's burst of laughter. Gong struck with a large number of fast beats (see *Ombak*).
Lit.: no. 163.

Bimpombu (Lower Congo). Small suspended bells used during dances.
Lit.: no. 280.

Bīn (*Mahatī Vīṇā*) (North India). The famous, now rare, North Indian *vīṇā*. It consists of a long bamboo tube upon which are placed 18-24 frets. To the lower side of the tube are attached two resonance gourds. The further south of India the instrument appears, the more is the lower gourd changed into an integrated resonance body. The instrument has four or five melody (metal) strings and 2-3 bourdon steel strings. The *bīn* is played (generally) by means of two wire ring plectra fastened on the index and middle fingers of the player's right hand. The tuning is:

Cf. *Mahatī Vīṇā*; *Vīṇā.*
Lit.: no. 254.

Bin (Assam). Fiddle with a coconut corpus. It has one silken string, and a small bow is used.
Lit.: no. 252.

Bīṇā (East India). Bengali term for *Vīṇā.*

Binakar (India). *Vīṇā* player.

Binaya (Nepal; Sikkim). Jew's harp made of bamboo. Also a group of about a dozen jew's harps, each one tuned differently. Cf. *Tung dyu.*

Binderi (Upper Volta). Drum made of gourd.
Lit.: no. 95.

Bindi (Congo). Cf. *Mbindu.*

Bindrabani-Sarang (*Sarang*) (North India). *Rāga* ascribed to the *Kafi thāta*, representing the actual *rāga Sarang.*
Tone material:
C D F G B c
c B♭ G F D C; *Vādis*: D, G
Lit.: no. 138.

Bindu (India). One of the ancient 10 basic ways of touching *vīṇā* strings (*dhatu*). The term indicates the long held sound of a vibrating string.
Lit.: no. 292.

Bindu Hērāḷi (South India). *Janya rāga* of the 15th *mēḷa* (*Māyāmāḷavagauḷa*).
Tone material:
C D♭ E D♭ E F G A♭ F G A♭ B c
c B A♭ G F E D♭ C
Lit.: no. 139.

Bindu Kalaṅga (South India). *Janya rāga* of the 16th *mēḷa* (*Chakravāka*).
Tone material:
C D♭ E F G A B♭ c
c B♭ G F E F D♭ E D♭ C
Lit.: no. 139.

Bindumālini (South India). *Janya rāga* of the 16th *mēḷa* (*Chakravāka*).
Tone material:
C E D♭ E F G B♭ c
c B♭ c A G E D♭ C
Lit.: no. 139.

Bine (Java). "Female" instruments of large size and low pitch. Smaller sized instruments of higher pitch are called *lake* ("male").
Lit.: no. 163.

Bingi (Assam – Bodo). Harp.
Lit.: no. 46.

Bingo (Malagasy Republic). Narrow bamboo-, cane-, or papaya-wood trumpet provided with a cattle horn as bell.
Lit.: no. 251.

Bingona (Malagasy Republic). Signal horn.
Lit.: no. 255.

Bingy (Malagasy Republic). Cylindrical drum.
Lit.: no. 251.

Bīnjōgī (North India; Punjab). The Sanskrit *tiktirī* and the Hindusthani *pūṅgī*. *Bīnjōgī* is a double clarinet type used by the snake charmers. The right hand tube (the melody pipe) has eight finger holes and the tube at the left side has one or two holes for producing the bourdon sound.
Lit.: no. 254.

Biṅkāvati (South India). *Janya rāga* of the 67th *mēḷa* (*Sucharitra*).
Tone material:
C E F♯ E G A♭ B♭♭ c
c B♭♭ A♭ G F♯ E D♯ C
Lit.: no. 139.

Binogh (Congo – Fang). Iron bells. Cf. *Enogh* (singular of *binogh*).
Lit.: no. 255.

Bin-sasara (Japan). Rattle made of a number of wooden discs used in Shinto and folk music.
Lit.: no. 185.

Binṣir (Arabia). The "third finger" in *'ud* playing.

Binṣir fi majrāhā (Arabia). See *Aṣab'.*

Bīn-sitār (India). A *bīn* used in and around Poona. It has 16 movable frets as they are used on the *sitār* with seven wire strings.
Lit.: no. 254.

Bin·t (*Bant*) (Egypt). Ancient bow harp with a small resonance corpus; the number of strings was variable, probably between five and seven.
Lit.: no. 100.

Binza (Gabon). Iron bell without clapper.
Lit.: no. 280.

Binzoṅga (Congo). The plural of *enzoṅga*. Cf. *Enzoṅga*.
Lit.: no. 255.

Bi-oh (Burma). See *Byo*.

Biola (*Mijue-mijue*) (Sumatra). See *Ketjapi* (Java).
Lit.: no. 254.

Bioran-druma (Ethiopia). Drumstick.
Lit.: no. 255.

Bipanchī Vīṇā (India; Bengal). See *Vipanchī Vīṇā*.

Bipat (Thailand). *Piphat*.

Biqā' (Arabia). Chanted lament.
Lit.: no. 76.

Biraḍai (South India). Tamil term for tuning peg (of *tanbura*, *vīṇā*, etc.).

Birha Gīt (Southeast India; Gond tribes). Song that expresses the grief of the bride when her beloved has to leave her.
Lit.: no. 134.

Bisah (Bali). Name of symbol in musical notation.
Lit.: no. 197.

Bīšah (Persia). Medieval flute.
Lit.: no. 77.

Bisak (Borneo – Dayak). Seven copper slabs of various thickness and length placed upon a wooden box. The slabs are beaten with thin ivory or wooden sticks.
Lit.: no. 255.

Bīsha (Mesopotamia). Medieval flute made of reed with seven or nine finger holes.
Lit.: no. 75.

Bisha (Persia). Ancient oboe type. Cf. *Bisah* (Persia).
Lit.: no. 254.

Bīsha-i mushta (Iran). Term for the *sheng*, the Chinese mouth organ.
Lit.: no. 78.

Bishur (*Bishshur*) (Mongolia). (1) A very slim conical oboe type with seven finger holes and one back hole. The mouthpiece, the lip supporting disk, and bell are made of metal. (2) The inner Mongolian *bishur* (*ordos*) indicates generally a transverse flute. Cf. *Bīsha* (old Persia); *Sona* (China); *Surna*; *Shahnāy* (India); *Suru-nai* (old Mongolia).
Lit.: no. 250.

Bishshur (Mongolia). See *Bishur*.

Bisino (Congo – Bayansi). Plural of *esino*.
Lit.: no. 255.

Bita (*Nabita*) (Congo). Drum.
Lit.: no. 190.

Bīṭāl (South India). *Janya rāga* of the 29th *mēḷa* (*Dhīraśaṅkarābharaṇam*).
Tone material:

C E D F G B A G B c
c B A G F E D C

Lit.: no. 139.

Bitete (Equatorial Africa; Congo – Teke). Plural of *i-tete*.
Lit.: no. 255.

Biti (Congo). *Marimba*; *sansa*.
Lit.: no. 255.

Bitu-uvu (Fiji Isl.). Transverse bamboo flute with seven finger holes: three in the middle, around the tube, two serving as mouth holes, near the closed ends, and two placed between the middle and both ends of the tube. The tones produced on the instrument are approximately A B C D a. The *bitu-uvu* can also be used as a nose flute. Cf. *Fango-fango.*
Lit.: nos. 184, 255.

Bitut (India). Drums.
Lit.: no. 255.

Biwa (Mongolia; Kalmucks). Term for the *dörwen chikhe khuur.*
Lit.: no. 61.

Biwa (Japan). The large lute of Japan imported from China in the 10th century. It has a flattened, pear-shaped wooden corpus, usually two (rarely three) halfmoon shaped resonance holes; the peg box is bent back almost at right angles to the neck. The instrument usually has four silk strings and four to five high frets. The strings are struck with a large triangular *bachi.* The *biwa* can appear in several sizes and shapes. Cf. *Bugaku biwa*; *Chikuzen biwa*; *Satsuma biwa*; *Heike biwa*; *Moso biwa*; and others.
Lit.: no. 185.

Biwapon (*Biwabon*) (Japan). Pan flutes.
Lit.: no. 255.

Bizug (Syria). Term for *Tanbur.*
Lit.: no. 255.

Bjn·t (Ancient Egypt). Ancient harp.
Lit.: no. 250.

Blero (Sunda District). See *Geseh.*

Blikan (Borneo – Dayak). Boat-shaped lute with two rotang strings and plucked with the fingernails.
Lit.: no. 254.

Bling (*Anak*) (West Java). See *Chikibung.*
Lit.: no. 163.

Blongsong (*Byur*) (Java). One of several terms for the *rebāb.* The *blongsong* neck is made entirely of ivory. Cf. *Pontang.*
Lit.: no. 163.

Blung (*Indung*) (West Java). Term for a low-pitched sound. See *Chikibung.*
Lit.: no. 163.

Bo (*Bok*) (Japan). Name of the 4th pipe of the *shō.*
Lit.: no. 225.

Bobi (*Foe*; *Semaku*) (Central Timor – Atoni). Bamboo flute without a mouthpiece and with four finger holes.
Lit.: no. 162.

Bobokon (Sunda District). See *Rebāb* (Sunda).

Bobre (Malagasy Republic; Mozambique). Music bow with resonator.
Lit.: no. 255.

Boč (Kurdistan). Neck of a string instrument.
Lit.: no. 255.

Boddheshela (Nepal). Religious songs sung by Buddhist monks and Hindu priests.
Lit.: no. 41.

Bodongo (Congo). Ground bow.
Lit.: no. 176.

Bodoran (Sunda District). Buffoon in theatrical performances. Cf. *Ogel.*
Lit.: no. 163.

Bog (*Bug*) (Tibet). Cf. *Sbug-chal* (*sbug-shal*).

Bōga Varāḷi (South India). *Janya rāga* of the 12th *mēḷa* (*Rūpāvatī*).
Tone material:
C D♭ E♭ F G B c
c B G F E♭ D♭ C
Lit.: no. 139.

Bogīni (South India). *Janya rāga* of the 41st *mēḷa* (*Pāvani*).
Tone material:
C E♭♭ F♯ G A B c
c B A G F♯ E♭♭ C
Lit.: no. 139.

Bogino-duu (Mongolia). "Short song" sung in fast tempo and in strict rhythm.

Bogir (New Guinea). Wooden slit-drum.
Lit.: no. 255.

Bok (Arabia). See *Buq.*

Bok (Japan). See *Bo.*

Bokallal (Algeria). Dance of the Berber.

Boku (Flores—Ende). Bamboo stamping tube. There are various names of this instrument: in Besisi (Malay Peninsula) it is called *ding teng khing*, in Mentawai *took took*, in Central Borneo *tekok*, in Sarawak *lalipok*, in West Java *kendang awi*, in Madura *dal ondel* or *tabbhuan boomboong*, in Bali *toompling* or *boomboong.*
Lit.: no. 166.

Bokufu (Japan). Notational system used for and by the narrators of the Heike Story (*Heikyoku*).
Lit.: no. 185.

Bōl (India). Derived from the Hindusthani *bōlna*, "to speak." Drum syllable, drum word. Each *bōl* represents one particular drumbeat (on *tablas*, *mṛdanga*), referring to a special hand position and stroke on the drum and, at times, to some rhythmic features performed by one or both hands. Fixed sequences of *bōls* constitute *thekas* drum phrases. Cf. *Jāti* (c).
Lit.: no. 136.

Bolange (*Susu*; *Koranko*) (Sierra Leone). Xylophone with 20 slabs placed on a small frame. Each slab has a small gourd resonator.
Lit.: no. 190.

Boleton (Philippines). Bamboo tube zither similar to the *valiha* of Madagascar. Three very thin strips are partly cut loose from the surface of the tube and strung across a bridge.
Lit.: no. 255.

Bolima (Congo—Ngando). Bow-lute.
Lit.: no. 176.

Bolon (Sierra Leone—Fula; Guinea—Malinke). Harp with three strings and an arched neck and a gourd resonator. Cf. *Seron.*
Lit.: no. 218.

Bol-tān (India). See *Khyāl.*

Bom (Vietnam). See *Cai Bom.*

Bombai (Japan). Term used by the Nishi-Hongan-ji sect for *shōmyō* (the "Brahman of the Indian chant"). Buddhist chant.
Lit.: no. 47.

Bomberdom (Flores—Ende). A "blowing gong." A thin bamboo tube is inserted into a plump bamboo section. When the player blows into the tube he can create three sounds: a very low one, its upper fifth, and octave. At times the *bomberdom* is used as a replacement of a gong. In the Manggaray the instrument is called *bambu mese.* Cf. *Gumbang* (*Bumbung*); *Serbung*; *Goöng awi.*
Lit.: no. 166.

Bombionko (Congo—Azande). Two-headed barrel drum.
Lit.: no. 26.

Bombo (Congo). Musical bow.
Lit.: no. 176.

Bomboli (West Africa; Senegal; Gambia). Clapper made of three wooden sticks used to drive away birds and monkeys.
Lit.: no. 255.

Bommalāṭṭam (South India). Puppet show.
Lit.: no. 261.

Bomo (Congo—Vili). A horizontally suspended wooden beam beaten with wooden sticks.
Lit.: nos. 190, 280.

Bompate (Congo—Kinshasa). Side-blown ivory horn.
Lit.: no. 28.

Bompete (Congo). Bow lute.
Lit.: no. 190.

Bompili (Congo-Brazzaville—Mbole). Clay pot used as a women's drum.

Bonang (Malaysia). A group of 10 bronze kettles placed in two rows horizontally on a flat wooden box.
Tuning and tone-names:

chi	*ruh*	*lu*	*mo*	*nem*
(C)	(E)	(F♯)	(A)	(B♭)
nem	*mo*	*lu*	*ruh*	*chi*
(B♭)	(A)	(F♯)	(E)	(C)

Other tunings may occur, e.g.:
C D E G A   A G E D C

Bonang (Java). Similar to the Malaysian group, the Javanese *bonang* is a double range of 10, 12, or 14 small bronze kettles organized in two times five or two times six kettles in *slendro* and two times seven in *pelog*. The kettles are placed horizontally with open sides downward on a criss-cross of strings held by a wooden stand. The wooden stand is called *ranchakan*, and the strings which support the gong-kettles are called *pluntur* or *janget*.

In the Jogya Kraton *gamelan*, earthenware resonance pots (called *kendil grabah*) are placed below the kettles.

The kettles of the higher octave are called *lanangan* ("male") and those producing sounds of the lower octave are called *wedokan* ("female"). The *lanangan* have a higher rim (*brunjung*) and the *wedokan* a lower one (*dempok*).

The arrangement of the kettles on the *ranchakan* is not in scalar order but can show several varieties, such as:

Pelog:	3′	5′	4′	2′	1′	6′	7′	(upper octave)
	7	1	2	6	4	5	3	(lower octave)
Slendro:	4′	3′	2′	1′	5′			(upper octave)
	1	2	5	3	4			(lower octave)
or:	4′	3′	2′	1′	5′			(upper octave)
	2	3	4	5	1			(lower octave)

Cf. *Pelog*; *Slendro*.

Small *bonangs* that have the kettles arranged in a single line are called *renteng*. These groups usually employ incomplete *pelog* scales. Cf. *Trompong* (Bali).
Lit.: no. 163.

Bonangan (Bali). Music played on the *bonang*.
Lit.: no. 197.

Bonang barung (Java). A set of kettles of the *bonang* ensemble that paraphrases the theme (cf. *genḍing sabetan*). *Bonang barung* kettles are tuned in medium range; *bonang panembung* stands one octave lower and *bonang panerus* one octave higher than *bonang barung*. The latter is used in the "strong playing" pieces. The other two sets of kettles, *bonang panembung* and *bonang panerus*, together with *genḍer panembung* represent "strong playing" instrumental groups.
Lit.: no. 163.

Bonang panembung (*Bonang penembung*) (Java). A large *bonang* tuned one octave lower than *bonang barung*.
Lit.: no. 163.

Bonang panerus (*Bonang penerus*) (Java). A smaller set of kettles tuned one octave higher than *bonang barung*.
Lit.: no. 163.

Bonang panerus (Malaysia). A set of 10 kettles placed horizontally in two rows and placed upon a wooden frame.

Bonda (Congo—Gombe). (1) Footed drum. Beaten for the accompaniment of dances. (2) Single headed cylindrical drum.
Lit.: no. 26.

Bondofo (West Africa—Mandingo). Antelope horn, blown laterally.
Lit.: no. 33.

Bondundu (Congo—Nkandu). Drum with one head. Cf. *Empete.*
Lit.: no. 26.

Bondung (Burma). Long drum.
Lit.: no. 255.

Bondyi (Burma). See *Segi.*

Bong (Vietnam). Drum in the shape of an hourglass. The drum has only one head.
Lit.: nos. 51, 296.

Bongele (Congo—Ngandu). Stick zither.
Lit.: no. 176.

Bongengu (Congo—Ntomba). Simple musical bow.
Lit.: no. 176.

Bonggang (East Java). See *Monggang.*

Bonginda (Congo—Topoke). Cylindrical drum with one head.
Lit.: no. 26.

Bong lang (*Kaw law*) (Laos). A vertically hung, popular xylophone with 12 keys. The instrument is of recent age.

Bongo-bongo (Nigeria—Daka). Simple musical bow.
Lit.: no. 176.

Bongoga (Congo—Bokete; Bosaka). Simple musical bow.
Lit.: no. 176.

Bongogo (Congo—Mbole). Simple musical bow.
Lit.: no. 176.

Bongolo (Congo—Bangandu). Barrel drum.
Lit.: no. 190.

Bong-so (Korea). See *So.*

Bongwabi (*Ndima*; *Dima*; *Gaza*) (Congo—Abangba). Drum. Cf. *Elembe.*
Lit.: no. 26.

Bon gyi (than) (Upper Burma). A pair of small barrel drums hung on straps around the neck of the player. The drums are beaten with his bare hands.
Lit.: no. 193.

Bonkendja (Congo—Ekonda; Nkundu). Drum. Cf. *Ndungu*; *Bankiya.*
Lit.: no. 26.

Bonkenge (Congo—Baloi). Pot-shaped drum.
Lit.: no. 26.

Bonnang (Java). See *Bonang.*

Bon odori (Japan). Folk dance performed at various festivities. It appears at the autumn equinox; it is the moonlight dance of peasants or of the fishermen on the seashore. Usually the dance has no instrumental accompaniment, but there are exceptions when flute, drum, and *samisen* are employed. These simple dances are *ondo* types, a large variety of community dances. Cf. *Obon.*
Lit.: no. 185.

Bon odori uta (Japan). Songs sung during work or during work games. Cf. *Bon odori.*
Lit.: no. 185.

Bonnon (Japan). See *Kansan.*

Bonsan (Japan). Buddhist hymns which have original Sanskrit (or Pali) texts or use Chinese translations of the original words.
Lit.: no. 185.

Bonto (Northeast Celebes). A trumpet imported from Ambon, consisting of two bamboo tubes. A narrow tube is inserted into a larger one, and changes of pitch are effected by sliding one tube.
Lit.: no. 132.

Boo (Liberia – Kpelle). Flute.
Lit.: no. 284.

Boomboong (*Toompling*) (Bali). See *Boku*; *Tabbhuan boomboong.*

Bo-pampane (South Africa). Cf. *Dikomana.*

Bōq (Arabia – Andalusia). Upright, straight trumpet.
Lit.: no. 255.

Bora (Australia). Initiation song of the aboriginals.

Bore (Turkey). Horn; trumpet. Also called *bure.* Cf. *Buri.*
Lit.: nos. 243, 255.

Bosta-nagar (Arabia). Sub *maqām* to *auj.* Its tone material is: *'irag*, *rast*, *duga*, *siga*, *jarka*, *saba*, *huseni*, *'ajam*, *kardan*, *shahnaz.*
Approximately:

B♭ (♭) C D E♭ (♭) F G♭ A B♭ c d♭

Lit.: no. 121.

Bote (Sierra Leone). Drum in the shape of a pot or vase.

Boti (Kenya). Wooden whistle.
Lit.: no. 29.

Bōtika (South India). *Janya rāga* of the 7th *mēḷa* (*Senāpāti*).
Tone material:

C E♭ F G A♭ B♭♭ c
c A♭ G F E♭ D♭ C

Lit.: no. 139.

Botuturu (Congo – Mbelo; Okongo). Drum.
Lit.: no. 26.

Boy (Mali – Dogon). Term for various drum types and dance.

Bozlak (Turkey). A specific melody type of *uzun hava.* The pieces are usually narrative or love songs.
Lit.: no. 243.

Bozūk (Turkey). A large *saz* (lute) with eight strings, played with a plectrum.
Lit.: no. 32.

Bradwom (Ghana – Akan). Songs sung during the puberty rites.
Lit.: no. 218.

Brag (Northeast New Guinea – Monumbo Papua). Sacred flute played by men only.
Lit.: no. 37.

Brahma (South India). Name of the 9th *chakra* in the system of the 72 *mēḷas.* Cf. *Rāga* (South India).
Lit.: no. 139.

Brahma Līlā (South India). *Janya rāga* of the 15th mēḷa (*Māyāmāḷavaguaḷa*).
Tone material:

C D♭ E F A♭ B c
c B A♭ G F E D♭ C

Lit.: no. 139.

Brahmatālam (*Bṛhattālam*) (South India). Large cymbals used at festive occasions in Hindu temples.
Lit.: no. 260.

Brahma vīṇā (North India). A name applied to various *tanbura* forms.

Brāhmi (South India). *Janya rāga* of the 46th *mēḷa* (*Śaḍvidhamārgiṇī*).
Tone material:
C D♭ E♭ F♯ A c
c A F♯ E♭ D♭ C
Lit.: no. 139.

Brāhmtāl (India). See *Tāla* (North India).

Bramā Taranginị (*B. Taranganị*) (South India). *Janya rāga* of the 51st *mēḷa* (*Kāmavardhanī*).
Tone material:
C D♭ E F♯ G A♭ B c
c G A♭ B G F♯ D♭ E F♯ D♭ C
Lit.: no. 139.

Branyak (Java). The proud character represented by a particular dancer in the *wayang wong* performances.
Lit.: no. 163.

Brekuk (*Bungkuk*) (Java). Ancient term for the *kenong* kettle. In the Hindu epos *Rāmāyaṇa* (300 B.C.) the kettle is called *kangsi.*
Lit.: no. 163.

Breng-breng (Java). A Chinese gong used in Java.
Lit.: no. 163.

Bṛhadghaṇṭa (India). Big brass bell placed at the entrance of Hindu temples.
Lit.: no. 261.

Bṛhati (India). Large *kinnari* with three strings and 14 frets.
Lit.: no. 261.

Bṛhattāḷam (*Brahmatālam*) (South India). Large cymbals used in religious services.
Lit.: no. 261.

Brihattālam (*Bṛhattāḷam*) (India). See *Brahmatālam.*

Brimbiri (West Sudan—Nuba). Lyre.

Brinda gānam (South India). Ensemble music. Three forms are distinguished: *uttama*, the entire ensemble performs (instrumentalists, singers); *madhyama*, only half the ensemble performs; *nritya kutapa*, a group of dancers perform.
Lit.: no. 261.

Britannia (Ghana). See *Agbadza.*

Bṛndāvana Dēśākshi (South India). *Janya rāga* of the 62nd *mēḷa* (*Riṣabhapriyā*).
Tone material:
C D E F♯ G F♯ A♭ c
c A♭ G F♯ E D C
Lit.: no. 139.

Bṛndāvana Kannaḍa (South India). *Janya rāga* of the 69th *mēḷa* (*Dhātuvardhanī*).
Tone material:
C E F♯ G A♭ c
c A♭ G F♯ E D♯ C
Lit.: no. 139.

Bṛndāvana Sāraṅga (South India). *Janya rāga* of the 22nd *mēḷa* (*Kharaharapriyā*).
Tone material:
C D F G B♭ c (C E♭ D F G B♭ c)
c B♭ G F D E♭ C
Lit.: no. 139.

Brudūvaka (South India). *Janya rāga* of the 24th *mēḷa* (*Varuṇapriyā*).
Tone material:
C D E♭ D F G A♯ B c
c B G F D C
Lit.: no. 139.

Brung (Java). See *Ḍog ḍog.*

Brunjung (Java). Gong kettles with high rims. Cf. *Bonang.*
Lit.: no. 163.

Brūravi (South India). *Janya rāga* of the 20th *mēḷa* (*Naṭabhairavī*).
Tone material:
C E♭ D E♭ F A♭ B♭ c
c B♭ A♭ G F E♭ D C
Lit.: no. 139.

Bshur ma (Tibet). "Strained," "filtered." Term referring to quick parlando features in the sacred chant.
Lit.: no. 143.

Btāyhī (Tunisia). See *Al Btāyhī.*

Bu (Western Torres Strait). Snail horn with lateral blowhole.
Lit.: no. 255.

Bubuwas (Timor; Alor; Ternate). Bull roarer. Cf. *Jata* (Flores).
Lit.: nos. 157-58.

Bu'd (Arabia). Old term for "interval."

Budbudiki (India). A very small *damaru.* It is used by snake charmers.
Lit.: no. 255.

Buddhavāhiṇī (South India). *Janya rāga* of the 68th *mēḷa* (*Jyōtisvarūpiṇī*).
Tone material:
C D♯ F♯ G A♭ B♭ c
c G F♯ E D♯ C
Lit.: no. 139.

Budhamanoharī (South India). *Janya rāga* of the 28th *mēḷa* (*Harikāmbhōji*).
Tone material:
C D E F E G c
c G F E C
Lit.: no. 139.

Budhamanōharī (South India). *Janya rāga* of the 29th *mēḷa* (*Dhīraśaṅkarābharaṇam*). The tone material of this *rāga* is the same as the one of *Budhamanōharī* of the 28th *mēḷa.*
Lit.: no. 139.

Budimba (Congo). See *Marimba.*

Budubuduke (India). Popular small *damaru* favored by traveling minstrels and fortune tellers. Cf. *Budbudiki*; *damaru.*
Lit.: no. 255.

Budung utas (written: *budugun utasun*) (Mongolia). The "thick string," the lower pitched string of the *khil-khuur.* The higher ("thin") string is called *närin utas* (written: *narin utasun*).
Lit.: no. 61.

Budyung (Philippines – Hanunoo). Bamboo trumpet. The term can also apply (by the Bukidnon) to a shell trumpet used for signalling.

-Bue (*buye*) (Japan). Term for flutes if a descriptive word precedes the term. See also *Fue* (*fuye*).

Buebalabala (New Hebrides; Leper Isl.). Panpipes with 6-7 tubes.
Lit.: no. 255.

Bug (Tibet). See *Bog.*

Bugaar (South Senegal – Kujamaat). Secular dance. One drummer beats three large drums (descending in pitch); a male chorus and one or several male solo singers take part. Facing the chorus are several women beating clappers.
Lit.: no. 122.

Bugaku (Japan). Ancient imported masked court dances performed still with traditional Indian gestures and accompanied by *gagaku* orchestral music. The *bugaku* dance were grouped into: *sanomai,* the "left side dances" (*tō-gaku*); *uhomai,* the "right side dances" (*koma-gaku*); *tsugaimai,* the "alternate dances," one left, one right.

The *bugaku* instrumental ensemble varied according to the items performed. If the item belonged to *tō-gaku,* two *da-daiko,* three *shō,* three *hichiriki* (no *biwa* and no *gaku-so*), *kakko, shoko, taiko* were used. If the piece belonged to *koma-gaku,* no *ryuteki* was used but the *koma-bue*; no *kakko* was played but the *san-no-tsuzumi.* The other wind and percussion instruments were the same as those stated in the *to-gaku* ensemble. Cf. *Gagaku.*
Lit.: no. 185.

Bugaku Biwa (Japan). A heavy pear-shaped lute with four silken strings and 4-5 frets and a peg box sharply bent backwards at right angle. The instrument is used in the accompaniment of later *bugaku* dances and is played with a small *bachi.*
Lit.: no. 226.

Bugaku fuye (*Bugaku bue*) (Japan). See *Ō-teki.*

Bugari (South India). Cane flute with five or six holes.
Lit.: no. 255.

Bughri (South India—Toda). Bamboo trumpet with a bell made of buffalo horn. Cf. *Bugari*; *Buguri.*
Lit.: no. 303.

Bu-hag (Tibet). Bass oboe with an almost globular bell.
Lit.: no. 255.

Buka (Flores; Manggaray). Flat gong without a central boss. See *Gong beri* (Java).
Lit.: no. 166.

Buka (Java). See *Bebuka.*

Bukaning genḍing (Java). See *Bebuka.*

Bukari (Papua). Bull roarer.
Lit.: no. 311.

Buki (Persia). Trumpet.
Lit.: no. 255.

Buktipriya (South India). *Janya rāga* of the 58th *mēḷa* (*Hemāvatī*).
Tone material:
C D F♯ G B♭ c
c B♭ A G F♯ E♭ D C
Lit.: no. 139.

Būl (Sudan; Uganda). Small cylindrical drum, beaten with a flexible leather striker.
Lit.: no. 108.

Būl ahank (Turkey). See *Nāy*; *Sūpurga.*

Bulo (Ghana). Ankle rattle consisting of a string to which tiny pellet bells are attached.

Bulo laelae (South Celebes). Rattle clapper beaten against a piece of heavy bamboo. In Flores the instrument is called *bulo palaeyang.*
Lit.: no. 166.

Bulo palaeyang (Flores). See *Bulo laelae.*

Bulo panggilu (South Celebes). A *tjuriga* type. Its rattling sound is believed to ward off and drive away evil spirits.
Lit.: no. 162.

Bulo-paseya-seya (Flores). See *Bulo-siya-siya.*

Bulo-siya-siya (Celebes; Makasar). A beating rod (switch) used to drive away bad demons, illness, and misfortune.
Lit.: no. 254.

Bulo-wok (Borneo—Kayan). Bird pipe without finger holes. Cf. *Nuren.*
Lit.: no. 255.

Bulu (Senegambia). Harp with 10 strings.
Lit.: no. 255.

Bulu decot (Siamese Malaysia). Low-pitched flute without any finger holes. It is used to call doves. The instrument is identical with the *bikut* and similar to the *foi mere.* Cf. *Dakoot.*
Lit.: no. 255.

Bulul (Kurdistan). Flute.
Lit.: no. 255.

Buluh ribut (Malaysia). One or more closed bamboo tubes with slits cut into their sides; stuck into the ground they become an Aeolian organ when the wind blows across the slits.
Lit.: no. 254.

Bülūr (Kurdistan). See *Bilyur.*

Bum-bun (New Guinea; Finschhafen). Wooden drum carved in the shape of an hourglass.
Lit.: no. 258.

Bum-bun (Borneo—Dayak). See *Bikut.*
Lit.: no. 254.

Bumbung (*Bunbung*) (Bali). One section of a bamboo stick open at one end, used as a stamping tube to accompany the *joged bumbung* dance (the harvest festival).
Lit.: no. 197.

Bumbung (Java). "Bamboo tube." (1) A primitive wind instrument consisting of two bamboo tubes. One is large and closed at the bottom, the other is thin and open. Through the latter the players blows into the stout tube. The result is a deep, resounding bass note. (2) See *Gumbeng.*
Lit.: no. 163.

Bummaworowa (North Ghana—Frafra). A wooden trumpet played at funerals of old men.
Lit.: no. 218.

Bumpa (Republic of Upper Volta; North Rhodesia). Primitive clarinet, also called *boumpa.*
Lit.: no. 50.

Bumumbu (Tanganyika—Washambala). Drum played by magicians.
Lit.: no. 130.

Bunanga (Mozambique—Thonga; Venda). Ensemble of 10 animal or seaweed horns.
Lit.: nos. 150-51.

Bunbung(an) (Java). Bamboo resonator placed under each slab of a *genḍer.*
Lit.: no. 163.

Buncacan (Philippines). A piece of bamboo shaped like a tuning fork. The handle is a bamboo tube closed by a node. When beaten against the hand a tone becomes audible, the pitch of which can be altered by closing a finger hole in the handle. Cf. *Ore-ore.*
Lit.: no. 255.

Bunchis (West Java). A small instrumental ensemble.
Lit.: no. 163.

Bunduma (Central and South Africa). See *Sansa.*

Bung (Bali). Resonator made of a bamboo tube.
Lit.: no. 197.

Bung (Burma). Cone-shaped drum made of wood.
Lit.: no. 255.

Bung-hse (Burma). Drum.
Lit.: no. 255.

Bungkuk (Java). See *Brekuk.*

Bungo-bushi (Japan). At the present time an almost obsolete form of narrative *shamisen* music. *Bungo-bushi* presented lively narrations of lovers whose relationships usually came to an end with a double suicide.

In Tokyo (before and after the Meiji restoration) there was a considerable wealth of narrative *shamisen* music. Of interest were three stylistic branches: *tokiwazu*, *tomimoto*, and *kiyomoto.* Furthermore there were the closely related styles of *shinnai*, *itchu-bushi*, and in the Kyoto-Osaka region *miyazono-bushi*, *gidayu-bushi*, and *kato-bushi*, as well as the *nagauta* and *sokyoku.* Cf. *Katarimono.* For further details see Lit. no. 295.

Bungo sagari-hi (Japan). *Taiko* pattern in *kabuki* music.
Lit.: no. 187.

Bungur (West Java; Cheribon). "The violet tone." The fourth note of the *pelog* system of Cheribon (Tjirebon). Cf. *Pelog.*
Lit.: no. 163.

Bunkafu (Japan). A simple modern *shamisen* tablature that uses Arabic numerals which denote semitones. The three strings of the instrument are indicated by three lines drawn horizontally from left to right.
Lit.: no. 185.

Bunkaka (Philippines). See *Buncacan.*

Bunraku (Japan). Puppet theater.
Lit.: no. 185.

Bunu (Sudan). Name of the *buru.*
Lit.: no. 95.

Bunun-glogu (Malay Peninsula – Semang). Nose flute with 2-8 (usually with four) finger holes.
Lit.: no. 313.

Būq (Persia; Sudan; Arabia). Brass horn.
Lit.: no. 108.

Būq (*Boq*) (Arabia). Long straight copper or brass trumpet. Cf. *Karranāy.*
Lit.: no. 255.

Buq al-nafīr (Arabia). Large brass or copper horn. Cf. *Buq.*

Būqāt (Arabia). Plural of *būq.*

Būq zamrī (Arabia). Medieval wind instrument (made of metal) with a beating reed.

Būra (India). The drone pipe of the *nāgasura.* Cf. *Ottu.*

Buranbar (Somali Republic). Home song sung by women.
Lit.: no. 98.

Burda (Algeria – Biskra). Funeral music.
Lit.: no. 110.

Bure (Turkey). See *Bore.*

Būrghū (Turkey). See *Būrū.*

Buri (Mongolia). See *Dung* (Tibet). Cf. *Bure.*
Lit.: no. 250.

Buri (Ancient India). Long straight copper war trumpet.
Lit.: no. 255.

Burifē (Nigeria; West Sudan – Mande; Soso). Wooden or ivory signal horn.
Lit.: no. 255.

Buro (Ghana; Goldcoast). Animal horn.

Burra (South India). Calabash resonator at the lower side of the *vīṇā.*
Lit.: no. 261.

Burra (South India). Clay drum with a tapering corpus. The wider end is covered with skin, the narrow end is open. The drum is employed by story tellers. The Telugu term *burra kathalu* means folk stories recited or chanted to the accompaniment of this instrument.

Burrakatha (South India). Folk theater performed by three persons.

Bur'-rting (Tibet). Temple gong. A small brass plate in triangular shape that produces a high, clear tone when beaten with a small hammer.
Lit.: no. 255.

Būrū (Turkey). Horn.
Lit.: no. 76.

Būrū (West Africa – Mandingo). Side-blown wooden or ivory horn.
Lit.: no. 33.

Buruburu (Torres Strait; North Australia). Small cylindrical drum with one skin. It is beaten with the bare hand.
Lit.: no. 255.

Burubush (South Africa – Korana Hottentots). Bull roarer. Cf. *Luvuvu.*
Lit.: no. 151.

Buruga (South India). Name of the *kurna.* Cf. *Banku* (see also *Karnā*).
Lit.: no. 255.

Burumamaramu (New Guinea). Bull roarer.
Lit.: no. 255.

Būrūsī (Turkey). General term for the (medieval) horn, trumpet.
Lit.: no. 81.

Būsah-lik (Middle East; Modern Egypt). *Maqām.* In Persian the name means "the kiss."
Tone material:

D E F G A B♭ c d

Lit.: no. 64.

Būsah-lik 'Ušayrān (Middle East). *Maqām.*
Tone material:

$\mathit{A}\ \overset{\flat}{\mathit{B}\flat}\ \mathrm{C}\ \mathrm{D}\ \overset{(\flat)}{\mathrm{E}}\ \mathrm{F}\ \mathrm{G}\ \mathrm{A}\ \overset{(\flat)}{\mathrm{B}}\ \mathrm{c}\ \mathrm{d}\ \overset{(\flat)}{\mathrm{e}}\ \mathrm{f}$

Lit.: no. 64.

Busalik (*Buselik*) (Arabia). *Maqām.*
Tone material:

$\mathrm{D}\ \mathrm{E}\ \overset{\flat}{\mathrm{F}}\ \mathrm{G}\ \mathrm{A}\ \mathrm{B}\flat\ \mathrm{c}\sharp\ \mathrm{d}$

Lit.: no. 64.

Buselik (*'Ushag*; *Busalik*) (Arabia). Tone name of a note approximately a quarter tone lower than *jarga* (in Egypt). See *Jagā* (*Yagā*); under its heading are listed all tone names within the interval of two octaves.

Bushāvali (South India). (1) The 64th *asampūrṇa mēḷa rāga* without *kaṭapayādi* prefix. (2) The 64th *asampūrṇa mēḷa rāga* with *kaṭapayādi* prefix was called *Bushāvati.* See *Rāga* (South India).
Lit.: no. 139.

Būshāvati (South India). See *Bushāvali.*

Bushe-bushe (Sahara; Sudan—Hausa). Wind instrument. Cf. *Fufe-fufedji.*
Lit.: no. 255.

Bushi (Japan). General term for Buddhist religious songs. These songs were never accompanied except by hand clapping. Only in recent times appeared drums in a simple accompaniment. During the Muromachi period (1332-1615) new *bushi* gained much popularity. They appeared as *joruri* types with licentious texts. These songs were called after their creators: *itchu-bushi* (after Miyaku Itchu of Kyoto), *bungo-bushi* (after Miyokoji Bungo), *kiyomoto-bushi* (after Kiyomoto Enjusai), and others. Eventually these songs with indecent and vulgar words were forbidden by the authorities.
Lit.: no. 185.

Busoi (North Borneo). Music bow with one rotang string. When played it is placed upon a resonance pot covered with a wooden plate (*aran*). The string is beaten with a small wooden stick.
Lit.: no. 18.

Busut (Borneo). The knob, boss, at the back of a gong. Cf. *Garantong*; *Tawak.*
Lit.: no. 255.

But sheau (Burma; Shan States—Palaung). Bamboo reed pipe with six finger holes in front and one rear hole. A free metal reed is placed in a hole of the wall.
Lit.: no. 252.

Butyu (South Africa—Bomvana). Horn (made of oxhorn) with lateral blowhole.
Lit.: no. 151.

Buye (Japan). See *Bue.*

Buyō (Japan). Classical dancing.

Buyong (Borneo; Brunei). Shell horn, used to call buffaloes.
Lit.: no. 255.

Buyut (Java). "Taboo." To certain persons in Banten (West Java) the listening to *gamelan* music is strictly *buyut* ("forbidden").
Lit.: no. 163.

Buzuk (Turkey). A big *tanbur* with six wire strings (tuned in pairs).
Lit.: no. 255.

Buzurg (Arabia). See *Jwab-sigā.*

Buzurg (Middle East). *Maqām.*
Tone material:
C D E♭ F G A B♭ c
Occasionally in descent:
G F♯ E D C
Lit.: no. 64.

Bwanzi (Congo; Nilotic Sudan). Board zither with bark resonator.
Lit.: no. 176.

Bwebalabala (New Hebrides; Leper Isl.). Panpipes with six or seven bamboo tubes.
Lit.: no. 255.

Byāg (South India). *Rāga.* (1) See *Behāg.* (2) *Byāg* stands also for *Hindusthani behāg*; *Karnāṭaka behāg.*
Lit.: no. 139.

Byāg (South India). *Janya rāga* of the 28th *mēḷa* (*Harikāmbhōji*).
Tone material:
C D E F G A B♭ c
c B♭ A B♭ G A F E D E C
Lit.: no. 139.

Byāgu (South India). See *Behāg.*

Byakushi (Japan). A clapper made of nine bamboo slabs strung on a cord. Cf. *Hakuhan.*
Lit.: no. 225.

Byang (Sunda District). A group of three *angklungs* used for bridal music. Also called *engklok*; *ganchang*; *tangklit.*
Lit.: no. 163.

Byo (Burma). Drum with two heads.
Lit.: no. 255.

Byong (Java). The term is derived from *rombyong*, "something with appendages." See *Genṭa* ("belltree").
Lit.: no 163.

Byo-toṅtsaṅ (Burma). Drum.
Lit.: no. 255.

Byur (Java). Fiddle with an ivory neck. See *Blongsong.*
Lit.: no. 163.

Bzi-shad (Tibet). "Fourfold *shad.*" See *Shad.*

C

Cācaputa (South India). See *Chāchaputa.*

Cağana (Turkey). Bell-tree.
Lit.: no. 243.

Ca Hue (Vietnam). Songs of Central Vietnam (of Hue); music of the literate people, always presented by female singers. The *Ca Hue* appear in three modal systems: *Bac* (North), *Nam* (South), and *Dung* songs. The *Bac* songs are believed to express joy and tranquillity, the *Nam* songs express sadness and pain, and the *Dung* songs show no specific character.

In the South, *Ca Hue* is called *Nhac Tai Tu*, "music of the amateurs." Cf. *Hat a dao*; *Dan tai tu.*
Lit.: no. 42.

Cai (Vietnam). The syllable *cai* appears as a prefix to various things, e.g., musical instruments: gong, rattle, bell, drum, lute, oboe, etc.

Cai ban ñac (Vietnam; the former Annam). A clapper made of three wooden slabs linked by hinges. They represent a dragon: the middle one is the "body, tail and head," the two outer slabs are the wings often ornamented with small bells and gaily painted in red and gold. When played the tail rests against the belt of the player and the two wings are beaten against the middle slab.
Lit.: nos. 254-55.

Cai bom (*Cai bōng*) (Vietnam; the former Annam). Medium sized barrel drum with two heads beaten with the bare hands. One of the tunable heads is provided with tuning paste. Cf. *Tapone* (Thailand); *Taphon* (Laos).
Lit.: nos. 254-55.

Cai canh (*Cai cañ*) (Vietnam). Gong with a flat broad boss, suspended from a wooden frame.
Lit.: no. 254.

Cai cap ke (Vietnam). Two small concave-shaped pieces of hardwood beaten against each other like castanets.
Lit.: no. 255.

Cai chac (*Cai hak*) (Vietnam). Hardwood sticks being clicked together by singing girls and dancers as accompaniment. Cf. *Hak; Sok yet* (Malaka).
Lit.: nos. 184, 255.

Cai chieng (*Cheng*) (Vietnam). Copper gong used as a signal instrument and as a bell for the dead. It is also beaten at executions, at military ceremonies and in the theater. There are two types of the *cai chieng*:

1. A large gong with a wide rim.
2. A small gong without any rim.

Both types are beaten with wooden sticks. Cf. *Kye tsi* (Burma).
Lit.: nos. 254-55.

Cai chuong (Vietnam). Small hand bell or copper gong.
Lit.: nos. 153, 255.

Cai chuong chua (Vietnam). Copper cymbals or bells used in temples and outdoor ceremonies.
Lit.: no. 255.

Cai chuong gang (Vietnam). Small globular temple bell with a pleasant, clean sound.
Lit.: no. 255.

Cai dan bão (Vietnam). A monochord consisting of a triangular or rectangular wooden box with one steel string. It is played by blind musicians with a bamboo plectrum.
Lit.: no. 250.

Cai dan day (Vietnam). Lute, a *taravansa* type, with a rectangular body, a long neck, and a rectangular resonance hole in its back. The instrument has three strings tuned to G D A and eight frets, and serves to accompany women singers.
Lit.: no. 254.

Cai dan nha tro (Vietnam; the former Annam). *Nha tro* means "female singer." A guitar with a trapezoid-formed corpus. It has three strings and 12 frets. The sound hole is in the back of the body.
Lit.: no. 255.

Cai dan nguyet (Vietnam). Popular guitar with a circular body (*nguyet* means "moon") with four thin silken strings tuned in pairs in a fifth. The log neck has eight frets which produce an anhemitonic pentatonic scale. Cf. *Ku* (Japan); *Wol kum* (Korea).
Lit.: no. 254.

Cai dan thap luc (*Cai dön tran*) (Vietnam). Zither with a body having a curved upper board and a flat lower one. The upper side represents Heaven, the lower one Earth. The instrument has 16 thin brass strings (*thap luc* means sixteen) that are strung across moveable bridges and are tuned in an anhemitonic pentatonic mode. Cf. *Cheng* (China).
Lit.: no. 254.

Cai dan ti (Vietnam). A lute with a slim, flat body similar to the Chinese *p'i-p'a*. It has four silken strings and 9-10 frets. The unusual tuning is: *G* C♯ E♭ G.
Lit.: nos. 153, 254.

Cai dön trañ (Vietnam). See *Cai dan thap luc.*

Cai hac (Vietnam). See *Cai chak.*

Cai ken (Vietnam). An oboe that consists of a wooden tube with 7-8 finger holes, a brass mouthpiece and a brass bell. Cf. *Ken.*
Lit.: no. 255.

Cai ken doi (Vietnam). A double oboe consisting of two cane or bamboo pipes. Each tube has seven finger holes. The noisy instrument is often played at funerals.
Lit.: no. 255.

Cai ken loa (Vietnam). *Loa* means "marine shell." The instrument consists of two *cai ken mot* glued together side by side. At times only one tube is used. The *cai ken loa* is used at funerals and its sound has been described as "ear splitting."
Lit.: no. 255.

Cai ken mot (Vietnam). One cylindrical shawm (occasionally two, glued together) with seven finger holes in front, one in the back.
Lit.: no. 255.

Cai khang (Vietnam). Triangular disc of bronze. Its sound is believed to remove depression and stupidity. Cf. *Bur'-rtin* (Tibet).
Lit.: no. 254.

Cai luang (Vietnam). See *Hat cai luong.*

Cai ma la (Vietnam). Flat gong with a low center and the rim bent downward.
Lit.: no. 254.

Cai mo (Vietnam). A block of camphor wood with slits carved into its form of a fish, frog, or fruit, lacquered red and gold and beaten with a mallet. It is used at night to announce the hours and appears also in instrumental ensembles. The *mo* has a poetic significance referring with its lovely soft tone to dark, humid nights. Cf. *Mu-yü*; *Moku-gyo*; *Ghāṭa* (South India).
Lit.: no. 254.

Cai mo nha chua (Vietnam). *Mo* means "wood," *nha* "house," *chua* "temple." A resounding block made of red-lacquered wood in the shape of an almond with gold-painted leaves. Its stem is used as a handle. During Buddhist services the priest beats alternately this instrument and a small bell. The bell is believed to invoke good spirits, and the *cai mo nha chua* is believed to drive away evil spirits.
Lit.: no. 255.

Cai nao-bat (Vietnam). Copper cymbals (the Chinese word for cymbals is *nao*). The instrument appears in three sizes. The largest one is used in the theater and at religious ceremonies.
Lit.: nos. 153, 254.

Cai nen (Cambodia). A set of 16 gong kettles similar to the *krewaiṅ* (Burma).
Lit.: no. 255.

Cai ñi (Vietnam). Spike fiddle with two silken strings tuned to a fifth. Its body is either part of a coconut shell or a section of bamboo. It is similar to the *t'i-ch'in* (China) or the *so-i* (Laos).
Lit.: no. 254.

Cai oṅ dich (Vietnam). Flute. It can appear as vertical or transverse, in various sizes. One vertically-blown type has seven finger holes.
Lit.: no. 153.

Cai sao (Vietnam). *Sao* indicates "singbird." A small bamboo pipe attached to a paper kite. The instrument produces a whistling sound when the kite flies in the wind.
Lit.: no. 254.

Cai sinh (Vietnam; the former Annam). A blind musician places a piece of bamboo between two toes of his left foot and clicks it with two thin sticks in order to mark the rhythm of his song.
Lit.: no. 255.

Cai tam (Vietnam). *Tam* = three. A spike lute with a heavy wooden corpus covered with snake skin. The instrument has three silken strings. It is closely related to the Chinese *san-hsien.* Cf. *Tro-u* (Cambodia).
Lit.: nos. 153, 254.

Cai than la (Vietnam). Small copper disc beaten with a wooden stick.
Lit.: nos. 153, 254.

Cai thieu canh (Vietnam). A set of 10 small round copper plates are suspended in a wooden frame. The instrument is related to the Chinese *yün-lo.* Its tuning is A B c# d# f g a b c'# d'#. The discs are beaten with a small wooden mallet.
Lit.: no. 254.

Cai tiu (Vietnam). A small copper pan, beaten with a wooden stick, is used in pagodas for marking the rhythm of prayer songs.
Lit.: no. 254.

Cai troṅ (Vietnam). *Troṅ* = drum. A large barrel drum with a lacquered body and two heads. It is suspended horizontally by means of a solid handle that is attached to an equally solid ring surrounding the body. The drum is beaten with a heavy wooden stick. See *Cai troṅ cai.* Cf. *Cai troṅ giaṅ.*
Lit.: nos. 153, 254.

Cai troṅ boc (Vietnam). A flat hand drum open on one side. It is beaten with a small wooden stick. Cf. *Cai troṅ gian.*
Lit.: no. 153.

Cai troṅ cai (Vietnam). *Cai* = big. Big drum in barrel shape, painted with red and gold lacquer. Used by priests and beaten with a wooden stick. Cf. *Cai troṅ.*
Lit.: no. 254.

Cai troṅ com (Vietnam). *Com* = boiled rice. A slim barrel drum. The name comes from the practice of pasting small patches containing boiled rice (and other ingrediences) on the drumheads in order to modify the sound. Cf. *Siyahi* (*Tabla*).
Lit.: no. 255.

Cai troṅ con (Vietnam). *Con* = child. A children's drum.
Lit.: no. 255.

Cai troṅ giaṅ (Vietnam). A small hand drum with a conically-shaped body. The lower (wider) side is open. The head is beaten with a small stick. In the orchestral ensemble the *cai troṅ giaṅ* plays together with the *cai troṅ.*
Lit.: nos. 153, 254.

Cai troṅ khān (Vietnam). A small drum with a lacquered barrel-shaped body and a handle.
Lit.: no. 254.

Cai troṅ manh (Vietnam). *Manh* = flat, thin. Tambourin. See *Cai troṅ met.*
Lit.: no. 255.

Cai troṅ met (Vietnam; the former Annam). *Met* = small, shell-like basket. A tambourine beaten with little wooden sticks. It is used in instrumental ensembles and by singers and magicians. See *Cai troṅ manh.*
Lit.: no. 184.

Cai troṅ tien co (Vietnam). "A little neck drum." A small drum with two heads. It is beaten with a stick and appears at the head of festival processions.
Lit.: nos. 184, 255.

Cai tu hoa (*Cai tu loa*) (Vietnam). A shell trumpet used as a signal instrument for the workers in the field. Its sound means a warning of danger.
Lit.: no. 255.

Cai xinh tien (Vietnam). *Tien* = clapper. A rattle clapper that consists of two small wooden slabs to the ends of which are attached several small coins. The slabs are rattled against each other by the left hand, and the right hand moves a third slab of wood with tooth-like projections across the first two.
Lit.: no. 255.

Cākāri (South India). See *Chākāri.*

Cākkyār kūttu (South India; Kerala). Term for the art of the *cakkyars*, dramatic story tellers, who perform *prabandham kūttu*, an elegant, dramatic form of story reciting. The stories are taken from the Hindu *Purāṇas.*
Lit.: no. 123.

Čallari (South India—Tamil). Cf. *Mañjīrā.*

Calung (*Chalung*) (Bali). A *gambang*-like instrument. Cf. *Jublag.*

Canang (*Čanang*) (Malaysia). A single or three knobbed gongs are placed horizontally upon a flat wooden box. A distinction is made between *canang anak* and *canang ibu* ("mother and son"). This terminology applies also to drums (e.g., *genḍang*) where one barrel as a smaller, the second a slightly larger diameter.
Lit.: no. 255.

Canang anak (Malaysia). Cf. *Canang.*

Canang ibu (Malaysia). Cf. *Canang.*

Čanang naga (Borneo—Dayak). "Snake gong" with richly ornamented surface. Its material is copper overlaid with black patina.
Lit.: no. 254.

Candra cūḍa (South India). See *Chandra chūḍa.*

Candra hasitam (South India). See *Chandra hasitam.*

Candrakānti (South India). See *Chandrakāntam.*

Candrakauśika (South India). See *Chandrakauśika.*

Candra Śrī (South India). See *Chandra Śrī.*

Candravadana (South India). See *Chandravadana.*

Cāndrikya (South India). *Chāndrikya.*

C'ang-glu (Tibet). Beer songs sung during wedding feasts.
Lit.: no. 62.

Cang-teu (Tibet). Also written *cang-tsang-teu.* Cf. *Damaru.*

Cang-tsang-teu (Tibet). Cf. *Cang-teu.*

Čaṅgu (South India—Kannarese). Jew's harp made of an iron hoop and a steel tongue.
Lit.: no. 254.

Canh (Vietnam). Cf. *Cai canh.*

Čank (*Chank*) (Persia). Ancient harp in triangular form with six strings. See also *Chang.*
Lit.: no. 255.

Čankela (*Chankela*) (North India). Rattle drum in the form of a *damaru.* Other names of this drum are *patpati* (Bengal), *Palototan* (Burma), *terbang* (Java).
Lit.: no. 254.

Čan teu (Tibet). Drum in the form of an hourglass made of two human skull bones. Held by a centrally attached handle; when turned, two strings with weighted ends rattle against the two drumheads. Cf. *Damaru.*
Lit.: no. 62.

Caping (Malaysia). Term for reeds and mouthpiece of the *serunai.* Cf. *Mali*; *Pipit.*

Cap-ke (Vietnam). See *Cai sinh.* Cf. *Cai cap ke.*
Lit.: no. 255.

Capuz (Turkey). Cf. *Cobza*; *Qūpūz.*
Lit.: no. 255.

Čāraṅki (South India). Tamil term for *Sāraṅgī.*

Caravibhāsini (South India). See *Charavibhāsini.*

Cāri (*Cāli*) (South India). Several of the numerous types of leg movements in Indian classical dance.

Carpare (Turkey). Percussion sticks.

Čartār (Persia). See *Chartār.*

Čārukeśi (South India). See *Chārukeśī.*

Cassuto (Angola—Ambundu). Scraper made of a hollow piece of wood and joined with a notched board. See *Quilando.*
Lit.: no. 190.

Čathurta (Vedic India). The fourth highest note of the Vedic chant, notated in one system with "4."
Lit.: no. 141.

Cathuśruti (India). Also *catuśśruti.* The interval of four *śrutis.*
Lit.: no. 138.

Caturambhā (South India). See *Chaturambhā.*

Catuśśruti (India). See *Catuḥśruti.*

Catuśśruti Dha (*Śuddha Ni*) (India). The tone name corresponding to *ālāpinī*, the 17th *śruti.* Cf. *Śruti.*
Lit.: no. 138.

Catuśśruti Ri (*Śuddha Ga*) (India). The note name corresponding to *Chandovatī*, the fourth *śruti*. Cf. *Śruti*.
Lit.: no. 138.

Caval (*Qawāl*) (Turkey). Vertically-blown flute.
Lit.: no. 190.

Çegane (Turkey). Three *zil* attached to a piece of wood.
Lit.: no. 229.

Ceṇḍa (South India; Kerala). A cylindrical drum used in *kathākaḷi* performances. Only one skin is beaten with slightly curved sticks. The drum is frequently used together with the *maddaḷa* (*mardaḷa*).
Lit.: no. 123.

Ćeng (Turkey). Cf. *Sheng*; *Cheng* (zither).

Ćengu (Turkey). See *Chengu*.

Chabara (*Para*) (Korea). Cymbals used in Buddhist ceremonial, by shamans and in military bands. The cymbals are called also *ja-bara* (*bara*) and occasionally *pal*.
Lit.: no. 179.

Chabbabeh (Arabia). Cf. *Shabbāba*.

Chac (*Chai chac*) (Vietnam). Bow.

Chachalappa (South Celebes). A *tjuriga* type. It drives away evil spirits.
Lit.: no. 162.

Chāchapuṭa (*Cācaputa*) (India). Ternary rhythm; mentioned in the *Nāṭyaśāstra*.
Lit.: no. 292.

Cha chiao (China—M 87; M 1174). A *la-pa* with a hooked bell. In Shanghai it is used at funerals, weddings and processions. In Shantung the instrument is called *hao*. Cf. *Huang la-pa* (Tibet).
Lit.: no. 1.

Chachin mori (*Jajin mori*) (Korea). Rhythmic mode; drum pattern:

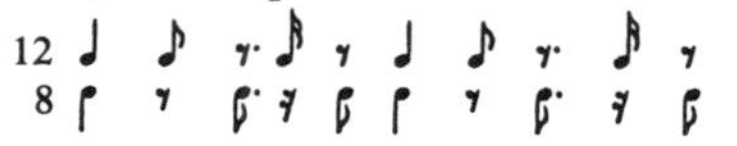

Lit.: no. 286.

Chachra (India). Circular wooden (occasionally iron) castanets. Cf. *Khattālī*.

Chadridal (India). See *Kanuna*.

Chaesu-gut (Korea). Cf. *Kut*.

Chaġāna (*Çaǧana*) (Iran; Persia). Ancient small metal cups attached to a fork-shaped metal holder, held in one hand. If the hand is closed into a fist the two little cups beat against each other.
Lit.: no. 243.

Chagane (*Chaghāna*) (Persia). See *Saghāne*.

Chagat (Bali). Sturdy wooden pillars that hold large gongs.
Lit.: no. 197.

Chäggum (Korea). Cymbals.
Lit.: no. 255.

Chaghāna (Persia; Afghanistan). Fiddle with a small circular body and three strings, played with a curved bow.
Lit.: no. 255.

Chaghāna (Turkey; Persia). Percussion stick used in the Janissary band. The stick was topped by a crescent with stars from which bells, jingles, and two horsehair tails were swinging.
Lit.: no. 78.

Chaghāna (Turkey). A simple 17th-century form of the percussion stick. It had three arms with tiny cymbals. It was also called *zilli masha* (jingling tongs). See *Saghane*.
Lit.: no. 81.

Chāghirtma dūduk (Turkey). "The crying flute." A 17th-century flute made of the bone of a crane.
Lit.: no. 81.

Chahārgāh (Persia). See *Dastgāh.*

Chahar-gāh (Arabia). (1) Cf. *Jaharkāh* (*Jargā*). (2) Modern Egypt: *tshahar-gah.*

Chahārmeḍrab (Iran). See *Dastgāh* (formal structure).

Chahār pāra (Iran; Arabia). Ancient, now almost obsolete, clappers made either of two wooden slabs or of two small clicking sticks held between the fingers of the dancers.
Lit.: no. 78.

Chai (Flores—Nage; Ngada District). An unaccompanied dance of young girls who form a wide circle and move with outstretched arms in a shuffling manner.
Lit.: no. 166.

Chaiṅ vaiṅ (*Tshaiṅ vaiṅ*) (Burma). 16-24 small two-headed tuned barrel drums are placed vertically in a low circular wooden framework. In the center of the circle squats the player who beats the drums with his bare hands.
Lit.: no. 254.

Chaite git (Nepal). Religious songs sung during the Chaitra period (March-April).
Lit.: no. 133.

Chajin mori (Korea). See *Chachin mori.*

Chak (*Kechak*) (Bali). A large chorus of men squatting on the ground recites in fast and gradually still accelerating tempo the syllables *chak* and *ke-chak.* This exciting performance of shouted syllables represents the accompaniment of the *sanghyang* (trance) dances.
Lit.: no. 197.

Chak (Korea). A broad gong or metal bell used in dance performances. Cf. *Cheng* (China).
Lit.: no. 52.

Chākāri (South India). *Janya rāga* of the 28th *mēḷa* (*Harikāmbhōji*).
Tone material:
C D E G B♭ A c
c B♭ A G F E D C
Lit.: no. 139.

Chakay (*Chakhē*; *Garathe*) (Thailand). A zither with three gut strings. Its body resembles the shape of a small crocodile. The Cambodian name of this instrument is *tak-he* and the Burmese name is *megyuṅ* or *migyauṅ.*
Lit.: no. 254.

Chakhē (*Chakay*) (Burma; Thailand). See *Tak-he.*

Chakkur (East Mongolia). See *Khöömiy.*

Cha-ko (China). Small cymbal with flat rim.
Lit.: no. 255.

Chakra (South India). Sanskrit: "wheel." A *chakra* represents one group of six *mēḷas.* There are 12 *chakras* in the system of 72 *mēḷas.* The names of the *chakras* are: *Indu* (1st *chakra, mēḷas* 1-6); *Netra* (2nd *chakra, mēḷas* 7-12); *Agni* (3rd *chakra, mēḷas* 13-18), *Veda* (4th *chakra, mēḷas* 19-24); *Bāṇa* (5th *chakra, mēḷas* 25-30); *Rutu* (6th *chakra, mēḷas* 31-36); *Rishi* (7th *chakra, mēḷas* 37-42); *Vasu* (8th *chakra, mēḷas* 43-48); *Brahma* (9th *chakra, mēḷas* 49-54); *Diśi* (10th *chakra, mēḷas* 55-60); *Rūdra* (11th *chakra, mēḷas* 61-66); *Āditya* (12th *chakra, mēḷas* 67-72).

A further grouping is the indication of the six *mēḷas* of each of the 12 *chakras.* The following mnemonic syllables are used:

1. *mēḷa* : *pa*
2. *mēḷa* : *śrī*
3. *mēḷa* : *go*
4. *mēḷa* : *bhu*
5. *mēḷa* : *ma*
6. *mēḷa* : *shā*

Cf. *Rāga* (South India).
Lit.: nos. 136, 139.

Chakradhari (South India). *Janya rāga* of the 20th *mēḷa* (*Naṭabhairavī*).
Tone material:
C D F E♭ G A♭ B♭ c
c A♭ G F E♭ D C
Lit.: no. 139.

Chakra Mañjari (South India). *Janya rāga* of the 56th *mēḷa* (*Śaṇmukhapriyā*).
Tone material:
C D E♭ F♯ A♭ G A♭ B♭ c
c A♭ G F♯ D C
Lit.: no. 139.

Chakra Pradīptā (South India). *Janya rāga* of the 22nd *mēḷa* (*Kharaharapriyā*).
Tone material:
C D E♭ G F A B♭ c (C D E♭ F G F A B♭ c)
c B♭ A F E♭ C
Lit.: no. 139.

Chakra Tulyam (South India). *Janya rāga* of the 64th *mēḷa* (*Mechakalyāṇī*).
Tone material:
C D F♯ G B c
c B A G F♯ E D C
Lit.: no. 139.

Chakravāka(m) (South India). (1) The name of the 16th *mēḷa*:
C D♭ E F G A B♭ c
(2) As a *rāga, Chakravāka* has the same tone material as stated in (1). Veṅkaṭamakhin (17th century) called *Chakravāka* by the name of *Toyavegavāhini*.
Lit.: no. 139.

Chaku (Persia). See *Cheku*.

Chalanāṭa (South India). (1) The name of the 36th *mēḷa*:
C D♯ E F G A♯ B c
(2) As a *rāga, Chalanāṭa* has the same tone material as stated in (1).
Lit.: no. 139.

Chalanāṭa (South India). Cf. *Nāṭa* (name of the 36th *asampūrṇa mēḷa*).

Chalanavarāḷi (South India). *Janya rāga* of the 20th *mēḷa* (*Naṭabhairavī*).
Tone material:
C D E♭ F A♭ B♭ A♭ c
c A♭ F E♭ D C
Lit.: no. 139.

Chalanī (South India). *Janya rāga* of the 35th *mēḷa* (*Śūlinī*).
Tone material:
C D♯ E F G A B A c
c B A F E D♯ C
Lit.: no. 139.

Chalapita gaḍing (Java). Ivory clapper.

Chal-chal (Sri Lanka – Tamil inhabitants). An iron tambourin frame without a membrane and with four pairs of jingles.
Lit.: no. 206.

Chale-meshk (Kurdistan). Bagpipe.
Lit.: no. 255.

Chalempung (*Chelempung*; *Tjelempung*) (Java; Sumatra; Borneo). (1) Psaltery. Cf. *Chelempung*. (2) One row *bonang* consisting of simple five to seven gongs used in Central Sumatra. The gongs are not imported from Java but instead from Singapore.
Lit.: nos. 254-55.

Chālījī mihtar (Turkey). Military musicians.
Lit.: no. 81.

Chalil (Israel – Hebrew). Flute, clarinet.

Chalintu (West Java). Notched flute with five finger holes.
Lit.: no. 163.

Chalonarang (Bali). Dance drama.

Chālpāra (Turkey). Clappers, castanets. The term is derived from the Persian *chārpāra*, "four pieces" of metal or wood.
Lit.: no. 81.

Chaluko (Tanzania – Gogo). Circumcision songs of girls. Cf. *Chasi*; *Chipande*.

Chalung (Java). (1) A xylophone made of 12, 14, or 16 bamboo tubes tied one after the other like a rope ladder. The instrument is suspended from a wall or a tree. The lower end is tied to the body of the player who beats the bamboo tubes with two sickle shaped sticks. (2) In the Garut district the term *chalung* indicates an instrumental ensemble (named after the instrument) which consists of several *chalungs*, a *tarompet*, a *goong awi* (or *goong buyung*), a *ketuk* (*awi*), and a *dogdog*. It performs at festivals of the circumcision ceremony. See also *Tjaluṅ*.
Lit.: no. 163.

Chalung (*Calung*) (Bali). Cf. *Jublag*.

Cham (Tibet). Ritual masked dance.
Lit.: no. 62.

Chāmaram (South India). *Janya rāga* of the 56th *mēḷa* (*Śaṇmukhapriyā*).
Tone material:
C E♭ D E♭ F♯ G B♭ c
c B♭ A♭ G F♯ E♭ D C
Lit.: no. 139.

Chāmaram (South India). See *Trimurti* (56th *asampūrṇa mēḷa*).

Chambaulani (South India). *Janya rāga* of the 61st *mēḷa* (*Kāntāmaṇi*).
Tone material:
C D F♯ E F♯ A♭ B♭♭ G c
c B♭♭ A♭ E D C
Lit.: no. 139.

Cham-dpon (Tibet). Chief dancer.

Chammarakriya (South India). *Janya rāga* of the 15th *mēḷa* (*Māyāmāḷavagauḷa*).
Tone material:
C D♭ E A♭ B c
c B A♭ G D♭ C
Lit.: no. 139.

Champaka Latā (South India). *Janya rāga* of the 19th *mēḷa* (*Jhaṅkāradhvani*).
Tone material:
C E♭ F A♭ B♭♭ c
c B♭♭ G F E♭ F D C
Lit.: no. 139.

Champaka Māli (South India). *Janya rāga* of the 17th *mēḷa* (*Sūryakānta*).
Tone material:
C D♭ E G A B c
c B A G E D♭ C
Lit.: no. 139.

Champaka Vidāri (South India). *Janya rāga* of the 28th *mēḷa* (*Harikāmbhōji*).
Tone material:
C F E F G B♭ A F G A B♭ A c
c B♭ A B♭ F A F E D E C
Lit.: no. 139.

Champar byed-pa (Tibet). Dancing.

Chamsaurija (Middle East; North Africa). Two (or more) parallel pipes, each with a single reed. The longer pipe produces the drone. Cf. *Urghan*; *Urghanūn*; *Urjan*.
Lit.: no. 215.

Chāmuṇḍi (South India). *Janya rāga* of the 63rd *mēḷa* (*Latāṅgī*).
Tone material:
C E D F♯ G B A♭ c
c A♭ B G F♯ E D C
Lit.: no. 139.

Chanang (Borneo – Dayak; Sumatra). Richly ornamented gong. Also *Tjanang*.
Lit.: no. 254.

Chanan(g) naga (*Čanaṅ naga*) (Borneo – Dayak). "Snake gong."
Lit.: no. 254.

Chanbar (Ancient Persia). Circular frame drum.
Lit.: no. 78.

Chanchalasasa Mallar (North India). Subordinate *rāga* to the *Kāfi thāta* and belonging to the *Mallar* group. The tone material consists of a combination of *Mallar* and *Kanada* features, with an added phrase that represents the *Chanchalasasa* characteristic.
Tone material:
C D F G B c
c B♭ A G F E♭ D C
Lit.: no. 138.

Chan-chung (China). Prayer bell.
Lit.: no. 255.

Chandana Gandhi (South India). *Janya rāga* of the 3rd *mēḷa* (*Gānumūrti*).
Tone material:
C D♭ E♭♭ G A♭ B c
c B A♭ G E♭♭ D♭ C
Lit.: no. 139.

Chandetan (Bali). Rice pounding music performed on very small cymbals in complex rhythm.
Lit.: no. 197.

Chandhikam (South India). *Janya rāga* of the 66th *mēḷa* (*Chitrāmbarī*).
Tone material:
C E F♯ A♯ B c
c B A♯ F♯ E C
Lit.: no. 139.

Chaṇḍika (South India). *Janya rāga* of the 20th *mēḷa* (*Naṭabhairavī*).
Tone material:
C D E♭ F A♭ B♭ c
c B♭ A♭ F E♭
Lit.: no. 139.

Chan dio (Thailand). "First level," "short version"; term used in rhythmical pattern of *phleng reo*.
Lit.: no. 208.

Chandra Chūḍa (*Candra Cūḍa*) (South India). *Janya rāga* of the 29th *mēḷa* (*Dhīraśaṅkarābharaṇam*).
Tone material:
C E F G A B c
c B A G F E C
Lit.: no. 139.

Chandra Chūḍapriya (South India). *Janya rāga* of the 18th *mēḷa* (*Hāṭakāmbarī*).
Tone material:
C E F G B A♯ B c
c B G F D♭ C
Lit.: no. 139.

Chandradāri (*Chhatradhāri*) (South India). *Janya rāga* of the 63rd *mēḷa* (*Latāṅgī*).
Tone material:
C E F♯ G F♯ G c
c B A♭ G F♯ E D C
Lit.: no. 139.

Chandradēśika (South India). *Janya rāga* of the 56th *mēḷa* (*Śaṇmukhapriyā*).
Tone material:
C D E♭ F♯ G F♯ A♭ B♭ c
c B♭ A♭ F♯ E♭ C
Lit.: no. 139.

Chandra Gāndhāram (South India). *Janya rāga* of the 8th *mēḷa* (*Hanumattōḍi*).
Tone material:
C D♭ E♭ F c
c B♭ F E♭ D♭ C
Lit.: no. 139.

Chandra Hasitam (South India). *Janya rāga* of the 28th *mēḷa* (*Harikāmbhōji*).
Tone material:
C D E F A B♭ c
c B♭ A F E D C
Lit.: no. 139.

Chandrajyōti (South India). *Janya rāga* of the 41st *mēḷa* (*Pāvani*).
Tone material:
C D♭ E♭♭ F♯ G A c
c A G F♯ E♭♭ D♭ C
Lit.: no. 139.

Chandrakalā (South India). *Janya rāga* of the 22nd *mēḷa* (*Kharaharapriyā*).
Tone material:
C D E♭ F G F A B♭ c
c A G F E♭ F C
Lit.: no. 139.

Chandrakant (North India). A subordinate *rāga* to the *Kalyan thāta*.
Tone material:
C D E G A B c
c B A G F♯ E D C; *Vādis*: E, B
Lit.: no. 138.

Chandrakāntam (*Candrakānti*) (South India). *Janya rāga* of the 65th *mēḷa* (*Mechakalyāṇī*).

Tone material:
C D E F# G A B c
c B A B G F# E D C
Lit.: no. 139.

Chandrakauns (North India). Subordinate *rāga* to the *Kāfi thāta.*
Three types of tone materials:
(a) C Eb F A Bb c
c Bb A F Eb C
(b) C Eb F Ab B c
c B Ab F Eb C
(c) C Eb F Ab Bb c
c Bb Ab G F Eb Db C; *Vādis*: F, C
Lit.: no. 138.

Chandrakauśika (South India). *Janya rāga* of the 29th *mēḷa* (*Dhīraśaṅkarabharaṇam*).
Tone material:
C D E F G F A B c
c A G F E C
Lit.: no. 139.

Chandra Kiraṇi (South India). *Janya rāga* of the 16th *mēḷa* (*Chakravāka*).
Tone material:
C E F G F A Bb c
c Bb A Bb G F E F Db C
Lit.: no. 139.

Chandra Maṇḍalam (South India; Telugu). Drum. Cf. *Chandrapirai.*
Lit.: no. 261.

Chandramaṇḍana (South India). *Janya rāga* of the 22nd *mēḷa* (*Kharaharapriyā*).
Tone material:
C D Eb F G F A Bb c
c Bb G F Eb F D C
Lit.: no. 139.

Chandrapirai (South India). A crescent-shaped frame drum with one parchment skin is fitted to the forehead of the player in such a manner that the concave part encircles partly the front of his head. It is beaten with a small stick and used at religious occasions.
Lit.: no. 261.

Chandra Prabhā (South India). *Janya rāga* of the 42nd *mēḷa* (*Raghupriyā*).
Tone material:
C Db Ebb F# G A# c
c A# G F# Ebb Db C
Lit.: no. 139.

Chandrarekha (South India). *Janya rāga* of the 15th *mēḷa* (*Māyāmāḷavagauḷa*).
Tone material:
C Db E G B Ab B c
c Ab G F E Db C
Lit.: no. 139.

Chandrarekha (*Chandrarēkhi*) (South India). *Janya rāga* of the 58th *mēḷa* (*Hemāvatī*).
Tone material:
C D Eb F# G A c
c A G F# Eb D C
Lit.: no. 139.

Chandrarēkhi (South India). See *Chandrarēkhā.*

Chandraśēkharapriya (South India). *Janya rāga* of the 14th *mēḷa* (*Vakuḷābharaṇam*).
Tone material:
C Db E G Ab Bb c
c Bb Ab G E Db C
Lit.: no. 139.

Chandra Śrī (*Candra Śrī*) (South India). *Janya rāga* of the 28th *mēḷa* (*Harikāmbhōji*).
Tone material:
C D E F G A Bb c
c Bb A G F E D C
Lit.: no. 139.

Chandravadana (*Candravadana*) (South India). *Janya rāga* of the 29th *mēḷa* (*Dhīraśaṅkarabharaṇam*).
Tone material:
C *B* C D E F G B c
c B A G F E D C
Lit.: no. 139.

Chandrika (South India). *Janya rāga* of the 18th *mēḷa* (*Hāṭakāmbarī*).
Tone material:
C Db E F G A# c
c A# G F E Db C
Lit.: no. 139.

Chandrika (South India). *Janya rāga* of the 21st *mēḷa* (*Kiravāṇi*).
Tone material:
C D E♭ G A♭ B c
c B A♭ G E♭ D C
Lit.: no. 139.

Chandrika Dhavaḷi (*Chandrika Gauḷa*) (South India). *Janya rāga* of the 15th *mēḷa* (*Māyāmāḷavagauḷa*).
Tone material:
C D♭ F G A♭ B c
c B A♭ G F E C
Lit.: no. 139.

Chandrikā Gauḷa (South India). *Janya rāga* of the 8th *mēḷa* (*Hanumattōḍi*).
Tone material:
C D♭ E♭ F G A♭ c
c A♭ G F D♭ C
Lit.: no. 139.

Chandrika Gauḷa (South India). *Janya rāga* of the 15th *mēḷa* (*Māyāmāḷavagauḷa*). See *Chandrika Dhavaḷi.*

Chāndrikya (*Cāndrikya*) (South India). *Janya rāga* of the 28th *mēḷa* (*Harikāmbhōji*).
Tone material:
C E F G A B♭ c
c B♭ A F D E D C
Lit.: no. 139.

Cha-nem (*Cha-nen*) (Tibet). See *Sgra-snyan.*

Chang (Turkey). Large bell with clapper.
Lit.: no. 255.

Chang (Central Asia—Kirgiz). Jew's harp. Cf. *Changko'uz.*
Lit.: no. 255.

Ch'ang (China—M 206). To sing. (The term for song is *ko.*) *Ch'ang* indicates also the vocal introduction of the *nan hsi.*

Chang (China; Shanghai Dialect). Cf. *K'in.*
Lit.: no. 255.

Chang (*Chank*) (Persia). Ancient triangular harp; the Arabic term is *jank.*
Lit.: no. 255.

Chang (*Ko'us*) (Afghanistan). Jew's harp made of metal, played by women.

Chaṅga (India). Ancient, now obsolete, harp. Cf. *Tsauṅ* (Burma).
Lit.: no. 254.

Changal (Turkey). Drumstick. Cf. *Dāwul.*
Lit.: no. 81.

Changdan (Korea). "Long-short." Fixed rhythmic patterns used in songs.

Chang-glu (Tibet). Cheerful and amusing songs.

Chang-go (Korea). Cf. *Chang-ko.*

Chang-gon (Korea). Drum with a cylindrical body. One of the two skins is beaten with a stick, the other with the bare hand. See *Chang-kun.*
Lit.: no. 255.

Chang-guk (Korea). Declamation, recitation of a dramatic text. The performer who recites, chants, or sings holds a fan in one hand and illustrates the chanted events with appropriate gestures. His performance can last one or two hours. *Chang-guk* means also opera consisting of alternating *pansori* vocal music interrupted by dramatic prose.
Lit.: nos. 179, 221.

Ch'ang hsiao (China—M 208; M 2619). The "song *hsiao.*" (1) *P'ai hsiao* type. Or playing the panpipes. (2) Vertical flute (T'ang period).
Lit.: nos. 137, 209.

Changiri (Japan). Small bronze gong without boss.
Lit.: no. 255.

Changkem (*Chlewekan*) (Java; Bali). "Mouth." The slit of the slit-drum. Cf. *Kulkul.*
Lit.: no. 163.

Chang-ko (*Chang-go*) (Korea). An hourglass-shaped drum with two (or one) heads. The body is made of metal. One skin, beaten with the left hand, is thick and produces a mellow sound. The other skin is thin, beaten with a small bamboo stick, and produces a bright sound. Occasionally only one skin is used and the other end of the drum remains open. The *chang-ko* is an old instrument and is used in all types of music. In shaman music both skins are beaten with sticks. Cf. *Chang-ku* (China); *Ō-tsuzumi* (Japan).
Lit.: nos. 52, 179.

Changko'uz (Western Central Asia). Cf. *Chang* (Afghanistan).

Changkriman (Bali). A simple verse form of Javanese origin. The singer performs a characteristic type of melody that is used for children's songs.
Lit.: no. 197.

Chang-ku (China—M 202; M 3479). "Staff drum." An hourglass-shaped drum beaten with the hands of the player. Its Japanese counterparts are the *ko-tsuzumi* and *ō-tsuzumi*. In Korea the name is *chang-ko*.

The Chinese instrument has also been called *wei* after the state of Wei, also *hsiang*, *hsi yao* ("thin waisted"), *ho*, or *cheng* ("principal"), indicating its leading function. It appears in processions in Shanghai, and probably also further south.
Lit.: no. 137.

Ch'ang-kuan (China). "Long reed pipe." A long, slim oboe with seven finger holes and one thumb hole. Its Cantonese name is *cheung-kwun*.
Lit.: no. 129.

Chang-kun (Korea). A clay pot beaten with a bamboo stick. At the beating end the stick is split into several thin parts. In the past the instrument was used for marking time. Cf. *Chang-gon; Fou* (China).
Lit.: no. 52.

Ch'ang-ti (China—M 213; M 6217). Long transverse flute of the Chin and Sung dynasties. Cf. *Tan-hsiao*.
Lit.: no. 255.

Chang-t'ou (China). Term used in Cantonese puppet plays. *Chang-t'ou* indicates "rod-head," meaning puppets guided by means of rods.
Lit.: no. 129.

Changu (South India; Kannarese). Cf. *Muchaṅga; Čaṅgu*.

Changura (*Kontrashica*) (Kurdistan). A large *tanbura* with four strings. (The *tanbura* of Georgia, U.S.S.R., has two or three strings and is called *chonguri*.)
Lit.: no. 255.

Chank (*Chang*) (Persia). (1) Ancient vertical, angular harp with 25 strings. Cf. *Chang*; *Kung-hu*. (2) Triangular psaltery with six strings. It was played with a plectrum. The instrument appears also in Afghanistan.
Lit.: no. 255.

Chankela (*Čankela*) (North India; Kashmir). A frame drum with two skins and a handle. Cf. *Patpati; Palototan*.
Lit.: no. 255.

Chan-ku (China—M 147; M 3479). A war drum in the shape of a barrel carried on a sling across the shoulder of a soldier. It is beaten by a second soldier who follows the first one. The instrument has the form of a small *t'ang-ku*.
Lit.: nos. 137, 209.

Chankun (Korea). See *Changkun*.

Chanṭang balung (Java). Bone rattle used in the Solo Kraton. Cf. *Kepyak*.
Lit.: no. 163.

Chanteng (Bali). Term for the bridge placed below the strings of the *rebāb*.
Lit.: no. 197.

Chan teu (Tibet). See *Čan teu*.

Ch'ao (China – M 253). "Bird's nest." A *sheng* with 19 pipes (also called *ta sheng*, "the big *sheng*").

Ch'ao ch'ü (China). An operatic type of Ch'ao-chou and Kwantung which employs the chorus beside the stereotyped operatic figures (*sheng*, *tan*, etc.).

Chap (Northeast Thailand). Large cymbals. See *Saeng.*
Lit.: no. 254.

Chapa (Japan). Cymbals used in *kabuki* music.
Lit.: no. 185.

Chāpa Ghaṇṭāravam (South India). *Janya rāga* of the 20th *mēḷa* (*Naṭabhairavī*).
Tone material:
C E♭ F G B♭
B♭ A♭ F E♭ D C
Lit.: no. 139.

Cha-pan (China [Mandarin Chinese]; *Chat-pan* [Cantonese]). See *P'ai-pan.*
Lit.: no. 129.

Chāpāra (Korea). Cymbals used at courtly festivities. Cf. *Chālpāra* (Turkey).
Lit.: nos. 52, 255.

Chap choa (Vietnam). A pair of cymbals used in *dai nhac.*
Lit.: no. 296.

Cha pei (Vietnam; Kampuchea; Phnom Penh). Popular big lute with a rectangular, occasionally heart-shaped, corpus. It has two (or four) strings and 11 frets.
Lit.: no. 43.

Cha pei thom (Vietnam; Kampuchea). A long-necked lute with a flat, circular, or heart-shaped corpus. The instrument has four gut strings tuned in pairs (scale steps 1, 5) played by means of little plectra affixed to the fingers of the player's right hand. The 11 frets produce a diatonic major scale. Cf. *Grajappi*; *Mohori.*
Lit.: no. 254.

Cha pei toch (Vietnam; Kampuchea). See *Cha pei.*

Cha-pen (China). Cf. *Chung-tu.*

Chaping buyuk (Java). Term for *kowangan.*
Lit.: no. 163.

Chap kuk (Persia). Cf. *Rast kuk.*

Chap lek (Thailand). Cymbals made of bronze.

Ch'a-po (China – M 109; M 4850). Brass cymbals. In Peking the large sized ones are called *ta ch'a-po* and the small ones *nao.*
Lit.: no. 209.

Chapuo (East Africa; Swaheli). Small barrel drum with two heads.
Lit.: no. 255.

Chapuo ya vumi (East Africa; Swaheli). Small drum with one head. The instrument is placed on three legs.
Lit.: no. 255.

Chappa (Japan). Cymbals.

Chapu tāla (South India). See *Tāla* (South India).
Lit.: no. 261.

Chāpu tōl (South India). The Tamil term for the middle ring on the right side head of the *mridangam.*
Lit.: no. 261.

Chara (Tanganyika – Washambala). A scrape stick with several notches and a resonance box. The stick is also called *kwacha.*
Lit.: no. 255.

Chara chaṇḍini (South India). *Janya rāga* of the 51st *mēḷa* (*Kāmavardhanī*).
Tone material:
C D♭ F♯ A♭ G A♭ c
c A♭ G E F♯ D♭ C
Lit.: no. 139.

Charajuki Mallar (North India). Subordinate *rāga* to the *Kafi thāta*; belonging in the *Mallar* group.
Tone material:
C D F G B c
c B♭ A G F E♭ (D) C
Lit.: no. 138.

Charana (South India). The third section of an art song (e.g., *kṛiti*); it usually is longer than the two preceding sections, the *pallavi* and *anupallavi*. Occasionally the melody of the *charaṇa* is the same as that of the *anupallavi*.
Lit.: no. 261.

Charāvaḷi (South India). *Janya rāga* of the 22nd *mēḷa* (*Kharaharapriyā*).
Tone material:
C D E♭ G A c
c B♭ A G E♭ D C
Lit.: no. 139.

Charavibhāsini (*Caravibhāsini*) (South India). *Janya rāga* of the 29th *mēḷa* (*Dhīraśaṅkarābharaṇam*).
Tone material:
C D F G F A B c
c B G F E D C
Lit.: no. 139.

Charavibhāsitam (South India). *Janya rāga* of the 65th *mēḷa* (*Mechakalyāṇī*).
Tone material:
C E F♯ G A B c
c A G F♯ E D C
Lit.: no. 139.

Chārbeiti (Iran; Khorāsān). See *Dūbeiti.*

Charb Lek (Thailand). Cymbals. Cf. *Piphat.*
Lit.: no. 49.

Charb Yai (*Charp Yai*) (Thailand). Two cymbals with broad rims. Cf. *Piphat.*
Lit.: nos. 49, 255.

Chārgā (North India; Kashmir). *Sitār* with six strings and 14 frets.
Lit.: no. 255.

Charik (Bali). A notational symbol that indicates the end of a section of a melody.
Lit.: no. 197.

Charik kalih (Bali). Double *charik.* Notational symbol that indicates the end of a melody.
Lit.: no. 197.

Charkhi (India). See *Charki.*

Charki (*Charkhi*) (India). Wooden rattle or drum used by children.
Lit.: no. 254.

Charmand (Armenia). String holder.
Lit.: no. 255.

Charp (Thailand). Cf. *Charb lek*; *Charb yai.*
Lit.: no. 49.

Charra (Tanganyika). Cf. *Chara.*

Chartar (Persia). "Four-stringer." A long lute with four strings. Cf. *Chikara* (North India; Punjab).
Lit.: no. 250.

Charuk (Bali). Ancient xylophone used in religious services. Outside of Bali the *charuk* is fallaciously called *saron.*
Lit.: no. 197.

Chārukeśī (*Cārukeśī*) (South India). (1) The 26th *mēḷa*:
C D E F G A♭ B♭ c
(2) As a *rāga* it has the same tone material as stated in (1). Veṅkaṭamakhin (17th century) called this *rāga Taraṅginī.*
Lit.: no. 139.

Chārukuntala (South India). *Janya rāga* of the 26th *mēḷa* (*Chārukeśī*).
Tone material:
C D E F A♭ B♭ c
c B♭ A♭ F E D C
Lit.: no. 139.

Charumera (Japan). A wooden or brass oboe with a widely flaring bell. It has seven finger

holes in front and one in the back. The instrument is used in the theater, in processions, and by itinerant vendors of sweets. The *charumera* is identical with the Chinese *so-na* and resembles the North Indian *sānāyī*.
Lit.: no. 225.

Chāru Vardhanī (South India). *Janya rāga* of the 15th *mēḷa* (*Māyāmāḷavagauḷa*).
Tone material:
C D♭ F G A♭ B c
c A♭ G F E D♭ C
Lit.: no. 139.

Chashtar (Persia). Six-stringed lute.
Lit.: no. 255.

Chasi (Tanzania – Gogo). Circumcision songs sung by old timers. Cf. *Chipande*; *Chaluko*.

Chātam (South India). *Janya rāga* of the 22nd *mēḷa* (*Kharaharapriyā*).
Tone material:
C E♭ F G A c
c B♭ A G F E♭ F D C
Lit.: no. 139.

Chat'han (Sibiria – Kachintzi). Primitive zither with seven strings and bridges made of ram bones. Cf. *Se* (China).
Lit.: nos. 220, 249.

Chat kulia (Southeast India; Bastar Muria Gond Tribe). Two small circular iron discs attached to the ends of a string of small shells. Dancing women clap the discs together like tiny cymbals. Cf. *Chitikelu*.
Lit.: no. 135.

Chat lima (Bali). Rhythmic unit consisting of five beats.

Chat nem (Bali). Rhythmic unit consisting of six beats.

Chat pan (China – Cantonese); *Cha-pan* (China – Mandarin). Cf. *P'ai-pan*.

Chat pitu (Bali). Rhythmic unit consisting of seven beats.

Chat telu (Bali). Rhythmic unit consisting of three beats.
Lit.: no. 197.

Chatsumi uta (Japan). Songs sung during work or work games.
Lit.: no. 225.

Chaturambhā (South India). *Janya rāga* of the 29th *mēḷa* (*Dhīraśaṅkarābharaṇam*).
Tone material:
C D E F A G A B c
c B A G F E D E C
Lit.: no. 139.

Chaturānanapriya (South India). *Janya rāga* of the 11th *mēḷa* (*Kokilapriya*).
Tone material:
C D♭ E♭ G A B c
c B A G E♭ D♭ C
Lit.: no. 139.

Chaturanga (India). Popular North Indian form consisting of a brief *khyāl*, *tarāna* (phrases that employ as text *bōl* syllables), *sargam* (passages of note names) and *trivata* (text represented by meaningless syllables).
Lit.: no. 261.

Chaturaṅgiṇī (South India). *Janya rāga* of the 66th *mēḷa* (*Chitrāmbarī*).
Tone material:
C F♯ E F♯ G B c (C D E F♯ G A♯ B c)
c B A♯ B G E F♯ E D C (c B G F♯ E D C)
Lit.: no. 139.

Chaturaṅgiṇī (South India). (1) The 66th *asampūrṇa mēḷa-rāga* without *kaṭapayādi* prefix. (2) The 66th *asampūrṇa mēḷa-rāga* with *kaṭapayādi* prefix. See *Rāga* (South India).
Lit.: no. 139.

Chatusra jāti (South India). Cf. *Tāla* (South India).

Chaugan (North India). In the closing section of the *dhrūpad*, the *chaugan* follows the *dugan*

and the *aḍ*. In the *chaugan* each note value is shortened to a quarter of its original. The *chaugan* may be followed by the *kuar* in which all note values are shortened to a sixteenth of their originals. Cf. *Theka*.
Lit.: no. 138.

Chauk-pauk (Burma). Tone name. See *Pattala*; *Hsaing-waing*.
Lit.: no. 198.

Chauk-pauk auk-pyan (Burma). Tone name. Below are listed the seven tone names used by the *hsaing-waing* ensemble:

1. *Chauk-pauk auk-pyan*. The first of seven tone names used by the *hsaing-waing* ensemble. Its equivalent in Burmese harp music is *du-raka* and the animal symbol for this note is the peacock.
2. *Than-lat auk-pyan*. The second of seven tone names used by the *hsaing-waing* ensemble. Its equivalent in Burmese harp music is *pyi-daw-byan* and the animal symbol for this note is the bull.
3. *Nga-bauk than-di*. The third of seven tone names used by the *hsaing-waing* ensemble. Its equivalent in Burmese harp music is *mying-zaing* and the animal symbol for this note is the goat.
4. *Than-bya tyaw, hsit-kyi* (*pat sabo*). The fourth of seven tone names used by the *hsaing-waing* ensemble. Its equivalent in Burmese harp music is *pale* and the animal symbol for this is the crane.
5. *Hsit-kyi auk-pyan* (*lei bauk*). The fifth of seven tone names used by the *hsaing-waing* ensemble. Its equivalent in Burmese harp music is *auk-pyan* and the animal symbol for this note is the cuckoo.
6. *Than gyat*. The sixth of seven tone names used by the *hsaing-waing* ensemble. Its equivalent in Burmese harp music is *chauk-thwe-nyun* and the animal symbol for this note is the horse.
7. *Than-yo* (*hkun-nathan-gyi*). The seventh of seven tone names used by the *hsaing-waing* ensemble. Its equivalent in Burmese harp music is *hnyin-lon* and the animal symbol for this note is the elephant.

Chauk-thwe-nyun (Burma). Cf. *Chauk-pauk auk-pyan*.

Chaunk (Tibet). Shell-horn.
Lit.: no. 255.

Chautāl (North India). See *Tāla*.

Chāyā Rudra (South India). See *Chhāyā Rudra*.

Ch'e (China – M 1045). Solmization syllable and notational symbol of the *kung-ch'e-p'u* system; assuming that *ho*, the basic note, is notated as the western note C, *ch'e* will represent the note G (the character M 1045 is usually read *ch'ih*, but in the present context it reads *ch'e*).
Lit.: no. 136.

Chechempres (West Java). Term for *kechicher* (bronze cymbals).
Lit.: no. 163.

Ch'e chuan (China – M 285; M 1436). "The removal of the viands," the fifth of the six stanzas of the Hymn in Honor of Confucius. The other stanzas are:

1. *Ying shen*
2. *Ch'u hsien*
3. *Ya hsien*
4. *Chung hsien*
6. *Sung shen*

Lit.: no. 136.

Cheeng (Ghanal). Zither with 11 strings.

Chegir (Bali). Sound (and pitch) produced by the *gong lanang*.
Lit.: no. 197.

Chegur (Bali). Sound produced by the *Gong wadon*.
Lit.: no. 197.

'Che hano ihu (Hawaii). Nose-flute with two finger holes.
Lit.: no. 37.

Chehezde (Persia). A lute with eight strings tuned in four pairs. Occasionally a ninth string is added, which supports the lowest sounding pair.
Lit.: no. 255.

Chekü (Persia). Plectrum, bow, drumstick.
Lit.: no. 255.

Chelempung (*Chalempung*) (Java). (1) A bamboo stick-zither with one or two strings. (2) A small instrumental ensemble named after two *chelempung* zithers. The ensemble consists of: a *rebāb*; two *chelempungs*, one called *kendang awi*, the other *ketuk awi*; and a *goong awi*. (3) A zither with 13 double metal strings. The corpus is a trapezoid teakwood box, the strings of which are plucked with the thumb nails. The function of the instrument is to paraphrase the melody. One of these zithers is tuned in the *slendro*, the other in the *pelog* scale. (4) The term is also used for a *bonang* used in Sumatra and parts of Borneo. It consists either of one row of five beating kettles, or of two rows, each having five kettles. Cf. also *Chalempung*.
Lit.: no. 163.

Chelempungan (Java). "Like a *chelempung*." A rare unusual zither type. See *Kowangan* (*gowangan*), *Chelempung* or *Chaping buyuk*, or *Tudung punduk*.
Lit.: no. 163.

Chelepita (Java – Solo Kraton). See *Gambang selukat* (2).

Ch'e ling (China – M 281; M 4056 [*fei ling*; M 1850, M 4056]). The Shanghai term for a whistling spinning top, favored during the 10th month and at the New Year.
Lit.: no. 209.

Cheluring (*Tjelurin̉*) (Java; Bali). Two or more bronze cups are nailed beside each other upon a wooden frame and are beaten with a thin iron stick. Similar to the *kemanak*, the instrument, which is rare in Java, is used in marking time.
Lit.: nos. 163, 197.

Chempala (Java). See *Keprak*.

Chempung (Sumatra). Gong.
Lit.: no. 162.

Chen (China). Pegs of a string instrument.
Lit.: no. 129.

Chen (China). Scrap stick with notches at its side. Cf. *Yü* (China).

Chenchu kāmbhōji (South India). *Janya rāga* of the 28th *mēḷa* (*Harikāmbhōji*).
Tone material:
C F E D G F A B♭ c
c B♭ G B♭ F E D C
Lit.: no. 139.

Cheṇḍa (*Cheṇḍamelam*) (South India; Malabar Coast). Barrel drum. A *kathakali* performance opens with a prelude (called *keli kottu*) played on the *cheṇḍa* (*cheṇḍamelam*), while the actual dance is accompanied by the less noisy *maddalam* (joined by gongs and cymbals). Cf. *Mardala*.

Cheṇḍamelam (South India). See *Cheṇḍa*.

Cheng (China – M 371). (1) General term for gongs and bells. (2) A specific gong, the sound of which ordered the troops to halt their advance. It was also used by priests. (3) Term used for the *t'ung-ku*, an inverted kettle gong. Cf. *Chak* (Korea); *Ching* (Korea).
Lit.: no. 137.

Cheng (China – M 369). A small zither with 10-16 brass (occasionally silk) strings which are strung across movable bridges. The instrument was used at festive and joyful occasions. Cf. *Se*; *Tai-chaing* (Korea); *Sō-no koto* (Japan).
Lit.: no. 137.

Chenga (India – Kandha). Frame drum.
Lit.: no. 255.

Chengcheng (*Tjeng-tjeng*) (Bali). Large cymbals used in the traditional *gamelan gong* and in

processions (*gamelan angklung*; *gamelan bebonang*). Cf. *Ke(ch)cher.*
Lit.: no. 197.

Chengkok (Java). (1) Melody; melodic line. (2) Final note or phrase. (3) Cf. *Kosok.*
Lit.: no. 163.

Chengkung (West Java). A *ketuk*, a light gong. Its heavier form is called *kebluk.*
Lit.: no. 163.

Cheng-pan (China – M 351; M 4885). Main beat (first beat, a term frequently used in operatic music). Also called *t'ou-pan* (M 6489; M 4885), "head beat," or *hung-pan* (M 2383; M 4885), "red heat." This beat appears usually in double meter. In four-beat measures the terms for the first beat can be *tseng-pan* (M 6769; M 4885) or *heh-pan* (M 2090; M 4885), "black beat."
Lit.: no. 136.

Cheng-sheng (China). Term for the stereotyped principal figure in the *yüan* drama. It represents the grand old man, the emperor, general, a man of wisdom and authority.

Cheng-tan (China). Stereotyped operatic role: the virtuoso female.

Cheng-t'ung-po (China – M 351; M 6619; Giles 9387). Large brass cymbals.

Chengu (India – Khanda). Term for *daf.* Cf. *Chenga.*
Lit.: no. 254.

Cheng-yen (China). "Main eye," the term indicates the third beat in a 4/4 meter. Cf. *Cheng-pan.*
Lit.: no. 136.

Chenik (Bali). High pitched; small in size. Cf. *Alit.*
Lit.: no. 197.

Chen-ku (China – M 322; M 3479). Army drum with two heads, in barrel form. Cf. *T'ang-ku.*
Lit.: no. 255.

Cheṅṅala (South India; Malayāḷam). Gong used in *kathakali* performances.
Lit.: no. 261.

Cheplanget (Kenya – Nandi). "The leopard." A water vessel covered with a skin, the middle of which is pierced by a stick which is rubbed with wet hands. Thus a humming sound is created. The instrument is used at the circumcision rituals of girls. No man and no uncircumcised woman may look at it.
Lit.: no. 255.

Cherewata (Ethiopia – Asmari). Spike fiddle with one horsehair string.
Lit.: no. 38.

Chermek (Kirgizstan). A small lute with two or three strings and eight gut frets. The Tadjiks call this instrument *dumburak.*
Lit.: no. 255.

Chētulāvaḷi (South India). *Janya rāga* of the 65th *mēḷa* (*Mechakalyāṇī*).
Tone material:

C D E D E F♯ G B A B c
c B A G F♯ D E D C

Lit.: no. 139.

Che-tzu (China – M 267; M 6942). A notational symbol in the *lü* notation used by Chiang K'uei (A.D. 1155-1229), a composer of the Sung period. The *che-tzu* indicates a microtonal or semitonal alteration of a note that appears either between two *ku-(hsi)* (E) or between two *ying-(chung)* (B). This middle note, having an ornamental function, can be shown as E Ⓕ E (*ku, che-tzu, ku*), or B ⓒ B (*ying, che-tzu, ying*), or E (Ė) E and B (Ḃ) B. For further information see Lit. no. 136.

Cheung-kwun (China – Cantonese). See *Ch'ang-kuan.*

Ch'e-yen (China – M 290; M 7400). "Cut-off eye" represents the second and fourth beats in common meter (4/4) when the notes are being held over from preceding beats. Cf. *Cheng-pan.*
Lit.: no. 136.

Cheza ngoma, randa, rukaruka (East Africa – Swahili). Dancing.

Chhac (Cambodia – Kampuchea). Bow.

Chham (Tibet). Religious dance performed by monks.
Lit.: no. 143.

Chhandōdarī (South India). *Janya rāga* of the 22nd *mēḷa* (*Kharaharapriyā*).
Tone material:
C E♭ D E♭ F G A B♭ G c
c B♭ A F E♭ D C
Lit.: no. 139.

Chhandovatī (India). Term for the fourth *śruti.* The corresponding note name is *catuśśruti ri* (or *śuddha ga*), as they were used in the past music theoretical treatises. Cf. *Śruti.*

Chha-nga (Tibet). Honorific form of *nga.*
Lit.: no. 143.

Chha-nyen (Tibet). Honorific term of *dra-nyen.*
Lit.: no. 143.

Chhatradhāri (South India). See *Chandradāri* (63rd *mēḷa*).

Chha-t'ri (Tibet). Honorific term of *t'ri-p'u.*
Lit.: no. 143.

Chhau (India – Orissa). Particular form of a dance drama which appears only in Orissa. *Chhau* is performed by men and boys who wear wooden masks. These dances can be observed in April (*chaitra*) during the spring festival. The music is sung by a choir accompanied by a *dhol.*
Lit.: no. 46.

Chhaya (North India). *Rāga* subordinated to the *Bilaval thāta.*
Tone material:
C D E (F) G A B c
c (B) (B♭) A G F E D C; *Vādis:* G, C
Lit.: no. 138.

Chhāyā (South India). *Janya rāga* of the 20th *mēḷa* (*Naṭabhairavī*).
Tone material:
C D E♭ D F G B♭ A♭ B♭ c
c B♭ G B♭ A♭ G F E♭ F D E♭ C
Lit.: no. 139.

Chhāyā bauḷi (South India). *Janya rāga* of the 8th *mēḷa* (*Hanumattōḍi*).
Tone material:
C D♭ E♭ F C G A♭ B♭ c
c B♭ G A♭ F E♭ D♭ C
Lit.: no. 139.

Chhāyā gauḷa (South India). *Janya rāga* of the 3rd *mēḷa* (*Ganamurti*).
Tone material:
C D♭ E♭♭ D♭ F G A♭ B c
c A♭ B G F E♭♭ C D♭ C
Lit.: no. 139.

Chhāyā gauḷa (South India). *Janya rāga* of the 15th *mēḷa* (*Māyāmāḷavagauḷa*).
Tone material:
C D♭ F G B c
c B A♭ G F E C D♭ C
Lit.: no. 139.

Chhāyā gauri (South India). *Janya rāga* of the 7th *mēḷa* (*Senāpāti*).
Tone material:
C D♭ F E♭ F G B♭♭ A♭ B♭♭ c
c B♭♭ A♭ G F E♭ F D♭ C
Lit.: no. 139.

Chhāyā kauśīka (South India). *Janya rāga* of the 15th *mēḷa* (*Māyāmāḷavagauḷa*).
Tone material:
C E D♭ E F G B c
c B A♭ G F E D♭ C
Lit.: no. 139.

Chhāyā māḷavi (South India). *Janya rāga* of the 7th *mēḷa* (*Senāpāti*).
Tone material:
C E♭ D♭ E♭ F G A♭ B♭♭ A♭ c
c B♭♭ A♭ G F E♭ F D♭ C
Lit.: no. 139.

Chhāyā māruva (South India). *Janya rāga* of the 49th *mēḷa* (*Dhavalāmbarī*).
Tone material:
C E Db E F# Ab Bbb Ab c
c Bbb Ab F# E Db C
Lit.: no. 139.

Chhāyā nārāyaṇi (South India). *Janya rāga* of the 6th *mēḷa* (*Tānarūpi*).
Tone material:
C G F G A# B c
c B A# B G F Ebb Db C
Lit.: no. 139.

Chhāyānāṭa (South India). (1) The 34th *asampūrṇa mēḷa rāga* without *kaṭapayādi* prefix. (2) The 34th *asampūrṇa mēḷa rāga* with *kaṭapayādi* prefix was called *Bhōgachhāyānāṭa*. See *Rāga* (South India).
Lit.: no. 139.

Chhāyānāṭa (*Bhōgachhāyānāṭa*) (South India). *Janya rāga* of the 34th *mēḷa*.
Tone material:
C D# E F G F G c
c Bb A Bb G F D# C
Lit.: no. 139.

Chhayanath(a) (North India). A subordinate *rāga* to *Kalyan thāta*.
Tone material:
C D E F G A B c
c Bb A G F E D C; *Vādis*: G, D
Lit.: no. 138.

Chhāyā Rudra (South India). *Janya rāga* of the 29th *mēḷa* (*Dhīraśaṅkarābharaṇam*).
Tone material:
C D F G F A B c
c A B G F E D C
Lit.: no. 139.

Chhāyā Saindhavi (South India). *Janya rāga* of the 11th *mēḷa* (*Kokilapriya*).
Tone material:
C Db Eb F G A G B c
c B A G F Eb Db C
Lit.: no. 139.

Chhāyā Sindhu (South India). *Janya rāga* of the 19th *mēḷa* (*Jhaṅkāradhvanī*).
Tone material:
C D F G Ab c
c Ab G F Eb D C
Lit.: no. 139.

Chhāyā Śobhitam (South India). *Janya rāga* of the 22nd *mēḷa* (*Kharaharapriyā*).
Tone material:
C D Eb F G A c
c Bb A G F A F D Eb D C
Lit.: no. 139.

Chāyataranginị (South India). *Janya rāga* of the 28th *mēḷa* (*Harikāmbhōji*).
Tone material:
C D F E F G Bb c
c Bb A G F E D C
Lit.: no. 139.

Chhāyā Tilak (North India). Subordinate *rāga* of the *Bilaval thāta*. It consists of a combination of *Chhayanath* and *Tilak Kamod*. The tone material and *vādis* are variable.
Lit.: no. 138.

Chhāyā Vardhini (South India). *Janya rāga* of the 69th *mēḷa* (*Dhātuvardhanī*).
Tone material:
C D# E F# Ab B c
c B Ab F# E D# C
Lit.: no. 139.

Chhāyāvati (South India). *Janya rāga* of the 17th *mēḷa* (*Sūryakānta*).
Tone material:

C D♭ E F A B c
c B A G F E D♭ C

Lit.: no. 139.

Chhāyāvati (South India). See *Supradīpam* (17th *asampūrṇa mēḷa*).

Chhāyā Vēḷa (South India). *Janya rāga* of the 3rd *mēḷa* (*Ganamurti*).
Tone material:

C D♭ E♭♭ D♭ F G A♭ B c
c A♭ B G F E♭♭ D♭ C

Lit.: no. 139.

Ch'hung (Kampuchea; Vietnam). Bell-shaped cymbals used for marking time.
Lit.: no. 153.

Chhusya (Nepal). A pair of cymbals, frequently used together with the *naya-khin* when important announcements have to be made.

Chi (Japan). Small bamboo cross flute with six or seven finger holes.
Lit.: no. 190.

Chi (Japan). Tone name of the pitch a fifth higher than the basic note of the *ryo* and *ritsu* scales.

Chi (China – M 430). A *chien-tzu*, indicating very fast tempo.
Lit.: no. 136.

Chi (*Ying ch'ing*) (China – M 481). Hemispherical brass bell used by Buddhists in Hangchow.

Chi (Korea). Scale: G A c d e.

Chi (Korea). Bamboo flute. See *Tchi*.

Chi (Malaysia – Johore). Tone syllable representing the first note of *wayang* scales. The frequently used pentatonic scales are: *chi* (e.g., C); *ru(h)* (E); *lu* (F with + above); *mo* (A); *nem* (B with ♭ above). Or: *chi* (C); *ru(h)* (D); *lu* (E); *mo* (G); *nem* (A).

Chi (Japan). Tone name; the equivalent of the Chinese *chih* (M 358f) of the ancient 5- and 7-tone scales. Cf. *Ryo*- and *Ritsu*-scales.
Lit.: no. 136.

Chia (China – M 586). Cf. *Hu-chia*.

Chia-chung (China – M 611; M 1503). "Pressed bell." One of the absolute pitches. The term represents the ninth fifth of the circle of fifths as demonstrated in the *lü-lü*. If the *huang-chung* is interpreted as C, *chia-chung* is E♭ (or D♯). Traditionally *chia-chung* was a *yin* (female) tone, used as basic note in Confucian hymns to be performed in the month of February. If used as a notational symbol only the first syllable, written *chia* (M 611), was used. Cf. *Lü*.
Lit.: no. 136.

Chia kuan (*Pei-li*; *Pi-li*) (China – M 586; M 3557). Old bamboo tube with heterophonic double reeds, resembling the *kuan tzu*. The bamboo tube of the *chia-kuan* and nine finger holes.
Lit.: no. 209.

Chia-kuan (China). In the formal structure of Chinese opera or puppet play *chia-kuan*, the "promotion petition" is the second staged invocation performed by a single person accompanied by gong, woodblock, and cymbals. The Cantonese term for *chia-kuan* is *ka-kwun*. Cf. *Tz'u-fu*.
Lit.: no. 129.

Chia-kuan lo (China). Cf. *Wu lo*. The Cantonese term is *ka-kwun lo*.

Ch'iang-ti (*Hu-ti*) (China – M 666; M 6217). A shepherd's flute. *Ch'iang* indicates tribes living in the west of China.
Lit.: no. 209.

Chiao (China – M 1174). Solmization syllable and notational symbol indicating the third note of the ancient 5- and 7-tone scales. Cf. *Kung* (M 3705), where the names and degrees of the two scales are listed.
Lit.: no. 137.

Chiao-feng-hsiao (China—M 719; M 1894; M 2619). The "teaching happiness *hsiao*." A *p'ai-hsiao* type.
Lit.: no. 137.

Chiao hsiang yüeh tui (China). Symphony orchestra.

Chiao-hsiao (China; Giles 1306, M 2169). Panpipes. Cf. *P'ai hsiao*.

Chiblon (*Siblon*; *Ketimpung*) (Java). The rhythmic beating of the hand on and in the water by bathing children. The term refers also to drum beating (*rarachiblon*, *rarasiblon*). *Chiblon* (*batangan*) indicated also a small drum used in dances. Cf. *Kendangan chiblon*.
Lit.: no. 163.

Chiblonan (Java). The free manner of drumming, called *kendangan chiblon*. In Sumatra this form is called *jamplakan*.
Lit.: no. 163.

Chibuk (Central Asia). Old shepherd's flute (pipe).
Lit.: no. 255.

Chi-ch'in (China). Popular zither consisting of a bamboo tube with five strings struck with a small hammer. The instrument has 13 frets. Cf. *Chi-chu*.

Ch'i-ch'in (China). See *Pan-hu*.

Chi-chu (China). Common zither similar to the *cheng*, tuned chromatically.
Lit.: no. 209.

Chi-chü (China). Recent operatic style.

Chidānandi (*Cidānandi*) (South India). *Janya rāga* of the 36th *mēḷa* (*Chalanāṭa*).
Tone material:

C D♯ E F G A♯ B c
c B A♯ B G F E F D♯ C

Lit.: no. 139.

Chieh-ku (China—M 779; M 3479). "Deer's skin drum," used in theatrical performances, opera, puppet shows, etc. Cf. *Kal-ko* (Korea).

Chieh-ku (China—M 795; M 3479). "Rhythm drum" (*chieh*, M 795, means "verse," "section"). The drum is used in theatrical performances.

Ch'ien-chin (China). A bowed or plucked lute with two strings. Around the neck and the strings is tied a silken loop that can be shifted up and down. The Cantonese term for this instrument is *ts'in-kam*.
Lit.: no. 129.

Chien k'ung-hou (China). See *K'ung-hou*.

Chieng (Vietnam; the former Annam). Gong of various sizes. The terms for its different parts are: *mat chieng*, copper plate; *vu*, central boss; *thanh chieng*, bent rim.
Lit.: no. 255.

Chien-ku (China—M 853; M 3479). Name of the *ying-ku* (M 7475; M 3479) of the Sui period. The *chien-ku* is a richly ornamented barrel drum that is placed upon a cart or a stand. Cf. *Kun-ko* (Korea).
Lit.: no. 137.

Chien-pan (China—M 837; M 4885). Rattle consisting of two slips of bamboo or red hardwood used by lepers and blind persons to warn the people of their approach.
Lit.: no. 137.

Chien-p'u (China). An abridged notational system that employs Arabic numerals. This manner of notating music has no relation to the Chinese musical culture. As it is very simple, it has gained considerable popularity.
Lit.: no. 136.

Ch'ien-tsou (China—M 919; M 6808). Musical prelude.

Chien-tzu (China—M 828; M 6942). About 200 tablature symbols that are employed in *ch'in* music. The *chien-tzu* indicate string, fret, and numerous technical matters, among which are plucking the string outward (away from the player) or inward, dynamics, harmonics, glissandos. For further information see Lit. no. 136.

Chien-tzu (China – M 865; M 6942). Brass horn with sliding tubes used on the theatrical stage and at funerals. (Military brass horns or trumpets were called *hao*.) Both *chien-tzu* and *hao* are *la-pa* types.

Chīfta Naqqāra (Turkey). See *Kūs*.

Chig (Tibet). See *Gcig*.

Chiganda (Tanzania – Gogo). Old dance before an elephant hunt.

Chih (China – M 358f). Solmization syllable and notational symbol indicating the fourth note (an interval of a fifth above *kung*) of the ancient 5- or 7-tone scales. Cf. *Kung* (M 3705), where the degrees of the two scales are listed.
Lit.: nos. 136-37.

Chih (Korea). See *Kung* (China – M 358 f).
Lit.: no. 136.

Chih (China – M 939). "The stopper." A wooden hammer used for striking the inside of the *chu*. See *Chu* (M 1379).

Ch'ih (China – M 1045). A symbol of the *kung-ch'e-p'u* notation. It represents a solmization syllable that signifies G, if *ho*, the first note of the scale, is interpreted as C. The pronunciation of this symbol (M 1045), if used in the *kung-ch'e* notational system, is not *ch'ih*, but *ch'e*.
Lit.: no. 136.

Ch'ih (China – M 1027). An ancient bamboo flute. Originally it was a vertical pitch pipe but (according to the *Erh Ya*, 3rd or 4th centuries B.C.) in later years it was blown transversely. The mouth hole is placed almost in the middle of the tube, which has 3-5 finger holes at both sides of the mouth hole.
Lit.: nos. 137, 250.

Ch'ih-pa kuan (China). "The eighteen inch *kuan*," also called *shu-ti*. This 16th-century *hsiao-kuan*, a vertically-blown flute with six finger holes, of which one is covered with a membrane.
Lit.: no. 209.

Chikāra (North India; Nepal). Bowed spike lute with three strings and five (or 3-9) resonance strings. The bow is called *sargi*. The Nepalese form of the instrument is a small *sārangī*. The three bowed strings are tuned to 1, 4, 5.
Lit.: no. 254.

Chikari (India). Bourdon strings of the *kacchapī vīṇā*.
Lit.: no. 255.

Chikenjenjo (Angola). Drum.

Chikhe (Mongolia). Written: *chikhin*. "Ear"; wooden pegs on the *khil-khuur*.
Lit.: no. 61.

Chikibung (*Dengdo*) (West Java). Term for the Javanese *chiblon*, a small drum. Its low sounds are called *blung* or *indung* and the high ones are *bling* or *anak*.
Lit.: no. 163.

Chiku-no-koto (Japan). Bamboo *koto* with 13 strings. The instrument is played by striking the strings with small bamboo sticks.
Lit.: no. 225.

Chikuzen Biwa (Japan). A *biwa* smaller than the *gaku biwa*. It has the usual set of four (or five) silken strings and five frets. The *bachi* is large and heavy. The instrument first appeared with the "blind priests" in the south of Kyushu, and was used by Buddhist priests in the performances of religious and magic songs. Cf. *Nagashimono*.
Lit.: no. 185.

Chilambu (South India). Cf. *Kaichilambu*.

Chilik (Java). See *Alit*.

Chilmandi (Turkestan). Popular tambourin in various sizes used for song accompaniments. In the south (Samarkand, Bukhara) it is known by its Persian name *dāīra*.
Lit.: no. 255.

Chi-lo (China). Gong employed in Buddhist services.
Lit.: no. 2.

Chim'umugizi (Ruanda). The distinguished drum, a symbol of royal importance.
Lit.: no. 26.

Chimwenyemwenyu (East Africa). Cf. *Kimwanyemwanye.*

Chin (China—M 1057a). Metal. The term refers to brass and copper instruments (gong, bells, etc.).

Ch'in (China—M 1103). The classical zither of China, the noble instrument of the poets, philosophers and scholars. Its origin is not known. Some vague information exists that the instrument was invented by one of the legendary emperors (probably Fu Hsi, ca. 2852 B.C.).

The corpus of the *ch'in* consists of two narrow wooden boards, one placed above the other. The upper board is slightly curved. The ancient *ch'in* had five silken strings; in later times it had seven tuned in an anhemitonic pentatonic manner, although recent tunings incline toward diatonic forms. The *ch'in* has no frets but has instead 13 inlaid or painted studs below the outermost string (lowest string). The studs, called *hui* (M 2354), in Korean called *hwi*, serve a purpose similar to frets on other zithers. The *hui* are placed in such a manner that the distances between them in both directions, to the right and left beginning from a central stud, become—with one or two minor exceptions—increasingly smaller. The following illustrates the spots indicated by the 13 *hui* of and after the Ming period (assuming that a string is tuned to the low C):

Open	*hui*:	13	12	11	10	9	8	7	6	5	4	3	2	1
string C		D	E♭	E	F	G	A	c	e	g	c′	e′	g′	c″

Another feature not visibly indicated on the instrument are the *fen* (M 1851), ten imaginary subdivisions between any two adjoining *hui*. The *fen* have to be learned by the player.

The ensemble *ch'in*, as it was used in the imperial palace and the Confucian temple, was played with a plectrum, and its music was notated by means of a simple tablature. The solo *ch'in*, however, was played with the bare finger tips in a delicate manner and was notated by a refined and highly complex tablature. For further details see Lit. no. 136.

Chi-na (China—M 411; M 4609). A small *so-na* with eight finger holes, called *k'ai-ti* in Peking and Shanghai.
Lit.: no. 209.

China Sampan (Sunda District). A "moon guitar" of Chinese origin (cf. *Yüeh-ch'in*), occasionally also called *kachapi.* It has four strings, a flat circular body, a short neck, and is played with a plectrum.
Lit.: no. 163.

Chinchem (Malaya—Temiar). Set of songs that accompanies ritual dances.
Lit.: no. 245.

Ch'in-ch'iang (China—M 1112; M 665). Music drama that originated probably in the 17th century and used a clapper orchestra that may have had its origin in Shensi. It became more and more popular a century later when the *yüeh-ch'in* was added to the clappers. Cf. *Ching-ch'iang*; *Pang-tzu.*

Chin-chi-chi (Japan). Small circular gong used by beggars and priests.
Lit.: no. 255.

Chin-daul (Turkestan). War drum.
Lit.: no. 255.

Chinditi (*Chiyenge*) (Former Equatorial Africa—Loango). Xylophone. See *Marimba.*
Lit.: no. 255.

Ching (China – M 1119). Stereotyped operatic actor type representing a powerful male figure with a painted face.

Ch'ing- (China – M 1171). "Clear." A prefix in the *lü* notation that indicates notes one octave higher: if *huang* (*chung*) is interpreted as middle C, the symbol *huang* with the prefix *ch'ing* indicates the note C one octave higher than the former.
Lit.: no. 136.

Ch'ing- (China – M 1171). In several instances (e.g., in the old five-tone- and old seven-tone-scales and their notational systems), the left side (half) of the *ch'ing* symbol may represent the rising of a note by a semitone. If *kung* is read as the western note C, *ch'ing kung* would be read as C♯. For further information see Lit. no. 136.

Ching (Korea). Cymbals of varying sizes used at festive occasions at the palace. Also *tjing.*
Lit.: no. 52.

Ch'ing (China – M 1164). (1) The famous sonorous stone slab. It is of great age and has the shape of a carpenter's square. If used as a single slab it is called *t'e ch'ing.* If used in groups, usually 16 tuned slabs, the instrument is called *pien-ch'ing.* The slabs were hung in two rows of eight from a wooden frame, and beaten with wooden sticks with padded ends. The *ch'ing* was used in the Confucian ritual and in the imperial palace.
(2) The same term has also been applied to brass or iron bowls of varying sizes. Singly or in groups they were used in Buddhist services and Taoist temples.
Lit.: nos. 137, 209.

Ching (Thailand). Brightly sounding small cymbals attached to the fingers of the player, used in classical music. Two forms of strokes are used: damped (d) and ringing (r). These strokes can occur in the following three patterns:

prop kai (rhythmic pattern)

1	2	3	4	1	2	3	4	1	2	3	4	1	2	3	4
			(r)				(d)				(r)				(d)

sam chan ("third level" extended version)

song mai ("two beats") (medium tempo)

1	2	3	4	1	2	3	4	1	2	3	4	1	2	3	4
	(r)		(d)		(r)		(d)		(r)		(d)		(r)		(d)

song chan ("second level" middle version)

phleng reo (fast song)

1	2	3	4	1	2	3	4	1	2	3	4	1	2	3	4
(r)	(d)	(r)	(d)	(r)	(d)	(r)	(d)	(r)	(d)	(r)	(d)	(r)	(d)	(r)	(d)

chan dio ("first level" short version)

Lit.: nos. 186, 203, 208.

Ching (China). One of the 10 orchestras of the T'ang period. See *Shih-pu-chi.*

Ching-ba (Tibet). See *Rguyd.*

Ching-ch'iang (China – M 665; M 1127). A noisy and commonplace operatic style greatly appreciated in Peking. This style, an *i-yang-ch'iang* form, had various names. In Szechwan and Hupeh it was called *ch'ing-hsi,* in Kwantung it was called *kao-ch'iang*, in the Hunan province *hsiaing-ch'ü*, in Kiangsi *kan'ch'ü* and in Szechwan, besides *ch'ing hsi*, also *ch'uan-ch'ü.* Cf. *Ti-fang-hsi.*
Lit.: no. 183.

Ch'ing-hsi (China – M 1169; M 2452). A recent (19th-20th century) highly popular operatic style, particularly of Hupeh and Szechwan. Its subjects represent historical romances which have little literary value. Only a limited number of melodies is used accompanied by strings, particularly by the *hu-ch'in.* Related varieties of the *ch'ing-hsi* are the styles of *erh-huang* and *hsi-p'i.* Their combination leads to the *p'i-huang* style. Cf. *Ching-ch'iang*; *Hu-tiao.*
Lit.: no. 183.

Ching-hu (China – M 1127; M 2167). The "first *hu-ch'in.*" *Ching-hu* is the Shanghai term of a fiddle with two strings. It is the leading "violin" of the Peking opera, where it is called *tan-ch'in.* The two strings of the instrument are tuned a fifth apart. The hair of the bow is strung between the two strings.
Lit.: no. 209.

Ching-I (China). "Subdued dress." The stereotyped figure of the leading female part (performed by a male actor-singer) of the Yüan drama (14th century).
Lit.: no. 83.

Ching-ku (China – M 1139; M 3479). Warning drum. It was beaten to announce the riding out of the emperor.
Lit.: no. 137.

Chin'go (Korea). See *Tchin-ko* (*Chin-ko*).

Chingongo (Former Equatorial Africa – Bavili). Two flat iron bells suspended from an iron stick. The bells are sounded in front of travelling distinguished persons, particularly when they were approaching human habitations.
Lit.: no. 255.

Chingraq (Turkey). Old small metal rattle of spherical shape.
Lit.: no. 81.

Ch'ing-sheng (China – M 1171; M 5748). "Clear (high) notes." The top octave range. The entire gamut is divided into three octaves: *cho-sheng* (the lowest), *chung-sheng* (the middle one), and *ch'ing sheng* (the bright, high one). Cf. *Kung-ch'e-p'u.*
Lit.: no. 136.

Ch'ing-tiao (China – M 1127; M 6298). The musical dramas of the capital, a combination of *erh-huang* and *hsi-p'i*, representing the national Chinese opera.
Lit.: no. 55.

Chingufu (French [former] Equatorial Africa – Loango). Drum; a deep wooden box that is open at the top and narrow and closed at the bottom. It is beaten with two padded sticks.
Lit.: no. 255.

Ch'ing-yang-ch'iang (China). 16th-century term for the regional operatic type of Anhwei. Cf. *Ti-fang-hsi.*
Lit.: no. 183.

Ch'ing-yüeh (China – M 1171; M 4129a). Pure native Chinese music.

Ch'ing-yüeh-hsiao (China – M 1171; M 2619; M 4129a). The *hsiao* (vertical flute) of the "clear and correct" (native) music. Cf. *P'ai-hsiao.*

Ch'in Han p'i-p'a (China). *P'i-p'a* with four strings and four frets. Cf. *P'i-p'a.*
Lit.: no. 209.

Chin-hsing (China). "Brilliant stars." Term for the 13 *hui* of the *ch'in.* "Stars that glitter in the moonlight."
Lit.: no. 93.

Chiniloi (Malaysia). Nose flute of the Senoi.
Lit.: no. 313.

Chin-kabai (Burma; Cambodia). Slim tall goblet drum.
Lit.: no. 252.

Chin-kang-t'ui (China – M 3272; M 6589). Small lute with three metal strings and 10 frets. (The term is also written M 1057, M 3268, Giles 12,184.)
Lit.: nos. 209, 255.

Chin-ko (*Tchin-ko*) (Korea). A large barrel drum placed horizontally on a wooden stand. As it is used in sacrificial ceremonies in the Confucian temple and not in the royal palace, it lacks the traditional ornamentation around its body.
Lit.: nos. 52, 179.

Chin-ku (*T-ch'eng-ku*) (China – M 1088; M 3479). A large barrel drum suspended in a frame and placed at the left side of the temple gate. At the Peking Confucian temple the frame was placed in the eastern pagoda. In other locations the drum was placed on a wooden stand. The *chin-ku* corresponded to a large bell hung in the western pagoda. This term is not to be mistaken for *chin-ku* (M 1057, M 3479), indicating a metal plate or stone slab.
Lit.: no. 209.

Chin-ku (China—M 1057; M 3479). A brass gong. At Hangchow it is called *tang-lo*; at Peking *t'ung'ku*.
Lit.: nos. 209, 255.

Chinmayi (South India). *Janya rāga* of the 16th *mēḷa* (*Chakravāka*).
Tone material:
C D♭ E F G F A B♭ c
c B♭ A B♭ G F E D♭ C
Lit.: no. 139.

Ch'in-p'u (China—M 1103; M 5386). Handbook for the *ch'in* player. These books exist since the Ming dynasty and were published by *ch'in* teachers in limited numbers, printed on inferior paper, as they were meant for *ch'in* students only. At the present time these *ch'in-p'u* have become rare.

A *ch'in-p'u* consists of the *fan-li* (introductory notes); followed by a chapter on pitches and their significance and a final chapter (*chih-fa*) on finger techniques and tablature. This latter part is often missing from the book, probably in order to prevent unqualified persons from having access. In the 19th century, however, there appeared *ch'in-p'u* in which were added to the tablature symbols transcriptions in the simple *kung-ch'e-p'u* side by side in parallel columns.
Lit.: nos. 93, 136.

Chinsete (Congo—Bemba). Drum carried under the left arm of the player and played with both hands.
Lit.: no. 26.

Ch'in-shih (China—M 1103; M 5820). The *ch'in* chamber. A suitable room or bower with a place of honor for the instrument. This room was set apart from the rest of the house and served for playing the *ch'in*.
Lit.: no. 93.

Chintāmaṇi (*Cintāmaṇi*; *Bhōga-Chintāmaṇi*; *Jaṭshrintāmani*) (South India). *Janya rāga* of the 7th *mēḷa* (*Senāvati*).
Tone material:
C D♭ E♭ F (C F) G A♭ B𝄫 c
(c B𝄫) c A♭ B𝄫 G F E♭ D♭ C
Lit.: no. 139.

Chintāmaṇi (South India). *Janya rāga* of the 56th *mēḷa* (*Śaṇmukhapriyā*).
Tone material:
C D G F♯ G A♭(+) B♭ c
c G A♭ G F♯ E♭ D C
In ascent the note *dha* (A♭) is often intoned sharp—an almost strong A-natural.
Lit.: no. 139.

Chintāramaṇi (South India). *Janya rāga* of the 52nd *mēḷa* (*Rāmapriyā*).
Tone material:
C E F♯ G A B♭
B♭ A G F♯ G E D♭ C *B♭*
The scale of this *rāga* has *niṣādantya* character.
Lit.: no. 139.

Chintlā (India). Large iron cymbals used in Central India (Bundelkhand).
Lit.: no. 261.

Chin-yang-jo (*Jinyang-jo*) (Korea). Rhythmic mode and drum pattern:

Bamboo strokes on *chang-ko*

Hand strokes on *chang-ko*

Lit.: no. 215.

Chipande (Tanzania—Gogo). Circumcision songs of boys.

Chipḷā (South India). Hardwood castanets. Occasionally *gejjai* are attached to the ends of the slabs. The *chipḷā* are used by *bhāgavatars* (reciters of religious texts and songs).
Lit.: no. 262.

Ch'i-pu-chi (China—M 508; M 579; M 5376). The seven orchestras of the Sui period (589-618). Cf. *Shih-pu-chi* (M 508; M 5376; M 5897).
Lit.: no. 137.

Chiranti (South India). *Janya rāga* of the 7th *mēḷa* (*Senāpati*).
Tone material:
C D♭ E♭ G A♭ B♭♭ c
c B♭♭ A♭ G E♭ D♭ C
Lit.: no. 139.

Chirashi (*Seme*) (Japan). The final parts of *nagauta* and *jōruri* performances. The latter is structured into the following sections: *oki*, *michiyuki*, *kudoki*, *monogatari*, *uta*, *odori*, *miarawashi*, and *chirashi* (*seme*).
Lit.: no. 185.

Chiri chawang(an) (Java; Sunda District). Notational symbol that indicates that from the point where the symbol is placed the *pancher* have to be beaten.
Lit.: no. 163.

Chirikara-byōshi (Japan). Rhythmic patterns played alternatively on the *ō-tsuzumi* and *ko-tsuzumi* in *kabuki* music.
Lit.: no. 185.

Chisanchi (Congo – Baluba). Term for *sansa*.

Chissori (Korea). "Performed solemnly and appealingly." Buddhist chant. Cf. *Pomp'ae*; *Kot-ch'aebi*; *Hossori*.
Lit.: no. 52.

Chitikelu (South India). Telugu term for wooden clapper. Cf. *Chat kulia*.
Lit.: no. 135.

Chitita (Angola). Men's dance. Cf. *Lundongo*.

Chitkul (Eastern Central India – Bastar Maria Gond). Small brass or iron discs linked in pairs at both ends of a string with shells. It is used by women at dances.
Lit.: no. 59.

Chitra Chandrikā (South India). *Janya rāga* of the 63rd *mēḷa* (*Latāṅgī*).
Tone material:
C E D F♯ G B A♭ c
c B A♭ F♯ E D C
Lit.: no. 139.

Chitra Mālikā (South India). *Janya rāga* of the 23rd *mēḷa* (*Gaurīmanōharī*).
Tone material:
C D E♭ F G A B c
c A G F D C
Lit.: no. 139.

Chitra Mandīra (South India). *Janya rāga* of the 15th *mēḷa* (*Māyāmāḷavagauḷa*).
Tone material:
C D♭ E F B c
c B A♭ G F E D♭ C
Lit.: no. 139.

Chitra Maṇi (South India). *Janya rāga* of the 11th *mēḷa* (*Kokilapriya*).
Tone material:
C D♭ F G A B c
c B A G F E♭ D♭ C
Lit.: no. 139.

Chitrāmbarī (South India). The 66th *mēḷa*:
C D E F♯ G A♯ B c
Is also used as a *rāga*.
Lit.: no. 139.

Chitrapādita (South India). *Janya rāga* of the 32nd *mēḷa* (*Rāgavardhanī*).
Tone material:
C E D♯ E F A♭ F G A♭ B♭ c
c A♭ G F D♯ E D♯ C
Lit.: no. 139.

Chitra Prabhanda (South India). A piece of music that contains a large number of ornaments.
Lit.: no. 261.

Chitraravam (South India). *Janya rāga* of the 30th *mēḷa* (*Nāgānandī*).
Tone material:
C D E F G A♯ B A♯ c
c B A♯ G F E C
Lit.: no. 139.

Chitrarūpi (South India). *Janya rāga* of the 4th *mēḷa* (*Vanaspāti*).
Tone material:
C D♭ E♭♭ F A c
c A F E♭♭ D♭ C
Lit.: no. 139.

Chitrasaurabham (South India). *Janya rāga* of the 30th *mēḷa* (*Nāgānandī*). Tone material is identical with that of *rāga Chitraravam.*
Lit.: no. 139.

Chitra Varāḷi (South India). *Janya rāga* of the 20th *mēḷa* (*Naṭabhairavī*).
Tone material:
C D E♭ D F G A♭ B♭ c
c B♭ F E♭ D C
Lit.: no. 139.

Chitsvarūpi (*Chitsvarūpiṇi*) (South India). *Janya rāga* of the 26th *mēḷa* (*Chārukeśī*).
Tone material:
C D E F G A♭ B♭ c
c B♭ A♭ G F E F D C
Lit.: no. 139.

Chitsvarūpiṇi (South India). See *Chitsvarūpi.*

Chittadyuti (South India). *Janya rāga* of the 65th *mēḷa* (*Mechakalyāṇī*).
Tone material:
C D F♯ G A B c
c B A G F♯ E D C
Lit.: no. 139.

Chittākarshiṇi (South India). *Janya rāga* of the 7th *mēḷa* (*Senāpāti*).
Tone material:
C D♭ E♭ F A♭ c
c A♭ F E♭ D♭ C
Lit.: no. 139.

Chiṭṭam (South India). The black paste that is applied to the right head of the *mṛdanga.*
Lit.: no. 261.

Chitta Mōdiṇi (*Chitta Mōhiṇi*) (South India). *Janya rāga* of the 10th *mēḷa* (*Nāṭakapriya*).
Tone material:
C D♭ E♭ F A c
c A F E♭ D♭ C
Lit.: no. 139.

Chitta Mōhiṇi (South India). See *Chitta Mōdiṇi.*

Chitta Rañjaṇi (South India). *Janya rāga* of the 22nd *mēḷa* (*Kharaharapriyā*).
Tone material:
C D E♭ F G A B♭ c
B♭ A G F E♭ D C (B♭ A G F D E♭ D C)
Lit.: no. 139.

Chitta Rañjillini (South India). *Janya rāga* of the 66th *mēḷa* (*Chitrāmbarī*).
Tone material:
C D E F♯ G A♯ c
c B G F♯ D E F♯ D C
Lit.: no. 139.

Chiṭṭa svara (South India). Note or notes serving for ornamentation, particularly in *kritis.*

Chitta tāna (South India). Exercise for the *vīṇā* player. Frequent playing of the *chitta tānas* is intended to improve the technique of the player.
Lit.: no. 261.

Chityatya (Tanzania – Makonde). Small *sansa* type with gourd resonator.

Chiyenge (Former French Equatorial Africa – Loango). Cf. *Chinditi.*

Chiyeyek (Java). See *Ke(chi)cher.*
Lit.: no. 163.

Chīz (North India). Under term for song; piece of music. Also written *cīz.*

Chīz (Kurdistan). Fiddle.
Lit.: no. 255.

Chizambi (South Africa – Venda). Musical bow with resonator.
Lit.: no. 151.

Chlewekan (*Changkem*) (Java). The slit of a slit-drum. Cf. *Kulkul.*
Lit.: no. 163.

Chloie (Central and South Vietnam, Cambodia, the former Annam). Transverse bamboo flute with seven finger holes. Cf. *Khloi*; *Klui*; *Cai sao.*
Lit.: no. 255.

Chnouē (Ancient Egypt). Short, noisy metal trumpet with a wide bell. Lit. no. 250 states that *chnouē* may be the Greek pronunciation of the Egyptian words *shnb* or *šneb.*

Cho (Burma). Simple songs of classical music.
Lit.: no. 185.

Cho (Korea). A small *saing* (*saenghwang*) with 13 pipes. Cf. *Sheng* (China); *Shō* (Japan).
Lit.: no. 52.

Cho (*Jo*) (Korea). Key, mode.

Ch'o (China). See *Chien-tzu.*

Chō (Japan). Melody pattern in *biwa* music. Each pattern (or melody) is numbered and when notated only its number is indicated.
Lit.: no. 185.

Chobo (Japan). Term for the (*gidayū*) musicians who are placed either off stage or above the stage in *kabuki* performances. In *kabuki* the *chobo* provide comments during the performance, while in puppet plays the musicians (singer and *shamisen* player) move the performance ahead with narration and music. Cf. *Shitikata.*
Lit.: no. 185.

Chob (India). Drumstick.
Lit.: no. 255.

Chochokan (East Java). See *Gembyangan.*

Chock (*Chuck*) (Korea). See *Chok.*

Chōdya (South India). Sporadic name of *laghu.*
Lit.: no. 261.

Chok (*Chock*; *Chuck*) (Korea). Notched bamboo flute of Chinese origin; vertically-blown. The instrument has six finger holes, one at the back. The *chok* is an *ah-ak* instrument. Cf. *Chu* (China).
Lit.: no. 52.

Chokekan (Central Java). Term for the numerous blind beggars who accompany their singing by beating the *rebāna* (or *terbang*).
Lit.: no. 163.

Cho-ko (Korea). Cf. *No-ko*; *Tsu-ku*; *Jwako.*

Chol-go (Korea). Cf. *Chol-ko.*

Chol-ko (*Chol-go*; *Tchul-ko*; *Chieh-ku*) (China—M 795; M 3479) (Korea). Medium-sized barrel drum resting obliquely on a wooden box. It is used in *ah-ak* and is placed on the terrace of the Confucian temple. The drum is beaten with the padded end of a heavy stick at the beginning and closing of the sacred hymn, and two beats are performed at the end of each 4-syllable verse.
Lit.: no. 52.

Chondong (Bali). "Servant maid." The third of the three girl dancers who perform the *legong.*
Lit.: no. 197.

Chōng-ak (Korea). Term for the refined ensemble music favored by the aristocracy.
Lit.: no. 179.

Chonge-chonge (Bali). Medium sized *cheng-cheng.*
Lit.: no. 197.

Chong-jae (Korea). Court dance. A speaker (*chuk-kanja*) introduces the dancers and narrates the subject of the dance. There are two parts: the traditional (Korean) and the imported ancient Chinese dance. These are slow movements performed in great dignity. In the past there was a considerable number of these classical dances (sword dance, priest's dance, drum dance, etc.). At the present time many of these dances have become obsolete.
Lit.: no. 179.

Chongka (Flores). See *Sanda.* Cf. *Danding.*

Chong-song (Korea). Serious vocal music.
Lit.: no. 179.

Chonguri (Kurdistan). *Tanbura* with two or three strings. Cf. *Changura.*

Chontang (East Java; Madura). An instrument that can be described as a five-toned bamboo *saron*, vaguely related to the *angklung.* It has five bamboo keys resting on a wooden frame. Cf. *Balibalian.*
Lit.: no. 163.

Choong-keum (*Choong-kum*; *Chottae*) (Korea). A medium sized transverse bamboo flute with six or seven finger holes, which have the same order as those of the somewhat larger *tae-kum.* At the present time the *choong-keum* has almost disappeared from use. Cf. *So-keum.*
Lit.: no. 179.

Choong-kum (Korea). Cf. *Choong-keum.*

Cho'or (Kirgizia). End-blown long flute closely related to the Kazakh *sybizga*, the Bashkir *kura*, and the Kalmuck *zurr.*
Lit.: no. 276.

Chop (Thailand). Small cymbals.

Chor (East Turkestan). (1) Ocarina, a toy for children. (2) Vertical flute with four finger holes. Cf. *Sybizga.*
Lit.: nos. 91, 254.

Ch'ö-(r)nga (Tibet). See *Ch'os-rnga.*

Ch'os-dung (Tibet). Sacred horn. Cf. *Ragdung.*
Lit.: no. 143.

Chosen (Japan). *Shamisen* type with a long neck, without any frets.
Lit.: no. 225.

Cho-sheng (China). "Muddy notes." The term refers to the lowest octave range. The entire gamut is divided into three octave ranges: *cho-sheng*, the lowest, *chung-sheng*, the middle one, and *ch'ing-sheng*, the high one. Cf. *Kung-ch'e-p'u.*
Lit.: no. 136.

Choshi (Japan). A very long prelude that precedes *bugaku* (music), usually *togaku*, and can appear either after the *netori* or replace it altogether. The *choshi* consists of a series of sections with irregular durations.
Lit.: no. 185.

Chōshigami (Japan). A small piece of tuning paper that is applied to the rear head of the *kotsuzumi.*
Lit.: no. 185.

Chōṣhi omoi (Japan). Observation of careful tuning, particularly the tuning of *shamisen* when performing *joruri.*
Lit.: no. 225.

Chōshi sadame (Japan). The proper way of voice-production when performing *joruri.* The teaching deals with the loudness or softness of the voice, which has to be well adjusted to the size of the hall.
Lit.: no. 255.

Ch'os rnga (Tibet). "Religious drum." A large barrel drum suspended in a wooden frame, or a small one with a flat cylindrical body pierced by a wooden handle which enables a person to carry the instrument. Cf. *Rnga.*
Lit.: no. 143.

Chottae (*Chot-tai*; *Choong keum*) (Korea). A long cross flute of bamboo with six finger holes and 1-2 non-stopped holes, of which one is covered by a thin membrane. Cf. *Tae-kum.*
Lit.: no. 179.

Ch'ou (China—M 1330). Stereotyped operatic actor figure of a clown with a painted ugly face.
Lit.: no. 183.

Choundake (India; Bengal). Term for *ānanda laharī.*

Choung (Former Cambodia; Vietnam). Cymbals.

Chu (China—M 1379). A percussion instrument in the form of a trough. The age of the *chu* is supposed to reach back into the Chou dynasty (1122-255 B.C.). The instrument consists of a rectangular wooden box, slightly wider at its open top than at the closed bottom. Inside the box, on the center of the bottom board, was anchored a movable hammer (*chih*). After the Sung dynasty (A.D. 960-1278) the hammer was detached. The box was painted green on three of its outer sides, and white on the fourth. The entire inside was painted black. Another way of painting the *chu* was: the four outside walls were painted blue, red, black, and white, respectively, and the inside of the box was painted yellow. The ancient instrument had a circular hole cut into the side wall facing west. Through it the player inserted his hand and moved the anchored hammer, beating the north wall in a east-north motion three times at the beginning of each verse of the Confucian hymn. The *chu* was placed at the east or north-east side of the Moon Terrace of the temple.
Lit.: no. 137.

Chu (China—M 1340). As a *chien-tzu* (*ch'in* tablature symbol), only the left side of the character is used. See *chien-tzu.*
Lit.: no. 136.

Chü (China—M 1541). "Sentence." The left hand side of the character (M 1541), which has been musical use since the Sung period (A.D. 960-1279), serves here as an indication of a brief pause of text and melody. It has the same function as *yün.*
Lit.: no. 136.

Ch'ü (China—M 1623). Literally "crooked," "wrong." In music the term originally referred to "simple songs," which ignored the stilted, sophisticated textual style of the past. The learned scholars used the term in order to express their contempt of simple songs. The term assumed increasingly a more respectable meaning, eventually referring to songs that were generally approved, and operatic arias, later also instrumental pieces, overtures, preludes, interludes, solo pieces, and others. Two types of *ch'ü* were distinguished: the *pei ch'ü*, the northern *ch'ü*, where the text was of greater importance than the musical accompaniment in which string instruments predominated. These lively bold songs were composed generally in a heptatonic mode and showed considerable rhythmic variety. The second type were the *nan-ch'ü*, the southern *ch'ü*, where the melody pre-dominated. Its accompaniment was provided by flute and percussion instruments. These were gentle songs composed in a purely anhemitonic pentatonic manner, and were in strict common (or rarely in double) meter. All these *ch'ü* appeared in three different ways:

1. *Ch'ü* sung at court; songs that were suitable for the entertainment of the highest nobility.
2. *Ch'ü* sung in cycles; the number of songs varied; there could have been as many as 40 songs in one cycle.
3. *Ch'ü* sung by learned scholars; songs often artful and amusing ones that were performed in conjunction with dancing.

All these *ch'ü* appeared in various sizes; the long ones consisted of numerous sections. The *ch'ü* can be described as the favorite musical form of the educated classes during and after the T'ang period.

Chü (China—M 1584). Term for an operatic style.
Lit.: no. 192.

Chu (Japan). See *Noh* (*Tsuyo*); *Yokyoku.*
Lit.: no. 185.

Chual (Flores). Cf. *Wale.*

Ch'uan-ch'ih (*Nan-ch'ü*) (China). A type of music drama that became fashionable by the end of the Yüan period (14th century) and during the Ming dynasty (1368-1644). The first celebrated drama of this category that found approval by the first Ming emperor and the nobility was *P'i-p'a-chi* ("The Story of the *P'i-p'a*"), a highly emotional work. In this form of

drama each act (occasionally there could be as many as 30 acts in one opera) was independent and had its own title. The *ch'uan-ch'ih* was the forerunner of the *k'un-ch'ü.* The texts of these dramas, originally in classical Chinese, eventually were infused with sections of popular, dialectal language in order to enable common people to comprehend them. These adjusted *ch'uan-ch'ih* were called *k'un-tiao.* Cf. *Ti-fang-hsi.*
Lit.: nos. 41, 55.

Ch'uan-ch'ü (China). Cf. *Ch'ing-ch'iang.*

Ch'üan-fu (China). See *Chien-tzu.*

Chuang (China). See *Chien-tzu.*

Ch'uan-ling (China). A rattle consisting of a hollow metal ring filled with little stones and kernels spun around a finger or a stick. Its noise announces the arrival of wandering magicians and physicians.
Lit.: no. 209.

Chubai (Japan). The middle hymn of a *kansan* group. The *chubai* was preceded by the introductory *shobai* and followed by the concluding *gobai.* See *Kansan.*
Lit.: nos. 53, 185.

Chubchīq (Arabia; Turkey; Turkestan). Term first used by Ibn Chaibi (15th century) for the Chinese *sheng* (M 5742). Cf. *Mushtaq ṣinī; Qāmish mizmār.*
Lit.: no. 81.

Chu che (Burma; Vietnam – Cambodia). Goblet drum. Smaller than the *chin-kabai.*
Lit.: no. 252.

Chuck (Korea). See *Chok.*

Chūḍāmaṇi (*Cūḍāmani*) (South India). *Janya rāga* of the 29th *mēḷa* (*Dhīraśaṅkarābharaṇam*). Tone material:

C D E F G A B c
c G B A F E C

Lit.: no. 139.

Ch'uen-kuan (China). See *Ch'un kuan.*

Ch'uen-ling (China). See *Ch'uan-ling.*

Chügür (Turkey; Persia). Lute with six strings and a long fretted neck. In Persia the neck is shorter.
Lit.: no. 81.

Ch'u-hsien (China – M 1390; M 2699). "The First Presentation of Offerings," being the second of the six stanzas of the "Hymn in Honor of Confucius." The other stanzas are:

1. *Ying-shen*
3. *Ya-hsien*
4. *Chung hsien*
5. *Ch'e-chuan*
6. *Sung-shen*

For notation and the entire text see Lit. no. 136.

Ch'ui (*Ku-ch'ui*) (China – M 1484). Drumsticks.

Ch'ui (China – M 1476a). Wind. Sound of music. The term indicates wind instruments or playing a wind instrument; playing and singing. Also M 1623a.

Ch'ui-ki-erh (China). Toy pipe.
Lit.: no. 255.

Ch'ui-la-pa (China). To blow a horn (bugle).

Chui-ta (Korea). Military music performed by two bands. The front band, large and noisy, employed oboes, trumpets, gongs, cymbals, and drums. The rear band, less noisy, consisted of oboes, transverse flutes, and drums.
Lit.: no. 179.

Ch'ui ti-tzu (China). Playing a flute.

Ch'uk (*Chuk*) (Korea). This *ah-ak* instrument is identical with the Chinese *chu* (M 1379). See *Tchouk.*
Lit.: no. 52.

Chuk (Korea). The fifth degree and notational symbol of the *kong-chuk-po.* Assuming that *hap* is the same as the western note C, *chuk* represents G.
Lit.: no. 136.

Chuk-chang-k'o (Korea). Cf. *Juk-jang-go.*

Chukkā (India). Medieval name for a wind instrument. The term appears in the *Saṅgīta ratnākara* (Śārṅgadeva, 1210-1247).
Lit.: no. 261.

Chu-ko-ku (China). Drum with a bronze kettle as body. Cf. *Daṅkī* (Tibet; Burma).
Lit.: no. 255.

Chūkyoku(sen) (Japan). Scale occasionally used in *shōmyō.*

Chul-ko (Korea). Cf. *Chol-ko.*

Chum-choe (the former Annam; Vietnam). Copper cymbals used in pagodas.
Lit.: no. 255.

Chumlak dunbalayī (Turkey). Earthenware kettledrum. In the 17th-century it was used in the procession of the Mahmal on the way to Mecca. Frequently the name *Dunbalāk* was used. The name *Dunbalāk* appeared in Persia, and *Dünbelek* in Turkey.
Lit.: no. 81.

Ch'un (China). "Lip." The edge above the slit on the *pu-yü.*
Lit.: no. 129.

Chün (China – M 1724). Common term for the 12 *lü* tones.

Chung (China – M 1503). To be distinguished from *chung*, M 1514, "cup," "goblet." *Chung* (M 1503) is the general term for a suspended bell that is struck from the outside. Cf. *Po-chung*; *Pien-chung*; *Ko-chung*; *Yung-chung*; *T'e-chung*.
Lit.: no. 137.

Chung (Korea). See *Yul-cha-po.*
Lit.: no. 136.

Chung (China – M 1509). See *Ch'ien-tzu.*
Lit.: no. 136.

Ch'ung (the former Cambodia; Vietnam). Cymbal.
Lit.: no. 254.

Chung-ak (Korea). Classical music imported from China for a small instrumental ensemble. Originally sacred Buddhist songs became in later periods purely instrumental music. The instruments used are: *komunko*, *kaya-kum*, two *hai-kum*, *t'ang-chuk*, *t'ang-p'iri*, *chang-ko.*
Lit.: no. 52.

Chung-chih (China). See *Chien-tzu.*

Chung-chung-mori (Korea). Rhythmic mode:

Bamboo strokes on *chang-ko*

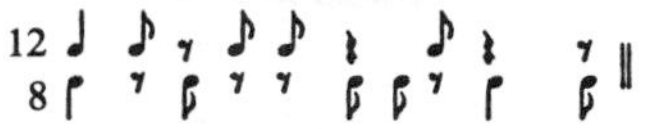

Hand strokes on *chang-ko*

Lit.: nos. 277, 286.

Chung-gum (Korea). See *Chung-keum.*

Chung-hsien (China – M 1500; M 2699). The third and last Presentation of Offerings, the fourth of the six stanzas of the "Hymn in Honor of Confucius." The other stanzas are:

1. *Ying shen*
2. *Ch'u-hsien*
3. *Ya-hsien*
5. *Ch'e-chuan*
6. *Sung-shen*

For notation and the entire text see Lit. no. 136.

Chung-kan-po (Korea). An early notational system that permits showing the durations of notes. The written form of the term *chung-kan-po* is of interest: M 1143 (the Chinese *ching*, "a well"), is read in Korean *chung* and its appearance resembles four tree trunks laid on the ground in such a manner as to indicate a square that creates the border of the opening of a well. Therefore the words *chung* and *kan* (in Chinese this character reads *chien*, is written as M 835, and means "among," "space between"). In the system of *chung-kan-po* are drawn sixteen rectangles, arranged like a ladder, where each rectangle represents a metrical unit (*chung-kan*). The 16 *chung-kan* form one *haeng* and each *haeng* is divided into six groups (*kang*) in the following manner:

:::::::::	first *kang* (with 3 metrical units)
....	second *kang* (with 2 metrical units)
:::::::::	third *kang* (with 3 metrical units)
:::::::::	fourth *kang* (with 3 metrical units)
....	fifth *kang* (with 2 metrical units)
:::::::::	sixth *kang* (with 3 metrical units)

For details see Lit. no. 136.

Chung-keum (*Chung-kum*; *chung-gum*) (Korea). Obsolete flute. Cf. *Sam-chuk*.

Chungklik (Bali). A simple xylophone. The slabs are placed across a deep resonance box.
Lit.: no. 197.

Chung-ko (Korea). A medium sized barrel drum with two heads. The drum rests vertically on a wooden stand, which allows the beating of one head only. The drum was used in sacrificial services to the God of War.
Lit.: no. 52.

Chung-lü (China). "Mean tube." Absolute pitch. The twelfth tone of the spiral of fifths as shown in the *lü-lü*. Traditionally *chung-lü* is a *yin* ("female") tone. It served as basic note in Confucian hymns performed in the month of April. When *chung-(lü)* appeared as a notational symbol only the first syllable (*chung*) was used.
Lit.: no. 136.

Chung mori (*Jung mori*) (Korea). Rhythmic mode and drum pattern. See *Chung-chung-mori. Cf. Chin-yang-jo.*
Lit.: no. 286.

Chung-sheng (China). "Middle notes." The middle octave range. The entire gamut is divided into three octave ranges: the highest is *ch'ing-sheng* and the lowest is *cho-sheng*. Cf. *Kung-ch'e-p'u*.
Lit.: no. 136.

Ch'ung-tu (China – M 1525; M 6520). An old form of the *p'ai-pan* rattle consisting of 12 bamboo (or wooden) slabs fastened together at one end. The beginnings of Confucian hymn texts were engraved in the slabs which, like a fan, were clicked together in order to indicate meter and rhythm at religious services. Originally *ch'ung-tu* signified a large piece of bamboo split several times at one end and struck with it against the ground. Cf. *Tok* (Korea).
Lit.: no. 250.

Chung-zong-song (Korea). "Muddy scale." The term refers to the chromatic scale.
Lit.: no. 145.

Ch'un-ku (China). The Cantonese term is *kuan-ku*. See *Pai-p'i-ku*.

Ch'un kuan (*La-pa*) (China – M 1493; M 3557). A simple bamboo shawm with six finger holes and a single reed. The range covers only the interval of one fifth. The instrument was used by toy vendors. The Peking name of the small *ch'un-kuan* is *kuan-tzu*. In Shantung two of these pipes were fitted together and called *tui-hsiao*.
Lit.: no. 209.

Ch'un-ling (China). See *Ch'uan-ling* (*Ch'uen-ling*).

Chunori (Japan). Two syllables performed on one beat in quick succession in *noh* music. This pattern, also called *shura-nori* ("battle rhythm"), was believed to create excitement. Cf. *Nori*.
Lit.: no. 187.

Ch'ü-p'ai (China – M 1623; M 4871). "Song label"; standard leitmotives that represent fixed modes or situations used in Chinese operas. These melodies were common property of the musicians and were well known to audiences. The *ch'ü-p'ai* were never sung but performed only instrumentally. Cf. *Ya-ti*.
Lit.: no. 136.

Chup en parri (West Pacific—East Caroline Isl., Ponape). Nose-flute. Cf. *Kash*; *Ang en tsuma.*
Lit.: no. 313.

Ch'ü-p'u (China). Music book. Notated material of songs, arias, instrumental pieces.

Churamanṭalam (South India). Board zither. Similar to the Arabic *qanun*. See *Sarmaṇḍal.*
Lit.: no. 254.

Churiga (South Celebes). See *Tjuriga.*

Churing (Bali). An obscure small *gangsa* type. The slabs are placed across a shallow resonance box.
Lit.: no. 197.

Churing (*Nggri-nggo*) (Flores—Manggaray). Tubular bamboo zither with 5-6 strings. Cf. *Gong-tondu.*
Lit.: no. 166.

Churinga (Australia—Aranda). Bull roarer. Cf. *Churunga.*
Lit.: nos. 37, 213.

Chūrṇika Vinodiṇi (South India). *Janya rāga* of the 66th *mēḷa* (*Chitrāmbarī*).
Tone material:
C D E F# G A# B c
c B A# B G F# E D C
Lit.: no. 139.

Churunga (Australia). See *Churinga.*
Lit.: no. 37.

Ch'u-tse p'i-"a (China). A *p'i-p'a* with five strings.

Chūtūvaḷi (South India). *Janya rāga* of the 56th *mēḷa* (*Śaṇmukhapriyā*).
Tone material:
C F# Eb F# G Ab Bb c
c Bb Ab G F# Eb D C
Lit.: no. 139.

Ch'ü-tzu (China). Lyric songs with lute or zither accompaniment. Cf. *Ch'ü.*

Ch'u-tz'u piao yen (China). Première; first performance.

Chu-uki (Japan). See *Nōh*; *Yowa.*

Chwago (Korea). See *Jwa-ko.*

Chyappa (Japan). A pair of small cymbals used offstage in accompanying dance, Chinese scenes in *kabuki* performances.
Lit.: no. 185.

Chyintat (Burma—Kachin). Long cylindrical drum.
Lit.: no. 252.

Chyo-kim (Korea). Grass flute.
Lit.: no. 252.

Cidānandi (South India). See *Chidānandi.*

Cintāmaṇi (South India). See *Chintāmaṇi.*

Citrā (India). See *Citrā Vīṇā.*

Citra Mālikā (South India). See *Chitra Mālikā.*

Citrapādita (South India). See *Chitrapādita.*

Citraravam (South India). See *Chitraravam.*

Citrasaurabham (South India). See *Chitrasaurabham.*

Citrā Vīṇā (Ancient India). *Vīṇā* with seven strings.
Lit.: no. 261.

Cīz (North India). See *Chīz.*

Coboro (*Kebero*) (Eritrea—Tigre). Barrel drum made from a hollowed log. The two heads are beaten with the bare hands.
Lit.: no. 38.

Cobuz (*Qubuz*) (Turkey). See *Cobza.*

Cobza (*Cobuz*) (Turkey). Lute with 4-10 strings and with a bent peg-board. It is played with a goose feather quill plectrum.
Lit.: no. 317.

Colangee (Sahara; Sudan – Hausa). See *Kalangu.*

Conchē (Vietnam – former Cambodia). Pipe.
Lit.: no. 255.

Condi (Congo – Abangba). Arched harp.
Lit.: no. 21.

Condong (Vietnam – former Cambodia). Bell.
Lit.: no. 255.

Cong (Tibet). Bell.
Lit.: no. 255.

Cong (Vietnam). Tone name. Cf. *Ho* (where tone names are listed).

Copong (Malaysia). Term for the attached bell of the *serunai.*
Lit.: no. 162.

Copuz (*Cobuz*) (Turkey). See *Cobza.*

Cora (West Africa; Guinea; Senegal; Gambia; Mali). Harp-lute with 21 strings. Cf. *Kasso.*
Lit.: no. 218.

C'os-dung (Tibet). Trumpet used in religious services.
Lit.: no. 255.

Courung-courung (Borneo). See *Gulung-gulung.*

Crap-fuong (Vietnam – former Cambodia). Clapper consisting of two rectangular pieces of wood beaten against each other. Cf. *Mohori.*
Lit.: no. 255.

Crop condong (Vietnam – former Cambodia). Clapper or hammer of a bell.
Lit.: no. 255.

Cūḍāmaṇi (South India). See *Chūḍāmaṇi.*

Cūlang (Philippines – Moro). Also *Kulang.* See *Barimbo.*

Cura (*Jura*) (Turkey). A small *saz* with a pear-shaped body, a long neck, three strings, and a variable number of frets.
Lit.: no. 243.

Čuramantalam (South India). See *Churamantalam.*

D

Daba (Malagasy Republic). Cylindrical drum.
Lit.: no. 251.

Dabbous (*Debbus*) (Arabia; Persia). "Club." Dervish rattle made of a club-shaped piece of wood, to which are linked chains and bells.
Lit.: no. 255.

Dabdāb (*Dardaba*) (North Africa; Morocco—Berber). Kettledrum. Cf. *Debdebe.*
Lit.: no. 70.

Dabke (Kurdistan). Term for *raqsa* (dance). Cf. *Govand.*
Lit.: no. 229.

Dabs (Ladakh). Large frame drum with one head.

Dabyl (Central Asia—Kirghiz). Frame drum, probably of Kazakh origin.
Lit.: no. 91.

Ḍaḍa (Central Java). "Breast." A tone name:

1. in Central Java as the third note of the *pelog* system (see also *Tengah*).
2. in Jombong Prabalingga as the third note of the *slendro* system.
3. in Java also as the fourth note of the modern *slendro* and as the fifth note of the modern *pelog* systems.

Quote: Lit.: no. 163.

Ḍaḍa (Malaysia). See *Tawak.*

Da-daiko (Japan). Two giant cylindrical drums, each with two heads. The skins produce no definite pitches but an impressive thunderous sound. They are beaten by two heavy lacquered sticks in a left-right sequence. The *da-daiko* are used in the imperial *gagaku* and frequently in *bugaku* dances (instead of the *tsuri-daiko*).
Lit.: nos. 185, 225.

Dadako (Timor). Bamboo zither with six strings.
Lit.: no. 162.

Dadaria (*Banbhajan*) (Southeast India; Maikal Hills—Gond). Forest songs of the young Gond people. Love songs with short verses; the boy sings one, the girl answers with another. There are numerous repetitions.
Lit.: no. 134.

Dadbari (Somali Republic). Dance song; dance of the men.
Lit.: no. 98.

Dadeli (South Africa). Cf. *Motaba.*

Dadi (Java). Cf. *Dados*; *Wirama tanggung.*

Dados (Java). Normal, correct tempo. Cf. *Wirama tanggung*; *Dadi.*

Dādra (India). Rhythmic mode resembling the western 6/8 meter. See *Tāla.*

Dāerah (India). Frame drum with one skin. Cf. *Dārā*; *Dāira.*

Daf (Turkey). Circular frame drum with thin metal discs inserted in slits in the rim. The *dā'ira* is very similar and often mistaken for the *daf.* According to Lit. no. 81, the *dā'ira* is provided with little bells or rings instead of metal discs.
Lit.: no. 81.

Daf (North India; Iran). Popular circular or octagonal frame drum without any jingling metal discs. The narrow rim is made of wood or iron. The single skin is held on the frame by leather straps tied on the lower side in star form. The instrument appears frequently at a festive time such as Holi in processions, and is also used to accompany folksongs.
Lit.: no. 255.

Daff (Persia). See North Indian *Daf.*

Daflī (*Dafrī*; *Daphla*; *Dhapla*; *Dapla*) (India). A rattle consisting of a pair of wooden plane shaped blocks with wooden handles having small round metal discs rattling within slots. The term refers also to the popular North Indian frame drum.
Lit.: no. 254.

Dafrī (India). See *Daflī.*

Daga (Java). See *Rebāb* (Java); the instrument is also called *sirah.*

Dagan (India). See *Dugan.*

Ḍagara (India; Bengal). A drum with a pear-shaped clay body. It is beaten with sticks and is played at weddings and religious festivities. See *Tikārā.*
Lit.: no. 255.

Ḍagelan (Java). Clownish comedy. See *Gembyakan.*

Dahare (*Dayere*) (Iran). Tambourin. See *Dā'ira.*
Lit.: no. 254.

Da-hao (China). Trombone.
Lit.: no. 255.

Dahīna (India). See *Daīna.*

Daibyōshi (Japan). "The grand time beater." A term usually used in *kagura* and *geza* music. It indicates a large barrel drum that rests horizontally on a heavy wooden stand. The drum is beaten with two heavy wooden sticks.
Lit.: nos. 185, 225.

Dai co (Vietnam). Big barrel drum.

Daijin-mai (Japan). Popular dance of the Edo period (A.D. 1615-1867).
Lit.: no. 187.

Daiko (Japan). See *Taiko.*

Daīna (India). Synonym for *tabla.*

Dai nhac (Vietnam). "Great music." Ceremonial music of Temple and Royal Palace performed by a large instrumental ensemble. The instruments of a *dai nhac* ensemble were: 4 *ken*, 2 *nhi*, 1 *trong nhac*, 1 *trong com*, 1 *bong*, 1 *sinh tien*, 1 *mo sung trau*, 1 set of *chap choa*, 1 set of *tam am la.*

At the present time the ensemble is reduced in size to: *ken* (*dam*) (oboe), (*dan*) *nhi* (fiddle), *trong* (drum), *chap choa* (cymbals), *sinh tien* (rattles), *sao* (flute).
Lit.: no. 296.

Dā'ira (Iran; North India). "Circle." Frame drum of Iran, Arabia, and Turkey with a circular or (rarely) octagonal frame. Cf. *Daf* (*Duff*); *Dahare.*
Lit.: no. 250.

Dāīra (Morocco; Algeria). See *Nuba.*

Ḍāirū (India). Popular name for *damaru.*
Lit.: no. 254.

Dai-shoko (Japan). The big *shoko*; a large gong, usually played together with the *da-daiko.* The *dai-shoko* rests upon a wooden platform.
Lit.: no. 185.

Dai trieu nhac (Vietnam). Music of the great assemblies; court music.

Dājina (*Qarīna*) (Arabia). A girl who sings in taverns.
Lit.: no. 308.

Ḍāk (North India). Large barrel drum. See *Ḍhol.*
Lit.: no. 198.

Dakado (*Beorla*) (East Timor). Bamboo tube zither.
Lit.: no. 190.

Daki (Southeast India; Orissa—Muria Bastar Gond). Frame drum of the Gond.
Lit.: no. 59.

Da k'in (China). See *Ta-ch'in.*

Dakoot (*Dakut*; *Dekoot*; *Dikoot*) (South and Central Sumatra). Bird whistle (a small tube without finger holes). Cf. *Bumbun* (Borneo).
Lit.: no. 167.

Dākṣāyaṇi (South India). See *Dākshāyaṇi.*

Dākshāyaṇi (South India). *Janya rāga* of the 15th *mēḷa* (*Māyāmāḷavagauḷa*).
Tone material:
C D♭ G A♭ B c
c B A♭ G D♭ C
Lit.: no. 139.

Dākshāyaṇi (South India). *Janya rāga* of the 29th *mēḷa* (*Dhīraśaṅkarābharaṇam*).
Tone material:
C D E F B A F G B c
c B A G F E D C
Lit.: no. 139.

Dakshina (India). Term for *tabla.*

Daku-dolo (Flores). Stick jumping dance game.
Lit.: no. 166.

Daku-in (Japan). See *Kwaigo-no-ben.*

Dakut (Southeast Asia). See *Dakoot.*

Dalang (Indonesia; Malaysia). The leader of the *wayang* drama. He speaks, sings, manipulates the marionettes, and directs the *gamelan.* See *Sutradhara.*
Lit.: no. 163.

Dalang tua (Malaysia). The old *dalang.*

Dalinzi (Congo; Ruanda—Bahavu). Drum.
Lit.: no. 26.

Dal ondel (*Tabbhuan boomboong*) (Madura; Sunda). See *Boku* (Flores).

Daluka (Sudan). Big cylindrical war drum.
Lit.: no. 255.

Dama (Burma). Barrel drum with two cowskin heads.
Lit.: no. 252.

Damai baja (Nepal). Instrumental ensemble consisting of two *sahanāī* (*mohali*), one of two instruments plays the melody, the other the drone; two *karnal* (*narsingha*), long trumpets straight or circular (or S-shaped); a *nagara*, *damaha*, *tyamko* (kettledrums); a *dholak*; *jhyamta* (cymbals).

Dāmāmā (North India; Afghanistan; Persia). A pear-shaped shallow kettledrum with a clay corpus and one skin. Cf. *Demāme*; *Tikārā*. Also *Damaha*.
Lit.: no. 255.

Daman (Ladakh). A pair of kettledrums, tuned a fifth apart.

Ḍamāram (South India). A couple of wooden drums in conical shape. One is beaten with a curved, the other with a straight stick. At the head of religious processions the drums are placed on top of a bullock and beaten by a boy who rides the animal and announces the coming of sacred symbols of the deity.
Lit.: no. 261.

Ḍamaru (India). An ancient clapper drum in the form of an hourglass. It is attributed to Shiva. A string ending in two knotted ends is wound around the waist of the drum's body. Next to the string with its two knotted ends is affixed a handle made of cloth or leather, which enables the player to shake the instrument to and fro and create a rattling sound that is believed to create magic.
Lit.: no. 255.

Ḍamaru (Tibetan; *Rnga-ch'un*) (Nepal; Tibet). In Tibet, occasionally also in Nepal, the hourglass shape of the drum is achieved by the use of two human skull bones joined together at the apexes. The two drumheads can be human or snakeskins, and now and then also parchment. Cf. *Čan teu*.
Lit.: no. 143.

Ḍamaruga (South India). A *damaru* type used during ceremonies and religious festivals in the temples of Mysore. The term *damarukam* is equally often used in places all over the south.
Lit.: no. 255.

Ḍamarukapriya (South India). *Janya rāga* of the 31st *mēḷa* (*Yagapriya*).
Tone material:
C D♯ E G A♭ B♭♭ c
c B♭♭ A♭ G E D♯ C
Lit.: no. 139.

Dambhākauśikam (South India). *Janya rāga* of the 65th *mēḷa* (*Mechakalyāṇi*).
Tone material:
C E F♯ G B c
c B G F♯ E D F♯ E C
Lit.: no. 139.

Dambōḷi (South India). *Janya rāga* of the 51st *mēḷa* (*Kāmavardhanī*).
Tone material:
C D♭ E G A♭ B c
c B F♯ E D♭ C
Lit.: no. 139.

Dambura (Afghanistan). (1) A folk lute with a long fretless neck and two strings. The sizes of the instrument vary: the Turkestani one is large, the Badakshani *dambura* is considerably smaller. (2) The term *dambura* can also be used to indicate a drum.
Lit.: no. 276.

Damburachi (Afghanistan). A *dambura* player.

Dami (*Jarami*; *Empet-empetan*) (Indonesia; Sunda District). Rice-stalk shawm. Its Hindu-Javanese name was *damyadamyan*. If a coconut leaf bell was attached it was called *ole-olean*. Cf. *De(r)men(an)*; *Ra'us woja*.
Lit.: no. 163.

Damiran (India). Term for *damaru*.

Dammāmah (India). One of the numerous terms for drum. The term is also applied for *tabla*.

Dammāmāt (Iraq). Ensemble of 4-5 players beating cylindrical drums.

Damong (Indonesia). Cf. *Demong*.

Dampha (India; Bengal). Octagonal frame drum used by beggars. It is very similar to the *dā'ira.*
Lit.: no. 254.

Damru (Southeast India; Bastar State—Gond tribes). See *Hulki mandri.*

Dāmya (South India). *Janya rāga* of the 59th *mēḷa* (*Dharmavatī*).
Tone material:
C D E♭ F♯ G A c
c B A G F♯ E♭ D C
Lit.: no. 139.

Damyadamyan (Java). Hindu-Javanese term for a small rice-stalk clarinet. Cf. *Ra'us woja* (Flores); *De(r)men(an).*
Lit.: no. 163.

Damyan (Nepal). An old lute with two double strings and one single, all of which were plucked with a plectrum. The wooden body is oval and the peg box is curved backward. The instrument was also popular in Tibet.

Dan (Japan). "Step." A term for section, scene, or variation. Combined with a numeral, it indicates which and how many sections are referred to: *ichidan*, *nidan*, *sandan*, *shidan*, *godan*, *rokudan*, *shichidan*, *hachidan*, *kudan.* A *dan* consists generally of 52 (54) *hyōshi* (measures, each having two beats), although there are deviations from this number.
Lit.: no. 225.

Dan (Southwest Pacific; Bismarck Archipelago; Admirality Isls.). Wooden drum.
Lit.: no. 84.

Dānakyū dūduyī (Turkey). Vertical reed flute with nine finger holes.
Lit.: no. 81.

Dāna Mañjari (South India). *Janya rāga* of the 46th *mēḷa* (*Śaḍvidhamārgiṇī*).
Tone material:
C E♭ F♯ A B♭ G A B♭ c
c B♭ A F♯ E♭ D♭ C
Lit.: no. 139.

Danāng (Andaman Isl.; Nicobar Isl.). A bamboo tube zither (*valiha*) with one string, three frets, and two resonance holes.
Lit.: no. 255.

Dāna Rakshasa (South India). *Janya rāga* of the 53rd *mēḷa* (*Gamanaśrama*).
Tone material:
C D♭ F♯ E G B c
c B A E D♭ C
Lit.: no. 139.

Danawase (*Dangaeshi*) (Japan). An instrumental piece, usually an interlude, played by two *kotos.* The first *koto* performs one (basic, original) tune (*honte*), and the second *koto* plays another melody (*kaede*) not newly invented, but another appropriate song tune. Both tunes are played in the same mode. If one *koto* plays a melody which lasts longer, the other will adjust to the same duration. Cf. *Kyōmono.*
Lit.: no. 185.

Danbal (Persia). Cf. *Denbal.*

Dan bāo (Vietnam; Annam). Cf. *Cai dan bāo*; *Phin nam tao*; *Dan dōc.*

Dan co (Vietnam). See *Dan nhi.*

Daṇḍā (India). (1) Iron sticks beaten against each other; used in dance music. In the Maratha region the sticks are called *ṭipri.* (2) *Daṇḍā* (*suthrā*), "stick of the Sutra." Rattle stick of the beggars.
Lit.: no. 254.

Daṇḍā (*Dhandi*). (3) Wooden (bamboo) tube. The term refers to the tube that serves as neck and fingerboard, along which are strung the strings of the *rudra vīṇā.* (4) Term for the tubes of wind instruments.

Dandā (Vietnam; Assam). Beating sticks.
Lit.: no. 46.

Daṇḍa hastam (Ancient India). One of a dozen *paṭaha vādyas* (drums).
Lit.: no. 255.

Dandana (Arabia). Singing.
Lit.: no. 73.

Ḍanḍang (Java). *Gembyakan* beat performed with both flat hands on both drumheads simultaneously.
Lit.: no. 163.

Dan day (Vietnam; Laos). See *Cai dan day.*
Lit.: no. 296.

Daṇḍayāna (South India). *Janya rāga* of the 50th *mēḷa* (*Nāmanārāyaṇī*).
Tone material:
C D♭ E G B♭ A♭ B♭ c
c B♭ A♭ G F♯ E D♭ E C
Lit.: no. 139.

Daṇḍi (India). The neck (also cross-bar) of plucked string instruments. Cf. *Daṇḍa* (3).
Lit.: no. 261.

Danding (*Dinde*) (Flores). Dance of the men. They walk and stamp around in a circle. Each dancer sings a line which is followed by the entire chorus. Drums provide the accompaniment. Cf. *Sanda*; *Chongka.*
Lit.: no. 166.

Dandiya (India; Rajasthan). War dance of the Rajput men.
Lit.: no. 46.

Dan doan (Vietnam). "Short necked lute." Vietnamese term for the Chinese *yüen-ch'in.* Also called *dan tao* ("Chinese lute").

Dan doc huyen (Thailand). See *Dan bao*; *Cai dan bao.*

Dang (Bali). Tone syllable. Cf. *Ding.* (All other tone syllables are listed under the heading of *Ding.*)
Lit.: no. 197.

Dang ageng (Bali). Tone syllable; the "great *dang*" (the low pitched *dang*). Cf. *Ding.*
Lit.: no. 197.

Dang alit (Bali). Tone syllable; the "small *dang*" (the high pitched *dang*). Cf. *Ding.*
Lit.: no. 197.

Dang chenik (*Dang tjenik*) (Bali). Tone syllable. The term has the same significance as *dang alit.*

Dang gede (Bali). The low-sounding *dang.*
Lit.: no. 197.

Dangaeshi (Japan). See *Danawase.*

Dangamut (Melanesia; Bismarck Archipelago). See *Garamut.*
Lit.: no. 255.

Dan gao (Vietnam). Bowed lute with two strings.

Dangḍang gula (Java). One of the meters of *tembang machapat.* See *Machapat.*
Lit.: no. 163.

Dangire (Japan). The dance finale (closing section) in *kabuki, nagauta.* Cf. *Mie.*
Lit.: no. 187.

Dango-khim (Nepal). A drum similar to the *dholak* and played in the same manner.

Dangori (Uganda). See *Nanga.*

Dangsa (Indonesia). See *Tari.*

Dang tjenik (Bali). See *Dang chenik.*
Lit.: no. 197.

Dan Hue (Vietnam). Music of Hue.

Danin (Liberia—Kpelle). Drum in the shape of an hourglass.
Lit.: no. 284.

Ḍaṅka (India). (1) The lower sounding of one of the two drumheads. (2) Drumstick. (3) A pair of conically-shaped drums carried on horseback. The drums were beaten by horsemen who led temple processions.
Lit.: no. 261.

Dankāmaṇi (South India). *Janya rāga* of the 28th *mēḷa* (*Harikāmbhoji*).
Tone material:
C D E F A B♭ c
c G F E F D C
Lit.: no. 139.

D'an karbi (North Nigeria—Hausa). A stick-beaten drum with two skins similar to the Yoruba *kannango*. See *Kuntuku*; *Gangan*.
Lit.: no. 293.

Daṅ-ki (Tibet; Burma). Kettle gong.
Lit.: no. 252.

Dan kim (Vietnam). See *Dan nguyet*.

Dan-mono (Japan). (1) Serious *koto* music organized in *dan*, without any vocal part. (2) A *nagauta* type, the text of which represents a dramatic plot.
Lit.: no. 187.

Dan nguyet (*Dan kim*) (Vietnam; Annam; Laos). Term for *cai dan nguyet*, a large lute with two silken strings. Cf. *Tam huyen*; *San hsien* (China).
Lit.: nos. 296-97.

Dan nha tro (Vietnam; Annam). See *Cai dan nha tro*.

Dan nhi (Vietnam). Also called *dan co*. Fiddle with two strings.

Dānṅo (Vietnam; Cambodia). Wooden bell beaten with several clappers suspended from a stick inside the bell.
Lit.: no. 252.

Dan tai tu (South Vietnam). "Music of the amateurs," "Music of the south." It is a mixture of traditional music (of Hue) and provincial form (Central Vietnam, Quang Nam, and Wuang Ngai). Cf. *Hat a dao*; *Ca Hue*.
Lit.: no. 297.

Dan tam (Vietnam). A pair of lutes, each with three strings.
Lit.: nos. 296-97.

Dan thap luc (Vietnam; Annam). See *Cai dam thap luc*.

Dan ti (Vietnam; Annam). See *Cai dan ti*.

Dan tinh (Vietnam). Lute. Cf. *Tinh tau*.
Lit.: nos. 296-97.

Danti Vasantam (South India). *Janya rāga* of the 51st *mēḷa* (*Kāmavardhanī*).
Tone material:
C D♭ F♯ A♭ B c
c A♭ B A♭ G F♯ E F♯ D♭ C
Lit.: no. 139.

Dan tranh (South Vietnam). Board zither with 16-17 wire strings running across movable bridges. The tunings of the instrument vary according to the mode of the piece performed:
C G B♭ c d f g ♭ c' d' f' g' ♭' c'' d'' f'' g''
D G A c d f (g) a c' d' f' g' a' a'' d'' f'' g''
C G A c d e g a c' d' e' g' a' c'' d'' e'' g''
Cf. *Chin* (China).
Lit.: nos. 215, 297.

Dan ty ba (*Dang ti ba*) (Vietnam). Lute with four strings. Cf. *P'i-p'a* (China).
Lit.: no. 215.

Danur vīṇā (India). A bowed *vīṇā*.
Lit.: no. 261.

Dao (*Tao*) (Northeast Thailand). The wind chest of the *kaen*.
Lit.: no. 203.

Dao (Vietnam). Cf. *Rao*.

Daola-daola (North Nias). Wooden stick-beaten drum.
Lit.: no. 255.

Dapka (Lebanon; Arabia). Dance. The performers move in a circle. Cf. *Ta'bir.*

Dapla (India). Clappers. See *Dafli.*
Lit.: no. 254.

Daphla (India). See *Dafli.*
Lit.: no. 254.

Dappu (South India). Telugu term for a circular frame drum with a cowhide membrane. Cf. *Daf*; *Tappu* (Tamil); *Patha* (Sanskrit).
Lit.: no. 254.

Daqqāqāt (Iraq). An ensemble of four women beating drums accompanying one singer.

Dara (North India; Kashmir). A stick rattle. Several iron rings ranged on a hook-shaped iron stick. Cf. *Bairaga*; *Khakkara*; *Daerah.*
Lit.: no. 255.

Dārā (India; Bengal). Circular frame drum. Cf. *Dāira*; *Dahare.*
Lit.: no. 255.

Darabch (written *darabchi*) (Mongolia). The tuning loop which is placed immediately below the peg box of the *khil-khuur.* The loop is tightly fitted around the neck and both strings. When moved the pitch of the strings is altered.
Lit.: no. 61.

Darābuka (Arabia). See *Darābukkeh.* Cf. *Deblek.*

Darābukkeh (*Darābuka*) (Arabia). A popular drum in the shape of a big clay or wooden goblet or vase. The body is usually ornamented. The wide end is covered with a membrane. The player holds the stem or neck of the vase-shaped drum under his arm, and beats the skin that covers the large end of the body with both hands. Another term for *darābukkeh* is *tabl.* Cf. *Darbuka.*
Lit.: no. 106.

Dāraka Vasanta (South India). *Janya rāga* of the 15th *mēḷa* (*Māyāmāḷavagauḷa*).
Tone material:
C E D♭ F G B c
c B G A♭ F E D♭ C
Lit.: no. 139.

Daramād (Persia). "To come in," "to appear," "to begin." The term denotes the opening *gusheh* in every *dastgāh* performance. E.g., *pishdaramād*, followed by *daramād-e aval*, first *daramād*; *daramād-e dovom*, second *daramād*; *daramād-e sevom*, third *daramād*; *daramād-e chaharom*, fourth *daramād*; *daramād-e panjom*, fifth *daramād.* All *daramād* forms are based on the *gusheh* material.
Lit.: no. 146.

Ḍarar-ḥiṣār (Arabia). See *Ḥiṣār-qaba.* Semitonal change of *yak-gah.* See *Jagā* (*Yagā*).
Lit.: no. 64.

Darārdhari (South India). *Janya rāga* of the 28th *mēḷa* (*Harikambhōji*).
Tone material:
C D E G A B♭ c
c B♭ A G E D C
Lit.: no. 139.

Ḍarb (Persia). Rhythmic mode. Piece of music which uses two rhythmic modes.
Lit.: no. 76.

Darbala (Arabia). Drum.

Darbāri-kanadā (North India). *Rāga* subordinated to the *Asavari thāta* and belonging in the *Kanadā* group.
Tone material:
C D E♭ F G A♭ B♭ c
c B♭ (A♭) G F (E♭) D C; *Vādis*: D, G
Lit.: no. 138.

Darbār(u) (South India). *Janya rāga* of the 22nd *mēḷa* (*Kharaharapriyā*).
Tone material:
C D F G A B♭ c
c B♭ A G F D E♭ D C (c B♭ A G F E♭ D C)
Lit.: no. 139.

Darbhakūlam (South India). *Janya rāga* of the 23rd *mēḷa* (*Gaurīmanōharī*).
Tone material:
C D E♭ F E♭ G A B c
c B A F E♭ D C
Lit.: no. 139.

Darbuka (Turkey; Algeria—Biskra). The instrument consists usually of a clay jug without a handle and a drum skin in place of its bottom. The jug is held under the player's left arm and the skin is beaten either on its rim or in its center by the right hand or by both hands.
Lit.: no. 243.

Darbūkha (*Deblek*) (Turkey). Goblet drum.

Dardaba (Arabia). See *Dabdāb*.

Dardara (Ancient India). Barrel drum.

Dardarika (India). Drum. Cf. *Godhika*.

Darga (Ancient Israel). Notational symbol used in biblical chant.
Lit.: no. 309.

Darhama (Mauritania). Gourd, drummed by women for the accompaniment of their songs. Cf. *Humbaldu*.
Lit.: nos. 190, 301.

Ḍāribūn (Arabia). Musicians; players.
Lit.: no. 66.

Dārij (Arabia). A variant of *tāwāshīh*. Cf. *Muwashah*.
Lit.: no. 171.

Dāriyāl (Afghanistan). Frame drum.

Darkūn (India—Mirzapur, U.P.). A rare musical bow, used only once during the year at religious ceremonies. A single fiber string is scraped.
Lit.: nos. 18, 254.

Darma (Afghanistan). See *Durma*.

Darphamañjari (South India). *Janya rāga* of the 53rd *mēḷa* (*Gamanaśrama*).
Tone material:
C E D♭ E F♯ G B c
c B A G F♯ E C
Lit.: no. 139.

Daru (Tibet). See *Damaru*.

Dāru (South India). A song with a text that tells a story. It is used in dramatic performances. The *daru* consists of three sections as they appear in art music: *pallavi*, *anupallavi*, and one or more *charanas*.
Lit.: no. 261.

Darubiri (*Kalinguang*) (New Guinea). Jew's harp made of wood or bamboo.
Lit.: no. 255.

Darway (Afghanistan). Shepherd's pipe.
Lit.: no. 255.

Darwīsh būrūsī (Turkey). Dervish horn, similar to the Persian *nafīr*.
Lit.: no. 81.

Darya (Afghanistan). Frame drum.
Lit.: no. 255.

Darz (North Africa; Algeria—Biskra). Love song (without any accompaniment).
Lit.: no. 20.

Dasar (Java). Pivotal tone. The melodic central point which has some similarity with the North Indian *vādi*, the *sa*, the *vishrantisthan*. A family of scales with the same *dasar* (and one or more common tones) is called *patet*.
The Sundanese terms for *dasar* are: *jawar*, *liwung*, *nyorog*, *panangis*, and *pamiring*.
Lit.: no. 163.

Dāsari Tappaṭṭai (South India). Tamil term for a frame drum with a calfskin membrane. It is used together with a gong and conch shell by the Pandarams and Dasaris.
Lit.: no. 261.

Dāsatīn (Arabia; Persia). "Hands," originally a Persian term, refers to frets of the *'ud* and *rubāb*. The Arabic term is also *'utāb*.
Lit.: no. 76.

Da-shōko (Japan). A large *shōko*. It is used together with the *da-daiko* at rare festive occasions.
Lit.: no. 185.

Dashtī (Persia). Among the *naghmeh* types, *Dashtī*, belonging to the *dastgāh Shur*, is one of the most important auxiliary forms. It often has the character of simple folk music. Its scale is approximately C D E F G A $\overset{\flat}{\text{B}}$ c in which the tone C represents the *ist* and E the *shahed*.
Lit.: no. 146.

Dasi (India). Dancing girls who worship the deity in sacred dances.

Dasiri (*Tamburi*) (India). See *Tumburu Vīṇā*.

Dast (Persia). "Hand," "fret." (Cf. *Dāsatīn*.) A term used in theoretical treatises to indicate finger positions on the (fretless) fingerboard of lutes.
Lit.: no. 250.

Dastaband (Persia). Customary game and dance of magicians holding hands and forming a circle.
Lit.: no. 244.

Dastān (Persia). Cf. *Dast*.

Dastgāh (plural: *Dastgāh-ha*) (Iran). Compositions using a particular melody type with fixed tone material and melody formulas. The *dastgāh* is similar to the Indian *rāga* and Arabian *maqām*.

The following are material scales of the *dastgāh-ha*:

Shūr and *nawā*

C $\overset{\flat}{\text{D}}$ E♭ F G A♭ B♭ c

Homāyun

C $\overset{\flat}{\text{D}}$ E F G A♭ B♭ c

Segāh ("the third")

C D $\overset{\flat}{\text{E}}$ F G $\overset{\flat}{\text{A}}$ B♭ c

Chahārgāh ("the fourth")

C $\overset{\flat}{\text{D}}$ E F G $\overset{\flat}{\text{A}}$ B c

Māhur and *rast panjgah* ("the fifth")

C D E F G A B c

Derived from or related to the *shūr*, similar to the *janya rāgas* of South India, are the following auxiliary types called *naghmeh* or *āwāz*: *abu atā*; *dashti*; *afshari*; and *bayote tork*.

Derived from *homāyun* is the *naghmeh esfahan*.

To each *dastgāh* and *naghmeh* are ascribed (ca. 20-50) short tunes, formulas (*gusheh*), which in their entirety are called *radif*. The performer selects a certain number of these melody formulas and produces his recital in the following order of five movements:

1. *Pīshdarāmad*, the prelude, which is not improvised but fixed and organized in rigid common meter (4/4), is performed by the instrumental ensemble. This ensemble consists of various instruments, often of a *setar*, *tar*, *santur*; also *nay*, *kamanjah*, and even several European instruments can be added. The drum is the Persian *tombak*.
2. *Chahārmeḍrab* is performed by one solo instrument, which is accompanied by the goblet drum *tombak* in strict 6/8 or 12/8 meter.
3. *Āwāz*, the song. At the present time *chahārmeḍrab* is often considered to be a part of the *āwāz*. The *āwāz* is the most important movement of the entire performance. It is sung and consists of several sections (*gushe-ha*), unmeasured and improvised. Every *gushe* is a complete feature by itself. Generally the *gushe-ha* are not in rigid meter (although there may be some measured exceptions). One instrument supports the vocal line. At the present time the unusual may happen only when instrumental music (without voice) is employed.
4. *Taṣnīf* (ballade) is a metrically fixed part, like the *pīshdarāmad*. The melody with

text is sung and is accompanied by the instrumental ensemble. It is a popular part, and often imitates popular western songs.

5. *Reng* is played in fixed rhythm by the ensemble or by solo instruments. The movement emphasizes dance character.

The metrical natures of *pīshdarāmad*, *taṣnīf*, and *reng* show a mixture of 6/8 and 3/4. The melodic material of these three movements is taken from the *radif*, the reservoir of fixed *gushe-ha*.
Lit.: no. 191.

Dastanagah (Northwest Pakistan; Baluchistan). Ballads.

Dāsumukhi (South India). *Janya rāga* of the 28th *mēḷa* (*Harikāmbhōji*).
Tone material:
C D F E F G A B♭ c
c A G F E D C
Lit.: no. 139.

Dāṭi Balam (South India). *Janya rāga* of the 65th *mēḷa* (*Mechakalyāṇī*).
Tone material:
C D E F♯ G A B c
c B A G E D C
Lit.: no. 139.

Daṭika Pañchamam (South India). *Janya rāga* of the 51st *mēḷa* (*Kāmavardhanī*).
Tone material:
C E D♭ E F♯ G F♯ B G c
c B A♭ G F♯ E D♭ C
Lit.: no. 139.

Daṭi Māñji (South India). *Janya rāga* of the 28th *mēḷa* (*Harikāmbhōji*).
Tone material:
C D E F G A c
c B♭ G F D C
Lit.: no. 139.

Dāṭu svara (India). A note distant by a large interval from the preceding one. Large interval.
Lit.: no. 261.

Datuur (Mongolia). Curved bow (of the *khil-khuur*) strung with horsehair.
Lit.: no. 60.

Dau (Vietnam; Annam). Bell used in religious ceremonies.
Lit.: no. 255.

Da'u kibi (Flores; Lio District). Rattling stamping stick with tinkling bells. In the Ende District the stick is called *ngasu*.
Lit.: no. 166.

Daulbe (Kurdisthan). Drum.
Lit.: no. 255.

Daule (*Dawal*) (Ethiopia). Sounding stone slab or bell of the Abyssinian and Egyptian Copts. The *daule* can be used only in the state church of Ethiopia. At any other occasions the bell has to be substituted by a *taqa*, a small zinc disc from which are suspended several copper rings. The *taqa* is beaten with a small wooden hammer.
Lit.: nos. 102, 184.

Daulika (South India). *Janya rāga* of the 1st *mēḷa* (*Kanakangi*).
Tone material:
C D♭ E♭♭ F G B♭♭ A♭ c
c B♭♭ A♭ F E♭♭ D♭ C
Lit.: no. 139.

Ḍaumya (South India). *Janya rāga* of the 32nd *mēḷa* (*Rāgavardhanī*).
Tone material:
C D♯ E F G A♭ B♭ G c
c B♭ A♭ G F E D♯ C
Lit.: no. 139.

Daur (Arabia). Basic cycle of each rhythm (rhythmic period), similar to the *avarta* of North India. Cf. *Iqa'āt*.
Lit.: no. 34.

Daurēyaṇi (South India). *Janya rāga* of the 53rd *mēḷa* (*Gamanaśrama*).
Tone material:
C D♭ E F♯ A B c
c B A F♯ E D♭ C
Lit.: no. 139.

Ḍaurū (India). Cf. *Ḍairū.*

Dauwala (Sri Lanka). Drum-shaped like a *damaru.*
Lit.: no. 255.

Davaḷai sangu (South India; Tamil). Ornamented conch shell blown at religious occasions, together with the *nāgasara.*
Lit.: no. 261.

Davalbas (Kirgizia). Kettledrum of Uzbek origin.
Lit.: no. 275.

Davaṇḍai (South India). Tamil term for a large stick-beaten *damaru*, used particularly in Māriyamman temples.
Lit.: nos. 260-61.

Ḍavaṇe (South India). Kannarese term for *damaru.*

Ḍavasam (South India). Drum.
Lit.: no. 261.

Davul (Turkey). Large drum. Cf. *Dawul.*

Davvi (South India). *Janya rāga* of the 13th *mēḷa* (*Gāyakapriya*).

Dawal (Ethiopia). See *Daule.*

Dawe gumgum (New Guinea). Mourning song.

Dawr (*Badaniyaḥ*) (Arabia). See *Muwashah.* Chant using a principal tune and a set of verses; see Lit. nos. 64 and 171.

Dāwud (Turkey). Large *nāy.*

Dāwūl (Turkey). Old large cylindrical drum with two heads. One is beaten with a stick (*changal*), the other with a flexible rod (*daynak*). Cf. *Duhul.*
Lit.: no. 81.

Dayan (India). Term for *tabla*, the tunable member of the drum pair.
Lit.: no. 136.

Dayarañjani (South India). *Janya rāga* of the 28th *mēḷa* (*Harikāmbhōji*).
Tone material:
C D F G A c
c B♭ A F E D C
Lit.: no. 139.

Dayāsyani (South India). *Janya rāga* of the 28th *mēḷa* (*Harikāmbhōji*).
Tone material:
C D F G B♭ A B♭ c
c B♭ A F E D C
Lit.: no. 139.

Dayāvatī (India). Music theoretical term for the fifth *śruti*. The corresponding note name is *prati ṣaṭśruti ri* (or *prati sādhāraṇa ga*). Cf. *Śruti.*
Lit.: no. 261.

Dayere (Iran). See *Dahare.*

Daynak (Turkey). A switch; a flexible thin rod, used to beat one skin of the *dawul.*
Lit.: no. 81.

Dayra (India; Bengal). See *Dāra*; *Dāira.*

Dayuray (Philippines; Mindanao). Small drum made of a part of a coconut shell or bamboo.
Lit.: no. 255.

Dbang-dung (Tibet). "Powerful tube." Small copper or brass trumpet used in several ceremonies of consecration. It produces one high, loud note. Cf. *Zangs-dung.*
Lit.: no. 143.

Dbu-mdzad-pa (pronounced: *um-dze-pa*) (Tibet). The master of the chant; the leader and instructor of the sacred chant performed by the monks of the monastery.
Lit.: no. 143.

Dbyangs (pronounced: *yang*) (Tibet). Sacred chant; singing hymns; song.
Lit.: no. 143.

Dbyangs-deb (pronounced: *yang-deb*) (Tibet). Song document; textbook. Cf. *Yang-deb.*
Lit.: no. 143.

Dbyangs-pa (Tibet). Singer.

Dbyangs-yig (pronounced: *yang-yig*) (Tibet). Musical notation; term for indicating vowels in grammatical writing. Buddhist song book (as used in monasteries).

Debayashi (Japan). The ensemble of the *nagauta*; *kabuki.* Singers and *shamisen* are placed slightly above the stage; dancers, drum, and flute appear in the back (on the level) of the stage.
Lit.: no. 185.

Debbus (Arabia; Persia). Cf. *Dabbous.*

Debdebe (Persia). Noise. A term that has been used for drum. Cf. *Dabdāb.*
Lit.: no. 255.

Deblek (South Turkey). Goblet-shaped drum beaten with the bare hands. Cf. *Darabuka*; *Deblet*; *Debuldek*; *Delbek*; *Dirimbekki*; *Dumbelek*; *Dünbelek.*
Lit.: no. 243.

Deblet (Turkey). Cf. *Deblek.*

Debtera (Ethiopia). A professional musician and teacher in the Ethiopian church.
Lit.: no. 218.

Debuldek (Turkey). Cf. *Deblek.*

Dedeco (Philippines). Panpipes.

Def (Turkey). Frame drum with one skin and circular jingles. Cf. *Duff.*
Lit.: no. 243.

Deff (Persia; Arabia). Tambourin in circular or octagonal shape. In Algeria the term indicates a rectangular frame drum with two skins. Cf. *Duff.*
Lit.: no. 255.

Deffe (Arabia). Drum skin.

Defik (Kurdisthan). Small tambourin.
Lit.: no. 255.

Degangande (West Africa; Upper Volta). Drum (in the Gurma language). Cf. *Ganga.*
Lit.: no. 95.

Deggwa (Ethiopia). Coptic hymns sung at church festivals.

Degung (West Java). (1) A group of 6-7 small gongs placed side by side horizontally on a low stand. The *degung* appears only in the *gamelan degung.* (2) Cf. *Surupan degung.* Cf. *Renteng.*
Lit.: nos. 159, 163.

Deha (Japan). Music that is played when the *shite* (the protagonist in the *noh* drama) appears in dignity and pomp on the stage. Also introductory *shamisen* music (*nagauta*) played off stage. Cf. *Dokkin.*
Lit.: no. 187.

Dehāḷi (South India). *Janya rāga* of the 16th *mēḷa* (*Chakravāka*).
Tone material:

C D♭ G A B♭ c
c B♭ A G D♭ C

Lit.: no. 139.

Deheniza (Gabon; Congo Republic—Baguana). A plectrum made of leather shaped like the sharp top of a lance.
Lit.: no. 255.

Dehol (*Dehul*; *Dohol*; *Duhul*) (Iran). Wooden cylindrical hand drum with two skins.
Lit.: no. 255.

Dehuk (Kurdisthan). Tambourin.

Dehul (Persia). Cf. *Dehol.*

Deiri-bayashi (Japan). Drum music linked to *nagauta.* It is played at entrances and exits, and characterizes actor and situation. Cf. *Maigoto-bayashi.*
Lit.: no. 187.

Dekana (Togo—Akasele). Trumpet.

Dekoot (South and Central Sumatra). Cf. *Dakoot.*

Del (Kurdisthan). Tambourin.
Lit.: no. 255.

Delbek (Turkey). Cf. *Deblek.*

Deldeleo (Cameroon Republic—Mafa). Drum of the Yoruba; a *koso* type.
Lit.: no. 293.

Deliko (East Africa; Somali Republic). Dance song performed by women.
Lit.: no. 98.

Delkashe (Arabia). A *maqām.* Cf. *Suz-nak.*
Lit.: nos. 64, 121.

Demāme (Persia). Kettledrum. See *Dāmāmā.*
Lit.: no. 255.

Demong (Java). A *saron* with seven keys. See *Saron demung.*
Lit.: no. 255.

Dempling (*Kedempling*) (West Java). Term for the (Javanese) *gambang gangsa.*
Lit.: no. 163.

Dempok (Java). Gong kettles with low rim. Cf. *Bonang.*
Lit.: no. 163.

Demung (Java). Of the four separate octave ranges of the *saron* group, *demung* is tuned to the third lowest octave ("tenor *saron*"). Cf. *Saron.* (The soprano *saron* is called *selento*, the alto bears the name *saron*, the tenor set is called *demung*, and the bass *slentem.*)
Lit.: no. 254.

Demung (Malaysia). Low octave range of the *saron.* Cf. *Saron.*

Demung gantung (Java). A *demung* formed like a *gender.* It is tuned one octave above the *slentem gantung* and plays the basic theme. It appears in the *gamelan klenengan.*
Lit.: no. 163.

Demung jemblung (Java). Idiophone consisting of five suspended bamboo tubes. Cf. *Jemblung.*
Lit.: no. 163.

Denaka (Malagasy Republic). Small barrel drum.
Lit.: no. 251.

Denbāl (*Danbul*; *Dunbal*) (Iran). Slim cylindrical drum with two heads.
Lit.: no. 77.

Denbere (Iran). *Tanbura.*

Dende (South Africa—Thonga; Venda). Musical bow. This instrument has numerous names. A few are: *tshitendje*; *tshikala*; *tshitendole*; *umakweyana*; *uhadi*; *nkoka*; *segwana*; *sekgapa.*
Lit.: nos. 150-51.

Den den daiko (Japan). Frame drum in the form of a fan with a handle. It has one skin and is beaten with a stick. The instrument is used by Buddhist monks.
Lit.: no. 255.

Dendun (Tunisia). Large cylindrical (or barrel) drum.
Lit.: no. 171.

Deng (*Beng*; *Bem* or *Bah*) (Java). Drum word denoting a stroke performed with four fingers close together on the edge of the large drum-head.
Lit.: no. 163.

Ḍeng (Bali). Tone syllable. Cf. *Ding* for a list of all tone syllables.
Lit.: nos. 197, 265.

Dengaku (Japan). "Field music." Comic dances of the rice planters accompanied by simple flutes and *taiko* and *ō-tsuzumi.* These popular performances absorbed elements from the Chinese opera, Buddhist mystery plays, and the *shōmyō* chant. When in the 13th century *dengaku* began to fade, a combination of *dengaku* and *sarugaku* formed the basis of the *noh* drama.
Lit.: no. 185.

Dengari (India; Bengal). See *Dindima.*

Dengdo (West Java). (1) Cf. *Chikibung.* (2) An old-fashioned simple manner of playing the Sundanese *rebāb.*
Lit.: no. 163.

Dengeng-dengeng (Toba District). Bull roarer. See *Jata* (Flores).
Lit.: no. 166.

Dengu-dengu (Flores—South Lionese District). Lullaby.

Denkenkelen (Ghana). Iron bells.

Denshō (Japan). A small *hontsuri-gane* (*han-shō*). A bell without clapper or gong used in Buddhist temples and in *kabuki.*
Lit.: no. 185.

Densi-git (Nepal). See *Bhailo-git.*

Denya (South Africa—Venda). The sound of male voices. Female voices: *sekene.*

Denyere (South Africa; South Rhodesia—Mashona). Lute. Cf. *Bania.*

Deo pata (Southeast India—Bastar State, Jhoria Muria Cond Tribe). Religious *gotul* song.
Lit.: no. 142.

Deph (India). See *Duff.*

Derabucca (*Derbuka*) (Egypt). Drum. In ancient Egypt the body was made of clay or gourd and covered with fish skin. Cf. *Darbuka.*
Lit.: no. 100.

Derbuka (Arabia). Cf. *Darbuka.*

Dere (Sumba). Drum with one head.
Lit.: no. 162.

Dereng (*Sakvā*) (India). Cf. *Śṛṅga.*

Derika (Arabia). Buffalo leather straps that are used to strike the *tabil turki* (Turkish drum).
Lit.: no. 255.

Derk (South China). A term for *so-na.*
Lit.: no. 255.

De(r)men(an) (Java). A rick-stalk aerophone with a beating reed. In the regency of Tegal the instrument is called *ilo-ilo-goto.* Cf. *Damyadamyan*; *Ole-olean*; *Dami*; *Ra'us woja*; *Kafoa*; *Wa.*
Lit.: no. 163.

Dernoboi (Sibiria—Yakutia). See *Shotang.*

Deru (Japan). "Going out." Entrance music of *kabuki, nagauta* performances.
Lit.: no. 187.

Des (North India). *Rāga* ascribed to the *Khamaj thāta.*
Tone material:
C D F G B c
c B♭ A G F (E♭) D C; *Vādis*: D, G
Lit.: no. 138.

Deśa gīta (Ancient India). Song; music of the humans (in contrast to the heavenly *deva gāndharvas).*

Dēśa kaku (South India). A foreign note introduced into a raga for ornamenting purposes.

Desakh (North India). See *Devsakh.*

Dēśākṣari (South India). See *Dēṣākṣiri.*

Dēśakshi (*Dēśakṣi*) (South India). *Janya rāga* of the 28th *mēḷa* (*Harikāmbhōji*).
Tone material:
C D E G A c
(C D E F G A c)
c B♭ A G F E D C
(c A F E F D C; also c B A G)
Lit.: no. 139.

Dēśakshi (*Dēśakṣi*) (South India). This *rāga* can be ascribed to the 28th or to the 29th *mēḷas.* Cf. *Dēśakshi* (*janya* of 28th *mēḷa*).

Dēśākṣī (South India). See also *Dēṣākṣirī* (35th *mēḷa*).

Dēśākṣī (South India). (1) The 35th *asampūrṇa mēḷa-rāga* without *kaṭapayādi* prefix. (2) The 35th *asampūrṇa mēḷa-rāga* with *kaṭapayādi* prefix was called *Sailadeśākṣī.* See *Rāga* (South India).
Lit.: no. 139.

Dēṣākṣirī (*Dēśākṣarī*) (South India). *Janya rāga* of the 35th *mēḷa* (*Śūlinī*).
Tone material:
C D♯ E F A c
c B A G F E F D♯ C
Also called *Dēśākṣī.*
Lit.: no. 139.

Dēśa Rañjani (South India). *Janya rāga* of the 31st *mēḷa* (*Yāgapriyā*).
Tone material:
C D♯ F G A♭ B♭♭ c
c B♭♭ A♭ G F D♯ C
Lit.: no. 139.

Dēśā Vāḷi (South India). *Janya rāga* of the 55th *mēḷa* (*Śyāmalāṅgī*).
Tone material:
C D E♭ F♯ B♭♭ A♭ c
c B♭♭ A♭ F♯ E♭ D C
Lit.: no. 139.

Deshakya (North India). See *Devsakh.*

Deshkar (North India). *Rāga* subordinated to the *Bilaval thāta.*
Tone material:
C D E G A c
c A G E D C; *Vādis*: A, E; *Vishrantisthan*: G
Lit.: no. 138.

Deśi (*Deshi*) (North India). *Rāga* subordinated to the *Asavari thāta.*
Tone material, three types:
(a) C D F G (B♭) B c
c (B) B♭ A♭ G F E♭ D C
(b) C D F G (B♭) B c
c (B) B♭ A G F E♭ D C
(c) C D F G (A B♭) B c
c (B A A♭) G F E♭ D C; *Vādis*: G, D
Lit.: no. 139.

Dēśī (South India). *Janya rāga* of the 28th *mēḷa* (*Harikāmbhōji*).
Tone material:
C D F G B♭ c
c B♭ A G F E D E C
Lit.: no. 139.

Dēśika Baṅgāḷa (South India). *Janya rāga* of the 8th *mēḷa* (*Hanumattōḍi*).
Tone material:
C D♭ E♭ G F A♭ B♭ c
c A♭ G F E♭ D♭ C
Lit.: no. 139.

Dēśika Rudri (South India). *Janya rāga* of the 9th *mēḷa* (*Dhēnuka*).
Tone material:
C F D♭ E♭ F G B c
c B G A♭ F E♭ D♭ C
Lit.: no. 139.

Desikhin (Nepal). (1) General term for drums. (2) Small barrel drum suspended from the player's neck, beaten with bare hands.
Lit.: no. 139.

Deśisimhāravam (South India). See *Simhārava* (58th *asampūrṇa mēḷa*).

Deśī(tāla) (Ancient India). See *Tāla* (I).

Des-Mallār (North India). *Rāga*. Obscure *Mallar* type ascribed to the *Kafi thāta*. The *rāga* consists of a combination of *Des* and *Mallar* elements. Numerous possibilities of combining the two ragas are shown, to some extent, in the following three versions:

1. *Des*
   C D F G B c
   Mallar
   c A B♭ G F G E♭ E♭ F D C
2. *Mallar*
   C D G F G B♭ A B c
   Des
   c B c d c d B♭ A G
   Mallar
   F G E♭ E♭ F D C
3. *Mallar*
   C (F) D G F G B♭ A B c
   Des
   c A B♭ G G G A F E D E *B* C

Vādis are flexible.
Lit.: no. 138.

Dēśmukhāri (South India). See *Dēsya Mukhāri*.

Destan (Turkey). Ballades. Structurally similar to the *koṣma*. Each line has seven or eight syllables. See *Semai* (Turkey).
Lit.: no. 243.

Dēśya Āndhāli (South India). *Janya rāga* of the 9th *mēḷa* (*Dhēnuka*).
Tone material:
C D♭ E♭ F G B A♭ c
c A♭ G F E♭ D♭ C
Lit.: no. 139.

Dēśya Baṅgāḷa (South India). *Janya rāga* of the 8th *mēḷa* (*Hanumattōḍi*). With the exception of placing the *vakra* feature in ascent above the note F, there is no difference between this *rāga* and *Dēśika Baṅgāḷa*.
Tone material:
C D♭ E♭ F G F A♭ B♭ c
c A♭ G F E♭ D♭ C
Lit.: no. 139.

Dēśya Bēgada (South India). *Janya rāga* of the 19th *mēḷa* (*Jhaṅkāradhvani*).
Tone material:
C E♭ F G c
c B♭♭ A♭ G F E♭ D C
Cf. *Dēśya Byāgaḍa*.
Lit.: no. 139.

Dēśya Byāgaḍa (South India). *Janya rāga* of the 19th *mēḷa* (*Jhaṅkāradhvani*).
Tone material:
C D E♭ F G c
c B♭♭ A♭ F E♭ D C
Although the names *Dēśya Bēgada* and *Dēśya Byāgaḍa* appear almost identical and could be considered to show only different readings of the same word, the two scales show a distinct difference in the use and deletion of the note G in descent.
Lit.: no. 139.

Dēśya Gānavāridhi (South India). *Janya rāga* of the 60th *mēḷa* (*Nītimatī*).
Tone material:
C D E♭ F♯ G A♯ B G c
c B c G F♯ E♭ D C
Lit.: no. 139.

Dēśyagauḷa (South India). *Janya rāga* of the 15th *mēḷa* (*Māyāmāḷavagauḷa*).
Tone material:
C D♭ C G A♭ B c
c B A♭ G C D♭ C
Lit.: no. 139.

Dēśya Gauri (South India). *Janya rāga* of the 5th *mēḷa* (*Manōrañjani*).
Tone material:
C D♭ E♭♭ F G A G B c
c A B G F E♭♭ D♭ C
Lit.: no. 139.

Dēśya Kalyāṇī (South India). *Janya rāga* of the 65th *mēḷa* (*Mechakalyāṇī*).
Tone material:
C D E F♯ G A G B c
c A G F♯ D C
Lit.: no. 139.

Dēśya Kamās (South India). *Janya rāga* of the 28th *mēḷa* (*Harikāmbhōji*).
Tone material:
C F E F G A B♭ c
c B♭ A G F E C
Lit.: no. 139.

Dēśya Kānaḍā (South India). *Janya rāga* of the 22nd *mēḷa* (*Kharaharapriyā*).
Tone material:
C D E♭ F A B♭ c
c B♭ G E♭ F D C
(Permissible is: c B♭ G B♭ c and
G A B♭ A G E♭ F D C)
Lit.: no. 139.

Dēśya Kāpi (South India). *Janya rāga* of the 22nd *mēḷa* (*Kharaharapriyā*).
Tone material:
C D F G B♭ c
c B♭ A B♭ G F E♭ D C
Cf. *Hindusthan Kāpi* (22nd *mēḷa*); the difference between the two *rāgas* rests in the interpretation of the performer.
Lit.: no. 139.

Dēśya Manoharī (South India). *Janya rāga* of the 22nd *mēḷa* (*Kharaharapriyā*).
Tone material:
C D E♭ F A c
c B♭ G F E♭ D C
Lit.: no. 139.

Dēśya Māruva (South India). *Janya rāga* of the 54th *mēḷa* (*Viśvambharī*).
Tone material:
C D♭ E F♯ B c
c B G F♯ E D♭ C
Lit.: no. 139.

Dēśya Mukhāri (*Dēśmukhāri*) (South India). *Janya rāga* of the 25th *mēḷa* (*Mārarañjanī*).
Tone material:
C D E D E F B♭♭ A♭ B♭♭ c
(C D E F G A♭ B♭♭ A♭ c)
c B♭♭ A♭ F G E D C
(c A♭ B♭♭ A♭ G F E D C)
Lit.: no. 139.

Dēśya Nārāyaṇi (South India). *Janya rāga* of the 6th *mēḷa* (*Tānarūpi*).
Tone material:
C D♭ E♭♭ F G B c
c B A♯ B G F E♭♭ D♭ C
Lit.: no. 139.

Dēśya Naṭakurañji (South India). *Janya rāga* of the 55th *mēḷa* (*Śyāmalāṅgī*).
Tone material:
C D E♭ F♯ G A♭ G B♭♭ c
c B♭♭ G A♭ G F♯ E♭ D C
Lit.: no. 139.

Dēśya Rēgupti (South India). See *Dēśya Rēvagupti.*

Dēśya Rēvagupti (*Dēśya Rēgupti*) (South India). *Janya rāga* of the 15th *mēḷa* (*Māyāmāḷavagauḷa*).
Tone material:
C D♭ E D♭ F G A♭ B c
c A♭ B A♭ G F E C
Lit.: no. 139.

Dēśya Śrī (South India). *Janya rāga* of the 58th *mēḷa* (*Hemāvatī*).
Tone material:
C D E♭ F♯ A B♭ A c
c B♭ A F♯ E♭ D C
Lit.: no. 139.

Dēśya Suraṭi (South India). *Janya rāga* of the 6th *mēḷa* (*Tānārūpi*).
Tone material:
C F D♭ E♭♭ F G A♯ B
G F E♭♭ D♭ C *B*
Lit.: no. 139.

Dēśyatōḍi (South India). *Janya rāga* of the 8th *mēḷa* (*Hanumattōḍi*).
Tone material (there are variants; a most frequently used form is):
C E♭ F G A♭ B♭ c
c B♭ A♭ G F E♭ D♭ C
Lit.: no. 139.

Ḍet (Java). *Gembyakan* beat. The rubbing of the large drumhead with four closed fingers.
Lit.: no. 163.

Dēvābharaṇam (South India). *Janya rāga* of the 49th *mēḷa* (*Dhavalāmbarī*).
Tone material:
C E D♭ E F♯ A♭ B♭♭ c
c B♭♭ A♭ B♭♭ G F♯ E D♭ C
Lit.: no. 139.

Dēvadāsi (India). "Slave of the gods." Female dancer who performs in Hindu temples. Other female dancers are called *rājadāsi*, *śivadāsi.*

Dēvagāndhāri (North India). *Rāga.* See *Dēvgāndhar.*

Dēvagāndhāri (South India). *Janya rāga* of the 29th *mēḷa* (*Dhīraśaṅkarābharaṇam*).
Tone material:
C D F G A c (C D E D F G A B c)
c B A G F E D C (c B A B A G F E D C)
Lit.: no. 139.

Dēva gāndharva (Ancient India). The heavenly music of the gods performed by the *gāndharvas* and *apsaras* (male and female celestial musicians).

Dēva ghōṣa priya (South India). See *Dēva ghōsha priya.*

Dēva ghosha priyā (South India). *Janya rāga* of the 28th *mēḷa* (*Harikāmbhōjī*).
Tone material:
A B♭ C D E F G A
A G F E D C *B♭ A*
Lit.: no. 139.

Dēvagiri (South India). *Janya rāga* of the 49th *mēḷa* (*Dhavalāmbarī*).
Tone material:
C D♭ F♯ G A♭ c
c B♭♭ A♭ G F♯ E D♭ E C
Lit.: no. 139.

Dēvagiri (South India). *Janya rāga* of the 51st *mēḷa* (*Kāmavardhanī*).
Tone material:
C D♭ F♯ G A♭ c
c B A♭ G F♯ C D♭ C
Lit.: no. 139.

Dēvagīrvāṇi (South India). *Janya rāga* of the 66th *mēḷa* (*Chitrāmbarī*).
Tone material:
C D E F# G c
c G F# E D C
Lit.: no. 139.

Dēvagauptam (*Dēva gupti*) (South India). *Janya rāga* of the 28th *mēḷa* (*Harikāmbhōji*).
Tone material:
C D E F G A Bb c
c A G F E C
Lit.: no. 139.

Dēvagupti (South India). See *Dēvaguptam.*

Dēvakānta (South India). *Janya rāga* of the 58th *mēḷa* (*Hemāvatī*).
Tone material:
C Eb F# G A G Bb c
c A G F# D C
Lit.: no. 139.

Dēvakōṭi (South India). *Janya rāga* of the 50th *mēḷa* (*Nāmanārāyaṇī*).
Tone material:
C Db F# E F# G Bb c
c Ab G F# Db E C
Lit.: no. 139.

Dēvakriya (South India). *Janya rāga* of the 22nd *mēḷa* (*Kharaharapriyā*).
Tone material:
(a) C D F G Bb c
c Bb A G F Eb D C
(b) C Eb D Eb F G Bb A c
c Bb A G F Eb D Eb C
Cf. *Dēvakriya* of the 20th *mēḷa.*
Lit.: no. 139.

Dēvakriyā (South India). *Janya rāga* of the 20th *mēḷa* (*Naṭabhairavī*).
Tone material:
C D Eb F Bb Ab Bb (c)
(c) G Ab F Eb D C *Bb*
Lit.: no. 139.

Dēvakurañji (South India). *Janya rāga* of the 27th *mēḷa* (*Sarasāṅgī*).
Tone material:
C D E F G Ab B c
c B Ab F E D C
Lit.: no. 139.

Dēva Kusumāvaḷi (South India). *Janya rāga* of the 60th *mēḷa* (*Nītimatī*).
Tone material:
C F# Eb F# G c
c B G F# Eb D C
Lit.: no. 139.

Dēva Kūṭam (South India). *Janya rāga* of the 25th *mēḷa* (*Mārarañjanī*).
Tone material:
C D E F G Ab Bbb c
c Ab G F D E D C
Lit.: no. 139.

Dēva Mālāka (South India). *Janya rāga* of the 43rd *mēḷa* (*Gavambōdhi*).
Tone material:
C Eb F# G Bbb c
c Bbb G Ab G F# Eb Db C
Lit.: no. 139.

Dēva Māḷavi (South India). *Janya rāga* of the 56th *mēḷa* (*Śaṇmukhapriyā*).
Tone material:
C D Eb F# G Ab Bb
Bb Ab G F# Eb D C
Lit.: no. 139.

Dēvamaṇi (South India). *Janya rāga* of the 33rd *mēḷa* (*Gāṅgeyabhushanī*).
Tone material:
C D# E G Ab B c
c B Ab G E D# C
Lit.: no. 139.

Dēvamanōharī (South India). *Janya rāga* of the 22nd *mēḷa* (*Kharaharapriyā*).
Tone material:
C D F G A B♭ c
c B♭ A B♭ G F E♭ D C
Lit.: no. 139.

Dēvamaya ṛūpa (India). The pictorial representation of a *rāga*. The musical characterization is called *nādamaya rūpa*. Cf. *Rāga* (IIIb); *Rāga-māla*.

Dēvamrita Varshiṇi (*Dēvamṛta Varṣiṇi*) (South India). *Janya rāga* of the 22nd *mēḷa* (*Kharaharapriyā*).
Tone material:
C D E♭ F B♭ A B♭ c
c B♭ A G F E♭ D C
Lit.: no. 139.

Dēvamṛta Vāhiṇi (South India). *Janya rāga* of the 64th *mēḷa* (*Vāchaspati*).
Tone material:
C E F♯ G B♭ A B♭ c
c B♭ A B♭ G F♯ E D C
Lit.: no. 139.

Dēvamṛta Varṣiṇi (South India). See *Dēvamrita Varshiṇi.*

Dēva Mukhāri (South India). *Janya rāga* of the 22nd *mēḷa* (*Kharaharapriyā*).
Tone material:
C D E♭ F G A B♭ c
c B♭ A F G F D E♭ F D C
Lit.: no. 139.

Dēvamukhi (South India). *Janya rāga* of the 28th *mēḷa* (*Harikāmbhōji*).
Tone material:
C D E G A c
c A G F E D C
Lit.: no. 139.

Dēva Nāyaki (South India). *Janya rāga* of the 69th *mēḷa* (*Dhātuvardhaṇī*). The scale of this *rāga* is identical with that of *rāga Chhāya Vardhiṇi* (69th *mēḷa*).
Lit.: no. 139.

Dēvarañjani (South India). *Janya rāga* of the 22nd *mēḷa* (*Kharaharapriyā*).
Tone material:
C E♭ D F G A B♭ c
c A G F E♭ D C
Lit.: no. 139.

Dēvarañjani (South India), *Janya rāga* of the 28th *mēḷa* (*Harikāmbhōji*). The scale of this *rāga* is identical with that of *Dēvamukhi* (28th *mēḷa*).
Lit.: no. 139.

Dēvarañjani (South India). *Janya rāga* of the 15th *mēḷa* (*Māyāmāḷavagauḷa*).
Tone material:
C F G A♭ B c
c B A♭ G F C
Lit.: no. 139.

Dēvarāṣṭram (South India). *Janya rāga* of the 69th *mēḷa* (*Dhātuvardhaṇī*).
Tone material:
C D♯ E F♯ G B c
c B A♭ G F♯ E D♯ C
Lit.: no. 139.

Dēva Sālagam (South India). *Janya rāga* of the 25th *mēḷa* (*Mārarañjanī*).
Tone material:
C E G A♭ B♭♭ c
c B♭♭ A♭ G F E D C
Lit.: no. 139.

Dēvaśramam (South India). *Janya rāga* of the 53rd *mēḷa* (*Gamanaśrama*). This *rāga* is identical with the *rāgas Daurēyaṇi* and *Haṃsānandi*, both ascribed to the 53rd *mēḷa*. Lit.: no. 139.

Dēvgandhar (*Dēvagandharī*) (North India). *Rāga* ascribed to the *Asavari thāta*. Despite of its obscurity, musicians speak of three types:

1. Actually *dvigandhar* ("two *gandhar*"), meaning the use of both forms: E and E♭.
2. The use of E♭ only.
3. *Gandhari rāga* combined with a typical *dēvgandhar* phrase (with E-natural): C D E F.

The tone material, subject to some alterations can be stated as follows:

C D E F G B♭ c
c B♭ A♭ G F E♭ D C; *Vādis*: A♭, E♭

Lit.: no. 138.

Devgiri-Bilaval (North India). *Rāga* ascribed to the *Bilaval thāta*.
Tone material:

C D E F G A B c
c B A G F E D C; *Vādis*: C, (A), G

Lit.: no. 138.

Dēvarñjani (North India). *Rāga* ascribed to the *Bhairav thāta*.
Tone material:

C F G A♭ (B) c
c B (B♭) A♭ G F C

Lit.: no. 138.

Devsakh (*Deshakya*; *Desakh*) (North India). *Rāga* ascribed to the *Kāfi thāta*.
Tone material:

C D E♭ F G B♭(+) C
c B♭ G F (E♭) D C; *Vādis*: F, C

Two types are in use:

1. Without the note A.
2. Rare, the note A is used occasionally.

Lit.: no. 138.

Deze (Rhodesia). Term for *sansa* with 21 iron tongues. The player holds the *deze* inside a large calabash resonator. Cf. *Mbila*.
Lit.: no. 151.

Dge-gling (Tibet). Large heterophonic double-reed instrument. *Dge-gling* means the same as *rgya-gling*.
Lit.: no. 255.

Dgyer-ba, glu dyer-ba (*Glu lin-pa*) (Tibet). To chant, sing. Also *ghyer-wa*.

Dha (India). Solmization syllable indicating the sixth degree of the heptatonic scale. *Dha* is the abbreviated form of the tone-name *dhaivata*. The tone-names of the heptatonic scale are listed under the heading of *Ṣaḍja* (*Sa*). Assuming that *sa* is interpreted as the western note C, *dha*, a sixth higher, will represent forms of the A degree (A♭, A, A♯) as demanded by the tone material of the *rāga* performed.
Lit.: no. 136.

Dhā (Nepal). Small barrel drum. One head is beaten with a stick, the other with the hand. Cf. *Naykin*.
Lit.: no. 46.

Dhairyamukhi (South India). *Janya rāga* of the 9th *mēḷa* (*Dhēnuka*).
Tone material:

C D♭ E♭ F G A♭ c
c B G F G D♭ C

Lit.: no. 139.

Dhairyōdari (South India). *Janya rāga* of the 20th *mēḷa* (*Naṭabhairavī*).
Tone material:

C E♭ F G B♭ c
c A♭ G F D E♭ D C

Lit.: no. 139.

Dhaivata (India). (1) See *Dha*. (2) See *Jāti*.

Dhaivatāntya (South India). Term for the scale of a *janya rāga* in which the highest note is *dha* of the middle octave range. Cf. *Dha*.

Dhaivatī (Ancient India). See *Jāti*.

Dhak (Nepal). A *ḍhōlak* beaten with a stick on one skin and with the hand on the other. The corpus is almost cylindrical. The drum is used at religious festivals. Cf. *Dhakka*.

Dhakka (*Dhak*) (India). Sanskrit term for *damaru.* The term has been used to denote both forms of drum: barrel and hourglass. Originally the *dhakka* was a war drum. At the present time it is used in religious ceremonies. Both skins are beaten with sticks.

Dhālivarāḷi (South India). See *Jhālavarāḷi.*

Dhālivarāḷi (South India). See *Varāḷi* (39th *asampūrṇa mēḷa*).

Ḍhālu (India). See *Gamak(a).*

Ḍhamāī (South India). Telugu term for drum (usually for *tabla*).
Lit.: no. 254.

Dha-man (Tibet). Ladakhi term for *lda-man.*

Dhāma Rañjani (South India). *Janya rāga* of the 15th *mēḷa* (*Māyāmāḷavagauḷa*).
Tone material:
C D♭ F G B A♭ c
c A♭ F G F D♭ E C
Lit.: no. 139.

Dhamartāl (India). See *Tāla.*

Dhāmavatī (South India). See *Dhaumyarāga* (59th *asampūrṇa mēḷa*).

Dhammal (North India). See *Dhris.*

Dhan (Nepal). Frame drum.

Dhanakriya Dhātu (South India). *Janya rāga* of the 20th *mēḷa* (*Naṭabhairavī*).
Tone material:
C D E♭ F G A♭ B♭ A♭ c
c A♭ G F E♭ D C
Lit.: no. 139.

Dhana pālinī (South India). *Janya rāga* of the 16th *mēḷa* (*Chakravāka*).
Tone material:
C D♭ E F G F G c
c B♭ A G F A F E D♭ C
Lit.: no. 139.

Dhanāsari (South India). *Janya rāga* of the 8th *mēḷa* (*Hanumattōḍi*).
Tone material:
C D♭ E♭ F G B♭ c
c B♭ A♭ G F E♭ D♭ C
Lit.: no. 139.

Dhanashri (North India). *Rāga* ascribed to the *Kāfi thāta.*
Tone material:
C E♭ F G B♭ c
c B♭ A G F E♭ D C
Lit.: no. 138.

Dhanḍi (India). See *Danḍa.*

Dhani (North India). *Rāga* ascribed to the *Kāfi thāta.*
Tone material:
B♭ C E♭ F G B♭ c
c B♭ G F E♭ (D) C; *Vādis*: E♭, B♭
Lit.: no. 138.

Ḍhankā (South India). Temple drum carried on horseback when used in religious processions.
Lit.: no. 261.

Dhanupriya (South India). *Janya rāga* of the 69th *mēḷa* (*Dhātuvardhaṇī*).
Tone material:
C D♯ E F♯ B c
c B G A♭ F♯ E D♯ C
Lit.: no. 139.

Dhanustata (India). Term for string instruments.
Lit.: no. 255.

Dhanyāsi (South India). *Janya rāga* of the 8th *mēḷa* (*Hanumattōḍi*).
Tone material:
C E♭ F G B♭ c
c B♭ A♭ G F E♭ D♭ C
Lit.: no. 139.

Dhapla (India). Cf. *Dafli* (*Daf*).

Dhara (India). *Gamaka.* Cf. *Varek.*

Dharaṇi Manōharī (South India). *Janya rāga* of the 29th *mēḷa* (*Dhīraśaṅkarābharaṇam*).
Tone material:

C D E F G B G c
c B A B G F E F D C

Lit.: no. 139.

Dharaṇi Priya (South India). *Janya rāga* of the 6th *mēḷa* (*Tānārūpi*).
Tone material:

C D♭ E♭♭ A♯ B c
c B A♯ E♭♭ D♭ C

Lit.: no. 139.

Dhara Pallavam (South India). *Janya rāga* of the 65th *mēḷa* (*Mechakalyāṇī*).
Tone material:

C D F♯ E F♯ G B c
c B A G F♯ E F♯ D E D c

Lit.: no. 139.

Dharmāṇi (*Dharminī*) (South India). *Janya rāga* of the 49th *mēḷa* (*Dhavalāmbarī*).
Tone material:

C D♭ E F♯ A♭ B♭♭ c
c B♭♭ A♭ F♯ E D♭ C

Lit.: no. 139.

Dharma Prakāśini (South India). *Janya rāga* of the 20th *mēḷa* (*Naṭabhairavī*).
Tone material:

C D F G B♭ c
c A♭ F E♭ D C

Lit.: no. 139.

Dharmavatī (South India). The 59th *mēḷa* scale:

C D E♭ F♯ G A B c

Lit.: no. 139.

Dharmiṇi (South India). *Janya rāga* of the 51st *mēḷa* (*Kāmavardhanī*).
Tone material:

C D♭ E F♯ A♭ B c
c B G F♯ A♭ F♯ E D♭ C

Lit.: no. 139.

Dharmiṇi (South India). See *Dharmāṇi.*

Dhātakunda (South India). *Janya rāga* of the 15th *mēḷa* (*Māyāmāḷavagauḷa*).
Tone material:

C D♭ F E F B A♭ B c
c A♭ G F D♭ C

Lit.: no. 139.

Dhāta Manōhari (South India). See *Dhātu Manōhari.*

Dhāṭi Mañjari (South India). *Janya rāga* of the 28th *mēḷa* (*Harikambhōji*).
Tone material:

C D E F G A c
c B♭ G F D C

Lit.: no. 139.

Dhātri (South India). *Janya rāga* of the 63rd *mēḷa* (*Latāṅgī*).
Tone material:

C D F♯ G A♭ B c
c B A♭ G F♯ D C

Lit.: no. 139.

Dhātu (India). Ten basic ways of touching *vīṇā* strings in ornamentation: *puṣpa*, *kala*, *tala*, *niṣkoṭita*, *unmṛṣta*, *repha*, *anubanda*, *anusvanita*, *bindu*, *avamṛṣta*.
Lit.: no. 292.

Dhātu (India). Section; component. E.g., the *dhrūpad* consists of four *dhātus* that follow the introductory *ālāp*: *sthāyī*, *antarā*, *sanchārī*, and *ābhog*.
Lit.: no. 261.

Dhātu Manōhari (*Dhāta Manōhari*) (South India). *Janya rāga* of the 22nd *mēḷa* (*Kharaharapriyā*).

Tone material:
C G F G A B♭ c
c B♭ G F E♭ D C
Lit.: no. 139.

Dhātu Pañchamam (South India). *Janya rāga* of the 69th *mēḷa* (*Dhātuvardhaṇī*).
Tone material:
C D♯ E F♯ G B G c
c B A♭ G F♯ D♯ E F♯ D♯ C
Lit.: no. 139.

Dhātupriya (South India). *Janya rāga* of the 63rd *mēḷa* (*Latāṅgī*).
Tone material:
C D G F♯ G A♭ c
c B A♭ G F♯ E F♯ D C
Lit.: no. 139.

Dhātupriya (South India). *Janya rāga* of the 69th *mēḷa* (*Dhātuvardhaṇī*).
Tone material:
C D♯ G F♯ G A♭ c
c B A♭ G F♯ E D♯ C
Lit.: no. 139.

Dhātuvardhaṇī (South India). The 69th *mēḷa*:
C D♯ E F♯ G A♭ B c
As a *rāga*, the *asampūrṇa* form (of the 69th *mēḷa*) is called *rāga Dhauta Pañchamam* with the following tone material:
C D♯ E F♯ G A♭ B c
c B A♭ G F♯ D♯ E C
For variants see Lit. no. 139.

Dhaulo (South India). Large barrel drum with two skins.

Dhaulika (not to be mistaken for *daulika*) (South India). *Janya rāga* of the 1st *mēḷa* (*Kanakāṅgī*).
Tone material:
C D♭ F G A♭ B♭♭ c
c B♭♭ A♭ G F E♭♭ D♭ C
Lit.: no. 139.

Dhaulikā Gauḷa (South India). *Janya rāga* of the 20th *mēḷa* (*Naṭabhairavī*).
Tone material:
C D F G A♭ B♭ c
c B♭ A♭ G F E♭ D C
Lit.: no. 139.

Dhaumyarāga (South India). (1) The 59th *asampūrṇa mēḷa-rāga* without *kaṭapayādi* prefix. (2) The 59th *asampūrṇa mēḷa-rāga* with *kaṭapayādi* prefix. It was called *Dhāmavatī*. See *Rāga* (South India).
Lit.: no. 139.

Dhaumya rāgam (South India). *Janya rāga* of the 59th *mēḷa* (*Dharmavatī*), identical with *rāga Dāmya* (59th *mēḷa*).
Lit.: no. 139.

Dhauṅsa (India). Kettledrum.
Lit.: no. 261.

Dhaurēyaṇi (South India). *Janya rāga* of the 45th *mēḷa* (*Śubhapantuvarālī*).
Tone material:
C D♭ E♭ F♯ B c
c B A♭ G F♯ E♭ D♭ C
Lit.: no. 139.

Dhautapañcham(a) (South India). (1) The 69th *asampūrṇa mēḷa-rāga* without *kaṭapayādi* prefix. (2) The 69th *asampūrṇa mēḷa-rāga* with *kaṭapayādi* prefix.
Lit.: no. 139.

Dhauta Pañchamam (South India). Representation of the 69th *mēḷa* of the old *asampūrṇa* system. See *Dhātuvardhanī*.
Lit.: no. 139.

Dhavaḷa Haṃsi (South India). *Janya rāga* of the 57th *mēḷa* (*Siṃhendramadhyama*).
Tone material:
C D F# G Ab c
c B Ab G F# Eb D C
Lit.: no. 139.

Dhavaḷa Kēsarī (South India). *Janya rāga* of the 8th *mēḷa* (*Hanumattōḍi*).
Tone material:
C Db Eb F G Ab Bb c
c Bb G F Eb C
Lit.: no. 139.

Dhavalāmbarī (South India). (1) The 49th *mēḷa*:
C Db E F# G Ab Bbb c
(2) Also as *rāga*. In the *asampūrṇa* system the name of the 49th *mēḷa* is *Dhavaḷāngam*.
Tone material:
C Db E F# G Ab c
c Bbb Ab G F# E Db C
Lit.: no. 139.

Dhavaḷāngam (South India). See *Dhavalāmbarī*.

Dhavalāṅgam (South India). See *Dhavalāṅgī* (49th *asampūrṇa mēḷa*).

Dhavaḷāṅgī (South India). *Janya rāga* of the 15th *mēḷa* (*Māyāmāḷavagauḷa*).
Tone material:
C Db E F G Ab G c
c B Ab G F E Db C
Lit.: no. 139.

Dhavaḷāṅgī (South India). *Janya rāga* of the 49th *mēḷa* (*Dhavalāmbarī*).
Tone material:
C F# E F# G Ab Bbb Ab c
c Bbb Ab G F# E Db C
Lit.: no. 139.

Dhavaḷāṅgī (South India). (1) The 49th *asampūrṇa mēḷa-rāga* without *kaṭapayādi* prefix. (2) The 49th *asampūrṇa mēḷa-rāga* with *kaṭapayādi* prefix was called *Dhavalāṅgam*. See *Rāga* (South India).
Lit.: no. 139.

Dhavaḷa Sarasīruham (South India). *Janya rāga* of the 44th *mēḷa* (*Bhāvapriyā*).
Tone material:
C Db Eb F# Ab G Bb c
c Bb Ab F# Eb Db C
Lit.: no. 139.

Dhavaḷa Vāhini (South India). *Janya rāga* of the 20th *mēḷa* (*Naṭabhairavī*).
Tone material:
C D Eb G Bb c
c Bb Ab G F Eb D C
Lit.: no. 139.

Ḍhēnkā (South India). A *kinnari* type with two coconut shells as resonators and cowrie shells used as frets.
Lit.: no. 261.

Dhēnuka (South India). The 9th *mēḷa*:
C Db E F G Ab B c
As *rāga*, which the orthodox musicians perform only in the morning. Veṅkaṭamakhin (17th century) called this *rāga* by the name of *Dhūnnibhinnaṣaḍja*.
Lit.: no. 139.

Dhermai (Nepal). Small, not tunable, barrel drum carried on a string around the player's neck.
Lit.: no. 46.

Dhīkaruṇi (South India). *Janya rāga* of the 52nd *mēḷa* (*Rāmapriyā*).

Tone material:
C D♭ F♯ D♭ F♯ E F♯ A G B♭ A B c
c B♭ A G F♯ E D♭ C
Lit.: no. 139.

Dhikr (*Tarīqa*) (Arabia). Dervish ceremonies: *maulawīya*, *'isāwīya*, *sa'dīya*, *bakāshīya*, *shādhilīya*.

Dhil (Modern Tunisia). *Maqām*.
Tone material:
G A $\overset{+}{\text{B}\flat}$ C D $\overset{\flat}{\text{E}}$ F G A $\overset{+}{\text{B}\flat}$ c d
Lit.: no. 64.

Dhīra Kaḷā (South India). *Janya rāga* of the 22nd *mēḷa* (*Kharaharapriyā*).
Tone material:
C D E♭ B♭ A c
c B♭ A G F E♭ D C
Lit.: no. 139.

Dhīrākāri (South India). *Janya rāga* of the 59th *mēḷa* (*Dharmavatī*).
Tone material:
C D E♭ F♯ G A B c
c A B G F♯ E♭ D C
Lit.: no. 139.

Dhīra Kuntaḷi (South India). *Janya rāga* of the 59th *mēḷa* (*Dharmavatī*).
Tone material:
C F♯ G A B c
c B A G F♯ E♭ D C
Lit.: no. 139.

Dhīramati (South India). *Janya rāga* of the 13th *mēḷa* (*Gāyakapriya*).
Tone material:
C D♭ F G A♭ c
c A♭ F D♭ E D♭ C
Lit.: no. 139.

Dhīramati (South India). *Janya rāga* of the 29th *mēḷa* (*Dhīraśaṅkarābharaṇam*).
Tone material:
C E D E F G F B A c
c B G A c G F E D C
Lit.: no. 139.

Dhīraśaṅkarābharaṇam (South India). (1) The 29th *mēḷa*:
C D E F G A B c
(2) As *rāga*; very popular.
Lit.: no. 139.

Dhīraśaṅkarābharaṇam (South India). *Asampūrṇa* form with *kaṭapayādi* prefix of the 29th *mēḷa-rāga*. See *Rāga* (South India).
Lit.: no. 139.

Dhīrasāvēri (South India). *Janya rāga* of the 69th *mēḷa* (*Dhātuvardhaṇī*).
Tone material:
C D♯ E F♯ G A♭ B c
c A♭ G F♯ E D♯ C
Lit.: no. 139.

Dhīra Svarūpi (*Dhīra Svarūpiṇi*) (South India). *Janya rāga* of the 49th *mēḷa* (*Dhavalāmbarī*).
Tone material:
C D♭ E F♯ G A♭ B♭♭ c
c A♭ B♭♭ A♭ G F♯ E C
Lit.: no. 139.

Dhīragadarśi (South India). *Janya rāga* of the 65th *mēḷa* (*Mechakalyāṇī*).
Tone material:
C D F♯ G A B A c
c B A G F♯ E F♯ C
Lit.: no. 139.

Dhīvakriya (South India). *Janya rāga* of the 49th *mēḷa* (*Dhalalāmbarī*).
Tone material:
C D♭ F♯ G A♭ c
c B♭♭ A♭ G F♯ E D♭ C
Lit.: no. 139.

Dhōl (*Dhōla*) (India). Barrel drum with two heads. It is popular in village music, weddings, and religious festivities. The *dhōl* has various names; a few are: *dhōlak(a)*, *dhōlakī*, *dhōlu*, *raṇa dhōl*, *khōl*.
Lit.: no. 255.

Dhōl (Southeast India—Gond tribes). Barrel drum. The Hill Maria Gond tribe place the drum horizontally on the ground. There are *dhōls* with only one skin; the other side of the barrel remains open. The skin is beaten with the hands of the player.
Lit.: no. 135.

Dhōla (India). See *Dhōl*.

Ḍhōlak (Nepal). A barrel drum related to the *mardalā* played with both hands.

Ḍhōlaka (India; Bengal). Popular barrel drum. See *Dhōl*.
Lit.: no. 254.

Ḍhōlakī (India; Deccan). A small ("female") *dhōl*, used by women.

Dholki (India). See *Dhōlaki*.

Dhōlu (India). See *Dhōl*.

Dhombaka (Afghanistan). Frame drum; occasionally also gong. Cf. *Donbek*.
Lit.: no. 255.

Dhomka (South India). See *Domka*.

Dhondhon (Nepal). Drum used by the Bhotiyas.

Dhris (North India). Folk dance; other popular dances are *sammi*, *bhangra*, and *dhammal*.
Lit.: no. 46.

Dhrūpad (North India). The old, serious North Indian form of the pure art song with religious text. It is performed to the accompaniment of the *tanbura* drone, and the drum has always to be the ancient *mṛdaṅga* (or the *pakhawaj*). The formal structure is:

1. *Ālāp*, performed by the soloist, accompanied by the *tanbura*. The drum is still silent.
2. *Asthāyī* (*sthāyī*); the drummer starts only one of the following *tālas*: *Chautāl*; *Dhamartāl*; *Surphakta* (*Sulphakta*), and *Tevra*. No other rhythmic modes are in use. With a few exceptions (e.g., *Vasanta rāga*), the melody moves mainly within the lower tetrachord of the scale.
3. *Antara* (cf. *Khyāl*), the melody moves to the upper region of the tetrachord.
4. *Sanchārī*, "alternation," where the melody moves within the entire range of lower and upper tetrachords, and "alternates" between both ranges.
5. *Ābhog*, the coda section which often ends with the opening part of the *asthāyī* or offers a new theme.

For further and more detailed information see my book, Lit. no. 138, pp. 124-26.

Dhruta (*Dhruta laya*) (India). Fast tempo.

Dhrutarūpa (South India). *Janya rāga* of the 34th *mēḷa* (*Vāgadhīśvarī*).
Tone material:
C D# E F G A c
c G F E F D# E C
Lit.: no. 139.

Dhruti Vardhani (*Druta Vardhanam*) (South India). *Janya rāga* of the 29th *mēḷa* (*Dhīraśaṅkarābharaṇam*).
Tone material:
C E F G A c
c B A G F D E D C
Lit.: no. 139.

Dhruva (India). See *Ābhōg*.

Dhruva tāla (South India). Cf. *Tāla* (South India).

Dhudka (India). An S-shaped brass horn consisting of two curved segments which can be turned into a semicircular or S-shaped form. *Dhudka* is the same instrument that in the past was called *rāṇaśṛnga* (*rāṇaśriṅga*), the war horn.

Dhulia mallar (North India). *Rāga* ascribed to the *Kāfi thāta* and *Mallar* family. It consists of features taken from *rāgas Des* and *Sarang* combined with *Mallar* features.
Tone material:
C D F G B c
c B♭ A G F E♭ D C
Lit.: no. 138.

Dhuli ka git (Southeast India; Gond tribes; Maikal Hills). Gond song sung when a girl gets married and leaves the home of her parents.
Lit.: no. 134.

Dhūmāla (South India). *Janya rāga* of the 42nd *mēḷa* (*Raghupriyā*).
Tone material:
C D♭ E♭♭ F♯ F♯ B
(B) G F♯ D♭ E♭♭ D♭ C
The scale of this *rāga* has *Niṣādāntya* character.
Lit.: no. 139.

Dhun (North India). Popular song.

Dhunnibhinnaṣaḍja (South India). See *Bhinnaṣaḍja* (9th *asampūrṇa mēḷa-rāga*). See *Dhēnuka*.

Dhūrjaṭipriya (South India). *Janya rāga* of the 30th *mēḷa* (*Nāganandī*).
Tone material:
C D F G A♯ B c
c B A♯ G F D C
Lit.: no. 139.

Dhurki (India; Bengal; Orissa). Humming pot (pot with a membrane, suspended from a string). When swinging the pot about, it creates a low humming sound. See *Megha*.
Lit.: no. 254.

Dhūrvāṅki (South India). *Janya rāga* of the 29th *mēḷa* (*Dhīraśaṅkarābharaṇam*).
Tone material:
C D F G A c
c B G A G F E D C
Lit.: no. 139.

Dhūsaravarṇi (South India). *Janya rāga* of the 19th *mēḷa* (*Jhaṅkāradhvani*).
Tone material:
C D G A♭ B♭♭ c
c B♭♭ A♭ G D C
Lit.: no. 139.

Dhusir (Southeast India; Bastar State; Muria Gond). Spike fiddle consisting of a body made of half a coconut and a bamboo handle with two horsehair strings. It is played with a bamboo bow.
Lit.: no. 59.

Dhvajakriyā (South India). *Janya rāga* of the 27th *mēḷa* (*Sarasāṅgī*).
Tone material:
C D E F G
c B G F E F D E D C
Lit.: no. 139.

Dhvajōnnatam (South India). *Janya rāga* of the 29th *mēḷa* (*Dhīraśaṅkarābharaṇam*).
Tone material:
C D E F A B c
c G F E D C
Lit.: no. 139.

Dhvani (Ancient India). Term for sound, the basis of music.
Lit.: no. 292.

Dhvaujeṅkaram (South India). *Janya rāga* of the 29th *mēḷa* (*Dhīraśaṅkarābharaṇam*).
Tone material:
C D E F A B c
c B A F E D C
Lit.: no. 139.

Dhyamaya (Nepal). A barrel drum beaten on one side with a twisted cane, on the other with the bare hand.

Di (China). See *Ti*.

Di (India). Also *duṇ*, *tuṇ*, *dụ*, *tụ*. Basic *tabla* stroke for the right hand. The fleshy bases of the 2nd, 3rd, 4th, and 5th fingers strike the outer rim of the *chanti* and create an "open" sound. For further information see Lit. no. 136.

Dị (India). See *Din.*

Diassa (North Rhodesia; also Republic of Upper Volta). Popular dances performed by a group of either men or women. The dancers are *zare* on their ankles.
Lit.: no. 50.

Dibinde (Mozambique—Tshopi). A xylophone (*mbila*) with 10 slabs. It resembles the smaller *tshilandzana.* Cf. *Didole*; *Tshikhulu.*
Lit.: nos. 150-51.

Dibo (New Guinea). Drum.
Lit.: no. 228.

Dibu (Congo—Bembe; Bwende; Sundi). Wooden bells that serve ritual purposes.
Lit.: no. 280.

Dich (Vietnam). Bamboo cross flute.
Lit.: no. 296.

Dicharuk (West Java). The lively, ornamented playing of the *kolenang* (*bonang*). Cf. *Dikemprang.*
Lit.: no. 163.

Dichela (South Africa—Pedi). Leg rattles made of strings of cocoons. Cf. *Amafohlwane*; *Umfece.*
Lit.: nos. 150-51.

Didilavy (Malagasy Republic). Musical bow with a gourd resonator. The single string is beaten with a stick.
Lit.: no. 18.

Didimbadimba (Congo—Baluba; Basongo). Cf. *Mbila.*
Lit.: no. 27.

Didjeridoo (Northwest Australia—Nyangumarda). Primitive long wooden (or bamboo) trumpet, painted colorfully according to ancient tradition. Occasionally it is blown into a tin can resonator. The name *didjeridoo* is used primarily by western travellers and is not the original one, although a large number of aboriginees have adopted it. The instrument is used for accompanying songs and it is believed to have magic qualities.
Lit.: no. 37.

Didole (South Africa—Tshopi). A large xylophone (*mbila*) with 10 slabs. Cf. *Tshilandzana*; *Dibinde*; *Thikulu.*
Lit.: nos. 150-51.

Dienguela (Republic of Upper Volta—Bisa). Music bow.
Lit.: no. 50.

Dieu (*Giong*) (Vietnam). Modal systems. *Bac* (literally: north) and *nam* (literally: south) represent in music not north and south, but modes that refer to the moods, sentiments, tempos, vaguely resembling the *rasa* concept of India. Cf. *-Hoi.*
Lit.: no. 297.

Dieu Bac (*Giong Bac*) (Vietnam). The term indicates three mode types (*-hoi*):

1. *-hoi bac* expresses a joyful mood (performed in fast tempo).
2. *-hoi quang* is the "Cantonese mood," a fantastic atmosphere.
3. *-hoi nhac* has a solemn, ceremonial atmosphere.

Dieu Oan (*-hoi Oan*) (Vietnam). Similar to a mode called *-hoi ai*, a mode expressing melancholy and sadness.
Lit.: no. 297.

Di'f (Arabia). Term for octave.

Diff (Arabia). Cf. *Deff.*

Diga (Congo—Akare). Clay drum.
Lit.: no. 26.

Digo chivoti (Kenya). Transverse flute.

Digongo (Togo—Akasele). Drum. Cf. *Gangsa.*
Lit.: no. 95.

Dikanmbo (Former French Equatorial Africa; Angola – Loango). Stamping tube.
Lit.: no. 280.

Dikemprang (West Java). The "quiet and gentle playing of the *kolenang*" – the beats occur at every *keteg*. Cf. *Dicharuk*.
Lit.: no. 163.

Dikomana (South Africa – Bagananoa). An ensemble of five kettledrums described as a "herd." The largest, *moradu* (big cow), dominates the group; the other four drums in increasingly smaller sizes are *pau*, *maditsi*, *to-diane*, and *bo-pampane*. The ensemble is (was) used at various occasions, fertility rites, battle ceremonies and (according to Kirby, Lit. no. 151) human sacrifice.
Lit.: nos. 150-51.

Dikoot (Serawak). See *Dikut*.

Dīkṣāṅgi (South India). See *Dīkshāṅgi*.

Dīkshāṅgi (South India). *Janya rāga* of the 46th *mēḷa* (*Śaḍvidhamārgiṇī*).
Tone material:
C D♭ C F♯ G A B♭ c
c B♭ A G F♯ E♭ C D♭ C
Lit.: no. 139.

Dikubila (Congo – Balunda). An hourglass-shaped drum.
Lit.: no. 26.

Dikut (*Gugul*) (Malaysia; Borneo). See *Bikut* (finger holes).
Lit.: no. 255.

Dilīpaka(m) (South India). *Janya rāga* of the 22nd *mēḷa* (*Kharaharapriyā*).
Tone material:
C D E♭ D F G B♭ A B♭ G A B♭ c
c B♭ A G F E♭ D C
(occasionally also: C D F G B♭ c
c B♭ G F E♭ D C)
Lit.: no. 139.

Dili-tüidük (Afghanistan – Turkmen). Single reed pipe.

Dilkas Hawran (Middle East). *Maqām*.
Tone material:
$\overset{+}{B\flat}$ C D $\overset{+}{E\flat}$ F G A $\overset{+}{B\flat}$ c d $\overset{+}{e\flat}$ f g a
Lit.: no. 64.

Dilkaśīdah (Middle East). *Maqām*.
Tone material:
G A B♭ C D $\overset{+}{E\flat}$ F G A $\overset{+}{B\flat}$ c d $\overset{+}{e\flat}$ f g a
Lit.: no. 64.

Dil-Nišin (Middle East). *Maqām*.
Tone material:
C D $\overset{+}{E\flat}$ F G A $\overset{+}{B\flat}$ c $\overset{(+)}{d\flat}$ e f g a $\overset{(+)}{b\flat}$
Lit.: no. 64.

Dilruba (North India). "The heart robber," a recent form of the *sārangī*; a bowed string instrument with two steel and two brass strings and 22 sympathetic strings. The instrument has 19 or 20 movable frets, and the wooden body can have various shapes: square, rectangular, or trapezoid.
Lit.: no. 248.

Dilrubab (Afghanistan). Term occasionally used for *dilruba*.

Dima (Congo). Term for *ndima*; *ndidi*.

Dimba (Lower Congo). Term for *sansa*. See also *Madimba*.
Lit.: nos. 27, 280.

Dimbek (Kurdisthan). Cf. *Dinbik*.

Dimbga (Africa). Cf. *Ndimbga*.
Lit.: no. 255.

Dimbila (Tanzania – Makonde). Log xylophone (six banana stalks are used).

Dimbu (Ghana). Song with accompanying rattles.

Dimukgemuk (Pacific; Marshall Isl.). Wooden sticks held by girls sitting in two rows facing each other. Each girl beats her stick against the one of her partner at the opposite side.
Lit.: no. 255.

Din (*Tin*; *Diṇ*; *Tiṇ*; *Dị*; *Tị*) (India). A *bol* indicating a basic *tabla* stroke for the right hand. The second finger, held stiffly above the drum head, is thrown against the *maidan*, and immediately after the stroke snaps back into its original position. For details, see Lit. no. 136.

Diṇ (India). See *Din.*

Dinadyuti (South India). *Janya rāga* of the 20th *mēḷa* (*Naṭabhairavī*).
Tone material:
C D E♭ F G B♭ c
c B♭ A♭ G F E♭ F D E♭ C
Lit.: no. 139.

Dinakarakānti (South India). *Janya rāga* of the 27th *mēḷa* (*Sarasāṅgī*).
Tone material:
C F E F G c
c B A♭ G F E C
Lit.: no. 139.

Dinbik (Kurdisthan). Frame drum. Cf. *Tunbuk*; *Donbek.*

Dinde (Flores). See *Sanda*; *Danding.*

Dindi (Flores — Pongkor). A song of praise to the ancestral spirits. It is sung by a precentor and a chorus.
Lit.: no. 166.

Ḍiṇḍima (India). An ancient drum (probably frame drum). The term appears already in the *Rāmāyāna.*
Lit.: nos. 184, 198.

Dindo (Congo — Gombe). Barrel drum. Cf. *Dundu.*
Lit.: no. 26.

Diṅ doṅ ti (Burma). Buffalo rattle. Three wooden clappers rattle in a trapezoid-shaped frame.
Lit.: no. 252.

Ding (New Guinea). "Long ghost." Long transverse flute with a piston that can alter its low pitch. The flute is used at circumcision rituals, and is played in pairs. The two instruments are tuned to different pitches.
Lit.: no. 255.

Ding (Bali). Tone syllable denoting the first tone of a scale. Below are shown all tone syllables of ritual ceremonial music (*gambang*) where seven tone are used: *ding*, *dong ageng* ("great *dong*," low pitched), *dang ageng*, *deng*, *dung*, *dang alit* ("small *dang*," high pitched), *dong alit.*
The popular theater (*gambuh*) uses: *ding*, *dong*, *deng*, *penyorog*, *dung*, *dang*, *pemero*. *Penyorog* and *pemero* are secondary notes and can be deleted. A *ding* may become any of five or seven notes, a variety of scales can be observed as shown below.

Basic scale, e.g.: E F G A B c d e f g a b

	E	F	G	A	B	c	d
Tembung	ding	dong	deng	penyorog	dung	dang	pemero
	A	B	c	d	e	f	g
Selisir	ding	dong	deng	penyorog	dung	dang	pemero
	B	c	d	e	f	g	a
Baro	ding	dong	deng	penyorog	dung	dang	pemero
	c	d	e	f	g	a	b
Lebeng	ding	dong	deng	penyorog	dung	dang	pemero

Cf. *Saih lima*; *Saih pitu*; *Pelog*; *Slendro*; *Saih angklung*. For other variants see Lit. no. 197.

Dingba (Congo). Musical bow or board zither of the Mangbetu.
Lit.: no. 176.

Dingdingti (Burma — Shan State). Square wooden cattle bell with three wooden clappers.
Lit.: no. 252.

Dinglye (Kampuchea). Tubular zither with 6-8 strings.
Lit.: nos. 156, 254.

Ding-sha (Tibet). A pair of deeply curved cymbals used by officiating Lamas. See *Mandira*; *Maha Mandira*; *Manjuri*.
Lit.: no. 255.

Ding teng-khing (Malay peninsula). See *Diṅ teṅkhiṅ*. Cf. *Boku* (Flores).

Dingwinti (Congo). Barrel-shaped humming pot covered with skin. In the center of the skin is fixed a piece of reed which is rubbed with the finger. See *Mwan'angulu*.
Lit.: nos. 255, 280.

Dinni (South India). Flat kettledrum.
Lit.: no. 255.

Dintara (India; East Bengal). Fiddle with three or four strings.
Lit.: no. 255.

Diṅ teṅkhiṅ (Malacca). "Quarrel bamboo sticks." Stamping and beating bamboo sticks in various sizes: *lemol* (bass) male, or *kuyn* (fathers); *kedol* (medium) females, or *gende* mothers; *kenon* (high-pitched) children. The latter sticks are now almost obscure.
Lit.: no. 254.

Diololi (West Africa; Senegal—Wolof). Bell.

Dipak (North India). *Rāga* ascribed to the *Bilaval thāta* (not to be mistaken for a *rāga* with the same name subordinated to the *Purvi thāta*).
Tone material:
C E F G A B c
c B♭ A G F E D C; *Vādis*: E (or C), F (or G)
This *rāga* is believed to create fire.
Lit.: no. 138.

Dipak (North India). *Rāga* ascribed to the *Purvi thāta*.
Tone material (the descending line is to be used first):
c G E D♭ C
C E (F♯) (G) (A♭) (B) c; *Vādis*: C, G
Lit.: no. 138.

Dīpakam (South India). *Janya rāga* of the 51st *mēḷa* (*Kāmavardhanī*).
Tone material:
C E F♯ G A♭ G c
c B A♭ B G F♯ E D♭ C
Lit.: no. 139.

Dīpar (South India). See *Dīparam*.

Dīparam (South India). *Janya rāga* of the 10th *mēḷa* (*Nāṭakapriya*).
Tone material:
C D♭ E♭ F G A B♭ c
c B♭ A B♭ G F E♭ D♭ C
Lit.: no. 139.

Dipchandi (India). See *Tāla*.

Dipela (South Africa—Bakwelo; Balubedu). Xylophone resembling the *mbila* of the Venda.
Lit.: no. 151.

Dīpika Vasantam (South India). *Janya rāga* of the 20th *mēḷa* (*Naṭabhairavī*).
Tone material:
C E♭ F G A♭ G B♭ c
c A♭ G F D C
Lit.: no. 139.

Dirada meta (Java). "The raging elephant." A stern, serious stretta part of the *gangsaran*. Cf. *Gangsaran*.
Lit.: no. 163.

Dirbuka (Arabia). Frame drum used by women.

Dīrgha (North India). "Long." Long-held note (*dīrgha svara*) with a duration of two metric units, as compared with *hrasva svara* (note lasting one metric unit). (All durational note values of North India are listed under the heading of *Anumātrā*.)
Lit.: no. 136.

Dīrghamaṅgali (South India). *Janya rāga* of the 47th *mēḷa* (*Suvarṇāṅgī*).
Tone material:
C D♭ F♯ G A c
c A G F♯ E♭ D♭ C
Lit.: no. 139.

Dirghānandiṇi (South India). *Janya rāga* of the 40th *mēḷa* (*Navanītam*).
Tone material:
G A B♭ C E♭♭ F♯ D♭ F♯ G B♭
A G F♯ E♭♭ D♭ C *B♭ A G*
Lit.: no. 139.

Dīrghataraṅgiṇi (South India). *Janya rāga* of the 20th *mēḷa* (*Naṭabhairavī*).
Tone material:
C E♭ F A♭ B♭ c
c B♭ A♭ G F E♭ F D E♭ D C
Lit.: no. 139.

Dīrghika (South India). *Janya rāga* of the 7th *mēḷa* (*Senāpāti*).
Tone material:
C D♭ E♭ A♭ B♭♭ c
c B♭♭ A♭ E♭ D♭ C
Lit.: no. 139.

Dirimbekki (Turkey). Cf. *Deblek*.

Dīṣaṇārati (South India). See *Dīshaṇārati*.

Dīshaṇarati (South India). *Janya rāga* of the 15th *mēḷa* (*Māyāmāḷavagauḷa*).
Tone material:
C D♭ E F A♭ B c
c B A♭ G A♭ F D♭ C *B A♭ B* C
Lit.: no. 139.

Dishi (Nepal—Newari). Drum with two heads. Cf. *Dhōlak*.
Lit.: no. 255.

Diśi (South India). *Diśi chakra*, name of the 10th *chakra* in the system of the 72 *mēḷas*. Cf. *Rāga* (South India).
Lit.: no. 139.

Dithlaka (Bechuanaland—Bangwaketse). Ensemble of a minimum of 10 reed pipes. The flutes have different lengths.
Lit.: nos. 150-51.

Diti (Lower Congo). Term for *sansa*.
Lit.: no. 280.

Ditumba (Congo—Basanga; Bena Lulua; Baluba). Ceremonial vase-shaped drum.
Lit.: no. 26.

Diungdiung (Senegal—Wolof). Big royal drum.
Lit.: no. 255.

Divikāmantini (South India). *Janya rāga* of the 20th *mēḷa* (*Naṭabhairavī*).
Tone material:
C E♭ D E♭ F G A♭ G c
c B♭ A♭ G F E♭ D C
Lit.: no. 139.

Diviṭi Vādyam (South India). Folk drum with two heads. The right hand skin is beaten with a straight stick, the left hand skin with a curved one.
Lit.: no. 261.

Divya Bauḷi (South India). *Janya rāga* of the 15th *mēḷa* (*Māyāmāḷavagauḷa*).
Tone material:
C D♭ E G B c
c A♭ G F E D♭ E C
Lit.: no. 139.

Divyābharaṇam (South India). *Janya rāga* of the 21st *mēḷa* (*Kiravāṇi*).
Tone material:
C D E♭ F G B c
c B G F E♭ D C
Lit.: no. 139.

Divya Gāndhāram (South India). *Janya rāga* of the 18th *mēḷa* (*Hāṭakāmbarī*).
Tone material:
C F D♭ G A♯ B c
c A♯ B G F E C D♭ C
Lit.: no. 139.

Divyagāndhāri (South India). *Janya rāga* of the 20th *mēḷa* (*Naṭabhairavī*).
Tone material:
C E♭ F G A♭ B♭ c (C E♭ D F G A♭ c)
c B♭ G F E♭ C (c A♭ B♭ A♭ G F E♭ D E♭ C)
Lit.: no. 139.

Divya Candhi (South India). *Janya rāga* of the 27th *mēḷa* (*Sarasāṅgī*).
Tone material:
C D F A♭ B E G c
c B A♭ G F E D C
Lit.: no. 139.

Divya Kuntala (South India). *Janya rāga* of the 48th *mēḷa* (*Divyamaṇī*).
Tone material:
C D♭ E♭ F♯ G A♯ c
c B A♯ G F♯ E♭ D♭ C
Lit.: no. 139.

Divyamaṇī (South India). (1) The 48th *mēḷa*:
C D♭ E♭ F♯ G A♯ B c
(2) As *rāga*.
Lit.: no. 139.

Divyamati (South India). *Janya rāga* of the 40th *mēḷa* (*Navanītam*).
Tone material:
C D♭ E♭♭ F♯ G A G B♭ c
c B♭ A G F♯ E♭♭ D♭ C
Lit.: no. 139.

Divyāmbari (South India). *Janya rāga* of the 27th *mēḷa* (*Sarasāṅgī*).
Tone material:
C G F G A♭ B c
c G B A♭ G F E D C
Lit.: no. 139.

Divyāmbari (South India). *Janya rāga* of the 40th *mēḷa* (*Navanītam*).
Tone material:
C E♭♭ D♭ E♭♭ F♯ G A G B♭ c
c B♭ A G F♯ E♭♭ D♭ C
Lit.: no. 139.

Divya Pañcam (South India). See *Divya Pañchama(m)*.

Divya Pañchama(m) (South India). *Janya rāga* of the 27th *mēḷa* (*Sarasāṅgī*).
Tone material:
C D E F C G F A♭ B c (C D E F G A♭ B c)
c B A♭ G F E D C
Lit.: no. 139.

Divyasēnā (South India). *Janya rāga* of the 58th *mēḷa* (*Hemāvatī*).
Tone material:
C D E♭ F♯ G A B♭ c
c B♭ A F♯ E♭ D F♯ E♭ C
Lit.: no. 139.

Divya Taraṅgiṇī (South India). *Janya rāga* of the 17th *mēḷa* (*Sūryakānta*).
Tone material:
C D♭ E F G c
c B A G F E D♭ C
Lit.: no. 139.

Divya Tōraṇi (South India). *Janya rāga* of the 61st *mēḷa* (*Kāntāmaṇi*).
Tone material:
C D E G A♭ c
c B♭♭ A♭ F♯ E D C
Lit.: no. 139.

Diwan (Arabia). "Assembly," "grouping." In music *diwan* represents collections of related *maqamāt*. The relationship between the *maqamāt* rests in the starting note or in additional common notes. Numerous Arabic music theorists have set up their own *diwans*.
Lit.: no. 121.

Diyānai (Arabia). Old double reed pipes (double *nay*). Cf. *Nay*.
Lit.: no. 81.

Djalupu (North Australia). Name for *didjeridu*.

Djandjingan (Borneo). See *Garantong*.

Djanger (Bali). See *Janger.*

Djanggar (Mongolia – Buryat). See *Geser Khan.*

Djaouak (Algeria). See *Juwak.*

Djarada (Australia). Love song.
Lit.: no. 57.

Djarupei (*Djerupai*) (Southeast Borneo). Single bamboo tube with a free beating tongue. It has four finger holes in front and one in back.
Lit.: no. 162.

Djebang-ari (Australia). Song and dance of the Northeast of Arnhem land. Characteristic of this song is a sudden interruption halfway until the song leader begins again.
Lit.: no. 57.

Djedjaok (Pulau-Pulay; Mentawai Isl.). Small bamboo jew's harp.
Lit.: no. 255.

Djimba (Belgian Congo). A *sanza* with a wooden melon-shaped body. Its top has five brass tongues.
Lit.: no. 255.

Djimpai (Borneo). See *Safe*; *Impai.*

Djoboko (Cameroon; Former French Equatorial Africa – Babinga). Favorite social dance. The music is provided by two choruses, one male and one female.
Lit.: no. 247.

Djodjo (Senegal – Fulble). Drum in the shape of an hourglass.
Lit.: no. 255.

Djoged (Bali). See *Joged.*

Djongkok (Bali). See *Jongkok.*

Djungga (West Sumba). Stick zither with one string.
Lit.: no. 162.

Djuring (Southeast Sumatra – Lampong). Jew's harp with a resonance bamboo tube.
Lit.: no. 255.

Djungkih (Borneo; Java; Sumatra). Jew's harp. See *Giriding.*

Dmag-dung (Tibet). War, hunting, or signal horn. Cf. *Mag-dung.*
Lit.: no. 255.

Do (India). Frame drum.
Lit.: no. 255.

Dō (Japan). Term for the wooden corpus of a musical instrument.
Lit.: no. 185.

Do (Oceania – Siar; Bilia). Slit-drum.
Lit.: no. 84.

Doal-doal bulo (North Sumatra). Bamboo (tube) zither with 4-6 strings.
Lit.: no. 156.

Dōbachi (Japan). "Copper cup." Temple gong shaped like a round cup that rests upon a pillow or wooden stand. It is beaten with a wooden stick. Cf. *K'ing.*
Lit.: no. 225.

Do bat (Burma). Small drum.
Lit.: no. 303.

Dobdab (Persia). Cf. *Debdebe.*

Doblang (Sunda District). An augmented *ogel* in the regency of Lebak.
Lit.: no. 163.

Dobon (New Guinea; Papua). Slit-drum.
Lit.: no. 84.

Do Butt (Burma). Short, small drums used in folk music played together with an oboe type, clappers, and cymbals.
Lit.: no. 252.

Dōbyoshi (Japan). "Copper time beaters." Brass cymbals of different sizes.
Lit.: no. 225.

Dodoan (West Java; Sunda District). Moderately quick tempo. Cf. *Wirama.*
Lit.: no. 163.

Dodoitsu (Japan). Popular light *shamisen* song (love song) of the geishas.

Dodot (Java). Cf. *Jamangan.*

Doeri (*Duri*) (North Nias). Jew's harp with one tongue. Cf. *Grinding.*
Lit.: nos. 163, 166.

Dof (Arabia). Tambourin. Cf. *Deff*; *Duff.*

Ḍogḍog (Java; Sunda District). A small *jedor* (in East Java it is called *reog*). The (Sundanese) *ḍogḍog* appears in various sizes. In small village orchestras the *ḍogḍogs* are used in one or two pairs. The larger drums of the pairs are called *brung*; *bangbrang* (*ambrang*); the smaller drums are called *tong* and the smallest *tilingting.* Cf. *Tong.*
Lit.: no. 163.

Ḍogḍog lojor (West Java). Ensemble consisting of drums and an *angklung*, used at festive occasions.

Doger (Java—Tasik District). Cf. *Lengger angklung.*

Dogori (Tanganyika—Zaramo). Footed drum.
Lit.: no. 255.

Dohol (Persia). Cylindrical drum with two heads. Cf. *Dehol.*
Lit.: no. 255.

Dohra (North India). A rhythmical drum phrase consisting of two *qaidas* in succession.
Lit.: no. 136.

Doirā (Afghanistan). Large frame drum with one head played by women.

Doka (Malagasy Republic; Southeast Coast). Bamboo rattle.
Lit.: no. 251.

Dokā (South India). *Janya rāga* of the 1st *mēḷa* (*Kanakāṅgī*).
Tone material:
C E♭♭ G A♭ B♭♭ c
c B♭♭ A♭ G E♭♭ C
Lit.: no. 139.

Dokaku (Japan). Copper trumpet with a long, extended cylindrical bell into which the narrow tube of the instrument can be inserted telescopically. The *dokaku* was used by the military and at funeral ceremonies. Cf. *Hao-t'ung* (China).
Lit.: no. 225.

Dokkin (Japan). Solo *shamisen* music. Cf. *Deha.*
Lit.: no. 187.

Dōko (Japan). Small brass or copper gong suspended from a wooden stand. Usually a set of three gongs is employed.
Lit.: no. 225.

Dokri (Sudan). "Spirit drum." Drum with two heads.
Lit.: no. 95.

Dola (Kurdistan). Drum with a cylindrical body.

Ḍōlak (India). Popular barrel drum with two heads.

Dolanan lare (Java). The singing of children.
Lit.: no. 163.

Dolbas (Central Asia; Kirghiz). Kettledrum.
Lit.: no. 91.

Doli-doli (Nias). Xylophone played only by girls. It is made of three or four wooden slabs laid across a hole in the ground. In the Mentawei Islands the instrument is called *tudukat* or *lelega*; in Central Borneo and South Celebes it is called *gendang-gendang*; the Batak people call it *garantung*; it does not appear in Flores.
Lit.: nos. 162, 166.

Dolla (South India). Kettledrum. Cf. *Dundubhi.*
Lit.: no. 254.

Dom (*Lori*) (East Iran). Low-cast travelling musicians.

Dombak (Persia). Cf. *Tombak.*

Dombra (Union of Soviet Socialist Republics; Kazakhstan; Kirgizia; Kalmykia). (1) Kazakh lute in various sizes generally with a round or oval body and 3-6 metal strings. (2) Kalmyk lute with a triangular body and movable frets. It has two single or two pairs of strings, plucked with a plectrum.
Lit.: no. 275.

Dömbra (*Dömbra*) (Afghanistan). See *Dombra.*

Dombuli (India). Bar; measure; type.

Domia (Liberia). Masked dancer who acts as a clown.

Domka (South India). Also called *Dhomka. Janya rāga* of the 13th *mēḷa* (*Gāyakapriya*). Tone material:

C E G A♭ B♭♭ c
c B♭♭ A♭ G E C

Lit.: no. 139.

Domo (Congo—Bangba; Mayogu). Arched harp. See *Domu.*
Lit.: no. 176.

Domog (Mongolia). Narrative song.

Domu (Congo—Mangbele). Arched harp.
Lit.: no. 255.

Don (*daun*) (Bali). Leaf; key; keys of a metallophone or xylophone.

Don (Annam; Vietnam). Term for musical instrument.

Donawa (Japan). A decorative rope of the *ō-tsuzumi* that has no function, in contrast to the other two ropes that influence the tension of the drumheads.
Lit.: no. 185.

Donbek (*Tonbak*) (Persia). Cup-shaped hand drum with one skin.
Lit.: no. 255.

Dōnen-bushi (Japan). 17th-century songs which served as accompaniments to dances.
Lit.: no. 225.

Dong (Bali). Tone syllable. See *Ding*, under which heading all tone-syllables are listed.

Donga (Java). Chanted prayer.

Dong ageng (Bali). "The great *dong*," the low sounding *dong*. Cf. *Saih pitu*; *Ding*, where all tone names are listed.
Lit.: no. 197.

Dong alit (Bali). "The small (high-pitched) *dong*." Tone syllable. See *Ding*, under the heading of which all tone-syllables are listed.
Lit.: no. 197.

Dong chenik (*Dong tjenik*) (Bali). Tone syllable; this term has the same significance as *dong alit.*

Ḍongḍing genḍing (Java). (1) Ornamentations or variation of the basic theme in *gamelan* music. (2) The structurally important points in a melody.
Lit.: no. 163.

Dongeldongel (Oceania; New Guinea). Musical bow. The player holds the string between his lips and lightly strikes it with a little stick held in one hand and plucks it with the other hand.
Lit.: no. 84.

Dong geḍe (Bali). The low sounding *dong*. See *Ding*, where all tone-syllables are listed. Cf. *Kidung*.
Lit.: no. 197.

Dongke (Borneo). See *Giridung*.

Dong tjenik (Bali). "The small *dong*." See *Dong chenik*. Cf. *Kidung*.

Dō nhac (Annam; Vietnam). Musical instrument.
Lit.: no. 255.

Don min (Burma – Highland). Zither. Cf. *Kim*.

Dono (Ghana – Ashanti). Drum in the shape of an hourglass.
Lit.: no. 95.

Don phong (Annam; Vietnam). Term for "organ."

Dontappo (Japan). Dance music.

Doogdooga (South India). See *Duguduga*.

Ḍootḍoot (Java; Solo). *Gembyang* beat. Four spread-out fingers of one hand strike the large drumhead, while the rest of the hand rests with its little finger on the rim of the drumhead. At the same time the smaller drum head is rubbed with the middle finger of the other hand.
Lit.: no. 163.

Dopa-dopa (Indonesia; Ternate). Bamboo clapper.
Lit.: no. 162.

Dōr (Arabia). Rhythmic period. A fixed sequence of simple rhythmical motives similar to the North Indian *āvarta*. Cf. *Iqā'*. Also term for *mauwal*.
Lit.: no. 34.

Dora (Japan; Korea). Small circular knobbed gong similar to the *lo* of China, where it was used by night watchmen to indicate the time and that "all's well."
Lit.: no. 255.

Dorungu (Congo – Anderimba pygmies). Board zither.
Lit.: no. 176.

Dörwen chikhe khuur (Mongolia – Sunit Mongols). "The *khuur* with four ears." A fiddle with a cylindrical (rarely hexagonal or octagonal) body. The front is covered with hide. The instrument has four strings, tuned in pairs to the interval of a fifth. The bow is drawn permanently between the string pairs (as in China). The Khorchin Mongols call this fiddle *khorae*, the Khalkha Mongals name it *khuur* or *khuuchin* and the Buryat Mongols call it *khuuchir*, *khor*, or *khur*, and the Kalmucks call it *biwa*.
Lit.: no. 61.

Dory (Malagasy Republic – Sakalava). Cylindrical drums played in pairs for ritual purposes. The *dory* is never to be touched by women. Cf. *Anakidory*.
Lit.: no. 251.

Dosa (Japan). See *Sona rappa*.

Dōsharahita Svarūpiṇī (South India). *Janya rāga* of the 63rd *mēḷa* (*Latāṅgī*). Despite its name, "free from any fault," this *rāga* is obscure. Three important South Indian sources (see Lit. no. 139) do not offer any specific details.
Tone material (vaguely):

G F♯ G A♭ B C E
D C *B A♭ G F♯ G*

Lit.: no. 139.

Dōshō (Japan). "Cave flute." Old and rarely used vertical flute with four finger holes. Cf. *T'ung hsiao*.
Lit.: no. 255.

Dotāra (North India). "Two stringer." A long necked lute with four strings tuned in pairs. The instrument has no frets and is played with a wooden plectrum.
Lit.: no. 46.

Doteku (Japan). Bronze gong in the shape of a bell. It is beaten with a wooden hammer.
Lit.: no. 255.

Do'uda (Flores; Manggaray). Xylophone with six attached keys. See *Preson*; *Garangtong*.
Lit.: no. 166.

Doula (India). See *Dhōl.*

Döwel (*Katchel*) (Ethiopia). Stone slabs suspended in wooden frames serving as church bells.
Lit.: no. 38.

Drabek (Algeria; Kabylia). Plural of *derbuka.* See *Darbuka.*

Draj (Tunisia). See *Al draj.*

Dra-nyen (*Dram-nyen*) (Tibet). Lute with three strings; synonym for *p'i-wang.* Cf. *Chha-nyen.*
Lit.: no. 255.

Dram-nyen (Tibet). See *Dra-nyen.*

Dravidian Music (South India). Music of ancient South India, of the Tamil speaking people. According to Lit. no. 261, the basic scale of the ancient system was the same as that of the present South India *harikāmbhoji.* The seven degrees of the scale were called: *kural*, *tuttam*, *kaikkilai*, *uzai*, *iḷi*, *viḷari*, *tāram*, *tuttam.*
Lit.: no. 261.

Dril-bu (Tibet). Bronze hand bell (clapper inside), essential in religious ceremonies.
Lit.: no. 143.

Dril-gzugs (Tibet). Body of the bell.

Dril-lca (Tibet). Bell clapper.

Dril srog-pa (Tibet). To ring a bell.

Dril-stegs (Tibet). The frame from which a bell is suspended.

Dritakāla (India). Fast tempo.

Drub (Tunisia). Rhythmical pattern used in coda sections:

or

Lit.: no. 171.

Druhiṇa priya (South India). *Janya rāga* of the 18th *mēḷa* (*Hāṭakāmbarī*).
Tone material:
C D♭ G A♯ B c
c B A♯ G D♭ C
Lit.: no. 139.

Druri dana (Indonesia). A bamboo buzzer (jew's harp) in the shape of a tuning fork with a handle that has two finger holes. The instrument is beaten with the right hand against the palm of the left. The finger holes in the handle alter the sound when closed or opened. The instrument has various shapes and numerous names such as: *genggon sakai*, West Borneo, Malacca; *sasesaheng*, Sangihe and Talau Islands; *baka-baka*, Ternate; *rere* or *talalu*, Celebes; *tatalu*, Banggai; *ore-ore*, Buton; *buncacan*, Philippines.
Lit.: nos. 162, 167.

Druta (*Kāla*) (India). The fast one of the three tempo indications. Used in Vedic chant and in South Indian art music. The other two tempo indications are: *vilambita*, slow, and *madhyama*, medium speed. Cf. *Drutam.*
Lit.: no. 261.

Drutam (*Durut*) (South India). "Quick." Durational note value. If the *laghu* is assumed to represent the metrical unit of one quarter note, the *drutam* will represent the duration of an eighth. (All durational note values of South India can be observed under the heading of *Anudrutam.*) Cf. *Akshara.*
Lit.: no. 136.

Druta Vardhanam (South India). See *Dhruti Vardhani.*

Druti (South India). *Janya rāga* of the 65th *mēḷa* (*Mechakalyāṇī*).
Tone material:

C D E G F♯ A B G A G c
c B A G F♯ D E F♯ E C

Lit.: no. 139.

Druti gati (India). See *Gati.*

Druva Kīrṇavam (South India). *Janya rāga* of the 43rd *mēḷa* (*Gavāmbōdhi*).
Tone material:

C D♭ F♯ G B♭♭ A♭ B♭♭ c
c B♭♭ A♭ G F♯ E♭ D♭ E♭ C

Lit.: no. 139.

Dsanādsel (*Tsanātsel*) (Ethiopia). A sistrum made of iron, occasionally also of precious metal. It is used in church service. The *dsanadsel* has the shape of a horseshoe, the two arms of which are linked by two metal rods on which hang several rings. The instrument is also called *isnasin.* Cf. *Seshet* (Egypt); *Sekhem.*
Lit.: no. 102.

Dsanasin (*Tsanasin*) (Ethiopia). See *Dsanādsel.*

Dsīr (Afghanistan). See *Zir.*

Du (India). See *Di.*

Du (Burma). Gong.

Dū ahank (Turkey). Double flute. Also called *nāy.*

Dub (Ancient South Mesopotamia). Ancient drum, either a frame drum or an hourglass-shaped instrument of the 3rd millenium B.C. Cf. *Tibbū*; *Timbutu.*
Lit.: no. 257.

Dūbeiti (Iran). Folksong.

Düblik (Turkey). Tambourin with little metal discs rattling in rectangular slits cut into the frame.
Lit.: no. 255.

Düdek (Turkey). See *Düdük.*

Dudi (South India). See *Edaka* (small drum of Coorg).

Dudu (Java). The extreme outer edge of a gong adjoining the *rechep.*
Lit.: no. 163.

Duduga (Republic of Upper Volta). Fiddle with one string.
Lit.: no. 50.

Düdük (*Düdek*) (Turkey). Beak flute with 6-8 finger holes. The term is also applied to other flute types.
Lit.: no. 255.

Duduk wuluh (*Megatruh*) (Java). One of the rhythmic patterns of *Tembang machapat.* See *Machapat.*

Dudunga (East India; Orissa). Cf. *Toila.*

Duff (*Daf*; *Deff*; *Tof*) (Middle East). General term for a flat frame drum with two skins. The frame can be square, octagonal, or circular.
Lit.: no. 81.

Dugā (*Du-gāh*; *Dukāh*) (Arabia). Tone name of the 5th main note. *Dugā* (in Persian) means the "second note" because *rast* (the 4th note) was and is often considered to be the first. (All tone names are listed under the heading of *Jagā* [*Yagā*].)
Lit.: no. 64.

Du-gāh (Arabia). See *Dugā.*

Du-gāh (Middle East). *Maqām.*
Tone material:

D $\overset{+}{E}\flat$ F $\overset{+}{G}\flat$ A $\overset{+}{B}\flat$ c $\overset{+}{d}\flat$ $\overset{+}{e}\flat$ f g a $\overset{+}{b}\flat$

Lit.: no. 64.

Dugan (*Dagan*; *Dugun*) (India). The closing section of many Indian art songs often is in a different *tāla* than that of the preceding melody. Cf. *Aḍ.*
Lit.: no. 136.

Dugduga (South India). Beggars' tambourine with a flat clay corpus and one skin with a friction stick. Another term for this instrument is *gubgubi*.
Lit.: nos. 17, 255.

Duggi (India). Drum.

Dugun (India). See *Dugan*.

Dügün (Turkey). Festive song (sung at weddings and circumcisions).

Duhūl (Persia). The equivalent of the Turkish *dāwūl*. Cf. *Dehōl*.
Lit.: nos. 171, 255.

Dukāh (Arabia). See *Dugā*.

Dukhūl al-btāyhī (Tunisia). Cf. *Al btāhyī*.

Dukhūl al-draj (Tunisia). Cf. *Al draj*.

Du-ko (Annam; Vietnam). See *Cai-nhi*.

Dukrrah (*Dukrah*) (Afghanistan). Kettledrum.
Lit.: no. 255.

Duku (Former French Equatorial Africa—Mandjia). Slit-drum.
Lit.: no. 21.

Dukulu (Congo—Dikongo). Small cylindrical drum.
Lit.: no. 280.

Düm (Turkey). Cf. *Uṣūl*.

Duma (Nigeria). See *Dunda*.

Duma(ṅ) (India). *Mādala* with a body of a truncated cone made of gray clay. Cf. *Mārdalā*.
Lit.: no. 254.

Dumba (Congo—Balese). Musical bow.
Lit.: no. 176.

Dumbak (Iraq). Also called *dumbash*. See *Durbakki*.

Dumbelek (Turkey). A pair of small kettle-drums. Cf. *Deblek*.
Lit.: no. 229.

Dumbing (New Guinea). A bamboo jew's harp.
Lit.: no. 255.

Dumbra (Afghanistan). Cf. *Dombra*.

Dumburak (Tadzhikstan). Cf. *Chermek* (Kirgizstan).

Dumilbaz (Kurdistan). Drum.
Lit.: no. 255.

Dumo (Congo—Mangbetu). Bow lute.
Lit.: nos. 21, 33.

Dumri (Southeast India; Bastar Muria Gond Tribe). Board zither with a gourd resonator.
Lit.: no. 59.

Dumtek (Afghanistan). Kettledrum.
Lit.: no. 157.

Dumūm (Islamic North Africa; Near East). A drum stroke that produces a dull and heavy sound, performed by striking the center of the drum head.
Lit.: no. 76.

Duṇ (India). See *Di*.

Dūnāy (*Kūshnāy*) (Persia). Double clarinet (double *nāy*). Cf. *Nāy*.
Lit.: no. 76.

Dunbāl (Persia). Cf. *Denbāl*.

Dunbalāk (Persia). Ancient small cylindrical drum. According to Lit. no. 76, a small kettle-drum. Cf. *Dünbelek*.
Lit.: no. 76.

Dunbaq (Persia). Old goblet drum.
Lit.: no. 77.

Dünbelek (Turkey). Tambourine; also kettle-drum. Cf. *Deblek*.
Lit.: no. 255.

Dunda (*Duma*) (Nigeria—Sokoto Province). Flute.
Lit.: no. 168.

Dunde (*Sosanru*; *Tutalo*) (Celebes). Stick zither with one string.
Lit.: no. 254.

Dundo (Africa; Swahili). The sound of beating a drum.

Dundu (West Africa; Mali; Guinea; Ivory Coast; Senegal). Drum. Cf. *Bia*; *Okworo*.
Lit.: no. 26.

Dundubhi (Vedic India). Sanskrit term for war drum, a large kettledrum beaten with two curved sticks. A later name of this drum (used in pairs in Iran, North and Central India) is *nagara* (*naqqara*), usually with a clay, less often with a copper corpus. In South India the term *dolla* represents the same drum.
Lit.: no. 250.

Dundubhipriya (South India). *Janya rāga* of the 48th *mēḷa* (*Divyamaṇī*).
Tone material:
C D♭ E♭ F♯ G A♯ B c
c B G F♯ E♭ D♭ C
Lit.: no. 139.

Dundufa (Sudan—Hausa). Cylindrical drum of the butchers and fish vendors.
Lit.: no. 95.

Dundum pata (Southeast India—Muria Gond Tribe). *Gotul* song of instructive character.
Lit.: no. 142.

Dundun (Nigeria—Yoruba). An hourglass-shaped tunable drum with two heads. Also an ensemble of *dundun* drums. It consists of *iya'lu*, "mother drum" or "talking drum," imitating the tonal inflections of spoken Yoruba, as the leading instrument. The other drums of the ensemble are called *omele* (*emele*) implying "supporting drum" or "following drum." Other terms referring to drums of the *dundun* ensemble are: *abaran*, *adesan*, *atele*, *gudugudu*, *isaju*, *isan'mele*, *karan*, *konkole*, *kerikeri*, *oriki*.
Lit.: nos. 215, 293.

Ḍunḍung (Java; Jogya). Term for a drum stroke performed with closed index, middle, and ring fingers in the center of the large drumhead. The sound produced is called *dung*.
Lit.: no. 163.

Dundusvana (Ancient India). One of the many Sanskrit terms for kettledrum.
Lit.: no. 254.

Dung (Tibet). General term for horn or trumpet. Cf. *T'ung*.
Lit.: no. 255.

Ḍung (Java; Sumatra). *Ḍung* or *genḍung* are terms for a drum stroke performed with three straight fingers on the center of the large drum head while the heel of the hand rests on the skin. See *Ḍunḍung*.
Lit.: no. 163.

Dung (Bali). Tone syllable; the 4th tone of *saih* 5, the 5th note of *saih* 7 of the *gambang* system. Cf. *Ding*, where all tone syllables are listed.
Lit.: no. 197.

Dung-che (*P'ab-che*) (Tibet). To strike (play) the cymbals.

Dung-chen (Tibet). "Great *dung.*" Long straight copper horns, each consisting of three sections. A pair of these horns is used in religious ceremonies. See *Rag-dung*. Cf. *Dung-dkar*.
Lit.: nos. 143, 255.

Dung-dkar (*Dung*) (Tibet). "White tube." A conch horn of Indian origin. It is used in various sizes. The term applies also to the bell of the great horn (*rag-dung*).

Dungga wo'o (West Sumba Isl.). Bamboo tube zither.
Lit.: no. 156.

Dungu (Congo – Basakata; Bakongo). Drum.
Lit.: no. 26.

Dunmang (Burma). Term for wind instrument.
Lit.: no. 255.

Dunsi-koni (West Africa; Upper Guinea). Lute. Cf. *Konimesin.*
Lit.: no. 33.

Du-raka (Burma). Tone name. See *Chauk-pauk auk-pyan* (*Thon-pauk*).

Durbakki (Arabia). Drum. Its Egyptian name is *derabucca*; the Iraqi name is *dumbak* or *dumbash.*
Lit.: no. 65.

Durban (Somaliland). Drum.
Lit.: no. 98.

Durbatudu (East India – Kanda). Short brass horn.

Durdha khyāyam (South India). *Janya rāga* of the 28th *mēḷa* (*Harikāmbhōji*).
Tone material:
C D F G A c
c B♭ G F D E F D C
Lit.: no. 139.

Durga (North India). *Rāga* ascribed to the *Bilaval thāta.*
Tone material:
C D F G A c
c A G F D C; *Vādis*: F, C
Lit.: no. 138.

Durga (North India). *Rāga* ascribed to the *Khamaj thāta.*
Tone material:
C E F A B c
c B♭ A F E C
Lit.: no. 138.

Duri (North Nias). Jew's harp with one tongue. Cf. *Rinding.*
Lit.: no. 255.

Durita Nivāriṇī (South India). *Janya rāga* of the 28th *mēḷa* (*Harikāmbhōji*).
Tone material:
C E D E F G F A c
c B♭ A G F E D E C
Lit.: no. 139.

Durma (Afghanistan). Shepherd's reed pipe. Instead of *durma* the term occasionally becomes *darma.*
Lit.: no. 255.

Durma (Java). One of the poetic meters of *tembang machapat*, usually occurring in battle songs. Cf. *Machapat.*
Lit.: no. 163.

Durraij (Arabia). Small, vase-shaped, single-headed drum.
Lit.: no. 76.

Duru (Nigeria – Yoruba). Lute with two strings of twisted goatskin. The corpus is half a calabash covered with skin. The strings are plucked with a plectrum.
Lit.: no. 293.

Ḍurūb (Old Arabia; Egypt). Rhythmic mode.
Lit.: no. 34.

Durun (Dahomey). Lute with a corpus made of half a coconut covered with snakeskin.
Lit.: no. 255.

Durut (South India). See *Drutam.*

Dūrvāhi (South India). *Janya rāga* of the 29th *mēḷa* (*Dhīraśaṅkarābharaṇam*).
Tone material:
C D F G A c
c B G A G F E D C
Lit.: no. 139.

Dusir (Southeast India; Gond Tribe; Abujhmar Mts.). Fiddle with two strings tuned a fourth apart. Each string is made of a bundle of horsehair.
Lit.: no. 135.

Dūtār (Persia; Turkestan; Afghanistan). Lute with a long neck and 15-16 movable frets. It has two strings tuned a minor third apart. The strings are played with a plectrum.
Lit.: no. 276.

Duteble (*Dutepil*) (Iran; Kudistan). Kettledrum played on horseback.

Dutiya bhairav (North India). An obscure *rāga* ascribed to the *Bhairav thāta*.
Tone material:
C E F G A♭ B c
c B A♭ G F E (F C) D♭ C
Lit.: no. 138.

Duu-dalga (Mongolia). Shaman songs of magic character.
Lit.: no. 24.

Duwabelas (Indonesia; Amboin). *Bonang* with 12 kettles. Also called *Gong duwabelas.*
Lit.: no. 163.

Duzele (Iran). Double clarinet with six finger holes on both pipes.

Dvaita Chintāmaṇi (*Dvaita Cintāmani*) (South India). *Janya rāga* of the 28th *mēḷa* (*Harikāmbhōji*).
Tone material:
C E F A B♭ c
c B♭ G A F E D C
Lit.: no. 139.

Dvaitānandi (South India). *Janya rāga* of the 28th *mēḷa* (*Harikāmbhōji*).
Tone material:
C D E F G c
c B♭ A B♭ G F D C
Lit.: no. 139.

Dvaita Paripūrṇi (South India). *Janya rāga* of the 28th *mēḷa* (*Harikāmbhōji*).
Tone material:
C D E F G A B♭
A G F D F E C
Lit.: no. 139.

Dvandvōtpala (South India). *Janya rāga* of the 28th *mēḷa* (*Harikāmbhōji*).
Tone material:
C E F G B♭ c
c B♭ G A G F E D C
Lit.: no. 139.

Dvayānūgam (South India). Described in Lit. no. 261 as a musical instrument. Cf. *Ubhayānugam.*

Dvigandhar (North India). "Two *gandhar.*" A *rāga* in which two *ga* (E and E♭) are used. See *Devgandhar.*

Dvijāvanti (South India). *Janya rāga* of the 28th *mēḷa* (*Harikāmbhōji*).
Tone material:
C D F E F G A c (C D E F G A B♭ c)
c B♭ A G F E D E C
Lit.: no. 139.

Dvimukhapriya (South India). *Janya rāga* of the 65th *mēḷa* (*Mechakalyāṇi*).
Tone material:
C E D F♯ G B c
c B A F♯ E D C
Lit.: no. 139.

Dvipavati (South India). *Janya rāga* of the 61st *mēḷa* (*Kāntāmaṇi*).
Tone material:
C D F♯ G A♭ B♭♭ c
c B♭♭ A♭ G F♯ D C
Lit.: no. 139.

Dviradagāmiṇi (South India). *Janya rāga* of the 66th *mēḷa* (*Chitrāmbarī*).
Tone material:
C D F♯ G A♯ B c
c B A♯ G F♯ D C
Lit.: no. 139.

Dvitāra (India). "Two strings." An *ektāra* (*yaktāra*) with two strings.
Lit.: no. 254.

Dvitīya (Vedic India). The second highest note of Vedic chant, notated as "2." For further information see Lit. no. 141.

Dvitīya pañchamam (South India). *Janya rāga* of the 69th *mēḷa* (*Dhātuvardhaṇī*).
Tone material:

C D♯ E F♯ G B G c
c B A♭ G F♯ D♯ E F♯ D♯ C

This scale is identical with that of *rāga Dhātu Pañchamam* (69th *mēḷa*).
Lit.: no. 139.

Dwan-dung (Tibet). Narrow copper trumpet.
Lit.: no. 255.

Dyanga (Congo and North Rhodesia—Baholoholo). Rattle made of a large calabash.
Lit.: no. 33.

Dyedye (Congo; North Rhodesia). Stick zither. Cf. *Seze.*
Lit.: no. 21.

Dyeli (Mali). Musician.

Dyuti Mālini (South India). *Janya rāga* of the 20th *mēḷa* (*Naṭabhairavī*).
Tone material:

C E♭ D E♭ F G B♭ A♭ B♭ c
c B♭ A♭ B♭ G F D C

Lit.: no. 139.

Dzedze (Congo). Swahili for *Seze.*
Lit.: no. 255.

Dzendze (Congo). Synonym term for *dzedze, nzeze, seze, zeze* (zither).
Lit.: no. 176.

Dzhang-ko (Korea). Cf. *Chang-ko.*

Dzhio (South Africa—Venda). A short vertical flute with conical bore, made of bone or wood. It produces two notes, usually a minor third apart.
Lit.: no. 151.

Dzilidzap (East Turkestan). Cf. *Sochiba.*

E

E (Japan). Term used in *koto* playing. Pressure on a string is applied below the bridge after the string has been struck (the result being a raised pitch). The pressure is maintained until the next note is played.
Lit.: no. 225.

Ebeg (West Central Java). Cf. *Reyog.*

Ebemm (Arabia). See *Bam.*

Ebero (North Australia). Bull roarer.
Lit.: no. 255.

Ebeje (Nigeria—Igbo). Metal rattle.

Ebiba (Uganda). Drum.
Lit.: no. 255.

Ebubu (Mesopotamia). See *Imbubu.*

Ebumi (Congo). Globular flute with two finger holes. Cf. *Kigwara*; *Ebundi.*
Lit.: no. 190.

Eburr (Uganda—Karamojong). Drum.

Ebwâq (Arabia). Trumpets.

Ecoc (Nilotic Sudan; Uganda—Lango). Conical end-blown flute made of animal horn.
Lit.: nos. 190, 302.

Eḍaka (India). A large *damaru.* One skin is beaten with a stick, the other with the hand.
Lit.: no. 255.

Eddenge (Uganda; Angola—Ganda). Vertical flute with one finger hole.
Lit.: no. 302.

Eddik le bodom (Micronesia; Truk). Nose flute.
Lit.: no. 313.

Edibu (*Dibu*) (Congo). Bell; jingle.
Lit.: no. 255.

Ediokeko (South Sumatra; Enggano Isl.). Metal jew's harp.
Lit.: no. 254.

Edir meṭṭu (South India). Movable bridge placed on a *tanbura* neck. The moving of the bridge enables the player to change the tuning without employing the pegs.
Lit.: no. 261.

Edjwa (Congo—Basangele). A conical drum with one head.
Lit.: no. 26.

Edo-bayashi (Japan). Music performed at a folk festival of Tokyo (formerly Edo). Cf. *Hayashi.*
Lit.: no. 215.

Edona (Uganda—Karamojong). Drum.

Edungu (Kenya—Samia). Lyre with eight strings.
Lit.: no. 302.

Eḍuppu (South India; Tamil). Starting point of a melody and its *āvārta.* The following types are distinguished: *sama eḍuppu*, when melody and *āvārta* begin simultaneously; *atīta eḍuppu*, when the melody begins earlier than the first beat of the *āvārta* (upbeat); *anagata eḍuppu*, when the *āvārta* starts first and the melody follows later. The term *eḍuppu* (*karana*) is also applied to the *ālāp.*
Lit.: no. 261.

Efam (Gabon Republic). A small bit of horn is placed into one nose-hole in order to create a particularly nasal sound to the singer's voice. Cf. *Abeng.*
Lit.: no. 255.

Eggwara (Uganda—Ganda; Lango). A conically-shaped end-blown gourd-trumpet. Occasionally it is also side-blown. *Kawundi* indicates the end-blown type, and *ekkondere* or *kondere* the side-blown forms.
Lit.: no. 302.

Ego (Central Flores). Wooden jew's harp. The instrument has numerous names, among them are: in Paluwe Island it is called *weda*; in Nage (Boawae) Mbai, *weto, kobeng*; in Ngada, *robe*; Central Timor, *knobe-oh*; Celebes, *rinda*; Sumba, *ngguinggi*; Manggaray (Flores), *nentu*; Rajong, *kombing.* Cf. *Genggo.*
Lit.: no. 166.

Egoboli (Uganda). Musical bow.
Lit.: no. 302.

Ei (Japan). Prefix to the note names *shō* and *u* indicating the *ritsu* character of the mode. *Ei-* has the same function as the sharp of western music: *ei-shō* is a semitone higher than *shō*, and *ei-u* is a semitone higher than *u.* Cf. *Ritsu.*

Ei (Japan). A musical (vocal) interpolation between the sections *ha* and *kyū* in *gagaku* music.

Ejin (West Africa; Gabon). Cf. *Njin.*

Eka (South India). Cf. *Tāla.*

Ēkāghrauṇi (*Ēkāgraṇi*) (South India). *Janya rāga* of the 28th *mēḷa* (*Harikāmbhōji*).
Tone material:

C D F G A B♭ c
c B♭ A B♭ G F E F D C

Lit.: no. 139.

Ēkāgraṇi (South India). See *Ēkāgrauṇi.*

Ēkākṣari (South India). See *Ēkākshari.*

Ēkākshari (*Ēkākṣari*) (South India). *Janya rāga* of the 15th *mēḷa* (*Māyāmāḷavagauḷa*).
Tone material:

C D♭ E F G A♭ B c
c B G F D♭ E F C

Lit.: no. 139.

Ēkalīla (South India). *Janya rāga* of the 15th *mēḷa* (*Māyāmāḷavagauḷa*).
Tone material:

C D♭ E D♭ F G B A♭ B G A♭ c
c A♭ G F E D♭ C

Lit.: no. 139.

Ēkaṇḍa Gōṭuvādyam (South India). A *gōṭuvādyam* (*vīṇā* type) made of one single block of wood. There exists also an *ēkāṇḍaṇḍi gōṭuvādyam.* It is made of one wooden block, but its head piece is made of a separate piece of wood.

Ēkāṇḍaṇḍi Gōṭuvādyam (South India). See *Ēkāṇḍa Gōṭuvādyam.*

Ēkāṇḍa Vīṇā (South India). Cf. *Ēkāṇḍa Gōṭuvādyam.*

Ēkānika (South India). *Janya rāga* of the 15th *mēḷa* (*Māyāmāḷavagauḷa*).
Tone material:
C F E F G A♭ B c
c B G F E D♭ C
Lit.: no. 139.

Ēkānta Vādyam (South India). *Ēkānta* (Sanskrit, "lonely place"). A string instrument resembling a *vīṇā*. It has a gentle, pleasing tone. Cf. *Ēkāṇḍa Gōṭuvādyam.*
Lit.: no. 261.

Ekara (Bali). Name for a notational symbol.
Lit.: no. 197.

Eka rāga mēḷa vīṇā (South India). A *vīṇā* with movable frets which can be set for the performance for any *rāga*. Cf. *Sarva rāga mēḷa vīṇā* (*Akhila rāga mēḷa vīṇā*).
Lit.: no. 261.

Ēkaśruṅgi (South India). *Janya rāga* of the 39th *mēḷa* (*Jhālavarāḷi*).
Tone material:
C D♭ E♭♭ F♯ E♭♭ D♭ G B A♭ B G A♭ G c
c B A♭ G F♯ E♭♭ D♭ C
Lit.: no. 139.

Eka tāla (South India). See *Tāla.*

Ēkatantri (South India). See *Ekkam.*

Ēkātantrikā (Ancient India). See *Ghoṣaka.*

Ēkatāra (India). Cf. *Ektār.*

Ekegogo (West Kenya—Kuria). Spike lute with one wire string.
Lit.: no. 299.

Ekende (Congo—Bangala). A *sansa* with nine tongues. Cf. *A-konde.*
Lit.: nos. 33, 255.

Ekere (Nigeria—Igbo). Slit-drum.

Ekereiko (Nigeria—Igbo). Xylophone.

Ekidi (Nilotic Sudan—Bari). Board zither.
Lit.: no. 176.

Ekidongo (Uganda—Nyoro). Arched harp with eight strings. Also called *Ekidongoli.*
Lit.: no. 302.

Ekidongoli (Uganda). Cf. *Ekidongo.*

Ekihako (Uganda). See *Kinanga.*

Ekinimba (Uganda—Kiga). Flute with two finger holes.
Lit.: no. 302.

Ekirei (Japan). Rattle.
Lit.: no. 225.

Ekiro (Japan). A set of three doughnut-shaped sleigh bells lined on a hook. The bells are used in *kabuki* and are intended to create a rustic atmosphere.
Lit.: no. 185.

Ekitulenge (Uganda; Congo). Musical bow.
Lit.: no. 302.

Ekkālam (South India). Tamil term for a straight copper or brass trumpet consisting of four parts fitted together like the sections of a telescope. The instrument was (is) used in religious processions and other ceremonies. Cf. *Rāṇaśṛṅga*; *Kālam.*
Lit.: no. 261.

Ekkam (*Ēkatantri*) (South India). Tamil term for a one stringed *vīṇā* with a coconut shell as resonator.
Lit.: no. 261.

Ekkondere (*Kondere*) (Uganda). Side-blown gourd trumpet. Cf. *Eggwara*; *Makondere.*
Lit.: no. 302.

Ekku jāru (South India). A musical ornament; an ascending glide.
Lit.: no. 261.

Ekoro (Senegal; Gambia). Lute with 18 strings. Cf. *Kasso.*
Lit.: no. 255.

Ektāl (India). See *Tāla.*

Ektār(a) (*Ekatāra*) (India). A beggar's lute with one wire string. Its corpus is a gourd and a bamboo stick serves as neck.
Lit.: no. 261.

Ekuara (French Congo). Little percussion sticks beaten against each other by dancers.
Lit.: no. 255.

Ekulu (Zaire — Bantu). Jingles; ankle and leg bells of the chiefs.
Lit.: no. 29.

Ekulu (Congo — Batetela). Drum.
Lit.: no. 26.

Ekutu (Nigeria — Yoruba). Side-blown antelope horn.
Lit.: no. 280.

Ekwe (Nigeria — Igbo). Term for drum, particularly slit-drum, with single or double slit.

Ēlaṅka Manōharī (South India). *Janya rāga* of the 37th *mēḷa* (*Sālaga*).
Tone material:
C D♭ E♭♭ F♯ G B♭♭ c
c B♭♭ G F♯ E♭♭ D♭ C
Lit.: no. 139.

Ēlaprabhāvam (South India). *Janya rāga* of the 29th *mēḷa* (*Dhīraśaṅkarābharaṇam*).
Tone material:
C D E F G A B A c
c B A G F D E D C
Lit.: no. 139.

Eldolem (Micronesia). Mourning chant.

Eleke (Congo; Zaire). Synonym for *sansa.*
Lit.: no. 255.

Elem (West Central Africa — Fan). Percussive music bow. Its string is held between the teeth of the player.
Lit.: nos. 21, 255.

Elembe (Congo — Ababua; Basoko). Drum. Cf. *Ndima*; *Bongwabi.*
Lit.: no. 26.

Elet (West Java). Flute with 4-6 holes.
Lit.: no. 255.

Elgasba (Arabia). Flute with nine finger holes, made of willow mood.
Lit.: no. 96.

Elgaita (Sudan — Hausa). See *Algaita.*

Elibo (West Africa; Fernando Po — Bubi). Wooden clapper.
Lit.: no. 255.

Elingingile (Uganda; Kenya — Ndo). Musical bow.
Lit.: no. 176.

Ellag (Ancient Mesopotamia; Sumer). Wooden horn. Also called *mekku-pukku.*
Lit.: no. 87.

Elo (Nigeria). Bell.

Elonga (West Africa; Togo — Akasele). Big drum.
Lit.: no. 255.

El-zehr (Arabia). See *Ṭabla el-darausha.*

Ema (Nigeria—Edo). Drum.
Lit.: no. 95.

Embaire (Uganda). Xylophone with 16 keys.
Lit.: no. 302.

Embat (Java). "To stretch." The term indicates slight deviations in the scales used in *laras sundari* and *laras larasati*. Cf. *Laras nyendari*.
Lit.: no. 163.

Embeg (Java). See *Kuda kepang*.

Embilitā (Ethiopia). See *Embiltā*.

Embiltā (Ethiopia). Bamboo or metal beak flute of the Galla. It has seven finger holes in two rows (three and four). There are several other flutes with the same name; they have two, three, and five finger holes.
Lit.: nos. 102, 218.

Embubu (Sumeria). Popular term for female flute players and their double flutes.
Lit.: no. 282.

Embuchi (Congo). Ivory horn with the blow hole near the side of the pointed end.
Lit.: nos. 184, 280.

Emele (*Omẹle*) (Nigeria). Cf. *Dundun*.

Emidiri (Uganda—Itesco). A couple of cylindrical drums.
Lit.: no. 29.

Empete (Congo). Drum with one head, widely known and used by numerous tribes (Ekota, Bakutu, Bosaka, Ekota, Mbole, etc.). Cf. *Bondundu*.
Lit.: no. 26.

Empet-empetan (West Java). A rice stalk shawm generally with a single reed, less often with double reeds. Other terms for this instrument are *dami* or *jarami* and *ole-olean* when it has a large cone-shaped bell made of coconut leaf.
Lit.: no. 163.

Empila (Central Africa—Baloi). Cylindrical drum.
Lit.: no. 26.

Emunak rua (Flores). Melody of a women's dance. Cf. *Roja*.
Lit.: no. 166.

Enanga (Uganda; Tanganyika; Congo). Term for various stringed instruments; arched harp with eight strings; musical bow; trough zither; general term for the European pianoforte and other imported string instruments.
Lit.: no. 302.

Endara (Congo—Azande). See *Kweningba*.

Endas (Java). See *Penchu*.

Endere (Uganda—Ganda). Reed or bamboo flute with four finger holes. The *endere*, also called *nyamulere*, is played in groups of five differently sized instruments.
Lit.: no. 302.

Endiga (Uganda—Ruli; Nyala). Xylophone with 16 slabs.
Lit.: no. 302.

Endingidi (Uganda). Spike fiddle with one string. Also *endingiri*. Cf. *Siilili* of the Gisii (Kenya).
Lit.: nos. 218, 302.

Endon-akum (Former French Congo). See *Mban-akum*.

Endor (Borneo). See *Krotong*.

Endumba (Congo; Uganda). Drum. Also called *libumba*.

Eneng-eneng (*Klenang*) (Java). The highest sounding row of *bonang* kettles.
Lit.: no. 163.

Engalabi (Uganda—Ganda). Cylindrical drum with a single head.
Lit.: no. 302.

Engboma (Congo – Budja). Cylindrical drum.
Lit.: no. 26.

Engei (Japan). See *Engeki.*

Engeki (Japan). Drama; theater; entertainment. In the 19th century the term was changed to *Engei.*

Engis (Cameroon). Rattle.

Engkerūrai (*Engkruri*) (Borneo – Sea Dayak). A mouth organ with free reed (similar to the Chinese *sheng*). It has a calabash wind chest and 6-8 bamboo pipes placed in circular form. Cf. *Kelurai*; *Khaen.*
Lit.: nos. 254-55.

Engket-engket (West Java). See *Rengkong.*

Engklok (Sunda District). (1) See *Indung.* (2) See *Byang.*

Engkok (Java). See *Engkuk.*

Engkruri (*Engkerūrai*) (Borneo – Dayak). A mouth organ (*sheng* type) with 6-8 pipes. Cf. *Keluri*; *Him.*
Lit.: no. 255.

Engkuk (*Kemong*) (Java). A pair of small, verti-cally suspended gongs used only in the *gamelan slendro. Engkuk* is tuned to *barang* and *kemong* to *nem.* Cf. *Kempyang*; *Kempyang slendro.*
Lit.: no. 163.

"English" (Ghana). See *Agbadza.*

Engoma (Central and South Africa). Cf. *Ngoma.*

Engsulu (Borneo – Dayak). See *Rudieng sulu.*

Ening (Java). See *Rebāb* (of Java).

Enkerbap (Borneo – Sea Dayak). Spike fiddle with two or three strings.
Lit.: no. 255.

Enkyoku (Japan). The opening of the old secular banquet music (and dance), the forerunner of *nagauta.* A second name for this banquet music was *enzui* ("drunken pools").
Lit.: no. 185.

Ennen (Japan). Old Buddhist temple and street theatricals of light character. *Ennen* appears also in *dengaku* and *sarugaku* and, in highly stylized form, in the *noh* drama.
Lit.: no. 185.

Enogh (Republic of Cameroon – Fan). Big iron bell.

Enoma (*Noma*) (Uganda). Drum.
Lit.: no. 255.

Ensegu (Uganda – Ganda). Rattle. Cf. *Akayamba*; *Musesegeto.*
Lit.: no. 302.

Enserunai (Borneo). See *Garadap.*

Ensuling (Java). See *Suling.*

Eñsulu (Borneo – Sea Dayak). Jew's harp made of copper.
Lit.: no. 254.

Entaala (Uganda – Ganda; Gwere). Xylophone with 12 slabs. Cf. *Amadinda.*
Lit.: no. 302.

Entara (Uganda). Xylophone.
Lit.: no. 302.

Entenga (Uganda – Baganda). Drum chime consisting of 12-15 drums. When performing melodies, four drummers are required.
Lit.: nos. 155, 218.

Entogal (Borneo). See *Gulong-gulong.*

Entoni (West Kenya – Kuria). Musical bow; at the present time almost obsolete.
Lit.: no. 299.

Entuning (West Borneo). Cf. *Pagan(g)*; *Satong*.
Lit.: no. 156.

Enzebe (Uganda; Congo). Percussion beam that is used in the accompaniment of the *kinanga*.
Lit.: no. 302.

Enzenze (Uganda). Stick zither with two or three strings and three frets. Cf. *Njenjo*; *Nzenze*; *Sese*; *Zenze*.
Lit.: no. 302.

Enzomba (Tanzania). Animal horn used for signalling. Cf. *Omwomba*.

Enzoṅga (Uganda; Congo — Fan). Small iron bells that Fan musicians attach to their wrists and ankles.
Lit.: no. 255.

Enzui (Japan). See *Enkyoku*.

Eqligh (Turkey). Small wooden castanet.
Lit.: no. 255.

Ērangōṭparai (South India). Simple drum (with one or two heads) used by farmers to recall cattle from grazing.

E'rāqye (Arabia). Shawm mostly used in Egypt. Its cylindrical tube has nine finger holes, seven in front and two at the back. The name shows that the instrument had its origin in Iraq.
Lit.: no. 255.

Erazhshtakan gortsi (Armenia). Term for musical instrument.

Erbābi (*Erbeb*) (Arabia; Indonesia; Sula Bese; Buru Isl.). Term for *rebāb*.
Lit.: no. 255.

Erbeb (Arabia). See *Erbābi*.

Ereg-ereg (Central Java). Bull roarer; whizzing low. See *(O)-wer-(o)-wer*.
Lit.: no. 163.

Ergion (Armenia). Term for organ.

Ergionaphol (Armenia). Term for organ pipe.

Erh-hsien (China — M 2663.3). A very popular spike fiddle with a wooden body. If the corpus is a cylindrical bamboo section, the instrument is called *hu-hu* (M 2155, M 2155). If the corpus is made of half a coconut shell, its name can be *t'i-ch'in*. The corpus can also have a hexagonal outline. In the south the instrument is called *yi-yin*. Its cylindrical bamboo body is open at the back. The hairs of the bow are strung between the two strings. Cf. *Hu-ch'in*; *Ko-ch'in*.
Lit.: no. 255.

Erh-hu (China — M 1751; M 2167). A fiddle with two silken strings and a hexagonal body covered with snakeskin. The strings are tuned a fifth apart, and the hair of the bow is strung between the two strings. The neck of the *erh-hu* is longer than that of the *erh-hsien*. At the present time the *erh-hu* is often provided with steel strings and used as a virtuoso instrument. Cf. *Erh-hsien*.
Lit.: no. 255.

Erh-huang (China — M 1751; M 2297). (1) A classical operatic style of the 19th-century. Its solemn, tragic plots deal with the lives of middle-class people. The music is much less noisy than that of the *pang-tzu* style. (2) Characteristic rhythm in Chinese opera. The *erh-huang* is represented by four (or two) beats, with the first beat accented.
Lit.: no. 136.

Erh-huang hu-ch'in (China). See *Erh-hsien* (*Hu-hu*).
Lit.: no. 255.

Erh-ku-tzu (China). See *Erh-hu*.

Erh-shou (China). "The second hand." A musician in the Hong Kong theater who plays the *sona*, the flute, and, if required, the *san-hsien*. Cf. *Ku-shou*; *Shang-shou*; *San-shou*.
Lit.: no. 129.

Eṛṛa jāru (South India). See *Ekku jāru.*

Eṛṛappaṭṭu (South India). Simple song of laborers sung by two persons (parties) alternately.
Lit.: no. 261.

Eršemma (Mesopotamia; Sumer). The syllables *er* and *šem* mean lament (song) and flute or drum respectively. *Eršemma* probably indicated a song (melody) performed during processions.
Lit.: no. 94.

Eru (Nigeria). See *Ewo.*

Eruma (Congo; Uganda—Amba). End-blown flute without any finger holes. Cf. *Oseke.*
Lit.: no. 302.

'Erzbar (Arabia). Obscure *maqām*; allegedly a mixture of tones of the scales *rast* and *ḥigāz.*
Lit.: no. 121.

Esandju (Congo—Mongo). Bow lute.
Lit.: no. 176.

Esandhōli (South India). *Janya rāga* of the 46th *mēḷa (Śaḍvidhamārgiṇī).*
Tone material:
C D♭ F♯ G B♭ c
c B♭ A G F♯ E♭ F♯ D♭ C
Lit.: no. 139.

Esāri (South India). *Janya rāga* of the 13th *mēḷa* (*Gāyakapriya*).
Tone material:
C D♭ E F G A♭ c
c B♭♭ A♭ G F E D♭ C
Lit.: no. 139.

Esembe (Congo—Ababua). Drum. Cf. *Ndima*; *Nduma.*
Lit.: no. 26.

Eseni (Nigeria—Ijaw). A series of dances, each having its own song and being accompanied by percussion sticks and single-headed pot drums.
Lit.: no. 218.

Esfahan (*Āwāz*) (Persia). See *Dastgah.*

Eshirtu (Ancient Mesopotamia). Harp with 10 strings.
Lit.: no. 87.

Esikulu (Angola). Kettledrum. Two sizes are in use: the bigger one, called *nkonzo a mpanzu*, and the smaller, *mtuta.* These drums appear together with trumpets at festivities and funerals. Cf. *Sikulu.*
Lit.: no. 280.

Esimben (*Furaaka*) (South Senegal). (1) Harp-lute with four strings. (2) Playing the harp-lute. (3) A solo singer alternates in his performance with the chorus.
Lit.: no. 122.

Esino (Congo—Bayansi). Bamboo scrape stick. Cf. *Bisino.*
Lit.: no. 255.

E-šir (South Mesopotamia; Sumer). "House of song." Name of a temple where music was performed.

Esrāj (*Esrār*) (India). A fiddle with a wooden waisted body and a broad, long fingerboard. It has five play strings (two made of steel, three of brass) and 13-15 metal resonance strings. Attached to the fingerboard are 16 movable frets. The tuning of the play strings is variable, e.g., f′ c c g′ C.
Lit.: nos. 254-55.

Esrār (India). See *Esrāj.*

Esudsu (Japan). Bronze temple hand bell.
Lit.: no. 258.

E-tabule (Sierra Leone—Temne). See *Atbal.*

Etida (Uganda—Itesyo). "Mad," "furious." A dance believed to create magic and cure illness. The accompaniment is provided by one drummer who beats two drums with wooden sticks.
Lit.: no. 29.

Etimoika (Easter Isl.). Bone clappers.
Lit.: no. 84.

Etokar (Sahara; Sudan—Tuareg). Drumstick. Cf. *Gangatan.*
Lit.: no. 255.

E-tsuzumi (Japan). "The elder"—a shoulder drum in the conventional shape of an hourglass. Cf. *Ō-tsuzumi.*
Lit.: no. 225.

Et'tebel (Sahara; Sudan—Tuareg). Drum.
Lit.: no. 255.

Etumba (Congo—Basonge). Wooden goblet-shaped drum.
Lit.: no. 26.

Etutu (Lower Congo). Flute.
Lit.: no. 255.

Etwie (Ghana—Akan). "Leopard"; a friction drum. The powdered drumhead is rubbed with a stick. The sound created imitates the snarl of a leopard.
Lit.: nos. 218, 258.

Eu (*Ō*) (Korea). "The stopper"; "the wooden tiger." A percussion instrument of the Confucian temple. The wooden form of a crouching tiger is placed upon a flat wooden box. The back of the tiger has twenty-seven "teeth." At the end of an instrumental item the player strikes the tiger on its head with a split bamboo stick, and immediately follows the beat with the running of the bamboo stick three times across the twenty-seven teeth. See *Yü.*
Lit.: no. 179.

Evongi (Lower Congo). Ocarina.

Ewa (Eastern New Guinea—Roro). Popular dance song. It is accompanied by double-headed drums.

Ewiri (Nigeria). Drum. See *Kete* (2).

E'wiu (New Zealand). See *Poretu.*

Ewo (*Eru*) (Nigeria). Iron percussion plate.

Eyin-erin (Nigeria—Yoruba). Elephant tusk horn, blown at important ceremonies.

Ezan (Turkey). The chanted call to prayer executed by the muezzin five times during the day.
Lit.: no. 243.

Ezel (Ethiopia). One of three liturgical modes. Cf. *Gheez.*
Lit.: no. 102.

Ezele (Sahara; Sudan—Tuareg). Dancing and singing.

F

Fa'ali (*Fa'ali laiti*) (Samoa). Slit-drum. Cf. *Pulotu.*
Lit.: no. 255.

Fa'ataupati (Polynesia; Samoa). Men's dance.

Fabresoro (West Africa; Mali—Bambara). Flute.

Fa-ch'ü (China). Popular music favored by rulers of the T'ang period (A.D. 618-906).
Lit.: no. 55.

Faḍla (*Baqiya*) (Arabia). Music theoretical term indicating the *limma*, the Pythagorean semitone. Cf. *Infiṣāl.*

Fagu-fagu (Samoa). Cf. *Siva-ofe.*

Fa hao-t'ung (China). Funeral trumpet, a large *hao* (*hao-t'ung*).
Lit.: no. 255.

Fakara (Ethiopia). War dances and hunting songs.
Lit.: no. 102.

Fan (China—M 1771). Solmization syllable and notational symbol. Assuming that *ho*, the basic note of the *kung-ch'e-p'u*, is C, *fan* is B, standing a major seventh higher.
Lit.: no. 136.

Fan-ch'i (China). See *Chien-tzu.*

Fanfami (North Nigeria—Hausa). Wooden trumpet. Cf. *Pampame.*
Lit.: no. 250.

Fang-ho (China). Cf. *Chien-tzu.*

Fang-hsiang (China—M 1802; M 2559). An obscure set of 16 iron slabs hung in two rows in a wooden frame. Cf. *Pang-hyang* (Korea).
Lit.: nos. 209, 250.

Fang-ku (China—M 1802; M 3479). Popular drum, allegedly tuned to the pitch of the *huang-chung.* If the drum was large, its body was made of clay. If the body was small, it was made of wood.
Lit.: no. 209.

Fango-fango (Marquesas; Fiji Isl.). Nose flute made of a section of bamboo closed at both ends. It has two blowholes at each end and four finger holes in the middle. Cf. *Bitu-uvu.*
Lit.: no. 255.

Fanke (Sierra Leone – Temne). Drum with a wooden body and two skins.

Fan-pai (China – M 1774; M 4865). Synonym for the Korean *pomp'ae* and the Japanese *shōmyō.*

Fan-yin (China – M 1773; M 7418). Harmonics used in *ch'in* preludes. Cf. *I* (M 2960).
Lit.: no. 93.

Faraḥ faza (Middle East). *Maqām* derived from *Nawā* (obscure in Iran).
Tone material:
G A B♭ C D E♭ F G A B♭ c d e♭ f g
Lit.: no. 64.

Faraḥ kazā (Modern Egypt). *Maqām.*
Tone material:
G A B♭ C D E♭ F G
Lit.: no. 64.

Faraḥ-nāk (Modern Egypt; Arabia). "May it cheer you up." Sub-*maqām* of *Auj.*
Tone material:
+B♭ C D +E♭ F♯ G A +B♭ c
Lit.: nos. 64, 121.

Farai (Nigeria; Niger; Chad; Ghana – Hausa). Wooden trumpet. Cf. *Rok'on fada.*

Farara (Malagasy Republic). Tree bark trumpet.
Lit.: no. 251.

Farara hazu (Malagasy Republic). Slit-drum.
Lit.: no. 251.

Faras (Arabia). "Horse"; the bridge on a string instrument.

Faritia (Nias). Small gong. Cf. *Gong.*

Fasil (Turkey). Secular music in the form of a cycle performed by vocal and instrumental musicians. Generally there are seven sections:

1. *Peşrev*
2. *Kār*
3. *Beste*
4. *Ağirsemai*
5. *Şarki*
6. *Yürük semai*
7. *Saz semai*

Peşrev and *saz semai* are instrumental items. The *peşrev* functions as prelude and the *semai* as coda. Items 2-6 are songs. *Kār* has eight-line strophes, the *beste* often contains meaning-less syllables. *Ağirsemai* and *yürük semai* have *semai* rhythms, and *şarki,* freely structured, indicates an art song.
Lit.: no. 243.

Fawn (Northeast Thailand). Term for traditional dancing.
Lit.: no. 203.

Fei-ling (China). See *Ch'e-ling.*

Fei-po (China). The Soochow flying cymbals. They are made to clash when having been thrown in the air.
Lit.: no. 209.

Feko (Flores). Vertically-blown flute. This instrument is used both singly and in pairs, particularly in East Flores. As a pair held at an angle and played by a single person, one flute, called "the woman," has seven stops, and the other flute, called "the man," has five stops. Cf. *Nuren*; *Fekor.*
Lit.: no. 166.

Fekor (Flores). Bamboo flute with a variety of finger holes and various names. Cf. *Feko*; *Nuren*; *Sunding.*
Lit.: no. 166.

Feku (Timor). Small club-formed ocarina.
Lit.: nos. 162, 168.

Felak (Afghanistan – Badakshan). Term for song or instrumental piece.

Feli (Liberia – Kpelle). Goblet-shaped drum with one head, held leaning to the legs of the player. The instrument is beaten with the hand.
Lit.: no. 284.

Fellahi (Turkey). Lute with an octagonal wooden body, a straight neck, and four strings.
Lit.: no. 248.

Fen (China). Cf. *Ch'in.*

Feng-cheng (*Fung-cheng*) (China). Zither made of a bamboo bow.
Lit.: no. 255.

Feng-ch'in (China). Term for the imported organ or harmonium.

Feng-ch'in-shih (China). Term for organist.

Feng-huang-hsiao (*Tung-hsiao*) (China—M 1894,20; M 2619). Literally the term refers to the male phoenix (*feng*) and its female counterpart (*huang*). As an instrument the term denotes an ancient single bamboo tube that belongs to a group of vertical flute, a system that points the way to the later *p'ai-hsiao.*
Lit.: no. 137.

Feng-ling (China). Wind bells hanging from the corners of eaves of pagodas and houses. The clappers are prolonged with thin leather straps in order to allow the wind to shake the clappers.
Lit.: no. 255.

Feng-shu k'ung-hou (China). See *K'ung-hou.*

Fen-k'ai (China). One of the numerous *chien-tzu.*

Fere-igba (Nigeria—Yoruba). Simple transverse flute with one finger hole.
Lit.: no. 33.

Fidla (East Africa—Swahili). Fiddle.

Fijiri (Arabia). Songs sung at night accompanied by drums.

Fik (Kurdisthan). Shawm; flute.
Lit.: no. 255.

Filimbi (East Africa—Swahili). Flute.

Filjān sāz (Turkey). A set of bowls filled with water and beaten with a thin stick. Cf. *Jaltarang* (India).
Lit.: no. 81.

Fillagori (India). See *Muralī.*

Fit-fit (Kurdisthan). Pipe.
Lit.: no. 255.

Floit ajar (Moluccas; Amboina). Long flute made of two bamboo tubes. The narrower tube is stuck into the bigger one in such a manner that the instrument can be made shorter or longer in order to create different pitches.
Lit.: no. 255.

Flolo (Timor). Rattle.
Lit.: no. 162.

Fodrahi (Nias). See *Tamburu*; *Fondrahi.*

Foé (Central Timor). Signal flute with four or six stops. See *Bobi.*
Lit.: no. 162.

Foi doa (Flores; Ngada). *Doa*, "double." Double flute. The two flutes are served by a single wooden mouthpiece. Each of the two flutes has three stops, and both flutes are tuned in unison. Cf. *Woi doa.*
Lit.: no. 166.

Foi dogo (Flores; Nage). Triple flute. Each of the two tubes at both sides of the central flute has three finger holes. The central tube is slightly longer than the two outer ones and has no finger hole.
Lit.: no. 166.

Foi duri udi (Flores; Ngada). Cf. *Huhe.*

Foi kedi (Flores; Ngada). A double flute. The two tubes are placed at an angle and converge in the player's mouth. Cf. *Woi doa.*
Lit.: no. 166.

Foi mere (Flores; Ngada). Bass flute. The player blows into a small tube placed at the side of the larger tube. The instrument has six finger holes and produces the following sounds: *F G G♯ A B♭ B* C. In Nage the name of this instrument is *woi mere*.
Lit.: no. 166.

Fondrahi (*Fodrahi*) (South Nias). A narrow long ceremonial goblet drum beaten with the fingers and palm of the hand.
Lit.: no. 254.

Fontomfrom (Ghana – Ashanti). "Talking drum" (kettledrum) of various forms and sizes.
Lit.: no. 241.

Forimo (Somaliland – Somali; Galla). Wooden pipe.
Lit.: no. 255.

Forud (Iran). Cadence. Motion of the melody toward the basic note. Transition from an improvised section into the structured main mode of the *dastgāh*.
Lit.: no. 146.

Fou (China – M 1905). Open clay vessel used as percussion instrument. The Korean pronunciation of the Chinese character is *bu* or *pu*.
Lit.: no. 137.

Fowa (South Africa). Rattle believed to cure a sick person if the instrument is tied to the leg of the patient. Cf. *Mafowa*.
Lit.: nos. 149-51.

Fu (China). Stereotyped operatic role: the aggressive, energetic male type.

Fu (Japan; the Chinese character is M 5386). "Notation." Japan has several notational systems: *go-on-fu*, *kari-fu*, *co-ma-fu*, *boku-fu*, *bunka-fu*, and others.
Lit.: no. 185.

Fu-ch'in (China). A type of *cheng* popular in Kiangsu.
Lit.: no. 255.

Fu-ching (*Mo*) (China). Cf. *Sheng* (M 5738).

Fue (*Fuye*) (Japan). Term for various flutes derived from the verb *fuku*, "to blow." In combination with a second word *fue* becomes *bue*. Cf. *Bue* (*Buye*).

Fufe-fufedji (Sahara; Sudan – Fulbe). Wind instrument. Cf. *Bushe-bushe* (of the Hausa).
Lit.: no. 255.

Fu-hakase (*Fu*) (Japan). A more distinct *shōmyō* notational system than the *ko-hakase*. *Fu-hakase* came into use during the middle of the 12th century.
Lit.: no. 47.

Fuhy (Vietnam; Annam). Scale used in instrumental music. It corresponds to the Japanese *ryosen* scale. In vocal music it corresponds to the Japanese *ritsusen* type.
Lit.: no. 153.

Fu'i-dole (Timor – Belu). Bamboo flute, open at both ends. Its blowhole is located in the center of the tube. Also called *fu'i tetek* or *fu'i latan*.
Lit.: no. 162.

Fu'i latan (Timor). See *Fu'i dole*.

Fu'i tetek (Timor). See *Fu'i dole*.

Fuji-yuri (Japan). A *kyōkusetzu*. A trill that begins with a slow and wide vibration, increases gradually in speed, and ends with a fast swinging within an interval that becomes increasingly smaller.

Fukarā (Ethiopia). Battle songs.

Fuk fuk (North Moluccas; Halmahera). Shell horns.
Lit.: no. 162.

Fukita (Japan). Cf. *Isso.*

Fukulu (Former North Rhodesia; Zambia—Batambwa). Barrel drum, formerly used in war, now in dances and sorcery.
Lit.: no. 26.

Fu-lai (China). "Helping to happen." Also called *li-pen*, "establishing a basis." *Fu-lai* is the name of the music ascribed to the mythical emperor Fu Hsi, who was often called the inventor of music and its instruments.

Fuli (Republic of Mali—Mandingo). See *Tuni.*

Fulu (Burma; Shan State). Mouth organ with free reeds, similar to the Chinese *sheng.* It has five cane pipes which are inserted in a calabash wind chest.
Lit.: no. 252.

Fumbo (Kenya—Jopadhola). Long cylindrical drum with one head.
Lit.: no. 302.

Fun (China). Clay pipe used in pairs.
Lit.: no. 255.

Funagaku (Japan). See *Gagaku.*

Fung cheng (China). See *Feng cheng.*

Fung kam (China). See *Yao chen.*

Fung k'in (China). See *Feng-ch'in.*

Fung huang hsiao (China). See *Feng huang hsiao.*

Fung ling (China). See *Feng ling.*

Fuqaishāt (Arabia). Castanets made of metal.
Lit.: no. 255.

Furaaka (Senegal). See *Esimben.*

Furi (Japan). A *kyōkusetzu.* A shake that is followed by a short note, a semitone or whole tone lower, and completed by a long note on the original pitch.

Furi (Niger region). Stopped long flute with three finger holes.
Lit.: no. 255.

Furin (Japan). "The wind bell." Small bells suspended from each of the four corners of the temple roof. Inside the bell hangs a broad, protruding clapper which is moved by the wind. Cf. *P'ung-kyong* (Korea); *Feng-ling* (China).

Furi-tsuzumi (Japan). "The shaking drum." A rattle used in processions. At the end of a stick five or six bell-rattles are attached to two small drums placed at 90 degrees, one above the other. When the stick is shaken the rattles beat the drumheads. Cf. *To-ko* (Korea); *T'ao-ku* (China).
Lit.: no. 225.

Furūdāsht (Arabia; Iran). See *Nauba.*

Furyū (Japan). Noisy popular street festivities, dances, masqueraderies, comic shows, used in *sarugaku* and in highly stylized form in the *noh* drama.

Fushi (Japan). (1) Melody. (2) The style of lyrically performed sections of the *noh* play. *Yowagin* indicates the gentle and soft style, and *tsuyogin* the energetic and war-like style.

Fushi-jiri (Japan). Closing ornament of a *nagauta* melody.
Lit.: no. 187.

Fushi-mawashi (Japan). Characteristic subtleties in the interpretation of *nagauta* melodies.
Lit.: no. 187.

Fushō (Japan). The seventh of the 12 ("chromatic") tones, usually transcribed as G♯ if the first tone (D) is *ichikotsu.* Cf. *Gagaku* (scales). The highest permissible pitch for singers.

Fusoku-furi (Japan). An event in *nagauta* performances when the voice appears without any noticeable accents, being "neutral" and not in time with the accompanying *shamisen*.
Lit.: no. 187.

Futaku (Japan). See *Feng-ling* (China).

Futa uta (Japan). "Second verse." See *Kumi*.

Fu t'o (or *Hsiao mou*) (China). Name of the music ascribed to the legendary ruler Shen Nung.

Fuye (Japan). General term for flute. Cf. *Fue*; *Bue*.
Lit.: nos. 53, 255.

Fuye no ana (Japan). Finger holes in the *fuye*.

Fuye no fuki kuchi (Japan). Mouth hole (blowing hole) of the *fuye*.
Lit.: no. 255.

Fuzoku (Japan). Folksongs admitted for (*gagaku*) performance at the imperial court.

G

Ga (Central African Republic; Ubangi). A dancer's rattle.
Lit.: no. 184.

Ga (Ghana—Ewe). Dance of the old men. In recent times the old dancers are joined by younger persons.
Lit.: no. 174.

Ga (India). Abbreviation for *gāndhāra*. The term indicates the third degree of a heptatonic scale. *Ga* can be the western E, if *sa* is taken as C.
Lit.: no. 136.

Gä (Burma; Southern Shan States). Buffalo horn with a cane reed mouthpiece. Cf. *Kwai.*
Lit.: no. 252.

Gabay (Somaliland). An unaccompanied song sung only by men in their private homes. The text consists of love lyrics.
Lit.: no. 98.

Gabbus (Tanzania; Zanzibar). A lute in the shape of the West African *rebāb* with 5-7 strings. Cf. *Gabus*; *Qūpūz*; *Gambus.*
Lit.: no. 249.

Gabguki (India). According to Lit. no. 261, a string instrument used by villagers of the Deccan.

Gablo (Somali Republic). Dance of the men. Cf. *Or.*
Lit.: no. 98.

Gabor (Bali). Ceremonial dance performed by women in the temple.
Lit.: no. 197.

Gabowie (South Africa—Hottentots). Lute consisting of a carved piece of wood across which are strung three strings.
Lit.: no. 255.

Gabus (South Africa—Korana Hottentots). Musical bow.
Lit.: no. 151.

Gada (South India). Derived from the Sanskrit *ghāṭa*, "jar," "pitcher." A large globular clay pot with a very short and narrow neck. The player holds the neck against his stomach and beats the pot with his hands. At the end of his performance he tosses the pot in the air and lets it smash into pieces.
Lit.: no. 254.

Gādar (India). Marwari term for *tūrya* (or *bheṛī*).

Gāḍi chakkai (South India). Tamil term for the two strips of wood that are placed on both sides of the fingerboard of the *vīṇā*.
Lit.: no. 261.

Gadodo (West Africa—Ewe). Cf. *Gawu*.

Gadza (Tanzania; Zanzibar). Rattle.
Lit.: no. 255.

Gadzo (Ghana—Ewe). Theatrical dance for young men. Originally a war dance of Togoland.
Lit.: no. 174.

Gafa (Northeast Africa—Galla). Antelope horn blown for dance music.
Lit.: no. 255.

Gaga (South New Guinea). Song sung at the forbidden *mayo* ceremony.

Gagah (*Lagu gagah*) (West Java). Vigorous, heroic style of resounding and impressive *gamelan* playing, and the strong and heroic character of acting in the *wayang wong* shows. Cf. *Alus* (the opposite of *gagah*). See also *Bapang* ("demonic"); *Ketek* ("monkey").
Lit.: no. 163.

Gagah kalang kinantang (Java). Strong and proud character portrayed by a figure in *wayang wong*. Cf. *Gagah*.

Gagah kambeng (Java). Strong character portrayed by a figure in *wayang wong*. Cf. *Gagah*.

Gagaku (Japan). *Ga*, "tasteful," "refined"; *gaku*, "music." The correct, refined, elegant ceremonial court music, the classical music particularly during the Heian Period (A.D. 794-1192).

Gagaku embraces a wide field of music with numerous styles, types and forms. It was divided into ancient music imported from India and Indo-China (*rinyu gaku*), the kingdoms of ancient Korea (*sankangaku*: *shiragi gaku*, *kudara gaku*, and *koma gaku*; in later periods all three styles were called *koma gaku*) and from China (*gigaku*; as T'ang music it was called *to gaku*). A group of purely orchestral pieces was *ko gaku* and *shin gaku*.

An important feature was *bu-gaku*, instrumental music performed to festive court dancing, masked dancing, and dancing at sacred shrines. Among the numerous types of *gagaku* were the *eikyoku* (later Japanese vocal, predominantly choral, music), and the *imayo*, popular songs sung and danced by girls. In later centuries the *imayo* were accepted by the imperial court and the nobility, as were also the *fuzoku* folksongs from various parts of the country. Other types were the *roei*, free recitations of Chinese poems (particularly favored during the Heian period), recitations with or without instrumental accompaniment, and the *utahiko*, free recitations of Japanese poems favored at New Year's festivities. In addition have to be mentioned the *saibara*, folk songs, usually love songs, elaborately arranged for voice and one instrumental ensemble generally consisting of *sho*, *hichiriki*, *oteki* (or *ryuteki*), *biwa*, and *koto* (*gaku-so*). Among other forms of *gagaku* were *tachigaku*, court music, performed standing, outdoors at special occasions; *igaku*, court music, performed seated, indoors; *michigaku*, music of the road, used for imperial processions and important funerals. *Gagaku* requires special portable drums: *funagaku* ("water music"), ship's music, performed on flat boats in ponds, rarely in rivers; *noborigaku*, music performed when the abbot mounts the pulpit at Buddhist ceremonies; *kudurigaku*, music performed when the abbot descends from the pulpit; *mairi-onjo*, entrance music into the imperial palace; *makado-onjo*, exit music performed at the close of important ceremonies.

The *gagaku* tone material, identical with the Chinese *lü*, has the following tone names (usually transcribed as the following Western notes):

Ichikotsu	D
Tangin	D♯

Hyōjō	E
Shōsetsu	F
Shimomu	F♯
Sōjō	G
Fushō	G♯
Ōshō	A
Rankei	A♯
Banshiki	B
Shinsen	c
Kamimu	c♯

The *gagaku* tone system employed six modes (see *Shōmyō*). The following list shows that the system consisted of three *ryo(sen)* and three *ritsu(sen)* scale forms:

Ichikotsuchō	D E F♯ . . A B . . d (*ryo* type)
Sōjō	G A B . . d e . . g (*ryo* type)
Taishikichō	E F♯ G♯ . . B c♯ . . e (*ryo* type)
Hyōjō	E F♯ . A B C♯ . e (*ritsu* type)
Oshikichō	A B . d e f♯ g a (*ritsu* type)
Banshikichō	B c♯ . e f♯ g♯ . b (*ritsu* type)

The modes employed in *to gaku* and *koma gaku*, "left and "right" music respectively, were—

Left music:

Ichikotsuchō	D E F♯ A B d
Hyōjō	E F♯ A B c♯ e
Sōjō	G A B d e g

Right music:

Koma-ichikotsuchō	E F♯ G♯ B c♯ e
Koma-hyōjō	F♯ G♯ B c♯ d♯ f♯
Koma-sōjō	A B c♯ e f♯ a

Modulation in *gagaku* can be done only from one *ryo* to another *ryo* mode, never from a *ryo* to *ritsu*. Rhythm in *gagaku* pieces employs common or duple meters. Slow pieces usually have eight rhythmic units within a measure, four in moderately fast, and two in fast pieces. In some fast pieces, alternating two and three beats can occur. The formal structure of numerous *gagaku* pieces usually consists of three (occasionally of two or even of one) movements. The three sections are called *jo*, introduction; *ha*, refined expression; and *kyū*, a fast end piece. This form can be observed in pure orchestral and dance pieces (*bugaku*) as well as in other types (*noh* music). The three main sections of a piece, *jo*, *ha*, and *kyū*, can be followed by the *nokorigaku* or a *choshi*. Orchestral pieces are usually introduced by a *netori*. For instrumentation details see *Bugaku*.
Lit.: nos. 53, 185, 225.

Gagaku-kyoku (Japan). An imperial *gagaku* department controlling and supervising court music and *kagura*. Cf. *Gagaku*.

Gagakuryō (Japan). The ancient imperial music office, established in the 8th century. Its function was to encourage and regulate the study and performance of the imported and fashionable music from China, Korea, Indo-China, India, and Central Asia. Cf. *Yüeh-fu* (China).
Lit.: no. 53.

Gagambangan (Java). "*Gambang* like"; a substitute for *gambang*.
Lit.: no. 163.

Gagana Bhūpāḷam (*Gagana Bhūpāḷi*) (South India). *Janya rāga* of the 21st *mēḷa* (*Kiravāṇi*).
Tone material:

C F E♭ F G A♭ B c
c B A♭ F E♭ D C

Lit.: no. 139.

Gagana Bhūpāḷi (South India). See *Gagana Bhūpāḷam*.

Gaganādari (South India). *Janya rāga* of the 54th *mēḷa* (*Viśvambharī*).
Tone material:

C D♭ E F♯ B c
c B A♯ F♯ E D♭ C

Lit.: no. 139.

Gagana Gāndhāri (South India). *Janya rāga* of the 40th *mēḷa* (*Navanītam*).

Tone material:

C D♭ E♭♭ D♭ F♯ G B♭ A B♭ c

c B♭ A G F♯ E♭♭ D♭ C

Lit.: no. 139.

Gagana Mayūri (South India). *Janya rāga* of the 51st *mēḷa* (*Kāmavardhanī*).

Tone material:

C F♯ E A♭ B c

c B A♭ F♯ G F♯ G F♯ E D♭ C

Lit.: no. 139.

Gaganāmbari (South India). *Janya rāga* of the 29th *mēḷa* (*Dhīraśaṅkarābharaṇam*).

Tone material:

C D E F G A B c

c B A G E D C

Lit.: no. 139.

Gagana Mōhini (South India). *Janya rāga* of the 64th *mēḷa* (*Vāchaspati*).

Tone material:

C E G A B♭ c

c B♭ G F♯ E C

Lit.: no. 139.

Gagana Rañjani (South India). *Janya rāga* of the 66th *mēḷa* (*Chitrāmbarī*).

Tone material:

C E F♯ G c

c A♯ B G F♯ E D C

Lit.: no. 139.

Gagana Sarasīruham (South India). *Janya rāga* of the 53rd *mēḷa* (*Gamanaśrama*).

Tone material:

C E D♭ E F♯ G A B

B A G F♯ E D♭ *B* C

This *rāga* has *Niṣādāntya* character.

Lit.: no. 139.

Gāgri (North India; Kashmir). A brass vessel. The player strikes the bulging body with copper rings which are placed on his fingers.

Lit.: no. 261.

Gah-gah (West Africa). A large hollow gourd with an orifice on top which is stamped against the ground.

Lit.: no. 223.

Gaikyoku (Japan). "Outside music." *Shakuhachi* music adapted from *shamisen* and *koto* repertory. Cf. *Shakuhachi*; *Honkyokū*; *Shinkyoku*.

Lit.: no. 185.

Ga'iṭa (Algeria; Morocco). Oboe. (Term for bagpipe in Spain, for pipe or flute in Brazil.) Cf. *Algaiṭa*; *Mizmār*. The term is also written *ghaiṭa*.

Gajānandini (South India). *Janya rāga* of the 30th *mēḷa* (*Nāgānandī*).

Tone material:

C D E F A♯ B c

c B A♯ F E D C

Lit.: no. 139.

Gaja Sāri (South India). *Janya rāga* of the 9th *mēḷa* (*Dhēnuka*).

Tone material:

C D♭ E♭ F G B A♭ c

c G F E♭ D♭ C

Lit.: no. 139.

Gaja Vardhanam (*Gaja Vardhani*) (South India). *Janya rāga* of the 29th *mēḷa* (*Dhīraśaṅkarābharaṇam*).

Tone material:

C E F A B c

c A G F E D C

Lit.: no. 139.

Gaja Vardhani (South India). See *Gaja Vardhanam.*

Gaja Vilaśita (South India). *Janya rāga* of the 29th *mēḷa* (*Dhīraśaṅkarābharaṇam*).

Tone material:

C D F E F B G A c

c B A F G F E D C

Lit.: no. 139.

Gajor (Java). Wooden frames from which gongs are suspended.

Lit.: no. 163.

Gajra (India). Cf. *Tabla.*

Gakki (Japan). Instrument.

Gakku daiko (Japan). Barrel drum.

Gakkuki (Japan). Significant instruments used in religious services: *biwa, hichiriki, kagura bue, kakko, kin-no koto, koma-bue, sanno tsuzumi, shaku-byoshi, shoko, sho-no fuye, taiko, yamato koto.*

Gakku no tsuzumi (Japan). Term for *tsuzumi* (hourglass-shaped drum).
Lit.: no. 139.

Gakpa (West Africa—Ewe). Cf. *Gawu.*
Lit.: no. 255.

Gaku (Japan). "Music." E.g., interlude performed by the *hayashi*, the instrumental ensemble (as used in the *noh* drama). *Gaku* appears also in *kabuki* performances. The *gaku* are several introductory *dan* followed by a coda.
Lit.: no. 185.

Gaku biwa (Japan). The oldest of the Japanese *biwa* types. It is used in *komagaku* (music of the right) of *gagaku.* The instrument has four silken strings and four frets and is played with a triangular *bachi.* A frequent tuning is: *A E A* C.
Lit.: no. 225.

Gakubu (Japan). The music department at the imperial palace in Tokyo. Cf. *Gagakuryo.*

Gaku-daiko (Japan). A flat bodied cylindrical frame drum with two heads beaten with two thin sticks and used off stage in *kabuki* performances.
Lit.: no. 185.

Gakunin (Japan). A distinguished title given to the highest class of well educated musicians, persons who were able to read and write musical notation, along with other qualities. The *gakunin* played in the imperial court orchestra of the Mikado.

The other classes of musicians, in descending order, were: the *genin, kengyō* and *kōtō*, and the *geishas.*
Lit.: no. 53.

Gaku-sō (*sōno koto* employed in *gagaku* music) (Japan). An ancient zither of Chinese origin used in *gagaku.* It had 12 or 13 strings running over sturdy bridges. Its rich tone caused the instrument to be used in solo parts, and eventually it led the way to the solo *koto.* The term for this instrument can also be simply *so.* Cf. *Shin-sō.*
Lit.: no. 53.

Gala (Ancient Mesopotamia; Sumer). Term for a musician who functions as a psalmist or priest in laments and at funerals. Cf. *Nar.*
Lit.: nos. 94, 282.

Gala (India; Gujarat). Cf. *Ranaśringa.*

Gala (North Moluccas; Halmahera). See *Gambus; Bangsil.*

Ǧalağil (Old Arabia; Persia). Cf. *Jalājil.*

Galak (Java). See *Greget saut.*

Galamutu (Bismarck Archipelago; St. Matthias Isl.). Slit-drum. Cf. *Garamut.*
Lit.: no. 84.

Galan (Iraq). Beduin fiddle made from an oil drum.

Galevu Kauhaumumu (Solomon Isl.). Panpipes consisting of one row with 11-13 bamboo pipes.
Lit.: no. 255.

Galevu ngungu (Solomon Isl.). Panpipes consisting of 50 bamboo pipes in two rows, usually accompanied by the *pupu horu* and *pupu galaga.*
Lit.: no. 255.

Galevu soniruka (Solomon Isl.). Panpipes with 40-44 bamboo pipes in two rows.
Lit.: no. 255.

Ġalimer (*Bem*) (Indonesia; Sunda District). (1) The second note of the *pelog* system of the Sunda District. (2) The second note of the *slendro* system of the Sunda District.
Lit.: no. 163.

Galimer (Java). "Great, low sounding." (1) The second note in *surupan melog.* (2) The second lowest octave (in a range of four octaves). Cf. *Petit* (West Java).

Galinquang (New Guinea). Jew's harp of bamboo. It has an unusually strong sound. Lit.: no. 255.

Galong (Java). A *suluk* usually performed after four specific *gendings* (Rina-rina, Sumirat, Maskumbang, Konda).

Galunggang petung (Java; Bali). One of the numerous *gambang* types.
Lit.: no. 197.

Gamak(a) (India). Musical ornament. Grace notes and other ornamental features were mentioned already in Vedic works and have been described and grouped in theoretical treatises since the *Bharatanāṭyaśāstra* (ca. 2nd century) up to the present time. Nārada in his *Saṅgīta Makaranda* (after the 7th century) lists 19 *gamakas*; Śārṅgadeva in his *Saṅgīta Ratnākara* (13th century) speaks of 15 ornaments; Ahobala in his *Saṅgīta Pārijāta* (18th century) mentions 17. At the present time usually 10 *gamakas* are enumerated. For further information see Lit. no. 262. In the *Saṅgīta Kaumudī*, a contemporary South Indian work written in Sanskrit (the Ms. is preserved in the O. M. Library of Madras), the following *gamakas* are listed:

1. *Ārohaṇa*, ascending order of notes.
2. *Avaroha*, descending order of notes.
3. *Ḍhālu*, intervals such as CG, CF, CE; also the playing of a high note on a basically low-pitched string.
4. *Sphurita*, stepwise formation such as CD, DE, EF, etc.
5. *Kampita*, repeated notes GGGGG, FFFFF, etc.; also trills.
6. *Āhata*, ascending pairs of notes CC, DD, EE, FF, or EF, FG, GA, AB, etc.
7. *Pratyāhata*, descending pairs of notes BB, AA, GG, or cB, BA, AG, etc.
8. *Tripuccha*, notes repeated three times: CCC, DDD, EEE, etc.
9. *Āndoḷita*; Lit. no. 261 describes this ornament: holding a note for a while, then pulling the string or gliding on it in order to produce a higher pitched note.
10. *Mūrchhanā*, quickly performed scale sequences: CDEFGAB, DEFGABc, etc.

Lit.: no. 238.

Gamakakriya (South India). *Janya rāga* of the 53rd *mēḷa* (*Gamanaśrama*).
Tone material:
C D♭ E F♯ G A c
c B A G F♯ E F♯ D♭ C
Lit.: no. 139.

Gamakakriyā (South India). (1) The 53rd *asampūrṇa mēḷa-rāga* without *kaṭapayādi* prefix. (2) The 53rd *asampūrṇa mēḷa-rāga* with *kaṭapayādi* prefix. See *Rāga* (South India).
Lit.: no. 139.

Gamakapriya (South India). *Janya rāga* of the 51st *mēḷa* (*Kāmavardhanī*).
Tone material:
C D♭ E F♯ G B A♭ c
c A♭ G F♯ E D♭ C
Lit.: no. 139.

Gamaka Sāmantam (South India). *Janya rāga* of the 45th *mēḷa* (*Śubhapantuvarālī*).
Tone material:
C E♭ F♯ G B c
c B A♭ G F♯ E♭ D♭ C
Lit.: no. 139.

Gamakha's (South Africa—Bergdama). Musical bow.
Lit.: no. 151.

Gāmākyam (South India). *Janya rāga* of the 23rd *mēḷa* (*Gaurīmanōharī*).
Tone material:
C D F G A B c
c B A G F E♭ G F D E♭ C
Lit.: no. 139.

Gamana Bhāskaram (South India). *Janya rāga* of the 29th *mēḷa* (*Dhīraśaṅkarābharaṇam*). Tone material:

C D E F G A G B c
c A G F E C

Lit.: no. 139.

Gamanakriya (South India). *Janya rāga* of the 53rd *mēḷa* (*Gamanaśrama*).
Tone material:

C D♭ F♯ G A B c
c B A G F♯ E F♯ D♭ C

Lit.: no. 139.

Gamana Lalita (South India). *Janya rāga* of the 15th *mēḷa* (*Māyāmāḷavagauḷa*).
Tone material:

C D♭ C E F G A♭ B A♭ c
c A♭ F E D♭ C

Lit.: no. 139.

Gamana Nirmaḷa (South India). *Janya rāga* of the 53rd *mēḷa* (*Gamanaśrama*).
Tone material:

C D♭ E F♯ G A B c
c B G F♯ D♭ C

Lit.: no. 139.

Gamanapriyā (South India). See *Gamanaśrama.*

Gamanaśrama (*Gamanapriyā*) (South India). The 53rd *mēḷa*:

C D♭ E F♯ G A B c

Veṅkaṭamakhin (17th century) called this *rāga* *Gamakakriya.* At the present time this name represents a *janya rāga* of the 53rd *mēḷa*.
Lit.: no. 139.

Gamana Taraṅgiṇi (South India). *Janya rāga* of the 20th *mēḷa* (*Naṭabhairavī*).
Tone material:

C D F E♭ F B♭ A♭ B♭ G A♭ B♭ c
c B♭ A♭ G E♭ D C

Lit.: no. 139.

Gambang (Bali). Special bamboo xylophone used during cremation rites. Cf. *Ding.*
Lit.: no. 197.

Gambang (Java; Borneo). A xylophone or metallophone; the instrument consists of an ornamented wooden trough upon which rest either wooden or metal slabs.
Lit.: no. 255.

Gambangan (Bali). A composition of the present time. It uses traditional *gambang* melodies.
Lit.: no. 197.

Gambang gangsa (*Gambang selukat*) (Java). An old multi-octave metallophone with 18 keys. There are some instruments with fewer. Cf. *Saron.*

Gambang kayu (Java). A *gambang* with wooden slabs, tuned either to *pelog* or *slendro.* In the Sunda Districts of West Java the *gambang kayu* produces sounds over four octaves. The very high one is called *petit*, the high one *manis*, the medium *galimer*, and the bass *gede.* This instrument appears also in Malaysia.
Lit.: no. 163.

Gambang kromong (West Java). An instrumental ensemble consisting of *gambang kayu*, *kromong*, *ohyan*, *gihyan*, *bangsing*, *kenong*, and *kendang*. It performs accompaniments to highly emotional songs.
Lit.: no. 163.

Gambang selukat (Java). (1) See *Gambang gangsa.* (2) In Solo Kraton this instrument is called *chelepita.*
Lit.: no. 163.

Gambhīra Nāṭa (South India). *Janya rāga* of the 36th *mēḷa* (*Chalanāṭa*).
Tone material:

C E F G B c
c B G F E C

This *rāga* is believed to express *vīra rasa*, heroic mood.
Lit.: no. 139.

Gambhīra Vāṇi (South India). *Janya rāga* of the 30th *mēḷa* (*Nāgānandī*).
Tone material:
C E G F G A♯ B c
c A♯ G F E D E D C
Lit.: no. 139.

Gambhīra Vasantam (South India). *Janya rāga* of the 8th *mēḷa* (*Hanumattōḍi*).
Tone material:
C F E♭ F D♭ E♭ F G B♭ A♭ B♭ G A♭ B♭ c
c A♭ G F D♭ C
Lit.: no. 139.

Gambhīriṇi (South India). *Janya rāga* of the 23rd *mēḷa* (*Gaurīmanōharī*).
Tone material:
C D E♭ F G A B A c
c B A G F E♭ D C
Lit.: no. 139.

Gāmbhīrya Ghōṣani (South India). *Janya rāga* of the 52nd *mēḷa* (*Rāmapriyā*).
Tone material:
C E D♭ G F♯ A B♭ c
c B♭ A G F♯ E D♭ E C
Lit.: no. 139.

Gāmbhirya Nāṭa (South India). *Janya rāga* of the 33rd *mēḷa* (*Gāṅgeyabhushanī*).
Tone material:
C E F G B c
c B G F D♯ C
Lit.: no. 139.

Gambuh (Java). One of the meters of *Tembang machapat*. Cf. *Machapat*.
Lit.: no. 163.

Gambuh (Bali). The ancient, classical theater based on old legends of court ceremonies concerning cremations, weddings, gods, and magic. *Gambuh* performances are rare at the present time. The performing ensemble consists of four *suling gambuh*, vertical flutes with six finger holes; one *rebab*, played by the leader of the group; one *kempur*, a large gong; a *kenong*, *klenang*, and *kadjar*, small gongs; and two *kendang* drums. The group has also one male who recites, two male singers, and several colorfully dressed male dancers. The music uses a heptatonic scale, similar to the *pelog* tone material. Cf. *Ding* (under the heading of this term are listed all basic tone names); *Semar pegulingan*.
Lit.: no. 197.

Gambuh Semar Pegulingan (Bali). Dance drama (*gambuh*, "drama"; *Semar*, "God of Love"). See *Semar Pegulingan*.
Lit.: no. 197.

Gambus (Sunda District; West Borneo). A plucked lute in the shape of the North African *rebāb*. Its pear-shaped body is covered with parchment. The *gambus* has three, six, or seven strings. The lowest, being single, is made of metal, while the other strings, made of silk, are tuned in pairs.
Lit.: nos. 162, 255.

Gambusi, Udi, Zeze (*yenye nyuzi sita*) (East Africa—Swahili). Lute.

Gambyong (Java). Cf. *Klenang*.

Gamelan (Java). An orchestra that appears not only in Java, but in the territory between Burma and Bali. It can be observed in a great variety of combinations of instruments. The word is derived from the verb *gamel*, "to handle," "to manipulate." A complete Javanese *gamelan* comprises instrument for both *pelog* and *slendro* systems, but there are ensembles that are tuned to only one of the two systems. There exist hundreds of *gamelans*—large ones, highly valuable ensembles, owned by rulers and wealthy persons, and very small and insignificant ones. Some of them are tuned to scales close to the western diatonic modes, others to widely different forms.

The functions of the *gamelan* instruments can be grouped as follows:

1. Theme playing instruments: *suling*, *rebāb*, *saron*, *demung*.

Gamelan

2. Paraphrasing, ornamenting instruments: *bonang* (*bonang barung*, *bonang panerus*), *gender*.
3. Ornamenting and filling in: *gambang kayu*, occasionally also *saron*.
4. Interpunctuation: *gong ageng*, *kenong*, *ketuk*, *kempul*, *kempyang*.
5. Drums: *kendang gending*.

JAVANESE GAMELAN INSTRUMENTS

Used in *pelog* and *slendro*:

Saron panerus
Saron barung (2 or 4)
Saron demung (mostly 2)
Saron slentem
Saron gangsa
Bonang panerus
Bonang barung
Bonang panembung

Used in *pelog*:	Used in *slendro*:
Gambang kayu (*bem*)	*Gambang kayu*
Gambang kayu (*barung*)	–
Gender panerus (*bem*)	*Gender panerus*
Gender panerus (*barung*)	–
Gender barung (*bem*)	*Gender barung*
Gender barung (*barung*)	
Gender panembung or *Slentem* (*gantung*)	
Kempyang	
	Engkuk
	Kemong

Ketuk
Kenong lanang (one or more)
Kenong japan
Kempul (one or more)
Gong suwukan (one or more)
Suling
Rebab
Chelempung
Gong kemodong
Gong ageng (one or two)
Kendang gending
Kendang chiblon
Ketipung
Bedug
Ke(chi)cher
Keprak
Kechrek
Kemanak

Lit.: nos. 158, 163.

NAMES OF FAMOUS *GAMELAN* ENSEMBLES

Many of these orchestras bear the title *Kyahi*, "venerable Sir," at times preceded by "kangjeng." Some of the names are: *Kanyut mesem*, "tempted to smile"; *Guntur madu*, "torrent of honey"; *Lipur tomba neng*, "consoling remedy, offering peace of soul"; *Udan asih*, "shower of love"; *Pamiwalkung*, "he who makes us forget even love"; *(H)arjanagara*, "the welfare of the country"; *Magunsih*, "practicing love."

Gamelan (Bali). (1) Instrumental ensemble (mostly percussion instruments). (2) An ensemble consisting of iron-keyed metallophones called *gamelan selundeng*.
Lit.: nos. 197, 265.

Gamelan (Malaysia). Both *gamelan* and the related *barongan-kuda-kepang* ensembles have their origins in Indonesia. The basic scale in Malaysia is *slendro* (in its pentatonic form). Its pitches differ slightly from those of the Indonesian *slendro*. *Wayang jawa* and *ludruk* ensembles (in Johore) employ the following basic scale (approximately the western equivalent):

Chi	C
Ruh	E
Lu	$\overset{+}{\mathrm{F}}$
Mo	A
Nem	$\overset{\flat}{\mathrm{B}}$

The *gamelan trengganu* (of Trengganu state) uses the following basic scale:

Chi	C
Ruh	D
Lu	E
Mo	G
Nem	A

Gamelan ajeng (West Java). A rare orchestra similar to the *renteng* ensemble. *Gamelan ajeng* has a considerable variety of instruments tuned to the *surupan ajeng* (scale). The instruments usually are: one *renteng* with 14 kettles, a *gambang gangsa* (*saron*) with 14 keys, two *ketuk*, *kendang*, *goong gede*, *goong leutik*, and *kekechrek*.
Lit.: no. 163.

Gamelan amen (Java). An ensemble that appears in the North of Central East Java. See *Gamelan sedit.*
Lit.: no. 163.

Gamelan angklung (Bali). An instrumental ensemble that customarily performs at the burning of the dead. It consists almost entirely of metallophones: two *rejong*, two small *kendang*, cymbals (if large, they are called *chengcheng*; if small they are called *richik*), one *kempul* (or *kempur*) tuned to a note outside the typical four-tone scale of the *gamelan angklung* (G $\overset{+}{A}$ $\overset{+}{B}$ d—*kempul* is tuned to e). In addition are used two drums (cymbals) and one or two gongs. It is remarkable to observe that the *gamelan angklung* has no real *angklung* among its instruments.
Lit.: no. 197.

Gamelan arja (Bali). Popular nightly theatrical shows, comedies with love songs, fun tunes, texts of sentimental and hilarious character. The music is performed by a small instrumental and vocal ensemble. The sung melodies are doubled by one or two flutes. The other instruments are drums, cymbals, and bamboo percussion instruments. The scales in use resemble to some degree *pelog*:

(a) C# D E G# A
(b) C# D# E# G# A

Lit.: no. 197.

Gamelan balas (Java). See *Gamelan mondreng.*

Gamelan baleganjur (Bali). An instrumental ensemble consisting of percussion instruments used in processions: two drums, three *chengcheng*, one *kemong*, and one *kempul.*
Lit.: no. 261.

Gamelan Bali (West Java). An orchestra similar to the *renteng* ensemble.
Lit.: no. 163.

Gamelan barong (*Gamelan bebarongan*) (Bali). A *gamelan* that plays for the *barong* dance drama. *Barong*, performed by two dancers, represents a mythological dragon. The music is based on a digressing five-tone *pelog* scale:

F# G# A c# d f#

This ensemble plays also the accompaniment of *chalonarang*, dance dramas.
Lit.: nos. 197, 265.

Gamelan barut (Java). See *Gamelan mondreng.*

Gameland bebonang (Bali). A *gamelan* consisting of gongs, cymbals, and drums, used in processions and martial music.
Lit.: no. 197.

Gamelan bebarongan (Bali). An ensemble used for the accompaniment of the *barong* (and *chalonarang*) dance dramas.
Lit.: no. 265.

Gamelan beling (Java). See *Gamelan sengganen.*

Gamelan bumbung (Java). *Gamelan* (also called *gumbang* or *gumbeng*) consisting of bamboo idiophones tuned in *slendro.*
Lit.: no. 163.

Gamelan bungbung (Bali). An obsolete village *gamelan* consisting of thick bamboo tubes of different lengths, each tube held by a single player who drops in turn the tube against a large bamboo pole lying on the ground and thus producing a crude sort of a tune. The instrument is of the same nature as the Javanese *bumbung.*
Lit.: no. 197.

Gamelan chalung (Java). A small group of instruments consisting of three *chalung*. Cf. *Chalung*; *Jublag*.
Lit.: no. 163.

Gamelan charabalen (*Gamelan talu*) (Java). A *gamelan* having 4-6 tones within the octave. It served as an "introductory gamelan" that performed signals and announced arrivals of important people.
Lit.: no. 163.

Gamelan charabali (Java). See *Gamelan charabalen.*

Gamelan chedit (Java). See *Gamelan sedit.*

Gamelan degung (West Java). A small instrumental ensemble that consists of the *degung*, a small group of hanging kettles and a *suling*, a *goong gede* (at rare times a *kendang*), and a *gambang gangsa* (*saron*).
Lit.: no. 163.

Gamelan djoger (Bali). A special *gamelan* accompaniment for public dancing girls.
Lit.: no. 250.

Gamelan gambang (Bali). An instrumental group basically the same as the *saron* ensemble. The figuration usually has eight tones to one melody tone. The melody, performed by two *gangsa*, usually shows the rhythm of the *gambang*: $^{5}/_{8} + ^{3}/_{8}$.
Lit.: no. 265.

Gamelan gambuh (Bali). The *gamelan* of the Balinese classical theater. The instruments employed are: four *suling gambuh* and one *rebab*, performing the melody (*gending*); one *kempur* and one *kajar* performs the main punctuation; one *kenyir* and one *kelenang* performs secondary punctuation; one *kendang lanang* and one *kendang wadon*, agogic instrument; one *rinchik*, four *gumanak*, and two *kangsi* performs additional percussion.
The *gamelan gambuh* in its music for the classical dance dramas employs the following tone materials:

Selisir:	(approx.)	C♯ D E G♯ A
Sunaren:	"	G A B d e (e♭)
Baro:	"	D E♭ F♭ A B
Lebang:	"	E F G♯ B c

Lit.: nos. 197, 265.

Gamelan gandrung (East Java; Banyuwangi District). A *gamelan* that consists of two fiddles, two *ketuk*, one gong, one *kendang*, one *klon(ch)eng* [*klun(ch)ing*]. At times the *angklung* is used in place of the fiddle(s). The ensemble provides the accompaniment of the Dance of the Seblang.
Lit.: no. 163.

Gamelan geḍah (Java). See *Gamelan sengganen.*

Gamelan gong (Bali). The most important and largest *gamelan* of Bali. Formerly it used to have about 40 players, hence it was called *gamelan gong geḍe*, the great *gamelan gong* ensemble. Now it varies in size and is used at all important religious occasions. It consists of the usual instrumental groups:

1. melody playing
2. figuration playing
3. punctuation playing
4. drums

For details cf. Lit. no. 197.

Gamelan gong kebyar (Bali). A modernized form of the traditional *gamelan gong.*
Lit.: no. 165.

Gamelan gumbeng (Java). Cf. *Gamelan bumbung.*

Gamelan janggrung (Java). See *Wong (ba)barang.*

Gamelan jiring (Java). See *Gamelan mondreng.* The *gender* in this ensemble have no sound tubes placed below the slabs.
Lit.: no. 163.

Gamelan klatan (Java). See *Gamelan klenengan.*

Gamelan klenengan (Java). A small *gamelan* without *bonangs* and often without *sarons.* If *sarons* are used, the ensemble is called *klenengan tengahan.*

The *gamelan klenengan* can be described as the typical *gamelan wayangan*, the *wayang* orchestra. Other names of the *gamelan klenengan* are *gamelan klonengan* in Pekalongan, Grobogan; *gamelan klatan* in Panaraga; *gamelan modong* in Tegal; and *gamelan klenyitan* in Jogya.
Lit.: no. 163.

Gamelan kodok ngorek (Java). Ancient *gamelan* using two notes in ritual services.

Gamelan krawang (Bali). A *gamelan* in which bronze instruments predominate.
Lit.: no. 197.

Gamelan lilingong (West Java). A *gamelan* that plays accompaniments of *wayang* performances. It consists of two *gambang kayu*, *kendang*, and a blown gong.
Lit.: no. 163.

Gamelan luang (*Gong luang*; *Gong saron*) (Bali). Ancient sacred ensemble consisting of several instruments: two *gangsa*, two *jegogan*, one *bamboo saron*, one 16-gong *trompong*, one *kendang wadon*, one *gong ageng*, one set of *cheng-cheng.* The following seven-tone scale is used:

approx. D♭ E♭ F G♭ A♭ B♭ c d♭

This *gamelan* was used in a few places in Bali when there was a death, a cremation, and the strewing of ashes in the sea.
Lit.: no. 197.

Gamelan miring (West Java). A *gamelan* tuned in a *miring* (deviating) form from the traditional manner. The West Javanese *miring* scales are related, more or less, to the (five-tone) *pelog* system. Lit.: no. 163 (p. 388 of vol. 1) mentions the following scales:

(a) I $_{150}$ II $_{131}$ III $_{397}$ IV $_{145}$ V $_{377}$ I'$_{\text{(cents)}}$

(b) I $_{113}$ II $_{150}$ III $_{402}$ IV $_{123}$ V $_{411}$ I'$_{\text{(cents)}}$

Lit.: no. 163.

Gamelan modong (Java). See *Gamelan klenengan.*

Gamelan mondreng (*Gamelan ringgeng*) (Java). A *gamelan* that performs music when the *mondreng* (girl dancers) render their dances. *Gamelan mondreng* is similar to *gamelan klenengan*, only that here instruments with *bonang* functions (ornamenting and paraphrasing) are used. *Gong kemodong* or *gong ringgeng* are used for concluding extended phrases. The keys of the *mondreng* (*ringgeng*) ensembles are made of iron. Cf. Lit. no. 163. Other names of *gamelan mondreng* are: *gamelan barut* (Jogya and Kedu); *gamelan balas* (Sragen and Magetan); *gumbeng wesi* (Demak); *gamelan timpleng* (Kudus); *gamelan jiring* (Tegal, Pemalang); *rinchikan* (Blora). Also the term *gamelan wesi* (the iron *gamelan*) has to be mentioned.

Gamelan munggang (*Gangsa patigan*) (Java). An archaic simple *gamelan* that produces three tones. It can be heard at night during the *sekaten* week. In a few places (e.g., Jogya) appear seven-tone ensembles with the name of *munggang.*
Lit.: no. 163.

Gamelan nyedit (Java). See *Gamelan sedit.*

Gamelan pejogedan (Bali). A small five-tone village ensemble consisting of two *rindik* (xylophones), two small *rindik*, one *kempur komodong* (bamboo slabs placed across a resonance vessel), one *kempli* (a 2-keyed xylophone often played by two persons), one set of *rinchik* (small cymbals), two *jejogan* (metallophones), and one single drum.

This village orchestra provides the music for the *joged* dance. *Joged*, a young girl, dances first alone until, after a little while, she is joined by male partners, one following the other. The *joged* scale is:

C	D♭	E♭	G	A♭
(*ding*)	(*dong*)	(*deng*)	(*dung*)	(*dang*)

Lit.: no. 197.

Gamelan pelegongan (Bali). See *Legong* (*gamelan*).

Gamelan pelog (West Java). An instrumental group that differs from the Central Javanese ensembles by having no metallophones, no *chelempung* (with metal strings), and using other *gamelan* instruments singly. The only exception, the *ketuk* (small kettle gongs), appear in pairs.
Lit.: no. 163.

Gamelan renteng (Indonesia; Sunda District). A village *gamelan* with a variable number of instruments. Its central feature is a *bonang* type called *kolenang renteng.* Furthermore can be used the *goong gede* (cf. *Gong gede*; *Gong ageng*) and *kendang*, *gambang gangsa*, *kempul*, *beri*; also a set of *chechempres.*
Lit.: no. 163.

Gamelan ringgeng (Java). See *Gamelan mondreng.*

Gamelan saronen (*Gamelan tetet*) (East Java). A *gamelan* that uses a *saronen*, *tetet* (a shawm) for playing the melody.
Lit.: no. 163.

Gamelan seḍit (Java). A *gamelan* ensemble without any *gender* instruments. The orchestra has various names: *gamelan nyedit*; *gamelan chedit*; *gamelan amen*; and, in Pemalang, *klenengang kaplok.*
Lit.: no. 163.

Gamelan sekati (Java). During the week when the mohammedan population honor the death of the Prophet, *gamelan sekati* is played uninterruptedly. Only during one night *gamelan sekati* is silent and *gamelan munggang* is played representing with its three notes the grief of the Prophet's daughter. This *gamelan* is also played at the circumcision of the boy child of the Prince, at the wedding of the first wife of the ruler, and during three Kraton festivals (*garebeg*). *Gamelan sekati* consists of the following instruments: two *gong ageng* (tuned to the notes *lima* and *nem*), one *bedug*, one *kempyang* (both its drums are tuned to *nem*), two *demung*, four *saron barung*, two *saron panerus*, the *trompong* type plays the melody, one double-row *bonang.*
Lit.: no. 158.

Gamelan selunding (Bali). A *gamelan* producing the most sacred music. Its predominating iron instruments are exclusively played by priests. In the *selunding* ensemble the figurations are also played by iron instruments.
Lit.: nos. 158, 265.

Gamelan semar pegulingan (Java). A gentle sounding ensemble that has become almost obscure. It was this orchestra, named after the Love God, that performed informally for distinguished members of the court. See *Semar pegulingan.*
Lit.: no. 163.

Gamelan sengganen (Java). A *gamelan* with instruments that have keys made of thick glass. Other names of this ensemble are: *gamelan beling* and *gamelan gedah.*
Lit.: no. 163.

Gamelan slendro (*Gamelan salendro*) (West Java). A *gamelan* that differs from the Central Javanese orchestras in the same way that *gamelan pelog* does.
Lit.: no. 163.

Gamelan talu (East Java). See *Gamelan charabalen.*

Gamelan tetet (Java). See *Gamelan saronen.*

Gamelan timpleng (Java). See *Gamelan mondreng.*

Gamelan tiruan (West Java). A pseudo-*gamelan* (*tiruan* mens substitute) that consists of a *goong buyung* (*gede*), a *goong buyung* (*leutik*), a *rebab*, a *saron* with iron keys (*saron beusi*), a *gambang*, and a *kechrek.* The *gamelan tiruan* is used at *wayang* shows and at dances (*tayuban*).
Lit.: no. 163.

Gamelan tumbug nem (Java). *Gamelans* are usually tuned either in *pelog* or *slendro*; if the note *nem* in the *pelog* and *slendro* ensembles is tuned to the same pitch (*tumbug* means "to coincide"), the term *gamelan tumbug nem* is applied.
Lit.: no. 163.

Gamelan wayangan (Java). See *Gamelan klenengan.* In *gamelan wayangan* the *gong ageng* is substituted by *gong suwukan*, or by *gong kemodong.*
Lit.: no. 163.

Gamelan wesi (Java). See *Gamelan mondreng.*

Gamti (Bismarck archipelago). See *Garamut*; *Kolamut.*

Gāna (India; Vedic Chant). Song; song book.

Gāna Lalita (South India). *Janya rāga* of the 3rd *mēḷa* (*Ganamurti*).
Tone material:
C E♭♭ F G A♭ B c
c B A♭ G F E♭♭ D♭ C
Lit.: no. 139.

Gāna Lōlam (South India). *Janya rāga* of the 29th *mēḷa* (*Dhīraśaṅkarābharaṇam*).
Tone material:
C D C F G B c
c B G A G F E F D C
Lit.: no. 139.

Gāna Mayūri (South India). Obscure *janya rāga* of the 51st *mēḷa* (*Kāmavardhanī*). The scale of this *rāga* is the same as that of *Gagana Mayūri*, with the exception of a shorter descent:
c B A♭ F♯ G F♯ E D♭ C
Lit.: no. 139.

Gānamūrti (South India). (1) The 3rd *mēḷa*:
C D♭ E♭♭ F G A♭ B c
(2) As a *rāga*, *Gānamūrti* is light in character and performers can take various liberties (*vakra* steps, occasional omissions of one or the other notes). Veṅkaṭamakhin (17th century) called this *rāga Sāmavarāli.* At the present time *Sāmavarāli* denotes a *janya* of the 3rd *mēḷa* (*Gānamūrti*).
Lit.: no. 139.

Ganang (Vietnam). Two cylindrical drums, both double-headed. One head is struck with a stick, the other with the hand.

Ganang (Kampuchea). Wooden drums; slit-drum.

Gānāṅgi (South India). *Janya rāga* of the 20th *mēḷa* (*Naṭabhairavī*).
Tone material:
C D F E♭ F G A♭ B♭ c
c A♭ B♭ A♭ F G F E♭ D C
Lit.: no. 139.

Gānapriya (South India). *Janya rāga* of the 19th *mēḷa* (*Jhaṅkāradhvani*).
Tone material:
C D E♭ F A♭ c
c A♭ F E♭ D C
Lit.: no. 139.

Gāna Sāmavarāli (South India). See *Sāmavarāli* (3rd *asampūrṇa mēḷa*).

Gāna Sindhu (*Ghāna Sindhu*) (South India). *Janya rāga* of the 15th *mēḷa* (*Māyāmāḷavagauḷa*).
Tone material:
C F E F G A♭ B A♭ c
c B A♭ G F E D♭ C
Lit.: no. 139.

Gāna Svabhāva (South India). *Janya rāga* of the 15th *mēḷa* (*Māyāmāḷavagauḷa*).
Tone material:
C D♭ F A♭ B G c
c A♭ B A♭ G F E D♭ C
Lit.: no. 139.

Gāna Varidhi (South India). *Janya rāga* of the 34th *mēḷa* (*Vāgadhīshvari*).
Tone material:
C F D♯ E F G A B♭ c
c A B♭ G F D♯ C
Lit.: no. 139.

Gāna Vasantam (South India). *Janya rāga* of the 22nd *mēḷa* (*Kharaharapriyā*).
Tone material:
C D E♭ F G B♭ A c
c B♭ A G F E♭ D C
Lit.: no. 139.

Ganchang (Indonesia; Sunda District). See *Byang.*

Gand (Ethiopia). See *Ghenta.*

Ganda (Kenya – Digo). Cylindrical drum with one open end.
Lit.: no. 28.

Ganda-ganda (Indonesia; Bonerate Isl., near Flores). A small kettledrum made of the shell of half a coconut.
Lit.: no. 254.

Ganda Madanam (South India). *Janya rāga* of the 53rd *mēḷa* (*Gamanaśrama*).
Tone material:
C D♭ F♯ G A c
c B A G F♯ A F♯ E D♭ C
Lit.: no. 139.

Gandaṅ (Borneo; Dayak). Barrel drum; kettledrum. Also called *gendang*; *gandang.*
Lit.: no. 255.

Gandaṅ bavoi (Borneo). See *Ageng.*

Gandang (Java; Malaysia; Borneo). See *Gendang*; *Gandaṅ.*
Lit.: no. 132.

Ganda Taraṅgiṇi (South India). *Janya rāga* of the 29th *mēḷa* (*Dhīraśaṅkarābharaṇam*).
Tone material:
C E D E F G A B c
c A B G F D C
Lit.: no. 139.

Gande (Africa). Cf. *Ganga.*

Gander (Java). See *Gender.*

Gāndhāra (India). (1) Tone name indicating the third degree of a heptatonic scale. Its abbreviation is *ga.* See *Ṣaḍja* (under which heading are listed all tone names). (2) See *Jāti* (*rasa*).
Lit.: nos. 136, 138.

Gāndhāra Gauḷa (South India). *Janya rāga* of the 15th *mēḷa* (*Māyāmāḷavagauḷa*).
Tone material:
C F E G A♭ B c
c B A♭ G E D♭ C
Lit.: no. 139.

Gāndhārapañchamī (Ancient India). See *Jāti.*

Gāndhārapriya (South India). *Janya rāga* of the 20th *mēḷa* (*Naṭabhairavī*).
Tone material:
C E♭ D F G B♭ c
c B♭ A♭ G F D E♭ F D C
Lit.: no. 139.

Gāndhārī (North India). *Rāga* ascribed to the *Asavari thāta.*
Tone material:
C D F G A♭ B♭ c
c B♭ A♭ G F E♭ D♭ C; *Vādis*: A♭, E♭
Lit.: no. 138.

Gāndhārodīcyava (Ancient India). See *Jāti.*

Gāndharva (*Devagāndharva*) (Ancient India). Semi-divine musicians; a group of celestial beings skilled in singing and playing instruments, mentioned in sacred texts together with their lovely musician wives, the *apsaras.*
Lit.: no. 292.

Gāndharva (Ancient India). Early term for music. Cf. *Gīta*; *Saṃgīta*; *Vādita*; *Gātha*; *Vādya* (*kārupravādana*).
Lit.: no. 292.

Gāndharva kannada (South India). *Janya rāga* of the 31st *mēḷa* (*Yāgapriyā*).
Tone material:
C D♯ E G A♭ c
c B♭♭ A♭ G F E F D♯ C
Lit.: no. 139.

Gāndharvam (South India). *Janya rāga* of the 42nd *mēḷa* (*Raghupriyā*).
Tone material:
F♯ G A♯ B C D♭ E♭♭
E♭♭ D♭ C *B G F♯* (G)
Lit.: no. 139.

Gāndharva Manōharī (South India). *Janya rāga* of the 26th *mēḷa* (*Chārukeśī*).
Tone material:
C D F G c
c B♭ A♭ F E D C
Lit.: no. 139.

Gāndharva Nārāyaṇi (South India). *Janya rāga* of the 24th *mēḷa* (*Varuṇapriyā*).
Tone material:
C F G A♯ B c
c B A♯ B G F E♭ C
Lit.: no. 139.

Gandrung (Java). A lively, popular dance. The *joged gandrung* is a love dance, always performed by a boy, never by a girl. Cf. *Joged.*
Lit.: no. 163.

Gaṇḍul (Java). A form of rubato in orchestral playing when the *rebāb* lags behind.

Gane (Japan). Gong; bell.

Ganegbaja (Dahomey; Ghana—Ashanti). Drum.
Lit.: no. 255.

Ganga (Morocco; Sudan; Nigeria—Hausa). (1) General term for a two-headed drum in various forms. All of their names end with *ganga*: *digongo*, *gonga*, *gongo*, *gande*, and others. (2) Kettledrum beaten with a knotted rope.
Lit.: no. 218.

Gangan (Nigeria—Yoruba). (1) An hourglass drum. (2) An ensemble of stick-beaten drums. It consists of:

1. *Gangan*, used by old men and musicians in traditional religious and dance performances.
2. *Adama* (*apala*), a drum popular with young persons.
3. *Kannango*, the smallest drum of the group, used in light entertainment.

Each drum has two tunable skins, an hourglass-shaped body, and a cylindrical waist. Young people who learn the "speaking" technique play the latter type of drum.
Lit.: nos. 293, 303.

Gangana (West Africa; Mali—Dogon). Iron bell.

Gangana (*Gangina*) (Assam—Bodo). Jew's harp made of bamboo.
Lit.: no. 46.

Gangatan (Sahara; Sudan—Tuareg). Term for drum in various shapes. The body can be made of clay or wood and has one or two skins. It is beaten with a club (*etokar*) or with leather straps and is used in diverse festivals and war dances.
Lit.: no. 255.

Gaṅgā Taraṅgiṇī (South India). *Janya rāga* of the 33rd *mēḷa* (*Gāṅgeyabhushanī*).
Tone material:
C D♯ E F G c
c B A♭ G F E F D♯ C
The present form of *Gāṅgeyataraṅginī*.
Lit.: no. 139.

Gaṅgā Taraṅgiṇī (South India). (1) The 33rd *asampūrṇa mēḷa-rāga* without *kaṭapayādi* prefix. (2) The 33rd *asampūrṇa mēḷa-rāga* with *kaṭapayādi* prefix. See *Rāga* (South India).
Lit.: no. 139.

Gāṅgeyabhushanī (*Gāṅgeyabhuṣanī*). (1) The 33rd *mēḷa*:
C D♯ E F G A♭ B c
(2) As *rāga*, it has the same tone material. Veṅkaṭamakhin (17th century) called this *rāga* *Gāṅgātaraṅgiṇī* or *Gaṅgeyataraṅgiṇī*.
Lit.: no. 139.

Gāṅgeyabhuṣanī (South India). See *Gāṅgeyabhushanī*.

Gāṅgeya Taraṅgiṇī (South India). See *Gāṅgeyabhushanī* and *Gāṅga Taraṅgiṇī*.

Gang-gaingi (*Hai-kum*; *Hae-kum*; *He-kum*) (Korea). A fiddle similar to the Chinese *hu-ch'in* and the Japanese *ko-kyu*. It has two silken strings strung very close to each other. Both strings are tuned to the same pitch. The corpus is a wooden cylinder or a small barrel. At the end of a long, slim, curved neck are two large pegs. The instrument, presumably of Mongolian origin, is used in Korea in indigenous music, in imported Chinese music, and in dance music.
Lit.: nos. 52, 179.

Ganggereng (Borneo—Dayak). A stick with leaves and seed kernels attached to its upper end. When stamped against the ground during dances it creates a rattling noise.
Lit.: no. 255.

Gangina (Assam). See *Gangana*.

Gangsa (Bali). "Bronze." The term indicates a one-octave metallophone, the keys of which are hung (*gantung*) or laid upon (*jongkok*) over a wooden block with resonance holes. The slabs are usually made of bronze, but there are instruments that have iron or bamboo slabs and are struck with a small mallet.
Lit.: nos. 197, 265.

Gang'sa (Philippines; Northern Luzon; Bontoc—Igorot). Gong. Ensemble of flat gongs. Cf. *Topayya*; *Itundak*.

Gangsa dasa (Bali). See *Gangsa gantung*.

Gangsa gantung (Bali). A *gangsa* with nine or 10 suspended keys. The nine-key instrument is called *gangsa siya*, the one with 10 keys is called *gangsa dasa*. The keys are struck with a little mallet.
Lit.: nos. 197, 265.

Gangsa jongkok (Bali). A *gangsa* or *saron* where the keys are not suspended, but each key rests on two pins and strips of rubber on top of the sound box. Cf. *Gangsa gantung*.
Lit.: nos. 197, 265.

Gangsal (Java). Cf. *Lima*; *Slendro*.

Gangsa patigan (Java). See *Gamelan munggang*.

Gangsaran (Java). A freely structured *gending* that represents an introduction to a piece in fast tempo. The *gangsaran* begins with one note (*gulu*) and all other instruments of the ensemble join in this pitch. When a high point of tension is reached the piece in fast tempo begins. Cf. *Merong*; *Gending parikan*.
Lit.: no. 163.

Gangsa senen (Java). Monday *gamelan*.

Gangsa setu (Java). Saturday *gamelan*.

Gangsa siya (Bali). The *gangsa gantung* with nine keys used in the *gamelan gong kebyar*. Cf. *Gangsa gantung*.
Lit.: no. 197.

Gangsingan (*Papanggalan*) (Java). A spinning top made of a cylindrical piece of bamboo pierced vertically by a thin stick. When spinning it creates a whistling sound.
Lit.: no. 163.

Gangurih (Mongolia—Kalmuck). Trumpet made of the arm-bone of a killed enemy.
Lit.: no. 255.

Ganhogui (Ghana—Ewe). Cf. *Atsiagbekor*.

Ganibri (North Africa; Morocco). See *Gnbri*; *Gunibri*.

Gaṇita Vinōdiṇi (South India). *Janya rāga* of the 16th *mēḷa* (*Chakravāka*).
Tone material:
C E F G B♭ c
c B♭ A G F E D♭ C
Lit.: no. 139.

Ganjel (Java). "Support." Bridge of a zither. In East Java it is called *tlapakan* ("foot sole").
Lit.: no. 163.

Ganjur (*Genjur*) (Java). Gong that creates a strongly vibrating sound. Cf. *Kempul.*
Lit.: no. 163.

Gankogui (Ghana—Ewe). A double bell without clappers. Two iron bells are linked together at the top.
Lit.: no. 128.

Ganoun (Arabia; Middle East). See *Qanun.*

Ganrang (Celebes—Macassar). Barrel drum. See *Gendang.*
Lit.: no. 255.

Gaṅsa (Java; Bali). Cf. *Gangsa.*

Gaṇṭa (South India—Tekugu). Hand bell. See *Ghaṇṭa.*

Gantung (Bali). "Hanging from," "suspending." A playing method in which the same note (or its octave) is repeated, usually in triplets. This method is also called *jantur* ("to lift," "to suspend").
Lit.: no. 163.

Ganvikpan (West Africa; Dahomey). A double metal bell. See *Gankogui.*
Lit.: no. 128.

Ganza (West Africa; Lower Guinea). Musical bow.
Lit.: no. 255.

Gapagala (*Gapimbi*) (Republic of the Congo). Drum. Drumming. Cf. *Ngoma.*
Lit.: nos. 28-29.

Gapeng (Caroline Isl.). Cf. *Gapenggapeng.*

Gapenggapeng (*Gapengapeng*; *Gapeng*) (Caroline Isl.—Ifaluk Atoll). Evocation.

Gapimbi (Southwest of the Republic of Congo). Term for *ngoma.* Also called *gapagala.*
Lit.: nos. 28-29.

Gāpriyanagam (South India). *Janya rāga* of the 12th *mēḷa* (*Rūpāvatī*).
Tone material:
C F G A♯ B c
c A♯ B G F E♭ D♭ C
Lit.: no. 139.

Gara (North India). *Rāga* ascribed to the *Khamaj thāta.* It is often described as a combination of phrases taken from the *rāgas Jhinjhoti*, *Pilu*, and *Khamaj.*
Tone material:
C D E F G A B c
c B♭ A G F E♭ D C; *Vādis*: E, (B)
Lit.: no. 138.

Gara-bageshri (North India). Obscure *rāga* consisting of a combination of phrases of the *rāgas Gara* and *Bageshri.*
Tone material (vague):
C D E F G A B♭ (c)
(c) B♭ A G F E♭ D C; *Vādis*: F, C
Lit.: no. 139.

Garadap (*Enserunai*) (Borneo—Dayak). A bowed string instrument. It is a crude imitation of the *rebāb*. The instrument has one or two strings made of fiber or copper wire. The body is either a gourd or a coconut shell with a movable bridge.
Lit.: no. 255.

Gara-gara (Java). A *wayang parwa* scene with ominous apparitions appearing at midnight, and representations of divine, mysterious figures.
Lit.: no. 163.

Gara-Kanada (North India). An obscure *rāga* that represents a combination of phrases taken from the *rāga Gara* and the *Kanada* family. The tone-material and the *vādis* are vague and flexible, as *Gara* itself is a combination of elements taken from the *rāgas Jhinjoti*, *Pilu*, and *Khamaj.*
Lit.: no. 138.

Garalāri (South India). *Janya rāga* of the 65th *mēḷa* (*Mechakalyāṇi*).
Tone material:
C D E F♯ A B c
c B A G E D C
Lit.: no. 139.

Garamudu (Oceania). See *Garamut.*

Garamut (Bismarck Archipelago; New Ireland) Also *Garmuth.* A wooden slit-drum. Other names of this drum are: *angremut, dangamut, galamutu, garamutu, geramo, gerom, karamut, kolamut, naramut, ngaramut, ngilamo, qaramut, tarremut.*
Lit.: nos. 84, 190, 255.

Garangtong (*Garanktum*) (Sumatra—Toba-Batak). Xylophone. Cf. *Tawak*; *Do'uda*; *Preson*; *Busut.*
Lit.: no. 255.

Garanton(g) (Southeast Borneo). Cf. *Tawak* (large gong).
Lit.: no. 159.

Garantung (Bali). The name of a *gambang*-like instrument used by the Batak people in the highlands of Sumatra. Cf. *Doli-doli.*

Ǧaras (Arabia). See *Jaras.*

Garathe (Thailand). Cf. *Chakay.*

Gārava Siṃhala (South India). *Janya rāga* of the 22nd *mēḷa* (*Kharaharapriyā*).
Tone material:
C E♭ D E♭ F G A B♭ G A G c
c B♭ G A G F E♭ D C
Lit.: no. 139.

Garaya (Republic of Niger; Nigeria—Hausa). Lute with two strings.

Garbha Līla (South India). *Janya rāga* of the 46th *mēḷa* (*Śaḍvidhamārgiṇī*).
Tone material:
C F♯ E♭ F♯ G B♭ A B♭ c
c B♭ A G F♯ E♭ F♯ E♭ D♭ C
Lit.: no. 139.

Garbha Śārdūlam (South India). *Janya rāga* of the 51st *mēḷa* (*Kāmavardhanī*).
Tone material:
C D♭ E F♯ B c
c B G A♯ G F♯ E D♭ C
Lit.: no. 139.

Garbi (Algeria; Biskra). See *Qarbi.*

Gar byed-pa (Tibet). Dance.

Gareng-gareng (Indonesia; Alor Isl.; Timor). Bull roarer. Cf. *Jata* (Flores).

Gardana (Persia). (1) Peg. (2) Musical instrument.
Lit.: no. 255.

Ǧarga (*Jarga*) (Arabia). *Maqām*; imported from Persia; identical with *sasgar.*
Lit.: no. 121.

Gargara (Vedic India). Obscure instrument (mentioned in *Rig Veda* 2:433; 8:69; 9; *Atharvaveda* 37,4). It could have been a lute, a *vīṇā*, a harp, or a bell, cymbals, and jingles.
Lit.: nos. 205, 250.

Gargēśvari (South India). *Janya rāga* of the 65th *mēḷa* (*Mechakalyāṇī*).
Tone material:
C D G A B c
c B A F♯ A G E D C
Lit.: no. 139.

Gariding (Borneo). See *Giriding.*
Lit.: no. 255.

Garigadya (South India). See *Gurugadya.*

Garika (India). Bow.

Garinding (Java). Bamboo pipe with a mouthpiece that contains a vibrating tongue.
Lit.: no. 255.

Garinga-taue (Northeast Africa; Nubia). Trumpet.

Garinge (Northeast Africa; Nubia). Flute.
Lit.: no. 255.

Garjam (South India). *Janya rāga* of the 17th *mēḷa* (*Sūryakānta*).
Tone material:
C E F A B c
c B A G F E D♭ C
Lit.: no. 139.

Gar-mk'an (Tibet). Dancer.

Garmut (*Garmuth*) (Oceania). See *Garamut.*

Garmuth (Pacific; Melanesia). Wooden slit-drum.
Lit.: no. 255.

Garode (Borneo – Dayak; Dusun). See *Garude.*

Garras (Southwest Africa – Bushmen). End-blown pipe made of an animal horn.
Lit.: no. 151.

Garsing (*Gissang*) (Nias). Wooden pipe.

Gar-stabs (Tibet). Dancing; dancing movement.

Garuḍadhvani (South India). *Janya rāga* of the 29th *mēḷa* (*Dhīraśaṅkarābharaṇam*).
Tone material:
C D E F G A B c
c A G E D C
Lit.: no. 139.

Garuḍapriya (South India). *Janya rāga* of the 45th *mēḷa* (*Śubhapantuvarālī*).
Tone material:
C F♯ G A♭ B c
c d♭ c B A♭ G F♯ D♭ E♭ D♭ C
Lit.: no. 139.

Garuḍa Varāḷi (South India). *Janya rāga* of the 59th *mēḷa* (*Dharmavatī*).
Tone material:
C D E♭ G B c
c B G F♯ E♭ D C
Lit.: no. 139.

Garuḍavardhani (South India). *Janya rāga* of the 45th *mēḷa* (*Śubhapantuvarālī*).
Tone material:
C D♭ E♭ F♯ B A♭ F♯ G A♭ B c
c B G F♯ D♭ C
Lit.: no. 139.

Garude (South Borneo – Dayak; Dusun). *Garude* (also *klaeddi*) is a mouth organ consisting of a bundle of bamboo tubes placed into a small gourd that serves as a wind chest. In North Borneo the instrument has eight pipes (four short ones and four long); in Southeast Borneo it has five short pipes and one long one.
Lit.: no. 255.

Garuding (Borneo). See *Giriding.*

Garyāl (North India; Persia). Gong.

Gasa-bin (Cameroon; Nilotic Sudan – Baia). Large slit-drum.
Lit.: no. 33.

Gaṣba (North Africa; Biskra). A long vertical wooden flute with 5-6 holes.
Lit.: no. 20.

Gat (North India). A rhythmical variation in the performance of a *khyāl.* It appears at twice the original speed. A further doubling of the tempo producing speed four times faster than that of the original is called *gat paran.*
Lit.: no. 136.

Gatambore (Borneo). See *Katamboṅ.*

Gat paran (North India). See *Gat.*

Gātha (Ancient India). Early term for religious chant; recent term: religious and secular recitation.
Lit.: no. 292.

Gāṭha (South India). Cf. *Gaḍa.*

Gāthika (India). The term indicates the use of only two notes in the performance of certain sections of the Vedic chant.
Lit.: no. 261.

Gati (India). Tempo. *Druti gati* means fast tempo; *Manda Gati*, slow tempo. Cf. Lit. no. 261.

Gaud (North India). *Rāga* which consists to a great extent of phrases from the *rāga* families *Mallār* and *Kanada.*
The flexible tone material can be:
C (D) (E♭) F G A B c
c (B♭) A G (F) (E♭) D C
Lit.: no. 138.

Gauḍa Mallāri (*Gauḍa Mallāru*; *Gauḷa Mallār*) (South India). *Janya rāga* of the 29th *mēḷa* (*Dhīraśaṅkarābharaṇam*).
Tone material:
C D F G A c
c B A F E D C
Lit.: no. 139.

Gauḍa Mallāru (South India). See *Gauḍa Mallāri.*

Gaudi (North India). An obscure *rāga* ascribed to the *Kalyan thāta. Gaudi* is often considered to be a type of *rāga Kedar.* It appears to consist of a combination of elements taken from the *rāgas Kedar*, *Bilaval*, *Sorat*, and *Mallār.*
The tone material is flexible and, among various possibilities, could be:
C F D G F G A B c
c B A B G A B♭ A G F E (D C)
Lit.: no. 138.

Gauḍīpantu (South India). See *Gaulīpantu.*

Gaud-mallār (North India). A *rāga* that can be ascribed either to the *Kafi* or to the *Khamaj thātas.* Generally there are five types of this *rāga*:

1. The note F is used as *vādi*; the scale uses E, never E♭.
2. G used as *vādi.* E is used (never E♭).
3. G used as *vādi.* E♭ is used (never E).
4. G used as *vādi.* Both E and E♭ can be employed.
5. Either F or G used as *vādi.* The scale avoids both E and E♭.

Tone materials:
(a) and (b) C D E F G A B c
c B♭ (A G A) E D C
(c) C D E♭ F G A B♭ (B) c
c B♭ A G F E♭ (D C)
(d) C D E F G A B c
c B♭ A G F E♭ (D C)
(e) C D F G A B c
c B♭ A G F D C
Lit.: no. 138.

Gaud-sarang (North India). A *rāga* usually ascribed to the *Kalyan thāta.*
Tone material:
C D E (F) F♯ G A B c
c B (B♭) A G F E D C
The characteristic feature of *Gaud-sarang* are the *vakra* (zig-zag) motions in ascent and descent; e.g.:
C E D F E G c
c A G E F D G E F D C; *Vādis*: E, A
Lit.: no. 138.

Gaula (South India). *Janya rāga* of the 15th *mēḷa* (*Māyāmāḷavagauḷa*).
Tone material:
C D♭ F G B c
(C D♭ E F D♭ F G B C)
c B G F D♭ E F E D♭ C
(c B G F E F D♭ C)
Lit.: no. 139.

Gaula Chandrika (South India). *Janya rāga* of the 7th *mēḷa* (*Senāpāti*).
Tone material:
C D♭ F G A♭ c
c B♭♭ A♭ G E♭ D♭ C
Lit.: no. 139.

Gauḷa gāndhāri (South India). *Janya rāga* of the 68th *mēḷa* (*Jyōtisvarūpiṇī*).
Tone material:
C D♯ E F♯ G A♭ c
c B♭ A♭ G F♯ E D♯ C
Lit.: no. 139.

Gauḷa Māḷavi (South India). *Janya rāga* of the 6th *mēḷa* (*Tānārūpi*).
Tone material:
C D♭ E♭♭ F G A♯ B G B c
c G A♯ B G F E♭♭ D♭ C
Lit.: no. 139.

Gauḷa Mallār (South India). See *Gauḍa Mallāri.*

Gaulan (India). Light, popular song. *Gaulan* implies "milkmaid." Her love songs and texts salute the god Krishna, who is often described as *gauli*, "cowboy."

Gauḷa Pañcamam (South India). See *Gauḷa Pañchamam.*

Gauḷa Pañchamam (*Gauḷa Pañcamam*) (South India). *Janya rāga* of the 24th *mēḷa* (*Varuṇa-priyā*).
Tone material:
C D F G B c
c B G F E♭ D C
Lit.: no. 139.

Gaulīpantu (*Gauḍīpantu*) (South India). *Janya rāga* of the 15th *mēḷa* (*Māyāmāḷavagauḷa*).
Tone material:
C D♭ E D♭ F G A♭ G B c
(C D♭ F G B c)
c B A♭ G F E D♭ C
(c B A♭ G F G A♭ F E D♭ C)
Lit.: no. 139.

Gau piti piti (Solomon Isl.; Florida Isl.). Pan flute; 13 bamboo pipes are placed around a central bourdon pipe.
Lit.: no. 255.

Gaupuchha (North India). "Cow's tail." A rhythmic phrase that, graphically shown, is believed to resemble the shape of a cow's tail.
Lit.: no. 136.

Gauri (North India). A *rāga* ascribed to the *Purvi thāta*. It must not be confused with *rāgas* with the same name (ascribed to the *Bilaval* and *Bhairav thātas*).
There are three versions:
(a) C D♭ E F♯ G A♭ (B) c
c (B) A♭ G F♯ E D♭ C
(b) C D♭ E F (F♯) G A♭ B c
c (B) A♭ G F♯ E D♭ C
(c) C D♭ E (F) F♯ G A♭ (A) B c
c B A (A♭) G F♯ (F) E D♭ C; *Vādis*: D♭, G
Lit.: no. 138.

Gauri (*Gauḍi*) (North India). *Rāga* ascribed to the *Bhairav thāta.*
Tone material:
C D♭ F G B c
c B A♭ G F E D♭ C; *Vādis*: D♭, G

Gaurī (South India). *Janya rāga* of the 15th *mēḷa* (*Māyāmāḷavagauḷa*).
Tone material:
C D♭ F G B c
c B A♭ G F E D♭ C
Lit.: no. 139.

Gaurī Bangala (South India). *Janya rāga* of the 9th *mēḷa* (*Dhēnuka*).
Tone material:
A♭ C D♭ F G A♭ B
A♭ H G E♭ D♭ C *B A♭* C
Lit.: no. 139.

GaurīGāndhāri (South India). *Janya rāga* of the 2nd *mēḷa* (*Ratnangi*).

Tone material:
C F D♭ E♭♭ F E A♭ B♭ A♭ c
c B♭ A♭ G F E♭♭ D♭ C
Lit.: no. 139.

Gaurī Kālam (South India). Brass trumpet with conical bore. The instrument is used in religious ceremonies. Cf. *Kālam*.
Lit.: no. 261.

Gaurī Kriya (South India). *Janya rāga* of the 60th *mēḷa* (*Nītimatī*).
Tone material:
C E♭ F♯ G A♯ B c
c B A♯ B G F♯ E♭ C
Lit.: no. 139.

Gaurīmanōharī (*Gaurīmonōharī*) (South India).
(1) The 23rd *mēḷa*:
C D E♭ F G A B c
(2) As *rāga* it has the same tone material as shown above. Veṅkaṭamakhin (17th century) calls this *rāga Gaurīveḷāvaḷī*.
Lit.: no. 139.

Gaurīmāruva (South India). *Janya rāga* of the 50th *mēḷa* (*Nāmanārāyaṇī*).
Tone material:
C D♭ F♯ G A♭ c
c B♭ A♭ G F♯ E D♭ E C
Lit.: no. 139.

Gaurīmonōharī (South India). See *Gaurīman-ōharī*.

Gaurī Niṣādam (South India). *Janya rāga* of the 71st *mēḷa* (*Kōsala*).
Tone material:
C E F♯ G B A c
c B A B G F♯ E C
Lit.: no. 139.

Gaurī Pantu (South India). *Janya rāga* of the 51st *mēḷa* (*Kāmavardhanī*).

Tone material:
C D♭ F♯ G B c
c B A♭ G F♯ A♭ F♯ E D♭ C
Lit.: no. 139.

Gaurī Sīmanti (*Gaurī Sīmantini*). *Janya rāga* of the 70th *mēḷa* (*Nāsikabhūṣanī*).
Tone material:
C D♯ E F♯ G A B♭ c
c B♭ G F♯ E C
Lit.: no. 139.

Gaurī Sīmanṭini (South India). See *Gaurī Sīmanti.*

Gaurī Vasantam (South India). *Janya rāga* of the 22nd *mēḷa* (*Kharaharapriyā*).
Tone material:
C D F G A B♭ c
c B♭ A G F D E♭ D C
Lit.: no. 139.

Gaurīveḷāvaḷī (South India). See *Gaurīman-ōharī.*

Gaurīveḷāvalī (South India). See *Veḷāvalī* (23rd *asampūrṇa mēḷa*).

Gaurkalyan (*Gorkikalyna*; not to be mistaken with *Gorakh-Kalyan*) (North India). *Rāga* ascribed to the *Kalyan thāta.*
Tone material:
C (D) E F♯ G (A) B c
c B A G (F) E D C; *Vādis*: E, B
Lit.: no. 138.

Gauruga (Mongolia; Persia). Drum (kettle-drum).
Lit.: no. 255.

Gautami (South India). *Janya rāga* of the 1st *mēḷa* (*Kanakāṅgī*).
Tone material:
C D♭ E♭♭ G A♭ B♭♭ c
c B♭♭ A♭ G E♭♭ D♭ C
Lit.: no. 139.

Gavāmbōdhi (South India). (1) The 43rd *mēḷa*:
C D♭ E♭ F♯ G A♭ B♭♭ c
(2) As *rāga*, several versions exist. The basic scale is the same as stated above but variants show, e.g., the complete deletion of the note B♭♭ (cf. *Añjanāvatī*).

Gavaṇtu (India). The projecting ivory ledge that separates the body of a *vīṇā* from the stem.
Lit.: no. 261.

Gavāsht (Arabia). A tone name indicating a note ca. 2/3 of a tone higher than *'iraq*. (All tone names within the range of two octaves are listed under the heading of *Jagā* [*Yagā*].) See *Gushat* (*Kushat*).

Ga-wa (New Guinea – Papua). A small musical bow with two strings. The player's mouth serves as resonator. The strings are plucked or strummed.
Lit.: no. 233.

Ǧawāq (Northwest Africa). A short beaked cane flute which is never used in a serious musical performance.
Lit.: no. 250.

Gawe (Java). See *Imbal.*

Gawi (Flores; Southern Lio). A dance, similar to the *teke* dance of the Nage people. The melody is started by one singer and joined after a few measures by a chorus.
Lit.: no. 166.

Gawu (*Gadodo*) (West Africa – Ewe). Kettle-drum.
Lit.: no. 255.

Gawukha (South Africa – Bushmen). Primitive zither consisting of a hollowed piece of wood covered with skin. It has one string.
Lit.: no. 151.

Gayakālāsini (South India). *Janya rāga* of the 30th *mēḷa* (*Nāgānandī*).
Tone material:
C D E F G A♯ c
c A♯ G F E D C
Lit.: no. 139.

Gāyakamandini (South India). *Janya rāga* of the 25th *mēḷa* (*Mārarañjanī*).
Tone material:
C D E F G A♭ c
c A♭ G F E D C
Lit.: no. 139.

Gāyakapriya (South India). (1) The 13th *mēḷa*:
C D♭ E F G A♭ B♭♭ c
(2) As a *rāga*, based on the same tone material. It was called in earlier systems by the name *Hejjuji*; when *kaṭapayādi* prefixes came into use it was called *Geyahejjaji.*
Lit.: no. 139.

Gāyakarañjani (South India). *Janya rāga* of the 29th *mēḷa* (*Dhīraśaṅkarābharaṇam*).
Tone material:
C D E F G A c
c A G F E D C
Lit.: no. 139.

Gāyana (Ancient Idia). Male singer. Cf. *Gāyikā.*

Gāyikā (Ancient India). Female singer. Cf. *Gāyana.*

Gayor (Java). A wooden frame in which a gong is suspended.
Lit.: no. 163.

Gaza (Congo – Azande). Large barrel drum. Cf. *Lari*; *Ndima*; *Kindri.*
Lit.: no. 184.

Gbedo (Dahomey). Drum made of a carved out tree trunk.
Lit.: no. 255.

Gbedu (Nigeria – Yoruba). *Gbedu* or *agba*, royal drum. Also an instrumental ensemble playing solemn, ceremonial music for royal processions and festivities.
Lit.: no. 293.

Gbee-kee (Liberia—Kpelle). Single-string bow lute.
Lit.: no. 284.

Gbegbetele (Liberia—Kpelle). Multiple bow lute.
Lit.: no. 284.

Gbelee (Liberia—Kpelle). *Sanza.*
Lit.: no. 284.

Gbere (Uganda). See *Oliko.*

Gbetu (Liberia). Masked dancer.

Gbingbe (Congo—Azande). See *Kweningba* (xylophone) without resonators.
Lit.: no. 249.

Gbo (Ivory Coast). Weeping; mourning songs.

Gbolo (Liberia—Kpelle). Paired, footed drums.
Lit.: no. 284.

Gbun-gbun (Liberia—Kpelle). Barrel drum beaten with wooden sticks. The drum is held between the knees or at the hip of the player.
Lit.: no. 284.

Gcig (*chig*) (Tibet). Notational symbol in Buddhist chant notation that indicates one (single or subdivided) beat.
Lit.: no. 143.

Gdangs (Tibet). Hymn in strict meter. The term is also applied to melody and music in general.
Lit.: no. 143.

Ge (Japan). Tone syllable in the *yokyōku* system. Cf. *Noh*; *Yokyōku.*
Lit.: no. 185.

Ge (*Gei*) (Japan). Name of the 15th pipe of the *shō*. Cf. *Shō.*
Lit.: no. 225.

Ge (*Kunka-da*; *Kada*) (Japan). Cf. *Wasan.*

Ge (*Ke*) (North India). *Bol* (drum syllable) performed on the closed *bayan* (*band bayan*) by the left hand. The heel of the hand remains on the rim of the drum while fingers 2, 3, 4, and 5, closely together, strike the *maidan.*
Lit.: no. 136.

Gebugan (Flores—West Java). Cf. *Main chachih.*
Lit.: no. 166.

Gebuki (Japan). "Summer blowing." A summer practice of Japanese musicians devised for the training of flute players in order to enable them to perform in any climate. See *Kan-geiko.*
Lit.: no. 225.

Geda (*keda*) (Flores). (1) Drum. See *Waning.* (2) *Geda* or *lambajawa* of Lio and Ende is the same as the *gedang* or *rebana* of Maumere (Flores).
Lit.: no. 166.

Gedang (Flores; Maumere). Small one-headed goblet-shaped drum. In Ende the drum is called *geda* or *lambajawa* and, in the Manggaray, *tutung* or *takitu.*
Lit.: no. 166.

Gede (Bali). Large; deep sound. The term referring to the opposite is *alit* (Sund.: *leutik*), "small," high pitched. In West Java *gede* indicates also the lowest of a range of four octaves. (Cf. *Petit*—West Java.) The Bali term for the lowest octave range is *ageng.*

Gedo (Congo—Bakongo pygmies). Musical bow.
Lit.: no. 176.

Gedombak (*gedu*; *gedumbak*) (Malaysia). Mushroom-shaped wooden drum with a single head made of goatskin. It is the same as the Siamese *thon* and the Cambodian *skor.*
Lit.: no. 19.

Gedu (Malaysia). See *Gedombak.*

Geduk (Malaysia). Generally a barrel drum standing in a slightly oblique (or vertical) position. The (upper) drumhead is called *baji* and the term for the body is *temalang.* There are two types of the drum—the *geduk ibu* and the *geduk anak*:

1. *Gedombak* (*geduk*) *ibu*, the lower-pitched drum.
2. *Gedombak* (*geduk*) *anak*, the higher-pitched drum.

Lit.: no. 217.

Gedzo (South Africa—Sotho). One of a four-drum group. The four drum names are: *gedzo* ("beating drum"—*gediza*), *beguri*, *tutumedjo*, and *magodi.*
Lit.: no. 151.

Ge'ez (Ethiopia). Cf. *Zēmā.*

Gegrumbungan (Malaysia). Huge wooden bells that are hung around the necks of bulls at the beginning of work in the fields.
Lit.: no. 254.

Gehong (Borneo—Bukar-Dayak). A barrel drum covered at one end with monkey skin and kept open at the lower end.

Gei (Japan). See *Ge.*

Geino (Japan). See *Minzoku-geino.*

Geisha (Japan). The lowest class (fourth class) of female musicians.
Lit.: no. 185.

Gejjai (India). Ankle bells worn by actors and dancers. See also *Shilambu.*
Lit.: no. 46.

Gejongan (Java). See *Bendrong.*

Gekin (Japan). See *Gekkin.*

Gekkin (Japan). Occasionally called the "miniature *biwa*" or the "moon-shaped *koto.*" It is of Chinese origin and is popular in Japan. It is a flat lute with two silken double strings tuned a fifth apart. The instrument has a circular body in which vibrates a resonating wire string. The *gekkin* has a short neck and 8-9 frets, four of which are placed upon the body, the rest on the neck. Songs sung to the accompaniment of the *gekkin* are generally of Chinese origin.

The frets produce the following notes if the two string pairs are tuned to C and G:

Fret	1st pair of strings	2nd pair of strings
Open strings	C	G
1st fret	D	A
2nd "	E	B
3rd "	F	c
4th "	G	d
5th "	A	e
6th "	c	g
7th "	d	a
8th "	f	c'

The instrument is played with a small ivory or tortoise-shell plectrum. Cf. *Wol-kum Yüeh-ch'in.* There exists also a six-string *gekkin* with a circular body, the string again tuned in pairs, and 16 frets.

Gekko (Japan). "Moon drum." A drum with a flat wooden body beaten with two wooden sticks in the same manner as the (*noh*) *taiko* is struck.
Lit.: no. 255.

Geko (Flores; Ende). Simple xylophone. Cf. *Preson.*

Gelang (Java; Sunda District). Sliding rings that regulate the tension of a *rarawat.*

Gelao (New Guinea—Papua). Flute played at circumcision ceremonies.
Lit.: no. 255.

Gelgel (Arabia). See *Gülgül.*
Lit.: no. 255.

Geliti (Lower Congo). Term for *sansa.*
Lit.: no. 280.

Gembi (Uganda – Mundu). Drum.

Gembri (Arabia). Old term for the two-stringed *gnbrī* (*gunibri*). Cf. *Gnbrī* (Morocco).

Gembyakan (Java). "To banter," "clownish," "having fun." Drumming pattern with an almost completely liberty for the player. In Solo it is called *ḍagelan* ("clownish"). Some of the funny beats are: *ḍanḍang*, *tulung*, *tungtung*, *ḍootḍoot*, *ḍet*.
Lit.: no. 163.

Gembyang (West Java). See *Setukat.*

Gembyangan (Java). Term for the octave interval; the added octave tone. Frequently called *sagembyangan.* In East Java it is called *chochokan* (the "corresponding" tone). The Sundanese term is *beulit.* For example: the range of the *gamelan* has six to seven octaves (*gembyangan*).
Lit.: no. 163.

Gembyung (West Java). Term for *terbang besar*, *terbang gembrung*, and *terbang ketimpring* (outside the regency of Lebak).
Lit.: no. 163.

Gem(p)ret (Java). See *Selompret.*

Genchlek (*Rusuh*) (Sunda District). Tempo indication: very fast. Cf. *Wirahma* (*Wirama*).

Genda (Flores – Manggaray). Frame drum. Cf. *Rebana.*
Lit.: no. 166.

Genḍang (Flores; Borneo – Dayak). Drum. See *Waning*. In Borneo: kettledrum. In Sumatra: drum with a pot-shaped body in conical form. Cf. *Kenḍang*; *Göndrang*; *Göndra.*
Lit.: no. 160.

Gendang (Malaysia). A drum with one or two heads. The body has the shape of an hourglass. The upper cone is narrower than the lower one. Cf. *Gordang.* The *gendang* can also have the shape that resembles that of the Indian *mṛdanga.*
Lit.: no. 255.

Gendang anak (Malaysia). Cf. *Geduk.*

Gendang batak (Malaysia). (1) A *valiha* of the Siamese Malayans. (2) An instrument with one string stretched between two pegs hammered into the ground. Beneath the string there is a hole in the ground covered with a palm leaf. Upon the palm leaf rests a small piece of wood that functions as a bridge. The string is beaten with two little wooden sticks.
Lit.: no. 255.

Gendang bawoi (Southeast Borneo – Dayak). "Pig drum." The instrument is no drum but a *valiha* with three (struck) strings.
Lit.: no. 255.

Gendang bulu (Sumatra – Batak). A *valiha* with three fiber strings that are strung along a piece of bamboo. The instrument is also called *gendang-gendang.*

Gendang-gendang (Central Borneo – Punan; South Celebes – Toala). Xylophone. See also *Gendang bulu*; *Gettung-gettung.*
Lit.: nos. 166, 254.

Gendang Ibu (Malaysia). See *Geduk.*

Gendang kling (Malaysia). An instrumental ensemble for dance music. It consists of one *serunai*, two drums (*gendang anak* and *gendang ibu*), two gongs (*gong jantan*, a large, and *betina*, a small one). The ensemble appears in the Northwest States, e.g., in Kedah of Malaysia.
Lit.: no. 217.

Gendang mara (Borneo – Dayak). A *gendang* (drum) with two skins. In contrast to the common *gendang* the larger skin (*bam*) is on top, the smaller one (*kampiang* or *sampiang*) below. Generally two such drums are used together: a louder sounding one (*panggulong*) and a weaker one (*paningka*). Both instruments are beaten with sticks.
Lit.: no. 255.

Gendang naubat (Malaysia). Big drum used at festive occasions.

Gendang nobat (Malaysia). See *Gendang naubat.*

Gendang panjang (Indonesia; Bangka). Big barrel drum.

Gendang pendek (Indonesia). Wooden drum with one skin.
Lit.: no. 255.

Gendang prang (West Borneo). War drum with two skins. Its body is slightly conically-shaped and mildly curved. The player beats the drum with his bare hands.
Lit.: no. 255.

Gendang rebāna (Malaysia). A cup-shaped drum with a wooden body and an open bottom. The single head is made of sheep skin.

Gendang toto (Borneo – Dayak). A very high-pitched drum. It has a wooden, cylindrical body and is beaten with the hand or a stick.
Lit.: no. 255.

Gende (Kedol – Malacca). Cf. *Din tenkhin.*

Gender (Bali). Metallophone with 10-15 thin slabs placed horizontally on a net. Below each slab is placed a tuned bamboo resonator tube. The range of the instruments extends for two octaves or slightly more. There are various types of the *gender*: *gender dasa* with 10 slabs, *gender telulas* with 13 slabs, and *gender limolas* with 15 slabs.
Lit.: nos. 197, 265.

Gender (Java). A metallophone consisting of 10-12 thin metal slabs placed upon a criss cross of strings and bamboo resonance tubes (*bunbungan*).

In recent times the bamboo tubes are replaced by metal or glass resonators. Four types are distinguished: *gender panerus*, *gender barung*, *gender slentem* (*slentem gantung* = *slentem*, with hanging keys), *gender demung* (*gantung*). *Gender* is also spelled *gendir.*
Lit.: no. 163.

Genderang (Malaysia). Drum.

Gender barangan (Bali). The *gender* that follows the leading instrument. A pair of small *genders*, small *trompongs* which are tuned an octave higher than the leading instrument.
Lit.: nos. 197, 265.

Gender barung (Java). A medium sized *gender* with bronze or bamboo slabs suspended over resonators is used in the "soft playing" parts, together with the *gender panembung* (of the lower octave range) and *gender panerus* (of the high octave range).
Lit.: no. 255.

Gender dasa (Bali). Gender with 10 slabs. See *Gender wayang.*
Lit.: no. 197.

Gender demung (*gantung*) (Java). A *gender* with the range of an octave that sounds an octave higher than *gender slentem.* It is used only in the *gamelan klenengan.*
Lit.: no. 163.

Gender lemprak (Java). A gender without any resonator tubes.

Gender limolas (Bali). A gender with 15 keys. See *Gender.*

Gender panembung (Java; Jogya). *Gender panembung* (*gender slentem*) is the large *gender* with bronze slabs which are tuned an octave lower than those of the *gender barung*, and two octaves lower than those of *gender panerus.*
Lit.: no. 163.

Gender panerus (Java). A small *gender*, the slabs of which are tuned one octave higher than those of *gender barung.* This set of thin bronze slabs belongs into the group of instruments that perform the "soft playing." Cf. *Gender panembung* (*gender slentem*); *Gender barung.*

Gender slentem (*Slentem gantung*; *Gender panembung*) (Java). A one-octave *gender.* Its tuning corresponds to the lowest octave of *gender barung.* In Pasuran it is called *slentem gandul*; in Jogya it is called *gender panembung.* This set of bronze slabs, suspended over resonators made of bamboo or metal, performs together with the *gender barung* and *gender panerus* the "soft playing" parts of the piece. Lit.: no. 163.

Gender telulas (Bali). *Gender* with 13 keys. Lit.: no. 197.

Gender wayang (*gender dasa*) (Bali). The instrumental ensemble used in the shadow plays (*wayang wong*). It consists of: four *genders*, each with 10 bronze slabs. Two of the *genders* are tuned one octave higher than the other two. Both pairs play the same theme. The tone material used is pentatonic, derived from *slendro.* In *gender wayang* the pieces always begin with *dong*, followed by *deng*, *dung*, *dang*, *ding*, and in the upper octave again: *dong*, *deng*, *dung*, *dang*, *ding.* In Western terms the pitches approach: F# G# B C# E and f# g# b c# e.
Lit.: nos. 197, 265.

Gending (Bali). Instrumental composition.

Genḍing (*Tabeuh*) (Java; Sundanese Isl.). (1) Instrumental composition. (2) The orchestral pieces of Javanese music are grouped into several categories: *genḍing ageng*; *genḍing tengahan* (*genḍing madya*); *genḍing alit*; *ladrang*; *ketawang.* Cf. *Lagu tandak.*

Genḍing ageng (Bali). A long drawn ceremonial instrumental piece which forms the major constituent part of the conventional *gamelan gong.* This composition has four or more *ketuk* beats per *kenongan.* These long orchestral works are grouped according to the *palets* within each *gongan*:

Tabuh besik	(*tabuh 1*)	within the	*gongan*
Tabuh roh	(*tabuh* 2)	"	"
Tabuh telu	(*tabuh* 3)	"	"
Tabuh pat	(*tabuh* 4)	"	"
Tabuh lima	(*tabuh* 5)	"	"
Tabuh nem	(*tabuh* 6)	"	"
Tabuh pitu	(*tabuh* 7)	"	"
Tabuh kutus	(*tabuh* 8)	"	"
Tabuh rohras	(*tabuh* 12)	"	"

Lit.: no. 197.

Genḍing ageng tengahan (*Genḍing tengahan*) (Java). A *genḍing ageng* composition where the *ketuk* beats appear closely together (*kerep*). Thus the *kenong* periods are rather brief (not more than 32 *keteg*).
Lit.: no. 163.

Genḍing alit (Java). A *genḍing tengahan* piece with four *kenongan* of 16 (or 32) *keteg* per *gongan*, but with only two *keṭuk* beats per *kenongan.*
Lit.: no. 163.

Genḍing alus (Java). A gently played *genḍing.* Cf. *Bebuka.*
Lit.: no. 163.

Genḍing angklung (Bali). Composition for the *gamelan angklung.*

Genḍing banyolan (Java). An amusing composition where comic unison choral singing (*gerongan*) is prominent. Cf. *Kendangan chiblon.*
Lit.: no. 163.

Genḍing bechat (Bali). Short and lively *gamelan gong* pieces.

Genḍing charabalen (Java). An ostinato of musical zigzag motion. See *Gamelan charabalen.* Several types are distinguished: *bali balen*, *pis(ah)an bali*, *g(l)angsaran*, *klumpung*, *lung gadung.*
Lit.: no. 163.

Genḍing gagah (Java). See *Genḍing sabetan.*

Genḍing gagahan (Java). See *Genḍing sabetan.*

Genḍing gembang (Bali). Compositions played during cremation rites by the *gambang* ensemble.
Lit.: no. 197.

Gendịng gangsaran (Bali). Short pieces belonging to the *gamelan gong* repertory played in fast tempo.
Lit.: no. 197.

Gendịng gong (Bali). The large material of compositions of the *gamelan gong* repertory. Also called *pegongan.*

Gendịng janturan (Java). See *Gendịng lambang sari taledekan.*

Gendịng kodok ngorek ayam sepenan(g) (Java). At rare occasions *saron*-type instruments join the *kodok ngorek.*
Lit.: no. 163.

Gendịng lambang sari taledekan (Java). A *gendịng* consisting of four *gongan* of unequal durations.
Lit.: no. 163.

Gendịng lambat(an) (Bali). Also called *gendịng ageng* or *adeng.* Pieces played in slow tempo.
Lit.: no. 197.

Gendịng lampah (*lampeh*) (Java). A *gendịng* in the form of *srepegan* (*sampak*) or *ayak-ayakan.*
Lit.: no. 163.

Gendịng lawas(an) (Bali). Old, classical *gendịng.*

Gendịng lokanonta (Java). *Lokanonta* refers to "heavenly music" played on invisible instruments. See *Gamelan munggang.*

Gendịng longgor (Bali). Several *gangsaran* (fast tempo) pieces used as closing music in the *gendịng ageng.*

Gendịng luang (Bali). Compositions performed by the *gamelan luang.*

Gendịng munggang (*Gendịng lokanonta*) (Java). See *Gamelan munggang.*

Gendịng parikan (Java). This *gendịng* is structurally and rhythmically free and cannot be listed among the standard forms. A similar type is *gendịng lampah.* Cf. *Gangsaran.*
Lit.: no. 163.

Gendịng pegambuhan (Bali). Pieces performed at the *gambuh* plays. They represent the basis of the *gamelan semar pegulingan* music.
Lit.: no. 197.

Gendịng pelegongan (Bali). Pieces from the *gambuh* repertory and adjusted as accompaniments of the *legong* dance.
Lit.: no. 197.

Gendịng sabetan (Sunda District). The vigorously and loudly sounding kettles and melodies of a *bonang.* The Javanese term is *gendịng gagah.*
Lit.: no. 163.

Gendịng taledekan (Java). A composition for the *taledek(an)* (girl dancers) in *patet manyura.*
Lit.: no. 163.

Gendịng tengahan (Java). See *Gendịng ageng tengahan.*
Lit.: no. 163.

Gendịr (Java). See *Gendẹr.*

Gendọng (Java). See *Bendrong*; *Kotekan.*

Gendoweng (Java). Ceremonial hand drum.

Gendreh kemasan (Java). See *Gendịng mianggong.*

Gendung (Java). See *Dung* (drum word).

Gengebe (French Congo—Mandia). Bell; jingle.
Lit.: no. 255.

Genggo (Flores; Larankuka District). Wooden jew's harp. It is called *ledo* in Riangwulu; *ego* (*weda*) in Maumere-Paluwe; *kobeng* in Mbai; *weto* in Nage; *robe* in Ngada; and *nentu* (*kombing*) in Manggaray.
Lit.: no. 166.

Genggong (Sumatra). Jew's harp. The same term is used in Malaysia.
Lit.: no. 160.

Genggong (Bali). Jew's harp made of bamboo; it is played in secular performances. If well played, it can produce four tones, hence mainly *angklung* pieces are played on the *genggong.*
Lit.: no. 197.

Genggong sakai (Malaysia—Siamese Malay people). See *Pare*; *Buncacan.*
Lit.: no. 254.

Genin (Japan). Title given to musicians who stand below the *gakunin* (*gakunen*) and above the *kengyo.* The *genin* represent professional musicians who are not as well educated as the *gakunin* and are unable to read notational symbols. Cf. *Gakunin.*
Lit.: no. 53.

Genjung (Sunda District). See *Indung.*

Genjur (Java). See *Ganjur.*

Genkin (Japan). A noun that indicates the "value" of an instrument: *ichi-genkin* (*koto*), a *koto* with one string; *ni-genkin* (with two strings); *san-genkin* (with three strings); etc.

Genkwan (Japan; Mongolia). A lute of Chinese origin with a flat, octagonal body and 11 frets on its long neck. The *genkwan* has 4 silken strings tuned to, e.g., C C G G, which are played with a small plectrum. Cf. *Shuang ch'in* (China); *Shigen*; *Ku.*
Lit.: nos. 225, 250.

Ge-no-chu (Japan). See scales: *Noh*; *Yowa*; *Tsuyo.*

Ge-no kuzushi (Japan). See *Noh*; *Yowa.*

Genrang (South Celebes). Large cylindrical drum.
Lit.: no. 162.

Genta (Malaysia). See *Rebana ibu.*

Genta (Bali). (1) Hand bell of bronze. It is used to indicate the endings of stanzas in sacred songs. Cf. *ghanta.*
(2) (Java). Bell tree. A thin wooden pole with sticks crosswise attached. On the sticks hang a number of small bells. The instrument is also called *klinting* or *byong*, also *kembang delima* ("pomegranate blossom"). In Bali it is called *gentorog.*
Lit.: no. 163, 197.

Gentora (Java). A small trumpet made of the leaf of a coconut palm.
Lit.: no. 163.

Gentorak (*gentorak*) (Bali). See *Genta* (Java).
Lit.: no. 265.

Gentoral (Bali). Bell tree.
Lit.: no. 265.

Geramo (New Guinea; Bismarck Archipelago). *Geramo* or *gerom.* A large wooden slit-drum. See *Garamut* (*garmuth*).
Lit.: no. 255.

Gerar (Somali Republic). Horse riding song. These songs are also sung, without accompaniment, inside the house when the women are absent.
Lit.: no. 98.

Gerema (New Guinea; Papua—Wenke). Wooden drum.

Gerin geri (Fiji—Viti). Drum.
Lit.: no. 255.

Gerom (New Guinea—Jabim; Bukaua). Wooden slit-drum used for signalling. Cf. *Geramo.*

Gerong(an) (Java). Unison male choir song; recently sung also by women with one man performing a solo.
Lit.: no. 163.

Gerremut (*Garamut*) (Melanesia; New Ireland). Wooden drum.
Lit.: no. 255.

Gershayim (Ancient Israel). Notational symbol used in biblical chant, indicating a weak disjunctive function.
Lit.: no. 309.

Ges (Somali Republic). Antelope horn. See *Gafa.*

Ge-sang-pa (Tibet). Cf. *Skad-bsang-pa.*
Lit.: no. 143.

Geseh (Java). An irregularity, a wrong note in a *gamelan* performance. The Sunda term is *blero.*

Geser Khan (Buryat Mongolia). Name of an epic song cycle. The Wolga Kalmucks call it *Djanggar.*
Lit.: no. 60.

Geso-geso (*Keso-keso*) (Celebes). Spike lute with one string.
Lit.: no. 132.

Gesong-gesong (Celebes). See *Geso-geso.*

Getang (Southeast Borneo—Dayak). Iron or silver rings placed around arms and legs of dancers.
Lit.: no. 255.

Getet (*Ndorobo getet*) (Uganda—Nandi kamasia). Drum.

Gettung-gettun (Sumatra—Batak). Tube zither with one or two strings. In North Sumatra the instrument is called *gendang-gendang.* In Nias its name is *gonra.*
Lit.: no. 254.

Geudumba (Indonesia; Atjeh). One-headed goblet-shaped drum. Cf. *Hareubab*; *Tataganing.*

Geyahejjaji (South India). See *Gāyakapriya.* See also *Hejjuji*, the 13th *asampūrṇa mēḷa.*

Geya nataka (South India). Village opera.

Geza (*Geza ongaku*) (Japan). "Lower place," off stage." *Geza* music is played off-stage behind a closed bamboo curtained window. It appears in *kabuki.* Usually it employs several drums, woodblocks, gongs, bells, cymbals, rattles, xylophone, two flutes, and *shamisen.*
Lit.: no. 187.

Geza-daiko (Japan). "*Geza* drum," the drum beaten off-stage in *kabuki* performances. See *Uta-daiko.*

Gezarke (Nubia). Term for *kissar.* See *Krar*; *Kerar.*
Lit.: no. 255.

Ghabe (*Ghaba*) (Arabia). Flute.
Lit.: no. 255.

Ghachaka (Afghanistan). Fiddle. Cf. *Ghizhak.*

Ghāḍa(m) (South India). See *Ghāṭa.*

Ghaḍam (Ancient India). See *Ghāṭa.*

Ghadi (Nepal). Small brass cymbals, smaller than the *babon.*
Lit.: no. 46.

Ghaida (Turkey). Mouth-blown bagpipe. Its chanter has seven finger holes. The instrument has a single drone.
Lit.: no. 255.

Ghaiṭa (Morocco; Algeria). The *ghaiṭa* (or *gā'iṭa*) is the Moroccan oboe. Two types can be observed: the older has a cylindrical tube with a single reed (this instrument may have been the *shihābī zūrnā* of Turkey). The other type has a conical bore and double reeds and can be considered to be the most important oboe type of North Africa. Cf. *Rai'tah.*
Lit.: nos. 76, 95.

Ghan (*Ghun*) (India). Gong.

Ghana (*Giṇḍi*) (India). General term for metallic idiophones are used in classifications of musical instruments in Sanskrit literature. See *Kaṃsāla.*

Ghanaja Ghana (South India). *Janya rāga* of the 22nd *mēḷa* (*Kharaharapriyā*).
Tone material:
C D F G A G B♭ c
c B♭ G A B♭ G F E♭ D C
Lit.: no. 139.

Ghana Kēśi (South India). *Janya rāga* of the 22nd *mēḷa* (*Kharaharapriyā*).
Tone material:
C D E♭ F G B♭ c
c B♭ A G F D C
Lit.: no. 139.

Ghana Nāyaki (South India). *Janya rāga* of the 65th *mēḷa* (*Mechakalyāṇī*).
Tone material:
C E F♯ B A G A B c
c B A G F♯ E D C
Lit.: no. 139.

Ghanāndōlika (South India). *Janya rāga* of the 28th *mēḷa* (*Harikāmbhōji*).
Tone material:
C E F A B♭ c
c B♭ A G F E D E C
Lit.: no. 139.

Ghāna Sindhu (South India). See *Gāna Sindhu.*

Ghāna Śobhitam (South India). *Janya rāga* of the 14th *mēḷa* (*Vakuḷabharaṇam*).
Tone material:
C D♭ E F A♭ B♭ A♭ c
c A♭ B♭ G F E D♭ C
Lit.: no. 139.

Ghāna Suprabhātam (South India). *Janya rāga* of the 65th *mēḷa* (*Mechakalyāṇī*).
Tone material:
C D F♯ G A c
c A G A B A G F♯ E D C
Lit.: no. 139.

Ghāna Śyāmaḷa (South India). *Janya rāga* of the 5th *mēḷa* (*Manōrañjanī*).
Tone material:
C D♭ F G A c
c B A G F E♭♭ D♭ C (*A* C)
Lit.: no. 139.

Ghāna tānam (South India). A *tāna* form produced on the *vīṇā*. The right hand plucks the string (one plucking; *miṭṭu*) and the left hand moves across several frets while the string still vibrates.
Lit.: no. 261.

Ghāna Taraṅgiṇi (South India). *Janya rāga* of the 29th *mēḷa* (*Dhīraśaṅkarābharaṇam*).
Tone material:
C D F G A B G c
c G B A F E C
Lit.: no. 139.

Ghāna Vādya (India). Percussion instruments made of metal.

Ghani (East Africa – Swahili). See *Imba*; *Lia*; *Vuma*; *Simulia kwa utenzi* (*kwa mashairi*).

Ghanna (Old Arabia). Singing.
Lit.: no. 65.

Ghanta (Bali). See *Genta.*

Ghaṇṭā (*Ghaṇṭāmaṇi*) (India). Cymbals; bells; small bronze bells used in religious service. Also called *ghaṇṭika.*
Lit.: nos. 250, 261.

Ghaṇṭā (South India). *Janya rāga* of the 8th *mēḷa* (*Hanumattōḍi*).
Tone material:
C E♭ D E♭ F G B♭ A♭ B♭ c
(C E♭ D E♭ F G B♭ c)
c B♭ A♭ G F E♭ D♭ C
Lit.: no. 139.

Ghaṇṭāmaṇi (India). Bell. See *Ghaṇṭā.*

Ghanṭāṇaman (*Ghottāṇam*) (South India). *Janya rāga* of the 57th *mēḷa* (*Siṃhendranad-hyama*).
Tone material:
C D E♭ F♯ A♭ B c
c B A♭ F♯ E♭ D C
Lit.: no. 139.

Ghantarava (South India). *Janya rāga* of the 2nd *mēḷa* (*Ratnangi*).
Tone material:
C D♭ C E♭♭ F G B♭ c
c B♭ A♭ G F E♭♭ D♭ C
Lit.: no. 139.

Ghaṇṭi (India). See *Ghaṇṭā*.

Ghaṇṭika (Indi). See *Ghaṇṭā* (bronze bell).

Gharghara (India). Sanskrit term for bell. A small bell is called *gharghharika*. Cf. *Gargara*.

Ghargharika (India). See *Gharghara*.

Ghaṛī (India; Bengal). A thick, simple, suspended bronze disc. It is beaten with a hammer at religious services.
Lit.: no. 250.

Ghaṛiyāl (India). See *Ghaṛī*.

Ghāṭa (India). Sanskrit term for a globular clay pot. It is beaten by the player in an elaborate manner with his fingers and palm, producing a variety of sounds. Other names are: *gāḍ(m)*, *kaṭṭivādyam*, *ghāṭam*. Cf. *Cai mo* (Annam).
Lit.: no. 250.

Ghāṭam (South India). Clay pot used in folk music where it serves to provide rhythmic accompaniment. The musical use of the *ghāṭam* is already mentioned in the ancient epic, the *Rāmāyāna*. The Pali term is *ghaṭī*.

Ghaṭi (India). See *Ghāṭam*.

Ghaṭita (South India). *Janya rāga* of the 64th *mēḷa* (*Vāchaspati*).
Tone material:
C D F♯ G B♭ c
c B♭ A G F♯ E D C
Lit.: no. 139.

Ghavavati (South India). *Janya rāga* of the 33rd *mēḷa* (*Gaṅgeyabhushanī*).
Tone material:
C D♯ E F G B c
c B A♭ G F E C
Lit.: no. 139.

Ghaychek (*Gheichak*) (Persia). Vertically held fiddle with four gut strings. It resembles the North Indian *sarinda*. The instrument appears also in Afghanistan and Pakistan.

Ghazāl (Egypt; Arabia). Bridge of the *kamānjah*.

Ghazal (North India). A love song with Urdu text. Frequently the melody is in *dadra tāla* (6/8). It is the Mohammedan counterpart of the Hindu *thumri*. The texts consist of short lyric love poems structured in simple couplets (e.g., AA, BA, CA, etc.). Cf. *Nauba*.
Lit.: no. 138.

Ghe (*Khe*) (North India). *Bol* (drum word) performed on the open (*khula*) *bayan* by the left hand. Either the second or third fingers, or both together, strike the *maidan*.
Lit.: no. 136.

Ghebomba (Gabon). Signal horn used in ritual services.

Ghedra (Morocco). Big hourglass-shaped clay drum.

Gheez (Ethiopia). One of three liturgical modes in Coptic chant (the other two are called *Araray* and *Ezel*). Curt Sachs (Lit. no. 257, p. 97) reports about the "Discouraging vagueness of all notes inside a fourth or a fifth and as a consequence, [researchers] will prefer to refrain from modal analysis."
Lit.: no. 102.

Gheichak (Persia). See *Ghaychek.*

Ghenddang (Small Sunda Isl.). Drum with two heads.
Lit.: no. 162.

Ghendhang (Lombok Isl.; Madura). Large cylindrical drum. See *Gendang.*
Lit.: no. 162.

Ghentā (Ethiopia). A small *qanā*, a shepherd's horn (made of cow's horn).
Lit.: no. 255.

Ghete (Egypt). Also called *gheta.* A clarinet type with 6-7 finger holes, a tin bell, and a single reed.
Lit.: no. 255.

Ghezarke (Ethiopia). Identical with *kissar.*

Ghichak (*Gichak*) (Persia). A *kamanja* type. Cf. *Ghizhak*; *Ghijjak.*
Lit.: no. 255.

Ghijjak (Turkestan). Fiddle with three strings. Cf. *Ghichak.*

Ghinā' (Arabia). Music; singing. In recent times the term denotes also an artistic type of *naṣb.*

Ghinā' (Arabia). See *Adhān.*

Ghinā' al-mutqan (Arabia). The term indicates a special feature of adapting a specific rhythm to the melody of a song which, originally, was free of the rhythm (*'arūḍ*) of the textual verse.
Lit.: no. 70.

Ghinā' murtajal (Arabia). An improvised song.

Ghirbāl (Arabia; Egypt). A circular frame drum having the shape of a sieve.

Ghirjek (Pamirs; Central Asia). *Ghirjek* or *girjek* is a fiddle similar to the *kemanje* with three strings (one made of metal).
Lit.: no. 255.

Ghiṭā (*Qaflah*) (Arabia). See *Muwashaḥ.*

Ghizhak (*Ghichak*) (Iran; Turkey). A large *kemanje* with eight additional sympathetic strings known in the 15th century. Cf. *Ghachaka*; *Ghichak*; *Ghordjek.*
Lit.: no. 190.

Ghochaī (Afghanistan). A peg of a string instrument.

Ghōradarsiṇi (South India). *Janya rāga* of the 36th *mēḷa* (*Chalanāṭa*).
Tone material:
C D♯ E F G A♯ c
c A♯ G F E D♯ C
Lit.: no. 139.

Ghordjek (Pamirs; Central Asia). *Kāmanja* with three strings. Cf. *Ghizhak.*

Ghoṣaka (Ancient India). *Ghoṣaka* or *ekantrikā.* A chordophone with one string.

Ghōṣākari (South India). See *Ghōshākari.*

Ghōṣaṇi (South India). See *Ghōshaṇi.*

Ghōṣavinōdini (South India). See *Ghōshavinōdini.*

Ghōshākari (*Ghōṣākari*) (South India). *Janya rāga* of the 32nd *mēḷa* (*Rāgavardhanī*).
Tone material:
C D♯ E F G A♭ c
c A♭ G F E D♯ C
Lit.: no. 139.

Ghōshamañjari (South India). *Janya rāga* of the 52nd *mēḷa* (*Rāmapriyā*).
Tone material:
C E G B♭ c
c B♭ G A B♭ G F♯ D♭ E D♭ C
Lit.: no. 139.

Ghōshaṇi (*Ghōshiṇi*; *Ghōṣaṇi*; *Ghōṣiṇi*) (South India). *Janya rāga* of the 16th *mēḷa* (*Chakravāka*).

Tone material:
C F E F G A B♭ A c
c B♭ A G F E F D♭ C
Lit.: no. 139.

Ghōshavinōdini (*Ghōṣavinōdinī*) (South India). *Janya rāga* of the 34th *mēḷa* (*Vāgadhīśvarī*).
Tone material:
C D♯ E F G A c
c A G F E D♯ C
Lit.: no. 139.

Ghōshiṇi (South India). See *Ghōshaṇi.*

Ghōṣiṇi (South India). See *Ghōshaṇi.*

Ghoshpāni (South India). *Janya rāga* of the 57th *mēḷa* (*Siṃhendramadhyama*).
Tone material:
C D E♭ F♯ G A♭ B c
c B A♭ F♯ E♭ D C
Lit.: no. 139.

Ghottāṇam (South India). See *Ghaṇṭaṇaman* (57th *mēḷa*).

Ghrutāchi (South India). *Janya rāga* of the 16th *mēḷa* (*Chakravāka*).
Tone material:
C D♭ F A B♭ c
c B♭ A F D♭ C
Lit.: no. 139.

Ghūghā (Sahara; Sudan—Hausa). Cf. *Goge*; *Goje.*

Ghughe (*Ghugha*) (Algeria; Morocco). A simple bowed string instrument. The body is shaped like a skin-covered bucket. The neck is a stick stuck through the corpus. The *ghughe* has one string made of horsehair and no peg for tuning.
Lit.: no. 250.

Ghumar (India; Rajasthan). Popular dance of the women.
Lit.: no. 46.

Ghun (India). See *Ghan.*

Ghunda (*-rud*) (Persia). Metal signalling trumpet.
Lit.: no. 255.

Ghunghunā (India). Little pellet bell.

Ghūṅghrū (*Ghuṅghurū*) (India). (1) Camel or bullock neck-bells used in the Punjab. (2) Bell-rattle placed around the foot ankles of dancers.
Lit.: no. 254.

Ghuṇṭa (India). See *Ghaṇṭā.*

Ghūrjari (South India). See *Gurjari.*

Ghurjari-tōḍi (North India). See *Gujri-tōḍi.*

Ghurumi-kiddi (*Gurumi*) (Sudan—Hausa). Lute.
Lit.: no. 255.

Ghuṭru (South India). Clay or wooden drum shaped in the form of a goblet. The wide opening is covered with a skin and the stem is open.
Lit.: no. 254.

Gwazhai (Afghanistan). Peg.

Ghyd (Tibet). The spelling of *rgyd*, "string."
Lit.: no. 255.

Ghyer-wa (Tibet). See *Dgyer-ba.*

Giao nhac (Vietnam). Music of the Heavenly Terrace; court music.

Giao phuong (Vietnam). Instrumental group which performed music for the former royal court.

Gichak (Persia). See *Ghichak.*

Gidayū-bushi (Japan). An important form of narrative *shamisen* music that had its origin in Osaka during the 17th century. It is music for the popular *bunraku* (puppet performances). The drama is shaped into five *dan*; the *gidayū-bushi* appears in eight sections: *oki*, the scene setting; *kudoki*, lyric part, lament, etc.; *monogatari*, the story evolves toward tension; *uta*, "song," or *odori*, "dance" the musical climaxes; *miarawashi*, the dramatic plot at its peak; *chirashi* or *seme*, resolution, conclusion.

The *gidayu* singer does not merely recite the story, but acts according to his music and provides an impressive melodramatic show. Cf. *Joruri*. See also *Bungo-bushi*.
Lit.: no. 185.

Gidayū-Samisen (Japan). A large sized *shamisen* occasionally used instead of the *chikuzen-biwa*.
Lit.: no. 255.

Gidirigo (Ghana). Cf. *Prempensua*.

Gi-irra (*Gi-gid*; *Gi-di*) (Sumeria). Obscure shepherd's shawms or flutes: *gi-irra*, "tube of lament"; *gi-gid*, "long tube"; and *gi-di*, "sounding tube."
Lit.: no. 94.

Gidzu (Uganda). Drum.
Lit.: no. 255.

Ǧiǧak (Afghanistan). Spike fiddle with two strings and a large bow, used by the Mountain Tadzhiks. A *ǧiǧak* with four strings is used in Uzbekistan and by the urban Tadzhiks.
Lit.: no. 276.

Gigaku (Japan). Masked play that originated in southern China (*Wu*) and became favorite at the Japanese court (*gagaku*) in the folk-lion dances. Cf. *Gagaku*.

Gigid (Mesopotamia; Sumeria). "Long cane." Probably a long vertical flute.
Lit.: nos. 190, 250.

Gihing (*giying*) (Bali). Term for an introduction of the *gending angklung* performed as a *gangsa* solo piece.
Lit.: no. 197.

Gihumurizo (*Nyampundu*) (Congo; Ruanda). Large royal drum.
Lit.: no. 26.

Gihyan (Sunda District). A large type of *ohyan*.
Lit.: no. 163.

Gilak (Bali). See *Kali*.

Gila āṭa (India). "Wet flour." See *Tabla*.

Gilgillepa (South India—Malayalam). Cf. *Jhunjhunā*.

Gili (Ubangi—Bwaka-Mabo). Drum.
Lit.: no. 26.

Gimba (Central Celebes—Torodja). Barrel drum.
Lit.: no. 254.

Gimbrede (*Gimbeī*; *Ginbrī*) (Morocco). See *Gnbri*.

Gimbrī (Morocco). See *Gnbrī*.

Ǧinā (*Jina*) (Arabia). Singing (in contrast to chanting, reciting prayers).
Lit.: no. 76.

Ginbrī (Morocco). See *Gnbrī*.

Gindai (Japan). A *koto* interchangeable with the *shichi-genkin*. The *gindai*, however, has 13 strings which are plucked by thumb and index finger of the right hand.
Lit.: no. 225.

Giṇḍi (India). Gong. See *Ghana*; *Kaṃsāla*.

Ginera (Egypt; Coptic). Late form of *k'nn'r* (lyre). Cf. *Kinnor*; *Kinnara*.
Lit.: no. 250.

Ging (Tibet). Small drum; beating of the small drum.

Ginger (Sudan – Ingassana). Lyre with a bowl-shaped body and five strings.
Lit.: no. 255.

Ginggung (Malaysia). *Ginggung* or *giridung*. See *Genggong*.

Gingiru (Mali – Dogon). Harp-lute.
Lit.: no. 303.

Gini (India; Orissa). Small cymbals.
Lit.: no. 255.

Ginnu (Mali – Dogon). Iron bell.
Lit.: no. 303.

Giong bac (South Vietnam). See *Dieu bac*.
Lit.: no. 297.

Giram(o) (Melanesia; New Guinea). Wooden slit-drum.
Lit.: no. 84.

Girbāl (*Ghirbāl*) (Arabia). "Sieve," large frame drum (now obsolete).

Giref (*Girif*; *Girift*) (Arabia). See *Nāy ghiref*.

Girgira (*Girgiri*; *Tavalaika*) (South India). Through a membrane that closes one side of a tin or a pasteboard cylinder is bound a string with a knot. When the player swings string and cylinder around, the membrane creates a peculiar vibrating sound.
Lit.: no. 17.

Giriri (South India). See *Girgira*.

Giridhara (South India). *Janya rāga* of the 28th *mēḷa* (*Harikāmbhōji*).
Tone material:
C D E F G B♭ c
c B♭ A G F E D C
Lit.: no. 255.

Giriding (*Garuding*; *Gariding*) (Borneo). Popular jew's harp.
Lit.: no. 255.

Girif (Arabia). See *Giref*.

Girift (Turkey). Term for small flutes, each with seven finger holes. Cf. *Nāy*.
Lit.: no. 81.

Girikarnika (South India). *Janya rāga* of the 3rd *mēḷa* (*Ganamurti*).
Tone material:
C D♭ F G A♭ B c
c B A♭ G F E♭♭ D♭ C
Lit.: no. 139.

Giri Kuntaḷi (South India). *Janya rāga* of the 72nd *mēḷa* (*Rasikapriyā*).
Tone material:
C D♯ E F♯ G F♯ E F♯ G c
c B A♯ B G F♯ E C
Lit.: no. 139.

Giring-giring (North Sumatra). Jingle; bell.

Girīśapriya (South India). *Janya rāga* of the 39th *mēḷa* (*Jhālavarāḷi*).
Tone material:
C D♭ E♭♭ F♯ G B c
c B G F♯ E♭♭ D♭ C
Lit.: no. 139.

Girjek (Pamir; Central Asia). See *Ghirjek*.

Gīrvāna (South India). (1) The 43rd *asampūrṇa mēḷa-rāga* without *kaṭapayādi* prefix. (2) The 43rd *asampūrṇa mēḷa-rāga* with *kaṭapayādi* prefix was called *Gīrvāni*. See *Rāga* (South India).
Lit.: no. 139.

Gīrvāṇi Padam (South India). *Janya rāga* of the 72nd *mēḷa* (*Rasikapriyā*).
Tone material:
C D# E F# G A# c
c B A# G F# E D# C
Lit.: no. 139.

Gīrvāṇapriya (South India). *Janya rāga* of the 29th *mēḷa* (*Dhīraśaṅkarābharaṇam*).
Tone material:
C D E F A c
c B A F E D C
Lit.: no. 139.

Gīrvāṇi (South India). (1) *Janya rāga* of the 43rd *mēḷa* (*Gavambōdhi*).
Tone material:
C Db Eb Db F# Eb F# Ab Bbb G Ab Bbb c
(C Db Eb Db F# Eb F# Ab Bbb G Bbb Ab c)
c Bbb Ab G F# Eb Db C
(2) The name of the 43rd *rāga* of the *asampūrṇa* system. See *Rāga* (South India).
Lit.: no. 139.

Gīrvāṇi (South India). Cf. *Gīrvāna* (43rd *asampūrṇa mēḷa*).

Girwa (*Puri*) (North India). Cf. *Tabla.*

Gisaba Rwanda (Congo; Ruanda). Drum.
Lit.: no. 26.

Gišak (Persia, 14th century). Ancient bowed lute of Turkmenia.
Lit.: nos. 320-21.

Gi-sal (Sumeria), **Gizallu** (Akkad.) (Ancient Babylon; Sumeria). Horn made of a dried fruit.
Lit.: no. 87.

Gisang (Korea). Dancing girl.

Gisarke (Sudan – Dongola). Term for *kissar.*
Lit.: no. 255.

Giš-ban (Sumeria). Term for a harp.
Lit.: no. 89.

Giš-H̱ar-H̱ar (Sumeria). Probably a string instrument.
Lit.: no. 87.

Gishikiso (*Nkiranwa*) (Ruanda-Urundi). Drum.
Lit.: no. 26.

Gissang (Nias). See *Garsing.*

Gita (Bali). Song; sacred chant.

Gīta (Ancient India). Early term for music. Later term for vocal music. Cf. *Gāndharva.*
Lit.: no. 292.

Gīta (India). Song. The term applies also to extensive works, e.g., *gīta govinda.*

Gītagani (India). Singer.

Gītālambana (South India). *Janya rāga* of the 28th *mēḷa* (*Harikāmbhōji*).
Tone material:
C D F E F A Bb c
c Bb F E D F E C
Lit.: no. 139.

Gītamohini (South India). *Janya rāga* of the 20th *mēḷa* (*Naṭabhairavī*).
Tone material:
C D Eb F Ab Bb c
c Bb Ab G F Eb D C
Lit.: no. 139.

Gītamūrti (South India). *Janya rāga* of the 33rd *mēḷa* (*Gāṅgeyabhushanī*). The scale (tone material) of this *rāga* is identical with that of its primary *rāga* (*Gāṅgeyabhushanī*).
Lit.: no. 139.

Gītanāṭaṇi (South India). *Janya rāga* of the 53rd *mēḷa* (*Gamanaśrama*).
Tone material:
C Db F# E F# G A B c
c B A G F# Db C
Lit.: no. 139.

Gītapriya (South India). *Janya rāga* of the 13th *mēḷa* (*Gāyakapriya*).
Tone material:
C D♭ E F G A♭ B♭♭ c
c A♭ G F E D♭ C
Lit.: no. 139.

Gītapriyā (South India). *Janya rāga* of the 63rd *mēḷa* (*Latāṅgī*).
Tone material:
C D E F♯ G A♭ B c G A♭ c
c B A♭ G F♯ D E D C
Not to be mistaken for *Gitapriyā* of the 13th *mēḷa*.
Lit.: no. 139.

Gītapriyā (South India). See *Gotrāri* (the 63rd *asampūrṇa mēḷa*).

Git-git (Philippines – Hanunoo). A small fiddle with three strings, related to the *rebāb*.
Lit.: no. 303.

Gitikam (East Java – Banyuwangi). Term for *main chachih*.
Lit.: no. 163.

Gizallu (Ancient Babylon). See *Gi-sal*.

Gkrego (Flores). See *Sego*.

G(l)ang-saran (Java). See *Genḍing charabalen*.

Glawn (Northeast Thailand). A prominent form of Lao poetry structured in stanzas of four lines.
Lit.: no. 203.

Glawng (Northeast Thailand). General term for drum.
Lit.: no. 203.

Glawng daloong (Thailand). A pair of barrel drums.
Lit.: no. 203.

Glawng hang (Northeast Thailand). "Tail drum." See *Glawng yao*.
Lit.: no. 203.

Glawng yao (*glawng hang*) (Northeast Thailand). "Long drum" in hourglass shape, with one head.
Lit.: no. 203.

Glekor (Flores). See *Nuren*.

Gling-bu (pronounced *ling-bu*) (Tibet). Vertical double or triple high-pitched wooden flutes, linked like a raft, with beak-mouthpieces. Each tube has 6-10 finger holes. The instrument is mainly used by shepherds. The *gling-bu* is the *limba* of Mongolia.
Lit.: nos. 250, 255.

Glompong (Java). See *Genḍing miaggong*.

Glu (*Mgur*; *Mgur-ma*) (Tibet). Profane term for song; tune.
Lit.: no. 143.

Glu-chung (Tibet). A little tune; ditty. Cf. *Glu*.

Glu-gar (Tibet). Dance songs sung alternately by two groups of dancers.
Lit.: no. 62.

Glu len-pa (Tibet). See *Tang-che*.

Glu lin-pa (Tibet). See *Dgyer-ba*.

Gnbrī (*Gunībrī*) (Morocco). Lute with 2-3 gut strings. The neck is fretless and the body is covered with ram hide. Cf. *Audd*.
Lit.: no. 255.

Go (Congo – Abandya; Azande; Basire). Barrel drum with one head, played with the bare hands.
Lit.: no. 26.

Go (or *Gong*) (Flores – Ngada). Gong of Javanese origin.

Go (South India). Mnemonic syllable of the 72 *mēḷas* scheme. It refers to the 3rd *mēḷa* of a *chakra*. See *Rāga* (South India). For other syllables see *Bhū*.
Lit.: no. 139.

Go (Dahomey). Calabash rattle.

Gō (Japan). Sets of melodic patterns played on the *chikuzen-biwa*.
Lit.: no. 185.

Gobai (Japan). Concluding section of the three parts of the *kansan* group.
Lit.: no. 185.

Gobais (Somali Republic). Flute. Also called *ulule*.
Lit.: no. 255.

Go bato (*Go beta*) (Flores; Ende). Tubular bamboo zither with 1-3 strings. The instrument is also called *riang wulu baba*. See *Gong tondu*.
Lit.: no. 156.

Gobi-gobi (South Nias). Bamboo tube zither.
Lit.: no. 156.

Gobyog (Java). A fast roll signal on the *kentongan* (alarm slit-drum) to call the people. A second meaning for *gobyog* is a small ensemble consisting of a *rebāb*, *kenḍang*, *kempul*, *kenong*, and *ketuk*. This group accompanies *ronggeng* dances.
Lit.: no. 163.

Gochnag (Armenia). A freely hung wooden board, beaten with two hammers, is used for signalling purposes.
Lit.: no. 255.

Go-dan (Japan). Five *dan*; five variations or sections of instrumental music (without vocal part) based on a leading theme. Cf. also *Roku-dan*; *Shichi-dan*; *Hachi-dan*; *Ku-dan*; etc. See also *Dan*.
Lit.: no. 185.

Godāri (South India). *Janya rāga* of the 39th *mēḷa* (*Jhālavarāḷi*).
Tone material:

C D♭ E♭♭ D♭ F♯ E♭♭ F♯ G A♭ B c
c B A♭ G F♯ E♭♭ D♭ C

Lit.: no. 139.

Goddan (Flores). Goblet drum. See *O-tsi* (Burma).
Lit.: no. 254.

Godhani (North India). Obscure *rāga*, possibly identical with *rāga Gorakh-kalyan*.
Tone material:

C (*B♭ A B♭*) C E F G (E F D) C A B♭ c
c B A F G F E D C

Lit.: no. 138.

Godhani-tōḍi (North India). Obscure *rāga*, not related to *Tōḍi*. It appears to consist of materials of the *rāga Barva* in the lower half of the octave and *rāga Bageshri* in the upper.
Lit.: no. 138.

Gōdha vināka (India). Obscure string instrument.
Lit.: no. 261.

Godhika (India). Drum. Its head is made of alligator (*godha*) skin.
Lit.: no. 261.

Gödumbas (Sumatra—Achin). A goblet-shaped hand drum.
Lit.: no. 255.

Goeika (Japan). Buddhist (*wasan*) hymns popularized into secular songs, particularly during the Muromachi period (14th-17th centuries). Another popular form of the *goeika* is performed by one solo singer and answered by a chorus. See the popular *ondo* (folk music).
Lit.: no. 185.

Goga dhol (India; Bastar State—Muria Gond). A small wooden or earthenware kettledrum covered with cowhide.
Lit.: nos. 59, 135.

Goge (Nigeria—Yoruba; Hausa). Bowed lute with one horsehair-string used in *sakara* ensembles. The curved bow is strung with horsehair. The instrument is also called *gonje* or *goje*; a Hausa term for it is *ghūghā*.
Lit.: nos. 95, 218.

Go gekkin (Japan). See *Gekkin* or *Gekin.*
Lit.: nos. 190, 255.

Gogen (Japan). Obsolete lute of Chinese origin with a round, flat corpus, a narrow neck, and four strings. Occasionally the term "ancient moon guitar" has been used.
Lit.: no. 185.

Gogeru (West Africa—Fulbe). Simple fiddle with two long and two (or one) short strings. The instrument has no bridge; the gourd body is covered with leather.
Lit.: no. 255.

Gogonjerenrai (India; Orissa). Primitive fiddle with two strings.

Go-in (*Go-sei*) (Japan). See *Kwaigo-no-ben.*

Going-going (South Africa—Bushmen). Bull roarer.
Lit.: no. 151.

Goje (West Africa). (1) See *Goge.* (2) A family of drums.
Lit.: no. 279.

Gojri-todi (North India). See *Gujri-tōḍi.*

Go-jū (*Sei-in*) (Japan). See *Kwaigo-no-ben.*

Gojū-in (Japan). "The fifty voices." A series of sounds produced by a singer on the five vowels (A, E, I, O, U) with open, closed mouth and several other modifications of each sung sound.
Lit.: no. 225.

Gok (Vietnam—Miau). Gong.
Lit.: no. 303.

Gokin (Japan). A five-stringed "*kin*" (*koto*). The strings are plucked with thumb and first finger of the right hand without any *tsume.*
Lit.: no. 250.

Gōkulamūrti (South India). *Janya rāga* of the 62nd *mēḷa* (*Riṣabhapriyā*).
Tone material:
C D E G A♭ c
c B♭ A♭ G F♯ E D C
Lit.: no. 139.

Golek menak (Java). See *Wayang golek.*

Golek purwa (Java). See *Wayang golek.*

Golgol (Arabia). See *Jüljül.*
Lit.: no. 255.

Gollabhāmā (South India). Telugu dance play.

Goly (Ivory Coast Republic—Baoule). Instrument with a single string.
Lit.: no. 303.

Goma (Malagasy Republic). Large cylindrical drum with a single head.
Lit.: no. 251.

Gomafu (*Gomaten*) (Japan). Musical notation of the Buddhist chant (*wasan*). The symbols are placed to the left side of the textual columns.
Lit.: no. 185.

Gōmaṇḍalam (South India). *Janya rāga* of the 28th *mēḷa* (*Harikāmbhōji*).
Tone material:
C D E D F G B♭ A G c
c B♭ A G F E D C
Lit.: no. 139.

Gomaten (Japan). See *Gomafu.*

Gombi (Congo—Azande; Makere). Stick zither.
Lit.: no. 176.

Gombri (Algeria—Biskra). "Mandoline" with two strings tuned to high E♭ and A. The strings are plucked with the hand; the A string provides the pedal note while the E♭ string serves as melody string.
Lit.: no. 20.

Gōmētikapriya (South India). *Janya rāga* of the 20th *mēḷa* (*Naṭabhairavī*).

Tone material:

C D E♭ G A♭ B♭ c

c B♭ A♭ G E♭ D C

Lit.: no. 139.

Gomgom (Java). A metallophone consisting of iron kettles of various sizes.
Lit.: no. 255.

Gomgon (South Africa). Cf. *Gora.*
Lit.: no. 190.

Gomukha (Ancient India). Shell horn ("cow-mouth horn"). A martial instrument mentioned in the Hindu epics *Rāmāyāṇa* and *Mahābhārata.*
Lit.: nos. 184, 255.

Gōmukhi (South India). *Janya rāga* of the 15th *mēḷa* (*Māyāmāḷavagauḷa*).
Tone material:

E D♭ C F G A♭ B c

c B A♭ G D♭ E C

Lit.: no. 139.

Gōmūtrakam (South India). *Janya rāga* of the 8th *mēḷa* (*Hanumattōḍi*).
Tone material:

C D♭ E♭ F G B♭ c

c B♭ A♭ G F E♭ D♭ C

Lit.: no. 139.

Goṅ (Borneo). Large gong.
Lit.: no. 254.

Gon (Japan). Name of the 8th pipe of the *shō.* Cf. *Shō.*
Lit.: no. 225.

Gōnang (Borneo). See *Gondang.*

Gondang (West Java). (1) The rice block stamping. Cf. *Kotekan*; *Bendrong*; *Tataganing.* (2) *Gondang* or *gōnang* in West Borneo: drum similar to the *gendang prang.* The *gondang* is smaller and is beaten with a curved stick called *pengombe.*

Gondang bulu (North Sumatra – Toba Batak). Bamboo (*bulu*) tube zither.
Lit.: no. 156.

Göndra (Java; Sumatra). Percussion instrument to scare away birds. Cf. *Göndrang*; *Cendang*; *Kendang.*
Lit.: no. 156.

Gondra hao (North Nias). "Bamboo drum." Bamboo tube zither.
Lit.: no. 156.

Göndrang (*Göndra*) (Sumatra). Big drum; its left side beaten with the hand, the right side with a small wooden stick. Cf. *Genḍang* (Sumatra).
Lit.: no. 255.

Gong (Malaysia). Large, vertically suspended low-pitched gongs.

Gong (Java; Borneo). Large gong. Cf. *Faritia*; *Saraina* (small gong).

Gong (New Guinea). Shell horn.

Gong (*gong ageng*) (Bali). The largest gong in the *gamelan gong* group.

Gonga (Congo – Mobenga). Double iron bell.
Lit.: no. 21.

Gongaa (North Africa; Libya). Drum beaten on one head with a stick and on the other with the hand.
Lit.: no. 255.

Gong ageng (Java). Also called *gong gede.* Large vertically suspended gong. Some of these large gongs bear names. Two are given below:

1. *Kangjeng Kyahi Lindu*, The Venerable Sir Earthquake.
2. *Kangjeng Kyahi Sima*, The Venerable Sir Tiger.

Lit.: no. 163.

Gongan (Bali). An entire melodic period, which ends with a gong stroke.
Lit.: no. 197.

Gongan (Java). The number of *kenong* beats per one *gongan* indicates into which structural category a composition is to be grouped. *Gongan* stands here for a formal, structural feature.

Gong anak (*Gong ibu*) (Malaysia). Heavy gong with a protruding boss. *Gong anak* has a higher sound than *gong ibu.* (*Anak* and *ibu* represent mother and son.)

Gong anggang-anggang (Java). *Anggang-anggang*, "touch gently." Cf. *Gong Kemodong.*

Gong ba'ung (Java). A gong that does not produce any *ombak* ("wave").
Lit.: no. 163.

Gong beri (Java). A small, almost flat knobless gong that is used for signalling and in warfare. The terms *beri* and *bende* are often interchanged. Instead of *beri* appears *bheri* or *bahiri* in Bali.
Lit.: no. 163.

Gong beri (Bali). A rare ensemble of percussion instruments.
Lit.: no. 265.

Gong besar (Java). A single large gong suspended from a wooden stand.

Gong betina (Malaysia). Medium-sized gong. See *Genḍang kling.*

Gong bumbung (*gumbeng*) (Java). See *Bomberdom* (Flores). Cf. *Serbung*; *Goong awi.*
Lit.: no. 159.

Gong duwabelas (Ambon; Moluccas). A *bonang* with four rows of eight kettles. Cf. *Gong sembilan.*
Lit.: no. 159.

Gong geḍe (*gong ageng*; *goong geḍe*) (Bali). (1) The largest gong of the orchestra. (2) The name for the large contemporary festive orchestra with about 50 players, used at temple festivities and for accompanying the *baris* (war) dance and the *topeng* (mask play) performed to glorify the Javanese ruler.

The orchestra is tuned to *selisir.* The melody is performed by the *trompong* and the drums are beaten with sticks. The *tabuh* differ from those of the *Semar Pegulingan*, and the gongs are larger than those of the *Semar Pegulingan* ensemble.
Lit.: nos. 163, 265.

Gong genḍer (Java). A pair of gongs suspended from a wooden frame.

Gong gentong (Java). See *Gong kemoḍong.*
Lit.: no. 163.

Gong guchi (Java; Bandawasa). Also called *Gong panggang.* See *Gong kemoḍong.*

Gong hoi (Thailand). A group of three (rarely five or seven) small gongs suspended (vertically) in a wooden frame. They are beaten with two padded sticks. The gongs are not tuned to specific pitches, but one sounds higher, one medium, and one lower. The *gong hoi* are not always used in the *pipat* ensemble. They are used only when sections of *Rāmāyāna* subjects are performed. See *Pipat*; *Thai.*

Gong Ibu (Malaysia). See *Gong Anak.*

Gongina (Assam — Garo). Bamboo jew's harp.
Lit.: no. 252.

Gong Jantan (Malaysia). Large gong. Cf. *Genḍang kling.*
Lit.: no. 217.

Gong Jemblok (Java). See *Gong jun*; *Gong kemoḍong.*

Gong Jun (Java). See *Gong kemoḍong.*
Lit.: no. 163.

Gong kebijar (Bali). See *Gong kebyar.*

Gong kebyar (Bali). Modernized form of *gamelan gong.* It presents lively pieces, with frequent changes of tempo and unison passages. The drums are beaten with the hands.
Lit.: nos. 197, 284.

Gong kemaḍa (Java; Jogya). Name of *gong kemoḍong.*
Lit.: no. 163.

Gong kemoḍong (*Gong kemaḍa*) (Java). A simple instrument that is frequently substituted for the *gong ageng* in *gamelan klenengan.* Two bronze slabs are hung horizontally above a heavy wooden sound box (called *grobogan*). The slabs are tuned to *lima* and *nem.* Occasionally there appears a *gong kemodong* with only on slab.

The instrument is called by various names:

1. East Java: *gong jun* or *gong jemblok.*
2. Kebumen: *gong gentong.*
3. Banyumas: *gong anggan.*
4. Panarukan, Bandawasa: *gong guchi* or *gong panggang.*
5. West Java: *goong buyung.*

Lit.: nos. 159, 163.

Gong kempul (Java). Single gong hung in a frame.
Lit.: no. 255.

Gong kemuḍa (*Gong kemaḍa*) (Java). See *Gong kemoḍong.*

Gong ko'e (*ko'e*, small) (West Flores). A small gong that has the shape of the Javanese *bonang.* The term can indicate one or several gongs.
Lit.: no. 166.

Gong lanang (Bali). Term for a "male" gong. It is smaller in size and higher in pitch than the second gong of a pair used in the *gamelan gong.* Cf. *Gong wadon*, the "female" gong.
Lit.: no. 197.

Gong luang (Bali). Also called *gong saron.* In this ensemble appear one or two bronze *saron.* They, together with a *trompong* and the little *kendang tumba* ("bug drum"), play the figuration of the theme. Cf. *Gamelan luang.*
Lit.: no. 265.

Gong mese (Flores). *Mese*, "big." A wide-rimmed gong used in the western mountains south of Ruteng. Cf. *Penontong* (Java).

Gong panggang (Java). See *Gong guchi*; *Gong kemodong.*

Gongo (Africa). Cf. *Digongo.*

Gong ringgeng (Java). Cf. *Gong kemodong.*

Gong saron (Bali). See *Gamelan luang.*

Gong sembilan (Moluccas; Banda). A *bonang*-formed group consisting of nine kettles. Cf. *Duwabelas*; *Tatabuhan.*
Lit.: no. 159.

Gong siyem (Java). See *Gong suwukan.*
Lit.: no. 163.

Gong suwukan (*Gong siyem*) (Java). A gong-formed instrument which in Central Java replaces the *gong ageng.* It is smaller than the *gong ageng.* The word *suwukan* indicates a rallentando feature. *Gong suwukan* (there can be one, two, rarely three) is struck when the music slows down toward the end of the *genḍing lampah* in *wayang* performances.
Lit.: nos. 158, 163.

Gong tondu (*Gong tundu*; *Banggi*) (Flores). A tubular zither with a varied number of strings and numerous names: in Larantuka the instrument is called *kolong-kolong*, or occasionally *laka do'o*, and has three or four strings; in Maumere, Sikka and on Paluwe its name is *santo* or *mapa* and has six, seven, or nine strings; in Ende its name is *gobato* and has three strings; in Ngada it is called *beko-beko* or *beko-fu'i* and has five strings; in the Manggaray it is called *nggri-nggo* or *churing* and has five or six strings.
Lit.: no. 166.

Gong tundu (Flores). See *Gong tondu.*

Gong wadon (Bali). Of a pair of gongs, the larger one in size and lower one in pitch, called the "female," is used in the *gamelan gong.* Cf. *Gong lanang.*
Lit.: no. 197.

Gong wong lek (Thailand). The term indicates the same or closely similar group as *gong wong yai.* The group has 16-18 small high-pitched gongs. It serves either to perform the main melody or to paraphrase parts of it. See *Pipat.*
Lit.: no. 49.

Gong wong yai (Thailand). On a low circular stand made of cane and rattan are placed 16 small gongs. The player sits in the center of the circle and strikes the gongs with two sticks which have their ends covered with buffalo hide. The *gong wong yai* plays the main melody in *pipat* performances. Cf. *Gong wong lek.*
Lit.: no. 49.

Gong yang (China). A single "male" gong that has no curved central boss.
Lit.: no. 255.

Gong yin (China). A single "female" gong with a curved central boss.

Gonje (West Africa). Fiddle with one string. Cf. *Goge.*

Gonra (North Nias). A *valiha* (bamboo zither) with one plucked string. See *Gettung-gettung*; *Gendang-gendang.*
Lit.: no. 254.

Go-on-fu (Japan). Early notation of the Buddhist chant. Cf. *Go-on-sanju.*
Lit.: no. 185.

Goöng (West Java). Term for gong.

Goöng awi (Sunda District). A common name of *gumbeng.*

Goöng buyung (West Java). *Buyung* means earthenware pot. Term for the Javanese *gong kemodong.*

Goöng gede (*Gong ageng*; *Gong gede*) (Java). Large vertically suspended bronze gong.
Lit.: no. 163.

Go-on-hakase (*Go-on-sanju*) (Japan). "Notation of the five sounds." Ancient Buddhist notational system consisting of three "layers" of five notes each:

shoju *C D E G A*
niju C D E G A
sanju c d e g a

This system came into use as *shōmyō* notation by the Tendai sect during the 9th century and by the Shingon sect in the 12th century.
Lit.: no. 185.

Goöng leutik (West Java). "Small gong." A West Javanese name for *kempul.*

Go-on-sanju (Japan). Cf. *Go-on-hakase*; *Go-on-fu.*

Gopati (South India). *Janya rāga* of the 42nd *mēḷa* (*Raghupriyā*).
Tone material:

C D♭ E♭♭ F♯ G A♯ B
(B) G F♯ E♭♭ D♭ C *B* (B A♯ F♯ D♭ E♭♭ D♭ C)

The scale of this *rāga* has *Niṣādāntya* character.
Lit.: no. 139.

Gopichand (India). Cf. *Gopi yantra.*
Lit.: no. 198.

Gōpikābharanam (South India). *Janya rāga* of the 43rd *mēḷa* (*Gavāmbōdhi*).
Tone material:

C D♭ E♭ F♯ G B♭♭ c
c B♭♭ G F♯ E♭ D♭ C

Lit.: no. 139.

Gōpikabhuṣaṇam (South India). *Janya rāga* of the 15th *mēḷa* (*Māyāmāḷavagauḷa*).

Tone material:
C D♭ F A♭ B c
c B A♭ F D♭ C
Lit.: no. 139.

Gōpika Kusumam (South India). *Janya rāga* of the 15th *mēḷa* (*Māyāmāḷavagauḷa*). This *rāga* uses the same tone material as *rāga Gōpikabhūṣaṇam.*
Lit.: no. 139.

Gopikāmanōrañjani (South India). *Janya rāga* of the 67th *mēḷa* (*Sucharitra*).
Tone material:
C D♯ E F♯ G B♭♭ c
c B♭♭ G F♯ E D♯ C
Lit.: no. 139.

Gōpika Tilakam (South India). *Janya rāga* of the 56th *mēḷa* (*Śaṇmukhapriyā*).
Tone material:
C D E♭ F♯ G B c
c B♭ G F♯ E♭ D C
Lit.: no. 139.

Gōpikavasant (North India). Obscure *rāga* of the *Asavari thāta.*
Tone material:
C E♭ F G A♭ B♭ c
c A♭ (B♭ A♭) F G (F) E♭ C
Lit.: no. 138.

Gōpika Vasanta (South India). *Janya rāga* of the 20th *mēḷa* (*Naṭabhairavī*).
Tone material:
C F G B♭ A♭ B♭ A♭ c
c B♭ A♭ G F E♭ C
Lit.: no. 139.

Gōpī yantra (India; Bengal). Also called *nandin.* A small wooden barrel with a skin at its lower end is topped by a forked bamboo stick. From the top of the bamboo stick down to the skin at the bottom of the barrel is strung one metal string which is plucked with a plectrum. By squeezing the fork the pitch can be altered to some extent. Cf. *Ananda lahari.*
Lit.: no. 255.

Gōpriya (South India). *Janya rāga* of the 62nd *mēḷa* (*Riṣabhapriyā*).
Tone material:
C D E F♯ A♭ B♭ c
c B♭ A♭ F♯ E D C
Lit.: no. 139.

Gora (South Africa – Hottentot). A mouth bow. The sounds are created by the breathing of the player on a quill which is attached to the string. The instrument had its origin with the Hottentots; only later was it adopted by other tribes (Bushmen, Bantu people, etc.). See *Gorra.* Cf. *Makwindi*; *Ugwala.*
Lit.: nos. 149, 151, 218.

Gorakh Kalyan (North India). A recently created *rāga.* It is subordinated to the *Bilaval thāta.* This *rāga* is related to the *Kalyan* and *Bilaval* materials.
Tone material:
C D F G A c
c B♭ A G F D C
Lit.: no. 138.

Gordi (Borneo). Cf. *Kledi.*

Gordang (Malaysia). See *Genḍang.*
Lit.: no. 254.

Gore (New Hebrides; Leper Isl.). Long bamboo flute with two finger holes in front and a third in the back. Cf. *Kaur.*
Lit.: no. 255.

Gorkikalyan (North India). See *Gaurkalyan.*

Goroṅ (Senegal – Wolof). Short drum.
Lit.: no. 255.

Gorr (Vietnam – Miao). Drum.
Lit.: no. 303.

Gorra (*Gora*; *Gurra*; *Goura*) (Africa – Bushmen). See *Gora.* The Bechuana term is *losiva*; the Basuto term is *lesiba.*
Lit.: no. 255.

Gorteh (Borneo). See *Garuding* (*Giriding*). Cf. *Kladde*; *Keluri.*

Go-sagari-roku-agari (Japan). "Lowered fifth and raised sixth." One of the *koto* tunings. This one represents a combination of *iwato* and *kumoi.* See *koto* (tunings).

Go-sei (Japan). "The five voices." The theory and study of singing the vowels A, E, I, O, U are combined with the notes of the pentatonic scale: *kyu*, *sho*, *kaku*, *chi* (or *cho*), and *U.* See *Kwaigo-no-ben.* Cf. *Go-in*; *Go-ju*; *Sei-in* ("clear voices"); *Jisei-in.*
Lit.: no. 225.

Gosh-darida (Iran). Term for tambourin.

Go-Shringa (India). See *Go-Śriṅga.*

Gosoq (Java). Bow.

Gō-śriṅga (India). Ancient cow-horn, blown at martial and sacred occasions.
Lit.: no. 254.

Got (North India). Cf. *Tabla.*

Goto (Japan). See *Koto.*

Gōtrāri (South India). *Janya rāga* of the 63rd *mēḷa* (*Latāṅgī*).
Tone material:
C D F# G A♭ c
c B A♭ G F# E D C
Lit.: no. 139.

Gotrāri (South India). (1) The 63rd *asampūrṇa mēḷa-rāga* without *kaṭapayādi* prefix. (2) The 63rd *asampūrṇa mēḷa-rāga* with *kaṭapayādi* prefix was called *gītapriyā.* See *Rāga* (South India).
Lit.: no. 139.

Gōttuvādyam (South India). See *Gōtuvādyam.*
Lit.: no. 215.

Gotul pata (Southeast India; Maria Gond tribe). The *gotul* is a religious "club house" and dormitory for the young people. *Gotul pata* means *gotul* song. There are numerous songs of this character.
Lit.: no. 142.

Gōṭuvādyam (*Gōttuvādyam*) (South India). A fretless *vīṇā*, also called *mahānāṭaka vīṇā*. It is used in dramatic and dance performances. The name *gōṭuvādyam* implies the stopping of strings with a *godu* (*kōḍu*), a wooden cylinder, held in the left hand. The player either plucks the strings with his right hand or with a plectrum. The instrument has a pear-shaped body and a hollow stem. The neck curves downward and beneath the neck is affixed a gourd resonator. The *gōṭuvādyam* has five play-strings and three drone strings. The five strings are tuned c c G C *G* and the three drone strings *C G* C. Seven sympathetic strings are strung below the play-strings along the *dandi* (stem).
Lit.: no. 261.

Goukha's (South Africa—Damara). Musical bow.
Lit.: no. 151.

Gourra (Africa). Cf. *Gora.*

Govand (Kurdisthan). Dance. Men and women hold each other by the hands and move in a semicircle.
Lit.: no. 229.

Goviḍambini (South India). *Janya rāga* of the 20th *mēḷa* (*Naṭabhairavī*).
Tone material:
C E♭ F G A♭ B♭ c
c A♭ G E♭ D C
Lit.: no. 139.

Gōvinda Dhanyāsi (South India). *Janya rāga* of the 63rd *mēḷa* (*Latāṅgī*).
Tone material:
C D E F# G A♭ c
c A♭ G F# E D C
Lit.: no. 139.

Gōvinda Nāyāraṇi (South India). *Janya rāga* of the 52nd *mēḷa* (*Rāmapriyā*).
Tone material:
C E F♯ G A B♭ c
c B♭ A G E D♭ C
Lit.: no. 139.

Gowangan (Java). See *Kowangan.*

Go weto (*Go beto*) (Flores). See *Baba.*

Graha (Ancient India). Initial note of a *rāga.*
Lit.: no. 138.

Graha bhēdam (*Graha svara bhēdam*) (South India). Method of creating new scales by shifting the tonic to another than the first place of the original scale.
Lit.: no. 261.

Grajappi (Thailand). Lute with four double strings (tuned in pairs) and a variable number of frets. In Cambodia this instrument is called *chapei thom.*

Gram (New Guinea). Cf. *Garamūt* (*Garamūth*).
Lit.: no. 84.

Grāma (Old India). "Village." The three basic scales of ancient music theory. Frequencies according to Lit. no. 261, p. 215:

sa grāma:	*sa*	*ri*	*ga*	*ma*	*pa*	*dha*	*ni*
	1	10/9	32/27	4/3	3/2	5/3	16/9
ga grāma:	1	10/9	32/27	4/3	40/27	5/3	16/9

Cf. *Mūrchhanās* (also concerning *ma grāma*).
Lit.: no. 138.

Grambyang(an) (*Griming[an]*) (Java). The gentle sounding of the *genḍer* that indicates the required pitch to the *dalang.*
Lit.: no. 163.

Grandha Taraṅgiṇi (South India). *Janya rāga* of the 29th *mēḷa* (*Dhīraśaṅkarābharaṇam*).
Tone material:
C E D E F G A B c
c A B G F E D C
Lit.: no. 139.

Grandha Vikṣēpam (South India). *Janya rāga* of the 22nd *mēḷa* (*Kharaharapriyā*).
Tone material:
C D E♭ F G A B♭ c
c A G E♭ D C
Lit.: no. 139.

Grantang (Bali). (1) Common term for the symbols used in musical notation. (2) A xylophone using bamboo tubes instead of wooden slabs. It is similar to the *angklung* of Banjuwangi (Java).
Lit.: nos. 136, 197.

Graw (Thailand). Slit-drum.
Lit.: no. 215.

Greget saut (*Galak*) (Java). The term indicates the peculiar mood, atmosphere, and emotion of a piece of music. Cf. *Ada-ada.*
Lit.: no. 163.

Griaule (Cameroon). Harp-lute.

Griming(an) (Java). See *Grambyang(an).*

Grinding (Java). Jew's harp made of a piece of reed with three tongues. Cf. *Doeri.*
Lit.: no. 255.

Grīṣmavaḷi (South India). *Janya rāga* of the 16th *mēḷa* (*Chakravāka*).
Tone material:
C D♭ E F G c
c B♭ A F E D♭ C
Lit.: no. 139.

Grobog (Java). A wooden resonance box supporting sticks (similar to a xylophone), variously tuned. The range extends for 3½ to 4 octaves.
Lit.: no. 254.

Grobogan (Java). The resonance boxes of various groups (e.g., *gong kemodong*) and of other metallophones (e.g., *saron*). In the boxes are placed clay pots which intensify the resonances.
Lit.: no. 255.

Grontolan (Java). Drum roll. The term is derived from *grontol* (cooked grains of maize). When poured out, the grains create a noise like a drum roll. See *Keter*.
Lit.: no. 163.

Grunong (Malaysia; Sarawak; Brunei). A round brass cowbell.
Lit.: no. 255.

Gsba (Arabia). See *Nāy*.

Gshang (Tibet). "Flat bell," obscure instrument of the Bön po.

Gsung (Tibet). Term for singing, speaking, voice, text.
Lit.: no. 143.

Gů (Burma; Southern Shan States). Horn. Cf. *Kwāi*.
Lit.: no. 252.

Gubar (Java). Ancient term for small, almost flat, gongs. Cf. *Munda*.
Lit.: no. 159.

Gubgubi (North India). Friction drum. Cf. *Dugduga*.
Lit.: no. 303.

Gubo (South Africa—Amazulu). Music bow with a gourd as resonance body.
Lit.: no. 18.

Gubu (Nyasaland). Xylophone.
Lit.: no. 26.

Gubuolukhulu (*Inkohlisa*) (South Africa). Cf. *Segwana*; *Imvingo*; *Ugubu*; *Uhadi*.
Lit.: no. 151.

Guda (Sumeria). Term for a low priestly class. Members of the priest's family were obliged to perform musical accompaniments.
Lit.: no. 94.

Gudi (Sumeria). Obscure musical instrument used at New Year ceremonies.
Lit.: no. 94.

Gudina pata karsana (Southeast India; Muria Gond Tribe). A *gotul pata*. Girls playing a game.
Lit.: no. 142.

Gudugudu (*Opon*) (Nigeria—Yoruba). The term for the accompanying kettledrum. It is tuned to a high pitch and has one skin. The drum belongs to the *dundun* ensemble. Cf. *Dundun*; *Bembe*.
Lit.: no. 293.

Guena (*Kwainya*) (Ryukyu Retto Isl.). A long narrative song sung by several women.

Guggu (Sudan; Congo—Azande). Slit-drum.
Lit.: no. 21.

Gughe (Algeria). Spike fiddle with one horse-hair string.
Lit.: no. 184.

Gugul (Malaysia; Sarawak). See *Dikoot*; *Dakoot*.

Guhapriya (South India). *Janya rāga* of the 16th *mēḷa* (*Chakravāka*).
Tone material:

C D♭ E F G F A B♭ c
c B♭ A G F E C D♭ C

Cf. *Gunapriya*; its ascent is identical with that of *guhapriya*. The descent of *gunapriya* shows the following form:

c A B♭ G F E C D♭ C

Lit.: no. 139.

Guharañjani (South India). *Janya rāga* of the 28th *mēḷa* (*Harikāmbhōji*).
Tone material:

C D C F G A B♭ c
c B♭ A B♭ G F E C

Lit.: no. 139.

Gui dounou (Republic of Guinea—Malinke). Floating gourd struck with two sticks.
Lit.: no. 303.

Gujjari (South India). See *Gurjari.*

Gujri-tōḍi (*Gurjari- Ghurjari-*, *Gojri-tōḍi*) (North India). *Rāga* subordinated to the *Tōdi thāta.*
Tone material:
C D♭ E♭ F♯ A♭ B c
c B A♭ G F♯ E♭ D♭ C; *Vādis*: A♭, E♭
Lit.: no. 138.

Guke (Uganda—Lugbara). Side-blown horn.

Ğülğül (Middle East). Frame drum with jingles.

Gulgul (Madura). Slit-drum. Cf. *Kulkul* (Bali).

Gulieng (Borneo). Bamboo beak flute with three finger holes.
Lit.: no. 255.

Gul'izar (Middle East). *Maqām.*
Tone material:
D E♭(+) F G A B♭(+) c d
Lit.: no. 64.

Gullāl (Algeria). Frame drum.
Lit.: no. 78-1.

Gulong-gulong (*Gulung-gulung*) (Borneo). Stamping bamboo stick. In Batanglupar it is called *ento gal*; in Tanah Laut, *kurong-kurong*; in Malay, *tugal.*
Lit.: no. 166.

Gulu (Tenggok) (Java). (1) Tone name. Its significance changes from one system and place to the other. In the *pelog* system in Central Java, Prabalingga, it is the second note. It is also the second note in the *slendro* system in Jombang, also in Prabalingga. It may become the third note of *slendro* and the fourth note of *pelog* (see *Pelog*; *Slendro*). (2) The term indicates also slit drum. Cf. *Jongga.*
Lit.: no. 163.

Gulu (Bali). See *Kulukul.*

Gulung-gulung (Borneo—Kapuas). (1) Rattle stamping stick. (2) An instrument that consists of seven bamboo tubes of different lengths. Each tube is used by a different player who holds the tube vertically and shakes it into a vessel. The sounds of the seven tubes are: *G B♭* C D F G A. Their names are: *sumah* (G), *pendanakinggi* (*B♭*), *pendana-gendah* (C), *tinki-besar* (D), *tangcup-besar* (F), *tinkie-hetjil* (G), *tangcup-hetjil* (A). The *gulung-gulung* is known as *tugal* in West Borneo and as *tongkat-krutak* in North Borneo.
Lit.: no. 184.

Gulupobe (New Guinea—Papua; Huli). Panpipes; bundles of bamboo tubes.
Lit.: no. 233.

Gü-lu sh'e-pa (Tibet). See *Sh'e-tang-wa.*

Gulutindi (Congo). See *Kilingila.*

Gumanak (*Kemanak*) (Bali). A small metal cylinder tapped with a metal stick, and used as a percussion instrument in the *gamelan gambuh.*
Lit.: no. 197.

Gumbang (*Gumbeng*) (Java; Sunda District). (1) See *Bumbung.* (2) *Gumbang* or *goong awi*, terms used in the Sunda District. See *Bomberdom* (Flores).
Lit.: no. 163.

Gumbeng (*Gumbang*; *Goong awi*) (Java). (1) A drum zither made of a piece of bamboo. A part of the wall of the tube is partly detached and serves as a string (*senteng*). In the regency of Kediri this zither is called *bumbung* ("bamboo tube"). (2) This term is also used for wind instruments.

Gumbeng wesi (Java). *Wesi* means "iron." See *Gamelan mondreng.*

Gumbrī (Morocco). See *Gnbrī* (*Gunībrī*).

Gummakāmbhōji (South India). *Janya rāga* of the 15th *mēḷa* (*Māyāmāḷavagauḷa*).
Tone material:
C D♭ E G A♭ B A♭ c
c B A♭ G F E D♭ C
Lit.: no. 139.

Gummaṭi (South India). Telugu term for pot drum used in village festivals. It provides accompaniment to the singing of popular ballads.
Lit.: no. 261.

Gummavaḷi (South India). *Janya rāga* of the 56th *mēḷa* (*Śaṇmukhapriyā*).
Tone material:
C D E♭ G A♭ B♭ c
c A♭ G F♯ E♭ D C
Lit.: no. 139.

Gumphita (*Humpita*) (India). See *Gamak(a)*.

Gumra (Southeast India). Cup-shaped drum; occasionally also goblet-shaped.
Lit.: no. 254.

Gu-mun-go (Korea). See *Ko-mun-ko*.

Gumyadyuti (South India). *Janya rāga* of the 29th *mēḷa* (*Dhīraśaṅkarābharaṇam*).
Tone material:
C D E G A B A G A c
c B A G F E D C
Lit.: no. 139.

Guna (India). String.

Gaṇabhūṣaṇi (South India). *Janya rāga* of the 37th *mēḷa* (*Sālaga*).
Tone material:
C D♭ E♭♭ F♯ G c
c G F♯ E♭♭ D♭ C
Lit.: no. 139.

Gunakali (North India). *Rāga* subordinated to the *Bilaval thāta* (another *rāga* with the same name is ascribed to the *Bhairav thāta*). *Gunakali* of the *Bilaval thāta* appears in two versions:
1. without the note B;
2. with the note B.

Tone material:
C D E (F) G A (B) c
c (B♭) A G (F) E D C; *Vādis*: C, G
Lit.: no. 138.

Gunakali (of the *Bhairav thāta*) (North India). See *Gunkari*.

Gunakari (North India). See *Gunkari* (*Bhairav thāta*).

Gunakiri (North India). See *Gunkari*.

Gunakriya (North India). See *Gunkari* (*Bhairav thāta*).

Guṇapriya (South India). See *Guhapriya*.

Gunbrī (Sudan; Arabia). See *Gunībrī*.

Gunda (Tanganyika – Washambala). Side-blown Kudu horn.
Lit.: no. 130.

Guṇḍakriya (South India). *Janya rāga* of the 15th *mēḷa* (*Māyāmāḷavagauḷa*).
Tone material:
C D♭ F G B c
c B G A♭ G F E D♭ C
Lit.: no. 139.

Gundang (Malaysia). See *Genḍang*.

Gundu (*Manikkāi*) (South India). (1) Tamil term for a small bead or round piece of wood fitted on the *tanbura* string near the bridge. It enables the player to achieve exact tuning. (2) Occasionally also a cylindrical piece of wood used for stopping (and gliding along) strings of the *gōṭusvādyam*.
Lit.: no. 261.

Guṇḍu tālam (South India). Also called *jālra*. A pair of brass cymbals.
Lit.: no. 261.

Guneman (Bali). An improvised prelude performed on a single solo instrument. It leads into the proper prelude (*pengawit*; *gihing*).
Lit.: no. 197

Gunghuru (*Gunguru*) (Ancient India). "Little bells, jingles." Foot rattle consisting of several rows of small round jingles fastened to a ring or strip of cloth. Other terms are: *kshudragh-haṇtikā*; *kinkinī*.
Lit.: no. 261.

Gungu (Tanzania). Song types.

Gunguma (Ethiopia—Galla). Drum.
Lit.: no. 102.

Gunguru (India). See *Gunghuru.*
Lit.: no. 261.

Gunībrī (*Gunbrī*) (Arabia; North Africa). Small popular bowed lute with one or two strings (also called *gnbrī*).
Lit.: nos. 215, 250.

Guninfu-bushu (Okinawa). Song sung before the ruler.

Guṇita Vinōdiṇi (South India). *Janya rāga* of the 16th *mēḷa* (*Chakravāka*).
Tone material:
C E F G (A) B♭ c
c B♭ A G F E D♭ C
This *rāga* is also known as *Gaṇita Vinōdiṇi.*
Lit.: no. 139.

Gunj dar (North India). "Echo effect." Cf. *Tabla.*

Gunkari (*Gunakari*; *Gunakali*; *Gunakiri*; *Gunakriya*) (North India). *Rāga* subordinated to the *Bhairav thāta.* (It must not be mistaken for *Gunakali* of the *Bilaval thāta.*)
Tone material:
C D♭ F G A♭ c
c A♭ G F D♭ C; *Vādis*: A♭, D♭
Lit.: no. 138.

Guntang (Bali). A bamboo zither with one string, used as a percussion instrument. A large sized *guntang* is used for punctuation and a small one for beating the rhythm.
Lit.: no. 197.

Gupek (Bali). A pair of small two-headed drums beaten with the hands and used in the *gamelan angklung* ensemble.
Lit.: no. 197.

Gup gaep (Northeast Thailand). A pair of wooden percussion blocks. Cf. *Mawlum gup gaep.*
Lit.: no. 203.

Gurban (*Gurbanghet*) (Ethiopia). Drum.
Lit.: no. 102.

Gurgbanghet (Ethiopia). See *Gurban.*

Gurjari (*Gujjari*; *Ghurjari*) (South India). *Janya rāga* of the 15th *mēḷa* (*Māyāmāḷavagauḷa*).
Tone material:
C D♭ E F G A♭ B c
c A♭ G F E D♭ C (c A♭ B G F E D♭ C)
Lit.: no. 139.

Gurjari-tōḍi (North India). See *Gujri-tōḍi.*

Gur-ma (Tibet). Religious song. Its honorific term is *sung-gur.*
Lit.: no. 143.

Gur-ma lem-pa (Tibet). See *Sh'e tang-wa.*

Gurra (South Africa). See *Gorra.*

Gurram (South India). A Telugu term (meaning "horse") for bridge of a string instrument. In Tamil the term is *kudirai* ("horse").
Lit.: no. 261.

Guru (South India). "Heavy." Term for a durational note value. If the *laghu* is assumed to be one quarter note (♩), the *guru* represents a half note (𝅗𝅥). (All other durational values are stated under the heading of *Anudrutam.*) Cf. *Akshara.*
Lit.: no. 261.

Guru druta(m) (South India). Durational note value: one *guru* plus one *drutam* (𝅗𝅥 + ♪). The other durational values are shown under the heading of *Anudrutam.*

Gurugadya (*Garigadya*) (South India). *Janya rāga* of the 56th *mēḷa* (*Śaṇmukhapriyā*).
Tone material:

B♭ C E♭ F♯ G A♭ B♭

B♭ A♭ G F♯ E♭ D C *B♭* C

Lit.: no. 139.

Gurujyōti (South India). *Janya rāga* of the 61st *mēḷa* (*Kāntāmaṇi*).
Tone material:

C D E F♯ A♭ c

c A♭ F♯ E D C

Lit.: no. 139.

Guru lagu (Bali). The final vowel of a verse line. Cf. *Guru wilangan*; *Kidung*; *Mekidung*.
Lit.: no. 265.

Guruma (New Guinea). Wooden drum. Cf. *Gerom*.
Lit.: no. 84.

Gurumi (Sahara; Sudan—Hausa). See *Ghurumi* (*Kiddi*).

Guruprakāśi (South India). *Janya rāga* of the 20th *mēḷa* (*Naṭabhairavī*).
Tone material:

C D E♭ F A♭ B♭ c

c B♭ A♭ G F D C

Lit.: no. 139.

Gurupriya (South India). *Janya rāga* of the 64th *mēḷa* (*Vāchaspati*).
Tone material:

C D E F♯ A B♭ c

c B♭ A F♯ E D C

Lit.: no. 139.

Guru wilangan (Bali). Number of syllables of one verse line. Cf. *Guru lagu*. Cf. also *Kidung*; *Mekidung*.
Lit.: no. 265.

Gushat (*Kushat*; *Gavāsht*) (Arabia). Tone name of a note approximately a semitone higher than *'iraq*. (A list of all tone names can be seen under the heading of *Jagā* [*Yagā*].)
Lit.: no. 64.

Gusheh (Persia; Iran). Rhythmically free, non-metric melodic formula that usually is limited to a compass of 4-5 notes. These formulas (*gusheh-ha*) are used in the composition of a *dastgāh* or *naghmeh* and, as there are numerous such formulas, every performer selects one or more *gusheh-ha* which can create characteristic features for his composition. Each *gusheh* has its own name.
Lit.: no. 146.

Gvaṇṭu (South India). A small ledge in the *vīṇā* structure, separating the body (*kudam*) from the neck (*daṇḍi*).
Lit.: no. 261.

Ǧwab (Arabia). "Answer." Term for an upper octave.

Gwaeng-ga-ri (Korea). The leader with a small gong directing *nong-āhk*.
Lit.: no. 221.

Gwale (Africa—Basuto). See *Koali*.
Lit.: no. 18.

Gwan'bal (Congo). See *Mushita*.

Gwaningba (Congo). See *Ninga*.

Gwanzu (West Africa—Ababua). Board zither.
Lit.: no. 21.

Gwara me akuta (Uganda—Lango). Straight side-blown wooden trumpet.
Lit.: no. 302.

Gyaku roku (Japan). Theoretical term indicating an interval of six semitone steps downward (a pure fourth).

Gya-ling (Tibet). Cf. *Rgya-gling*.

Gyer-k'a (Tibet). Set of bells.

Gyilli (Ghana). Xylophone.

Gyō (Japan). See *Kyū*.

Gyō (Japan). Cf. *Yü* (China, the "wooden tiger").

Gyōdō (Japan). Important section of the regular Buddhist service when the priests sing and drop symbolic lotus petals.
Lit.: no. 185.

Gyoyū (Japan). Groups of musical amateurs (*miasobi*) who prospered at the court during parts of the Heian period.

Gytarah (Arabia; Sudan – Nubia). See *Qitara*; *Kissar.*

H

Hā (South Africa – Bushmen). Cf. *Gorra.*
Lit.: no. 151.

Ha (Japan). A musical and dramatic form; *ha* signifies the extended middle part (development) of *noh* and *nagauta.* The entire structure is called *jo-ha-kyū* in which *ha* represents the long middle part. It consists of the 2nd, 3rd, and 4th *dan* (scenes). In the 2nd *dan* the first song (*issei*) is presented. This is usually followed by the *michiyuki* ("going on the road") when the *shite* slowly comes from the back through a passage to the stage. Recitatives (*mondo*) follow in the 3rd *dan.* The 4th *dan* contains the *kuri* and *kuse*, dances with songs; the songs are performed in a high register and the dances are greatly stylized, performed by the protagonist. The 4th *dan* is concluded by the *rongi* (end of piece) performed by the *shite* and *waki.* Frequently *ha* ends with a song performed by the chorus (*nakairi*). The chorus song can lead to the finale part (*kyū*) of the drama. At times a comic interlude without music, spoken in common language (*kyōgen*), is inserted before the *kyū* begins.
Lit.: no. 185.

Habajanai (Assam – Bodo). Wedding dance.
Lit.: no. 43.

Habak (Korea). "Combined music." Court orchestra and its grand music using various instruments and chimes: *hai kum*, *achaeng*, *p'iri*, *taegum*, *tangjok*, *chang-ko*, *jwa-ko*, *p'yongjong* (*p'yen-chong*), *p'yon'gyong* (*p'yen-kyeng*).
Lit.: no. 287.

Habara (Arabia). Term used by medieval Jewish poets for *maqām.* The word signifies also tone, note, and sound. Cf. *Naġma* (*Naghma*).
Lit.: no. 121.

Hac (Annam). *Cai hac.* See *Cai chak.*

Hachi (Japan). Name of the 10th pipe of the *shō.* See *Shō.*
Lit.: no. 225.

Hachi-dan (Japan). "8 *dan*" – eight sections or variations (without singing), based on a leading theme. Cf. *Go-dan*; *Roku-dan*; *Shichi-dan*; *Ku-dan*; *Dan.*
Lit.: no. 185.

Hachi-hyōshi (Japan). Eight beats. Cf. *Ya-hyōshi.*

Hachi-kake (Japan). See *Kake.*

Ḥād (Arabia; Iran). The fifth and highest string of the *'ūd*. Cf. *Maṭlaṭ*; *Maṭna*; *Zīr*.
Lit.: no. 255.

Ḥadd (Arabia). The term is the same as *ḥad*. Al-Farabi (A.D. 9-10 centuries) calls *ḥadd* the "extreme string." It is placed above the first of the four other strings of the *'ūd*.

Ḥāddat al-awsāṭ (Arabia). Tone name (as used by Al-Kindī) and notated with the Arabic letter *kāf* (K), which, when transcribed into western notation, can be the note G.
Lit.: no. 69.

Ḥaddat al-muqaddamāt (Arabia). Tone name (as used by Al-Kindī) and notated with the Arabic letter *wāw* (W), which, when transcribed into western notation, can be the note D.
Lit.: no. 69.

Hade (South Africa—Bantu; Zulu). Musical bow.
Lit.: no. 18.

Haegum (Korea). See *Hai-keum.*

Haekum (Korea). See *Hai-keum.*

Haeng (Korea). See *Chung-kan-po.*

Haggum (Korea). See *Hai-keum.*

Hahel (*Henhoel*) (Nicobar Isl.). Nose flute.
Lit.: no. 313.

Hāhōri (*Hāhūri*) (South India). *Janya rāga* of the 20th *mēḷa* (*Naṭabhairavī*).
Tone material:

C D E♭ D F G A♭ B♭ A♭ c
c B♭ A♭ F E♭ D C

Lit.: no. 139.

Hāhūri (South India). See *Hāhōri.*

Haiau (Malaysia). Tube zither with three or four rattan strings.
Lit.: no. 254.

Hai-keum (*Hae-kum*; *Haekum*; *Haegum*; *Haigum*) (Korea). A fiddle with two silken strings and a narrow, cylindrical corpus. The horsehair of the bow is drawn between the two strings which are tuned to the interval of a fifth. The Chinese name of this instrument is *hu-ch'in*; the Japanese name is *kokyū*. The *hai-keum* has maintained its popularity and is used in all types of music. Cf. *Gang-gaingi.*
Lit.: no. 179.

Hai-lo (China—M 2014; M 4111). A large sea shell (conch) with the blowhole broken (or cut) into its apex. The instrument is used for signalling, for serving in Buddhist ritual, by soldiers and watchmen. The Japanese name is *hora* and the Korean name is *sora.*
Lit.: no. 250.

Haimavati (South India). *Janya rāga* of the 19th *mēḷa* (*Jhankāradhvanī*).
Tone material:

C D F G B𝄫 c
c B𝄫 G F D C

Lit.: no. 139.

Hairan (North Iraq). See *Lawko.*

Haiyaṅgavīnam (South India). *Janya rāga* of the 40th *mēḷa* (*Navanītam*).
Tone material:

C D♭ E𝄫 F♯ A B♭ c
c B♭ A F♯ E𝄫 D♭ C

Lit.: no. 139.

Haka (*peruperu*) (New Zealand—Maori). Posture dance, vigorous, warlike, danced by old and young, guided by a leader who shouts out key words that are answered by a chorus. The stamping of feet, slapping thighs, and clapping hands provide the rigid rhythmical foundation.

The *haka* dance instills fear with a variety of threatening poses. *Haka koiri* is the dance with swaying movements. *Haka tutohu* is danced in wedge formation.
Lit.: nos. 37, 185, 228, 298, 315.

Hakapoponge (Solomon Isl.). See *Mou hatingaa nge'o.*

Hakase (Japan). "Learned doctor." General term for *shōmyō* notation. Cf. *Ko-hakase*; *Fuhakase*; *Meyasu*; *Hom-bakase.*
Lit.: no. 47.

Haka tutohu (New Zealand – Maori). See *Haka.*

Hakep (Java). Mouthpiece.

Haku (Japan). See *Pak* (Korea); *P'ai-pan* (China).

Hakuhan (*Hukuhan*) (Japan). A wooden rattle consisting of small slabs tied together in fan shape. Cf. *Byakushi.*
Lit.: no. 225.

Halam (*Khalam*) (Gambia – Wolof). Lute with four or five horsehair strings.
Lit.: nos. 201, 206.

Halay (Turkey). Round dance performed to the music of the *davul-zurnā*.
Lit.: no. 243.

Hālāyūdhapriya (South India). *Janya rāga* of the 44th *mēḷa* (*Bhāvapriyā*).
Tone material:
C E♭ F♯ G A♭ c
c A♭ G F♯ E♭ C
Lit.: no. 139.

Ḥalḥallatu (Ancient Mesopotamia). Term for reed pipe. Cf. *Ḥalīl.*
Lit.: no. 87.

Ḥalīl (Ancient Israel). An obscure wind instrument; either a flute or an oboe or a clarinet. *Ḥalīl* means "hollow" ("pierced") and indicates a pipe. The term probably refers to a double pipe such as an aulos type. Cf. *Ḥalḥallatu*; *Abūb(a).*
Lit.: no. 250.

Ḥalilu (Mesopotamia; Akkadian). See *Nā.*

Halleloth (Yemen – Jews). Solemn song parts (psalm verses) used to introduce and conclude ceremonial songs. Cf. *Zafat.*

Halumukhi (South India). *Janya rāga* of the 33rd *mēḷa* (*Gāṅgeyabhushanī*).
Tone material:
C D♯ F G A♭ B c
c B A♭ F E D♯ C
Lit.: no. 139.

Hallisaka (South India). Dance. One man leads a group of women.
Lit.: no. 261.

Hama (*Opak oron*) (Flores). A round-dance (*hama* means "stamping") stamped by the men. The stamping can be, e.g., l. r. l. r. r. Cf. *Roja.*
Lit.: no. 166.

Ha-ma (China – Giles 4199). A humming pot made of clay in the shape of a frog. A horsehair string is strung through the pot's (open) bottom which is covered with paper. The paper is rubbed with wet fingers whereby a sound is produced that resembles the croaking of a frog.
Lit.: nos. 209, 255.

Hama roja (East Flores). "Stamping-singing." A round-dance performed by women. The sung accompaniment is based on an ancient song with a text in a language that is understood only by a few of the very old women.
Lit.: nos. 166, 301.

Hambalan (Sunda District). See *Wilah* (Java).

Ham-chi-ak (Korea). "Entire Influence of the King's Virtue Music." *Ah-ak* in honor of the spirits of the earth. It is believed to represent the music of the legendary Chinese emperor Yao.
Lit.: no. 136.

Hami (New Guinea – Huon Gulf region). Drum in the shape of an hourglass. Cf. *On.*
Lit.: no. 25.

Ḥāmila (Arabia; Iran). String holder.

Hamir(a) (North India). *Rāga* subordinated to the *Kalyan thāta.*
Tone material:
C D E F F♯ G A B c
c B B♭ A G F E D C
Lit.: no. 138.

Hamīrkalyāṇī (South India). *Janya rāga* of the 65th *mēḷa* (*Mechakalyāṇī*).
Tone material:
C G F♯ G A B c
c B A G E F♮ D C
Lit.: no. 139.

Hamono (Japan). A *nagauta* type; its text emphasizes the poetic element and usually does not convey a particular plot. Cf. *Danmono.*
Lit.: no. 187.

Haṃsa (South India). *Janya rāga* of the 15th *mēḷa* (*Māyāmāḷavagauḷa*).
Tone material:
C D♭ F G A♭ c
c A♭ G F D♭ C
Lit.: no. 139.

Haṃsa Bhāṣiṇī (South India). *Janya rāga* of the 24th *mēḷa* (*Varuṇapriyā*).
Tone material:
C E♭ F A♯ B c
c B A♯ F E♭ D C
Lit.: no. 139.

Haṃsa Bhōgi (South India). *Janya rāga* of the 38th *mēḷa* (*Jalārṇava*).
Tone material:
C D♭ E♭♭ F♯ A♭ B♭ c
c B♭ A♭ G F♯ E♭♭ D♭ C
Lit.: no. 139.

Haṃsabhramari (South India). *Janya rāga* of the 58th *mēḷa* (*Hemāvatī*).
Tone material:
C D E♭ F♯ G A c
c B♭ A G F♯ E♭ D C
Lit.: no. 139.

Haṃsa Bhūpāḷam (South India). *Janya rāga* of the 24th *mēḷa* (*Varuṇapriyā*).
Tone material:
C D E♭ F G c
c B A♯ B G F E♭ C
Lit.: no. 139.

Haṃsa Bhūṣaṇi (South India). *Janya rāga* of the 24th *mēḷa* (*Varuṇapriyā*). A *rāga* generally considered to be identical with *Haṃsa Bhāṣiṇī*, excepting some minute differences. For information see Lit. no. 139.

Haṃsa Bhūshavāḷi (South India). *Janya rāga* of the 55th *mēḷa* (*Śyāmalāṅgī*).
Tone material:
C *B♭♭* C D E♭ F♯ G A♭ B♭♭
B♭♭ A♭ G F♯ (F♯) E D♭ E C
This scale has *Niṣādāntya* character.
Lit.: no. 139.

Haṃsadhvani (South India). *Janya rāga* of the 29th *mēḷa* (*Dhīraśaṅkarābharaṇam*).
Tone material:
C D E G B c
c B G E D C
Lit.: no. 139.

Haṃsa Dīpakam (South India). *Janya rāga* of the 23rd *mēḷa* (*Gaurīmanōharī*).
Tone material:
C D E♭ F A c
This *rāga* is also called *Hāsya Dīpakam*.
Lit.: no. 139.

Haṃsa Dīparam (South India). *Janya rāga* of the 42nd *mēḷa* (*Raghupriyā*).
Tone material:
C Db Ebb F♯ G B G c
c B G A♯ B G F♯ Ebb Db C
Lit.: no. 139.

Haṃsa Gamani (South India). *Janya rāga* of the 52nd *mēḷa* (*Rāmapriyā*).
Tone material:
C E F♯ G Bb A c
c Bb A G F♯ A G F♯ E Db C
Lit.: no. 139.

Haṃsa Gāndhāri (South India). *Janya rāga* of the 25th *mēḷa* (*Māraranjanī*).
Tone material:
C D E F G c
c Bbb Ab G F Ab G E D C
Lit.: no. 139.

Haṃsa Gandharvam (South India). *Janya rāga* of the 30th *mēḷa* (*Nāgānandī*).
Tone material:
C D E F G c
c B A♯ B G F D C
Lit.: no. 139.

Haṃsa Ghaṇṭanam (South India). *Janya rāga* of the 35th *mēḷa* (*Śūlinī*).
Tone material:
C D♯ E F G A B c
c B G F E F D♯ C
Lit.: no. 139.

Haṃsa Ghaṇṭāravam (South India). *Janya rāga* of the 20th *mēḷa* (*Naṭabhairavī*).
Tone material:
C D Eb F Eb F G Bb Ab Bb G Ab Bb c
c Bb Ab Bb G Bb Ab F Eb D Eb F Eb D C
Lit.: no. 139.

Haṃsagiri (South India). *Janya rāga* of the 72nd *mēḷa* (*Rasikapriyā*).

Tone material:
C D♯ E F♯ G A♯ B c
c B G A♯ B G F♯ C
Lit.: no. 139.

Haṃsa Gīrvāṇi (South India). *Janya rāga* of the 55th *mēḷa* (*Śyāmalāṅgī*).
Tone material:
C D Eb F♯ G Ab c
c Ab G F♯ Eb C
Lit.: no. 139.

Haṃsa Kambhōji (South India). *Janya rāga* of the 14th *mēḷa* (*Vakuḷābharaṇam*).
Tone material:
C Db E F Ab Bb c
c Bb Ab G F Db C
Lit.: no. 139.

Haṃsa Kōsala (South India). See *Haṃsa Kōsali*.

Haṃsa Kōsali (South India). *Janya rāga* of the 70th *mēḷa* (*Nāsikabhūṣaṇī*).
Tone material:
C D♯ E F♯ G A Bb A c
c Bb A G F♯ E F♯ C
Lit.: no. 139.

Haṃsa Mañjari (South India). *Janya rāga* of the 15th *mēḷa* (*Māyāmāḷavagauḷa*).
Tone material:
C Db E G Ab c
c B G F Db C
Lit.: no. 139.

Haṃsa Nādam (South India). *Janya rāga* of the 60th *mēḷa* (*Nītimatī*).
Tone material:
C D F♯ G A♯ B c
c B A♯ B G F♯ D C
Lit.: no. 139.

Haṃsānandi (South India). *Janya rāga* of the 8th *mēḷa* (*Hanumattōḍi*).
Tone material:
C D♭ E♭ F A♭ B♭ c
c B♭ A♭ F E♭ D♭ C
Lit.: no. 139.

Haṃsānandi (South India). *Janya rāga* of the 53rd *mēḷa* (*Gamanaśrama*).
Tone material:
C D♭ E F♯ A B c
c B A F♯ E D♭ C
Cf. *rāgas Daurēyaṇi* and *Dēvaśramam*, both ascribed to the 53rd *mēḷa*.
Lit.: no. 139.

Haṃsa Nārāyaṇi (South India). *Janya rāga* of the 51st *mēḷa* (*Kāmavardhanī*).
Tone material:
C D♭ E F♯ G c
c B G F♯ E D♭ C
Lit.: no. 139.

Haṃsa Naṭani (South India). *Janya rāga* of the 13th *mēḷa* (*Gāyakapriya*).
Tone material:
C E F G c
c G F E D♭ C
Lit.: no. 139.

Haṃsanibhōgi (South India). *Janya rāga* of the 29th *mēḷa* (*Dhīraśaṅkarābharaṇam*).
Tone material:
C D E F G A B c
c B A F E D F E C
Lit.: no. 139.

Haṃsa Nīlāmbari (South India). *Janya rāga* of the 39th *mēḷa* (*Jhālavarāḷi*).
Tone material:
C D♭ E♭♭ F♯ A♭ B c
c B G A♭ F♯ E♭♭ D♭ C
Lit.: no. 139.

Haṃsa Nisāri (South India). *Janya rāga* of the 32nd *mēḷa* (*Rāgavardhanī*).
Tone material:
C D♯ F G A♭ c
c B♭ A♭ G F E D♯ C
Lit.: no. 139.

Haṃsa Pañchamam (South India). *Janya rāga* of the 21st *mēḷa* (*Kiravāṇi*).
Tone material:
C E♭ F G B A♭ B G c
c B A♭ F E♭ D C
Lit.: no. 139.

Haṃsa Prabhāvaḷi (South India). *Janya rāga* of the 55th *mēḷa* (*Śyāmalāṅgī*). This *rāga* is identical with *Haṃsa Bhushavali* (55th *mēḷa*).
Lit.: no. 139.

Haṃsapriyā (South India). *Janya rāga* of the 24th *mēḷa* (*Varuṇapriyā*).
Tone material:
C E♭ D F G B A♯ B c
c B A♯ G F E♭ D C
Lit.: no. 139.

Haṃsa Rasāḷi (*Haṃsa Rasāvaḷi*) (South India). *Janya rāga* of the 41st *mēḷa* (*Pāvani*).
Tone material:
C D♭ E♭♭ F♯ A G A B c
c B A G F♯ E♭♭ C
Lit.: no. 139.

Haṃsa Rasāvaḷi (South India). See *Haṃsa Rasāḷi*.

Haṃsa Śrēṇi (South India). *Janya rāga* of the 28th *mēḷa* (*Harikāmbhōji*).
Tone material:
C D E G A c
c B♭ G F E C
Lit.: no. 139.

Haṃsa Vāridhi (South India). *Janya rāga* of the 13th *mēḷa* (*Gāyakapriya*).
Tone material:
C D♭ F G A♭ c
c A♭ G F D♭ C
Lit.: no. 139.

Haṃsa Veḷāvaḷi (South India). *Janya rāga* of the 42nd *mēḷa* (*Raghupriyā*).
Tone material:
C D♭ E♭♭ F♯ G A♯ G B c
c B G F♯ E♭♭ D♭ C
Lit.: no. 139.

Haṃsa Vinōdini (South India). *Janya rāga* of the 29th *mēḷa* (*Dhīraśaṅkarābharaṇam*).
Tone material:
C D F G A B c
c B A F E D C
Lit.: no. 139.

Hamzah (Islamic North Africa; Near East). A sudden brief stop of the song; the voice is interrupted by a closure of the glottis.
Lit.: no. 6.

Han (Japan). A heavy wooden board suspended at the entrance of Zen monasteries and beaten with a wooden hammer if somebody wishes the gate to be opened. The *han* serves also as a signalling instrument, calling the monks into the assembly hall.
Lit.: no. 185.

Ḥanafī (Arabia). Religious songs.
Lit.: no. 76.

Hanagasa odori (Japan). An old popular dance in which the participants wear hats or large umbrellas decorated with flowers. This dance still exists in folk festivals.
Lit.: no. 185.

Hanamichi (Japan). A ramp; a passage that leads from the back of the theater to the *kabuki* stage.
Lit.: no. 187.

Hana ni ireru (Japan). Term for a particular nasal voice production. The term is often considered as a *kyokusetzu*, although it does not indicate a melodic formula.

Handap (Java; Sunda District). *Hanḍap* or *nganḍap* denotes a "lower" tone according to the Javanese concept. The same term, *hanḍap*, described in the western languages, will indicate a higher tone. Similarly the term *luhur* in the Javanese world means "higher tone," and in the western languages implies a lower tone.
Lit.: no. 163.

Handja (West Africa—Fan). A xylophone in a bamboo frame.
Lit.: no. 33.

Haneru (Japan). A term in *koto* music. It indicates an upward (outward) motion of the 1st or 2nd fingers. The full surface of the *tsume* is not employed; only its edge strikes the strings. Cf. *Sukui.*
Lit.: no. 225.

Hang (Japan). Notational symbol used in *minshin gaku.*
Lit.: no. 136.

Hanihani (New Zealand—Maori). Song of abuse, of insulting character.

Haṅkluṅ (Java). See *Angklung.*

Han-koto (Japan). A "half-*koto*"; a small *koto* used in the past by travelling people.
Lit.: no. 225.

Han-kumoi (Japan). "Half *kumoi*," *koto* tuning, a mixture of *hirajoshi* and *kumoi*.
Lit.: no. 225.

Hanokahā (South India). *Janya rāga* of the 22nd *mēḷa* (*Kharaharapriyā*).
Tone material:
C D E♭ D F G B♭ A B♭ c
c B♭ A B♭ G F D E♭ F D C
Lit.: no. 139.

Han-ryo – han-ritsu (Japan). Half *ryo* (scale), half *ritsu* (scale).

Hansadhvani (North India). A rare *rāga* ascribed to the *Bilaval thāta*. Its tone material is the same as that of the South India *Haṃsadhvani*. The *vādis* are C and E.
Lit.: no. 138.

Han shō (Japan). See *Denshō*.

Hanskankani (North India). See *Haunskankani.*

Hanteki (Japan). See *Mu-yü*; *Moko* (Korea); Cf. *Mokugyo.*

Hanumantōḍi (South India). See *Hanumattōḍi.*

Hanumatōḍi (South India). See *Hanumattōḍi.*

Hanumattōḍi (South India). (1) The 8th *mēḷa*:
C D♭ E♭ F G A♭ B♭ c
(2) As *rāga*: popular, to be performed in the evening. Veṅkaṭamakhin (17th century) called this *rāga Janatōḍi.* Despite several characteristic phrases shown in Lit. no. 138, the performer is not obliged to use them and has considerable liberty. The tone material is the same as that of the *mēḷa*.
Lit.: no. 139.

Hao (China – M 2064). "To summon." Also *hao-t'ung.* Term for the *la-pa* with a flat mouthpiece. In Peking it was used in pairs at funerals.
Lit.: no. 255.

Hao-kwun (China – Cantonese term). See *Hou-kuan.*

Hao talla (Burma). Long bamboo tube. It consists of eleven telescopically joined sections. The bell is made of buffalo horn.
Lit.: no. 252.

Hao-t'ung (*Hao*) (China – M 2064; M 6637). A straight slim cylindrical copper or brass trumpet with a wide, flat mouthpiece and hardly any bell. The upper part of the tube can be pushed into the lower in a telescopic manner. The *hao-t'ung* is used as a signal trumpet and in processions. It should not be confused with the *la-pa*, the *cha-chiao*, and others, all of which have distinctly curved bells. Cf. *Dokaku.*
Lit.: nos. 225, 255.

Hap (Korea). First basic note and notational symbol of the *kong-chuk-po.* Cf. *Kung-ch'e-p'u* (China).
Lit.: no. 136.

Hapai (Sumatra – Achin). Term for *rebāb.* Also called *hapa'i.*
Lit.: no. 258.

Hap-cha-po (Korea). Zither (mainly *hyon-kum*) tablature. This system, patterned after the Chinese *chien-tzu*, is a highly complex tablature of East Asia. For details see Lit. no. 136.

Hapetan (*Husapi*; *Hasapi*) (Sumatra – Toba Batak). Lute with boat-shaped corpus and two fiber strings. Cf. the Sundanese *Kachapi.*
Lit.: no. 254.

Happu (Japan). Ancient large, flat drum of Chinese origin. The body is filled with rice powder. The drum hangs in a large wooden frame which shows a pattern of flame-like ornaments.
Lit.: no. 225.

Harabhūṣaṇi (South India). *Janya rāga* of the 39th *mēḷa* (*Jhālavarāḷi*).

Tone material:
C E♭♭ F♯ G B c
c B G F♯ E♭♭ C

Hāradhāriṇi (South India). *Janya rāga* of the 37th *mēḷa* (*Sālaga*).
Tone material:
C E♭♭ F♯ G A♭ c
C A♭ G F♯ E♭♭ C
Lit.: no. 139.

Haranarthana (South India). *Janya rāga* of the 35th *mēḷa* (*Śūlinī*).
Tone material:
C D♯ C D♯ F G B A B c
c B A B F E D♯ E C
Lit.: no. 139.

Harēnapi (South India). *Janya rāga* of the 42nd *mēḷa* (*Raghupriya*).
Tone material:
C E♭♭ F♯ G A♯ c
c A♯ G F♯ E♭♭ C
Lit.: no. 139.

Hareubab (North Sumatra; Atjeh). A set of small drums identical with *tataganing*. Cf. *Geudumba*.

Harib (Tibet). Cf. *Sur-na*; *Rgya-gling*.

Harichandrapriya (South India). *Janya rāga* of the 72nd *mēḷa* (*Rasikapriyā*).
Tone material:
C D♯ F♯ A♯ B c
c B A♯ F♯ D♯ C
Lit.: no. 139.

Haridarpam (South India). *Janya rāga* of the 28th *mēḷa* (*Harikāmbhōji*).
Tone material:
C D E F G A B♭ c
c A G F D C
Lit.: no. 139.

Hariharamōhiṇi (South India). *Janya rāga* of the 22nd *mēḷa* (*Kharaharapriyā*).
Tone material:
C D E♭ F G A B♭ c
c B♭ A G F C
Lit.: no. 139.

Harihari (New Zealand—Maori). See *Hautu*.

Harikāmbhōji (South India). (1) The 28th *mēḷa*:
C D E F G A B♭ c
(2) As *rāga, Harikāmbhōji* is very popular, performed frequently. Some of its *janya rāga*s show considerable deviations from the primary tone material. Veṅkaṭamakhin (17th century) called this *rāga Harikēdaragauḷa* (in which the notes E and A are deleted in ascent).
Lit.: no. 139.

Harikathā (*Kālakshepa*) (India). A religious, musical performance, very similar to the *bhajana*. In contrast to the *bhajana*, the *harikathā* usually has no choir. It employs a small instrumental group and one leading singer.

Harikēdaragauḷa (South India). See *Kāmbhōji* (28th *asampūrṇa mēḷa*).

Harikēdāram (South India). *Janya rāga* of the 28th *mēḷa* (*Harikāmbhōji*).
Tone material:
C D E F G A B♭(+) c B♭ c
c B♭ c B♭(+) A G F E D C
Lit.: no. 139.

Hariṇākṣi (South India). *Janya rāga* of the 70th *mēḷa* (*Nāsikabhūṣaṇī*).
Tone material:
C D♯ F♯ A B♭ c
c B♭ A F♯ D♯ C
Lit.: no. 139.

Harinārāyaṇi (South India). *Janya rāga* of the 22nd *mēḷa* (*Kharaharapriyā*).
Tone material:
C F E♭ F G A B♭ A c (C D E♭ F G F A B♭ c)
c B♭ G F E♭ D C
Lit.: no. 139.

Harinārāyaṇī (South India). *Janya rāga* of the 28th *mēḷa* (*Harikāmbhōji*).
Tone material:
C D E F G F A B♭ c
c B♭ G F E D C
Lit.: no. 139.

Hāriṇāśvā (India). The second of the ancient *mūrchhanās* derived from the *mā-grāma*. Cf. *Mūrchhanās.*
Lit.: no. 261.

Haripriya (South India). *Janya rāga* of the 27th *mēḷa* (*Sarasāṅgī*).
Tone material:
C D E F G c
c B A♭ G F E C
Lit.: no. 139.

Harṇōtrikam (South India). *Janya rāga* of the 29th *mēḷa* (*Dhīraśaṅkarābharaṇam*).
Tone material:
C D E F G A B c
c B A B G F D C
Lit.: no. 139.

Harusi (Tanganyika; Wanyamwezi). Wedding tune played on a *sanza.*
Lit.: nos. 28-29.

Hasapi (*Husapi*) (Sumatra – Karo-Batak). See *Kulchapi.* Cf. *Kachapi* (Sunda).

Hashigakari (Japan). Passage between the back and the stage of the *noh* theater.
Lit.: no. 185.

Hasino (Ghana). The leader of the chorus.

Hasosroth (*Hazozroth*) (Ancient Israel). Hebrew term for two silver trumpets. There may have been several types and functions of these instruments: used before the assembly of people, used for leading, guiding purposes, used when a victory occurred, used during a siege, battle against a city, used when battling enemies.
Lit.: no. 250.

Hastini (South India). *Janya rāga* of the 37th *mēḷa* (*Sālaga*).
Tone material:
C D♭ F♯ G A♭ c
c A♭ G F♯ D♭ C
Lit.: no. 139.

Hāsya (India). "Laughter." One of the nine emotions (*rasas*) expressed in music. Cf. *Navarasa*; *Rasa.*
Lit.: nos. 140, 235.

Hāsya Bhūṣaṇi (South India). *Janya rāga* of the 24th *mēḷa* (*Varuṇapriyā*).
Tone material:
C D E♭ F A♯ B c
c B G E♭ D C
Lit.: no. 139.

Hāsya Dīpakam (South India). See *Haṃsa Dīpakam.*

Hāsya Gāndhāri (South India). *Janya rāga* of the 25th *mēḷa* (*Mārarañjanī*).
Tone material:
C D E F G c
c B♭♭ A♭ G A F E D C
This *rāga* is practically identical with *Haṃsa Gāndhari.* A minute difference in descent may occur only occasionally and appears to be of no importance.
Lit.: no. 139.

Hat- (Vietnam). Prefix indicating festival songs: *hat quan ho*, *hat trong quan*, and others. These songs are sung in dialogue form at seasonal celebrations.
Lit.: no. 296.

Hat a dao (Vietnam). Learned music of the North. The "song of women singers." A limited repertory of several songs performed by professional singers (solo and group). The performance of these songs is subject to strict rules and regulations.
Lit.: no. 296.

Hāṭakabharaṇam (South India). *Janya rāga* of the 21st *mēḷa* (*Kiravāṇi*).
Tone material:

C D E♭ F G A B c
c B G F D F E♭ C

Lit.: no. 139.

Hāṭakāmbarī (South India). (1) The 18th *mēḷa*:

C D♭ E F G A♯ B c

(2) Veṅkaṭmakhin (17th century) called this *rāga Jayaśuddhamāḷavi* (which has the same scale as the 18th *mēḷa*).
Lit.: no. 139.

Hatakangi (South India). *Janya rāga* of the 47th *mēḷa* (*Suvarṇāṅgī*).
Tone material:

C D♭ E♭ F♯ A B c
c B A F♯ E♭ D♭ C

Lit.: no. 139.

Hāṭaka Varāḷi (South India). *Janya rāga* of the 28th *mēḷa* (*Harikāmbhōji*).
Tone material:

C D F G A c
c B♭ A G F E D E C

Lit.: no. 139.

Hat bo (Vietnam). Popular theatrical songs and gestures.
Lit.: no. 296.

Hat boi (Vietnam). See *Hat tuong*.

Hat cai luong (Vietnam). The modern music of the popular theater of the South.
Lit.: no. 296.

Hat cheo (Vietnam). Music of the folk theater.
Lit.: no. 296.

Hatong (West Java). Bamboo panpipes. (The name is probably derived from the Chinese *hsiao-t'ung*.) The instrument is usually played in pairs: the large *hatong* with 10-14 pipes and the small one with 2-3 pipes. The pipes are tied together side by side like a raft. The large *hatong* is described as *indung*, the small one as *anak*. The pipes are tuned either to *slendro*, *pelog*, or *miring*. Cf. *Tote* (Central Borneo).
Lit.: no. 163.

Hatong honghong (West Java). See *Hatong ijen.*

Hatong ijen (*Hatong honghong*) (West Java). *Hatong* with a single pipe.
Lit.: no. 163.

Hatong manuk (West Java). The "bird *hatong*," a short bamboo flute used to imitate bird calls.
Lit.: no. 163.

Hatong pan(g)ajak (West Java). *Hatong* with three pipes.

Hatong sekaran (West Java). *Hatong* with two pipes.

Hat quan ho (Vietnam). Festival song.
Lit.: no. 51.

Hat ru (Vietnam). Lullaby.

Hat sam (Vietnam). Song sung by blind men.
Lit.: no. 51.

Hatsiatia (*Hatsyiatsya*) (Ghana—Ewe). A song or instrumental piece that introduces a club dance (*ahiavui*).
Lit.: no. 128.

Hatsu (Japan). See *Batsu.*

Hat trong quan (Vietnam). Festival song.
Lit.: no. 51.

Hat tuong (*Hat boi*) (Vietnam). Music of the traditional theater; at the present time almost obsolete.
Lit.: no. 296.

Hatzozroth (Ancient Israel). See *Hasosroth* (*Hazozroth*).

Hau kwoon (South China; Canton). Mouth tube. A simple heterophonic double reed instrument.

Haunskankani (North India). A *rāga* ascribed to the *Kafi thāta.* Its material consists of elements from the *rāgas Tilang* and *Bhimpalasi.* The flexible tone material can be:

Tilang — B C E F G G B c; *Bhimpalasi* — e♭ e♭ d c c B♭ A G F G F

Tilang — E E F G; *Bhimpalasi* — E♭ D C

Lit.: no. 138.

Hauta (Japan). "Short song." Popular song accompanied by *shamisen* and *shakuhachi.* At the present time the term is used for all types of short songs with *shamisen* accompaniment. While the *hauta* text usually conveys a story, the one of the *kouta* does not. Cf. *Kumiuta.*

Hautu (*Harihari*) (New Zealand—Maori). Chant that regulates the timing of the strokes in rowing a boat.

Hāvavilāsini (South India). *Janya rāga* of the 69th *mēḷa* (*Dhātuvardhaṇī*).
Tone material:

C D♯ F♯ G A♭ c
c A♭ G F♯ D♯ C

Lit.: no. 139.

Hawā'i (Persia; Khorasan; Turkmenia). Instrumental piece in form of a free fantasy. Cf. *'Amal.*

Hawar-hawar (Sumatra—Batak). A cymbal used to accompany the dance of the local sorcerer.
Lit.: no. 288.

Hawis (*Awis*) (Java). Beats placed "far apart." The subdivision of phrases by means of interpunctuation is expressed by the numbers of beats. The longest temporal unit lasts from one heavy *gong* to the next (*gongan*). This duration represents *hawis* because the two *gong* beats are "far apart." The subdivisions of the same temporal united are marked by the *kempul*, which resounds three times, the *kenong* four times, and the *ketek* eight times (every two heart beats). All this happens during the same temporal unit and occurs again in the next phrase. This pattern can change in various places. Cf. *Arang.*
Lit.: no. 163.

Ḥawzī (Middle East). *Maqām.*
Tone material:

D $\overset{+}{\text{E}\flat}$ F G A $\overset{+}{\text{B}\flat}$ c d

Lit.: no. 64.

Hayabue (Japan). A *noh* interlude used in *nagauta* performances.
Lit.: no. 187.

Haya-byōshi (Japan). Common meter (4/4) in moderate tempo, employed in *gagaku.* Cf. *Nobe-byoshi*; *Ose-byoshi*; *Tada-byoshi*; *Yatara-byoshi.*
Lit.: no. 185.

Hayagaki (Japan). One of two short basic melody patterns played on the *gaku-so.* The second pattern is called *shizugaki.*
Lit.: no. 185.

Hayagati (South India). *Janya rāga* of the 17th *mēḷa* (*Sūryakānta*).
Tone material:

C E F G F A B c
c B A G F E D♭ C

Lit.: no. 139.

Haya-kaki (Japan). Term in *koto* playing. It indicates two *kaki* played one after the other in quick succession.
Lit.: no. 225.

Hayaku (Japan). Term in *koto* playing that indicates a shortening of a rhythmical feature into half of its metrical value and a speeding up of the original tempo.
Lit.: no. 225.

Hayān (Middle East). *Maqām.*
Tone material:

C D E♭ F♯ G A♭ B c d $\overset{+}{\text{e}\flat}$ f g a $\overset{+}{\text{b}\flat}$

Lit.: no. 64.

Hayariuta (Japan). Popular short-lived city music. Cf. *Ryūkoka.*
Lit.: no. 185.

Hayashi (Japan). Instrumental ensemble consisting of one flute, one or several drums, and occasionally a gong. The *hayashi* plays village music (*sato-kagura*) and provides the music in *kabuki*, *nagauta*, and *noh* performances.

If the term *hayashi* is preceded by a word or syllable it becomes *-bayashi*, as in *edo-bayashi* or *matsuri-bayashi.*
Lit.: no. 215.

Hayashi-kata (Japan). "The accompanying party." The modern theater orchestra. It consists of two *shamisen*, one flute, three drums (*uta-daiko*, *ō-tsuzumi*, *ko-tsuzumi*), plus two reciters. As a female ensemble the *shita-kata* employs the same instruments but has no reciters.
Lit.: no. 225.

Hayawatari (Japan). Drum pattern used in *kabuki* music.
Lit.: no. 187.

Hazaj (Arabia). Bright, cheerful songs generally in uninterrupted double meter. Cf. *Sinād.* Was classified into three types: *naṣb*, *sinād*, and *hazaj.* Singing. Cf. *Dōr*; *Ramal.*
Lit.: nos. 34, 73.

Hazolahi (*Manandria*) (Malagasy Republic). Wooden drum with two heads, played in pairs.
Lit.: no. 254.

Hazozroth (Ancient Israel). See *Hasosroth.*

Hazumu (Japan). A term in *koto* playing. Lit. no. 225, p. 127, states: "a short phrase in frequent use, composed of the 10th string dotted, followed by the ninth and eighth [strings]."

Hcham-po (*Hcham-pa*) (Tibet). A dancer (religious).

Hdur-ma (Tibet). "Thick." This term is used in Tibetan Buddhist service and indicates that the chant is slow and "dark," but has some rhythmical character.
Lit.: no. 143.

Hechchu kaṭṭai (South India). Tamil term for a high-pitched *mṛdanga.*
Lit.: no. 261.

Heh-chih-pan (China—M 986; M 2090; M 4885). See *T'ou-chih-pan.*

Heh-pan (China—M 2090; M 4885). See *Tseng-pan.*

Heike biwa (Japan). The *biwa* used for playing the accompaniment of heroic recitations. Particularly recitations about the famous Heike and Genji clans, the troubles of Heike, and the drowning of the emperor Antoku. Like the other *biwa* types, this instrument has four silken strings and 4-5 frets. Cf. *Biwa*; *Satsuma biwa.*
Lit.: no. 185.

Heikyoku (Japan). The singing of the (200 verses) Heike Story. This is accompanied by the *heike biwa.* In the past the *heikyoku* led to the *joruri*, narrative *shamisen* music. Cf. *Bokufu.*
Lit.: no. 185.

Hei-mu-pan (China). See *Pang-tzu.*

Hejjaji (South India). See *Gāyakapriya* and *Hejjuji.*

Hejjuji (*Hejjaji*) (South India). *Janya rāga* of the 13th *mēḷa* (*Gāyakapriya*).
Tone material:
C D♭ E F G A♭ c
c A♭ G F E D♭ C (c B♭♭ A♭ G F E D♭ C)
Lit.: no. 139.

Hejjuji (South India). (1) The 13th *asampūrṇa mēḷa-rāga* without *kaṭapayādi* prefix. (2) The 13th *asampūrṇa mēḷa-rāga* with *kaṭapayādi* prefix was called *geyahejjaji.* See *Rāga* (South India).
Lit.: no. 139.

He Koauan (New Zealand). Pipe made of a whale tooth.
Lit.: no. 255.

Heko-odori (Japan). Cf. *Samurai-odori.*

He-kum (Korea). See *Hae-kum*; *Hai-kum.*

Hēlaprabhata (South India). *Janya rāga* of the 29th *mēḷa* (*Dhīraśaṅkarābharaṇam*).
Tone material:
C D E F G A B A c
c A B A G F E D C
Lit.: no. 139.

Hel-hel (Nicobar Isl.). Ring flute (see *Nuren*). Cf. *Lolowe.*
Lit.: no. 166.

Heliḍamuthaḍughi (India; Bengal). Bagpipe.
Lit.: no. 255.

Hēma Bhūṣaṇi (South India). *Janya rāga* of the 33th *mēḷa* (*Gāṅgeyabhushanī*).
Tone material:
C D# E F A♭ B c
c B A♭ F E D# C
Lit.: no. 139.

Hēmakriya (South India). *Janya rāga* of the 20th *mēḷa* (*Naṭabhairavī*).
Tone material:
C D E♭ F G A♭ B♭ c
c B♭ A♭ G F D E♭ F D C
Lit.: no. 139.

Hēmalatā (South India). *Janya rāga* of the 60th *mēḷa* (*Nītimatī*).
Tone material:
C D E♭ F# A# c
c A# F# E♭ D C
Lit.: no. 139.

Hēma Māndāra (South India). *Janya rāga* of the 28th *mēḷa* (*Harikāmbhōji*).
Tone material:
B♭ C *B♭* C D F E F G A B♭
B♭ A G F E D C *B♭ A*
Lit.: no. 139.

Hēmāmbari (South India). *Janya rāga* of the 55th *mēḷa* (*Śyāmalāṅgī*).
Tone material:
C D E♭ F# A♭ c
c A♭ F# E♭ D C
Lit.: no. 139.

Hēmāmbari (South India). *Janya rāga* of the 58th *mēḷa* (*Hemāvatī*).
Tone material:
C D E♭ F# G A B♭ c
c G F# E♭ D C
Lit.: no. 139.

Hēmāṅgi (South India). *Janya rāga* of the 54th *mēḷa* (*Viśvambharī*).
Tone material:
C D♭ E F# A# c
c A# F# E D♭ C
Lit.: no. 139.

Hēmāpiṅgaḷa (South India). *Janya rāga* of the 41st *mēḷa* (*Pāvani*).
Tone material:
C *B* C D♭ E♭♭ F# B A B G c
c G F# E♭♭ D♭ C
Lit.: no. 139.

Hēmāpriya (South India). *Janya rāga* of the 58th *mēḷa* (*Hēmāvatī*).
Tone material:
C D E♭ F# A c
c A F# E♭ D C
Lit.: no. 139.

Hēmārṇavam (South India). *Janya rāga* of the 51st *mēḷa* (*Kāmavardhaṇī*).
Tone material:
C E F# G A♭ B c
c B A♭ F# E D♭ C
Lit.: no. 139.

Hēma Sāraṅga (South India). *Janya rāga* of the 28th *mēḷa* (*Harikāmbhōji*).
Tone material:
C D E F G A B♭ G A G c
c G F E D C
Lit.: no. 139.

Hēmāvāhini (South India). *Janya rāga* of the 58th *mēḷa* (*Hēmāvatī*).
Tone material:
C D G F# G A B♭ c
c A G F# E♭ C
Lit.: no. 139.

Hēmāvaḷi (South India). *Janya rāga* of the 22nd *mēḷa* (*Kharaharapriyā*).
Tone material:
C D E♭ F A c
c B♭ G F E♭ D E♭ C
Lit.: no. 139.

Hēmāvanti (South India). See *Hēmāvatī.*

Hēmāvantiṇi (South India). See *Hēmāvatī.*

Hēmāvati (South India). Also *Hēmāvanti*; *Hēmāvantiṇi*. The 58th *mēḷa*:
C D E♭ F# G A B♭ c
Rāga Hēmāvati has the same tone material as the 58th *mēḷa.*
Lit.: no. 139.

Hemkalyan (North India). *Rāga* ascribed to the *Bilaval thāta.*
Tone material:
C (D) E (F) G A (B) c
c (B) A G F E D C; *Vādis*: C, G
Lit.: no. 138.

Hen- (Japan). Similar to the western "flat," the prefix *hen* indicates the lowering of a note by a semitone. *Hen-chi* is a semitone below *chi*, and *hen-kyū* a semitone below *kyū.* Cf. *Ryo* (scale).
Lit.: nos. 136, 185.

Heng-chok (Korea). Cylindrical cross flute with three or four front finger holes and 1-2 thumbholes.
Lit.: no. 52.

Hengemono (Japan). A series of *kabuki* dances in which the dancer changes his costume and with it the entire mood five to seven times. The *hengemono* gained great popularity during the first half of the 19th century. The term can also be *henkeimono*, referring to a *kabuki* performance in which the actor-singer changes from a human being to a ghost.
Lit.: no. 187.

Heng-ti (China—M 2106; M 6217). Term for the transverse flute in the Shantung province.
Lit.: no. 255.

Henhoel (Nicobar Isl.). Or *hahel.* Nose flute.
Lit.: no. 255.

Hen-kyū (Japan). Tone name of the 7th degree of the *ryo* scale.
Lit.: no. 136.

Hennon (Japan). Literally, "changing tones." A mode used in modulations. It consists of a combination of *ritsu* and *ryo* scales. Cf. *shōmyō.*

Henong (Java). Synonym for *gambang gangsa.*

Hera (Mozambique). *Sansa* played in ancestral ritual.

Hērambhapriya (South India). *Janya rāga* of the 66th *mēḷa* (*Chitrāmbarī*).
Tone material:
C D F# A# B c
c B A# F# D C
Lit.: no. 139.

Heravoa (Malagasy Republic). One-stringed fiddle.
Lit.: no. 251.

Herrauu (*Lokango voatovo*) (Malagasy Republic). A zither, similar to the African *seze.* Cf. *Heravoa.*
Lit.: no. 251.

Hevehe (*Beure hevehe*) (Gulf of Papua). Bull roarer. Also *hevoa hevoa bobo-bobo.*
Lit.: no. 311.

Hi (Japan). (1) See *Hii.* (2) The term *hi* denotes an instrument made of porcelain in the shape of a tea cup, struck with a small stick.

Hia ma (China). See *Ha ma.*

Hiang (China). See *Hsiang.*

Hib phleng (Thailand). A harmonium; musical box.
Lit.: no. 255.

Hibiligizo (Congo; Ruanda—Bashi). Small drum used for dance music.

Hib phleng dit (Thailand). Pianoforte.

Hib phleng jai (Thailand). Organ.

Hib phleng kuan (Thailand). Barrel organ.

Hichi (Japan). See *Shichi.*

Hichiriki (Japan). "Sad-toned tube." A small, noisy heterophonic double-reed *gagaku* instrument made of wood or bone. It has seven holes in front and two in the back. The long reeds are called *shita.* On account of its penetrating tone it often is the lead instrument of *togaku* and *komagaku* ensembles. A larger form of this instrument is called *ō-hichiriki.* Cf. *P'i-ri* (Korea); *Pi-li* (China).
Lit.: nos. 225, 255.

Ḥidā' (Arabia). Bedouin caravan song with an old rhythmic pattern (horse movement).
Lit.: no. 34.

Hiddujjoth (Yemen—Jews). Popular songs sung after the marriage ceremony.

Hien (China). Dialectal form of *hsien* (M 2661), denoting "string."
Lit.: no. 255.

Hii (Japan). Name of the first *shō* pipe. Cf. *Shō*

Lit.: no. 225.

Hija (Old Arabia). Satire; originally incantation in rhymed prose (called *saj'*).
Lit.: no. 70.

Ḥijāz (*Ṣaba*) (Arabia). Tone name of a note a semitone higher than *jargā.* (A list of all tone names and tones through two octaves can be seen under the heading of *Jagā* [*Yagā*].)
Lit.: no. 64.

Ḥijāz (Arabia). (1) A very popular Arabic *maqām.* Its name originates from the region of Mecca and Medina. The Muezzin's call to prayer is usually chanted in this *maqām. Ḥijāz* is also the mode used in numerous folk melodies. Only in Yemen it is not in use at all. El-Kholay (Lit. no. 56) calls *ḥijāz* the little *nahawand.* The scale of this *maqām* is:

D E♭ F♯ G A B♭ c d (e f)

(2) *Ḥijāz* (bis), a second form (cf. Lit. no. 65), described as an *āwāz*, has the following scale:

C E♭♭ E♭ F G♭ B♭♭ B♭ c

(according to Ṣafī al Dīn, 13th century, reported by Farmer, Lit. no. 65.)
Lit.: no. 121.

Ḥijāzi (Middle East). *Maqām.*
Tone material:

D E♭ F♯ G A $\overset{(+)}{B\flat}$ c d

Lit.: no. 64.

Ḥijāzī (Modern Tunisia). *Maqām.*
Tone material:

C D E♭ F♯ G A B♭ c d

Ḥijāzi of modern Egypt has the same scale, except B♭ which is raised to $\overset{+}{B\flat}$.
Lit.: no. 64.

Ḥijāzī 'Ušayrān (Middle East). *Maqām.*
Tone material:

A $\overset{+}{B\flat}$ C D $\overset{+}{E\flat}$ F♯ G A

Lit.: no. 64.

Ḥijāz-kār (Arabia). *Maqām.* It is called "son of Hijaz," but appears to be of foreign origin, perhaps Turkish. In Egypt this *maqām* is considered to be related to *rast* (and *mahur*). Its scale according to Lit. no. 121 is:

C D♭ $\overset{+}{E\flat}$ F G A♭ $\overset{+}{B\flat}$ c $\overset{+}{d\flat}$ e

The intonation of the note E varies from one place to the other.
Lit.: nos. 64, 121.

Ḥijāz-kār-kurdī (Middle East). *Maqām.*
Tone material:
C D♭ E♭ F G A♭ B♭ c
The *maqām* is also used in modern Egypt.
Lit.: no. 64.

Hik (New Guinea). Big drum.
Lit.: no. 255.

Hikiren (Japan). Term in *koto* playing that indicates a sliding across several (1-6, 1-10) strings.
Lit.: no. 225.

Hi-kyoku (Japan). (1) "Secret music" of the highest class. It can be performed only by those who have attained the performer's final certificate. (2) Performances of *bugaku* dances are to be given only at very important occasions.
Lit.: no. 225.

Hilu (Indonesia; Alor Isl.). Flute.
Lit.: no. 162.

Him (Siam). Mouth organ with 5-10 pipes. Cf. *Engkruri.*

Himāṅgi (South India). *Janya rāga* of the 8th *mēḷa* (*Hanumattōḍi*).
Tone material:
C D♭ E♭ F G A♭ B♭ A♭ c
c B♭ G A♭ F E♭ D♭ C
Lit.: no. 139.

Himavāluka (South India). *Janya rāga* of the 45th *mēḷa* (*Vanaspāti*).
Tone material:
C E♭♭ F G A c
c A G F E♭♭ C
Lit.: no. 139.

Himavardhani (South India). *Janya rāga* of the 8th *mēḷa* (*Hanumattōḍi*).
Tone material:
C D♭ F G B♭ c
c B♭ A♭ G F A♭ F E♭ D♭ C
Lit.: no. 139.

Himene (Tahiti). Form of polyphonic singing (the term being derived from "hymn"). The Hawaiian term (*himeni*) refers to songs that are not linked with *hula* dancing.
Lit.: no. 215.

Hiṃkāra (*Humkara*) (Vedic India). The chanting of the sacred syllable *hum* at the beginning and between sections of the Sāmavedic chant.
Lit.: no. 119.

Hīmkarī (South India). *Janya rāga* of the 24th *mēḷa* (*Varuṇapriyā*).
Tone material:
C D E♭ F G A♯ c
c A♯ G F E♭ D C
Lit.: no. 139.

Ḥimyārī (Arabia). Songs of the Himyarites (Arab tribe). Cf. *Ḥanafī.*
Lit.: no. 76.

Hin (Senegambia—Wolof). Log drums standing upright. There are three sizes. The *hin* are drums belonging to the chief and are destroyed when he dies.
Lit.: no. 200.

Hiṅ (Burma; Shan States). Bronze bell of a flat beehive form, with a wooden clapper inside.
Lit.: no. 252.

Hinaburi (Japan). Folk songs of rural character.

Hindchu (Central Africa). See *Mobeke.*

Hindī darāy (Ancient Persia). Indian bell.
Lit.: no. 77.

Hindol (North India). Famous *rāga* ascribed to the *Kalyan thāta.*
Tone material:
C E F♯ A B A c
c B A F♯ E C; *Vādis:* A, E
Lit.: no. 138.

Hindōḷa(m) (South India). *Janya rāga* of the 20th *mēḷa* (*Naṭabhairavī*).
Tone material:
C F E♭ F A♭ B♭ c
c B♭ A♭ F E♭ C
Lit.: no. 139.

Hindōḷa Darbār (South India). *Janya rāga* of the 32nd *mēḷa* (*Rāgavardhanī*).
Tone material:
C E F G c
c B♭ A♭ G F D♯ C
Lit.: no. 139.

Hindōḷa Dēśākṣi (South India). *Janya rāga* of the 68th *mēḷa* (*Jyōtisvarūpiṇī*).
Tone material:
C *B♭* C D♯ E F♯ G A♭ (B♭)
B♭ A♭ G F♯ E D♯ C
The scale of this *rāga* has *Niṣādāntya* character.
Lit.: no. 139.

Hindōḷa Dēśika (South India). *Janya rāga* of the 10th *mēḷa* (*Naṭakapriyā*).
Tone material:
C F D♭ E♭ F G A B♭ c
c G B♭ A F E♭ D♭ C
Lit.: no. 139.

Hindōḷa Kannaḍa (South India). *Janya rāga* of the 31st *mēḷa* (*Yāgapriyā*).
Tone material:
C E F A♭ B♭♭ c
c B♭♭ G A♭ F E C
Lit.: no. 139.

Hindōḷa Kāpi (South India). *Janya rāga* of the 32nd *mēḷa* (*Rāgavardhanī*).
Tone material:
C D♯ E F G F G c
c B♭ A♭ G F E C
Lit.: no. 139.

Hindōḷa Mālavi (South India). *Janya rāga* of the 33th *mēḷa* (*Gāṅgeyabhushanī*).
Tone material:
C F G A♭ B A♭ c
c B A♭ F G F D♯ C
Lit.: no. 139.

Hindōḷa Mōhanam (South India). *Janya rāga* of the 36th *mēḷa* (*Chalanāṭa*).
Tone material:
C D♯ F G A♯ c
c B G F D♯ C
Lit.: no. 139.

Hindōḷa Nāyaki (South India). *Janya rāga* of the 33rd *mēḷa* (*Gāṅgeyabhushanī*).
Tone material:
C F E F G c
c B A♭ G F E F D♯ C
Lit.: no. 139.

Hindōḷa Sāraṅga (South India). *Janya rāga* of the 32nd *mēḷa* (*Rāgavardhanī*).
Tone material:
C D♯ E F G c B♭ c
c B♭ A♭ G B♭ A♭ F E F D♯ C
Lit.: no. 139.

Hindōḷa Sāvēri (South India). *Janya rāga* of the 33rd *mēḷa* (*Gāṅgeyabhushanī*).
Tone material:
C E F G F A♭ B c
c B G A♭ F D♯ C
Lit.: no. 139.

Hindōḷavasanta(m) (South India). *Janya rāga* of the 20th *mēḷa* (*Naṭabhairavī*).
Tone material:
C E♭ F G A♭ B♭ A♭ c
c B♭ A♭ G F E♭ A♭ F E♭ C
Lit.: no. 139.

Hindōḷavasantam (South India). *Janya rāga* of the 22nd *mēḷa* (*Kharaharapriyā*).
Tone material:

C E♭ F G B♭ A c

c B♭ A F E♭ D E♭ C (c B♭ A G F A F E♭ C)

Lit.: no. 139.

Hindol-bahar (North India). An obscure *rāga*. It represents a combination of *Hindol* and *Bahar* phrases.
The flexible tone material can be:

Hindol

C E F♯ A

Bahar

B♭ A B c B♭ A B♭

Hindol

A F♯ E C

Lit.: no. 138.

Hindol-pancham (North India). See *Pancham*.

Hindustan Kāpi (*Hindusthāni Kāpi*) (South India). *Janya rāga* of the 22nd *mēḷa* (*Kharaharapriyā*).
Tone material:

C D F G B♭ c

c B♭ A B♭ G F E♭ D C (several variants are in use)

Lit.: no. 139.

Hindusthāni Behāg (South India). See *Behāg*.

Hink (Egypt; Coptic). See *Stychon*.

Hirādhāriṇi (South India). *Janya rāga* of the 64th *mēḷa* (*Vāchaspati*).
Tone material:

C E F♯ G A c

c A G F♯ E C

Lit.: no. 139.

Hirajōshi (Japan). A prevalent tuning of the *koto*. See *Koto* (tunings); cf. *Kin-jū*.
Lit.: no. 225.

Hira-nori (Japan). A frequently occurring feature in *noh* performances when the five and seven syllables line of the text is distributed among eight beats in the following manner:

Beats (top)

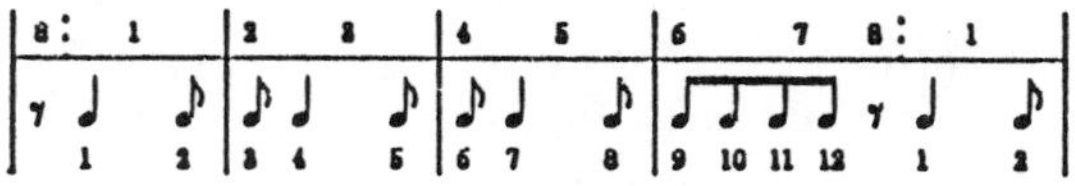

Textual syllables (bottom)

This relationship between text and music can appear either during a single 8-beat phrase, or it can extend repeatedly throughout the composition. See *Utai*. Cf. *Jibyoshi*.
Lit.: nos. 187, 204.

(H)irim-(h)irim (Java). See *Irim-irim*.

Hiriyula (New Guinea—Papua). Jew's harp made of bamboo.
Lit.: no. 233.

Hiroiji (Japan). One of the *ōzatsuma* patterns. See *Ōzatsuma*.
Lit.: no. 187.

Hirri (Republic of Upper Volta—Bisa). Terra cotta whistle in globular form with three finger holes.
Lit.: no. 50.

Hiru-jushi (Japan). A *jushi* performed in the afternoon.
Lit.: no. 185.

Ḥiṣār (*Hissār*; *Shuri*) (Arabia). "The enclosed, reduced one." Name of a tone about a semitone higher than *nawā*. (A list of all tone names and notes through two octaves can be seen under the heading of *Jagā* [*Yagā*].)
Lit.: no. 121.

Ḥiṣār (Middle East; Egypt). *Maqām*.
Tone material:

D E F G♯ A B♭ c♯ d

As a genuine Egyptian *maqām* the scale shows few variants:

D E♭(+) F G♯ A B♭ c♯ d

Lit.: nos. 64, 121.

Ḥiṣār-qaba (*Darār-ḥiṣār*) (Arabia). Tone name of a note a semitone higher than *jagā* (*yagā*). (A list of all tone names and notes through two octaves can be seen under the heading of *Jagā* [*Yagā*].)
Lit.: nos. 64, 121.

(H)isen-(h)isen (Java). A group of instruments within the *gamelan* ensemble (*gong, kenong, ketuk, kempul*) which represent and play the musical ornamentation.
Lit: no. 163.

(H)isen-(h)isen (Java). See *Isen-isen.*

Hissār (Arabia). See *Ḥiṣār.*

Hitabhāsini (South India). *Janya rāga* of the 18th *mēḷa* (*Hāṭakāmbarī*).
Tone material:
C D♭ E F G B A♯ B c
c B G F E D♭ C
Lit.: no. 139.

Hitapriya (South India). *Janya rāga* of the 28th *mēḷa* (*Harikāmbhōji*).
Tone material:
C D E F A B♭ c
c B♭ A B♭ G F D E C
Lit.: no. 139.

Hitotsu-gane (Japan). Small gong used at religious occasions. Buddhists employed its sound to mark verses of prayers. A smaller form is called *matsumushi.*
Lit.: no. 185.

Hito uta (Japan). "First verse." See *Kumi.*

Hitoyogiri (Japan). "One joint cut." A vertical flute; in size similar to the *shakuhachi*. It has four holes on top and one at the back. It is smaller than the *shakuhachi* and its range is higher. The instrument is used by Buddhists.
Lit.: no. 185.

Hitsu-no-koto (Japan). An ancient zither supposed to be the first one that came across from China. The instrument originally had 50, later 25, 23, and finally 20 strings. Cf. *Se*; *So-no-koto*; *Kin-no-koto.*
Lit.: nos. 225, 255.

Hiuen (China). Distorted form of *hsüan.*
Lit.: no. 255.

oHiva (South Africa – Herero). Term for wind instrument.
Lit.: no. 255.

Ḥizam-a Siga (Arabia). Cf. *'Auj* (*'Auǧ*).

Hkun-nathan-gyi (Burma). Tone name. See *Pat-tala*; *Hsaing-waing*; *Than-yo.*

Hladiṇi (South India). *Janya rāga* of the 64th *mēḷa* (*Vāchaspati*).
Tone material:
C E F♯ G B♭ c
c B♭ G F♯ E C
Lit.: no. 139.

Hna-pauk (*Pat-sabo*) (Burma). See *Pat-tala*; *Hsaing-waing*; *Than-hman.*

Hne (*Kaya*) (Burma). Oboe type (*sānāyī* form) in various sizes. Some of these instruments have huge dimensions. Curt Sachs reports (Lit. no. 254, p. 157) that the blowing of such an enormous instrument is so exhausting that the player needs the help of a second man (*nauktaiṅ*) to stand behind him, against whom he can lean and find support. The smaller *hne* appear in groups of five in the Burmese orchestra.
Lit.: nos. 252, 254.

Hnyin (Burma). Small mouth organ (with free reeds) used at funerals and during mourning.

Hnyin-lon (Burma). Cf. *Chauk-pauk auk-pyan.*

Ho (China – M 2115). Term used for *hsiao-ho*, denoting a *sheng* with 13 pipes.

Ho (China—M 2117). The first basic note (and symbol) of the *kung-ch'e-p'u* (notational system). In the present report *ho* is interpreted as the western note C, but as it is a solmization symbol it can be represented by any other note as well.

Assuming that *ho* is the western note C, the other notes of the *kung-ch'e-p'u* are: *ho* C, *hsia ssu* D♭, *ssu* D, *hsia yi* E♭, *yi* E, *shang* F, *kou* F♯, *ch'e* G, *hsia kung* A♭, *kung* A, *hsia fan* B♭, *fan* B, *liu* upper c, *hsia wu* d♭, *wu* d, *hsia yi* e♭, *yi* e.
Lit.: no. 136.

Hō (*Mō*) (Japan). The second pipe of the *shō* which is a silent pipe. See *Shō.*
Lit.: no. 225.

Ho (Vietnam). (1) The name of the first note of the basic scale. All note names of this scale are: *ho* (e.g.) C, *xu•* D, (*xu•* E♭), *xang* F, *xe* G, *cong* A, *oan* (B♭), *liu* c, *u* d. (2) *Ho-*. As prefix indicates a work song: *ho do ta kea go*, a woodcutter's song; *ho khoan*, a ferry man's song.

Ho'ae ae (Hawaii). Love chant.
Lit.: no. 215.

Hōbalo (Somalia). Dance and song performed by men. Usually it is danced by two persons while the rest of the men stand around and sing and beat the rhythm by clapping hands—never by drumming. The names of such dances vary according to the song sung by the chorus. Each dance is introduced by the *or.* Cf. *Gablo.*
Lit.: no. 98.

Ho do keo go (Vietnam). Woodcutter's song. See *Ho.*
Lit.: no. 51.

Ho du (West Africa; Upper Volta). Lute.

Ho du chi (Vietnam). Weaver's song.

Ho dua linh (Vietnam). River funeral songs.
Lit.: no. 51.

Hoeng-ji (Korea). Cf. *Tae-kum.*

Hōgaku (Japan). Native Japanese *shamisen* music, particularly for dancing.
Lit.: no. 185.

Hogoi (*Hogro*; *Ngor*; *Song gor*) (Vietnam). Barrel drum.

Hogro (Vietnam). See *Hogoi.*

Hohoang (West Java). A bull roarer made of coconut leaf. Cf. *Kekinchiran.*
Lit.: no. 163.

Hoi (Flores; Nage of Ngada). Panpipes. Four unbound small bamboo tubes closed at one end are held vertically. The player blows across the open upper ends.
Lit.: no. 166.

Hoi (Vietnam). Modal distinction. Cf. *Bac.*
Lit.: no. 296.

Hoi Ai (South Vietnam). Mode *dieu nam*, expressing sadness, melancholy.
Lit.: no. 297.

Hoi Bac (Vietnam). Mode expressing joy. Cf. *Bac.*
Lit.: no. 297.

Hoi-ch'eung (China). (Cantonese term.) See *K'ai-ch'ang.*

Hoi Dao (South Vietnam). Mode *dieu bac* expressing serene solemnity. Cf. *Bac.*
Lit.: no. 297.

Hoi nhac (Vietnam). A modal nuance derived from *dieu bac* expressing fantasy. The *nhac* pieces are played in the theater and during ceremonies.
Lit.: no. 297.

Hoi Oan (South Vietnam). Mode. Vaguely ascribed to *dieu bac*, *dieu nam*, expressing sadness.

Hoi quang (Vietnam). A modal nuance derived from *dieu bac* expressing fantasy. Cf. *Dieu Bac.*
Lit.: no. 297.

Hoi-teuk-i (Korea). Pipe made of bark.
Lit.: no. 255.

Hoi tong baat yam (China). Cantonese term. Cf. *Woo tip kam.*

Hoi xuan (Vietnam). Mode derived from *dieu nam*, expressing serenity and calm.
Lit.: no. 297.

Hojok (Korea). Heterophonic double-reed instrument with a conical tube. Cf. *Nal-na-ri*; *T'aep-yongso.*
Lit.: no. 221.

Hokai gane (Japan). Bronze cymbals.

Hokeo (Sandwich Isl.—Hawaii). See *Pa-ipu.*

Ho khoan (Vietnam). Ferryman's songs.
Lit.: no. 51.

Hokiokio (*Hokioko*) (Hawaii). Nose-blown globular calabash flute with two or three finger holes. Cf. *Ipu hokiokio.*
Lit.: nos. 84, 278.

Ḥoḳḳah (Egypt). The coconut corpus of the *kamānjah.*

Hokke-daiko (Japan). A *taiko* with a handle. (The *Hokke* are a Buddhist sect.)
Lit.: no. 255.

Ho-köi (Korea). Trumpet.
Lit.: no. 255.

Hoko ni 'au (Malaita; Solomon Isl.). Panpipe-bundle.
Lit.: no. 318.

Ho-kuan (China—M 2117; M 3557). Double flute; two vertically-blown tubes, each with five finger holes.
Lit.: no. 137.

Hokum (India; Muria Gond of Bastar State). Hunting horn.
Lit.: no. 59.

Hokyo (Japan). See *Kei.*

Hōkyoko (Hawaii). See *Ipu hōkyoko.*

Ho mai day (Vietnam). Name of a scale. Cf. list of basic scales shown under the heading of *Bac.*

Homayun (Persia). See *Dastgah.*

Hom-bakase (*Hom-pu*) (Japan). Notational system used in *shōmyō* that indicates distinct pitches for the first time. The system originated in the 13th century.
Lit.: no. 47.

Hom-pu (Japan). See *Hom-bakase.*

Hōmrōng (Thailand). Introductory music; an invocation of the gods. This music appears at the opening of a ceremony or festivity. See *Khōn-nōnrōng.*
Lit.: no. 208.

Honchirashi (Japan). The final, concluding movement. Cf. *Kumi-uta.*

Hon-chōshi (Japan). The tuning of string instruments, particularly *shamisen*, has the characteristic of the interval of a fourth between the first and second strings, followed by a fifth between the second and third strings; e.g., B E b (1 4 8). This tuning pattern is not applied on the *kokyū.*
Lit.: no. 185.

Ho nen (Vietnam). Digger's songs.
Lit.: no. 51.

Hong (Nepal). Straight brass horn (conical bore).

Hōn'ga (Korea). Cf. *Tungga.*

Hong-chok (Korea). A transverse bamboo flute with 3-4 finger holes in the front, 1-2 holes in the side, and 1 in the back. One hole near the mouth hole is covered with paper. The instrument is used in classical music. Cf. *Ch'ih* (China—M 1027); *Fuye* (Japan).
Lit.: no. 52.

Honji (Japan). One of the stereotyped *ozatsuma* melodic patterns played on the *shamisen.*
Lit.: no. 185.

Honkyoku (Japan). Original pieces that constitute the basis of *shakuhachi* music. Cf. *Shakuhachi*; *Gaikyoku*; *Shinkyoku.*
Lit.: no. 185.

Hon-pu (Japan). "Principal score" indicating the fingering in *gagaku* music. Cf. *Kana-fu.*

Honte (Japan). See *Danawase.*

Hontirasi (Japan). See *Jiuta.*

Hontsuri-gane (Japan). Small hanging bell (or gong) in temples, in *kabuki*, and used for various signalling purposes usually to indicate the passage of time. Cf. *Denshō.*
Lit.: no. 185.

Ho O (Vietnam). Irrigation workers' songs.
Lit.: no. 51.

Hoon (*Hun*) (Korea). (*Hsün*, China—M 2908). A globular clay flute with its blowhole on top. It has five finger holes. When all holes are stopped the instrument produce the *huang-chung*. By appropriate fingering and half-stopping the following notes can be produced: C, C♯, D, D♯, E, F, F♯, G, G♯, A, A♯, B. The instrument was used in *ah-ak* (palace and Confucian temple). It was imported from China during the 12th century.
Lit.: nos. 137, 179.

Ho qay voi (Vietnam). Masons' songs.
Lit.: no. 51.

Hora (Japan). Shell trumpet used by Buddhist priests. Cf. *Hai-lo* (China); *Sora* (Korea).

Horagai (Japan). Conch shell trumpet used in folk music.

Horaneva (Sri Lanka). See *Horanoa.*

Horanoa (Sri Lanka). Oboe (*sanayi*) type.
Lit.: no. 254.

Hora-no-kai (Japan). See *Rappakai.*

Hori (India). Popular religious Hindu songs sung at the Holi festival. Of interest are the *hori-dhamar* songs (*hori* in *dhamar-tāla*), old folk melodies allegedly of the Mathura region.
Lit.: no. 138.

Ho-shen-t'ou (China). "Monk's head," a small drum with a single skin used in regional operas (*kao-ch'iang*) of Kwantung.
Lit.: nos. 129, 183.

Ho-sho (Japan). Wooden transverse flute with six finger holes.
Lit.: no. 255.

Hōshō (Japan). Later type of the *noh* drama in which Zen features are noticeable. Similar forms appear in *noh* types called *kanze* (the first school), *komparu*, *kita*, and *kongo.*
Lit.: no. 185.

Hosho (Rhodesia—Shona mbira). Gourd rattles.
Lit.: no. 22.

Hosori (Japan). Fashionable songs of the 17th century.
Lit.: no. 225.

Hossori (Korea). Songs chanted with open voice, reflecting the mercy of the Buddha in simple manner. Cf. *Chissori*; *Kot-ch'aebi*; *Pomp'ae.*
Lit.: no. 178.

Hotar (*Hotar* or *Hotri*) (Ancient India). Priest who performs the sacrificial ceremony and chants Vedic prayers.

Hou khin (Mongolia). See *Ohyan* (Sunda Isl.).

Hou-kuan (China). Short oboe consisting of a cylindrical tube with seven finger holes and one thumb hole. Recently it was accepted in Cantonese puppet opera music. The Cantonese name is *hao kwun.*
Lit.: no. 129.

Ho xa lua (Vietnam). Rice cutters' song.
Lit.: no. 51.

Ho yin hsüeh (China). Harmony (the study of harmony), a modern colloquial term.

Hpa:zi (Burma). "Frog cylinder," *shan kauṅ-chet.* Bronze kettle gong. Cf. *Pāzi.*
Lit.: no. 254.

Hrasva (India). "Short," *hrasva svara*; "short note," short syllable. Cf. *Mātrā*; *Dīrgha*; *Parvan.*
Lit.: no. 136.

Hrida Tāntiṇi (South India). *Janya rāga* of the 50th *mēḷa* (*Nāmanārāyaṇī*).
Tone material:
C D♭ E F♯ G B♭ A♭ c
c B♭ A♭ G F♯ E C
Lit.: no. 139.

Hṛśyakā (India). The seventh of the ancient *mūrchhanās* derived from the *Ma-grāma.*

Hsaing-waing (*Pat-waing*) (Burma). The largest (tuned) drum ensemble used at festive occasions. It can consist of several groups: drum chimes (*pat-waing*), gong chimes (*kyi-waing, maung-zaing*), oboe (*hne*), drums (*chauk-lon bat*), barrel drum, and *sahkun* and *pat-ma.* Punctuating instruments, slit drum (*hyauk*), clapper (*walet-hkok*), cymbals (*yagwin*), small cymbals (*si*), and large gong (*maung*). Cf. *Pat-waing.*

Hsia (China—M 2520). This prefix, used in *kung-ch'e-p'u*, lowers the following note by a semitone. If *ssu* is read as the note D, *hsia-ssu* is D♭, *hsia-yi* is E♭, etc.
Lit.: no. 136.

Hsia-fan (China). Assuming that *ho*, the basic note of *kung-ch'e-p'u*, is C, *hsia-fan*, the "lowered" *fan* is B♭.
Lit.: no. 136.

Hsia-kung (China). (This *kung* [M 3697] must not be mistaken for *kung* [M 3705].) Assuming that *ho*, the basic note of the *kung-ch'e-p'u*, is C, *kung* (M 3697) is A, hence *hsia-kung* is A♭.
Lit.: no. 136.

Hsiang (China—M 2562). A drum pillow, a not-tunable "drum" made of a leather bag filled with chaff; occasionally it is a small barrel filled with straw.
Lit.: no. 137.

Hsiang-ch'ih (China—M 1045; M 2560). A redwood stick struck with a short piece of wood. In Peking two *hsiang-ch'ih* preceded the coffin at funeral processions.
Lit.: no. 209.

Hsiang-chü (China—M 1593; M 2565). See *Ching-ch'iang.*

Hsiang-pan (China—M 2565; M 4885). Brass plate carried on a string and struck with a wooden stick. It was used by Buddhist priests and by peddlers in Hangchow.
Lit.: no. 209.

Hsiao (China—M 2619). Vertical bamboo flute of great age. It has five or more finger holes in front and one in the back. The term is also used to signify the *p'ai hsiao.* Cf. *T'ung-hsiao.*
Lit.: no. 137.

Hsiao ch'ü (China—M 1623; M 2605). Small tunes. Cf. *Ch'ü.*

Hsiao ho (China—M 2115; M 2605) "Small harmony." Often simply called *ho*, a *sheng* with 13 reed pipes. Cf. *Sheng*.

Hsiao ku (China). "Little drum." A small circular frame drum that is beaten with a thin rod.
Lit.: no. 209.

Hsiao Kuan (China—M 2605; M 3557). Sixteenth-century flute with six holes, one covered with a paper membrane. Cf. *Ch'in-pa kuan*.
Lit.: no. 209.

Hsiao lo (China). (*Hsiao lo* is the Mandarin, *siu lo* the Cantonese form of the term.) A small gong. See *Wu lo*.

Hsiao mou (China). See *Fu t'o*.

Hsiao sheng (China). Stereotyped operatic role of the young man. See *Sheng* (M 5738).

Hsiao t'ung (*T'ung hsiao*) (China). Cf. *Hsiao*.

Hsia-ssu (China). Cf. *Hsia*.

Hsia-wu (China). "Lowered *wu*." Assuming that *ho*, the basic note of the *kung-ch'e-p'u*, is C, *wu* is d, a ninth higher, and *hsia-wu* is d♭.
Lit.: no. 136.

Hsia-yi (China). Cf. *Hsia*.
Lit: no. 136.

Hsi-ch'in (China—M 1103; M 2425). A simple fiddle with two strings. It resembles the *hu-ch'in*.

Hsi-ch'ü (China). "Theater and song," "music-drama." (1) The great classical opera of Peking. (2a) The local opera typical of the province where it originates. It is classical in character, presenting an old tradition, but is less impressive and smaller than the Peking opera. (2b) The recent folk opera, simple and lively, presenting country life. Its music contains folk songs.
Lit.: no. 83.

Hsieh-tzu (China). Prelude, prologue of the northern *tsa-chü*.

Hsien (China—M 2661). String. The term was used in the Chinese classics to denote string instruments, particularly zithers. Bowed instruments did not appear in ritual and ceremonial music.
Lit.: no. 137.

Hsien-chih (China). "The all-pervading influence." Name of the music ascribed to the first human emperor Huang Ti, the creator of the *lü-(lü)*.
Lit: no. 137.

Hsien-t'ao (China). Obscure lute with a round corpus, a long neck, 12 frets, and four strings.
Lit.: no. 209.

Hsien-tzu (China). "The strings." Also called *san hsien* ("three strings"). A lute with a small, circular corpus, a long neck, three strings, no frets. The *hsien tzu* is played with a plectrum and is the favorite lute of blind beggars. It also appears among instruments in theatrical shows and processions.
Lit.: no. 209.

(Ḥsīn) 'Ajam (Modern Tunisia). *Maqām*.
Tone material:

C D E♭(+) F G A B♭(+) c d

(the + over E♭, the (+) over B♭)

Lit.: no. 64.

(Ḥsīn) Aṣl (Modern Tunisia). *Maqām*.
Tone material:

B♭(+) C D E♭(+) F G A B♭ c d

Lit.: no. 64.

Hsing-erh (China—M 1759; M 2772). A pair of hemispherical cymbals used in religious services. A second name of *hsing erh* is *p'eng chung*.
Lit.: no. 209.

(Ḥsīn) Nīriz (Modern Tunisia). *Maqām*.
Tone material:

B♭(+) C D E♭(+) F G A B♭ c

Lit.: no. 64.

(Ḥsīn) 'Ushayrān (Modern Tunisia). *Maqām*. Tone material:

A $\overset{+}{B\flat}$ C D $\overset{+}{E\flat}$ F G A B♭ c d e♭

Lit.: no. 64.

Hsi-p'i (China). (1) A recent operatic style related to the *chin-ch'iang* and *pang-tzu* (*ch'iang*). The accompanying instrument is the *hu-ch'in*, the two strings of which are tuned one whole tone higher than those in the classical *erh-huang* style. Cf. *Erh-huang*.

(2) A characteristic rhythmic Chinese opera. It always has an upbeat; in a common four-beat feature the upbeat consists of two beats; in a two-beat feature it is one beat.

Lit.: nos. 136, 183.

Hsit-kyi auk-pyan (*Lei-bauk*) (Burma). See *Chauk-pauk auk-pyan*.

Hsi-wen (China—M 2434; M 7142). Operatic style that originated during the Yüan period, ca. 15th century. It represented a free, relaxed theatrical performance in which the lute was the accompanying instrument. Cf. *Tsa-chü*.

Lit.: no. 183.

Hsi-yüan (China—M 2452; M 7731). Noisy theaters where shows were presented uninterruptedly and during which tea and refreshments were offered. These theaters were of varying size.

Lit.: no. 183.

Hsüan (China—M 2887). The terms *hsüan* or *t'ien* (M 6362) were used if the ornamented *ying-ku* had several small drums attached to its body.

Lit.: no. 137.

Hsüan-ssu (South China). Suspended puppet (Cantonese term).

Lit.: no. 129.

Hsüan-tzu (China). See *Pao-chün-chih*, Shantung term: small gong of the blind.

Lit.: no. 137.

Hsün (China—M 2908). A Chinese "ocarina"—a globular flute made of baked clay or porcelain, with six finger holes: one at the apex, three in front, and two below. It was used at Confucian ceremonies where two *hsün* players were placed at the west and east sides of the hall. They played in unison with the *hsiao*. See *Koon* (Korea).

Lit.: no. 137.

Hsü-pan (China—M 2851; M 4885). "The board of orderliness." A board suspended on the gate of a monastery beaten with a heavy club to call the monks to meetings, to announce the arrival of visitors, and other important events.

Lit.: no. 209.

Ḥthen-pa (Tibet). "To draw out." This term is used when a "drawing out" of the notational curve and melody is required by adding a higher pitched note. The "drawing out" does not extend the duration of the notes but indicates a widening of the melodic range.

Lit.: no. 143.

Hu (Melanesia; Admirality Isl.). Bamboo nose flute.

Lit.: no. 313.

Hu (China). *Hu* music. See *Hu yüeh*.

Hua-chiao (China—M 1174; M 2212). A wind instrument, probably a double reed with three finger holes.

Lit.: no. 209.

Hu'a ha'u (Flores; Nage District). See *Orupi*. Cf. *Nggoa-nggao*.

Hua-ku (*Yao-ku*) (China—M 2212; M 3479). Barrel drum used in Confucian temples, in theaters, and in popular music. The *hua-ku* appears in various sizes. Formerly it was known as *ya-ku* or *yao-ku*.

Lit.: nos. 184, 209.

Hua-mei chiao-tzu (China—M 700; M 2222; M 4391; M 6939). *Hua-mei* is the name of a thrush. A bamboo whistle that imitates birds' voices. In Shantung the whistle was called *hua-mei-shao-erh* (M 1759; M 2222; M 4391;

M 5676). The term *shao erh* means a toy whistle made of clay.
Lit.: no. 209.

Hua-mei-shao-erh (China). See *Hua-mei-chiao-tzu.*

Huang-chung (China—M 1503; M 2297). "Yellow bell." Absolute pitch. It represents the first and most important tone of the circle of fifths as shown in the *lü-lü.* If used as a notational symbol only the first syllable is used (*huang*, M 2297).
Lit.: no. 136.

Huang lapa (Tibet). A *cha-chiao* used by Tibetan monks.
Lit.: no. 255.

Huan t'ou (China). A rattle of beggars and travelling barbers. It consists of two iron pincer-shaped arms.
Lit.: no. 209.

Hua-pu (China). See *Ya-pu.*

Hua-Tan (China). "Flower." A standard type of operatic actor-singer of the *yüan* drama. The term indicates either the second wife, or a courtesan, or the beautiful and shrewd slave girl. (All female parts were performed by men.) *Hua tan* was often simply called *tan.*

Hu-chia (China). An old term for reed pipe made of bark or leaves coiled into a tube. The Peking instrument was called *chia* (M 586).
Lit.: no. 209.

Hu-ch'in (China—M 1103; M 2167). A large variety of popular fiddles, probably of Central Asian origin. The corpus of the *hu-ch'in* is a small cylinder or cup made of bamboo, wood, or coconut. The slim neck pierces the body. Two silken strings are tuned a fifth apart and are played with a bow, the hair of which passes between the two strings. A few of the many names of the instrument are: *ching-hu*, *erh-hsien*, *ehr-hu*, *hai-keum* (Korea), *hui-hu*, *hu-hu*, *kei-kin* (Japan), *pan-hu*, *sadung* (Thailand), *ssu-hu*, *ta-hu-ch'in*, *tan*, *tan-ch'in*, *t'i-ch'in.*
Lit.: no. 250.

Ḥudā (Arabia). Caravan song.
Lit.: no. 76.

Huḍukka (South India). Small drum having the shape of an hourglass.
Lit.: no. 261.

Huhe (Flores—Mbai; Ngada). Flute with a central hole. In Nage (Ngada) it is called *foi duri udi.* Both ends of the tube are open. The player blows across the center hole and the player's opening or closing the holes at both ends of the tube create a variety of sounds. The instrument is generally played by young girls. Occasionally extra holes are cut into the tube near both ends of the instruments.
Lit.: no. 166.

Hu-hu (*Pang-tzu-erh-hu-ch'in*) (China—M 2663.3). A *hu-ch'in* popular in Shensi. The term *hu-hu* is applied to fiddles with bodies made of bamboo, coconut, or wood. Cf. *T'i-ch'in*; *Erh-hsien.*
Lit.: no. 255.

Hui (Korean: *Hwi*) (China—M 2354b). The term indicates the 13 inlaid round mother of pearl studs, occasionally also painted, placed below the outermost (lowest sounding) string of the *ch'in.* The *hui* serve a purpose similar to frets on other zithers and lutes; theoretically they are numbered from right to left. The stopping of the lowest string of the *ch'in* at the places indicated by the *hui* produces the following notes:

Open string	*hui*: 13	12	11	10	9	8	7	6	5	4	3	2	1
(C)	D	E♭	E	F	G	A	c	e	g	c′	e′	g′	c″

Lit.: no. 136.

Hui-hu (China). A fiddle of the same type as the *hu-ch'in* but smaller in size. The instrument is popular in and around Hangchow.
Lit.: no. 255.

Hui mori (Korea). Rhythmic mode; drum pattern.

Hujanī (Egypt). Caravan songs. Cf. *Ḥidā*; *Rakbānī.*

Hukh (Pak; Admirality Isl.). Nose flute.

Hukuhan (Japan). See *Hakuhan.*

Hula (Hawaii). Traditional dance.
Lit.: no. 215.

Hula 'ala'apapa (Hawaii). Formal dance.

Hula 'ili 'ili (Hawaii). Traditional dance in which small stones are held by the dancer. The rubbing of two stones (one held in each hand) creates an accompanying noise.
Lit.: no. 37.

Hula ipu (Hawaii). Drum made of a large gourd.
Lit.: no. 37.

Hula kālā'au (Hawaii; Sandwich Isl.). Dance accompanied by song and wooden percussion sticks. Two wooden sticks are beaten against each other.
Lit.: no. 84.

Hulakaya (India). Tambourin.
Lit.: no. 255.

Hula kuolo (Hawaii). Kneeling dance.

Hula 'ulī'ulī (Hawaii). Gourd-rattle dance.

Hulidzap (Turkestan). Cf. *Sochiba.*

Hulki (Southeast India; Muria Gond Tribe). Gotul dance of boys and girls. The *gotul* is a club of the Gond youngsters. Almost every village has such a club in which boys and girls meet every night, sing and dance, and spend the night together.
Lit.: no. 134, 142.

Hulki māndri (Southeast India; Bastar State; Muria Gond Tribe). An hourglass-shaped drum with two lizard skin heads. Other names of the drum are *damru* and *ojha parra.* See *Mandri.*
Lit.: no. 59.

Hulki pata (Southeast India; Jhoria Muria Gond Tribes). Dance song. The dance imitates the movements of a snake.
Lit.: no. 142.

Hulur (Southeast India; Gond Tribes). Transverse bamboo flute with four finger holes. It produces the notes ca. G A B d.
Lit.: no. 135.

Hu-lu sheng (China). Mouth organ.

Hulwane (South Africa – Venda). See *Tuku.*

Humbaldu (Nigeria – Fut). Dried hand-beaten gourd. Its aperture can be closed or opened by the player in order to vary the sound. The instrument is used to accompany songs of the women. Cf. *Darhama.*
Lit.: no. 190.

Humkāra (Vedic India). See *Hiṃkāra.*

Humpita (India). Cf. *Gumphita* (*Gamaka*).

Hun (Korea). Egg-shaped clay flute with five or six finger holes (four in front and two in the back). The instrument is used in the *ah-ak* ensemble. Cf. *Hsün* (China – M 2908).
Lit.: no. 52.

Hunarmand (Kurdistan). Term for musician. See also *Sazandeh.*
Lit.: no. 229.

Hunga (Angola). Musical bow. Cf. *Hungo.*
Lit.: no. 18.

Hungo (West Africa – Malinke). Musical bow.
Lit.: no. 18.

Hung-pan (China). See *Cheng-pan.*
Lit.: no. 136.

Hun-pu-sze (China). A lute with (two) three or four strings. The name is probably derived from *qubuz*. Cf. *Hu-po*; *Qubuz*.
Lit.: nos. 5, 78.

Hu-po (China). Slim lute with a small pear-shaped corpus and a long neck. The instrument has four strings. Cf. *Qubuz*.
Lit.: no. 209.

Huqqe (Arabia). Corpus, *kemanje*.
Lit.: no. 255.

Hurava (Papua—Orokolo). Bull roarer.
Lit.: no. 311.

Hurka (*Huruka*) (India). Cf. *Damaru*.

Huro (Rhodesia—Shona mbira). High (non-verbal) yodelling style.
Lit.: no. 22.

Huruk (India). Also *Huruka*. Cf. *Ḍamaru*.

Husago (Ghana—Ewe). Ritual dance for Yeve, the god of thunder. It is accompanied by the drums *sogo*, *kidi*, and *kaganu*, the bell and rattle *gankogui* and *axatse*. There are seven dances for Yeve; besides *husago* there are *sovu*, *soga* (*sogha*), *adavu*, *afovu*, *agovu*, and *avelevu*.
Lit.: nos. 128, 174.

Ḥusainī (Arabia). *Maqām*. See *Ḥusaynī*.

Huṣāni (South India). *Husēni*.

Husapi (*Hapetan*) (Sumatra—Batak). Lute. Cf. *Kachapi* (Sundanese lute).
Lit.: no. 254.

Ḥusaynī (Middle East). *Maqām*.
Tone material:

D $\overset{+}{\text{E}\flat}$ F G A (A♭) B♭ (B) c d

Lit.: nos. 64-65.

Ḥusaynī (Modern Egypt). *Maqām*.
Tone material:

D $\overset{+}{\text{E}\flat}$ F G A $\overset{+}{\text{B}\flat}$ c d

Lit.: no. 64.

Ḥusaynī 'Uśayrān (Middle East). *Maqām*.
Tone material:

A B♭ C E $(\overset{+}{\text{E}\flat})$ $\overset{+}{\text{F}}$ G A

Lit.: no. 64.

Husēni (*Huśāni*; *Uśāni*; *Uśēni*) (South India). *Janya rāga* of the 22nd *mēḷa* (*Kharaharapriyā*).
Tone material:

C D E♭ F G A B♭ c
c A G F E♭ D C

Lit.: no. 139.

Ḥusēnī (*Ḥusaynī*; *Hussenī*) (Arabia). (1) A tone name of a main tone, one octave higher than *'ashirān* (*'ushayrān*). (A list of all tone names and tones through two octaves can be seen under the heading of *Jagā* [*Yagā*].) (2) *Ḥusēnī*, *maqām*.

A $\overset{+}{\text{B}\flat}$ c d; A G F $\overset{+}{\text{E}\flat}$ D

If *Ḥusēnī* ends with the note D (*duga*) the *maqām* is called *Ḥusēnī kar duga* (*Ḥusēnī* based on the tone *duga*). If the melody uses the note *ajam* (B♭), the *maqām* is called *Ḥusēnī bayat*. A sub-*maqām* of *Ḥusēnī* is *maqām Suz-dal*, "The burnt heart."
Lit.: no. 56.

Ḥusēnī Bayat (Arabia). See *Ḥusēnī*.

Ḥusēnī kar duga (Arabia). See *Ḥusēnī*.

Husseini-Kanada (North India). A rare *rāga* ascribed to the *Kafi thāta*.
Tone material:

C D (E♭) F G A $\overset{+}{\text{B}\flat}$ c
c B♭ A G F E♭ D C

Lit.: no. 138.

Ḥussenī (Arabia). See *Ḥusēnī*.

Hutamba (Sierra Leone). Drum (hourglass type).

Hu-ti (China—M 2167; M 6217). "Foolish flute." A shepherd's flute with four or five finger holes. Cf. *Ch'iang ti*.
Lit.: no. 209.

Hu-tiao (China). Operatic style favored by actor-singers of Anhwei. It prepared the road for the *ch'ing hsi*, the "theater of the capital city."

Hu-yüeh (China—M 2167; M 4129). Foreign, barbarian music imported into China from Central Asia, particularly during the Sui and T'ang dynasties, incorporated in the ensembles and musical activities of the *yüeh-fu*, the imperial music office.
Lit.: no. 136.

Ḥuzām (Middle East). *Maqām.*
Tone material:
+
E♭ F G A♭ (B♭) B c d e♭ f♯ g

Ḥuzam (Modern Egypt). *Maqām.*
Tone material:
+
E♭ F G A♭ B c d e♭
Lit.: no. 64.

Hwach'ong (Korea). Buddhist chant with Korean text, using secular melodies and rhythms.

Hwang (Korea). See *Yul-cha-po.*
Lit.: no. 136.

Hwarang (*Yanjung*) (Korea). Male musicians who accompany female shamans (*tan'gol*).
Lit.: no. 287.

Hwi (Korea). Korean term of the Chinese *hui.*

Hwi-kum (Korea). See *Kaya-kum.*

Hyang-ak (Korea). The Korean indigenous classical music performed at the royal court. Its melodies have hexatonic character. The essential instruments of the *hyang-ak* ensemble were: *komunko*, *kaya-kum*, *hyang p'i-p'a*, *tae-gum*, *hyang-p'iri*, and one of the old drums. When all instruments are silent, the *a-chaeng* is played.
Lit.: no. 136.

Hyang-pal (Korea). Curved cymbals often used in folk music. Cf. *Hyang-ryong*. See *Ja-bara.*
Lit.: no. 52.

Hyang p'il-lyul (Korea). The Korean *p'iri.* the instrument is a little larger than the *t'ang p'il-lyul.* It is made of bamboo and has seven finger holes. Cf. *P'iri.*
Lit.: no. 52.

Hyang p'i-p'a (Korea). The Korean indigenous "provincial" lute, which at the present time is almost obsolete. The instrument had five strings, 10 (occasionally 11-12) frets, and was tuned to (e.g.) C E F A c. The *hyang p'i-p'a*, whose body was slightly slimmer than that of the *t'ang p'i-p'a*, was played with a bamboo plectrum.
Lit.: nos. 52, 179.

Hyang-p'iri (Korea). A heterophonic double reed instrument indigenous of Korea. It has seven finger holes in front and one at the back. The tones produced are:

A♭ B♭ c d♭ e♭ f g♭ a♭ b { c' d♯ / c♯' f' }

The instrument is slightly smaller than its imported Chinese counterpart, the *t'ang-p'iri.*
Lit.: no. 179.

Hyang-ryong (Korea). A small bell (or cymbal) used at dances. Cf. *Hyang-pal.*
Lit.: no. 52.

Hyauk (Burma). Small slit-drum beaten with a stick.

Hyaw (Burma). Large two-headed drum.

Hymn in Honor of Confucius (China). The hymn has six stanzas: *ying shen* (receiving the approaching spirit); *ch'u hsien* (first presentation of offerings); *ya hsien* (second presentation of offerings); *chung hsien* (third and last presentation); *ch'e chuan* (removal of the viands); *sung shen* (escorting the spirit back). For notation and entire text see Lit. no. 136, pp. 82-83.

Hyōjō (Japan). One of the six *gagaku* modes. Cf. *Sō-no-koto* (Tunings). *Hyōjō* is the tone name of the third of the 12 chromatic tones, usually transcribed as E. Below is shown the entire chromatic scale, beginning with D: D (*ichikotsu*); D# (*tangin*); E (*hyōjō*); F (*shosetsu*); F# (*shimomu*); G (*sojo*); G# (*fusho*); A (*osho*); A# (*rankei*); B (*banshiki*); c (*shinsen*); c# (*kamimu*). The *hyōjō* mode (*gagaku*) is:

E F# (G) A B c# (d) e

All six *gagaku* modes can be seen under *Gagaku* (the six modes).

Hyon-ak (Korea). An ensemble of string instruments.

Hyon-cha (Korea). A long necked lute with three strings. Now very rarely used. Cf. *San-hsien* (China); *Shamisen* (Japan).
Lit.: no. 52.

Hyon-kum (*Hyen-keum*) (Korea). See *Komunko.*
Lit.: no. 136.

Hyōshi (Japan). Rhythm; measure; rhythmical mode; clappers. *Hyōshigi*, wooden clappers; *shakubyōshi*, wooden clappers (court singing); *hyōshitori*, the person who beats time; a single time unit; a rhythmic mode. See *Yo-hyōshi* (*Shi-hyōshi*); *Ya-hyōshi* (*Hachi-hyōshi*); *Mu-hyōshi* (*Roku-hyōshi*); *Tadabyōshi* (three beats). Cf. *Kage*; *Kumi.*
Lit.: no. 225.

Hyōshiban (Japan). Teaching method used by the instructor beating drum rhythms with a couple of fans on a wooden box (*hyōshiban*).
Lit.: no. 185.

Hyōshigi (Japan). Two wooden blocks of hard wood beaten against each other or against the floor as clappers. Their sound in the theater, when beaten on the floor in fast speed, is supposed to signify confusion, battle, and rough style. Cf. *Aragoto.* The term implies also "wooden time beaters." They are used in *kabuki*, *nagauta* off-stage, indicating the number of minutes before a performance begins. When the curtain rises and falls, a series of fast clicks is produced.
Lit.: no. 215.

Hyōshitori (Japan). See *Hyōshi.*

Hyōshi-uchi (Japan). "The rule of emphasis." The singer has to mark tempo and meter by clicking his fan (*hyōshi-ogi*).
Lit.: no. 225.

Hyottoko (Japan). A masked character of a folk dance. His performance is called a "bumpkin dance."
Lit.: no. 185.

Hyun-kum (*Hyon-kum*) (Korea). See *Komunko.*

Hyup (Korea). See *Yul-cha-po.*
Lit.: no. 136.

I

I (Korea). See *Yul-cha-po.*
Lit.: no. 136.

I (China—M 2960). A short *ch'in* prelude that precedes a piece of music of the same mode (*tiao*). This *tiao-i* ("mode meaning") is similar to a brief (Indian) *ālāp.* The *tiao-i* often ended with *fan-yin* ("floating sounds") harmonics. During the Ming period the *tiao-i* were notated in *ch'in* handbooks. In later times they were deleted. These preludes appeared also in the ceremonial court music of Japan. See *Netori* or *Torine.*
Lit.: no. 93.

Iba (Ancient Egypt). Simple, jingling sistrum in form of a horseshoe with a handle. Also called *sehem.* See also *Sesheshet.*
Lit.: no. 250.

Ibeka (West Africa; Gabon—Bakele). A *sansa.*
Lit.: no. 33.

Ibgakare (East Africa; Mozambique). Lute with one fiber string. The corpus is covered with parchment.
Lit.: no. 255.

Ibi (Sudan). Drum.
Lit.: no. 95.

Ibihozo (Central Africa; Ruanda). Lullaby.

Ibrik (Arabia). Also called *'unk.* Neck of the *'ud.*
Lit.: no. 255.

Ibu (Malaysia). See *Gong anak*; *Gong ibu.*

Ibuma (Nigeria—Igbo). Large iron bell.

Ichi (Japan). Name of the 11th pipe of the *sho.*
Lit.: no. 225.

Ichiban-daiko (Japan). An old pattern of *ōdaiko* drumming performed at the beginning of a *kabuki* performance.
Lit.: no. 185.

Ichi-genkin (Japan). Also called *suma-koto.* A *koto* with one string. The "frets" on the soundboard are either inlaid or merely painted.
Lit.: no. 255.

Ichikata (Japan). *Biwa* school of the Kamakura period (late 12th century). A second school was the *Yasaka.* The *Ichikata* school emphasized special musical interpretations, while the *Yasaka* school stressed original, correct textual presentations.
Lit.: no. 185.

Ichikotsu (Japan). The first and basic of the 12 (chromatic) tones, usually transcribed as the western note D. See *Shōmyō*; *Gagaku*.
Lit.: no. 185.

Ichikotsu-chō (Japan). The *ichikotsu* mode used in *shōmyō* and *gagaku*: D E F♯ (G G♯) A B (c c♯) d.
Lit.: no. 185.

Ichi-no tsuzumi (Japan). Also called *ikko*. A small drum in the shape of an hourglass. Cf. *Ni-no tsuzumi*.
Lit.: no. 225.

Ichiotsu (Japan). (1) *Ritsusen* form. Cf. *Sō-no koto* (tunings). (2) *Ryosen* form. Cf. *Sō-no koto* (tunings).
Lit.: no. 225.

Ichi sagari (Japan). *Shamisen* tuning. See *Shamisen*.
Lit.: no. 291.

Ichy'umwe (Ruanda). Royal drum.
Lit.: no. 26.

Ichibitiku (Nigeria – Lala; Ghana). Drum.
Lit.: no. 128.

Icilongo (*Ixilongo*) (South Africa – Zulu). A bamboo trumpet with a hooked bell made of an oxhorn, imitating European trumpets. The term *icilongo* is applied also to any European trumpet or horn. Cf. *Ixilongo* (*impempe*).
Lit.: no. 151.

Icombi (Uganda). Trumpet with a gourd as bell.
Lit.: no. 302.

Ida (Sudan – Edo). A drum shaped in the form of an hourglass. The Yoruba treat the *ida* as a royal instrument. Cf. *Kalengo* (Nigeria).
Lit.: no. 95.

Iḍaibāri (*Bāri*) (South India). Tamil term for a double oboe (*nagasvaram*). The small form of this instrument is called *timiri*, and the large one *bāri*.
Lit.: no. 261.

Iḍakka (South India). A drum in the form of a spool with two heads that are fastened by ropes to the corpus in a zigzag pattern. The player can alter the pitch by adjusting the ropes.
Lit.: no. 261.

Idan (Arabia). The plural of *'ūd*.

Idan bupe (Nigeria; Benin region – Yoruba). Drum. Cf. *Koso*.
Lit.: no. 293.

Ideteta (Uganda – Teso). Drum chime consisting of five drums.

Idi (*Odi*) (Nigeria – Igbo). Hourglass drum.

Idje (*Idzdzai*; *Idzibile*) (Congo – Balendu). Drum.
Lit.: no. 26.

Idudu egu (*Udu*) (Nigeria – Ibo; Edo). Clay pot beaten by women.
Lit.: nos. 190, 223.

Idzdzai (*Kibili*) (Congo – Bahema). Barrel drum used for dancing and signalling. Cf. *Idje*.
Lit.: no. 26.

Idzibile (Congo). See *Idje*.

Iemoto (Japan). The system of various degrees (ranks with certificates) of performing musicians. The term refers also to the principal of the school where these degrees can be obtained.
Lit.: no. 215.

Igaku (Japan). See *Gagaku*.

Igba (Nigeria – Yoruba). See *Aha*.

Igbin (Nigeria – Yoruba). Drum with a cylindrical corpus and one skin. The lower end is open. The drum rests on a small pedestal. It is used at religious festivals.
Lit.: nos. 293, 303.

Igbombo (Congo—Nepoko Pygmies). A ground bow consisting of a rattan string attached with one end to the elastic bow stick. The other end of the string is fastened to a piece of bark laid over a pit. The player plucks the string with one hand and beats the bark with a stick held in the other hand, thus producing some accompaniment to the singing of a partner.
Lit.: no. 176.

Igemfe (*Igenxe*; *Igerre*; *Igexhle*) (South Africa—Zulu). (1) A notched flute made of two pieces of cane. The thinner tube is stuck into the wider one. These instruments are used in pairs; the two are tuned a semitone apart. The higher pitched flute is called "female," the lower one "male." (2) A transverse flute similar to the *tshitiringo*.
Lit.: nos. 150, 190.

Igenxe (South Africa—Zulu). See *Igemfe.*

Igerre (South Africa—Zulu). See *Igemfe.*

Igexhle (South Africa—Zulu). See *Igemfe.*

Īggīw (Mauritania). Professional musician.

Igihumulizo (Central Africa; Ruanda). See *Indahura.*

Igo (Nigeria—Igbo). Xylophone.

Igubu (South Africa). See *Gubo.*

Ihango (Congo—Mbuti). Zither with six or seven strings.
Lit.: no. 220.

Ihara (Tahiti). Percussion tube placed horizontally on the ground and struck with two wooden sticks.
Lit.: no. 7.

Ihembe (Central Africa; Ruanda). Side-blown antelope horn.

Iholere (*Mushereko*) (Ruanda—Bashi). Side-blown antelope horn, occasionally made of ivory. It is used to accompany dances and songs.
Lit.: no. 190.

Ihumke (Japan—Ainu). Lullaby. Its refrain is sung in falsetto.

'I'i (Hawaii). An articial tremolo produced by the singer in order to express a highly emotional mood.
Lit.: no. 215.

Ijala (Nigeria—Yoruba). Songs of the hunters.
Lit.: no. 218.

Ikake (Japan). See *Kake.*

Ikembe (Central Africa; Ruanda). *Sansa* with 11-13 keys.

Ikere (West Kenya—Kuria). One of the *iribogwe* made of bamboo. It is transversely blown by young men.
Lit.: no. 299.

Ikibiswi (West Kenya—Kuria). The smallest flute of the *iribogwe* flutes.
Lit.: no. 299.

Iki-gae (Japan). "Return of breath." A breathing technique, from measure to measure a regular in- and exhaling.

Ikimbe (Congo—Ngundi). Term for *sansa.* See *Ikembe.*
Lit.: no. 21.

Ikimea (Flores). Dance.
Lit.: no. 166.

Ikinyuguri (Central African; Ruanda). Gourd rattle.

Ikinimba (Uganda). Mouthpiece of the *umukuri.*
Lit.: no. 200.

Ikisandasanda (Congo; Urundi). Long wooden flute with three finger holes.
Lit.: no. 255.

Ikivuvu (Congo). See *Inanga.*

Ikko (Japan). See *Ichi-no tsuzumi.*

Ikliğ (Turkey). Old spike fiddle with two or three strings.

Ikoka (Congo—Lokalo). Musical bow.
Lit.: no. 176.

Ikokolo (Uganda—Gishu). Trough or pot beaten with sticks or hands.
Lit.: no. 302.

Ikolo (Nigeria). See *Ikoro.*

Ikondi (*Ikondo*) (Kenya—Nandi). Large antelope horn.
Lit.: no. 255.

Ikoro (Sudan; Nigeria). Very large double slit-drum used at funerals.
Lit.: no. 94.

Ikoro uta (Nigeria—Igbo). Double slit-drum.

I-kuan-hsia (China). Clarinet.
Lit.: no. 255.

Ikulu (North Rhodesia—Lala). Big drum of the leader.
Lit.: no. 128.

Ikur (Congo—Badinga; Badzing). Signal drum.
Lit.: no. 26.

Ikuta jiuta (Japan). See *Jiuta.*

Ikuta-koto (Japan). A recent *koto* type (since ca. 1930) with 17 strings. The delicately built instrument is favored by lady amateur players.
Lit.: nos. 185, 225.

Ikwemgbo (Nigeria—Igbo). Large xylophone.

Il (Korea). The third note (and its notational symbol) of the *kong-chuk-po.* Assuming that *hap* is interpreted as the western note C, *il* represents E♭ or E (as demanded by the mode used by the performer).
Lit.: no. 136.

Ilaittāḷam (South India). See *Ilattāḷam.*

Ilat (Indonesia; Sunda District). See *Kachapi.*

Ilattāḷam (*Ilaittāḷam*) (South India). A pair of small brass cymbals used in *kathakali* performances.
Lit.: no. 261.

Iḷi (South India). The term for the note *pa* in ancient Tamil terminology. It is used to denote the interval of a fifth.
Lit.: no. 261.

'Ili'ili (Hawaii). Stone rattle; specific rhythm produced by this instrument.
Lit.: no. 278.

Ilimba (Congo—Balamba). Xylophone.
Lit.: no. 26.

Il-ji (Korea). Cf. *Tae-kum.*

'Ilm-i mūsīqī (Turkey). Theory of music.
Lit.: no. 81.

Ilo-ilo-goto (Java). See *De(r)men(an).*
Lit.: no. 163.

Ilongo (Congo—Nkundo). A goblet- or pot-shaped drum made of clay.
Lit.: no. 26.

Iloṅma (Assam—Garo). A bamboo cross flute with three finger holes.
Lit.: no. 252.

Ilpirra (*Ulbura*) (South Australia). Trumpet of the aboriginals. The instrument is a hollow, five feet long, piece of tree through which the performer sings. The sound has ritual meaning.

Im (Korea). See *Yul-cha-po.*
Lit.: no. 136.

Imālāt (Arabia). Long held vocal tones.

Imana (North India). See *Kalyan.*

Imangu (Congo–Balamba). A heavy large drum with two heads used in battles and during funerals. Cf. *Mangu.*
Lit.: no. 26.

Imayō (Japan). "Present style songs." The word "present" refers to the 10th century, when *imayō* songs and dances of the imperial court had gained much popularity.
The early *imayō* were *wasan* hymns performed by Buddhist monks with adjusted and popularized texts. At the present time the *imayō* have disappeared. Cf. *Zōgei.*
Lit.: no. 185.

Imba (Africa; Zanzibar). Swahili term for "to sing."

Imbal (Java). "To repeat." *Imbal* is played by two musicians on the *sarong demung.* One plays the first halves (*gawe*) of the notes of the theme, the other one plays the second halves (*ngiṇtil*).
Lit.: no. 163.

Imbalanyi (Uganda–Gishu). Wooden board beaten with drumsticks.
Lit.: no. 302.

Imbande (South Africa–Zulu). Also written *imbhande.* A small flute with a conical bore. The instrument is made of a bird's leg bone. It has no finger holes.
Lit.: no. 151.

Imbeni (North Rhodesia). Traditional dance.
Lit.: no. 128.

Imbhande (South Africa). See *Imbande.*

Imbila (Transvaal–Matabele). Xylophone. Cf. *Ilimba*; *Mbila.*
Lit.: no. 255.

Imbingi (Assam; Burma). Bamboo clarinet with three finger holes.
Lit.: no. 252.

Imbongi (South Africa–Zulu). Court singer who performs *izibongo.*

Imbubu (Mesopotamia; Akkad.). Also called *malilu.* An ancient term for a long cane pipe with a double reed. Cf. *Gi-gid*; *Ebubu.*
Lit.: no. 87.

Imele (Congo). Bow lute.
Lit.: no. 176.

Imiguza (*Imiguzza*) (South Africa–Xhosa). A rattle made of dried gourds tied to the waist of the dancer.
Lit.: no. 151.

Impai (Borneo). Lute with two strings. Its body can have the shape of a boat, but the instrument appears in various shapes. Cf. *Sapeh*; *Blikan*; *Safe*; *Djimpai*; *Kasapi.*
Lit.: no. 254.

Impandula (South Africa–Zulu). Cf. *Ipandula.*

Impango (North Rhodesia–Ila; Tongo). Song performed by women only.
Lit.: no. 99.

Impempe (*Ixilongo*) (South Africa–Zulu; Xhosa). Vertically-blown flute. Cf. *Ncongolo.*
Lit.: no. 151.

Impuruza (*Impuruzza*; *Ishako*) (Congo–Bahutu). Drum with a conically-shaped body.
Lit.: no. 26.

Imvingo (*Uqwabe*). Musical bow. Its Zulu names are *inkohlisa* or *unkoka.* The Swaziland term is *umakweyana* (the "maiden's instrument").
Lit.: no. 151.

Imzad (Mali). Fiddle.

In (Japan). Or *In-sen*, "soft mode." Scale; mode used particularly in old *shakuhachi* music:

D E♭ F G A B♭ c d

Variants:

D E♭ G A B♭ d (of the Edo Period, 1603-1868)

D E♭ G A c d

D E G A c d

Cf. *Yō*.
Lit.: no. 185.

Iṇai (South India). Ancient Tamil term for *vādī*. See *Rāga*.

Inakabue (Japan). "Country flute." A melody played on the bamboo flute (in a *nagauta* performance) in order to create a rustic country atmosphere. Cf. *Kusabue*.
Lit.: no. 187.

Inakapriya (South India). *Janya rāga* of the 22nd *mēḷa* (*Kharaharapriyā*).
Tone material:

C D E♭ F A B♭ c

c Bv A F Ev D C

Lit.: no. 139.

Inang (Sunda District). "Breast." Movable bridges. Cf. *Rebāb* (Sundanese); *Kachapi*.

Inanga (*Ikivuvu*) (Congo; Ruanda-Urundi—Barundi). A boat-shaped psaltery. The strings are strung across a trough.
Lit.: no. 176.

Inavardhani (South India). *Janya rāga* of the 39th *mēḷa* (*Jhālavarāḷi*).
Tone material:

C Dv Ew Fc G Av c

c B Av G Fc Ew C

Lit.: no. 139.

Incwala (Swaziland). A royal ceremony where special dance songs (*incwala*) are performed with numerous dramatic religious features.

Indahura (Central Africa; Ruanda). Drum of the *ingoma* ensemble (led by the *ishakwe*). Other names of these drums are: *indamutsa*; *igihumulizo*. *indahura* can mean also flute.

Indamutsu (Central Africa; Ruanda). See *Indahura*.

Indandala (Zambesi River area—Ila). Small drum.
Lit.: no. 255.

Indhvi (North India). Cf. *Tabla*.

Indingidi (Congo; Rundi). Fiddle with one string.
Lit.: no. 176.

Indip (Congo—Badzing). Barrel drum with one head.
Lit.: no. 26.

Indrapriya (South India). *Janya rāga* of the 1st *mēḷa* (*Kanakangī*).
Tone material:

C Ew F Av Bw c

c Bw Av F Ew C

Lit.: no. 139.

Indrapriya (South India). *Janya rāga* of the 24th *mēḷa* (*Varuṇapriyā*).
Tone material:

C D Ev F Ac B c

c B Ac F Ev D C

Lit.: no. 139.

Indrapriya (South India). *Janya rāga* of the 54th *mēḷa* (*Viśvambharī*).
Tone material:

C Dv E Fc G Ac c

c Ac G Fc E Dv C

Lit.: no. 139.

Indravaṃsa (South India). *Janya rāga* of the 29th *mēḷa* (*Dhīraśaṅkarābharaṇam*).
Tone material:

C E F A B c

c B G A F E D C

Lit.: no. 139.

Indravardhanam (South India). *Janya rāga* of the 29th *mēḷa* (*Dhīraśaṅkarābharaṇam*).
Tone material:
C D E F G A B c
c A F E D C
Lit.: no. 139.

Indu (South India). Name of the 1st *chakra* in the system of the 72 *mēḷas*. Cf. *Chakra.*

Indubhōgi (South India). *Janya rāga* of the 46th *mēḷa* (*Ṣaḍvidhamārgiṇī*).
Tone material:
C Ev Dv Ev Fc G A c
c Bv A Bv G Fc Ev Dv C
Lit.: no. 139.

Indu chakra (South India). The name of the first *chakra* in the system of the 72 *mēḷas*. Cf. *Rāga* (South India); *Mēḷa*.

Indu Dhanyāsi (South India). *Janya rāga* of the 46th *mēḷa* (*Ṣaḍvidhamārgini*).
Tone material:
C Ev Fc A Bv c
c Bv A G A Fc Ev Dv C
Lit.: no. 139.

Indu Dhavaḷi (South India). *Janya rāga* of the 21st *mēḷa* (*Kiravāṇi*).
Tone material:
C D Ev F C F G Av B c
c B Av G F Ev C
Lit.: no. 139.

Indu Gaulika (South India). *Janya rāga* of the 28th *mēḷa* (*Harikāmbhōji*).
Tone material:
C D E F G A Bv c
c A Bv G A F E D F E C
Lit.: no. 139.

Indughaṇṭārava(m) (South India). *Janya rāga* of the 20th *mēḷa* (*Naṭabhairavī*).
Tone material:
C Ev F G Av G Bv
Bv Av G F Ev D C
Lit.: no. 139.

Indu Gīrvāṇi (South India). *Janya rāga* of the 42nd *mēḷa* (*Raghupriyā*).
Tone material:
C Dv Ew Fc G c
c B G Ac B G Fc Fc Ew Dv C
Lit.: no. 139.

Indu Hāvaḷi (South India). *Janya rāga* of the 21st *mēḷa* (*Kiravāṇi*).
Tone material:
C D Ev F C C G B Av c
c B Av G F Ev C
Lit.: no. 139.

Indu Kānti (South India). *Janya rāga* of the 53rd *mēḷa* (*Gamanaśrama*).
Tone material:
C Dv E Fc G A c
c A G Fc E Dv C
Lit.: no. 139.

Indumati (South India). *Janya rāga* of the 51st *mēḷa* (*Kāmavardhanī*).
Tone material:
C E Fc Av B c
c B Av Fc E C
Lit.: no. 139.

Indung (*Jong-jrong*; *Genjung*) (Sunda District). The two biggest and low-pitched *angklungs* of an ensemble of nine (with or without other types of instruments). The two next higher pitched *angklungs* are called *ambruk*; the next higher one is called *engklok*; the next higher two are called *pancher* and the final and highest two are called *roel* (or *anak*).
Lit.: no. 163.

Indung (West Java). See *Blung.*

Indureru (East Africa – Nandi). Wooden horn.
Lit.: no. 255.

Indu Sāraṅganāṭa (South India). *Janya rāga* of the 8th *mēḷa* (*Hanumattōḍi*).
Tone material:
C Dv Ev F G F Av Bv c
c Av G F Ev Dv C
Lit.: no. 139.

Indu Sītala (South India). *Janya rāga* of the 4th *mēḷa* (*Vanaspāti*).
Tone material:

C Dv Ew F G A Bv A c

c A Bv G F Ew Dv C

Lit.: no. 139.

Indu Vardhanam (South India). *Janya rāga* of the 29th *mēḷa* (*Dhīraśaṅkarābharaṇam*). This *rāga* is probably identical with *Indravardhanam*. The only difference appears in ascent:

C D E F G A B G c

c A F E D C

Lit.: no. 139.

Infiṣāl (*Baqiva*) (Old Arabia). Music theoretical term that signifies a large semitone (114 cents).

Ingetsu (Japan). See *Koto* (parts).
Lit.: no. 225.

Inggil (Java). Thin, high-pitched sounds.
Lit.: no. 163.

Ingilīz būrūsī (Turkey). An English brass trumpet (17th century).
Lit.: no. 81.

Ingoma (Central Africa; Ruanda). (1) Drum with two heads. (2) Ensemble of nine drums. (3) Dance.

Ingondjo (Congo—Bombesa). Drum. See *Lilenga*.
Lit.: no. 26.

Ingonga (West Congo). Musical bow.
Lit.: nos. 28-29.

Ingqongqo (South Africa—Bantu; Xhosa). Ground drum of various shapes.
Lit.: no. 151.

Ingungu (South Africa—Zulu). Obsolete drum consisting of a basket with a skin stretched over its opening. The body of this drum can also be a barrel.
Lit.: no. 151.

Injua (*Njua*) (North Rhodesia—Ila). A rattle, serving as signal instrument.
Lit.: no. 255.

Iningiti (Central Africa; Ruanda). Fiddle with one string.

Inkinge (South Africa—Pondo; Xhosa). Musical bow played by women and young shepherds. Cf. *Lugube*. (The Zulu name is *isitontolo*.)
Lit.: no. 151.

Inkohlisa (South Africa—Zulu). Musical bow. Cf. *Isiqoqomana*; *Isiqwemqwemana*; *Gubuolukhulu*; *Segwana*; *Imvingo*; *Ugubu*.
Lit.: no. 151.

In-kyeng (Korea). Bell.

Inma (South Australia). Term for music used by the aboriginals.

Insei (Japan). Ancient term for blind *koto* players.
Lit.: no. 185.

In-sen (Japan). See *In*.

Insimbi (Africa—Zambesi Kafir). Plucked idiophone, a *sansa* type.
Lit.: no. 184.

Intambula (South Africa; Swaziland). Simple drum consisting of a pot-shaped vessel and goatskin serving as head that is not attached to the pot but held in place by an assisting person. The drum, beaten with sticks by one or two persons, is used in exorcism.
Lit.: nos. 151, 190.

Inting (Bali). The second largest iron instrument used in the *gamelan selunding*.
Lit.: no. 197.

Intiqālāt (Arabia). Modulations.

In yimbo (North Rhodesia – Ila; Tonga). Song type.
Lit.: no. 99.

Inzirā (Ethiopia). See *Nzira.*

Inzogera (Central Africa; Ruanda). Ankle rattles used by dancers.

Ipandula (South Africa – Ndebele). A small whistle flute. Its Zulu name is *impandula*; the Sotho name is *phatola.*
Lit.: no. 151.

Ipch'ang (*Sonsori*) (Korea). "Standing songs." Folk songs performed by travelling groups of Buddhists. The songs were accompanied by the *changgo* and joined by acrobatic dancers. At present the *ipch'ang* are sung by professionals. These songs were not always of a decent nature.
Lit.: no. 287.

Ipe (*Ikpe*) (Nigeria – Yoruba). Ivory horn of conical shape.
Lit.: no. 293.

Ipiano (South Africa). See *Utiyama.*

Ipili (Congo – Wasangola). Globular flute with two finger holes.
Lit.: no. 33.

Ipopa (*Maumwakodi*) (North Rhodesia – Ila). Big drum beaten by two men.
Lit.: no. 255.

Ippaki-ni (Japan – Ainu). A flat piece of wood with a hole over which is placed a piece of skin. When blown through the hole the skin vibrates and creates sounds similar to animal cries.
Lit.: no. 255.

Ipu (Hawaii). A large calabash, upon which is attached a small one, is pounded against the ground and beaten with the fingers. Several rhythmic patterns are produced that are used as accompaniments of the ceremonial and profane *hula.*
Lit.: no. 278.

Ipu hōkyokyo (Hawaii). A nose-blown calabash flute with two or three finger holes. See *Hōkyokyo.*
Lit.: no. 215.

Ipu hula (Hawaii). Stamping vessel (*ipu* = calabash).
Lit.: no. 7.

Iqā' (Arabia). Rhythm; rhythmic pattern; mode. Cf. *Hazaj*; *Dōr.*
Lit.: no. 34.

Īqā'āt (plural: "rhythms") (Arabia; Persia). Rhythmic modes of the Arabian and Persian music theories of the past.

Rhythmical features specified by names, particularly features of the past, provide us with numerous variants and differing interpretations which cause considerable obstacles if clear, individual definitions are wanted. The flexibility of the modes, the variety in rhythmical beats, the patterns in their, at times, complicated usage, show astonishing diversities.

A few of the hundreds of names of rhythmical modes are mentioned below: *hazaj*; *ramal*; the first and second *thaqīl*; *thaqīl* indicates a serious, slow tempo although its pattern can be: 1st *thaqīl* ♫ |♪ 𝄾 ♫ |♪ 𝄾 ♫ |♪ and 2nd *thaqīl* ♬ |♩. ♫ |♩. ♫ etc. indicate the movement of a horse. In contrast to *thaqīl* are the popular and vivid patterns with the name *khafīf.*

Other names of variants are: *al-thaqīl al-awal*; *al-thaqīl alp-thānī*; *al-makhūri* (a variation of the second *thaqī*); *khafīf al-ramal*; *khafīf al-khafīf*; *īqa' ba'ira basseet*; *īqa' fakhit waurash*; *ī'qa' moudawar*, and many others.

At the present time traditional music is rhythmically free or linked with the metric features of poetry.
Lit.: no. 65.

Iqāma (Arabia; Middle East). Call to prayer chanted inside the mosque by the *muezzin* (*mu'adhdhin*). The call to prayer chanted on top of the minaret is called *adhān*.

Iqliq (Turkestan; Arabia). Ancient term for *kamanje*, a spike fiddle with two, three, or four strings, now obsolete.
Lit.: no. 81.

Irama (Java). Tempo.

'Irāq (Arabia). The third main note of the Arabic scale. (A complete list of tone names and notes through two octaves is shown under the heading of *Jagā* [*Yagā*].)

'Irāq (Arabia; Middle East; Egypt). *Maqām*. *Maqām 'Irāq* is very closely related to *maqām Sigā*. *'Irāq* stands a fourth lower than *Sigā*; *maqām 'Irāq* uses the same scale as *maqām Sigā*. The types of *'Irāq* are distinguished: *'Irāq-Siga* (the *Sigā*-related *maqām*) and *'Irāq-Ṣaba*. This latter type is called in Egypt *'Irāq-Dugā* because its scale begins with the note *dugā*. The *'Irāq* scale is:

$\overset{+}{B}$v C D $\overset{+}{\mathrm{E}}$v F $\overset{(+)}{\mathrm{F}}$ G A $\overset{+}{\mathrm{B}}$v

(*'Irāq-Sigā*, using the *Siga* scale.) In *'Irāq-Saba* the note G is lowered to ca. Bv ($\overset{+}{\mathrm{F}}$).
Lit.: no. 64.

'Irāq (Modern Tunisia). *Maqām*.
Tone material:

G *A* $\overset{+}{B}$v C D $\overset{+}{\mathrm{E}}$v F G A Bv

'Irāq-al-'ajam (Islamic North Africa). One of the Moroccan *nawbat* performed in the early morning.

'Irāq Aṣl (Tunisia). An identical *maqām* of *'Irāq* of modern Tunisia.

'Irāqīa (Arabia). An oboe popular in Egypt, with a large double reed, seven finger holes in the front, and two thumb holes at the back.
Lit.: no. 184.

Īravati (South India). *Janya rāga* of the 64th *mēḷa* (*Vāchaspati*).
Tone material:

C D Fc G A c
c A G Fc E D C

Lit.: no. 139.

Iravuppan (South India). *Rāgas* that are supposed to be performed during the night only. Cf. *Pagal pan*; *Poduppan*.
Lit.: no. 261.

Irchi (Kirgizia). Singer.
Lit.: nos. 275-76.

Iribogwe (West Kenya – Kuria). Cross flutes used in cattle herding: *umwere*; *ikere*; *ikibiswi*.
Lit.: no. 299.

Irim-irim (*[H]irim-[h]irim*) (Java). When the Prince of the *wayang* performance has decided to relax from his work as a ruler, and when he walks toward the harem, the *irim-irim*, a *suluk* is performed.
Lit.: no. 163.

Iritingo (West Kenya – Kuria). Bowl lyre with eight strings. It is slightly smaller than the bowl type (*obokano*) of the Gusii. Cf. *Obokano*.
Lit.: no. 299.

Irkhā' (Arabia). Microtone; ca. quarter tone.
Lit.: no. 65.

Irna (Southeast India – Muria Gond). Clapper bell fastened to the back of a dancer.
Lit.: no. 59.

Iroe (Japan). A short dance performed by dancing girls. It serves as a preparation for the following part of the main dance of the *noh* drama.
Lit.: no. 187.

Iro modori (Japan). "Colored *modori*." A *kyokusetzu*, a *modori* in which the central of the three notes is replaced by two shakes produced by pressure applied to the vocal cords.
Lit.: no. 47

Irrilku (Southeast New Guinea—Motu). Nose or conventional flute with two finger holes. Lit.: no. 313.

I-sā (Central Congo). Clapper. Lit.: no. 255.

Īśagauḷa (South India). *Janya rāga* of the 7th *mēḷa* (*Senāpāti*). Tone material:

C F E♭ F G A♭ B♭♭ c
c A♭ G A♭ F E♭ D♭ C

Lit.: no. 139.

Īśagiri (South India). *Janya rāga* of the 69th *mēḷa* (*Dhātuvardhaṇī*). Tone material:

C D♯ E F♯ G A♭ B
B A♭ G F♯ E D♯ C *B* C

The scale of this *rāga* has *Niṣādāntya* character. Lit.: no. 139.

Iśaivēḷāḷar (South India). Dancing girls. Lit.: no. 261.

Isaju (Nigeria). See *Dundun*; *Bembe*. *Isaju* is also spelled *issaju*.

Isaka (Nigeria—Igbo). Basket rattle.

Īśamanōhari (South India). *Janya rāga* of the 28th *mēḷa* (*Harikāmbhōji*). Tone material:

C D E F G A B♭ c
c B♭ A G F D F E D C

Lit.: no. 139.

Isambu (Africa; Victoria Lake; Baziba). A gourd or animal horn with the blowhole on its side. Lit.: no. 255.

Isankuni (South Africa—Pondo). Musical bow. Lit.: no. 151.

Isan'mele (Nigeria). See *Dundun*.

Isanzi (Central Congo—Teke). Term for *sansa*. Lit.: no. 280.

Īśapriya (South India). *Janya rāga* of the 66th *mēḷa* (*Chitrambarī*). Tone material:

C D E F♯ G A♯ c
c A♯ G F♯ E D C

Lit.: no. 139.

Isa ura (Flores; Ende). Flute. Lit.: no. 166.

'Isāwīya (Arabia). See *Dhikr*.

Isbāhān (Modern Tunisia). *Maqām*. Tone material:

G A B♭(+) C D E♭(+) F G A B♭ c♯ d

Cf. *Iṣfāhān*. Lit.: no. 64.

Iselwa (North Zululand). Rattle. Lit.: no. 151.

Isenan (Java). The filling-in instruments. See *Panerusan*. Lit.: no. 163.

Isen-isen (Java). The ornamenting and variating instruments of the *gamelan*. Lit.: no. 163.

Iṣfāhān (Arabia; Persia). (Persian: *Ispāhān*.) *Maqām*; "the son of *Ḥijaz*," popular in Persia. It uses the tone material of *Ḥijaz* and always has the note G as its basis:

G D E♭(+) F♯ G A B♭ c d (G F E♭(+) D / F♯ E♭ D

Lit.: nos. 64, 121.

Iṣfahānak (Middle East). *Maqām*. Tone material:

D E♭(+) F♯ (F) G (G♭) A B♭ c d

Lit.: no. 64.

Ish (Mongolia). Written: *eshi*. The neck of the *khil kuur*, a long stick carrying two strings. Lit.: no. 60.

Ishako (Congo). See *Impuruza*; *Ishakwe*.

Ishakwe (Central Africa; Ruanda). Leading (solo) drum of the *ingoma* ensemble (flute and drum).

Ishkarti (Northeast Sudan; Nubia). Tambourin.

Ishoku sashi (Japan). "Consideration of rank." The voice of the singer has to be adjusted to the character and rank of the person whom the singer addresses in his song, whether he sings to a warrior or a lady, a saintly man or a laborer.
Lit.: no. 225.

Isigodhlo (South Africa – Xhosa). Animal horn blown from the side.
Lit.: no. 151.

Isigubu (South Africa). A large barrel or cylindrical drum.
Lit.: no. 151.

Isikehlekehle (South Africa – Swazi). Bowed tube zither. Cf. *Tsijolo.*
Lit.: no. 151.

Isikunjane (South Africa – Xhosa). Rattle tied to the legs of the dancers.
Lit.: no. 151.

Isiqomqomana (South Africa – Zulu). Musical bow. Cf. *Isitontolo*; *Penda.* Also *isiqemq-wemana*, the same as *inkohlisa*.
Lit.: no. 151.

Isitontolo (*Isiqomqomana*) (South Africa – Swazi; Zulu). Musical bow.
Lit.: no. 151.

Isnasin (Ethiopia). Sistrum. Cf. *Dsanadsel.*
Lit.: no. 38.

Ispahān (Arabia; Persia). *Maqām.* The Persian term for *Iṣfahān.*

Isquitra (East Turkestan). Globular clay flute with two finger holes.
Lit.: no. 267.

Issaju (Nigeria). See *Isaju.*

Issei (Japan). The first song of the *ha* section (of a *noh* play). The melody moves within the low and middle ranges of the vocal gamut.
Lit.: no. 185.

Issei-itchō (Japan). An *issei* for voice and drum. In this instance the drum represents the entire *hayashi* ensemble.
Lit.: no. 185.

Issō (Japan). School of *noh* flute playing. Other well-known schools are *Morita* and *Fukita.*
Lit.: no. 185.

Ist (Persia). The note on which melodies end.

Istiftākh (Tunisia). See *Al Istiftākh.*

Istihlālu-dh-dhīl (Modern Tunisia). *Maqām.*
Tone material:

G A $\overset{+}{B\flat}$ C D $\overset{+}{E\flat}$ F G A $\overset{+}{B\flat}$ c d $\overset{+}{e\flat}$ f

Lit.: no. 64.

Istri (*wedokan*) (Java). "Female"; a term applied to the lower pitched *bonang* kettles and to one of the low pitched *rebāb* strings. The *laranangis* ("weeping virgin") too can be used instead of *istri.* See *Rebāb.*
Lit.: no. 163.

Īśvarī (South India). *Janya rāga* of the 6th *mēḷa* (*Tānārūpi*).
Tone material:

C D♭ E♭♭ F G A♯ c
c A♯ G F E♭♭ D♭ C

Lit.: no. 139.

Itag (*Jitag*; *Jatag*) (Mongolia). Cf. *Yatag.*

Itchō (Japan). A part of *noh* music that is performed by one or several singers and one drummer.
Lit.: no. 185.

Itchō-ikkan (Japan). A part of *noh* music performed by one flute, a drum, and a singer. The singer may join the two instruments.
Lit.: no. 185.

Itchu (Japan). *Shamisen* narrative music.
Lit.: no. 187.

Itchū-bushi (Japan). An old *shamisen* form of narrative songs. Cf. *Bungo-bushi.*
Lit.: no. 187.

Itemelo (Tanzania). A drum that is beaten to announce the death of a chief.
Lit.: no. 218.

I-tete (Congo – Teke). Small bell. Cf. *Bitete.*
Lit.: no. 255.

Itikili (Uganda – Lugbara). A toy ground bow.
Lit.: no. 302.

Itomaki (Japan). The three large ivory or wooden pegs of the *shamisen.*
Lit.: no. 185.

I-tse (China – M 2982; M 6746). "Equalizing rule." Absolute pitch (*lü*), representing the ninth tone of the circle of fifths as shown in the *lü-lü.* Traditionally a *yang* (male) tone, *I-tse* was used as a basic note in Confucian hymns performed in the month of July. If used as a notational symbol, only the first syllable, *I* (M 2982), was used.
Lit.: no. 136.

Itulasi (Samoa). Drum.
Lit.: no. 84.

Itumbilongonda (*Itumbolongonda*) (Congo – Bokote; Beloko). Ground bow or musical bow.
Lit.: no. 176.

Itundak (*Tinebtebak*) (Philippines – Karao). Gong ensemble (*gangsa*). It consists of seven gongs: one *salaksati*, three *maleok*, two *banengbeng*, *sitot.* Each gong type plays its own rhythm.

Ivenge (*Umtshingo*; *Umtshingi*) (South Africa – Zulu; Pondo). Cf. *Ncongolo.*
Lit.: no. 151.

Ivom (Nigeria). See *Alo.*

Iwato (Japan). The 3rd principle tuning of the *koto.* Cf. *Koto* tuning.
Lit.: no. 225.

Iwato (Japan). A specific drum pattern in *kabuki* performances.
Lit.: no. 187.

Ixilongo (South Africa – Xhosa). Also *impempe.* Trumpet of the Zulu (cf. *Icilongo*), a vertical flute of the Xhosa (cf. *Umtshingo*). Cf. *Ncongolo.*
Lit.: no. 151.

Iya'lu bata (Nigeria – Yoruba). Cf. *Bata.*

Iya'lu kete (Nigeria – Yoruba). Cf. *Kete.*

Iya'lu (Nigeria – Yoruba). "Mother drum." Principal drum. Cf. *Akika*; *Omolu*; *Oriki*; *Dundun*; *Apesin*; *Bembe.*
Lit.: no. 218.

Iya'lu bembe (Nigeria). Cf. *Bembe.*

Iyamaombe (Congo – Balamba). Cylindrical or barrel drum beaten in initiation rites.
Lit.: no. 26.

I-yang-ch'iang (China – M 665; M 3016; M 7265). Common popular operatic style; chorus scenes (*pang-ch'iang*), originating in I-yang of the Chianghsi (Kiangsi) province. Cf. *Ti-fang-hsi*; *Ching-ch'iang.*
Lit.: no. 183.

Iyup-iyup (West Java; Alas District). Term for *dermenan.* See *Ra'us woja.*
Lit.: no. 176.

Izambilo (Africa – Zulu). Xylophone; term for marimba.
Lit.: no. 255.

Izeze (Congo; Urundi). Fiddle with one string.
Lit.: no. 176.

Izibongo (South Africa – Zulu). Songs the texts of which are poetic expressions of praise. Cf. *Imbongi.*

J

Jabā (India; Bengal). Long wooden plectrum occasionally used in *sarōd* playing.

Ja-bara (Korea). See *Chabara. Ja-bara* (*bara*) is the same as the Chinese *po*, a cymbal of varying sizes used in Buddhist temples and by military bands. It is also favored by the shamans in Mongolia. See *Tong-pal.*
Lit.: no. 179.

Jadaghara (India; Bengal). War drum. The term signifies also the trumpeting sound of elephants.

Jagā (*Yagā*; *Yak-gāh*) (Arabia; Persia; Egypt). In Persian: "the first." The tone name of the first main note, the basis of various scales. There is no common basic scale that would serve as foundation of Arabic music. Scales with various microtonal features such as those of Turkey, Syria, Iraq, and Egypt differ noticeably from the almost diatonic western types of Tunisia, Algeria, and Morocco. Scale and tone names may be the same in different areas, but pitches and intervals differ from one place to the other.

The following chart (see pp. 296-97) represents a theoretically established material scale with 24 microtones in the octave, displaying tone names and approximate pitches within the gamut of two octaves.
Lit.: nos. 56, 202, 257.

Jagā (*Yak-gāh*) (Arabia). *Maqām.*
Tone material:

G A $\overset{+}{B\flat}$ C D $\overset{+}{E\flat}$ (E) F (F♯) G

Lit.: no. 64.

Jagābharaṇam (South India). *Janya rāga* of the 64th *mēḷa* (*Vāchaspatī*).
Tone material:

C D F♯ E F♯ G A B♭ c

c B♭ A G F♯ E F♯ D C

Lit.: no. 139.

Jagadambari (South India). *Janya rāga* of the 52nd *mēḷa* (*Rāmapriyā*).
Tone material:

C E F♯ G A B♭

B♭ A G F♯ G E D♭ C *B♭* C

The scale of this *rāga* has *niṣādāntya* character.
Cf. *rāga Chintāramaṇi* (52nd *mēḷa*).
Lit.: no. 139.

Jagadbari (South India). *Janya rāga* of the 54th *mēḷa* (*Viśvambharī*). (A variant of *Jagadambari* of the 52nd *mēḷa*.)
Tone material:

C E F♯ G A♯ B

B A♯ G F♯ G E D♭ C *B* C

The scale of this *rāga* has *niṣādāntya* character.
Lit.: no. 139.

MATERIAL SCALE

Theoretically Established, with 24 Microtones in the Octave

Pitch	*Egypt*	*Arabia*	*Syria*	
G	*Jagā* (*Yagā*)	*Yak-gāh*	*Ja-gā*	Persian: "The first"
	Nam ḥiṣār (*qaba ḥiṣar*)	*Nim qarār-ḥiṣār*	*Nam ḥiṣār*	
	Ḥiṣār qaba	*Ḍarār ḥiṣār*	*Ḥiṣār*	
	Taq ḥiṣār qaba (*shurī*)	*Tiq-qarār-ḥiṣār*	*Taq ḥiṣār*	
A	*'Ashirān*	*'Ushayrān*	*'Ashirān*	
	Nam-'ajam-'ashirān	*Nim-'ajam-'ushayrān*	*Nam 'ajām*	
	'Ajam-'ashirā	*'Ajam-'ushayrān*	*'Ajām*	
+ *B*♭	*'Irāq*	*'Irāq*	*'Irāq*	
	Nam gushat	*Nim gavāsht*	*Kawasht*	
	Gushat (*Kushat*)	*Gavāsht*	*Taq kawasht*	
C	*Rāst*	*Rāst*	*Rāst*	Persian: "The straight tone"
	Nam-zarkala (*Nam-zirkulah*)	*Nim-zirgūlah*	*Nam zarkala*	
	Zarkala (*Zirkula*)	*Zirgulah*	*Zarkala*	
	Taq-zarkala (*Taq-zirkula*)	*Tik-zirgūlah*	*Taq zarkala*	
D	*Dugā*	*Du-Gāh* (*Dukāh*)	*Dugā*	"The second"
	Nam Kurdī (*Hahawānd*)	*Nim Kurdī*	*Nam Kurdī*	
	Kurdī	*Kurdī*	*Kurdī*	
+ E♭	*Sigā*	*Sah-Gāh* (*Sikāh*)	*Sigā*	"The third"
	Nam būselik	*Nim būsalik*	*Buselik*	"The kiss"
	Būselik (*'Ushaq*)	*Busālik*	*Taq buselik*	
F	*Jargā*	*Charhar-gāh* (*Chaharkāh*)	*Jahargā*	"The fourth"
	Nam hijaz	*Nim hijaz* (*'Araba*)	*'Araba*	
(F♯)	*Ḥijāz* (*Ṣaba*)	*Ḥijāz*	*Ḥijāz*	
	Taq-hijāz (*Taq-ṣaba*)	*Tik-ḥijāz*	*Taq-ḥijāz*	
G	*Nawā*	*Nawā*	*Nawa*	Arabian: kernel; "The center of reason." Persian: "The one full of sound."
	Nam ḥiṣār	*Nim-ḥiṣār*	*Nam ḥiṣar*	
	Ḥisār (*shurī*)	*Ḥisār*	*Ḥisār*	
	Taq-hisār	*Tik-ḥiṣār*	*Taq-ḥiṣār*	
A	*Ḥusēnī*	*Ḥusaynī* (*Ḥussenī*)	*Ḥusēni*	Arabian: named after Holy Ḥusēni Ibn Ali.
	Nam 'ajam	*Nim 'ajam Ḥusaynī*	*Nam 'ajām*	
	'Ajam (*Noiriz*)	*'Ajam Ḥusaynī*	*'Ajam* (*Ḥussaynī*)	
+ B♭	*'Auj*	*'Auj* (*'Irāq*)	*Aug*	Persian: *Auk*, "The high one."

MATERIAL SCALE—(*continued*)
Theoretically Established, with 24 Microtones in the Octave

Pitch	*Egypt*	*Arabia*	*Syria*	
	Nam māhūr	*Nim-nihuft (Nim-māhūr)*	*Nahaft*	
	Māhūr (Nahaft)	*Nihuft*	*Taq-nahaft*	
c	*Kardā*	*Kardān (Kirdān)*	*Mahūr*	Persian: "The frontier"
	Nam shāh'nāz	*Nim shāh'nāz*	*Nam shah'nāz*	
	Shāh'nāz	*Shah'naz*	*Shah'naz*	
	Taq-shāh'nāz	*Tik-shāh'nāz*	*Taq-shah-nāz*	
d	*Muḥajer*	*Muḥayir*	*Muḥajer*	Arabian: "The whimsical"
	Nam-sunbula	*Nim-sumbulaḥ*	*Sunbula*	Persian: "The rose"
	Sunbula (Zawal)	*Sunbulaḥ*	*Zawāl*	
+eb	*Jwab-Sigā (Bazruq)*	*Buzurg*	*Buzruq*	
	Jwab-nam-būselik	*Nim-jāwāb-būsalik*	*Ḥusēni-shad*	
	Jwab-būselik	*Jawāb-būsalik*	*Taq-ḥusēni-shad*	
f	*Jwab-Jargā (Māhūrāni)*	*Māhūrān*	*Māhūrāni*	Arabian: "Trotting horse"
	Jwab-nam-ḥijāz	*Nim-jawāb-ḥijāz*	*Jwab-nam-ḥijaz*	
	Jwab-ḥijāz-ṣaba	*Jawāb-hijāz*	*Jwab-hijaz*	
	Jwab-taq-ḥijaz (ṣaba)	*Tik-jawāb-ḥijāz*	*Jwab-taq-ḥijaz*	
g	*Jwab Nawā*	*Ramal Tūtī*	*Ramal Tuti*	

Jagadīśvari (South India). *Janya rāga* of the 34th *mēḷa* (*Vāgadhīśvarī*).
Tone material:

C D# E F A Bb c

c Bb A F E D# C

Lit.: no. 139.

Jagajhampa (India). Sanskrit and Bengali term for a small wooden tube drum with two heads that are beaten with sticks. In the South this drum is called *naguar*.
Lit.: no. 254.

Jagamaṇi (South India). *Janya rāga* of the 20th *mēḷa* (*Naṭabhairavī*).
Tone material:

C D F Eb F Ab Bb G Ab Bb c

c G F Eb D C

Lit.: no. 139.

Ja-gaṇa (South India). See *Ashta gaṇas*.

Jagāṅgana (South India). *Janya rāga* of the 42nd *mēḷa* (*Raghupriyā*).
Tone material:

C Db Ebb F# G B A# B c

c B G F# Db Ebb F# Db C

Lit.: no. 139.

Jaganmanōhari (South India). *Janya rāga* of the 29th *mēḷa* (*Dhīraśaṅkarābharaṇam*).
Tone material:

C E F G A B c

c A G F E D E C

Lit.: no. 139.

Jaganmāta (South India). *Janya rāga* of the 30th *mēḷa* (*Nāgānandī*).

Tone material:

C E G A♯ B c

c B A♯ G E C

Lit.: no. 139.

Jaganmohana (South India). (1) The 38th *asampūrṇa mēḷa-rāga* without *kaṭapayādi* prefix. (2) The 38th *asampūrṇa mēḷa-rāga* with *kaṭapayādi* prefix. See *Rāga* (South India).
Lit.: no. 139.

Jaganmōhanam (South India). *Janya rāga* of the 38th *mēḷa* (*Jalārṇava*).
Tone material:

C D♭ F♯ G A♭ c B♭ c

c B♭ A♭ G F♯ E♭♭ D♭ C

Lit.: no. 139.

Jaganmōhanī (South India). See *Jaganmōhinī.*

Jaganmōhinī (South India). Also called *Jaganmōhanī. Janya rāga* of the 15th *mēḷa* (*Māyāmāḷavagauḷa*).
Tone material:

C E F G B c

c B G F E D♭ C

Lit.: no. 139.

Jāgaṭe (*Jēgaṭe*) (South India). Kannarese term. See *Jegaṇṭa.*

Jaharkāh (*Chahar-gāh*) (Arabia). "The fourth." Tone name. (All tone names within the range of two octaves are listed under the heading of *Jagā* [*Yagā*].) Cf. *Jargā.*

Jait (*Jayat*; *Jet*) (North India). (Not to be mistaken for *Jayat-Kalyan.*) *Jait* is ascribed to the *Marva thāta.*
Its tone material shows the following forms:

(a) C D♭ E G A (B) c
 c A G E D♭ C

(b) C D♭ E F♯ G A (B) c
 c A G F♯ E D♭ C

(c) C D♭ E F♯ G (A♭) A (B) c (d)
 c A (A♭) G F♯ E D♭ C

Lit.: no. 138.

Jait-Kalyan (North India). See *Jayat-Kalyan.*

Jaitshankara (North India). Obscure *rāga.* It is a combination of the materials of either the *rāgas Shankara* and *Jait* or *Shankara* and *Jayat Kalyan.*
Lit.: no. 138.

Jajin mori (Korea). See *Chachin mori.*

Jājīvasantam (South India). *Janya rāga* of the 29th *mēḷa* (*Dhīraśaṅkarābharaṇam*).
Tone material:

C D E F G A B c

c A G F D E C

Lit.: no. 139.

Jakhē (Thailand). Zither with three strings struck with an ivory plectrum. Its head has the shape of a crocodile.

Jakki (South India). Temple drum.
Lit.: no. 261.

Jakkulu (South India). Dancers, singers belonging to a specific class.
Lit.: no. 261.

Jaksa (Java). "The judge." The gong whose sound divides the compositions into (audible) sections.
Lit.: no. 163.

Jaladhara-Kedar (North India). *Rāga* ascribed to the *Bilaval thāta.*
Tone material:

C D F (F♯) G A (B) c

c (B) A G F D C; *Vādis*: F(G), (D)

Lit.: no. 138.

Jalajamukhi (South India). *Janya rāga* of the 68th *mēḷa* (*Jyōtisvarūpiṇi*).
Tone material:

C D♯ E F♯ G A♭ c

c B♭ A♭ B♭ G F♯ D♯ E C

Lit.: no. 139.

Jalajavāsini (South India). *Janya rāga* of the 27th *mēḷa* (*Sarasāṅgī*).
Tone material:
C E F G B c
c B A♭ G F D C
Lit.: no. 139.

Jalājil (*Jaljil*) (Arabia). Bells.
Lit.: no. 70.

Jālaprabala (South India). *Janya rāga* of the 29th *mēḷa* (*Dhīraśaṅkarābharaṇam*).
Tone material:
F G A B C D E F
F E D C *B A G F*
This *rāga* has *madhyamāntya* character.
Lit.: no. 139.

Jalasugandhi (South India). *Janya rāga* of the 38th *mēḷa* (*Jalārṇava*).
Tone material:
C D♭ E♭♭ F♯ G A♭ c
c A♭ G F♯ E♭♭ D♭ C
Lit.: no. 139.

Jālatarāṅgam (South India). See *Jāltarāng*.

Jaler (Java). String. See *Rebāb*.

Ja-ling (Tibet). Pronunciation of *Rgya-gling* (*rGya-gling*).

Jaljil (Arabia). See *Jüljül*.

Jalōddhati (South India). *Janya rāga* of the 29th *mēḷa* (*Dhīraśaṅkarābharaṇam*).
Tone material:
C D F G B c
c A G F D E F D C
Lit.: no. 139.

Jalōdharam (South India). *Janya rāga* of the 63rd *mēḷa* (*Latāṅgī*).
Tone material:
C D E F♯ G A♭ B c
c B A♭ B G E F♯ E D C
Lit.: no. 139.

Jālra (*Guṇḍu tālam*) (India). Pair of cymbals of various sizes. Cf. *Brahmatālam*.
Lit.: no. 260.

Jāltarāng (South India; *Jālatarāṅgam*) (India). Chime of porcelain cups filled with water to various levels in order to achieve a required scale. The cups are placed in a semicircle around the player who strikes them with thin wooden sticks. The number of cups varies: usually there are 14-18 producing a scale between two to three octaves.

Jamangan (*Dodot*) (Java). A velvet robe, richly ornamented, in which the *rebāb* is preserved.
Lit.: no. 163.

Jambala (*Tambala*) (Nepal). Term for the Indian *tabla* pair.
Lit.: no. 46.

Jambukriya (South India). *Janya rāga* of the 29th *mēḷa* (*Dhīraśaṅkarābharaṇam*).
Tone material:
C E D F G B c
c B G B F E D C
Lit.: no. 139.

Jām dunbalayī (Turkey). Kettledrum. Its corpus is made of glass.
Lit.: no. 81.

Jamisen (Japan; Ryu-kyu). A three-stringed lute type resembling the *shamisen*. It became popular during the 16th century. The instrument came from the Ryu-kyu islands and is believed to have had its origin in the *san-hsien* of China.
The *jamisen* has a similar corpus as the *shamisen*, rectangular with rounded corners or in oval shape, and was first covered with snake-skin, later with cat-skin. It has a long slim neck, three silken strings, large lateral pegs, no frets, and is played with an ivory or tortoise shell plectrum. The tuning of the strings is generally in *honchōshi* (1, 4, 8). See *Shamisen*.
Lit.: nos. 185, 225.

Jamplakan (Java). See *Chiblonan.*

Janaka mēḷa (*Janaka rāga*) (South India). A parent form (cf. *Mēḷa*) that has *krama sampūrṇa* (straight heptatonic) ascent and descent scales. The term has the same significance (primary *rāga*) as *mēḷa* (*mēḷakarta*). See *Rāga* (South India).
Lit.: no. 139.

Janaka(rāga) (South India). Old South Indian term for parent *rāga.* Traditionally each *janaka* has five wives and four sons, and each son has one wife. At present *janaka rāga* and *mēḷa rāga* have the same meaning. See *Rāga* (South India).
Lit.: nos. 138-39.

Janākarṣaṇi (South India). *Janya rāga* of the 16th *mēḷa* (*Chakravāka*).
Tone material:
C D♭ E G F A B♭ c
c B♭ A G F E A F E D♭ C
Lit.: no. 139.

Janānandi (South India). *Janya rāga* of the 40th *mēḷa* (*Navanītam*).
Tone material:
C D♭ E♭♭ F♯ A c
c A F♯ E♭♭ D♭ C
Lit.: no. 139.

Janānandini (South India). *Janya rāga* of the 20th *mēḷa* (*Naṭabhairavī*).
Tone material:
C D E♭ D E♭ F G B♭ A♭ G B♭ c
c B♭ A♭ G F D E♭ F D C
Lit.: no. 139.

Janāndōḷika (South India). *Janya rāga* of the 22nd *mēḷa* (*Kharaharapriyā*).
Tone material:
C D E♭ D E♭ F G B♭ A G B♭ c
c B♭ A G F D E♭ F D C
Lit.: no. 139.

Janani (South India). *Janya rāga* of the 52nd *mēḷa* (*Rāmapriyā*).
Tone material:
C D♭ E F♯ G A B♭ c
c B♭ A G F♯ E D♭ E C
Lit.: no. 139.

Janarañjaṇi (South India). *Janya rāga* of the 29th *mēḷa* (*Dhīraśaṅkarābharaṇam*).
Tone material:
C D E F G A G B c
c A G F D C
Lit.: no. 139.

Janasammōdini (South India). *Janya rāga* of the 28th *mēḷa* (*Harikāmbhōji*).
Tone material:
C D E G A B♭ c
c B♭ A G E D C
Lit.: no. 139.

Janatōḍi (South India). See *Tōḍi* (South India). Also see *Tōḍi* (8th *asampūrṇa mēḷa*).

Janavarāḷi (South India). *Janya rāga* of the 15th *mēḷa* (*Māyāmāḷavagauḷa*).
Tone material:
C E D♭ E F A♭ B A♭ c
c B A♭ G F E F D♭ E F D♭ C
Lit.: no. 139.

Jangala (North India). See *Jangla.*

Jaṅgala (South India). *Janya rāga* of the 29th *mēḷa* (*Dhīraśaṅkarābharaṇam*).
Tone material:
A B C D E F G A B
B G F E D C *B A*
This *rāga* has *niṣādāntya* character.
Lit.: no. 139.

Janger (*Djanger*) (Bali). A sequence of traditional folk dances accompanied by songs with meaningless textual syllables sung in unison by a group of children. The instrumental accompaniment consists of: two *gender*, one *suling*, a

kajar and *klenang*, one *lemana*, and a *tjeng-tjeng*. The dancers (girls and boys) sit on the floor, forming a rectangle and sing, while moving their upper bodies, hands, arms, and heads. Cf. *Sanghyang*.
Lit.: no. 197.

Janget (Java). See *Bonang* (*Pluntur*).

Jangla (*Jangala*) (North India). A rare *rāga* ascribed to the *Asavari thāta*.
Tone material:
C D (E) F G A♭ (A) B♭ c d
c B♭ A♭ G F E♭ D C
Lit.: no. 138.

Jangula (North India). A rare *rāga* ascribed to the *Bhairav thāta*.
Tone material:
C D♭ E F G A♭ (A) B c
c B (B♭) (A) A♭ G F E D♭ C
Lit.: no. 138.

Janil (Micronesia; Satawal). Bamboo or mangrove root tube used as nose flute.
Lit.: no. 313.

Jañjhūṭi (*Juñjhūṭi*) (South India). *Janya rāga* of the 28th *mēḷa* (*Harikāmbhōji*).
Tone material:
A C D E F G A B♭
A G F E D C *B♭ A G A* C
Lit.: no. 139.

Jank (*Cank*; *Chank*) (Persia; Afghanistan). A dulcimer in triangular form (rarely rectangular) with six strings played with sticks or plectrum. (In the *Kitāb al-adwār* of Safī al-Dīn 'Abd al-Mu'min [d. 1294], a manuscript preserved in the National Library Cairo, a *jank* is depicted with 34 strings.) Cf. *Wann*.
Lit.: no. 254.

Jank (Turkey). Bell.

Jank miṣrī (Egypt). Triangular harp dating back to the 11th century.
Lit.: no. 65.

Jantarungrai (East India; Orissa). Stick zither. Its resonance corpus is held against the chest of the player. The upper end of the zither stick is held between the lips of the player.

Jantur (Java). See *Gantung*.

Jānudvaya (South India). *Janya rāga* of the 28th *mēḷa* (*Harikāmbhōji*).
Tone material:
C D E F B♭ c
c A G F E D C
Lit.: no. 139.

Janya (South India). A subordinate *rāga* derived from one of the 72 *mēḷas* (*mēḷakarta rāgas*).

Janya sampūrṇa (South India). A *janya rāga* which employs all seven notes within the octave.
Lit.: no. 139.

Japka (Korea). See *Chapka*.

Jarami (*Dami*) (Indonesia; Sunda District). A rice-stalk clarinet. The tube has 2-3 finger holes. The instrument is called by various names: in Nias it is called *lai waghe*; in the Toba district, *oli-oli*; in the Sunda district, *jarami* or *dami*; in Central Java, *de(r)men(an)*. Among the Sa'dan Torajas it is called *om-om*; in the Northwest Toraja district, *pe-peon*; in the Alas district, *iyup-iyup*; in East Sumbawa, *kafu*. The ancient rice-stalk clarinet in Hindu-Javanese literature was called *damya-damyan*.
Lit.: no. 163.

Jaran Kepang (Central Java). Cf. *Reyog*.

Jaran sirig (Bali). Simple melody.
Lit.: no. 197.

Jaras (*Ǧaras*) (Arabia). Small bell.
Lit.: no. 255.

Jaraśēkharam (South India). *Janya rāga* of the 28th *mēḷa* (*Harikāmbhōji*).
Tone material:
C D E F G A B♭ c
c B♭ A G F B♭ A F E D F E C
Lit.: no. 139.

Jargā (Arabia). See *Jaharkāh.*

Jargā (*Chahar-gāh*; *Jahar-kāh*; *Ǧarǧā*) (Arabia; Persia). The Persian term indicates the fourth main note of the scale. In Arabic music the term refers to the seventh main note of the scale. (A complete list of notes and tone names can be seen under the heading of *Jagā* [*Yagā*].) As *maqām, Jargā* is identical with *maqām Sasgar.*
Tone material:

C D E♭(+) F G A B♭ c

Lit.: no. 121.

Jariang (Northeast Thailand). Khmer singing that resembles *lao mawlum.*
Lit.: no. 203.

Jarīgha (India). Large temple-cymbals.

Jarupei (Southeast Borneo). Small bamboo flute with three finger holes.
Lit.: no. 255.

Jata (*Gareng-gareng*) (Flores; Ende). Bull roarer; whizzing bow. A variety of names is in use: in Nias, *riwi-riwi-löchö*; in the Toba district, *dengeng-dengeng*; in Cental Java, *(o)-wer-(o)wer* or *ereg-ereg*; in the Sunda district, *kekinchiran*; in Timor, Alor, Ternate, *bubuwas*; in the Malay Peninsula, *berbaling, baling* (*balling-balling*).
Lit.: no. 166.

Jaṭādhari (South India). *Janya rāga* of the 52nd *mēḷa* (*Rāmapriyā*).
Tone material:

C E D♭ F♯ G A B♭ c
c B♭ A G E D♭ C

Lit.: no. 139.

Jatag (*Jataga*) (Mongolia). A zither of the western and Khalka Mongols and of the Volga Kalmucks. The Chakhar Mongols call it *itag* or *jitag* (*yitag*). In Central Asia and Iran it is called *yaduga.* The *jatag* is a long, rectangular box that shows a downward angle at one end. The instrument has 12 silken strings; the Volga Kalmucks use 7-8 metal or gut strings. The strings are never stopped but always used open. The Sunit Mongols tune the zither:

The instrument is played either with thumb and forefinger or with two plectra (called *khume*, nail).
Lit.: no. 61.

Jataga (Mongolia). See *Jatag.*

Jāti (Ancient India). (1) An ancient term that represented seven *śuddha* (pure) and 11 *vikṛta* (modified) scales. The *śuddha jātis* differed from the *mūrchhaṇās* in possessing the following characteristic features and thus were the forerunners of the *rāgas*: *graha*, the initial note; *nyāsa*, the final note; *aṁśa*, the central (stressed) note; *apanyāsa*, the secondary final note. See Lit. no. 261.

The seven *śuddha jātis* were named after the seven tone names: *ṣāḍjī*, *ārṣabhī*, *gāndhārī*, *madhyamadī*, *pañchamī*, *dhaivatī*, and *naiṣādī*. Each of these seven tones functioned as *nyāsa* (final note).

The 11 *vikṛta jātis* showing various modifications (except the *nyāsa* notes) were called: *ṣāḍjamadhyamā*, *ṣāḍjakaiśikī*, *ṣāḍ-jodīcyavati*, *gāndhārodīcyavā*, *madhyamodīcyavā*, *raktagāndhāri*, *āndhrī*, *nāndayantī*, *gandhārapañchamī*, *karmāravī*, *kaiśikī*. These *vikṛta jātis* were constructed by combining sections of the *śuddha jātis.*

(2) Each *aṁśa* of a *jāti* was linked with a *rasa* as shown below (cf. Lit. no. 292): *ṣāḍja*

and *ṛṣabha*, heroism, fury and wonder; *gāndhāra*, pity; *madhyama* and *pañchama*, mirth and love; *dhaivata*, disgust and terror; *niṣāda*, pity.

(3) In South India the term *jāṭi* is still in use, particularly referring to characteristics of rhythmic modes (cf. *Tāla*).
Lit.: nos. 136, 140.

Jatilan (Java). Dance play with music. Cf. *Reog* (2).
Lit.: no. 163.

Jatisvaram (India). The second dance of the *bharata nāṭyam* performance. It represents the praise of the deity. Musically this section is of interest because a *rāga-malika* is presented. The singer employs solmization syllables as text and is accompanied by a cross flute, a jew's harp, a barrel drum, and a reed box (*śruti*). The dance provides the performer with the opportunity of showing her art of musical interpretation.

Jatra (India). Audience singing in operatic folk performance.

Jaṭshrintāmaṇi (South India). See *Chintāmaṇi.*

Jauḍa Gāndhāri (South India). *Janya rāga* of the 68th *mēḷa* (*Jyōtisvarūpiṇī*).
Tone material:
C D# E F# G A♭ c
c B♭ A♭ G F# E D# C
Lit.: no. 139.

Jauje (North Nigeria—Hausa). Drum with two heads beaten with a stick. It is similar to the *gangan* of the Yoruba.
Lit.: no. 293.

Jaumin (New Guinea—Kate). Hourglass drum.
Lit.: no. 25.

Jaunpuri (*Jivanpuri*; *Yavanapuri*) (North India). *Rāga* ascribed to the *Asavari thāta.*
Tone material:
C D F G A♭ B♭ c
c B♭ A♭ G F E♭ D C
Lit.: no. 138.

Javā (India). See *Jawā.*

Jāvali (South India). A *shabdam* of cheerful but religious character; usually a love story of Krishna is presented in a form similar to the *tappa* of North India. *Jāvali* appears as the third item of the *bharata nāṭyam* performance.

Javanika (South India). *Janya rāga* of the 18th *mēḷa* (*Hāṭakāmbarī*).
Tone material:
C D♭ E G A# B c
c B A# G E D♭ C
Lit.: no. 139.

Javata (Tanganyika—Washambala). Side-blown animal horn.
Lit.: no. 130.

Javōnnati (South India). *Janya rāga* of the 29th *mēḷa* (*Dhīraśaṅkarābharaṇam*).
Tone material:
C D E G A B G c
c B G A G F E D C
Lit.: no. 139.

Jawā (*Javā*) (India). A wooden plectrum that is used when playing certain lutes that need not be plucked at all occasions but can be bowed as well. Other lutes that are never bowed and have to be plucked at all occasions have to use the *mizrab*, a wire plectrum.
Lit.: nos. 163, 254.

Jawa (New Guinea). See *Wōn-wōn.*

Jawāb (Arabia). An antiphon to the *tarjī'*. An opening brief melody and a concluding section; both create a musical frame to the *tarjī'*.
Lit.: no. 76.

Jawāb-būsalik (*Jwab-būselik*) (Arabia). Tone name of a note approximately a semitone higher than *jwab-sigā* (*buzurg*). (A list of all tone names and notes through two octaves can be seen under the heading of *Jagā* [*Yagā*].)

Jawāb-ḥijāz (Arabia). See *Jwab-ḥijāz-ṣaba.*

Jawar (Java). Also *biasa* ("normal"). One of the (theoretically 45) *surupan melog* scales, beginning with *singgul*:

Tones in approx. cents (top)

I 120	II 150	III	[IV]	390
singgul	*galimer*	*panelu*	(*liwung*)	

Tone names (bottom)

Tones in approx. cents (top)

V 120	VI	[VII]	420 I
kenong	*barang*	(*sorong*)	

Tone names (bottom)

Liwung and *sorog* are auxiliary tones. See *Surupan melog.*
Lit.: no. 163.

Jawil (Java; Sunda District). A gently and only incidentally intoned sound. *Jawil* is the term for an intermediate tone that would have to appear between the IV (*kenong*) and V (*barang*) scale degrees of the *slendro* system of the Sunda District.
Lit.: no. 163.

Jawwāq (Algeria). See *Juwak.*

Jaya (India). Ancient flute.
Lit.: no. 255.

Jayabharaṇam (South India). *Janya rāga* of the 17th *mēḷa* (*Sūryakānta*).
Tone material:
C D♭ E F G A B c
c A B G F D♭ E F D♭ C
Lit.: no. 139.

Jayābharaṇi (South India). *Janya rāga* of the 27th *mēḷa* (*Sarasāṅgī*).
Tone material:
C E F G F D E F G c
c B A♭ G F D C
Lit.: no. 139.

Jayabhēri (South India). Victory drum.
Lit.: no. 261.

Jayadhakka (India). Big drum used in battle and at festivals.
Lit.: no. 255.

Jayaghanta (India). Large bell used in battle and during festivals.
Lit.: no. 255.

Jayākṣari (South India). *Janya rāga* of the 22nd *mēḷa* (*Kharaharapriyā*).
Tone material:
C E♭ F G A c
c B♭ A G F E♭ D E♭ D C
Lit.: no. 139.

Jayamañjari (South India). *Janya rāga* of the 22nd *mēḷa* (*Kharaharapriyā*).
Tone material:
C E♭ G A B♭ c
c B♭ G A G F D E♭ D C
Lit.: no. 139.

Jayamanoharī (South India). *Janya rāga* of the 22nd *mēḷa* (*Kharaharapriyā*).
Tone material:
C D E♭ F A c
c B♭ A F E♭ D C
Lit.: no. 139.

Jayamōhanam (South India). *Janya rāga* of the 53rd *mēḷa* (*Gamanaśrama*).
Tone material:
C E F♯ G A c
c B A G F♯ E D♭ C
Lit.: no. 139.

Jayanārāyaṇi (South India). *Janya rāga* of the 22nd *mēḷa* (*Kharaharapriyā*).
Tone material:
C D E♭ F G A c
c B♭ A G F E♭ D C
Lit.: no. 139.

Jaya Nrityam (South India). Victory dance.

Jayanta Sēna (South India). *Janya rāga* of the 22nd *mēḷa* (*Kharaharapriyā*).
Tone material:
C E♭ F G A c
c B♭ A G F E♭ C
Lit.: no. 139.

Jayantaśrī (South India). *Janya rāga* of the 20th *mēḷa* (*Naṭabhairavī*).
Tone material:
C E♭ F A♭ B♭ c
c B♭ A♭ F G F E♭ D C
Lit.: no. 139.

Jayant Mallar (North India). A rare and obscure *rāga* which is ascribed to the *Kafi thāta* and belongs to the *Mallar* family of *rāgas*. It consists of combinations of (*rāga*) *Jayjayvanti* and (*rāga*) *Mallar* phrases.
The tone material can be (e.g.):
C D F D G B♭ G F G c
c B♭ A B♭ G E F D E♭ D C; *Vādis*: G, C
Lit.: no. 138.

Jayarāma (South India). *Janya rāga* of the 28th *mēḷa* (*Harikāmbhōji*).
Tone material:
C D E F G A B♭ c
c B♭ A G F E C
Lit.: no. 139.

Jayasāraṅga (South India). *Janya rāga* of the 57th *mēḷa* (*Siṃhendramadhyama*).
Tone material:
C D E♭ F♯ G F♯ A♭ B c
c B A♭ F♯ G A♭ F♯ E♭ D C
Lit.: no. 139.

Jayasāveri (South India). *Janya rāga* of the 5th *mēḷa* (*Manōrañjanī*).
Tone material:
C F D♭ E♭♭ F G A B
A G F E♭♭ D♭ C *B* C
Lit.: no. 139.

Jayashringa (*Jayaśṛṅga*) (India). See *Ranaśṛṅga*.
Lit.: no. 255.

Jaya Sindhu (South India). *Janya rāga* of the 2nd *mēḷa* (*Ratnangi*).
Tone material:
C D♭ E♭♭ F G c
c G B♭ A♭ F E♭♭ D♭ C
Lit.: no. 139.

Jayaśrī (South India). *Janya rāga* of the 21st *mēḷa* (*Kiravāṇi*).
Tone material:
C D E♭ F G A♭ B A♭ c
c B A♭ G F E♭ D C
Lit.: no. 139.

Jayaśrīkanthi (South India). *Janya rāga* of the 46th *mēḷa* (*Śaḍvidhamārgiṇī*).
Tone material:
C E♭ F♯ G A B♭ c
c B♭ A G F♯ E♭ C
Lit.: no. 139.

Jayaśuddhamāḷavi (South India). See *Hāṭakāmbarī*. See also *Śuddhamāḷavi* (18th *asampūrṇa mēḷa*).

Jayaśuka (South India). *Janya rāga* of the 71st *mēḷa* (*Kōsala*).
Tone material:
C D♯ E F♯ G A B c
c A G F♯ E F♯ D♯ C
Lit.: no. 139.

Jayat (North India). See *Jait*.

Jayat-Kalyan (*Jait-*; *Jet-Kalyan*) (North India). *Rāga* ascribed to the *Kalyan thāta*.
Tone material:
C E G c
c (A) G E D C
Lit.: no. 138.

Jayavēlavaḷi (South India). *Janya rāga* of the 43rd *mēḷa* (*Gavāmbōdhi*).
Tone material:
C D♭ E♭ F♯ A♭ G A♭ B♭♭ c
c B♭♭ A♭ F♯ E♭ D♭ C
Lit.: no. 139.

Jayjayvanti (North India). *Rāga* ascribed to the *Khamaj thāta.* Two types are distinguished:

1. *Jayjayvanti, Sorath-anga,* the older type, considered to be the genuine *Jayjayvanti* form. It resembles *rāga Sorath.*
2. *Jayjayvanti, Bageshri-anga,* resembling *rāga Bageshri,* of recent origin.

Tone materials:

(a) *Sorath* *Khamaj* *Kafi*
B C D F G B c c B♭ A G F E D E♭ D C

(b) *Bageshri* *Kafi*
C A B♭ D E F A B♭ c c B♭ A B F E D E♭ D C
Vādis: D, G

A brief *kafi* passage appears usually in the descent of both types.
Lit.: no. 138.

Jede (Flores; Nage District). Festive dance performed by women when buffaloes are slaughtered.
Lit.: no. 166.

Jeḍor (Java; Sunda District). A large conical one-headed drum.
Lit.: no. 163.

Jeḍoran (Java). Cf. *Jeḍor*; *Slawatan.*

Jegaṇṭa (South India). Telugu term for a single circular metal disc that hangs in the entrance of a temple and is beaten by every devotee who enters. Other names of this disc are: *ghaṛī*; *ghaṛiyāl*; *ghaṛiyāval*; *śegaṇḍi* (in Tamil); *jegaṭe*; *jāgaṭe* (in Kannarese).
Lit.: no. 254.

Jegogan (Bali). The sound and instruments of a *gamelan* ensemble which perform the "cantus firmus" in long held notes.
Lit.: nos. 197, 265.

Jejaok (Indonesia; Mentawei Isl.). Jew's harp.
Lit.: no. 255.

Jejilava (Malagasy Republic). Musical bow.
Lit.: no. 251.

Jejy (Malagasy Republic; Uganda). Stick zither.
Lit.: no. 251.

Jele-masha (Turkey). Metal clapper.
Lit.: no. 255.

Jeljel (Persia). See *Jinjil.*

Jemblok (East Java). See *Gong jemblok*; *Gong kemodong.*

Jemblung (Java). A *gamelan* with bamboo instruments that accompany the *wayang jemblung.* In use are: *gong suwukan* (*jemblung*), *kempul, kenong, ketuk, demung, saron, kendang, gumbeng* (*bumbung*).
Lit.: no. 163.

Jeme (Congo – Balesa-Basa). Drum.
Lit.: no. 26.

Jeneng (*Watangan*) (Java). See *Rebāb* (Java).

Jengglong (West Java). A typical West Javanese *gamelan* consisting of seven kettles tuned in *pelog* and six tuned in *slendro.* The sounds produced represent the gamut of the lowest of the four octaves of the *gamelan.* Cf. *Kedemung*; *Saron*; *Peking.* Also called *saron jengglong.*
Lit.: no. 159.

Jengking (Java). A *suluk* (of *slendro patet sanga*) performed when a saint and a sage make an appearance. In Solonese performances *suluk jengking* is also performed during love scenes.
Lit.: no. 163.

Jeru gender (Bali). The musicians (placed behind the *dalang*) who accompany the *wayang* play.
Lit.: no. 197.

Jerupai (Borneo). A woodwind instrument with a free-beating reed.
Lit.: no. 157.

Jet (North India). A *rāga.* See *Jait.*

Jetashri (*Jetshri*) (North India). *Rāga* ascribed to the *Purvi thāta.*
Tone material:
C E F# G B c
c B Ab G F# E Db C; *Vādis*: E, B
Lit.: no. 138.

Jet-Kalyan (North India). See *Jayat-Kalyan.*

Jetshri (North India). See *Jetashri.*

Jeu (Japan). See *Ju.*

Jhālakēśari (South India). *Janya rāga* of the 45th *mēḷa* (*Śubhapantuvarālī*).
Tone material:
C Db F# G Ab B c
c Ab G F# Db C
Lit.: no. 139.

Jhālamañjari (South India). *Janya rāga* of the 22nd *mēḷa* (*Kharaharapriyā*).
Tone material:
C D Eb G A Bb c
c Bb G A G F D C D D
Lit.: no. 139.

Jhalārṇava (South India). (1) The 38th *mēḷa*:
C Db Ebb F# G Ab Bb c
(2) As *rāga* it uses the same scale.
Lit.: no. 139.

Jhālavarāḷi (South India). (1) The 39th *mēḷa*:
C Db Ebb F# G Ab B c
(2) As *rāga* it uses the same scale. Veṅkaṭamakhin (17th century) called this *rāga Dhālivarāḷi.*
Lit.: no. 139.

Jhallaka (India). Sanskrit term for cymbal. Cf. also *Jhampatāla.*

Jhallarī (*Jhallri*; *Jhalli*) (India). Cymbal.
Lit.: no. 254.

Jhalo (Indonesia; Ceram). Drum.
Lit.: no. 255.

Jhampa (India). See *Tāla* (North India); *Tāla* (South India).

Jhampatāla (India). See *Jhallaka.*

Jhamre (*Salaju*) (Nepal). Short love song in question and answer form.
Lit.: no. 133.

Jhaṇākāri (South India). *Janya rāga* of the 63rd *mēḷa* (*Latāṅgī*).
Tone material:
C D E F# G B Ab c
c Ab G F# D E D C
Lit.: no. 139.

Jhanjh (North India). Small cymbal with a flat rim and curved center.
Lit.: no. 250.

Jhānjha (India). See *Jhanjh.* The term indicates a pair of small, almost bell-shaped cymbals. Cf. also *Tāla.*
Lit.: no. 250.

Jhañjhana (India). Rattle (made of various materials). Cf. *Ravularavulā.*
Lit.: no. 254.

Jhanjhkhanjanī (India). Small frame drum with jingles inserted into its frame.
Lit.: no. 254.

Jhaṅkārabhramarī (South India). (1) See *Jhaṅkāradhvani.* (2) *Janya rāga* of the 19th *mēḷa* (*Jhaṅkāradhvani*).
Tone material:
C D Eb F G Ab Bbb Ab c
(C Eb D Eb F G Ab Bbb c)
c Bbb Ab G F Eb D C
Lit.: no. 139.

Jhaṅkārabhramarī (South India). (1) The 19th *asampūrṇa mēḷa-rāga* without *kaṭapayādi* prefix. (2) The 19th *asampūrṇa mēḷa-rāga* with *kaṭapayādi* prefix. See *Rāga* (South India).
Lit.: no. 139.

Jhaṅkāradhvani (South India). (1) The 19th *mēḷa*:

C D E♭ F G A♭ B♭♭ c

(2) As *rāga*, the same tone material is used in ascent and descent as shown above. Veṅkātamakhin (17th century) called this *rāga Jhaṅ kārabhramarī*.
Lit.: no. 139.

Jhaṅkāra śīla (South India). *Janya rāga* of the 29th *mēḷa* (*Dhīraśaṅkarābharaṇam*).
Tone material:

C D E F A B c
c B A F E D C

Lit.: no. 139.

Jhaṅkāravāṇi (South India). *Janya rāga* of the 20th *mēḷa* (*Naṭabhairavī*).
Tone material:

C E♭ D E♭ F G B♭ c
c B♭ A♭ G F D C

Lit.: no. 139.

Jhaṅkāri (South India). *Janya rāga* of the 19th *mēḷa* (*Jhaṅkāradhvani*).
Tone material:

C D E♭ F G A♭ c
c A♭ G F E♭ D C

Lit.: no. 139.

Jhaptāl (India). See *Tāla*.

Jharālata (South India). *Janya rāga* of the 29th *mēḷa* (*Dhīraśaṅkarābharaṇam*).
Tone material:

C D E F G A c
c B A G E D C

Lit.: no. 139.

Jharapuñjari (South India). *Janya rāga* of the 15th *mēḷa* (*Māyāmāḷavagauḷa*).
Tone material:

C D♭ E F A♭ B c
c B A♭ G F D♭ F E C

Lit.: no. 139.

Jhāriḍāp (East India; Bengal). (1) Pear-shaped clay drum with one head. (2) Small kettledrum. See *Ṭikārā*.
Lit.: nos. 254-55.

Jhiaure gīt (Nepal). Short love song. Cf. *Jhamre*.
Lit.: no. 133.

Jhilli (India). Sanskrit term for kettledrum (with metal kettle).

Jhinjhoti (North India). *Rāga* ascribed to the *Khamaj thāta*.
Tone material:

C D E F G A (B♭) B c
c B♭ A G F E D C; *Vādis*: E, A

Lit.: no. 138.

Jhīnāvaḷi (South India). *Janya rāga* of the 39th *mēḷa* (*Jhālavarāḷi*).
Tone material:

C E♭♭ D♭ E♭♭ F♯ G A♭ B A♭ c
c B A♭ G F♯ E♭♭ D♭ C

Lit.: no. 139.

Jhumar (North India; Baluchistan). Folk dance performed by hand clapping women or men in circular formation. There are several types of *jhumar*.
Lit.: no. 46.

Jhumbarī (India). Simple lute type.

Jhunjhuna (India). A gourd-shaped rattle used by children. The vessel of the rattle is made of wood or clay and is filled with seeds or small stones. Cf. *Kiri-kiri*; *Jhanjhana*.
Lit.: no. 255.

Jhyamta (North India). Dialectal term for cymbals; also used for drums. Cf. *Jhañjha*.

Ji (in Chinese writing: M 6198) (Japan). (1) Basic melodies of *noh* music played by the *nōhkan*. (2) The chorus of the *noh* play. (3) Group of *ōzatsuma* tunes played on the *shamisen* or derived from its music; motives used as basic material in recitatives in *nagauta*. (4) A set of drum patterns. Cf. *Kakari*.
Lit.: no. 185.

Ji (in Chinese writing: M 4953; M 5738) (Japan). Bridges on the *koto*.
Lit.: no. 185.

Ji (in Chinese writing: M 5598) (Japan). A *wagon* melodic pattern. Cf. *San*; *Oru*; *Tsumu*.
Lit.: no. 185.

Jiang (China). Term for *ch'in* in the Shanghai dialect.
Lit.: no. 255.

Jibyōshi (Japan). A set of complex rules and explanations how to combine textual lines of the *noh* play, consisting of certain numbers of syllables with different numbers of fixed musical beats. For further information see *Hira-nori*.
Lit.: no. 185.

Jiḍor (Malaysia). Barrel drum placed horizontally upon a wooden stand. The drum is also called *Jeḍor*. See *Bajiḍor*.

Jifti (Arabia). Term for *zummara*; the instrument is called *jifti* when the two pipes have the same length and equal number of finger holes.

Jigashira (Japan). The leader of the chorus of the *noh* play. He establishes and controls the tempo of the performance.
Lit.: no. 185.

Jigi-jigi (Uganda – Alur). A toy ground bow.
Lit.: no. 302.

Jimba (Congo – Aruwimi). *Sansa* with five brass tongues. Also term for *madimba*.
Lit.: nos. 27, 255.

Jinā (Arabia). Pan flutes consisting of seven or more pipes.
Lit.: no. 255.

Jin daiko (Japan). See *Taiko*.

Jindai rappa (Japan). Spherical clay horn.
Lit.: no. 255.

Jindai sudsu (Japan). Pair of small bells.

Jindra (*Jaler*) (Java). See *Rebāb* (Java).

Jindu (South India). *Janya rāga* of the 17th *mēḷa* (*Sūryakānta*).
Tone material:

C F G F A c
c B A F G F E D♭ C

Lit.: no. 139.

Jineman (Java). Soft music (*jinem* = "quiet," "modest").

Jing (Korea). Gong. Also called *na*. (See the Chinese *Lo*.) The large *jing* was beaten to signal to the army the order of retreat; the small *jing* was used to order the troops to march ahead.
Lit.: no. 179.

Jiṅgalābhairavī (South India). See *Jinglābhairavī*.

Jin gane (Japan). Bronze gong with the shape of a bell. It was beaten with wooden sticks and served as signalling instrument in war. At the present time it is used in some religious services.
Lit.: no. 255.

Jingai (Japan). Cf. *Hora*.

Jinge (Congo – Gombe of Busu-Djoana). Stick zither.
Lit.: no. 176.

Jiṅgla (South India). *Janya rāga* of the 20th *mēḷa* (*Naṭabhairavī*).
Tone material:

C D E♭ F G A♭ B♭ A♭ G c
c B♭ A♭ G F E♭ D C

Lit.: no. 139.

Jiṅglābhairavī (South India). Also written: *Jiṅgalābhairavī*. *Janya rāga* of the 32nd *mēḷa* (*Rāgavardhanī*).
Tone material:

C E F G F A♭ c
c B♭ A♭ G F E F D♯ C

Lit.: no. 139.

Jingun (Borneo). See *Stobeong*.

Jinimuni (Nepal). Triangle.
Lit.: no. 46.

Jinjeram (Ghana). Musical bow.

Jinjil (Kurdistan). Small bell, jingle. Cf. *Jeljel* (Persia).
Lit.: no. 255.

Jinjīvi (India). See *Puñji.*

Jinku (Japan). Folk song.

Jinontra (Java). The protruding spokes of a water wheel click against suspended pieces of bamboo tuned in different pitches.
Lit.: no. 163.

Jins (Arabia). The lowest tetrachord of the scalar material of a *maqām.*

Jinyang jo (Korea). See *Chiṇ yang jo.*

Jirba (Arabia). Bagpipe of Kuwait.

Jisei-in (Japan). "The second clear voices." Among numerous sung syllables, the *jisei-in* represent a group of vocal sounds (beside the *goju-in*, "the fifty voices"). See *Kwaigo-no-ben.*
Lit.: no. 225.

Jitag (Mongolia). Cf. *Yatag (Itag).*

Jiuta (Japan). *Jiuta*, originally *shamisen* music of Kyoto (in contrast to that of Tokyo). In *koto* music the *jiuta* style grew and added the *shamisen.* The instrumental sound became emphasized and was more important than the vocal part. A third instrument was added, either the *kokyū* or the *shakuhachi.* This trio was called *sankyoku.* In the 19th century the *ikuta jiuta* was created (by Kengyo), a style in which a second *koto* was added to the first. This type of *koto* music was named *kyōmono* (after the place of its origin, Kyoto). The impressive dance of the geishas of Kyoto (*kyōmai*) still has the *kyōmono* ensemble as its musical accompaniment.

The *jiuta* in the 18th century evolved into various instrumental and vocal forms. A simple form consisted of the following sequence: *mae-uta*, introductory song; *tegoto*, instrumental interlude; *ato-uta*, concluding song. This form evolved eventually into: *maebiki*, instrumental introduction; *mae-uta*, opening song.

The first *tegoto*: *tsunagi*, transition from *mae-uta* to *tegoto*; *tegoto*, long instrumental interlude; *nakatirasi*, lively instrumental section; *hontirasi*, instrumental closing; *naka-uta*, song between the first and second *tegoto.*

The second *tegoto*: *tegoto*, instrumental transition; *tirasi*, instrumental closing; *ato-uta*, closing song.
Lit.: no. 185.

Jivan-bhairav (*Asavari-bhairav*) (North India). *Rāga* ascribed to the *Bhairav thāta.* It is called occasionally *Asavari-bhairav* because one phrase can be used in this *rāga* that resembles *Asavari.*
Tone material:

C D♭ E F G A♭ B c
c B A♭ G F G E♭ D♭ C; *Vādis*: F, C
Asavari

Lit.: no. 138.

Jivanpuri (North India). See *Jaunpuri.*

Jivantika (South India). *Janya rāga* of the 17th *mēḷa (Sūryakānta).*
Tone material:

C D♭ F G A B c
c B A G F D♭ C

Lit.: no. 139.

Jīvantini (South India). *Janya rāga* of the 48th *mēḷa (Divyamaṇī).*
Tone material:

C F♯ G A♯ B c
c B G F♯ E♭ C

Lit.: no. 139.

Jīvantikā (South India). See *Jīvantini* (48th *asampūrṇa mēḷa).*

Jīvantini (South India). The 48th *asampūrṇa mēḷa-rāga* without *kaṭapayādi* prefix. Also the 48th *asampūrṇa mēḷa-rāga* with *kaṭapayādi* prefix was called *Jīvantikā.* See *Rāga* (South India).
Lit.: no. 139.

Jīvarañjani (South India). *Janya rāga* of the 2nd *mēḷa* (*Ratnangi*).
Tone material:
C D♭ E♭♭ F A♭ B♭ c
c A♭ G F E♭♭ D♭ C
Lit.: no. 139.

Jīvaratnabhūṣaṇi (South India). *Janya rāga* of the 38th *mēḷa* (*Jalārṇava*).
Tone material:
C D♭ E♭♭ F♯ G A♭ B♭ A♭ c
c B♭ A♭ G F♯ E♭♭ D♭ C
Lit.: no. 139.

Jivika Vasanta (South India). *Janya rāga* of the 22nd *mēḷa* (*Kharaharapriyā*).
Tone material:
C D F G A B♭ A c
c B♭ G F D C
Lit.: no. 139.

Jjembe (Uganda – Ganda). Horn.
Lit.: no. 302.

Jñanabōdhini (South India). *Janya rāga* of the 10th *mēḷa* (*Naṭakapriya*).
Tone material:
C D♭ E♭ A B♭ c
c B♭ A E♭ D♭ C
Lit.: no. 139.

Jñānadāyaki (*Jñānadāyiki*) (South India). *Janya rāga* of the 4th *mēḷa* (*Vanaspāti*).
Tone material:
C D♭ E♭♭ A B♭ c
c B♭ A E♭♭ D♭ C
Lit.: no. 139.

Jñanasvarūpiṇī (South India). *Janya rāga* of the 6th *mēḷa* (*Tānārūpi*).
Tone material:
C D♭ E♭♭ G A♯ c
c A♭ G D♭ E♭♭ C
Lit.: no. 139.

Jñotnāpriya (South India). *Janya rāga* of the 5th *mēḷa* (*Manōrañjanī*).
Tone material:
C D♭ E♭♭ A B c
c B A E♭♭ D♭ C
Lit.: no. 139.

Jō (Japan). Name of the 5th pipe of the *shō*. Cf. *Shō*.
Lit.: no. 225.

Jo (Japan). Introductory part in free rhythm of various types of musical compositions, e.g., of the *noh* dramas. *Jo* is the first *dan* (scene) in which appear on the stage the *waki* (side character), after him the *shite* (protagonist) and further actors (*tsure*). They introduce themselves to the audience and begin the *mondo* (dialogue in question and answer form). For the other parts of the play, see *Ha* the development, and *Kyū* the concluding section, the resolution, or revelation of the plot. Cf. *Noh*; *Gagaku*.
Lit.: no. 185.

Jo (Japan). Notes of the *noh* tone material. See *Yokyōku*.
Lit.: no. 185.

Jobal (Ancient Israel). See *Jubal*.

Jog (North India). A vague *rāga* which can appear in two versions:
1. using materials from the *rāgas Malkouns* and *Naiki-Kanada*, or:
2. using materials of the *rāgas Nath* and *Nand*.

Both versions use the notes E and B as *vādis*.
The flexible tone material can be:
C E F G A (B♭) B c (G - c)
c B♭ A♭ F E♭ F C E♭ C (or: G E F D C)
Naiki-Kanada
Lit.: no. 138.

Joged (Bali). A popular noisy flirting street dance performed by a girl who invites persons from the audience to join her. The instrumental ensemble accompanying the dance consists of four *rindik*, two *suling*, one *kendang*, *tjeng-tjeng*, and a *tawa-tawa*.
Lit.: no. 265.

Joged (Flores—Mbai). A dance accompanied by the *rebanas.*
Lit.: no. 166.

Joged (Java). Dance. It consists of four sections:

1. *Pokok*, principal dance.
2. *Kubahan*, secondary dance, "ornamentation."
3. *Gandrung*, love dance performed by a boy.
4. *Tayub*, free, improvised dance.

Lit.: no. 163.

Joged Bumbung (Bali). Dance performed by women at harvest festivals. The music too is produced by women, each using a *bumbung*, a bamboo tube, pounding the tube against a wooden podium or plank in one of the rice-pounding rhythms and patterns. The four bamboo tubes are of different lengths and create various sounds.
Lit.: no. 197.

Joged gandrung (Java). See *Joged* (Java).

Joged kubahan (Java). See *Joged.*

Joged pokok (Java). See *Joged.*

Joged tayub (Java). See *Joged.*

Jōgī (South India). *Janya rāga* of the 15th *mēḷa* (*Māyāmāḷavagauḷa*).
Tone material:
C D♭ F G A♭ c
c A♭ B A♭ G F D♭ F E D♭ C
Lit.: no. 139.

Jogibhairavī (South India). *Janya rāga* of the 28th *mēḷa* (*Harikāmbhōji*).
Tone material:
C D E F G B♭ A B♭ c
c A G F D E D C
Lit.: no. 139.

Jōgisāveri (South India). *Janya rāga* of the 15th *mēḷa* (*Māyāmāḷavagauḷa*).
Tone material:
C D♭ F G A♭ c
c B A♭ G E D♭ C
Lit.: no. 139.

Jogiya (North India). *Rāga* ascribed to the *Bhairav thāta.*
Tone material:
C D♭ F G A♭ c
c B (B♭) A♭ G F D♭ C; *Vādis*: F, C
Lit.: no. 138.

Jo-Ha-Kyū (Japan). Term indicating the formal structuring into three sections of the *noh* drama and similar musical forms. The introductory part is called *jo*, the elaborated middle part is called *ha* and the final concluding part *kyū*. Cf. *Gagaku*; *Nagauta*; *Noh*. See also *Jo*; *Ha*; *Kyū.*
Lit.: no. 215.

Jojo (Senegal). Drum.
Lit.: no. 190.

Jokyoku (Japan). See *Yōkyoku.*

Jomo (Congo—Modjombo). Drum used to accompany dances; it is played together with the *mongondo.*
Lit.: no. 26.

Jongga (*Gulu*) (Bali). See *Gulu*; *Kulkul.*

Jongga (Central Java). Term for *gulu*, the second note of the *slendro* and *pelog* systems.
Lit.: no. 163.

Jong-jrong (Sunda District). See *Indung.*

Jongka (Sunda Isl.; Sumba). Stick zither with one string.
Lit.: no. 220.

Jongkok (*Djongkok*) (Bali). "Laid upon." Cf. *Gangsa.*

Jorah (Borneo). See *Stobeong.*

Joru (North India). Medium tempo.

Jōruri (Japan). Narrative songs usually in form of recitatives with *shamisen* accompaniment which punctuates, and at times illustrates, the vocal line with appropriate sounds. *Jōruri* was most successful in the puppet theater. The highest developed form appeared in the 17th century *gidayū*. At recent times the *jōruri* of Kyoto and Osaka are much enjoyed by audiences, while the *edo joruri* receives far less appreciation. In the north of Japan some early types of *jōruri* still survive: *ko-jōruri*; *oku-jōruri* and *okumi-jōruri*, simple narrative forms. Cf. *Sugagaki*.
Lit.: nos. 53, 187.

Jōruri-nagauta (Japan). The term indicates borrowed *jōruri* items used in *nagauta* performances.
Lit.: no. 187.

Jōsīla (South India). *Janya rāga* of the 20th *mēḷa* (*Naṭabhairavī*).
Tone material:
C D G A♭ B♭ c
c A♭ G F E♭ D C
Lit.: no. 139.

Jotirāga (South India). See *Jotishmati*.

Jotishmati (South India). (1) The 68th *asampūrṇa mēḷa-rāga* without *kaṭapayādi* prefix. (2) The 68th *asampūrṇa mēḷa-rāga* with *kaṭapayādi* prefix; it was called *Jotirāga*. See *Rāga* (South India).
Lit.: no. 139.

Jou (China). See *Chien-tzu*.
Lit.: no. 136.

Jō-uki (Japan). See *Noh*.

Jozēr (Ancient Israel). Vocal interpolation to the *Shema Yisrael* prayer. Cf. *R'shuth*.
Lit.: no. 12.

Ju (*Jeu*) (Japan). Name of the 16th pipe of the *shō*. Cf. *Shō*.
Lit.: no. 225.

Ju (China—M 3153). "Flesh." Children used as puppets in southern puppet shows.
Lit.: no. 129.

Jubal (*Jobel*) (Ancient Israel). Term for *shofar*.
Lit.: no. 12.

Jubari gīt (*Juwari kheliako*) (Nepal). A chain of *jhiaure* songs in the form of questions and answers.
Lit.: no. 133.

Jublag (*Chalung*) (Bali). *Jublag* denotes the second largest slab of the one-octave metallophones that constitute the *gender* group. Cf. *Tabuh*.
Lit.: no. 197.

Ju-i (China). Cf. *Chien-tzu*.
Lit.: no. 136.

Jui-pin (China—M 3175; M 5259). "Luxuriant vegetation." An absolute pitch (*lü*). It is the seventh tone of the circle of fifths as shown in *lü*. If *jui-pin* is used as a notational symbol, only the first syllable (*jui*, M 3175) is used.
Traditionally it was a *yang* (male) tone and was used as basic note in Confucian hymns which were performed in the month of May.
Lit.: no. 136.

Jujāhuḷi (South India). *Janya rāga* of the 28th *mēḷa* (*Harikāmbhōji*).
Tone material:
C F E F G A B♭ c
c B♭ A G F E C
Lit.: no. 139.

Jujahuri (South India). Variant of *Jujāvaḷi*.
Lit.: no. 139.

Jujāvaḷi (South India). *Janya rāga* of the 13th *mēḷa* (*Gāyakapriya*).
Tone material:
C F E F G A♭ B♭♭ c
c A♭ B♭♭ G F (E) C
Lit.: no. 139.

Ju-ju (Nigeria—Yoruba). Tambourine with one skin. It has jingles in the circular frame.
Lit.: no. 293.

Jū kake (Japan). See *Kake.*

Juk-jang-go (*Chuk-chang-ko*). A bamboo stamping tube.
Lit.: no. 181.

Julāv (South India). *Janya rāga* of the 29th *mēḷa* (*Dhīraśaṅkarābharaṇam*).
Tone material:
G B C D E F G
G F E D C *B* (*A G*)
Lit.: no. 139.

Julavu (South India). *Rāga* identical with *rāga Julāv.*

Jüljül (Arabia). Bells. Tambourin.
Lit.: no. 255.

Ju-man (China). Cf. *Chien-tzu.*
Lit.: no. 136.

Jungga au (Indonesia; East Sumba Isl.). Bamboo tube zither.
Lit.: no. 156.

Junggotan (Malaysia; Sarawak). Jew's harp.

Ju-ni-ritsu (Japan). See *Gagaku.*

Jungjung mori (Korea). See *Chung chung mori.*

Jungmori (Korea). See *Chung mori.*

Jungwa (Northeast Thailand). "Rhythm."
Lit.: no. 203.

Juñjhūṭi (South India). See *Jañjhūṭi.*

Junk (Arabia). Harp.
Lit.: no. 255.

Junpachi (Japan). Theoretical term signifying an interval of eight semitones upward (an ascending fifth).
Lit.: no. 225.

Junroku (Japan). Theoretical term signifying an interval of six semitones upward (an ascending fourth).
Lit.: no. 225.

Jura (Turkey). See *Cura.*

Jura (Arabia). See *Zamr el-soghair.*
Lit.: no. 255.

Jūrā zūrnā (Turkey). Small oboe, favored by the Kurds of Erzerum. Similar to the Egyptian *zamr al-sughayyir.*
Lit.: no. 81.

Jūrā zūrnā (Kurdistan; Egypt). Small *zūrnā* of the Kurds and of modern Egypt.
Lit.: no. 65.

Juring (Sumatra; Lampong). Jew's harp made of bamboo.
Lit.: no. 255.

Juru (Ivory Coast Republic—Baoule). An instrument with five strings.
Lit.: no. 303.

Juru memacha (Bali). A reciter that chants *kawi* texts in a *kekawin* performance. (*Kawi* is the old Javanese-Sanskrit literary language.)
Lit.: no. 197.

Jurusian (*Mariri*) (Indonesia; Aru Isl.). Tube zither with two strings.
Lit.: nos. 156, 220.

Juru tandak (Bali). A singing commentator who remarks on the drama during its performance. His singing is added occasionally to the *gamelan pelegongan.*
Lit.: no. 197.

Jūśaṅgadā (South India). *Janya rāga* of the 28th *rāga* (*Harikāmbhōji*).

Tone material:

C D E F G B♭ A c

c A F E C

Lit.: no. 139.

Jushi (Japan). Popular and comic Buddhist New Year's entertainments that appear in *sarugaku* and, in a highly stylized form, in *noh* performances. Cf. *Hiru-hushi.*
Lit.: no. 185.

Jūwāk (*Juwāq*) (Algeria—Berber). A *shabbaba*, a beak flute, with 5-6 finger holes. Occasionally a 7th hole appears at the back. The tuning is variable and differs from one place to the other. Cf. *Pisha.*
Lit.: no. 255.

Juwāq (Algeria). See *Juwāk.*

Juwari kheliako (Nepal). See *Jubari gīt.*

Juz (Islamic North Africa; Middle East). Strophe.

Juza (Iraq). Small spike fiddle with four strings.

Juzale (Iraq; Kurdistan). Double barreled flute, or double clarinet, each tube having six finger holes.
Lit.: no. 229.

Jvālākēśari (South India). *Janya rāga* of the 29th *mēḷa* (*Dhīraśaṅkarābharaṇam*).
Tone material:

C D F A B c

c B A F E D C

Lit.: no. 139.

Jwab-būselik (Arabia). See *Jawāb-būsalik.*

Jwab-ḥijāz-ṣaba (*Jawāb-ḥijaz*) (Arabia). Tone name of a note a semitone higher than *jwab-jargā.* (A list of all tone names and tones through two octaves can be seen under the heading of *Jagā* [*Yagā*].)

Jwab-jargā (*Māhūrāni*; *Māhūrān*) (Arabia). Tone name of a main note one octave higher than *jargā.* (A list of all tone names and tones through two octaves can be seen under the heading of *Jagā* [*Yagā*].)

Jwab-nam-būselik (*Nim-jāwāb-būsalik*) (Arabia). Tone name of a note approximately ¼ tone lower than *jwab-būselik.* (A list of all tone names and tones through two octaves can be seen under the heading of *Jagā* [*Yagā*].)

Jwab-nam-ḥijāz (*Nim-jāwāb-ḥijaz*) (Arabia). Tone name of a note approximately ¼ tone lower than *jwab-ḥijāz-ṣaba.* (A list of all tone names and tones through two octaves can be seen under the heading of *Jagā* [*Yagā*].)

Jwab nawā (*Ramal tūtī*) (Arabia). Tone name of the highest main note, two octaves above *jagā.* (A list of all tone names and tones through two octaves can be seen under the heading of *Jagā* [*Yagā*].)

Jwab-sigā (*Bazruq*; *Buzurq*) (Arabia). Tone name of a main note one octave higher than *sigā.* (A list of all tone names and tones through two octaves can be seen under the heading of *Jagā* [*Yagā*].)

Jwab-taq-ḥijāz (ṣaba) (*Tik-jawāb-ḥijāz*) (Arabia). Tone name of a note approximately ¾ tone higher than *jwab-jargā.* (A list of all tone names and tones through two octaves can be seen under the heading of *Jagā* [*Yagā*].)

Jwago (Korea). See *Jwa-ko.*

Jwa-ko (Korea). (Also *Jwago*; *Chwago*; *Cho-ko.*) A flat barrel-shaped frame drum. It is hung from a wooden stand and beaten with a heavy stick. The instrument is used in dance music, never in serious musical performances.
Lit.: no. 179.

Jyabisen (Japan; Amami Isl.). A simple *shamisen* type.
Lit.: no. 157.

Jyo (Japan). The Japanese term for the Chinese *yü* (the "tigerbox").

Jyōtirañjani (South India). *Janya rāga* of the 61st *mēḷa* (*Kāntāmaṇi*).
Tone material:
C D E F# G Ab Bbb c
c Bbb Ab G F# E F# D C
Lit.: no. 139.

Jyōtiṣmati (South India). *Janya rāga* of the 68th *mēḷa* (*Jyōtisvarūpiṇī*).
Tone material:
C D# E F# G c
c Bb Ab G F# D# E C
Lit.: no. 139.

Jyōtisvarūpiṇi (South India). The 68th *mēḷa*:
C D# E F# G Ab Bb c
The *rāga* with the same name has the same tone material as shown above.
Lit.: no. 139.

K

Ka (Japan). "Single pressure." Raising the pitch by a semitone by applying pressure on the string (*koto*). Cf. *Koto*; *Osu.*
Lit.: no. 225.

Ka (Korea). Fret (*ka*).

Kā (Arabia). Soft; gentle (drumbeat).

Ka (Turkey). Cf. *Usul.*

Ka (Africa; Mali—Dogon). Side-blown trumpet.
Lit.: no. 303.

Ka'ara (Oceania; Cook Isl.). Slit-drum beaten with two sticks.
Lit.: no. 84.

Kaba (New Guinea). Cylindrical drum with one head and a wooden corpus.
Lit.: no. 255.

Kabacha (India). Simple curved horn consisting of sections, without a noticeable bell.
Lit.: no. 254.

Kabak (Turkey). Fiddle.

Kabak Kemençe (Turkey). Spike fiddle with three strings.

Kabar (Arabia). Ancient single-headed drum.
Lit.: no. 78.

Kabaro (Ethiopia). Sacred big barrel drum. The Galla call it *nagārit* when it is used for dances.
Lit.: nos. 102, 255.

Kabarome (Uganda—Mbuti Pygmies). Musical bow or *sansa.*
Lit.: no. 302.

Kābe (Equatorial Africa). Magical song sung by men accompanied by drums, horns, and clapping of hands. Its magic is believed to attract alligators.
Lit.: no. 247.

Kabirizi (Uganda; Urundi). Sacred drum.

Kabiry (Malagasy Republic). A double reed instrument.
Lit.: no. 251.

Kabisli (Assam; Burma—Khasi). Bamboo cross flute with six finger holes.
Lit.: no. 252.

Kabosa (*Kabosi*) (Malagasy Republic). Lute with three or four pairs of strings.
Lit.: nos. 250-51.

Kabosi (Southeast Celebes—Maronene; Borneo—Butong). Plucked or bowed lute with one brass strings. Related to the *gabus* (Zanzibar).
Lit.: no. 254.

Kabuki (Japan). A highly popular form of Japanese bourgeois theater. It became known and increasingly appreciated about the end of the 16th century. While the early *kabuki* was of doubtful repute and had to be prohibited for a while, the later *Kabuki* (cf. *Yaro-kabuki*) became acceptable to all audiences and represented a synthesis of every theatrical type of the land. *Noh* plays were shortened and the *noh hayashi* was altered by the appearance of the increasingly dominating *shamisen*. *Joruri* lost some of its distinction and charm when it was adjusted to the *kabuki* taste. The same happened to the *gidayu* and other dramatic and narrative *shamisen* forms. *Kabuki* performances gained increasing popularity over the original sources, whether they were the distinguished *noh*, puppet shows, or any other theatrical types. *Kabuki* was and is performed without masks but uses a wealth of colorful costumes. Since 1650, when the somewhat more respectable *kabuki* used the *shamisen* and its *kouta* and *kumiuta*, new forms came into existence such as the *edo-nagauta* which later became the musical mainstay of the *kabuki* theater.
Lit.: no. 185.

Kabus'u (East Africa—Swahili). Term for *gabus*. The gut strings of this music bow are called *tari*.
Lit.: no. 255.

Kacarāga (South India). See *Kacharāga*.

Kacchapī Vīṇā (*Kachuya Sitar*) (India; Indonesia). The "tortoise vina." The body of this instrument has little or no similarity with the shape of a tortoise. *Kacchapa* or *kaccha* represent the Sanskrit term for a tree (*cedrela toona*), the wood of which is used for the building of *sitars* or furniture. The *kacchapī vīṇā*, a popular instrument, is a *sitar* type with seven metal strings (two of which are bourdon strings) plucked with a wire plectrum. The broad neck has usually 16 frets.

Numerous names used in Malaysia and Indonesia refer to the same or similar instrument. Among them, *katjapi* (*kachapi*), *ketjapi* (*kechapi*), *kutjapi* (*kuchapi*) apply to lute or board zither types. In Sumatra the instrument is called *husapi* or *hapetan*. In East Celebes the name is *kasapi* and in South Celebes *kachapin*.
Lit.: no. 254.

Kā:chabpi (Siam). A large lute with three strings, 12 frets, and a circular corpus. The plectrum is made of copper or horn.
Lit.: no. 255.

Kachapi (*Kechapi*) (Indonesia; Sunda District Toba Batak; South Celebes). A zither consisting of a narrow trough-shaped wooden box (called *raraga*) which is strung with 6-18 strings. Inside the box is a wooden stick (*ilat*, "tongue") which reinforces the structure. The strings run across moveable bridges (*inang*). The instrument is played by plucking the strings with index finger and thumb.
Lit.: no. 255.

Kachapin (South Celebes). See *Kacchapi*.

Kacharāga (*Kacarāga*) (South India). *Janya rāga* of the 27th *mēḷa* (*Sarasangi*).
Tone material:

C D E G A♭ B c
c A♭ G F D C

Lit.: no. 139.

Kācha Vīṇā (India). A recent *sitar* with a glass fingerboard, six wire strings, and 11 resonance strings. The Bengali term can be *kancha bīṇā*.
Lit.: no. 254.

Kachibong (West Java). See *Renteng*.

Kachintzi (Sibiria). See *Chat'han*.

Kach-tehendor (Southeast India; Bastar State). Iron jew's harp of the Muria Gond.
Lit.: no. 59.

Kachuya Sitar (India). See *Kacchapi Vīṇā.*

Kachva (India). A rare *sitar* type, difficult to play. It has two strings (tuned in the interval of a third) and two higher-pitched bourdon strings.
Lit.: no. 255.

Kada (*Kunka-da*) (Japan). Cf. *Wasan.*

Kadamba (South India). Term for the *trisra jātai* form of *Jhampa tāla*. See *Tāla* (South India).
Lit.: no. 136.

Kādambiṇi (South India). *Janya rāga* of the 16th *mēḷa* (*Chakravāka*).
Tone material:
C D♭ E F G A B♭ c
c B♭ A F D♭ E F E C
Lit.: no. 139.

Kādambiṇi (South India). *Janya rāga* of the 19th *mēḷa* (*Jhaṅkāradhvani*).
Tone material:
C D E♭ G A♭ B♭♭ c
c B♭♭ A♭ G E♭ D C
Lit.: no. 139.

Kadana Kutūhalam (*Kathana Kutūhalam*) (South India). *Janya rāga* of the 29th *mēḷa* (*Dhīraśaṅkarābharaṇam*).
Tone material:
C D F A B E G c (C D F B A G B c)
c B A G F E D C
Lit.: no. 139.

Kadanam (South India). *Janya rāga* of the 27th *mēḷa* (*Sarasāṅgī*).
Tone material:
C F G A♭ B c
c B A♭ G F C
Lit.: no. 139.

Kadaram (South India). *Janya rāga* of the 21st *mēḷa* (*Kiravāṇi*).
Tone material:
C E♭ F A♭ B c
c B A♭ F E♭ C
Lit.: no. 139.

Ka-de (*Ge*) (Japan). See *Kunka-da* of *Wasan.*

Kadia m'buji (Congo—Kasai; Bena-Lulua). Hourglass drum.
Lit.: no. 26.

Kadimbwa (Mozambique—Nyungwe). Musical bow.

Kadjar (Bali). See *Kajar.*

Kaduar (New Guinea; Humbold Bay). Wooden slit-drum.
Lit.: no. 84.

Ka duitara (Burma). Lute with four silken strings. The body has the shape of a cube.
Lit.: no. 252.

Kã:i dung (Siam). Little bell.
Lit.: no. 255.

Kaḍuntuḍi (South India; Kerala). Drum used in *kathakali* performances.

Kaede (Japan). The second *koto* and *koto*-part in *koto* duets. Cf. *Honte*; *Danawase.*
Lit.: no. 185.

Ka'eke'eke (*Oh'eke'eke*) (New Zealand; Tahiti). Bamboo stamping tubes. See *Pahu*; *Putatara.*
Lit.: no. 215.

Kaen (Northeast Thailand). A mouth organ in four sizes. The instrument has raft form and free beating reed pipes. The four sizes of the *kaen* are: *kaen hok* (six pipes); *kaen jet* (14 pipes); *kaen baet* (16 pipes); *kaen gao* (18 pipes). See *Kaen* (*khaen*) *wong.* See also *Khen*; *Kyen.*
Lit.: no. 203.

Kaen baet (Northeast Thailand). See *Kaen.*

Kaen gao (Northeast Thailand). See *Kaen.*

Kaen hok (Northeast Thailand). See *Kaen.*

Kaen jet (Northeast Thailand). See *Kaen.*

Kaen wong (North Thailand). A *kaen* ensemble.

Ka fang muri (East Bengal – Khassiya). A crude *sānāyi.*
Lit.: no. 255.

Kafi (North India). *Thāta* and *rāga*. *Thāta Kafi*:
C D E♭ F G A B♭ c
As *rāga*, *Kafi* is light, popular, and shows a flexible tone material:
C D E♭ (E) F G A B♭ (B) c
c (B) B♭ A G F (E) E♭ D C; *Vādis*: G, C
Lit.: no. 138.

Kafi-Kanada (North India). A rare *rāga* ascribed to the *Kafi thāta.* There are two versions:
1. "*Kafi* style"
C D E♭ F G B♭ G B♭ c
c B♭ G F G A G E♭ D C
2. "*Bageshri* style"
C D E♭ F G E♭ F A B c
c B♭ A F E♭ F D C; *Vādis*: G, C
Lit.: no. 138.

Kafo (Nigeria; Western Sudan – Hausa; Fulbe). Small side-blown horn. Cf. *Rok'on fada.*

Kafoa (East Sumbawa). See *Ra'uswoja* (Flores).
Lit.: no. 163.

Kafu (East Sumbawa). See *Kafoa.*

Kagami dora (Japan). Circular mirror gong.
Lit.: no. 255.

Kagan (Ghana – Ewe). Small barrel drum with one head.
Lit.: no. 128.

Kaganu (Ghana – Ewe). See *Kagan.*

Kage (Japan). Half a *kobyōshi.* See *Hyōshi.*
Lit.: no. 225.

Kagen-gaku (Japan). Private dance performances in the imperial palace.
Lit.: no. 225.

Kagok (Korea). Vocal music. Art songs. *Kagok* represents a group of 26 items, the performance of which may last several hours. *Kagok* became popular in the 14th century. In the present time it has become very rare. The texts of the songs deal with pleasant subjects. The songs were performed by one female and a few male singers, and were accompanied by a small instrumental group in which the following instruments appeared: *komunko*, *kayakum*, *yangkum*, *sae-p'iri*, *tae-kum*, *tanso*, *hae-kum*, and *changko.*
There are variants in the instrumental accompaniments and there exist several *kagok* pieces that are sung without any instrumental accompaniment. For examples see Lit. no. 136 (*Man tae-yup*; *Chung tae-yup*).

Kagura (Japan). "Divine music." Shinto music. It appears as *mi-kagura*, the courtly form, and as *sato-kagura*, the *kagura* of the village.
Kagura probably developed from two types of sacred song: the *o-uta*, "grand singing," in which the chorus sang sitting and the *tachi-uta*, in which the singers stood on the steps of the temple.

Kagura-bayashi (*Matsuri-bayashi*). Festival music.

Kagurabue (*Yamatobue*). The Shinto flute. It is made of bamboo, has six finger holes, and is blown transversely. The instrument produces the following scale: D E F♯ G A c, or a plain anhemitonic form. Two types of this flute are distinguished: *kagurabue* (used in *kagura* music) and *azumabue*, smaller than the former, used in *azuma asobi.*
Lit.: no. 53.

Kagura Daiko (Japan). A *taiko* with a wooden flat cylindrical corpus.
Lit.: no. 255.

Kagura sutsu (Japan). Small bell-tree.

Kaha (*Kahal*) (Nepal). Slim, straight copper trumpet used at religious ceremonies when dead bodies are taken to the burning ground.
Lit.: no. 254.

Kāhaḷam (India). Malāyaḷam term for *rāṇaśṛṅga.*

Kahaḷe (India). Kannarese term for *rāṇaśṛṅga.*
Lit.: no. 46.

Kahao Vakai (Polynesia; Solomon Isl.). Game song accompanied by hand clapping.
Lit.: no. 319.

Kāhea (Hawaii). The spoken introduction that leads to the beginning of the *hula* dance. These spoken calls advise the dancers to be ready and to pick up the wooden sticks which had been placed in front of each participant.
Lit.: no. 215.

Kāholo (Hawaii). A dance step in the *hula* dance.
Lit.: no. 215.

Kai-ak-ko (Korea). Zither; also small fiddle. Cf. *Kaya-ko.*
Lit.: no. 255.

Kaiamba (Malagasy Republic). Bamboo rattle. Cf. *Kajamba.*
Lit.: no. 251.

Kaiavuru (Oceania; Papua—Elema). Bull roarer.
Lit.: no. 311.

K'ai-ch'ang (China—M 3204; M 218). "Opening the performance," the invocation of blessings. The *k'ai-ch'ang* (its Cantonese term is *hoi-ch'eung*) is the prelude to various stage plays, opera and puppet dramas. Cf. *Tz'u-fu.*
Lit.: no. 129.

Kaichilambu (South India). Metal rattle in the shape of an oval ring, used in temples of village deities.
Lit.: no. 261.

Kai hui (Indonesia; Timor Isl.). Vertically-blown, conically-shaped flute. It has only one finger hole.
Lit.: no. 254.

Kai-kai (Polynesia). Recitations accompanying games.

Kai-kāṭṭuka (South India; Kerala). "Hand-showing." Prescribed hand movements used by the Nambudiri Samavedins when performing *sāman.*
Lit.: no. 119.

Kaikavaśi (South India). *Janya rāga* of the 60th *mēḷa* (*Nītimatī*).
Tone material:
C D E♭ F♯ G A♯ B c
c B G F♯ E♭ D C
Lit.: no. 139.

Kaikkiḷai (South India). Old Tamil term for the note *ga* (*gāndhāra*, the 3rd degree of a heptatonic scale).

Kaiko (Japan). An antiquated broad, short *kakko.* It was carried in processions on the left shoulder and played with the left hand. The instrument was called "the third processional instrument" (the *ni-daiko* being the first and the *ni-shōko* the second processional instrument).
Lit.: no. 255.

Kaikoṭṭikaḷi (South India; Kerala). Folk dance performed by women and girls.
Lit.: no. 261.

Kai-Lakṣaṇa (South India; Kerala). "Hand indication." Prescribed hand movements used when chanting the *Sāmaveda* in Kotuntirapulli village. See *Kai-kāṭṭuka.*
Lit.: no. 119.

Kaimaṇi (South India). Small bells (or cymbals) used in religious services in temples and private homes.
Lit.: no. 261.

Kaioraora (New Zealand—Maori). Songs similar to the *patere.* The *kaioraora*, however, are songs predominantly of abusive and defamatory character. Cf. *Tumoto.*

Kairāta Vīṇā (India). A stick zither with one gourd corpus, 6-7 frets, and 3-4 wire strings tuned to F C (*G*) *C*.
Lit.: nos. 220, 254.

Kaiśika (South India). *Janya rāga* of the 22nd *mēḷa* (*Kharaharapriyā*).
Tone material:
C E♭ F A B♭ c
c B♭ A F E♭ F D C
Lit.: no. 139.

Kaiśiki (India). (1) Interval by a "hair's breadth"—term used in theoretical works. (2) See *Jāti.*

Kaiśikī-Ni (India). See *Ṣaṭśruti Dha.*

K'ai-ti (China—M 3205; M 6217). Peking term for a small *so-na.* The Shantung term is *wa-waerh.* Cf. *Ki-na* (China).
Lit.: no. 209.

Kaitiri (South India). Hourglass drum.

Kaivasi (South India). *Janya rāga* of the 58th *mēḷa* (*Hemāvatī*).
Tone material:
C D E♭ F♯ G A B♭ c
c B♭ G F♯ E♭ D C
Lit.: no. 139.

Kaivēṇi (South India). *Janya rāga* of the 61st *mēḷa* (*Kāntāmaṇi*).
Tone material:
C D F♯ G A♭ c
c A♭ B♭♭ A♭ F♯ G A♭ G F♯ E D C
Lit.: no. 139.

Kajamba (Tanganyika—Wabondei). Bamboo rattle. Cf. *Kaiambe.*
Lit.: no. 130.

Kajar (*Kadjar*) (Bali). Small gong with sunken boss used in the *gambuh*, *semar pegulingan*, and similar ensembles.
Lit.: no. 197.

Kajirei (Japan). Rattle made of three hollow metal rings hung on a bent wire.
Lit.: no. 255.

Kajon (Bali). See *Kajonan.*

Kajonan (Bali). The first figure design that becomes visible in a *wayang* performance. It has an oval shape and represents a tree.
Lit.: no. 197.

Kak (Korea). Tone name. The equivalent of the Chinese *chiao* (ancient five or seven tone scale with *kung* as starting point).
Lit.: no. 136.

Kakagoe (Japan). Drum words; drummer's calls.
Lit.: no. 215.

Kakaki (*Kakati*) (West Sudan). Long straight metal trumpet which symbolizes the majesty of the ruler. Cf. *Rok'on fada.*
Lit.: no. 255.

Kākaḷam (South India). Tamil term for *rāṇaśṛṅga.*

Kakalari (Congo—Logo). Ground zither.
Lit.: no. 176.

Kākalī (India). "Low," "peaceful." The term is used in theoretical works indicating "flat" of a sound. Cf. *Kākalī Ni.*
Lit.: no. 86.

Kākali (South India). *Janya rāga* of the 55th *mēḷa* (*Śyāmalāṅgī*).

Tone material:
C D E♭ F♯ B♭♭ c
c B♭♭ G F♯ E♭ D C
Lit.: no. 139.

Kākalī Ni (India). The tone name corresponding to *ugrā*, the 21st *śruti*. Cf. *Śruti.*
Lit.: no. 138.

Kakandika (Nigeria). Rattle.

Kakanika-kanika (Malagasy Republic). See *Rondro.*
Lit.: no. 251.

Kākapāda(m) (South India). "Crow's foot." Durational note value of four *matras* (𝅝). The other durational note value of South Indian music are listed under the heading of *Anudrutam.* Cf. *Akshara.*
Lit.: no. 261.

Kakari (Japan). (1) Group of *ōzatsuma* patterns (tunes and motives). Cf. *Ji* (*Ōzatsuma* patterns). (2) "In the manner of style of . . ." (parlando).
Lit.: no. 187.

Kakati (Sudan—Nupe). Also *kakaki.* Long, straight metal trumpet.
Lit.: no. 95.

Kakawen (Java). See *(Ka)kawin.*

Kakawihan (Java). "Imitation singing"; false, contrived singing. Cf. *Tembang kaäyeunaän.* "Modern" vocal music.
Lit.: no. 163.

Kakawihan barudak (Sunda District). Children's songs.

(Ka)kawin (Java). A *suluk* that is performed by the *dalang* when a *wayang* fighter appears. (The Sundanese term is *kakawen.*)
Lit.: no. 163.

Kaké (Japan). Term in *koto* playing that indicates one of six frequently used five-note passages:

to kaké: 7 8 6 7 *to*

i kaké: 8 9 7 8 *i*

kin kaké: 9 10 8 9 *kin*

ju kaké: 6 7 5 6 10 *ju*

hachi kaké: 4 5 3 4 8 *hachi*

roku kaké: 2 3 1 2 6 *roku*

Lit.: no. 225, p. 127.

Kakeeke (Hawaii). (1) Bamboo flute. (2) Percussion tube made of bamboo.
Lit.: no. 7.

Kakegoe (Japan). Drum calls in *noh* and *kabuki* performances.
Lit.: no. 185.

Kakeit (Timor). Jew's harp.
Lit.: no. 162.

Kakeji (Japan). One of the *ōzatsuma* patterns.

(Ka)kembangan (Java). Cf. *Kembangan*; *Sekaran.*

Kakhara (Java). Rattle stick with jingles, carried by beggars.

Kaki (Japan). Term in *koto* playing. It indicates that the player, with one motion, strikes two adjoining strings.
Lit.: no. 225.

Kaki (Nigeria). Trumpet.

Kakiawase (Japan). "To adjust plucking." A term used by string players for an introduction or prelude (*gagaku* music). Cf. *Netori.*

Kakko (Japan). A small ancient drum beaten with two knobbed sticks by the leader of the *togaku* (cf. *bugaku*) orchestra. The drum probably had its origin in Central Asia. The *kakko* has the appearance of an hourglass, which is caused by the two protruding heads attached to a central metal cylinder. The drum is placed horizontally on a wooden stand. There are three (traditional) ways of striking the *kakko* heads: *katakarai*, *mororai*, and *sei.* The Korean name of this drum is *kalko*. Cf. *O-kakko.*
Lit.: no. 225.

Ka könshau (*Ka shakurian*) (Assam; Burma). Brass cymbals.
Lit.: no. 252.

Kakonti (Indonesia; Sula Isl.). An idiophone made of one bamboo segment, an instrument that roughly resembles a tuning fork. The large part is cut in the form of a fork, and the shorter end, the handle, a tube, has two holes (at opposite sides). The player beats the fork against his hand and is able to alter the sound by opening or closing the holes in the handle. The same or similar types of this instrument bear various names: *rerre* (Central Celebes); *genggong sakai* (Malacca); *tulumpe* (Tonapuh); *ore-ore* (Buton); *ta-uto* (Talaut; Bangai); *buncacan* (Philippines).
Lit.: nos. 132, 254.

Kakoshi (Angola—Masongo; Congo—Holo). Fiddle with three strings.
Lit.: no. 255.

Ka ksiṅ (Assam; Burma). Wooden barrel drum.
Lit.: no. 252.

Kaku (Japan). Tone name; the equivalent of the Chinese *chiao* of the ancient five and seven tone scales. Cf. *Ryo*; *Ritsu.*

Kakubh (North India). See *Kukubh.*

Kaku-goto (Japan). The ancient square *koto.* It had a rectangular ornamented corpus with 25 strings and was plucked with a hard wooden *tsume.*
Lit.: no. 225.

Kaku-koto (Japan). See *Kaku-goto.*

Kakulonkeun (Java). *Lagam kulon.*

Kakulumbumba (Angola; Congo—Lunda). Musical bow.
Lit.: no. 176.

Kakva (Assam—Garo). Cymbals.
Lit.: no. 254.

Ka-kwun-lo (China). Cantonese term for *chia-kuan.*

Ka-kwun-lo (China). Cantonese term for *wu-lo.*

Kala (Bali). Old formal term for cymbals.
Lit.: no. 197.

Kala (India). One of the ancient 10 basic ways of touching *vīṇā* strings (*dhātu*): the two thumbs touch two strings simultaneously.
Lit.: no. 292.

Ka'la'au (Hawaii). The dancer clicks two small wooden sticks against each other.
Lit.: no. 37.

Kalābharaṇam (South India). *Janya rāga* of the 28th *mēḷa* (*Harikāmbhōji*).
Tone material:
C D E F G A B♭ c
c A G E D C
Lit.: no. 139.

Kalābharaṇi (South India). *Janya rāga* of the 52nd *mēḷa* (*Rāmapriyā*).
Tone material:
C E D♭ E F♯ G B♭ A B♭
B♭ A G F♯ E D♭ C *B♭* C
This *rāga* has *niṣādāntya* character.
Lit.: no. 139.

Kalābhogi (South India). *Janya rāga* of the 69th *mēḷa* (*Dhātuvardhaṇī*).
Tone material:
C D♯ E F♯ G A♭ G c
c A♭ F♯ G F♯ E D♯ C
Lit.: no. 139.

Kalagaḍā (*Kaltaḍā*) (South India). *Janya rāga* of the 13th *mēḷa* (*Gāyakapriya*).
Tone material:
C D♭ E G A♭ B♭♭ c
c B♭♭ A♭ G E D♭ C
Lit.: no. 139.

Kalagaḍa (South India). *Janya rāga* of the 16th *mēḷa* (*Chakravāka*).
Tone material:
C D♭ E G A B♭ c
c B♭ A G E D♭ C
Lit.: no. 139.

Kalah (Siam). A small bamboo slit-drum, split open at one side. It is beaten with two sticks. The drum appears throughout Malaysia and on numerous islands of the southern Pacific ocean.
Lit.: no. 255.

Kalāhaṃsa (South India). See *Kalahans.*

Kalāhaṃsa (South India). (1) The 31st *asampūrṇa mēḷa-rāga* without *kaṭapayādi* prefix. (2) The 31st *asampūrṇa mēḷa-rāga* with *kaṭapayādi* prefix; it was called *Kalāvati.* See *Rāga* (South India).
Lit.: no. 139.

Kalāhaṃsagamini (South India). *Janya rāga* of the 8th *mēḷa* (*Hanumattōḍi*).
Tone material:
C D♭ E♭ F G B♭ c
c B♭ G F E♭ D♭ C
Lit.: no. 139.

Kalahans (*Kalāhaṃsa*) (South India). *Janya rāga* of the 31st *mēḷa* (*Yāgapriyā*). The tone material of this *rāga* is identical with that of its primary *rāga* (*Yāgapriyā*). One slight and unimportant difference can be that in descent *Kalahans* now and then deletes the note E.
Lit.: no. 139.

Kāḷakam (South India). One of numerous Tamil terms for the *rānaśṛṅga* (war-horn).
Lit.: no. 254.

Kalākaṇṭha (South India). *Janya rāga* of the 7th *mēḷa* (*Senāpāti*).
Tone material:
C E♭ G A♭ B♭♭ c
c B♭♭ A♭ G E♭ C
Lit.: no. 139.

Kalākaṇṭhatvani (South India). *Janya rāga* of the 26th *mēḷa* (*Chārukeśī*).
Tone material:
C D E G A♭ B♭ C
c B♭ A♭ G E D C
Lit.: no. 139.

Kalākaṇṭhi (South India). *Janya rāga* of the 13th *mēḷa* (*Gāyakapriya*).
Tone material:
C D♭ F G A♭ B♭♭ c
c B♭♭ A♭ G F D♭ C (c B♭♭ A♭ c F D♭ F E♭ C)
Lit.: no. 139.

Kālakṣēpa(m) (South India). A series of songs combined with prose and occasional dance. The work is based on stories from the *Purāṇa*s and the two Hindu epics, the *Mahābārata* and the *Rāmāyaṇa*. Cf. *Abhanga*; *Harikathā.*

Kāḷam (South India). Tamil term for *rāṇaśṛṅga* (war-horn). Cf. *Gauri-kāḷam*; *Ekkalam.*
Lit.: no. 261.

Kāḷam (South India). *Yāzh*, ancient harp. The *perungalam*, a big *yāzh*, allegedly had 100 strings.
Lit.: no. 261.

Kalama (North India). Bamboo shawm with seven finger holes.
Lit.: no. 254.

Kalāmūrti (South India). *Janya rāga* of the 44th *mēḷa* (*Bhāvapriyā*).
Tone material:
B♭ C D♭ E♭ F♯ G c
c B♭ A♭ G F♯ E♭ D♭ C
Lit.: no. 139.

Kalanba (Congo – Togbo; Mono). Xylophone with 10 wooden slabs. See *Karangba.*
Lit.: no. 27.

Kalangu (*Kalungu*; *Colangee*) (West Africa – Hausa). Small hourglass-shaped drum with two heads, considered to be a royal instrument.
Lit.: nos. 118, 293.

Kalangual (West Africa – Fulbe). Hourglass-shaped drum. See *Kuba.*
Lit.: no. 95.

Kalangwa (Congo – Ngbandi). Xylophone with five wooden slabs. Cf. *Kalanba.*
Lit.: no. 27.

Kaḷānidhi (South India). *Janya rāga* of the 22nd *mēḷa* (*Kharaharapriyā*).
Tone material:
C D E♭ F C G F A B♭ c
c B♭ A G F E♭ D C
Lit.: no. 139.

Kālanirnika (South India). *Janya rāga* of the 63rd *mēḷa* (*Latāṅgī*).
Tone material:
C E F♯ G B A♭ c
c G F♯ E D C
Lit.: no. 139.

Kalāpini (South India). *Janya rāga* of the 12th *mēḷa* (*Rūpāvatī*).
Tone material:
C E♭ F G A♯ c
c A♯ G F E♭ C
Lit.: no. 139.

Kalāsāvēri (South India). *Janya rāga* of the 8th *mēḷa* (*Hanumattōḍi*).
Tone material:
C D♭ E♭ G B♭ c
c B♭ A♭ F E♭ D♭ C
Lit.: no. 139.

Kā:la so (Siam). Mandoline type.
Lit.: no. 255.

Kalāsvarūpi (South India). *Janya rāga* of the 22nd *mēḷa* (*Kharaharapriyā*).
Tone material:
C D E♭ F G A B♭ G c
c B♭ G F E♭ D C
Lit.: no. 139.

Kālā'au (Hawaii). Wooden percussion sticks used in the accompaniment of the *hula* dance.
Lit.: nos. 215, 278.

Kalandin (Africa). A string instrument with a gourd resonator.
Lit.: no. 215.

Kalāvasanta (South India). Also *Kalika Vasanta. Janya rāga* of the 43rd *mēḷa* (*Gavambōdhi*).
Tone material:
C E♭ F♯ G A♭ B♭♭ c
c B♭♭ G F♯ D♭ C
Lit.: no. 139.

Kalāvatī (South India). See *Yāgapriyā.* Cf. also *Kalāvatī* (16th *mēḷa*). See *Kalahaṃsa* (31st *mēḷa*).

Kaldei (Borneo). See *Kledi*; *Kladdi.*

Kalambete (Congo – Holo). A fiddle with two or three strings.
Lit.: no. 176.

Kalengo (Nigeria – Yoruba). Hourglass drum. Cf. *Ida.*
Lit.: no. 293.

Kalgo (Korea). See *Kal-ko.*

Kalhāru (South India). *Janya rāga* of the 22nd *mēḷa (Kharaharapriyā).*
Tone material:
C D F E♭ F G A G c
c A G F D C
Lit.: no. 139.

Kali (*Gilak*) (Bali). Frequently repeated short motives. See *Batel.*
Lit.: no. 265.

Kalibaboe (Indonesia; Ternate). See *Koka.*

Kaligo (Nyasaland – Chinyanja). Musical bow. Cf. *Gubu.*
Lit.: no. 190.

Kalih (*Kaleh*) (Java). See *Loro.*

Kālika (South India). *Janya rāga* of the 22nd *mēḷa (Kharaharapriyā).*
Tone material:
C D E♭ G A B♭ c
c B♭ A G E♭ D C
Lit.: no. 139.

Kaliki (South India). *Janya rāga* of the 13th *mēḷa (Gāyakapriya).*
Tone material:
C D♭ E F G A♭ B♭♭ c
c B♭♭ A♭ G F D♭ C
Lit.: no. 139.

Kalindaja (South India). *Janya rāga* of the 14th *mēḷa (Vakuḷābharaṇam).*
Tone material:
C D♭ E F G B♭ c
c B♭ G F E D♭ C
Lit.: no. 139.

Kālindi (South India). *Janya rāga* of the 15th *mēḷa (Māyāmāḷavagauḷa).*
Tone material:
C D♭ E G A♭ B c
c B A♭ G E D♭ C
Lit.: no. 139.

Kālindi (South India). *Janya rāga* of the 23rd *mēḷa (Kharaharapriyā).*
Tone material:
C D E♭ F G B♭ c
c B♭ G F E♭ D C
Lit.: no. 139.

Kaling (Bali). A clay resonator of the *kempur kōmōdong.*
Lit.: no. 197.

Kalinga (Congo – Bahavu; Ruanda). Royal drum made of a hollow tree trunk. According to tradition a new drum is always made for every new ruler, and the head of the preceding dead chief has to be placed into the corpus of the drum.
Lit.: no. 26.

Kalingda (North India). See *Kalingra.*

Kalingra (*Kalingda*) (North India). A *rāga* ascribed to the *Bhairav thāta.* It has a light, pleasant character, and the *vādis* are of no consequence.
Tone material:
C D♭ E F G A♭ B c
c B A♭ G F E D♭ C
Lit.: no. 138.

Kalinguang (*Darubiri*) (New Guinea). Bamboo jew's harp.

Kalirangwe (Africa; Lake Nyasa region). Music bow.
Lit.: no. 255.

Kalivasantam (South India). *Janya rāga* of the 43rd *mēḷa (Gavāmbōdhi).*
Tone material:
C D♭ E♭ F♯ G A♭ c
c B♭♭ G F♯ E♭ D♭ C
Lit.: no. 139.

Kal-ko (*kalgo*) (Korea). A drum similar to the *chang-ko,* with an hourglass-shaped metal corpus. Both drumheads are beaten with sticks. In the past the instrument was used frequently; at the present time it has become almost obsolete. Cf. *Kakko* (Japan); *Chieh-ku* (China). Cf. also *Thoko*; *Tsuzumi.*
Lit.: nos. 52, 225.

Kallōla(m) (South India). *Janya rāga* of the 18th *mēḷa* (*Hāṭakāmbarī*).
Tone material:
C G A# B c (C E F G A# B c)
c B A# B G F E C
Lit.: no. 139.

Kallōla Baṅgala (South India). *Janya rāga* of the 31st *mēḷa* (*Yāgapriyā*).
Tone material:
C D# F G Ab Bbb c
c Bbb G Ab F E D# C
Lit.: no. 139.

Kallōla Dhvani (South India). *Janya rāga* of the 17th *mēḷa* (*Sūryakānta*).
Tone material:
C Db F E F G B A B c
c B A G F B A F E C Db C
Lit.: no. 139.

Kallōla Sāvēri (South India). *Janya rāga* of the 25th *mēḷa* (*Mārarañjanī*).
Tone material:
C D F G Ab c
c Bbb Ab G F E D C
Lit.: no. 139.

Kalopannatā (India). The third of the seven *mūrchhanās* (derived from the *ma-grāma*).
Lit.: no. 261.

Kalove (Solomon Isl.; Florida Isl.). Music bow with two strings.
Lit.: no. 84.

Kalowongan (Java). Group of *gamelan* instruments that perform the coloring design of the piece. Cf. *Gamelan*.
Lit.: no. 163.

Kaltaḍā (South India). See *Kalagaḍā*.

Kalū (Akkad). Cf. *Gala* (Sumer).

Kalumba (North Rhodesia – Ila). Music bow.
Lit.: no. 255.

Kalung (Central Africa – Mbum). Arched harp.
Lit.: no. 21.

Kalungu (West Africa). See *Kalangu*.

Kalur (Uganda – Copi). Vertical flute with one finger hole. Cf. *Kilu*; *Kiluka*.
Lit.: no. 302.

Kaluri (*Kledi*) (Borneo – Dayak). See *Kläddi*.

Kalutang (Philippines – Hanunoo). (1) Percussion stick. (2) Bamboo xylophone of the Tirurai.
Lit.: nos. 215, 303.

Kalwaking (India – Bastar Muria Gond). Small globular rattles tied around the ankles of dancers.
Lit.: nos. 59, 134.

Kalyala (Congo – Umda; Tshokwe). Fiddle with three strings.
Lit.: no. 176.

Kalyan (*Yaman*; *Yemen*; *Imana*; *Yamuna*) (North India). *Thāta* and *rāga*.
Tone material:
C D E F# G A B c
c B A G F# E D C; *Vādis*: E, B
Lit.: no. 138.

Kalyan (*thāta*) (North India). See *Thāta*.

Kalyāṇa Dāyini (South India). *Janya rāga* of the 65th *mēḷa* (*Mechakalyāṇī*).
Tone material:
C D E F# A B c
c B A F# E D C
Lit.: no. 139.

Kalyāṇa Gauri (South India). *Janya rāga* of the 39th *mēḷa* (*Jhālavarāḷi*).
Tone material:
C Db Ebb Db F# G Ab B c
c Ab G Ebb Db C
Lit.: no. 139.

Kalyāṇa Kēsari (South India). *Janya rāga* of the 13th *mēḷa* (*Gāyakapriya*).
Tone material:
C D♭ E G A♭ c
c A♭ G F E D♭ C
Lit.: no. 139.

Kalyāṇa Taraṅgini (South India). *Janya rāga* of the 22nd *mēḷa* (*Kharaharapriyā*).
Tone material:
C F E♭ F G F B♭ A B♭ c
c B♭ A B♭ G A G F E♭ F D E♭ C
Lit.: no. 139.

Kalyāṇa Vasanta (South India). *Janya rāga* of the 21st *mēḷa* (*Kiravāṇi*).
Tone material:
C E♭ F A♭ B c
c B A♭ G F E♭ D C
Lit.: no. 139.

Kalyāṇa Vasanta (South India). *Janya rāga* of the 22nd *mēḷa* (*Kharaharapriyā*).
Tone material:
C E♭ F G A B♭ c
c A c B♭ G F E♭ D C
Lit.: no. 139.

Kalyāṇī (*Mechakalyāṇī*) (South India). (1) The 65th *asampūrṇa mēḷa-rāga* without *kaṭapayādi* prefix. (2) The 65th *asampūrṇa mēḷa-rāga* with *kaṭapayādi* prefix. The form was called *Śantakalyāṇī*. See *Rāga* (South India).
Lit.: no. 139.

Kam (New Guinea; Tami Isl.). Drum in hourglass shape.
Lit.: no. 25.

Kam (South China; Canton). See *Woo tip kam.*

Kamala (South India). *Janya rāga* of the 23rd *mēḷa* (*Gaurīmanōharī*).
Tone material
C E♭ F A B c
c B A F E♭ C
Lit.: no. 139.

Kamalābharaṇam (South India). *Janya rāga* of the 45th *mēḷa* (*Śubhapantuvarālī*).
Tone material:
C D♭ E♭ F♯ G B A♭ c
c B A♭ G B A♭ F♯ E♭ D♭ C
Lit.: no. 139.

Kamalāmanōharī (South India). *Janya rāga* of the 27th *mēḷa* (*Sarasāṅgī*).
Tone material:
C E F G B c
c B A♭ G F E C
Lit.: no. 139.

Kamala Mōhanam (South India). *Janya rāga* of the 28th *mēḷa* (*Harikāmbhōji*).
Tone material:
C D F G B♭ A c
c A G F E D C
Lit.: no. 139.

Kamala Nārāyaṇi (South India). *Janya rāga* of the 55th *mēḷa* (*Śyāmalāṅgī*).
Tone material:
C D F♯ G A♭ B♭♭ c
c B♭♭ A♭ G F♯ E♭ F♯ D C
Lit.: no. 139.

Kamala Pañchamam (South India). *Janya rāga* of the 15th *mēḷa* (*Māyāmāḷavagauḷa*).
Tone material:
C G F E F G A♭ B c
c A♭ G F E D♭ C
Lit.: no. 139.

Kamalapāṇi (South India). *Janya rāga* of the 70th *mēḷa* (*Nāsikabhūṣaṇī*).

Tone material:

C D♯ E F♯ G A c

c A G F♯ E D♯ C

Lit.: no. 139.

Kamālapati (South India). *Janya rāga* of the 6th *mēḷa* (*Tānārūpi*).
Tone material:

C E♭♭ G A♯ B c

c B A♯ G E♭♭ C

Lit.: no. 139.

Kamalāptapriya (South India). *Janya rāga* of the 51st *mēḷa* (*Kāmavardhanī*).
Tone material:

C D♭ E F♯ G A♭ c

c A♭ G F♯ E D♭ C

Lit.: no. 139.

Kamalāsanapriya (South India). *Janya rāga* of the 24th *mēḷa* (*Varuṇapriyā*).
Tone material:

C D E♭ G A♯ B c

c B A♯ G E♭ D C

Lit.: no. 139.

Kamalasūna (South India). *Janya rāga* of the 38th *mēḷa* (*Jalārṇava*).
Tone material:

C D♭ E♭♭ F♯ G B A♭ c

c B♭ G A♭ G F♯ E♭♭ D♭ C

Lit.: no. 139.

Kamalataraṅgiṇi (South India). *Janya rāga* of the 20th *mēḷa* (*Naṭabhairavī*).
Tone material:

C D E♭ F G A♭ B♭ c

c B♭ A♭ G F D C

Lit.: no. 139.

Kamala Vasantam (South India). *Janya rāga* of the 37th *mēḷa* (*Sālaga*).
Tone material:

C D♭ E♭♭ D♭ C F♯ G A♭ B♭♭ c

c B♭♭ A♭ G F♯ E♭♭ D♭ C

Lit.: no. 139.

Kamala Vilasita (South India). *Janya rāga* of the 29th *mēḷa* (*Dhīraśaṅkarābharaṇam*).
Tone material:

C D F G A B c

c B A B G F E F D C

Lit.: no. 139.

Kamalika Vasantam (South India). *Janya rāga* of the 37th *mēḷa* (*Sālaga*).
Tone material:

C D♭ E♭♭ D♭ F♯ G A♭ B♭♭ c

c B♭♭ A♭ F♯ E♭♭ D♭ C

Lit.: no. 139.

Kamalini (South India). *Janya rāga* of the 1st *mēḷa* (*Kanakāṅgī*).
Tone material:

C D♭ E♭♭ F G B♭♭ c

c B♭♭ G F E♭♭ D♭ C

Lit.: no. 139.

Kamalini (South India). *Janya rāga* of the 30th *mēḷa* (*Nāgānandī*).
Tone material:

C E F A♯ B c

c B A♯ F E D C

Lit.: no. 139.

Kamalōttaram (South India). *Janya rāga* of the 65th *mēḷa* (*Mechakalyāṇī*).
Tone material:

C F♯ G A B c

c B A G F♯ C

Lit.: no. 139.

Kamalu (South India). *Janya rāga* of the 60th *mēḷa* (*Nītimatī*).
Tone material:

C E♭ F♯ A♯ B c

c B A♯ F♯ E♭ C

Lit.: no. 139.

Kamān (North Africa; Middle East). Abbreviation for *kamānjah.*

Kamānjah (Persia; Arabia; Egypt). Large spike fiddle with two strings. The instrument is spread over a large area (North Africa, Near East, South Asia, Celebes, etc.).
Lit.: no. 100.

Kamānjah a'jūz (Egypt; Near East). (1) "Old fiddle"—spike fiddle with two hair strings tuned to (e.g.) A and E. It has a small coconut body that is covered with snakeskin and has a long, richly ornamented neck.
(2) In Turkestan and Kashmir the instrument has three or four strings; occasionally it is provided with a set of sympathetic wire strings strung below the bowed strings. The tuning of the main strings varies: C G C, C G d, and other forms.
Lit.: no. 250.

Kamānjah farkh (*Sogaī*; *Sojaīr*; *Kemānje farq*). "Detached *kamānjah*." A small spike fiddle with a small coconut corpus and two hair strings tuned to E and B.
Lit.: no. 250.

Kamānjah rūmī (Near East). (1) "Byzantine fiddle." A fiddle with a pear-shaped corpus and three gut strings. The middle string serves as a drone, the two outer strings are stopped with the fingernails. (2) Another form of the instrument has 4-6 gut strings and 4-6 resonance strings.
Lit.: no. 250.

Kamānjah taqtī (Arabia). A *kamānjah a'jūz* with a trapezoid-shaped body and three strings.
Lit.: no. 255.

Kāmarañjari (South India). *Janya rāga* of the 45th *mēḷa* (*Śubhapantuvarālī*).
Tone material:
C D♭ E♭ D♭ F♯ G A♭ B c
c B A♭ F♯ E♭ D♭ E♭ C
Lit.: no. 139.

Kāmarupi (South India). *Janya rāga* of the 52nd *mēḷa* (*Rāmapriyā*).
Tone material:
C E F♯ G F♯ A B♭ G c
c B♭ A G F♯ E D♭ C
Lit.: no. 139.

Kamasu (South India). See *Khamās.*

Kamaṭadhvajam (South India). *Janya rāga* of the 55th *mēḷa* (*Śyāmalāṅgī*).
Tone material:
C D E♭ F♯ G A♭ B♭♭ c
c A♭ G F♯ E♭ D E♭ C
Lit.: no. 139.

Kāmavardhanī (South India). (1) The 51st *mēḷa*:
C D♭ E F♯ G A♭ B c
(2) As *rāga*, the same tone material as stated above. Veṅkaṭamakhin called this *rāga Kaśīrāmakriyā* in the *asampūrṇa mēḷa* system.
Lit.: no. 139.

Kambala (Sudan). Initiation dance performed by men.

Kāmbhōji (South India). *Janya rāga* of the 28th *mēḷa* (*Harikāmbhōji*).
Tone material:
C D E F G A c
c B♭ A G F E D C
Lit.: no. 139.

Kāmbhōji (South India). (1) The 28th *asampūrṇa mēḷa-rāga* without *kaṭapayādi* prefix. (2) The 28th *asampūrṇa mēḷa-rāga* with *kaṭapayādi* prefix was called *Harikedāragauḷa*. Cf. *Rāga* (South India).
Lit.: no. 139.

Kambi (Congo—Nkundo). Musical bow.
Lit.: no. 176.

Kambre (Nigeria; Senegal—Wolof; Mandingo). A small slim lute consisting of a hollowed piece of wood that serves as corpus, and a neck with a thin slab of iron and rattling rings. The instrument has 3-4 horsehair strings.
Lit.: no. 254.

Kami bue (*Fue*) (Japan). See *Kami koto.*

Kami (New Guinea—Yatmul). Bamboo stick stamped against the ground during initiation rites.
Lit.: no. 84.

Ka mien (East Bengal; Assam—Khasi). A long wooden jew's harp. See *Rinda.*
Lit.: no. 255.

Kamigata-hagauta (Japan). Term for an older form of *nagauta* of Ōsaka and Kyōto.
Lit.: no. 187.

Kami koto (Japan). "The divine *koto*" and the *kami bue* are said to have been the few remnants of an early, indigenous form of Japanese music.
Lit.: no. 250.

Kamimu (Japan). The twelfth of the 12 chromatic tones, usually transcribed as the upper c#, assuming that the first note, *ichikotsu* is interpreted as D. (All the twelve note names are listed under the heading of *Hyōjō.*)

Kāmini (South India). *Janya rāga* of the 2nd *mēḷa* (*Ratnangi*).
Tone material:
C D♭ E♭♭ G A♭ B♭ c
c B♭ A♭ G E♭♭ D♭ C
Lit.: no. 139.

Kamisama (Japan). Term for masks which represent god and spirits. They are shown in rustic processions and religious performances.
Lit.: no. 185.

Kammaji (South India). *Janya rāga* of the 28th *mēḷa* (*Harikāmbhōji*).
Tone material:
C F E F G A B♭ c
c B♭ A G F E F C
Lit.: no. 139.

Kamod (*Kamoda*; *Kamodi*; *Kamodika*) (North India). *Rāga* ascribed to the *Kalyan thāta.*
Tone material:
C D E F (F#) G A c
c B (B♭) A G F D C; *Vādis*: G, D
Lit.: no. 138.

Kāmodamāruva (South India). *Janya rāga* of the 65th *mēḷa* (*Mechakalyāṇī*).
Tone material:
C E F# G A B c
c B A G F# E C
Lit.: no. 139.

Kāmodnāṭ (South India). *Janya rāga* of the 65th *mēḷa* (*Mechakalyāṇī*).
Tone material:
C D G A c
c E F# G D C
Lit.: no. 139.

Kamodnath (North India). Obscure *rāga*; a combination of *Kamod* and *Nath* (*rāgas*).
Tone material (flexible):
C D E F G c
c A G B G E F D C; *Vādis* (possibly): C, G
Lit.: no. 138.

Kampa (Vedic India). "Trembling." A shaking, trill-like production of the voice, often employed in the Sāmavedic chant. *Kampa* is never notated, and appears as a traditional feature.
Lit.: no. 119.

Kamphāk (Thailand). Recitatives and dialogues used in *khon* performances.

Kampiang (*Sampiang*) (Borneo). See *Gendang mara.*

Kampita (India). See *Gamak(a)*; a musical ornament, a shake with a narrow or wide compass.
Lit.: no. 261.

Kaṃsāla (India). Marathi and Kannarese term for *kaṃsya.*
Lit.: no. 250.

Kāṃsara (India). Bengali term for *kaṃsya.*
Lit.: no. 254.

Kāṃsari (South India). *Janya rāga* of the 8th *mēḷa* (*Hanumaṭṭōḍi*).
Tone material:
C E♭ D♭ E♭ F G B♭ c
c B♭ A♭ G F E♭ D♭ C
Lit.: no. 139.

Kāṃsatālo (*Kaṃsa*) (South India). Pali term for *kaṃsya.*

Kāṃsya (India). Rare flat signal-gong without any boss and with a narrow rim. See *Peddagaṇṭa.*
Lit.: no. 254.

Kamya (South India). *Janya rāga* of the 5th *mēḷa* (*Manōrañjanī*).
Tone material:
C D♭ E♭♭ G A B c
c B A G F E♭♭ D♭ E♭♭ C
Lit.: no. 139.

Kan (Japan). When playing octaves, the upper note is called *kan*, the lower one *ryō*. See *Awaseru.*
Lit.: no. 225.

Kaṇ (*Kaṇ Pakkam*) (South India). (1) The right-hand drumhead of the *mṛdanga* (the drumhead that bears the patch of black tuning paste). (2) The holes in the rims of the two *mṛdanga* heads through which the braces are strung.
Lit.: no. 261.

Kana (Solomon Isl. – Malaita). To sing. Song. Divination song.
Lit.: no. 318.

Kanaḍapriya (South India). See *Kannapriya* (63rd *mēḷa*).

Kanaḍa Rāgas (North India). *Kanaḍa* indicates Carnatic, the name of a former province of the South, between the eastern ghats and the Coromandel coast, later included in the Madras Presidency. The *Kanaḍa rāgas* of the North, similar to other families such as the *Mallar rāgas*, are ascribed to the *Asavari* and *Kafi thātas.*
The *Kanaḍa* group consists of: *Abhogi* (*Kanaḍa*), *Adana-Kanaḍa*, *Bageshri-Kanaḍa*, *Darbari-Kanaḍa*, *Devsakh* (related to the *Kanaḍa* group), *Husseini-Kanaḍa*, *Kafi-Kanaḍa*, *Kaushik-Kanaḍa*, *Naiki-Kanaḍa*, *Shahana-Kanaḍa*, *Sugharai-Kanaḍa*, *Suha-Kanaḍa.*
Lit.: no. 138.

Kānaḍa (South India). *Janya rāga* of the 22nd *mēḷa* (*Kharaharapriyā*).
Tone material:
C D E♭ F A B♭ c
c B♭ c A G F G E♭ F D C
Lit.: no. 139.

Kana-fu (Japan). Kana-letter notation. The letters refer to rhythmical and metrical features while the numbers used in *hon-pu* indicate pitches (fingering) (used particularly in *gagaku*). Cf. *Hon-pu.*

Kaṇaka (South India). *Janya rāga* of the 13th *mēḷa* (*Gāyakapriya*).
Tone material:
C E F A♭ B♭♭ c
c B♭♭ A B F E C
Lit.: no. 139.

Kanaka Bhavāni (South India). *Janya rāga* of the 66th *mēḷa* (*Chitrāmbarī*).
Tone material:
C F♯ E F♯ G A♯ B c
c B G F♯ D C
Lit.: no. 139.

Kanaka Bhūṣavāḷi (South India). *Janya rāga* of the 58th *mēḷa* (*Hemāvatī*). The scale of this *rāga* is identical with that of its primary *rāga*, *Hemāvatī.*
Lit.: no. 139.

Kanaka Candrikā (South India). See *Kanaka Chandrikā.*

Kanaka Cāri (South India). See *Kanakachāri.*

Kanaka Chandrikā (South India). *Janya rāga* of the 28th *mēḷa* (*Harikāmbhōji*). The scale of this *rāga* is identical with that of its primary *rāga*, *Harikāmbhōji.*
Lit.: no. 139.

Kanakachāri (South India). *Janya rāga* of the 31st *mēḷa* (*Yāgapriyā*).
Tone material:
C D# E F G Bbb c
c Bbb G F E D# C
Lit.: no. 139.

Kanaka Dīparam (South India). *Janya rāga* of the 45th *mēḷa* (*Śubhapantuvarālī*).
Tone material:
C Eb F# G Ab G B
(B) Ab G F# Eb Db C *B* C
This *rāga* has *niṣādāntya* character.
Lit.: no. 139.

Kanakādri (South India). *Janya rāga* of the 9th *mēḷa* (*Dhēnuka*).
Tone material:
C Db Eb G Ab B c
c B Ab G Eb Db C
Lit.: no. 139.

Kanaka Ghaṇṭa (South India). *Janya rāga* of the 65th *mēḷa* (*Mechakalyāṇī*).
Tone material:
C E D E F# G B A c
c B G F# D E F# D C
Lit.: no. 139.

Kanakagiri (South India). *Janya rāga* of the 66th *mēḷa* (*Chitrāmbarī*).
Tone material:
C D E F# G c B c
c B A# B G F# E C
Lit.: no. 139.

Kanaka Gīrvāṇi (South India). *Janya rāga* of the 67th *mēḷa* (*Sucharitra*).
Tone material:
C D# F# G F# Ab Bbb c
c Ab G F# D# C
Lit.: no. 139.

Kanaka Jyōtiṣmati (South India). *Janya rāga* of the 72nd *mēḷa* (*Rasikapriyā*).
Tone material:
C F# G A# B c
c B A# G F# C
Lit.: no. 139.

Kanaka Kusumāvaḷi (South India). *Janya rāga* of the 61st *mēḷa* (*Kāntamaṇi*).
Tone material:
C D E F# G Ab c
c Ab G F# E D C
Lit.: no. 139.

Kanakāmbarī (South India). *Janya rāga* of the 1st *mēḷa* (*Kanakāṅgī*).
Tone material:
C Ebb Db Ebb F G Ab Bbb Ab c
c Bbb Ab G F Ebb Db C
Lit.: no. 139.

Kanakāmbarī (South India). (1) The 1st *asampūrṇa mēḷa-rāga* without *kaṭapayādi* prefix. (2) The 1st *asampūrṇa mēḷa-rāga* with *kaṭapayādi* prefix. See *Rāga* (South India).
Lit.: no. 139.

Kanakāmbarī-Phenadyuti (South India). The two older systems of South Indian *mēḷa-rāgas*. See *Rāga* (South India).
Lit.: no. 139.

Kanaka Nāsāmi (South India). *Janya rāga* of the 62nd *mēḷa* (*Riṣabhapriyā*).
Tone material:
C D E D F# G Ab Bb c
c Bb Ab G F# E D C
Lit.: no. 139.

Kanakāṅgī (South India). (1) The 1st *mēḷa*:
C Db Ebb F G Ab Bbb c
(2) As *rāga*, rarely performed; traditionally to be played in the morning. The *rāga* has the same tone material as the *mēḷa*. Veṅkaṭamakhin called this *rāga Kanakāmbarī*.
Lit.: no. 139.

Kanakāṅgī-Ratnāṅgī (South India). Name of the present, generally accepted system of the 72nd *mēḷas*. Each *mēḷa* in this system is *krama sampūrṇa* and has a *kaṭapayādi* prefix. See *Rāga* (South India).
Lit.: no. 139.

Kanaka Nirmada (South India). *Janya rāga* of the 67th *mēḷa* (*Sucharitra*).
Tone material:
C D♯ E F♯ G F♯ A♭ c
c B♭♭ A♭ G F♯ E D C
Lit.: no. 139.

Kanaka Rasāḷi (South India). *Janya rāga* of the 51st *mēḷa* (*Kāmavardhanī*).
Tone material:
C D♭ E F♯ A♭ B c
c A♭ G F♯ E D♭ C
Lit.: no. 139.

Kanaka Siṃhāravam (South India). *Janya rāga* of the 61st *mēḷa* (*Kāntāmaṇi*).
Tone material:
C E F♯ G B♭♭ c
c B♭♭ A♭ G F♯ D C
Lit.: no. 139.

Kanaka Śrīkaṇṭhi (South India). *Janya rāga* of the 60th *mēḷa* (*Nītimatī*).
Tone material:
C D E♭ F♯ G c
c B A♯ B G F♯ D C
Lit.: no. 139.

Kanaka Varāḷi (South India). *Janya rāga* of the 22nd *mēḷa* (*Kharaharapriyā*).
Tone material:
C D F G B♭ c
c B♭ A B♭ G F E♭ D C
Lit.: no. 139.

Kanakavasantam (South India). *Janya rāga* of the 20th *mēḷa* (*Naṭabhairavī*).
Tone material:
C E♭ F G B♭ A♭ C
c B♭ A♭ G F E♭ D C
Lit.: no. 139.

Ka-nākrā (Assam; Burma). Vertically standing barrel or kettledrum with a wooden body. Cf. *Naqqāra* (Arabia).
Lit.: nos. 46, 252.

Kananga (Solomon Isl.). See *Ose*.

Kanango (Nigeria—Yoruba). Small hourglass drum.
Lit.: no. 95.

Kanbile (Belgian Congo; Ituri Forest). Mirliton pipe with membrane.
Lit.: nos. 28-29.

Kanbiwa (Japan). *Biwa*.

Kāñcanāṅgi (South India). See *Kānchanāṅgi*.

Kāncani (South India). *Kānchani*.

Kāñcha Bīṇā (*Kācha Vīṇā*) (India; Bengal). "Glass lute." A *sitar* with a grooved neck that is covered by a glass fingerboard, below which is placed a set of sympathetic brass strings. This unusual instrument is acoustically of little satisfaction.
Lit.: no. 254.

Kāñchanamāla (South India). *Janya rāga* of the 49th *mēḷa* (*Dhavalāmbarī*).
Tone material:
C D♭ E F♯ G B♭♭ c
c B♭♭ G F♯ E D♭ C
Lit.: no. 139.

Kāñchanāṅgi (South India). *Janya rāga* of the 19th *mēḷa* (*Jhaṅkāradhvani*).
Tone material:
C D E♭ F G B♭♭ c
c B♭♭ G F E♭ D C
Lit.: no. 139.

Kāñchanāṅgi (South India). *Janya rāga* of the 55th *mēḷa* (*Śyāmalāṅgī*).
Tone material:
C D E♭ F# G A♭ c
c A♭ G F# E♭ D C
Lit.: no. 139.

Kāñchanāvati (South India). *Janya rāga* of the 44th *mēḷa* (*Bhāvapriyā*).
Tone material:
C D♭ E♭ F# G B♭ c
c B♭ G F# E♭ D♭ C
Lit.: no. 139.

Kānchani (*Kāncani*) (South India). *Janya rāga* of the 31st *mēḷa* (*Yāgapriyā*). The scale of this *rāga* is identical with that of *Yāgapriyā*. Nevertheless, numerous South Indian theorists list the two *rāgas* separately.
Lit.: no. 139.

Kanching (Indonesia; South Celebes). (1) A *tjuriga* rattle that is believed to ward off evil spirits. (2) Instead of an iron rattle the term can also indicate brass cymbals, the sound of which is also believed to drive away evil phantoms, bad weather, illness, and malevolence.
Lit.: nos. 132, 162.

Kan-chü (China—M 3239; M 1593). Operatic style originating in the Province of Kianghsi. See *Ching-ch'iang*; *Ti-fang-hsi.*

Kanda (Congo—Balunda). Large drum of the chief.
Lit.: no. 26.

Kāndadruma (South India). *Janya rāga* of the 29th *mēḷa* (*Dhīraśaṅkarābharaṇam*).
Tone material:
C E F A F B c
c B F E D C
Lit.: no. 139.

Kandang (Malaysia). Drum.

Kāṇḍajvalana (South India). *Janya rāga* of the 51st *mēḷa* (*Kāmavardhanī*).
Tone material:
C D♭ F# G B c
c B A♭ G F# E D♭ C
Lit.: no. 139.

Kandara (West New Guinea). Hourglass drum.
Lit.: no. 190.

Kandarapriya (South India). *Janya rāga* of the 18th *mēḷa* (*Hāṭakāmbarī*).
Tone material:
C D♭ E F G A# B c
c B A# G B G F D♭ C
Lit.: no. 139.

Kandarpa Manōhari (South India). *Janya rāga* of the 5th *mēḷa* (*Manōrañjanī*).
Tone material:
C D♭ E♭♭ G A B c
c B A G E♭♭ D♭ C
Lit.: no. 139.

Kandāvaḷi (South India). *Janya rāga* of the 61st *mēḷa* (*Kāntāmaṇi*).
Tone material:
C E D E F# G A♭ B♭♭ c
c A♭ G F# E D C
Lit.: no. 139.

Kandingan (Philippines). Wedding dances.

Kandiri-kandiri (Congo—Balese). Musical bow.
Lit.: no. 176.

Kandō (Japan). Notation of the beginning of a *koto* piece indicated by a small circle.
Lit.: no. 225.

Kane (*Gane*) (Japan). Bell; small gong used in rustic music.
Lit.: no. 215.

Kang (Korea). Cf. *Chung-kan-po.*

Kanga (Uganda—Alur; Congo—Logo). (1) Short side-blown trumpet of the Alur. (2) End-blown trumpet of the Logo. (3) Set of five short trumpets. Cf. *Agwara.*
Lit.: no. 302.

'Kan'gan (South Africa—Bantu). Musical bow with a single string; borrowed from the Bushmen. Cf. *Penda.*
Lit.: no. 151.

Kangata (Japan). The ensemble of musicians who perform *bugaku.*
Lit.: no. 215.

rKang-dung (pronounced *kang-dung*) (Tibet). "Bone tube"; a trumpet made of human thigh bone, occasionally provided with a copper or brass mouthpiece and a trumpet-shaped bell. See *Rkang-gling* (*rkang-gling*). Cf. *Stag dung.*
Lit.: no. 255.

Kan-geiko (Japan). The winter practice of the Japanese musician during the 30 days of the *kan* season (Jan. 5 to Feb. 6) when the player has to practice in the cold from 4 a.m. on. The idea is to train the musician to be able to perform in any climate. See *Gebuki.*
Lit.: no. 225.

Kangen (Japan). The instrumental ensemble of *gagaku.*

Kangere (Congo—Warega). Globular flute with one finger hole.
Lit.: no. 33.

Kangkanong (Southeast Borneo). Small *garantong* (*tawak*).

rKang-gling (pronounced *kang-ling*) (Tibet). A high-pitched pipe made of a human tibia. Bones of criminals or persons who died by violence are preferred when manufacturing these instruments. The term is also applied to an eagle-bone pipe with seven finger holes. Cf. *Stag-gling.*
Lit.: nos. 143, 255.

Kangoma (Congo—Batshoko). Also called *ngoma.* Small drum used by children.
Lit.: no. 26.

Kāngsara (*Kangsi*) (India; Bengal). Gong with an inverted rim. Cf. *Brekuk* (Java).
Lit.: nos. 159, 184.

Kangsi (Bali). At the ends of sticks are attached bells or cup-shaped cymbals in pairs. In the *gambuh* orchestra these sticks are stamped against the floor.
Lit.: no. 197.

Kāngsī (Java). Ancient term for *bonang.*

Kang-t'ou (*Ta-wang*) (China). A conically-shaped brass or bronze horn. It was used in funeral processions and in the Yung Ho Kung, the Peking Lama Temple.
Lit.: nos. 209, 255.

Kan(g)-t'ung (China—M 3211; M 6611). The Chinese form of the Tibetan *rKang-dung.* The term is used for the "Lama trumpet." See *Kang-t'ou.*

Kan-guri (Japan). See *Noh*; *Tsuyo.*

Kanhi (Vietnam). Fiddle made of a turtle shell with two strings.
Lit.: no. 43.

Kani (Liberia—Kru). Triangular frame psaltery with seven fiber strings. Cf. *Oba.*
Lit.: no. 255.

Kañjabhavapriya (South India). *Janya rāga* of the 68th *mēḷa* (*Jyōtisvarūpiṇī*).
Tone material:
C D# E F# G Bb c
c Bb G F# E D# C
Lit.: no. 139.

Kañja Puñji (South India). *Janya rāga* of the 46th *mēḷa* (*Śaḍvidhamārgiṇī*).
Tone material:
C Db Eb F# G Bb A c
c Bb A G F# Eb Db C
Lit.: no. 139.

Kanjeri (South India). Also called *kanjira.* Small frame drum.

Kanjin-noh (Japan). Old popular public benefit *noh* performances employing a *hayashi* consisting of one *noh* flute and three drums.

Kanjira (South India). See *Kanjeri.*

Kanjrī (North India). Frame drum. Cf. *Bendir* (North Africa).

Kaṅkaṇālaṅkāri (South India). *Janya rāga* of the 52nd *mēḷa* (*Rāmapriyā*).
Tone material:
C E G A Bb c
c Bb A G F# E Db C
Lit.: no. 139.

Kankan-chōshi (Japan). Old name for the Chinese anhemitonic pentatonic scale.
Lit.: no. 185.

Kankobele (North Rhodesia—Ila). *Sansa.*
Lit.: no. 255.

Kannaḍa (South India). *Janya rāga* of the 29th *mēḷa* (*Dhīraśaṅkarābharaṇam*).
Tone material:
C E F G F A B c (C D E F G F A B [c])
c B c A G F E F D C (c A G F G E F D [c])
Lit.: no. 139.

Kannaḍa Baṅgāḷa (South India). *Janya rāga* of the 15th *mēḷa* (*Māyāmāḷavagauḷa*).
Tone material:
C Db F E F G Ab c (C Db F E F Ab G Ab c)
c Ab G F E Db C
Lit.: no. 139.

Kannaḍa Bhōgi (South India). *Janya rāga* of the 50th *mēḷa* (*Nāmanārāyaṇī*).
Tone material:
C Db E F# G Bb Ab Bb c
c Bb Ab F# E Db E C
Lit.: no. 139.

Kannaḍa Bhōmaṇi (South India). *Janya rāga* of the 70th *mēḷa* (*Nāsikabhūṣaṇī*).
Tone material:
C D# E F# G A Bb c
c Bb A F# E D# F# E C
Lit.: no. 139.

Kannaḍa Darbar (South India). *Janya rāga* of the 33rd *mēḷa* (*Gāṅgeyabhushanī*).
Tone material:
C D# E F Ab G c
c B Ab G F D# C
Lit.: no. 139.

Kannaḍa Dīparam (South India). *Janya rāga* of the 44th *mēḷa* (*Bhāvapriyā*).
Tone material:
C Db Eb F# Ab Bb c
c Bb Ab G Ab F# Eb Db C
Lit.: no. 139.

Kannaḍa Gauḷa (*Kannaḍa Gauḷi*) (South India). *Janya rāga* of the 22nd *mēḷa* (*Kharaharapriyā*).
Tone material:
C D Eb F G Bb c
c Bb A G F Eb C
Lit.: no. 139.

Kannaḍa Gauḷi (South India). See *Kannaḍa Gauḷa.*

Kannaḍa Kurañji (South India). *Janya rāga* of the 49th *mēḷa* (*Dhavalāmbarī*).
Tone material:
C E Db E F# G Ab Bbb c
c Ab G F# Db C
Lit.: no. 139.

Kannaḍa Mallār (South India). *Janya rāga* of the 20th *mēḷa* (*Naṭabhairavī*).
Tone material:
C Eb F G Ab c
c Bb Ab F Eb C
Lit.: no. 139.

Kannaḍa Māruva (South India). *Janya rāga* of the 53rd *mēḷa* (*Gamanaśrama*).
Tone material:
C E F# G A B c
c B A G F# E C
Lit.: no. 139.

Kannaḍamu (South India). *Janya rāga* of the 38th *mēḷa* (*Jalārṇava*).
Tone material:
C Ebb F# Ab Bb c
c Bb Ab F# Ebb C
Lit.: no. 139.

Kannaḍa Pañcama (South India). See *Kannaḍa Pañchama.*

Kannaḍa Panchama (South India). *Janya rāga* of the 26th *mēḷa* (*Chārukeśī*).
Tone material:
C D E F G Bb c
c Bb Ab Bb Ab G F E D C
(c Bb Ab Bb G F E C)
Lit.: no. 139.

Kannaḍa Sālavi (South India). *Janya rāga* of the 8th *mēḷa* (*Hanumattōḍi*).
Tone material:
C Eb F G Ab c
c Bb Ab F Eb C
Lit.: no. 139.

Kannaḍa Saurāshṭram (South India). *Janya rāga* of the 10th *mēḷa* (*Nāṭakapriya*).
Tone material:
C Db F Eb F G A Bb c
c Bb A G F Eb C
Lit.: no. 139.

Kannaḍa Saurāṣṭram (South India). See *Kannaḍa Saurāshṭram.*

Kannaḍa Varāḷi (South India). *Janya rāga* of the 22nd *mēḷa* (*Kharaharapriyā*).
Tone material:
C D F G Bb c
c Bb A Bb G Eb D C
Lit.: no. 139.

Kannaḍa Vēḷāvaḷi (South India). *Janya rāga* of the 48th *mēḷa* (*Divyamaṇī*).
Tone material:
G B C Db Eb F# G
G F Eb Db C *B A# B G*
The scale of this *rāga* has *pañchamāntya* character.
Lit.: no. 139.

Kanname (Japan). Carvings on the inside of the wooden body of the drum which are believed to enhance the tone of the instrument.
Lit.: no. 185.

Kannango (Nigeria—Yoruba). See *Gangan.*
Lit.: no. 293.

Kannapriya (*Kanaḍapriya*) (South India). *Janya rāga* of the 63rd *mēḷa* (*Latāṅgī*).
Tone material:
C D E F# G F# Ab B c
c Ab B G F# E D C
Lit.: no. 139.

Kannāre (Arabia). See *Kinnāre.*

Kano (Equatorial Africa—Kouya). Women's chorus and dance accompanied by an iron bell and three drums beaten by young men. The song celebrates the birth of twins.
Lit.: nos. 39, 247.

Kaṉ Pakkam (South India). See *Kaṉ.*

Kansambi (Congo—Warega). *Sansa.*
Lit.: nos. 21, 33.

Kansan (Japan). *Shōmyō*; Buddhist hymns with original Chinese texts. There are four categories of *kansan*:

1. *Bombai* (or *bai*). This term referring to the ancient Sanskrit (or Pali) texts can denote the entire *shōmyō.* As *kansan* the *bombai* indicates three sections: the *shobai* (introduction), the *chubai* (middle part) and the *gobai* (conclusion).
2. *Sange.* The three sections, in ABA form, entitled "The Scattering of Flowers." While the A section stays unchanged, the B section is variable and subject to change depending on the Buddha who is to be honored.
3. *Bonnon.* "The Brahmanic Voice."
4. *Shakujo.* "The Priest's Staff."

Cf. *Bonsan*; *Wasan.*
Lit.: nos. 53, 185.

Kansara (India; Bengal). Gong; a large *kaṅsi.*
Lit.: nos. 255.

Kansavar (North India). Gong.

Kanshingiri (Congo—Bambemba). A drum used during the initiation rites of women.
Lit.: no. 26.

Kaṅsi (*Kansara*) (India). Gong with inverted rim.
Lit.: no. 255.

Kansilemba (Congo—Warega). Hand bell.
Lit.: no. 21.

Kansu-ch'iang (China—M 3223; M 5509; M 665). Operatic style. See *Pang-tzu* (*ch'iang*).

Kānsya tāla (Ancient India). Cymbals.

Kānta Dhanyāsi (South India). *Janya rāga* of the 8th *mēḷa* (*Hanumaṭṭōḍi*).
Tone material:

C E♭ F G B♭ c
c B♭ A♭ G B♭ G F E♭ D♭ C

Lit.: no. 139.

Kānta Dhruma (South India). *Janya rāga* of the 29th *mēḷa* (*Dhīraśaṅkarābharaṇam*). Identical with *rāga Kandadruma* (29th *mēḷa*).

Kāntāmaṇi (South India). (1) The 61st *mēḷa*:

C D E F♯ G A♭ B♭♭ c

(2) As *rāga*: in the *asampūrṇa* system *Kāntāmaṇi* was represented by the name *Kuntala.*
Lit.: no. 139.

Kānta Mañjari (South India). *Janya rāga* of the 37th *mēḷa* (*Sālaga*).
Tone material:

C D♭ E♭♭ F♯ A♭ B♭♭ c
c B♭♭ c A♭ G B♭♭ A♭ F♯ D♭ E♭♭ D♭ F♯ E♭♭ D♭ C

Lit.: no. 139.

Kāntaraka Pani (South India). *Janya rāga* of the 1st *mēḷa* (*Kanakāṅgī*).
Tone material:

C E♭♭ F G B♭♭ c
c B♭♭ G F E♭♭ C

Lit.: no. 139.

Kānta Rākshasa (South India). *Janya rāga* of the 45th *mēḷa* (*Śubhapantuvarāḷī*).
Tone material:

C D♭ E♭ D♭ F♯ G A♭ B c
c A♭ G F♯ E♭ D♭ C

Lit.: no. 139.

Kāntā Ratna (South India). *Janya rāga* of the 61st *mēḷa* (*Kāntāmaṇi*).
Tone material:

C D F♯ G B♭♭ A♭ c
c B♭♭ A♭ G F♯ E D C

Lit.: no. 139.

Kānti (South India). *Janya rāga* of the 38th *mēḷa* (*Jalārṇava*).
Tone material:
C D♭ E♭♭ F♯ G B♭ c
c B♭ G F♯ E♭♭ D♭ C
Lit.: no. 139.

Kantilan (Bali). Term for the two-part *gangsa* figuration, also called *kantilan* (referring to the small one-octave metallophones of the *gender* group). Cf. *Koṭekan.*

Kantimati (South India). *Janya rāga* of the 31st *mēḷa* (*Yāgapriyā*).
Tone material:
C D♯ E F G c
c G F E D♯ C
Lit.: no. 139.

Kantimati (South India). *Janya rāga* of the 60th *mēḷa* (*Nītimatī*).
Tone material:
C D E♭ F♯ G c
c A♯ G F♯ E♭ D C
Lit.: no. 139.

Kantisvarūpiṇi (South India). *Janya rāga* of the 61st *mēḷa* (*Kāntāmaṇi*).
Tone material:
C D E F♯ A♭ B♭♭ c
c B♭♭ A♭ F♯ E D C
Lit.: no. 139.

Kantom (Borneo). Tube zither with six strings. Cf. *Pagang.*

Kanūn (*Qānūn*) (Turkey). Plucked zither with a trapezoid body. Each tone is produced by triple (gut) strings, and all 72-75 strings are organized into 24 groups. Cf. *Qānūn.*

Kanuna (India). The Indian form of the *qānūn* with 22 wire strings. Cf. *Kātyāyana vīṇā.*
Lit.: no. 254.

Kanya Mālini (South India). *Janya rāga* of the 29th *mēḷa* (*Dhīraśaṅkarābharaṇam*).
Tone material:
C D C E F G F A B c
c B A F E D C
Lit.: no. 139.

Kanyāvitāna (South India). *Janya rāga* of the 31st *mēḷa* (*Yāgapriyā*).
Tone material:
C E F G A♭ B♭♭ c
c B♭♭ G F E D♯ E D♯ C
Lit.: no. 139.

Kanzabu (Ancient Babylon). See *Kitmu.*

Kanze (Japan). The first school of the *noh.*
Lit.: no. 185.

Kao-chang (China—M 3290; M 182). Concluding music performed at official festivals by an ensemble of ten instruments and two dancers.
Lit.: nos. 55, 227.

Kao-ch'iang (China—M 3290; M 665). Operatic style representing regional dramas, particularly of Kwantung. The texts are in dialectal village styles. The music is not refined but has become very popular. See *Ching-ch'iang*; *Ti-fang hsi.*
Lit.: no. 183.

Kao-kao (Java). Small drum of Chinese origin. The instrument has two painted skins which are beaten with wooden sticks.
Lit.: no. 184.

Kao-pien lo (China) The Cantonese term is *kou-pin-lo.* Cf. *Ta-lo.*

Kaotari (Japan). A *jamisen* covered with snake-skin. It comes from the Ryu-kyu islands, has three strings and no frets.
Lit.: no. 225.

Kapa (Solomon Isl.—Bellona Isl.). Song.
Lit.: no. 246.

Kapat (North Philippines). Cf. *Topayya.*

Kāpi (South India). See *Karṇaṭaka Kāpi.*

K'api (East Tibet). A jew's harp made of bamboo. Three types are distinguished:

1. *P'o kä*, "male tone."
2. *Din kä*, "middle tone."
3. *Ton mo kä*, "female tone" (high pitched).

The Lepcha term of this instrument is *teng-dyu*.
Lit.: nos. 62, 255.

Kāpi Jaṅgla (South India). *Janya rāga* of the 22nd *mēḷa* (*Kharaharapriyā*).
Tone material:
C *B*♭ C D E♭ F
F E♭ D C *B*♭ *A* *B*♭ C
Lit.: no. 139.

Kapila (South India). *Janya rāga* of the 12th *mēḷa* (*Rūpāvatī*).
Tone material:
C D♭ E♭ G A♯ B c
c B A♯ G E♭ D♭ C
Lit.: no. 139.

Kāpinayāraṇi (South India). *Janya rāga* of the 28th *mēḷa* (*Harikāmbhōji*).
Tone material:
C D F G A B♭ c
c B♭ A G F E D C
Lit.: no. 139.

Kappore (Japan). Geisha songs derived from basic Shinto music. When performed by geishas the songs lost their serious Shinto character and assumed a humorous, entertaining nature.

Kāpyā Nagam (South India). *Janya rāga* of the 12th *mēḷa* (*Rūpāvatī*).
Tone material:
C D♭ E♭ F G c
c B A♯ G F E♭ D♭ C
Lit.: no. 139.

Kāra (Sudan). *Tanbur* with two gut strings.
Lit.: no. 184.

Kārā (India; Bengal). Cone-shaped drum with two heads.
Lit.: no. 255.

Karabib (Morocco; Sudan). A pair of castanets consisting of two small metal discs that are fastened on a string ornamented with shells.
Lit.: no. 255.

Karadisamela (South India). A temple *nāgara* with a large conically-shaped kettle.
Lit.: no. 255.

Karadsamila (South India). See *Karadisamela.*

Karagam (South India). Folk dance in which a pot is balanced on the dancer's head. The pot is gradually filled with rice. *Karagam* is the ancient (Tamil) *kudakuttu*.
Lit.: no. 261.

Karaharapriyā (South India). See *Kharaharapriyā*.

Karaka (South India). *Janya rāga* of the 15th *mēḷa* (*Māyāmāḷavagauḷa*).
Tone material:
C E G A♭ B c
c B A♭ G E C
Lit.: no. 139.

Karakia (New Zealand – Maori). Ritual magic songs, exorcistic incantations to placate the deity or beg for a favor.
Lit.: nos. 37, 228.

Karalādhari (South India). *Janya rāga* of the 46th *mēḷa* (*Śaḍvidhamārgiṇī*).
Tone material:
C D♭ E♭ F♯ A B♭ c
c B♭ A F♯ E♭ D♭ C
Lit.: no. 139.

Karamut (*Garamut*) (Melanesia; Bismarck Archipelago; Duke of York Isl.). Wooden slit-drum.
Lit.: no. 255.

Karan (Ancient Babylon). Sumerian term for trumpet.
Lit.: no. 87.

Karan (Nigeria). See *Dundun.*

Karana (India). Dance figure (gesture) of the *bharata-nāṭyam.*
Lit.: no. 46.

Karaṇā (India). Straight copper or brass trumpet. See also *Karnā.*
Lit.: no. 249.

Karanga (*Marae*) (New Zealand—Maori). Shouts, called or sung. Cf. *Marae.*
Lit.: no. 228.

Karangba (Congo). See *Kalanba.*

Karaning (West Africa—Mandingo). Spike fiddle (*ngenge*).
Lit.: no. 190.

Karaṇi (South India). *Janya rāga* of the 22nd *mēḷa* (*Kharaharapriyā*).
Tone material:
C E♭ G A B♭ c
c B♭ A G E♭ C
Lit.: no. 139.

Karañjakam (South India). *Janya rāga* of the 28th *mēḷa* (*Harikāmbhōji*).
Tone material:
C F G A B♭ c
c B♭ A G F C
Lit.: no. 139.

Karapāni (South India). *Janya rāga* of the 23rd *mēḷa* (*Gaurīmanōharī*).
Tone material:
C D E♭ G A B c
c B A G E♭ D C
Lit.: no. 139.

Karatagan (Java; Suda District). Sundanese term for *srepegan* and *sampak.* Cf. *Srepegan.*
Lit.: no. 163.

Karātala (*Kartali*) (India). Rattle with small round thin rattling brass discs inserted into four openings cut into two wooden bars in the shape of carpenter's planes that are beaten against each other.
Lit.: no. 254.

Karatāla (India; Bengal). Cymbals with bent rim.
Lit.: no. 255.

Karatoyam (South India). *Janya rāga* of the 7th *mēḷa* (*Senāpāti*).
Tone material:
C D♭ E♭ F G B𝄫 c
c B𝄫 G F E♭ D♭ C
Lit.: no. 139.

Karatoyam (South India). *Janya rāga* of the 56th *mēḷa* (*Śaṇmukhapriyā*).
Tone material:
C F♯ G A♭ B♭ c
c B♭ A♭ G F♯ C
Lit.: no. 139.

Karatsaka (Malagasy Republic; Majunga Region). Percussion beam. Cf. *Tsikaretika.*
Lit.: no. 251.

Karatu (Celebes). Wooden goblet-shaped drum used in sacred rites.
Lit.: no. 132.

Karawitan (Java). Traditional music played by the *gamelan* ensemble.

Kar-ba (Tibet). See *Dril-bu.*

Kārchilambu (South India). Hollow metal (mostly iron) rings placed around the ankles of dancers. The rings contain rattling small stones.
Lit.: no. 261.

Kardān (*Kirdān*) (Arabia; Middle East). A tone name. In Persian the term indicates "frontier," "border," and signifies a tone one octave higher than *rāst.* It is the 11th main note of the rising scale (or the 8th note if *rāst* is considered to be the first tone). (All tone names within the range of two octaves are listed under the heading *Jagā* [*Yagā*].)

As a *maqām Kardān* has the following scale:
D E♭(+) F G A B♭(+) c d
Lit.: no. 64.

Kardaniya (*Āwāz*) (Arabia). Henry G. Farmer (Lit. no. 65, p. 185) reports the scale of this *maqām*, as stated by Safī al-Dīn 'Abd al-Mu'min al-Baghdadi (13th century) in the following manner:

C D F♭ F A♭♭ G A c♭ c

Lit.: no. 65.

Kare (Bali). See *Main chachih* (Flores).
Lit.: no. 197.

Kareng (West Java). See *Karinding*.
Lit.: no. 163.

Kar gyin (Burma). Ancient battle song and war dance. (*Kar* means "shield of warriors.")

Kari fu (Japan). An 18th-century *go-on fu* (and *meyasu*) notational system of the Buddhists. While the *go-on fu* was a simple way of notation where each notational line or curve represented one or two notes, the *kari fu* showed extensive lines and curves annotated with numerous letters placed (vertically) below the lines and curves. Cf. *Meyasu*.
Lit.: no. 185.

Karim (East India; Orissa). Frame drum.

Karinding (West Java). The West Javanese term for *rinḍing* (Java). In the Tasik District the instrument is called *karinding* only if it is made of wood. If it is made of bamboo it is called *kareng*.
Lit.: no. 163.

Kär-i-tälān (Kurdistan). Bridge (on a string instrument).
Lit.: no. 255.

Karkaba (Morocco – Genaua). Iron castanets.
Lit.: no. 255.

Karkarī (India). Sanskrit term of an obscure instrument of ancient India, mentioned in the *Rig Veda* and *Atharvaveda*. Probably a bell or jingles and much less likely a lute. Cf. *Gargara*.
Lit.: no. 250.

Karma (Southeast India – Maikal Hills). The Gond and Baiga tribes call *karma* a song and dance that symbolizes the bringing home of green branches and fruit from the jungle. The *karma* songs, similarly to the *dadaria*, are sung in a question and answer form.
Lit.: no. 134.

Karmāravī (Ancient India). See *Jāti*.

Karmata Karsana (Southeast India – Muria Gond Tribe). *Gotul* song sung at a girls' game.
Lit.: no. 142.

Kārmukhāvati (South India). *Janya rāga* of the 59th *mēḷa* (*Dharmavatī*).
Tone material:

C D E♭ F♯ A B c
c B A F♯ E♭ D C

Lit.: no. 139.

Karmuvu (South India). *Janya rāga* of the 44th *mēḷa* (*Bhāvapriyā*).
Tone material:

C E♭ F♯ A♭ B♭ c
c B♭ A♭ G F♯ E♭ D♭ C

Lit.: no. 139.

Karnā (*Qarna*) (Persia; North India). Metal trumpet. In India the instrument consists of a heavy straight or curved tube. Cf. *Karana*; *Karnal* (Nepal); *Banku*; *Buruga*; *Kurna*.
Lit.: no. 255.

Karṇabhūṣan (South India). *Janya rāga* of the 70th *mēḷa* (*Nāsikabhūṣaṇī*).
Tone material:

C D♯ E F♯ A B♭ c
c B♭ A F♯ E D♯ C

Lit.: no. 139.

Karṇabhūṣaṇi (South India). *Janya rāga* of the 16th *mēḷa* (*Chakravāka*).

Tone material:
C D♭ E A B♭ c
c B♭ A G F E D♭ C
Lit.: no. 139.

Karnal (Nepal). Trumpet made of copper or brass. Cf. *Karṇa.*

Karṇarañjaṇi (South India). *Janya rāga* of the 22nd *mēḷa* (*Kharaharapriyā*).
Tone material:
C D E♭ F E♭ G A c
c B♭ A G F E♭ D C
Lit.: no. 139.

Karṇāṭa Jōgi (South India). *Janya rāga* of the 17th *mēḷa* (*Sūryakānta*).
Tone material:
C D♭ E F G A c
c B A G F D♭ C
Lit.: no. 139.

Karṇāṭaka Andhāḷi (South India). *Janya rāga* of the 14th *mēḷa* (*Vakuḷābharaṇam*).
Tone material:
C E D♭ F G A♭ B♭ c
c B♭ G F E D♭ C
Lit.: no. 139.

Karṇāṭaka Behāg (South India). See *Karṇāṭaka Byāg.*

Karṇāṭaka Byāg (*Karṇāṭaka Behāg*) (South India). *Janya rāga* of the 28th *mēḷa* (*Harikāmbhōji*).
Tone material:
C D E F G A B♭ c
c B♭ A B♭ G A F E D E C
Lit.: no. 139.

Karṇāṭa Kadamba (South India). *Janya rāga* of the 53rd *mēḷa* (*Gamanaśrama*).
Tone material:
C D♭ F♯ G A c
c B A G F♯ E D♭ C
Lit.: no. 139.

Karṇāṭaka Dēvagāndhāri (South India). *Janya rāga* of the 21st *mēḷa* (*Kiravāṇi*).
Tone material:
C E♭ F G A♭
A♭ G F E♭ D C, *B* C E♭ F E♭ D
Lit.: no. 139.

Karṇāṭaka Dēvagāndhāri (South India). *Janya rāga* of the 22nd *mēḷa* (*Kharaharapriyā*).
Tone material:
C D C E♭ F G A G B♭ c
c B♭ A G F E♭ D C
Lit.: no. 139.

Karṇāṭaka Kāpi (*Kāpi*) (South India). *Janya rāga* of the 22nd *mēḷa* (*Kharaharapriyā*).
Tone material:
(a) C D E♭ F D G F G A B♭ c
c B♭ A G F E♭ D C
(b) C D E♭ F G A B♭ c
c B♭ A G F E♭ F D C
Lit.: no. 139.

Karṇāṭaka Mañjari (South India). *Janya rāga* of the 54th *mēḷa* (*Viśvambharī*).
Tone material:
C D♭ F♯ G A♯ B c
c B A♯ G F♯ G E D♭ C
Lit.: no. 139.

Karṇāṭaka Sāranga (South India). *Janya rāga* of the 15th *mēḷa* (*Māyāmāḷavagauḷa*).
Tone material:
C D♭ E F G A♭ B c
c A♭ F G F E D♭ C
Lit.: no. 139.

Karṇāṭaka Surati (South India). *Janya rāga* of the 4th *mēḷa* (*Vanaspāti*).

Tone material:
C D♭ E♭♭ F G A c
c B♭ A G F D♭ C
Lit.: no. 139.

Karṇāṭaka Taraṅgiṇi (South India). *Janya rāga* of the 61st *mēḷa* (*Kāntāmaṇi*).
Tone material:
C D E F♯ G B♭♭ c
c G F♯ E D C
Lit.: no. 139.

Karṇikādhari (South India). *Janya rāga* of the 20th *mēḷa* (*Naṭabhairavī*).
Tone material:
C D E♭ F G A♭ B♭ c
c B♭ A♭ G F D E♭ C
Lit.: no. 139.

Karṇika Rañjani (South India). *Janya rāga* of the 20th *mēḷa* (*Naṭabhairavī*).
Tone material:
C D E♭ F G F A♭ B♭ c
c B♭ A♭ G F E♭ D C
Lit.: no. 139.

Ka-roko (Sierra Leone—Temne). Drumstick.
Lit.: no. 255.

Karombi (Indonesia; Sa'dang-Toraja). Small wooden jew's harp.

Karotugal (Java). Term for fast tempo. Cf. *Wirama siji*; *Loro*; *Telu*; *Papat*.
Lit.: no. 163.

Karpūramu (South India). *Janya rāga* of the 30th *mēḷa* (*Nāgānandī*).
Tone material:
C F G A♯ B c
c B A♯ G F C
Lit.: no. 139.

Karranāy (Turkey). Long curved trumpet. Other terms: *shaipūr*, *būq*.

K'ar-rnga (Tibet). Gong.

Karruli (India). Ancient obscure percussion instrument.
Lit.: no. 255.

Kartal (Assam). Wooden clapper.
Lit.: no. 46.

Kartāl (Nepal). Rattle consisting of six pairs of tiny, flat brass cymbals placed in a wooden frame.
Lit.: no. 46.

Karunā (India). One of the nine emotions (*rasas*) (pathos; compassion). Cf. *Navarasa*; *Rasa*.
Lit.: no. 140.

Karunakai (South India). *Janya rāga* of the 63rd *mēḷa* (*Latāṅgī*).
Tone material:
C F♯ G A♭ B A♭ c
c B A♭ G F♯ C
Lit.: no. 139.

Karuṇapriya (South India). *Janya rāga* of the 37th *mēḷa* (*Sālaga*).
Tone material:
C D♭ E♭♭ F♯ B♭♭ A♭ G B♭♭ c
c B♭♭ A♭ G F♯ E♭♭ D♭ C
Lit.: no. 139.

Kārupravādana (Ancient India). Term indicating the art of playing musical instruments.
Lit.: no. 292.

Karuvali (South India). *Janya rāga* of the 24th *mēḷa* (*Varuṇapriya*).
Tone material:
C E♭ G A♯ B c
b B A♯ G E♭ C
Lit.: no. 139.

Kāryamati (South India). *Janya rāga* of the 20th *mēḷa* (*Naṭabhairavī*).
Tone material:
C D E♭ G A♭ c
c B♭ A♭ G F A♭ F E♭ D C
Lit.: no. 139.

Kās (Egypt). General term for small and large cymbals. See *Sajjat.*
Lit.: no. 255.

Kas (Angola). Primitive marimba. Cf. *Marimba.*
Lit.: no. 255.

Kasa (Korea). A ballade type of song accompanied by the *tae-kum*, *chang-ko*, occasionally also by the *sae-p'iri* (cf. *Hyang-p'iri*) and *haikeum.*

The *kasa* repertoire is limited to 12 items; several are strophic and some are freely composed. The rhythm of the *kasa* is in six beats. An abbreviated form of *kasa* is called *sijo.*

Ḳaṣaba (*Ḳashsha*) (Arabia). Term for reeds, single or double.

Kasai (Nepal). See *Naya khin.*

Kasai baja (Nepal). See *Naya-khin.*

Kasambonaṅ (Borneo). See *Katambon*; *O-tsi* (Burma).

Kasanga (Southeast Africa; Lourenco Marques Bay Area). Term for *sansa.*
Lit.: no. 255.

Kasapi (Southeast Borneo). Cf. *Sapeh*; *Safe.*

Kāsāt (Arabia). Bowl-shaped cymbals in various sizes, from small finger cymbals to large bowl-shaped instruments. Cf. *Ku'ūs*; *Sajjat.*
Lit.: no. 76.

Kasayi (Congo; Ruanda). *Sansa* with 17 metal tongues, nine at the right side and eight at the left. Cf. *Likembe.*
Lit.: nos. 201, 303.

Kase (Japan). An extra fret added to the neck of the *uwajōshi shamisen*, the obbligato *shamisen.* This enables the player to play his occasionally elaborate part an octave higher than on other *shamisen* in *nagauta* music.
Lit.: no. 187.

Kase (Persia). Bowl, cymbal, bowl-shaped corpus.
Lit.: no. 255.

Kash (East Caroline Isl.; Ponape). General name for nose flutes in various forms. See also *Ang en tsuma*; *Chup en parri*; *Parri chup en rò.*
Lit.: no. 313.

Ka shakurian (Burma). See *Ka konshau.*

Kashakwe (Congo—Warundi). Drum.
Lit.: no. 26.

Kashane (South Africa—Balubedu). Musical bow with one string.
Lit.: no. 151.

Kā-sharati (India; Khasi Hills). Flute with six (or seven) finger holes.

Kashila (Congo—Balamba). Cylindrical drum with two heads, beaten with the hands of the player.

Kashira (Japan). Characteristic drum technique (drum cadencing pattern) performed on the *taiko* in *noh* and *nagauta* music.
Lit.: nos. 185, 187.

Kāshīrāmakriya (*Kāśīrāmakriya*) (South India). *Janya rāga* of the 51st *mēḷa* (*Kāmavardhanī*). Tone material:

C E D♭ E F♯ G A♭ B c
c B A♭ G F♯ E D♭ C

Lit.: no. 139.

Kashiwaba (Japan). Cf. *Koto* parts.

Ḳashsha (Arabia). See *Ḳaṣaba.*

Kāshṭa Tarang (South India). A xylophone consisting of 15 wooden cups (or slabs) arranged in the form of a *jaltarang.* The *kāshṭatarang* cups are tuned when manufactured, and are never to be filled with water as is done with the *jaltarang.*
Lit.: no. 261.

Kāshyapī (South India). *Janya rāga* of the 8th *mēḷa* (*Hanumaṭṭōḍi*).
Tone material:
C D♭ E♭ G A♭ B♭ c
c B♭ A♭ G D♭ C
Lit.: no. 139.

Ka si (Burma; Shan State). "Frog drum." Four pairs of frogs are depicted as ornaments on the tops of four kettle gongs. This set is also called *kaun chet.*
Lit.: no. 198.

Kasik (Turkey). Wooden spoons used as rattles (castanets).
Lit.: no. 157.

Kasingkil (Philippines). Dance performed between several bamboo posts. It is called "Royal Fan Dance."

Kāśīrāmakriya (South India). See *Kāshīrāmakriyā*; *Kāmavardhanī*; *Rāmakriyā* (51st *asampūrṇa mēḷa*).

Kāśmīra (South India). *Janya rāga* of the 6th *mēḷa* (*Tānārūpi*).
Tone material:
C D♭ E♭♭ G A♯ B c
c B A♯ G E♭♭ D♭ C
Lit.: no. 139.

Kasso (West Africa). Harp-lute with a gourd as resonance body, a long straight neck from which are strung strings to varying number to a stick attached to the corpus at right angles. Cf. *Kilara.*
Lit.: nos. 190, 255.

Kassuto (Congo). A small wooden scrape box, the lid of which shows the carving of a ladder. The player scrapes the ladder with a wooden stick.
Lit.: no. 255.

Kastratang (India). See *Jaltarang.*

Kāśyapī (South India). See *Kāshyapī.*

Katabachi (Japan). Sequence of *obachi* beats played accelerando and crescendo. The "crowding" of these beats is called *kūwaheru.*

Katakapriya (South India). Also called *Khadgapriya. Janya rāga* of the 1st *mēḷa* (*Kanakāṅgī*).
Tone material:
C E♭♭ D♭ E♭♭ F G A♭ G B♭♭ c
c A♭ G A♭ F E♭♭ D♭ C
Lit.: no. 139.

Katakyi (Ghana). Royal ivory horn. Cf. *Kakaki.*
Lit.: no. 95.

Katala (Sumba). Gong.
Lit.: no. 159.

Katambon (*Kasambonaṅ*) (Borneo). Simple goblet drum. Cf. *Gatambore*; *Katambore*; *Tabir.*
Lit.: no. 254.

Katambore (Borneo). See *Katamboṅ.*

Ka taṅmuri (Assam; Burma). A small bamboo beak flute with seven finger holes.
Lit.: no. 252.

Katanto (Africa; Dahomey). Drum music played at rites of planting and harvesting.
Lit.: no. 218.

Kaṭapayādi sankhya (South India). System of using the Sanskrit letters, particularly the Devanagiri letters *ka*, *ṭ*, *pa*, and *yā* for various purposes of classification.

The four groups of consonants of the Devanagari alphabet are used in the following manner:

1. *Kādinava* group

K	KH	G	GH	NG	CH	CHH	J	JH	(JN)
1	2	3	4	5	6	7	8	9	0

2. *Tādinava* group

Ṭ	ṬH	Ḍ	ḌH	Ṇ	T	TH	D	DH	(N)
1	2	3	4	5	6	7	8	9	0

3. *Pādipancha* group

P	PH	B	BH	M
1	2	3	4	5

4. *Yādiashṭa* group

Y	R	L	V	S	SH	S	H	(LH	KSH	DNY)
1	2	3	4	5	6	7	8	0	0	0

The correct number of a *mēḷa* in the system of 72 is obtained by using the two first consonants of the *mēḷa* name in any of the four groups of letters and inverting their sequence. An example may illustrate this procedure: e.g., the *mēḷa-rāga* name *Yāgapriyā*. Its two first consonants are *Y* and *G*. The theorist and musician who wish to establish the correct number within the system of the 72 *mēḷas* will take the numbers of the first two consonants, *Y* and *G*. Consulting the list of the four letter groups the number 1 stands for *Y* and the number 3 for *G*. The final step is now to revert the numbers: 1 3 is turned into the number 31. This number (31) is the correct number of *Yāgapriyā* in the system of the 72 *mēḷas* (of the *Kanakāṅgi-Ratnāṅgi* system).

In a few instances when, in the place of the second consonant, conjunct consonants appear, it is important to observe that occasionally the first of the two conjunct consonants is counted. But in *rāgas* with the names *Chakravāka*, *Divyamani*, *Viśvambhari*, *Simhendramadhyama*, and *Chitrāmbari* the second of the conjunct consonants has to be counted.

For details see my books, Lit. nos. 136 and 139. Cf. *Chakra.*

Katarai (Japan). Several beats performed in accelerando by the left stick on the *kakko.* Generally the series of beats is concluded by a *sei.*
Lit.: no. 225.

Katarimono (Japan). Narrative style accompanied by *shamisen* music. The other style in which music alone is elaborated without any narrative character is called *utaimono.*
Lit.: no. 187.

Katāuba (Indonesia; Mentawai Isl.). Goblet drum. Cf. *O-tsi* (Burma).
Lit.: no. 254.

Katchel (Ethiopia). A small *döwel.*
Lit.: no. 38.

Kathakali (South India; Kerala). South West Indian story play, performed by masked and heavily made up male dancers. It is a complex folk art with intricate dance motions and gestures. The music is performed by a male singer who relates the story and by drummers (*maddala* players) who stand to the right side of the stage. The plays represent religious and legendary subjects emphasizing heroic and romantic events. Cf. Lit. no. 123.

Kathana kutūhalam (South India). See *Kadana kutūhalam.*

Kaṭhinya (South India). *Janya rāga* of the 22nd *mēḷa* (*Kharaharapriyā*).
Tone material:

C D F G A B♭ c
c B♭ A G F D C

Lit.: no. 139.

Katiboke (Southwest Malagasy Republic). Slit-drum.
Lit.: no. 251.

Katiwul (West Java). Term for *kempul.* In Indramayu these gongs are also called *weleri* or *goong leutik* (small gong).
Lit.: no. 163.

Katjapi (Java; South Celebes). Also *kachapi.* See *Ketjapi*, *Kacchapi.* A large cylindrical drum.
Lit.: no. 162.

Katjapin (South Celebes). Boat-shaped lute.
Lit.: no. 254.

Katlo (North Philippines). Cf. *Topayya.*

Katō-bushi (Japan). Narrative *shamisen* songs of the 18th century. Songs of a fishmonger can still be heard occasionally. Cf. *Katarimono*; *Bungo-bushi.*
Lit.: no. 225.

Katongga (Sunda; Bima). Bamboo stamping stick. The term has been used also for a simple xylophone. Cf. *Katongga kayu.*
Lit.: no. 162.

Katongga kayu (Sunda; Bima). Simple xylophone. In Central Timor it is called *sene ha'u.* This type appears in Eastern Flores as *preson, letor, geko.*
Lit.: nos. 162, 166.

Katral (Ancient Babylon; Akkad.). Cymbals.
Lit.: no. 87.

Kattalam (South India). *Janya rāga* of the 63rd *mēḷa* (*Latāṅgī*).
Tone material:
C F♯ G A♭ B c
c B A♭ G F♯ C
Lit.: no. 139.

Kattivadiyam (South India). Tamil term for *gāda* (*gāṭha*).
Lit.: no. 254.

Katumba ka vidye (Congo – Baluba-Shankadi). Small goblet drum.
Lit.: nos. 26, 190.

Katumbeng (Malaysia – Dayak). Drum.
Lit.: no. 255.

Katumbi (Congo – Bena-Lulua of Kasai). Drum with a cylindrical corpus.
Lit.: no. 26.

Katungu (Congo – Wasongola). Musical bow used only by women.
Lit.: nos. 21, 33.

Kātyāyaṇa Vīṇā (India). Ancient board zither. Cf. *Kānūna*; *Sārmaṇḍal* (Marathi term); *Śatatantrī vīṇā*; *Svaramaṇḍala* (*Surmaṇḍal*).
Lit.: no. 292.

Kātyayānī (South India). *Janya rāga* of the 62nd *mēḷa* (*Riṣabhapriyā*).
Tone material:
C D E F♯ G B♭ c
c B♭ G F♯ E D C
Lit.: no. 139.

Kaula (*Mujaguzo*) (Uganda; Angola). The royal drum of the (Wa)-Ganda.
Lit.: no. 255.

Kaumāri (South India). *Janya rāga* of the 11th *mēḷa* (*Kokilapriya*).
Tone material:
C D♭ E♭ F G A c
c B A G F E♭ D♭ C
Lit.: no. 139.

Kaumati (South India). *Janya rāga* of the 5th *mēḷa* (*Manōrañjani*).
Tone material:
C D♭ E♭♭ G A B c
c B A G F E♭♭ D♭ C
Lit.: no. 139.

Kaumōda (South India). *Janya rāga* of the 65th *mēḷa* (*Mechakalyāṇī*).
Tone material:
C D E F♯ B c
c B F♯ E D C
Lit.: no. 139.

Kaun chet (Burma – Shan State). Cf. *Ka si.*

Kaunjangera (Angola). Dance, drum.

Ḳauns (Arabia). See *Ḳos.*

Kauns (*Kaunsadhvani*; *Koshadhvanī*) (North India). *Rāga* ascribed to the *Bilaval thāta*; very rare.
Tone material:
C E F A c
c B (B♭) A (F) E C
Lit.: no. 138.

Kaunsadhvani (North India). See *Kauns.*

Kaunsi (North India). See *Kaushik-kanada.*

Kaur (New Mecklenburgh; New Britain; Bismarck Archipelago). (1) Stopped pan-flutes. (2) Notched long flute of Neupommern. Cf. *Khor*; *Gore*; *Korr.*
Lit.: no. 255.

Kaushik-Kanada (*Kaunsi*) (North India). *Rāga.* There are two types:

1. ascribed to the *Asavari thāta.*
2. ascribed to the *Kafi thāta.*

The *vādis* are the same in both types: F and c (C).
Tone material:

(a) C (D E♭) F (G) A♭ $\overset{+}{\text{B}\flat}$ c
c B♭ A♭ (G) F E♭ D C

(b) C (D E♭) F G A $\overset{+}{\text{B}\flat}$ c
c B♭ A G F E♭ D C

Lit.: no. 138.

Kauśikikanada (South India). *Janya rāga* of the 20th *mēḷa* (*Naṭabhairavī*).
Tone material:
C E♭ F A♭ B♭ c
c B♭ A♭ F E♭ D F E♭ D C
Lit.: no. 139.

Kauśilakam (South India). *Janya rāga* of the 20th *mēḷa* (*Naṭabhairavī*).
Tone material:
C D E♭ F G B♭ A♭ c
c B♭ A♭ F E♭ C
Lit.: no. 139.

Kauss (Turkey; Turkestan). Fiddle in the shape of a large wooden spoon. The corpus and neck are made of one piece. It has two horsehair strings and no bridge.
Lit.: no. 255.

Kaustubhapriya (South India). *Janya rāga* of the 71st *rāga* (*Kōsala*). The scale of this *rāga* is identical with that of *rāga Jayaśuka* (71st *mēḷa*).
Lit.: no. 139.

Kaval (Turkey; Central Asia). Vertical open flute used in folk music. Cf. *Düdük.*
Lit.: no. 243.

Kavardham (South India). *Janya rāga* of the 43rd *mēḷa* (*Gavambōdhi*).
Tone material:
C E♭ F♯ A♭ B♭♭ c
c B♭♭ A♭ F♯ E♭ C
Lit.: no. 139.

Kaved (Israel; Samaria). Cf. *Qal.*

Kāvya chitra (South India). *Janya rāga* of the 20th *mēḷa* (*Naṭabhairavī*).
Tone material:
C E♭ D E♭ F G A♭ G B♭ c
c B♭ G F D C
Lit.: no. 139.

Kawa (Japan). Drum skins (*noh* drums).
Lit.: no. 185.

Kawālī (North India). Folk music of the Islamic North. The songs have Urdu texts and are accompanied by the *dholaka.* The *kawal* do not use any string instruments.
Lit.: no. 46.

Kawasht (Syria). See *Nam* (*nim*) *gushat*; *Nim gavasht.*

Kawat (Java). Wire string. See also *Rebāb* (Java and Bali).
Lit.: no. 197.

Kawi (Bali). (1) The ancient formal literary language using numerous elements of old Javanese and Sanskrit. (2) Vocal music (Sunda Districts). Cf. *Kekawin.*

Kawih (Sunda District; Bali). Song of a woman soloist with *gamelan degung.*

Kaw law (Northeast Thailand). Xylophone.
Lit.: no. 203.

Kawng (*Mong*) (Northeast Thailand). Small bronze gong, generally used in pairs suspended in a wooden box.

Kawö (Burma – Shan State; Kwanhai-Palaun). Double pipe made of bamboo with free beating metal reeds. It consists of a melody pipe with seven finger holes and one thumbhole. The drone pipe has no finger holes.
Lit.: no. 252.

Kawundi (Uganda). Cf. *Eggwara.*

Kayā (Burma). Large oboe type. Cf. *Hne.*
Lit.: no. 254.

Kaya-geum (Korea). Cf. *Kaya-gum*; *Kaya-kum*; *Kaya-ko.*

Kaya-ko (*Kaya-keum*; *Kaya-kum*) (Korea). Long board zither of Korean origin with 12 strings. Each string is strung across its own tall movable bridge. The instrument is used not only in classical music but also, with slight changes in tuning, in folk and *sanjo* music. The instrument was also called *hwi-kum*, the old "*hui*" zither.
Lit.: nos. 136, 179.

Kayamba (Kenya). Rattle in the shape of a flat box.

Kayanda (Rhodesia – Ba Ila; Congo – Balamba; Bayeke). Drum.
Lit.: no. 26.

Kayapriya (South India). *Janya rāga* of the 4th *mēḷa* (*Vanaspāti*).
Tone material:
C D♭ E♭♭ G A B♭ c
c B♭ A G E♭♭ D♭ C
Lit.: no. 139.

Kayī (India). The body of the *vīṇā* or lute instruments.

Kayitalama (Ceylon). Flat cymbals.
Lit.: no. 206.

Kayoma (Uganda – Amba). Board zither. The instrument has one single *rattan* string.
Lit.: no. 302.

Kayon (Bali). The "stage tree" used in shadowplays. It symbolizes various features: storm, lightning, fire, rains, and other heavenly and divine events. On ancient Indian sculptures, particularly on stupas, the Bodhi tree represented the Buddha, his throne and related features. A similar significance may be found in Southeast Asian shadowplays. When the tree appears alone it generally means a change of scenery or the end of the play.

Kazaduratan (Philippines). Dance of the women.

Kazān (Arabia). Musical instrument.

Ka zi (*Ka si*) (Burma). See *Hpa:zi*; *Ka si.*

Kazo (Japan – Aino). Simple drum with one head.

Ke (Japan). The "twisted sharp," a term employed in *koto* music. After a string has been struck it is twisted by thumb and first finger in such a manner that its sound is raised by a semitone. Then the pressure is released and the string is allowed to continue its vibration on the original pitch.
Lit.: no. 225.

Ke (North India). See *Ge* (North India).

Kebero (South Ethiopia). Name of the *coboro.* See *Coboro.*
Lit.: no. 38.

Keblūk (West Java). Cf. *Chengkung.*
Lit.: no. 163.

Kebyar (Bali). Music for the *kebyar*, a dance in modern style. A single boy dancer fashions his movements freely to the music of the *gamelan.*
Lit.: no. 197.

Kechak (*Ketjak*; *Chak*) (Bali). A male chorus of about 150 men provides the accompaniment of the ritualistic trance dance called *sanghyang.* The men of the chorus sit on the floor and shout in unison syllables such as *ke cha-ka*, *cha-ka*, *ke*, also *chu-ku*, *chu-ku* in an exciting crescendo and accelerando. Occasionally the *ke-chak* (*kechak*) can be employed in secular performances. See also *Chak.*
Lit.: no. 197.

Kechapi (Borneo). The term signifies the same instrument as *kachapi* of the Sunda District. Cf. also *Ketjapi.*
Lit.: no. 156.

Ke(chi)cher (*Kecher*) (Java; Bali). In East Java, *kencher*; in Grobogan, *chiyeyek*. Two small bronze cymbals. The Balinese term is *cheng-cheng, ke(n)-chek, richik*.

Kechrek (*Kepyak*) (Java). Two small iron discs tied loosely together and used as a rattle. Usually the *kechrek* is attached to the wall of the *kotak* in order to enable the player to rattle the *kechrek* plates with his toes.
Lit.: no. 163.

Kechruk (Java—Majakerta). Cf. *Angklung*.
Lit.: no. 163.

Keda (Flores). Cf. *Geda*.

Kedah Makyong (Malaysia). Dance drama (at the present time almost obsolete).

Kedang (East Flores—Larantuka). Jew's harp made of iron. In the Sunda Archipelago the same instrument is made of bamboo or palm-wood.
Lit.: no. 166.

Kedang bebanchian (Bali). A particular manner of playing one drum, in which the main accents of "female" and "male" drums are combined. Generally it is employed in *joged* and *gandrung*.
Lit.: no. 197.

Kēdār (*Kidar*; *Kēdāri*; *Kēdārika*) (North India). *Rāga* ascribed to the *Kalyan thāta*. In legends it was believed that *Kēdār*, when performed correctly, can melt stones, prison walls (hence jailers readily offered to teach the prisoners how to sing this *rāga* for a suitable remuneration), and heal diseases.
Tone material:
C F (F♯) G A (B) c
c B (B♭) A G F♯ (F) D C; *Vādis*: F, c
Lit.: no. 138.

Kēdāra (*Kedaram*) (South India). *Janya rāga* of the 29th *mēḷa* (*Dhīraśaṅkarābharaṇam*).
Tone material:
C F E F G B c
c B G F E D C (c B G F E F A F E D C)
Other probably descents are:
c B G A G F E D C
c B G F G A F D C
Lit.: no. 139.

Kēkāragaula (South India). *Janya rāga* of the 28th *mēḷa* (*Harikāmbhōji*).
Tone material:
C D F G B♭ c
c B♭ A G F E D C
Lit.: no. 139.

Kēdāranāṭa (South India). *Janya rāga* of the 27th *mēḷa* (*Sarasāṅgī*).
Tone material:
C D E F G B G c
c B G F E D C
Lit.: no. 139.

Kedari (North India). See *Kedar*.

Kedarika (North India). See *Kedar*.

Kedar-nath (North India). *Rāga* consisting of a combination of *Nath* and *Kēdār* materials.
Lit.: no. 138.

Kedempling (West Java). Cf. *Dempling*.

Kedemung (*Saron Kedemung*) (Sunda District). The "tenor" range of a 4-octave range *gamelan*. (The other ranges are called: the highest, *peking*; the "alto," *saron*; the "bass," *jengglong*.)
In West Java *kedemung panerus* (not to be mistaken for the Javanese *saron panerus*), means *saron demung*. In Indramayu the term *penurung* is used.
Lit.: no. 163.

Kedire (Borneo). See *Kledi*.

Kedol (*Gende*) (Malacca—Singapore; Malaysia). Cf. *Diṇ teṅkhiṅ*.

Kedondolo (South Africa—Bakwebo). Musical bow.
Lit.: no. 148.

Kedzangi (Ghana). See *Agbadza.*

Kee (Liberia—Kpelle). Gourd rattle.
Lit.: no. 284.

Keembe (Uganda—Kikuya). Drum.
Lit.: no. 255.

Kehido (Sumba). Bamboo flute.
Lit.: no. 162.

Kei (*Hokyo*) (Japan). A small bronze (or gold) Buddhist temple-gong that hangs in a wooden frame at the right side of the altar. Its shape, described as "fish-mouthed," consists of two rhombically-shaped plates linked with their narrow sides.
Lit.: nos. 185, 255.

Keikin (Japan). A spike fiddle imported from China. Its body is a bamboo segment covered with snakeskin. The instrument has four silken strings tuned in pairs to a fifth (or fourth), and the horsehair of the bow is strung between the two pairs of strings. Cf. *Kokyū*; *Kokin*; *Seiteki*; *Hu-ch'in* (China).
Lit.: nos. 225, 255.

Keisu (China). A *dōbachi* (Japanese temple gong) used by several Chinese sects.
Lit.: no. 255.

Kejo (Flores). Dance.

Kekawin (Bali). Reciting and chanting of texts in ancient Javanese taken from the two Hindu epics, the *Mahābhārata* and the *Rāmāyaṇa*. Each line is provided with a translation from Kawi into colloquial Balinese. Cf. *Kawi.*
Lit.: nos. 197, 265.

Keke (Nigeria—Yoruba). Two flat bamboo sticks are clicked against each other. Other terms for *keke* are: *keke-were*; *pa-pe*; *oparun.*
Lit.: no. 293.

Kekechrek (West Java). Term for the Javanese *kechrek* when it consists of more than two rattling plates.
Lit.: no. 163.

(K)eketek (Java; Jogya). A drum word that indicates a stroke with one finger, middle or index, on the rim of a small drumhead. The sound produced is called *tong* or *pen* (as related in Lit. no. 163, pp. 205-06.)

Keke-were (Nigeria). See *Keke.*

Kekinchiran (Sunda District). A bull roarer, made of other material than coconut leaf. See *Jata* (Flores). Cf. *Hohoang.*
Lit.: no. 163.

Kekreng (Southeast India; Bastar State—Muria Gond). An iron or bamboo scraper.
Lit.: no. 59.

Kelantan Makyong (Malaysia). Traditional dance drama.

Kele (Sierra Leone—Mende; Dahomey—Naga). Slit-drum; drum.
Lit.: no. 303.

Kele (Mali—Dogon). Transverse flute.

Keledin (*Kledi*) (Borneo—Dayak). See *Kläddi.*

Keleli (Africa; Chad). Plucked lute with 2-3 strings.

Kelen (Liberia—Kpelle). Large slit-drum.
Lit.: no. 284.

K'elen (Sudan—Temne). Temne term for the great Mandingo drum; a hollowed-out tree trunk that serves as a canoe is turned upside down and beaten like a drum.
Lit.: no. 95.

Kelenang (Bali). Small gong together with the *kempli* (a second small gong) are used for additional (musical) punctuation.
Lit.: nos. 197, 265.

Keḷi-koṭṭa (South India; Kerala). Vigorous drumming announcing the beginning of the *kathakali* performance at sunset. Cf. *Cheṇḍa.*
Lit.: no. 123.

K(e)liningan (West Java). Term for the Javanese *genḍer.*
Lit.: no. 163.

Kelir (Java). The *wayang* screen.
Lit.: no. 163.

Kelleli (Sahara—Teda of the Tibesti region). A primitive lute made of a metal pan covered with skin. Only men are allowed to play this instrument.
Lit.: no. 301.

Kelong (Celebes). Short popular lyrical song.
Lit.: no. 166.

Kelosok (Borneo). Dancing shield ornamented with Chinese coins fastened to its sides. The shield is used by the Dayak people during their dance.
Lit.: no. 255.

Kelurai (*Klurai*) (Borneo—Dayak). A mouth organ with seven pipes. Pipes 1-6 (F A $\overset{+}{B\flat}$ c f $\overset{\flat}{g}$) are melody pipes, pipe 7 plays the bourdon note. Cf. *Kladdi.*
Lit.: nos. 163, 254.

Kemaga (Java). A term that indicates that certain ways of performing are forbidden. For instance, if *klenengang* is played with the *kendang* (drum) but without gong, this practice is prohibited. It is called *kemaga.*
Lit.: no. 163.

Kemān (*Kaman*) (Persia). Bow.

Kemanak (Java). Obsolete percussion instrument consisting of two bronze (or iron) banana-shaped parts that are beaten crosswise against each other.
Lit.: no. 168.

Kemānjah (*Kemānje*) (Arabia; Egypt). See *Kamānjah.*

Kemānjah (Arabia; Persia; Afghanistan). Also *kemānǧeh.* The term is generally used for the *kamānjah a'jūz.*
Lit.: no. 255.

Kemānje (Arabia). See *Kemānjah.*

Kemānje a'jūz (Arabia; Iran). See *Kamānjah a'juz.*

Kemānje rūmī (Arabia; Iran). See *Kamājah rūmī.*

Kemānje soghair (Arabia; Iran). See *Kamānjah farkh.*

Kemānje taqti (Arabia; Iran). See *Kamānjah taqti.*

Kema rodi (Flores). Working songs sung by a leader and chorus of road workers.
Lit.: no. 166.

Kembangan (Java; Bali). Ornamental passages; a "flowery" treatment of the melody. Cf. *Sekaran.*
Lit.: nos. 163, 197.

Kembang delima (Java). See *Genta* (Java).

Kembang kirang (Bali). A rare instrumental ensemble playing purely pentatonic music.
Lit.: no. 265.

Kembe (Central Africa; Sahara). Term for *sansa.*
Lit.: nos. 201, 215.

Kemenak (Bali). See *Gumanak.*

Kemenche (*Kemençe*) (Turkey; Iran). Bowed lute with three strings. The instrument has a pear-shaped body.
Lit.: no. 243.

Kemenche rūmī (Turkey). Fiddle with three strings. The strings are stopped sideways with the fingernail as it is done when the Indian musician plays the *sarangi.* Cf. *Kamānjah rūmī.*
Lit.: no. 243.

Kemin (India). Marine-shell trumpet.

Kemkem (Ethiopia; Coptic). Drum; tambourin.
Lit.: no. 255.

Kemong (Java). Small vertically hanging gong. It is always used together with the *engkuk.* The two instruments are beaten alternately.
Lit.: no. 163.

Kemong (*Ken[t]ong*) (Bali). Small vertically suspended gong used in *gamelan pelegongan.*
Lit.: nos. 197, 265.

Kempiang (West Java). (1) Two small gongs tuned to *nem* and *barang* (tonic and fifth). (2) The term can also denote a *terbang.*
Lit.: no. 255.

Kempli (Bali). (1) A small gong used for producing secondary punctuation. (2) In *gamelan pejogedan* the term *kempli* indicates a special two-keyed xylophone. The two bamboo slabs are called *kempli* and *kempyung.*
Lit.: nos. 159, 162, 197.

Kemprongan (West Java). Itinerant theater. See *Ketuk tilu.*

Kempul (Central and East Java; Bali). (1) Gong suspended freely in a wooden frame, sounding an octave higher than *gong suwukan* and an octave lower than *kenong.* Occasionally *kempul* gongs are called by the old name *ganjur* (or *genjur*). When there is only one *kempul* in the *gamelan*, it will be tuned to the note *nem* (or *lima*). In West Java this gong is called *katiwul*, *weleri*, or *gong leutik.* Cf. *Penontong.* (2) Cf. *Kempur* (Bali); *Hawis.*
Lit.: nos. 163, 265.

Kempur (*Kempul*) (Bali). Large gong performing secondary punctuation in the *gamelan gong.* See *Gamelan angklung.*
Lit.: no. 159.

Kempur kōmōdong (Bali). A large slice of bamboo hung over the opening of an earthenware vessel. This instrument occasionally appears in the *gamelan pejogedan.*
Lit.: nos. 197, 265.

Kempyang (*Kompyung*) (Bali). The higher sounding of two small gongs, placed in a frame. Both gongs are called *ponggang.*

Kempyang (Java). Two kettle gongs used as *pelog* instruments. Both can be tuned to *nem*, or one to *nem*, the other to *barang*, and, more recently, to *lima* and *nem.* Both kettles are beaten simultaneously.
Lit.: no. 163.

Kempyang (Java – Jogya). Drum word. It indicates a swiftly performed, clicking beat executed by the middle finger and index on the rim of the small drumhead. Cf. *Tong.*
Lit.: no. 163.

Kempyang slendro (Java). Gong in the form of a *bonang* (gong), tuned to the note *barang.* The kettle is used instead of the *engkuk* and *kemong* in the *jogya kepatihan.*
Lit.: no. 163.

Kempyong (*Kompyong*) (Bali). Term for the lower sounding of the two *ponggang* gongs (*kompyong* or *kompyung*). Cf. *Kempyang.*

Kempyung (Java). "Inversion." The inversion of *kempyung* (interval of a fourth) is called *salah gumun* ("out of the way agreement").
Kempyung indicates also one of the two-keyed xylophone *kempli* in *gamelan pejogedan.* One bamboo key is called *kempli*, the other *kempyung.*
Lit.: no. 163.

Kemrapyang (*Kencheng*) (Java). Bright drum sound in contrast to a dull sound (*kendo*).

Ken (Japan). Small "gong" made of porcelain. Beaten with a wooden stick.

Ken (Vietnam). Oboe with a wooden bell. There are four *ken* playing in *dai nhac*.
Lit.: nos. 296-97.

Ken (*Khen*) (Former Annam; Laos; Vietnam). Mouth organ (similar to *sheng*) with 14 or less diatonically tuned pipes. Two pipes are used to play the bourdon bass. Three sizes are distinguished: *ken tieu* (small); *ken trung* (medium); *ken dai* (large). Cf. *Cai ken*.
Lit.: no. 255.

Kenadi (Alor; Indonesia). Bamboo tube zither.
Lit.: no. 156.

Ke nangi (Flores—Ende; Lio). Elegy, Dirge. Also called *nangi 'ta mata*.
Lit.: no. 166.

Kenawak (East Java). Term for *kemanak*.
Lit.: no. 163.

Ke(n)chek (Bali). Medium sized cymbals used in the *kebyar* dance. See also *Ke(chi)cher*.
Lit.: no. 197.

Kencheng (Java). See *Kemrapyang*. The Balinese term is *cheng-cheng*.

Kencher (East Java). See *Ke(n)chek*; *Ke(chi)-cher*.

Kendai (Japan). The wooden stand upon which is placed text and notated music.
Lit.: no. 225.

Kenḍang (Bali). A conically-shaped, two-headed drum beaten with a stick. The *kenḍang* usually appears in pairs. One drum is larger and is called *wadon* ("female"), while the other is smaller and bears the name *lanang* ("male"). If a *kenḍang* is beaten without a stick it is called *genḍang gupekan*. If one drum is beaten with a stick it is called *kenḍang pegongan*. Cf. *Genḍang*; *Gönḍrang*.
Lit.: nos. 162, 197, 265.

Kenḍangan (Bali; Java). Term for drumming.

Kenḍangan (Java). Also *tilam*. The term indicates the skin (buffalo intestine or bladder parchment) that covers the belly of the *rebāb*.

Kenḍangan bibaran (Java). *Bibar*; *bubar*, "to complete," "finish." Drum pattern beaten at the end of a *wayang* or festival performance.
Lit.: no. 163.

Kenḍang awi (Java). A *chelempung* that is used as a *kenḍang*. Cf. *Chelempung*.

Kenḍang awi (West Java). Stamping bamboo tube of Tasikmalaya. In the Bandung district it is called *kinchir* ("reel"). Cf. *Boku* (Flores).
Lit.: no. 163.

Kenḍang batangan (*Batangan*) (Java). Drum used in the *gamelan* when dances are to be accompanied. The instrument is a large barrel drum, richly ornamented.
Lit.: no. 163.

Kenḍang besar (Java). Large drum in the form of a *mṛdanga*.

Kenḍang chiblon (Java). Barrel drum similar to the *kenḍang genḍing* but smaller in size. It appeared in the *gamelan* ensemble in 1870 and was used for the *nguyu-uyu* on the day or evening before the festivity. The playing of the *kenḍang chiblon* is less restricted by rules than that of the *kenḍang genḍing*. See *Chiblon*.
Lit.: no. 163.

Kenḍang genḍing (Java). A large drum with a wooden body. Its shape is either that of a truncated cone or full bellied. Of the two drum heads the larger one is struck by the right, the smaller by the left hand.
Lit.: no. 163.

Kenḍang gupekan (Bali). *Kenḍang* without a beater. Cf. *Kenḍang pegongan.*

Kenḍang jemblung (Java). A thick bamboo tube, open at both ends, the node slightly above the middle. It is beaten with a *tabuh.*
Lit.: no. 163.

Kenḍang lanang (Bali). See *Kenḍang.*

Kenḍang leutik (*Kolanter*) (West Java). "The little *kendang.*" It is identical with the Javanese *penuntung* or *ketipung.*
Lit.: no. 163.

Kenḍang pegongan (Bali). *Kenḍang* with the beater. Cf. *Kenḍang gupekan.*
Lit.: no. 265.

Kenḍang penchak (Java; West Java). See *Penchak.*

Kenḍang tumba (Bali). "Bug drum." A very small drum, hence its name.
Lit.: no. 265.

Kende (West Africa—Kissi). Slit-drum. Cf. *Kemanak.*
Lit.: no. 168.

Kenḍil grabah (Java). A group of earthenware resonance pots. See *Bonang.*
Lit.: no. 163.

Kendo (Java). The Malay word *kendor* means "slack," "flabby." Dull drum sound.

Kendo (Gabon). Bell.

Keneku (Flores). Term for playing the *remba.*
Lit.: no. 166.

Kengere (Uganda—Madi; Alur; Congo—Waundi). (1) Cylindrical drum with a single head, played by a woman. (2) Royal drum of the Alur (Uganda). (3) Horn (made of cow horn) of the Warundi (Congo).
Lit.: nos. 26, 190, 302.

Kengyō (Japan). The honorary rank of the third class of blind musicians. Those persons who have received the title *kengyō* ("maestro"), are permitted to wear wide trousers. These musicians play popular music. Cf. *Gakunin*; *Genin*; *Koto*; *Geishas.*
Lit.: no. 185.

Kenite (Flores). A zither with six, seven, or nine strings. In East Flores (Larantuka) the instrument is called *santo.* In Maumere it has the same name or *mapa*, also *nggo nggri.* In Riangwulu (East Flores) it is called *surondopi.* In Ende (Lio) it is called *reketora.* In the Head of Flores the instrument generally has three strings; the *santo* of Larantuka has seven and the *nggo nggri* has six (or seven) strings.
Lit.: no. 166.

K'enne (Korea). Ancient small drum.
Lit.: no. 255.

Kenoṅ (Malaysia; Malacca). Stamping drum. See *Diṅ teṅkhiṅ.*

Kenong (Malaysia). (1) A group of six bronze kettles placed horizontally across a flat wooden box in a rectangular form.
(2) Four brass slabs are placed across a wooden box. The tuning of the slabs is c B♭ A E (the notes *chi*, *nem*, *mo*, *ruh*). Another set consisting of three kettles is tuned to *E D C.*
Lit.: no. 217.

Kenong (*Loloran*) (Sunda District). (1) The fifth note of the *pelog* system (Sunda District). (2) Term for the Javanese *lima*, the fourth main note of the *slendro* system (Sunda District). (3) A foreign tone, not belonging to the scale. Cf. *Salah gumun.* (4) Note in *surupan melog* (Java).

Kenong (Java). The name of a well known interpunctuating *gamelan* instrument which, when there is only one specimen of it in the ensemble, always produces the tone *kenong* (*lima*). The instrument is a single large kettle

with a high rim. The kettle produces a high, clear sound when beaten with a short wooden stick. Cf. *Hawis.* The instrument can also be called: *kenong wayang*, *kenong ringgitan*, *kenong playon.*
Lit.: no. 159.

Kenongan (Java). The *kenong* "cuts." The markings of subdivisions in large gong periods (*gongan*), performed on the *kenong.*
Lit.: no. 159.

Kenong japan (Java). A large flat *kenong* that sounds an octave below the common *kenong.* It is considered to be "female." Cf. *Kenong lanang.*
Lit.: no. 163.

Kenong lanang (Java). The term represents the common *kenong. Lanang* means "male" and is used to distinguish the instrument from the large *kenong japan* (allegedly introduced by a Japanese sovereign).
Lit.: no. 163.

Kenong penongtong (Java). See *Penongtong.*

Kenong playon (Java). A *kenong* tuned to the note *nem.* It has interpunctuating function.
Lit.: no. 163.

Kenong ringgitan (Java). High Javanese term for *kenong wayangan.*
Lit.: no. 163.

Kenong wayangan (Java). See *Kenong playon. Kenong* tuned to *nem.*

Kenteng (Java). String.
Lit.: no. 255.

Kenṭong (Java). Term for the alarm signals beaten on a slit-drum or slitted wooden box (*kenṭongan*) to inform people that some crime has been committed or that people are called for a meeting. The type of crime is indicated by the number of beats. Cf. *Kenṭong loro*, *Kenṭong telu*, *Kenṭong pat*, and *Kenṭong titir*, *Kenṭong pinchang.* A roll on these slit-drums (*gobyog*) signifies the call for meeting of the people. Cf. *Kenṭongan.*
Lit.: no. 163.

Kenṭongan (Java). The slit-drums mentioned under the heading of *kenṭong.* If the drum is made of bamboo it is called *tetekan.* Cf. *Kukulan gantang.*
Lit.: no. 162-63.

Kenṭong loro (Java). See *Kenṭong.*

Kenṭong pat (Java). See *Kenṭong.*

Kenṭong pinchang (Java). See *Kenṭong.*

Kenṭong telu (Java). See *Kenṭong.*

Kenṭong titir (Java). See *Kenṭong.*

Kentrung (Java). The accompaniment of a song sung by a man advising young girls about good manners and cleanliness. The accompaniment is performed by a *terbang* and a *kendang* (the name of the song is called *prawang kenya*).
Lit.: no. 163.

Kentung-kentung (Malaysia). Wooden slit-drum. Cf. *Kentong.*
Lit.: no. 163.

Kenut (Java). A single slab of a *saron.*

Kenyir (Bali). A small *gangsa* with three keys, all tuned to the same pitch, is struck with a triple-headed hammer. The *kenyir* is used in the *gamelan gambuh.*
Lit.: nos. 197, 265.

Keo pata (Southeast India—Hill Maria Gond Tribe). Religious *gotul* song. See *Gotul pata.*
Lit.: no. 142.

Kep (Thailand). Variations on a melody.

Kepala Copong (Malaysia). Term for the widely flaring bell of the *serunai.*

Kepatihan (Indonesia). See *Titilaras Kepatihan.*

Keplakan (*Kepuakan*) (Bali). Bamboo rattle. According to Lit. no. 197, also a pair of large cymbals.
Lit.: no. 197.

Keplep (West Java). Cf. *Kohkol.*
Lit.: no. 163.

Keprak (Java). A small wooden box (or tube) with a slit. The box is beaten with a wooden hammer called *chempala* or *tabuh keprak.* The instrument is used for accompaniments of dances.
Lit.: no. 163.

Kepuakan (Bali). See *Keplakan.* The rattle is used to frighten birds.

Kepyak (Java). See *Kechrek.* The term *kepyak* is used in *wayang* performances; it usually means a rattle. *Kepyak* can also be applied to a clapper made of buffalo bones. These clappers can be made also of wood, iron, and ivory.
Lit.: no. 163.

Kepyak (West Java). A group of three *bonang.* One is tuned to *barang* and the other two to *singgul.*
Lit.: no. 163.

Keran-non-konin (Liberia—Kpelle). Harp-lute.
Lit.: no. 284.

Keranting (Malaysia—Orang Temiar). Tube zither with up to 20 strings.
Lit.: no. 255.

Kerar (*Krar*) (Erithrea; Ethiopia). See *Kissar.* Lyre with 10 strings, tuned in pairs.
Lit.: no. 102.

Kerek (Java). See *Bajang.*

Keren (Ancient Israel). Term for animal horn. Cf. *Shofar.*

Kerep (Java). Close together (rhythmically), such as the *keṭuk* beats. See *Gending ageng tengahan.*
Lit.: no. 163.

Kereshmeh (Iran). "Nod," "sign." After a rhythmically free *gusheh* section in a *dastgāh* performance, the *kereshmeh* section is metrically structured.
Lit.: no. 146.

Keretata (Southeast Pacific; Mangareva Isl.). Slit-drum.
Lit.: no. 84.

Keretok (Malaysia). Cattle bell made of palm tree wood.
Lit.: no. 255.

Keretok-krebau (Thailand; Malaya). Wooden buffalo bell.
Lit.: no. 255.

Kerikeri (Nigeria—Yoruba). Low pitched, hourglass-shaped drum of the *dundun* ensemble. Cf. *Bembe.*
Lit.: no. 303.

Kerilong (Sumatra—Benkulen). Transverse flute with six finger holes.
Lit.: no. 255.

Kering (Sunda District). Fast tempo. See *Wirahma* (*wirama*).
Lit.: no. 163.

Keriten (South Africa—Qung Bushmen). Rattle placed around the ankles of male dancers.
Lit.: no. 151.

Kerō (Japan). Small, high pitched drum of the *taiko* type. It is suspended from the neck of the player and is used in processions marking time in music.
Lit.: nos. 225, 255.

Keronaru (Sierra Leone—Fula). Lute with six strings.

Kerunai (Borneo). See *Kläddi* (*Kledi*).

Keruri (Borneo). See *Kläddi* (*Kledi*).

Kēsaranāṭa (South India). *Janya rāga* of the 27th *mēḷa* (*Sarasāṅgī*).
Tone material:
C D E F G B c
c B G F E D C
Lit.: no. 139.

Kēsāravaḷi (South India). *Janya rāga* of the 17th *mēḷa* (*Sūryakānta*).
Tone material:
C D♭ F G A B c
c A G E D♭ C
Lit.: no. 139.

Kēsaravālōkam (South India). *Janya rāga* of the 58th *mēḷa* (*Hemāvatī*).
Tone material:
C D F♯ G A c
c B♭ A G F♯ E♭ D C
Lit.: no. 139.

Kēsarī (South India). *Janya rāga* of the 25th *mēḷa* (*Mārarañjanī*).
Tone material:
C D E F G F A♭ G c
(C D E F G F A♭ G A♭ c)
c B♭♭ A♭ G F E D C
(c A♭ B♭♭ G F E D C)
A third ascent can be:
C F E F E D E F G A♭ c
Lit.: no. 139.

Kēśarikriya (South India). *Janya rāga* of the 51st *mēḷa* (*Kāmavardhanī*).
Tone material:
C D♭ E F♯ A♭ F♯ G B c
c B G F♯ D♭ F♯ E C
Lit.: no. 139.

Kesekawan (Indonesia; Indramayu). Tone name indicating the second main note of the *slendro* system (of Indramayu). Cf. *Slendro* (table C).
Lit.: no. 163.

Kesekawan (Java). "Four." The fourth note.

Kesetunggal (Indonesia; Indramayu). See *Kesetunggil.*

Kesetunggil (*Kesetunggal*) (Indonesia; Indramayu). The fifth note of the *slendro* system of Indramayu (in Javanese the term can indicate the first tone of the scale). Cf. *Slendro.*

Kesi (Malaysia). A pair of small cymbals.

Keso-keso (Celebes). Bowed lute. In Buginese the instrument is called *gesong-kesong.* Cf. *Geso-geso.*
Lit.: no. 162.

Kesubi (Japan). Specific drum beat on the *taiko.*

Ket (Armenia). Metrical unit in liturgy. It can be compared with the *mātrā* of India or with the quarter note of the West. *Sugh* represents a whole note (four *ket*) and *zoigket* a half note (two *ket*).
Lit.: no. 101.

Ketadu (Sumba). Boat-shaped lute.
Lit.: no. 162.

Kētakāṃkuśa (South India). *Janya rāga* of the 68th *mēḷa* (*Jyōtisvarūpiṇī*).
Tone material:
C D♯ F♯ G F♯ A♭ B♭ c
c A♭ F♯ E D♯ C
Lit.: no. 139.

Kētakapriya (South India). *Janya rāga* of the 64th *mēḷa* (*Vāchaspati*).
Tone material:
C E F♯ G B♭ c
c B♭ A G F♯ E D C
Lit.: no. 139.

Kētanāvaḷi (South India). *Janya rāga* of the 67th *mēḷa* (*Sucharitra*).
Tone material:
C D♯ E F♯ B♭♭ G A♭ c
c B♭♭ A♭ F♯ G F♯ E C
Lit.: no. 139.

Kētāramañjari (South India). *Janya rāga* of the 60th *mēḷa* (*Nītimatī*).
Tone material:
C E♭ F♯ G B c
c B A♯ G F♯ E♭ D C
Lit.: no. 139.

Ketawak (Malaysia). Gong.

Ketawang (*Genḍing*) (Java). A *genḍing alit* composition which has 16 *keteg* per *kenongan.* The 16 *keteg* consist of only two *ketuk* beats and the *gongan* has two *kenongan* beats. The second part of this composition is of the *ladrang* type. When this part is played separately (in both *slendro* or *pelog*) it is called *kenḍangan lahela.*
Lit.: no. 163.

Kete (Ghana). Vertical flute with four finger holes.
Lit.: no. 206.

Kete (Nigeria – Yoruba). Popular drum with a wooden corpus. Its upper part is cylindrical, the lower is that of a rounded calabash. The *kete* ensemble consists of three drums: *iya'lu kete*, the leading drum; *two ewiri* drums, smaller than the *iya'lu kete*. At times there are two additional drums added, each with two (or one) heads: *omele ako* (beaten with the hand) and *omele kenkele* (beaten with a stick).

Kete (Ghana – Ashanti). Music of the Ashanti rulers performed by drums (*kete*). Occasionally there are introductory pieces performed by a chorus and several flutes.
Lit.: no. 218.

Ketek (*Keteg*) (Java). The smallest time unit ("heartbeat"). In Sundanese the term is *takol.* Also *dami* is used (not to be mistaken for *dami*, the rice-stalk shawm).
Lit.: no. 163.

Ketek (West Java). "Monkey" character in dances.

Keteng-keteng (North Sumatra – Karo Batak). A bamboo tube zither.
Lit.: no. 156.

Keter (Java). A particular manner of playing *gambang kayu* (also called *ṭuṭukan rangkep*) that sounds like a drum roll. *Keter* is also called *grontolan* ("like a roll on a drum"). Cf. *Ṭuṭukan rangkep*; *Toyamili.*
Lit.: no. 163.

Ketimpung (Java). See *Chiblon.*

Ketipluk (Bali). Term for *klontong.*

Ketipung (*Ketobong*) (Java). Small barrel drum. It corresponds to the *marvas* of Sumatra. See also *Penuntung.* Cf. *Kenḍang leutik*; *Kolanter.*
Lit.: no. 163.

Ketjak (Bali). See *Kechak.*

Ketjapi (*Kechapi*; *Katjapi*; *Kachapi*) (Java; Sumatra). A wooden boat-shaped zither with 2-16 wire strings. In Sumatra the *ketjapi* (also called *biola* or *mijue-mijue*), also with a boat-shaped body, is a lute with two gut or brass strings.
Lit.: no. 254.

Ketobong (*Ketipung*) (Borneo). A cylindrical or cup-shaped drum used by priests for healing diseases and driving away evil spirits. See *Sobang.*
Lit.: no. 255.

Ketoprak (Java). A popular theatrical (musical) performance of recent origin in which Javanese fairy tales are enacted to a musical accompaniment called *wreksatama* ("precious, noble wood").
Lit.: no. 163.

Ketsü (Assam – Naga). A straight, narrow trumpet made of a tree root.
Lit.: no. 252.

Keṭuk awi (Java). A *chelempung* that functions as a *keṭuk.* See *Chelempung* (2).
Lit.: no. 163.

Keṭuk kintel (Java). A *keṭuk* tuned to the note *gulu.*

Keṭuk kungkang (Java). *Keṭuk* tuned to the note *barang.*

Kaṭuk tilu (West Java). An instrumental ensemble that accompanies the *ronggeng* dance. It consists of three *keṭuk*, a *kenḍang*, a gong *rebāb* or *tarompet.* The same ensemble without the *rebāb* is called *banjet.* It often appears in the Sukabumi district. Another ensemble with the same function is the *amben.* It consists of a *rebāb*, two *saron*, three *keṭuk*, a *kenḍang*, *kenḍang leutik*, two gongs and a *kekechrek.* Its players are called *panjak.* In the district of Cheribon the group is called *kemprongan.*
Lit.: no. 163.

Ketungan (Bali). Rice pounding music.
Lit.: no. 197.

Keum (Korea). See *Kum.*

Kēyachāradhāriṇi (South India). *Janya rāga* of the 20th *mēḷa* (*Naṭabhairavī*).
Tone material:
C D E♭ F G B♭ c
c B♭ G F E♭ D C
Lit.: no. 139.

(K)fu'i dole (Timor). A flute similar to the *huhe* (Flores) but longer. There are no extra holes near the two ends of the tube. The instrument is also called *(k)fu'i tetek* and *(k)fu'i latan.*
Lit.: no. 166.

(K)fu'i latan (Timor). See *(K)fu'i dole.*

(K)fu'i tetek (Timor). See *(K)fu'i-dole.*

Kgabudubudu (South Africa—Pedi). Cf. *Kgabududu*; *Luvuvu.*

Kgabududu (South Africa). A bull roarer. Cf. *Luvuvu.*
Lit.: no. 148.

Khab (Tibet). "Needle." Notational curve with a sharp edge. For details see Lit. no. 143.

Khabab (Arabia). Cf. *Ḥidā.*

Khabun (Burma). See *Khobun.*

Khaḍgadhāriṇi (South India). *Janya rāga* of the 8th *mēḷa* (*Hanumattōḍi*).
Tone material:
C D♭ G A♭ B♭ c
c B♭ A♭ G D♭ C
Lit.: no. 139.

Khadyōta kānti (South India). *Janya rāga* of the 32nd *mēḷa* (*Rāgavardhanī*).
Tone material:
C D♯ F A♭ B♭ c
c B♭ A♭ F D♯ C
Lit.: no. 139.

Khadyōtapriya (South India). *Janya rāga* of the 8th *mēḷa* (*Hanumattōḍi*).
Tone material:
C D♭ F A♭ B♭ c
c B♭ A♭ F D♭ C
Lit.: no. 139.

Khaen (Thailand). See *Kaen*; *Khaen wong.*

Khaen (kaen) wong (Thailand). Mouth organ ensembles. Cf. *Kaen.*

Khafīf (Tunisia). See *Al khafīf.*

Khafīf al-khafīf (Old Arabia). See *Īqā'āt.*

Khafīf al-ramal (Old Arabia). See *Īqā'āt.*

Khafīf al-thaqīl (Old Arabia). See *Īqā'āt.*

Khagarājitam (South India). *Janya rāga* of the 20th *mēḷa* (*Naṭabhairavī*).
Tone material:
C D F G B♭ c
c B♭ A♭ G F G A♭ G E♭ D C
Lit.: no. 139.

Khais (South Africa; Hottentot). Drum made of a wooden pot-shaped vessel covered with goatskin. It is played only by women.
Lit.: no. 151.

Khajari (India). Songs similar to the *bhajana* with erotic-religious texts, accompanied on the *dholak* and by the *majīra*.
Lit.: no. 46.

Khakkara (Central Asia). An old Buddhist stick rattle. It has metal rings attached to its upper end. Also called *dorje*. Cf. *Bairāga*; *Dara*.
Lit.: no. 219.

Khalam (Senegal; Gambia—Wolof). See *Ḥalam*. In Senegal, Mali, and Guinea *khalam* means a lute, generally with three strings, occasionally with two or five. The strings are made of horsehair.
Lit.: nos. 33, 218.

Khāli (India). See *Tāla*.

Kham (Iran). "Bent." Trumpet; cymbals or drum.
Lit.: no. 255.

Khamaj (North India). Also called *Khammaja* or *Khambhojika*. *Thāta* and *rāga*.
Tone material:
C D E F G A (B♭) B c
c (B) B♭ A G F E D A; *Vādis*: E, B♭
Lit.: no. 138.

Khamaj thāta (North India). See *Thātas*.

Khamaji (North India). Obscure *rāga*. Its material consists of *Jhinjhoti* and *Khamaj* elements.
Tone material:
C D E F G B c
c (B) B♭ A G F E C; *Vādis* (probably): E, B
Lit.: no. 138.

Khamaka (India). Rustic drum of the present time.

Khamās (*Kamāsu*) (South India). *Janya rāga* of the 28th *mēḷa* (*Harikāmbhōji*).
Tone material:
C F E F G A B♭ c (C E F G A B♭ c)
c B♭ A G F E D C (B♭ c B♭ A G F E C)
Lit.: no. 139.

Khambavati (North India). *Rāga* ascribed to the *Khamaj thāta*. Three types are distinguished.
Tone material:
(a) C D F G A c
c B♭ A G (F) (E) C
(b) C E F G A B c
c B♭ A G (F) (E) C
(c) C E F A B c
c (B) (B♭) A (G) (F) (E) C; *Vādis*: E, B
Lit.: no. 138.

Khambhojika (North India). See *Khamaj*.

Khammaja (North India). See *Khamaj*.

Khamphak (Thailand). The subject of a *Khōn* performance.

Khāṃsya (India). Metal disc suspended in the entrance gates of Hindu temples for the devotees to ring upon entering.

Khan (Siam). Bow.
Lit.: no. 255.

Khānah (*Silsilah*) (Arabia). See *Muwashah*.

Khanda jāti (South India). See *Tāla*.

Khaṇdika (South India). See *Aḍi*.

Khang (Vietnam). See *Cai khang*.

Kha-nga (Tibet). Gong.

Khangari (India). See *Khanjani*.

Khanh (Annam). Small gong or bell.
Lit.: no. 255.

Khanh-da (Cambodia). Sonorous stone disc.
Lit.: no. 43.

Khanjan (Nepal). A tambourin with a high frame. The instrument appears also in Bengal.

Khanjanī (East India; Manipur). A pair of small cymbals. The term applies also to *khanjan*, also *khanjarī* or *khanjri*. Cf. *Khanjan*. The *khanjanī* can also be a single small wooden drum.
Lit.: no. 46.

Khanjri (India). See *Khanjanī*.

Khâqânī kus (Turkey). See *Kūs* (Turkey).
Lit.: no. 81.

Khara (Burma). Horn.
Lit.: no. 255.

Kharaharapriyā (*Karaharapriya*) (South India). (1) The 22nd *mēḷa*:

C D E♭ F G A B♭ c

(2) Popular *rāga*. Veṅkaṭamakhin called this *rāga Śri* or *Śrīrāga*. The tone material is identical with that of the 22nd *mēḷa*.
Lit.: no. 139.

Khararañjani (South India). *Janya rāga* of the 28th *mēḷa* (*Harikāmbhōji*).
Tone material:

C D E F G A c B♭ c
c B♭ A G F E C *B♭ A B♭* C

Lit.: no. 139.

Kharbī (Tunisia). A fast moving end-piece of the *nauba*.

Kharq (Arabia). Peg hole.

Kharunhāmon-lim (Burma). A shell trumpet.
Lit.: no. 255.

Kha's (South Africa—Korana Hottentot). "Hunting bow"; musical bow.
Lit.: no. 151.

Khat (North India). Rare *rāga* ascribed to the *Asavari thāta*. Its tone material consists of elements of *Asavari*, *Bhairav*, and *Mallār* elements.
Tone material:

C (D) E♭ F G A♭ B♭ (B) c
c (B) (B♭) (A) A♭ G F (E) (E♭) (D) (D♭) C

Lit.: no. 138.

Khatm (Tunisia). See *Al-khatm*.

Khattālī (India; Bengal). A pair of short iron sticks, one stick beaten against the other, in the manner of castanets. Cf. *Chachra*; *Karatāla*.
Lit.: no. 254.

Khat-tōḍi (North India). *Rāga* ascribed to the *Tōḍi thāta* or, if *Khat* material predominates, to the *Asavari thāta*.
Tone material is vague:

C D F G A♭ B♭ (B) c
c B A♭ G F♯ E♭ D♭ C; *Vādis*: A♭, E♭

Lit.: no. 138.

Khayāl (North India). See *Khyāl*.

Khazneh (Arabia; Egypt). Head; peg box (often made of ivory) of the *kamanjah*.

Khe (North India). See *Ghe*.

Khecharāṅgi (South India). *Janya rāga* of the 15th *mēḷa* (*Māyāmāḷavagauḷa*).
Tone material:

C D♭ F E F A♭ B c
c A♭ B G F E D♭ C

Lit.: no. 139.

Khem-kalyan (North India). Rare *rāga*; probably ascribed to the *Kalyan thāta*.
Tone material:

C D E F♯ G A B c
c B A G F♯ E D C

The *vādis* are identical with those of *rāga Kalyan*.
Lit.: no. 138.

Khen (Annam). See *Ken*.

Khen (Laos). A mouth organ that sounds like a bagpipe. It usually consists of two bunches each with seven long pipes with silver tongues. All pipes are placed in a calabash windbox with a mouthpiece. The instrument is played by blowing into the mouthpiece or by sucking the air out in order to obtain an uninterrupted sound. The tuning is: *A B♭* C D E F G A B♭ c d e f g. The lowest pipe serves as a drone. See also *Kaen.*
Lit.: no. 153.

Khenqekhenge (South Africa—Zulu). Rattle generally used by children.
Lit.: no. 151.

Khil (Khalka Mongolia). Cf. *Khil-khuur.*

Khilāvaḷi (South India). *Janya rāga* of the 22nd *mēḷa* (*Kharaharapriyā*).
Tone material:
C D E♭ F G c
c B♭ G F E♭ D C
Lit.: no. 139.

Khil-khuur (written: *kili kugur*) (Monglia—Sunit Mongols). A heavy fiddle with a trapezoid (or circular) wooden body, a long neck, and two horsehair strings tuned a fifth apart. The peg box is usually ornamented and presents the shape of a horsehead. In Khalka Mongolia the instrument is called *khil.* The Buriat and Khorchin Mongols call it *khur.* Cf. *Ta hu-ch'in*; *Budung utas*; *Närin utas.*
Lit.: no. 61.

Khin (Nepal). Term for *mṛdanga.*

Khinṣir (Arabia). Term for the fourth finger (in *'ud* playing).

Khinṣir fī majrā al-binṣir (Arabia). See *Aṣab'.*

Khinṣir fī majrā al-wuṣtā (Arabia). See *Aṣab'.*

Khiriu khiriu (Madagascar). Bell.

Khloi (Cambodia). Bamboo flute with seven finger holes. See *Khlui* (Thailand).
Lit.: no. 255.

Khloi toch (Cambodia). High-pitched noisy vertical bamboo flute with six finger holes. See *Khloi.*

Khloi thom (Cambodia). Low-pitched bamboo flute. See *Khloi.*

Khlui (Thailand). Small vertical flute (made of bamboo, wood, or ivory) with 6-7 finger holes, one covered with a thin membrane. The flute is used in the *mahori* ensemble. Cf. *Khloi* (Cambodia).
Lit.: no. 254.

Khmo (Cambodia). Gong.

Khobun (*Khābun*) (Burma). Drum.

Khokar (North India). Obscure *rāga.* There are two indistinct versions:

1. a combination of elements taken from *Khamaj* and *Bihagda.*
2. a vague firm, as shown by R. N. Vaze in his *Sangit Kala Pradesh* (Calcutta, 1982).

Tone material (flexible):
C E F G A c
c B♭ A G A F G E F E (D) C
Lit.: no. 138.

Khol (India). Barrel drum with a clay body and two skins. Cf. *Dhōlaka.*
Lit.: no. 250.

Khola bayan (India). "Open *bayan,*" a drum word. For details see Lit. no. 136. Cf. *Ghe*; *Bol.*

Khōn (Thailand). A category of the classical dance in which the performers wear masks in different colors. The colors represent: red (*phrot*) for Bharata; green (*rama*); gold (*lak, lakshman*); purple (*satrud* [*satrughna*]).

The chorus is called *kon* (*khon*) *phak.* The accompanying orchestra, consisting of five players (at the present time it is a variable number), is led by the *ranat* player. The performances show scenes from the *Rāmāyāna.* The text-translations into Thai language are called *Ramakien.*

The numerous masks represent five forms of the *khon*:
1. *khon klangplaeng.*
2. *khon rong nok* (*khon nung rao*).
3. *khon na co.*
4. *khon rongnai.*
5. *khon chak.*

Lit.: no. 207.

Khōn chāk (Thailand). A modernized variety of the *khōn* with much singing and elaborate scenery. It shows a distinct organization of the play into acts and scenes.
Lit.: no. 207.

Khōng (Siam; Burma). General term for gong, bell, and kettledrum.
Lit.: no. 255.

Khōng hui (Cambodia). A group of three gongs tuned to different pitches.
Lit.: no. 43.

Khōng khu (Thailand). Gong.
Lit.: no. 159.

Khōng lek (Siam; Burma). A *krewaing* with 21 small gongs.
Lit.: no. 255.

Khōng long (Burma). Big bell.

Khōng long tshan (Burma). Clapper (rattle).

Khōng malo (Thailand). Gong.

Khōng mong (Thailand). A suspended bronze gong.

Khōng ñai (Laos). Gong chime. Cf. *Khong vong yai.*
Lit.: no. 190.

Khōng noi (Laos). The Lao term for *khong vong lek.*

Khōng rao (Thailand). Gong.
Lit.: no. 159.

Khōng thom (Cambodia). Chime of 17 bell-shaped high-pitched gongs. They are beaten with sticks. The tuning closely resembles the western diatonic major scale, with the lowest note being tune to approximately the Western middle C. Cf. *Pip-hat.*
Lit.: no. 254.

Khōng toch (Cambodia). Chime of 16 small bell-shaped gongs beaten with small sticks. For tuning, see *Khōng thom.*

Khōng vong (Laos; Luang Prabhang; Thailand). 8-16 small gongs placed upon thin ropes stretched on top of a circular wooden stand.
Lit.: nos. 43, 159.

Khōng vong lek (Thailand). Chime of 18 high-pitched gongs. Cf. *Khōng vong yai.*
Lit.: no. 49.

Khōng vong yai (Thailand). Chime consisting of 16 gongs tuned lower than the *khong vong lek*, placed on a low circular frame.
Lit.: no. 49.

Khōn klang plaeng (Thailand). A variety of the *khōn.* An open air performance of masked dancers who represent battle scenes. The accompanying music has martial character. Cf. *Khōn.*
Lit.: no. 207.

Khōn nā cō (Thailand). Masked play acted before a white cloth screen. It has the character of a shadow play. Originally this type of play served as an in-between show between the acts. At the present time it has become an independent form of play. See *Khōn.*
Lit.: no. 207.

Khōn nang rao (*Khon nung rao*) (Thailand). See *Khon rōng nōk*; *Khon.*

Khōn nōnrōng (Thailand). A variety of the *khōn* shown on the first day when the introductory performances are given. This introductory music is called *homrong* (*khōn nōnrōng*). On the second day the main show is presented.
Lit.: no. 207.

Khōn nung rāo (*Khon nangrāo*) (Thailand). See *Khōn rong nok.*

Khōn phāk (Thailand). The chorus that recites the *khamphak* (the story of the *khōn*). There are several types: the *kabya*, *ceraca*, *rai*, and others. See *Khon.*
Lit.: no. 207.

Khōn rōngnai (Thailand). Masked play of the court. Elaborately staged. See *Khon.*

Khon rōng nōk (*Khōn nangrāo*) (Thailand). *Khon* performance on a stage. There is no singing, only recitatives and dialogues. Two *pipat* bands play on either end of the stage.
Lit.: no. 207.

Khöömiy (*Chakkur*) (East Mongolia). Throaty singing.
Lit.: no. 60.

Khor (New Hebrides; Aurora Isl.). Bamboo flute. Cf. *Gore*; *Kaur.*
Lit.: no. 255.

Khor (Mongolia—Buriat Mongols). Term for *Dörwen chikhe khuur.*
Lit.: no. 60.

Khorāḍak (*Khorāḍhāk*) (North India; Persia). Small kettledrums of Persian origin. The body of these drums is made of clay. The *khorāḍak* are used in pairs and beaten with the hands. The left side drum is tuned to a lower pitch than the right side.
Lit.: nos. 184, 254.

Khorae (Mongolia—Khorchin Mongols). Term for the *dörwen chikhe khuur.*
Lit.: no. 61.

Khore (New Hebrides—Aurora Isl.). Long bamboo flute.

Khouy (Laos). Bamboo flute.
Lit.: no. 43.

Khouy lip (Thailand). High-pitched, noisy vertical bamboo flute.
Lit.: no. 43.

Khouy pen ah (Thailand). Low-pitched bamboo flute. Used at solemn occasions. Cf. *Khloi.*
Lit.: no. 43.

Khram (Assam). Conically-shaped drum with two heads. It is believed that it has magical properties. An ensemble of four of these drums is called *nauksvebon.*
Lit.: no. 252.

Khrekhroṅ (Burma). Jew's harp.
Lit.: no. 255.

Khruaṅ dit (Siam). String instrument.

Khruaṅ ma:hori (Siam). Musical instrument.

Khruaṅ pao (Siam). Wind instrument.

Khruaṅ saī (Thailand). Instrumental ensemble consisting of strings, *khlui*, and percussion instruments.

Khryāng sāi (Thailand). An instrumental ensemble consisting of *sō duang*, *sō ū*, and *jakhē.* At times a *sō sām sāi* is added, and a flute, *thōn*, *rammanā*, and hand cymbals.

Khshe (Cambodia). String.

Khudra ghaṇṭa (India). Small *ghaṇṭa*, used for beating time.

Khudra kātyayāna viṇā (India). Small *kātyayāna vīṇā* (*kanuna*) with 14-18 strings. The word *khudra* stands here for *kshudra.*

Khui (Laos). Shawm with free reeds.
Lit.: no. 254.

Khula bayan (India). See *Khola bayan.*

Khumak (Persia). Also *khummak.* Small drum.
Lit.: no. 255.

Khumb (Persia). Trumpet.

Khumbgwe (South Africa—Venda). A combination of a *shiwaya* and a reed flute with three finger holes. The Kranga people call this unusual instrument *ombgwe.*
Lit.: no. 151.

Khume (Mongolia). "Nail" plectrum. The term indicates that two plectra are used in playing the *jatag*. The plectra have little leather caps to be placed on thumb and forefinger, from which protrude little pieces of horn which pluck the strings.
Lit.: no. 61.

Khum-muhra (Persia). Shell-horn.

Khur (Mongolia—Buriat and Khorchin Mongols). Fiddle. See *Khil-khuur.*
Lit.: no. 61.

Khut māndri (Bastar State; India-Gond). Conical or cylindrical two-headed *māndri.* Cf. *Māndri.*
Lit.: no. 59.

Khuuchir (Mongolia). See *Dörwen chikhe khuur*; *Khil khuur* (*Kuur*).

Khuur (Mongolia). Cf. *Pi-wang* (Tibet).

Khwak-khwang (Burma). Cymbal.
Lit.: no. 255.

Khwalimili (Nepal). Pair of small cymbals.
Lit.: no. 133.

Khyāl (North India). The light art song of North India. The *khyāl* is said to have had its origin in the 15th century with Mahmud Sharqi of Jaunpur. This creation became a free imitation of the ancient and dignified *dhrūpad.*
The formal structure of the *khyāl* is:

1. The *ālāp*. This introductory part is performed only by the soloist and the *tanbura* player. The drummer is silent.
2. The *asthāyī* represents the formal beginning of the *khyāl.* With it starts the *tabla* player, and from now on is the song rhythmically organized.
3. The *antara* shows a change in the melody, a moving up into the higher regions of the octave. After the *antara* follows:
4. A repetition of the *asthāyī.*
5. The "proper or big *ālāp.*" This section is performed with the drums in contrast to the opening *ālāp*: (a) The *rāga ālāp*, a rhythmified *ālāp* type; (b) the *rūpaka ālāp*, a miniature representation of the entire *khyāl*, presenting a short *asthāyī*, *antara*, *sanchārī*, and *ābhog*. These sections are sung usually to the syllables "ah," or "nah."
6. Occasionally appears now the repetition of the entire *asthāyī* and *antara.*
7. The *bol-tans. Tana* is a fioritura, melodic figuration, combined with textual syllables: small *bol-tans* are followed by big, extensive ones (big *bol-tans*).
8. A further interpolation of *asthāyī* and *antara* can be used here, but is often deleted.
9. The "real and proper *tans.*" These are complex variations and figurations.
10. As conclusion can be observed either a new, short song with its own *asthāyī* and *antara*, or simply the first *āvarta* of the original *asthāyī.*

For detailed information see my book, Lit. no. 138, pp. 27-35.

Khyū (Burma). Small globular bell; string with small round bells.
Lit.: no. 255.

Ki (Japan). Demon. One of five traditional subjects used in the *noh* drama (the other four are: *shin*, *nan*, *nyo*, and *kyo*).

Ki (Marquesas Isl.). Whistle flute, probably of European origin.
Lit.: no. 84.

Kiami-natik (Arabia). Melismatic song, probably of Turkish origin. Cf. also *Nakish*; *Semai*.
Lit.: no. 110.

Kiba (South Africa—Sotho). Cf. *Moromthwana.*

Kibanda (Congo—Babunda; Bakwese; Bapende). *Sansa.* Cf. *Kimbanda.*
Lit.: no. 33.

Kibbi (Northeast Congo—Bongo). Conical drum.
Lit.: no. 21.

Kibili (Congo). See *Idzdzai.*

Kibinja (*Kibinǧa*) (Tanzania—Swahili). Pipe.

Kibiti (West Africa). *Sansa.*
Lit.: no. 280.

Kibitiko (Congo—Basanga; Bayeke). Drum.
Lit.: no. 26.

Kibudikidi (Angola; Congo—Bwende). Small slit-drum.
Lit.: no. 157.

Kibugander (Kenya—Kisigi). Lyre with five strings.
Lit.: no. 218.

Kibulu kinteta (Congo—Bakongo). Cylindrical drum.
Lit.: no. 26.

Kichak (Bali). Tiny cymbals used in some *angklung* ensembles. The term refers also to the rhythmic patterns performed by the cymbals.

Kichi (East Turkestan). Cf. *Sochiba.*

Kidar (North India). See *Kedar.*

Kidete (Congo). Cane flute with four finger holes.

Kidi (Ghana—Ewe). Vertical barrel drum with one head, beaten with two sticks. Cf. *Sogo*; *Atsimevu.*

Kidi (Chad). Two-headed drum beaten by blacksmiths.

Kidideka (Malagasy Republic). Bamboo concussion sticks.
Lit.: no. 251.

Kidimba (Congo—Baluga). Term for *madimba.*
Lit.: no. 27.

Kidiyo (Uganda—Amba). Cow- or ivory-horn.
Lit.: no. 302.

Kidrar (Ethiopia). See *Kirar*; *Kinnor*; *Masonquo.*

Kidung (Bali). Festive temple songs with texts and meters in the middle Javanese language. For notating *kidung* songs, symbols are used, the names of which are: *ding* (E), *dong gede* (F), *dang gede* (G), *deng* (A), *dung* (B), *dang tjenik* (c), *dong tjenik* (d). For further details see Lit. no. 136, pp. 168-69. See also *Mekindung.*

Kiendu (Southwest Belgian Congo—Kasai). Wooden slit-drum.

Kifumwale (East Africa—Swahili language). String.

Ki-gae (Japan). Change of breath in *shō* playing; referring to successions of chords.

Kigan (Japan). Buddhist prayer chant.

Kignit (Ethiopia). Term that indicates a specific pentatonic tuning of the *krar.* The word *kignit* actually refers to "song."
Lit.: no. 144.

Kigoma (East Africa—Swahili). Term for small drum.

Kigulu (Solomon Isl.; Norfolk Isl.). Music bow with two fiber strings.
Lit.: no. 255.

Kigunda (East Africa — Swahili). See *Baragumu.*

Kigwara (Uganda — Gishu; Gwere; Nyole). Globular flute with two finger holes. Other names of the instrument are *ebumi* and *ebundi.*
Lit.: no. 302.

iKihuha (East Africa — Burundi). Simple cow horn.
Lit.: no. 255.

Kiiki (Africa; Chad — Teda). See *Kiki.*

Ki'ipā (Hawaii). Instrumental prelude and interludes during a *hula* dance.
Lit.: no. 215.

Kikadi (Congo — Eastern Kasai Province). Song type.

Kikasa (*Tshikasa*) (Congo — Baluba; Basanga). Drum.
Lit.: no. 26.

Kiki (Africa; Chad). Fiddle with one string.

Kikilo (Congo — Dongo). Ground zither.
Lit.: no. 176.

Kikira (India). Small bells.

Ki kohe puru (Marqueses Isl.). Nose flute. See *Ko'e.*
Lit.: nos. 190, 313.

Kikomfi (Congo — Manyema). Cylindrical slit-drum.
Lit.: no. 21.

Kikongwe (Kenya — Washambala). Short cylindrical flute. See also *Wikongwe.*
Lit.: no. 130.

Kiḷai (South India). Ancient Tamil term for *samvādī.*

Kilando (Lower Congo). Calabash with slits beaten like a drum.

Kilangay (Southwest Madagascar). Slit-drum.

Kilara (Senegambia — Wolof). Large harp-lute. Cf. *Kasso.*
Lit.: no. 255.

Kilembe (Tanganyika). See *Ngoma.*

Kili (Congo — Azande). Wooden bell. In the Medje language it is called *negpwapwo.*
Lit.: no. 184.

Kiliba (Congo — Wasongola). Wooden rattle.

Kilibongo (Congo — Azo; Andemaderi). Musical bow. See also *Kilingbindiri*; *Kilingila.*
Lit.: no. 176.

Kilingbindiri (Congo — Dongo). Musical bow.
Lit.: no. 176.

Kilingila (Congo — Logo). Musical bow. Also called *gulutindi.*
Lit.: no. 176.

Kilu (Uganda — Aoli). Term for the *kalur.* See also *Kiluka.*
Lit.: no. 302.

Kiluka (Uganda — Alur). Term for the *kalur.*
Lit.: no. 302.

Kiluku (South India). Tamil term for rattle.

K'im (China; Amoy). Ancient term for *ch'in.*

Kim (Burma). Mouth organ.
Lit.: no. 303.

Ki-ma (Tibet). Term for the Chinese *ch'in*, and for a Tibetan zither with seven strings that imitates the Chinese instrument (the latter is mentioned in literary works).
Lit.: no. 255.

Kimasa (Uganda—Soga). A rare arched harp with eight strings.
Lit.: no. 302.

Kimbal (Philippines). Drum with a conically-shaped body.

Kimbanda (Congo—Bahuana; Bakwese; Bambala; Batetela). *Sansa.* Cf. *Kibanda.*
Lit.: no. 21.

Kimbandu (Congo—Bayaka). Goblet drum beaten during male initiations.
Lit.: no. 26.

Kimbolo (Malagasy Republic). Bamboo percussion beam. See *Tsikaretika.*
Lit.: no. 251.

Kimonji (Japan). One of the *ozatsuma* patterns. Cf. *Ikioiji.*
Lit.: no. 185.

Kimwanyemwanye (East Africa). Wooden fiddle with two (or one) strings in the shape of a pot with a handle. Cf. *Tid.*
Lit.: no. 254.

Kin (Japan). (1) Term for *koto.* Cf. *Ichi-gen-kin*; *Kin-no-koto*; *Ni-gen-kin*; *San-gen-kin.* (2) The 13th string of the *koto.*
Lit.: nos. 225, 255.

Kin (Japan). Buddhist gong or bell, usually in bowl form. Cf. *Uchinarashi.*
Lit.: no. 185.

Kin (South Africa—Bergdama). Rattle consisting of cocoons attached with strings to the legs of male dancers.
Lit.: no. 151.

K'in (China). See *Ch'in.*

Kinaban (Philippine Isl.—Hanunoo). Jew's harp.
Lit.: no. 303.

Kinanda (Congo; Tanganyika; Uganda). Zither of various shapes. Cf. *Kindanda.*
Lit.: no. 176.

Kinanda (East Africa—Swahili). Term used also for pianoforte. *Kinanda cha mkono*, term for accordion; *kinanda santuri*, term for harmonium.

Kinandi-kinubi (Central Africa). A "devil's harp," a lyre type.
Lit.: no. 255.

Kinanga (*Ekihako*) (Uganda—Mugiba). Arched harp with seven strings. Cf. *Enzebe*; *Adungu.*
Lit.: no. 302.

Kinanṭi (Java). One of the poetic meters of *tembang machapat*, usually occurring in love songs. Cf. *Machapat.*
Lit.: no. 163.

Kinchir (West Java). See *Kenḍang awi.*

Kind (Korea). Occasional term for *kon-ko*; *kun-ko.*

Kindanda (*Kinanda*) (Central Africa). A term with various meanings: in Swahili it signifies "instrument"; in the East, a zither in various shapes; in the Congo, a lute of the *nanga* type with a fiddle-shaped body (with hips) and with 3-4 fiber strings; generally the term also means *sansa.*
Lit.: no. 255.

Kinditi kia nsi (Congo—Bembe). Large *sansa* with a rectangular resonator. It is played while the player is walking.
Lit.: nos. 190, 280.

Kinditi kiantele kia mbasa (Congo—Bembe). Small *sansa.* It is played while the player is walking.
Lit.: nos. 190, 280.

Kindja (Congo—Nzakara). Rattle worn by dancers on arms and legs.
Lit.: no. 33.

Kindri (Congo – Logo). Cylindrical drum with a single head. Cf. *Gaza*; *Ndima*; *Lari.*
Lit.: no. 26.

Kindu (Congo – Logo). Lyre type.
Lit.: no. 21.

K'ing (China). Term occasionally used for *ch'ing* (M 1164): a sounding stone generally made of nephrit and shaped in the form of a carpenter's square. See *Ch'ing.* The term *k'ing* can also be applied to a cup-shaped metal gong. In Japan this instrument is called *dōbachi.*

King (India). (1) In the Punjab the term stands for "bow." (2) In a wider sense the term is applied to a *bīn* (in Lahore). It is an instrument with one string and 7-8 bridges.
Lit.: no. 254.

Kingira (Iran). See *Kinguri.*

Kingoma kya nkisi (Lower Congo). Small drum with two heads.
Lit.: no. 280.

Kinguri (India). A zither with four strings, consisting of two calabashes linked by a frame. At the present time only one calabash and one string are used.
Lit.: no. 255.

Kingwa ndikila (Congo – Bembe). Stick zither with one string.
Lit.: nos. 190, 280.

Kin jū (Japan). Third variant of *hirajōshi* tuning. See *Koto* (Tuning).

Kin kake (Japan). See *Kake.*

Kin-kang-t'ui (China). See *Chin-kang-t'ui.*

Kinkinī (Ancient India). Sanskrit "little bell." Cf. *Guṅghurū*; *Salangai.*
Lit.: nos. 255, 260.

Kinkoto (Congo – Diki-diki). Clapperless bell made of sheet metal.
Lit.: no. 280.

Kin-ku (China). See *Chin-ku.*

King-tiao (China). See *Ching-t'iao.*

Kinguvu (Southwest Belgian Congo – Kasai area). Suspended slit-drum.
Lit.: no. 29.

Kinnarāvaḷi (South India). *Janya rāga* of the 35th *mēḷa* (*Śūlinī*).
Tone material:
C D♯ E G A B c
c B A F E D♯ C
Lit.: no. 139.

Kinnāre (*Kannāre*) (Arabia; also Indonesia). Term for a stick zither. The name is related to *kinnor.*

Kinnarēśapriya (South India). *Janya rāga* of the 10th *mēḷa* (*Nāṭakapriya*).
Tone material:
C D♭ E♭ G A B♭ c
c B♭ A G E♭ D♭ C
Lit.: no. 139.

Kinnārī (South India). Stick zither with two or three metal strings, 11-12 high frets, and three resonators. Two smaller gourds are attached near the ends of the stick and one large gourd is fastened to the middle of the stick. The *kinnā rī* is the favored instrument of beggars.
Lit.: no. 254.

Kinnārī vīṇā (India). This instrument has nothing to do with the stick zither (*kinnārī*). It is a *sitar* type with 5-7 strings. Its body has the form of half an ostrich egg. *Kinnārī vīṇā* is just a fancy type and term and has no consequence in serious musical practice.
Lit.: no. 254.

Kin no koto (*Hitsu no koto*) (Japan). One of the early Japanese names for the imported Chinese *ch'in.*
Lit.: no. 53.

Kinnōr (Ancient Israel). "The harp of King David." A lyra, the *k.nn.r* of ancient Egypt. The instrument had a variable number of sheep gut strings (3-12), usually 10 (five courses, each of two strings). The shape of the *kinnor* was rectangular or trapezoid. The strings were plucked with the bare fingers except when accompanying dances, when a plectrum was used. Cf. *Kannār*; *Kinnāra*; *Kinyra*; *Knr.*
Lit.: nos. 89, 250.

Kinor (Ancient Israel). See *Kinnōr.*

Kinteta (Congo—Bakongo). Barrel drum.
Lit.: no. 280.

Kinubi (East Africa—Swahili language). Harp.

Kinyo (*Kisaeng*) (Korea). Professional female entertainer. The term has the same meaning as *geisha* in Japan.

Kinyra (Ancient Egypt). See *Kinnōr.*

Kiondo (Congo—Baholoholo). Cylindrical slit-drum.
Lit.: no. 21.

Kipāntsona (Madagascar). Tambourin; cymbal.
Lit.: no. 255.

Kipokan (Kenya—Nandi). Lyre with five strings and one spare string.

Kiprah (*Nglana*) (Java). "Toilet dance." Cf. *Bedug.*

Kiragutse (Ruanda). Royal drum.
Lit.: no. 26.

Kirān (Old Arabia). Lute.
Lit.: no. 76.

Kiraṇa Bhāskara (South India). *Janya rāga* of the 22nd *mēḷa* (*Kharaharapriyā*).
Tone material:
C D E♭ F B♭ c
c B♭ A G F A F E♭ D C
Lit.: no. 139.

Kiraṇāvaḷi (South India). *Janya rāga* of the 21st *mēḷa* (*Kiravāṇi*).
Tone material:
C D E♭ F G A♭ B c
c A♭ G F E♭ D C (c G F E♭ D C)
Lit.: no. 139.

Kiraṇāvali (South India). (1) The 21st *asampūrṇa mēḷa-rāga* without *kaṭapayādi* prefix. (2) The 21st *asampūrṇa mēḷa-rāga* with *kaṭapayādi* prefix. See *Rāga* (South India).
Lit.: no. 139.

Kiraṇi (South India). *Janya rāga* of the 51st *mēḷa* (*Kāmavardhanī*).
Tone material:
C D♭ E F♯ G B A♭ B c
c B A♭ F♯ E D♭ C
Lit.: no. 139.

Kirar (*Kidrar*) (Ethiopia). Synonym of *masanquo.* Cf. *Kinnōr.*

Kirari (North Nigeria—Hausa). Repertory of fixed verbal-musical patterns.
Lit.: no. 112.

Kiravāṇi (South India). (1) The 21st *mēḷa*:
C D E♭ F G A♭ B c
(2) As *rāga*: the same tone material as shown above. Veṅkaṭamakhin called the *rāga Kiraṇāvaḷi.*
Lit.: no. 139.

Kirdān (Arabia). See *Kardān.*

Kirembe (Uganda—Ruwenzori area). Drum. Cf. *Ngaidja.*

Kiri (Japan). The end section of a *noh* drama performed by the chorus.
Lit.: no. 187.

Kirik hava (Turkey). "Fractured melody." Short songs in rigid meter with strictly syllabic text. Often used as dance music.

Kiri-kiri (South India). Kannarese term for *jhunjhuna.*
Lit.: no. 254.

Kiringi (Guinea; Sierra Leone—Soso). Wooden slit-drum made of a carved-out tree stump closed at both ends. The wooden part between the slits is beaten with sticks provided with rubber heads. Cf. *Balaḥ.*
Lit.: no. 184.

Kirisen (Japan). A large *shamisen* type with three strings. The rectangular corpus of the instrument has rounded edges and is covered with parchment. A small *gekkin* plectrum (made of tortoise shell) is used. Cf. *Taisen.*
Lit.: no. 225.

Kiroha (Solomon Isl.). A water game, during which songs are sung to the accompaniment of beaten or stamped bamboo tubes.
Lit.: no. 318.

Kirr-kishi (Southeast India). A simple scraper; a carved notched wooden stick is scraped with a piece of bamboo.
Lit.: nos. 59, 134-35.

Kīrtana (India; Bengal). A religious, mystical song. Its text refers to legends dealing about Krishna and Radha. See also *Saṅkīrtana*; *Bhajana.*

Kīrtana(m) (South India). An important art song of sacred character. The texts are generally in Sanskrit.

The formal structure is the same as that of the *kriti.*

Kīrtibhānu (South India). *Janya rāga* of the 67th *mēḷa* (*Sucharitra*).
Tone material:
C D♯ E F♯ G A♭ G c
c B♭♭ A♭ G F♯ E D♯ C
Lit.: no. 139.

Kīrtipriya (South India). *Janya rāga* of the 1st *mēḷa* (*Kanakāṅgī*).
Tone material:
C D♭ F G A♭ c
c B♭♭ A♭ G F E♭♭ D♭ C
Lit.: no. 139.

Kīrtivijaya (South India). *Janya rāga* of the 61st *mēḷa* (*Kāntāmaṇi*).
Tone material:
C D E F♯ G B♭♭ A♭ c
c B♭♭ A♭ G F♯ E D C
Lit.: no. 139.

Kisachi (Congo—Basongo). *Sansa.* Cf. *Kisanchi*; *Kisanji*; *Kisansi.*
Lit.: no. 21.

Kisaeng (Korea). Later term for the early *kinyo.*

Kisanchi (Congo—Dembo; Mahungo). *Sansa.*
Lit.: no. 21.

Kisanji (Angola—Mbundi). *Sansa* with inlaid rattle.
Lit.: no. 255.

Kisansi (Congo—Baluba; Hemba). *Sansa.*
Lit.: no. 21.

Kisirka (Nubian Desert). Term for *kissar.*

Kissar (Arabia; Ethiopia; Northeast Africa). A lyre. The name is derived from *kithara.* The instrument has the shape of a bucket and is covered with raw leather. It has two arms and a crossbar which holds five strings made of camel gut. The tuning generally is 5 1 2 3 6. Cf. *Krar*; *Kerar.*
Lit.: no. 255.

Kissara barbarieh (Nubian desert). See *Qitara barbarieh.*

Kisumba (Angola). Term for the *wambi* (Congo).

Kita (Japan). Cf. *Hōshō* (*noh* drama).

Kitimplik (West Java). A small *terbang*.
Lit.: no. 163.

Kitingbi (Congo—Balese; Mangbetu; Mdo; Dongo). Musical bow.
Lit.: no. 176.

Kitingi (Congo—Mamvu). Musical bow.
Lit.: no. 176.

Kitiran (Japan). Bull roarer generally used by children.

Kitmu (*Kanzabu*) (Ancient Babylon). Single beating reed pipe with covered mouthpiece.
Lit.: no. 87.

Ki-tong (Siam). See *Keretok*.

Kitsantsona (Madagascar). Cymbal; tambourin.
Lit.: no. 255.

Kitsarakara (Congo—Bembe). A pair of rattles.
Lit.: no. 280.

Kitsatsa (Congo). See *Masaka*.
Lit.: no. 280.

Kitsika (Congo—Bembe). Bell worn by women during rites praying for the protection of a newborn child.
Lit.: nos. 190, 280.

Kitumba (Congo). See *Umukunto*.

Kivudi-vudi (Congo—Kikongo). Also called *vudi-vudi*. A wooden trumpet.
Lit.: no. 280.

Kiyamba (Zanzibar). Rattle.
Lit.: no. 255.

Kiyari (Japan). Working song of lumbermen and other manual laborers who lay down the foundations of new buildings.

Kiyomoto (Japan). Lyrical narrative *shamisen* music. See *Bungo-bushi*.
Lit.: no. 187.

Kizami (Japan). A *kabuki taiko* pattern. The same pattern occurs in *noh* music.
Lit.: no. 187.

Kizugo (Kenya—Washambala). Wooden double bell in the shape of an hourglass.
Lit.: no. 130.

Kläddi (*Kledi*) (Borneo—Dayak). A mouth organ with six or eight bamboo (reed) pipes inserted into a small gourd that functions as a wind chest. Cf. *Garuding*; *Keluri*; *Giriding*; *Gorteh*; *Kaldei*.
Lit.: nos. 162, 254.

Klama (Ghana). Songs accompanied by three drums and bell.

Klang (Thailand). Tone name. Cf. *Thang*.

Kledi (Borneo). See *Kläddi*.

Klekor (Flores). See *Nuren*.

Klenang (*Kelenang*) (Bali). Small, high-pitched gong struck on the off-beats.
Lit.: no. 197.

Klenang (Java). (1) "Male." The high-sounding row of gong kettles in the *bonang* (the low sounding gongs, the "female" row, is called *gambyong*). See *Bonang*. (2) See *Eneng-eneng*.
Lit.: no. 163.

Klenengan genḍer (Java). See *Klenengang kaplok* (tuned to *slendro* or *pelog*, or *miring*).

Klenengan kaplok (Java). Also called *gamelan sedit*. The term signifies iron *klenengan* (in Pemalang) from which the *genḍer*s are missing (but a *saron* may be included in the ensemble). If the *genḍers* are used, the small ensemble is called *klenengan genḍer*.
Lit.: no. 163.

Klenengan tengahan (Java). A medium type of *gamelan klenengan* that uses sarons. See *Gamelan klenengan tengahan*.

Klentangan (Bali). See *Rejong*.

Klenteng (Bali). Old term for *rejong* (*reong*) as found in the *gamelan angklung*.
Lit.: no. 197.

Klentengan (Bali). The part which is performed by the *rejongs* of the *gamelan angklung*. The *rejong* part (*kajar* passages) are played on the surfaces and not on the bosses of the gongs.
Lit.: no. 197.

Klenti (Bali). Old term for *kempli*.

Klentong (Java). A bronze, oval cattle bell.
Lit.: no. 255.

Kliningan (West Java). Term for *gender*.

Klinṭing (Java). See *Genta*.
Lit.: no. 163.

Klinṭingan (Java). Pellet bells.

Kloboto (Ghana). See *Klodzie*.
Lit.: no. 128.

Klodzie (*Kloboto*) (Ghana – Ewe). Barrel drum with one head and an open bottom.
Lit.: no. 128.

Kloie (Cambodia). Bamboo flute.

Klōṅ (Thailand). Drum.

Klon(ch)eng (*Klun(ch)ing*) (Java). Triangle; used in the *gamelan gandrung*.
Lit.: no. 163.

Klōng khāek (Thailand). Long cylindrical drum, beaten with the hand.

Klōṅ khek (Malaysia). "Foreign drum." Long barrel drum with a wooden, slightly curved body. It is beaten with a wooden stick.
Lit.: no. 254.

Klōṅ poṅ piṅ (Thailand). Drum in the shape of an hourglass. It has a wooden body and one head.
Lit.: no. 255.

Klōng thad (Thailand). A barrel-shaped drum that rests vertically on the floor. The (upper) drum head is covered with a circular patch of paste (similar to the Indian *tabla* and *mṛdanga*). The drum appears in pairs or in three, and different but not clearly tuned sounds are produced. The *klong thad* is beaten with sticks with padded ends. See *Piphat*.
Lit.: no. 49.

Klonṭang (Java). See *Klotak*.

Kloṅ ta roti pote (Siam). Drum with two heads.

Klontong (Java). A small barrel-shaped drum with a handle. The two heads are covered with snakeskin. The *klontong* has a similar structure as the *damaru*; when it is shaken two little balls on strings hit the drumheads. In Bali the instrument is called *ketipluk*.
Lit.: no. 163.

Klōṅ tuā miā (Thailand). High-tuned drum.

Klōṅ yai (Thailand). Two or three barrel drums richly decorated. They are beaten with two wooden sticks.
Lit.: no. 255.

Klotak (Java). Also *Klonṭang*. Bells made of wood.

Klū (Burma – Shan States; Padaung). A bamboo beak flute with five holes (four in front, one in the back). Both ends are open.
Lit.: no. 252.

Kluï (Cambodia). Bamboo flute vertically-blown. Cf. *Cai sao*.

Klui (Vietnam). Bamboo flute.

Klumpung (Java). See *Genḍing charabalen.*

Klun(ch)ing (Java). See *Klon(ch)eng.*

Klung kung (Bali). A tube zither with one string. In the middle of the tube is a hole that is covered with thin wood and beaten with a stick.
Lit.: no. 220.

Klurai (Borneo). See *Keluri.*

Kneya (North Africa—Biskra). Chant; song. Either a rubato song without drums, or a fixed rhythm song with drums sung by one or two persons. It is accompanied either by *zawaq* or by *gasba.* The singer himself plays the *darbuka.* The meter of the song can be $^3/_4$, $^4/_8$, or $^6/_8$.
Lit.: no. 20.

Knite (Timor). Horn.

K.nn.r (*Knr*) (Ancient Egypt). Lyra. The instrument and the name have been borrowed from the Semitic word *kinnōr.* Cf. *Kinnōr*; *Kannāre*; *Kinnāre*; *Kinyra*; *Ginēra*; *Bagannā.*
Lit.: no. 100.

Knobe oh (Timor). Bamboo jew's harp. See *Ego.*
Lit.: no. 162.

Ko (Korea). See *Yul-cha-po.*

Ko (Korea). Drum. See Chinese *Ku* (M 3479).

Ko (China—M 3364; see also M 208.9). To sing; songs; melody.

Koa (Northeast New Guinea). Cross flute used in male initiation rites. The flute is played in pairs; it appears in two varieties, with none or with one finger hole.
Lit.: no. 312.

Koala (South Africa—Lesotho). See *Koali.*

Koali (South Africa—Lesotho). Simple music bow. Cf. *Gorra.*
Lit.: no. 255.

Koauau (New Zealand—Maori). Ancient vertically-blown wooden or bone flute with three finger holes. The instrument has various sizes and can be mouth-blown or nose-blown. Cf. *Putorino.*
Lit.: nos. 7, 37, 84, 313.

Kōba (Old Persia). Hourglass drum.

Kōbe (India—Kota). Term for *ranaśṛṅga.*
Lit.: no. 254.

Kobeng (Flores—Mbai). Jew's harp made of palmwood. Cf. *Genggo*; *Ego.*
Lit.: no. 166.

Kobira (Belgian Congo; Ituri Forest—Bantu). Dance of the master of ceremonies (circumcision ritual) and one helper.
Lit.: no. 28-29.

Koboz (*Kobuz*) (Arabia; Kirgizia). A short necked lute with 3-5 strings and seven frets. Cf. *Cobza*; *Kobyz*; *Qabus*; *Qubuz.*
Lit.: no. 31.

Kobuz (Arabia; Kirgizia). See *Koboz.*

Kobyōshi (Japan). Subdivision of *hyōshi.* See *Hyōshi.*
Lit.: no. 225.

Kobyz (Turkestan; Kirgizia Tatar). A simple *sārangi* type.
Lit.: no. 250.

Kochak (Kurdistan). Religious, ceremonial dancer.

Ko-ch'ing (*Ko-k'ing*) (China—M 3364; M 1164). "The singers' stone," or "stone chime." An obscure ancient instrument composed of 12 or 24 stone slabs which are cut in unusual forms

(fish, heart, happy cloud, bat, dragon, etc.), vaguely similar to the *pien-ch'ing*. The stones are not hung in two series (*ying* and *yang*) but in chromatic order.
Lit.: no. 2.

Ko-chung (China – M 3364; M 1503). "Singers' bell chime." Similar to the *pien-chung*, which sounded an octave higher, the *ko-chung* was the companion of the *ko-ch'ing*. It had either 12 or 24 bells (of rectangular form or bent into crescent-shaped size). It is reported that the instrument intoned the appropriate pitch before each textual syllable – a long held tone – of the Confucian hymn. See *Ko-ch'in*.
Lit.: no. 137.

Koḍa (South India). Also called *kuṭa*. The Kannarese term for the earthenware percussion pot. The term is derived from the Sanskrit *ghāṭa*.
Lit.: no. 254.

Ko-daiko (Japan). A small *ō-daiko* used in the *kagura* orchestra and at processions. In processions it is carried on a long pole and in the orchestra it rests upon a wooden stand. It is beaten with one or two wooden sticks.
Lit.: nos. 225, 255.

Kodama (Japan). Drum effect in *kabuki* that imitates echo sounds as perceived in the mountains.
Lit.: no. 185.

Kōdan (*Rakugo*) (Japan). Narrating of serious or humorous events.

Koden-kyōku (Japan). *Shakuhachi* music imported from South China by the Buddhist priest Kakushin in the 13th century.
Lit.: no. 291.

Kodili (Solomon Isl.; Norfolk Isl.). Music-bow consisting of a bamboo stick with one fiber string.
Lit.: no. 255.

Ko-ding (Philippines – Ibaloi). Jew's harp made of metal or bamboo.

Koḍok ngorek (Java). "The croaking frog." A *gamelan* similar to *gamelan munggang* with tone material of two (rarely three) notes. After a few beats the *bedūg* of the ensemble suddenly performs a *salahan* for a few measures, usually consisting of a sharp crescendo and a few syncopated fast strokes.
Lit.: no. 163.

Kōḍu (South India). Cf. *Gōṭuvādyam*.

Ko'e (Cook Isl.; Mangareva; New Zealand). Nose-flute (also called *kofe*). See also *Ki kohe puru*.
Lit.: no. 84.

Ko erh nai (China). Term for the imported *qanun*.
Lit.: no. 78.

Kofe (Polynesia). See *Ko'e*.
Lit.: no. 313.

Kofen (Ghana – Ga). Animal horn. Cf. *Akofe*.
Lit.: no. 95.

Ko-gaku (Japan). See *Kwangen-gaku*; *Gagaku*.

Ko-hakase (Japan). Ancient notational system of the Nara and Heian periods (8th-12th centuries). The system employed lines that (to a certain degree) indicated the rise and fall of the melody. Cf. *Shōmyō*.
Lit.: no. 47.

Kohkol (West Java). Slit-drum. A group of small bamboo slit-drums. Cf. *Keplek*. See *Kulkul* (Bali).
Lit.: no. 163.

Koholo (Persia). See *Karna*.

Ko-hsiao (China – M 3364; M 2619). The "song *hsiao*" (pipe; pipes), used in military music. It accompanies and plays the songs sung by soldiers.
Lit.: no. 137.

Ko-iso (Japan). See *Koto* (parts).

Kojiki and **Nihongi** (*Nihon shoki*) (Japan). "Record of ancient matters." Chronicle containing ancient literary collections (about 250 items), folk and religious songs of the 8th century.

Kojime (Japan). A secondary rope on the *ko-tsuzumi* and *ō-tsuzumi* that is wound through the five strands that fasten each part of the drum head to the body.
Lit.: no. 185.

Kojin-biwa (Japan). The music of 12th-century traveling Buddhist priests who sang their magic songs in order to liberate the village from evil and illness caused by local deities. *Kojin*, the name of a kitchen deity, refers to this type of music (*Kojin-biwa*).

Ko Jōruri (Japan). See *Jōruri.*

Koka (*Kalibaboe*) (Indonesia; Ternate). Bowed lute with a long bamboo neck and a body of half a coconut shell.
Lit.: no. 162.

Kōkilabhāshaṇi (South India). *Kōkila Bhāshiṇi.*

Kōfila Bhāshiṇi (*Kokilabhāṣiṇi*; *Kōkilabhāshaṇi*) (South India). *Janya rāga* of the 29th *mēḷa* (*Dhīraśaṅkarābharaṇam*).
Tone material:
C D E F G A B c
c B G F E F D C
Lit.: no. 139.

Kōkiladhvani (South India). *Janya rāga* of the 28th *mēḷa* (*Harikāmbhōji*).
Tone material:
C D E F A B♭ A c (C D E F A B♭ c)
c B♭ A B♭ G F E D C
Lit.: no. 139.

Kōkila Dīpakam (South India). *Janya rāga* of the 23rd *mēḷa* (*Gaurīmanōharī*).
Tone material:
C E♭ F A B c
c B A F E♭ D C
Lit.: no. 139.

Kōkila Dīparam (South India). *Janya rāga* of the 43rd *mēḷa* (*Gavambōdhi*).
Tone material:
C D♭ E♭ F♯ B♭♭ A♭ c
c B♭♭ A♭ F♯ E♭ D♭ C
Lit.: no. 139.

Kōkila Dīptam (South India). *Janya rāga* of the 43rd *mēḷa* (*Gavambōdhi*).
Tone material:
C D♭ E♭ F♯ G A♭ c
c B♭♭ G F♯ E♭ D♭ C
Lit.: no. 139.

Kōkila Gāndharvam (South India). *Janya rāga* of the 31st *mēḷa* (*Yāgapriyā*).
Tone material:
C E F A♭ c
c A♭ G F D♯ E C
Lit.: no. 139.

Kōkila Gīrvāṇi (South India). *Janya rāga* of the 43rd *mēḷa* (*Gavāmbōdhi*).
Tone material:
C D E♭ F♯ G A♭ c
c B♭♭ F♯ E♭ D♭ C
Lit.: no. 139.

Kōkila Kāmavardhani (South India). *Janya rāga* of the 11th *mēḷa* (*Kokilapriya*).
Tone material:
C E♭ F G F B A B c
c B G A F E♭ C
Lit.: no. 139.

Kōkilam (South India). *Janya rāga* of the 16th *mēḷa* (*Chakravāka*).
Tone material:
C D♭ E F A B♭ c
c B♭ A F E D♭ C
Lit.: no. 139.

Kōkilānandi (South India). *Janya rāga* of the 56th *mēḷa* (*Śaṇmukhapriyā*).
Tone material:
C E♭ F♯ A♭ B♭ c
c B♭ A♭ G F♯ E♭ C
Lit.: no. 139.

Kōkilanāṭa (South India). *Janya rāga* of the 36th *mēḷa* (*Chalanāṭa*).
Tone material:
C D♯ E F G A♯ B c
c B G F E D♯ C
Lit.: no. 139.

Kōkila Pañcham(am) (South India). *Janya rāga* of the 39th *mēḷa* (*Jhālavarāḷi*).
Tone material:
C E𝄫 D♭ G A♭ B c (C D♭ E𝄫 G A♭ B c)
c B A♭ G F♯ E𝄫 D♭ C
Lit.: no. 139.

Kōkila Pratāpam (South India). *Janya rāga* of the 26th *mēḷa* (*Chārukeśī*).
Tone material:
C E F G F A♭ B♭ c
c B♭ G F E C
Lit.: no. 139.

Kōkilapriya (South India). (1) The 11th *mēḷa*:
C D♭ E♭ F G A B c
(2) As *rāga*: the same tone material as in the *mēḷa*. Veṅkaṭamakhin (17th century) called this *rāga Kokilārāva(m)*.
Lit.: no. 139.

Kōkilārāva(m) (South India). *Janya rāga* of the 11th *mēḷa* (*Kōkilapriya*).
Tone material:
C D♭ E♭ D♭ F G A B c
c B A G F E♭ D♭ C
Lit.: no. 139.

Kōkilārāvam (South India). (1) The 11th *asampūrṇa mēḷa-rāga* without *kaṭapayādi* prefix. (2) The 11th *asampūrṇa mēḷa-rāga* with *kaṭapayādi* prefix. See *Rāga* (South India).
Lit.: no. 139.

Kōkila Svarāvaḷi (South India). *Janya rāga* of the 41st *mēḷa* (*Pāvani*).
Tone material:
C D♭ E𝄫 F♯ A B c
c A F♯ E𝄫 D♭ C
Lit.: no. 139.

Kōkilavarāli (South India). *Janya rāga* of the 28th *mēḷa* (*Harikāmbhōji*).
Tone material:
C D F G A c
c B♭ A F G F E D E C
Lit.: no. 139.

Kōkila Vardhani (South India). *Janya rāga* of the 15th *mēḷa* (*Māyāmāḷavagauḷa*).
Tone material:
C F E G A♭ B c
c B A♭ F E D♭ C
Lit.: no. 139.

Kokin (Japan). A spike fiddle of Chinese origin with a square corpus and two strings. The *kokin* is related to the Chinese *hu-ch'in* and the *erh-hsien*. It has a large bow, the hairs of which are either strung between the two strings or are detached from the instrument. Cf. *Keikin*; *Kokyu*; *Nisen*.
Lit.: nos. 185, 225.

Ko-k'ing (China). See *Ko-ch'ing*.

Kokkara (South India). See *Kokkurai*.

Kokkurai (*Kokkara*) (South India). A scraping instrument consisting of an iron cylinder not quite closed, with teeth filed along its edges. The player, usually a magician, scrapes the rims with a small iron stick.
Lit.: nos. 59, 255.

Koko (East Indonesia; Nias). Bamboo zither.
Lit.: no. 162.

Koko (Congo — Dendi). Whistle with two finger holes.
Lit.: no. 33.

Kokolo (Lower Congo). A *nanga* (arched harp).
Lit.: no. 21.

Kokondi (*Popondi*) (Indonesia; Moluccas). See *Tuba pondi.*

Kokoprak (Java). Several bamboo tubes that rattle against a bamboo cross bar are set up as scarecrows in the rice fields.
Lit.: no. 163.

Kokpworo (Congo). See *Okporo.*

Kokun (Korea). See *Hü-ch'in* (China).

Kokun (Japan). Spike fiddle identical with the *kei kin.* Cf. *Kokyū*; *Kokin.*

Kokyoku (Japan). Short songs performed during the comic entr'actes (*kyōgen*) of the *noh* dramas.
Lit.: no. 185.

Kokyū (Japan). A spike fiddle with two (also three or four) strings. The body has an almost quadrangular shape covered on both sides with parchment. The instrument is played with a bow, the hair of which is not strung between the strings. The two top strings of the four-stringed instrument are always tuned in unison. The tuning of the *kokyū* can be: normal (*san sagari*): G c f f; rare (*hon choshi*): C F, c c; rare (*niagari*): C G c c. The *kokyū* appears in *koto* ensembles, in puppet shows, and is favored by beggars. An ensemble such as *kokyū*, *shamisen*, and drums can be heard often in the pleasure districts of Tokyo.

A three-string *kokyū* was used in the early 18th century. When the violin was imported from the West, the *kokyū* almost disappeared. Cf. *Keikin*; *Kokin.*
Lit.: no. 185.

Kōlāhala(m) (South India). *Janya rāga* of the 29th *mēḷa* (*Dhīraśaṅkarābharaṇam*).
Tone material:

C G F E F G A B c
c B A G F E D C

Lit.: no. 139.

Kolamut (Bismarck Archipelago). Also called *gamti.* See *Garamut.*
Lit.: no. 84.

Kolangi (Africa). See *Kalangu.*

Kolanter (West Java). Name of the *keṭipung.* See *Kenḍang leutik*; *Penunṭung.*

Kōlaphaṇi (South India). *Janya rāga* of the 30th *mēḷa* (*Nāgānandī*).
Tone material:

C D E F A♯ G B c
c A♯ F E D C

Lit.: no. 139.

Kōlāṭṭam (South India). Folk dance. Every dancer holds in his hand a wooden stick and strikes the stick of the dancer next to him. All dancers form a wide circle.
Lit.: no. 261.

Kolenang (West Java). Term for *bonang.* In Banten the instrument is called *kromong* (a single row of kettles) or *renteng.*
Lit.: no. 163.

Kolendang (West Java). Term for *kemanak.*
Lit.: no. 163.

Kolilo (Cook Isl.). Also called *koriro.* Slit-drum.
Lit.: no. 84.

Kolintang (Celebes). Gong chime. A *bonang* identical with the *tatabuan.*
Lit.: no. 254.

Kol-i-pärdä (Kurdistan). Term for the narrow groove at the right side of the neck in the *tanbur.*
Lit.: no. 255.

Kol-kola (Lesser Sunda—Kisar). Wooden percussion tube with slit.
Lit.: no. 254.

Kolla (Sahara—Teda). Drum with two heads of which only one is used. The drum is beaten by men when they accompany dances of the women.
Lit.: no. 301.

Kologo (Ghana). Lute.

Kolokocho (Kenya—Washambala). Dancers' rattle.
Lit.: no. 130.

Kolong-kolong (Flores; Larantuka). Also called *Laka do'o.* Tube-zither. Cf. *Gong-tondu.*
Lit.: no. 219.

Kolongwe (Congo—Bena-Kalundwe). Two-headed drum.
Lit.: no. 26.

Kolotok (West Java). A wooden type of the Javanese *genta.*
Lit.: no. 163.

Koma (Kenya—Washambala). Jew's harp.
Lit.: no. 130.

Koma (Japan). Term for the bridge on the *kokyū* and *shamisen.*

Komabue (*Koma-fue*) (Japan). A small, slim cross flute with six finger holes imported from Korea. The instrument was used in *Komagaku.* Cf. also *Ryūteki.*
Lit.: no. 185.

Komagaku (Japan). Term for the music of Koguryo (one of the medieval provinces of Korea). There are several styles in this imported court music, particularly *shiragi gaku* and *kudara gaku.* Cf. *Gagaku. Komagaku* was and is called "The right side music" (performed at the right hand side of the Confucian temple). For instruments used in *komagaku* see *Bugaku.*
Lit.: nos. 53, 185.

Koma-hyōjo (Japan). One of the scales used in *gagaku.*

Komai (Japan). Early dance of *kabuki.*
Lit.: no. 187.

Koma-ichikotsuchō (Japan). One of the scales used in *gagaku.* See *Gagaku.*

Komal (North India). "Flat." Term and symbol for lowering the pitch of certain notes by a semitone. Only the notes *re* (*ri*), *ga*, *dha*, and *ni* can be lowered. The *komal* symbol is a short horizontal line placed below the tone syllable (written in *nagari* script). In South India the flattening is not notated. The performing musician has to know the exact intonation.
Lit.: no. 136.

Kōmalāṅgi (South India). *Janya rāga* of the 26th *mēḷa* (*Chārukeśī*).
Tone material:
C D E F G B♭ c
c B♭ A♭ F E D C
Lit.: no. 139.

Kōmalāṅgi (South India). *Janya rāga* of the 27th *mēḷa* (*Sarasāṅgī*).
Tone material:
C D E F A♭ B c
c B G F E D C
Lit.: no. 139.

Komal-desi (North India). *Rāga* ascribed to the *Āsāvari thāta.* It is popular and subject to several variants.
Tone material:
C D F G A♭ B♭ c
c B♭ A♭ G F E♭ D♭ C; *Vādis*: G, D
Lit.: no. 138.

Komali (South India). *Janya rāga* of the 63rd *mēḷa* (*Latāṅgī*).
Tone material:
C D E F♯ G B A♭ F♯ G c
c A♭ B F♯ E D C
Lit.: no. 139.

Koma-sōjō (Japan). One of the scales used in *gagaku.* See *Gagaku.*

Komba (Congo—Budu). Arched harp.
Lit.: no. 176.

Kombing (Flores). Jew's harp. Cf. *Genggo*; *Nentu.*
Lit.: no. 166.

Kom boat (Vietnam—Moi). Mouth organ.
Lit.: no. 305.

Kombu (India). Term in Tamil, Malayalam, and Kannarese for *śṛṅga*. See also *Kahale*.
Lit.: nos. 254, 260.

Kommu (South India). Telugu term for *rānaśṛṅga*. Cf. *Kombu*.

Komosō (Japan). Term for wandering Buddhist priests, often former samurai without swords, who carried the *shakuhachi*, a heavy flute, that could also be used as weapon.
Lit.: no. 185.

Komparu (Japan). Cf. *Hōshō*.

Kompyung (Bali). See *Kempyong*.

Kömsöl (Korea). Term for the Chinese *p'i-p'a*.
Lit.: no. 255.

Komungo (Korea). See *Komunko*.

Komunko (*Komungo*; *Hyon-kum*) (Korea). The distinguished zither, the "black *ko*" (or *kum*), is the Korean counterpart of the Chinese *ch'in*. The instrument deviates in several aspects from the Chinese *ch'in*; of its six silken strings only the second and third string run across the 16 frets, while the fourth string is placed high above the body that, although the frets extend below it, they cannot be touched. Strings 1, 4, 5, and 6 remain open and are not fretted. The tuning and playing as well as the notation are complex and require detailed explanations. For further information the reader is referred to my book, Lit. no. 136, pp. 301-51. See also Lit. no. 52. Cf. *Yamato goto*; *Tae-chaing*.

Komusō (Japan). Cf. *Komoso*.

Komuz (Kirgizia; Afghanistan). A lute with a slim, pear-shaped body and a narrow neck with three gut strings and no frets. The terms *kobus*, *kobys*, *qobuz* indicate similar instruments throughout Central Asia, which appear as fiddles, lutes, and zithers.
Lit.: nos. 91, 275.

Kon (Northeast Thailand). Term for the classical dance drama.
Lit.: no. 203.

Koṇa (India). Ancient term for plectrum used in playing the *vipañcī vīṇā*. The term applies also to wooden carved sticks used in beating drums (e.g., the *dundubhi*).

Kōṇakombu (South India). Brass horn in S-shape. Cf. *Kombu*, which usually has a crescent shape.

Koncha-khin (Nepal). A cylindrical clay- or wood-drum with one skin. The other end is open.

Konde (Africa—Republic of Upper Volta). Lute with two strings.
Lit.: no. 50.

Kondele (East Africa—Kisiba; Uyamtura). Flute with four finger holes.
Lit.: no. 313.

Kondere (*Ekkondere*) (Uganda). Side-blown gourd trumpet. Cf. *Eggwara*; *Makondere*.

Kondi (Sierra Leone). *Sansa* with 5-6 tongues.

Kondu (Congo—Azande). Arched harp.
Lit.: no. 176.

Kone (Liberia—Kpelle). Iron idiophone. For information, see Lit. no. 284.

Konene (Uganda—Madi). Gourd *mirliton*.
Lit.: no. 302.

Kong (Korea). The sixth scale degree and notational symbol of the *kong-chuk-po*. Assuming that *hap* is the western C, *kong* represents A or A♭ as required by the mode.
Lit.: no. 136.

Kong (Japan). See *Minshin gaku.*
Lit.: no. 185.

Konga (Congo—Bolia). Drum.
Lit.: no. 26.

Kong chok (China). A stout bamboo tube used by night watchmen for signalling. When beaten, the tube creates a penetrating sound.
Lit.: no. 255.

Kong-chuk-po (Korea). Notational system derived from the Chinese *kung-ch'e-p'u.* The written symbols are the same as the Chinese but the pronunciation of the tone names is different:

Chinese	(e.g.)	Korean	(e.g.)
ho	C	*hap*	C
ssu	D	*sa*	D♭, D
yi	E	*il*	E♭, E
shang	F	*sang*	F
kou	F♯	*ku*	F♯
ch'e	G	*chuk*	G
kung	A	*kong*	A♭, A
fan	B	*pum*	B♭, B
liu	c	*yuk*	c
wu	d	*o*	d♭, d, d♯

In contrast to the Chinese system, the symbols and names of the *kong-chuk-po* are devoid of affixes that indicate the flat, natural, or sharp forms of notes.
Lit.: no. 136.

Kong-hu (Korea). An ancient angular harp with 12 strings. Cf. *Tadegoto.*
Lit.: no. 52.

Kong keh (Assam—Ao-Naga; East Bengal). Primitive fiddle with a small cylinder of bamboo as body. The instrument has one fiber string. The bow is called *lish.*
Lit.: no. 254.

Kongo (Japan). Cf. *Hōshō.*

Kongo (Congo—Ashira). Music bow with a part of a climbing plant used as a string. It is attached to one end of the stick; the other end is held in the mouth of the player who beats it with his right hand holding a small wooden stick.
Lit.: no. 255.

Kongoma (Sierra Leone). Large *sansa.*

Kong thom (Vietnam; Cambodia). A set of 17 bells (diatonically tuned through 2⅓ octaves) arranged on a wooden stand in a circle around the player. The bells are struck with wooden sticks. Cf. *Mohori.*
Lit.: nos. 153, 159.

Kong toch (Vietnam; Kampuchea). Medium low pitched bell harmonica consisting of 16 bells diatonically tuned (C-c-c'-d'). Cf. *Mohori.*
Lit.: nos. 153, 159.

Konimesin (Africa; Upper Guinea). Harp-lute with a gourd or wooden body and four strings.
Lit.: no. 33.

Konin (Liberia—Kpelle). Triangular frame zither.
Lit.: no. 284.

Konkakhin (Nepal). Drum in the shape of a jug. The single head is beaten with the hands.
Lit.: no. 46.

Konkole (Nigeria). See *Dundun.*

Konkoma (Liberia—Kpelle). Two- or three-pronged *sansa* with box resonator.
Lit.: no. 284.

Koṅ-koṅ (Malacca—Oran Mentera; Oran Belenda). Simple xylophone with four slabs.
Lit.: no. 255.

Kon-kpala (Liberia—Kpelle). Musical bow.
Lit.: no. 284.

Kono (Liberia—Kpelle). Slit wooden or bamboo idiophone.
Lit.: no. 284.

Konroṅ (Burma – Shan States). Wooden cattle bell with several (up to five) clappers.
Lit.: no. 254.

Kontrashica (Kurdistan). See *Changura.*

Kooauau (New Zealand – Maori). Small vertical wooden or bone flute with three finger holes.

Koombi-koombi (Ternate near Halmahera). A *tondu.*
Lit.: no. 166.

Koonti (Flores). Cf. *Main chachih* (whip game).

Kopiak (*Koprak*) (Bali). A bamboo slit-drum.
Lit.: no. 197.

'Kopo (South Africa – Bushman). Cf. *Segwana.*
Lit.: no. 149.

Kopok-kopok (Malaysia). Small cymbals.

K'opong (Tibet). Also *Sgra-snyan.* See *Beda.*

K'opong srog-ce (Tibet). Playing the 3-stringed lute.

Koprak (Bali). See *Kopiak.*

Kopuz (Turkey). Name of ancient spike fiddle (also used as lute), related to the *baglama.* Cf. *Koboz.*
Lit.: no. 243.

Kora (Republic of Mali; Senegambia). Musical bow; harp-lute with 16-18 strings. The instrument appears in various forms under several names: *seron, bolon, ekorro, gore, gorra.*
Lit.: nos. 33, 303.

Korei (Japan). Rattle with iron jingles placed on an (iron) frame.
Lit.: no. 258.

Kori (Nigeria). Rattle.

Koriro (South Pacific; Cook Isl.). See *Kolilo.*

Kornai (Turkestan). Straight brass horn; always played in pairs. Cf. *Quarna.*
Lit.: no. 255.

Koro (Mali – Dogon). Percussion board.
Lit.: no. 303.

Koron (Iran). Notational symbol that indicates the flattening of a note.

Korr (*Kaur*) (New Mecklenburgh – Kalil). Panflutes.

Korra (Flores). Also *sason.* Cf. *Corra; Remba.*

Korro (Republic of Mali – Mandingo). Harp with 18 strings. Cf. *Kora.*
Lit.: no. 255.

Kos (*Ḳauns*) (Arabia; Egypt). Bow of the *kāmanjah* and *rebāb.*

Kōs (*Kös*) (Iran; Turkey). Large kettledrum. See also *Kūs.*
Lit.: no. 255.

Kosaburōfu (Japan). *Shamisen* tablature using Arabic numerals written in vertical rows. Cf. *Bunkafu.*
Lit.: no. 187.

Kōsala(m) (South India). The 71st *mēḷa*:

C D♯ E F♯ G A B c

The *rāga* with the same name has the same tone material as shown above.
Lit.: no. 139.

Kosekan (Java). *Kosek* = stirring peeled rice by hand in a basket. Drumming pattern of more ornamental character than the serious *kendangan.*
Lit.: no. 163.

Koshadhvani (North India). See *Kauns* (North India).

Kōshiki (Japan). Form of Buddhist chanting employing *bonsan*, *kansan*, and *wasan*. Of interest are the Chinese texts pronounced in polysyllabic Japanese.
Lit.: no. 185.

Ko-sho (Japan). Beehive-shaped bell without a clapper, suspended in a frame.
Lit.: no. 258.

Koṣma (Turkey). Love songs, songs describing nature with 11 syllables in each line. The songs have 3-6 strophes, each strophe with four lines. Cf. *Kozhma.*
Lit.: no. 243.

Koso (Nigeria—Yoruba). One-skin drum, tunable and hand-beaten, with an hourglass-shaped corpus and a cylindrical waist, used for certain festivals and to honor distinguished persons. The *koso* drum, of various sizes, is decorated with small brass bells.
Lit.: no. 293.

Kosoguri (Japan). The highest pitch in *noh* singing. Cf. *Yokyōku.*
Lit.: no. 185.

Kosok (*Kosoq*) (Java). The bow used in *rebāb* playing. At times it is also called *chengkok.* The bow's wooden part is called *rangkung* and its hair is called *yoga.*
Lit.: no. 163.

Kosoq (Java). See *Kosok.*

Kosso (Nigeria). See *Kotso.*

Koṭak (Java). A chest containing the *wayang* requisites.

Kot-ch'aebi (*Pakkat-ch'aebi*) (Korea). "Song of outside musicians." Buddhist chant sung by trained singers, often called from the outside, from another temple. The texts are Chinese and are poetically structured in quatrains and are melodic *hossori* or rare *chissori* and show elaborate forms.
Lit.: no. 287.

Kotek (Java). Small hand drum.
Lit.: no. 255.

Koṭekan (*Bendrong*; *Genḍong*) (Java). Rice pounding music. On moonlit nights a group of women pound rhythmical patterns.
Lit.: no.163.

Koṭekan (*Paketan*) (Bali). General term for two-part *gangsa* figuration; also interchangeable with *kantilan.*
Lit.: no. 197.

Kōtō (Japan). The lowest musical degree given to professional musicians; also to blind musicians who perform popular music. The *kōtō* of the past were not allowed to wear wide trousers as sign of their profession. Cf. *Gakunin*; *Genin*; *Kengyō*; *Geishas.*

Koto (Japan). The national distinguished zither imported from China during the 9th century. The instrument went through several changes and differs now considerably from the Chinese prototype (*ch'in*). The basic form is an oblong, slightly curved, sound board strung with 13 silken strings across high flexible bridges. The player plucks the strings with three ivory plectra (*tsume*), which look like elongated fingernails, fitted on his thumb and the first and second finger tips of his right hand. At the present time this distinguished instrument appears mainly in the ancient *kagura* and *saibara* music. The many *koto* schools of the past established numerous tunings. A few of them are listed on pages 388-89.

The three prinicpal tunings are *hirajoshi*, *kumoi*, and *iwato.* The mixed tunings are represented by *han-kumoi* and *go-sagari-roku-agari.* In *han-kumoi*, strings 1-7 are taken from the *hirajōshi* scale, while strings 8-12 are taken from *kumoi.* In *go-sagari-roku-agari*, strings 1-7 show *iwato* tuning and strings 8-12 *kumoi* tuning. In both tunings the 13th string is g♯.

Parts of the instrument bear the following names: the upper part (of the board) is called the sea-shore, *ō-iso*; the lower part is called the lesser shore, *ko-iso*; the oval tortoise shell at the

Hirajōshi
strings:
1 2 3 4 5 6 7 8 9 10 11 12 13

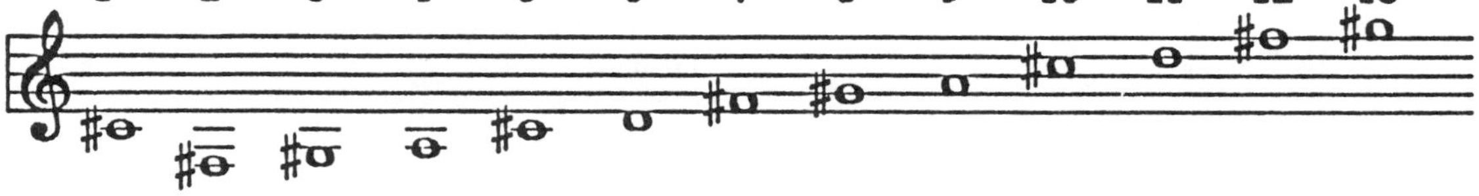

Akebono

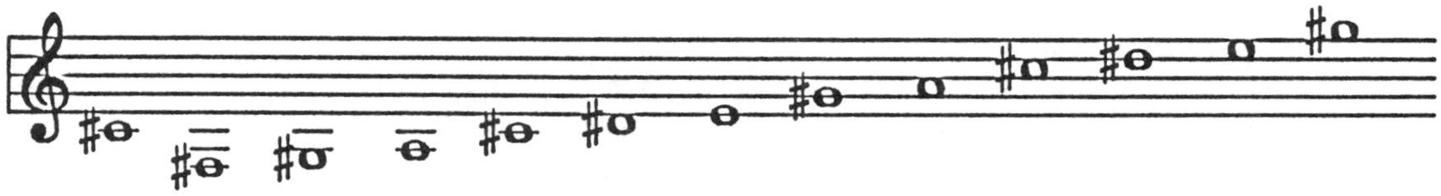

Kumoi

Han-Kumoi

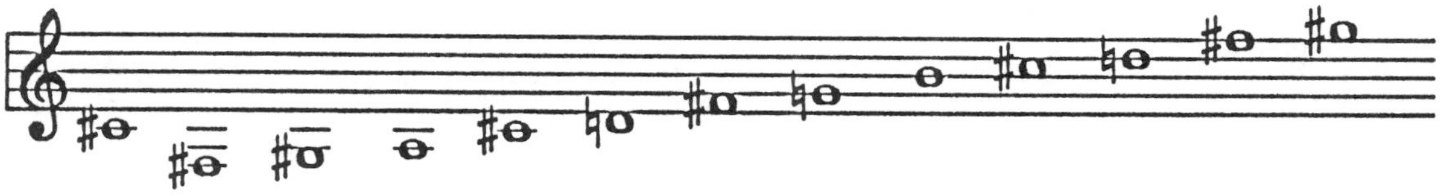

Iwato

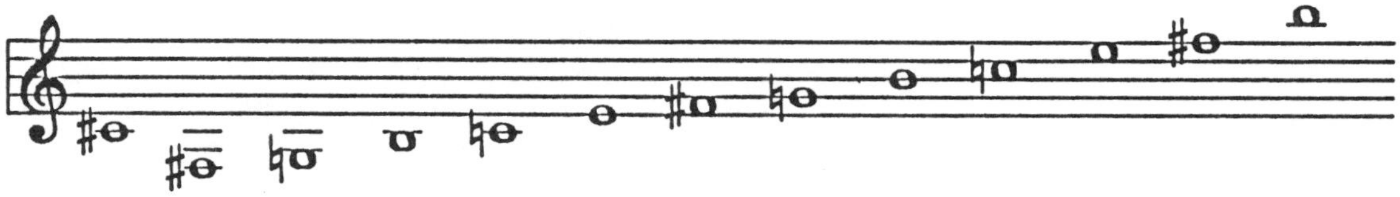

Go-Sagari-Roku-Agari

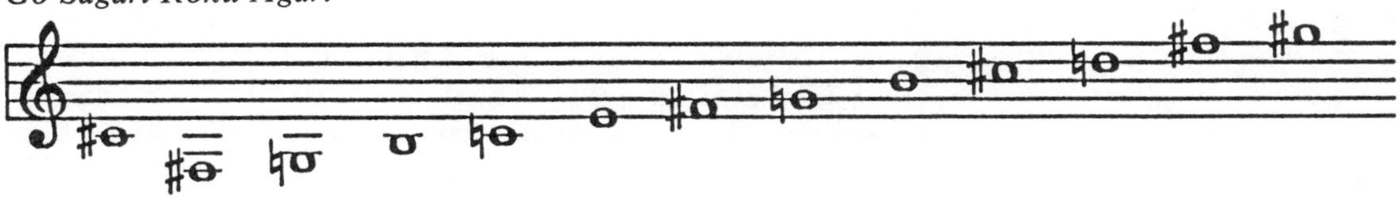

right end of the upper surface is called the sea, *umi*; the long bridge at the right end is the dragon's horn, *ryōkaku*; the long bridge at the left end is called the horn of cloud or angel's seat, *temmyō*; the angular projection at the right end is called the dragon's forked tongue, *ryō-ni shita*; the other end is called the dragon's tail, *kashi waba*; the cavity at the right end of the lower surface is the hidden moon, *ingetsu*; the bowl-shaped place at the left end, *marigata.*

The following terms indicate various *koto* types: *wagon*; *gaku-so*; *ichigenkin* (*suma-koto*); *nigenkin* (*yakumon*, *yakumo-koto*); *akikire-koto*; *azuma-koto*; *chiku-no-koto*; *han-koto*; *hitsu-no-koto* (*kin-no-koto*); *ikuta-koto*; *kaku-koto* (*kaku-goto*); *kundara-koto*; *sage-koto*; *shiragi-koto*; *so-no-koto*; *sho-hitsu-no-koto*; *taki-koto*; *tsuma-koto*; *ya-koto*; *yamada-koto*; *yamato-koto*; *yayoi-koto*; *yakumo-koto* (*nigenkin*); *san-gen-kin*; *go-kin*; *roku-kin*; *shichi-gen-kin*; *yō-kin.*
Lit.: no. 185.

Kotoba (Japan). "Words." The prose parts of the *noh* text. *Kotoba* is recited, not chanted nor spoken. The presentation is highly stylized in an exquisitely elaborate form of recitation. The lyrical counterpart of *kotoba* is *fushi* ("melody").

Koto-no-ji (Japan). Bridge used on the *koto.*
Lit.: no. 255.

Koto-no-o (Japan). Strings used on the *koto.*
Lit.: no. 255.

Koto-no-tsume (Japan). Plectrum used in *koto* playing.

Kotor (Southeast India—Muria Gond). Small portable wooden slit-drum.
Lit.: no. 135.

Kotso (*Kosso*) (North Nigeria—Hausa). One-headed snare drum in hourglass form. It has the same function as the *koso* of the Yoruba.
Lit.: nos. 255, 293.

Kotsu (Japan). See *Yotsu.*

Kō-tsuzumi (Japan). Also *oto-tsuzumi.* A small drum in the shape of an hourglass. It is carried on the right shoulder, held there with the left hand and beaten with the right. The *kō-tsuzumi* is important in the *noh* ensemble. It is called the "younger" while the *ō-tsuzumi*, slightly larger, held on the left hip, being called the "elder drum," is struck energetically. Cf. *Ō-tsuzumi.*
Lit.: nos. 185, 225.

Koṭṭu (South India). Term implies movable frets.

Koṭṭu maddalam (South India). Temple drum.
Lit.: no. 261.

Koṭṭumaṇi (South India). A cluster of bells used in Hindu temples.
Lit.: no. 261.

Ko-turu (Liberia—Kpelle). War horn.
Lit.: no. 284.

Kou (China). See *Chien-tzu.*
Lit.: no. 136.

K'ou (China—M 3434). "Mouth." The slits on the *pu-yü.*
Lit.: no. 129.

Kou (China—M 3409). Tone name and notational symbol. Assuming that *ho*, the basic note of the *kung-ch'e-p'u*, is the western C, *kou* represents the note F#. *Kou* appears in the official scale of the Yüan dynasty (14th century): C D E F F# G A B c.
Lit.: no. 136.

Kouauau (New Zealand—Maori). Obsolete open flute with three finger holes.
Lit.: no. 228.

K'ou-ch'in (China—M 3434; M 1103). Iron jew's harp played by street boys in Peking (the instrument is unknown in Shanghai).
Lit.: no. 209.

Kouitra (Algeria). See *Kuitra* (2).

Koulintaugau (North Borneo—Sandakan). Group of 10 gongs.
Lit.: no. 255.

Koulou (Dahomey). Horn whistle.

Kou-pin-lo (China). Cantonese term; the Mandarin term is *kao-pien-lo*. See *Ta-lo*.

Ko-uta (Japan). "Small song." Short *shamisen* song which became popular during the Muromachi (Ashikaga) period (14th-17th centuries) and became the favorite song of the geishas. The *ko-uta* in the 18th century contributed much to the evolution of *jōruri*. Cf. *Ha-uta*; *Utazawa*; *Utaimono*; *Jōruri*; *Kumiuta*; *Hauta*.
Lit.: no. 187.

Ko'uz (Western Central Asia). Cf. *Chang* (Turkey) (2).

Kove (New Hebrides Isl.). Panpipes with three bamboo tubes.
Lit.: no. 255.

Kowangan (*Gowangan*) (Java). This now very rare and unusual instrument has the appearance of a bamboo hut or tent that can be worn by a player as a huge hat. Inside a number of fiber strings are strung and tuned in pitches (vaguely resembling *slendro* tuning). In addition the hut contains two flat bamboo rods on unequal lengths. When strings and tops of bamboo rods are plucked, sounds are produced which resemble a *gamelan*. Cf. *Chelempungan*. For details see Lit. no. 163, pp. 200-01.

Koy na bala (Congo—Bapende). "Village leopard." A friction drum. It is played during initiation rites.
Lit.: no. 33.

Ko-yuri (Japan). See *Ō-yuri*.

Kozhma (Turkey). Love songs, social songs. Also *Koşma*.

Kpai (Congo—Mamvu; Balese). Board zither with resonator.
Lit.: no. 176.

Kpa-ndu (Ivory Coast). Slitted, hollow iron cylinder beaten with a small iron stick.
Lit.: no. 255.

Kpanligan (Dahomey). A court minstrel who chants poems of praise and chants glorious episodes of the past, to the accompaniment of a double bell.
Lit.: no. 218.

Kpe (West Africa; Togo). Horn; ivory.

Kpedimba (Congo—Azande). Term for *kweningba*.

Kpe-kee (Liberia—Kpelle). Container; rattle.
Lit.: no. 284.

Kpene-kee (Liberia—Kpelle). Double slit idiophone.
Lit.: no. 284.

Kpeninga (Congo—Azande). Term for *kweningba*.

Kpete (Ghana). See *Agbadza*.

Kple (Ghana). The music of the religious cult of the Ga of Ghana. The dance is called *kpledzo.*
Lit.: no. 218.

Kpledzo (Ghana). See *Kple.*

Kpolo (Congo). Big bell.
Lit.: no. 255.

Kpomeghe (Ghana). See *Agbadza.*

Kpwokolo (Congo—Balese). Simple musical bow.
Lit.: no. 176.

iKpwokpwo (Congo). See *Papakungbu.*

Kpworo (Congo—Banza). Conical drums played in pairs at dances and funerals. Cf. *Ta ngo.*
Lit.: no. 26.

Krajappī (Thailand). Lute with a body in the form of a tortoise shell. The instrument has four strings and is played with a plectrum.

Krajavali (South India). *Janya rāga* of the 4th *mēḷa* (*Vanaspāti*).
Tone material:
C D♭ F G A B♭ c
c A G F D♭ C
Lit.: no. 139.

Krakab (North Africa). Long castanets of North Arabs.
Lit.: no. 255.

Kralu (Celebes). Primitive goblet drum. Cf. *O-tsi* (Burma).
Lit.: no. 254.

Kram (Assam—Garo). Large drum with two heads of different sizes. The drum can be taken outside the house only at very festive occasions.
Lit.: no. 254.

Krama (India). Straight; step by step, uninterrupted scale.

Krama sampūrṇa (South India). Fully heptatonic scale. The term is used in theoretical descriptions of scales. *Krama* means regular, orderly; its opposite is *vakra*, zigzag.

Kranting (Malacca). A tube zither widely popular in Southeast Asia.
Lit.: nos. 156, 255.

Krap fuong (Cambodia). Wooden clappers.
Lit.: no. 255.

Krap puan(g) (Thailand). A clapper consisting of six wooden slabs tied together at one end. The two outer slabs are thick and slightly curved.
Lit.: no. 254.

Krar (*Kerar*) (Ethiopia). A 6-string lyre with a bowl-shaped body. Its tuning can be D E♭ G A♭ c C. The *krar* is used in secular music and is played by men and women.
Lit.: nos. 144, 218.

Krawang (Bali). "Bronze." The *gamelan krawang* is an ensemble composed of bronze instruments.
Lit.: no. 197.

Krempeng(an) (Bali). High pitched, dry drum sounds produced by striking the rim of the drum head with the fingertips. Cf. *Krumpung(an).*
Lit.: no. 197.

Krenon(g) (*Kyenon*) (Burma). Small brass gong.
Lit.: no. 255.

Kre-tsaṅ (*Krenan*) (Burma). Gong without boss.
Lit.: no. 255.

Kre-tsi (Burma). Triangular gong. See *Lan kan* (Thailand).

Kre-waiṅ (*Krevaing*; *Krewong*) (Burma; Thailand). A group of 16 small gongs placed upon a circular low stand around the player. The kettles are tuned one octave higher than the ones of *ranatlek.* Cf. *Cai nen.*
Lit.: no. 255.

Krewong (Burma). See *Kre-waiṅ*.

Kri (Sudan). An Agni term for drum.
Lit.: no. 95.

Kriah (Ancient Israel). The calling, singing of the Bible and the older parts of the Talmud.
Lit.: no. 12.

Kriḍāmati (South India). *Janya rāga* of the 45th *mēḷa* (*Śubhapantuvarālī*).
Tone material:
C D♭ E♭ F♯ G A♭ B c
c A♭ G E♭ D♭ C
Lit.: no. 139.

K'rims-dung (Tibet). Trumpet used in courts of justice.
Lit.: no. 190.

Krish (Turkey). Gut string.
Lit.: no. 255.

Krishmaf (South India; Pondicherry). Nose flute with three holes.
Lit.: no. 255.

Krishna-Beh (Nepal). See *Beh*.

Krishnalīlā (South India). Dance plays based on legends about Krishna.
Lit.: no. 46.

Krishṇaveni (*Kṛṣṇaveni*) (South India). *Janya rāga* of the 15th *mēḷa* (*Māyāmāḷavagauḷa*).
Tone material:
C D♭ E F G B c
c B G F E D♭ C
Lit.: no. 139.

Kriti (*Kṛti*) (South India). Name of the important art song form of South India. The *kriti* consists of the introductory *ālāpa*, followed by the *pallavi* and *anupallavi* and *charaṇa*. There can be more than one *charaṇa*. The form corresponds to the northern *dhrūpad* and *khyāl*. The texts of the *kriti* can be both sacred or secular. Cf. *Dhrūpad*; *Khyāl*.
Lit.: no. 86.

Kritsa-kritsa (Malagasy Republic). Bamboo rattle.
Lit.: no. 190.

Kriya (India). Counting beats. Meter. The *sasabda kriya* is the counting of beats audibly. The *nissibda kriya* is the counting without any audible beating and clapping.

Kriyanga rāga (India). A *rāga* suitable for theatrical performance.

Kriyāvati (South India). *Janya rāga* of the 54th *mēḷa* (*Viśvambharī*).
Tone material:
C D♭ E F♯ G A♯ B c
c B A♯ G F♯ E D♭ E C
Lit.: no. 139.

Kriyā Virāmam (South India). *Janya rāga* of the 17th *mēḷa* (*Sūryakānta*).
Tone material:
C D♭ E D♭ F G B A c
c B A G F A F E D♭ C
Lit.: no. 139.

Krob (Malay Peninsula – Sakai). Tube zither.
Lit.: no. 156.

Kroboto (Ghana – Ewe). Drum with one head. Cf. *Atsiagbekor*.
Lit.: no. 174.

Krodhā (India). Term for the 9th *śruti*. The corresponding note name is *pratiśuddha ma* (term used in music theory). Cf. *Śruti*.
Lit.: no. 138.

K'ro h'cham-pa (Tibet). Dancer wearing a frightening mask in religious performances.

Krol-dong (Tibet). Big bell.

Kromo (Borneo – Sea Dayak). A group (usually seven) of sonorous small stone discs suspended from a wooden frame. The same term is applied when, instead of stone discs, gongs or wooden slabs are used. Cf. *Kolenang*; *Bonang* (West Java).
Lit.: no. 254.

Kromong (*Bonang*) (Malaysia). Metallophone. Ten brass slabs are placed across a box in two rows. The tuning is:

bb	a	f#	e	c
nem	*mo*	*lu*	*ruh*	*chi*
C	E	F#	A	Bb
chi	*ruh*	*lu*	*mo*	*nem*

Kromong (Borneo; South Sumatra). A *bonang* consisting of wooden or stone slabs or small gongs. Cf. *Chalempung.*
Lit.: nos. 159, 254.

Kronchong (Sunda District). Also *Krontjong.* (1) A term for various imported instruments from the West: mandoline, violin, guitar, ukulele, etc., and the music performed on them. (2) A native *kronchong*: a copy of a narrow, slim Portuguese 5-stringed guitar with rear pegs. The term also implies imported folk music of the past (16th-17th centuries).
Lit.: no. 163.

Krong (Thailand). Bamboo drum.
Lit.: no. 254.

Krontjong (Sunda District). See *Kronchong.*

Kroto (Borneo – Land Dayak). Beak flute with five front holes.
Lit.: no. 255.

Kroton(g) (Borneo – Land Dayak). Xylophone with six wooden slabs or bamboo tubes. Cf. *Konkon*; *Tjalun* (Java).
Lit.: no. 254.

K'rovah (Ancient Israel). Sung interpolation in prayers. Cf. *R'shuth.*
Lit.: no. 12.

Kṛṣṇaveni (South Idia). See *Krishṇaveni.*

Kṛti (South India). See *Kriti.*

Kruert (Thailand). Tone name. Cf. *Thang.*

Kru harp (Guinea – Toma; Liberia – Kru). Zither with strings strung in a triangular wooden frame. See also *Kani*; *Toa*; (*Oba*).
Lit.: nos. 118, 303.

Krumba (Nias). Beaten tube zither of Borneo, Philippines, and the entire archipelago. Cf. *Agong.*
Lit.: no. 255.

Krumpung(an) (Bali). Drum sounds deeper in pitch than those of the *krempeng.*
Lit.: no. 197.

Kruṣṭa (Vedic India). (1) The highest sound of the Vedic chant notated as 1 or 11 in the Sāmavedic (Kauthuma) notation; the other notes, in descending sequence, are: 2, 3, 4, 5, (6). The *kruṣṭa* has been described as a note that is heard and used only by the gods. (2) Term for a hand gesture (*kai-lakṣaṇa*) and musical sound of the chant linked with the syllable *kru* (of the Jaiminīya syllable notation of South India – Kerala).
Lit.: no. 141.

Kṣadrākṣi (South India). See *Kshadrākshi.*

Kṣana Prabha (South India). See *Kshana Prabha.*

Kṣaṇika (South India). See *Kshaṇika.*

Kṣapā (South India). See *Kshapā.*

Kṣēpiṇi (South India). See *Kshēpiṇi.*

Kshadrākshi (*Kṣadrākṣi*) (South India). *Janya rāga* of the 46th *mēḷa* (*Śaḍvidhamārgiṇī*).
Tone material:

C Db F# Eb Db F# G A Bb c
c Bb G A G F# Eb Db C

Lit.: no. 139.

Kshana Prabha (*Kṣana Prabha*) (South India). *Janya rāga* of the 1st *mēḷa* (*Kanakangi*).
Tone material:

C Ebb F G Ab c
c Ab G F Ebb C

Lit.: no. 139.

Kshaṇika (South India). *Janya rāga* of the 8th *mēḷa* (*Hanumattōḍi*).
Tone material:
C E♭ F G A♭ c
c A♭ G F E♭ C
Lit.: no. 139.

Kshapā (*Kṣapā*) (South India). *Janya rāga* of the 29th *mēḷa* (*Dhīraśaṅkarābharaṇam*).
Tone material:
C D E F G B c
c B F E D C
Lit.: no. 139.

Kshēmakari (South India). *Janya rāga* of the 58th *mēḷa* (*Hemāvatī*).
Tone material:
C D F♯ A B♭ c
c B♭ A F♯ D C
Lit.: no. 139.

Kshēpiṇi (*Kṣēpiṇi*) (South India). *Janya rāga* of the 12th *mēḷa* (*Rūpāvatī*).
Tone material:
C E♭ F G A♯ c
c A♯ G F E♭ C
Lit.: no. 139.

Kshudraghaṇtikā (Ancient India). See *Guṅghurū*.

Kshudrā Kātyāyaṇa Vīṇā (India). A small *satatantrī vīṇā* (of Bengal) with a flat calabash body and a soundboard with 18 steel strings.
Lit.: no. 254.

Kṣitiḥ (India). Term for the 14th *śruti*. The corresponding note name is *pratiśuddha dha*, a term used in theoretical treatises. Cf. *Śruti*.

Kṣobhiṇī (India). Term for the basic *śruti* of the 22 microtonal intervals within the octave. *Kṣobhiṇī* represents the note *sa*. Cf. *Śruti*.

Kśudrā Kātyāyaṇā Vīṇā (India; Bengal). See *Kshudrā Kātyāyaṇā Vīṇā*.

Ku (Korea). The augmented fourth note and notational symbol used by the *kong-chuk-po*. Assuming that *hap* represents the western C, *sang* would be F and *ku* F♯. See *Kong-chuk-po*.

Ku (China). See *Ch'in-pu*.

Ku (China). General term for "drum." Some of the Chinese drums are: *chang-ku*, *chen-ku*, *hsiao-ku*, *hua-ku*, *lo-ku*, *man-t'ou-ku*, *pa-fang-ku*, *pang-ku*, *pan-t'ang-ku*, *shu-ku*, *t'ang-ku*, *t'ao-ku*, *tien-ku*, *tsin-ku*, *tsu-ku*, *yao-ku*, *ying-ku*, *yü-ku*.

Ku (China). Term for corpus of string instruments.

Ku (Japan). The 13th pipe of the *shō*.

Ku (Japan). A flat lute with four strings similar to the *genkwan*. The instrument has a circular corpus and nine frets. The body is richly ornamented. The tuning is variable. Cf. *Wol-kum* (Korea); *Can dan Ṅuyet* (Vietnam).
Lit.: nos. 225, 255.

Ku (Japan). The spots (interruptions) where in a sung melody the performer can take breaths. Cf. *Kobyōshi*.
Lit.: no. 225.

Kü (Kurdistan). Peg.

Kuan (China—M 3557a). "Tube," "reed." Originally a small vertical flute without any fingerholes, tuned to one of the 12 *lü*. In later periods the term represented not only various flutes, but numerous oboe types of varying sizes. See *Kuan-tzu*. Cf. *T'ou-kuan*; *Shuang-kuan*; *Hichiriki* (Japan).
Lit.: nos. 137, 209.

K'uang (China). Term for the body of the barrel-shaped *ku*.

Kuan-ku (South China). Cantonese term for *ch'ü-ku*.

Kuan-tzu (China—M 3557; M 6939). (1) The Peking name of a small cylindrical shawm with seven holes in front and two in the back. It is blown by means of a coarsely made reed and is used in funeral or marriage processions. It produces approximately the following notes: C D E F F♯ G A B c d e f. Cf. *Tui-hsiao*; *Ch'un-kuan*. (2) *Kuan-tzu* means also the pipes of the *sheng*, particularly the 12-pipe *sheng*.

Kuar (India). Cf. *Chaugan*.
Lit.: no. 138.

Kūbā (Arabia; Persia). An ancient 2-headed drum with an hourglass-shaped body. At the present time it is known as *ṭabl mukhannath*. See also *Kalangual*; *Kalungu*; *Lūnga*.
Lit.: no. 95.

Kubahan (Java). Cf. *Joged*.

Kubar (New Guinea; Geelvin Bay). Shell trumpet with lateral blowhole.
Lit.: no. 184.

Kuchapi (Philippines; Mindanao; Maranao). See *Kacchapi*; *Kachapi*.

Kuchchi (South India). Drumstick.

Kuchi-jamisen (Japan). Solmization syllables used in notation and teaching *shamisen* music. The syllables are placed to the left of the notated music column and indicate open string, down-stroke, up-stroke, stopped string, pizzicato, etc.
Lit.: nos. 185, 187.

Ku-ch'in (*Ku-k'in*) (China). A jew's harp (first mentioned in the 12th century). Cf. *K'ou-ch'in*.
Lit.: no. 250.

Kuchipudi (South India). Theatrical performance in which the actors sing and dance. The accompaniment is provided by musicians who are placed on the stage. This dance style is named after the village Kuchipudi of Andhra Pradesh. At times the performance is called *bhama-kalapam*, the story of Krishna and the *gopi*.

Ku-ch'ui (China). Drumstick. Also ceremonial music of the Han dynasty.
Lit.: no. 255.

Ku-ch'ui-hsiao (China—M 3479; M 1476; M 2619). The drum music *hsiao*.
Lit.: no. 137.

Kud (North India; Jammu; Kashmir—Dogra). Popular dance with Pahari music, prevalent around Bhardawah and Kishtwar.

Kuda (Japan). A heavy ivory cylinder that prolongs the fingernail of the middle finger of the left hand. It is used to stop the (single) string of the *ichi-gen-kin*.
Lit.: no. 255.

Kuda kepang (*Jaran kepang*) (Java). A dance play. In the play appear hobby horses (*kuda*, *jara*) made of basket work (*kepang*) occasionally covered with leather (*lumping*). Cf. *Kuda lumping*. The musical accompaniment of the play is provided by a varying number of instruments: one *selompret*, two *angklungs*, a *terbang*, *reog* (*ḍogḍog*).
Lit.: no. 163.

Kuda-kuda (West Java; Sunda District). The low wooden stand upon which the *kenḍang* rests.
Lit.: no. 163.

Kuḍakuttu (South India). Tamil term for *karagam*.

Kuda lumping (Java; Sunda District). See *Kuda kepang*.

Kudam (South India). "Bowl," corpus, of the *vīṇā*. General term for resonator of string instruments.
Lit.: no. 261.

Kudan (Japan). "Nine *dan*," nine variations, sections (without singing) based on a leading theme.

Kudara-gaku (Japan). Name of the music of Paekche (one of the medieval kingdoms of Korea). The name implies also the imported music. See *Gagaku.*
Lit.: no. 185.

Kudara-koto (Japan). The old Korean *koto* with an animal-head ornamenting one end. Cf. *Shiragi-koto*; *So-kong-hu* (Korea).
Lit.: no. 225.

Kudeketera (Rhodesia—Shona Mbira). Speaking in a sing-song manner. This presentation of texts and songs is considered by local musicians as music.
Lit.: no. 22.

Kudi (Nigeria—Yoruba). Cf. *Omele abo*; *Bata.*

Kudirai (South India). See *Gurram.*

Kudlung (Philippines—Hanunoo). Bamboo zither.
Lit.: no. 303.

Kudoki (Japan). The section (song) in which the lyric beauty of the melody is more emphasized than the text. The *kudoki* can be found in numerous narrative compositions (*jōruri*, *nōh*, *kabuki*, *nagauta*, etc.).
Lit.: no. 187.

Kudre (Congo—Mombutu; Momvu). Conical drum. Cf. *Udre.*
Lit.: no. 26.

Kudrekene (*Kudrenene*) (Congo). Ground zither.
Lit.: no. 176.

Kudrenene (Congo). See *Kudrekene.*

Kudru-gu (Congo—Kilima; Andemanza). Ground zither.
Lit.: no. 176.

Kudu (Congo—Mundo). A lyre type.
Lit.: no. 176.

Kudüm (Turkey). Term for the *nakkāra* when used in sacred music. Cf. *Nakkare.*

Kudurigaku (Japan). See *Gagaku.*

Kudyapi (Philippines—Hanunoo). Lute (? *kachapi*).
Lit.: no. 303.

Kuei (China). See *Chien-tzu.*
Lit.: no. 136.

K'uei-fu (China—M 3667; M 1939a). Drumsticks made of clay used to beat the *t'u-ku.*
Lit.: no. 137.

K'uei-lei hsi (China). Puppet theater.

Kufo (West Cameroon). Court and ceremonial music.

Kugo (Japan). Obsolete ancient harp (of the 12th century) with 23 strings. The instrument was probably imported from East Turkestan and was related to the *k'ung-hu* of China.
Lit.: no. 52.

Kuhotora imirya (Congo). Term for the *inanga* (trough zither of Ruanda and Urundi).
Lit.: no. 255.

Ku-hsi (China—M 3453; M 2465). "Old, purified." Absolute pitch; the fifth tone of the circle of fifths as shown in the *lü-lü.* If used as a notational symbol only the first syllable (*ku*) was used.
Lit.: no. 136.

Kuimba (*Uimbaji*) (East Africa—Swahili). Singing.

Kuimbi (Angola; Loango District). See *Nkwimbi.*

Kuina (Kenya—Nandi). Horn.
Lit.: no. 255.

Kuitra (*Kouitra*) (Northwest Africa; Algeria). Lute with four double gut strings and a calabash corpus. The plectrum is made of a feather. The tuning is *G* D A e.
Lit.: nos. 34, 255.

Kujamba (Tanganyika – Washambala). Rattle made of cane.
Lit.: no. 130.

Kujanmōhanam (South India). *Janya rāga* of the 16th *mēḷa* (*Chakravāka*).
Tone material:
B♭ C E D♭ E F G A c
c B♭ A G E D♭ C
Lit.: no. 139.

Kūkāt (Mongolia). Eight modes brought by the Mongols into Islamic lands (14th century).
Lit.: no. 76.

Kukau (New Zealand – Maori). Jew's harp.
Lit.: no. 7.

K'u-k'in (China). See *Ku-ch'in.*

Kukokoteza sauti (East Africa – Swahili). See *Uvumi. . . .*

Kukubh (*Kukubha*; *Kakubh*) (North India). *Rāga* ascribed to the *Bilaval thāta*. It appears in two versions: as a combination of elements taken from the *rāgas Jayjayvanti* and *Alahiya-Bilaval* and as a combination of *Jhinjhoti* and *Alahiya-Bilaval.* The second version is very rare.
Tone material:
C D E F G A B c
c (B) (B♭) A G F E D C; *Vādis*: F, C
Lit.: no. 138.

Kukuḍa (South India). *Janya rāga* of the 15th *mēḷa* (*Māyāmāḷavagauḷa*).
Tone material:
C D♭ E G A♭ B A♭ c
c B A♭ G F D♭ C
Lit.: no. 139.

Kukulan gantang (Java). Hindu-Javanese term indicating the *kenṭongan.*
Lit.: nos. 163, 190.

Kukumā (Sahara; Sudan). Scraping instrument.
Lit.: no. 255.

Kula Bhūṣani (South India). See *Kula Bhūshaṇi.*

Kula Bhūshaṇi (*Kula Bhūṣani*) (South India). *Janya rāga* of the 21st *mēḷa* (*Kiravāṇi*).
Tone material:
C D E♭ F G B c
c A♭ G F E♭ D C
Lit.: no. 139.

Kulaṃkaṣa (South India). See *Kulamkasha.*

Kulamkasha (*Kulaṃkaṣa*) (South India). *Janya rāga* of the 1st *mēḷa* (*Kanakāṅgī*).
Tone material:
C D♭ F A♭ B♭♭ c
c B♭♭ A♭ F D♭ C
Lit.: no. 139.

Kulang (*Culang*) (Philippines – Moro). Cf. *Barimbo.*

Kulapavitra (South India). See *Kulapavitri.*

Kulapavitri (*Kulapavitra*) (South India). *Janya rāga* of the 28th *mēḷa* (*Harikāmbhōji*).
Tone material:
C E F A G B♭ c
c B♭ G F D C
Lit.: no. 139.

K'ulen (Sierra Leone – Temne). Flute.

Kulepa gane (*Nunut*) (New Ireland). A wooden block with three slits and heavy tongues. When rubbed the instrument can produce four different sounds.
Lit.: nos. 37, 84.

Kulibao (Philippines – Ilonggot). See *Litlit.*

Kulimbet (Philippines—Ibaloi). An instrumental ensemble consisting of two long barrel drums and one gong. Two dancers perform a healing dance around a pig that has to be sacrificed.

Kulintang (South Philippines). Instrumental ensemble consisting of gongs similar to the *bonang* types of Java and several drums.
Lit.: no. 186.

Kuḷir (South India). Pot-shaped drum.

Kulit perut lembu (Malaysia). See *Rebāb* (Malaysia).

Kulkul (Bali). Bamboo or wooden slit-drum used for signaling. The various parts of the drum, referring to the human body, are: *sirah* (head); *gulu* or *jongga* (neck); *chlewekan* (*changkem*) (slit, actually mouth); *lambe* (side edges, actually lips). The Sundanese name of the drum is *kohkol*; the Madurese name is *gulgul*. In other places the name is *titir*, referring to Javanese rice-block stamping parties.
Lit.: nos. 163, 197.

Kultjapi (Indonesia). See *Kulchapi*; *Lagija*.

Kulkulan (Bali). The sounding of the *kulkul*. A drumming feature consisting of rhythmic patterns beaten on the *kulkul* to *kopiak* (*koprak*) accompaniment.
Lit.: no. 197.

Kum (*Keum*) (Korea). Small zither (cf. the Chinese *Ch'in*) with seven strings, without any frets. It is tuned to C D E G A c d. The instrument was used only in imported Chinese ritual music.
Lit.: no. 179.

Kuma (India). Straight brass trumpet used in temples and in religious services.

Kumambang (*Mas Kumambang*) (Java). One of the poetic meters of *Tembang machapat* generally occurring in songs, the texts of which deal with nostalgia, longing for home.
Lit.: no. 163.

Kumanak (Bali). Rattle stick.
Lit.: nos. 197, 265.

Kumāradyuti (South India). *Janya rāga* of the 28th *mēḷa* (*Harikāmbhōji*).
Tone material:
C D E F B♭ A B♭ c
c B♭ A G D C
Lit.: no. 139.

Kumāra Lila (South India). *Janya rāga* of the 20th *mēḷa* (*Naṭabhairavī*).
Tone material:
C F G A♭ B♭ G B♭ c
c B♭ A♭ G F E♭ D C
Lit.: no. 139.

Kumāra Rañjani (South India). *Janya rāga* of the 25th *mēḷa* (*Māraran̄janī*).
Tone material:
C D E F A♭ B♭♭ c
c B♭♭ A♭ F E D C
Lit.: no. 139.

Kumārapriya (South India). *Janya rāga* of the 3rd *mēḷa* (*Gānamūrti*).
Tone material:
C D♭ E♭♭ A♭ B c
c B A♭ E♭♭ D♭ C
Lit.: no. 139.

Kumba (Java). The curving of the boss on top of a gong.

Kumbhavādya (South India). Kannarese term for a pot-shaped drum. A large number of various terms are in use for this instrument (cf. Lit. no. 254). Cf. *Gāḍa*; *Ghāṭa*.

Kumbhinī (South India). *Janya rāga* of the 2nd *mēḷa* (*Ratnangi*).
Tone material:
C D♭ E♭♭ A♭ B♭ C
c B♭ A♭ E♭♭ D♭ C
Lit.: no. 139.

Kumbhiṇī (South India). *Janya rāga* of the 41st *mēḷa* (*Pāvanī*).
Tone material:

C E♭♭ D♭ E♭♭ F♯ G B A B c

c B G F♯ E♭♭ D♭ C

Lit.: no. 139.

Kumbhinī (South India). See *Prabhāvati* (41st *asampūrṇa mēḷa*).
Lit.: no. 139.

Kumbi-kumbi (Indonesia; Ternate). Ground zither in form of a bamboo music-bow with one metal string.
Lit.: no. 162.

Kumbili (Congo). Musical bow also called *gambili, kambili.*
Lit.: no. 176.

Kūmhuan (Korea). Acrobatic ball play according by flute and drum. Cf. *Taemyōn.*

Kumi (Japan). A type of *koto* music; it is less ponderous than the severe *dan-mono* form, although written in similar sections. The sections of the *kumi* are called *uta* (verse) and are numbered: *hito-uta* (first verse), *futa-uta* (second verse), *mi-uta* (third verse), *yo-uta* (fourth verse), *itsu-uta* (fifth verse), *mu-uta* (sixth verse), etc. Each verse is divided into eight sections and each section into eight *hyōshi* (measure). Cf. *Kumi-uta.*
Lit.: no. 225.

Kumitang (Philippines). Tagalog dances in a pantomimic fashion.
Lit.: no. 186.

Kumiuta (Japan). A suite form that originated in the 16th century by the Tsukushigoto school. The form began with *shamisen* music, later led to alternating *koto* and vocal items (cf. *Ko-uta*), resulting in suites at times consisting of 10 pieces. In the late 17th and 18th centuries these suites appeared in *kabuki* performances. The structure of the *kumiuta* is as follows: *maebiki*, instrumental introduction; *maeuta*, first song; *tegoto*, instrumental interlude; *atouta*, final song.

Further extensions to the *kumiuta* form were: one or more *tegoto* (interludes), a *nakauta* (middle song), *makura* (introduction), *tsunagi* (transition), *naka-chirashi* (middle climax), and the *honchirashi* (real finale).
Lit.: no. 187.

Kummi (South India). Tamil name of folk dance performed by girls. The musical accompaniment is provided by *kummi pāṭṭu* songs.

Kumoi (Japan). The second principal *koto* tuning. See *Koto* tunings. *Kumoi* (or *kumoi joshi*) means the "cloud" tuning because the first tune learned by the *koto* pupil in this particular tuning is *kumo-no-ye*, the "Song of the Clouds."
Lit.: no. 185.

Kumoi-jōshi (Japan). See *Kumoi.*

Kumpee (Northeast Thailand). A palm leaf manuscript.
Lit.: no. 203.

Kum-po (Korea). Korean zither book written in the same manner as the Chinese *ch'in-p'u.* There are numerous such books, such as the famous *An-sang kum-po* (16th-17th centuries), and the *Yang-kum shin-po* (1610).
Lit.: no. 136.

Kumpul (Malaysia). (1) A set of large gongs suspended from a wooden frame. There are several types of *kumpul.* (2) In another *kumpul* (combined with *gong kumbang*) two bronze tubes are suspended above a wooden resonance box.

Kumudābharaṇam (South India). *Janya rāga* of the 38th *mēḷa* (*Jalārṇava*).
Tone material:

C D♭ E♭♭ F♯ G B♭ A♭ c

c A♭ B♭ G F♯ E♭♭ D♭ C

Lit.: no. 139.

Kumudapriya (South India). *Janya rāga* of the 51st *mēḷa* (*Kāmavardhanī*).
Tone material:
C D♭ E F♯ G c
c B A♭ B G F♯ E C
Lit.: no. 139.

Kumudapriya (South India). *Janya rāga* of the 22nd *mēḷa* (*Kharaharapriyā*).
Tone material:
C D E♭ F G c
c B♭ A B♭ G F E♭ C
Lit.: no. 139.

Kumudvatī (India). Name of the second *śruti.* The corresponding note name is *śuddha ri* (music theoretical term). Cf. *Śruti.*

Kumunko (Korea). See *Komunko.*

Kumurere (Uganda—Gishu). Wooden or bamboo flute with two finger holes.
Lit.: no. 302.

Kumuthiṇi (South India). *Janya rāga* of the 67th *mēḷa* (*Sucharitra*).
Tone material:
C D♯ E F♯ G A♭ c
c A♭ G F♯ E D♯ C
Lit.: no. 139.

K'un (China). Term in Amoy dialect for *ch'in* (M 1103).

K'un-ch'iang (China). Modified, modernized *k'un-ch'ü* drama. See *K'un-ch'ü.*

K'un-ch'ü (China—M 3679; M 1623; *K'un-ch'iang*). "Songs of the men of K'un-shan." This important drama originated in the 16th century in K'un-shan (Kiangsu Province). In its early form it was a simple popular drama. Later it became the subtle, elegant drama (*ya-pu*), fashionable and appreciated by the educated classes. Among the instruments used are the dominating *ti-tzu*, the *kuan* (single reed), *p'i-p'a* (four strings), *tung-hsiao*, *yüeh-ch'in*, and the *san-hsien.* Cf. *Ch'uan-ch'i.*
The k'un-ch'ü can be described as the 20th-century operatic style. Its plots have literary value and the subjects are subtle. There exists a large variety of melodies in this style. Rhythmically the *k'un-ch'ü* music shows a surprisingly rigid character.
Lit.: no. 183.

Kunda (Lower Congo—Bwende; Sundi; Yombe). Wooden double bell with 1-3 clappers in each bell.
Lit.: no. 280.

Kundamalika (South India). *Janya rāga* of the 22nd *mēḷa* (*Kharaharapriyā*).
Tone material:
C D E♭ G A B♭ c
c B♭ A G F E♭ D C
Lit.: no. 139.

Kundi (India). Drumstick (punjabi).

Kundi (*Kundu*) (Northeast Congo—Zande). Arched harp (*nanga* type) with five strings. Cf. *Nkundi.* The term is also applied to a xylophone (Congo—Kabba).
Lit.: nos. 10, 176.

Kundu (Congo). See *Kundi.*

Kundu (New Guinea). A drum with one head, the body having the shape of an hourglass, used with rattles at dances.
Lit.: no. 215.

Kundung (Nigeria). Xylophone.

Kunduri (*Kundur*) (Southeast India—Hill Maria and Muria Gond). Slim cylindrical drum. It is used at religious festivals and dances and is beaten with both hands.
Lit.: no. 135.

Kundye (West Africa; Republic of Guinea—Soso). Fiddle with one horsehair string. Cf. *Ngime.*
Lit.: no. 255.

Kune tsuzumi (Japan). A wooden ring imported from South China, used as a percussion instrument. It is beaten with a wooden stick.
Lit.: no. 225.

Kung (China—M 3705 宫) (not to be mistaken for *kung* M 3697 below). Ancient solmization syllable and notational symbol indicating the first degree of the old 5- and 7-tone scales. Assuming that *kung* represents the western note C, the five (seven) notes of the scales are:

kung	C	
shang	D	
chiao	E	(since the Ming period, *chiao* is F)
pien-chih	F♯	
chih	G	
yü	A	
pien-kung	B	

Lit.: no. 137.

Kung (China—M 3697 工) (not to be mistaken for *kung* M 3705 above). Solmization syllable and notational symbol of the first note of *kung-ch'e-p'u*. Assuming that *ho* is the western note C, *kung* (M 3697) is A. See *Kung-ch'e-p'u*. Lit.: no. 136.

Kung (Korea). Solmization syllable and notational symbol representing the first note of pentatonic and heptatonic scales. If *kung* is represented by the western note C, the other notes are: *sang* (D, D♭); *kak* (E, E♭, [also F]); *chi* (G); *U* (A, A♭).

Kung (China). Finger hole (in Fuhchan dialect). Lit.: no. 255.

Kung-ch'e-p'u (China—M 3697; M 1045; M 5386). The most frequently used notational system. It came into use probably during the Sung dynasty (960-1279), perhaps even earlier, and remained in full use since the Yüan period (1260-1368).

Its symbols denote relative pitches. If the first note is read as the western C, the following notes are:

ho	C	
hsia-ssu	D♭	
ssu	D	(in South China: *shih*)
hsia-yi	E♭	
yi	E	
shang	F	
kou	F♯	
ch'e	G	
hsia-kung	A♭	
kung	A	(This *kung*—M 3697—must not be mistaken for *kung*—M 3705)
hsian-fan	B♭	
fan	B	
liu	c	
hsia wu	d♭	
wu	d	
hsia-yi	e♭	
yi	e	

The *kung-ch'e* symbols cover a gamut of three octaves. In practice, however, the entire range was and is never used. The three octaves are called: *cho-sheng* ("lowest notes"); *chung-sheng* ("middle notes"); *ch'ing-sheng* ("highest, clear notes").

The basic scale of the Yüan dynasty was: C D E F F♯ G A B; the basic scale of the Ming and post-Ming periods was: C D F G A c. For further details see Lit. no. 136.

K'ung cheng (China—see, e.g. M 3722; M 369). A double humming top consisting of two *ti-ko-tzu* mounted on a wooden stick. Lit.: nos. 190, 209.

Kung ch'en kuan (China—M 3710; M 336; M 3557). A 16th-century flute with six finger holes. Lit.: no. 209.

K'ung-hou (China—M 3727; M 2141). A harp imported from Persia, now obsolete, an instrument that was never fully accepted in the Far East. It had 25 strings and, allegedly appeared in three forms:

1. *Chien-k'ung-hou*, ancient obscure harp with 12 strings.
2. *Feng-shu k'ung-hou*, ancient obscure arched harp with 16 strings.
3. *Wo k'ung-hou*, ancient obscure zither with 12 strings (probably erroneously shown as a flat positioned *chien-k'ung-hou*).

Lit.: no. 250.

Kung long (Thailand). Cf. *Bendrong* (Java). Lit.: no. 163.

Kungu (Congo—Warega). Zither.
Lit.: no. 21.

Kunguleme (Congo—Baluba-Hemba). Musical bow.
Lit.: no. 21.

Kunka-da (*Ka-da* or *Ge*) (Japan). See *Wasan.*

Kun-ko (Korea). A large ornamented barrel drum that came from China in the 12th century. In later centuries it became obsolete. A wooden supporting pillar is pierced through the middle of the body of the *kun-ko.* On top of the corpus, as a continuation of the pillar, stands a miniature wooden ornamental pavillion of two stories curtained by silks and decorated with tassels. On top of the pavillion appears a wooden crane with spread out wings. See *Sakko.*
Lit.: no. 179.

Kuṅkumāmbari (South India). *Janya rāga* of the 15th *mēḷa* (*Māyāmāḷavagauḷa*).
Tone material:
C D♭ E F G A♭ B c
c A♭ G F E D♭ C
Lit.: no. 139.

Kuntala (South India). *Janya rāga* of the 16th *mēḷa* (*Chakravāka*).
Tone material:
C D♭ E F G A B♭ c
c A B♭ G F E F D♭ C
Lit.: no. 139.

Kuntala (South India). See *Kāntāmaṇi.*

Kuntala (South India). (1) The 61st *asampūrṇa mēḷa-rāga* without *kaṭapayādi* prefix. (2) The 61st *asampūrṇa mēḷa-rāga* with *kaṭapayādi* prefix. See *Rāga* (South India).
Lit.: no. 139.

Kuntala Bhavāni (South India). *Janya rāga* of the 67th *mēḷa* (*Sucharitra*).
Tone material:
C D♯ E F♯ G F♯ G c
c B♭♭ A♭ B♭♭ G F♯ D♯ C
Lit.: no. 139.

Kuntala Bhōgi (South India). *Janya rāga* of the 41st *mēḷa* (*Pāvani*).
Tone material:
C D♭ E♭♭ F♯ A G B c
c B A B F♯ E♭♭ D♭ C
Lit.: no. 139.

Kuntala Dhanyāsi (South India). *Janya rāga* of the 47th *mēḷa* (*Suvarṇāṅgī*).
Tone material:
C D♭ E♭ F♯ G F♯ A B c
c B A B G F♯ E♭ D♭ C
Lit.: no. 139.

Kuntala Dīparam (South India). *Janya rāga* of the 48th *mēḷa* (*Divyamaṇī*).
Tone material:
C F♯ G A♯ B c
c B A♯ B G F♯ E♭ C
Lit.: no. 139.

Kuntala Ghaṇṭāṇam (South India). *Janya rāga* of the 70th *mēḷa* (*Nāsikabhūṣaṇi*).
Tone material:
C D♯ E F♯ G F♯ G c
c B♭ G F♯ D♯ C
Lit.: no. 139.

Kuntala Gīrvāṇi (South India). *Janya rāga* of the 68th *mēḷa* (*Jyōtisvarupiṇī*).
Tone material:
C D♯ E F♯ G A♭ B♭ c
c A♭ F♯ G F♯ E D♯ C
Lit.: no. 139.

Kuntala Kāmbhōji (South India). *Janya rāga* of the 13th *mēḷa* (*Gāyakapriya*).
Tone material:
C E F G A♭ B♭♭ A♭ c
c B♭♭ A♭ G F E C
Lit.: no. 139.

Kuntala Kusumāvaḷi (South India). *Janya rāga* of the 65th *mēḷa* (*Mechakalyāṇī*).
Tone material:
C D E F♯ G F♯ G c
c B A B G F♯ E C
Lit.: no. 139.

Kuntala Rama (South India). *Janya rāga* of the 53rd *mēḷa* (*Gamanaśrama*).
Tone material:
C D♭ E G A c
c B A G F♯ E D♭ C
Lit.: no. 139.

Kuntala Rañjani (South India). *Janya rāga* of the 68th *mēḷa* (*Jyōtisvarūpiṇī*).
Tone material:
C D♯ F♯ G B♭ A♭ B♭ c
c B♭ A♭ G F♯ E D♯ C
Lit.: no. 139.

Kuntala Sāraṅga (South India). *Janya rāga* of the 17th *mēḷa* (*Sūryakānta*).
Tone material:
B C D♭ E F G A B
A G F E D♭ C *B*
Lit.: no. 139.

Kuntala Siṃhāravam (South India). *Janya rāga* of the 69th *mēḷa* (*Dhātuvardhaṇī*).
Tone material:
C D♯ F♯ G F♯ A♭ B c
c A♭ G F♯ D♯ C
Lit.: no. 139.

Kuntala Śrīkaṇṭhi (South India). *Janya rāga* of the 65th *mēḷa* (*Mechakalyāṇī*).
Tone material:
C E F♯ G A B c
c B G F♯ E D C
Lit.: no. 139.

Kuntala Svarāvali (South India). *Janya rāga* of the 46th *mēḷa* (*Śaḍvidhamārgiṇī*).
Tone material:
C E♭ F♯ G A B♭ c
c B♭ A B♭ G F♯ E♭ D♭ C
Lit.: no. 139.

Kuntalavarāḷi (South India). *Janya rāga* of the 28th *mēḷa* (*Harikāmbhōji*).
Tone material:
C F G A B♭ A c
c B♭ A G F C
Lit.: no. 139.

Kun-tiao (China – M 3676; M 6298). Interpolated features in the *ch'uan-ch'ih* performances. These texts were in popular, common language, in contrast to the general classical text. The reason for using these interpolations was to make the story comprehensible to the common large audiences who did not understand enough of classical, literary Chinese.
Lit.: no. 183.

Kuntigi (Republic of Niger; North Nigeria – Hausa). Simple lute with one string.

Kunting (West Sudan – Mandingo). Harp-lute with three strings.
Lit.: no. 255.

Kuntuku (North Nigeria – Hausa). Drum with one skin. It is used together with the *kalangu* and *d'an karbi*, both Hausa drums, each with two skins.

Kuo-men (China – M 3730; M 4418). Interlude.

Kup (Thailand). To sing according to linguistic tones; the term can also imply unaccompanied singing in alternation with instrumental interludes.
Lit.: no. 203.

Ku-pi (China). Drum skin.

Kuping (Java). Drum skin.

Kupingan (Java). See *Rebāb* (Java).

Kupu (North Rhodesia; Congo – Babembe). Musical bow.
Lit.: no. 21.

Kura (Mongolia – Bashkiria). Vertical flute. Cf. *Zurr.*
Lit.: no. 60.

Kural (India). Double flute; mouth- or nose-blown.
Lit.: nos. 190, 313.

Kural (South India). The note *sa* in ancient Tamil terminology. Cf. Dravidian music.

Kurama-jishi (Japan). Special *koto* tuning.

Kurañjalōchani (South India). *Janya rāga* of the 3rd *mēḷa* (*Gānamūrti*).
Tone material:
C D♭ E♭♭ F G c
c B G F E♭♭ D♭ C
Lit.: no. 139.

Kurañjī (South India). *Janya rāga* of the 29th *mēḷa* (*Dhīraśaṅkarābharaṇam*).
Tone material:
C *B* C D E F G A
A G F E D C *B* C
Kurañjī is a *dhaivatāntya rāga*. In the lower octave range the note *ni* (*B*) is often taken as a *B*♭.
Lit.: no. 139.

Kuravanji (South India). Popular dance drama.
Lit.: no. 261.

Kurbi (West Sudan). Harp with five strings.

Kurdī (Iraq; Arabia). From the province of Kurdistan. Tone name of a note about a semitone higher than *dugā* (*du gāh*, *dukāh*). A list of all tone names and tones through two octaves can be seen under the heading of *Jagā* (*Yagā*). *Kurdī* as *maqām*: D E♭ F G A B♭ c d (see Lit. no. 64); it appears also in modern Egypt.

Kure (New Guinea). Wooden drum.
Lit.: no. 255.

Kureke (Arabia). Big drum; tamtam.
Lit.: no. 255.

Kūrēśam (South India). *Janya rāga* of the 65th *mēḷa* (*Mechakalyāṇī*).
Tone material:
C D E F♯ G B c
c B A G F♯ D C
Lit.: no. 139.

Kure tsuzumi (Japan). An ancient (probably Southern Chinese) idiophone consisting of a wooden ring beaten with sticks.
Lit.: no. 225.

Kūrgā (Mongolia). Giant kettledrum. Cf. *Ṭabl al-kabīr.*

Kurga (Arabia). Large kettledrum usually used in pairs. Cf. *Ṭabl al-kabīr.*
Lit.: no. 71.

Kuri (Japan). Scale degree in *noh* music. Cf. *Noh*; *Tsuyo*; *Yowa*; *Ha*; *Kuse.*

Kurka (India; Persia). Cf. *Kurga* (Arabia; Persia).
Lit.: no. 78.

Kurma (India; Bengal). Excessive religious dances.

Kūrma vīṇā (India). Ancient obscure fiddle with a tortoise-shaped body.
Lit.: no. 261.

Kurna (India). Large trumpet.
Lit.: no. 261.

Kuromisu (Japan). The black bamboo blind that hides the off-stage (*geza* room) from the *kabuki* theater hall.
Lit.: no. 187.

Kurong-kurong (Borneo – Tanah Laut). See *Gulong-gulong.*

Kursī (Arabia). String holder.
Lit.: no. 255.

Kurtar (India). Rattle clapper consisting of a wooden block with two wide slits. In the slits hang two small thin brass discs that rattle when the instrument is shaken.
Lit.: no. 255.

Kurube (Upper Nile—Bongo). *Kissar* with six strings.
Lit.: no. 255.

Kurudēśyam (South India). *Janya rāga* of the 65th *mēḷa* (*Mechakalyāṇī*).
Tone material:
C D E F# A B c
c B A F# E D C
Lit.: no. 139.

Kurugu (New Guinea). Sacred wooden flute with one finger hole. The upper end is ornamented with the carved head of a human with hairs, or an animal. The instrument is made of an egg-shaped clay vessel.
Lit.: no. 37.

Kuruḷa (India). See *Gamak(a).*

Kurunku (Ghana—Akan). A lament performed by a solo voice with choral accompaniment.
Lit.: no. 218.

Kurunkuzhal (South India). (1) Short flute. (2) Short *nāgaswaram* of Kerala. Cf. *Neḍunkuzhal.*
Lit.: no. 261.

Kuruvañji (South India). Popular dance-play performed by female dancers.

Kuryapi (Philippines). Lute with two strings.

Kūs (Turkey; Persia). A large kettledrum beaten with two club-shaped sticks. The corpus is made of metal and the head is covered with a net in order to avoid too much vibration. Cf. *Tabīra.* The drum is also called *khāqānī kūs*, after Kāqā, a Chinese, who was believed to be the patron of this instrument. The medium sized kettledrum is called *qudūm* (beaten with sticks). *Naqqāra* is the small kettledrum. It is held by the left hand and beaten with the right. The gypsies in Turkey call it *na'ra.* When the *naqqāra* is played in pairs it is called *chīfta naqqāra*.
Lit.: no. 81.

Kusabue (Japan). "Grass flute"; the term represents also a rustic flute melody. See *Inkabue.*
Lit.: no. 187.

Kuśa Vāhiṇi (South India). *Janya rāga* of the 65th *mēḷa* (*Mechakalyāṇī*).
Tone material:
C D E D F# G F# A B c
c B A G F# E D C
Lit.: no. 139.

Kuse (Japan). In the fourth *dan* of the play, the last *dan* of the exposition in *nohgaku*, appear two important sections: the *kuri* and *kuse.* The *kuri* (named after the highest note of the *noh* range) is of musical importance, while the *kuse* represents a climax of the drama expressed by an elaborate dance. See *Ha* (*Noh*).
Lit.: no. 187.

Kusemai (Japan). Ancient dance and its music. Cf. *Kuse.*

Kushat (Arabia). See *Gushat.*

Kushaura (Rhodesia—Shona). Solo part; lead part.
Lit.: no. 22.

Kūshnāy (Central Asia; Turkestan—Sart). Double clarinet. Cf. *Dūnāy.*
Lit.: no. 190.

Ku-shou (China). The orchestra leader of the Hong Kong theater who plays a wooden clapper and beats a small drum. Cf. *Shang-shou*; *Erh-shou*; *San-shou.*

Kuśīlava (Ancient India). Actor, clown.

Kussir (Turkey). Turkish *kissar*.
Lit.: no. 255.

Kusuma Bhavāni (South India). *Janya rāga* of the 68th *mēḷa* (*Jyōtisvarūpiṇī*).
Tone material:
C D♯ F♯ G A♭ c
c B♭ A♭ F♯ G F♯ D♯ C
Lit.: no. 139.

Kusumabhōgi (South India). *Janya rāga* of the 50th *mēḷa* (*Namanārāyaṇī*).
Tone material:
C D♭ E F♯ A♭ B♭ c
c A♭ B♭ A♭ F♯ E D♭ E C
Lit.: no. 139.

Kusumabhramari (South India). *Janya rāga* of the 34th *mēḷa* (*Vāgadhīśvarī*).
Tone material:
C D♯ E F G F A B♭ c
c B♭ A G F D♯ C
Lit.: no. 139.

Kusumacandrikā (South India). See *Kusumachandrika.*

Kusumachandrikā (South India). *Janya rāga* of the 32nd *mēḷa* (*Rāgavardhanī*).
Tone material:
C D♯ F E G A B♭ c
c A♭ G F D♯ C
Lit.: no. 139.

Kusuma Dhāriṇi (South India). *Janya rāga* of the 25th *mēḷa* (*Mārarañjanī*).
Tone material:
C D E G A♭ B♭♭ c
c B♭♭ A♭ G E D C
Lit.: no. 139.

Kusumāgraṇi (South India). *Janya rāga* of the 65th *mēḷa* (*Mechakalyāṇī*).
Tone material:
C E D E F♯ B A G A B c
c B A G F♯ D E D C
Lit.: no. 139.

Kusumajā (South India). *Janya rāga* of the 19th *mēḷa* (*Jhaṅkāradhvani*).
Tone material:
C E♭ F G A♭ c
c A♭ G F D C
Lit.: no. 139.

Kusuma Jyōtiṣmati (South India). *Janya rāga* of the 69th *mēḷa* (*Dhātuvardhaṇī*).
Tone material:
C D♯ F♯ E F♯ G A♭ B c
c A♭ B A♭ G F♯ D♯ C
Lit.: no. 139.

Kusumakallōlam (South India). *Janya rāga* of the 32nd *mēḷa* (*Rāgavardhanī*).
Tone material:
C G F D♯ E F G c
c A♭ G F E F D♯ C
Lit.: no. 139.

Kusumākara (South India). See *Kusumāvali* (71st *asampūrṇa mēḷa*).

Kusuma Mārutam (South India). *Janya rāga* of the 17th *mēḷa* (*Sūryakānta*).
Tone material:
C F G A B c
c B A G F E D♭ E F C
Lit.: no. 139.

Kusumāṅgi (South India). *Janya rāga* of the 16th *mēḷa* (*Chakravāka*).
Tone material:
C D♭ C G A B♭ c
c B♭ A G F E D♭ C
Lit.: no. 139.

Kusumapriya (South India). *Janya rāga* of the 27th *mēḷa* (*Sarasāṅgī*).

Tone material:

C D E F G A♭ B c

c B G F E D C

Lit.: no. 139.

Kusumarañjani (South India). *Janya rāga* of the 37th *mēḷa* (*Sālaga*).

Tone material:

C D♭ F♯ G A♭ B♭♭ c

c B♭♭ A♭ B♭♭ G F♯ E♭♭ D♭ C

Lit.: no. 139.

Kusumasāraṅga (South India). *Janya rāga* of the 27th *mēḷa* (*Sarasāṅgī*).

Tone material:

C D E F G A♭ B c

c B G F E D C

Lit.: no. 139.

Kusumasāraṅga (South India). *Janya rāga* of the 56th *mēḷa* (*Śaṇmukhapriyā*).

Tone material:

C D F♯ G A♭ B♭ c

c B♭ A♭ G F♯ E♭ D C

Lit.: no. 139.

Kusumāvaḷi (South India). *Janya rāga* of the 38th *mēḷa* (*Jalārṇava*).

Tone material:

B♭ C D♭ E♭♭ F♯ G A♭ B♭

(B♭) A♭ G F♯ E♭♭ D♭♭ C

Lit.: no. 139.

Kusumāvali (South India). (1) The 71st *asampūrṇa mēḷa-rāga* without *kaṭapayādi* prefix. (2) The 71st *asampūrṇa mēḷa-rāga* with *kaṭapayādi* prefix. It was called *Kusumākara.* See *Rāga* (South India).

Lit.: no. 139.

Kusumavāli (*Kusumākara*) (South India). *Janya rāga* of the 71st *mēḷa* (*Kōsala*).

Tone material:

C E F♯ G A c

c B A G F♯ E F♯ D♯ C

Lit.: no. 139.

Kusuma Vichitra (*Kusuma Vicitra*) (South India). *Janya rāga* of the 29th *mēḷa* (*Dhīraśaṅkarābharaṇam*).

Tone material:

C D F B A G B c

c B A G F E D C

Lit.: no. 139.

Kumāra Vilasita (South India). *Janya rāga* of the 29th *mēḷa* (*Dhīraśaṅkarābharaṇam*).

Tone material:

C F E F A B G A B c

c B A G F A F E D C

Lit.: no. 139.

Kut (*Gut*) (Korea). Shamanist ceremonial music: for a dead person the term is *ogu-gut*; for a household, *chaesu-gut*; and for a village, *sonang-gut* (*pyolsin-gut*).

Lit.: no. 287.

Kuṭa (South India). Cf. *Koda.*

Kuṭa (South India). Kannarese term for *ghāṭa*.

Lit.: no. 254.

Kūṭam (India; Malabar Coast). The *kuṭa* of the South is provided with a string that is strung from the bottom of the pot to a detached cup. A wooden stick or small board is affixed to the cup and is used to stretch the string. The string is beaten with a little stick. Cf. *Pulluvam Kutam.*

Lit.: no. 260.

Kutapa (*Vadya vrinda*) (India). Vocal and instrumental ensemble of the ancient theater.

Kutapa (India). Instrumental ensemble. *Tata kutapa*, string ensemble; *avanaddha kutapa*, drum ensemble. For further information see Lit. no. 260.

Kutjapi (*Kuchapi*) (Java). See *Ketjapi*; *Kacchapi.*

Kut kori (Korea). Rhythmic mode; drum pattern.

Bamboo strokes on the *chang-ko*

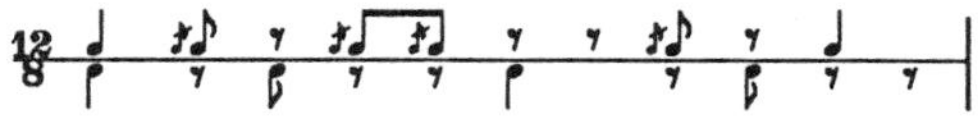

Hand strokes on the *chang-ko*

See *Sam-hyon.*
Lit.: no. 286.

Kutsi-biwa (Japan). Jew's harp.
Lit.: no. 255.

Kutsinhira (Rhodesia—Shona). The second section of a piece of music.

Kutšuk (Middle East). *Maqām.*
Tone material:

D $\overset{+}{\text{E}\flat}$ F G A $\overset{+}{\text{B}\flat}$ c d

Lit.: no. 64.

Kutu (French Equatorial Africa—Kuyu). Lively pantomimic funeral dance.
Lit.: no. 29.

Kuṭumbini (South India). *Janya rāga* of the 64th *mēḷa* (Vāchaspati).
Tone material:

C E F♯ A G A B♭ c
c B♭ G F♯ E D C

Lit.: no. 139.

Ku-um (Korea). "Mouth-sound." A simple, rather inefficient notational system that uses the full *lü* names irrespective of their original significance. The syllables of the *lü* names (both syllables of each name are used) are set to the notes of a hymn, but musically there is no connection between the *lü* syllables and the actual notes performed.
Lit.: no. 136.

Ku'ūs (Middle East). Ancient bowl-shaped cymbals. Cf. *Kāsāt.*
Lit.: no. 76.

Kuvalayābharaṇam (South India). *Janya rāga* of the 14th *mēḷa* (*Vakuḷābharaṇam*).
Tone material:

C D♭ E F A♭ B♭ c
c B♭ A♭ F E D♭ C

Lit.: no. 139.

Kuvalayānandi (South India). *Janya rāga* of the 16th *mēḷa* (*Chakravāka*).
Tone material:

C D♭ E F B♭ A B♭ G B♭ c
c B♭ A F E C

Lit.: no. 139.

Kuwaheru (Japan). See *Katabachi.*

Kuwasht (Arabia). *Āwāz.* According to Ṣafī al-Dīn'Abd al Mu'nim al-Baghdadi (13th century), reported in Lit. no. 65, was: C E♭♭ F♭ F A♭♭ A♭ B♭♭ c♭ c. Cf. *Maqām.*

Kuwing (Sunda District). See *Singgul.* Tone name; the first note of the *pelog* system (Sunda districts). Cf. *Patapet*; *Panatup.*
Lit.: no. 163.

Kuwītra (diminutive of *Kaitara*; *Kitara*) (North Africa; Morocco). A small unfretted long-necked lute with four pairs of gut strings, played with a quill plectrum.
Lit.: no. 78.

Kuyn (*Lemol*) (Malacca). Cf. *Din tenkhiṅ.*

Kuyō (Japan). A category of Buddhist chant sung during the offerings.

Kuze-gene (Congo—Balese). Ground zither.
Lit.: no. 21.

Kuzhal (South India). Heavy transverse flute with eight finger holes. In Tamil the term *vangiyam* is used.
Lit.: no. 261.

Kuzure (Japan). Melody pattern played on the *satsuma biwa* during battle scenes.
Lit.: no. 185.

Kvachit Prayōga (India). Cf. *Bahula Prayōga.*

Kwacha (East Africa). See *Chara.*

Kwa da ban tse (China). Castanets of China.
Lit.: no. 255.

Kwadi (South Bechuanaland). Term for *gorra* (*gora*).
Lit.: no. 151.

Kwāi (Burma; South Shan States). Open buffalo horn. A small tongue is attached near the narrow end.
Lit.: no. 252.

Kwaigo-no-ben (Japan). A listing used in studies of voice-production that shows and explains the manifold combining of vowels, consonants, syllables with tones, performed with closed or open mouth, and shows how to achieve a distinct pronunciation of the texts. This listing indicates vowels and syllables produced in the throat, on the back teeth, on the teeth, tongue, lips; it refers to clear voice, half-thick voice, thick voice, and others. Some of the terms are: *go-sei* (*go-in*), the "five voices"; *go-ju* (*sei-in*), the "fifty voices"; *daku-in*, 20 "thick voices"; *jisei-in*, five "second clear voices"; *handaku-in*, five "half-thick voices." Cf. *Ryo*; *Ritsu.*
Lit.: no. 225.

Kwainya (Ryūkyū Isl.). Cf. *Guena.*

Kwanak (Korea). Music of the court.
Lit.: no. 215.

Kwanga (Congo). See *Makwanga.*

Kwangdae (Korea). Wandering street singers.

Kwangengaku (Japan). Orchestral music of *gagaku.* It can be grouped into:
1. *Ko-gaku*, "ancient music."
2. *Shin-gaku*, "new music."

Cf. *Gagaku.*

Kwa-sang-chung (Korea). "Clear one above the frets." Name of the 4th open string of the *Hyon-kum.* See *Komunko.*
Lit.: no. 136.

Kwatha (South Africa—Venda). Term for various horns (e.g., sable antelope). Cf. *Lepapata.*
Lit.: no. 151.

Kwa woe chung (Korea). "Clear one outside the frets." Name of the 5th (open) string of the *hyon-kum.* Cf. *Komunko.*
Lit.: no. 136.

Kwayen (Japan). "Flames." Painted red flames which surround the phoenix and the dragon ornaments on large drums.

Kwelli (Africa; Chad). Drum with a cylindrical body and two heads.

Kwendibe (Congo—Aimeri). Musical bow.
Lit.: no. 176.

Kwengwe (*Kweningba*) (Congo—Nbandi; Azande). A hardwood xylophone with a variable number of slabs. The Azande use a large number of names for the instrument: *bangi*, *endara*, *gbingbe*, *kbedimba*, *kpeninga*, *kwengwe*, *linz*, *manza*, *mozunga*, *ndara*, *paningba*, *pendibe*, *queniba.*
Lit.: no. 27.

Kweningba (Congo). See *Kwengwe.*

Kwii-turu (Liberia—Kpelle). Western horn (trumpet).
Lit.: no. 284.

Kwororo (*Pakwulo*) (Congo—Banza). Slim, almost cylindrical drum.
Lit.: no. 26.

Kwun-tzu (China). Cantonese term for *kuan-tzu.* Cf. *Tui-hsiao.*

Kya (Kenya; Tanganyika—Akamba). Stamping tube. Cf. *Muvungu.*
Lit.: no. 181.

Kyahi guntur madu (Java). A *gamelan sekati* of the Jogya kraton.
Lit.: no. 163.

Kyahi henem (Java). A *gamelan sekati* of Solo kraton.
Lit.: no. 163.

Kyahi kodok ngorek (Java). *Gamelan* played during fights between tiger and buffalo (in the past this was a public amusement).

Kyahi munggang (Java). A *gamelan sekati* of Paku Alaman, Jogya.

Kyahi naga ilaga (Java). A *gamelan sekati* of Jogya kraton.

Kyahi patalon (Java). A three-tone *gamelan* ensemble of the Solonese kraton. It is similar to *gamelan munggang* and *kodok ngorek.* It is called a *gangsa setu* and was played every Saturday.
Lit.: no. 163.

Kyahi sepuh (Java). A *gamelan sekati* of Solo kraton.
Lit.: no. 163.

Kyahi suka rame (Java). The old sultan's *gamelan sekati* at Banten.
Lit.: no. 163.

Kyahi surak (Java). A *gamelan slendro* of the Jogya kraton with a high sounding *barang.* It is played for the mounting of the guards and several festivities.
Lit.: no. 163.

Kyak (Kirgizia). Fiddle with two (occasionally also with four) strings.
Lit.: no. 275.

Kyamancha (Armenia). A small fiddle with the form of a banjo. Cf. *Kamānjah.*

Kyedi (Burma). Buddhist bell.
Lit.: no. 303.

Kyen (Burma—Shan State; Karen). Mouth organ consisting of ten cane pipes (with metal reeds) arranged in a circular bundle stuck into a bottle-shaped gourd. Cf. *Kaen*; *Khaen wong*; *Sheng.*
Lit.: no. 252.

Kye-nong (Burma). Small gong.
Lit.: no. 250.

Kye-tsi (Burma). Bronze (brass) disc in a circular or vaguely triangular shape. It can represent the outline of a mountain, a cloud, or a dragon. Cf. *Cai chieng*; *Bur'rting.*
Lit.: nos. 252, 254.

Kye-vaing (Burma). A gong chime consisting of 16-18 (also 21) gongs. See *Krewain.* Cf. *Khong vong lek*; *Bonang*; also *Kyi-waing* or *Kyi-naung.*
Lit.: nos. 252, 254.

Kyiak (Central Asia; Kirgizia). Fiddle with a bowl-shaped body and two horsehair strings. Its curved horsehair bow is covered with tar.
Lit.: no. 91.

Kyi-naung (Burma). See *Kye-vaing.*

Kyo (Japan). "Madness." One of the five traditional subjects used in the *noh* dramas. The other four are: *shin*, *nan*, *nyo*, *ki.*

Kyo (Burma). "String." Elementary piece for young zither and lute students.

Kyobang-ko (Korea). Large flat barrel drum resting horizontally upon a wooden stand.

Kyōgen (Japan). "Mad words." Comic interludes, comic actors, in *noh* performances. Cf. *Ha.* See *Gidayu bushi.*
Lit.: no. 185.

Kyōgen-kata (Japan). A special stagehand who rattles wooden clappers (*hyōshigi*) in rough scenes (*aragoto*) of *kabuki* plays.
Lit.: no. 185.

Kyō-ke (Japan). A type of *wasan* with Japanese text. Originally the *kyo-ke* were songs intended to awaken saintly sentiments. Later they became prayers to the Buddha. There are two types of *kyō-ke*:

1. *Sam-bun*, prayer songs with free poems as texts.
2. *Ritsu-go*, prayers with ruled words taken from sacred texts.

Kyō-kei (Japan). Suspended circular brass disc.
Lit.: no. 258.

Kyōkusetzu (*setzu*) (Japan). Melodic formulas that are lined up, one after the other in sequences in the forming of *shōmyō* melodies.
Some of the formulas are: *yuri*, *yuri-age*, *ō-yuri*, *ko-yuri*, *yuri-ori*, *fuji-yuri*, *yuri-kake-kiru*, *asa-ori*, *sori*, *sugu*, *makuri*, *uchitsuke*, *modori*, *iro-modori*, *furi*, *suteru*, *hana-ni-ireru*.

Kyōmai (Japan). Impressive dance of Kyōto geishas.

Kyōmono (Japan). A duet for two *koto* zithers. Each instrument plays its own melody. This technique originated in Kyōto and has been a characteristic particularly of the Ikuta school of the late 17th century.
Lit.: no. 185.

Kyo pang-ko (Korea). A flat barrel drum placed horizontally on a wooden stand. It is struck by two dancers (in the "drum dance") and not by musicians.
Lit.: nos. 52, 179.

Kyōto (Japan). Temple musicians who had come from Kyōto to be in charge of *bugaku* music.

Kyū (*Gyo*) (Japan). The sixth pipe of the *shō*. Cf. *Shō*.
Lit.: no. 225.

Kyū (Japan). (1) The final part of *gagaku*, *nagauta*, and *noh* performances. *Kyū* starts with the *machiutai* ("waiting song") which is followed by the 5th *dan* in which an *issei* (song) and *mondō* (recitative) appear. The following dance (*mai*) is the climax of the drama because here the audience is shown the real identity of the protagonist (*shite*). The dance is followed by a short piece called *waka* that leads to the choral ending, the *kiri*. Cf. *Jo-ha-kyu*. (2) The first note of the scale (*ryo*; *ritsu*). See *Gagaku* (the scale is generally transcribed as the Western D mode—not C). (3) Bow of string instruments.

L

La (India). Name of a basic *tabla* (r.h.) stroke. The 4th finger tip gently strikes the border of the *siahi* and remains on the drum head after the stroke. For further information see Lit. no. 136.

Lā (Thailand). Cf. *Rūang.*

Laala (Sierra Leone—Fula). Rattle. Cf. *Wansamba.*
Lit.: no. 190.

La'au (Hawaii). Concussion stick, an almost obsolete instrument. Cf. *Pakuru.*
Lit.: no. 7.

Laba (Flores; Nage). Barrel drum similar to the Indian *dhōl*, beaten with two wooden sticks. Cf. *Lambajawa.*
Lit.: no. 163.

Laba dera (Flores; Ngada District). Broad, one-headed hand-beaten drum. The Central Manggaray term for this drum is *tembang.*
Lit.: no. 166.

Laba-go (Middle and West Flores). A small ensemble of five gongs of the Javanese *bonang* type and one *laba* (drum). The gongs are tuned: B♭ c d♭ e♭ f.
Lit.: no. 159.

Laba toda (*Laba wai*) (Flores; Nage). (1) See *Wani(ng).* Cf. *Toda.* (2) A one-headed, high, narrow bamboo drum standing on short legs. The instrument is beaten with wooden sticks.

Laba wai (Flores). See *Laba toda.*

Labak (Persia). Flute.
Lit.: no. 255.

Labbanātu (Ancient Babylon; Akkadian). Trumpet.
Lit.: no. 87.

Labu (Celebes). Free reed mouth organ.
Lit.: no. 43.

Lachari-Tōdī (North India). Rare *rāga* ascribed to the *Tōdī-thāta.* The *rāga* has little relation to *Tōdī*, but stands closer to *rāga Desi.*
Tone material (flexible):

C D E♭ E F G A♭ A B♭ B c

c B B♭ A A♭ G F E E♭ D C; *Vādis*: F, C

Lit.: no. 138.

Lachhasakh (North India). A rare and obscure *rāga* ascribed to the *Bilaval thāta.*
Tone material:
C (D) E F G A (B♭) B c
c (B, B♭) A G F E D C
Lit.: no. 138.

La-ch'in (China – M 1103; M 3756). A bowed zither with 10 pairs of silk strings tuned pentatonically. Cf. *La-k'in*; *Achaeng.*
Lit.: no. 209.

Ladakeh (India). Rattle drum in *damaru* shape.
Lit.: no. 255.

Ladrang (Java). A *genḍing* in which the repeated series of four *kenong* beats within a large gong-period (*gongan*) indicates the form and character of the composition. The *ladrang* structure (as shown in Lit. no. 163, p. 300) shows the following pattern:

ketuk	*wela*	*ketuk*	*kenong*
ketuk	*kempul*	*ketuk*	*kenong*
ketuk	*kempul*	*ketuk*	*kenong*
ketuk	*kempul*	*ketuk*	*kenong*
			gong ageng

Cf. *Kenḍangan ladrang.*
Lit.: no. 163.

Lae (Northeast Thailand). Singing by Buddhist monks.
Lit.: no. 203.

Lae-lae (South Celebes). A long bamboo pole struck with two bamboo switches. Cf. *Siya-siya.*
Lit.: no. 132.

Lagalogo (Nigeria). Bell.

Lagam Bandung (Java). See *Tembang kaayeunaan.*

Lagam chiawian (Java). See *Tembang kaayeunaan.*

Lagam kulon (West Java). "Western *kulon*," a type of *tembang kaayeunaan*, the modern style of singing which the systems *melog* and *nyorog* are used. Another term for *lagam kulon* is *kakulonkeun*, mainly used in Chianjur.
Lit.: no. 163.

Lagam wetan (Java). See *Lagam chiawian.*

Laga ukar (Flores; Sikka). A special type of wood used for making xylophones. Cf. *Doli-doli*, xylophones made of this material.
Lit.: no. 166.

Laggi (North India). Term for the repetition of one *vibhaga* which appears often in popular music in which *sām* and *khāli* are of little importance.
Lit.: no. 136.

Laghu (South India). "Short" – durational note value. The *laghu* is often taken as the basis of metrical units and can be equated to the quarter note of Western music (other durational note values have been listed under the heading of *Anudrutam*). In North India *laghu* is expressed by the term *mātrā.*
Lit.: no. 136.

Laghu drutam (South India). The durational note value of a *laghu* plus one *drutam* (♩‿♪).
Lit.: no. 136.

Lagija (*Lagiya*) (Indonesia; Nias). Bowed spike lute. In the Batak regions the instrument is called *katjapi* (*kachapi*), *hasapi*, *hapetan*; in Karo *kultjapi* (*kulchapi*).
Lit.: no. 162.

Lag-na (Tibet). Large frame drum with a broad, richly ornamented wooden frame. The frame is pierced vertically by a wooden pole. The drum has two skins and is beaten by a sickle-shaped stick.

Lagon (Java). Melodies with preceding and following recitatives in *wayang* performances. Cf. *Paṭetan*; *Sendon*; *Suluk.*
Lit.: no. 163.

Lagu (Bali). (1) Melody; tune. (2) Name of a symbol in musical notation.
Lit.: no. 197.

Lagu blai-blai berjalan (Malaya). See *Wayang-kulit* (Malaya).

Lagu bertabuh (Malaya). See *Wayang kulit* (Malaya).

Lagu dalang berkhabar (Malaysia). See *Wayang kulit* (Malaya).

Lagu dewa panah (Malaysia). See *Wayang kulit* (Malaya).

Lagu gagah (Java). Term for vivace, energetic. Cf. *Gagah.*

Lagu gamelan (Sunda District). A *genḍing.* See *Lagu tandak.*

Lagu gung (Flores). Gong melody.

Lagu hulubalang (Malaysia). See *Wayang kulit* (Malaya).

Lagu jalan gede (Java). Street song.

Lagu kelong (Flores). *Lagu* (melody), *Kelong* is a term used in the south of Celebes for a popular poem, mostly of erotic character.

Lagu kuda (Flores). Music that accompanies the dance of a small horse.

Lagu leuleuy (West Java; Sunda District). See *Leuleuy.*

Lagu mati geduk (Malaysia). See *Lagu penutup.*

Lagu Mbai (Flores; Mbai of Ngada). "Song of Mbai," a two-voiced canon built upon a drone.

Lagu menari (Flores). Accompaniment to a women's dance played by a *laba-go* ensemble.

Laguni (Celebes). A metal or wooden disc is beaten with a stick of ebony. It is used to ward off evil spirits, illness, and other disasters.

Lagu pa' dogol (Malaysia). See *Wayang kulit* (Malaya).

Lagu penutup (*Lagu mati geduk*) (Malaysia). See *Wayang kulit* (Malaya).

Lagu perang (Malaysia). See *Wayang kulit* (Malaya).

Lagu sindir (Flores). A derisive, insulting song with diverse insinuations.

Lagu tandak (Sunda District). Compositions for the accompaniment of dances. At times they are wrongly called *lagu gamelan* or simply *genḍing.*
Lit.: no. 163.

Lagu t'o maha siku (Malaysia). See *Wayang kulit* (Malaya).

Lagu tukar dalang (Malaysia). See *Wayang kulit* (Malaya).

Laḥan (Israel; Middle East). Hebrew term for melody.

Laḥn (Arabia). Secular melody. Cf. *Adhdhan* (*Aḏān*).
Lit.: no. 70.

Lai (Northeast Thailand). An improvisation that uses characteristic motives, rhythms within fixed pentatonic modes. The term is used in conjunction with *kaen* improvisations such as *lai yai*, *lai sootsanaen*, *lai bo sai*, *lai soi*, and *lai noi.* Cf. *Noi*; *Lum.*
Lit.: no. 203.

Lai haroba (Northeast India). One type of *manipuri* dance performed by a male and a female temple dancer in the months of March and April. Cf. *Rāsa Līlā.*

Lai noi (Northeast Thailand). Cf. *Noi*; *An nungsü.*

Lai waghe (Nias). Rice-stalk oboe. See *Ra'us woya* (Flores).

Lai yai (Northeast Thailand). Cf. *An nungsü.*

Lak (Thailand). See *Khon.*

Lakado (Timor). Tube zither with three strings. The Laga people on East Timor call the instrument *be orla.* On Wetar (north of Timor) it is called *agiht.* See *Tabuan* (*Tagbuan*); *Laka do'o.*
Lit.: no. 254.

Laka do'o (Flores). (1) A tube zither; an imitation of the western guitar. (2) Cf. *Kolong-kolong*; *Gong tondu.*
Lit.: no. 166.

Lakalaka (Polynesia—Tonga). Popular dance performed by large groups of men and women. It is a dance in which poetic speech is interpreted by gestures. The accompaniment is polyphonic singing.

Lakawn (Northeast Thailand). A Siamese dance drama.
Lit.: no. 203.

Lake (Java). "Male"; instruments of smaller size and higher pitch than those called *bine* ("female").
Lit.: no. 163.

Lakhon (Thailand). The classical dance drama, a second dramatic form beside the *khon.* Originally the *lakhon* was danced by men only. Women joined the performance in the middle of the 19th century. Only dancers who represent demons, monkeys, and other unusual figures have to wear masks. All other dancers are unmasked. While in *khon* performances the text is recited by a chorus, in *lakhon* it is sung. It is performed at festive occasions. At the present time six varieties of the drama can be observed (although there may have been more in the past):

1. *Lakhon nok.*
2. *Lakhon nai.*
3. *Lakhon derk damban.*
4. *Lakhon nora chatri.*
5. *Lakhon phang tang.*
6. *Lakhon sepha.*

Lit.: no. 207.

Lakon dekr damban (Thailand). Variety of *lakhon.* The dancers speak and sing; usually there is no chorus. The name means: "*lakhon* performed at the Derk Damban Theater."
Lit.: no. 207.

Lakhon nai (Thailand). Variety of *lakhon.* A court dance play performed by women. Originally it was called *lakhon nang nai,* "performed by the actresses of the court." The orchestra is a percussion ensemble consisting of 10-14 members. The subjects are taken from the Hindu epics.
Lit.: no. 207.

Lakhon nang nai (Thailand). See *Lakhon nai.*

Lakhon nok (Thailand). A popular variety of *lakhon* with fast, farcical actions. The play contains simple popular songs. Its orchestra is a small percussion ensemble (*wong piphat khrerang ha*).
Lit.: no. 207.

Lakhon nora chatri (Thailand). The oldest form of *lakhon.* The subjects are taken from the Buddhist jatakas. The actors dance, sing, and speak. In the past only men were performing. Recently men and women were employed. The musical accompaniment was provided by two drums. Recently, when the cast was increased and men and women appeared, a percussion ensemble was in use.
Lit.: no. 207.

Lakhon phan tang (Thailand). A variety of *lakhon* using foreign subjects. The performers are men and women, but they do not sing. A chorus accompanies the play; only the dancers may speak. The orchestra is a small percussion ensemble.
Lit.: no. 207.

Lakon sepha (Thailand). A variety of *lakhon*, a dance drama linked with "sepha," a Thai word derived from *seva* (Sanskrit: *siva*). *Lakhon sepha* represents a kind of worship by men and women. The music consists of songs of praise of the deity. The orchestra consists of a sundry variety of instruments.
Lit.: no. 207.

Laki (Borneo). Cf. *Telarli.*

La-k'in (China). See *La-ch'in.*

Lakkhat (Burma). Drumstick.
Lit.: no. 255.

Lakshmi-tōdī (*Laxmi-tōdī*) (North India). *Rāga* ascribed to the *Tōdī thāta*. It has little relationship with *Tōdī*.
Tone material (flexible):
C D E♭ E F G A♭ (B♭) c
c (B♭) A A♭ G F E♭ D D♭ C;
Vādis (flexible): G, (c)
Lit.: no. 138.

Lal (Sudan). See *Bal.*

Lalango (Congo – Apagi beti). Musical bow.
Lit.: no. 176.

Lalat (North India). See *Lalit.*

Laler menggeng (Java). See *Genḍing mianggong.*

Lali (Tonga; Fiji Isl.; New Hebrides). Wooden slit-drum in various sizes.
Lit.: no. 84.

Lālibalā (Ethiopia). Night singers.

Lalibaloch (Ethiopia). Songs of the descendents of a brotherhood of lepers. These songs are to be sung only at night and are believed to protect the singers from leprosy and evil spirits.
Lit.: no. 102.

Lali ni meke (Fiji Isl.). Small wooden slit-drum used together with stamping tubes and singing as accompaniment of the *meke* dance.
Lit.: no. 37.

Lalipok (Borneo; Sarawak – Land Dayak). See *Boku* (Flores).
Lit.: no. 255.

Lalis (Fiji Isl.). Wooden signalling drum.
Lit.: no. 255.

Lalita (North India). See *Lalit.*

Lalit (*Lalita*; *Lalat*) (North India). *Rāga* ascribed either to the *Marva* or *Bhairav thātas.*
Tone material:
C D♭ E F F♯ A B c
c B A F♯ F E D♭ C; *Vādis*: F, c
Lit.: no. 138.

Lalitā (South India). *Janya rāga* of the 15th *mēḷa* (*Māyāmāḷavagauḷa*).
Tone material:
C D♭ E F A♭ B c
c B A♭ F E D♭ C D♭ C
Lit.: no. 139.

Lalitā (South India). *Janya rāga* of the 17th *mēḷa* (*Sūryakānta*).
Tone material:
C D♭ E F A B c
c B A F E D♭ C
Lit.: no. 139.

Lalitadīparam (South India). *Janya rāga* of the 42nd *mēḷa* (*Raghupriyā*).
Tone material:
C D♭ E♭♭ F♯ G A♯ B c
c B A♯ B G F♯ E♭ D♭ C
Lit.: no. 139.

Lalitagāndhari (South India). *Janya rāga* of the 22nd *mēḷa* (*Kharaharapriyā*).
Tone material:
C D E♭ F G B♭ c
c B♭ G F E♭ F D C
Lit.: no. 139.

Lalita-gauri (North India). A *rāga* ascribed to the *Marva thāta*. It can be described as a combination of *Gauri* (*Purvi thāta*) and *Lalit* elements.
Tone material:
C D♭ F (F♯) G A B c
c B A G (F♯) F E D♭ C; *Vādis*: vague
Lit.: no. 139.

Lalita-gauri (South India). *Janya rāga* of the 15th *mēḷa* (*Māyāmāḷavagauḷa*).
Tone material:
C D♭ E F G A♭ B c
c A♭ G E D♭ C
Lit.: no. 139.

Lalitaghāndravam (South India). *Janya rāga* of the 30th *mēḷa* (*Nāgānandī*).
Tone material:
C D E F̊ G A♯ B c (+ above F)
c B G E D C
Lit.: no. 139.

Lalitakōsaḷi (South India). *Janya rāga* of the 69th *mēḷa* (*Dhātuvardhaṇī*).
Tone material:
C D♯ E F♯ G A♭ B A♭ c
c B A♭ G F♯ E F♯ D♯ C
Lit.: no. 139.

Lalitakriya (South India). *Janya rāga* of the 15th *mēḷa* (*Māyāmāḷavagauḷa*).
Tone material:
C D♭ E F G F A♭ B c
c B A♭ F E D♭ C
Lit.: no. 139.

Lalitamanoharī (South India). *Janya rāga* of the 22nd *mēḷa* (*Kharaharapriyā*).
Tone material:
C E♭ F G A B♭ c
c B♭ G F E♭ G C
Lit.: no. 139.

Lalitamāruva (South India). *Janya rāga* of the 37th *mēḷa* (*Sālaga*).
Tone material:
C D♭ E♭♭ F♯ G A♭ B♭♭ c
c B♭♭ A♭ F♯ E♭♭ D♭ C
Lit.: no. 139.

Lalitapañcham (South India). *Janya rāga* of the 15th *mēḷa* (*Māyāmāḷavagauḷa*).
Tone material:
C D♭ E F A♭ B c
c B A♭ F G F E D♭ C
Lit.: no. 139.

Lalitasiṃhāravam (South India). *Janya rāga* of the 9th *mēḷa* (*Dhēnuka*).
Tone material:
C D♭ E♭ F G c
c B F E♭ D♭ C
Lit.: no. 139.

Lalitasiṃhāravam (South India). *Janya rāga* of the 59th *mēḷa* (*Dharmavatī*).
Tone material:
C D E♭ F♯ G c
c B G F♯ E♭ D C
Lit.: no. 139.

Lalitaśrīkanti (South India). *Janya rāga* of the 9th *mēḷa* (*Dhēnuka*).
Tone material:
C D♭ E♭ F G A♭ B♭ c
c B A♭ G F A♭ F E♭ D♭ C
Lit.: no. 139.

Lalitatōḍī (South India). *Janya rāga* of the 3rd *mēḷa* (*Gānamūrti*).
Tone material:
C D♭ E♭♭ F G c
c B A♭ F E♭♭ D♭ C
Lit.: no. 139.

Lalit-pañcham (North India). *Rāga* ascribed to the *Bhairav thāta*. It is related with the *rāgas* *Lalit* and *Pañcham*.
Tone material:
C D♭ E F (F♯) A♭ B c
c B A♭ G (F♯) F E D♭ C; *Vādis*: F, c
Lit.: no. 138.

Lamako (Malagasy Republic). Castanets made of bones.
Lit.: no. 251.

Lamba (Sumba). Drum with one head.
Lit.: no. 162.

Lamba (Senegambia). Large drum.
Lit.: no. 255.

Lambajawa (Flores—Mbai). Two-headed barrel drum. In Nage it is called *laba* ("drum"). In Ngada its name is *laba dera.*
Lit.: no. 166.

Lamba rangkap (Bali). The old performance style in which the figuration tones in *gamelan* music overlap only little with each other and thus produce a thin sound contrary to the full and rich sound of the *renjab.* Cf. *Renjab.*
Lit.: no. 265.

Lambat (Bali). Slowly. See *Gending lambat.*

Lambe (Bali). See *Kulkul.*

Lambe (Java). "Lip." The outer bottom edge of a gong. *Lambe* means also the side edges of a slit on a (slit) drum.
Lit.: no. 163.

Lambung (Java). "Flank." The sides of a slit-drum. Cf. *Kulkul* (Bali).

Lampah (Java). "Walk," "gait," "distance"—length of a song-line measured by the number of text syllables.
Lit.: no. 163.

Lampahan (*Wayang gambuh*). *Wayang* plays; their subjects are taken from the great Hindu epics (*Mahābhārata* and *Rāmāyaṇa*). Only in some rare instances (*wayang gambuh*) are subjects used that have other origins than the Hindu epics.
Lit.: nos. 197, 265.

Lanang (Bali). A "male" *kenḍang* drum tuned a whole tone higher than the *wadon.*
Lit.: no. 197.

Lanangan (Java). "Male"—the high-pitched gong kettle row of the *bonang.*
Lit.:no. 163.

Lanchar (West Java; Sunda). See *Wirahma.* A tempo taken not too slowly.
Lit.: no. 163.

Landai (Afghanistan). Folk couplet.

Langen asmara; Langen pranasmara (Java). Two types of dance opera (*langendriya*) both performed by female dancers. *Langen asmara* is accompanied by *gamelan slendro*; *langen pranasmara* uses *gamelan pelog.*
Lit.: no. 163.

Langen wanara (Java). *Langen* = entertainment; *wanara* = monkeys. Dance opera using subjets from the *Rāmāyaṇa.*

Langi (Polynesia; Samoa; Tonga; Cook Isl.; New Zealand; British Solomon Isl.). Songs sung by a chorus. The texts deal with a variety of subjects: from the Sanga ritual, of sacred nature, to erotic, scornful, and mocking pieces.
Lit.: no. 319.

Langkara (Malaysia). Kettledrum.
Lit.: no. 255.

Lang kwang (Burma).
Lit.: no. 255.

Langlayan peteng (Sunda District). See *Peteng.*

Langorao (Malagasy Republic). See *Langoro.*

Langoro (*Langorao*; *Langorany*) (Malagasy Republic). Cylindrical drum with two heads.
Lit.:no. 251.

Langorony (Malagasy Republic). See *Langoro.*

Lankadahan-sarang (North India). *Rāga* that can be ascribed to the *Kafi thāta*. It consists of a combination of *Sarang* and *Kanada* elements.
Tone material:
C D F G B c
c B♭ A G F (E♭) D C
Lit.: no. 138.

Lan kaṅ (Thailand). Triangular bronze disc. Cf. *Kre-tsi* (Burma).
Lit.: no. 255.

Lankeshri (North India). Obscure *rāga*. It consists of elements taken from the *rāgas Khamaj*, particularly *Rageshri* and *Jhinjhoti*. A scale cannot be defined distinctly as it varies according to the performer's preference of any of the constituent features taken from the indicated *rāgas*.
Tone material (possible):
C E F G A B c
c B♭ A G F E D C
Lit.: no. 138.

Lantoy (Philippines – Palawan; Batac). Nose flute.
Lit.: no. 313.

Lantuy (Philippines – Hanunoo). Flute. Cf. *Lantoy*.
Lit.: no. 303.

Lao sheng (China – M 3833; M 5738). Stereotyped operatic role: the old man. Cf. *Wai*. See *Sheng* (China – M 5738).

Lao mawlum (Northeast Thailand). Singing; singer, of Laos.

La-pa (China – M 3758.1). (1) Long slim straight brass trumpet with a very slight conical bore and a large bell. The tube consists of two or three sections which can be pushed together like a telescope. The *la-pa* was used for military signalling purpose. Cf. *Rapa* (Japan); *Rapal* (Mongolia); *Napal* (Korea); also *Nabal* (Korea); *Ah-tu cha chiao* (China). (2) The term stands as synonym for *ch'un-kuan*.

Lapinka (Iraq). Conch shell.

Laputa (Iran). See *Lavut* (Turkey).

Larachiblon (Java). Distorted term of *rarachiblon*.

Laranangis (Java). See *Rebāb* (Java).

Laras (Bali). Scale. Cf. *Saih*.

Laras (Sunda District). Term for the Javanese *patet* (in *pelog* and *slendro*).

Laras (Java). The general Javanese "concert pitch" which often comes close to the western tone B. Absolute pitches do not exist in the region, and the basic tone *nem* is intoned frequently about a semitone lower (B♭). The term *laras* is derived from the word *nglaras*, "to tune."
Lit.: no. 163.

Lari (Congo – Mangbetu). Also called *kindri*. Drum. Cf. *Gaza*.
Lit.: no. 26.

Larimva (Congo – Logo). Drum played alternately with the *bili*. Cf. *Bia*.
Lit.: no. 27.

Lasaki (South India). *Janya rāga* of the 14th *mēḷa* (*Vakūlābharaṇam*).
Tone material:
C D♭ E G B♭ c
c B♭ G E D♭ C
Lit.: no. 139.

Lāsyapriya (South India). *Janya rāga* of the 43rd *mēḷa* (*Gavāmbōdhi*).
Tone material:
C D♭ E♭ F♯ G c
c G F♯ E♭ D♭ C
Lit.: no. 139.

Latāṅgī (South India). The 63rd *mēḷa*:
C D E F♯ G A♭ B c
The *rāga* uses the same notes.
Lit.: no. 139.

Latantapriya (South India). *Janya rāga* of the 1st *mēḷa* (*Kanakāṅgī*).
Tone material:
C D♭ F G A♭ c
c A♭ G F D♭ C
Lit.: no. 139.

Latowe (Celebes). Nose flute.
Lit.: no. 313.

Lauḥ (Arabia; Iran). Resonator.

Lauka (*Lelet*) (New Ireland). See *Nunut.*
Lit.: no. 84.

Laure (Ivory Coast Republic—Baoule). Iron percussion disc in form of a horseshoe.
Lit.: no. 33.

Lauta (North Africa; West Asia). Small unfretted lute.
Lit.: no. 78.

Lāvaṇi (India). Improvised vocal music of Maharashtra in the form of ballads accompanied by a *tuntina* and a *deph.* Cf. *Nilāvani.*
Lit.: no. 272.

Lavta (Turkey). Term for lute.
Lit.: no. 243.

Lavayuvati (South India). *Janya rāga* of the 12th *mēḷa* (*Rūpāvatī*).
Tone material:
C D♭ E♭ F A♯ B c
c B A♯ F E♭ D♭ C
Lit.: no. 139.

Lavut (Turkey). Lute.

Lawas (Bali). "Old." *Gending lawasan*; old compositions performed in classical or ancient style.
Lit.: no. 197.

Lawk (North Iraq). See *Lawko.*

Lawko (Kurdistan; North Iraq). Improvised songs; described as pure, unspoiled. Cf. *Hairan.*
Lit.: no. 229.

Laxmi-tōdī (North India). See *Lakshmi-tōdī.*

Laya (India). Tempo. Three *layas* are distinguished: *vilambita laya*, slow tempo; *madhya laya*, medium, moderate tempo; and *druta laya*, fast tempo.
Lit.: no. 262.

Laya bansī (*Laya vaṃśī*) (India). Long flute with seven holes.
Lit.: no. 255.

Layano tabage (New Guinea—Papua; Huli). Drum. Its body is made of layano tree wood.
Lit.: no. 233.

Laya vaṃśī (India; Bengal). See *Laya bansī.*

Lazimah (Middle East; North Africa). Instrumental motive interpolated between sections and strophes.

Lda-man (Tibet). A pair of copper kettledrums used at secular occasions.
Lit.: no. 255.

Lea (Flores; Ngada). Dance of a man and a woman. The man is trying to snatch an ornament from the woman. The people surrounding the dancers stand in a circle and stamp with their feet.
Lit.: no. 166.

Leaflegbe (Ghana). See *Nyayito.*

Lebang (*Lebeng*) (Bali). Scale used in *gambuh semar pegulingan*: E F G♯ B c (c♯). Cf. *Semar pegulingan.*
Lit.: no. 163.

Lebeng (Bali). See *Lebang.*

Leboxa (South Africa—Sotho). Cf. *Moromthwana.*

Lebung-lebung (South Celebes). See *Serubay.*

Lechaka (South Africa – Bechuana Land). Pipe without a finger hole. At the lower end is a movable piston; when moved it alters the pitch. Lit.: no. 255.

Ledo (Flores). See *Genggo.*

Ledor (Flores – Lio). Simple xylophone. See *Preson.*
Lit.: no. 166.

Legane (Japan). Small bronze bell.
Lit.: no. 255.

Legong (Bali). A sacred classical dance performed by two (or three) small girls. The accompanying music is provided by the full *gamelan* (*legong gamelan*), without *trompong* and the *gender* functions as leading instrument. The girls represent the ruling pair, a third girl represents the *chondong* (lady in waiting) who hands the pair fans. Cf. *Nandir.*
Lit.: no. 197.

Lei-bauk (Burma). Tone name. See *Pat-tala*; *Hsaing-waing.*

Lei-ku (China – M 3479; M 4236). "Thunder drum." A cluster of small kettledrums, all suspended from a frame; the little drumheads, placed in a circular arrangement, are turned downward and outward.
Lit.: no. 137.

Leiwah (Arabia). Dance-song of Central African origin.

Lekhitlane (South Africa – Basutoland). End-blown flute.
Lit.: no. 151.

Lekolilo (South Africa – Basutoland; Sotho). End-blown flute. Cf. *Umtshingi*; *Mokoreie*; *Nkongolo.*
Lit.: no. 151.

Lekope (South Africa; Transvaal – Sotho; Pedi). (1) Musical bow of the Sotho, played only by women and girls. (2) Music bow of the Pedi played only by men.
Lit.: no. 151.

Lekwon (Congo). Cf. *Wambi.*

Lelega (Mentawei Isl.). Simple xylophone. Cf. *Tundukut*; *Tudukat.*

Lelempale (Indonesia; Toraja District). A whizzing bow. See *Jata* (Flores).
Lit.: no. 166.

Leleo (Northeast Celebes). Reed pipe made in three sizes. Cf. *Pu pai*; *Lolodio.*
Lit.: no. 132.

Lelol (Indonesia; Sunda District). Ornamented phrase. The term indicates the modern ornamental style of playing the Sundanese *rebāb.* The related term for glissando is *leotan*, which can be applied to vocal and *suling* music as well.
Lit.: no. 163.

Lemana (Bali). Large kettledrum.

Lemāna (Ethiopia – Galla). Bamboo flute of the Galla.
Lit.: nos. 102, 255.

Lemol (*Kuyn*) (Malacca; Singapore). Cf. *Diṅ teṅkhiṅ.*

Lēngā (Central African Republic). Slit-drums.

Lengger Angklung (Java). An instrumental ensemble identical with the Sundanese *badut.* This type of orchestra is called *doger* in the Tasik district.
Lit.: no. 163.

Lenggo (West Java). A play with song and dance of Djakarta. The songs are accompanied by three *robana* (*terbang*) and one or two *rebāb* and a Chinese *yüeh-ch'in.*

Lengope (South Africa—Chwana). Musical bow. Cf. *Lugube.*
Lit.: no. 151.

Lengwane (South Africa—Bakgatla; Pedi). Flute made of goat or sheep bone.
Lit.: no. 151.

Le(n)yepan (West Java; Sunda District). Very slow tempo. See *Wirahma.*

Leotan (Java; Sunda District). See *Lelol.*

Lepakusu (Congo). See *Nemurambi.*

Lepapata (South Africa—Chwana). A ceremonial side-blown horn made of a bone of the sable antelope. It is used during warfare and at circumcision rites.
Lit.: no. 151.

Lepet (Java). See *Rebāb.*

Leqso (Ethiopia). Mourning-, wailing-song.
Lit.: no. 102.

Lera (Africa; Niger). Long flute with 4-6 holes.
Lit.: no. 255.

Lēra (Morocco). A jew's harp. A vibrating tongue is attached to the closed end of a tube. When blowing through the opposite open end the tongue vibrates and produces a sound.
Lit.: no. 255.

Leri (Upper Nile—Logo). Cylindrical drum.
Lit.: no. 26.

Leriyo (Uganda—Kakwa). Term for various drums.
Lit.: no. 302.

Lesiba (*Lesiva*) (South Africa—Basuto). Term for *gorra* (*gora*).

Lesiva (South Africa). See *Lesiba.*

Lethlakanoka (South Africa—Bakgatla). Whistle (reed pipe) played by boys. Cf. *Naka ya lethlaka.*
Lit.: no. 151.

Letlot (Indonesia; Kai Isl.). Bamboo slit-drum.
Lit.: no. 162.

Letor (Flores). Simple xylophone. See *Preson.*
Lit.: no. 166.

Leuleuy (*Lagu leuleuy*) (West Java; Sunda District). Softly. In gentle mood.
Lit.: no. 163.

Leutik (*Petit*) (Sunda District). Small. See *Alit*; *Gede.* The high octave (register).

Leyepan (West Java). Dignified, slowly performed dance.

Li (China). See *Chien-tzu.*
Lit.: no. 136.

Lia (East Africa—Swahili). See *Imba*; *Ghani.*

Liang ken hsien erh (China). *Erh-hu* (of Peking).

Libumba (Congo). See *Endumba.*

Lichaka (South Africa—Bechuana). Piston flute; a signal instrument.
Lit.: no. 10.

Liduku (Uganda—Gishu). Raft-zither.
Lit.: no. 302.

Lien (China). See *Chien-tzu.*
Lit.: no. 136.

Lien-hua-lo (China—M 2212; M 4013; M 4129a). A rattle made of four short bamboo pieces tied together. Coins are tied between the pieces. The name *lien-hua-lo* is supposed to be the refrain of a song ("lotus song") that is accompanied by this rattle.
Lit.: no. 209.

Lifogo (Congo – Topoke). Cylindrical drum.
Lit.: no. 26.

Ligangale (Sudan – Tobote). Drum. Cf. *Ganga.*
Lit.: no. 95.

Ligatik (Micronesia – Hok). Bamboo nose flute.
Lit.: no. 313.

Ligeh (Northeast Thailand). Popular theater; the texts are improvised.
Lit.: no. 203.

Ligo (Congo – Mbwaka). Xylophone.
Lit.: no. 190.

Ligombo (Tanzania – Hehe). Trough zither with six strings and a large gourd resonator.

Ligoshu (South Africa – Swazi). Rattle. Cf. *Ndjele.*
Lit.: no. 151.

Ligubu (South Africa – Swazi). Musical bow. Cf. *Segwana*; *Uhadi.*
Lit.: no. 151.

Likembe (East Congo; Ruanda; Urundi). Term for *sansa.*
Lit.: no. 200.

Lik haanga (Kenya). A long, side-blown trumpet (horn) made of a wooden tube and a cow horn.
Lit.: no. 302.

Liku (Northwest Pakistan; Baluchistan). Love song.

Likuma (Cameroon). "Initiation ceremony" – head drum.
Lit.: no. 29.

Līlāraṅgani (South India). *Janya rāga* of the 4th *mēḷa* (*Vanaspāti*).
Tone material:
C F D♭ E𝄫 F G c
c B♭ A G F E𝄫 D♭ C
Lit.: no. 139.

Līlāvati (South India). *Janya rāga* of the 55th *mēḷa* (*Śyāmalāṅgī*).
Tone material:
C D E♭ F♯ G c
c G F♯ E♭ D C
Lit.: no. 139.

Līlāvinōdiṇi (South India). *Janya rāga* of the 63rd *mēḷa* (*Latāṅgī*). The scale of this *rāga* is identical with that of its primary *rāga* (*Latāṅgī*).
Lit.: no. 139.

Lilemo (Congo – Topeke). Drum.
Lit.: no. 26.

Lilenga (Congo – Lalia of Tshuapa District). Cylindrical drum. Cf. *Ingondjo*; *Limbitji.*
Lit.: no. 26.

Lilimba (Congo – Baluba-Hemba). Xylophone.
Lit.: no. 21.

Lilis (South Mesopotamia; Sumeria). Ancient term for a large sacred goblet drum that rests on a stand.
Lit.: no. 87.

Lilissu (Akkad). Sacred drum. Cf. *Lilis.*
Lit.: no. 282.

Lima (Java). "Five." (1) Besides being the name of an important note the term can be used in certain systems for "foreign tone." (2) The 3rd tone of *slendro* in Banjermasin and Madura. (3) The 4th tone of *slendro* in Majakerta; Banyawangi; Prabalingga; Jombang (also called *gangsal* in Central Java). (4) The 5th tone of *pelog* in Central Java; Majakerta (also called *gangsal*). The 5th tone of *pelog* in Cheribon; Prabalingga (also called *loloran*). The 5th tone of modern *slendro.* (5) The 7th tone of modern *pelog* (also called *gangsal*). See *Slendro*; *Pelog.*

Limba (Mongolia). Term for flute—transverse, occasionally also vertical. The transverse flute, open at the bottom, has 12 stops. One hole is covered by a paper membrane which influences the sound. Seven holes are fingered, four holes serve for tuning purposes. The vertical *limba* is rare. Cf. *Gling-bu* (Tibet); *Ti-tzu* (China).
Lit.: no. 60.

Limba (Uganda—Madi). Side-blown wooden trumpet.
Lit.: no. 302.

Limba (East Central and South Africa). Small plucked idiophone. A *sansa* type with 5-25 iron or bamboo tongues fixed on top of a resonator box. Cf. *Malimba*; *Madimba*; *Marimba*; *Lulimba.*
Lit.: no. 28.

Limbitji (Congo—Bombesa). Cylindrical drum. Cf. *Lilenga.* The *limbitji* of the Bangandu is played during the dances of women.
Lit.: no. 26.

Limbombe (Congo—Mobango). Cylindrical drum. Cf. *Litenda.*
Lit.: no. 26.

Limbu (Mongolia). Vertical flute of the Ordos Mongols.

Limele (Congo—Saka). Bow lute.
Lit.: no. 176.

Lina (India). See *Gamak(a).*

Linbut (New Guinea; New Britain). See *Tutupele.*
Lit.: no. 37.

Lin-chung (China—M 1503; M 4022). "Forest bell." Absolute pitch; the second tone in the circle of fifths. Assuming that the *huang-chung* represents the western note C, *lin-chung* will be G. Traditionally *lin-chung* is a *yin* ("female") tone and is used as the basic note in Confucian hymns performed in the month of June. If this tone is used as notational symbol, only the first syllable is used: *lin* (M 1503). See *Lü-lü.*
Lit.: no. 136.

Lindai (Afghanistan). Bow.

Ling (China—M 4056). Hand bell with clapper attached to its inside (if the bell is struck from the outside it is called *chung*). Cf. *Feng-ling*; *Ling-tang*; *Lo-to-ling-tang*; *Ma-ling.*
Lit.: no. 255.

Ling bu (*Gling-bu*) (Tibet). Shepherd's flute.

Lingile (Congo—Bombesa). Drum. Cf. *Lilenga.*
Lit.: no. 26.

Lingita (Congo—Gombe). Term for the *ndundu.*
Lit.: no. 26.

Ling-tang (China—M 4056; M 6093). Iron bell in the shape of a *po-chung*, used by oil vendors in Shantung.
Lit.: no. 255.

Ling-tzu (China—M 4058; M 6939). A small *tang-lo*, a gong used by vendors.

Linz (Congo—Azande). See *Kweningba.*
Lit.: no. 27.

Li-pen (China). See *Fu-lai.*

Li-p'i (China). Concluding court music ending with a masque dance of the Sui period (A.D. 589-618).
Lit.: no. 227.

Lipombo (Congo—Boa). Musical bow.
Lit.: no. 176.

Lirih (Java). Softly (piano).

Lish (East Bengal). Cf. *Konkeh.*

Līt (Gambia; Senegal—Wolof). Flute or shawm.

Litenda (Congo—Mobango). Drum. Cf. *Limbombe.*
Lit.: no. 26.

Litlit (Kulibao) (Philippines—Ilonggot). Fiddle with three strings.

Litumba (Zambia; Lake Gangweulu area). Drum.
Lit.: no. 26.

Litungu (Kenya—Logoli). A lyre with six strings. Cf. *Liduku.*
Lit.: no. 218.

Liu (China—M 4185). Solmization syllable and notational symbol. Assuming that *ho*, the first note of the *kung-ch'e-p'u*, is the western C, *liu* is c, an octave higher.
Lit.: no. 136.

Liu sheng (China). A very simple *sheng.*

Livika (Bismarck Isl.; New Ireland). See *Nunut.*

Liwung (Indonesia; Sunda Isl.). See *Bungur.*

Liwung (Java). "Dizzy," "amorous," "thoughtful." (1) Note in *surupan melog.* (2) Scale in *Surupan melog* which begins with *liwung*:

iv	v	vi	(vii)
liwung	*kenong*	*barang*	—
x	i	ii	iii
pamiring	*singgul*	*galimer*	*panelu*

Pamiring and *panelu* are auxiliary notes.
Lit.: no. 163.

Lo (China—M 4107). A brass gong without a boss. It can have varying sizes and is struck with a mallet. It announces the arrival of visitors and is used in religious services; also in the theater, at processions, funerals, weddings, and for various signalling purposes. Cf. *Ching* (Korea).
Lit.: nos. 137, 209.

Loanga (Congo). Iron double bell.

Lōhaja (India). The metallic sound produced by gongs, cymbals, and other related metal idiophones.
Lit.: no. 262.

Lohāti (*Māwāloti*) (India). See *Nissan.*

Lohenga (Congo—Batatela). Battle drum beaten with the hands. Lit. no. 190 relates that in the past, fingers of dead enemies were placed inside the drum and the hands (of the enemies) were suspended from the exterior.
Lit.: nos. 26, 190.

Lōkadīparam (South India). *Janya rāga* of the 46th *mēḷa* (*Śaḍvidhamārgiṇī*).
Tone material:
C D♭ E♭ F♯ G B♭ A B♭ c
c B♭ A F♯ G F♯ E♭ D♭ C
Lit.: no. 139.

Lokanga (Malagasy Republic). Fiddle imitating the European violin. The term is also applied to the *seze* (Kenya).
Lit.: nos. 33, 255.

Lokangambazaha (Malagasy Republic). "Guitar."
Lit.: no. 255.

Lokangavava (Malagasy Republic). Jew's harp. See *Lokangabazaha.*
Lit.: no. 251.

Lokanga voatava (Malagasy Republic). Stick zither. See *Seze*; *Lokangambazaha*; *Lokangavava.*
Lit.: no. 251.

Lokanko (Zambia; Lake Banweulu region—Babisco). Slit-drum.
Lit.: no. 280.

Lokapriya (South India). *Janya rāga* of the 13th *mēḷa* (*Gāyakapriya*).
Tone material:
C D♭ E F A♭ B♭♭ c
c B♭♭ A♭ F E D♭ C
Lit.: no. 139.

Lokarañjani (South India). *Janya rāga* of the 52nd *mēḷa* (*Rāmapriyā*).
Tone material:
C E F♯ G F♯ A B♭ c
c B♭ A B♭ G F♯ E D♭ C
Lit.: no. 139.

Lokilo (Congo – Basengele; Bolia). Drum. Cf. *Ndungu.* The Bolia *lokilo* has a cylindrical shape, one head, and is used as a war drum.
Lit.: no. 26.

Lokiro (Congo – Nkundo). Drum. Cf. *Lokilo.*
Lit.: no. 26.

Lokole (Belgium Congo – Balolo). Wooden slit-drum. Cf. *Nkole-nkole.*

Lokombe (Congo – Batetela; Wasangola). Trapezoid-formed slit-drum. Cf. *Lukumbi.*
Lit.: nos. 21, 176.

Lokombi (Upper Congo). Bow-lute, a *wambi* type, with a round corpus and five fiber strings.
Lit.: no. 255.

Lo-ku (China). Gong and drum of vendors.

Lōlākchi (South India). *Janya rāga* of the 36th *mēḷa* (*Chalanāṭa*).
Tone material:
C D♯ E F A♯ c
c A♯ F E D♯ C
Lit.: no. 139.

Lolo (Australia; West Torres Str.). A *padatrong* (rattle).
Lit.: no. 255.

Lolob (New Guinea; Admirality Isl.). Wooden slit-drum.
Lit.: no. 255.

Lolodio (Celebes). See *Leleo.*

Lolehan (Java). The open (lower) side of a gong.

Loloran (Indonesia; Cheribon). "The second tone." See *Lima* (5th note of *pelog*).
Lit.: no. 163.

Loloran (Indonesia; Sunda District). See *Kenong.*
Lit.: no. 163.

Lolowe (Celebes; Toraja). Simple bamboo flute. Cf. *Tulali*; *Tujali*; *Banchi banchi*; *Surune ndrawa* (South Nias).
Lit.: no. 132.

Lomba (Java). Tempo indication: andante.

Lonfembe (Congo River area – Wangata). Arched harp.
Lit.: no. 21.

Longa (Angola). Double iron bell beaten with wooden sticks in honor of chiefs.
Lit.: no. 255.

Longa (North Togo – Akasele). Large drum.
Lit.: no. 255.

Longombe (Congo-Kinshasa – Nkundo). Large bow harp.
Lit.: no. 176.

Longgor (Bali). Drumming in fast tempo. A number of compositions in the *gamelan gong.* See *Gending longgor.*
Lit.: no. 197.

Longser (West Java). See *Utuk-ubruk.*

Lontana (North Rhodesia; Congo – Bambamba). Musical bow.
Lit.: no. 21.

Lontar (Bali). Handwritten book consisting of tal palm leaves.
Lit.: no. 197.

Lontore (Upper Volta – Bisa). Cross flute with four holes.
Lit.: no. 50.

Lontyeng (Java). Bell.
Lit.: no. 255.

Lo-pan (China). See *T'i-tang.*

Lopu (Polynesia; Samoa; Tonga; Cook Isl.; New Zealand; British Solomon Isl.). Songs sung at the yearly sacred ritual. The songs are accompanied by stamping of bamboo tubes.
Lit.: no. 318.

Lo(r)loran (Java). The second tone of a scale. Cf. *Pamindo.*

Lori (East Iran). See *Dom.*

Loro (*Kaleh*) (Java). Moderate tempo. Cf. *Wirama siji*; *Karotugel*; *Telu*; *Papat.*

Lo-sau (China; Canton). See *Lu-shao.*

Losiva (*Lesiva*; *Lesiba*) (South Africa). Bechuana word for *gorra* (*gora*).

Loterokuma (Uganda—Acoli). Arched harp with five (occasionally seven) strings.
Lit.: no. 302.

Lo-to-ling-tang (China—M 4056; M 4127; M 6093; M 6448). Camel bell with an oval opening and a wooden clapper.

Lotong (*Tutung*) (Sarawak). Bamboo tube zither.
Lit.: no. 156.

Lo tsoi (China). Dialectal term for shell trumpet.

Lu (Malaysia). Tone syllable representing the third note of several scales (*wayang*). See *Chi* for complete scales.

Lü-(lü) (China—M 4280; M 4297). Literally "lawful pipe," "standard tube." Absolute pitches of ancient Chinese music arranged in a spiral of absolute fifths. As a matter of fact, the pitches did change during the many centuries. For details see Lit. no. 136.

When notated, only the first syllable of each *lü* is used. Below are given the complete two-syllable *lü* names. If the first tone is assumed to be the Western note C, all other *lü* are:

Huang-chung (M 1503; M 2297)	C	The Five Basic *Lü*
Lin-chung (M 1503; M 4022)	G	
T'ai-ts'u (M 6020; M 6840)	D	
Nan-lü (M 4280; M 4620)	A	
Ku-hsi (M 2465; M 3453)	E	
Ying-chung (M 1503; M 7477)	B	The Seven Auxiliary *Lü*
Jui-pin (M 3175; M 5259)	F#	
Ta-lü (M 4280; M 5943)	C#	
I-tse (M 2982; M 6746)	G#	
Chia-chung (M 611; M 1053)	D♭	
Wu-i (M 2960; M 7180)	A#	
Chung-lü (M 1505; M 4280)	E#	

Ideological Grouping

The *Yang Lü* (male *lü*)	*Ascribed to the month of*
Wu-i (A#)	September
I-tse (G#)	July
Jui-pin (F#)	May
Ku-hsi (E)	March
T'ai-ts'u (D)	January
Huang-chung (C)	November
The *Yin Lü* (female *lü*)	
Yin-chung (B)	October
Nan-lü (A)	August
Lin-chung (G)	June
Chung-lü (E#)	April
Chia-chung (D#)	February
Ta-lü (C#)	December

Lü-lü (China). For details see *Lü* and Lit. no. 136.

The *lü* names in Korean music:

Hwang	(e.g.) C
Tae	C#
Thae	D
Hyup	D#
Ko	E
Chung	F

Yu	F#
Im	G
I	G#
Nam	A
Mu	A#
Ung	B

The Japanese equivalents of the *lü*:

Shinsen	(e.g.) C
Kamimu	C#
Ichikotsu	D
Tangin	D#
Hyojo	E
Shosetsu	F
Shimomu	F#
Sojo	G
Husho	G#
Oshiki	A
Rankei	A#
Banshiki	B

Lubang jerit (Malaysia). Term for the single hole at the back of the *serunai* tube.

Lubang petit (Malaysia). Term for the seven finger holes on top of the *serunai* tube.

Lubembe (Congo—Lunda; Basonge; Baluba-Hemba). Iron double bell. Cf. *Rubembe.*
Lit.: no. 21.

Ludaya (Uganda—Gishu herders). Cross flute.
Lit.: no. 302.

Ludi (Lower Congo—Sundi). Wooden trumpet used to frighten away elephants.
Lit.: no. 280.

Lu-dim-ma (Sumeria). A group of persons who had various (non-musical) professions. But, in addition, they functioned also as musicians who played in funeral services and lamentations.
Lit.: no. 94.

Lue (Polynesia). Dance songs accompanied by clicking sticks or by beating a slit-drum. These songs are not linked with the *sanga* ritual; they start in slow tempo and gradually accelerate.
Lit.: no. 319.

Lugaya (*Milango*) (Tanzania—Sukuma). Big drum.
Lit.: no. 218.

Lugoma (Ruanda—Bashi; Angola—Ambunda). Large drum.
Lit.: no. 255.

Lugube (South Africa—Venda). Also called *gabus.* Musical bow played by girls and young women.
Lit.: no. 151.

Lugumba (Congo—Kongo). Conical drum.
Lit.: no. 26.

Luhenga (Congo—Bajok; Batatela). Short-stemmed goblet drum with a nailed head. It is beaten with the hands.
Lit.: no. 190.

Luḥūn (Arabia). Term used by Al-Kindi (9th century) for modes.

Luhur (Java). See *Handap.*

Luk (Siam). Bell clapper.
Lit.: no. 255.

Lukembi (Congo—Ituri Forest tribes). *Sansa.*
Lit.: no. 303.

Lukeme (Uganda—Acoli). Term for *sansa.*
Lit.: no. 302.

Lukonde (Belgian Congo—Bakuba). A *wambi* with eight strings.
Lit.: no. 190.

Lu-ku (China—M 3479; M 4181). Street drum. Cf. *Noko* (Korea); *Yin-ku.*

Lukumbe (Congo). (1) Bow lute. The *lukumbe* of the Teke and Lali has five strings, that of

the Bakuba has eight. (2) The *lukumbe* can also be a cylindrical drum of the Wasangola, and a friction drum of the Bambala and Bashongo. Cf. *Koy na bala.*
Lit.: nos. 26, 33, 176, 280.

Lukumbi (Congo-Kinshasa—Batetela). Wooden slit-drum. Cf. *Lokombe.*
Lit.: nos. 21, 176.

Lulanga (Congo—Bashi; Fuliri). Wooden trough zither with eight fiber strings. The tuning is approximately C E G A♭ B♭ c d♭ e♭.
Lit.: no. 176.

Lulimba (North Mozambique—Yao). *Sansa.*
Lit.: no. 255.

Luddi (North India). Folk dance. Referring to movements imitating field work. Cf. *Dhris.*

Ludi (Congo—Kikongo). Wooden trumpet.

Lulanga (Congo). Trough zither with eight strings.
Lit.: no. 190.

Lum (Northeast Thailand). (1) One of two basic scales: G A C D E g (the other scale is A C D E G, called *an nungsü* [*lai yai*], or, when transposed: D F G A C [*lai noi*]). (2) "To sing" accordingly to word tones in Lao. (3) Term for a long story, usually about a person, told in verse, such as *Lum prawet*, the story of Prince Westsundawn.
Lit.: no. 203.

Luma (Uganda; Ruwenzori Mts.; Bundibugyo Village). Vertical bamboo flute. It produces one note. The *luma* is played in groups.
Lit.: no. 29.

Lumbamba (Congo—Kongo). A small cylindrical drum with two heads.
Lit.: no. 280.

oLumbendo (Southwest Africa). Primitive whistle flute imitating the European recorder.
Lit.: no. 255.

Lum dut (Northeast Thailand). Folk song accompanied by a large drum.
Lit.: no. 203.

Lum tang sun (Northeast Thailand). To sing rhythmically, as opposed to *lum tang yao* (Laos), to sing parlando.
Lit.: no. 203.

Lunat (New Ireland). See *Numut.*

Lundongo (Angola). Men's dance of the Kuvali. Cf. *Chitita.*

Lunga (Sudan). Large drum in Mossi and Akasele languages. Hourglass drum in Agni, Dyoula, and Huela languages. Cf. *Kūbā.*
Lit.: nos. 95, 190.

Lung ch'ih (China). "Dragon pond"; the bigger one of the two resonance holes in the bottom of the *ch'in* body.

Lung-ching-ti (China—M 1126; M 5248; M 6217). Obsolete cross flute with eight finger holes.
Lit.: no. 209.

Lung gaḍung (Java). See *Gending charabalen.*

Lung-ku (China—M 3479; M 4258). "Dragon drum." Drum mounted on a stand ornamented with dragons. Cf. *Ryong-ko* (Korea).
Lit.: no. 78.

Lungoma (Angola—Ambundu). Large long hand drum.

Lungo ndolo (Congo—Kongo). Cylindrical drum.
Lit.: nos. 26, 280.

Lung-ti (China—M 4258; M 6217). "Dragon flute." Transverse flute adorned with a dragon's head or (and) tail. This adornment was not permitted to appear on other, ordinary instruments. The *lung-ti* were used in Confucian ceremonies and were played together with the (vertically-blown) *hsiao.*
Lit.: no. 209.

Lung-t'ou-ti (China—M 4258; M 6217; M 6489). "Dragon head flute." Transverse flute with six finger holes. Beyond the mouth hole are several additional holes generally used for ornamental purposes (such as tying tassels into them).
Lit.: no. 137.

Lungunga (Congo—Bembe). Musical bow.
Lit.: no. 26.

Lungungu (Congo). Musical bow.
Lit.: no. 176.

Lunko (Congo—Bali). Musical bow.
Lit.: no. 21.

Lunkufi (Congo—Eastern Kasai Province). Slit gong.
Lit.: no. 200.

uLu-nkwindi (South Africa). Musical bow.

Lunsi (Ghana). Dagbari term for one or several hourglass drums.
Lit.: no. 218.

Luntang (Philippines). Several vertically suspended wooden beams beaten like a large xylophone.
Lit.: no. 186.

Lunuot (New Ireland). Friction idiophone. Cf. *Nunut.*
Lit.: nos. 84, 190.

Lunut (North New Mecklenburgh). A *kulepa gane.* Cf. *Nunut.*

Lunyege (Ruanda—Bashe). Rattle.
Lit.: no. 190.

Luoü (Assam—Naga). Angami term for a double flute made of a bamboo tube with three nodes. Two nodes are at both ends of the tube and the 3rd node divides the tubes into two sections. Thus two flutes, a fifth apart in pitch, are created. The flutes have no finger holes.
Lit.: no. 252.

Lupita (*Chelupita*) (Bali). A wooden clapper.
Lit.: no. 197.

Lupondo (Congo—Basonge; Baluba; Batatela). Goblet drum.
Lit.: no. 26.

Lurah genḍing (Java). The principal musician of an ensemble.

Lure (Flores). See *Feko* (2).

Luru (Uganda—Lubara). Trumpet made of a bottle-shaped gourd.
Lit.: nos. 190, 302.

Luruh (Java). An actor's humble, modest character in the *wayang wong.*
Lit.: no. 163.

Luruh (*Laras*; *Larasati*). "Soft," "gentle." The term is used to describe a *gamelan* in which the intervals *barang-gulu* (in *slendro*) and *penunggul* (*bem*)—*gulu* (in *pelog*) are exceptionally small: in *slendro* less than 240 cents and in *pelog* about 100 cents.
Lit.: no. 163.

Lusengo (Ruanda—Warundi). Signal horn yielding two tones.
Lit.: no. 33.

Lusese (Congo—Luntu). Stick zither.
Lit.: no. 176.

Lu shao (China). Double reeds. In Cantonese the term is *lo-sau.*

Lü-shih (China—M 4297c; M 5783). An 8-line stanza of five or seven syllables. Cf. *Tz'u*; *Ch'ü.*

Lusinga (Congo). Bow-lute with four or five bows. Cf. *Nsami.*
Lit.: no. 280.

Lusuba (Congo—Baluba-Hemba). Musical bow.
Lit.: no. 21.

Lusukia (Congo—Wasongola). Term for *sansa.*

Lu-t'ao (China—M 4181; M 6151). Cf. *No-to* (Korea).

Lutar (North Africa—Berber). Lute with three strings tuned to F C g. Cf. *Lauta.*
Lit.: no. 65.

Lūṭūriyā (*Lūṭūriyān būrūsī*) (Turkey). "Ship's trumpet." A brass tube blown by Christian sailors.
Lit.: no. 81.

Lūṭūriyān būrūsī (Turkey). See *Lūṭūriyā.*

Luveve (South Africa—Swazi). Conical flute vertically blown.
Lit.: no. 151.

Luvuvu (*Tshivhilivhi*) (South Africa). Bull roarer of the Venda. The Pedi call the instrument *kgabududu* or *kgabudubudu*. The Sotho call it *sevuruvuru*, the Zulu *mapembe*, the Xhosa, who use a spinning disk bull roarer call it *uvuru.*
Lit.: no. 151.

Lwimbo (Zambia). Music.

Lyuli (Kurdistan). Flute.

M

Ma (China—M 4310). Lit. "horse." Bridge on string instruments, particularly on fiddles.

Mā (Burma—Shan State). (1) Long closed vertical bamboo flute (of various sizes). The instrument has no finger holes. (2) Panpipes with four stopped pipes.
Lit.: no. 252.

Ma' (Ancient Egypt). See *Mat.*

Ma (India). Abbreviation for *madhyama. Ma,* a tone syllable, represents the fourth degree of a scale (if *sa* is the western C, *ma* is F). In North India two terms are in use: *ma śuddha* for F natural; *ma tivra* for F♯.
Lit.: no. 136.

Mā (South India). One of the mnemonics applied to the 72 *mēḷas.* It indicates the 5th *mēḷa* of each *chakra* (the other syllables can be seen under the heading of *Bhū*). Cf. *Rāga* (South India).
Lit.: no. 139.

Ma (Japan). Interval; pause.

Maamad (Ancient Israel). See *Pijut.*

Maaravoth (Ancient Israel). Vocal addition to the evening prayer. Cf. *R'shuth.*
Lit.: no. 12.

Ma'āzif (singular *mi-zaf*) (Arabia; Iran). Stringed instruments.

Mabādī (Arabia). Tonic note (in lute playing). See *Majrā.*

Mabilango (Belgian Congo—Bantu). Friction drum.
Lit.: no. 29.

Macham garongan (Java). "The tiger's roar." A large *terbang.* The smaller sizes of this instrument are called *kempyang.*
Lit.: no. 163.

Machapat (Java). Cf. *Tembang machapat.* The following free *machapat* meters are quoted from Lit. no. 163, vol. 1, p. 125. The formulas consist of series of numbers and letters. The numbers indicate the quantity of syllables of each textual line. The letters, placed below the numbers, show the final vowels in each line. The formulas are:

Dangḍang gula:	10	10	8	7	9	7	6	8	12	7
	i	a	e(o)	u	i	a	u	a	i	a

Sinom:	8	8	8	8	7	8	7	8	12
	a	i	a	i	i	u	a	i	a

Asmarandana:	8	8	8	8	7	8	8
	i	a	o(e)	a	a	u	a

Kinanṭi:	8	8	8	8	8	8
	u	i	a	i	a	i

Pangkur:	8	11	8	7	12	8	8
	a	i	u	a	u	a	i

Durma:	12	7	6	7	8	5	7
	a	i	a	a	i	a	i

Midjil (*Mijil*):	10	6	10	10	6	6
	i	o	e	i	i	u

Mas kumambang:	12	6	8	8
	i	a	i	a

Puchung:	12	6	8	12
	u	a	i	a

Megatruh (= *Duduk wuluh*):	12	8	8	8	8
	u	i	u	i	o

Gambuh:	7	10	12	8	8
	u	u	i	u	o

Juru demung:	8	8	8	8	8	8	8
	a	u	u	a	u	a	u

Wirangrong:	8	8	10	6	7	8
	i	o	u	i	a	a

Balabak:	12	3	12	3	12	3
	a	e	a	e	a	e

Machiutai (Japan). "Waiting song." Entr'acte, interlude after the *ha* section and before the beginning of the *kyū* section of the *noh* drama.
Lit.: no. 185.

Machol (Ancient Israel). Round dance of women. The dance is accompanied by drums.
Lit.: no. 12.

Machunga (Nepal; Sikkim). Small iron jew's harp.
Lit.: no. 133.

Madā (Afghanistan). Street singer (and his singing) of religious character.

Māḍagam (South India). Name of the tuning pegs of the *yāzh.*
Lit.: no. 261.

Mādal (Nepal). A two-headed clay drum played with both hands. Cf. *Mārdala*; *Mādel.*
Lit.: nos. 46, 254.

Mādalā (India). See *Mārdala.*
Lit.: no. 254.

Madantī (India). Term for the 18th *śruti.* The corresponding note name is *prati ṣatṣruti dha* (*prati kaiśikī ni*). Cf. *Śruti.*
Lit.: no. 261.

Maddaḷa (South India – Kerala). Large *mṛdaṅga* used in *kathakaḷi* performances.
Lit.: no. 254.

Maddu (India). Ancient percussion instrument.

Madel (Sikkim – Lepcha). Two-headed barrel drum. See *Madal* (Nepal).
Lit.: no. 133.

Madela (India). Drummer.

Madenda (West Java). See *Surupan madenda.*

Mader (Arabia). Beduin song.

Madgalatūrya (India; Sanskrit). Festival instrument.
Lit.: nos. 205, 255.

Madhavamanōharī (South India). *Janya rāga* of the 57th *mēḷa* (*Siṃhendramadhyama*).
Tone material:

C E♭ D E♭ F♯ G B A♭ B c
c B A♭ F♯ E♭ D C

Lit.: no. 139.

Mādhavapriya (South India). *Janya rāga* of the 12th *mēḷa* (*Rūpāvatī*).
Tone material:

C E♭ F G A♯ B c
C B A♯ G F E♭ C

Lit.: no. 139.

Madhavi (South India). *Janya rāga* of the 21st *mēḷa* (*Kiravāṇi*).
Tone material:
C F E♭ F G A♭ B c
c B A♭ G F C F E♭ D C
Lit.: no. 139.

Mādhi (South India). *Janya rāga* of the 22nd *mēḷa* (*Kharaharapriyā*). This *rāga* can be assumed to be identical with *raga Madhyamāvati* (22nd mēḷa). As some South Indian writers list the two *rāgas* separately there may exist some minute differences in performing them, although no difference is known to this writer. As *Mādhi* is stated separately, the same policy is applied in this work. See *Madhyamāvati*.
Lit.: no. 139.

Madhmādi (North India). See *Madhvamādi-sarang*.

Madhukari (India). Ancient wind instrument.
Lit.: no. 255.

Madhukāri (South India). *Janya rāga* of the 50th *mēḷa* (*Nāmanārāyaṇī*). The scale of this *rāga* is identical with that of *rāga Nāmanārāyaṇī*.
Lit.: no. 139.

Madhurālāpa (South India). *Janya rāga* of the 28th *mēḷa* (*Harikāmbhōji*).
Tone material:
C D E A B♭ c
c B♭ A E D C
Lit.: no. 139.

Madhya (*Madhya laya*) (India). Medium; moderate tempo.

Madhya Kāla (India). See *Madhya laya*.

Madhyama (South India). Cf. *Brinda gānam*.

Madhyama (India). Abbreviation: *ma*. Sanskrit tone name. See *Ṣaḍja*, under which heading are listed all tone names. Also see *Saptaka* in Vedic chant. Cf. *Tritīya*. Also see *Jāti* (*rasa*).
Lit.: nos. 136, 138.

Madhyamadī (Ancient India). See *Jāti*.

Madhyamadī-sarang (North India). Also called *madhmādi*. Obscure *rāga* belonging to the *sarang* family. The *rāga* was "revived" recently.
Tone material:
C D F G B♭ c
c B♭ G F D C
Lit.: no. 138.

Madhyamāvati (*Madhumāvati*) (North India). An obscure *rāga* consisting of features taken from the *rāgas Jhinjhoti* (or *Khamaj*), and *Sindhura*. The tone material cannot be defined distinctly as it varies according to the performer's preference of any of the constituent features taken from the indicated *rāgas*.
One form of tone material can be:

Sindhura	*Khamaj*
C D F E♭ D E♭ C	F G B c
Sindhura	*Jhinjhoti*
c d B♭ A G A F	G F G E D E C

The *vādis* are probably C and G. See also *Mādhi*.
Lit.: no. 138.

Madhyamāvati (South India). *Janya rāga* of the 22nd *mēḷa* (*Kharaharapriyā*).
Tone material:
C D F G B♭ c
c B♭ G F D C
Lit.: no. 139.

Madhyamāntya (South India). A *rāga* of this type has its scale shifted from *sa*, *ri*, *ga*, etc., to *ma*, *pa*, *dha*, etc., a fifth below, whereby the highest note becomes *ma* (F) of the middle octave range.

Madhyamodīcyavā (Ancient India). See *Jāti*.

Madhya Saptaka (India). "Middle octave." Cf. *Mandra saptaka*; *Tara saptaka*.
Lit.: no. 136.

Madih (Arabia). That part of a song (verse) in which the person to whom the poem is addressed is praised.

Madilan (Persia). See *Medilan ārā*.

Madimba (Congo-Kinshasa; Uganda—Bakuba; Baluba). Widely popular xylophone with a variable number of wooden slabs and gourd resonators. Cf. *Amadinda*; *Dimba*; *Jimba*; *Kidimba*; *Madiumba*; *Malimba*.
Lit.: no. 27.

Madinda (Congo; Uganda). See *Amadinda*.
Lit.: no. 302.

Maditsi (South Africa). Cf. *Dikomana*.

Madiumba (Lower Congo; Angola). Xylophone (also *sansa*) with nine tongues (slabs).
Lit.: no. 280.

Mādlā (India; Maharashtra). Cf. *Mardalā*.

Mae (Japan). Formal transition between two sections in *nagauta* performed by voice, *shamisen*, and *tsuzumi*.
Lit.: no. 187.

Maebiki (Japan). Instrumental introductory music of *jiuta*, *kumiuta*. Cf. *Kumiuta*.
Lit.: no. 187.

Maemae (New Zealand—Maori). Death chants.

Maeuta (Japan). Opening song (with instrumental accompaniment) that follows an instrumental introduction (*maebiki*). Cf. *Jiuta*; *Kumiuta*.
Lit.: no. 187.

Mafow(n)a (South Africa—Thonga). Rattles tied around the legs of dancers. Cf. *Fowa*.
Lit.: no. 151.

Mafuaton ya sauti katika kuimbe au kupiga ngoma (East Africa—Swahili). See *Wimbo*; *Sauti*. . . .

Māgadhi (South India). *Janya rāga* of the 34th *mēḷa* (*Vāgadhīśvarī*).
Tone material:
C D♯ F G A B♭ c
c B♭ A G F D♯ C
Lit.: no. 139.

Magak (Java). A type resembling the *salahan* feature.
Lit.: no. 163.

Ma gaṇa (South India). See *Ashta gaṇas*.

Magaudi (India). *Tanbur*.
Lit.: no. 255.

Mag-dung (Tibet). See *Dmag-dung*, army trumpet.
Lit.: no. 125.

Mage ling (Kampuchea). Small bell.

Maghiiti (*Saka*) (Solomon Isl.). Strophic solo songs.
Lit.: no. 246.

Mago (Burma—Shan State). Jew's harp made of bamboo.
Lit.: no. 252.

Magodi (South Africa). One of the synonyms of *gedzo*.
Lit.: no. 151.

Magondo (Congo—Mondjembo; Bongo). Xylophone.
Lit.: no. 21.

Ma-grāma (India). One of the fundamental scales of ancient Indian music theory (*ma* functions here as first note, but *sa* remains the final note).
Lit.: no. 138.

Magri sumpi (Burma—Shan State). Double cane-pipes with metal reeds. The melody pipe has four finger holes and two thumbholes. The drone pipe is narrower and has no finger holes.
Lit.: no. 252.

Maguḍi (South India). Tamil term for a snake charmer's pipe made of an oblong gourd with two small cane tubes ending in reeds. One tube performs the drone, the other the melody. Cf. *Puñji*; *Bhujanga svaram*. See also *Tiktirī*. If the instrument is nose-blown it is called *nāsa-jantra*.
Lit.: no. 260.

Magyaun (Laos; Cambodia). Reference to the Sanskrit *makara*, "crocodile." *Magyaun* is a crocodile-shaped zither with two strings and eight frets.
Lit.: no. 41.

Mahāl (Arabia). String holder (of the *qanun*).

Mahāmandirā (India). The big *mandirā*.

Mahā nāgarā (India). The big *nāgarā*. See *Nahabat*.

Mahānāṭaka (India). See *Vichitra vīṇā*; *Rudra vīṇā*; *Gōṭvādyam*.

Mahā paṭaha (India). Large battle drum.

Mahāri (South India). Dancing girls.

Mahati (South India). *Janya rāga* of the 43rd *mēḷa* (*Gavāmbōdhi*).
Tone material:
C E♭ F♯ G A♭ B♭♭ c
c B♭♭ A♭ G F♯ E♭ C
Lit.: no. 139.

Mahatī vīṇā (*Bīn*) (North India). The famous Indian stick zither, rarely used at the present time. Often the word *vīṇā* suffices to indicate this distinguished instrument. It has two large resonance gourds, 4-5 melody strings of metal strung across 18-24 movable frets, and two or three thin bourdon strings which are placed on the side of the stick. The strings are plucked with a *mizrab*. Cf. *Naradiya vīṇā*; *Rañjanī vīṇā*.
Lit.: nos. 250, 254.

Mahea (Malagasy Republic). Ankle rattle.
Lit.: no. 251.

Mahfil (India). Gathering for unrestricted music making.
Lit.: no. 234.

Mahila (South India). *Janya rāga* of the 6th *mēḷa* (*Tānarūpi*).
Tone material:
C E♭♭ F G A♯ B c
c B A♯ G F E♭♭ C
Lit.: no. 139.

Mahonyera (Rhodesia—Shona mbira). Low, non-verbal humming style.
Lit.: no. 22.

Mahorathuk (Siam). Kettledrum with copper body.
Lit.: no. 255.

Mahōrī (Thailand; Cambodia). Ensemble of lutes, xylophones, gongs, drums, vertical flutes, and a group of string instruments: *sāw sam sai*, *sāw duang*, *sāwu* (*sāw ōo*), *chakay*, *grajappi*. Cf. *Sō duang*; *Sō ū*; *Jakhē*; different spellings.
Lit.: no. 186.

Mahpah (Ancient Israel). Notational symbol used in biblical chant, indicating a conjunctive function (the Latin *acutus*).
Lit.: no. 309.

Maḥsor (Ancient Israel). The festive prayer book which contains the frequently sung hymns.
Lit.: no. 12.

Mahulas (Malaysia). See *Rebāb* (Malay).

Māhūr (Middle East). Tone name of a note approximately an octave higher than *rast*. In Egypt this tone is called *kardan*. (The list of all tone names which can be seen under the heading of *Jagā* [*Yagā*].)

Māhūr (Middle East; Persia; Syria). The Syrian *maqām Māhūr* has the same tone material as the Egyptian *maqām Ḳardan*. The scale is the same as that of *rast*: $\overset{\flat}{B}$ C D $\overset{\flat}{E}$ F G A B♭ c d e♭. *Māhūr*, "the trotting," is said to be of Persian origin. It is well known in Persia but rarely, or not at all, in Arabia.

Maqām Māhūr begins with the note *kardan* (c), then the melody gradually descends to the note *rast* where the performance can come to an end. Slight differences in intonation ($\overset{\flat}{B}$ and B♭; $\overset{\flat}{E}$ and e♭) do appear and can be compared to features in the old synagogue modus "Adonay Moloch."
Lit.: no. 121.

Māhūr (Persia). See *Dastgāh*.

Māhūrān (Arabia). See *Jwab-jargā*. Also *Māhūrāni*.

Māhūrāni (Arabia). "The little *Māhūr*," a *maqā m* performed a fifth higher than *Māhūr*. *Mā hūrāni* was imported from Persia. See also *Jargā*; *Sasgar*.
Lit.: no. 121.

Māhūri (South India). *Janya rāga* of the 29th *mēḷa* (*Dhīraśaṅkarābharaṇam*).
Tone material:
C D E D C G B
B A G F E D C
Lit.: no. 139.

Māhūri (South India). Also *Mukavina*; *Mohori*. A small-sized oboe with 7-8 finger holes. The moderately-sized bell is made of metal. Cf. *Nāgāśuram*, a large oboe.
Lit.: no. 254.

Mai (New Hebrides—Leper Isl.). Bamboo flute with two finger holes.
Lit.: no. 255.

Mai (Japan). Dance. E.g., section of the *noh* drama. See *Kyū*.
Lit.: no. 187.

Mai bok bek (Northeast Thailand). A percussion instrument made of two pieces of wood.
Lit.: no. 203.

Maidan (North India). "Open space." Cf. *Tabla*.

Maigainai (Assam). Harvest dance.
Lit.: no. 46.

Maigoto-bayashi (Japan). Drum music of *nagauta*, accompanying dances. Cf. *Deiri-bayashi*.
Lit.: no. 187.

Main chachih (*Ujungam*) (Flores). A Malay term for the Whip Duel, a violent dance performed by two men accompanied by gongs, one or two xylophones, and, occasionally, a drum. All instruments are played by young girls. In the Manggaray *main chachih* can be called *parise*. When one dancer is struck in the duel, he acknowledges it by a *koonti*, a closing song, or by a *Pachih*, a challenging or mocking song.
Lit.: no. 163.

Main puteri (Malaysia). Healing service, a (musical) ceremonial.

Mairi-onjo (Japan). See *Gagaku*.

Mait (Ancient Egypt). See *Mat*.

Maitai talla (Assam—Naga). Long slim bamboo trumpet.

Majimba (Congo—Ruanda-Urundi). Xylophone. Cf. *Madimba*.
Lit.: no. 27.

Majīra (*Manjīra*) (India). Small cymbals. Also called *jhalrī*.
Lit.: no. 46.

Majrā (Arabia). See *Maqām*.

Majrā (Old Arabia). "Course." The melodic modes (*aṣābi*) were classified according to their course (*majrā*) as either in the *binṣir* (third finger; i.e., with the major third) or *wuṣṭā* (middle finger; i.e., with the minor third).
The courses were named after their tonics (*mabādī*) such as *mutlaq*. . . , *sabbāba* . . . , etc. There were eight of these modes. Cf. *Aṣab'*.
Lit.: no. 70.

Majruda (Libya). Song with a vigorous rhythmic character, accompanied by clapping of hands. Its Lebanese, Syrian, Jordan term is *murabba'*. The audience usually joins singing the refrain.

Makado-onjo (Japan). See *Gagaku*.

Makaji (Congo—Baluba). Xylophone with nine slabs.
Lit.: no. 303.

Makam (Turkey). Term for the Arabic *maqām.*

Makarālapriya (South India). *Janya rāga* of the 15th *mēḷa* (*Māyāmāḷavagauḷa*).
Tone material:
C D♭ E A♭ B c
c B A♭ E D♭ C
Lit.: no. 139.

Makasa (Malagasy Republic – Soalala District). Rattle.
Lit.: no. 251.

Makata (Congo – Ituri Forest). Nine percussion sticks.
Lit.: no. 303.

Makhuri (Arabia). Arabic popular rhythm, a variation of the second *thaqil.* Cf. *Iqa'at.*

Makhweyane (South Africa – Swazi). Cf. *Umakhweyana.*

Makkow (South Africa – Batlaping). Rattle. Cf. *Mathlo.*
Lit.: no. 151.

Makkuri (Japan – Ainu). A jew's harp played only by women.
Lit.: no. 185.

Mak-mak-jo (Korea). Cf. *Tae-kum.*

Mako (Solomon Isl.). Sitting songs (strophic form).
Lit.: no. 246.

Mako hakahaahine (Solomon Isl.; Bellona Isl.). A dance originally danced by women is now performed by men only.
Lit.: no. 246.

Makondere (Uganda – Banyoro; Ruanda Urundi – Tutsi). Ensemble of side-blown gourd-horns of the ruler. The horns are played at every new moon. Cf. *Ekkondere*; *Kondere.*
Lit.: no. 29.

Mak-t'ung (Tibet). See *Mag-dung* (*Dmag-dung*).

Makura (Japan). Brief introduction to an extensive interlude in the *kumi-uta.*
Lit.: no. 187.

Mākūrī (Arabia). Cf. *Ramal.*

Makuri (Japan). A melodic formula, in which *asa-ori* is followed by *sori.* Cf. *Kyōkusetzu.*

Makutadhāriṇi (South India). *Janya rāga* of the 22nd *mēḷa* (*Kharaharapriyā*).
Tone material:
C D E♭ A B♭ c
c B♭ A E♭ D C
Lit.: no. 139.

Makwanga (*Kwanga*; *Mavonda*) (Lower Congo – Yombe). Panpipes with four, six, or eight stopped pipes, bound together in raft form.
Lit.: no. 280.

Makwindi (South Africa – Swaziland). Term for *gora.*

Makyong (Malaysia). Instrumental ensemble consisting of one *serunai*, and (or) a *rebāb*, drums, and gongs.

Māla (Liberia – Kpelle). Dance.
Lit.: no. 284.

Malahari (South India). *Janya rāga* of the 15th *mēḷa* (*Māyāmāḷavagauḷa*).
Tone material:
C D♭ F G A♭ c
c A♭ G F E D♭ C
Lit.: no. 139.

Malāhī (Arabia). Old term for musical instruments (9th-12th centuries).

Malakat (Ethiopia). A long straight or slightly curved bamboo trumpet covered with skin and provided with seven finger holes. The tube ends in a calabash or copper bell.
Lit.: nos. 102, 218.

Malandiya (Arabia). Ancient (obscure) instrument used for signalling in battles.
Lit.: no. 255.

Malashri (North India). Rare *rāga* ascribed to the *Kalyan thāta*. Three versions are in use:
1. with F# in descent;
2. F# as lightly touched ornament;
3. the notes C, E, G are essential.

All others are "hidden" in descending, gliding steps.
Tone material:
C E G F# E G (B) c
c B G (F#) E G; *Vādis*: G, c
Lit.: no. 138.

Mālava (North India). See *Mālavi*.

Mālava (South India). *Janya rāga* of the 15th *mēḷa* (*Māyāmāḷavagauḷa*).
Tone material:
C Db E F G Ab B c
c B Ab G F E Db C
The scale of this *rāga* is identical with that of its primary *rāga*.
Lit.: no. 139.

Mālavagauḷa (South India). (1) The 15th *asampurna mēḷa-rāga* without *kaṭapayādi* prefix. (2) The 15th *asampurna mēḷa-rāga* with *kaṭapayādi* prefix was called *Māyāmāḷavagauḷa*. See *Rāga* (South India).
Lit.: no. 139.

Mālavapañcham (South India). *Janya rāga* of the 15th *mēḷa* (*Māyāmāḷavagauḷa*).
Tone material:
C Db E F G B c
c B Ab G F E Db C
Lit.: no. 139.

Mālavaśrī (South India). *Janya rāga* of the 10th *mēḷa* (*Nāṭakapriya*).
Tone material:
C Eb F G Bb A Bb c
c Bb A G F Eb C
Lit.: no. 139.

Mālavaśrī (South India). *Janya rāga* of the 22nd *mēḷa* (*Kharaharapriyā*).
Tone material:
C Eb F G Bb A Bb G A Bb c
c Bb A G F Eb C
Lit.: no. 139.

Mālavatāriṇi (South India). *Janya rāga* of the 45th *mēḷa* (*Śubhapantuvarālī*).
Tone material:
C Eb F# G Ab B c
c B Ab G F# Eb C
Lit.: no. 139.

Mālavi (South India). *Janya rāga* of the 28th *mēḷa* (*Harikāmbhōji*).
Tone material:
C D E F G Bb F A Bb c
c Bb A Bb G F E F D C
Lit.: no. 139.

Malāwī (*Melwī*) (Arabia; Iran). Tuning pegs of the *kemanja*. Peg box.
Lit.: no. 255.

Malayajālapini (South India). *Janya rāga* of the 7th *mēḷa* (*Senāpāti*).
Tone material:
C Db Eb F Ab c
c Ab F Eb Db C
Lit.: no. 139.

Mālayamāruta (South India). *Janya rāga* of the 16th *mēḷa* (*Chakravāka*).
Tone material:
C Db E A Bb c
c A G F E C Db C
Lit.: no. 139.

Maleok (Philippines). Cf. *Itundak*.

Malgunj (*Malgunji*) (North India). *Rāga* ascribed to the *Kāfi thāta*.
Tone material:
C D E F A Bb B c
c Bb A G F Eb D C
Lit.: no. 138.

Malhar (North India). See *Mallār.*

Mali (Malaysia). Mouthpiece of the *serunai.*

Maligaura (North India). *Rāga* ascribed to the *Marva thāta.* Three versions are in use:

1. With the use of the note A only.
2. With the use of A♭ only.
3. With the use of the notes A and A♭.

The *rāga* consists of elements taken from *Shrī rāga* and *rāga Puria.*
Tone material can be:

C D♭ E F♯ G (A♭) A B c
c B (A) A♭ G F♯ D D♭ C

Lit.: no. 138.

Malilū (South Mesopotamia; Akkadian). Flute. See *Imbubu.*

Malimba (*Madimba*) (Congo—Bapende; Bambana). Xylophone with 17 (or fewer) keys fixed to a frame. Below each key is a gourd resonator. The Bango-Bango people (Congo) use the same xylophone but without resonators. Cf. *Manja.*
Lit.: nos. 27, 29.

Ma-ling (China—M 4056; M 4310). "Horse bell." A semi-spherical brass bell with an iron clapper suspended from the necks of horses. In Hangchow the term for the bell is *tu-ling* ("single, simple bell").
Lit.: no. 255.

Malinga (Congo). Frame drum.

Malkouns (*Malkauns*; *Malkous*) (North India). *Rāga* ascribed to the *Bhairavi thāta.*
Tone material:

C E♭ F A♭ B♭ c
c B♭ A♭ F E♭ C

Lit.: no. 138.

Mallār (*Malhar*) (North India). *Rāgas.* This family of *rāgas* is generally ascribed to the *Kafi thāta* and its *rāgas* are performed during the monsoon, the rainy season. There are several phrases that are characteristic of the entire family: C D C / B♭ A B c / C F D G / B♭ F G.
The names of the *Mallar rāgas* are:

Megh Mallār	*Mirabai ki Mallār*
Miyan ki Mallār	*Naiki Mallār*
Gaud Mallār	*Jayant Mallār*
Śuddh Mallār	*Charujuki Mallār*
Nath Mallār	*Des Mallār*
Sur Mallār	*Chanchalasasa Mallār*
Ramdasi Mallār	*Dhulia Mallār*
Rupamanjari Mallār	

Lit.: no. 138.

Mallār(u) (South India). *Janya rāga* of the 22nd *mēḷa* (*Kharaharapriyā*).
Tone material:

C D F E♭ F G A G A c
c A G F D C (c A G F E♭ F D C)

Lit.: no. 139.

Mallikāmōda (South India). *Janya rāga* of the 40th *mēḷa* (*Navanītam*).
Tone material:

C E♭♭ F♯ G A B♭ c
c B♭ A G F♯ E♭♭ C

Lit.: no. 139.

Mallikāvasantam (South India). *Janya rāga* of the 15th *mēḷa* (*Māyāmāḷavagauḷa*).
Tone material:

C E F G B c
c B A♭ G F E D♭ C

Lit.: no. 139.

Malluj (Sudan; Upper Nile—Dinka). A *zummara* (double pipe with a reed mouthpiece) with four or six finger holes.
Lit.: no. 255.

Malongu (Congo—Balese). Board zither.
Lit.: no. 176.

Malshiri git (Nepal). Religious song that celebrates Durga's victory over the demons.
Lit.: no. 133.

Maluf (Tunisia). Term for art music.

Maluha (North India). *Rāga* ascribed to the *Bilaval thāta*.
Tone material:
C D F G B c
c A G F D C
Lit.: no. 138.

Maluha-Kedar (North India). *Rāga* ascribed to the *Bilaval thāta*.
Tone material:
C E F G B c
c B A G F E D C; *Vādis*: C, F
Lit.: no. 138.

Malume (Congo—Luba). Xylophone.
Lit.: no. 303.

Malvi (*Malava*) (North India). *Rāga* ascribed to the *Purvi thāta*. This *rāga* is little known. Its melodies usually begin with the upper note c (*sa*) and progress in a descending line.
Tone material:
c B G F♯ E D♭ C
C E F♯ A♭ c
Lit.: no. 138.

Mamanis (Java). Sweet; lyrical.
Lit.: no 163.

Mamanis (Sunda District). See *Barang*.

Mamapu (Samoa). Large bamboo tubes are tied with their open ends into a basket. The basket is beaten with sticks or shaken.
Lit.: no. 255.

Mamban-tetsu-no-fuye (Japan). Long iron flute with five finger holes in front and one in the back.
Lit.: no. 255.

Mambira (*Marimba*) (Mozambique). Xylophone, used to provide music for dancing.

Mambunong (Philippines). War dance performed by two male dancers.

Mam-ma-lie (Australia). Bull roarer.
Lit.: no. 255.

Mampembe (South Africa—Zulu). Spinning disc (bull roarer).
Lit.: no. 151.

Mamuat (Cambodia; Khmer). Northeast Thailand term for *mawlum pee fah*.
Lit.: no. 203.

Man (Burma; Shan State; Padaung). Panpipes (20 bamboo pipes).
Lit.: no. 252.

Mānābharaṇi (South India). *Janya rāga* of the 27th *mēḷa* (*Sarasāṅgī*).
Tone material:
C D E G F A♭ B c
c B A♭ G E D C
Lit.: no. 139.

Manandria (Malagasy Republic). See *Hazolahi*.

Manangis (Java). Scale in *surupan melog* beginning with the note *galimer*:

II	III	x	(iv)
galimer	*panelu*	*panangis*	(*liwung*)
V	VI	VII	(X)
kenong	*barang*	*sorog*	*pamiring*

Pamiring and *kenong* are auxiliary notes.
Lit.: no. 163.

Manas (Kirgizia). Chanted epic poem.
Lit.: no. 275.

Manasijapriya (South India). *Janya rāga* of the 16th *mēḷa* (*Chakravāka*).
Tone material:
C D♭ E F G F A B♭ c
c A B♭ G F E D♭ C
Lit.: no. 139.

Mānaskagāmiṇī (South India). *Janya rāga* of the 16th *mēḷa* (*Chakravāka*).
Tone material:
C D♭ E F B♭ c
c B♭ F E D♭ C
Lit.: no. 139.

Mānavātī (South India). (1) The 5th *mēḷa*:

C D♭ E♭♭ F G A B c

(2) As *rāga Mānavātī* has the same tone material as that of the *mēḷa*. Veṅkaṭamakhin (17th century) called this *rāga Manōrañjanī*.
Lit.: no. 139.

Mand (North India). *Rāga* ascribed to the *Bilaval thāta*.
Tone material:

C D E F G A B c
c B A G F E (D) C

Pandit Bhatkhande is of the opinion that all notes of the *Mand* scale have a *vakra* (zig-zag) character (Lit. no. 138, p. 148):

C E D F E G F A G B A c
c A B G A F G E F C

Lit.: no. 138.

Mānd (South India). *Janya rāga* of the 29th *mēḷa* (*Dhīraśaṅkarābharaṇam*).
Tone material:

C E F G A c
c B A G F E D C

Lit.: no. 139.

Mandā (India). Term for the third *śruti*. The corresponding note name is *praticatuśśruti* (or *pratiśuddha ga*), term used in the past in music theoretical works. Cf. *Śruti.*

Manda gati (India). See *Gati.*

Mandakini (South India). *Janya rāga* of the 1st *mēḷa* (*Kanakāngi*).
Tone material:

C D♭ E♭♭ F B♭♭ c
c B♭♭ F E♭♭ D♭ C

Lit.: no. 139.

Mandal (India). See *Mādāla.*
Lit.: no. 254.

Maṇḍalāgrapāṇi (South India). *Janya rāga* of the 17th *mēḷa* (*Sūryakānta*).
Tone material:

C D♭ G A B c
c B A G D♭ C

Lit.: no. 139.

Mandamari (South India). *Janya rāga* of the 22nd *mēḷa* (*Kharaharapriyā*).
Tone material:

C D F G A c B♭ c
c A G F E♭ D C

Lit.: no. 139.

Māndar (*Mandari*) (India—Kherwar). Sacred drum in kettle or barrel form, used by native tribes in Central India.
Lit.: no. 254.

Mandaram (India). Name of the lowest string of the *tanbura.* The string is tuned to the lowest *Sa* (C).
Lit.: no. 262.

Mandāri (*Mandar*) (Southeast India—Muria Gond tribes in the Abujhmar Mountains). Term for *kunduri.*
Lit.: no. 135.

Mandāri (South India). *Janya rāga* of the 50th *mēḷa* (*Nāmanārāyaṇī*).
Tone material:

C D♭ E F♯ G B♭ c
c B♭ G F♯ E D♭ C

Cf. *Mandāri* (of the 51st *mēḷa*).
Lit.: no. 139.

Mandāri (South India). *Janya rāga* of the 51st *mēḷa* (*Kāmavardhanī*).
Tone material:

C D♭ E F♯ G B c
c B G F♯ E D♭ C

Cf. *Mandāri* of the 50th *mēḷa.*
Lit.: no. 139.

Mandhāsini (South India). *Janya rāga* of the 52nd *mēḷa* (*Rāmapriyā*).
Tone material:

C D♭ E F♯ G F♯ A B♭ c
c B♭ A G F♯ E F♯ D♭ C

Lit.: no. 139.

Mandi (East India; Orissa). Brass gong.

Mandileh (India; around Multan; Agra). Rattle rings worn by dancing boys around their ankles.
Lit.: no. 255.

Mandira (*Tālā*) (North India). Small half-spherical cymbals used for ringing the hours and for accompaniment of dancing. (Large cymbals are called *mahāmandirā*.) The Tibetan name of these cymbals is *ding-sha*. Cf. *Munjira*.
Lit.: no. 255.

Mandola (*Mandora*) (North Africa). Moorish guitar with a pear-shaped body and six double strings.

Mandora (Arabia). See *Mandola*.

Mandra (Vedic India). Deeply resounding drum (mentioned in *Rig Veda* 9, 69,2).

Mandra (India). See *Saptaka*. The lowest of three octaves (*mandra saptaka*) of the gamut of music. The middle octave is called *madhya saptaka* and the high one *tāra saptaka*.
Lit.: no. 136.

Mandra (or *pañchama*) (Vedic India). The second lowest note of the vedic chant notated with "5."
Lit.: no. 141.

Māndri (Southeast India – Muria Gond; Jhoria Muria Gond). Either an hourglass-shaped drum (*hulki māndri*) or a barrel-shaped one (*khut mā ndri*).
Lit.: no. 59.

Maṅgalagauri (South India). *Janya rāga* of the 3rd *mēḷa* (*Gānamūrti*).
Tone material:
C F G A♭ B c
c B G A♭ F E♭♭ D♭ C
Lit.: no. 139.

Maṅgalakaiśika (South India). *Janya rāga* of the 15th *mēḷa* (*Māyāmāḷavagauḷa*).
Tone material:
C F E F G F A♭ B c
c B A♭ G F E D♭ C
Lit.: no. 139.

Maṅgalakari (South India). *Janya rāga* of the 64th *mēḷa* (*Vāchaspati*).
Tone material:
C D G F♯ G A B♭ c
c B♭ A G A D C
Lit.: no. 139.

Mangalapratha (South India). *Janya rāga* of the 48th *mēḷa* (*Divyamaṇī*).
Tone material:
C E♭ F♯ G A♯ B c
c B A♯ G F♯ E♭ C
Lit.: no. 139.

Mangol (Java). See *Rebāb* (Java).

Mangu (Congo – Bazimba). Truncated barrel drum. Cf. *Imangu*.
Lit.: no. 26.

Mangu (Java; Sunda District). "Dull," "absent-minded," "in love." As a musical term *mangu* signifies an intermediate tone between *bem* (the second note) and *panelu* (the third note, both of the *slendro* system of the Sunda District). Cf. *Slendro*.

Mangval (Congo – Bongo). Antelope horn with three finger holes.
Lit.: no. 255.

Maṇi (India). Tamil term for *ghaṇṭa* (hand bell).
Lit.: no. 254.

Mani (Turkey). Term for *semai* with one strophe or 4-6 lines, each having seven syllables. The melody is improvised and usually is presented in a contest of singers.
Lit.: no. 243.

Maṇikkāi (South India). See *Guṇḍu*.

Manimāyi (South India). *Janya rāga* of the 27th *mēḷa* (*Sarasāṅgī*).
Tone material:
C D E F G A♭
G F E D C *B*
Lit.: no. 139.

Mānini (South India). *Janya rāga* of the 47th *mēḷa* (*Suvarṇāṅgī*).
Tone material:
C E♭ F♯ G A B c
c B A G F♯ E♭ C
Lit.: no. 139.

Mānini (South India). *Janya rāga* of the 66th *mēḷa* (*Chitrāmbarī*).
Tone material:
C D E F♯ A♯ c
c A♯ F♯ E D C
Lit.: no. 139.

Ma-ni-pa (Tibet). Travelling singers and story tellers who present similar themes as those of the *ache-lhamo*.
Lit.: no. 62.

Manipuri (Northeast India). Classical dance of religious character. Cf. *Lai haroba*; *Rāsa līlā*.

Maṇiraṅgu (South India). *Janya rāga* of the 22nd *mēḷa* (*Kharaharapriyā*).
Tone material:
C D F G B♭ c (C D F E♭ F G B♭ c)
c B♭ G F E♭ D C
Lit.: no. 139.

Manis (West Java). Second highest octave (in a gamut of four octaves). Cf. *Petit* (West Java).
Lit.: no. 163.

Manja (Congo—Ngbandi; Sango; Bwaka). Also called *banjanga*. Xylophone with 10-13 wooden slabs. Cf. *Malimba*; *Manjanga*; *Manza*; *Menza*.
Lit.: no. 26.

Manjaira (*Manǧaira*) (Syria). Bamboo long-flute with six holes.
Lit.: no. 255.

Manjanga (Congo). Cf. *Manja*.
Lit.: no. 27.

Mañjari (South India). *Janya rāga* of the 22nd *mēḷa* (*Kharaharapriyā*).
Tone material:
C E♭ D E♭ F G B♭ A B♭ c
c B♭ A G F E♭ D C
Lit.: no. 139.

Māñji (South India). *Janya rāga* of the 20th *mēḷa* (*Naṭabhairavī*).
Tone material:
C D E♭ F G A B♭ c
(C E♭ D E♭ F B♭ A B♭ c)
c B♭ A♭ G F E♭ D C
(c B♭ c G A♭ G F E♭ D C)
Lit.: no. 139.

Mañjīrā (*Majīra*) (India). Hindusthani term for *mandira*. Cf. *Nūpura*; *Čallari*.

Mañjula (South India). *Janya rāga* of the 36th *mēḷa* (*Chalanāṭa*). The scale of this *rāga* is identical with that of its primary *rāga* (*Chalanāṭa*).
Lit.: no. 139.

Manjuri (Nepal). A pair of small cymbals played together with the *mādal*.

Manodharma sangita (India). Freely improvised music.

"Man of War" (Ghana). See *Agbadza*.

Manohar (North India). A little known *rāga* (of recent origin) subordinated to the *Purvi thāta*.
Tone material:
C (E) (F♯) A♭ c
c B A♭ G F♯ E D♭ C; *Vādis*: E, A♭
Lit.: no. 138.

Manōhari (South India). *Janya rāga* of the 22nd *mēḷa* (*Kharaharapriyā*).
Tone material:
C E♭ D E♭ F G A c
c A G F E♭ D C
Lit.: no. 139.

Manol (Java). Peg.
Lit.: no. 255.

Manora (Thailand). Syncopated rhythms used in South Thailand.

Manōrajanī (South India). *Janya rāga* of the 5th *mēḷa* (*Mānavātī*).
Tone material:
C D♭ F G A B c
c B A G A F E♭♭ D♭ C
Lit.: no. 139.

Manōrañjanī (South India). (1) The 5th *asampūrṇa mēḷa-rāga* without *kaṭapayādi* prefix. (2) The 5th *asampūrṇa mēḷa-rāga* with *kaṭapayādi* prefix. Cf. *Rāga* (South India).
Lit.: no. 139.

Mansu (Ancient Babylon). Akkad term; see *Me-ze.*

Mansūr (Iran; Turkey). A medium-sized modern *nay.* Cf. *Qiz.*
Lit.: no. 255.

Man-t'ou-ku (China—M 3479; M 4340; M 6489). "Loaf of steamed bread." A small drum resting on a folding stand. The name describes the shape. The drum appears frequently in theatrical performances of the South.
Lit.: no. 209.

Mantsakota (South Africa—Venda). Wooden reed pipe used in ritual activities. Cf. *Sitlanjani.*
Lit.: no. 151.

Mantshomane (South Africa—Thonga). Also *ubhababa.* Magicians' frame drum, beaten with a stick.
Lit.: no. 151.

Manya (South India). *Janya rāga* of the 1st *mēḷa* (*Kanakāngi*).
Tone material:
C E♭♭ F G A♭ B♭♭ c
c B♭♭ A♭ G F E♭♭ C
Lit.: no. 139.

Manyini (Sudan—Bongo). Straight wooden tuba trumpet).
Lit.: no. 255.

Manyōshū (Japan). "Collection of Ten Thousand Leaves." A large anthology of poems compiled in the 8th century. Among the 4496 poems from the period A.D. 313-765, 262 are *nagauta* types. In numerous poems can be found references to musical matters.
Lit.: no. 188.

Manyura (Java). The term is derived from the Sanskrit word *mayura* ("peacock"), and indicates a moderately high register in singing and playing.
Lit.: no. 163.

Manza (Congo—Azande; Abondja). Xylophone with 5-10 wooden slabs and resonators. Cf. *Manja*; *Kweningba.*
Lit.: no. 27.

Manzh (North India). An obscure *rāga* that consists of elements taken from the *rāgas Bilaval*, *Khamaj*, and *Mand* (North India). Its *vādis* are E and A. The tone material and scales cannot be defined distinctly as they vary according to the performer's preference of any of the constituent features taken from the three indicated *rāgas.* For further information see Lit. no. 138.

Mao karsana (Southeast India—Muria Gond tribe). *Gotul* song for the bison hunting game.
Lit.: no. 142.

Maotoru (Japan). Term in *koto* music indicating "rest," "pause."
Lit.: no. 225.

Mapa (East Flores). Cf. *Kenite*; *Santo.*
Lit.: no. 220.

Mapiku (Tanzania—Makonde). Masked dancers (at circumcision ritual).

Mapobaulo (North Rhodesia—Ila; Tonga; Bantu speaking tribes). War songs sung by men.
Lit.: no. 99.

Maqāla (Arabia). Rhythm.

Maqām

Maqām (Arabia; Islamic Orient). The term has two related meanings:

1. The musical tone, sound, note which Jewish writers and poets translated with the terms *qōl* or *habara*. The Egyptian is *naqma* or *naghma*, the Persian term is *dastgāh*, the Algerian term is *ṭaba*.
2. The meaning indicates a melody pattern consisting of a fixed tone material (which can often be shown in scale form) combined with characteristic phrases and ornaments.

Maqām originally signified a stage or platform from where poet-singers used to recite at the time of the Kalifs. Gradually the term denoted that which was performed on the podium. All these compositions have to contain distinctive phrases and passages of a specific *maqām*, otherwise they were considered to be of little value and called unmusical.

The forerunners of the *maqāmāt* were the eight finger-modes (*aṣābi*) of Al-Iṣfahānī (in his *Kitāb al-aghānī al-kabīr*, 10th century). The finger-modes referred to *'ud* playing and were grouped according to the "course" (*majrā*) with the *wusṭā*, the middle finger producing the minor third, or *binṣir*, the third finger, producing the major third. These finger-modes were in use up to the 11th century and led to the evolution of the 12 *maqāmāt* and six secondary modes called by Persian names, the *awāzāt*. Turkmen had modes called *shu'ab* and in the 15th century 48 modes, called *shudūd*.

A number of *maqāmāt* differ from each other only by the order of the notes—while the basic tone-material remains the same. This can be observed in the *maqāmāt Rast* and *Nawā*, *Rehaw* and *Bayat*, *Ḥijāz* and *Ispahan* and *Shahwrak*. The same material scale, if started a fourth, fifth, or octave higher can create a different *maqām*.

The old Arabic music theorists and literati divided the *maqāmāt* into "fathers" and "sons." There are several "father-son" lists. Below are shown a few:

Fathers:	Sons:	
1. *Rāst*	*Mahur*	
2. *Bayat*	*Rehaw*	
3. *Ṣaba*	*Ispahan*	generally known
4. *Ḥijāz*	*Buselik*	generally known
5. *'Ushaq*	*'Ashiran*	generally known
6. *Siga*	*Sasgar*	generally known
7. *'Iraq*	*Ḥijāz-kar*	generally known
8. *Auj*	*Jarka*	lesser known
9. *Ḥusēnī*	*Mahurani*	lesser known
10. *Nawā*	*Shuri*	lesser known
11. *'Ajam*	*Shawrak*	lesser known
12. *Nahawānd*	*Shāh'nāz*	lesser known
13.	*Raml*	lesser known

The order of the "fathers" (which are well known) changes with time and author. The *Diwan* of Israel Nağara of Damascus (16th century) shows the following order of the *maqāmāt*:

1. *Rast*
2. *Mahur*
3. *Ḥusēni*
4. *Sunbuli*
5. *Ṣaba*
6. *Siga*
7. *'Iraq*
8. *Auj*
9. *Nawā*
10. *Nev-ruuz*
11. *Buselik*
12. *Jarga*
13. *'Usal*

A Diwan from Aleppo (1906) has:

1. *Rast*
2. *Mahur*
3. *Nahawānd*
4. *'Ajām*
5. *Bayat*
6. *Ḥusēni*
7. *'Ashiran*
8. *Rehaw*
9. *Ṣaba*
10. *Siga*
11. *Ḥijāz*

Muhammed Kamel el-Kholay in his *Musiqa esh-Sharqije* (ed. 1905) offers the following list:

1. *Rast*
   - (a) *Suz-di-lara*
   - (b) *Sasgar*
   - (c) *Suz-nak*

   } Persian derivations of *Rast*
2. *Kardan*
3. *Ḥijāz-kar*
4. *Nahawānd*
   - (a) *Neuter*
   - (b) *Nigriz*
   - (c) The Great *Nahawand*
   - (d) *Turz-neuin*

   } Persian derivations of *Nigriz*
5. *Bayati*
6. *Buselik*
7. *'Ushaq*

8. *Ḥijāz*
9. *Ṣaba*
10. *Siga*
    (a) *Shu'ar* — Persian-derived type
11. *Jarka*
    (a) The Little *Mahur* — Persian derived-type
12. *Jaga* (*Nawā*)
    (a) *Faraḥfaza* — Persian derived of Nawa
13. *Ḥusēni*
14. *Suz-dal*
15. *'Ajām* (*'Ajām-, 'Ashiran, 'Ajam-'Ashiran*)
16. *Shauq-afza*
17. *'Iraq*
18. *Aug̃* (*Auj*)
19. *Raḥat-il-aruh*
    (a) *Auj-ara*
    (b) *Farahnak*
    (c) *Basta-nigar*
    } Persian-derived types

There are only seven *maqām* types of real Arabic origin: *'Iraq, Bayat, 'Ushaq, Ṣaba, Ḥijāz, Nawā, Sasgar. Maqāmāt* and *Awāzāt* listed by Safī al-Dīn (13th century; Lit. no. 65). The *maqāmāt* are: *'Ushshāq, Nawā, Būsalik, Rāst, 'Irāq, Iṣfahān, Zīrāfkand, Buzurk, Zankūla, Rahāwī, Ḥusainī, Ḥijāz.* The *Awāzāt* are: *Kuwasht, Kardānīyā, Naurūz, Nihuft, Muhaiyar al-Ḥusain, Ḥijāz* (II).

Maqāmāt of Modern Tunisia: *Dhīl, Rasdu-dh-Dhīl, Istihlālū-dh-Dhīl, Mujannabu-dh-Dhīl, Rahāwī, Rasd* (*Rast*), (*Ḥsīn*) *Nīriz*, (*Ḥsīn*) *'Ajam*, (*Ḥsīn*) *Aṣl*, (*Ḥsīn*) *Ṣabā*, (*Ḥsīn*) *'Ushayrān, Ḥijāzi, 'Ushshāq, Ṣabā, 'Irāq, Muḥayir 'Irāq, Ramal, Aṣbu'ayn, Nawā, 'Iraq, Aṣl, Rāmal-Māyah, Isbāhān, Sikah, Māyah, 'Ajam, 'Ajam 'Ushayrān, Mazmūm, 'Arḍawi, Muḥayir Sīkah.*

Maqāmāt of Modern Egypt: *Yak-gāh, Faraḥ-Kazā, 'Ushayrān, Sūz-i-Dil, 'Ajam-Ushshayrān, 'Irāq, Faraḥ-nāk, Rāhat-al-Arwak, Bastah-nigār, 'Auj-'Āra* (*'Awj-'Āra*), *Rast, Sūz-nāk, Sūz-dil-'arā, Nagrīz, Tarz-Nwīn, Nihawand, Nawathar, Ḥijāz-kār, Bayātī, Ḥusaynī, Qar-jigar, Ḥijāzī, Ṣa-bā, Kurdī, Būsah-lik, Sah-yāh, Huzām, Musta'ār, Tshahār-gāh* (*Chahār-gāh*).

Popular *maqāmāt* of Iraq-Kurdistan:

Auj: $\overset{\flat}{B}$ C D E♭ F G A $\overset{\flat}{B}$

Awahār: C D E♭ F G $\overset{\flat}{A}$ $\overset{\flat}{B}$ c

Dasht: G $\overset{\flat}{A}$ B c d e♭ f g

Ḥijāz kār Kurd: C D♭ E♭ F G A♭ B♭ c

Kurdi: G $\overset{\flat}{A}$ B♭ c d e f g

Lāmi: G A♭ B♭ c d♭ e♭ f g

Nahawānd: C D E♭ F G A B c / c B (B♭). . . .

Rast: C D $\overset{\flat}{E}$ F G A $\overset{\flat}{B}$ c

Lit.: no. 121.

Maqām Delkashe (Arabia). See *Sūz-nāk.*

Maqāṭi' (Arabia). Rests; Pauses.

Maqrūn (*Mijwiz*) (Islamic North Africa). Double reed pipe.
Lit.: no. 78.

Mār (Ancient Persia). Simple oboe type.
Lit.: no. 78.

Marābba (*Murabba*) (Arabia). "Quadrangle." A *rebāb* with one string. Both sides of the flat body are covered with skin.
Lit.: no. 255.

Maradika (Moluccas; Sula Isl.). Bamboo tube zither.
Lit.: no. 156.

Marae (New Zealand—Maori). Literally, "village square." Calls of welcome or farewell shouted or partly sung, performed by women. Cf. *Karanga*; *Powhiri*; *Poroporoaki.*
Lit.: no. 195.

Marakatabhūṣaṇi (South India). *Janya rāga* of the 38th *mēḷa* (*Jalārṇava*).
Tone material:

C E♭♭ F♯ G A♭ B♭ c

c B♭ A♭ G F♯ E♭♭ C

Lit.: no. 139.

Marāladhvani (South India). *Janya rāga* of the 2nd *mēḷa* (*Ratnangi*).
Tone material:
C E♭♭ F G A♭ B♭ c
c B♭ A♭ G F E♭♭ C
Lit.: no. 139.

Marālagāmini (South India). *Janya rāga* of the 9th *mēḷa* (*Dhēnuka*).
Tone material:
C D♭ E♭ F B c
c B F E♭ D♭ C
Lit.: no. 139.

Māranārāyaṇī (South India). *Janya rāga* of the 50th *mēḷa* (*Nāmanārāyaṇī*).
Tone material:
C E D♭ E F♯ G A♭ c
c A♭ G F♯ E D♭ C
Lit.: no. 139.

Marapo (South Africa—Chwana). Rattle made of bones. Two bones (usually from cattle) are held in one hand and clicked against each other. The Zulus call this type of rattle *amatambo*.
Lit.: no. 151.

Māraranjanī (South India). (1) The 25th *mēḷa*:
C D E F G A♭ B♭♭ c
(2) As *rāga*: the same tone material is used. Veṅkaṭamakhin (17th century) called this *rāga Śarāvati*.
Lit.: no. 139.

Marawat (Ethiopia). Church bells.
Lit.: no. 102.

Marāwe (Syria; Armenia). A group of small bells attached to a metal (often silver) disc which is carried about on a stick. The instrument is used by Kopts, Syrian, and Armenian Christians.
Lit.: no. 255.

Marbāb (Moluccas). Term for *rebāb*.
Lit.: nos. 131, 254.

Mardalā (*Marddalā*; *Madalā*) (South India). A drum with two heads. Its clay corpus has the appearance of two truncated cones joined at their wide bases. The term is also used as synonym for *mṛdanga*.
Lit.: no. 254.

Mardd (Coptic). Responsorial of sacred singing.

Marddalā (India). See *Mardalā*.

Mārgadēśika (South India). *Janya rāga* of the 15th *mēḷa* (*Māyāmāḷavagauḷa*).
Tone material:
C D♭ E (F) G A♭ c
c A♭ G E D♭ C
Lit.: no. 139.

Mārgadēśika (South India). *Janya rāga* of the 15th *mēḷa* (*Māyāmāḷavagauḷa*).
Tone material:
C D♭ E G A♭ c
c A♭ F G E D♭ C
Lit.: no. 139.

Mārgahindōḷa (South India). *Janya rāga* of the 20th *mēḷa* (*Naṭabhairavī*).
Tone material:
C D E F G A B♭ c (E and A in ascent)
c B♭ A♭ (G) F E♭ C (A♭ and E♭ in descent)
Lit.: no. 139.

Mārgahindōḷa (South India). *Janya rāga* of the 22nd *mēḷa* (*Kharaharapriyā*).
Tone material:
C D E♭ F G A B♭ c
c B♭ A F E♭ C
Lit.: no. 139.

Mārga (Ancient India). See *Tāla* (I).

Marghūla (Islamic North Africa). See *Mukassarah*.

Mārgī (India). The fifth of the seven ancient *mūrchhanās* derived from the *ma-grāma*. See *mūrchhanās*.
Lit.: no. 86.

Marīchika (South India). *Janya rāga* of the 13th *mēḷa* (*Gāyakapriya*).
Tone material:
C E F G A♭ B♭♭ c
c B♭♭ A♭ G F E C
Lit.: no. 139.

Marigata (Japan). See *Koto* parts.

Marimba (Africa). African xylophone. Below each wooden slab is placed a resonator calabash. The instrument can be found in West Africa, South Cameroons, Congo, Zambezi District, and in the North Transvaal. Cf. *Balak*; *Balangi*; *Budimba*; *Chinditi*; *Izambilo*; *Kas*; *Madimba*; *Madinda*; *Mbila*; *Mihambi*; *Silimba*.
Lit.: no. 255.

Maringa (Congo—Azande). *Sansa* or harp.
Lit.: no. 176.

Mariri (Indonesia; Aru Isl.). Term for *Jurusian*.

Mari-uta (Japan). Song of girls playing ball; songs sung during work and work games.
Lit.: no. 250.

Mārjanī (India). Term for the 13th *śruti*. The corresponding note-name is *pa*. Cf. *Śruti*.
Lit.: no. 86.

Maromena (Malagasy Republic). See *Beabobo*.

Maromogny (Malagasy Republic). Side-blown ritual shell horn.
Lit.: no. 251.

Maroto (Congo—Mamvu; Mambutu). Friction drum played for ritual dances. It is made of a cylinder of sticks over which a skin is stretched. Women are not permitted to see this instrument. Cf. *Najoroto*; *Akunde*.
Lit.: no. 184.

Marovany (Malagasy Republic). See *Valiha*.

Marsia (North India). Urdu term indicating songs about saints who had been killed in religious fights.

Mārtāndapriya (South India). See *Māruvabaṅgaḷa*.

Marthiya (Arabia). Pre-Islamic term for lament; mourning songs.

Māru (South India). See *Māruva*.

Māru-behag (North India). A rare, obscure *rāga*.
Tone material:
C (D) E (F) F♯ G (A) B c
c B A G F♯ (F) E D C
Lit.: no. 138.

Māruva (South India). *Janya rāga* of the 15th *mēḷa* (*Māyāmāḷavagauḷa*).
Tone material:
C E F G A♭ B A♭ G c
c B A♭ G F E D♭ C
(c B A♭ G F A♭ F G F E D♭ C)
Lit.: no. 139.

Māruva (*Māru*) (South India). *Janya rāga* of the 51st *mēḷa* (*Kāmavardhanī*).
Tone material:
C D♭ E F♯ A♭ B c
c B A♭ F♯ E D♭ C
Lit.: no. 139.

Māruvabaṅgaḷa (*Mārtāndapriya*) (South India). *Janya rāga* of the 39th *mēḷa* (*Jhālavarāḷi*).
Tone material:
C G F♯ G A♭ B c
c B A♭ G F♯ E♭♭ D♭ C
Lit.: no. 139.

Māruvachandrikā (South India). *Janya rāga* of the 38th *mēḷa* (*Jalārṇava*).
Tone material:
C D♭ E♭♭ F♯ G A♭ B♭
B♭ A♭ G F♯ E♭♭ D♭ E♭♭ C
This *rāga* has *niṣādāntya* character.
Lit.: no. 139.

Māruvadēśi (South India). *Janya rāga* of the 48th *mēḷa* (*Divyamaṇī*).

Tone material:
C D♭ E♭ F♯ G c
c G A♯ B G F♯ E♭ D♭ C
Lit.: no. 139.

Māruvadēśika (South India). *Janya rāga* of the 11th *mēḷa* (*Kokilapriya*).
Tone material:
C E♭ F G A G B c
c B A G F G F E♭ D♭ C
Lit.: no. 139.

Māruvadhanyāsi (South India). *Janya rāga* of the 22nd *mēḷa* (*Kharaharapriyā*).
Tone material (one form):
C E♭ F G A B♭ A G F G B♭ c
c B♭ A G F A (G) F E♭ (D E♭) C
Probably also:
C E♭ F G A c
c B♭ A G F E♭ D C
Lit.: no. 139.

Māruvagauḷa (South India). *Janya rāga* of the 43rd *mēḷa* (*Gavāmbōdhi*).
Tone material:
C D♭ E♭ G F♯ A♭ B♭♭ c
c B♭♭ A♭ G F♯ E♭ D♭ C
Lit.: no. 139.

Māruvagauri (South India). *Janya rāga* of the 46th *mēḷa* (*Ṣaḍvidhamārgiṇī*).
Tone material:
C E♭ D♭ E♭ F♯ G A B♯ c
(c) A G F♯ D♭ C *B♭*
Lit.: no. 139.

Māruvakannaḍa (South India). *Janya rāga* of the 35th *mēḷa* (*Śūlinī*).
Tone material:
C D♯ F E F G B c
c B G F D♯ E D♯ C
Lit.: no. 139.

Māruvanārāyaṇi (South India). *Janya rāga* of the 47th *mēḷa* (*Suvarṇāṅgī*).
Tone material:
C D♭ E♭ F♯ G A c
c A B G F♯ D♭ E♭ C
Lit.: no. 139.

Māruvavasantam (South India). *Janya rāga* of the 45th *mēḷa* (*Śubhapantuvarālī*).
Tone material:
C F♯ E♭ F♯ G A♭ B c
c B G A♭ F♯ E♭ D♭ C
Lit.: no. 139.

Marva (*Marava*) (North India). *Thāta* and *rāga*. As *rāga* its tone material is:
(C) D♭ E F♯ A B (c)
c (B) A F♯ G D♭ C; *Vādis*: D♭, A♭ [(♭) (♭)]
Lit.: no. 138.

Mārvāri dō-tāra (India). A two-stringed instrument of the Marwaris. Both strings produce the same note.
Lit.: no. 261.

Marvas (*Marwas*) (Sumatra). Small drum with two heads. Cf. *Ketipung* (Java).
Lit.: nos. 162, 164.

Marva thāta (North India). See *Thātas*.
Lit.: no. 138.

Marwas (Sumatra). See *Marvas*.

Maśak (*Mośuk*) (India). Hindusthani term for *nagabaddha*.

Masaka (Congo). Rattle consisting of a calabash (fitted into a basket) and filled with coconut shells. Cf. *Kitsatsa*.
Lit.: no. 255.

Masaka titti (India). Simple bagpipe that produces one drone note. The player who is also the story teller blows air into the bag until it is filled. Then he sings the story while he allows the bag to slowly empty and produce the drone note. When the bag is empty he begins again, first to blow into the bag and then to sing the story.
Lit.: no. 261.

Masake (Belgian Congo). See *Masaka*.

Maseke (*Masake*) (Belgian Congo—Bangala). Footed drum made of a wooden tube; its top is covered with iguana skin.
Lit.: no. 33.

Masenqo (Ethiopia). Small spike fiddle with one string; a minstrel instrument.

Mashak (India). The Hindusthani term for skin bag. A mouth-blown bagpipe. Its single chanter usually has seven finger holes. The Tamil term for the instrument is *śruti.* Cf. *Śruti upāṅga*; *Nāgabaddha.* See also *Moshuk.*
Lit.: nos. 15, 262.

Mashar (Turkey). Large frame drum. The instrument has no jingles in its frame.

Mashirkya (Sahara; Sudan—Hausa). String instrument.
Lit.: no. 255.

Ma shuddha (North India). F-natural, if *sa* is assumed to be C.
Lit.: no. 136.

Mashq (Pakistan). Bagpipe with two reed pipes.

Mashura (Egypt). "Enchanted." A double clarinet strongly resembling the *zummāra.* In the *zummāra* the reed is directed toward the front opening of the tube, while in the *mashura* it faces the opposite direction. The instrument has four finger holes.
Lit.: nos. 103, 255.

Masinko (Ethiopia). Fiddle with one string. It has a wooden body covered with goatskin.
Lit.: no. 218.

Mas kumambang (Java). One of the meters of *Tembang machapat.* See *Machapat.*

Masonquo (Ethiopia). A lyre with a bowl-shaped body and six strings. In Ethiopia it is believed to have been the harp of King David (called *kirar* or *kidrar* in Shoa Province). Cf. *Kinnor.*
Lit.: no. 38.

Massaneqo (Ethiopia). A popular type of a (bowed) *rebāb* with one string. Its body has the form of a square box. The Galla term for this instrument is *timbo.*
Lit.: no. 102.

Masseri (Celebes). See *Messeri.*

Massunda (South Congo). Music bow. The string is made to vibrate when scraped with the jagged stick of the bow.
Lit.: no. 280.

Mat.t (*Ma'*; *Mait*; *Met*) (Ancient Egypt). Common term for flutes and reed instruments. The long cane or metal flute was vertically-blown and had 2-6 finger holes. The oboes were shorter and appeared always in pairs. One tube was the drone pipe, the other produced the melody. The number of finger holes on the oboes was variable. The later name of this instrument is the Persian term *nāy.* In North Africa (western part) it is *qaṣaba* (*quaṣṣāba*).
Lit.: nos. 100, 250.

Matalam (South India). Tamil term for *mādalā* (*mardala*).
Lit.: no. 254.

Matali (Uganda). Frame drum.
Lit.: no. 302.

Mata titiram (Bali). "Wood-dove's eye." A notational symbol in the form of a circle. It indicates the final gong sound produced at the end of a phrase.
Lit.: no. 197.

Maṭaḷam (South India). See *Mādalā.*

Mataṅgagāmini (South India). *Janya rāga* of the 10th *mēḷa* (*Nāṭakapriya*).
Tone material:
C E♭ F G A B♭ c
c B♭ A G F E♭ C
Lit.: no. 139.

Mat chieng (Vietnam; Annam). The flat copper surface-part of the *chieng* (gong).
Lit.: no. 255.

Mathlath (Arabia). See *Matlat.*

Mathnā (Arabia). See *Maṭnā.* Cf. *'Ud.*

Mathlo (*Makkow*) (South Africa—Chwana). Leg rattles used by male dancers.
Lit.: no. 151.

Mathotse (North Transvaal). Rattle. Cf. *Njele.*
Lit.: no. 151.

Ma-t'i-ku (China). See *Pai-p'i-ku.*

Ma tivra (North India). Scale degree. The note *ma* being raised by a semitone; it represents the Western note F♯ if *sa* is assumed to be C. Cf. *Ma shuddha.*
Lit.: no. 136.

Maṭlat (*Mathlat*) (Arabia). "The third"—the third highest (or second-lowest) string pair of the *'ud.*

Maṭnā (*Mathna*) (Arabia). The second highest string pair of the *'ud.*

Mātrā (*Hrasva*) (North India). The basic metrical unit, usually interpreted as the Western quarter note. The South Indian equivalent is the *laghu.* See *Akshara.*
Lit.: no. 136.

Matsarīkrita (India). The fifth of the seven ancient *mūrchhanās*, derived from the *sa-grāma.*
Lit.: no. 86.

Matsumushi (Japan). "Pine insect." Small gongs or bells used in *kabuki* off-stage. See *Hitotsu-gane.*
Lit.: no. 185.

Matsuri (Japan). See *O-matsuri* (festivals to celebrate the arrival of seasons).

Matsuri bayashi (Japan). Shinto folk-festival instrumental ensemble and music. Cf. *Hayashi.*
Lit.: no. 215.

Mattakāsini (South India). *Janya rāga* of the 27th *mēḷa* (*Sarasāṅgī*).
Tone material:
C D E A♭ B c
c B A♭ E D C
Lit.: no. 139.

Mattakōkila (South India). Rare and vaguely defined *janya rāga* of the 28th *mēḷa* (*Harikāmbhōji*).
Tone material:
C D A G B♭
A G C D C B♭ C
Lit.: no. 139.

Matuli (Tanzania—Pangwe). Dance. The participants form a circle surrounding the accompanying drums.

Matulika (South India). *Janya rāga* of the 26th *mēḷa* (*Chārukeśī*).
Tone material:
C D F G A♭ B♭ c
c B♭ A♭ G F D C
Lit.: no. 139.

Matulika (South India). *Janya rāga* of the 27th *mēḷa* (*Sarasāṅgī*).
Tone material:
C D E F B c
c B F E D C
Lit.: no. 139.

Matutu (Congo—Bakongo). Funeral drum.
Lit.: no. 26.

Maṭya (South India). Cf. *Tāla.*

Maulawīya (Turkey). The oldest Dervish ceremony (13th century) consisting of 13 movements:

1. *Na'at sherīf*	(Praise of the Prophet)
2. *Pīshrev*	("Overture")
3. *Salām-i awwal*	(First salutation)
4. *Salām-i thani*	(Second salutation)
5. *Salām-i thālith*	(Third salutation)
6. *Tarannum sāz*	(instrumental item)
7.-10.	(instrumental items)

11. *Salām-i rābi'*	(Fourth salutation)
12. *Ṣong pīshrev*	(Second overture)
13. *Ṣong tarannum*	(final instrumental item)

Lit.: no. 79.

Ma'ulu'ulu (Polynesia; Samoa). Dance that interprets a poem. Cf. *Lakalaka.*

Maumwakidi (Rhodesia—Ila). See *Ipopa.*

Maung (Burma). Large gong, vertically suspended.

Maung saing (Burma). Gong chimes. Twelve gongs suspended in three frames: three gongs in one frame, four medium-sized gongs in a second, five small ones in a third. *Maung saing* can also consist of 18-19 small gongs arranged in five rows: 3, 3, 4, 3, 5 (6).
Lit.: no. 303.

Mauno (New Guinea). Gong.

Mauṣul (Egypt). Wind instruments.

Mauwal (*Dōr*; *Ad-dōr*) (Egypt). Monologue and dialogue, partly chanted in free rhythm.
Lit.: no. 100.

Mauwashahat (Egypt). Flowing song, rhythmically free.
Lit.: no. 100.

Mauzūn (Arabia). Metrical poetry.

Mavonda (Congo). See *Makwanga.*

Mawāda'ed-desātin (Arabia). Frets.
Lit.: no. 255.

Mawāl (Arabia; Kurdistan). Song in free rhythm. See *Muwāl.*

Mawālī (Arabia). Instrumental musicians; usually freedmen of foreign origin (e.g., Iran).

Māwāloti (*Lohāti*) (India). See *Nissan.*

Mawāše'et (Ethiopia). Coptic liturgical hymn sung at funerals.

Mawlum (Northeast Thailand). A traditional singer; his song.
Lit.: no. 203.

Mawlum ching choo (Northeast Thailand). A form of *mawlum glawn* sung by two men and one woman.
Lit.: no. 203.

Mawlum glawn (Northeast Thailand). A common form of *mawlum* sung by one man and one woman.
Lit.: no. 203.

Mawlum gup gaep (Northeast Thailand). A *mawlum* sung by one person who accompanies himself with two pairs of *hup gaep.*
Lit.: no. 203.

Mawlum jot (Northeast Thailand). An old form of *mawlum glawn* in which two singers compete by asking each other questions.
Lit.: no. 203.

Mawlum lüang (Northeast Thailand). A form of *mawlum pün* in which the singer acts out the story by changing his costume.
Lit.: no. 203.

Mawlum moo (Northeast Thailand). Serious theater.
Lit.: no. 203.

Mawlum pee fah (Northeast Thailand). A ceremony in which old women perform magic by singing and dancing in order to help a person who had been made sick by evil spirits.
Lit.: no. 203.

Mawlum plün (Northeast Thailand). A burlesque form of theater.
Lit.: no. 203.

Mawlum pün (Northeast Thailand). The chanting of epic-length stories.
Lit.: no. 203.

Mavonda (Congo). See *Makwanga.*

Māyāh (Middle East; Modern Tunisia). *Maqām.* Tone material:

Middle East: $\overset{+}{E}$♭ F G A B♭ c d $\overset{+}{e}$♭

Modern Tunisia: *A* $\overset{+}{B}$♭ C D $\overset{+}{E}$♭ F G A B♭ B c

Lit.: no. 64.

Māyāmāḷavagauḍa (South India). See *Māyām-āḷavagauḷa.*

Māyāmāḷavagauḷa (South India). (1) The 15th *mēḷa*, frequently used and very popular. It resembles closely the North Indian *rāga Bhairav.* Tone material:

C D♭ E F G A♭ B c

(2) As *rāga* the same scale as that of the 15th *mēḷa* is employed. (3) Also called *Mālavagauḷa* (the 15th *asampūrṇa mēḷa*).
Lit.: no. 139.

Māyāpratīpam (South India). *Janya rāga* of the 22nd *mēḷa (Kharaharapriyā).*
Tone material:

C F E♭ F G A B♭ c

c A G F E♭ D C

Lit.: no. 139.

Māyātaraṅgiṇi (South India). *Janya rāga* of the 28th *mēḷa (Harikāmbhōji).*
Tone material:

C D F E F G F B♭ c

c B♭ A G F E D C

Lit.: no. 139.

Māyāvinōdini (South India). *Janya rāga* of the 34th *mēḷa (Vāgadhīśvarī).*
Tone material:

C D♯ E A B♭ c

c B♭ A E D♯ C

Lit.: no. 139.

Ma'yong (Malaysia). Drama that includes beside spoken prose, stylized dancing, choral and solo singing.

Mayu (South Australia). Aboriginal (indefinite) term for rhythm and melody.

Mayūradhvani (South India). *Janya rāga* of the 45th *mēḷa (Śubhapantuvarāḷī).*
Tone material:

C D♭ F♯ G A♭ B c

c B A♭ F♯ E♭ D♭ C

Lit.: no. 528.

Mayūrī (North India). Long-necked lute, generally bowed. It has the form of an *esrar*; the body and neck have the shape of a peacock (the Sanskrit word *mayura* means "peacock"). See also *Tāyuś*; *Ṭāūs.* Cf. *Bālasarasvati.*

Mazhar (Egypt; Turkey; Arabia). Large frame drum with one head and without snare strings. In its frame are inserted rattle rings instead of jingling discs. Cf. *Mi'zafa.*
Lit.: no. 250.

Mazim (Morocco; Algeria; Tunisia). Rhythmic mode.

Mazin (Assam – Naga). A bamboo jew's harp.
Lit.: no. 252.

Mazmūm (*Mezmūm*) (Modern Tunisia). *Maqām.*
Tone material:

C D $\overset{+}{E}$♭ F G A B♭ c d

Lit.: no. 64.

Mazoko (Lower Congo). See *Nzau.*

Mbabi (Congo – Abangba). Drum.
Lit.: no. 26.

Mba'e (Congo). See *Mbe(i).*

M'bagga (Congo – Bobango). Harp.
Lit.: no. 33.

Mbamba nsia (Congo – Bembe). Antelope horn that produces a whistling sound.
Lit.: no. 280.

Mbambi (Congo – Kikongo). Whistle or flute.
Lit.: no. 280.

Mbana (Congo – Mangbetu). Side-blown antelope horn. Also called *mbema.*
Lit.: no. 21.

Mbaṅ-akum (French Congo – Fan). Mirliton in the form of a wooden box.
Lit.: no. 255.

Mbandu (Congo – Kikongo). Small drum. The Angola term is *mbande* (drum; dance).

Mbanju (North Congo). Psaltery.
Lit.: no. 255.

Mbarang (Java). Performance.

Mbaru genḍang (Flores – Manggaray). The drumhouse where drums are stored. These drums are used in order to obtain the approval and goodwill of the ancestors.
Lit.: no. 166.

Mbasa (Angola). Vertical flute with conical bore, without any finger holes.
Lit.: nos. 21, 280.

Mbasa (Congo – Banziri). Xylophone.
Lit.: no. 280.

oMbeda (Southwest Africa – Zulu; Dwakwanyama). Mutilated form of the word "trumpet."
Lit.: no. 255.

Mbe(i) (*Mba'e*) (New Guinea; former Kaiser Wilhelmsland). A bamboo flute; blown horizontally.
Lit.: no. 255.

Mbe(i) (West Africa – Fan). Drum with one head. *Mbejn* (Gabon), vertical drum with a conically-shaped body.

Mbeka (Flores). Lute. Also called *sato.* See *Robeka.*

Mbema (Congo). See *Mbana.*

Mbeta (Tanzania – Luguru). Flute ensemble. Each flute is differently tuned and produces only one note.
Lit.: no. 218.

Mbichi (Congo – Bangala). Term for *sansa.*

Mbila (*Mbira*) (Congo – Basongo; Senegal; South Africa; Rhodesia – Venda Tshopi; Ethiopa – Karanga). Term for xylophone. The Tshopi call the instrument also *muhambi*, and in Rhodesia the term *deze* can be used. Cf. *Imbila*; *Dipela*; *Tshikhulu.*
Lit.: no. 151.

Mbili (Gambia; Ghana – Mandingo). Wooden drum.
Lit.: no. 95.

Mbilip (Senegal – Wolof). Flute.
Lit.: no. 255.

'Mbilta (Ethiopia). Vertically-blown metal or wooden flute without any finger holes, played in sets of three *mbiltas.*
Lit.: no. 38.

Mbindu (Lower Congo). A narrow double-headed drum with a conically-shaped body. Cf. *Bindi.*
Lit.: no. 280.

Mbira (South Africa – Vakaranga'Makalaka'). *Sansa.* An idiophone with tuned wooden or metal tongues attached to a resonator box. Cf. *Mbila.*
Lit.: nos. 218, 255.

Mbira dzavadzimu (Africa; Rhodesia – Shona). *Mbira* of the ancestral spirits.
Lit.: no. 22.

Mbi ta ni tanga (Fiji Isl.). Bamboo nose flute with eight finger holes.
Lit.: no. 255.

Mbiu (East Africa – Swahili). See *Baragumu.*

Mbizi (East Tanganyika—Zaramo). Small wooden clapper.
Lit.: no. 255.

Mbobila (West Africa). Term for *sansa.*
Lit.: no. 280.

Mbocho (French Congo). Bell.

Mbombu (*Pivora*) (Central Africa—Bobati). Large bell without a clapper, struck from the outside.
Lit.: no. 184.

Mbom-mvet (Cameroon). A *mvet* player.

Mbonda (Congo—Mbole; Bosaka; Gombe; Bahutu). Large drum. Cf. *Ta ngo.*
Lit.: no. 26.

Mbonga (Central Africa). Metal bell.
Lit.: no. 21.

Mbott (Kampuchea). Mouth organ consisting of a variable number of bamboo pipes with free reeds and a gourd serving as a wind chamber. Cf. *Sheng.*
Lit.: no. 254.

Mbrunau (Admirality Isl.—Mouk). Nose flute.
Lit.: no. 313.

Mbudikidi (West Africa). Wooden slit-drum.
Lit.: no. 280.

Mbugi (Kenya—Washambala). Iron anklet rattle worn by male dancers.
Lit.: no. 130.

Mbuki (Congo—Balunda; Batshoko). Small drum beaten by sorcerers.
Lit.: no. 26.

Mbutu (Uganda—Ganda). A mushroom-shaped drum.
Lit.: no. 33.

Mbutu (Nigeria—Efik). *Sansa.* Its tongues are made of cane.
Lit.: no. 33.

Mebachi (Japan). The left-side beat and drumstick ("female beat"), softly performed on the *taiko.* Cf. *Obachi*; *Morobachi.*
Lit.: no. 255.

Mechabaṅgāḷa (South India). *Janya rāga* of the 44th *mēḷa* (*Bhāvapriyā*).
Tone material:
C D♭ E♭ F♯ G B♭ c
c A♭ G F♯ E♭ D♭ C
Lit.: no. 139.

Mēchabauḷi (South India). *Janya rāga* of the 15th *mēḷa* (*Māyāmāḷavagauḷa*).
Tone material:
C D♭ E G A♭ c
c B A♭ G F E D♭ C
Lit.: no. 139.

Mēchagāndhāri (South India). *Janya rāga* of the 34th *mēḷa* (*Vāgadhīśvarī*).
Tone material:
C D♯ E F G A B♭ c
c B♭ A B♭ G F E D♯ C
Lit.: no. 139.

Mēchakalyāṇī (*Kalyāṇī*) (South India). The 65th *mēḷa*:
C D E F♯ G A B c
As *rāga*: Veṅkaṭamakhin (17th century) calls it *Śantakalyāṇī.*
Lit.: no. 139.

Mēchakāmbhōji (South India). *Janya rāga* of the 43rd *mēḷa* (*Gavāmbōdhi*).
Tone material:
C D♭ E♭ F♯ A♭ B♭♭ c
c B♭♭ G A♭ F♯ E♭ D♭ C
Lit.: no. 139.

Mēchakaṅgi (South India). *Janya rāga* of the 53rd *mēḷa* (*Gamanaśrama*).
Tone material:
C D♭ E F♯ G A B c
c B G A G F♯ E D♭ C
Lit.: no. 139.

Mēchakannaḍa (South India). *Janya rāga* of the 50th *mēḷa* (*Nāmanārāyaṇī*).
Tone material:
C F♯ G A♭ B♭ c
c B♭ A♭ G F♯ E C
Lit.: no. 139.

Mēchamanōharī (South India). *Janya rāga* of the 45th *mēḷa* (*Śubhapantuvarālī*).
Tone material:
C E♭ F♯ G A♭ G B c
c B A♭ F♯ E♭ D♭ C
Lit.: no. 139.

Mēchasāvēri (South India). *Janya rāga* of the 42nd *mēḷa* (*Raghupriyā*).
Tone material:
C D♭ F♯ G B c
c B G F♯ E♭♭ D♭ C
Lit.: no. 139.

Mecharu (Bali). See *Sangkah.*

Medet (Bali). See *Rebāb.*

Medilen ārā (*Madilan*) (Iran). Fiddle with two necks (invented in 1883 by Mirza Galam Husseyn).
Lit.: no. 255.

Medzang (Gabon—Pahouin; Bakele). Xylophone with seven slabs. Cf. *Menzan*; *Menzi.*
Lit.: no. 33.

Me'etu'upaki (Polynesia; Tonga). Dance of standing men.

Megaṅ me bongo (French Congo). A music-stick used as a children's toy.
Lit.: no. 255.

Megatruh (*Duduk wuluh*) (Java). One of the meters of *tembang machapat.* See *Machapat.*
Lit.: no. 163.

Megh (North India). See *Megh-mallār.*

Mēgha (North India). Small friction drum. The player swings the drum around like a bull roarer, on a string which penetrates the drum membrane. In Orissa the instrument is called *dhurki.*
Lit.: no. 254.

Megh(a) (*Megha rāga*) (South India). *Janya rāga* of the 13th *mēḷa* (*Gāyakapriya*).
Tone material:
C D♭ F G B♭♭ (A♭ G)
c B♭♭ A♭ G F D♭ C
Lit.: no. 139.

Megh-mallār (*Megha-mallar*; *Megh*) (North India). *Rāga* that belongs to the *mallār* family and is ascribed to the *Kāfi thāta.* Three versions are in use:
(a) C D F G (B♭) B c
c B♭ G F D C
(b) C D F G (B♭) B c
c B♭ G F (E♭) D C
(c) C D F G (A) B c
c B♭ A G F D C; *Vādis*: C, F
Lit.: no. 138.

Mēgharāgam (*Mēgharañjani*) (South India). *Janya rāga* of the 13th *mēḷa* (*Gāyakapriya*).
Tone material:
C D♭ F G B♭♭ A♭ G c
c B♭♭ A♭ G F D♭ C
Lit.: no. 139.

Mēgharañjani (South India). *See Mēgharāgam.*

Mēgharañji (South India). *Janya rāga* of the 15th *mēḷa* (*Māyāmāḷavagauḷa*).
Tone material:
C D♭ E F B c
c B F E D♭ C
Lit.: no. 139.

Mēghrañjani (North India). *Rāga* ascribed to the *Bhairav thāta.*
Tone material:
[*B* C] D♭ E F (F♯) B c
c B (F♯) F E D♭ C; *Vādis*: F, C
Lit.: no. 138.

Megyuṅ (*Mi gyaun*; *Mingas*; *Patola*) (Burma). An antiquated zither which is plucked with an ivory plectrum. The instrument has three silk or gut or metal strings strung across 8-10 movable bridges. The body of the zither has the shape of a crocodile. Cf. *Takhe*; *Chak-he*. Lit.: no. 255.

Mehterhane (Turkey). Term for the imperial military band linked with Janissary music. The ensemble became obsolete in the final quarter of the 19th century. The band consisted of 54 players and employed the following rhythm instruments: four types of *zhil* (bells and cymbals), *saghāne* (jingle tree), *naqqāra* (a pair of small kettledrums), and *davul* (large drum). Lit.: no. 243.

Meijiwiz (*Mijwiz*) (Syria). Double shawm with a single reed and six holes in each pipe. Lit.: no. 255.

Mejra (India; Punjab). Term for *mandirā*.

Meke (Fiji Isl.). Popular traditional dance accompanied by singing, the *lali ni meke*, and stamping tubes. Lit.: no. 215.

Mekidung (Bali). The chanting of poems of the Middle Javanese period at sacred festivals. The *kidung* poems are structured in various modes which are characterized by the number of syllables (*guru wilangan*) and the last vowel of each line (*guru lagu*). For instance, the *sinom* mode (as shown in Lit. no. 265) is:

8	—	a
8	—	i
8	—	o
8	—	i
7	—	i
7	—	u
7	—	a
8	—	i
4	—	u
8	—	a

This mode indicates that the first line of the poem has 8 syllables and the final vowel of the line is "a." The second line, too, has 8 syllables and the final vowel is "i," and so forth.

The *kidung* were notated in palm-leaf books. The degrees of the notes were called:

ding (e.g., as Western note:)	E
dong gede	F
dang gede	G
deng	A
dung	B
dan tjenik	c
dong tjenik	d

Lit.: no. 265.

Mekku-pukku (Ancient Mesopotamia; Akkad). See *Ellag*. Lit.: no. 75.

Mek mulung (Malaysia). Instrumental ensemble. See *Makyong*.

Mēḷa (South India). Abbreviation of *mēḷakarta*, parent scale (the equivalent of *thāta* of North India). South Indian music theory distinguishes 72 *mēḷas* and to each of the *mēḷas* are ascribed subordinate *janya rāgas*. For further and detailed information see *Rāga* (South India).

Mēḷagam (South India). *Janya rāga* of the 37th *mēḷa* (*Sālaga*).
Tone material:

   C Db Ebb F# Ab Bbb c
   c Bbb Ab F# Ebb Db C
Lit.: no. 139.

Mēḷakarta (South India). See *Mēḷa*.

Mēḷāpaka (India). See *Ābhōga*.

Melappadaṃ (South India). Virtuoso drumming in *kathakali* performances. It accompanies songs from the *Gīta Gōvinda*. For examples see Lit. nos. 123, 139.

Mēḷa-rāga (South India). See *Mēḷakarta-rāga*. Cf. *Mēḷa*.

Melāwee (Egypt). The pegs of the *kemānjeh*, *qānūn*, *'ūd*.

Mele (Hawaii). (1) Chant, distinguished from song, called *mele oli*, not linked with dance. (2) Chant that serves as accompaniment of the *hula* dance, called *mele hula*.
Lit.: no. 215.

Mele hula (Hawaii). See *Mele*.

Mele oli (Hawaii). See *Mele*.

Melo (Flores—Ngada). (1) Bamboo stamping stick. (2) Dance performed by a single male who wears a mask of goat's hair in front of his eyes and holding a long bamboo stamping stick in his hand. The dance consists of tripping and hopping steps, to and fro, in fast rhythm, along a piece of bamboo which lies on the ground.
Lit.: no. 166.

Melog (West Java). Five-tone scales with the notes (in ascending order): *singgul*, *bem*, *panelu*, *kenong*, *barang*, *singgul leutik*. Lit. no. 163, p. 395 states that the *melog* vary to some degree but can be approximated to (roughly transcribed):

I		II		III		V		VI		I'
		+		+				+		
C	120	D♭	150	E♭	390	G	120	A♭	490	c

See *Surupan Melog*. A corresponding simple five- or six-tone scale is *nyorog*.

Melung (Flores). A joyful (secular) dance for men and women.
Lit.: no. 166.

Melwī (Arabia). The head peg of a *kemānjeh*. See *Malāwī*.
Lit.: no. 255.

Mempo (South Africa). Cf. *Motaba*.
Lit.: no. 151.

Mēn (singular form of *Minnīm*) (Israel). Hebrew term for sheep gut string.

Mena'anim (Ancient Israel). Rattles made of metal or bone.

Menari (Flores—Nage). Festive dance.
Lit.: no. 166.

Menari kuda (Flores—Nage District). Festive dance of the women.

Mendet (Bali). See *Rejang*.

Mendzen (Cameroon). Xylophone with gourd resonators.

Menghi (South India). See *Tavalaika*.

Menoreh (Java). A form of *wayang wong*; it consists of *jiḍor*, *terbang*, *kenḍang*, and *keprak*.
Lit.: no. 163.

Menur (Java). The top of the neck of the Javanese *rebāb*.
Lit.: no. 255.

Menza (Congo—Abandja). See *Manja*.

Menzaṅ (*Anzaṅ*) (French Congo—Fan). Marimba with 10 slabs tuned to approximately: *A B* C D E F G A B c.
Lit.: no. 255.

Menzi (Congo—Abandja). Xylophone with seven slabs. Cf. *Menzaṅ*; *Medzang*.
Lit.: no. 21.

Mepadu (Bali). "Competing." A festival competition of *gamelan gong kebyar* ensembles.
Lit.: no. 197.

Merdap (Sumatra—Batak). Term for *rebāb*.

Merewa (Ethiopia—Amhara). Struck sounding-stone or wooden slab.
Lit.: no. 218.

Meri-kari (Japan). In *shakuhachi* or *hichiriki* playing, tones are used which lie between the ones created by the full use of the finger holes. By partly covering the finger holes the player distinguishes three types of *meri* (low) and three of *kari* (high), whereby the differences are not semitonal but microtonal. Thus *meri-kari*, representing an unusual but traditional and characteristic feature of *gagaku*, consists first

of a deliberate slight lowering of a certain pitch, followed by a smooth upward glide passing through the original pitch toward a point slightly higher. This practice is considered to be of rare beauty.
Lit.: no. 185.

Meriyasu (Japan). Serious, quiet vocal interludes in *nagauta* music, having the character of short melancholy songs.
Lit.: no. 187.

Meromero (West Australia). Bull roarer used during the ceremony of puberty initiation.
Lit.: no. 255.

Merong (Java). The introductory section of a *genḍing*. Cf. *Gangsaran*; *Munggah*.
Lit.: no. 163.

Mershem (South India). Name of an ancient mode (mentioned in the *Shilappadikaram*).
Lit.: nos. 45.

Meshek (India). Cf. *Tubrī*; *Tiktirī*.
Lit.: no. 255.

Messel (Arabia). An erroneous interpretation of the Arabic term *mithl* ("the thing compared," "the same") led to the meaningless "messel system" which referred to third-tones and faulty measurements of intervals.
Lit.: no. 173.

Messeri (*Masseri*) (Celebes). Stomach dance.
Lit.: no. 259.

Met (Ancient Egypt). See *Mat*.

Metsang (Iran). *Tanbura* with two strings. Cf. *Tanbura*.
Lit.: no. 255.

Mettet (Indonesia; Madura). The fifth note of the *slendro* system (of Madura). Cf. *Slendro* (Java).

Meṭṭu (South India). Tamil and Telugu terms for frets on the *vīṇā*.
Lit.: no. 254.

Metziltayim (Ancient Israel). Pair of cymbals. Cf. *Tziltzelim*.

Mevada (North India). *Rāga* ascribed to the *Bilaval thāta*. It has a light character and is popular.
Tone material:
C D (E) F G A B c
c B A G F E D C; *Vādis*: F, C
Lit.: no. 138.

Mevlit (*Mevlut*) (Turkey). Liturgic melody. Its text deals with the birth of the Prophet.

Mevlut (Turkey). See *Mevlit*.

Mey (Turkey). Obscure short cone-shaped oboe with big reeds and often without any bell.
Lit.: no. 243.

Meyasu (Japan). Notational system used by the Tendai sect when notating *shōmyō*. *Meyasu*, "easy to the eyes," avoids the numerous annotations that occur in *karifu*. *Meyasu* is a mnemonic system and cannot be read without the singer's previous knowledge of the outline of the melody.
Lit.: nos. 47, 185.

Meyatva (Ancient India). "Measurableness." The determination of durations of syllables (*akṣara*).
Lit.: no. 292.

Meydan sazi (Turkey). A lute (*saz*) with 12 strings, played with a plectrum.
Lit.: no. 32.

Me-ze (Sumeria). An obscure instrument, probably a frame drum (or tambourine), not of Sumerian origin.
Lit.: nos. 87, 94.

Mfuhlulu (South Africa—Bavendaland). Term for *tshihoho*.
Lit.: no. 151.

Mganda (East Africa—Swahili). Conical drum with one head, used at festivals.
Lit.: no. 255.

Mghani (East Africa—Swahili). Professional singer.

Mgrin dbyangs (Tibet). "Throat singing." The term indicates a rough and throaty sound. The term represents also changes of pitch if the sound is prolonged.
Lit.: no. 143.

Mgur (*Mgur-ma*) (Tibet). Honorific term for *glu. Mgur* stands particularly for chant and hymn.
Lit.: no. 143.

Mgur, Mgur snyan-pa (*Gur-ma*) (Tibet). Pleasant voice; song. E.g., *mgur-bum*, the 100,000 songs (hymns) (*mgur*) of Milarepa.

Mhroktsaṅ (Burma). Drum.
Lit.: no. 255.

Mhutthokara (*Mhutthotantshatamyo*) (Burma). Horn.
Lit.: no. 255.

Miarawashi (Japan). The penultimate section of the *joruri* sequence.
Lit.: no. 187.

Miasobi (*Gyoyū*) (Japan). Groups of amateur musicians who performed during the Heian period (A.D. 794-1192). Their music consisted of Chinese pieces and newly created vocal items.
Lit.: no. 185.

Michigaku (Japan). See *Gagaku*.

Michiyuki (Japan). A composition that is used as entrance music for the dancer in *jōruri*, *kabuki*, *nagauta*, and *noh*. Cf. *Ha*; *Noh*.
Lit.: no. 185.

Mididi (West Congo; Eastern Kasai Province). Long drum.
Lit.: no. 201.

Midimu (Tanzania—Makua). Dancers who wear face masks. Cf. *Isingyago*.

Midimu ya muha (Tanzania—Makua). Dancers who wear small face masks, usually worn over the foreheads. Cf. *Isinyago*.

Midjil (*Mijil*) (Java). One of the poetic meters of *tembang machapat*, generally occurring in love songs. See *Machapat*.
Lit.: no. 163.

Miḍrāb (*Midhrāb*; *Mizrāb*) (Arabia; North India). Plectrum used in *'ūd* playing. Cf. also *Rise* (*risheh*), a piece of a vulture's feather.
Lit.: no. 255.

Mie (Japan). The final scene in the *dangire* set up by the *kabuki* dancers. The music for the scene is played by all instruments. When the players start Japanese audiences, knowing this feature, begin applauding. A similar end section appears in *nagauta*.
Lit.: no. 185.

Mié (Liberia). Sound of a singer or a choir.

Mien (China—M 4497). "Face." The side of the *pang-tzu* (*pu-yü*) where two slits are cut into the wooden blocks.
Lit.: no. 129.

Mieu nhac (Vietnam). Music of the palace and temple. Court music.

Mi-gyauṅ (Burma). "Alligator." A zither with three wire or gut strings. The body resembles the shape of a crocodile. Cf. *Chakay*; *Megyuṅ*.
Lit.: no. 254.

Mihambi (Africa). See *Marimba*.

Mihtar dūduyī (Turkey). Imperial court flute (recorder) employed in the palace household musical exercises.
Lit.: no. 81.

Mijil (*Midjil*) (Java). One of the meters of the *Tembang machapat*. See *Machapat*.
Lit.: no. 163.

Mijue-mijue (Sumatra). Zither. See *Ketjapi*; *Biola.*
Lit.: no. 163.

Mijwiz (Middle East). See *Maqrūn*; *Mujwiz.*
Lit.: no. 78.

Mi-kagura (Japan). Music and dance performed in the Shinto shrine and imperial palace by the *mikomai*, female temple dancers. See *Kagura.*
Lit.: no. 185.

Mike (Solomon Isl.). Jew's harp made of bamboo.
Lit.: no. 255.

Miko (Uganda—Kiganda). The transposing of a melody on a five-tone xylophone into the five available modes.
Lit.: no. 218.

Mikomai (Japan). Ancient sacred dances performed by women at Shinto shrines of Kyoto, Nara, and Ise. Each dancer carries a *suzu.*
Lit.: nos. 53, 185.

Milango (Tanzania—Sukuma). See *Lugaya.*

Milha (Arabia; Persia). Musical instrument.
Lit.: no. 255.

Min-ak (Korea). Folk music. Songs about home, simple love songs, songs about the moon, spring, the beloved, etc.
Lit.: no. 52.

Minalōchana (South India). *Janya rāga* of the 5th *mēḷa* (*Manōrañjanī*).
Tone material:
C D♭ E♭♭ F G A B G c
c B A F E♭♭ D♭ C
Lit.: no. 139.

Mīna sāraṅgī (India; Bengal). "Fish *sāraṅgī.*" A fiddle resembling an *esrār* made of a long calabash.
Lit.: no. 248.

Mīnḍ (*Ghasīṭ*) (India). Glide; an uninterrupted ascent or descent from one note to another.

Mindachna pata (Southeast India—Jhoria Muria Gond tribe). *Gotul* dance song. Cf. *Gotul pata.*
Lit.: no. 142.

Mingas (Burma). See *Megyun* (*Mi gyaun*).

Ming-chih (China—M 4524). See *Chien-tzu.*
Lit.: no. 136.

Minggah (Java). The high voice register.
Lit.: no. 163.

Minnīm (*Minīm*) (Israel). Hebrew term for sheep-gut-strings. Cf. *Mēn.*
Lit.: no. 255.

Minshin-gaku (Japan). Imported (also imitated) Chinese Ming (and Ch'ing) music; popular in Japan during the late 19th century.
Lit.: no. 136.

Min-teki (Japan). An ancient vertical flute with six finger holes.
Lit.: no. 255.

Minyō (Korea; also Japan). Folk songs.

Minzoku-geino (*Geino*) (Japan). All forms and types of folk theater and dance.
Lit.: no. 185.

Miohachigane (Japan). Cf. *Dōbachi.*

Mipil (Bali). The stretta-like closing section of a movement which concludes with a final phrase in the opening tempo.
Lit.: no. 197.

Mirabai-ki Mallār (North India). A *rāga* belonging to the *Mallār* family. It is ascribed to the *Kāfi thāta.* This *Mallār* of *Mirabai* consists of elements taken from the *rāgas* *Adana-Kanada* and *Mallār* passages.
Tone material:
C D E F G A B c
c B♭ A♭ G F E♭ D C
Lit.: no. 138.

Mirambura (Australia). A thick stick made of redwood.
Lit.: no. 255.

Mirdang (India). See *Mṛdaṅga* (*Mridanga*).

Mirh (Bengal). See *Mīnd.*

Miring (Java). Deviating; wrong.

Miritum (*Sabitum*) (Sumeria). Obscure musical instruments. The names imply instruments from Sabum and Ma'eri.
Lit.: no. 94.

Mir-sang (Iran; Afghanistan). Shell trumpet.
Lit.: no. 255.

Miskal (Turkey). Panpipes.

Misrā (Islamic North Africa). Also called *'ajiz.* Half a line of a verse; a section of *abyat.*
Lit.: no. 6.

Miśra (India). Cf. *Miśrita.*

Miśra jāti (South India). See *Tāla.*

Miśrita (*Miśra*) (India). See *Gamak(a).*

Mithqāl (Turkey). Panpipes. See *Mūsīqāl.*
Lit.: no. 81.

Mitrabhāviṇī (South India). *Janya rāga* of the 65th *mēḷa* (*Mēchakalyāṇī*).
Tone material:
C D E F♯ G A B c
c A G F♯ E D C
Lit.: no. 139.

Mitrakirani (South India). *Janya rāga* of the 15th *mēḷa* (*Māyāmāḷavagauḷa*).
Tone material:
C D♭ E F G A♭ B c
c A♭ G F E D♭ C
Lit.: no. 139.

Mitrarañjāni (South India). *Janya rāga* of the 25th *mēḷa* (*Mārarañjanī*).
Tone material:
C D E F G A♭ c
c B♭♭ A♭ G F E D C
Lit.: no. 139.

Mitsuji (Japan). A new pattern of accompaniment in *noh* music that creates a contrast by interrupting the preceding stereotyped form of accompaniment.
Lit.: no. 187.

Miṭṭu (South India). A single plucking motion on the *vīṇā.*

Mitu (India). Wire plectrum placed on fingers for playing the *vīṇā.*
Lit.: no. 215.

Mi-uta (Japan). "Third verse." See *Kumi.*

Miyan-ki Mallār (North India). *Rāga* belonging to the *Mallār* group, ascribed to the *Kāfi thāta.* Allegedly the *rāga* was created by Miyan Tansen, court musician of Akbar the Great.
Tone material:
C F D G B♭ A B c
c B♭ A B♭ G F G ^{F}E♭ ^{F}E♭ ^{F}E♭ F D C;
Vādis: C, F
Lit.: no. 138.

Miyan-ki Sarang (North India). A serious *rāga* ascribed to the *Sarang* family, subordinated to the *Kāfi thāta.* Allegedly the *rāga* was created by Tansen, court musicians of Akbar the Great.
Tone material:
C D F G A B♭ (B) c
c B♭ A G F D C; *Vādis*: D, C, or G
Lit.: no. 138.

Miyan-ki Tōdī (North India). *Rāga* ascribed to the *Tōdī thāta.* It is often stated that this *rāga* was created by Tansen, court musician of Akbar the Great. There are different opinions regarding the use of the note G in this *rāga.* Generally it is treated weakly or omitted in ascent (of

Miyan-ki Tōdī), but there are musicians who disagree and maintain that the note G can be used fully and that there is no difference between the *rāgas Tōdī* and *Miyan-ki Tōdī*.
Tone material:

    ♭   (♭)   +
C D♭ E♭ F♯ (G) A♭ B c

c B A♭ (G) F♯ E♭ D♭ C; *Vādis*: A♭, E♭
Lit.: no. 138.

Miyazono-bushi (Japan). See *Bungo-bushi*.

Mi'zaf(a) (*Mizhar*; *Mazhar*) (Arabia; Iran). (1) Kettle- or framedrum. (2) Ancient type of zither or harp allegedly with 5, 7, or 12 strings. Cf. *Ma'āzif* (plural of *mi'zaf*).
Lit.: nos. 76, 109.

Mizhar (*Mazhar*) (Old Arabia). Tambourine. Cf. *Mi'zafa*.
Lit.: nos. 76, 250.

Mizhavu (South India—Kerala). A vessel made of clay or copper, used only in sacred services (Koothu, the discourses of the Puranas and Koodiyattam, the presentation of Sanskrit dramas) in Hindu temples of Kerala. The neck of the vessel is covered with parchment and the instrument serves to produce percussion sounds.
Lit.: no. 236.

Mizmār (Arabia; Middle East). A popular oboe generally with 6-8 finger holes. The Persian term for this instrument is *ṣūrnāya*; the Algerian and Moroccan term is *ghaiṭa* (*ǧa'iṭa*); the Tunisian term is *zūqra*; the Egyptian terms are *aba* (from "hautbois," the large oboe) and *sibs* (the small oboe). Cf. *Zamr*; *Zummārah*.
Lit.: nos. 107, 250, 255.

Mizmār al-muthannā (Arabia). Double *mizmar*.
Lit.: no. 78.

Mizmār al-muzawwaj (Arabia). Double *mizmar*.

Mizmār baladi (Egypt). Folk oboe with 10 finger holes.

Mizmār dūduyī (Turkey). Obsolete panpipes in various sizes.
Lit.: no. 81.

Mizmāru 'l-qasab (Iran). Panflutes.
Lit.: no. 255.

Mizrāb (North India). Plectrum made of steel wire. It is placed on the index and middle fingers of the right hand of the player and is used in *vīṇā* playing, particularly in the use of the *mahatī-vīṇā* of North India. Cf. *Miḍrāb* (*Midhrāb*).
Lit.: no. 255.

Mizwid (North Africa). Bagpipe that accompanies choir singing.

Mjolo (Tanganyika—Washambala). Ankle bells in the form of crescents.
Lit.: no. 130.

Mk'ar-wa gsil (Tibet). Stick with bells used by begging monks.

Mkinda (Tanganyika—Washambala). Drum with cylindrical corpus and two heads. When used to accompany dances it is suspended from the neck of the player. When performing ritual music it is placed in the player's lap.
Lit.: no. 130.

M'kul (French Congo). See *Nku*.

Mkwiro (East Africa—Swahili). Drumstick.

Mlampah (Java). See *Balunganing genḍing*.

Mleng (*Pleng*; *Resik*) (Java). "True." If all intervals of a *gamelan* are tuned perfectly alike (not *silir*).
Lit.: no. 163.

Mna'an'īm (Ancient Israel). Hebrew term for rattle. Cf. Bible (2nd Book of Samuel), probably indicating the Egyptian *sistrum*.
Lit.: no. 250.

Mngoli (Africa—Nyanja of Nyasaland). Wooden lute with one string.

Mo (China—M 4593). See *Chien-tzu.*

Mo (China—M 4546). Term used for *sheng* in operatic performances, particularly during the Yüan period (A.D. 1280-1368). Cf. *Sheng* (M 5738); *Nan-hsi.*
Lit.: no. 183.

Mo (Malaysia). Tone syllable representing the fourth degree of *wayang-* (and other) scales. See *Chi* for scales.

Mo (Annam). See *Cai mo.*

Mō (Japan). See *Hō.*

Mobeke (Central Africa). Whistle of the Pygmies.

Mochaṅga (India; Bengal). See *Murchaṅg.*

Modeku (Congo—Azande). *Sansa.*
Lit.: no. 184.

Modewwer (Arabia). "The round," a string instrument of the *qānūn* type.
Lit.: no. 255.

Modimba (Congo—Basonge). Slit-drum.
Lit.: no. 21.

Modjoko (Congo—Gombe). Cf. *Bonda* (2).
Lit.: no. 26.

Modori (Japan). A *kyōkusetzu.* In *ryo* modes the same note is produced three times (in succession) by a deep, guttural sound with short interruptions between each note, all in the same breath. In *ritsu* modes the middle of the three notes is raised.
Lit.: no. 47.

Moghni (Arabia). "The satisfying one." Ancient *qānūn* type.
Lit.: no. 255.

Mo gia tri (Vietnam). Wooden drum beaten for punctuation in Buddhist cantillation.

Moglo (*Mogolo*) (Ghana). Lute with three strings.

Mohali (Nepal). A *sānāyī* type with seven finger holes used by the Khusliya caste. Also *Sahanai.*
Lit.: no. 255.

Mohalli (Nepal). See *Mohali.*

Mohambu (Central Africa; Nyasaland—Wahenga). Tall drum of conical shape with a single head. Two of these drums are used to accompany the *vimbuza* dance.
Lit.: no. 155.

Mōhana (*Mōhanakalyāṇī*) (South India). *Janya rāga* of the 28th *mēḷa* (*Harikāmbhōji*).
Tone material:
C D E G A c
c A G E D C
Veṅkatamakhin (17th century) places this *rāga* under the heading of the 65th *mēḷa.* Tulajā (in his *Saṅgīta Sārāmṛta,* 18th century) calls this *rāga Mōhanakalyāṇī* or *Śuddhakalyāṇī* (with several variants in the descending line), also in the 65th *mēḷa.*
Lit.: no. 139.

Mōhanakalyāṇī (South India). See *Śuddhakalyāṇī.*

Mōhanmallār (South India). *Janya rāga* of the 1st *mēḷa* (*Kanakangi*).
Tone material:
C D♭ E♭♭ F A♭ B♭♭ A♭ c
c A♭ B♭♭ A♭ G F E♭♭ D♭ C
Lit.: no. 139.

Mōhananāṭa (South India). *Janya rāga* of the 9th *mēḷa* (*Dhenuka*).
Tone material:
C D♭ E♭ F G A♭ B A♭ c
c A♭ B A♭ G F E♭ D♭ C
Lit.: no. 139.

Mohea (*Mouhaia*) (Malagasy Republic). Rattle.
Lit.: no. 251.

Mohori (Kampuchea). The mildly sounding women's orchestra. It does not perform in theatrical plays but specializes a form of gentle chamber music for the sovereign. It consists of: *roneat-ek*, *roneat-thum*, *roneat-dec*, *kong-thom*, *kong-toch*, *tro-u*, *tro-khmer*, *takhe*; *chapey-thom*, *chapey-toch*, *ronmonea*, *crap-fuong*. Cf. *Pip-hat*.

Mohori (Kampuchea—in the Phnom Penh Palace). Orchestra of 11 players. Tuning about:
C (D) E♭ F G (A♭) B♭ c and C (D) E F G A B♭ c
Lit.: no. 43.

Mohori (*Luang Prabhang*) (Laos). Orchestra of eight players. Tuning about:
C D $\overset{+}{\text{E}}$ G $\overset{+}{\text{A}}$ c; or: C $\overset{\flat}{\text{D}}$ $\overset{\flat}{\text{E}}$ $\overset{\flat}{\text{G}}$ $\overset{\flat}{\text{A}}$ c
also: C D $\overset{+}{\text{E}\flat}$ $\overset{+}{\text{F}}$ $\overset{+}{\text{G}}$ $\overset{+}{\text{A}}$ $\overset{+}{\text{B}\flat}$ c
Lit.: no. 43.

Mohori (India). A *sānāyī* with seven finger holes.
Lit.: no. 254.

Mohra (*Mukhrā*) (North India). In the last *āvarta* (called *mohra*) of a piece of art music, there has to appear the *tia*, a brief rhythmical passage performed three times in succession in such a manner that the final note of the third passage coincides with the concluding *sam* of the drummer. Cf. *Tia*.
Lit.: no. 136.

Mohur (India; Bengal). See *Tāyuś*.

Mokanga (India; Bengal). See *Muchanga*.

Mokita (Congo—Mongo; Doko). Footed drum with a cylindrical body.
Lit.: no. 26.

Mokkin (Japan). Xylophone with 13-16 slabs placed across a wooden trough. The slabs are beaten with two knobbed thin sticks. The instrument is often used in comic scenes off-stage in *kabuki* performances.
Lit.: no. 226.

Moko (Korea). "Wooden fish." A small, carved wooden slit-drum beaten with a stick. It appears in almost all Buddhist monasteries where it is used for marking punctuation and tempo in chanted prayers. Occasionally it is used in the theater. See *Mokugyo* (Japan); *Mu-yü* (China).
Lit.: no. 52.

Moko (Alor Isl. Indonesia). Kettle gong.
Lit.: no. 162.

Mokoreire (*Mokoreie*; *Mokoreile*) (South Africa—Bechuanaland; Bangkwaketse). Vertically-blown cane flute. Cf. *Ncongolo*.

Mokthak (Korea). Small wooden slit-drum used by priests and beggars. Although it has some small insignificant variants, it is basically the same as the *moko* (Korea), the *mu-yü* (China) and the *mokugyo* (Japan).
Lit.: no. 52.

Mokugyo (Japan). See *Moko* (Korea).
Lit.: nos. 53, 185.

Mokuri (Japan). Jew's harp. See *Mukkuri*.

Moletsi (South Africa—Sotho). Chief dancer who plays the *tsusi* (flute). Cf. *Motaba*.

Mo lo (China; Canton). Term for the Mandarin word *wu lo*.

Molo (Nigeria—Hausa). Slim, long lute with three horsehair strings.

Molo (Nigeria—Oyo-Yoruba; Congo—Mbum). *Agidigbo*. Plucked idiophone belonging to the *mbira* (*sansa*) family. The popular *molo* consists of a box with five or more tongues.
Lit.: nos. 21, 293.

Molos (Bali). "Simple." The simple, direct melody-part with which a second figurative line intertwines.
Lit.: no. 197.

Mombye (Congo—Bateke). Footed drum with a cylindrical body.
Lit.: no. 26.

Momongan (Java). Copper cymbal.
Lit.: no. 255.

Mōn (Thailand). Term that indicates a musical system in which six or seven notes are used. These notes belong to the basic heptatonic scale with equidistant intervals. Cf. *Thai.*

Mon (Burma). See *Talaing.*

Monāqeb-khvān (Iran). Medieval public performer of the Shi'ites. The Sunnite public performer was called *fazā'il-kvān.*

Monchol (Bali). The central rounded boss of a gong.

Mondai (Japan). Cf. *Mondō.* In several scenes of *noh* dramas occur the *mondo* dialogues in form of questions and answers, presented in the manner of recitatives.
Lit.: no. 187.

Mondo (Tanganyika; Angola). Wooden drum with two quadratic holes which are linked by a slit.
Lit.: no. 280.

Mondreng (Java). Girl dancers. Cf. *Gamelan mondreng.*
Lit.: no. 163.

Mong (*Ketuk*) (Malaysia). Single horizontally-placed gong over a flat, rectangular wooden box. The gong has a pleasant, low-pitched sound.

Mōng (*Mowng*) (Burma; Thailand). A gong with upturned rim suspended from a wooden tripod. The term can also mean a gong chime (also called "Chinese gong"). Cf. *Piphat*; *Kawng.*
Lit.: no. 252.

Mongam-mongang (South Celebes). A *tjuriga* type.
Lit.: no. 162.

Monggawa (West Java). Energetic, large-step, rough dance.

Mongenda (Congo – Bosaka). One or two drums tied together.
Lit.: no. 26.

Mongele (Congo – Saka). Stick zither.
Lit.: no. 176.

Monggang (*Ponggang*; *Bonggang*) (East Java). A *bonang* of one-octave range. The kettles are arranged in one row.
Lit.: no. 163.

Mongondo (Congo – Modjombo). A slit-drum together with a second drum (the *jomo*), providing dance music.
Lit.: no. 26.

Mongungu (Congo – Bakumu; Bapopoie). Cylindrical drum.
Lit.: no. 26.

Monkela (Congo – Balesa-Basakata). Ceremonial drum used only in very solemn rituals and important formalities.
Lit.: no. 26.

Monkita (Congo – Balesa-Basakata). Drum of the local chiefs. See *Monkela.*

Moṅkoṅ (Java). The stick used for beating the slabs of the *gambang.*
Lit.: no. 255.

Monogatari (Japan). Narrative section. Cf. *Gidayū bushi* (*Jōruri*). Interpolated comedy between the acts of serious drama. Cf. *Kyōgen.*
Lit.: no. 187.

Montro Madura (Java). *Genḍing.* See *Genḍing miangong.*

Monu (Australia). See *Tundum.*

Monzen-kokyū (Japan). Street music.

Monzo (Congo—Wasongola; Tofoke). Side-blown horn.
Lit.: no. 33.

Moqadameh (Iran). Rhythmically free, slow and stately introduction. See *Pīshdarāmad.*

Mora (Southeast India—Muria Gond tribe of Bastar State). Term for *sānāyī.*
Lit.: no. 59.

Morachaṅgu (South India—Telugu language). Also *morchiṅgu.* See *Murchaṅg.*

Moradu (South Africa—Bagananoa). Cf. *Dikomana.*

Moraxoxakiba (South Africa—Sotho). One of a set of seven flutes. Cf. *Moromthwana.*
Lit.: no. 151.

Morita (Japan). Cf. *Isso.*

Moriunkar (Australia). Elliptically-shaped bull roarer, used to drive away evil spirits during circumcision ceremonies. Cf. *Churinga.*
Lit.: no. 255.

Morka (Ethiopia—Sidamo). Xylophone with six or seven slabs.
Lit.: no. 127.

Morobachi (Japan). Sequence of *mebachi* and *obachi*:

Beats:	1	2		4		2
	.	.	3	.	1	.
			mebachi		*obachi*	

Cf. *Mu hyōshi.*

Moromthwana (South Africa—Sotho). One of the following set of seven flutes: *moromthwana, moraxoxakiba, kiba, tatedi, phalola, theme, leboxa.*
Lit.: no. 151.

Moropa (South Africa—Botswana). Wooden conical drum.
Lit.: no. 255.

Mororai (*Rai-rai*). Alternate strokes performed on the *kakko* with both sticks, beginning slowly and accelerating into a roll.
Lit.: no. 225.

Morothloane (Africa—Basutoland). Ankle rattle.
Lit.: no. 151.

Moroto (South Africa). Also *sente.* Cf. *Motaba.*
Lit.: no. 151.

Mōrshiṅgu (South India). See *Muchaṅga.*

Morupa (South Africa). Humming pot with its membrane pierced by a stick which causes it to vibrate.
Lit.: no. 151.

Morin-khuur (*Khil-khuur*) (Mongolia). Fiddle with two strings; the top of its long neck shows a carved horse-head. The wooden circular or trapezoid body is covered with goatskin.
Lit.: no. 60.

Moshembe da (Sudan). Dance that exorcises sickness and drives away evil spirits. It is accompanied by a lyre (*bangia*) and four gourd trumpets (*penah*).

Moshuk (*Maśak*) (India). Hindusthani term for *nagabaddha.* Cf. *Mushag.*

Moshupiane (South Africa—Pedi). A bowl-shaped wooden friction drum secretly played by old women during the initiation ceremony of young girls.
Lit.: nos. 151, 280.

Moska (India). See *Nāgasara*; *Nāgasuram.*

Mōsō biwa (Japan). "The blind priest's *biwa.*" An old small *biwa* with four silken strings and five high frets. Cf. *Biwa.*
Lit.: no. 185.

Mossena (Arabia). "Air." The term for the second highest string of the ancient 4-stringed *'ud*.
Lit.: no. 255.

Mossundro (Malagasy Republic). Cylindrical drum.
Lit.: no. 251.

Mosumba (Gabon). Drum.

Motaba (South Africa—Sotho). Set of five flutes: high-pitched, *moroto* (*sente*), *pekudi*, *dadeli*; principal instrument, *tsusi*; bass flute, *mempo*.
Lit.: no. 151.

Motashāwi (*Motasābi*) (Arabia). Strings tuned in unison.

Moteghayer (Persia). Stressed note that must not be altered during the performance of a *dastgāh*.

Mothlatsa (South Africa—Bakgatla). Flute. See *Naka ya phatola*.
Lit.: no. 151.

Moti (New Guinea). Drum in the shape of an hourglass.
Lit.: no. 25.

Motki (*Motaki*) (North India). Rare *rāga* ascribed to the *Bhairavi thāta*. It consists of phrases from the *rāgas Sarang*, *Bhairavi*, *Mallār*, and a characteristic *Motki* feature. Tone material:

C D E♭ F G A B♭ (B) c
c B♭ A G F E♭ D♭ C; *Vādis*: G, C

Lit.: no. 138.

Motoa (South Africa—Sotho). A very small vertically-blown flute made of bird bone.
Lit.: no. 151.

Mots (Central Celebes; Timor). Slim bamboo clarinet with four finger holes.
Lit.: no. 254.

Motsellets (Arabia). "Water." The second lowest string of the ancient 4-stringed *'ud*, consisting of 48 silk threads.
Lit.: no. 255.

Mouhaia (Malagasy Republic). See *Mohea*.

Mou hatingaa nge'o (Solomon Isl.; Bellona Isl.). Variety of voices in the "polyphonic" singing of the islanders: *nge'o panguunguu*, "voice deepest"; *nge'o hakatootonu*, "voice straight" (medium); *nge'o makanga*, "voice higher"; *nge'o hakahaahine*, "voice high" (women's); *to'o ki 'angunga*, upward movement of voice; *tuku ki ngango*, downward movement of voice; *songongi*, very deep; *to'o hakatoontonu*, "singing straight," or on a level tone; *okeoke*, vibrato, "to shake, swing back and forth"; *hakapoponge*, "ending ee (EE)" with a shake.
Lit.: no. 246.

Mouleya derie (Syria; Iraq). Sad song with a row of quatrains. The text relates that lovers are separated from each other. Cf. *Nayel*.
Lit.: no. 44.

Mowng (Burma). See *Mong*.

Mozika (Malagasy Republic). "Music"; musical instruments.
Lit.: no. 255.

Mozika fitsiofina (Malagasy Republic). Flute.
Lit.: no. 255.

Mozungu (Congo—Azande). See *Kweningba*.
Lit.: no. 27.

Mpalampala (South Africa—Swazi; Zulu). Side-blown horn. Cf. *Shipalapala*; *Upondo*; *Phalaphala*.
Lit.: no. 151.

Mpandala (Belgian Congo—Basonga). Side-blown wooden horn.
Lit.: no. 255.

Mpats'ibihugu (Uganda). The drum of the sovereign.
Lit.: no. 26.

iMpeta (Northwest Rhodesia). Horn.
Lit.: no. 255.

Mpetshanga (Congo). See *Mushits.*

Mpiga fidla (Africa; Zanzibar). Swahili term for fiddler.

Mpiga filimbi (Africa; Zanzibar). Swahili term for flutist.

Mpiga kinanda (Africa; Zanzibar). Swahili term for organ player.

Mpiga kinubi (East Africa—Swahili). Lute-, harp-, zither-player.

Mpiga tarumbeta (Africa; Zanzibar). Swahili term for trumpeter.

Mpolomono (Congo—Bembe). Side-blown wooden trumpet.
Lit.: no. 280.

Mpovila za londe (Lower Congo). Small wooden clapper. See *Ndingi.*
Lit.: no. 280.

Mpungi (Congo—Kikongo; Angola). Elephant tusk. Horn.
Lit.: no. 280.

Mpungwe (East Africa). Zither with five strings.
Lit.: no. 255.

Mpwita (Congo—Mbala). Humming pot with friction stick.
Lit.: no. 255.

uMqangala (South Africa; Natal). Music bow.
Lit.: no. 255.

Mṛdaṅga (India). See *Mṛidaṅga.*

Mṛdāni (South India). *Janya rāga* of the 26th *mēḷa* (*Chārukeśī*).
Tone material:
C D E A♭ B♭ c
c B♭ A♭ E D C
Lit.: no. 139.

Mridaṅga (*Mṛdaṅga*) (India). The ancient drum is mentioned in Sanskrit literature as early as 400 B.C. Its name means "earthen or clay-drum" (Sanskrit: *mrdanga*; Hindu: *mridaṅga*; Tamil: *mritaṅgam*; Prakrit: *muinga*; Pali: *mutingo*). The body of the two-headed drum has the shape of two frusta of cones linked together with their broad bases. In most instances the profile of the drum is not angular but gently curved. The outline of the body (slightly slimmer at both ends) has caused some Indian drummers to call the simple rhythmical pattern (♪ ♩ ♪) by the name of the drum.

The drumheads of the *mridaṅga*, on both sides of slightly unequal sizes, are held and stretched by leather straps. The bigger skin is tuned to *sa*, the basic note of the *rāga* to be performed, and the smaller skin can be tuned either to the upper fourth or fifth, or even the upper octave of *sa*. In modern practice the smaller skin is tuned to *sa* while the bigger one produces a note that has a lower pitch and is not always distinct.

Today *mridaṅgas* are used only in the performance of certain *tālas* such as *Tivratāl*, *Sultāl*, *Chautāl*, *Dhamar Tāl*, and *Jhaptāl*. *Dhrūpad* performances must be accompanied invariably by *mridaṅgas*, while the *Khyāls* and music of lighter nature require the popular *tabla* pair.
Lit.: nos. 136, 138.

Mridya (East Africa). Swahili term for shepherd's "flute" (a shawm).
Lit.: no. 255.

Mritaṅgam (South India). Tamil term for *mridaṅga.*

Mrugākshi (South India). *Janya rāga* of the 8th *mēḷa* (*Hanumattōḍi*).
Tone material:
C D♭ E♭ F B♭ c
c B♭ F E♭ D♭ C
Lit.: no. 139.

Mrugākṣi (South India). See *Mrugākshi.*

Mrwāsī (Iraq). Small drum with two heads.

Msaddar (Tunisia). See *Al Msaddar.*

Mshad (Tunisia). See *Al Mshad.*

Mṣiltayim (Israel). Ancient Hebrew term for *ṣelṣlim.*

Msomari (Tanganyika – Washambala). Oboe with six or seven finger holes.
Lit.: no. 130.

Msondo (East Africa; Swahili). Large footed drum in the shape of a mortar.
Lit.: no. 255.

Msunyunho (Tanzania). Dance performed during the harvesting of the ripe millet and maize in May. This dance is also performed in January after the rainy period. Another type of this dance can be observed by a group of young boys. Cf. *Ndualala.*

Mtangala (North Rhodesia; West Nyasa L. – Nyanja). Music bow played by women.
Lit.: no. 255.

Mtorilo (Kenya). See *Mululi.*

Mu (Korea). See *Yul-cha-po.*

Mu (*Hyung*) (Korea). "Military string." The name of the sixth open string of the *hyon-kum.* Cf. *Komunko.*
Lit.: no. 136.

Mu'aabaka (Solomon Isl.; Bellona Isl.). Group dance song in which women take part.
Lit.: no. 246.

Mu'adhdhin (Arabia). The one who calls the believers to prayer. Cf. *Adhdhān* (*Aḏān*).

Muai (Solomon Isl.). A small plucked instrument made of galip almond from which a tongue is cut out. The instrument is believed to create love-magic.

Mu'allaqāt (Arabia). "Treasured poems," sung or recited during contests of musicians and poets.
Lit.: no. 76.

Muana (Congo – Bakongo). Cylindrical drum.
Lit.: no. 280.

Muanza (East Africa – Wanika). Humming pot (friction drum).
Lit.: no. 17.

Mubango (Uganda – Ganda). Percussion beam beaten with wooden sticks.
Lit.: no. 302.

Muchaṅga (India). Sanskrit *mukha,* "mouth"; *chaṅga,* "plucked instrument." Iron jew's harp. The instrument is called *mochaṅga* in Bengali, *murchaṅg* or *muṅhchaṅg* in Hindosthani, *morachaṅgu* or *morchiṅgu* in Telugu, *mōrshiṅgu* in Tamil, and *chaṅgu* in Kannarese.
Lit.: no. 254.

Muchongoyo (Mozambique). Ensemble consisting of three two-headed drums.

Muda'af al ramal (Arabia). Rhythm of Persian origin:

Lit.: no. 65.

Mudang (Korea). The drum and gong player who in villages exorcise harmful spirits.
Lit.: no. 277.

Mudawwar (Arabia). "Round." Probably a *qanūn* with a circular body.

Mudidi (Congo – Bena-Lulua). Goblet drum.
Lit.: no. 26.

Mudji (*Muji*) (South Australia). Bull roarer.
Lit.: no. 255.

Mudrā (India; Vedic time). "Seal," "sign." The hundreds of hand and finger positions used by reciters of the *Sāmaveda*, and body, limb, and hand positions used in Indian dance. The *mudrās* can also appear as textual signature of the composer, singer, of his pseudonym, of the *rāga* and *tāla* used, of the teacher, the patron, the structural form of the song, and of numerous other connotations.

The *mudrās* appear not only in Indian and Buddhist Central Asia, but East Asia as well.
Lit.: nos. 216, 264.

Mudrita (India). See *Gamak(a).*

Muezzin (Arabia). See *Mu'adhdhin.*

Mughann (Arabia). Ancient term for musician, reciter, singer.
Lit.: no. 70.

Mughannī(yūn) (Arabia). Male musicians (singers).
Lit.: no. 66.

Mughannīyāt (Arabia). Hired female musicians (singers).
Lit.: no. 66.

Mughnī (Iran). Obsolete string instrument of the 14th century (see Lit. no. 250, p. 258). It was supposed to be a combination of zither and lute with a very broad neck and 39 open strings.
Lit.: no. 250.

Mūḥaiyar al-Ḥusain (*Āwāz*) (Arabia). An obscure *maqām* which has been described as *Bayāt*, but performed one octave higher (see Lit. no. 65). Cf. *Muḥayer.*
Lit.: no. 121.

Muhambi (South Africa – Tshopi). See *Mbila.*

Muḥayer (*Muḥavir*) (Arabia). "The wonderful," "the whimsical." The term indicates the 12th tone of the scale (or the 9th tone if *rast* is considered to be the first tone). As *maqām* the tone material is:

D $\overset{+}{E\flat}$ F G A $\overset{+}{B\flat}$ c d

Lit.: no. 64.

Muḥayir 'Iraq (Modern Tunisia). *Maqām.* Tone material:

C♯ D E $\overset{+}{F}$ G A $\overset{+}{B\flat}$ c d

Lit.: no. 64.

Muḥayir Sīkah (Modern Tunisia). *Maqām.* Tone material:

D E♭ F♯ G A B♭ c d e♭ f♯ g

Lit.: no. 64.

Mu-hyōshi (*Roku-hyōshi*) (Japan). A six-beat meter used in *Bugaku*:

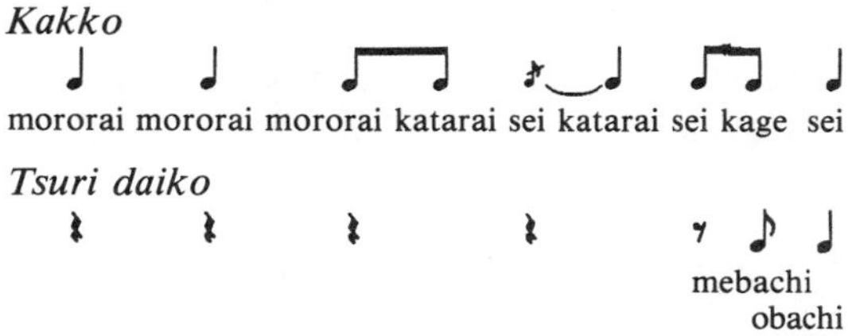

Lit.: no. 250.

Muinga (South India). Prakrit term for *mridaṅga.*

Mujaguzo (Uganda; Angola). Also *muǧaguzo.* The 93 cup-shaped royal drums of various sizes.
Lit.: no. 255.

Mujannab (Arabia). Slightly higher (¼ or ½ tone) than the sound of the open *'ud* string. The note is not yet called *sabbāba*, the one created by the first finger on the string, but is produced by a very slight touching. Cf. *Mutlaq*; *Sabbāba.*
Lit.: no. 76.

Mujannabu-dh-Dhīl (Modern Tunisia). *Maqām.* Tone material:

G A♭ B C D $\overset{+}{E\flat}$ F G A♭ B c d e♭

Lit.: no. 64.

Mujegereza (Ruanda – Bashi). Rattles made of dried fruits. A small number of the rattles are fastened to a stick.
Lit.: no. 190.

Muji (*Mudji*) (South Australia). Bull roarer used at puberty ceremonies.
Lit.: no. 255.

Mujwiz (Arabia). Double clarinet. Cf. *Mijwiz.*

Muka (Malaysia). See *Rebāb* (Malaya).

Mukaja (India; Bengal). Tambourin.
Lit.: no. 255.

Mukande (Angola). Masked dancing.

Mukassarah (*Marghūlah*) (Islamic North Africa). The repetition of the same note in order to avoid any pause in the melody.

Mukavina (*Mukhavīnā*) (South India). Cf. *Sānāyī.*
Lit.: no. 260.

Muk-brogon (Australia). See *Tundum.*

Mukhapriya (South India). *Janya rāga* of the 11th *mēḷa* (*Kokilapriyā*).
Tone material:
C D♭ E♭ F A B c
c B A F E♭ D♭ C
Lit.: no. 139.

Mukhārī (South India). *Janya rāga* of the 22nd *mēḷa* (*Kharaharapriyā*).
Tone material:
C D F G A B♭ A c (C D F G B♭ c)
c B♭ A (A♭) G F E♭ D C
Lit.: no. 139.

Mukhavīṇā (South India—Khota). Oboe with eight finger holes, similar to the *nāgasvaram*, but smaller. The instrument is played during certain night services in Hindu temples.
Lit.: nos. 46, 262.

Mukhrā (North India). Characteristic phrase in songs. See *Mohra.*
Lit.: no. 136.

Mukko (Japan). A very rare psaltery of the Aino in the form of a sword with five strings.
Lit.: no. 255.

Mukkuri (Japan—Ainu). Also *mokuri.* A wooden or bamboo jew's harp played by women.
Lit.: no. 255.

Mu-ko (Korea). A large drum suspended in a frame; it is beaten by two players.
Lit.: no. 52.

oMuko (Southwest Africa—Herero). String.

Mukoko (Lower Congo). Slit-drum.
Lit.: no. 280.

Mukonzi (Congo—Bembe; Sundi). (1) Slit-drum beaten with two sticks. (2) Cylindrical drum with one head.
Lit.: no. 280.

Mukta (South India). Cf. *Amukta.*

Muktambari (South India). *Janya rāga* of the 1st *mēḷa* (*Kanakāngi*).
Tone material:
C D♭ E♭♭ F G B♭♭ c
c B♭♭ A♭ F E♭♭ D♭ C
Lit.: no. 139.

Muktayi (*Nyāsa*) (South India). See *Ālāp.*

Muktitāyani (South India). *Janya rāga* of the 64th *mēḷa* (*Vāchaspati*).
Tone material:
C E F♯ G A B♭ c
c B♭ A G F♯ E C
Lit.: no. 139.

Mukumbi (Congo—Bwende). A scraper. A notched stick is moved across a piece of vibrating animal skin that is placed across the slit of a wooden drum. Cf. *nKumbi.*
Lit.: no. 280.

Mukupele (Congo—Balunda). Drum. See *Mukupila.*

Mukupila (Congo—Bambala; Basuku; Batshoko). An hourglass drum with two heads. Cf. *Mukupele.*
Lit.: no. 190.

Mukurapōla (South India). *Janya rāga* of the 24th *mēḷa* (*Varuṇapriyā*).
Tone material:
C D E♭ A♯ B c
c B A♯ F E♭ C
Lit.: no. 139.

Mukwanga (Congo – Bakongo; Bembe). Rattle made of a calabash. It is used in ritual ceremonies. Cf. *Mkwanga.*
Lit.: no. 280.

Muk-yü (China). Cantonese term for the Mandarin *mu-yü*. See *Pang-tzu.*

Mulimba (Congo – Baluba-Hembe). Also *nkumoi.* A slit-drum.
Lit.: no. 21.

Mulizi (Ruanda – Bashi). Also *shwegu.* A cane flute with two finger holes.
Lit.: no. 218.

Multani (North India). *Rāga* ascribed to the *Tōdi thāta*. Its scale is the same as that of *Tōdi* but the treatment of the individual notes is different.
Tone material:
C E♭ F♯ G B c
c B A♭ G F♯ E♭ D♭ C; *Vādis:* G, C
Lit.: no. 138.

Mululi (*Mtorilo*) (Kenya – Washambala). Flute with 2-6 finger holes.
Lit.: no. 130.

Mumbeta (Lower Congo – Babembe). Term for a small *ndungu.*

Mumbiki wa ngoma (Congo – Bapende). Goblet drum.
Lit.: no. 26.

Mun (Burma). Gong.

Munach (Ancient Israel). Notational symbol (in the form of a low placed comma) used in biblical chant, indicating a conjunctive function (the equivalent of the Latin *gravis*).
Lit.: no. 309.

Munchang (North India). See *Murchang.*

Munda (Java). Hindu-Javanese term for the small gong types. Cf. *Gubar.*
Lit.: no. 159.

Mundur (Sunda District). Also *turun.* Term for rallentando, ritenuto. Cf. *Suwuk.*

Mu-nenga (*Ru-nenga*). General term for musical instrument.
Lit.: no. 255.

Munfasil (Islamic North Africa). Disjunct (in poetry and song).

Munggah (Java). Term for the coda part of a *genḍing*. It usually has twice as many *keṭuk* beats in each *kenongan* as in the *merong*. Cf. *Potok.*
Lit.: no. 163.

Munggang (Java). See *Gamelan munggang.*

Mungubire (Congo – Wavira). Cylindrical drum. Both heads are covered with lizard skin.
Lit.: no. 26.

Mungungi (Congo – Bambala; Basuku). Drum played for dancing.
Lit.: no. 26.

Muṅh-chaṅg (North India). See *Murchang.*

Mun-hyŭn (Korea). "Civil string." The first open string of the *hyon-kŭm.* Cf. *Komunko.*
Lit.: no. 136.

Munjira (India; Bengal). See *Mandira.*

Munkamba (*Munkandu*; *Munsaku*) (Congo – Kikongo). A small *ndungu.* Also *nkandu.*
Lit.: no. 190.

Munkoko (Lower Congo). Slit-drum.
Lit.: no. 280.

Mu-nkugi (Former French Congo). Bell.

Munkunku (Lower Congo—Sundi). Tulip-shaped, clapperless bell.
Lit.: no. 280.

Munkwaka (Congo—Bembe; Dondo). Scraper.
Lit.: no. 280.

Muno (New Guinea). Funeral song. Cf. *Ratara*; *Rano.*

Munsaku (Congo). See *Munkambo*; *Ndungu.*

Munsasi (Congo). See *Munsiasi.*

Munsenkele (Congo). Barrel drum.
Lit.: no. 26.

Munshid (Arabia). Chant of a group of Dervishes.

Munsiasi (Congo—Bembe). Small *nsembu.*
Lit.: no. 280.

Munswangala (Lower Congo). A long *ndungu.*
Lit.: no. 280.

Muntshintshi (South Africa—Thonga). Footed drum.
Lit.: no. 151.

Mupimpi (Congo—Wasongola). One-headed drum.
Lit.: no. 151.

Mupunpi (Congo—Wasongola). Obscure drum made of a hollowed-out tree trunk.
Lit.: no. 33.

Muqaddamāt al-muqaddamāt (Arabia). Tone name (as used by Al-Kindī, 9th century), notated with the Arabic letter *jīm* (*J*), usually transcribed into western notation as the note B.
Lit.: no. 69.

Muqarran dunbalayī (Turkey). Paired kettle-drums. The two drummers are believed to come from Mecca.
Lit.: no. 81.

Murabba' (Old Arabia). "Square." An ancient form of *rabāb* with a quadrangular or rectangular body and one horsehair string.
Lit.: no. 70.

Murabba' (Lebanon; Syria). See *Majruda.*

Muraja (Ancient India). Drum, standing vertically; the term implies also tambourin.

Murajavādhini (South India). *Janya rāga* of the 25th *mēḷa* (*Mārarañjanī*).
Tone material:
C D E F B♭♭ c
c B♭♭ F E D C
Lit.: no. 139.

Murakkabah (Islamic North Africa). Multiple grace notes. Cf. *Basītah.*

Muralī (India). Transverse bamboo flute with 6-8 finger holes. Cf. *Murli*; *Vaṅśa*; *Zangskar.*
Lit.: nos. 46, 254.

Muraṣṣa' (Iran; Khorasan; Turkmenia). Instrumental piece in the form of a fantasy. Cf. *'Amal.*
Lit.: no. 76.

Murasu (South India). Tamil term for drum. Three types were distinguished: *nyāya murasu* (drum of judgement), *tyāga murasu* (drum beaten during a sacrifice), *vira murasu* (battle drum).
Lit.: no. 262.

Mūrchhanā (Ancient India). (1) Obsolete heptatonic scales. One of the oldest sources of Indian music theory (*Bharatanāṭyaśāstra*, ca. 200 B.C.) presents the scales in two groups (*grāmas*). The *sa-* and *ma-grāmas.* Actually there were three groups: the *sa-*, *ma-*, and *ga-grāmas.* The third, however, was believed to contain scales used only by the gods, hence they were not supposed to be used by humans (see *grāma*). Each *grāma* (literally, "village") contains seven *mūrchhaṇās*. The first seven of these scales of the *sa-grāma* were:

Uttara mandrā	(first note: *sa*)	approx.: C mode
Rajanī	(" " : *ni*)	" : B "
Uttarayatā	(" " : *dha*)	" : A "
Suddhaśaḍjā	(" " : *pa*)	" : G "
Matsarīkrita	(" " : *ma*)	" : F "
Asvakrāntā	(" " : *ga*)	" : E "
Abhirudgatā	(" " : *ri*)	" : D "

The other seven *mūrchhaṇās* of the *ma-grāma* were:

Sauvīrī	*(first note: ma)*	approx.: F mode
Hariṇāśva	(" " : *ga*)	" : E "
Kalopannatā	(" " : *ri*)	" : D "
Śuddha Madhyā	(" " : *sa*)	" : C "
Mārgī	(" " : *ni*)	" : B "
Pauravī	(" " : *dha*)	" : A "
Hṛśyakā	(" " : *pa*)	" : G "

(2) See *Gamak(a)*.
Lit.: nos. 86, 292.

Murchaṅg (North India). Circular iron jew's harp; also called *chang* ("harp"). Cf. *Chaṅgu*; *Mochaṅga*; *Munchaṅg*; *Muchaṅga*; *Mursing*.
Lit.: no. 254.

Muri (Small Sunda Isl.). Clarinet made of palm leaf.
Lit.: no. 162.

Muri aṭanta (South India; Kerala). *Kathakaḷi* term for *Tripuṭa tāla* (*trisra jāti*).
Lit.: no. 262.

Murlī (Southeast Iran; West Pakistan—Baluchistan). Term for the *muralī*, a cross flute with six finger holes. Also term for double clarinet with eight finger holes.
Lit.: no. 258.

Murlu-murlu (Australia—Warramunga). Bull roarer. Cf. *Churunga*.
Lit.: no. 37.

Mursing (North India). See *Murchaṅg*.

Murtajal (Arabia) Musical. Improvisation.
Lit.: no. 73.

Muruas (Arabia). Small cylindrical drum with two heads.

Murukkaṇi (South India). Tamil term for the tuning peg on the *yāzh*, *tanbura*, and *vīṇā*. Cf. *Māḍagam*.
Lit.: no. 262.

Murumbu (South Africa; Basutoland—Venda; Pedi; Chwana; Sotho). Conical drum with one head played by women (described as "alto drum").

Musāfiq (Arabia). Ancient small cymbals. Cf. *Shūqaifāt*.
Lit.: no. 78.

Musaḥḥir (Middle East). Announcer who chants signals and wakes people during Ramadan.

Musenkele (Congo—Basanga). Drum used at funeral dances.
Lit.: no. 26.

Musesegoto (Uganda—Konjo). Rattle. Cf. *Ensegu*.
Lit.: no. 302.

Mushag (Burma). Bagpipe with a double-reed pipe and 3-5 finger holes. Cf. *Maśak* (North India); *Mośuk*.
Lit.: no. 254.

Mushekera (Congo—Wanande). Trumpet.
Lit.: no. 26.

Mushereko (Ruanda—Bashi). See *Ihloere*.

Mushits (*Gwan'bal*; *Mpetshanga*) (Congo—Babunda). Drum.
Lit.: no. 26.

Musht̤ (Arabia). Bridge-tail piece (of the *'ud*).

Mushta (*Mushtaq*) (Iran). Ancient mouth organ with five reed pipes, probably of Chinese origin.
Lit.: no. 76.

Mushtāq ṣinī (Arabia; Iran). Old Persian term for the Chinese *sheng*. Cf. *Qāmish mizmār*; *Chubchīq*.
Lit.: no. 81.

Mushta-yi ṣinī (Iran). See *Mushtāq ṣinī*.

Mūsika (Arabia). Piece for military band.
Lit.: no. 73.

Mūsīqāl (*Mithqāl*) (Turkey). Panpipes. The Egyptian term is *shu'aibīya*.
Lit.: nos. 76, 255.

Mūsīqār (Arabia; Turkey). See *Mūsīqāl*.

Mūsīqāy (Arabia). Organ.

Musokolome (Uganda—Sogo). Ground bow.
Lit.: no. 302.

Musta'ār (Middle East). *Maqām*.
Tone material:
$\overset{+}{E\flat}$ F♯ G A B♭ c d $\overset{+}{e\flat}$
Egypt. "The borrowed one."
$\overset{+}{E\flat}$ F♯ G A B♭ c d♯ $\overset{+}{e\flat}$
Lit.: nos. 64, 121.

Mustahsin (Turkey). Large modern *nāy*.
Lit.: no. 81.

Mustazad (Arabia; Iran). See *Nauba*.

Muṭabbiq (Arabia). See *Muṭbiq*.

Mutanda (Congo—Bangango). Musical bow.
Lit.: no. 33.

Muṭbiq (Arabia). Double clarinet. Cf. *Mijwiz*; *Mujwiz*.

Mutiĕttu (South India). Ancient dance-play.
Lit.: no. 123.

Mutiṅga (India). Prakrit term for *mridaṅga*.
Lit.: no. 254.

Mutingo (South India). Pali term for *mridaṅga*.

Muṭlaq (Arabia). (1) Bourdon string. (2) The sound produced by the bourdon string. Cf. *Mujannab*.
Lit.: no. 255.

Muṭlaq fī majrā-binṣir (Arabia). See *Aṣab'*.

Muṭlaq fī majrā al-wuṣtā (Arabia). See *Aṣab'*.

Mutoto (Congo; Ruanda; Urundi—Balunda). Goblet-shaped drum.
Lit.: no. 26.

Muṭrib (Mesopotamia). Instrumentalist, musician (14th century).
Lit.: no. 75.

Muṭrib (Iran; Arabia). An ensemble (musicians) of the Mevlevi order of the Dancing Dervishes. The instruments were 2-3 reed flutes and two pairs of kettledrums. Cf. *Ālātī*.

Mutshakatha (South Africa). Dancer's leg rattles. See *Thuzo*.
Lit.: no. 151.

Mutumbi (*Mutumbwe*) (Congo—Baholoholo). Drum with one head.
Lit.: no. 26.

Mu-uta (Japan). "Sixth verse." See *Kumi*.

Muvungu (Kenya). Obsolete term for *kya*.

Muwāl (*Mawāl*) (Arabia). Vocal improvisations. Cf. *Taqsim*.

Muwashaḥ (*Muwashshaḥ*) (Arabia). A strophic song, similar to a Western medieval *ballade*. It is based upon the structure of the text (poem) and is performed by alternating chorus and solo voice. The instruments used in its performance are: *ṭabl* (drum), *'ūd* (lute), *kamān* or *kamānjah* (fiddle). If there are no instruments used, *taṣfiq* (handclapping) is applied. The formal structure of the *muwashaḥ* shows three sections:

1. *Dawr* ("turn," "cycle") or *badaniyah* ("body") in which one line of the poem is presented. This is followed by a repetition of the *dawr* with the next line of the poem.
2. *Khānah* ("inn," "square of the chessboard") or *silsilah* ("chain," "series") which presents a new melody which may return to the *dawr* melody.
3. *Qaflah* ("closing," "key") or *rujū* ("return") or *ghitā* ("cover"). In this section new lines of the poem are used but, musically, the *dawr* melody is repeated.

Lit.: no. 6.

Muwashshaḥ (Arabia). See *Muwashaḥ.*

Muwattar (Old Arabia). A stringed instrument; probably a lute. Cf. *Kirān.*
Lit.: no. 76.

Muyang (Southeast India; Bastar State—Muria Gond). Small round brass or iron jingles fastened to the backs of dancers.
Lit.: no. 59.

Mu-yü (China—M 4593; M 7668). "Wooden fish." A block of camphor wood, hollowed out and shaped like a human skull. It is painted red and gold. It is beaten by priests to mark time in the recitation of prayers. The Cantonese term for *mu-yü* is *muk-yü*. See *Pang-tzu*; *Ao-yü*; *Moko* (Korea); *Moku-gyo* (Japan).
Lit.: nos. 137, 250.

Muziki (*Ngoma*) (East Africa—Swahili). Music.

Muzumbi (Kenya—Kasai area). *Sansa.*
Lit.: no. 280.

Mvet (Cameroon; Central Africa). Stick zither with 5-8 strings. Also called a "fan harp" made of the rib of a raffia palm from which the strings are detached. The term *mvet* applies also to zither music and dance.
Lit.: nos. 218, 280.

Mveul (Gabon—Pahouin). Bow lute with four strings.
Lit.: no. 33.

Mvumvuni (Lower Congo—Bembe). Side-blown signal horn.
Lit.: no. 280.

Mwakasa (Lower Congo). Rattle. It is believed to possess magical properties.
Lit.: no. 280.

Mwan'angūlū (Congo—Kikongo). See *Dingwinti.*

Mwandu (North Rhodesia—Ila). Friction drum.
Lit.: no. 255.

Mwanzo (wa ngoma na kuimba) (East Africa—Swahili). Prelude, overture.

Mwemvo (Lower Congo). Vertically-blown flute without finger holes.
Lit.: no. 280.

Mwimba (North Rhodesia). Small drum played while walking.
Lit.: no. 26.

Mwi-mbaji (Zanzibar). Swahili term for "singer."

Mying-zaing (Burma). Cf. *Chauk-pauk auk-pyan.*

Mzungu (Tanganyika—Wampare). Bamboo stamping tube. Each dancer carries two tubes.
Lit.: nos. 130, 181.

N

Nā (Ancient Babylon—Sumer). Also called *ḥalilu.* A reed pipe.
Lit.: no. 87.

Na (India). Basic tabla stroke for the right hand. Performed in the same manner as *ta*, but with lesser force, and the tip of the straight, stiffened second finger stays on the *chanti* after the stroke. For further information see Lit. no. 136.

Na (Korea). See *Nagak.*

Naama (Egypt). Also *naghma.* Term for *maqām.* Cf. *Habara*; *Qōl.*

Naat (North India). Religious song with Urdu text.

Nabal (*Napal*) (Korea). Slim, long, conically-shaped brass trumpet consisting of three parts that fit into each other like a gently bent telescope. Cf. *Rag-dung* (Tibet); *La-pa* (China).
Lit.: no. 179.

Nabara (Arabia). In singing a glottal hiatus. Also called *nabra.*

Nabhomani (South India). *Janya rāga* of the 40th *mēḷa* (*Navanītam*).
Tone material:
C D♭ E♭♭ D♭ F♯ G c
c B♭ A G F♯ E♭♭ D♭ C
Lit.: no. 139.

Nabhomani (South India). (1) The 40th *asampūrṇa mēḷa-rāga* without *kaṭapayādi* prefix. (2) The 40th *asampūrṇa mēḷa-rāga* with *kaṭapayādi* prefix. See *Rāga* (South India).
Lit.: no. 139.

Nabhōmārgiṇi (South India). *Janya rāga* of the 16th *mēḷa* (*Chakravāka*).
Tone material:
C E F G A B♭ c
c A G F E D♭ C
Lit.: no. 139.

Nabiba (Congo—Mombutu). Conical drum with two heads.
Lit.: no. 26.

Nabita (Congo—Mangbele; Mangbetu; Makere; Momvu). Also called *tshembe.* Drum with two laced heads.
Lit.: no. 26.

Nablā (*Nevel*; *Nebel*) (Ancient Israel). Lyre; harp.

Nabra (Old Arabia). Interval. See *Nabara.*

Nachuni (*Nautchumi*) (India). Hindi term for dancing girl.

Naek (Sunda). Accelerando. Cf. *Seseg(an)* (Java).

Nādabhramam (South India). *Janya rāga* of the 64th *mēḷa* (*Vāchaspati*).
Tone material:
C G F# Bb c
c Bb A G F# E C
Lit.: no. 139.

Nādabhramari (South India). *Janya rāga* of the 37th *mēḷa* (*Sālaga*).
Tone material:
C Ebb Db Ebb F# G Ab Bbb
(Bbb) Ab G F# Ebb Db C *Bbb*
This *rāga* has *niṣādāntya* character.
Lit.: no. 139.

Nādācintāmaṇi (South India). See *Nādāchintāmaṇi.*

Nādāchintāmaṇi (South India). *Janya rāga* of the 22nd *mēḷa* (*Kharaharapriyā*).
Tone material:
C Eb F G Bb A Bb c
c Bb A G F Eb D Eb C
Lit.: no. 139.

Nādamaya rūpa (India). See *Dēvamaya rūpa.*

Nādāmūrti (South India). *Janya rāga* of the 22nd *mēḷa* (*Kharaharapriyā*).
Tone material:
C Eb F A Bb c
c Bb G F D Eb C
Lit.: no. 139.

Nādanāli (South India). *Janya rāga* of the 8th *mēḷa* (*Hanumattōḍi*).
Tone material:
C Db Eb F G Bb c
c Bb Ab G F Eb Db C
Lit.: no. 139.

Nādanāmakriyā (South India). *Janya rāga* of the 15th *mēḷa* (*Māyāmāḷavagauḷa*).
Tone material:
C Db E F G Ab B (C Db F E F G Ab B)
B Ab G F E Db C *B*
This *rāga* has *niṣādāntya* character.
Lit.: no. 139.

Nādanapriya (South India). *Janya rāga* of the 22nd *mēḷa* (*Kharaharapriyā*).
Tone material:
C Eb D F A Bb c
c Bb G F Eb D C
Lit.: no. 139.

Nādanapriya (South India). *Janya rāga* of the 27th *mēḷa* (*Sarasāṅgī*).
Tone material:
C F E F G Ab B c
c B Ab G F E D C
Lit.: no. 139.

Nādarūpi (South India). *Janya rāga* of the 6th *mēḷa* (*Tanarūpi*).
Tone material:
C Db Ebb F A# B c
c B A# F Ebb Db C
Lit.: no. 139.

Nādasvaram (South India). Recent term for *nāgasvaram.*
Lit.: no. 262.

Nādasvarūpi (South India). *Janya rāga* of the 27th *mēḷa* (*Sarasāṅgī*).
Tone material:
C E F G E Ab B c
c B Ab G F E D C
Lit.: no. 139.

Nādataraṅgiṇī (South India). *Janya rāga* of the 22nd *mēḷa* (*Kharaharapriyā*).
Tone material:
C G F D Eb D C
c G Bb A G F Eb D C
Lit.: no. 139.

Nādavinōdini (South India). *Janya rāga* of the 27th *mēḷa* (*Sarasāṅgī*).
Tone material:
C D E F G A♭ B c
c B c A♭ G F E D C
Lit.: no. 139.

Nādeśvara vīṇā (India). Loudly sounding *vīṇā*. A modern form of the *kacchapi vīṇā* with a body of the size and shape of the Western violin without resonance holes. The instrument has nine strings which are played with a metal plectrum (occasionally also bowed).
Lit.: no. 254.

Nādī (India). Sanskrit term for pipe.

Nādika (South India). *Janya rāga* of the 33rd *mēḷa* (*Gāṅgeyabhushanī*).
Tone material:
C D♯ E F B c
c B F E D♯ C
Lit.: no. 139.

Naek (Sunda). Term for accelerando. Cf. *Seseg*; *Sesegan*.

Naek turunna sora (Sunda District). Seven-tone scale (intervals shown in cents):
I 156 II 156 III 210 IV 156 V 156 VI 156 VII 210 I
Its basic tones, I, II, III, V, VI, are called *sora lelugu*.
Lit.: no. 163.

Nafa (Samoa; Tonga Isl.). Large wooden slit-drum. Cf. *Naffa*; *Nawa*. Beaten with two wooden sticks.
Lit.: no. 84.

Nafari (India). Small straight trumpet.
Lit.: no. 255.

Naffa (Tonga Isl.; Samoa). See *Nafa*.
Lit.: no. 7.

Nafīr (*Nefīr*; *Anfār*) (Turkey; Iran; Kurdistan; Arabia). An old straight trumpet with cylindrical bore without any finger holes or ventils. Particularly the small straight one is in contrast to the *karna*. At the present time the term *nafīr* signifies a cow's horn played by the Dervishes of the Baktashi sect. The *nafīr* is also called "Persian horn." See *Darwīsh būrūsī*.
Lit.: no. 34.

Nāgabaddha (North India). A mouth-blown bagpipe with double pipes. The southern type has only one bourdon pipe. Cf. *Mośuk*; *Maśak*; *Śruti-upanga*; *Bhazana-śruti*.
Lit.: no. 255.

Nāgābāṣiṇi (South India). *Janya rāga* of the 30th *mēḷa* (*Nāgānandī*).
Tone material:
C E D E F A♯ B c
c B G F D C
Lit.: no. 139.

Nāgābharaṇam (South India). See *Nāgānandī*.

Nāgābharaṇam (South India). See *Sāmantam* (30th *asampūrṇa mēḷa*).

Nāgābharaṇi (*Nāgābharṇi*) (South India). *Janya rāga* of the 27th *mēḷa* (*Sarasāṅgī*).
Tone material:
C D E F G F G c
c A♭ G F E D C
Lit.: no. 139.

Nāgābharṇi (South India). See *Nāgābharaṇi*.

Nāgabhōgi (South India). *Janya rāga* of the 39th *mēḷa* (*Jhālavarāḷi*).
Tone material:
C D♭ E♭♭ F♯ G A♭ B
(B) A♭ G F♯ E♭♭ D♭ C *B*
This *rāga* has *niṣadāntya* character.
Lit.: no. 139.

Nāgabhūpāḷam (South India). *Janya rāga* of the 23rd *mēḷa* (*Gaurīmanōharī*).
Tone material:
C D E♭ F B c
c B F E♭ D C
Lit.: no. 139.

Nāgabhūṣaṇī (South India). *Janya rāga* of the 29th *mēḷa* (*Dhīraśaṅkarābharaṇam*).
Tone material:
C D F G A c
c B A G F D C
Lit.: no. 139.

Nāgachandrika (*Nāgachudāman*) (South India). *Janya rāga* of the 17th *mēḷa* (*Sūryakānta*).
Tone material:
C E F G A B c
c B A G F E C
Lit.: no. 139.

Nāgachudāman (South India). See *Nāgachandrika.*

Nāgadhvani (South India). *Janya rāga* of the 29th *mēḷa* (*Dhīraśaṅkarābharaṇam*).
Tone material:
(a) C D C F E F G B A F G B A B c
c B A B G F E C D C
(b) C D C F E F G B (c)
c B A B G F E C
Lit.: no. 139.

Nāgadīpakam (South India). *Janya rāga* of the 21st *mēḷa* (*Kiravāṇi*).
Tone material:
C D E♭ F G c
c B A♭ F E♭ C
Lit.: no. 139.

Nāgadīparam (South India). *Janya rāga* of the 38th *mēḷa* (*Jalārṇava*).
Tone material:
C D♭ E♭♭ F♯ A♭ B♭ c
c B♭ A♭ B♭ F♯ E♭♭ D♭ E♭♭ C
Lit.: no. 139.

Nāgagāndhāri (South India). *Janya rāga* of the 20th *mēḷa* (*Naṭabhairavī*).
Tone material:
C D E♭ F G A♭ B♭
B♭ A♭ G F E♭ D C (*B♭*)
Lit.: no. 139.

Nāgagāndharvam (South India). *Janya rāga* of the 31st *mēḷa* (*Yāgapriyā*).
Tone material:
C D♯ F G A♭ B♭♭ A♭ c
c A♭ B♭♭ G F D♯ C
Lit.: no. 139.

Nāgaghaṇṭam (South India). *Janya rāga* of the 39th *mēḷa* (*Jhālavarāḷi*).
Tone material:
C E♭♭ D♭ E♭♭ F♯ B A♭ c
c B A♭ F♯ (E♭) D♭ E♭♭ C
The note E♭ in descent (between F♯ and D♭) is used only ornamentally. The proper intonation of the third degree of this scale has to be E♭♭.
Lit.: no. 139.

Nāgagiri (South India). *Janya rāga* of the 71st *mēḷa* (*Kōsala*).
Tone material:
C E F♯ G A c
c A G F♯ E C
Lit.: no. 139.

Nāgagīrvāṇi (South India). *Janya rāga* of the 55th *mēḷa* (*Śyāmalāṅgī*).
Tone material:
C D E♭ F♯ A♭ B♭♭ A♭ c
c B♭♭ A♭ G F♯ E♭ D C
Lit.: no. 139.

Nāgahindōḷam (South India). *Janya rāga* of the 33rd *mēḷa* (*Gāṅgeyabhuṣanī*).
Tone material:
C E F G c
c B A♭ G F D♯ C
Lit.: no. 139.

Nagak (Korea). Shell trumpet used in military bands. Also called *na*.

Nāgakuntali (South India). *Janya rāga* of the 66th *mēḷa* (*Chitrāmbarī*).
Tone material:
C D E F♯ G B c
c B G A♯ B G F♯ E D C
Lit.: no. 139.

Nāgamani (South India). *Janya rāga* of the 10th *mēḷa* (*Nāṭakapriya*).
Tone material:
C D♭ E♭ F G A c
c A G F E♭ D♭ C
Lit.: no. 139.

Na-gaṇa (South India). See *Ashṭa gaṇas*.

Nāgānandī (*Nāgānandinī*) (South India). The 30th *mēḷa*:
C D E F G A♯ B c
As *rāga*: Veṅkaṭamakhin calls this *rāga Nāgābharaṇam* and shows the following scale:
C D C F E F G A♯ B c
c B A♯ B G F E (D C)
At the present time the tone material is the same as that of *Nāgānandī*.
Lit.: no. 139.

Nāgapañcamam (South India). See *Nāgapañchamam*.

Nāgapañchamam (South India). *Janya rāga* of the 23rd *mēḷa* (*Gaurīmanōharī*).
Tone material:
C A F G B c
c A F E♭ D C
Lit.: no. 139.

Nāgaprabhāvali (South India). *Janya rāga* of the 55th *mēḷa* (*Śyamalāṅgī*).
Tone material:
C E♭ F♯ G A♭ B♭♭ c
c B♭♭ A♭ F♯ E♭ D C
Lit.: no. 139.

Nāgarā (Nepal; Turkestan; India). A pair of small clay drums beaten with wooden sticks. Each drum has one skin stretched across the opening of a shallow earthenware or copper kettle.
Lit.: nos. 46, 254.

Nāgarājam (South India). *Janya rāga* of the 12th *mēḷa* (*Rūpāvatī*).
Tone material:
C D♭ E♭ F G A♯ c
c A♯ G F E♭ D♭ C
Lit.: no. 139.

Nāgari (South India). *Janya rāga* of the 22nd *mēḷa* (*Kharaharapriyā*).
Tone material:
C D F G A B♭ c
c B♭ A G F E♭ C
Lit.: no. 139.

Nagarit (*Kabara*) (Ethiopia). Kettledrums, the symbol of power, were beaten with sticks for the ruler or high dignitaries. For the emperor the *nagarit* were made of silver, for high officials copper was used, for officials of lower rank wooden kettles were employed. When the emperor inspected the army or was involved in warfare, 88 silver *nagarit* were beaten. A Ras could use only 44 drums and other officials 22. The Coptic church, too, employs a large number of these drums.
Lit.: no. 102.

Nāgasāmantam (South India). *Janya rāga* of the 13th *mēḷa* (*Gāyakapriya*).
Tone material:
C D♭ G F G A♭ c
c A♭ G F D♭ C
Lit.: no. 139.

Nāgasara (*Nagsar*; *Nāgasaram*; *Nāgasvaram*) (India). Conically-shaped double oboe made of metal or wood. It has seven finger holes. Cf. *Iḍaibāri*; *Ottu*; *Timiri*; *Bāri*; *Būra*.
Lit.: no. 255.

Nāgasvaram (India; Andhra Desa). Snake charmer's pipe with a single reed. The drone pipe is called *būra*. Cf. *Nāgaśuram*.

Nāgasarasīrūham (South India). *Janya rāga* of the 54th *mēḷa* (*Viśvambharī*).
Tone material:
C E F♯ G c
c B A♯ B G F♯ D♭ C
Lit.: no. 139.

Nagashi (*omote*) (Japan). "To flow." A term in *koto* (or *shamisen*) playing that indicates a sliding of the first finger across the strings.
Lit.: no. 225.

Nagashimono (Japan). Interlude played on the *Satsuma-* and *Chikuzen-biwa*. Or, music for voice and *Chikuzen-biwa*.
Lit.: no. 185.

Nāgasuram (India). Large oboe with a large metal bell. Cf. *Nāgasara*.
Lit.: no. 254.

Nāgasvaram (*Nāgaswaram*) (South India). See *Nāgasara(m)*.

Nāgasvarāli (South India). *Janya rāga* of the 28th *mēḷa* (*Harikāmbhōji*).
Tone material:
C E F G A c
c A G F E C *A* C
Lit.: no. 139.

Nāgataranjiṇi (South India). *Janya rāga* of the 18th *mēḷa* (*Hāṭakāmbarī*).
Tone material:
C D♭ E F G B c
c B G A♯ G F E C
Lit.: no. 139.

Nagauta (Japan). "Long song." Type of classical music for voice and *shamisen* accompaniment. Originally *nagauta* was music for *kabuki* dancing. Later it became independent of dance and appeared on the concert stage. *Nagauta* are lyric or dramatic art songs. The accompanying *hayashi* consists of *shamisen*, flute and drum, occasionally with gong or cymbal. This small group provides also instrumental interludes. There are various types: song emphasizing the melody, songs that serve as dance music, and dramatic songs that illustrate the character of the drama. Cf. *Kabuki*.
Lit.: no. 187.

Nāgavāhiṇi (South India). *Janya rāga* of the 63rd *mēḷa* (*Latāṅgī*). The scale of this *rāga* is identical with that of its primary *rāga Latāṅgī*.
Lit.: no. 139.

Nāgavarāḷi (South India). *Janya rāga* of the 8th *mēḷa* (*Hanumattōḍi*).
Tone material:
D♭ C E♭ D♭ E♭ F G A♭
(*B*♭ C E♭ D♭ E♭ F G A♭)
G F E♭ D♭ C *B*♭ (C)
Lit.: no. 139.

Nāgavēlavali (South India). *Janya rāga* of the 40th *mēḷa* (*Navanītam*).
Tone material:
C D♭ E♭♭ F♯ A c
c B♭ A F♯ E♭♭ D♭ C
Lit.: no. 139.

Nage-bushi (*Tsugi-bushi*) (Japan). 17th-century short popular songs of Kyoto.
Lit.: no. 225.

Nāgesar (India). See *Nāgasuram*.

Nagbhin (*Nagbin*) (North India; Nepal). Brass (copper) trumpet in the form of a twisted snake.
Lit.: no. 254.

Nagham (Arabia). Modes.

Naghāra (Turkey). See *Naqqāra.*

Naghareh (Iran). A pair of large kettledrums.

Naghma (Egypt). Musical notes. See *Maqām*; *Qōl*; *Habara*; *Naama*; *Dastgāh.*

Naghmah (*Naghmeh*) (Iran). See *Dastgāh.*

Nagla (North Ghana—Kassena-Nankani). Flute and drum music played at funerals.
Lit.: no. 218.

Nāgma (Afghanistan). Dance tune.

Nagmeh (Iran). See *Naghmah*; *Dastgāh.*

Nāgrā (Assam—Garo). Ritual clay drum.
Lit.: no. 254.

Nagrīz (Middle East; Modern Egypt). *Maqām.* Tone material:

C D E♭ F♯ G A B♭ c

Cf. *Nigrīz.*
Lit.: no. 64.

Nāgsar (India). See *Nāgasuram.*

Naguar (South India). South Indian term for the *jagajhampa* drum. Cf. *Pāni.*
Lit.: no. 254.

Nahabat (*Nahabet*) (India). Kettledrum(s). Cf. *Maha Nāgarā*; *Sahib Nahabat.*
Lit.: no. 254.

Nahaft (Arabia). (1) Tone name—all tone names within the range of two octaves are listed under the heading of *Jagā* (*Yagā*). See *Mahur.* (2) Also *nihuft.* An obscure *maqām* believed to be similar to *Nawā.*
Lit.: no. 121.

Naham (Arabia). Singer who entertains fishermen during their work at sea.

Nahawānd (Arabia). See *Nam kurdī.*

Nahawand (Middle East). A *maqām* named after Nahavand, a city in West Iran. Its scale is:

C D E♭ F G A♭ $\overset{+}{B\flat}$ c

Sub-*maqām* types related to *Nahawand* are: *Neuter* (the "Greek *Nahawand*"); *Nigriz* (the "Turkish *Ḥijāz*"); the Great *Nahawand*; *Turez-Neuin* (the "New Way"). Cf. *Ḥiṣar.* Derivatives from *Nahawand*:

Neuter: C D E♭ F♯ G A♭ $\overset{+}{B\flat}$ c

The Great *Nahawand*: G A B♭ c d e♭ f♯ g

Turez-neunin: C D♭ E♭ F $\overset{+}{G\flat}$ A B♭ c d♭ $\overset{+}{e\flat}$ f $\overset{+}{g\flat}$

In ascent are used the notes: *rast*, *zirkula*, *kurdi*, *jarka*, *ṣaba*, *ḥusēni*, *'ajam*, *kardan*, *shahnaz*, *jawab-siga* (or *sunbula*, *jawab-jarka*, *jwab-ṣaba*). In descent appear: *'ajam-'ashiran*, *shuri*, *jagā.*
Lit.: no. 121.

Nai (Turkey). See *Nāy.*

Nai (Afghanistan). General term for pipe (flute or shawm).

Naiki-Kanada (North India). *Rāga* ascribed to the *Kafi thāta*. Occasionally the *Sarang* background is noticeable.
Tone material:

C D E♭ F G $\overset{+}{B\flat}$ c
c B♭ G F E♭ D C

Lit.: no. 138.

Naiki-Mallār (North India). A rare *rāga* ascribed to the *Kafi thāta*. The *rāga* belongs to the *Mallār* family. It consists of a combination of *Naiki-Kanada* and *Mallār* material.
Tone material:

C F D G B♭ A B c
c B♭ G B♭ G E♭ E♭ E♭ F G F D C D C;
Vādis: F, C

Lit.: no. 138.

Naiṣādī (Ancient India). See *Jāti.*

Nai-sarbagi (Uzbeks). See *Sarbasnai.*

Nait (Turkey). Prayer sung in solo form as introduction to a religious celebration.
Lit.: no. 243.

Najdī (Middle East). *Maqām.*
Tone material:

F G A B♭(+) c d e♭(+) f

Lit.: no. 64.

Najoroto (Congo—Makere). Truncated barrel drum. Cf. *Maroto.*
Lit.: nos. 26, 184.

Naka (South Africa—Bamalete; Chwana). Also *pala.* Vertical bone or reed flute.
Lit.: no. 151.

Naka (South Africa—Sotho; Balubedu; Chwana; Ndebele). The Ndebele use this term for an entire reed-flute ensemble.
Lit.: no. 151.

Naka-chirashi (Japan). The climax; a centrally placed interlude in the *kumiuta* cycle.
Lit.: no. 187.

Na-kag (*Sora*) (Korea). Shell trumpet which produces only one note. It was used in Buddhist temples. Cf. *Hai Lo*; *Hora.*
Lit.: no. 179.

Nakah (Bali). The repetition of a part of a melody; a da capo motion to the beginning of a section.
Lit.: no. 197.

Nakairi (Japan). Chorus song; an interlude in the *noh* play performed between *ha* and *kyū.*
Lit.: no. 185.

Na-ka-la (China). Term for *nāghārā* (Turkey).
Lit.: no. 78.

Nakamunsale (Uganda—Ganda). Side-blown horn.
Lit.: no. 302.

Naka no yurushi (Japan). "Intermediate license." License given to professional musicians. Cf. *Ura no yurushi.*
Lit.: no. 225.

Nakāra (India; Punjab). Kettledrum with a shallow clay body, beaten with wooden sticks. Cf. *Tarshā.*

Naka tirasi (Japan). See *Jiuta.*

Nakauta (Japan). Central song of the *kumiuta.* See *Jiuta.*
Lit.: no. 187.

Naka ya lethlaka (South Africa; Transvaal—Pedi). Reed flute. Cf. *Tshitiringo*; *Naka.*
Lit.: no. 151.

Naka ya makoditsane (South Africa—Pedi). See *Naka ya phatola.*
Lit.: no. 151.

Naka ya phatola (South Africa; Transvaal—Pedi; Venda). Whistle flute. Cf. *Mothlatsa.*
Lit.: no. 151.

Naka ya sefako (South Africa—Pedi). End-blown whistle flute. Cf. *Pala.*

Nakhaprakāśini (South India). *Janya rāga* of the 52nd *mēḷa* (*Rāmapriyā*).
Tone material:

C D♭ E F♯ G A B♭ A c
c A B♭ G F♯ E D♭ C

Lit.: no. 139.

Nakhuna (Iran). Plectrum.

Nakish (Arabia). Also *semai.* Melismatic song (probably of Turkish origin).

Nakkāre (Turkey). Small kettledrum. When used in sacred music it is called *kudüm.* See *Naqqārā.*

Nakki (South India). Kannarese term for a steel plectrum, often in form of a ring, placed on the index finger. Cf. *Mizrāb.*
Lit.: no. 262.

Nakotība (Northeast Timor). Wooden goblet drum.
Lit.: no. 254.

Nakṣatramāla (South India). See *Nakshatramāla.*

Nakshatramāla (South India). *Janya rāga* of the 18th *mēḷa* (*Hāṭakāmbarī*).
Tone material:
C D♭ E A♯ B c
c B A♯ E D♭ C
Lit.: no. 139.

Nakula (India). Sanskrit term for musical instrument.
Lit.: no. 255.

Nakuloshthi (India). Sanskrit term for musical instrument.
Lit.: no. 255.

Nal(a) (India). (1) Kettledrum used on horseback. (2) Pipe.

Nalanganjur (Java). A two-toned variant of *kodok ngorek.* It uses the notes *gulu* and *ḍaḍa* in the low register and can be played by any *gamelan.*
Lit.: no. 163.

Nalangsa (*Sedih*) (Sunda District; West Java). "Melancholy mood."
Lit.: no. 163.

Nalikānti (South India). *Janya rāga* of the 27th *mēḷa* (*Sarasāṅgī*).
Tone material:
C E D F G B c
c B G F E D C
Lit.: no. 139.

Nalinābhumaṇi (South India). *Janya rāga* of the 58th *mēḷa* (*Hemāvatī*).
Tone material:
C D F♯ G A B♭ c
c B♭ A B♭ G F♯ D C
Lit.: no. 139.

Nalināhaṃsi (South India). *Janya rāga* of the 35th *mēḷa* (*Śūlinī*).
Tone material:
C D♯ E F G B A c
c B A G F D♯ C
Lit.: no. 139.

Nalinakusumāvaḷi (South India). *Janya rāga* of the 69th *mēḷa* (*Dhātuvardhaṇī*).
Tone material:
C D♯ E F♯ G c
c B A♭ B G F♯ D♯ C
Lit.: no. 139.

Nalinasukhi (South India). *Janya rāga* of the 34th *mēḷa* (*Vāgadhīśvarī*).
Tone material:
C F E F G A B♭ A c
c B♭ A G F E F D♯ C
Lit.: no. 139.

Nallari (Korea). See *T'ae-p'yong-so.*

Nal-na-ri (Korea). Conical oboe with seven finger holes in front and one in the back. See *So-na.*

Nam (Vietnam). "South." Modal system (*dieu*). Next to *bac* ("north"). *Nam* ("south") is the other important system. While the *bac* compositions are performed in fast tempo, the *nam* (and *oan*) are rendered in slow tempo. Name of a scale. See list of scales shown under the heading of *Bac.*
Lit.: no. 297.

Nam (*Bam*) (South Borneo; Banjermasin). The fourth note of the *slendro* system (of Banjermasin). Cf. *Slendro* (Table C).

Nam- (*Nim-*) (Arabia). Prefix to the name of a note indicating that its intonation is supposed to be approximately a quartertone lower than the fixed main tone (e.g., *ḥijāz* [F♯] and *nam-ḥijāz* [about F̊]). A list of all tone names and notes through two octaves can be seen under the heading of *Jagā* (*Yagā*). Cf. *Taq.*
Lit.: no. 34.

Nam (Korea). See *Yul-ch-po.* Cf. *Nan-lü* (China).

Nam (Java). See *Nem.*

Namaddu (Uganda – Gwere). Ensemble of five tuned drums.
Lit.: no. 218.

Nāmadeśi (South India). See *Narmada* (50th *asampūrṇa mēḷa*).

Nam ai (*Hue*) (Vietnam). Scale. See list of scales shown under the heading of *Bac.*

Nam-'ajām (Arabia). Also *nim-'ajām ḥusaynī*. Tone name of a note ca. ¼ tone lower than *'ajam* (*ḥusaynī*). A list of all tone names and notes through two octaves can be seen under the heading of *Jagā* (*Yagā*).
Lit.: no. 64.

Nam-'ajām (Arabia). See *Nam-'ajām-'ushayran.*

Nam-'ajām-'ashiran (*Nam-'ajām-'ushayrān*) (in Syria this tone is called *nam-'ajām*) (Arabia). Tone name of a note ca. ¼ tone lower than *'ajām-'ashiran.* A list of all tone names and notes through two octaves can be seen under the heading of *Jagā* (*Yagā*).
Lit.: no. 64.

Namalanga (Congo – Bapopoie). Hand bell.
Lit.: no. 21.

Namalua (North Rhodesia – Mashuku-Lumbwe). Friction drum.
Lit.: no. 255.

Nāmanārāyaṇī (South India). The 50th *mēḷa*:
C D♭ E F♯ G A♭ B♭ c
As *rāga* the same scale is used (as shown above).
Lit.: no. 139.

Namarue (New Guinea – Bare'e). Jew's harp.

Nambongo (Congo – Mangbetu). Side-blown ivory horn.
Lit.: no. 21.

Nam-buselik (*Nim-busalik*) (Arabia). Tone name of a note ca. ¼ tone lower than *busalik* (*'ushaq*). A list of all tone names and notes through two octaves can be seen under the heading of *Jagā* (*Yagā*).
Lit.: nos. 34, 64.

Nam-gushat (*Nim-gavāsht*; *Kawasht*). Tone name of a note ca. ¼ tone lower than *gushat.* A list of all tone names and notes through two octaves can be seen under the heading of *Jagā* (*Yagā*).
Lit.: nos. 34, 64.

Nam-ḥijāz (*Nim-ḥijāz*) (Arabia). Tone name of a note ¼ tone lower than *ḥijāz* (in Syria this note is often called *'araba*). A list of all tone names and notes through two octaves can be seen under the heading of *Jagā* (*Yagā*).
Lit.: nos. 34, 64.

Nam-ḥiṣār (*Nim-ḥiṣār*; *Nim-qarār-ḥiṣār*; *Ḥiṣārqaba*) (Arabia). Tone name of a note ¼ tone lower than *ḥiṣār* (*shurī*). A list of all tone names and notes through two octaves can be seen under the heading of *Jagā* (*Yagā*).
Lit.: nos. 34, 64.

Namigaeshi (Japan). "Waves coming and going." A term in *koto* playing. *Namigaeshi* consists of glides across all strings (1-*kin*) and back to one; this is done once or twice. It always ends with an upward *nagashi* or with a *hikiren* from string 1 to strings 5, 6.
Lit.: no. 225.

Nāmita (India). See *Gamak(a).*

Nam-Kurdī (*Nahawānd*; *Nim-Kurdī*) (Arabia). Tone name of a note ca. ¼ tone lower than *kurdi* (in Egypt this note can be called *nahawānd*). A list of all tone names and notes through two octaves can be seen under the heading of *Jagā* (*Yagā*).
Lit.: nos. 34, 64.

Nam-māhūr (*Nim-māhūr*; *Nim-mahuft*) (Arabia). Tone name of a note ca. ¼ tone

lower than *māhūr* (*nihuft*) (in Syria this note can be called *nahaft*). A list of all tone names and notes through two octaves can be seen under the heading of *Jagā* (*Yagā*).
Lit.: nos. 34, 64.

Namna ya tarumbeta (East Africa; Zanzibar). Swahili term for bassoon.

Namna ya zeze (Zanzibar). Swahili term for zither.

Namongu (Sumba). Gong.

Nam-shāh'nāz (*Nim-shāh'nāz*) (Arabia). Tone name of a note ca. ¼ tone lower than *shah'naz*. A list of all tone names and notes through two octaves can be seen under the heading of *Jagā* (*Yagā*).
Lit.: nos. 34, 64.

Nam-sunbula (*Nim-sumbulaḥ*) (Arabia). Tone name of a note ca. ¼ tone lower than *sunbula* (in Syria this note is called *sunbula*). A list of all tone names and notes through two octaves can be seen under the heading of *Jagā* (*Yagā*).
Lit.: nos. 34, 64.

Namukenge (Congo—Bapopoie). Board zither.
Lit.: no. 21.

Namwarki (Micronesia; Ponape). The chief who is privileged to beat the drum.

Nam-zarkala (*Nam-zirkula*; *Nim-zirgulah*) (Arabia). Tone name of a note ca. ¼ tone lower than *zarkala*. A list of all tone names and notes through two octaves can be seen under the heading of *Jagā* (*Yagā*).
Lit.: nos. 34, 64.

Nan (Japan). Literally, "man," "ghost," "warrior." One of the five traditional subjects appearing in the *noh* drama (the other four subjects are: *shin*, *nyo*, *kyo*, and *ki*).

Nan-ch'ü (China—M 4620; M 1623). See *Ch'ü*; *Ch'uan-ch'ih*.

Nand (*Nanda*; *Anandi*) (North India). Rare *rāga* ascribed to the *Bilaval thāta*.
Tone material:
C E (F) F♯ G A c
c B A G (F♯) E D C; *Vādis*: probably C and G
Lit.: no. 138.

Nānda (India). Flute.
Lit.: no. 255.

Nāndayanti (Ancient India). See *Jāti*.

Nāndī (Ancient India). Prayer song asking for blessing.

Nandin (India). See *Gopi yantra*; *Gopichand*.
Lit.: no. 198.

Nandir (Bali). An old dance, performed by three boys. Cf. *Legong*.
Lit.: no. 197.

Nanduṇi (South India; Trivandrum). Lute with a slim body, two strings, and seven frets. The instrument is played with a plectrum.
Lit.: no. 254.

Nang (Thailand). Term for drum beat. See *Song na*.

Nanga (Tanganyika). Trough zither. Also arched harp with 5-8 gut strings. Cf. *Enanga*; *Inanga*.
Lit.: no. 206.

Nangara (Africa; Chad—Kanembu). Large drum with two heads. Cf. *Kwelli*; *Kidi*.

Nanga ya danga (South Africa—Venda). End-blown flute made of the bone of a vulture.
Lit.: no. 151.

Nangaya davhi (South Africa—Venda). Wooden flute.
Lit.: no. 151.

Nanga ya mathanga (South Africa – Venda). "Reeds in a circle." Reed-flute ensemble that can consist of 22 instruments.
Lit.: no. 151.

Nanga ya ntsa (South Africa – Venda). Whistle.

Nang ek (Northeast Thailand). The leading female in *mawlum moo.*
Lit.: no. 203.

Nangi 'ta mata (Flores). Cf. *Ke nangi.*
Lit.: no. 166.

Nangka (Borneo). Shaft of the *ketobong* (*ketipung*).
Lit.: no. 255.

Nang-ma (Tibet). Ancient songs performed in religious, serious dance-plays.
Lit.: no. 143.

Nang rawng (Northeast Thailand). The second leading female in *mawlum-moo.*
Lit.: no. 203.

Nang-talung (Northeast and South Thailand). Cf. *Angtalung*; *Nung daloong.*

Nan-hsi (China – M 4620; M 2452). "Southern drama." An early dramatic form that originated in the southern Chekiang province during the 12th century. It led to the *tsa-chü* in Wen-chou. It became popular and later was considered to be a genuine forerunner of the Peking opera. See *Ch'ang.*
Lit.: no. 183.

Nan-hu (China – M 4620; M 2167). The "southern" fiddle with a cylindrical body, a slim neck, and two silken strings. The hair of the bow is strung between the two strings. Cf. *Hu-ch'in.*

Nani phulaune git (Nepal). Cradle song.
Lit.: no. 133.

Naniwa-bushi (Japan). Popular narrative songs accompanied by the *shamisen.* Cf. *Katarimono.*
Lit.: no. 185.

Nan-lü (China – M 4620; M 4280). "Southern tube." The name of an absolute pitch. It is the fourth tone of the circle of fifths as shown in the *lü-lü* system. Traditionally *nan-lü* is a *yin* (female) tone. It was used as the basic note of Confucian hymns performed in the month of August. If the tone is represented by a notational symbol, only the first syllable was used: *nan* (M 4620).
Lit.: no. 136.

Nantanapriya (South India). *Janya rāga* of the 72nd *mēḷa* (*Rasikapriyā*).
Tone material:
C D# F# A# B c
c B A# F# D# C
Lit.: no. 139.

Nanto (Japan). Hereditary temple musicians who originally came from Nara. Their activities were concerned with the ancient *kagura.*
Lit.: no. 225.

Nao (China – M 4641). Noisy cymbals. See *Nao-po.* Cf. *Nyo* (Korea).
Lit.: no. 137.

Nao-bat (Former Annam). See *Cai Nao-bat.*

Nao-chin-chieh (China – M 4646; M 1057; Giles 1434). Rattle consisting of 4-5 oblong iron slabs hung loosely on two strings.
Lit.: no. 209.

Nao-po (China – M 4641; M 5325). A Hang-chow term for two large brass cymbals used by Buddhist priests and in the theater. Cf. *Yin-ch'ing.*
Lit.: no. 209.

Naos (Egypt). An ancient sistrum, the upper half of which representing the outline of a tiny Naos, a temple. See *Seshesht.*
Lit.: no. 250.

Napal (Korea). Long, slim metal trumpet consisting of three sections which can be telescoped into each other when the instrument is not in use. Cf. *La-pa* (China); *Ra-pa* (Japan).
Lit.: no. 52.

Napuṃsaka (India). A now obscure term for "neutral" *rāgas* (neither "male" nor "female") as mentioned by Nārada, author of *Saṅgīta Makaraṇda* (written between the 7th and 11th centuries).
Lit.: no. 138.

Napura (*nupura*) (India). Rattle consisting of hollow copper or iron rings containing small metal particles or tiny stones.
Lit.: no. 184.

Naqāra (North Africa). Small clay kettledrum.
Lit.: no. 255.

Naqqāra (North Africa; Arabia; Iran; Turkey; Ethiopia; North India). Term for a pair of small kettledrums, each with a deep copper or wooden kettle and beaten with wooden sticks. These drums have numerous names among them may be mentioned: *anaka* (India); *kus* (Turkey); *dumbelek* (Turkey); *mahā-nāgarā* (India); *nāgarā* (India); *nāgarit* (Ethiopia); *nāgra* (Assam); *naguar* (South India); *naqqarya* (Arabia); *na'ra* (Turkey). Cf. *Dundubhi. Naqqāra* can also mean simply "percussion instrument."
Lit.: nos. 250, 254.

Naqqārya (Arabia). Two large flat kettledrums carried on the back of a camel. The lower pitched one is placed at the player's right, the higher pitched one at his left. Both drums are struck with wooden sticks.
Lit.: no. 250.

Naqr (Arabia). Tambourin.

Naqrazān (Arabia). Two shallow small kettledrums carried on the back of a donkey. Cf. *Naqqarya.*
Lit.: no. 255.

Naqsh (Iran; Khorasan; Turkmenia). Instrumental piece rich in musical ornamentation. Cf. *'Amal.*

Nāqūr (Arabia). Shawm; horn (according to the Koran, *nāqūr* and *ṣūr* are the instruments which will produce the "last trumpet sound").

Naqūs (Arabia; Ethiopia). A metal hand bell attached to a board or a stick. It is struck with a metal stick and is used in religious services of the Copts and other Christians living in Arab countries.
Lit.: no. 255.

Nar (Sumeria). Term (rank) of a singer or musician-priest who performs hymns praising gods and kings.
Lit.: nos. 94, 281.

Nar (Central Asia). Vertical flute.

Na'ra (Turkey). See *Kus.*
Lit.: nos. 81, 255.

Narabhairavī (South India). See *Naṭabhairavī.*

Nāradiya vīṇā (India). The southern name of the *mahatī vīṇā.*

Naramut (Bismarck Archipelago; New Britain). Term for *garamut.*
Lit.: no. 84.

Nārāsam (South India). *Janya rāga* of the 18th *mēḷa* (*Hāṭakāmbarī*).
Tone material:

C D♭ E F A♯ c
c A♯ F E D♭ C

Lit.: no. 139.

Narashringa (Nepal). Copper horn.
Lit.: no. 255.

Nārāyaṇadēśadi (South India). *Janya rāga* of the 20th *mēḷa* (*Naṭabhairavī*).
Tone material:

C D C E♭ F G A♭ G B♭ c
c B♭ A♭ G F G A♭ G F E♭ D C
(c B♭ A♭ G F E♭ D C)

Lit.: no. 139.

Nārāyaṇagauḷa (South India). *Janya rāga* of the 28th *mēḷa* (*Harikāmbhōji*).
Tone material:
C D F G B♭ A B♭ c
c B♭ A G F E D C
Lit.: no. 139.

Nārāyaṇi (North India). Rare *rāga* ascribed to the *Khamaj thāta*.
Tone material:
C D F G A c
c B♭ A G F D C; *Vādis*: D, G
Lit.: no. 138.

Nārāyaṇi (South India). *Janya rāga* of the 28th *mēḷa* (*Harikāmbhōji*).
Tone material:
C D F G A c
c B♭ A G F D C
Lit.: no. 139.

Nares-juẖ (*Nares-jux*) (Northwest Sibiria). "Musical wood." Lyre of the Ostyaks, called *sangkultap* among the Vogul. Most probably the only surviving lyre in Asia. It has a rectangular corpus, five gut strings diatonically tuned, and is played (plucked) with both hands. Also called *pannang-jux.*
Lit.: nos. 8, 250.

Narik (*Narek*) **Kendang** (Bali). A sudden lively stringendo drumming during the performance of the *mipil* section.
Lit.: no. 197.

Nārī-moṅ (Burma). A gong that is struck in order to indicate the hours.
Lit.: no. 255.

Närin utas (written: *narin utasun*) (Mongolia). "Thin string"; a string of the *khil kuur*, tuned a fifth higher than the *budung utas.*
Lit.: no. 61.

Narirītigauḷa (South India). See *Naṭabhairavī.*

Narmadā (South India). *Janya rāga* of the 50th *mēḷa* (*Nāmanārāyaṇī*).
Tone material:
C D♭ E F♯ A♭ B♭ c
c B♭ A♭ F♯ G E D♭ C
Lit.: no. 139.

Narmadā (South India). (1) The 50th *asampūrṇa mēḷa-rāga* without *kaṭapayādi* prefix. (2) The 50th *asampūrṇa mēḷa-rāga* with *kaṭapayādi* prefix. It is called *Nāmadeśi.* See *Rāga* (South India).
Lit.: no. 139.

Narsiṅgā (India). Hindi term for *rāṇaśṛṅga.*

Narsingha (Nepal). Copper trumpet blown during marriage processions. Cf. *Raṇaśṛṅga.*

Narśṛṅga (*Narshriṅga*) (India). See *Rāṇaśṛṅga.*

Nartaka (Ancient India). Dancer.

Nartaki (South India). *Janya rāga* of the 28th *mēḷa* (*Harikāmbhōji*).
Tone material:
C D F G A c
c B♭ A F D C
Lit.: no. 139.

Nāru (Ancient Mesopotamia). See *Nar* (Sumeria).

Nāsa jantra (South India). Term for nose flute. See *Magudi.* Cf. *Tiktirī.*

Nāsāmani (South India). *Janya rāga* of the 70th *mēḷa* (*Nāsikabhuṣaṇī*).
Tone material:
C D♯ E F♯ G F♯ G c
c B♭ A B♭ G F♯ D♯ C
Lit.: no. 139.

Nāsāmaṇi (South India). (1) The 70th *asampūrṇa mēḷa-rāga* without *kaṭapayādi* prefix. (2) The 70th *asampūrṇa mēḷa-rāga* with *kaṭapayādi* prefix. See *Rāga* (South India).
Lit.: no. 139.

Naṣb (Arabia). Secular song. A more or less artistic form of the simple *ḥuda'*. Songs are classified into three categories: *naṣb*, *sinād*, and *hazaj*.

Nashā'id (Arabia). Religious hymns.

Nashīd (Arabia). In the past, a nasal way of singing psalms in very free rhythm. In recent times rhythm has been applied. In Andalusia the *nashīd*, in the manner of recitative, was used to open a concert.
Lit.: no. 76.

Nashīd (Yemen — Jews). Bride's song of lament.

Nāsikabhūṣaṇi (South India). The 70th *mēḷa*:

C D♯ E F♯ G A B♭ c

Lit.: no. 139.

Na't (Afghanistan). Religious songs; qur'anic cantillation.

Naṭa (Ancient India). Actor-dancer.

Nāṭa (South India). *Janya rāga* of the 36th *mēḷa* (*Chalanāṭa*).
Tone material:

C D♯ E F G A♯ B c
c B G F D♯ C

Lit.: no. 139.

Nāṭa (South India). (1) The 36th *asampūrṇa mēḷa-rāga* without *kaṭapayādi* prefix. (2) The 36th *asampūrṇa mēḷa-rāga* with *kaṭapayādi* prefix. It was called *Chalanṭa*. See *Rāga* (South India).
Lit.: no. 139.

Naṭabhairavī (*Narabhairavī*) (South India). (1) The 20th *mēḷa*. (2) As *rāga*: it has the same tone material as that of (1). Veṅkaṭamakhin (17th century) called this *rāga Narirītigauḷa*, in which the note A♭ is omitted in ascent.
Lit.: no. 139.

Nāṭābharaṇam (South India). *Janya rāga* of the 10th *mēḷa* (*Nāṭakapriya*).
Tone material:

C D♭ E♭ F G A G B♭ c
c B♭ A G F E♭ F D♭ C

Lit.: no. 139.

Nāṭābharaṇam (South India). (1) The 10th *asampūrṇa mēḷa-rāga* without *kaṭapayādi* prefix. (2) The 10th *asampūrṇa mēḷa-rāga* with *kaṭapayādi* prefix. See *Rāga* (South India).
Lit.: no. 139.

Nāṭakapriya (South India). (1) The 10th *mēḷa*:

C D E♭ F G A B♭ c

(2) As *rāga*: to be performed in the evening or at night. Veṅkaṭamakhin (17th century) called this *rāga Nāṭabharaṇam*. The tone material is the same as that of the *mēḷa*.
Lit.: no. 139.

Nāṭakurañji (South India). *Janya rāga* of the 28th *mēḷa* (*Harikāmbhōji*).
Tone material:

C D E F A B♭ c (C D E F B♭ A B♭ c)
c B♭ A F E C (c B♭ A F E D E C)

Lit.: no. 139.

Nāṭanavēlavaḷi (South India). *Janya rāga* of the 39th *mēḷa* (*Jhālavarāḷi*).
Tone material:
C D♭ F♯ G A♭ B c
c B G F♯ E♭♭ D♭ C
Lit.: no. 139.

Nāṭanāyāraṇi (South India). *Janya rāga* of the 28th *mēḷa* (*Harikāmbhōji*).
Tone material:
C D E F A B♭ A c
c B♭ A G F E F D C
Lit.: no. 139.

Nat-chin (Burma). Brief songs sung when celebrating spirits.

Nath (*Nat*) **Rāga** (North India). Important *rāga* performed at night. It is ascribed to the *Bilaval thāta*.
Tone material:
C D E F G A c
c B (B♭) A G F E D C
Lit.: no. 138.

Nath-Bihag (North India). *Rāga* ascribed to the *Bilaval thāta*. It is combination of features taken from the *rāgas Nath* and *Bihag*.
Lit.: no. 138.

Nath-Bilaval (North India). A morning *rāga* which represents a combination of features taken from the *rāgas Nath* and *Bilaval*. It is ascribed to the *Bilaval thāta*.
Tone material:
C D E F G A B c
c B (B♭) A G F E D C; *Vādis*: F, C
Lit.: no. 138.

Nathendra (South India). Flute with seven finger holes.
Lit.: no. 262.

Nath-Kamod (North India). A *rāga* ascribed to the *Bilaval thāta*. It was (and is) performed almost exclusively by the pupils of the late Aladiya Khan of Bombay. As the name indicates, this *rāga* consists of a combination of features taken from *rāgas Nath* and *Kamod*.
Lit.: no. 138.

Nath-Mallār (North India). A *rāga* ascribed to the *Kafi thāta* and belongs to the *Mallār* family. The characteristic of this *rāga* is the combination of *Nath* material with the typical *Mallār* phrase c A B♭ G.
Tone material:
C D E F G A B c
c B♭ A G F E D C; or,
C D (E♭) E F G A B c
c B♭ A G F E (E♭) D C; *Vādis*: F, C
Lit.: no. 138.

Nath-Narayan (*Nattanarayani*) (North India). An important *rāga* with a fierce character. It is ascribed to the *Bilaval thāta*.
Tone material:
C D E F G A c
c A G F (E) D C; *Vādis*: F, C
Lit.: no. 138.

Natori (Japan). Professional name (title). After a student has passed some rigorous tests and paid a substantial fee, he eventually is given a professional name which generally includes part of his teacher's name.
Lit.: no. 185.

Nat puja (Assam). Sword dance.
Lit.: no. 46.

Nauba (*Nuba*) (Islamic North Africa; Morocco; Algeria). A "round" of musician-singers. A suite of vocal and instrumental pieces performed by a group of musicians (originally minstrels at the Abbasid court, A.D. 749-1258). Each member of this group took his turn and performed his favorite piece (cf. *Ador*).

Before the 14th century the *nauba* consisted of four movements: *qaul* (*qal*), *ghazal*, *tarana*, and *furudāsht*. Later, cultivated in Andalusia and at recent times preserved in Morocco and Algeria, the *nauba* became vocal: a cantata of usually nine movements, all in the same tonality. With the *mustazad* added, all items were vocal but were provided with instrumental preludes (*tariqa*) and an introductory, overture-like *pishrev* (*peshref*) or *bashrau*. At the present time there still exists in Morocco the tradition of 11 *naubas*.

Principally the *nauba* consists of the following movements: the first, a prelude, performed by a singer without drum accompaniment. It is called *daira* ("circle"), the 2nd and 3rd movements are instrumental pieces, the 4th, 5th, and 6th are songs, the 7th is instrumental, the 8th, is a set of songs and the 9th is a single concluding song.

Beside the western ("Andalusian") *nauba* of Morocco, Algeria, and Tunisia, has to be mentioned the eastern *nauba*. This suite consists generally of eight movements:

1. *Taqsīm*, an instrumental improvised introduction.
2. *Bashraf*, an instrumental item consisting of four or five parts (*khānas*).
3. *Samā'i*, an instrumental item consisting of three or four parts.
4. *Tawāshīḥ*, several *mūwashshāt* (vocal items) sung by the performing ensemble.
5. *Qaṣīda*, vocal piece. The singer accompanies this improvised item on the *'ūd*.

The second part of the *nauba*:

6. *Tahmīla*, a light fantasy of instrumental sections.
7. *Dawr*, a vocal item in three parts.
8. *Qafla*, first part of the end piece performed in unison by singers and players; *dārij*, coda.

Lit.: nos. 76, 110, 257.

Nauba (*Maluf*) (Tunisia). Suite consisting of 10 movements; the names of the movements are: *al istiftākh*, *al masaddar*, *al abyāt*, *al btāyhī*, *al tushiyah*, *al mashad*, *al barwal*, *al draj*, *al khafīf*, *al khatm*.
Lit.: no. 171.

Naubat (Arabia). Instrumental music performed at weddings.

Naubat (North India). "The nine players." Term for a *shahnay* ensemble.
Lit.: no. 46.

Naubat (*Damāmā*) (Malaya). The big drum of the sovereign. Cf. *Gending*; *Mahanagāra*; *Nahabat*.
Lit.: no. 254.

Nauḥ (Arabia). Elegy.
Lit.: no. 76.

Nauksvebon (Burma). See *Khram*.

Nauktaiṅ (Burma). A person who assists the *hne* (*kayā*) player when he becomes exhausted from the strenuous playing of the huge oboe. Cf. *Hne*.
Lit.: no. 254.

Naurūz (*Āwāz*) (Arabia). *Maqām*.
Tone material:

C E♭♭ E♭ F A♭♭ A♭ B♭ c

According to Ṣafī al-Dīn 'Abd al-Mu'min al-Baghdadi, 13th century.
Lit.: no. 65.

Nautanki (North India). The performance of the buffoon who comically or sarcastically describes local conditions during a dramatic show.

Nautch (India). Hindi term for dance entertainment: a dance group, usually a female dancer and four musicians.
Lit.: no. 46.

Nava (*Nawā*) (Iran). See *Dastgah*.

Navahand (Arabia). *Maqām*.
Tone material:

G A B♭ c d e♭ f g

Cf. *Nawa*.
Lit.: no. 270.

Navanītam (South India). (1) The 40th *mēḷa*:

C D♭ E♭♭ F♯ G A B♭ c

(2) *Rāga*; same tone material as that of *mēḷa*.

Navanītapañcamam (South India). See *Navanītapañchamam*.

Navanītapañchamam (South India). *Janya rāga* of the 24th *mēḷa* (*Varuṇapriyā*).
Tone material:

C E♭ F A♯ G A♯ B c
c B G F D C

Lit.: no. 139.

Navarasa (India). Nine emotions linked with music:

1. *Sringāra*, love.
2. *Hāsya*, laughter.
3. *Karunā*, pathos, compassion.
4. *Raudra*, singer.
5. *Vira*, heroism.
6. *Bhayānaka*, fear
7. *Bībhatsa*, disgust
8. *Adbhuta*, surprise, wonder.
9. *Sānta*, tranquillity, peace.

Among further *rasas* can be found: *bhakti*, "devotion"; *vātsalya*, "affection toward children." Cf. *Rasa*; *Bhava*.
Lit.: no. 262.

Navarasabaṅgāḷa (South India). *Janya rāga* of the 47th *mēḷa* (*Suvarṇāṅgī*).
Tone material:
C D♭ E♭ F♯ A G A B c
c B A F♯ E♭ C
Lit.: no. 139.

Navarasagandhāri (South India). *Janya rāga* of the 50th *mēḷa* (*Nāmanāyāyaṇī*).
Tone material:
C D♭ E F♯ G F♯ A♭ B♭ c
c B♭ A♭ F♯ E D♭ C
Lit.: no. 139.

Navarasakalānidhi (South India). *Janya rāga* of the 28th *mēḷa* (*Harikāmbhōji*).
Tone material:
C D F G c B♭ c
c A G F E D C
Lit.: no. 139.

Navarasakannaḍa (South India). *Janya rāga* of the 28th *mēḷa* (*Harikāmbhōji*).
Tone material:
C E F G c
c B♭ A F E D C
Lit.: no. 139.

Navarasakuntavarāḷi (South India). *Janya rāga* of the 40th *mēḷa* (*Navanītam*).
Tone material:
C F♯ G A B♭ c
c B♭ A G A F♯ E♭♭ D♭ C
Lit.: no. 139.

Navarasāndhāli (South India). *Janya rāga* of the 49th *mēḷa* (*Dhavalāmbarī*).
Tone material:
C E D♭ E F♯ G A♭ c
c A♭ G F♯ E D♭ E C
Lit.: no. 139.

Navaratnabhūśaṇi (South India). *Janya rāga* of the 63rd *mēḷa* (*Latāṅgī*).
Tone material:
C D E F♯ G A♭ c
c B A♭ G F♯ E D C
Lit.: no. 139.

Navaratnavilāsam (South India). *Janya rāga* of the 22nd *mēḷa* (*Kharaharapriyā*).
Tone material:
C D F G B♭ c
c B♭ A G E♭ D C
Lit.: no. 139.

Navaroj (*Navaroju*) (South India). *Janya rāga* of the 29th *mēḷa* (*Dhīraśaṅkarābharaṇam*).
Tone material:
G A B C D E F G
G F E D C *B A G*
This *rāga* has *pañchamāntya* character.
Lit.: no. 139.

Navasūtika (South India). *Janya rāga* of the 8th *mēḷa* (*Hanumattōḍi*).
Tone material:
C D♭ E♭ A♭ B♭ c
c B♭ A♭ E♭ D♭ C
Lit.: no. 139.

Nawā (Arabia). Tone name of the upper octave of *Jagā* (*Yagā*). A list of all tone names and notes through two octaves can be seen under the heading of *Jagā* (*Yagā*).

Nawā (Arabia). *Maqām* well known in Arabia and Iran. Its name means "the center of reason" (the Persian meaning would be "full of sound"). *Nawā* is one of the seven genuine Arabic *maqamāt*. Its tone material used frequently by oriental Jews in their Friday evening prayers. Tone material:

G A B♭(+) c d e♭(+) f g (or f♯ g)

Nawā melodies never move to the upper octave. The Persians distinguish two types: the big and the small *nawā*. The tone material of big *nawā* is shown above. The material of small *nawā* is:

G A♭ B♭ c d e♭(+) f g

Lit.: nos. 64, 121.

Nawā (Modern Tunisia). *Maqām*.
Tone material:

A *B♭*(+) C D E F(+) G A B c d

Lit.: no. 64.

Nawa (Java). See *Rebāb* (Java).

Nawa (South Pacific—Tonga; Niue). Slit-drum. Cf. *Nafa* (*Naffa*).
Lit.: no. 84.

Naw'athar (Modern Egypt; Middle East). *Maqām*.
Tone material:

C D E♭ F♯ G A♭ B c

Lit.: no. 64.

Nawba (West Central Sahara). Tuareg term for *nauba*.

Nawek (East Java). Term for the *kemanak*.
Lit.: no. 163.

Nāy (Arabia; Iran; North India). (1) General term for vertical and transverse flutes and reed pipes. (2) Long vertical cane flute with 6-7 finger holes. (3) The *nāy* players of Turkestan and Kashmir use a small transverse flute with 5-6 finger holes. (4) The name *nāy* is also applied to a few string instruments, e.g., *nāy tunbur*. (5) There are numerous names for the large variety of this instrument: *baṭṭāl*, *baṭṭāl-i dāwudī*, *būl ahank*, *dāwud*, *diyānai*, *dū-ahank*, *dūnāy*, *girift*, *kūshnāy*, *manṣūr*, *mustaḥsin*, *nāy-abyaḍ*, *nāy-asnad*, *pīsha*, *qīz*, *sarhang*, *shāh*, *sūpurga*, *sūryanāy*, *zarbasnāy*.
Lit.: no. 34.

Nāy abyad (Turkey). "The white *nāy*" (flute). Cf. *Nāy*.

Nayaga (Java). See *Niyaga*.

Nāy aswad (Turkey). "The black *nāy*," a reed pipe. Cf. *Nāy*.

Naya-khin (Nepal). A drum similar to the *dhyamaya*. Instead of a twisted cane a wooden bar is used as a drumstick. The drumming is called *kasai baja* (Kasai's music). Cf. *Chhusya*.

Nāyakī (South India). *Janya rāga* of the 20th *mēḷa* (*Naṭabhairavī*).
Tone material:

C D (C) F G A♭ B♭ A♭ G c
c B♭ A♭ G F E♭ D C

Lit.: no. 139.

Nāyakī (South India). *Janya rāga* of the 22nd *mēḷa* (*Kharaharapriyā*).
Tone material:

(a) C D F G A B♭ A c
c B♭ A G F E♭ D C
(b) C D F G B♭ A G c
c B♭ A G F D E♭ D C

Lit.: no. 139.

Nāyanam (India). See *Nāgasuram*.

Naye (Arabia). Flute.

Nayel (Syria; Iraq). Sad song lamenting the absence of the beloved. Cf. *Mouleya derie*.

Nāy erbab (Arabia). Bagpipe.
Lit.: no. 255.

Nāy ghiref (Arabia). Small *nay.*

Nāy-i-anban (Iran). Bagpipe.

Nāy-i-aswad (Iran). An ancient term for the *nāy-siyāh.*
Lit.: no. 77.

Nāy-i balābān (Turkey). A single reed pipe. Cf. *Balābān.*
Lit.: no. 72.

Nāy-i chādūr (Turkey). See *Ayyūb būrūsī.*
Lit.: no. 81.

Nāy-i narm (Iran). Beak-flute.
Lit.: no. 77.

Nāy-i safid (Iran). "White *nāy.*" Flute. Cf. *Nāy-i siyāh.*

Nā-i siyāh (*Nāy siyāh*) (Iran). "The black *nāy,*" a reed pipe. Cf. *Nāy-i safid.*
Lit.: no. 76.

Nāy jiraf (Egypt). A very short *nāy.*
Lit.: no. 76.

Naykin (Nepal). Small barrel drum, similar to the *dhā.*

Nāy labek (Iran). Cf. *Sūt.*

Nāy mus (Iran). Pan flutes.
Lit.: no. 255.

Nayrūz Rāst (Middle East). *Maqām.*
Tone material:
C D $\overset{+}{E\flat}$ F G $\overset{+}{A\flat}$ B♭ c (also: C D E F G $\overset{+}{A\flat}$ $\overset{\flat}{B\flat}$ c)
Lit.: no. 64.

Nāy shāh (Iran; Egypt). The royal (big) *nāy.*

Nāy siyāh (*Nāy-i siyāh*) (Iran). "The black *nāy,*" also called *zamr-siyāh nāy.* Cf. *Nāy; Nāy-i aswad.*
Lit.: no. 65.

Nāy tunbūr (Arabia; Middle East). A *tunbūr* with two strings tuned a fourth apart.
Lit.: no. 76.

Nāy zunāmī (West Islamic countries). An early *nāy* named after its builder Zunam. In recent times the term became *zulami.*
Lit.: no. 78.

Nāz-i Niyāz (Middle East). *Maqām.*
Tone material:
D $\overset{+}{E\flat}$ F G A $\overset{+}{B\flat}$ c d
Occasionally the note G is changed to $\overset{\flat}{G}$.
Lit.: no. 64.

Nchabagome (Ruanda). Judgement drum struck when the accused is found guilty.
Lit.: no. 26.

Ncwa (Uganda). See *Nsegu.*

Ndaku (Congo). Small bell.
Lit.: no. 255.

Ndaludali (East Tanganyika—Zaramo). Music bow with one string.
Lit.: no. 10.

Ndamutsu (Ruanda). Royal drum.
Lit.: no. 26.

iNdandala (Northwest Rhodesia). Small drum.
Lit.: no. 242.

Ndara (Uganda—Alur; Congo—Andekobe). (1) Xylophone with eight wooden slabs; cf. *Kweningba* (Uganda). (2) Board zither (Congo).

Ndavni (Fiji Isl.—Viti Levu). Marine shell trumpet.
Lit.: no. 190.

Ndembo (Congo—Loango). Ritual (kettle)-drum.
Lit.: no. 280.

Ndenda (Senegal—Wolof). Drum.

Ndeo (Flores—Ende, Lio). To sing; song.
Lit.: no. 166.

Ndidi (*Dima*) (Lower Congo—Sundi). Barrel drum. See *Gaza.* Cf. *Elembe.*
Lit.: no. 26.

Ndima (Congo—Abarambo). Drum. Cf. *Gaza*; *Dima*; *Elembe.*
Lit.: no. 26.

Ndimbga (*Ndimga*) (South Rhodesia—Shuna). Music bow with resonator.
Lit.: no. 255.

Ndingi (Lower Congo). See *Mpovila za londe.*
Lit.: no. 280.

Ndjele (Mozambique). Thonga hand rattle (calabash with stick attached). The Venda name is *tsele*, the Swazi name is *ligoshu.*
Lit.: no. 151.

Ndjembo (Congo; Stanley Pool—Bateke). Guitar type. It has five strings played with a plectrum.
Lit.: no. 255.

iNdjua (Northwest Rhodesia—Ila). Rattle consisting of a tin filled with small stones. The tin is attached to a stick.
Lit.: no. 255.

Ndomo (Tanzania). Musical bow.
Lit.: no. 215.

Ndöna (*Akadankama*) (Cameroon—Fan). Musical bow.

Ndonga (Java). Passages from the Koran recited.

Ndongo (*Ntongoli*) (Uganda—Ganda; Soga; Faṅ). (1) Ganda bowl lyre with eight strings. (2) Pluriarc of the Faṅ.
Lit.: no. 33.

Ndono (Tanganyika—Wanyamwezi; Nyamwezi). Music bow.
Lit.: no. 255.

Ndorobo getet (Uganda). See *Getet.*

Ndualala (Tanzania). Small bells beaten during the *msunyunho* dance.

Nduma (Congo). (1) Conical drum of the Langbase. (2) Cylindrical drum of the Banziri. (3) Barrel drum of Mono. The body contains a rattling stone or, in the past, a finger cut off the hand of a killed enemy. Cf. *Esembe.*
Lit.: nos. 26, 190.

N'dundu (Congo—Bapote; Gombe). Drum with two heads.
Lit.: no. 26.

Ndungu (Lower Congo—Dunde; Ekonde). Single headed drum.
Lit.: no. 280.

N'dwele (Congo—Balesa-Basakata). Signal and war drum.
Lit.: no. 26.

Nebel (Ancient Israel). See *Nablā*; *Nevel.*

Nebuguwu (Congo—Malele). Drum that accompanies the ruler on his travels.
Lit.: no. 26.

Nedomu (Congo—Mangbetu). Arched harp. Cf. *Neduma.*
Lit.: no. 176.

Neduku (Congo). See *Nendime.*

Neduma (Congo—Meje). Arched harp. Cf. *Nedomu.*

Neḍunkuzhal (South India). Long flute (the term for the short flute is *kurunkuzhal*).
Lit.: no. 261.

Nefes (Turkey; Iran). Hymn with mystic undertones.

Nefīr (Middle East). See *Nafir.*

Negariti (Ethiopia). Drum. Cf. *Nagarit.*

Nei (China). The lower-pitched string of two fiddle-strings. Cf. *Wai.*

Nei (Central Asia). Cf. *Nay.*

Nei-anbun (Iran). Fars term for bagpipe.

Nei-ko (Korea). The term is derived from the Chinese *t'ao-ku.* The *nei-ko* consisted of a complex of six small suspended drums, painted black and arranged horizontally around a wooden stick like a wheel, each spoke being a small drum. Of the six drums only one was struck, while the other five were not beaten at all.
Lit.: no. 137.

Neipāli (South India). See *Nepali.*

Nei-to (Korea). Three small barrel drums horizontally placed, one above the other, pierced diametrically by one vertical handle. Each drum was struck like a *damaru.*
Lit.: no. 137.

Nem (Java). "Six." (1) First note of the modern *slendro* and the modern *pelog* systems. (2) A favorite *patet* of the music of the Royal Court of Jogyakarta. (3) The sixth tone of *pelog* in Central Java, Cheribon, Prabalingga, and Majakerta. The sixth tone of *slendro* in Central Java, Jombang, Prabalingga, Banyuwangi, Majakerta. (4) See *Laras.*
Lit.: no. 163.

Nem (Malaysia). Tone syllable representing the fifth note of *wayang* (and related scale systems). See *Chi* for complete scales.

Nembongo (Congo – Mangbetu). Ivory horn with lateral blowhole.
Lit.: no. 190.

Nembutsu (Japan). Cf. *Nembutsu-odori.*

Nembutsu-odori (Japan). Exorcistic folk dance of Buddhist origin. Priests beat gongs while dancing the *nembutsu* (the calling of the name of Buddha). Although women can dance *nembutsu*, the dancing of men and women is kept apart. Instruments used for the *nembutsu* accompaniment are flute, *shamisen* and, when available, a variable number of percussion instruments. *Nembutsu-odori* can be considered to be the predecessor of *kabuki.*
Lit.: no. 185.

Nemurambi (*Lepakusu*) (Congo – Mangbetu). Slit-drum.
Lit.: no. 21.

Nendime (*Neduku*) (Congo – Abarambe). Drum with two heads.
Lit.: no. 26.

Nenggara (Malaysia). Kettledrum.

Nengilsi (Assam – Garo). Cymbals.
Lit.: no. 254.

Nengoniki (Congo – Makere). Stick zither.
Lit.: no. 176.

Neṅilsi (Assam – Garo). See *Nengilsi.* Cf. *Mandirā.*

Nentu (Flores – Ruteng). Also *Kombing.* Jew's harp. See *Genggo* (*Ego*).
Lit.: nos. 163, 166.

Nēpālagauḷa (South India). *Janya rāga* of the 15th *mēḷa* (*Māyāmāḷavagauḷa*).
Tone material:

C D♭ E F A♭ B c
c B A♭ F E D♭ C

Lit.: no. 139.

Nēpāli (*Neipali*) (South India). *Janya rāga* of the 36th *mēḷa* (*Chalanāṭa*).
Tone material:

C D♯ E G A♯ B c
c B A♯ G E D♯ C

Lit.: no. 139.

Nepathya (India). The back space of a theatrical stage. Cf. *Rangapitha.*

Neshīd (Egypt). Patriotic marching song of recent origin.
Lit.: no. 100.

Netori (*Torine*) (Japan). "To dress the tone"; a short mood-setting prelude in slow tempo in *gagaku.* In instrumental pieces the *netori* begins with the *shō* playing a short melody, which is followed by the playings of the *hichiriki* (and *kakko*), *biwa,* and *koto.* In dances the *netori* represents the *jo* section.
String players call this prelude *kakiawase.* At festive occasions (*bugaku*) the *netori* is substituted by the bigger *choshi.* Cf. *Gagaku.*
Lit.: no. 185.

Netra (*chakra*) (South India). Name of the 2nd *chakra* in the system of the 72 *mēḷas.* Cf. *Rāga* (South India); *Mēḷa.*
Lit.: no. 139.

Neur (Thailand). Term for melody.
Lit.: no. 58.

Neuter (Arabia). "The Greek *Nahawand,*" a sub-*maqām* of *Nahawānd.*
Tone material:

C D E♭ F♯ G A♭ $\overset{+}{\text{B}\flat}$ c

This material is the same as that of *maqām Ḥiṣar.* The latter begins with *rast.*

Neve (Solomon Isl.). Jew's harp. Cf. *Mike.*

Nevel (*Nebel*) (Ancient Israel). Hebrew term used by Flavius Josephus (1st century A.D.) for an obscure instrument with 12 strings plucked with the bare fingers. It could have been a harp, a zither, or a lyre.
Lit.: no. 250.

Nevruuz (Persia). "The new day"; a *maqām* that is identical with the Arabic *maqām 'Ajam.*

Ney (Turkey). The Arabic *nāy.* An open, long, vertically-blown flute that is used in art music.
Lit.: no. 243.

Ney-ko (Korea). See *Nei-ko* (Korea).

Nfīr (Arabia; Turkey; Iran). See *Nafīr.*

Nga (Tibet). Drum. The honorific term is *chha-nga.*

Ngab (Pacific; New Ireland; New Mecklenburgh). Jew's harp.
Lit.: no. 255.

Nga-bauk (Burma). Tone name. See *Pat-tala; Hsaing-waing; Than-hman; Than-yo chauk-pauk.*

Nga-bank auk-pyan (Burma). See *Than-yo chauk-pauk.*

Nga-bauk than-di (Burma). See *Chauk-pauk auk-pyan.*

Nga-ch'ung (Tibet). Term for *damaru.*

Ngaidja (Uganda). A long *kirembe.*

Ngala (Tanganyika—Bahaya). *Sansa* used in groups of four.
Lit.: no. 190.

Ngalage (West Java). Dance of old men and women when preparing harvesting rice. The dance is accompanied by the *kachapi.*

Ngalamba (Sunda District). Extremely slow tempo. See *Wirama.*

aṄgalamu (New Guinea—Nakanai). Wooden drum.
Lit.: no. 255.

Ngalana (West Java). Rough, lively dance similar to the *monggawa.*

Ngalir (Senegal—Wolof). Trumpet.

Nganda (East Africa—Swahili). See *Mganda.*

Ngandap (Java). Low register. See *Ngisor.*
Lit.: no. 163.

Ngangibaka (*Tububaka*) (Solomon Isl.). Strophic songs sung while pulling ropes.
Lit.: no. 246.

Nga-pa (Tibet). Drum skin.

Ngaplak (Java). Cf. *Salahan.*

Ngarabi (Africa; Victoria Lake). Drum made of a part of a hollow tree trunk with a lizard-skin head.
Lit.: no. 255.

Ngaramut (Pacific; Bismarck Archipelago). See *Garamut.*

Ngaren (Bali). Syncopated playing of a melody instrument.
Lit.: no. 197.

Ngasu (Flores; Ende). Stamping stick; little bells fastened to the upper end. See *Da'u kibi.*
Lit.: no. 166.

Ngateh (Bali). Strict unison (not an octave apart).
Lit.: no. 197.

Nga-yo (Tibet). Drumstick.

Ngbandje (Congo—Mbuja). Board zither. Cf. *Neduma.*
Lit.: no. 176.

Ngechek (Java). Short, pointed, forceful bowing on the *rebāb.*
Lit.: no. 163.

Ngeḍasih (Java). A term derived from *keḍasih,* "singing bird." A Jogya manner of orchestral playing where the main melody is closely followed by the *rebāb.*
Lit.: no. 163.

Ngedegwu (Nigeria—Igbo). Xylophone.

Ngekik (Java). Glissandos on the *rebāb* from low, middle, to high registers.
Lit.: no. 163.

Ngeku (Nepal). A buffalo horn.

Ngelenge (Igbo). Xylophone. See *Odome.*

Ngelik (Java). The playing in a high register (e.g., *rebāb* playing). The sudden move of a part of a melody into a higher register.
Lit.: no. 163.

Ngenchot (Java). Muffling (with the left hand) the keys of a metallophone (e.g., the *saron*):
muffled: ♫ open: ♩
Cf. *Pitet.*
Lit.: no. 163.

Ngenḍelong (Java). Cf. *Salahan.*

Ngenge (Sierra Leone—Fula). Spike fiddle with a single string of hair. See *Karaning.*
Lit.: no. 190.

Nge'o hakahaahine (West Pacific; Solomon Isl.). See *Mou hatingaa nge'o.*

Nge'o hakatootonu (West Pacific; Solomon Isl.). See *Mou hatingaa nge'o.*

Nge'o makanga (West Pacific; Solomon Isl.). See *Mou hatingaa nge'o.*

Nge'o Panguuguu (West Pacific; Solomon Isl.). See *Mou hatingaa nge'o.*

Ngepinjal (*Pinjalan*) (Java). A method of playing (e.g., the *gambang kaju*) whereby the right hand of the player beats twice as many notes as the left.
Lit.: no. 163.

Ngere (Former French Equatorial Africa—Teke). Big musical instrument.
Lit.: no. 255.

Ngetetang (Bali). See *Rebāb.*

Ṅgetundo (Kenya—Nandi). A friction drum. Also a bull roarer. Used in circumcision ceremonies.
Lit.: no. 255.

Ngga (Flores; Ende). Gong of Javanese origin. Cf. *Nggo.*
Lit.: no. 166.

Nggeri-go (Flores). See *Churing*; *Gong tondu.*

Nggoa-nggao (Flores; Ngada). Small bamboo clarinet without any finger holes. Cf. *Orupi*; *Hu'a-ha'u.*
Lit.: no. 166.

Nggo nggri (Flores; Manggaray). Tubular bamboo zither with five or six strings.
Lit.: no. 156.

(Ng)gorong-gorong (*Wai wonta*) (Flores). See *Uwe kotang.*

Nggungga (Sumba). Wooden jew's harp.
Lit.: no. 162.

Nggungi (*Nggunga*) (Sumba). See *Ego.*

Nghang (Burma). Trumpet; horn.
Lit.: no. 255.

Ngibing (Bali). A courting dance in which a dancing girl invites a male spectator to dance. The young man is usually not trained in the dance and has to improvise his part. The young girl dancer makes amusing advances to him.
Lit.: no. 197.

Ngilamo (Bismarck Archipelago; West New Britain). See *Garamat.*

Ngime (West Africa—Mandingo; Sarakole). Fiddle. Cf. *Kundye.*
Lit.: no. 184.

Nginā (Israel). Hebrew term for the Arabic *maqām.*

Ngiṇtil (Java). "Following like a shadow." See *Imbal.*

Ngisor (Java). Low register. Cf. *Ngandap.*

Ngiwesio ngimongin (Uganda). A song in which the singer praises his ox and other cattle.

Ngkratong (Borneo—Dayak). Psaltery with four strings placed vertically on top of a bird-shaped box.
Lit.: no. 255.

Ngkul (Cameroon). Slit-drum.

Nglana (Java). See *Kiprah*; *Bedug.*

Nglaras (Java). The tuning of a gong.

N'go (Congo—Ngbandi). Drum. Cf. *Leri.*
Lit.: no. 26.

Ngoa-ngao (Flores; Ngada). See *Orupi.*

Ngodo (Mozambique—Chopi). A dance that consists of 9-11 movements. Its music is performed by a large group of xylophones and several percussion instruments.
Lit.: no. 218.

Ngoma (East Africa; Zanzibar—Swahili). Drum; dance. See also *Muziki.*

Ngoma (North Central Tanganyika—Wanyamwezi; South Africa; Angola—Venda). Tubular drum beaten with the hands and used in the magic of healing. In South Africa the *ngoma* has the shape of a kettledrum. Cf. *Kangoma* (Congo).
Lit.: nos. 29, 255.

Ng'oma (Tanzania). Dance of women. It is performed when a boy has his circumcision, when a girl had come to the end of her first menstrual period, and frequently also at weddings.

Ngombang (Java). After having played *sirep* (softly), the term *ngombang* indicates a return to the normal intensity of sound.
Lit.: no. 163.

Ngombi (Congo—Bwake; Gabon—Tsogho). Arched harp with eight or 10 strings.
Lit.: nos. 21, 218.

Ngomfi (Lower Congo—Bembe). Bow lute with five strings.
Lit.: no. 280.

Ngomo (Congo). Harp with eight strings. Also cylindrical drum of the Bosaka (Congo).
Lit.: no. 26.

Ngong (Burma). Gong.
Lit.: no. 255.

Ngonga (Congo—Teke). Metal or wooden bell.
Lit.: nos. 255, 280.

Ngonge (Congo—Batatela). War drum.
Lit.: no. 26.

Ngongi (Congo—Bakongo). Iron bell struck with a stick.
Lit.: no. 280.

Ngor (Vietnam). See *Hogoi*. Two-headed barrel drum.

Ngoret (Bali). A brief rapidly performed scale within the range of an octave, serving as an ornament to a following important note.
Lit.: no. 197.

Ngrachik (*Ngranchak*) (Java). A method of playing three successive ascending steps in anapaest meter. Cf. *Nyaruk*.
Lit.: no. 163.

Ngrengrengan (Java). The early, opening part of a composition where the prescribed tempo is not yet clearly established.
Lit.: no. 163.

Nguchekan (Bali). Brief syncopated portions of the melody.
Lit.: no. 197.

Ngumbi (Congo—Azande). Stick zither.
Lit.: no. 176.

Ngunda (Congo—Yombe). Globular flute with 2-6 finger holes.
Lit.: no. 280.

Ngunga (Congo—Kikongo). Metal bells.
Lit.: no. 280.

Ngungkung (Java). The playing in the middle register of an instrument (e.g., the *rebāb*).
Lit.: no. 163.

Ngungu (Congo-Mayombe; Angola—Luanda). Slit drum of the Mayombe and musical bow of the Luanda.
Lit.: no. 280.

Nguomi (Gabon—Teke; Congo—Kukuya). Harp zither.
Lit.: no. 280.

Nguru (New Zealand—Maori). Small, vertically-blown conical flute (or nose flute) made of wood or bone, with 2-3 front holes and one in the rear. The number of finger holes varies.
Lit.: nos. 7, 228.

Ngu tu nhac (Vietnam). Music of the five sacrifices. Court music.

Nguyet (Vietnam). Moon-shaped lute.
Lit.: no. 296.

Nguyu-uyu (*Uyon-uyon*; *Klenengan*) (Java). Concert performance of *gamelan* music.
Lit.: no. 163.

Ngwalala (Congo—Sundi). Vertical flute without any finger holes. Cf. *Nsembu*.
Lit.: no. 280.

Ngwana (Congo). Drum with a conical corpus.
Lit.: no. 280.

Ngwaya (Tanzania—Pangwa). Dance accompanied by large hourglass drums.

Ngwen (Congo—Yan). Bow-lute.
Lit.: no. 176.

Ngwingwingwe (Congo; Angola). Bull roarer.
Lit.: no. 280.

Ngwombi (Congo—Teke). Bow-lute.
Lit.: no. 176.

Ngwomi (Kenya—Kikuyu). Stick zither.
Lit.: no. 280.

Ngwomo (Gabon—Mbama; Wumbu). Bow-lute.
Lit.: no. 280.

Ngwosto (Congo—Mbum). Musical bow.
Lit.: no. 176.

Nhac (Vietnam). Name of a scale. See list of scales shown under heading of *Bac.*

Nhac cai cach (Vietnam). Modernized music influenced by Western styles. Cf. *Tan nhac.*

Nhac dai noi (Vietnam). "Music of the Palace." Cf. *Nha nhac*; *Quan nhac.*
Lit.: no. 296.

Nha nhac (Vietnam). "Elegant music"; the equivalent of the Chinese *ya yüeh* (M 7222; M 4129a). The instrumental ensemble consists of: four *ong dich*, two *dan nhi*, two *dan nguyet*, two *dan tam*, one *dan ty ba*, one *trong cai*, one *tam am la*, one *sinh tien.*
Lit.: nos. 42, 296.

Nhac tai tu (Vietnam). Music of amateurs. Cf. *Ca Hue.*

Nhi (Vietnam). Fiddle with two strings, used in *dai nhac.*
Lit.: no. 296.

Nhip (South Vietnam). To beat time (strong beat). The weak beat is called *lai.*

Ni (India). Tone syllable. Abbreviation of *niṣāda*, the seventh degree of the heptatonic scale. If *sa* is interpreted as C, *ni* means B.
Lit.: no. 136.

Ni-agari (Japan). (1) The tuning of string instruments with the characteristics of a fifth followed by a fourth; e.g., A E a. (2) Name of a *shamisen* piece that uses this tuning. Cf. *Kokyū*; *Shamisen.*

Ni'au-kani (Hawaii). A jew's harp made of bamboo with a detached tongue that is tied to the wooden basis.
Lit.: nos. 37, 277.

Nibaddha (India). See *Anibaddha.*

Nibiles (Ethiopia). Trumpet or bagpipe.
Lit.: no. 102.

Nichik (Bali). The smallest of the *chengchengs*; their particular rhythmical pattern.
Lit.: no. 197.

Nichin (Japan). A *koto* with six strings and a circular corpus. Inside the body is stretched a vibrating iron wire.
Lit.: no. 225.

Nidaiko (Japan). A processional portable *daiko* carried on a long, wooden lacquered pole by two carriers. The two drumheads protrude beyond the cylindrical body.
Lit.: no. 225.

Nidhana (Vedic India). The fifth section of a *stoma.* The term represents the closing part of a hymn that ends with the syllable "om." All three officiating priests (*prastotar*, *udgātar*, *pratihartar*) chant this part together.
Lit.: no. 141.

Nigamasañjāri (South India). *Janya rāga* of the 70th *mēḷa* (*Nāsikabhūṣaṇī*).
Tone material:

C E F♯ G A B♭ c
c B♭ A B♭ G F♯ D♯ C

Lit.: no. 139.

Nigenkin (Japan). A two-stringed *koto*. Both strings are tuned to the same pitch and are plucked with a heavy cylindrical *tsume*. Cf. *Yakumon* (*Yakumo-koto*).
Lit.: no. 185.

Nigrīz (Arabia). "The Turkish *Ḥijāz*"—a sub-*maqām* of *Nahawānd*.
Tone material:

C D E♭ F♯ G A B♭ c (or: A $\overset{+}{\mathrm{B}\flat}$ c)

Cf. *Nagrīz*.
Lit.: no. 121.

Nīharādri (South India). *Janya rāga* of the 2nd *mēḷa* (*Ratnangī*).
Tone material:

C E♭♭ G A♭ B♭ c
c B♭ A♭ G E♭♭ C

Lit.: no. 139.

Nīharam (South India). *Janya rāga* of the 51st *mēḷa* (*Kāmavardhanī*).
Tone material:

C E F♯ A♭ B c
c B A♭ F♯ E C

Lit.: no. 139.

Nihāwand (Middle East; Modern Egypt). *Maqām*.
Tone material:

C D E♭ F G A♭ B♭ c

Lit.: no. 64.

Nihāwand-Kabīr (Middle East). *Maqām*.
Tone material:

C D E♭ F♯ G A♭ B♭ c

Lit.: no. 64.

Nihāwand-Rumi (Middle East). *Maqām*.
Tone material:

C D E♭ F G♭ A B♭ c / c d♭ e d♭ c B A♭ G . . .

Lit.: no. 64.

Nihoihagi (Japan). Bronze cymbals.
Lit.: no. 184.

Nihongi (*Nihon shoki*) (Japan). See *Kojiki*.

Nihuft (*Nahaft*) (Arabia). Tone name. See *Māhūr*.

Nihuft (Middle East). *Maqām*.
Tone material:

A $\overset{+}{\mathrm{B}\flat}$ C D E $\overset{+}{\mathrm{F}}$ G A $\overset{+}{\mathrm{B}\flat}$ c d $\overset{+}{\mathrm{e}\flat}$ f g a

Lit.: no. 64.

Nihuft (Arabia). *Maqām*.
Tone material:

C E♭♭ F♭ F G B♭♭ B♭ c

Stated in Lit. no. 65, according to Ṣafī al-Dīn 'Abd al-Mu'min al Baghdadi (13th century).

Nijū (Japan). The middle octave range as notated in the *go-onfu* system. The low octave range is called *shojū* and the upper octave range *sanjū*.
Lit.: no. 185.

Nijū-ōshi (Japan). Term in *koto* playing that indicates a "double pressure" on the string, which raises the original pitch by a whole tone.
Lit.: no. 225.

Ni-kin (Japan). See *Ni-chin*.

Nīlakaṇṭhapriya (South India). *Janya rāga* of the 34th *mēḷa* (*Vāgadhīśvarī*).
Tone material:

C D♯ E G A B♭ c
c B♭ A G E D♯ C

Lit.: no. 139.

Nīlamani (South India). *Janya rāga* of the 27th *mēḷa* (*Sarasāṅgī*).
Tone material:

C D F G A♭ B c
c B A♭ G F D C

Lit.: no. 139.

Nīlāmbari (North India). *Rāga*. A variant of *rāga Kafi*.
Lit.: no. 138.

Nīlāmbari (South India). *Janya rāga* of the 28th *mēḷa* (*Harikāmbhōji*).

Tone material:
C D E F G A G B♭ c
c B♭ G F E D E C
(c B♭ G A B♭ G F E D E F E C)
Lit.: no. 139.

Nīlāṅgi (South India). *Janya rāga* of the 55th *mēḷa* (*Śyāmalāṅgī*).
Tone material:
C D E♭ F♯ A♭ B♭♭ c
c B♭♭ A♭ F♯ E♭ D C
Lit.: no. 139.

Nilāvaṇi (South India). Tamil term for *Lāvaṇi*.

Nīlavēni (South India). *Janya rāga* of the 20th *mēḷa* (*Naṭabhairavī*).
Tone material:
C D E♭ F G A♭ B♭ A♭ c
c A♭ G F E♭ D C
Lit.: no. 139.

Nim- (Arabia; Persia). See *Nam-*.

N'imah (Ancient Israel). Melody sung in the public reading of sacred texts.
Lit.: no. 12.

Nim-'ajam (*Ḥūsaynī*) (Arabia). Tone name. See *Nam-'ajam-ḥūsaynī.*

Nim-'ajam-'ushayrān (Arabia). Tone name. See *Nam-'ajam-'ashirām.*

Nīmapriya (South India). *Janya rāga* of the 63rd *mēḷa* (*Latāṅgī*).
Tone material:
C D F♯ E F♯ A♭ G A♭ c
c B A♭ G F♯ E G F♯ E D C
Lit.: no. 139.

Nimba (Japan). "The dog dance." A *sato-kagura* folk dance.
Lit.: no. 185.

Nim-būsalik (Arabia). Tone name. See *Nam-būselik.*

Nim-gavasht (Arabia). Tone name. See *Nam-gushat.*

Nim-ḥijāz (Arabia). Tone name. See *Nam-ḥijāz.*

Nim-ḥiṣar (Arabia). Tone name. See *Nam-ḥiṣar.*

Nim-jāwāb-būsalik (Arabia). Tone name. See *Jwab-nam-būselik.*

Nim-jāwāb-ḥijāz (Arabia). Tone name. See *Jwab-nam-ḥijāz.*

Nim-kurdī (Arabia). Tone name. See *Nam-kurdī.*

Nim-māhūr (Arabia). Tone name. See *Nam-māhūr.*

Nim-nihuft (Arabia). Tone name. See *Nam-māhūr.*

Nim-qarar-ḥiṣār (Arabia). Tone name. See *Nam-ḥiṣār.*

Nim-shāhnāz (Arabia). Tone name. See *Nam-shāh'nāz.*

Nim-sunbulaḥ (Arabia). Tone name. See *Nam-sunbula.*

Nim-zirgūlah (Arabia). Tone name. See *Nam-zarkala.*

Ninai daiko (Japan). The *taiko* of *gagaku* carried about in processions. Only one of the two heads is beaten with sticks.
Lit.: no. 185.

Nincho (Japan). The leading male court dancer who offers wine to the Shintō gods.
Lit.: no. 185.

Nindo (Tanzania – Gogo). Choral singing; praise and festive dance. Accompanied by the *ndulele* (side-blown animal horn) and *mlanzi* (cross flute).
Lit.: no. 218.

Ninga (*Gwaningba*) (Congo – Azande). Musical bow.
Lit.: no. 176.

Ninkairna (India). Small *nāgasara.*

Ni-no-tsuzumi (Japan). An ancient hourglass-shaped drum. It probably was slightly larger than the *ichi-no-tsuzumi.* The drum is no longer in use.
Lit.: no. 225.

Nirañjani (South India). *Janya rāga* of the 10th *mēḷa* (*Nāṭakapriya*).
Tone material:
C D♭ E♭ F G A c
c B♭ A G F E♭ D♭ C
Lit.: no. 139.

Nirhāri (South India). *Janya rāga* of the 33rd *mēḷa* (*Gāṅgeyabhushanī*).
Tone material:
C D♯ F A♭ B c
c B A♭ F D♯ C
Lit.: no. 139.

Nīriz (Tunisia). *Maqām.* See [*Ḥsīn*] *Nīriz.*

Nirjhārini (South India). *Janya rāga* of the 31st *mēḷa* (*Yāgapriyā*).
Tone material:
C D♯ G A♭ B♭♭ c
c B A♭ G D♯ C
Lit.: no. 139.

Nirmalāṅgi (South India). *Janya rāga* of the 30th *mēḷa* (*Nāgānandī*).
Tone material:
C D F G A♯ c
c B A♯ B G F E D C
Lit.: no. 139.

Niṣāda (India). See *Nishāda.*

Nisen (Japan). Fiddle of Korean origin with two strings. It is almost identical with the *kokin.*
Lit.: no. 225.

Nishābūr (Middle East). *Maqām.*
Tone material:
+
(B♭)
D E F♯ G A B♭♭ c d e♭ f g
Lit.: no. 64.

Nishābūrak (Middle East). *Maqām.*
Tone material:
(G♯) +
D E F♯ G A B♭ c d
Lit.: no. 64.

Nishāda (India). Sanskrit tone name. Cf. *Ṣaḍja*, under which heading are listed all Indian tone names. Also see *Jāti.*
Lit.: no. 136.

Nishāda (South India). *Janya rāga* of the 60th *mēḷa* (*Nītimatī*).
Tone material:
C E♭ D F♯ G c
c B A♯ F♯ G B G F♯ E♭ D C
Lit.: no. 139.

Nishādam (South India). *Nishāda rāga*, 60th *asampūrṇa mēḷa.*
Lit.: no. 139.

Nishadāntya (South India). A *rāga* has *nishadāntya* character when the highest note of its scale is *ni* of the middle octave range.
Lit.: no. 139.

Nishādi (*Niṣādi*) (South India). *Janya rāga* of the 65th *mēḷa* (*Mechakalyāṇī*).
Tone material:
C D F♯ G A B c
c B A G F♯ D C
Lit.: no. 139.

Ni-shōko (Japan). The portable *shōko.* Two men carry the drum on a long pole in processions.
Lit.: no. 225.

Niṣkoṭita (India). One of the ancient 10 basic ways of touching *vīṇā* strings (*dhātu*); *niṣkoṭita* indicates a stroke with the left thumb.
Lit.: no. 292.

Nissan (Southeast India—Muria Gond of Bastar State). Large, single headed drum played with two sticks. Cf. *Lohāti*; *Māwāloti.*
Lit.: no. 59.

Nitalaprakāśini (South India). *Janya rāga* of the 14th *mēḷa* (*Vakulābharaṇam*).

Tone material:
C F G A♭ B♭ c
c B♭ G F D♭ E C
Lit.: no. 139.

Nītimatī (South India). The 60th *mēḷa*:
C D E♭ F♯ G A♯ B c
Rāga Nītimatī has the identical tone material.
Lit.: no. 139.

Nīvāram (South India). *Janya rāga* of the 41st *mēḷa* (*Pāvani*).
Tone material:
C E♭♭ F♯ A B c
c B A F♯ E♭♭ C
Lit.: no. 139.

Niyaga (*Nayaga*) (Java). Musician, particularly drummer.

Nizhalaṭṭam (South India). Tamil term for a popular shadow play produced by leather puppets. The accompaniment consists of prose and songs. The Telugu term is *tolu bommalu.*
Lit.: no. 262.

Nizhalkuttu paṭṭu (South India). Songs sung during the performance of a *nizhālaṭṭam.*

Nja (Nigeria – Werre). Arched harp.
Lit.: no. 21.

Nja (Nigeria – Igbo). Leg rattle.

Njaga (Congo – Gbea-Manja). Xylophone.
Lit.: no. 21.

Njele (South Africa – Thonga). Rattle.
Lit.: no. 151.

Njembo (Congo – Bateke). Bow lute.
Lit.: no. 21.

Njenjo (Congo; Lake Tumba region). Stick zither. Cf. *Nzenze.*
Lit.: no. 190.

Njin (*Ejin*) (Gabon – Fan). Transverse flute with one finger hole.

Njingiri (Kenya). Pellet bells fastened to the belt of a dancer.

Njua (North Rhodesia). See *Injua.*

Nkaku (South Africa – Thonga). Cf. *Nkoka.*

Nkandu (Congo). See *Ndungu*; *Munkambo.*

Nkango (Cameroon – Tikar). Musical bow. Cf. *Nkungu.*
Lit.: no. 21.

Nkenke (Congo – Bwende). Small wooden side-blown trumpet.
Lit.: no. 280.

Nkili (Angola). Dance accompanied by drum and hand clapping.

Nkoka (*Nkaku*) (South Africa – Thonga). Musical bow. Cf. *Dende.*

Nkoko (Lower Congo – Vili). Slit-drum.
Lit.: no. 280.

Nkole-nkole (Congo – Balolo). See *Lokole.*

Nkongolo (South Africa – Bomvana). Vertically-blown conical flute open at both ends. Among the various names of the instruments are: *umtshingo* (or *ivenge*), called by the Zulu; *umtshingosi*, called by the Swazi; *umtshingi*, called by the Pondo (or *ivenge*); *ixilongo*, called by the Xhosa (or *impempe*); *lekolilo*, called by the Sotho; *mokoreire*, called by the Bangkwaketse.
Lit.: no. 151.

Nkonjo (Congo Republic – Mpongwe). Two-headed drum.
Lit.: no. 255.

Nkonko (West Africa – Vili; Yombe; Bwende; Sundi). Slit-drum.
Lit.: no. 280.

Nkonzo a mpanzu (Angola). See *Esikulu.*

Nkraton (Borneo—Sea Dayak). Harp zither with four strings.
Lit.: no. 254.

Nku (West Africa—Fan). Slit-drum.
Lit.: no. 255.

Nkul (Gabon). Slit-drum of large size.

Nkumbi (Congo). Cf. *Mukumbi.*
Lit.: no. 280.

Nkumoi (Congo). Term for *mulimba.*
Lit.: no. 21.

Nkundi (Congo—Azande). See *Kundi.*
Lit.: no. 176.

Nkungu (Angola). Musical bow with one fiber string which is struck with a small wooden stick.
Lit.: nos. 180, 280.

Nkwagasho (Tanganyika—Washambala). Scraper.
Lit.: no. 130.

Nkwaka (Lower Congo—Sundi). Scraper; notched stick.
Lit.: no. 280.

Nkwanga (Congo). See *Swanga.* Cf. *Mukwanga.*

Nkwimbi (*Kuimbi*) (Angola—Loango). Scraper.
Lit.: no. 255.

N'lapa (Malagasy Republic). Barrel drum with one head.
Lit.: no. 252.

Nnawuta (Ghana). Double bell; the two bells are of different sizes.

No (Thailand). Oboe type with seven finger holes in front and one at the back. Cf. *Sona.*
Lit.: no. 255.

Nobat (Malay Peninsula). The ceremonial band of the sovereign. The number of instruments varies from one place to the other. The Trenganu band, for instance, consists of a kettledrum (*nenggara*), two additional drums (*gendang nobat*), one horn (*nafiri*), one oboe (*serunai*), and two small cymbals (*kopok-kopok*).

Nobut (India). The term is derived from the Arabia *naubat. Nobut* represents a very large kettledrum. Cf. *Cai nao-bat*; *Naubat.*

Nobe-byōshi (Japan). Eight beats performed in slow tempo (*Gagaku*). Cf. *Haya-byōshi.*
Lit.: no. 185.

Noborigaku (Japan). See *Gagaku.*

Nodivu (South Africa—Kafir). Bull roarer.
Lit.: no. 255.

Nodo (Korea). See *Noto.*

Nogo (Korea). See *Noko.*

Noh (Japan). The highly refined and stylized lyric drama of Japan. Its history dates back into the middle ages. Two of the several origins of the *noh* are the *dengaku* ("field music" of rural festivals) and the *sarugaku* ("monkey music," pantomime and dance without song, a comic, often vulgar form, both originating in the 12th to 14th centuries). By the middle of the 14th century the old *dengaku* had absorbed dances and pantomimes from *sarugaku*, and *sarugaku* had accepted *dengaku* features, thus becoming a form called *sarugaku no noh*, later simply called *noh.*

Since the 16th century the subjects of the *noh* dramas were grouped into five categories:

1. *shin* (god)
2. *nan* (man, ghost, warrior)
3. *nyo* (woman, wig-play)
4. *kyo* (madness)
5. *ki* (demon)

At the present time there exist about 250 *noh* dramas representing several schools. The music is preserved in several notational systems.

A *noh* play is organized into three sections: *jo* (introduction), *ha* (development), *kyū* (conclusion). The texts contain Buddhist sayings, more or less obscure formulas, and refer to ancient songs and poetry. They are written in prose (*kotoba*) or in verse (*utai*). The prose sections are recited and the verse sections are sung. The music is built upon a number of melodic formulas. These phrases are known to the educated listener and have a function similar to that of the Chinese *ya-ti*, or, vaguely similar to the Leitmotives of the West. The instrumental *noh* ensemble (*hayashi*) consists of the *nohkan* and three drums (*ko-tsuzumi*, *ō-tsuzumi*, and *taiko*). The rhythms performed by the *hayashi* are free in recitatives and show several fixed patterns in the sung and instrumental music: *ō-nori*, *chū-nori*, and *hira-nori*.

The actors are the *shite*, the protagonist, and *tsure* (additional performers). When each actor appears on the stage he introduces himself. Furthermore has to be mentioned the *waki* (side character).

For further information see Lit. no. 185. For scale material used in *noh* music see *Yokyōkū*.
Lit.: no. 306.

Noh-fue (Japan). See *Nohkan*; *Ōteki*.

Nohgaku (Japan). See *Noh*.

Nohkan (Japan). A large bamboo cross flute of the *noh hayashi*. The instrument has seven front finger holes. It is lacquered red on the inside of the tube and black on its outside. The *nohkan* is the only instrument of the ensemble that can perform melodies (introductory music, dance tunes) and follow closely the screams, sighs, and moans of the acting singer. It also provides the required pitch for the chorus.
Lit.: no. 185.

Noi (Thailand). One of the five *kaen* modes, *lai noi*, following the pitches of the *an nungsü* scale. The five modes are:

Lai sootsanaen	*G A* C D E G A
Lai ho sai	C D F G A c
Lai soi	D E G A B d
Lai yai	*A* C D E G A
Lai noi	D F G A c d

Cf. *Lum*.
Lit.: no. 203.

Nōkan (Japan). See *Nohkan*.

No-ko (Korea). Two large barrel drums, one above the other at right angles, are placed within a wooden frame. The barrels are painted red and were used in processions to and from the places of sacrificial ceremonies. Cf. *Lu-ku* ("street drum" China); *No-to*; *Cho-ko*.
Lit.: no. 179.

Nokorigaku (Japan). Types of court music. Each of its various sections is performed by a specific group of instruments (e.g., only strings are used for concluding features). See *Gagaku*.
Lit.: no. 185.

Nokukwane (South Africa – Chwana). Musical bow.
Lit.: no. 151.

Noma (Tanganyika – Mbwari). See *Enoma*.

Nong-ahk (Korea). Simple rural band music played by peasants. Usually it is outdoor music performed at festivities of transplanting or harvesting rice. The ensemble consists of various percussion instruments and a *sona* (conical oboe).
Lit.: no. 179.

Nongsok (Bali). See *Rebāb*.

Nori (Japan). A rhythmic pattern in *noh* music based upon a certain number of syllables used within an 8-beat musical phrase. A two-syllable pattern in one beat is called *chūnori*. Seven and five syllables within an 8-beat phrase is called *hira-nori*. Cf. *Jibyōshi*.
Lit.: no. 187.

Norito (Japan). Unaccompanied chanting in Shinto service.

Nork (Thailand). Tone name. Cf. *Thang*.

Nosbug (India). See *Śruti upāṅga*. Bagpipe producing the drone note.

No-to (*Nodo*) (Korea). Two small barrel drums, one above the other, are placed horizontally at right angles to each other and are pierced by a stick. Cords hang from the drums and when the stick is twirled the thick ends of the cords hit the drumheads in a *damaru* fashion. The body of the *no-to* is smaller than that of the *no-ko*. Cf. *Lu-t'ao*.
Lit.: no. 179.

Notto (Japan). Drum pattern in *noh* and *kabuki* music.
Lit.: no. 187.

Nritta (*Nṛtta*) (Ancient India). Sanskrit term for dancing, gesticulation. Generally the term indicates the pure dance without any symbolism.

Nritya (*Nṛtya*) (Ancient India). Sanskrit term for acting, dancing. It indicates the knowledge and ability of dancers concerning the *abhinaya* and the footwork. The term implies acting and the expressive dance. Cf. *Śabdam* (*Bharata Nāṭyam*).

Nritya kutapa (South India). Cf. *Brinda ganam*.

Nsakala (Lower Congo). See *Sakala*.

Nsambi (Angola—Ndembo). Bow lute with 4-5 strings. Cf. *Lusinga*; *Ngomfi*.
Lit.: no. 280.

Nsansi (Lower Congo). *Sansa* or rattle.
Lit.: no. 280.

Nsatong (Cameroon—Tikar). Xylophone.
Lit.: no. 21.

Nsegu (*Ncwa*) (Uganda—Nyoro; Toro; Nkole). Vertical flute with conical bore, played from its wide end.
Lit.: no. 305.

Nseke (Uganda—Ganda). Rattle used during dances.
Lit.: no. 33.

Nsembu (Congo Republic—Bembe; Bongo). Conically-shaped, vertically-blown flute without any finger holes. Cf. *Ngwalala*.
Lit.: no. 280.

Nsengu (Uganda—Amba; Konjo). Wooden flute with conical bore.
Lit.: no. 302.

Nsense (Ethiopia). Stick zither.

Nsiba (Lower Congo—Bembe). Also *Ludi*. Wooden trumpet or flute.
Lit.: no. 280.

Nsimbi (Africa; Zambezi river area). Iron *sansa*.

Ntahera (Ghana—Ashanti). The chief's 5-7 ivory horns.
Lit.: no. 218.

Ntamba (Lower Congo—Bwende). Also *kikongo*. Side-blown wooden trumpet.
Lit.: nos. 190, 280.

Ntanda (Malavi). Nine tuned drums played in secret ancestral cult.

Ntandu (Congo). Barrel drum with one head.
Lit.: no. 26.

Ntara (Uganda; Nyoro District). Xylophone.
Lit.: no. 29.

Ntenga (Uganda). Drum chorus of the Gande.
Lit.: no. 304.

Ntimbo (Uganda—Nyoro; Toro). Goblet-shaped hand drum.
Lit.: nos. 218, 302.

Ntongoli (Uganda). See *Ndongo*.

Ntshinda (Congo—Ekota; Bahutu). Drum.
Lit.: no. 26.

Ntuantuangi (Celebes—Poso; Toradja). Shell trumpet with lateral blowhole.
Lit.: no. 132.

Ntubu (Lower Congo—Vili). Percussion gourd.
Lit.: no. 280.

Ntufu (Former Belgian Congo; Ituri Forest—Bantu). Pipe.
Lit.: no. 29.

Ntumpani (Ghana—Ashanti). Barrel drum with one head that protrudes beyond the rim of the body. It is beaten with wooden sticks and is used as "chief talking drum." Cf. *Atukpani*; *Atumpani.*
Lit.: no. 241.

Ntuta (Angola). See *Esikulu.*

Ntuta (Congo). Barrel drum.
Lit.: nos. 26, 280.

Nuba (Islamic North Africa; Middle East). See *Nauba.*

Nuba (Algiers; Biskra). (1) A suite of musical pieces. (2) A single item. (3) There are various types, e.g., wedding *nuba*; *nuba* of Sidi Abd-al-Kader; *nuba* of the Marabu of Constantine; religious forms of *nuba*; *nuba* from Algiers.

Nugara (Sudan). Village dance performed by men and women together, in contrast to dances in towns where men and women perform separately.

Nulei (Liberia—Kpelle). Term for "song."
Lit.: no. 284.

Numena (Flores; Ende). Grass blade shawm.
Lit.: no. 166.

Numpuk (Bali). Ornamental feature in *trompong* playing.

Nung bramo tai (Northeast Thailand). Term for *nung da loong.*
Lit.: no. 203.

Nung daloong (Thailand). Shadow puppet theater.
Lit.: no. 203.

Nungneng (North Sumatra—Toba Batak). Bamboo tube zither. Cf. *Tanggetong.*
Lit.: no. 156.

Nungu nange (Flores; District of Maumere). Story presented in dramatic, theatrical form.

Nungungu (Congo—Bapopoie; Mangbetu). Tubular slit-drum.
Lit.: no. 21.

Nunib (South Africa—Berg-Dama). Vertically-blown whistle made of the upper part of a springbok horn.
Lit.: nos. 151, 190.

Nunut (Bismarck Isl.; New Ireland). A large friction idiophone made of a wooden block. It has three crosscuts which form the upper surface of four large wooden teeth. Cf. *Alaunut*; *Kulepa ganeg*; *Lauka*; *Livika*; *Lunat*; *Lunuot.*
Lit.: nos. 37, 84.

Nūpura (*Napura*) (Ancient India). Iron foot rattle consisting of a tube in the form of an oval ring containing little rattling stones. The ring is slipped on the dancer's foot ankle. Other terms for this rattle, believed to possess magic powers, are *manjīra*, *tulākoti*, and *pālipada.*

Nuqairāt (Syria; North Africa—Berber). Small kettledrums.
Lit.: no. 34.

Nuqaisāt (North Africa—Berber). Finger cymbals.

Nuren (East Flores—Larantuka). Also *feko*; *welo.* A flute with a variable number of finger holes. In East and Central Flores the *nuren* has five, rarely six, holes. In West Flores it has occasionally four, only occasionally six or three holes. In Riangwulu the instrument is called *klekor*, in Maumere *glekor*, in Lio of Ende *feko*, and in the Manggaray *sunding.*
Lit.: no. 166.

Nur Sarang (North India). *Rāga* ascribed to the *Kafi thāta*; a member of the *Sarang* family. Three types are distinguished.
Tone material:
(a) C D F♯ G B c
c B G F♯ D C
(b) C D F♯ G B c
c B (B♭) G F♯ (F) D C
(c) C D F♯ G (A) B c
c B (B♭) A G F♯ (F) D C; *Vādis*: D or C, G
Lit.: no. 138.

Nuṣf ṭanīn (Arabia). Old term for semitone.

Nuuha (Solomon Isl. – Malaita). Song.
Lit.: no. 318.

Nuuha iisisu (Solomon Isl. – Malaita). Love songs.
Lit.: no. 318.

Nuzha (Arabia; Persia). Ancient rectangular psaltery with 64 strings.
Lit.: nos. 78, 250.

Nvatt (Kampuchea – Bönon). Jew's harp made of copper.
Lit.: no. 254.

Nwakpo (Nigeria). Bamboo flute with five finger holes.

Nxonxoro (South Africa – Qung Bushman; Venda; Thonga). Instrument made of a semi-circular bow with one string made of grass. This musical bow is made to vibrate by rubbing it with a stick. One end of the bow is held in the player's mouth. Cf. *Tshizambi*; *Zambi.*
Lit.: no. 151.

Nyaado (Ghana – Ga). A ritual drum.
Lit.: no. 218.

Nyachah (Bali). A short rhythmic pattern in *chengcheng* performances.
Lit.: no. 197.

Nyading (Bali). *Gambang* ornamentation.

Nyalawat (Sunda District). Term for the Javanese *slawatan.*
Lit.: no. 163.

Nyalendro (Sunda District). See *Kachapi.*

Nyalit (Bali). Changing into the high register of a musical instrument. See *Penyalit.*
Lit.: no. 197.

Nyampundu (Congo). See *Gihumurizo.*

Nyamulere (Uganda; Congo). See *Endere.*
Lit.: no. 302.

Nyandet (Bali). A syncopated rhythmic feature in *chengcheng* and rice-pounding music.
Lit.: no. 197.

Nyangsih (Bali). See *Nyachah.*

Nyaruk (Java). The playing (e.g., on the *gambang kayu*) of three successive notes in descending order in anapaestic form. Cf. *Ngrachik.*
Lit.: no. 163.

Nyasa (Ancient North India). Final note (a term used in theoretical writings).

Nyāsa (South India). Also *muktayi.* See *Ālāp.*

Nyāstaraṅga (India). This unusual instrument consists of two short brass trumpets, the mouth-pieces of which are covered with a thin but strong spider-egg skin. The singer places each mouthpiece against the right and left sides of his throat. The sound created adds a reedy coloring to the voice.
Lit.: no. 254.

Nyatiti (Kenya – Luo). See *Thum.*

Nyatria (West Java). Fast-moving dance.

Nya won (Assam – Naga). Horn.
Lit.: no. 252.

Nyayito (Ghana—Ewe). Funeral dance. Also called *tobaha*, *leaflegbe*, *akpaluvu*.
Lit.: no. 128.

Nyenḍal (Java; Solo). A free excited way of bowing the *rebāb* with frenzied strokes.
Lit.: no. 163.

Nyenḍari (Java; Solo). The free, recent method of *rebāb* playing in ensemble performances (in contrast to *ngeḍasih*).
Lit.: no. 163.

Nyen-nyen (Liberia—Kpelle). Metal rattles.
Lit.: no. 284.

Nyerodin (Bali—Karangasem). Playing in two parts.
Lit.: no. 197.

Nyibro palit (Nepal; Sikkim—Lepcha). Double flute, vertically blown. Each tube has six finger holes.

Nyimbo zz pungwa (Tanzania). Praise songs to influence the spirits and protect the singers from their enemies.

Nyi n'go (Congo—Ngbandi). A conical drum with two heads (identical with *sila*).
Lit.: no. 26.

Nyis-shad (Tibet). "Double *shad.*" See *Shad.*

Nyo (Japan). "Woman," "wig-play." One of five traditional subjects used in the *noh* drama (the other four subjects are: *shin*, *nan*, *kyo*, *ki*).

Nyo (Korea). Small cymbals. Cf. *Nao* (China).
Lit.: no. 52.

Nyo-pai-glu (Tibet). Riddle songs performed alternatingly when suitors are required to answer singing long series of questions.
Lit.: no. 62.

Nyorog (Java). A *surupan melog* scale beginning with *kenong*:

V	VI	VII	
kenong	*barang*	*sorog*	
I	II	III	X
singgul	*galimer*	*panelu*	*panangis*

Singgul and *panangis* are auxiliary tones.

Nyorog (West Java). A scale consisting of: *singgul*, *bem*, *bungur*, *kenong*, *barang*, and *singgul leutik.* The approximate western sounds are: C D♭ F G A♭ c. Cf. *Melog.*
Lit.: no. 163.

Nyorog Handap (Java). Scale in *surupan melog* that begins (1) with *barang*:

VI	VII	X	(I)
barang	*sorog*	*pamiring*	
II	III	X	IV
galimer	*panelu*	*panangis*	*liwung*

Galimer and *liwung* are auxiliary notes. (2) A scale that begins with *Panelu*:

III	X	IV	(V)
panelu	*panangis*	*liwing*	
VI	VII	X	I
barang	*sorog*	*pamiring*	*singgul*

Singgul and *barang* are auxiliary notes.
Lit.: no. 163.

Nyorog Malang (West Java). See *Surupan Madenda.*

Nyorog Rangu rangu (West Java). See *Surupan Madenda.*

Nyorog Wisaya (West Java). See *Surupan Madenda.*

Nzangwa (West Africa). Also *nzanza.* Term for *sansa.*
Lit.: no. 280.

Nzau (*Mazoko*) (Lower Congo—Kuta). Rattle used during circumcision dances.
Lit.: no. 280.

Nzegh akom (Congo). Conical flute blown across the wide end.

Nzenze (Ruanda – Bashi). Stick (bar) zither with two strings. Cf. *Enzenze*; *Njenjo*; *Seze*; *Zenze*.
Lit.: no. 176.

Nzeze (Congo – Ngombe). Bar zither; identical with *nzenze*.

Nzira (*Inzira*) (Ethiopia). A kithara with three strings. Cf. *Bagana*.
Lit.: nos. 102, 255.

Nzobo (Congo – Azande). Ankle bells in pellet form.
Lit.: no. 184.

Nzoko (Lower Congo). Cylindrical drum with a single head.
Lit.: no. 280.

Nzolo (Congo – Basiri). Small iron bell attached to the top of the bow of a *bagili*.

Nzonga (West Africa – Fan). Small iron bell tied to the hand or foot of a magician.

Nzundu (Congo). Rattle made of iron nails.
Lit.: no. 280.

O

O (Korea). A tone name of the *kong-chuk-po*. Assuming that *hap* (the first note of the scale) is C and *yuk*, its upper octave, c, *O* represents the notes d, also d♭ and d♯, as required by the mode of the performed item.
Lit.: no. 136.

Ŏ (Korea). The "wooden tiger" placed upon a wooden box. The tiger has 27 notches at its back which are scraped with a bamboo stick that is spliced into several thin, elastic ends at the front. The Ō is an *ah-ak* instrument. Its Chinese name is *yü* (M 7650); the Japanese name is *gyo*.
Lit.: nos. 52, 179.

Oan (Vietnam). (1) Tone name. Cf. *Ho* (where all tone names are listed; see also *Bac*). (2) See *Bac* (*Hoi Oan*), country songs (of *Ca Hue*).

Oapoh (Flores). Dance similar to the *teke*, but faster in tempo and more violent in its movements.
Lit.: no. 166.

Oat (Thailand). Tone name. Cf. *Thang*.

Oba (Sierra Leone). See *Kani*.
Lit.: no. 255.

Obachi (Japan). The right side ("male") drumstick of the *tsuri-daiko*, energetically used. Cf. *Mebachi*.
Lit.: no. 225.

Oba rede (Flores—Sikka District). Lively drum rhythm (in anapaestic meter) believed to express joy and, at the end of ceremonies, to drive away evil spirits and vermin from the crops in the fields.
Lit.: nos. 11, 166.

Obene (Ghana). Dance.
Lit.: no. 218.

Obokano (West Kenya—Gusii). Large bowl lyre with eight strings. Cf. *Iritingo*.
Lit.: no. 299.

Obon (Japan). Popular folk festival with chorus singing and dancing. Cf. *Bon-odori*.
Lit.: no. 185.

Obukano (West Kenya). See *Obokano*.

Obulere (Uganda—Sogo). Small panpipes with a variable number of pipes (8-13).
Lit.: no. 302.

Obute (Uganda—Acoli). Side-blown horn.
Lit.: no. 302.

Obwaso (Tanzania). Songs of buffalo hunters.

Obwoshe (Tanganyika—Bahaya). Fiddle with one horsehair string. Played by men only.

Ochet-ochetan (Bali). A specific type of figuration in *kebyar* music.
Lit.: no. 197.

Ochingufu (West Africa). See *Chingufu.*

Ō-Daiko (Japan). Large barrel drum that rests upon a wooden stand. It is beaten with two stout wooden sticks. The drum is used in folk and *kagura* music. Cf. *Taiko* (*Daiko*).

Odalan (Bali). Temple festival held twice during the year.

Oḍava (*Auḍava*) (North India). See *Rāga.*
Lit.: no. 138.

Oḍav-Devgiri (North India). *Rāga.* A rare form of *Devgiri-Bilaval*, ascribed to the *Bilaval thāta.* Tone material:

C D E G A c
c A G E D C

Lit.: no. 138.

Odeguiliguili (Nigeria—Ibo). Bull roarer.
Lit.: no. 223.

Odi (Uganda—Kakwi; Madi; Lugbara). Lyre with 4-5 strings. Cf. *Idi* (Nigeria).
Lit.: no. 302.

Odi (*Idi*) (Nigeria—Igbo). Hourglass-shaped drum.

Oḍissi (India; Orissa). Local dance play.

Odo (Nigeria—Igbo). Ivory horn. See *Opi.*

Odoko (Flores). A piece of music, usually played in two voices, in canonic form with a drone.
Lit.: no. 166.

Odome (*Ngelenge*) (Nigeria). Large xylophone.

Odori (Japan). The central section of the classic *joruri* structure, representing a dance-like interlude played on the *shamisen.* Cf. *Bon-odori*; *Nembutsu-odori.*
Lit.: no. 185.

Odoriji (Japan). Dance section in *nagauta* and *joruri.*
Lit.: no. 187.

Odori kudoki (Japan). A 17th-century dance performed at special parties (*kabuki*).
Lit.: no. 187.

Odori-uta (Japan). A *nagauta* type combined with a dance performance, particularly in the *kabuki* theater.

Odurugya (Ghana). Long cane flute.

O-e-o-e (Hawaii). A whirled friction drum that consists of a hollow nut or calabash swung around on a string.
Lit.: no. 37.

Ogane (Japan). Large Buddhist bell suspended in a separate pagoda close to the temple, struck by a horizontally-swinging heavy pole. Its sound marks the hours and announces the New Year and other important events.
Lit.: no. 185.

Oganga (Sudan). Drum.
Lit.: no. 95.

Oga onijo (Nigeria—Yoruba). Chief dancer.
Lit.: no. 293.

Oga onilu (*Ogalu*) (Nigeria—Yoruba). Master drummer.
Lit.: no. 293.

Ogboni (Nigeria). Royal drums.
Lit.: no. 293.

Ogel (Sunda District). An ensemble of four (6) angklungs (*angklung ubrug*) and four *ḍogḍogs*. It accompanies the performing buffoons (*bodoran*).
Lit.: no. 163.

Ogele (Nigeria—Igbo). See *Ogene.*

Ogene (Nigeria—Igbo). Also *ogele*; *ogeni.* Iron bell without clapper. The bell can be single or double.

Ogeni (Nigeria—Igbo). See *Ogene.*

Ōgibyōshi (Japan). Beating meter and rhythm with a fan.
Lit.: no. 185.

Ogidan (Dahomey—Nago). Drum.
Lit.: no. 303.

Ogidigbo (Nigeria—Yoruba). An almost obsolete slit-drum.

Ogido (Nigeria—Yoruba). Hand-beaten drum with a single skin.

Ogo buru (Mali—Dogon). Side-blown trumpet.
Lit.: no. 303.

Ogu-gut (Korea). Cf. *Kut.*

Ogung (Sumatra). Barrel drum. Cf. *Gordang.*

Ogung-ogung bulu (North Sumatra—Toba Batak). Bamboo zither.
Lit.: no. 156.

Ohe Hano (Hawaii). Bamboo nose flute with four finger holes.
Lit.: no. 255.

Ohe ke eke (Hawaii). Bambo stamping tube.
Lit.: no. 181.

Ō-hichiriki (Japan). Large *hichiriki* with nine finger holes. See *Hichiriki.*
Lit.: no. 255.

Ohiva (South Africa—Herero). Obsolete animal horn.
Lit.: no. 151.

Ohonji (Angola). Mouth-held musical bow.

Ohsi (Burma; Southern Shan States). Goblet drum. The Burmese term is *o-tsi.*
Lit.: no. 252.

Ohyan (Sunda District). Also *rebab batok kechil*; *gihyan.* A fiddle of Chinese origin. It has two strings, a long neck, and a small corpus made of half a coconut. Cf. *Hu-ch'in.*
Lit.: no. 163.

O-hyen-kum (Korea). "Five-stringer." See *Go-kin.*

Ō-iso (Japan). See *Koto* (parts).

Oiwake (Japan). Originally a popular song of pack-horse drivers; later sung by workers at herring fisheries. It was accompanied by a *shakuhachi* player. Usually the *oiwake* was and is named after the places where it is sung (e.g., *matsumae-oiwake*). Cf. *Min-yō*; *Yagibūshi.*

Oja (Nigeria—Igbo). End-blown flute with two finger holes.

Oja-ufele (Nigeria—Igbo). *Ugene* with one finger hole.

Ojha parra (Southeast India—Gond of the Bastar State). See *Hulki mandri.*

Ō-kakko (*Dai-byoshi*) (Japan). The large *kakko* (drum) used in *kagura* and *kabuki* music.
Lit.: no. 225.

Okame (Japan). A pantomimic comic dance presented by a woman. The music is played by a *hayashi.*

Okanga (Nigeria—Igbo). A two-headed cylindrical drum.

Okawa (Japan). See *Ō-tsuzumi.*

Ok-che (Korea). Marble flute. Cf. *Yü-ti.*

Okedō (Japan). Barrel-shaped drum used in *kabuki* (*geza*) and folk music. Beaten with two sticks.
Lit.: no. 185.

Okeoke (Solomon Isl.). See *Mou hatingaa nge'o.*

Oki (Japan). Introductory part of *kabuki* dance. Cf. *Nagauta*; *Joruri.*
Lit.: no. 187.

Okike (Nigeria – Igbo). Ivory horn. Cf. *Opi.*

Okiribongo (Gabon Republic – Koyo). Harp-zither. Cf. *Mvet.*
Lit.: no. 280.

Oki-uta (Japan). Theatrical prelude.

Okobolo (Nigeria – Igbo). Large xylophone.

Okoco (Uganda – Acoli). Rattle made of the upper shell of a tortoise with a few small iron chains attached, tied to the arm of a male dancer.
Lit.: no. 302.

Okonko (West Africa; Guinea). Percussion clay pot with a side aperture.
Lit.: no. 223.

Okoroko (Nigeria – Igbo). Leg rattle.

Okpokolo (Nigeria – Igbo). Small bamboo slit-drum.

Okporo (Congo – Mono; Banda). Also *kokpwero.* Barrel drum. A conical drum of the Banda. Cf. *Bia.*
Lit.: nos. 21, 26.

Oku-jōruri (Japan). Musical folk narrative without any accompaniment. Only the singer beats his fan against his hand and thus produces a rhythmical background. See *Jōruri.*
Lit.: no. 187.

Okumi joruri (Japan). See *Jōruri.*

Oku no yurushi (Japan). "The innermost license." The third diploma issued in the regular course of *koto*, *kokyu*, or *shamisen* playing. This entitles the student to lower the first string of his *koto* by one octave in all modes. Cf. *Ura no yurushi*; *Omote no yurushi.*

The successful completion of the fourth, the highest, course, entitles the student to use the name of his teacher and, having become a professional musician, to establish this on a sign-board and open his own school.
Lit.: no. 225.

Okuterananga (*Enanga*) (Uganda; Tanganyika). A zither or a harp.
Lit.: no. 190.

Okuyimba (East and Central Africa). Three part music performed by one voice and two instruments.
Lit.: no. 155.

Okwo-agida (Nigeria – Igbo). Bamboo slit-drum.

Okwo-mata (Nigeria – Igbo). Bamboo slit-drum.

Okworo (congo – Togbo). Drum. See also *Opporo*; *Dundu.*
Lit.: nos. 21, 26.

Ola (New Guinea – Ngaing). Ritual dance (in honor of birth, death, initiation, and marriage) performed by men and women during the first night when the spirits of the dead are believed to appear. The dance is accompanied by the playing of simple trumpets.
Lit.: no. 177.

O le fa'a (Samoa). See *O le polotu.*

Ole olean (West Java). See *Empet-empetan*. Cf. *De(r)men(an)*.
Lit.: no. 163.

Oleg (Bali). Ritual dance performed by a group of women.
Lit.: no. 197.

O le polotu (Samoa; Tonga). Also *o le fa'a*; *alii la iti*. Percussion board, beaten when songs are sung.
Lit.: no. 84.

Oli (Talaud Isl.). Jew's harp.
Lit.: no. 162.

Oliko (Uganda—Madi). Also *gbere*. Conical, vertical gourd flute.
Lit.: no. 302.

Oli-oli (West Java; Toba District). Rice stalk shawm. See *Ra'us woja* (Flores).
Lit.: no. 166.

Olodero (Uganda—Alur). Dance music accompanied by a percussion stick (*olodero*) and by an *adungu*.
Lit.: no. 302.

Olubeye (Uganda—Nyole). Rattle made of dried fruits.
Lit.: no. 302.

Olukula (Tanganyika). See *Amokoderi*.

Olwet (Uganda—Acoli). Trumpet in various forms.
Lit.: no. 302.

Omakola (West Angola). Scraper stick played by women.
Lit.: no. 280.

O-matsuri (*Matsuri*) (Japan). Folk festivals that greet the arrivals of spring, midsummer, harvest (autumn), and winter. Many of the popular *sata-kagura* folk dances are performed at these occasions. The dances are: *okame*, "comic woman's dance"; *hyottoko*, "bumpkin dance"; *nimba*, "dog-dance"; *shishi-odori*, "lion's dance."
Lit.: no. 185.

Ombak (Java). "Wave." Term for the acoustical waves when a (large) gong is beaten slowly and gently. The depth and fullness of the gong's venerated sound is called *ulem*. Cf. *Pengumbang*.
Lit.: no. 163.

Ombak banyu (Sunda District). "Undulating water." See *Bima gumuyu*. Cf. *Ombak*.

Ombi (Guinea; Republic of Africa). A trough-shaped wooden resonance box, covered with leather. It has an upward curving neck and 4-8 fiber strings. Cf. *Bulu*; *Bambur*.
Lit.: no. 33.

Ombgwe (South Africa—Karanga). Vertical flute with 2-3 finger holes. The flute is not only blown but sung into. Cf. *Khumbgwe*.
Lit.: no. 151.

Ombiwe (South Africa). See *Ombgwe*.

Omele (*Emele*) (Nigeria). Cf. *Dundun*.

Omele abo (*Kudi*) (Nigeria—Yoruba). Also *kudi*. Stick-beaten cylindrical drum slightly bigger than the *omele ako*. It belongs to the *dundun* ensemble. Cf. *Bata*.
Lit.: no. 293.

Omele abo iyu'lu (Nigeria—Yoruba). Cf. *Bata*.

Omele ako (Nigeria—Yoruba). Cf. *Bata*. *Omele ako* is a high-pitched drum with two heads, hand beaten, and with a conical corpus. It belongs to the *dundun* and *kete* ensembles.
Lit.: no. 293.

Omele kenkele (Nigeria—Yoruba). A stick beaten drum belonging to the *kete* ensemble.
Lit.: no. 293.

Omolu (Nigeria—Yoruba). A globular earthenware pot drum with one head named after a water and fertility deity, in whose honor it is played. *Omolu* also represents an ensemble of drums that consists of *iya'lu* (the leading drum); *apesin*; *omele ako*; *omele abo*.
Lit.: no. 293.

Omoro (Ryukyu Isl.). Obsolete religious and ceremonial songs.

Omote (Japan). See *Nagashi*.

Omote no yurushi (Japan). "Front license." The first diploma in the regular course in *koto*, *kokyu*, or *shamisen* playing. Cf. *Ura no yurushi*; *Oku no yurushi*.
Lit.: no. 225.

Ompochawa (Ghana—Ashanti). *Sansa* with wooden tongues.
Lit.: no. 255.

Omudage (Ruanda). Musical bow.
Lit.: no. 302.

Omugoboli (*Egobolo*) (Uganda). Musical bow.
Lit.: no. 302.

Omukuri (Uganda—Kiga; Nkole). Flute with four finger holes.
Lit.: no. 302.

Omuleri (Tanganyika—Bahaya). Whistle flute with eight finger holes.

Omvok (Congo). See *Ongo*.

Omwomba (Tanzania). Wooden hunting horn. Cf. *Enzomba*.

Oñ (New Guinea—Yabim). Drum with an hourglass-shaped body. Cf. *Amban*; *Hami*; *Kam*; *Moti*; *Onum*; *Wonggang*.
Lit.: no. 25.

On ahk (Korea). Serious (instrumental) music with sung text.

Ondo (Japan). Popular Buddhist folk songs, folk hymns, in which a solo singer and a chorus perform alternately. Cf. *Goeika*.
Lit.: no. 185.

Ong dich (Vietnam). Transverse flute. Cf. *Cai on dich*.
Lit.: no. 296.

Onge (Melanesia). See *Giram(o)*.

Ongo(la) (*Omvok*) (Former French Congo—Fan). Simple iron bell.
Lit.: no. 255.

Ongoma (South Africa—Herero). Rare barrel drum.
Lit.: no. 151.

Onikete (Nigeria—Yoruba). A *kete* drummer.
Lit.: no. 293.

Oni no mai (Japan). Devil dances (performed in Shinto ceremonies).

Ong tieu (Annam). Flute.

Onna Kabuki (Japan). "Women's *kabuki*," an early form.
Lit.: no. 187.

Ōnori (Japan). One syllable sung to one beat (in *noh* music). Cf. *Chunori*.
Lit.: no. 187.

O'o (Solomon Isl.—Malaita). Slit-drum.
Lit.: no. 318.

Oñum (New Guinea—Kate). Drum. Cf. *Oñ*.
Lit.: no. 25.

Oobar (Australia). A hollow tree trunk, or an appropriately large piece of wood used as a drum.
Lit.: no. 303.

Oo-hse (Burma). See *Ozi*.

Oöi (Northwest Borneo—Sea Dayak). See *Sigittuad.*

Ompochawa (West Africa—Ashanti). A *sansa* with wooden tongues.
Lit.: no. 255.

Oompoochawa (West Africa). See *Ompochawa.*

Opak oron (Flores). Round dance of men. Cf. *Hama.*
Lit.: no. 166.

Opanda (Nigeria—Igbo). A *sansa* with a box resonator.

Oparun (Nigeria). Also *pape.* See *Keke.*

Opi (Sudan; Nigeria). A long calabash flute; in Nigeria it is a cow- or ivory-horn.
Lit.: no. 95.

Opi-ukwu (Nigeria—Igbo). Wooden flute.

Opi-nta (Nigeria—Igbo). Bamboo flute.

Opon (Nigeria—Yoruba). See *Gudugudu.*

Opporo (Congo—Togbo). Cylindrical drum.
Lit.: no. 26.

Opuk agoya (Uganda—Acoli). Harp with five or seven strings.
Lit.: no. 302.

Or (Somaliland). The call to dance of the men (*gablo*). The call is performed immediately before the beginning of the actual dance, and can be rhythmically free or can employ a traditional tune. Each dance has its own *or.* The *or* singer stands apart from the dancers and does not join them. When the actual dance begins the dancing men, functioning as a chorus, provide the melody.
Lit.: no. 98.

Oranda-chōshi (Japan). An old name for the major mode of the West.
Lit.: no. 185.

O'rdu (Sudan). Harp-lute.
Lit.: no. 33.

Oreh (Southeast Celebes). Term for *rebāb.*

Ore (Uganda—Made). Triangular harp with five or seven strings.
Lit.: no. 190.

Oreh (Southeast Celebes). See *Arababu.*
Lit.: no. 132.

Ore-ore (Southeast Celebes). Name for the *buncacan* (of the Philippines). It has the form of a tuning fork. The sound can be altered by closing or opening a finger hole in the handle. Cf. *Buncacan*; *Genggong sakai.*
Lit.: no. 254.

Orghoul (Arabia). See *Yaroul.*

Ori (Japan). "Breaking." A very brief *koto* motive, usually used between arpeggios and echo effects, played with the fingers of the left hand.

Orikai (India). Ornament (*gamak*).

Oriki (Nigeria—Yoruba). Solo *dundun* music played on the *iya'lu dundun. Oriki* represents recitations of praise-poetry linked with drum music. See *Dundun*; *Iya'lu dundun.*

Oriori (New Zealand—Maori). Songs sung by parents and grandparents for the children. These songs can be lullabies and tell the child of his noble ancestors. Occasionally the *oriori* can be a teaching song.
Lit.: no. 228.

Orkes melayu (Indonesia). "Malay orchestra" (*dung-det*), a modern popular instrumental ensemble employed for entertainment. It appears all over the archipelago.

Oro (New Zealand—Maori). The central tone about which a melody moves.
Lit.: no. 228.

Orodo (Uganda—Madi). Harp with five or seven strings.
Lit.: no. 302.

Orogunchara (West Kenya—Gusii). Side-blown cow horn. Used as accompaniment, together with the *rirandi* of funeral music.
Lit.: no. 299.

Oroshi (Japan). Drum (*taiko*) pattern.

Oru (Japan). A melodic pattern of *wagon* music. Cf. *San*; *Ji*; *Tsumu*.
Lit.: no. 185.

Orugōru (Japan). Five bells of varied sizes suspended from a wooden board. Originally the bells were used in Buddhist services, later they appeared also in *kabuki* shows whenever a rustic mood and a countryside effect were required.
Lit.: no. 185.

Orupi (Flores; Ende). A short single or double bamboo clarinet without any finger holes. In Nage it is called *hu'a ha'u*; in Badjawa, Were, and Todabelu of Ngada it is called *nggoa-nggao*.
Lit.: no. 166.

Oruto (Kenya). Lute.

Osae (Japan). Several pitches of the *yokyōku* tone system.
Lit.: no. 185.

Osameru (Japan). *Taiko* drumming phase, which comes to a stop with both sticks left resting on the drumhead.
Lit.: no. 185.

Ose (Solomon Isl.). To sing a *kananga*, a song with indecent text.
Lit.: no. 246.

Ose-byōshi (Japan). *Gagaku* pieces played in fast double meter. Cf. *Haya-bhōshi*.
Lit.: no. 185.

Oseke (Uganda—Alur). Flute.
Lit.: no. 302.

Osha (Nigeria—Igbo). Basket rattle.

O'shaq (Algeria). *Maqām*.
Tone material:
A B c d e f# g a
Cf. *'Ushshaq*.
Lit.: no. 64.

Ōshiki (Japan). Mode in use by the Shingon and Tendai sects. Cf. *Sō-no-koto* (tunings): A B d e f# a. Cf. *Shōmyō*.
Lit.: nos. 185, 225.

Ōshiki-chō (Japan). Cf. *Gagaku* (mode).
Lit.: no. 185.

Oshirabe (Japan). Before the *shite* enters (in the *jo* section of the *noh* drama) the *hayashi* (one flute and three drums) play a short introductory prelude. *Oshirabe* types appear also in *kabuki* performances.
Lit.: no. 187.

Ōshō (Japan). The eighth of the 12 chromatic tones (usually transcribed as the Western note A). This pitch is too high for the average singer and is believed to create an ugly sound (*uragoe*).
Lit.: no. 225.

Osobuki (Japan). Short pipe of bamboo or metal with either six or no finger holes.

Osu (Japan). "To press." A term used in *koto* playing when a string has to be pressed below the bridge in order to sharpen the tone by one semitone (*ritsu*). Commonly this procedure is called *ka*.
Lit.: no. 225.

Ot chung mori (Korea). Rhythmic mode:

Bamboo strokes on the *chang-ko*

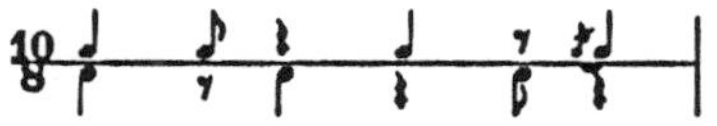

Hand strokes on the *chang-ko*

Lit.: no. 286.

Otea (Tahiti). Dance.
Lit.: no. 215.

Ō-teki (*Ryūteki*; *Yoko-bue*) (Japan). A medium-sized transverse cane flute of Chinese origin. Its tube is tightly wound with lacquered string and has 6-7 finger holes. The *ō-teki* was used in the *tōgaku* ensemble. See *Ryūteki*; *Nohkan*.
Lit.: nos. 185, 225, 291.

Otekra (Assam). A bamboo cross flute with two finger holes near its lower end.
Lit.: no. 252.

Otongoli (Uganda – Gwere). Arched harp with six strings.
Lit.: no. 302.

Oṭot (West Java). See *Rengkong*.

Oto-tsuzumi (Japan). "The younger." An hourglass drum carried on the left shoulder and beaten with the fingers of the right hand. See *Ko-tsuzumi*. Cf. *Ō-tsuzumi*.
Lit.: no. 225.

Otou (India). See *Panchama Otu*.

Ō-tsi (*Ō-zi*) (Burma). Goblet drum (see *Ohsi*). The instrument has a considerable number of names. Several are: *fondrahi* (*fondraki*) in Nias, *goddan* in Flores, *katambon* (*kasambonan*) in Borneo, *katāuba* in Mentavi Islands, *kralu* in Celebes, *nākotība* in Northeast Timor, *thon* (*thong*) in Siam, *tron* (*trong*) in Cambodia, *tihal* in East Timor and Letti, *tivele* in Sermata, *tīval* (*tifa*, *tīfal*) in Tanembar and Kei, *tuba* in Buru and Sula-Besi.
Lit.: no. 254.

Otsu (Japan). The fourteenth pipe of the *shō*. Cf. *Shō*.
Lit.: no. 225.

Ō-tsuzumi (*E-tsuzumi*; *Okawa*) (Japan). "The elder" drum in hourglass shape. It is related to the *ko-tsuzumi* but has a larger body. Its heads are made of cowhide. The *ō-tsuzumi* is played as a hip drum, is beaten with three fingers of the right hand, and is used in *noh* and *kabuki* music. Cf. *Chang-ku* (China); *Chang-ko* (Korea).
Lit.: no. 185.

Ottu (India). The drone pipe of the *nāgasara* (*nāgasuram*). It has four or five finger holes and the tube is slightly longer than the melody pipe. Cf. *Bura*.
Lit.: no. 260.

Otu (*Ottu*) (India). See *Panchama Otu*.

'Otu haka (Polynesia; Tonga). Dance of sitting men and women.

Oukpwe (Upper Guinea). See *Embuchi* (Congo).

O-um-yak-po (Korea). "Five-sounds-abbreviated-notation." A simple notational system that came into use during the reign of King Sae-cho (15th century). No absolute pitches are given. Above and below the central note *kung* (the Chinese M 3705) are placed the numerals 1, 2, 3, 4, 5 (in Chinese or Korean script) with the "up" (M 5669) or "below" signs (M 2520). *Sang* ("up") means "above *kung*" and *sa* ("below") indicates the lower part of the scale, below *kung*.
The chart on the following page shows the use of the *o-um-yak-po* tone names in the four basic modes of *ah-ak*. For details see Lit. no. 136, pp. 125-26.

Ō-uta (Japan). See *Kagura*.

Outa (*Outa otji humba*) (South Africa – Damara). Musical bow.
Lit.: no. 18.

Ōutadokoro (Japan). A section of the *gagakuryō*, established in the 9th century, dealing with ancient songs and dances. Cf. *Wagaku*.
Lit.: no. 53.

O-UM-YAK-PO TONE NAMES
Ah-ak modes

Tone names	*Pyong-cho*	*Pyong-cho Kae-myon-cho*	*U-cho*	*U-cho Kae-myon-cho*
Sang o [5]	c	c	f	f
Sang sa [4]	A	B♭	d	e♭
Sang sam [3]	G	G	c	c
Sang i [2]	F	F	B♭	B♭
Kung	C	C	F	F
Sa il [1]	*A*	*B♭*	D	E♭
Sa i [2]	*G*	*G*	C	C
Sa sam [3]	*F*	*F*	*B♭*	*B♭*
Sa sa [4]	*D*	*E♭*	*G*	*A♭*
Sa o [5]	*C*	*C*	*F*	*F*

Outa otji humba (South Africa). See *Outa* (South Africa).

Ovambo (South Africa). Musical bow. Cf. *Lukombe.*
Lit.: no. 151.

Ove (Polynesia; Mangaia). Slit-drum.

Ovis (India). Marāṭha song (long epic text).

(O)wer-(o)wer (Central Java). Bull roarer; cf. *Jata* (Flores); whizzing bow.

Oyara (Nigeria—Igbo). Wooden double bells. Cf. *Ugbom-eze.*

Oye (Nigeria—Yoruba). See *Tioko.*

Oyo (Nigeria—Igbo). Basket rattle.

Ō-yuri (Japan). "Grand *yuri*" is a *kyōkusetzu. Ō-yuri* is a *yuri* (in *ryo*) preceded by a held note that is followed by ascending trills. In the *ritsu* mode the feature is called *ko-yūri* ("little *yūri*"). It, too, begins with a held note that is followed by a slow trill that gradually increases in speed and rises in tempo. Cf. *Yūri-ori*; *Fuji-yuri.*
Lit.: no. 185.

Ozashiki (Japan). Music detached from *kabuki* and performed in concert-form without any dancing.
Lit.: no. 187.

Ozashiki nagauta (Japan). Concert form of *nagauta* music without dancing. Cf. *Ozashiki.*
Lit.: no. 187.

Ōzatsuma (Japan). In *nagauta* pieces stereotyped melodic fragments are used (each fragment having its own name) that are remnants from an early *shamisen* music called *ōzatsuma bushi.* The entire lot of these fragments is called "the 48 *ōzatsuma te.*"
Lit.: no. 187.

Ōzatsuma bushi (Japan). Old narrative (*joruri* types) *shamisen* music. Parts of it are frequently used in *nagauta.*
Lit.: no. 187.

Ogatsuma te (Japan). See *Ōzatsuma.*

Ozi (Burma). A wooden pot-shaped drum with a black and red lacquered body. It is held under the arm and beaten with the hand. Cf. *O-tsi.*
Lit.: no. 255.

Ozi (Nigeria – Igbo). A one-headed drum used at funerals.

Ozila (Cameroon). Initiation dance.

Ozohahi (South Africa – Herero). Ankle rattles worn by women.
Lit.: no. 151.

P

P'a (*Pa*) (China — M 4830). The plucking in an inward direction of lute and zither strings. Cf. *P'i.*

Pa (India). Abbreviation of *pañcama* (*pañchama*). The tone syllable represents the fifth degree of a heptatonic scale (e.g., G if *sa* is C). *Pa* cannot be altered by a semitone; *sa* and *pa* remain unchanged in all scales of North and South India. *Pa* corresponds to the 13th *śruti Mārjanī*. Cf. *Śruti.*

Pa (Ghana; Upper Volta). Arched harp.
Lit.: no. 21.

Pa (Thailand). Drum beat on the *tapone* struck with the right hand. The flat hand strikes the drumhead and remains on the drum, producing a short, dull sound.

Pa (South India). One of the six mnemonics that indicates the first *mēḷa* of each *chakra* (the six syllables are: *pā*, *śrī*, *go*, *bhū*, *ma*, and *shā*). When these syllables are used in combination with the names of the *chakras*, the Indian theorist can easily determine any number of the 72 *mēḷas*. See *Rāga* (South India).
Lit.: no. 139.

Paakuru (New Zealand — Maori). See *Pakuru.*

Pa'amon (Ancient Israel). Hebrew term for small jingling bells attached to the high priest's garment.
Lit.: no. 250.

Paatere (New Zealand — Maori). Songs sung by slandered women who answer in nasty language.

P'ab-che (Tibet). See *Dung-che.*

Pacat (Malaysia). See *Rebāb* (Malaysia).

Pacchimā (Nepal). Barrel drum with two heads.
Lit.: no. 46.

Pa chiao ku (China). See *Pa fang ku.*

Pachih (Flores). See *Main Chachih.*

Pāda (Vedic India). "Foot"; quarter verse of a regular stanza; a portion of a verse.
Lit.: no. 292.

Padam (South India). *Padam inimal* . . . the 4th (or 5th) dance of the *bharata nāṭyam* series. It indicates a number of gestures (*abhinaya*) and is sung by a woman.

Padatrong (West Torres Street). Rattle consisting of sticks tied together.
Lit.: no. 255.

Paddhati (India). System; practice.

Pādi (*Pahāḍi*) (South India). *Janya rāga* of the 15th *mēḷa* (*Māyāmāḷavagauḷa*).
Tone material:
C D♭ F G B c
c B G A♭ G F E D♭ C
Lit.: no. 139.

Padingbwa (Congo—Kinshasa). Loose key xylophone without any resonator.

Padmabhavani (South India). *Janya rāga* of the 69th *mēḷa* (*Dhātuvardhaṇī*).
Tone material:
C D♯ E F♯ G A♭ c
c B A♭ G F♯ E D♯ C
Lit.: no. 139.

Padmakānti (South India). *Janya rāga* of the 62nd *mēḷa* (*Riṣabhapriyā*).
Tone material:
C D E F♯ G A♭ B♭ c
c B♭ G F♯ E D C
Lit.: no. 139.

Padmamukhi (South India). *Janya rāga* of the 57th *mēḷa* (*Siṃhendramadhyama*).
Tone material:
C D E♭ F♯ A♭ B c
c A♭ G F♯ E♭ C
Lit.: no. 139.

Padmarāgam (South India). *Janya rāga* of the 27th *mēḷa* (*Sarasāṅgī*).
Tone material:
C D E F G A♭ B c
c B A♭ G F E C
Lit.: no. 139.

Padmini (South India). *Janya rāga* of the 16th *mēḷa* (*Chakravāka*).
Tone material:
C D♭ F G A B♭ c
c B♭ A F D♭ C
Lit.: no. 139.

Padumalai (South India). Name of an ancient mode mentioned in the *Shilappadikaram*.
Lit.: no. 45.

Padya (India). See *Pāda*.

Pa fang ku (*Pa chiao ku*) (China). Octagonal frame drum (with jingles), covered with snakeskin.
Lit.: no. 258.

Pagal paṇ (South India). *Rāgas* that are to be performed during the day. See *Iravuppaṇ*; *Poduppaṇ*.
Lit.: no. 261.

Pagan(g) (Borneo—Loṅ Kiput). Tube zither with six strings.
Lit.: no. 254.

Pagolo (New Britain). Also *Pangolo*. Music bow played by women.
Lit.: nos. 18, 206.

Pagugu (Nigeria—Yoruba). Stamping tube. It is believed to represent a dead person and is used in funeral rites.
Lit.: no. 223.

Pahāḍī (North India). Light popular *rāga* ascribed to the *Bilaval thāta*.
Tone material:
(C D) F G A B♭ c d (e) f
f (e) d c B♭ A G F; *Vādis*: F, C
Lit.: no. 138.

Pahāḍī (South India). See *Pādi*.

Pahawang (Southeast Borneo). See *Babandi*.

Pah pung (Vietnam—Miau). Stamping tube.
Lit.: no. 303.

Pahu (Oceania). (1) General term for membrane drums. Frequently the instruments are long, cylindrical, standing drums with shark-skin heads beaten with the hand. The term appears throughout the vast region of Polynesia. In its northern region (Hawaii) and in its center (Tahiti) the drum can have various sizes. In the Southwest (New Zealand) the Maori use the term to indicate slit-drums beaten with a wooden stick or mallet.

(2) Occasionally *pahu* signifies gongs and bells.
Lit.: nos. 7, 84, 255, 311.

Pahuu (New Zealand). Wooden gong of the Maori. Generally used in war in order to alarm the men when danger is near.

Pahu hula (Hawaii). Broad drum with one membrane. The body rests upon a supporting socle.
Lit.: no. 37.

Pahul (West Java). The bridge on a bamboo *chelempung* with one or two strings. A central vibrating bridge is called *sumbi.*
Lit.: no. 163.

Pahu vanano (French Polynesia; Marqueses Isl.). One-headed drum with a long slim wooden body.
Lit.: no. 255.

Pai (Japan). See *Bai.*

Pai (China). Spoken parts that start scenes of the *tsa-chü.*
Lit.: no. 182.

Pai ah (Kampuchea). Small bamboo shawm with six front holes.
Lit.: no. 43.

P'ai-hsiao (China—M 4870; M 2619). A rank of pipes (*hsiao*), panpipes, of ancient origin. Originally the instrument had 10, later 12, 16, 23, and at the present time 16 small pipes (*kuan*) tuned to: A B C♯ D♯ F G A B A A♯ G♯ F♯ E D C *B*♭ *A*♭.

A box imitating the form of the wings of the bird phoenix, in which the pipes are placed, has been added during the Yüan period (1264-1368). Cf. *So* (Korea).
Lit.: nos. 1, 137.

Paiku (Burma). Xylophone with bamboo slabs.

Painjani (India). Jingle.

P'ai-pan (*P'e-pan*) (China—M 4986; M 4886). A popular clapper consisting of three wooden slabs, each hung with one end on a silken string. The player beats two slabs against the third with a twist of his hand. The clapper is used in theatrical shows, also by traders, mendicants, and at funerals. The rattle has many names; a few are: *p'ak-pan* (Cantonese), *cha-pan*, *chat-pan* (Cantonese), *pan-tzu*, *pan.* Cf. *Ch'ung-tu*; *Shou-pan.*
Lit.: no. 209.

Pai-p'i-ku (China). A small barrel drum with two heads, suspended between three wooden posts. It is used in theatrical, puppet, and similar shows. Its Cantonese name is *pak-k'ei-ku.* Other names of this drum are: *shuang-p'i-ku* (Mandarin), *sheung-p'ei-ku* (Cantonese), *ch'ün-ku* (Mandarin), *kuan-ku* (Cantonese), and *ma-t'i-ku* (Mandarin; "horse-hoof drum").
Lit.: no. 129.

Pak (*P'ai-pan* [China]; *Haku* [Japan]) (Korea). A clapper in the shape of a fan consisting of six wooden (rarely ivory) slabs tied together at one end. The player rattles five slabs held in one hand against one slab in the other hand. The instrument was already in use in the 11th century and was rattled once at the beginning of a Confucian hymn and thrice at its end. *Pak* has to be considered as an *ah-ak* instrument.
Lit.: no. 52.

Pakasanapriya (South India). *Janya rāga* of the 70th *mēḷa* (*Nāsikabhūṣaṇī*).
Tone material:

C D♯ F♯ G A B♭ c
c B♭ A G F♯ D♯ C

Lit.: no. 139.

Pa-keha (New Zealand). "Western songs" adjusted and harmonized in thirds and sixths for choral singing of the Maori.
Lit.: no. 228.

Paketan (Bali). Term for *kotekan* (Bali).
Lit.: no. 197.

Pakha sarani (India). "Side strings." Strings that run outside the fingerboard and serve to produce bourdon sounds.

Pakhawāj (North India). The *mṛdaṅga* of the Urdu-speaking North. Occasionally the drum appears in a slightly smaller form than the ancient *mṛdaṅga* of the South.

Pakhe dumbā (Burma—Shan State). Oboe made of a conical tube of wood with six finger holes—four in front and two in the back.
Lit.: no. 252.

Paking (Borneo; Alor). Split bamboo zither. In Central West Timor the zither is called *sene-kaka.*
Lit.: no. 132.

Paking alu (Flores). Cf. *Alu.*

Pakkat-ch'aebi (Korea). See *Kot-ch'aebi.*

P'ak-pan (China). Cantonese term for wooden clapper. See *P'ai-pan.*

Pak-p'ei-ku (China). Cantonese term for *pai-p'i-ku.*

Pa-kua (China—M 4845; M 3514). The eight trigrams shown in the *I Ching* (Chinese Classics). These trigrams refer also to the eight materials of which musical instruments were made.
Lit.: no. 137.

Pakuda (Andaman Isl.). Beating-board that lies on the floor and is beaten with the heel of the foot.
Lit.: no. 254.

Pakuru (New Zealand). A pair of obsolete hardwood concussion sticks of the Maori. Cf. *La'au.*
Lit.: no. 7.

Pakwulo (Congo). See *Kwororo.*

Pal (Korea). See *Chabara.*

Pala (South Africa—Venda; Chwana). Vertical flute type made of the horn of an impala. Cf. *Naka ya sefako*; *Naka.*
Lit.: no. 151.

Palamajarī (*Phalamañjarī*) (South India). *Janya rāga* of the 22nd *mēḷa* (*Kharaharapriyā*).
Tone material:
C E♭ F A c
c B♭ A G F E♭ F D C
Lit.: no. 139.

Palankha (North India). A brief rhythmic phrase that is believed to represent the outline of the top of a palanquin: ♩ ♪ ♩.
Lit.: no. 136.

Palasi (North India). A rare *rāga* ascribed to the *Kafi thāta.*
Tone material:
C E♭ F G B♭ c
c B♭ G F E♭ D C
Lit.: no. 138.

Palawakiya (Bali). Epic prose (particularly the *Mahabharata* in its Kawi version) recited. Now performed with instrumental interludes played by the *gamelan gong kebyar.*
Lit.: no. 197.

Palayi (Philippines). Gong.

Paldong (Philippines). Flute with three (4) finger holes. Cf. *Tongali.*

Pale (Burma). Cf. *Chauk-pauk auk-pyan.*

Palemahan (*Songgabuwana*) (Java). See *Rebāb* (Java).

Palet (*Paletan*) (Bali). *Palet* means a group, a unit, a set of something to be indicated by a second word. One can observe the use of *palet* of verses, gongs, etc.
Lit.: no. 197.

Pālika (South India). *Janya rāga* of the 23rd *mēḷa* (*Gaurīmanōharī*).
Tone material:
C D E♭ A B c
c B A E♭ D C
Lit.: no. 139.

Pālini (South India). *Janya rāga* of the 14th *mēḷa* (*Vakulābharaṇam*).
Tone material:
C D♭ E A♭ B♭ c
c B♭ A♭ E D♭ C
Lit.: no. 139.

Pālipada (Ancient India). See *Nūpura.*

Pallavi (South India). The first section of an art song (*kriti* or *kirtana*). It is preceded by the introductory *ālāpa*. The *pallavi* corresponds to the *sthāyī* (*asthāyī*) of the North Indian *dhrūpad* or *khyāl.*

Pallim (Korea). Dramatic action.

Paloea (Sumatra). See *Palua.*

Palook (Philippines). Ensemble of seven gongs. Cf. *Gangsa.*

Palototan (Lower Burma—Pegu). Rattle drum (resembling the *damaru*) used by children as a toy. Cf. *Paṭpaṭi*; *Terbang*; *Čankela.*
Lit.: no. 255.

Pal-pal-jo (Korea). *Tae-kum.*

Palta (North India). A rhythmic elaboration of a *dohra.*
Lit.: no. 136.

Palua (Sumatra—Batak). Bamboo flute with five finger holes.
Lit.: no. 255.

Pa-lwe (*Pillui*) (Burma). Cf. *Pu-lwe.*
Lit.: no. 15.

Pamangkat (Java). See *Bebuka.*

Pamanis (Sunda). "Secondary tone"; also called *panyumbang* or *senggol nyimpang.* In Bali it is called *pemero.*
Lit.: no. 163.

Pambai (South India). Drum. Cf. *Panaba.*
Lit.: no. 260.

Pambe (India). Kettledrum, used only in Hindu temples. Cf. *Pambai*; *Panabe.*

Pāmbunāgasuram (South India). Tamil term for the (Sanskrit) *tiktirī*, a raucous double clarinet used by mendicants and snake charmers.
Lit.: no. 254.

Pamindo (Java). "The second tone." In Indramayu the term signifies the fourth tone of the *slendro* system.
Lit.: no. 163.

Pamiring (Sunda District). (1) Intermediate tone between *singgul* (the first) and *bem* (or *galimer*), (the second tone) of the *slendro* system of the Sunda District. (2) Intermediate tone between *sorog*, the seventh, and *singgul leutik*, the first tone of the next higher octave of the *pelog* system of the Sunda District. Cf. *Surupan melog.*
Lit.: no. 163.

Pam-me (Burma). Large *bung.*
Lit.: no. 255.

Pampame (West Africa—Fulbe). Long, wooden trumpet. Cf. *Fanfami.*
Lit.: nos. 190, 255.

Pāmulanāgasaramu (South India). Telugu term for (Sanskrit) *tiktirī*. Cf. *Pāmbunāgasuram*.

Pan (*Pang*) (China—M 4886). A wooden idiophone consisting of a rectangular wooden block. A tongue is cut into the upper surface of the block and is linked with the block on one side only. The player beats the tongue and makes it rattle against the block. Occasionally there are some *pan* with two tongues. Cf. *P'ai-pan*.
Lit.: no. 255.

Panaba (India). Drum with a wooden conical body and one skin. Cf. *Pambe*.

Panangis (Sunda District). (1) Intermediate tone between *panelu*, the third and *bungur*, the fourth tones of the *pelog* system of the Sunda District. (2) The intermediate tone between *panelu*, the third, and *kenong*, the fourth, tones of the *slendro* system of the Sunda District. (3) *Panangis* (Java), "the weeping tone." Cf. *Surupan melog*.

Paṇava (Ancient India). Drum with an hourglass-shaped body.

Pañcama (*Pañchama*; abbreviated: *pa*) (India). Sanskrit tone name. See *Pa*.

Pañcamāntya (South India). *See Pañchamantya*.

Pañcamūrti (South India). *Janya rāga* of the 64th *mēḷa* (*Vāchaspatī*).
Tone material:
C D E F♯ G A B♭
B♭ A G F♯ G E D C *B♭*
This scale has *niṣādāntya* character.
Lit.: no. 139.

Pañchali (South India). *Janya rāga* of the 15th *mēḷa* (*Māyāmāḷavagauḷa*).
Tone material:
C D♭ F G A♭ B c
c B A♭ G F D♭ C
Lit.: no. 139.

Pañchālika (South India). *Janya rāga* of the 2nd *mēḷa* (*Ratnangi*).
Tone material:
C E𝄫 F G B♭ c
c B♭ G F E𝄫 C
Lit.: no. 139.

Pancham (*Hindol-pancham*) (North India). An important *rāga* ascribed to the *Marva thāta*. There are two types of this *rāga*.
Tone material:
(Ia) C E F F♯ A c
c B A F♯ F E C
(b) C D♭ E F F♯ A c
c B A F♯ F E D♭ C
(II) C D♭ E F F♯ G A B c
c B A G F♯ F E D♭ C; *Vādis*: F, C
Lit.: no. 138.

Pañchama (Vedic India). See *Mandra* (Vedic chant).

Pañchama (South India). Also *Pañcama*. *Janya rāga* of the 22nd *mēḷa* (*Kharaharapriyā*).
Tone material:
C D A G B♭ c
c B♭ A G F E♭ D C
Lit.: no. 139.

Pañchamāntya (South India). A scale in which the highest note has to be *pa* (G) of the middle octave range (assuming that *sa* is C).

Panchama otu (India). Metal or wooden trumpet.
Lit.: no. 255.

Pañchamī (Ancient India). See *Jāti*.

Pancher (Sunda District). See *Indung*.

Panchkalyan (North India). *Rāga* ascribed to the *Kalyan thāta*. The name refers to a combination of five *Kalyan* types: *Yaman Kalyan*, *Shyam Kalyan*, *Suddh Kalyan*, *Hemkalyan*, and *Hamir Kalyan*. The tone material is indistinct on account of the variable mixture of elements used. *Vādis*: C, G.
Lit.: no. 138.

Panchtal-khin (Nepal). A *mṛdaṅga* type. To its middle is attached a small kettledrum. Both drumskins of the *mṛdaṅga* and the one of the small kettledrum are beaten with both hands alternatively.

Panchtār (*Pañctar*) (Persia; Turkestan; Afghanistan). "A fivestringer"—a *tanbur* with five strings. Cf. *Tanbūr*.
Lit.: no. 255.

Panda (*Panda-panda*) (Zanzibar—Swahili). Horn.

Pandir (Armenia). *Tanbur*.

Pandur (Sumeria). "Pan-tur" ("small bow?"). *Tanbura*.
Lit.: no. 250.

Pane (East India; Orissa). Heterophonic double reed instrument.

Panelu (Sunda District). (1) Tone name of the third note (*pelog*) of the Sunda Districts, third note (*slendro*), Sunda District, Indramayu. (2) Term for the Javanese *dada*. See also *Sanga*. Cf. *Surupan melog*.
Lit.: no. 163.

Panembung (Java). Xylophone type used in *gamelan*.

Panerus (West Java). See *Kedemung*.

Panerusan (Java). *Gamelan* instruments used for paraphrasing and ornamenting.
Lit.: no. 163.

Pang (China—M 4912). Wooden slit-drum in various sizes and forms used by night watchmen, but also by cooks who beat the drum with a wooden stick. Also called *t'o*. Cf. *Pan*.

Pang (Korea). "Playstring." Name of the second (fretted) string of the *hyon-kum*. Cf. *Komunko*.
Lit.: no. 136.

Pangaba (India; Bengal). Conically-shaped wooden drum with a single head. See *Panaba*.
Lit.: no. 190.

Pangakeppan (Java). "Mouthpiece."

Pangalay (Philippines—Tausug). Wedding dance.

Pangapit (Java). The flanking kettledrums set separately by the side of the *lurah gending* (leading musician).
Lit.: no. 163.

Pang-ch'iang (China—M 4914; M 665). Operatic chorus. Frequently used in *i-yang-ch'iang*.
Lit.: no. 183.

Pangeset (Sunda District). See *Rebāb* (Sunda).

Panggal awi (*Panggalan*) (West Java). Also *Papanggalan*. A bamboo spinning top. Cf. *Gangsingan*.
Lit.: no. 157.

Panggul (Bali). Term for hammer; mallet used in striking drums, metallophones, bells, gongs, and other percussion instruments.
Lit.: no. 197.

Panggulong (Java). A resounding *gendang mara*.

Pang-hyang (Korea). Sixteen iron slabs hung in a large wooden frame in two rows and beaten with a wooden mallet. It is identical with the Chinese *fang-hsiang*. The instrument came to Korea during the 12th century and has been described as belonging to the "nine barbarian orchestras," which points to a Central Asian origin.
Lit.: nos. 52, 179.

Pāngi (*Pāṅi*) (South India). Kannarese term for the Sanskrit *jagajhampa*.
Lit.: no. 254.

Pangkat (Sunda District). Introduction (to *gamelan* music). Cf. *Bebuka.*
Lit.: no. 163.

Pangkat nḍawah (Java). The conclusion of the first introduction of a *gending* (*merong*) which leads to the next section.
Lit.: no. 163.

Pang-kiang (Korea). Wind bell. Its clapper has the shape of a fish.
Lit.: no. 255.

Pangkon (*Tlapakan*) (Java). The wooden frame that holds the metal slabs of the *saron.*

Pangkonan (Sunda District). Octave.

Pang-ku (China—M 4912; M 3479). Frame drum. Its single head is made of cow skin. The drum rests on a bamboo tripod and is struck with two light bamboo sticks. The instrument has been used frequently in the instrumental ensemble of the Peking opera.
Lit.: no. 209.

Pangkur (Java). One of the poetic meters of the *tembang machapat*, generally used in battle songs. See *Machapat.*
Lit.: no. 163.

Pango (Kenya—Wahili; Wasamba). A resonating bowl-shaped psaltery.
Lit.: no. 255.

Pangolo (New Britain). See *Pagolo.*

Pāṅgrā See *Puṅgī.* Cf. *Tiktirī.*

P'an-gro (Tibet). Resonating box.

Pang-tzu (China—M 4912; M 6939). (1) Rectangular wooden block with two slits on each side. It is used in opera and puppet play and is beaten with wooden sticks. Among the numerous names are: *pong-tzu* (Cantonese), *pu-yü* (Mandarin), *puk-yü* (Cantonese), *sha-ku* (Mandarin), *sa-ku* (Cantonese, "pebble," "shaman"), *hei-mu-pan* (Mandarin, "the blackwood time keeper"), *mu-yü* (Mandarin, "wooden fish"), *muk-yü* (Cantonese).
Lit.: nos. 129, 255.

Pang-tzu-ch'iang (China—M 4912; M 6939; M 663). An operatic style that came into fashion during the last two centuries. *Pang-tzu* means "drum-sticks" and indicates the prevalence of percussion instruments in heroic plots and pantomimic battle scenes. The performances were done outdoors because the noise was too much inside a hall. *Pang-tzu* was also called *ch'in-ch'iang* (Shensi) and *kan-su ch'iang* (Kansu). Cf. *Ti-fang hsi*; *Hsi-p'i.*
Lit.: no. 183.

Pang-tzu hu-ch'in (China). See *Hu-hu.*

Pang-tzu ti (China). A small *ti* used together with the *pang-tzu.*
Lit.: no. 209.

Pangul (Korea). One or several wind bells suspended from roofs of temples, palaces, even private homes. The Chinese term is *fen-ling*, the Japanese is *futaku.*
Lit.: no. 52.

Pan-hu (China). A rare type of *hu-ch'in.* In Shantung the instrument is called *ch'i-ch'in.*
Lit.: no. 209.

Pāni (South India). Kannarese term for *naguar.*
Lit.: no. 254.

Pāṇighna (Ancient India). People who clap their hands to mark accents in the recitation of the (white) *yajurvēda.*
Lit.: no. 254.

Paningba (*Paningbwa*) (Congo—Azande). Term for *kweningba.*

Paningka (Indonesia; Dayak). A softly sounding *genḍang mara.*
Lit.: no. 255.

Panjabi (North India). See *Tāla.*

Panjak (West Java). See *Keṭuk tilu.*

Panjam (East Turkestan). Cf. *Sochiba.*

Panjang (*Panutup*) (Indonesia; Indramayu). The first note of the *slendro* system in Indramayu.
Lit.: no. 163.

Panjang (Java). A long key.

Panj-gāg (Middle East). *Maqām.*
Tone material:

C D E F♯ G A B♭(+) c d e♭(+) f g

Lit.: no. 64.

Panj-gāh (Persia). See *Dastgāh.*

Pan-ku (China—M 4885; M 3479). Shanghai term for *pang-ku*: a flat barrel drum with two heads. Cf. *Pang-ku.*
Lit.: nos. 209, 255.

P'ansori (Korea). A popular form of dramatic musical entertainment during the 18th and 19th centuries. A singer narrates a dramatic tale and performs appropriate motions with his fan and occasionally dances. He is accompanied by one drummer who beats the *puk.*

Pan-t'ang-ku (China). Wooden frame drum with one skin.
Lit.: no. 209.

Pantheru (Ceylon). Frame rattle.
Lit.: no. 46.

Pantu (Java). *Gambang gangsa* type. See *Saron.*
Lit.: no. 163.

Pantun (Malaysia; North Sumatra). (1) A quatrain. (2) The Sundanese *Pantun* is an epic partly recited, partly sung by the people of Atjeh Province. It is accompanied by a *kachapi.*

Pantun (East Borneo). A stick with a thick end, covered with wax. It is used to beat the *garantong* (signal gong).
Lit.: no. 255.

Pantuvarālī (South India). *Janya rāga* of the 51st *mēḷa* (*Kāmavardhanī*). The scale of this *rāga* is identical with one of its primary *rāga Kāmavardhanī.*
Lit.: no. 139.

Pantuvarālī (South India). (1) The 45th *asampūrṇa mēḷa-rāga* without *kaṭapayādi* prefix. (2) The 45th *asampūrṇa mēḷa-rāga* with *kaṭapayādi* prefix. It was called *Saivapantuvarālī.* See *Rāga* (South India).
Lit.: no. 139.

Pan-tzu (China). See *P'ai-pan.*

Panunggul (*Penunggul*) (Java). A popular term used for *bem* in the *pelog* system. *Panunggul* stands 250 cents above *barang* (of *pelog*) and 415 cents above *nem.* Cf. *Pelog.*
Lit.: no. 163.

Panutup (Indonesia; Indramayu). (1) See *Panjang.* (2) The name of the closing tone; it refers to the 1st note (*pelog*) in the Sunda Districts and the 1st note (*slendro*) in Indramayu.
Lit.: no. 163.

Panyumbang (Sunda District). See *Pamanis.*

Pao (China—M 4938). "The fold in the arms." The traditional term for carrying the *ch'in.*
Lit.: no. 93.

Pao (New Zealand—Maori). Improvised entertaining gossip-songs in the form of couplets.

Paoa (Tahiti). Simple tribal song.

Pao chün chih (China—M 4955; M 1715; M 932). Small gong often used by blind peddlers. In Shantung it is called *hsüan-tzu.*
Lit.: no. 209.

Pao poroporoaki (New Zealand—Maori). Farewell songs.

Pao whaiaipo (New Zealand—Maori). Love songs.

Pao whakautu (New Zealand—Maori). Song answering slander and mockery.

Papa (Solomon Isl.—Bellona Isl.). Musical sounding board beaten with two sticks for dance accompaniment.
Lit.: no. 246.

Papa hai 'atua (Solomon Isl.). The beating of the wooden sounding board to praise and invoke the gods.
Lit.: no. 246.

Papa hehi (Hawaii). A small wooden boat-shaped bowl (or board) played with the foot of the player, while his arms beat the rhythm sticks (*ka'la'au*) against each other.
Lit.: nos. 37, 278.

Papakungbu (*ikpwokpwo*). Ground bow.
Lit.: no. 176.

Papan (New Guinea). Oval bull roarer.
Lit.: no. 255.

Papanggalan (West Java). See *Panggal awi.*

Papat (*Sekawen*) (Java). Very slow tempo. Cf. *Wirama siji*; *Karotugel*; *Loro*; *Telu.*
Lit.: no. 163.

Papatet (Java). "The limiting tone." In West Java: the first tone of the *pelog* material (*singgul*).
Lit.: no. 163.

Papatet panatup (Sunda District). See *Singgul.*

Pa-pe (Nigeria). See *Keke.* Also called *oparun.*

Papenchelut (West Java). See *Pihul.*

Papuwi (*Pupuwi*; *Puwi-puwi*) (Flores). Bamboo clarinet with four finger holes. Cf. *Perere.*
Lit.: no. 166.

Para (Africa; Niger region). Angular harp.

Para (Java). The outer edge of a gong which is bent inward.
Lit.: no. 163.

Para (Korea). See *Chabara.*

Parabhrutāviṇī (South India). *Janya rāga* of the 20th *mēḷa* (*Naṭabhairavī*).
Tone material:
C D G A♭ B♭ c
c B♭ A♭ G D C
Lit.: no. 139.

Paraj (North India). *Rāga* ascribed to the *Purvi thāta*. *Paraj* is a night *rāga*.
Tone material:
c B A♭ G F♯ (F) E D♭ C
C (D♭) E F♯ (G) A♭ B c; *Vādis*: c, G
Lit.: no. 138.

Paraju (South India). *Janya rāga* of the 15th *mēḷa* (*Māyāmāḷavagauḷa*).
Tone material:
C (D♭) E F G A♭ B c
c B A♭ G F E D♭ C
Lit.: no. 139.

Parakapzuk (Armenia). Bagpipe with two pipes and five holes in each pipe. Cf. *Tulum.*
Lit.: no. 15.

Paralak (West Java). A stout papaya clapper. See *Perelek*; *Bendi rojo muku* (Flores).
Lit.: no. 163.

Parand (North India). Drum variation; an elaborated "filled up" *theka*, maintaining the basic structure of the *tāla*. Cf. *Tabla*; *Theka.*

Parapanda (South Africa—Macaranga; Karanga). Large (animal) horn with a frightening sound. Cf. *Phalaphala* (Venda).
Lit.: no. 151.

Pärdä (Iran). Frets.

Parda-dār (*Mo'areke-gir*) (Iran). Street singer who recites religious or didactic songs.

Pare (Celebes—Kulavi). "Tuning fork" idiophone. A medium-sized bamboo stick is cut at its end into a fork. When the fork is beaten against the hand of the player a tuning fork sound is produced that is subject to change of pitch and intensity of sound when the holes cut into the handle are closed or opened. There are various names for this instrument: in Malacca, *genggong sakai*; in Tonapuh, *tulumpa*; in Central Celebes, *rerre* (or *re-re*); in Buton, *ore-ore*; in Talaut, Bangai, *ta uto*; on the Philippines, *buncacan*.
Lit.: no. 254.

Paridhi (South India). *Janya rāga* of the 69th *mēḷa (Dhātuvardhaṇī)*.
Tone material:
C D♯ E G A♭ B c
c B A♭ G E D♯ C
Lit.: no. 139.

Parisé (Flores—Manggaray). Term for *main chachih*.

Parōdha (South India). *Janya rāga* of the 29th *mēḷa* (*Dhīraśaṅkarābharaṇam*).
Tone material:
C D F A B c
c B A F F C
Lit.: no. 139.

Parrai (South India). Tamil term for drum. Cf. *Parrang*.
Lit.: no. 59.

Parrang (Southeast India; Bastar State). Small drum in hourglass form of the Muria Gond tribe. The body is made of clay and covered with cowhide (two heads). The instrument is also called *parrai*, *parrayin*, and *tori parra*.
Lit.: no. 59.

Parri chup en ro (Micronesia; Ponape). Nose flute. Cf. *Kash*; *Ang en tsuma*; *Chup en parri*.
Lit.: no. 313.

Parua (Melanesia; New Guinea—Kilenge). Drum.
Lit.: no. 255.

Parvan (Ancient India; Vedic India). A section of the *Sāmavedic* chant consisting of a number of textual syllables (*akshara*), long (*dīrgha*) or short (*hrasva*), always filling one *parvan* that can be sung within one breath.

Pārvati (South India). *Janya rāga* of the 72nd *mēḷa* (*Rasikapriyā*).
Tone material:
C D♯ F♯ G A♯ B c
c B A♯ G F♯ D♯ C
Lit.: no. 139.

Pasinḍèn (Java). The female, rarely also male, choirs providing the accompaniment to the *beḍaya-*, *serimpi*-dances.
Lit.: no. 163.

Pasu (West Polynesia—Tokelau). Cylindrical drum.
Lit.: no. 84.

Pasu (Java). Part of the gong where the flat surface begins to tilt. Cf. *Rai*; *Tikel*; *Wideng*.
Lit.: no. 163.

Paśupatipriya (South India). *Janya rāga* of the 29th *mēḷa* (*Dhīraśaṅkarābharaṇam*).
Tone material:
C D F G F A c
c A G F D F C
Lit.: no. 139.

Pasyak (Philippines). See *Bulu dekot* (Siam).

Paṭ (*Patbo*) (Burma). Small cylindrical tunable drum. Usually several of these drums are placed in a circle around the player. Cf. *Pat-mah*; *Pat-waing*.

Paṭ (*Thoṅk*) (India). Staccato.

Pata (Flores). Song (*tampata* = "to sing"). Lit.: no. 166.

Patadip (North India). See *Patadipaki.*

Patadipaki (*Patadip*; *Pradipaki*) (North India). An afternoon *rāga* ascribed to the *Kafi thāta.* Three types are distinguished: with E♭, B; with E, B in ascent and E♭, B♭ in descent; with E in ascent, E♭ in descent, B in both, ascent and descent.
Generalized tone material:
C E♭ F G B♭ c
c B♭ A G F E♭ D C; *Vādis*: C, F
Lit.: no. 138.

Pāṭaha (India). Ancient term for various types of drum. Cf. *Pāṭaka* (Sanskrit).
Lit.: no. 254.

Paṭaha vādya (India). Drum music.

Pāṭaka (India). Sanskrit drum ("divider"). Cf. (Bengali): *Pataha.*
Lit.: no. 255.

Patala (Burma). See *Pattalā.* The term means the same as Javanese wooden *gambang.*

Pātaladhari (South India). *Janya rāga* of the 48th *mēḷa* (*Divyamaṇī*).
Tone material:
C D♭ E♭ F♯ A♯ c
c A♯ F♯ E♭ D♭ C
Lit.: no. 139.

Pātalāmbari (South India). *Janya rāga* of the 52nd *mēḷa* (*Rāmapriyā*).
Tone material:
C D♭ E F♯ A C
c A F♯ E D♭ C
Lit.: no. 139.

Patamanjari (North India). See *Patmanjri.*

Patarageshri (North India). Rare *rāga* ascribed to the *Khamaj thāta.*
Tone material:
C E F G B c
c B A F E (D) C
Lit.: no. 138.

Patbo (Burma). Small cylindrical drum. The term *patbo* is used occasionally for bell. Cf. *Patsha.*
Lit.: no. 255.

Pate (Ocenia; Ellice Isl.; Loyalty Isl.; Samoa; Viti). Small slit-drum.
Lit.: no. 84.

Patere (New Zealand—Maori). Song sung by women in fast tempo in reply to unfair, slanderous gossip. Also recitation songs with historical tales. Cf. *Kaioraora.*
Lit.: no. 228.

Paṭet (Java). "To curb," "to limit." Pentatonic modes derived from the two basic tone systems, *slendro* and *pelog.* In each *paṭet* are three notes that have to be emphasized.

Paṭet derived from *slendro*	Emphasized notes
slendro patet nem	*nem, gulu, lima*
slendro patet sanga	*gulu, lima, nem*
slendro patet manyura	*dada, nem, gulu*

Paṭet derived from *pelog*	Emphasized notes
pelog patet lima	*gulu, lima, bem (penunggul)*
pelog patet nem	*nem, gulu, lima*
pelog patet barang	*dada, nem, barang*

Secondary form: *patet pelog nyamat* is a transferred *slendro patet manyura* in which *bem* predominates. *Barang miring*, a "polymodal" form.

In *wayang* performances *slendro patet nem* represents childhood; *slendro patet sanga* represents the maturity of life; *slendro patet manyura* is used to represent old age.

Each *patet*, the moodmaker, the "taste" of the *genḍing*, is used during a specific time period of a nightly *wayang* performance:

slendro patet nem
pelog patet lima } between evening and midnight

slendro patet sanga } between midnight and 3 a.m.
pelog patet nem
slendro patet manyura } between 3 a.m. and sunrise
pelog patet barang
Lit.: no. 163.

Paṭetan (Java). Cf. *Senḍon*; *Lagon*.

Paṭet Slendro (Java). The Central Javanese *slendro paṭets* are always placed in the manner of *jawar* scales. There are three varieties: *paṭet nem*; *paṭet sanga*, and *paṭet manyura*.
Lit.: no. 163.

Patha (India). Sanskrit term for the circular frame drum. Cf. *Tappu* (Tamil); *Dappu* (Telugu).

Pāṭhya (Vedic India). Vedic texts presented in recitative manner.
Lit.: no. 16.

Patih (Java). "The prime minister" of the *gamelan* ensemble, the *kendang* (drum).
Lit.: no. 163.

Pati-tal (Assam). Small flat cymbals.
Lit.: no. 46.

Pat-mah (Burma). Suspended barrel drum (*pat*).
Lit.: no. 252.

Patmanjari (North India). *Rāga* ascribed to the *Kafi thāta*. It is an afternoon *rāga*. A second type of this *rāga* is ascribed to the *Bilaval thāta*. The following two tone materials are used at the present time:

(a) C D F G B♭ c
c B♭ A (G) F E♭ D C

(b) C D E♭ E F G (A) B♭ c
c B♭ A (G) F E♭ D C; *Vādis*: C, G

Lit.: no. 138.

Patmanjri (*Patamanjari*; *Patmanjari*; *Bangal-bilaval*) (North India). This form of *Patmanjari*, ascribed also to the *Bilaval thāta*, has the following tone material:

C D E F G A (B) c
c B A G F E D C; *Vādis*: C, G

Lit.: no. 138.

Pāto (Iraq). Long cylindrical one-headed drum.

Patokan (Sunda District). Fundamental notes, the framework of all *gamelan* pieces.

Patola (Burma; Assam). "Crocodile zither." See *Megyun* (*Mi gyaun*).

Paṭpaṭī (India). A north Indian two-headed rattle drum (related to the *damaru*) used by beggars and children. Cf. *Palototan*; *Terbang*; *Čankela* (Kashmir).
Lit.: no. 255.

Pat-pyo (Burma). Term for a large group of songs, mostly old, popular court songs but often combined with modern material.

Patsa (Burma). See *Patsha*; *Patbo*.

Pat sabo (Burma). Cf. *Than-bya tyaw*; *Hsit-kyi*; *Chauk-pauk auk-pyan*. See also *Than-yo chauk-pauk*; *Pattalā*.

Patsha (*Patsa*) (Burma). Identical with *patbo*.

Pat sin wo sao (South China). "Blessings of the Eight Immortals"—a chanted prayer for longevity accompanied by a *sona* and various percussion instruments.
Lit.: no. 129.

Pattalā (Burma). Xylophone with 18-24 bamboo slabs placed above a resonance trough. The most often used is the *pattalā* with 21 slabs suspended over a boat-like resonator. The note names used in *pattalā*, occasionally also in *hsaing-waing* music are:

Than-hman	(ca. C)
Nga-bauk	(F)
Hna-pauk (*Pat sabo*)	(B)
Chauk-pauk	(E)
Thon-pauk	(A)
Hkun-nathan-gyi	(D)
Lei-bauk	(G)

Cf. *Ranat-ek* (Thailand); *Hsaing-waing*.
Lit.: no. 198.

Pattchak (Korea). Cf. *Antchak.*

Patt-waing (Burma). A circle formed by 21 drums. The player sits in the center and strikes the drums with his hands. The tuning of the drums is approximately:

C B C E F G B c e f g a b c′ d′ e′ f′ g′ a′ b′ c″

Patutan (Bali). Correct tuning.

Pat-waing (*Hsaing-waing*) (Burma). See *Patt-waing.*

Pa'u' (Oceania; Cook Isl.). Identical with *pahu.*

Pau (South Africa – Bagananoa). Cf. *Dikomana.*

Pau (Burma; Shan State). Jew's harp made of bamboo.
Lit.: no. 252.

Pauravī (India). The sixth of the seven *mūrchhanas*, derived from the *ma-grāma.*

Pāva (*Pāwa*) (India). Cross flute with six finger holes.
Lit.: no. 255.

Pāvanakari (South India). *Janya rāga* of the 41st *mēḷa* (*Pāvani*).
Tone material:

C D♭ E♭♭ F♯ A B c
c B A F♯ E♭♭ D♭ C

Lit.: no. 139.

Pāvani (South India). The 41st *mēḷa*:

C D♭ E♭♭ F♯ G A B c

As *rāga, Pāvani* has the same tone material as shown in the *mēḷa.*
Lit.: no. 139.

Pāwa (India). See *Pava.*

Paya (West Polynesia – Pukapuka). Drum.
Lit.: no. 84.

Pa-yin (China – M 4845; M 7418). "The eight sounds," created by the eight materials from which musical instruments were made. The eight materials are: stone, metal, silk, bamboo, wood, skin, gourd, and earth (clay).
Lit.: no. 137.

Pay-shur (Persia). See *Pay-sutur.*

Pāzi (Thailand – Karen). A large bronze kettle gong, richly ornamented. The flat bottom of the kettle shows outlines of animal figures. Cf. *Hpa zi.*
Lit.: no. 254.

Péat cong (Kampuchea). Metallophone with bronze slabs.
Lit.: no. 255.

Peddagaṇṭa (South India). Telugu term for a flat gong used for signalling purposes. Other terms for this gong are: *kamso, kamsatalo* (Pali); *kāṃsara* (Bengali); *kaṃsāla* (Marathi).
Lit.: no. 254.

Pecah (Thailand). See *Pekah.*

Pegineman (Bali). An improvised solo prelude played on a *gender.*
Lit.: no. 197.

Pegongan (Bali). See *Gending gong.*

P'eg-rdob (Tibet). Small brass disc, struck at religious dances.
Lit.: no. 255.

Pei-ch'ü (China – M 4974; M 1623). See *Ch'ü.*

Pei- (China – M 5000). "Double." A prefix used in the *lü* notation (since the Manchu dynasty, 1644-1911). It indicates the notes of the lowest octave range. Assuming that the *huang-chung* (M 2297; M 1503) is the middle C of the West, *pei-ying* (M 5000; M 7477) will indicate the note B, a semitone below the *huang-chung.*
Lit.: no. 136.

Pei ah (Kampuchea; Khmer orchestra). Small oboe.

Pei-ch'ü (China – M 1623; M 4974). Cf. *Ch'ü.*

Pei-li (China – M 4992; M 3929). "Sad tube." The ancient *kuan* with a reed mouthpiece. The Korean prototype is *p'i-ri.*
Lit.: no. 137.

Pei-pok (Former Cambodia). Transverse flute.
Lit.: no. 43.

Pei toch (Kampuchea – Khmer related). A heavy oboe in the shape of a *sanayi*, the tube widens out in the center. The *pei toch* has six finger holes and produces a penetrating sound. Other terms used for this instrument are *sra-lay* (Thailand), *pi-chava* (Thailand), *hne* (Burma), *sernei* (Malaya).
Lit.: no. 43.

Pekah (Thailand). Lute with a coconut body and two wire strings.
Lit.: no. 255.

Pekak (Java). See *Pitet.*

Pekang (Malaysia). The high octave range of the *saron.* Cf. *Saron.*

Pekin(g) (Sunda District). The highest of the four octave ranges. See *Titil* (West Java). Cf. *Saron.*
Lit.: no. 163.

Pekko (Korea). Big drum; also flat drum (cylindrical shape) fastened to a wooden handle. It is used by Buddhist priests.
Lit.: no. 255.

Pekudi (South Africa). Cf. *Motaba.*

Pele (Liberia – Kpelle). Term for performance. E.g., *lon-pele* means a (musical) performance for the birth of a child; *feli-pele* means the performance with a goblet drum.
Lit.: no. 284.

Pelegongan (Bali). Ensemble derived from the *semar pegulingan* that performs the accompaniment of the *legong.*
Lit.: no. 265.

Pella (Celebes; South Toraja District). Cf. *Pellé.*

Pellaṅkōvi (South India). Telugu term for the ancient *vāṃsī.* Cf. *Bansi.*

Pelle (Celebes). Clarinet identical with the *serubay.* Cf. *Pelle dawa*; *Adan.*

Pelo (Java). The name of a tone that is alien to the regular scale.
Lit.: no. 163.

Pelog (Central Java). The two important systems are the pentatonic *slendro* and the heptatonic *pelog.* The latter has been described as "female."

The *pelog* scale, which in the past may have consisted of approximately major thirds and semitones, now shows various forms in one region or the other. Cents which are shown below illustrate the various changes:

cents: 165 250 120 150
nem — *barang* — *penunggul (bem)* — *gulu (jongga)*

270 130 115
dada (tengah) — *pelog* — *lima (gangsal)* — *nem*

The scale can begin with any degree. The following starts with *bem*:

120 150 240
bem — *gulu* — *dada* — *pelog*

120 150 270
lima — *nem* — *barang* — *bem alit*

Patet forms in *pelog* are: *pelog patet lima*, *pelog patet barang*, *pelog patet manyura*, *pelog patet bem* (East Java: *lima* and *nem*). Two examples are shown below:

Pelog patet barang (in East Java it is called *pelog miring*):

	lima	*new*	*barang*	*(bem)*	*gulu*	*dada*
ca.:	A	B♭	C	–	E	F

Pelog patet bem:

	bem	*gulu*	*dada*	*(pelog)*	*lima*	*nem*
ca.	D	E♭	F	–	A	B♭

The list on the following page, quoted from Lit. no. 163, p. 102, shows the various tone names of the *pelog* system at different locations.

Pelog Krawitan (Java; Kudus District). Term for *pelog bem* (Java). Cf. *Pelog.*

Pelog Miring (East Java). Term for *pelog barang.* Cf. *Pelog.*

Pelonchong (Borneo). Beating bamboo tubes placed in two sections. The tubes are struck with a stick.
Lit.: no. 166.

Pelong (Sunda District). Term for the Javanese *pelog* system.

Pemero (Bali). Term for one of the two secondary notes of the *saih pitu* scale. The term is derived from *pembero*, *bero*, "false." These two secondary tones appear in the following spots (X):

ding dong deng (X) *dung dang* (X) *ding alit*
Lit.: no. 197.

Pemetit (Bali). A very small *gambang.*

Pemungkah (Bali). *Bunkah* means "to open up." The introductory music played to a *wayang* performance when the puppets are being readied in the wings before the screen.
Lit.: no. 197.

Pen (Korea). A term that means "flat" by a semitone. For instance, *pen kak* signifies A♭ (*kak* meaning the note A).

Pen (Java; Joya). Cf. Tong; *(Ke)ketek.*

Pena (*Pena Khomba*) (Burma; Manipur). A fiddle with a coconut body and a single string made of a bundle of hairs. A small bow made of cane or, in a few instances, of iron; its strung hair is provided with several jingles.
Lit.: no. 252.

Penah (East Sudan). A family of primitive wind instruments made of gourds. The largest is called "mother," the next smaller "father," and the rest are called "(two) children."

Penangkep (Bali). Term for octave.

Penarik (*Penarek*) (Bali). (1) Term for *batel maya.* (2) The two smallest *gambangs* of a *gamelan* (bamboo xylophones).
Lit.: no. 197.

Pencak silak (Malaysia). Instrumental ensemble identical with *makyong.*

Penchak (West Java; Sunda District). A dance imitating the fencing motions of a fighting cat. It is accompanied by a small ensemble consisting of two *kendangs*, one *tarompet*, and one *kempul.*

Penchu (*Pentju*) (Java). The boss of a gong is called *endas* ("head") by the gong smiths. The top of the *penchu* is called *ucheng*, the rounding of the boss *kumba*, the sunk part around it *wideng(an).*

Penda (South Africa). Music bow with one string; resonance is created by placing one end of the bow in the mouth of the player. The Bantu (on the coast) call this instrument *'kan'gan*, the Venda name is *tshigwana* or *tshivhana*, the Sotho (Transvaal) call it *lekope*, the Sotho of Basutoland call it *setolotolo*, the Thonga name is *sekgapa*, the Swazi *isitontolo*, the Zulu *isitontolo* or *isiqomqomana*, and the Karanga call it *tshipendani.*
Lit.: no. 151.

Pendana-besar (Borneo). See *Gulung-gulung.*

Pendana-gendah (Borneo). See *Gulung-gulung.*

Pendana-kinggi (Borneo). See *Gulung-gulung.*

Pendibe (Congo – Azande). Term for *kweningba.*
Lit.: no. 27.

PELOG TONE NAMES

Tones	*Central Java*	*Sunda District*	*Cheribon*	*Prabalingga*	*Majkerta*
I	bem penunggul	singgul kuwing papatet panatup	bem	sorog pengasih	sorog
II	gulu (H. J. Jongga)	galimer bem (singgul)	sedasa penggulu	gulu tenggok	tengah tenggok
III	dada tengah	panelu sanga	sanga panelu	dada	sanga
Vocal*		panangis			
IV	pelog	bungur liwung sorog gede	bungur	pelog	pelog
V	lima (H. J. Gangsal)	kenong loloran	lima loloran	lima	lima gangsal
VI	nem	barang laras mamanis	laras nem surupan apik	nem	nem
VII	barang	sorog sorog kuwing	barang	barang	barang
Vocal*		pamiring			
I′	bem alit	singgul leutik	bem alit		

* Intermediate tone.

Penem (Bali). A small metallophone which is used in pairs in the *gamelan selundeng*.
Lit.: no. 197.

Penembung (*Bonang Panembung*) (Java). In the complete *gamelan* there are three *bonangs* which differ from each other in the range. The lowest range is called *bonang penembung*, the medium range *bonang barung*, and the highest *bonang panerus*.
Lit.: no. 254.

Penerus (*Panerus*) (Java). Cf. *Panembung*.

Pengalian (*Pengalihan*) (Bali). A freely improvised prelude to a piece in classical form performed by the two important *genders* of the *gamelan pelegongan*.
Lit.: no. 197.

Penganten anyar (Java). See *Rebāb* (Java).

Pengaras (Bali). Introductory music to the second section of the *gending ageng*.
Lit.: no. 197.

Pengasih (Indonesia; Prabalingga). Tone name. It indicates the first note of the *pelog* system as used in Prabalingga.

Pengawak (Bali). After the introduction (*pengalian*) follows the *pengawak*, the first part of the main body of a composition in classical form. The *pengawak* is followed by a faster section called *pengechet* (*pengetjet*).
Lit.: no. 265.

Pengawit (Bali). *Kawit* = "to begin." The solo introduction that points out the theme to the musicians of the ensemble. See *Gihing*.
Lit.: no. 197.

P'eng-chung (China—M 5064; M 1514). See *Hsing-erh*.

Pengechet (Bali). "Body." The second movement of (the "body" of) a classical composition; the *pengechet* usually follows the *pengawak*, although some *gendings* do begin and end with the *pengechet*. Cf. *Pengawak*.

Pengedé (Bali). The large two xylophones (*rindik*) used in the *gamelan pejogedan*.
Lit.: no. 197.

Pengelik (Bali). A contrasting section of the melody. The *pengelik* appears in a higher register than the first part of the melody which is in the middle or low range. Cf. *Penyalit*.

Pengèntèr (Bali). A large *gambang* which is used in the *gamelan* ensemble.

Pengetog, pengetog (Bali). Transitional music, rhythmically strong, that links two movements of a *legong* composition. The transition begins slowly and gradually accelerates to the faster tempo of the dance.
Lit.: no. 197.

Pengetjet (*Peniban*) (Bali). See *Pengawak*.

Penggulu (*Gulu*) (Indonesia; Cheribon). See *Sedasa*.

Pengipuk (Bali). Part of a dance suite that represents music to a love scene.

Pengisep (Bali). "The sucker." The smaller, higher pitched pair of *genders* in the *wayang* orchestra. Cf. *Pengumbang*.
Lit.: no. 197.

Pengiwa(n) (*Peniba[n]*) (Bali). The last repetition of the *pengawak* section in the *gending ageng*. This repetition shows distinct melodic and rhythmic changes.
Lit.: no. 197.

Pengomba (Borneo). See *Gondang*.

Pengumbang (Bali). The lower pitched *gender* of the *wayang* ensemble (also called *kumbang*, "bumble bee"). *Pengumbang* is also called "the ones that hum." Cf. *Pengisep*.
Lit.: no. 197.

Penjipu (Borneo – Sea Dayak). See *Penyipu.*

Penjorog (Bali). Also *penyorog.* Cf. *Saih pitu*; *Pemero.*

Penna (India; Manipun). Simple fiddle.

Penontong (*Kenong penontong*) (Central Java). Wide rimmed gong, smaller than the *kempul.* Besides appearing in some ensembles, the gong is used for signalling purposes.
Lit.: no. 163.

Pen Pata (South India; Maria Gond tribe). Religious *gotul* song.
Lit.: no. 142.

Pensol (Malaysia – Senoi). Nose flute.

Penṭat (Java). See *Rebāb* (Java).

Pentju (Java). See *Penchu.*

Pentre (Ghana). Gourd drum. Cf. *Bentere.*

Penunggul (*Panungul*; *Penungul*) (Java). The third note of the modern *pelog* system. See *Panungul.* Also first note of the Central Javanese *pelog* scale (cf. *Bem*). Cf. *Pelog* (list of tone names).

Penungka (Bali). Musical introduction to some *wayang* performances.

Penunṭung (*Keṭipung*) (Java). A small drum (*gendang*) with either a truncated or round-bellied body, beaten together with the *kendang-gending* – used in *ladrang* and *ketawang* compositions. Frequently one musician plays both drums. See *Kedang leutik*; *Kolanter.*
Lit.: no. 163.

Penurung (West Java). See *Kedemung* of Indramayu.

Penyachah (Bali). A member of the *gender* group with a range of one octave. Its thin metal slabs are tuned an octave higher than those of the *jublag.*
Lit.: no. 197.

Penyalit (Bali). A section of a composition that exhibits a sudden change in sound character. E.g., if the preceding part of the music was performed with drums, the *penyalit* would suddenly avoid any drum sound. Cf. *Nyalit.*
Lit.: no. 197.

Penyelag (Bali). Interlude played by the solo *trompong*, linking movements of the *gending ageng.*
Lit.: no. 197.

Penyelah (Bali). A short, detached piece of music performed, as an insert, before the sections of an interlude.
Lit.: no. 197.

Penyalat (Bali). Medium sized *gambang.*

Penyipu (Borneo – Sea Dayak). Ocarina type with two holes.
Lit.: no. 255.

Penyorog (Bali). Term for one of the two secondary notes intercalated in the *saih pitu* (scales). The term is derived from *sorog*, "to insert." The second of these notes is called *pemero.* Cf. *Sorog* (Sunda District), *Penyorog* (Bali), *Sora geganti* (Sunda District).
Lit.: no. 197.

Penyumu (Bali). Solo introduction to a composition.

Penyuwud (Bali). Coda, closing section. The term appears frequently in *legong* suites.

Pepeon (Flores). See *Ra'us woya.*

Pepet (Bali). Name of a notational symbol.

Pepet wuno nio (Flores; Ende). "A *pereret* made of coconut leaves." A shawm made of a coconut leaf turned into a conical spiral instrument. The edges of the end serve as heterophonic double reeds.
Lit.: no. 166.

Pepetengan (Sunda District). See *Peteng.*

Pera (India). Sanskrit term for "musical instrument."

Perelek (West Java; Sunda District). A delicate form of papaya clapper. See *Paralak* and *Bendi rojo muku* (Flores).
Lit.: no. 166.

Perere (Flores). Bamboo clarinet without finger holes of the Manggaray. It is made of spirally-wound coconut-palm leaves.
Lit.: no. 166.

Pereren (Bali). Brief carefully worked out instrumental pieces played in the popular *gamelan arja* performances as preludes and accompaniments of songs.
Lit.: no. 197.

Pereret (Bali). Term for the obsolete *serunai* (*seruni*). Cf. *Perere* (Flores); *Selompret* (Java).

Peret (Java). The "clown," a stereotyped figure in the Javanese dance dramas. Cf. *Sori-tekes.*

Peretitala (Bali). Short stanzas appearing in *wayang* plays.

Peria mēlam (South India). An ensemble consisting of several *nagasaram* and percussion instruments. Cf. *Nautch.*
Lit.: no. 43.

Perungalam (South India). See *Kalam.*

Peruperu (New Zealand—Maori). See *Haka.*

Pesandon (Timor Kupang; Roti). Split bamboo zither consisting of a semi-spherical sound box and seven strings.
Lit.: no. 166.

Pese (Solomon Isl.—Bellona Isl.). Songs accompanied by hand clapping.
Lit.: no. 246.

Pese hakasa'amoa (Solomon Isl.). Hand clapping way in the Samoan way: two groups of a choir sing antiphonically the refrain and the leader performs the verse. Cf. *Tau baalogha.*
Lit.: no. 246.

Peshkar (North India). The opening drum phrase, usually a *qaida* or half of a *qaida*, in a *khyāl* performance. Cf. *Khyāl.*
Lit.: no. 136.

Peshref (Middle East). Prelude played by an instrumental ensemble. The "prelude" appears also in the middle of a sequence, e.g., in Turkish religious music, in a piece that begins with *ezan*, followed by a *mevlid* and *nait.* Then follows the *pesrev* which is followed by an *aying* and *yür-ük semai* and a brief *peṣrev* that concludes the sequence.
Lit.: no. 243.

Peṣrev (Turkey). See *Peshref.*

Pesinden (Java). A female solo singer performing with the *gamelan.*
Lit.: no. 215.

Peteng (West Java; Sunda District). Term for the Javanese *sundari* (*sundaren*), the combination of kite and vibrating string, called *langlayan peteng* or *pepetengan.*
Lit.: no. 163.

Petit (West Java). "Tail," "extremity." The highest octave range. The *gambang kayu* has four octaves: the highest is called "*petit*" (or "*leutik*" [small]), the next lower one is called *manis*, the next *galimer*, and the lowest *gede.* Cf. *Tong* (3) (Java).
Lit.: no. 163.

Petruk ngaṇḍul (Java). A particular way of beating the *bonang* and *gambang kayu.* The left hand strikes one and the right another tone. This sequence is performed in quick alternating succession. Cf. *Ṭuṭukan rangkap.*
Lit.: no. 163.

Petuduh (Bali). One of two medium-sized metallophones in the *gamelan selundeng*.
Lit.: no. 197.

Peurih (West Java). Painful; doloroso.

Peureut (Sunda District). Term for pegs. See *Rebāb* (Sundanese).

Pewayangan (Bali). Five tone scale:
E F♯ G♯ B c♯
Lit.: no. 265.

Pey (Former Cambodia). Small flute. See *Pi* (Thailand).

Phach (Vietnam). (1) Bamboo time beater. (2) Term indicating tempo, time units (*phach*). *Phach don*, e.g., means "fast tempo."

Phaladāyaki (South India). *Janya rāga* of the 64th *mēḷa* (*Vāchaspati*).
Tone material:
C E F♯ G A B♭ c
c A B♭ G E F♯ E D C
Lit.: no. 139.

Phalamañjarī (South India). See *Palamajarī.*

Phalaphala (South Africa—Pedi; Venda). Side-blown (sable antelope, occasionally also other material) horn. Cf. *Mpalampala*; *Shipalapala*; *Lepapata*; *Parapanda.*
Lit.: no. 151.

Phan (Vietnam). Mouth organ. Cf. *Kaen* (Thailand).
Lit.: no. 184

Phalola (South Africa—Sotho). Cf. *Moromthwana.*
Lit.: no. 151.

Phan-gro (Tibet). Resonance box.

Phatola (South Africa—Sotho). "Split-horn" whistle. Cf. *Ipandula.*

Phen (Thailand). Mouth organ with 6, 14, 16, and 18 pipes. Cf. *Kaen.*
Lit.: no. 43.

Phenadyuti (South India). (1) See *Ratnangi.* (2) *Janya rāga* of the 2nd *mēḷa* (*Ratnangi*).
Tone material:
C D♭ F G A♭ B♭ c
c B♭ A♭ F E♭♭ D♭ C
Lit.: no. 139.

Phenadyuti (South India). (1) Second *asampūrṇa mēḷa-rāga* without *kaṭapayādi* prefix. (2) The same with *kaṭapayādi* prefix. See *Rāga* (South India).
Lit.: no. 139.

Phin nam tao (Thailand). Monochord. Cf. *Dan doc huyen*; *Sa diu.*

Phlēng chā (Thailand). "Slow song." Term for slow tempo.
Lit.: no. 208.

Phlēng lā (Thailand). Farewell song. Cf. *Hōmrōng.*
Lit.: no. 208.

Phlēng reo (Thailand). Rhythmical pattern in fast tempo.
Lit.: no. 208.

Phong oar (Thailand). Tone name. Cf. *Thang.*

Phring (Thailand). A series of drum beats on the rims of the *tapone* heads performed by both hands. The beats of the left hand are stronger than those of the right. Immediately after this series some open sounds on the drum are produced. Cf. *Song na.*
Lit.: no. 208.

Phroet (Thailand). Drum beats on the *tapone* performed by both hands in the same manner in *phring.* In *phroet* the sound is dulled immediately after the drumheads are struck.
Lit.: no. 208.

Phrued (Thailand). Drum beats on the *tapone* performed by both hands in the same manner as *phring*. In *phrued* the hands remain on the drumheads and create dull, closed sounds. Cf. *Phroet*.
Lit.: no. 208.

Phunga (*Ponga*) (Nepal). A long copper trumpet. The Newari call it an instrument of the gods.
Lit.: no. 255.

Phuong cheo (Vietnam). Popular theater of ancient origin.
Lit.: no. 296.

Phyed rnga (Tibet). Drum with one head.

Phyen kyung (Korea). Litophone. See *Pien ch'ing* (China).
Lit.: no. 248.

Pī (Thailand). A raucous sounding shawm made of wood, ivory, or marble. It has six finger holes. The instrument is made in various sizes. The largest now in use is called *pi-nai*.
Lit.: no. 255.

P'i (China—M 5151). The plucking of string (lute, zither) in a forward direction. The plucking in the opposite direction is *p'a* (M 4830). Cf. *P'i-p-a* (*P'i-pa*).

Pi (China—M 5074). An ancient war drum.
Lit.: no. 137.

Pi (China—M 5115). A circular jade disc with a probable musical significance.
Lit.: no. 137.

Piah (Laos). Stick zither with four wire strings.
Lit.: no. 254.

Pia'u (Indonesia; Pulau-Pulau Isl.; Mentawai). Term for *pepet wuno nio*.
Lit.: no. 166.

Pi-ba (Tibet). See *P'i-p'a*.

Pibat (Burma—Shan State). Double pipe made of cane with metal tongues. The melody pipe has four finger holes in front and one in the back. The bourdon pipe is thinner and has no holes.
Lit.: no. 252.

Pib-pib (Sumatra). Flute of the Atjeh made of burnt clay.
Lit.: no. 255.

Pi chawa (Thailand). Term for the Javanese *zurna* (an oboe type). The former Cambodian name is *sralay*, the Malayan name is *sernei*.
Lit.: no. 254.

Pichung lingkup (West Java). An ensemble consisting of five large *terbang gembrung*.

Pien- (China—M 5245). "To change," "to alter." A prefix to the note *kung* and *chih* that lowers the pitch by a semitone. If *kung* is the note C and *chih* G, *pien-kung* becomes B and *pien-chih* F# (under the heading of *Kung* [M 3705] are listed all notes of the system under consideration).
Lit.: no. 136.

Pien-chih (China—M 5245; M 358f). See *Pien-*.
Lit.: no. 137.

Pien-ch'ing (China—M 5231a; M 1164). Stone chimes. In the Han dynasty (3rd century B.C. to 3rd century A.D.) the instrument consisted of two rows of 16 stone slabs each in the form of a carpenter's square. In later times the number of slabs changed to 19, 14, 21, and 24. The slabs, all of the same length and width, but of different thickness, were tuned to the 12 *lü*. The upper row displaying *yang* ("male") pitches, was, in descending order, tuned to:

A# G# F# E D C *B♭ A♭*

The lower row displaying *yin* ("female") pitches, to:

B A G F D# C# *B A*

Cf. *Lü*.
Lit.: nos. 106, 137, 250.

Pien-chung (China—M 5231a; M 1503). A bell chime similar to the *pien-ch'ing.* It consisted of a large ornamented wooden frame with two rows of suspended bells. In the past there were 12, also 6 and 9, 24, 14, and, in later periods, most frequently 16 (8 in each row). The bells, of different sizes, were tuned in the same manner as the slabs of the *pien-ch'ing.* In the Confucian temple the *pien-chung* was placed at the East side in a line with the *po-chung.* Each bell of the *pien-chung* was struck together with each chanted note (and textual syllable) of the Confucian hymn.
Lit.: nos. 137, 209.

Pien-kung (China—M 5245; M 3705). See *Pien-.*

P'i-huang (*Ch'ing-hsi*) (China—M 5142; M 2297). Term for the style of the national Peking opera. The constituent styles are *hsi-p'i* and *erh-huang.* Cf. *Ch'ing tiao*; *Ti-fang hsi.*

Pihul (*Papenchelut*) (West Java). The boss of the gong. Cf. *Penchu* (Java).

Pi-java (Thailand). See *Bee chawa.*

Pi jum (Thailand). Oboe type. Cf. *Pi erh*; *Pi nai.*

Pijut (Ancient Israel). Hymn singing. An earlier term was *maamad.*
Lit.: no. 12.

Pik (Kurdistan). Small reed flute.
Lit.: no. 229.

Pi-lava (Thailand). See *Bee chawa.* Term also used for *pi-nai.*

Pi-li (China—M 5136; M 3920). "Sad tube." A cylindrical bamboo oboe type that may have had its origin in a Tatar instrument, the sound of which was used to frighten horses away. The *pi-li* had nine finger holes in the past; at present 7-8 holes are favored. Cf. *Tan kuan*; *T'ou kuan*; *Pei-li*; *P'iri* (Korea); *Hichiriki* (Japan).

Pillāṅgōvi (South India). Kannarese term for the ancient *vāṃsī.* Cf. *Baṅsi.*

Pillāṅkulal (South India). Tamil term for the ancient *vāṃsī.* Cf. *Baṅsi.*

Pillui (Burma). Bamboo flute. See *Pa-lwe.* Cf. *Khloi.*

Pilu (North India). Popular light *rāga* ascribed to the *Kafi thāta.* Tone material is variable. *Vādis*: E♭, B.
Lit.: no. 138.

Piluli (Asam—Naga). A straight wooden trumpet without bell or mouthpiece.
Lit.: no. 252.

Pilu pilu (Southwest Pacific; New Caledonia). Circle dance. The inner of three circles of dancers moves slowly, the second one moves faster, and the outer circle moves very fast.
Lit.: no. 259.

Pin (Indonesia; Sula Isl.). Flute.
Lit.: no. 162.

Pin (*Süng*) (Northeast Thailand). Plucked lute with 2-4 strings and 5-8 frets.
Lit.: no. 203.

P'in (Thailand). Stick zither with two metal strings. Cf. *P'in-namao*; *Sa diu.*
Lit.: no. 250.

Pina (China). See *Feng huang hsiao.*

Pi-nai (Thailand). See *Pī.*

Pināka (India). Actually *pinākī vīṇā.* A North Indian music bow without resonance body.
Lit.: no. 255.

Pinākiṇi (South India). *Janya rāga* of the 18th *mēḷa* (*Hāṭakāmbarī*).
Tone material:
C D♭ F G A♯ B c
c B A♯ G F D♭ C
Lit.: no. 139.

Pinanyo-wan (Philippines). Dance to entertain a young couple.

Ping (China – M 5286). Handle; simple rod or neck stuck through the corpus of a lute or fiddle.

Pingoru (Papua – Orokaiva). Musical bow or a jew's harp.
Lit.: no. 84.

P'ing-ts'e (China – M 5303; M 6754). Notational symbols that indicate linguistic inflections and the correlation between them and melodic inflections, which particularly during the Sung period (A.D. 960-1279) resulted in fixed, preset tonal patterns in which the rising and falling of the melody had to correspond with the up and down of textual syllables.
Lit.: no. 136.

Pinjalan (Java). "To play like a flea," meaning a jumping about in music.
Lit.: no. 163.

P'in namao (Thailand). Stick zither with one string.
Lit.: no. 220.

Pin paet (Former Cambodia; Khmer). Court music and the court orchestra. Cf. *Piphat*; *Pinpat.*

Pinpat (Northeast Thailand). A Lao term for the classical Thai ensemble *piphat*.
Lit.: no. 203.

Pi orh (Thailand; Kampuchea). An oboe type made of one piece of wood, ivory, or marble, with a conical bore and a bellied outline. It has six finger holes. The tube has no bell. The old Cambodian term for this instrument is *sralay*. Cf. *Pi chawa*; *Pi-nai*; *Serunai.*
Lit.: no. 254.

P'i-p'a (China – M 5157.1). Also *p'i-pa*. During the Han period (202 B.C. – A.D. 220) the borders of China extended as far west as the Caspian sea. Musical instruments from the West were imported – an important one was the *p'i-p'a*, a short lute (erroneously called "balloon guitar"). The instrument has a short neck and a pear-shaped corpus. Usually it has four silken strings (which represent the four seasons) tuned to 1, 4, 5, 8. There are *p'i-p'a* types with more strings (up to 13). The instrument has 11 frets of which the chromatic ones are never, or very rarely, utilized. The highest sounding string is used for melody playing. There exists no notation for the *p'i-p'a*. It is played with a plectrum, excepting some recent smaller types which are plucked with the fingers. Cf. *Chin Han p'i-p'a*; *Chin p'i-p'a*; *Chin kan t'ui*; *Ch'u-tse p'i-p'a*; *T'ang p'i-p'a*; *Ti-ba.*
Lit.: no. 250.

Pīpa (Iraq). Large drum placed upright upon a stand.

Pipat (Thailand). See *Piphat.*

Pi-phat (Thailand). The conventional instrumental ensemble, the "classical" orchestra of the land. It consists of the following instruments: *pi nai*, *ranat ek*, *ranat thong ek*, *gong wong yai*, *gong wong lek*, *ranat thum*, *ranat thong*, *tapone*, *song na*, *klong thad*, *gong hoi*, *chark lek*, *charb yai*, *ching*, *mong.* The anhemitonic tone material of this music is ca.:

E♭ G♭ A♭ B♭ d♭

Piphat (Kampuchea). The large theater orchestra of the land. Its instruments were played only by male musicians: *roneat-thum*, *roneat dec*, *kong-thom*, *kong-toch*, two *chloie*, *sralay*, *tro-khmer*, *ch'hung*, *sompho*, *sangna*, *sco-thom*, *thong*, *ronmonea.* Cf. *Mohori.*
Lit.: nos. 49, 153.

Piphat (Laos). Instrumental ensembles.

Pi-pi (Tibet). Obscure toy pipe, not used in musical performances.

Pipit (Malaysia). Term for the reeds of the *serunai.*

Pipo (Eastern New Guinea – Papua). Jew's harp made of bamboo.
Lit.: no. 190.

Pi pyu (Burma; Shan State). Bamboo ring flute with seven finger holes: six in front and one in the back.
Lit.: no. 252.

P'iri (Korea). Popular oboe made of bamboo or willow wood, with a large mouthpiece. The instrument has seven finger holes in front and one at the back. Three types of *p'iri* are distinguished:
1. *Tang-p'iri* (*tang p'il-lyul*), the Chinese oboe used in religious ceremonies.
2. *Hyang-p'iri* (*hyang p'il-lyul*), the Korean oboe used in folk music.
3. *Sei-p'iri*, a slender, gentle sounding instrument used in folk music.

Lit.: no. 52.

Piring buru (Turkey). Brass trumpet.
Lit.: no. 81.

Piripity (Malagasy Republic). Drum.
Lit.: no. 251.

Pis(ah)an bali (*Pisang bali*) (Java). See *Gending charabalen.*

Pi saw (*Khlui*) (Thailand; Vietnam). Long bamboo clarinet with one free beating metal reed and six or seven finger holes.
Lit.: nos. 51, 186.

Pisha (Iran; Turkey). Recent term for the old *bisha*, a small transverse flute or a slim oboe (*surnaya*). Cf. *Bishur*; *Shahnay.*
Lit.: no. 190.

Pi sha'nai (*Sralai*) (Former Cambodia). Oboe.
Lit.: no. 43.

Pishdaramad (Persia). The section which appears in strict, slow and stately tempo before the first *daramad* (*dar* = door; *amad* = it enters). Cf. *Dastgāh.*
Lit.: no. 320.

Pishrey (Persia). Overture to a *nauba.*

Pi-so (Thailand). Reed-flute.

Pisui (South China Sea; Hainan Tao). Bamboo tube zither with six (or fewer) strings.
Lit.: no. 156.

Pitale (Australia; Cape York). Song.

Pitet (*Pekak*). The muting of vibrating keys (e.g., on the *saron*) with thumb and forefinger of the left hand. See also *Ngenchot.*
Lit.: no. 163.

Pitikilangy (Malagasy Republic). Ground zither.
Lit.: no. 251.

Pitorka (South India). See *Piturka.*

Pitu (Ancient Babylon; Akkad). Hooked reed pipe.
Lit.: no. 87.

Pitu (Lower Congo). Wooden pipe (Portuguese *apito*).
Lit.: no. 255.

Pitu (Java). Seven. The seventh scale degree of the *pelog* scale. All seven numbers are: *siji*, *loro*, *telu*, *papat*, *lima*, *nem*, *pitu.* When the numbers are recited, one syllable of each numberword is used: *ji*, *ro*, *lu*, *pat*, *ma*, *nem*, *pi* (*tu*).

Piturka (South India; Bastar State—Muria Gond). (1) A large bell (cowbell type). (2) Slit-drum.
Lit.: no. 59.

Pivora (Central Africa). See *Mbombu.*

Pi-wang (Tibet). Lute with two or three strings tuned in fourths. Cf. *P'i-p'a*; *Khuur* (Mongolia).

Pi-wang rgyud-gsum (Tibet). *Pi-wang* with three strings.

Pi-wang rgyud-mang (Tibet). *Pi-wang* with many strings.

Plak kendang (Bali). Noisy drum stroke indicating the end of a melodic phrase.

Planchak (Java). See *Trachak.*

Plandang (South Mindanao – Bagobo). Bamboo flute with five finger holes.
Lit.: no. 255.

Plangkan (Java). (1) A wooden stand on which the *rebāb* is placed when not played. The *plangkan* is often beautifully ornamented. (2) The long spike (foot) on which the *rebāb* stands when played. See *Rebāb.*
Lit.: no. 163.

Plang lakorn (Thailand). Theater music.
Lit.: no. 58.

Plataran (Java). Group of instruments within the *gamelan* ensemble. This group represents the "open field," the more or less neutral musical background.
Lit.: no. 163.

Plāvita (India). See *Gamak(a).*

Playon (Java). Jogya term for all *srepegan* (*sampak*) forms (music of the *wayang* plays) with the exception of the final fight called *sampak galong* (Jogya).

Plenchung (Java). Musical formula. *Suluk plenchung* is a typical phrase that presents the final note (notes).

The *suluk plenchung* is intoned by the *dalang* when the scene comes to an end and the army appears. The spectators are thereby informed that the next scene will take place elsewhere.
Lit.: no. 163.

Pleng (*Resik*) (Java). See *Mleng.*

Pleng look groong (Northeast Thailand). Westernized popular songs sung in Bangkok and other cities.
Lit.: no. 203.

Pleng look toong (Thailand). Popular songs based on folk melodies.

Pleret (Java). See *Selompret.*
Lit.: no. 163.

Plesedan (Java). "Tones that have slid down." Tones created by partly covering a finger hole (e.g., on the *suling*).
Lit.: no. 163.

Pluntur (*Janget*) (Java). See *Bonang.*

Pluta (*Vṛddha*) (North India). (1) Durational note value of three *matras* (♩.). (Other durational note values of North India can be seen under the heading of *Anumatra.*) (2) *Pluta* (*plutam*) ("augmented") indicates a durational note-value (of South India) of three *matras* (♩.). (The other South Indian durational note values are shown under the heading of *Anumatram.*) Cf. *Akshara.*
Lit.: no. 136.

Po (China – M 4850). Brass cymbals used mainly in the theater (opera, puppet shows). The cymbals are beaten several times at the end of each verse (stanza). The Cantonese name is *poot.* Cf. *Tong pal* (Korea).
Lit.: no. 250.

Po (China). See *Chien-tzu.*
Lit.: no. 136.

Po-chung (China – M 5325; M 1503). A large bell hung in a wooden frame used in Confucian service. When the *po-chung* was struck, the *t'e-ch'ing*, tuned to the same note, had to answer. Ancient China used twelve *po-chung*, each bell tuned to one of the twelve *lü.*
Lit.: no. 137.

Poduppan (South India). *Rāgas* that can be performed at any time of the day or night.

Poeng Mang (Thailand). Term for the *song na* drum when used for accompanying songs. Cf. *Song na.*

Po-fu (China—M 5323; M 1919). "Strike—tap." An ancient small barrel drum that rests on a low wooden stand. In the Confucian temple there are two, one at the left, the other at the right side of the hall. The drum is beaten with the right hand, then with the left, and with both hands simultaneously. These drum sounds are produced at the end of each verse of the hymn answering the two sounds of the *tsu-ku*.
Lit.: no. 137.

Poh (Bali). Name of a notational symbol.

Poi (New Zealand—Maori). Dances of women who swing light balls on strings above their heads. *Poi* also refers to the dance itself and the accompanying song. The songs are sung only by girls.
Lit.: no. 298.

Poik (Israel-Hebrew). Drum.

Pokido (Belgian Congo). A *sansa* made of human skull bones. On its top are fixed five tongues placed across a bridge.
Lit.: nos. 21, 33.

Poko (Java). *Pokok* = stem. The starting note; principal tone. Cf. *Dasar.*

Pokok (Bali). *Pokok gending.* The nuclear fundamental theme of a *gending.*

Pokok (Java). Principal dance; basic dance. See *Joged.*
Lit.: no. 163.

Pokpok (*Opop*) (North Philippines). Cf. *Topayya.*

Pokul-logun (Indonesia; Nias). Tube psaltery.
Lit.: no. 255.

Polayol (Bali). The teaching of the classical dance.
Lit.: no. 197.

Po-lit (Sikkim—Lepcha). Transverse flute.

Polo (Congo—Banza). Cylindrical drum. Cf. *Bia.*
Lit.: no. 26.

Polos (Bali). See *Molos.*

Pomp'ae (Korea). Ritual Buddhist chant based on Chinese texts, both in language and poetic form. It appears in two styles: *hossori* (simple chant) and *chissori* (long, solemn chant). *Pomp'ae* corresponds to *bombai* in Japan.
Lit.: no. 178.

Pomsa (Africa; Lower Niger). Lute with two strings.
Lit.: no. 255.

Pone (South Africa—Ndebele). Bowed tube zither. Cf. *Tsijolo.*
Lit.: no. 151.

Ponga (Angola). Ivory horn. Also called *apunga.*

Ponga (Nepal). See *Phunga.*

Ponggang (Bali). Two small horizontally placed gongs of the old *gamelan gong* and the almost vanished *gamelan semar pegulingan.*
Lit.: no. 197.

Ponggang (East Java; Prabalingga). Identical with *monggang.*

Pong-tzu (China). Cantonese term for *pang-tzu.*

Ponggawa dangah (Sunda District). Male character, a "village warrior" of the *wayang* play.

Ponggawa lungguh (Sunda District). Male character, the "great fighter" of the *wayang* play.

Ponitu (New Zealand—Maori). Nose flute.
Lit.: no. 318.

Pontang (Java). Term for *rebāb*; its neck and bottom are made of ivory, the middle of the body is made of buffalo horn. Cf. *Blongsong.*
Lit.: no. 163.

Poo (*Pu*; *Chang-kun*) (Korea). A large polished bowl made of baked clay that was struck with a split bamboo stick. The sounds served to mark time. This bowl was also part of a group of bowls, each tuned to a different pitch. At the present time only one bowl is used in the ensemble of Confucian temple music.
Lit.: no. 179.

Poo-rai (Northeast Thailand). The antagonist opposing the leading hero in *mawlum moo.*
Lit.: no. 203.

Poot (China). Cantonese term for the Mandarin *po.*

P'o-pan (China). Clappers made of six slabs of hardwood, tied together at one end. Cf. *P'ai-pan*; *Ch'un-tu*; *Shou-pan.* See *Hakuhan* (Japan).
Lit.: no. 52.

Popondi (Central Celebes). Stick zither with one string.
Lit.: no. 162.

Popondi (*Kokondi*) (Indonesia; Moluccas). See *Tuba pondi.*

Popor kangduwur (Java). Also *umpak ngingil.* See *Rebāb* (Java).

Popor kangngisor (*Umpak ngandap*) (Java). See *Rebāb.*

Poretu (New Zealand – Maori). Also *e'wiu.* Flute; nose flute.
Lit.: no. 313.

Poroporoaki (New Zealand – Maori). *Marae* of farewell.
Lit.: no. 84.

Porutu (*Whio*) (New Zealand – Maori). Vertical wooden flute with three finger holes and an occasional thumbhole in the back. Men play this flute to catch the attention of young women.
Lit.: nos. 7, 84.

Poti-poti (New Zealand – Maori). See *Pu tatara.*

Potok (Java). "Equal." The term indicates that the number of beats (*ketuk*) in the *merong* and *munggah* are equal.
Lit.: no. 163.

Po-(tzu) (China). See *Chien-tzu.*
Lit.: no. 136.

Powhiri (New Zealand – Maori). Welcoming dance (*marae*).
Lit.: no. 84.

Poya (India). Sanskrit term for wind instrument.

Prabhanda (India). Sanskrit term for composition. Such an ancient work consisted of a variable number of sections. The common division into four sections (*dhatus*) was: *udgrāha*, *mēlāpaka*, *dhrūva*, and *ābhōga.*
Lit.: no. 231.

Prabandham kūttu (South India; Kerala). See *Cākkyār kūttyu.*

Prabhat (*Prabhat-bhairav*) (North India). Slow and dignified morning *rāga* which has the same tone material as *rāga Bhairav* with a slight deviation in descent (F♯).
Tone material:
C D♭ E F G A♭ B c
c B A♭ G (F♯) F E D♭ C; *Vādis*: F, C
Lit.: no. 138.

Prabhāvali (South India). *Janya rāga* of the 41st *mēḷa* (*Pāvani*).
Tone material:
C D♭ F♯ G A B c
c B A G F♯ D♭ E♭♭ D♭ C
(c B A F♯ G F♯ D♭ E♭♭ D♭ C)
Lit.: no. 139.

Prabhāvali (South India). (1) The 41st *asampūrṇa mēḷa-rāga* without *kaṭapayādi* prefix. (2) The 41st *asampūrṇa mēḷa-rāga* with *kaṭapayādi* prefix, called *Kumbhinī*. See *Rāga* (South India).
Lit.: no. 139.

P'rad-gling (Tibet). Small transverse metal flute. Its correct name is *p'red-gling-bu*.

Pradipaki (North India). See *Patadipaki*.

Pradipika (North India). *Rāga*; the same as *rāga Malashri* (using the note B).
Lit.: no. 138.

Pra ek (Northeast Thailand). The leading male actor of *mawlum moo*.
Lit.: no. 203.

Praharas (North India). Performance times of the *rāgas*. See North Indian *Rāgas*.
Lit.: no. 138.

Prāk-prasiddha rāga (India). See *Adhuna prasiddha rāga*.

Pranasmara (Java). See *Langen asmara*.

Praṇavākari (South India). *Janya rāga* of the 64th *mēḷa* (*Vāchaspati*).
Tone material:
G A Bb A Bb C D E F# G
G F# E D C *Bb A Bb* C
The scale of this *rāga* has *pañcamantya* character.
Lit.: no. 139.

Pra rawng (Northeast Thailand). The second leading male actor of the *mawlum moo*.
Lit.: no. 203.

Prasāriṇī (India). Old term for the 11th *śruti*. The corresponding note name is *prati antara ma*. Cf. *Śruti*.

Prasāriṇī Vīṇā (India). "Complete *vīṇā*." A *sitar* type with one gourd as corpus. The long neck carries five metal strings. Next to it is a second, thin and shorter neck without resonance body. It also has five wire strings which are tuned an octave higher than the first set. Each neck has 16 frets. The instrument is played with a wire plectrum.
Lit.: no. 254.

Prastāva (Vedic India). The first section of a *stoma* (Vedic hymn) started by the *prastotri*, the assistant priest, humming the sacred syllables.
Lit.: no. 141.

Pratāpa (South India). *Janya rāga* of the 50th *mēḷa* (*Nāmanārāyaṇī*).
Tone material:
C E F# G Ab Bb c
c Bb Ab G F# C Db C
Lit.: no. 139.

Pratāpachintāmani (*Pratāpacintāmani*) (South India). *Janya rāga* of the 28th *mēḷa* (*Harikāmbhōji*).
Tone material:
C E F G F A Bb c
c Bb A G F E F D C
Lit.: no. 139.

Pratāpahaṃsi (South India). *Janya rāga* of the 31st *mēḷa* (*Yāgapriyā*).
Tone material:
C E F G Bbb Ab Bbb c
c Bbb Ab G F E F D# C
Lit.: no. 139.

Pratāpakōkilam (South India). *Janya rāga* of the 30th *mēḷa* (*Nāgānandī*).
Tone material:
C G F G A# B c
c B G F D# C
Lit.: no. 139.

Pratāpanāṭa (South India). *Janya rāga* of the 28th *mēḷa* (*Harikāmbhōji*).
Tone material:
C D E F A G A Bb c
c Bb A G F E C
Lit.: no. 139.

Pratāparudhri (South India). *Janya rāga* of the 28th *mēḷa* (*Harikāmbhōji*).
Tone material:
C F E F G A B♭ c
c B♭ G F E F D C
Lit.: no. 139.

Pratāpasāraṅga (South India). *Janya rāga* of the 71st *mēḷa* (*Kōsala*).
Tone material:
C D♯ E F♯ G A c
c B A G F♯ E C
Lit.: no. 139.

Pratāpavarāli (South India). *Janya rāga* of the 28th *mēḷa* (*Harikāmbhōji*).
Tone material:
C D F G A G c (C D F G c)
c A G F E D C
Lit.: no. 139.

Pratāpavasantam (South India). *Janya rāga* of the 12th *mēḷa* (*Rūpāvatī*).
Tone material:
C F D♭ E♭ F G B c
c B G F D♭ C
Lit.: no. 139.

Prathama (Vedic India). The highest note used in Vedic chant. It was notated as "1."
Lit.: no. 141.

Prati (South India). Literally, "opposite." The term denotes in South Indian music the equivalent of "sharp." E.g., *prati ma* indicates a sharp *ma* (F♯, if *sa* is C).
Lit.: no. 136.

Pratiantara Ga (India). The note name corresponding to *raktika*, the 7th *śruti*. Cf. *Śruti*.

Pratiantara Ma (India). The note name corresponding to *prasāriṇī*, the 11th *śruti*. Cf. *Śruti*.

Praticatuśśruti Dha (*Pratiśuddha Ni*) (India). The note name corresponding to *sandīpinī*, the 16th *śruti*. Cf. *Śruti*.

Praticatuśśruti Ri (*Pratiśuddha Ga*) (India). The note name corresponding to *mandā*, the 3rd *śruti*. Cf. *Śruti*.

Pratihāra (Vedic India). The 3rd section of a *stoma*. The first priest is joined by the *pratihartri* (second priest) in chanting the sacred syllables.
Lit.: no. 141.

Pratihāri (South India). *Janya rāga* of the 46th *mēḷa* (*Ṣaḍvidhamārgiṇī*).
Tone material:
C D♭ F♯ G A B♭ c
c B♭ A G F♯ D♭ C
Lit.: no. 139.

Pratikaiśiki Ma (India). The note name corresponding to *prītiḥ*, the 12th *śruti*. Cf. *Śruti*.

Pratikaiśikī Ni (India). See *Prati ṣaṭśruti Dha*. Cf. *Śruti*.

Prati kākalī Ni (India). The tone name corresponding to *ramyā*, the 20th *śruti*. Cf. *Śruti*.

Prati Ma (India). Name for the 12th *śruti* above *acyuta ṣaḍja*, or *prītiḥ* above *kṣobhiṇī* (C above F♯). Cf. *Śruti*.

Pratisādhāraṇa Ga (India). See *Prati ṣaṭśruti*.

Pratiṣaṭśruti (*Pratisādhāraṇa Ga*) (India). The note name corresponding to *dayāvatī*, the 5th *śruti*. Cf. *Śruti*.

Prati ṣaṭśruti Dha (*Prati kaiśiki Ni*) (India). The tone name corresponding to *madantī*, the 18th *śruti*. Cf. *Śruti*.

Pratiśuddha Dha (India). The note name corresponding to *kṣitiḥ*, the 14th *śruti*. Cf. *Śruti*.

Pratiśuddha Ga (India). See *Praticatuśśruti Ri*.

Pratiśuddha Ma (India). The note name corresponding to *krodhā*, the 9th *śruti*. Cf. *Śruti*.

Pratiśuddha Ni (India). See *Praticatuśśruti Dha.*

Pratiśuddha Ri (India). The note name corresponding to *tīvra*, the 1st *śruti.* Cf. *Śruti.*

Pratiti (South India). *Janya rāga* of the 35th *mēḷa* (*Śūlinī*).
Tone material:
C D♯ F A B c
c B A F D♯ C
Lit.: no. 139.

Pratyāhata (India). See *Gamak(a).*

Pravālajoti (South India). *Janya rāga* of the 28th *mēḷa* (*Harikāmbhōji*).
Tone material:
C D F G A B♭ c
c B♭ A B♭ G F E C
Lit.: no. 139.

Praveshaka (Ancient India). Prologue leading to the beginning of the drama when the actors are presented.

Prawang Kenya (Java). Name of a song offering advice to young virgins. See *Kentrung.*
Lit.: no. 163.

P'red-gling-bu (Tibet). Small transverse (*p'red*) flute—usually made of metal. Cf. *P'rad-gling.*

Prempensua (*Gidirigo*) (Ghana). *Sansa* type.

Preng-ba (Tibet). See *Rgyud.*

Prèson (East Flores). Xylophone with 4-6 loose keys. The instrument has various names, a few given below:

lètor	in Sikka
lèdor, lètor	in Lio, Maumere
géko	in Endé
ridu	in Ngada
do'u da	in the Manggaray

Lit.: no. 166.

Prītiḥ (India). Term for the 12th *śruti.* The corresponding note name is *pratikaiśiki ma* (term used in the past in music theory). Cf. *Śruti.*

Priyatarṣaṇi (South India). See *Priyatarshaṇi.*

Priyatarshaṇi (South India). *Janya rāga* of the 27th *mēḷa* (*Sarasāṅgī*).
Tone material:
C D F A♭ B c
c B A♭ G F D C
Lit.: no. 139.

Prop kai (Thailand). Rhythmical drum pattern. It shows the common meter in which every fourth beat is accented and provided with a *ching* (hand cymbals) stroke.
Lit.: no. 208.

Psali (*Ṭuruḥat*) (Egypt; Coptic). Responsorial sacred song consisting of 16-20 strophes (each strophe having four lines). The answers are sung by the choir. Each *psali* begins with a strophe on Coptic language.

Psanter (Israel-Hebrew). Piano.

Pu (Korea). See *Poo.*

Pu (New Zealand—Maori). Flute.
Lit.: no. 7.

Pu (Hawaii). Shell used as signal horn.
Lit.: no. 278.

Pu-a (Hawaii). Nose flute in globular form. The instrument has two or three finger holes.
Lit.: no. 313.

Puan (Borneo). Cf. *Telarli.*

Puchuk (Sunda District). See *Rebāb* (Sundanese).

Puchung (Java). One of the meters of *tembang machapat.* See *Machapat.*
Lit.: no. 163.

Pucuk Rebong (Malaysia). See *Rebāb* (Malaysian).

Puepava (New Hebrides). Panpipes.
Lit.: no. 255.

Puh (*Pupuh*) (Bali). Notated melody with or without text.
Lit.: no. 197.

Pu hau re roa (New Zealand). See *Pu tatara.*

Pu heko heku (Polynesia; Marquesas Isl.). Nose flute.
Lit.: no. 255.

Pu hoho (New Zealand). See *Pu torino.*

Pühuri (Indonesia; Isl. of Ceram—Alifu). Triton shell horn.
Lit.: no. 255.

Pu ihu (Polynesia; Marquesas Isl.). Nose flute.
Lit.: no. 313.

Pü'ili (Hawaii). Bamboo beating sticks, rattled against each other.
Lit.: nos. 255, 278.

Puita (Congo—Bambala; Bahungana). Friction drum.
Lit.: no. 17.

Pujāri Kaichilambu (South India). Temple rattle made of a small iron tube bent into an oval ring, filled with little stones. The rattle is used in pairs, either placed around both ankles of the dancer or held in his two hands, and is gently shaken.

Puji (India). Nose double flute. The two pipes are stuck into a gourd.

Puk (Korea). (1) General term for drum. (2) Barrel drum used for accompaniment of the dramatic *p'ansori.*
Lit.: no. 52.

Pukaea (New Zealand—Maori). Wooden trumpet with a free wooden tongue called *tohe-tohe* ("tonsil") inside the tube near the lower end. The *pukaea* is used as signal instrument. The instrument is also called *putahoro.*
Lit.: nos. 7, 84.

Pu kihi (New Zealand—Maori). Cf. *Tetere.*

Pukku (Akkad). See *Ellag* (Sumeria).

Pukuta yemnga (Andaman Isl.). Percussion board.
Lit.: no. 198.

Puk-yü (China). Cantonese term for *pang-tzu.*

Pu la'i (Hawaii). Simple leaf oboe.
Lit.: no. 278.

Pulala (Philippines; Mindanao—Montese). Bamboo oboe.
Lit.: no. 255.

Pulavan kuḍam (South India; Malabar). Friction drum. Cf. *Pulluva kudam.*
Lit.: no. 254.

Pulik (Malaya). Clay flute.
Lit.: no. 255.

Pulluva kuḍam (South India). A monochord. A string is stretched from the bottom of a clay pot through a membrane that covers the top of the pot, to a small half gourd. The player presses a stick against the string in order to maintain the tension. Also *pulluvam kuṭam.* Cf. *Kuṭam.*
Lit.: no. 255.

Pulotu (Samoa). Small wooden slit-drum. Cf. *Fa'ali.*
Lit.: no. 255.

Pu-lwe (Burma). Long bamboo flute with seven finger holes in the front and one in the back. An extra hole (front) is covered with paper as it is done in the Chinese *ti-tzu.*

Pum (Korea). The seventh degree and symbol of the *kong-chuk-po.* Assuming that *hap* is C, *pum* represents B or B♭ as required by the mode of the piece performed. Cf. *Kong-chuk-po.*

Pumliṅga (India). An ancient term for main *rāgas*. At the present time the term is obscure. It appeared in the music theoretical work *Saṅgita Makaranḍa* written sometime between the 7th and 11th centuries.
Lit.: no. 138.

Pu-moana (New Zealand—Maori). See *Pu tatara.*

Pum-piang (Philippines). Bell.
Lit.: no. 255.

Puṅgī (*Pangra*) (India). Simple double clarinet used by snake charmers. Cf. *Tiktirī*; *Binjogi.*

Pung-ku (China). Drum beaten by the leader of the orchestra. Cf. *Pang-ku.*

P'ung-kyong (Korea). See *Furin* (Japan); *Feng-ling* (China).
Lit.: no. 52.

Punin (Hawaii). A small kettledrum. Its body is made of a calabash.
Lit.: no. 37.

Pūniu (Hawaii). Small drum with a coconut body which is covered with fishskin. The drum is fastened to the leg of the player, hence often described as a "kneedrum."
Lit.: nos. 7, 37, 84, 215.

Puñji (India). A long *maguḍi* that consists of a brass tube placed next to two reed pipes.
Lit.: no. 262.

Punnāgavarāḷi (South India). *Janya rāga* of the 8th *mēḷa* (*Hanumattōḍi*).
Tone material:

B♭ C D♭ E♭ F G A♭ B♭
B♭ A♭ G F E♭ D♭ C *B*♭

Lit.: no. 139.

Puntong palit (Nepal; Sikkim—Lepcha). Bamboo cross flute with four finger holes.

Pu-pai (Central Celebes; Toraja District). Bamboo clarinet. See *Pupui.* Cf. *Leleo.*
Lit.: no. 254.

Pupakapaka (New Zealand—Maori). A *pu-tatara* with a long mouthpiece.
Lit.: no. 7.

Pupu galaga (Solomon Isl.—Florida Isl.). Bamboo flute without finger holes.
Lit.: no. 255.

Pupuh (Bali). Melody; tune.
Lit.: no. 265.

Pupu horu (Solomon Isl.). Vertical bamboo flute with three finger holes near the lower end.
Lit.: no. 255.

Pupui (Sumatra). Bamboo clarinet without bell. It has 6-7 finger holes. Other names of this instrument are given below:

sigu mbava	on Nias
mots	in Celebes and Timor
bansi	in Flores
pu-pai	in the Toraja District
pupuwi	in Menangkabau

Cf. *Mots.*
Lit.: no. 167.

Pupul pandum (Southeast India—Jhoria Muria Gond). *Gotul* song sung when the first fruits of the urat pulse are eaten.
Lit.: no. 142.

Pupuwi (*Puwi-puwi*) (Flores; Manggaray). Bamboo clarinet made of grass leaves. Cf. *Pupui*; *Papuwi.*
Lit.: no. 166.

Purab (North India). A light, popular song. *Purab* is a dialect spoken in and about Benares and Lucknow.

Purappād (South India; Kerala). Dance prelude to a *kathakali* performance ("setting forth") indicating the begin after the opening *tōdayam*.
Lit.: nos. 123, 232.

Purba (North India). A rare evening *rāga* ascribed to the *Marva thāta*. It consists of a combination of features taken from the *rāgas Purvi*, *Puria*, and *Marva.*

Tone material:

C D♭ E F♯ A B c

c B A F♯ E D♭ C

Lit.: no. 138.

Puri (*Girwa*) (North India). Cf. *Tabla*.

Puria (*Puriya*; *Purya*) (North India). An evening *rāga* ascribed to the *Marva thāta*.
Tone material:

(C) D♭ E F♯ A (B) c

c B A F♯ E D♭ C

Lit.: no. 138.

Puria-dhanashri (North India). An evening *rāga* ascribed to the *Purvi thāta*.
Tone material:

C D♭ E F♯ G A♭ B c

c B A♭ G F♯ E D♭ C

Lit.: no. 138.

Pūrṇabhairavī (South India). *Janya rāga* of the 20th *mēḷa* (*Naṭabhairavī*).
Tone material:

C D E♭ F A♭ B♭ A♭ c

c B♭ A♭ G F E♭ D C

Lit.: no. 139.

Purṇacandrikā (South India). See *Purṇachandrikā*.

Pūrṇachandrikā (South India). *Janya rāga* of the 29th *mēḷa* (*Dhīraśaṅkarābharaṇam*).
Tone material:

C D E F G A G c

c B G F D E F D C

(c B G A G F E F E D C)

Lit.: no. 139.

Pūrṇakalānidhi (South India). *Janya rāga* of the 22nd *mēḷa* (*Kharaharapriyā*).
Tone material:

C E♭ F G A B♭ c

c A G F E♭ D♭ C

The note D♭ in descent is a characteristic feature.
Lit.: no. 139.

Pūrṇalalita (South India). *Janya rāga* of the 19th *mēḷa* (*Jhaṅkāradhvani*).
Tone material:

C D E♭ D F G c

c B♭♭ A♭ G F E♭ D C

Lit.: no. 139.

Pūrnaniṣādam (South India). *Janya rāga* of the 63rd *mēḷa* (*Latāṅgī*).
Tone material:

G A♭ B A♭ C A E F♯ G

G F♯ E D C *B A♭ G*

The scale of this *rāga* has *pañchamantya* character.
Lit.: no. 139.

Pūrnapañcham (South India). *Janya rāga* of the 15th *mēḷa* (*Māyāmāḷavagauḷa*).
Tone material:

C D♭ E F G A♭

A♭ G F E D♭ C

Lit.: no. 139.

Purṇaṣaḍja (South India). *Janya rāga* of the 20th *mēḷa* (*Naṭabhairavī*).
Tone material:

C D E♭ F G B♭ c (C G F G A♭ G c)

c B♭ G F E♭ D C (c B♭ A♭ F E♭ D C)

Lit.: no. 139.

Purṇaṣaḍja (South India). *Janya rāga* of the 22nd *mēḷa* (*Kharaharapriyā*).
Tone material:

C D E♭ F B♭ c

c B♭ G F E♭ D C

Lit.: no. 139.

Pūrṇasvarāvali (South India). *Janya rāga* of the 12th *mēḷa* (*Rūpāvatī*).
Tone material:

C E♭ F G A♯ B c

c A♯ B G F D♭ E♭ C

Lit.: no. 139.

Pūrvagauḷa (South India). *Janya rāga* of the 29th *mēḷa* (*Dhīraśaṅkarābharaṇam*).
Tone material:

C D F E D F G B A B c

c B A G F E D C

Lit.: no. 139.

Purvakalyan (North India). A rare *rāga* ascribed to the *Marva thāta*. It consists of a combination of phrases taken from the *rāgas Marva* and *Kalyan*.
Tone material:
B D♭ E F♯ G A B c
c B A B F♯ E D♭ C
Lit.: no. 138.

Pūrvakalyāṇī (South India). Also *Pūrvikalyāṇī*. *Janya rāga* of the 53rd *mēḷa* (*Gamanaśrama*).
Tone material:
C D♭ E F♯ G A B c (C D♭ E F♯ G A B A c)
c B A G F♯ E D♭ C
Lit.: no. 139.

Pūrvakannaḍa (South India). *Janya rāga* of the 5th *mēḷa* (*Manōrañjanī*).
Tone material:
C D♭ E♭♭ F G F G c
c A B A G F E♭♭ D♭ C
Lit.: no. 139.

Pūrvamukhāri (South India). *Janya rāga* of the 22nd *mēḷa* (*Kharaharapriyā*).
Tone material:
C F E♭ F G A B♭ A c
c B A F E♭ D C
In descent appears B-natural.
Lit.: no. 139.

Pūrvarāmakriya (South India). *Janya rāga* of the 10th *mēḷa* (*Nāṭakapriya*).
Tone material:
C D♭ E♭ F G B♭ A B♭ c
c B♭ G A F E♭ D♭ C
Lit.: no. 139.

Purvaranga (India). Invocations used as preludes performed behind the curtain of the stage. They were followed by the *bahir gīta*.

Pūrvasālavi (South India). *Janya rāga* of the 19th *mēḷa* (*Jhaṅkāradhvani*).
Tone material:
C E♭ F A♭ B♭♭ c
c B♭♭ A♭ G F D C
Lit.: no. 139.

Pūrvasindhu (South India). *Janya rāga* of the 5th *mēḷa* (*Manōrañjanī*).
Tone material:
C E♭♭ F G c B c
c A G F G E♭♭ D♭ C
Lit.: no. 139.

Pūrvavarāḷi (South India). *Janya rāga* of the 3rd *mēḷa* (*Gānamūrti*).
Tone material:
C D♭ F G A♭ c
c B A♭ G F E♭♭ D♭ C
Lit.: no. 139.

Purvi (North India). Serious *thāta rāga* to be performed at the time of sunset.
Tone material:
C D♭ E F♯ (G) A♭ B C
c B A♭ G F♯ E D♭ C
Lit.: no. 138.

Pūrvī (South India). *Janya rāga* of the 15th *mēḷa* (*Māyāmāḷavagauḷa*).
Tone material:
C E D♭ E F G A♭ B A♭ G c
c B A♭ G F E G F E D♭ C
Lit.: no. 139.

Pūrvī (North India). See *thātas*.

Pūrvikalyāṇī (South India). See *Pūrvakalyāṇī*.

Purya (North India). See *Puria*.

Pusaka (Java). *Pusaka Bendè*, "sacred *bende*," a gong. Four of these instruments are used in the Jogya Kraton. Some of their names are "rain of scent," "he who drives away the foe," "Lord Tiger."
Lit.: no. 163.

Puṣakalyāṇi (South India). See *Pusha Kalyāṇi*.

Pusha Kalyāṇi (South India). *Janya rāga* of the 54th *mēḷa* (*Viśvambharī*).
Tone material:
C D♭ E F♯ G A♯ B c
c B G F♯ E D♭ C
Lit.: no. 139.

Pushkaraṇī (*Puṣkaraṇī*) (South India). *Janya rāga* of the 8th *mēḷa* (*Hanumattōḍi*).
Tone material:
C E♭ F G A♭ B♭ c
c B♭ A♭ G F E♭ D♭ C *B♭* (C)
Lit.: no. 139.

Pushpalatīkā (*Puṣpalatīkā*) (South India). *Janya rāga* of the 22nd *mēḷa* (*Kharaharapriyā*).
Tone material:
C D E♭ F G B♭ c
c B♭ G F E♭ D C
Lit.: no. 139.

Pushpavasantam (*Puṣpavasantam*) (South India). *Janya rāga* of the 2nd *mēḷa* (*Ratnangi*).
Tone material:
C D♭ E♭♭ F G A♭ B♭ c
c A♭ B♭ G F E♭♭ D♭ C
Lit.: no. 139.

Puṣkaraṇī (South India). See *Pushkaraṇī.*

Puṣpa (India). One of the ancient basic ways of touching *vīṇā* strings (*dhātu*): the little finger, combined with the thumb, is called flower (*puṣpa*).
Lit.: no. 292.

Puṣpalatīkā (South India). See *Pushpalatīkā.*

Puṣpavasantam (South India). See *Pushpa-vasantam.*

Putahoro (New Zealand – Maori). See *Pukaea.*

Putara (New Zealand – Maori). See *Pu tatara.*

Pu tatara (*Putara*; *Tetere*) (New Zealand – Maori; Tahiti). Shell trumpet. In Tahiti a long mouthpiece is inserted into the shell. Cf. *Pu hau re roa*; *Pukaea.*
Lit.: no. 84.

Putorino (New Zealand – Maori). Wooden double trumpet. Also long "flute" with a central mouth hole, richly ornamented. One end is closed. Cf. *Pu tatara.*
Lit.: nos. 37, 228.

Putrika (South India). *Janya rāga* of the 29th *mēḷa* (*Dhīraśaṅkarābharaṇam*).
Tone material:
C D E A B c
c B A E D C
Lit.: no. 139.

Puttari (South India). *Janya rāga* of the 64th *mēḷa* (*Vāchaspati*).
Tone material:
C E F♯ G A B♭ c
c B♭ A F♯ E C
Lit.: no. 139.

Putura putura (New Zealand – Maori). Wooden bass trumpet used in battles.
Lit.: no. 255.

Putut gelut (Java). A particular manner of beating the *bonang* and *gambang kayu* signifying the "struggling disciples of the hermit." Both hands alternately beat the same tone in quick succession. Cf. *Tutukan rangkep.*
Lit.: no. 163.

Pututue (Polynesia; Marquesas Isl.). Nose flute.
Lit.: no. 313.

Puukaaea (New Zealand – Maori). Wooden signal trumpet blown in time of war.

Puun (Malaysia; Sarawak). Large gong.

Puurorohuu (New Zealand – Maori). Bull roarer.

Puutaatara (*Puu Moana*) (New Zealand – Maori). Shell trumpet.

Puutoorino (New Zealand – Maori). See *Putorino.*

Puwi-puwi (Java). The term *puwi-puwi* applies to almost all Indonesian oboe and clarinet types. The Javanese instrument (clarinet) has six finger holes in front and one at the back. In South Celebes the *puwi-puwi* is an oboe,

identical with the Javanese *selompret.* In Flores the *puwi-puwi* is a clarinet type. Cf. *Sarune* (oboe type of Central Sumatra). See *Serubay.*
Lit.: no. 132.

Pu-yü (China). See *Pang-tzu* (wooden drum). Cf. *Puk-yü.*

Pwe (Burma). Public theater. Marionette play accompanied by clappers, cymbals, gong and drum, several barrel drums, and a raucous sounding oboe.

Pworu (Congo – Bobati). Double or single bell. Cf. *Aporo* (Congo).
Lit.: no. 184.

Pwupworo (Congo – Babanga; Mono-bundu). Conical drum with two heads.
Lit.: no. 26.

P'yag-mt'san (Tibet). Performance of religious dances.

Pyan cho (*jo*) (Korea). Changing mode; altered mode.

Pye (Burma; Shan State). Jew's harp made of bamboo.
Lit.: no. 252.

Pyi-daw-byan (Burma). Cf. *Chauk-pauk auk-pyan.*

Pyi-krap (Burma; Shan State; Kachin). Cane flute with four or six finger holes in the front and one rear thumbhole.
Lit.: no. 252.

Pyi sun (Burma; Shan State). Vertical bamboo whistle flute. The instrument has five holes in front and one at the back.
Lit.: no. 252.

P'yon-chong (*P'yen-chong*) (Korea). Bell chimes. In an ornamented wooden frame are suspended 16 bells in two rows (of eight). The tuning of the upper row of bells is G♯ chromatically rising to d♯, and the lower row: G chromatically descending to C. The instrument was imported from China during the 12th century. Cf. *Pien-chung* (China).
Lit.: nos. 52, 179.

P'yong-kyeng (*P'yon-kyong*; *P'yen-kyeng*) (Korea). Stone chimes. In an ornamented wooden frame are suspended 16 marble (or jade, or soapstone) slabs in two rows (of eight). The tuning is the same as that of the *p'yon-chong.* Cf. *Pien-ch'ing.*
Lit.: nos. 52, 179.

Pyong-cho (Korea). One of the four important modes used in *ah-ak.* For all modes see *O-um-yak-po.*
Lit.: no. 136.

Pyong-cho kae-myon-cho (Korea). One of the four important modes used in *ah-ak.* For all modes see *O-um-yak-po.*
Lit.: no. 136.

P'yong-jong (Korea). See *P'yen chong.*

Pyolsin-gut (*Sonang-gut*) (Korea). See *Kut.*

Pywe (Burma). Flute.
Lit.: no. 255.

Q

Qabā (Egypt). Term for the *zamr*.
Lit.: no. 109.

Qabā dūduk (Turkey). Large recorder, flageolet. The term indicates the *ṭūṭik* of the Turkmen and the *ṭūṭak* of the Persians.
Lit.: no. 81.

Qabā-ḥiṣār (Arabia). See *Nam-ḥiṣar.*

Qabā zurnā (Turkey). Obsolete *zurnā* with seven finger holes in front and a rear thumbhole.
Lit.: no. 190.

Qabūs (Arabia). Lute with six strings played with a plectrum. Cf. *Qūbūz.*
Lit.: no. 78.

Qaḍīb (Arabia; Persia). A small wooden percussion stick that is struck against the palm of the hand or against resounding wooden or metal objects in order to beat a given rhythm.
Lit.: no. 76.

Qaflah (Arabia). Also *rujū*; *ghiṭā*. See *Muwashah.*

Qaida (North India). A fixed elaboration of a *tāla*. It provides the basic material for complex rhythmical variations.
Lit.: no. 136.

Qaināt (*Qiyān*) (Arabia). Hired singing girls.
Lit.: no. 66.

Qākel (Ethiopia). A simple bell rattle used by Coptic priests. It consists of five tiny bells or jingles fastened to a small piece of leather which is tied to the back of the hand.
Lit.: no. 184.

Qal (Israel; Samaria). A light, distinctly rhythmic manner of singing, in contrast to the heavy, recitative style called *kaved.*

Qalam (Arabia). Reed pipe.

Qalqal (Arabia). Jingles.
Lit.: no. 71.

Qāmish mizmār (Turkey). Term for the Chinese *sheng* (M 5742).
Lit.: no. 81.

Qanā (*Qarna*) (Ethiopia). Cow or antelope horn used as instrument by shepherds. Cf. *Qarn.*
Lit.: no. 102.

Qanbūs (South Yemen). Hadramaut name for *qabūs.*

Qanda (Ethiopia). Conical drum with two heads.
Lit.: no. 255.

Qānūn (Arabia; North Africa). A psaltery consisting of a wooden trapezoid-shaped box which has two or three rosette-formed resonance holes. The instrument has 63-78 gut strings tuned in groups of three. It is played with a small wire plectrum (*riṣe*). Cf. *Mughnī* (Persia); *Santīr.*
Lit.: nos. 66, 255.

Qaramut (New Britain). Term for *garamut.*
Lit.: no. 84.

Qarāqib (North Africa). Also called *qarqabu.* Plate-shaped castanets joined in pairs by leather thongs.
Lit.: no. 190.

Qarbi (Algeria; Biskra). Song with rubato features.
Lit.: no. 20.

Qarīna (Arabia). See *Dājina.*

Qarjiġār (Middle East). *Maqām.*
Tone material:
D $\overset{+}{\text{E}}\flat$ F G A♭ B c d
Lit.: no. 64.

Qarn (Arabia; Persia). A long curved horn.
Lit.: no. 255.

Qarnā (Ancient Babylon). Aramaic term for horn. Cf. *Keren.*
Lit.: no. 250.

Qarnā (Persia). Long metal horn, often in the shape of the letter S. Cf. *Keren.*
Lit.: no. 254.

Qaṣ'a (Lybia). Large wooden plate in the form of a cymbal. It is used to accompany a choir.

Qaṣa'a (Arabia). (1) An oval, shallow kettle-drum. (2) The rounded back of the *'ud.* Cf. *Tabl al-markab.*
Lit.: no. 70.

Qaṣab (Arabia). Tube; shawm.

Qaṣaba (Tunisia; Algeria; Morocco). Cane flute; the Algerian *qaṣaba* ("reed") indicates a vertical cane tube, a *nay*, with five or six finger holes placed on the tube in two groups. Cf. *Gaṣba.*

Qaṣā'id (Arabia). Odes of considerable length sung in the desert.
Lit.: no. 76.

Qasba (Arabia). See *Qaṣaba.*

Qasha (Arabia). Double reed.

Qāshiq (Arabia; Persia). "Wooden spoon" with small bells attached to its opening. This small rattle is beaten with a little stick.
Lit.: no. 255.

Qaṣīdah (Arabia; North Africa). A classical poem (extended ode of the past) sung in recitativic form by a solo singer with *'ud* accompaniment at social gatherings.
Lit.: nos. 66, 171.

Qaṣṣ (Arabia). The story teller.
Lit.: no. 73.

Qaul (*Qal*). See *Nauba.*

Qaus (Arabia; Turkestan). Bow. The term is also applied to a fiddle with two strings.
Lit.: no. 255.

Qavāl (Turkey; Turkestan). Shawm. This instrument, also written *qawal*, appears in Egypt and Turkey as a rustic flute (or shawm). The tube is made of wood with 6-7 finger holes and is the favorite of peasants and shepherds in Asia Minor and North Africa.
Lit.: nos. 81, 105.

Qawwālī (North India). Sufi songs performed at festivals honoring the many Sufi saints. They are performed as group or solo songs.

Qeddasē (Ethiopia). Liturgical (Coptic) missal.

Qeita (Algeria; Biskra). A wooden oboe with 6-7 finger holes. It has a very penetrating sound. A particular manner of playing can be observed when the player aims at a continuous sound without any interruption. He inhales through his nose and simultaneously presses air into the instrument from his fully blown cheeks. The scale produced is not steady; the player can alter the pitches at will.
Lit.: no. 20.

Qenie (Ethiopi). Features in the liturgical (Coptic) chant that strongly resemble the tropes of European plainchant of the 10th-12th centuries.
Lit.: no. 102.

Qirā'a (Arabia; Iraq). The reading, reciting, chanting of the Koran.

Qiṭ'a (Arabia). Old term for ballade.

Qītārā (*Qīthārā*) (North Africa; Arabia). The term (*kithara*) refers to the west African *'ud.*
Lit.: nos. 78, 249.

Qīṭarah barbariyah (Sudan). A Nubian or *barābra kissar*, a bowl-formed lyra. The instrument can be found in various sizes.
Lit.: no. 108.

Qiyān (Arabia). See *Qaināt.*

Qīz (Turkey). Medium-sized modern *nāy.* Cf. *Mansūr*; *Shāh.*
Lit.: no. 81.

Qōl (Arabia). Term used by oriental Jewish poets for *maqām*. Other terms are *habara* and *naama* (*naghma*). The latter term is used in Egypt.
Lit.: no. 121.

Qopūz (*Qobūs*) (Central Asia). (1) Turkey: lute with one or two strings. (2) Afghanistan (Kazaks, Kirghiz) lute with one string. When after 1000 A.D. the instrument was provided with a bow, its name changed into *rabāb* (*rebāb*).
Lit.: no. 250.

Qōshnāy (Minor Asia; Afghanistan—Uzbek). Turki term for double reed pipes.
Lit.: no. 76.

Qowus (Central Asia). See *Qopus* (*Qobus*).

Qowus (Kirgisia). Jew's harp made of iron with a tongue that extends beyond the frame. Cf. *Qopus.*
Lit.: no. 255.

Qṣeida (Algeria; Biskra). Religious song in praise of a derwish. It is sung only by men and accompanied in fixed rhythm by the *darbuka.*
Lit.: no. 20.

Qṣīda (Arabia). *Qaṣīda.*

Quand (Ethiopia). See *Qanā.*

Quang (*Quang-dōng*, "fantasy") (South Vietnam). Music of Central Vietnam referring to *quang-nam* and *quang-ngai.* Cf. *Dan-tai-tu.*

Quang (Vietnam). Songs in Cantonese style (of *Ca Hue*).

Quan Nhac (*Nha Nhac*; *Nhac Dai Noi*) (Vietnam). Aristocratic, distinguished music.
Lit.: nos. 296-97.

Quatchel (Ethiopia). Rattle used in religious services.

Qūbūz (*Qūpūz*) (Turkey). A formerly popular minstrel lute with five double strings. At the present time it is almost obsolete. In other parts of the East (Middle East, Southeast Asia, East Africa, etc.) the *qūbūz* is still in use. Cf. *Cobza*; *Koboz.*
The term *qūbūz* can also indicate a fiddle. Cf. *Hu-po*; *Hun-pu-sze*; *Qopuz.*

Qudūm (Arabia; Turkey). Kettledrum of medium size beaten by dervishes with club-shaped sticks (*Zakham*). Cf. *Dunbalak*.

Queng (New Guinea). Shell trumpet.
Lit.: no. 268.

Queniba (Congo). Xylophone. Cf. *Kweningba.*

Quilando (Angola—Ambundu). Also *cassuto*. Calabash scraper.
Lit.: no. 280.

Quira'at (Arabia). Chanting, reciting the Koran (Quran).
Lit.: no. 234.

Qulāq (Turkey). Bell of a wind instrument, e.g., the flaring bell of the *zūrnā*.
Lit.: no. 81.

Qullal (Maghrib; Morocco). Goblet drum.

Qurmah (Arabia). A double clarinet. One tube has six finger holes; the other has none and performs the bourdon accompaniment. Cf. *Arghul*; *Zummarah.*

Qurnaita (Syria). General term for reed-blown instruments.
Lit.: no. 81.

Qurnāṭa (Turkey). Term for clarinet.

Qushma (Iran; Khorasan). Double clarinet. See *Duzele.* Cf. *Qoshnai* (Uzbek).

Quṣṣāba (Arabia). Ancient term for tube: flute-, oboe-, or clarinet-types. The Persian term is *nāy*. Cf. *Qaṣāba.*

Quṣṣāba (Arabia). See *Qaṣāba.*

Quwāl (North Africa). Frame drum. Cf. *Gullāl* (Algeria).
Lit.: no. 78.

Quyen (Former Annam). Flute.
Lit.: no. 255.

R

Raatte (Egypt). A belt made of sail cloth in which are fastened small rattles. The belt is used by Egyptian dervishes.
Lit.: no. 255.

Rabāb (North India; Pakistan). This instrument, now rare in India, is probably of Persian origin. It is a short-necked lute on which neck and body are linked without any indentation. It has three gut strings and one copper string; occasionally the highest string is doubled. The instrument has a variable number of resonance strings. This type of *rabāb* is usually played with a plectrum and only rarely with a bow. Cf. *Rudra Vīṇā.*
Lit.: no. 46.

Rabābah (Egypt). Term for *rebāb*. In Egypt and Arabia the instrument is a fiddle with a rectangular body and one string.
Lit.: no. 250.

Rabāb al-mōgannī (Egypt). See *Rabāb el-mughannee.*

Rabāb el-mughannee (Arabia). The "singer's fiddle," a *rebāb* with two strings. Its first string is tuned to the tonic, the second to the upper fifth.
Lit.: no. 250.

Rabab assa'ir (*Rabāb ash-sha'ir*) (Egypt). See *Rabāb ash-sha-'er.*

Rabāb esh-sha-'er (Arabia). The "poet's fiddle" has one string. The body has a trapezoidal shape.
Lit.: no. 250.

Rabābi (Arabia). Fiddler.

Rabāna (Sumatra; Sunda District; Flores; Celebes; Malaysia). Also *Rebāna.* Frame drum of wood or clay. Cf. *Arabāna*; *Ravana*; *Terbang.*
Lit.: nos. 132, 166.

Rabāni (Ceylon). Singhalese term for a drum played only by women.
Lit.: nos. 255, 290.

Rabbār (East Africa; Somali Republic). Dance song (performed by women).

Rabbās (Somaliland). Dance of the men accompanied by clapping hands. At the present time the dance has lost its popularity.
Lit.: no. 98.

Rabekin (Hottentot; Southwest Africa). Lute with 3-4 strings.
Lit.: no. 255.

Rabōb (North India; Afghanistan). *Rebāb* type (*sarōd*) with four gut strings, bowed or plucked. Cf. *Robāb*.
Lit.: no. 250.

Ra-cho (Tibet). Horn.

Rad'he (Arabia). Beduin song.

Radif (Iran). *Radif* = "row" indicating the entire repertory of (art) music of several hundred short melodies handed down by oral tradition. These melodies appear in parts in all seven *dastgāh-ha* and in the five *naghmeh* forms. The rhythms of the melodies are based on poetic meters. The *radif* need not be exactly the same with every performer. Recently endeavors were made to establish one national comprehensive *radif*, but, for the time being, the result was not satisfactory to the leading musicians of the land.
Lit.: no. 146.

Radoh (Sumatra—Bengkulu). Frame drum.

Radop (Malaysia). Drum.

Raft (Afghanistan). "Going." The melodic progress away from the basic note, preparing another *āmad*.
Lit.: no. 276.

Rag (North India). See *Rāga*.

Rāga (Hindi and dialectal: *Rag*; South India: *Rāgam*) (India). The term is derived from the Sanskrit *raṅga* ("color," "color of mood," "atmosphere"). As a musical term it first appeared in the Sanskrit work *Bṛhaddeśi* by Matanga who lived some time between the 5th and 7th centuries. The concept *rāga* (or its dialectal form *rag*) means melody type or melody pattern. Theoretically there were hundreds of *rāgas* and even at the present time there are still numerous *rāgas* in use. Each *rāga* has a rigidly fixed tone material, scale, zig-zag (*vakra*) features, characteristic phrases, stressed and weak notes (*vādī, vishrantisthan, anuvādī, vivādī*), typical intonations and essential ornaments (*gamakas*).

After various endeavours to organize the many *rāgas*, North Indian musicians grouped them under the headings of *thātas*, South Indian musicians under the headings of *mēḷas* (*mēḷa-kartas*, or *janaka-mēḷas-*, "parent-*rāgas*").

After numerous endeavours in the past to group the *rāgas* into orderly systems, North Indian *rāgas* have been efficiently grouped by Pandit Bhatkhande in his work *Hindusthani Sangit Paddhati* (Bombay, 1940) into a set of 10 *thātas* (*thāta-rāgas*), parent *rāgas*. All these *rāgas* are represented by heptatonic scales. (For details see *Thāta* of North India and, further below, *Mēḷa* of South India.)

Numerous *rāgas* were placed into fixed three-hour periods (*praharas*) when they were supposed to be performed. There were (occasionally there still are) *rāgas* to be sung or played at sunrise, noon, afternoon, at sunset, evening, early and late at night, and before sunrise.

Furthermore, one observes *rāgas* to be performed at certain seasons: spring, summer, autumn, winter, and at the rainy season. The term *rāga-mala* indicates poetic descriptions of the significance and mood of *rāgas*. This resulted in an interesting iconography and similar related features that show *rāgas* in visual forms in colorful paintings.

Each *rāga* is performed to the accompaniment of a bourdon bass, usually played on the *tanbura*. If the tone material of the *rāga* contains the note *pa* (e.g., G) above the basic note *sa* (C), the tuning of the *tanbura* has to be G c c C. If the note *pa* (G) does not occur, but the fourth above the basic note, the note F above C (*ma* above *sa*), the bourdon sound will be F c c C. If neither G nor F are used in certain *rāgas* (e.g., *Hindol*), the bourdon sound uses the major seventh above C: B c c C.

For formal structure used in *rāga* performances see *Dhrūpād* and *Khyāl*.

The ten *thāta-rāgas*:

1. *Kalyan*:	C D E F♯ G A B c
2. *Bilaval*:	C D E F G A B c
3. *Khamaj*:	C D E F G A B♭ c
4. *Bhairav*:	C D♭ E F G A♭ B c
5. *Purvi*:	C D♭ E F♯ G A♭ B c
6. *Marva*:	C D♭ E F♯ G A B c
7. *Kafi*:	C D E♭ F G A B♭ c
8. *Asavari*:	C D E♭ F G A♭ B♭ c
9. *Bhairavi*:	C D♭ E♭ F G A♭ B♭ c
10. *Todi*:	C D♭ E♭ F♯ G A♭ B c

For further information see my book, Lit. no. 138, pp. i-20.

The eight *praharas*:

Time	*Thāta-rāga*
1. 7-10 a.m.	*Kalyan*; *Bilaval*
2. 10-1	*Bhairavi*; *Todi*; *Asavari*; *Kafi*
3. 1-4 p.m.	*Kafi*; *Todi*
4. 4-7	*Purvi*; *Marva*; *Bhairav*
5. 7-10	*Kalyan*; *Bilaval*
6. 10-1	*Khamaj*; *Kafi*
7. 1-4 a.m.	*Asavari*; *Bhairavi*
8. 4-7	*Purvi*; *Marva*; *Bhairav*

There are numerous other arrangements as far as performance time is concerned. For further information see O. C. Gangoly, *Rāgas and Rāginis* (Bombay, 1935).

The names of *rāgas* are derived from various sources. Some receive their names from the Sanskrit tone names *ṣaḍja*, *ṛṣabha*, *gāndhāra*, *madhyama*, etc., and thus become *Ṣaḍji*, *Arṣabhi*, *Gāndhāri*, *Madhyamadi*, etc. Other *rāga* names are derived from the names of Indian tribes such as *Ābhīrī*, *Āndhrī*, *Gūrjarī*, *Sāverī*, etc. Others come from the seasons and times of the day: *Megh* indicates the rainy season; *Vasant* (in Bengali: *Basant*) means spring; *Shrī* refers to the autumnal harvest festival which has a pronounced religious character; *Panchamā* implies spring when the Indian cuckoo produces its single note, *panchama*. *Shyām-kalyān* may imply evening *Kalyān*. Some *rāga* names are or include mutilated words or syllables. *Sankīrṇa rāgas* are mixed *rāgas* which were in fashion several centuries after Bharata's time. *Sankīrṇa* eventually became *Sankara* (*Shankara*), thus assuming an entirely different meaning. Other *rāga* names utilize the names of animals, trees, and flowers: *Bihāgḍā* is derived from the bird's name *vihaṅgadā*; *Kokila* from the Indian cuckoo; *Hansadhvani* comes from *haṃsa-dhvani*, the "voice of the swan"; *Pilu* may be derived from the local name of a tree (*salvadora indica*), and a number of *rāgas* are named after famous musicians and kings. A large number of essential North and South Indian *rāgas* (names and tone materials) are mentioned in this book. For detailed information, see Lit. no. 138.

Rāga (*Rāgam*) (South India). Since the 16th century the *rāgas* of the Karnatic South underwent several groupings into *mēḷas* (*mēḷakartas*, "unifiers") and into subordinate *janya rāgas*.

The present system consists of 72 *mēḷas* which in theory can be grouped into three categories. The first one represents the *Kanakāṅgi-Ratnāṅgi* system containing only *sampūrṇa* (complete heptatonic) scales. This system is in general used at the present time, and the list of its *mēḷas* is shown below. The second and third systems contain *asampūrṇa* scales (not necessarily heptatonic); one is older and one of more recent age. These systems are not in use and are not shown in this book. If required they can be seen in my book, Lit. no. 139 (introduction).

The 72 *mēḷas* are organized into 12 *chakras* ("wheels") of six scales *mēḷas* each, and each *chakra* has its own name. These names may be seen under heading of *Chakra* (cf. also Lit. no. 136).

All 12 *chakras* have the following notes in their lower tetrachords. The unchanged notes of the first six *chakras* (*mēḷa* 1-36) are C, F, and G, while the unchanged notes of the second six *chakras* (*mēḷa* 37-72) are C, F♯, and G.

First six *chakras*		Second six *chakras*	
I:	C D♭ E♭♭ F	VII:	C D♭ E♭♭ F♯
II:	C D♭ E♭ F	VIII:	C D♭ E♭ F♯
III:	C D♭ E F	IX:	C D♭ E F♯
IV:	C D E♭ F	X:	C D E♭ F♯
V:	C D E F	XI:	C D E F♯
VI:	C D♯ E F	XII:	C D♯ E F♯

Chakra	*Mēḷas*
I	1 2 3 4 5 6
II	7 8 9 10 11 12
III	13 14 15 16 17 18
IV	19 20 21 22 23 24
V	25 26 27 28 29 30
VI	31 32 33 34 35 36
VII	37 38 39 40 41 42
VIII	43 44 45 46 47 48
IX	49 50 51 52 53 54
X	55 56 57 58 59 60
XI	61 62 63 64 65 66
XII	67: G A♭ B♭♭ c
	68: G A♭ B♭ c
	69: G A♭ B c
	70: G A B♭ c
	71: G A B c
	72: G A♯ B c

LIST OF *MĒḶAS*
Kanakāṅgi-Ratnāṇgi system

Sampūrṇa mēḷas
(The modern system with *kaṭapayādi* prefixes)

Kanakāṅgi	Kharaharapriyā
Ratnāṅgī	Gaurīmanoharī
Gānamūrti	Varuṇapriyā
Vanaspātī	Māraranjanī
Mānavāti	Chārukeśī
Tānarūpi	Sarasāṅgī
Senāvati	Harikāmbhojī
Hanumaṭṭoḍi	Dhīraśaṅkarābharaṇa
Dhenuka	Nāgānandinī
Nāṭakapriya	Yāgapriyā
Kokilapriyā	Rāgavardhanī
Rupavati	Gāṅgeyabhūṣaṇi
Gāyakapriya	Vāgadhīśvarī
Vakulābharanam	Śūlinī
Māyāmālavagauḷa	Chalanāṭa
Chakravākam	Sālagam
Sūryakāntam	Jalārṇavam
Hātakāmbari	Jhālavarāli
Jhaṅkāradhvanī	Navanītam
Naṭabhairavī	Pāvani
Kiravāni	Raghupriyā

Gavāmbodhi	Hemavatī
Bhavapriya	Dharmavatī
Śubhapantuvarālī	Nītimatī
Śadvidhamārgiṇī	Kāntāmaṇi
Suvarṇāṅgī	Riṣabhapriya
Divyamaṇī	Latāṅgī
Dhavalāmbarī	Vāchaspati
Nāmanārāyaṇī	Mechakalyāṇī
Kāmavardhanī	Chitrāmbarī
Rāmapriyā	Sucharitra
Gamanaśrama	Jyotisvarūpini
Viśvambarī	Dhātuvardhani
Śyāmalāṅgī	Nāsikabhūṣanī
Śaṇmukhapriyā	Kosalam
Simhendramadhyāma	Rasikapriyā

For detailed information see Lit. no. 139. See *Chakra*; *Kaṭapayādi.*

Rāgachandrika (South India). *Janya rāga* of the 17th *mēḷa* (*Sūryakānta*).
Tone material:

C D♭ E F G A c
c A G F E D♭ C

Lit.: no. 139.

Rāgachūdāmaṇī (*Rāgacūdāmaṇī*) (South India). *Janya rāga* of the 32nd *mēḷa* (*Rāgavardhanī*).
Tone material:

C D♯ E F G c
c B♭♭ A♭ F D♯ E C

For variants see Lit. no. 139.

Rāgachūdāmani (South India). (1) The 32nd *asampūrṇa mēḷa-rāga* without *kaṭapayādi* prefix. (2) The 32nd *asampūrṇa mēḷa-rāga* with *kaṭapayādi* prefix. See *Rāga* (South India). Lit.: no. 139.

Rāgacūdāmani (South India). See *Rāga-chūdāmani.*

Rāga-mālā (India). Literal and pictorial representation of *rāgas*. There are several schools in India that teach this art. Cf. *Dēvamaya rūpa.*

Rāga-mālika (India). A composition using a row ("garland") of *rāgas*. This form is in contrast to to all other serious types of art music. A *rāgamālika* can be observed in the *jatisvaram*, the second movement of the *bharata nāṭyam* performance.

Rāgamañjari (South India). *Janya rāga* of the 25th *mēḷa* (*Mārarañjanī*).
Tone material:
C D E F A♭ c
c A♭ F E D C
Lit.: no. 139.

Rāgamūrti (South India). *Janya rāga* of the 3rd *mēḷa* (*Gānamūrti*).
Tone material:
C D♭ E♭♭ F A♭ B c
c B A♭ F E♭♭ D♭ C
Lit.: no. 139.

Ra-gaṇa (South India). See *Asta gaṇas.*

Ragapañcaram (South India). See *Rāgapañcharam.*

Rāgapañcharam (South India). *Janya rāga* of the 28th *mēḷa* (*Harikāmbhōji*).
Tone material:
C D F G A B♭ A c
c B♭ A F D C
Lit.: no. 139.

Rāgarañjani (South India). *Janya rāga* of the 7th *mēḷa* (*Senāpāti*).
Tone material:
C D♭ E♭ G B♭♭ c
c B♭♭ G E♭ D♭ C
Lit.: no. 139.

Rāgavardhanī (South India). The 32nd *mēḷa*:
C D♯ E F G A♭ B♭ c
In the past this *rāga* was called *Rāgachūḍamani.* At the present time it is a *janya rāga* of the 32nd *mēḷa.*

Rāgavardhanī (South India). Cf. *Ālāp.*

Rāgavasant (South India). Obscure *janya rāga* of the 14th *mēḷa* (*Vakuḷābharaṇam*).
Tone material:
C D♭ F G B♭ A♭ c
c B♭ A♭ F G F E D♭ C
Lit.: no. 139.

Rāgavinodini (South India). *Janya rāga* of the 28th *mēḷa* (*Harikāmbhōji*).
Tone material:
C D E F A c
c A F E D C
Lit.: no. 139.

Rag-dung ("brass tube"; *Dung-chen* ["big tube"]) (Tibet). A pair of long straight copper horns. Each horn consists of three sections which can be telescoped together when the instrument is not in use. When played the *rag-dung* rests upon a stand. The two horns are supposed to be tuned in unison. For further information see Lit. no. 143. Cf. *Nabal.*

Rageshri (North India). A rare and serious *rāga* ascribed to the *Khamaj thāta*. It is to be performed at night.
Tone material:
C E F A B c
c B♭ A F E D C; *Vādis*: E, B
Lit.: no. 138.

Rāgiṇī (North India). "Wife of a *rāga*." The term was used mainly for purposes of classification. It appeared first in a Sanskrit work entitled *Pañcamasara-samhita*, probably dating of the period between the 7th and 11th centuries. The author (Nārada?) is uncertain. At the present time the term *rāgiṇī* has become obsolete.
Lit.: no. 138.

Raghulīlā (South India). *Janya rāga* of the 42nd *mēḷa* (*Raghupriyā*).
Tone material:
C F♯ D♭ G F♯ E♭♭ F♯ G F♯ D♭ F♯ G B c
c B A♯ B G F♯ E♭♭ F♯ D♭ C
(c B A♯ B G F♯ E♭♭ F♯ D♭ F♯ E♭♭ D♭ C)
Lit.: no. 139.

Raghulīlā (South India). (1) The 42nd *asampūrṇa mēḷa-rāga* without *kaṭapayādi* prefix. (2) The 42nd *asampūrṇa mēḷa-rāga* with *kaṭapayādi* prefix was called *Ravikriyā*. See *Rāga* (South India).
Lit.: no. 139.

Raghupriyā (South India). The 42nd *mēḷa*:
C D♭ E♭♭ F♯ G A♯ B c
As *rāga* the same tone material is used.
Lit.: no. 139.

Ra-gvin (Burma). See *Ya-gvin*.

Rāḥa(t)-il-arawaḥ (*Rāḥat-il-aruh*). "The calmer of the mind." An Egyptian *maqām*:
$\overset{+}{B\flat}$ C D E♭ F♯ A B♭
The Syrian name of this *maqām* is *Baghdadi*.
Lit.: nos. 64, 121.

Rāḥat Fazā (Middle East). *Maqām*.
Tone material:
G A B♭ C D E♭ F♯ G A $\overset{+}{B\flat}$ c d
Lit.: no. 64.

Rāḥat-il-aruḥ (Egypt). See *Rāḥat-il-arawaḥ*.

Rahāwi (Middle East). *Maqām*.
Tone material:
C D $\overset{+}{E\flat}$ (F♯) F G A $\overset{+}{B\flat}$ c
Lit.: no. 64.

Rahāwī (Tunisia). *Maqām*.
Tone material:
A B♭ C D E♭ F G A B♭ c
Lit.: no. 64.

Rai (Java). The flat part of the gong surface that adjoins the *tikel*.
Lit.: no. 163.

Raijo (Japan). A musical pattern performed by the *noh hayashi*.
Lit.: no. 187.

Rai-rai (Japan). See *Mororai*.

Ra'īsat al-awsāṭ (Arabia). Tone name (as used by Al-Kindi, 9th century). It is notated with the Arabic letter *ha* (H), at times transcribed into Western notation with the note (e.g.) E.
Lit.: no. 69.

Rai'ṭah (*Reīta*; *Rhei'ta*) (North Africa). Small, slim oboe used particularly at marriages and circumcision processions.
Lit.: no. 294.

Raja (Java). "King"; the *rebāb* played by the leader of the *gamelan*.

Rājadāsi (India). Female temple dancer. See *Dēvadāsi*.

Rajanī (India). The second of the seven ancient *mūrchhanās* derived from the *sa-grāma*. Cf. *Mūrchhanā*.

Rajaz (Old Arabia). Unrhymed poetry.

Rajori dewangata (Flores; Ende). A papaya shawm. Its Javanese name is *sompret*. It consists of a bent papaya stem, closed at one end. Into the tube is cut a narrow slit which vibrates when the player blows into the open end of the instrument.
Lit.: no. 163.

Rakb (Middle East). *Maqām*.
Tone material:
D $\overset{+}{E\flat}$ F $\overset{+}{G\flat}$ A B♭ c d
Lit.: no. 64.

Rakbānī (Iraq). Caravan songs. Cf. *Hujanī* (*Hujaynī*); *Ḥidā*.

Raket (Java). See *Sori-tekes*; *Nayang wwang*.

Ra:khaṅ (Thailand). Bell.

Ra:khaṅ samrab nuṅ (Thailand). Glockenspiel.

Raktā (India). Term for the 15th *śruti*. The corresponding note name is *śuddha dha* (a term used in the past music theory). Cf. *Śruti*.

Raktagāndhārī (Ancient India). See *Jāti*.

Raktikā (Ancient India). Term for the 7th *śruti*. The corresponding note name is *prati antara ga* (a term used in the past music theory). Cf. *Śruti.*

Raktimārgaṇi (South India). *Janya rāga* of the 52nd *mēḷa* (*Rāmapriyā*).
Tone material:
C G F♯ A B♭ c
c B♭ A G F♯ G E D♭ C
Lit.: no. 139.

Rakugo (Japan). Popular monologue comedy. Cf. *Kodan.*
Lit.: no. 185.

Raloba (Malagasy Republic). Percussion beam. Cf. *Tsikaretika.*
Lit.: no. 251.

Ral-pa (Tibet). See *Beda.*

Rama (Thailand). See *Khon.*

Rama'kie (South Africa – Hottentot-Bushman). Simple lute with four strings. It has a small round body and a broad neck.
Lit.: no. 151.

Ramakien (Thailand). See *Khon.*

Ramakriya (South India). *Janya rāga* of the 51st *mēḷa* (*Kamavardhanī*). The scale of this *rāga* is identical with that of its primary *rāga* (*mēḷa*) *Kamavardhanī.*
Lit.: no. 139.

Rāmakriya (South India). (1) The 51st *asampūrṇa mēḷa-rāga* without *kaṭapayādi* prefix. (2) The 51st *asampūrṇa mēḷa-rāga* with *kaṭapayādi* prefix was called *Kāśirāmkriyā.* See *Rāga* (South India).
Lit.: no. 139.

Rāmakuntala (South India). *Janya rāga* of the 67th *mēḷa* (*Sucharitra*).
Tone material:
C D♯ E F♯ G A♭ B♭♭
B♭♭ A♭ G F♯ E D♯ C *B♭♭*
The scale of this *rāga* has *niṣādāntya* character.
Lit.: no. 139.

Rāmakusumāvaḷi (South India). *Janya rāga* of the 61st *mēḷa* (*Kāntāmaṇi*).
Tone material:
C E F♯ G B♭♭ c
c B♭♭ A♭ G F♯ E D C
Lit.: no. 139.

Ramal (Middle East). *Maqām.*
Tone material:
$\overset{+}{E\flat}$ F G $\overset{+}{A\flat}$ B♭ c d $\overset{+}{e\flat}$
Lit.: no. 64.

Ramal (Tunisia). *Maqām.*
Tone material:
B♭ D E♭ F♯ G A B♭ c d
Lit.: no. 64.

Ramal (*Al-ramal*; *Ramel*). (1) Festive rhythmic mode (described by Al Kindi, 9th century, by Al Farabi, 10th century).

Cf. *Hazaj.*
(2) Later form:

Cf. *Iqa'at.*
Lit.: no. 76.

Rāmalīlā (South India). Dance-play about *rāma.*
Lit.: no. 46.

Rmala-Māyah (Modern Tunisia). *Maqām.*
Tone material:
G A $\overset{+}{B\flat}$ C D $\overset{+}{E\flat}$ F G A
According to Lit. no. 186 the tone material varies in adjoining countries:

Tunisia:	e d c♯ $\overset{\flat}{B\flat}$ A G F♯ E
Algeria:	A B c d e f♯ g a
Morocco:	E F♯ G A B c d e (called *O'shaq*)

Lit.: no. 186.

Ramal Tūtī (Arabia). See *Jwab nawā.*

Ramāmanoharī (South India). *Janya rāga* of the 52nd *mēḷa* (*Rāmapriyā*).

Tone material:

C D♭ E F♯ G A B♭ A c

c B♭ A G F♯ E D♭ C

Lit.: no. 139.

Rāmamanohari (South India). (1) The 52nd *asampūrṇa mēḷa-rāga* without *kaṭapayādi* prefix. (2) The 52nd *asampūrṇa mēḷa-rāga* with *kaṭapayādi* prefix. See *Rāga* (South India). Lit.: no. 139.

Ramam lum dut (Laos). Frame drum.

Ramanī (South India). *Janya rāga* of the 63rd *mēḷa* (*Latāṅgi*).
Tone material:

C E F♯ G B c

c B G F♯ E C

Lit.: no. 139.

Rāmapriyā (South India). The 52nd *mēḷa* and *rāga*:

C D♭ E F♯ G A B♭ c

Lit.: no. 139.

Rambu (Melanesia). Wooden drum.
Lit.: no. 255.

Ramdasi Mallār (North India). Subordinated *rāga* to the *Kafi thāta*. It belongs to the *Mallār* family.
Tone material:

(*B♭*) C D E F G A B c

c B♭ G F (E♭) D C; *Vādis*: F,C

Lit.: no. 138.

Rameh (Flores). Festivity with song and dance.
Lit.: no. 166.

Ramel (Arabia). See *Ramal* (*Raml*).

Rāmgiri (South India). *Janya rāga* of the 68th *mēḷa* (*Jyotisvarupinī*).
Tone material:

C D♯ E F♯ G A♭ B♭ c

c A♭ B♭ A♭ G F♯ E D♯ C

Lit.: no. 139.

Bamkali (North India). *Rāga* ascribed to the *Bhairav thāta*. It ought to be performed in the morning. There are four types of *Ramkali*:

1. The notes F and B are avoided in ascent.
2. Using the *Bhairav* scale throughout.
3. The notes F, F♯, B♭, and B are used.
4. The notes E and E♭ are used; this type is very rare.

The average tone material is:

C D♭ E F G A♭ B c

c B (B♭) A♭ G (F♯) F E D♭ C;

Vādis: G or A♭; C or D♭

Lit.: no. 138.

Ramkavāmbari (South India). *Janya rāga* of the 67th *mēḷa* (*Sucharitra*).
Tone material:

C D♯ F♯ G A♭ c

c A♭ G F♯ D♯ C

Lit.: no. 139.

Ramkie (South Africa—Korana; Hottentot; Bushman). Simple lute, occasionally bowed, mostly plucked, an imitation of the 18th-century imported Portuguese guitar. The instrument usually has three strings; a few tribes use four strings. Cf. *Xguthe*.
Lit.: no. 151.

Raml (Arabia; Syria). "The sandy one." A lesser known subordinate *maqām*, a "son" probably of *rast*, that is used in some middle sections of performances. Its material, confined within the range of a fifth, is:

$\overset{+}{\text{E}\flat}$ F♯ G A♭ $\overset{+}{\text{B}\flat}$

Cf. *Ramal*.
Lit.: no. 121.

Rammanā (Thailand). Frame drum.

Rampak sekar (Sunda District). Women's chorus.

Ramyā (India). Term for the 20th *śruti*. The corresponding note name is *prati-kākalī ni* (term used in past Indian music theory).

Raṅ (Assam—Garo). Bronze kettle gong.
Lit.: no. 252.

Ranad (Thailand). See *Ranat*.

Raṇa Dhōl (India). War drum, barrel form. Cf. *Dhōl.*

Rāṇasīṅgaḍum (India). Gujarati term for *rāṇaśṛṅga.*

Rāṇaśṛṅga (*Rānashriṅga*) (India). Ancient S-shaped war horn, made of brass with conical bore. It is provided with rings at the four joints where the tube curves. Cf. *Śṛṅga*; *Narsinga*; *Kombu*; *Kommu.*
Lit.: no. 254.

Ranāt ēk (Thailand). High-pitched xylophone with 21 (or 22) wooden slabs which rest on a slightly curved trough. The trough is richly ornamented with ivory or mother of pearl. The slabs are beaten with two knobbed sticks and produce a range of three octaves. See *Piphat.*
Lit.: no. 49.

Ranāt lek (Thailand). See *Ranāt thong ēk.*
Lit.: no. 49.

Ranāt ēk lek (Thailand). High-pitched metallophone with a rectangular box resonator. Rectangular iron keys are used to imitate the form of a xylophone.

Ranāt thong ēk (Thailand). Metallophone with 21 steel keys structured in the same manner as *ranāt ēk.*
Lit.: no. 49.

Ranāt thong thum (*Thum lek*) (Thailand). Metallophone with 17 steel slabs. See *Piphat.*
Lit.: no. 49.

Ranāt thum (*Thume mai*) (Thailand). Xylophone with 17 slabs tuned one octave lower than the *ranat ēk*. See *Piphat.*
Lit.: no. 49.

Ranāt thum lek (Thailand). Low-pitched metallophone with a rectangular box resonator. The instrument has rectangular iron keys. Cf. *Ranāt ēk lek*; *Ranāt thong thum.*

Ranchakan (*Rantjakan*) (Java). Wooden stand to support *gender* and *bonang* instruments.
Lit.: no. 163.

Randa (East Africa – Swahili). See *Cheza ngoma*; *Randa rukaruka.*

Ran(g) (Burma). Small flat gong.

Ran(g) (Assam – Garo). Flat gong. A condemned person has to pay his punishment with *ran(g)*. The higher his rank the more gongs are believed to be in his possession.
Lit.: no. 250.

Raṅganāyaki (South India). *Janya rāga* of the 1st *mēḷa* (*Kanakāṅgī*).
Tone material:
C D♭ E♭♭ G A♭ c
c A♭ G E♭♭ D♭ C
Lit.: no. 139.

Raṅgapitha (India). The front part of the theatrical stage. Cf. *Nepathya.*

Raṅgarōhiṇi (South India). *Janya rāga* of the 70th *mēḷa* (*Nāsikabhūṣaṇī*).
Tone material:
C D♯ F♯ G B♭ c
c B♭ G F♯ D♯ C
Lit.: no. 139.

Raṅgasirsha (India). A backstage platform which occasionally was used by actors taking part in the performance behind the scene.

Raṅgavalli (South India). *Janya rāga* of the 37th *mēḷa* (*Sālaga*).
Tone material:
C D♭ E♭♭ F♯ A♭ c
c A♭ F♯ E♭♭ D♭ C
Lit.: no. 139.

Rangi (New Zealand – Maori). Dance melody.
Lit.: no. 37.

Rangi paakuru (New Zealand). Dance melodies sung to the accompaniment of the *paakuru.*

Rangkep (Sunda District). Tempo indication: "double," meaning "slowly." Cf. *Wirahma.*
Lit.: no. 163.

Rangkep (Bali). "Double." Twice as slowly.

Rangkung (Java). See *Rebāb*; *Kosok.*

Rang nat (Laos). Xylophone of the *mohori* orchestra.
Lit.: no. 43.

Rajanī (India). Term for the 6th *śruti.* The corresponding note name is *śatśruti ri* (*śadhāraṇa ga*), terms used in music theory of the past. Cf. *Śruti.*

Rañjani (South India). *Janya rāga* of the 59th *mēḷa* (*Dharmavatī*).
Tone material:
C D E♭ F♯ A c
c B A F♯ E♭ C D♭ C
Lit.: no. 139.

Rañjanī Vīṇā (India). "The coloring *vīṇā.*" Term for the *mahati vīṇā* with five melody strings, two bourdon steel side strings, and 16 frets. Cf. *Kacchapi vīṇā.*
Lit.: no. 255.

Rankei (Japan). The ninth of the 12 Japanese (chromatic) tones transcribed as A♯ (if the first tone, *ichikotsu*, is read as D). See *Gagaku.*

Rankoan (Melanesia; Admirality Isls.). Nose flute.
Lit.: no. 313.

Rante (Java; Jogya). Low range.

Rantjakan (Java). See *Ranchakan.*

Rano (New Guinea – Waropen Coast). Songs about myths sung canonically by men in boats. Cf. *Ratara.*

Rao (South Vietnam). Improvised prelude (also called *zao*). In the North the introduction is called *dao.*

Rapa (Japan). See *La-pa* (China); *Napal* (Korea); *Rapal* (Mongolia).
Lit.: no. 53, 250.

Rapa'i (Sumatra – Atjeh). Spike lute. A *rebāb* type. The instrument has numerous names, a few are given below:

erbābi	in Sula-Besi and Buru
arabābu	in Halmahera
merbāb	in Goron (Goram)
rabāb; *rebāb*	in Java
merdap	in Batak
rebop	in Gajo

Lit.: no. 254.

Rapakai (Japan). See *Rappakai.*

Rapal (Mongolia). A long brass trumpet. Cf. *Rapa*; *La-pa.*

Rapana (Sumatra; Atjeh). Tambourin. Cf. *Rabana*; *Rebana.*

Rapapa (Congo – Bari). Lyre.
Lit.: no. 176.

Ra-pol (Sierra Leone – Temne). Term for string.
Lit.: no. 255.

Rappa (Japan). Straight slim brass horn, occasionally called "foreigner's flute."
Lit.: no. 225.

Rappakai (Japan). Conch horn with a cup shaped mouthpiece. Cf. *Hora-no-kai.*
Lit.: nos. 255, 258.

Raqabe (Arabia). Term for the neck of a lute.
Lit.: no. 255.

Raqqāṣa (Iran). Ancient term for female dancer. Also *raqqāṣūn* is used.
Lit.: no. 66.

Raqṣ (West Asia; Israel). Beduin dance. In antiquity the term was used to indicate the forbidden dance. In Arabia, also Kurdistan, the term signified dance with a prelude by a *mawal.*
Lit.: no. 229.

Rarachiblon (*Rarasiblon*) (Java). "The *chiblon*-playing girl." See *Chiblon.*

Raraga (Sunda District). See *Kachapi.*

Rarasiblon (Java). See *Chiblon.*

Raraup (Borneo—Dayak). Copper cymbals.
Lit.: no. 255.

Rarawat (West Java). The tightening straps on the Sundanese *kendang.* (The sliding rings are called *gelang*, the wooden stand on which the drum rests is called *kuda-kuda.*)
Lit.: no. 163.

Ra's (Arabia). The head of the *'ud.*

Rasa (Ancient India). "Flavor." The feeling, mood of a poem, drama, dance, and music. Generally the following *rasas* were listed: love, fear, heroism, pathos, wonder, terror, loathsomeness, and spiritual peace. Cf. *Bhāva.* See *Rāga.*
Lit.: no. 138.

Rasagūcham (South India). *Janya rāga* of the 1st *mēḷa* (*Kanakāṅgī*).
Tone material:
C D♭ E♭♭ G B♭♭ c
c B♭♭ G E♭♭ D♭ C
Lit.: no. 139.

Rasakalānidhi (South India). *Janya rāga* of the 16th *mēḷa* (*Chakravāka*).
Tone material:
C G F A B♭
(B♭) A G F E D♭ C *B♭*
Lit.: no. 139.

Rasali (*Rasāvali*) (South India). *Janya rāga* of the 4th *mēḷa* (*Vanaspāti*).
Tone material:
C D♭ F G A B♭ c
c A G D♭ C (*B♭* C)
Lit.: no. 139.

Rāsa līlā (India). Religious form of the *manipuri* dance. Its several types deal with the relationship between Krishna, Radha, and the Gopis. Cf. *Lai haroba.*

Rasamañjari (South India). *Janya rāga* of the 72nd *mēḷa* (*Rasikapriyā*).
Tone material:
C D♯ E F♯ G A♯ B c
c B G F♯ D♯ C
Lit.: no. 139.

Rasamañjari (South India). (1) The 72nd *asampūrṇa mēḷa-rāga* without *kaṭapayādi* prefix. (2) The 72nd *asampūrṇa mēḷa-rāga* with *kaṭapayādi* prefix. See *Rāga* (South India).
Lit.: no. 139.

Rasāvali (South India). See *Rasali.*

Rasavinōdini (South India). *Janya rāga* of the 52nd *mēḷa* (*Rāmapriyā*).
Tone material:
C E F♯ G A B♭ A c
c B♭ A G F♯ E C
Lit.: no. 139.

Rasd (*Rast*) (Modern Tunisia). *Maqām.*
Tone material:
G A C D E F G A $\overset{+}{B\flat}$ c
Lit.: no. 64.

Rasdu-dh-dhīl (Modern Tunisia). *Maqām.*
Tone material:
C D $\overset{+}{E\flat}$ $\overset{+}{F}$ G A $\overset{+}{B\flat}$ c d
Lit.: no. 64.

Rasia gīt (Nepal). Rustic love song sung during work in the field.
Lit.: no. 133.

Rasika (India). A music "taster," a teacher-critic, an examiner.

Rasikapriyā (South India). The 72nd *mēḷa*:
C D♯ E F♯ G A♯ B c
The *rāga* with the same name uses the identical tone material.
Lit.: no. 139.

Rasikarañjani (South India). *Janya rāga* of the 16th *mēḷa* (*Chakravāka*).
Tone material:

C D♭ E G A c
c A G E D♭ C

Lit.: no. 139.

Rāst (Arabia). "The straight note." (1) Tone name. (A list of all tone names and notes within the range of two octaves can be seen under the heading of *Jagāga* [*Yagā*].) (2) A *maqām* that begins and ends with the note *rāst* (usually transcribed as the western note C). Generally *rāst* is considered to be the first *maqām* that opens the *diwan* and the concert. The name *rāst* is Persian and may be derived from Rasht, the name of a North Persian town. Although professional musicians favor the *maqām*, it never became popular and always stayed a "Persian" art *maqām*. When performed, ornaments, trills, and coloraturas are to be avoided and the tempo has to stay dignified.
The *rāst* scale is:

C D $\overset{+}{E\flat}$ F G A $\overset{+}{B\flat}$ c

Cf. *Māhūr*.
Lit.: nos. 64, 121.

Rāst (Egypt). *Maqām* with the following scale: *rāst*, *duga*, *siga*, *jarka*, *nawa*, *ḥiṣār*, *auj*, *kardan*.

C D $\overset{+}{E\flat}$ F G A♭ $\overset{+}{B\flat}$ c

Sub maqāms are: *Suz-dil-'āra*, *Suz-nak*, and *Sasgar*, the "son of *'Ajam*."
Lit.: nos. 56, 121.

Rāst (Iran). See *Dastgah*.

Rāst Jadīd (Middle East). "The new *rāst*." *Maqām*.
Tone material:

C D $\overset{+}{E\flat}$ $\overset{(\sharp)}{F}$ G A $\overset{+}{B\flat}$ c

Lit.: no. 64.

Rāst kabīr (Middle East). *Maqām*.
Tone material:

C $\overset{(\sharp)}{D}$ $\overset{+}{E\flat}$ F G A $\overset{+}{B\flat}$ c

Lit.: no. 64.

Rāst kuk (Iran). The correct tuning of string instruments (e.g., *santur*). A tuning a fourth lower than *rast kuk* is called *chap kuk* ("left tuning").

Rāst-Shanbar (Arabia; Iran). *Maqām*: identical with *rāst* but characterized by the *shanbar* rhythm.
Lit.: no. 121.

Rata (Java). "Even," "medium." The term indicates a *gamelan* in which the intervals *baranggulu* (in *slendro*) and *penunggul* (*bem*)-*gulu* (in *pelog*) are of average (medium) size. Cf. *Luruh*; *Srigak*; *Laras lugu*.

Ratara (New Guinea). Song sung by women at marriages and childbirth. Cf. *Rano*; *Muno*.

Rateli gīt (Nepal). Wedding songs sung by relatives of the bridegroom while he is on his way to his bride.
Lit.: no. 133.

Rati (South India). See *Sāramati*.

Ratichandrikā (South India). *Janya rāga* of the 52nd *mēḷa* (*Rāmapriyā*).
Tone material:

C D♭ E F♯ G A c
c B♭ A G F♯ E D♭ C

Lit.: no. 139.

Ratika (South India). *Janya rāga* of the 47th *mēḷa* (*Suvarṇāṅgī*).
Tone material:

C E♭ D♭ E♭ F♯ G A B c
c B A G F♯ E♭ D♭ C

Lit.: no. 139.

Ratipatipriya (South India). *Janya rāga* of the 20th *mēḷa* (*Naṭabhairavī*).
Tone material:

C D E♭ G B♭ c
c B♭ G E♭ D C

Lit.: no. 139.

Ratipriyā (South India). *Janya rāga* of the 62nd *mēḷa* (*Riṣibhapriyā*).
Tone material:
C D F# E D F# G Bb Ab Bb c
c Bb Ab G F# E D C
Lit.: no. 139.

Ratipriyā (South India). See *Ratnabhānu* (62nd *asampūrṇa mēḷa*).

Ratnabhanu (South India). *Janya rāga* of the 62nd *mēḷa* (*Riṣabhapriyā*).
Tone material:
C D F# E D F# G Bb Ab Bb c
c Bb Ab Bb c Bb Ab G F# E D C
(c Bb Ab G F# E C D C)
Lit.: no. 139.

Ratnabhānu (South India). (1) The 62nd *asampūrṇa mēḷa-rāga* without *kaṭapayādi* prefix. (2) The 62nd *asampūrṇa mēḷa-rāga* with *kaṭapayādi* prefix called in the past *Ratipriyā*. See *Rāga* (South India).
Lit.: no. 139.

Ratnabhūṣaṇi (South India). *Janya rāga* of the 13th *mēḷa* (*Gāyakapriya*).
Tone material:
C Db E F G c
c G F E Db C
Lit.: no. 139.

Ratnagarbha (South India). *Janya rāga* of the 45th *mēḷa* (*Śubhapantuvarālī*).
Tone material:
C Db Eb F# B c
c B F# Eb Db C
Lit.: no. 139.

Ratnakānti (South India). *Janya rāga* of the 63rd *mēḷa* (*Latāṅgī*).
Tone material:
C D E F# G B c
c B G F# E D C
Lit.: no. 139.

Ratnakari (South India). *Janya rāga* of the 28th *mēḷa* (*Harikāmbhōji*).
Tone material:
C E F G Bb A Bb c
c Bb A G F D C
Lit.: no. 139.

Ratnamani (South India). *Janya rāga* of the 27th *mēḷa* (*Sarasāṅgī*).
Tone material:
C F E F D E F G Ab B c
c B Ab G F E D C
Lit.: no. 139.

Ratnāmbari (South India). *Janya rāga* of the 64th *mēḷa* (*Vāchaspati*).
Tone material:
C E F# G c
c Bb A G F# D C
Lit.: no. 139.

Ratnāṅgi (South India). The 2nd *mēḷa*:
C Db Ebb F G Ab Bb c
As *rāga* the same material is used. Veṅkaṭamakhin (17th century) called this *rāga* *Phenadyuti*. See *Rāga* (South India).
Lit.: no. 139.

Raudra (India). "Anger." One of the nine emotions (*rasas*) expressed in music. Cf. *Navarasa*; *Rasa*.

Raudrī (India). Term for the 8th *śruti*. The corresponding note is *antara ga*, a term used in music theory of the past. Cf. *Śruti*.

Raupyanaga (South India). *Janya rāga* of the 12th *mēḷa* (*Rūpāvati*).
Tone material:
C F G A# B c
c B G F Eb Db C (also: c A# B G F Eb Db C)
Lit.: no. 139.

Raupyanangam (South India). (1) The 12th *asampūrṇa-mēḷa-rāga* without *kaṭapayādi* prefix. (2) The 12th *asampūrṇa-mēḷa-rāga* with *kaṭapayādi* prefix was called *Rūpāvāti*. See *Rāga* (South India).
Lit.: no. 139.

Rau-rau (Malaysia). Bamboo rattle used by fishermen.

Ra'us woja (Flores—The Manggaray). Rice stalk clarinet with 2-3 finger holes. The instrument has numerous names: *lai waghe* in Nias, *oli-oli* in the Toba District (West Java), *dami* or *jarami* in the Sunda District, *de(r)men(ian)* in Central Java, *om-om* by the Toradja people (Sa'dan), *wa* in Atjeh (Sumatra), *pe-peon* in the Gayo District, *iyup-iyup* in the Alas districts, *kafu* in East Sumbawa, *damyadamyan* (an ancient Hindu-Javanese name).
Lit.: no. 163.

Ravaṇa (Moluccas). Term for *rabāna*.

Rāvaṇahasta (India). "The hand of Ravana." This Sanskrit term implies nothing else but a *sarangi* with six strings. The name *rāvaṇahasta* probably refers to the upper part of the neck which resembles the form of an outstretched hand. Cf. *Rāvaṇastron*.

Rāvaṇahatta (India; Rajasthan—Bhil). Obsolete fiddle with two horsehair strings and a body made of a coconut shell. Below the two main strings are strung several (3-13) sympathetic wire strings. Cf. *Rāvaṇastron*; *Rāvaṇatta*.

Rāvaṇastron (India). An obscure ancient fiddle with two strings and a small cylindrical corpus covered at the top and open at the bottom. The instrument is almost unknown and not in use by Indian professional musicians. Cf. *Rāvaṇahasta(m)*; *Rovana*.
Lit.: no. 255.

Rāvaṇatta (West India). A fiddle with hemispherical body of coconut, a parchment belly, two strings attached to lateral pegs. The bow passes between the strings. Cf. *Rāvaṇahatta*.

Ravekinge (South Africa—Hottentots; Bushman). Primitive lute, generally plucked, rarely bowed. Cf. *Ramkie*; *Xguthe*.

Ravicandrikā (South India). See *Ravichandrika*.

Ravichandrikā (South India). *Janya rāga* of the 28th *mēḷa* (*Harikāmbhōji*).
Tone material:
C D E F A B♭ A ♭
c B♭ A F E D C
Lit.: no. 139.

Ravikiraṇi (South India). *Janya rāga* of the 16th *mēḷa* (*Chakravāka*).
Tone material:
C E F B♭ A B♭ c
c B♭ A G F E D♭ C
Lit.: no. 139.

Ravikriyā (South India). See *Raghulīlā* (42nd *asampūrṇa mēḷa*).

Raviprabhāvali (South India). *Janya rāga* of the 38th *mēḷa* (*Jalārṇava*).
Tone material:
C D♭ E♭♭ F♯ A♭ c
c A♭ G F♯ E♭♭ D♭ E♭♭ C
Lit.: no. 139.

Ravipratāpi (South India). *Janya rāga* of the 70th *mēḷa* (*Nāsikabhūṣaṇi*).
Tone material:
C D♯ E F♯ A c
c A F♯ E D♯ C
Lit.: no. 139.

Ravipriya (South India). *Janya rāga* of the 57th *mēḷa* (*Siṃhendramadhyama*).
Tone material:
C D E♭ F♯ B c
c B F♯ E♭ D C
Lit.: no. 139.

Ravisvarūpiṇī (South India). *Janya rāga* of the 63rd *mēḷa* (*Latāṅgī*).
Tone material:
C E F♯ G A♭ B c
c B A♭ G F♯ E C
Lit.: no. 139.

Ravula-ravula (India). Marthi term for rattle. Cf. *Jhañ-jhana.*

Rawāsīn (Ancient Persia; Khorasan; Turkmenia). Popular instrumental piece. See *Tarā'iq.*

Rāwī (Old Arabia). Reciter.

Rawnaq Numa (Middle East). *Maqām.*
Tone material:
+   (♭)   (♯) +
B♭ C D♯ E F♯ G A B♭ c d e
Lit.: no. 64.

Raysakanada (North India). An obscure *rāga* consisting of phrases taken from the *rāgas Naiki-kanada* and *Bahar.* The tone material cannot be stated distinctly as it varies according to the performer's preference of any of the constituent features taken from the indicated *rāgas*. The *vādis* usually are: C, G.
Lit.: no. 138.

Razfa (Arabia). Popular songs sung at weddings by a chorus.

Réa (East Flores). The Manggaray term for a flat bamboo or rattan ring placed as a part of a mouthpiece around the node of a flute. Cf. *Nuren*; *Klekor*; *Glekor*; *Feko*; *Sunding.*
Lit.: no. 166.

Rebāb (*Rabāb*) (North Africa; Turkey; Arabia; Iran; Southeast Asia). Generic term for bowed lutes in the Islamic world. The widely popular spike fiddle appears in manifold shapes. Its corpus can be rectangular, circular, boat-shaped, pear-shaped, hemispherical, pandore-like, or with open chest. The rectangular instrument usually has one gut string, often provided with an extra peg for a second string. The handle is round and pierces the body. Its lower end, a spike, can be of wood or of iron.

The one-string *rebāb* of Egypt bears the name *rabāb-esh-shā'er*, the "poet's fiddle." When there are two strings (tuned a fifth apart, the lower one tuned to the key-note of the *maqām* performed), the instrument is called *rabāb-el-mughannee*, the "singer's fiddle." A very closely related fiddle with a hemispherical body and a Persian name, is the *kamānjah.* It is the best known bowed instrument in the Middle East, Turkestan, and Kashmir.

The North African *rebāb* has a wooden, narrow, boat-shaped corpus, the peg box of which is bent backward at right angles of the neck. The instrument has two strings: one is a gut string and the other is made of twisted goat or camel hair. Another, less elaborate form is the *amizad* of the Algerian Tuareg and the Moroccon Sus-shluh. The latter call the instrument *ribab.* This has one or two strings made of horsehair.

The corpus of the Egyptian *rebāb* consists of a trapezoidal frame, the front and back of which are covered with skin, resembling the shape of an angular frame drum, a simple neck, and one or two strings made of horse, goat, or camel hair. The *rebāb* (*rabob*; *robab*; *rubāb*) of Afghanistan generally has a pear-shaped body, three double strings, and one metal string, below which are strung several metal resonance strings.

The *rebāb* of Malaysia is a spike fiddle with three strings. The various parts of the instrument are: peg box and top of the neck, *pucuk rebong*; the pegs, *mahulas* ("ears"); the neck, *batang* ("stem"); strings, *tali*; bridge, *pacat*; body, *muka*; resonance hole, *susu*; front of the corpus, *kulit perut lembu* ("skin of the cow's belly").

The *saw tai* of Thailand is a very beautifully built *rebāb* type decorated with ivory or mother of pearl. It has three strings.

The Cambodian instrument, *tro khmer*, has a similar shape and an equally beautiful appearance. Cf. *Saw sam sai.*

On the Philippines one finds a small *rebāb* type with three strings. The Javanese *rebāb*, usually played by the leader of the *gamelan* ensemble, has a heart-shaped wooden corpus and a long neck with long pegs. The instrument has two copper wire strings tuned to the notes *gulu* and *nem* or *penunggul* (*bem*) and *lima.* The corpus shows at its back a circular ornament of small holes. Its front is covered with buffalo intestine or bladder parchment. The various parts of this spike fiddle are: the back, *pentat*; the little ornamental holes at the back, *nawa*; back and sides of the instrument, *batok*; belly, *babad*, *kenḍangan*, or *tilam*; the spike, *sikil* ("foot"); the widened lower end of the spike, *palemahan* (*lemah* = "foot") or *songgabuwana* (*sungga* ["standard"]; *buwana* ["world"]). The lowest point of the spike is called *tunjung.* The neck is *jeneng* or *watangan*; the upper part of the neck, *daga* or *sirah* ("head"); the top of the head, *menur.* The broadening of the lower part of the neck is called *popor kangduwur* (*umpak ngingil*) and the widened part of the *sikil* is called *popor kangngisor* (*umpak ngandap*).

The two copper strings are called *kawat*: the first is called *jindra* or *jaler* ("male"), the second *laranangis* ("weeping virgin") or *istri* ("female"). The pegs are called *mangol*, the knob of each peg is *kupingan* ("ear"), the teak wood bridge *santen* or *srenten.* A folded banana leaf functions as a mute which is called *ening*, *sumping*, or *srawing.* Both strings together are called *penganten anyar* ("the new bridal couple").

The bow is called *kosok* or *chengkok*; its wooden part is *rangkung* and the hair *yoga.* See also *Blongsong*; *Ponṭang.*

The *rebāb* of Sumatra has a curved wooden body covered with skin. A stick is pushed through the corpus and at its lower end it forms a blunt spike. The lowest end of the spike is a button that serves as string holder.

The Balinese instrument is of much lesser importance than the Javanese *rebāb.* Roughly it has the same size and features. See Lit. no. 197.

The parts of the Balinese instrument are: the loose bow, *sarad*; the pushed bow, *nongsok*; the drawn bow, *medet.* The full bowing of long sustained tones of unequal speed and pressure is called *ngetetang.* The *rebāb* is usually found in the *gambuh* ensemble where it plays unison with the *sulings.*

The Sundanese *rebāb* differs from the Javanese by the material of the sound box. The Sundanese is always made of wood, the Javanese generally of coconut shell and rarely of wood. The parts of the Sundanese instrument are: neck, *tihang*; upper part, *puchuk*; body, *bobokon*; sound "board" (made of buffalo bladder), *wangkis*; the bridge, *inang* ("breast"); pegs, *peureut* ("to wring"), bow, *pangeset.*
Lit.: nos. 132, 163, 254.

Rebābah (Egypt). Fiddle with a pear-shaped body and with two strings.

Rebāb batok besar (West Java). A large *ohyan.*

Rebāb batok kechil (Sunda District). See *Ohyan.*

Rebāna (*Geda*) (Flores). Frame drum of various sizes introduced by the Mohammedans into Islamic parts of the Indonesian region. It is beaten during prayers. Other names are *geda* in Lio; *genda* in the Manggaray.
Lit.: no. 254.

Rebāna (Sunda District). Also *Rabāna*; *Robāna.* See *Terbang.*

Rebāna Ibu (Malaysia). Large frame drum. In the frame are placed jingles (*genta*); the body (*baluh*) is covered with goatskin. Cf. *Rebāna peningkah.*

Rebāna peningkah (Malaysia). A frame drum with jingles. It is smaller than the *rebāna ibu.*

Rebang (Flores). See *Remba.*

Rebong (Bali). Music accompanying love scenes in the *wayang* play.
Lit.: no. 197.

Rebŏp (Sumatra—Gayo). Term for *rebāb.*

Rechep (Java). The incline of the outer edge of a gong (following the *pasu*).

Redang (Flores; Maumere). A dancing rattle mounted on a stick. The rattle is made of a dried coconut shell filled with small stones. Lit.: no. 166.

Redap (Southwest Sumatra). Drum; term for *terbang.*

Redep (Java). See *Tabang-tabang*; *Terbang.* Cf. *Rebāna.*

Redep (Sumatra; West Coast). Term for *rebāna* (Flores).

Rēgupti (South India). See *Rēvagupti.*

Rehaw (Arabia). *Maqām*. The name *Rēhaw* is said to refer to the city of Urfa (Edessa). This *maqām* has the same scale as *Bayat* and is little known in Egypt. A melody in *Rēhaw* should begin with the note *nawa* (e.g., G), turn then to *duga* (D) and end with *jarga* (F). Singers of Aleppo call *Rēhaw* "Son of Huseni"; other singers state that its origin is *Bayat.* A simplified pattern that shows the tone material is:

G A B♭ c (d) c B♭ A G F ($\overset{+}{\text{E}}$♭ C D)

Lit.: no. 121.

Rehu (New Zealand – Maori). Flute.

Rei (Japan). Buddhist handbell (with clapper). Lit.: no. 185.

Reisei (Japan). Melodic pattern in *shamisen* music.
Lit.: no. 187.

Rejang (Bali). Also *mendet*. A festive ceremonial dance-procession performed in the temple by unmarried girls.
Lit.: no. 197.

Rejong (Bali). Also *rijong*; *reyong*. An instrument that consists of two small metal kettles (differently tuned) attached to both ends of a wooden stick in such a manner that they can vibrate freely when beaten. The player has the stick lying across his lap. Generally two *rejongs* are in use and perform the following four notes with the kettles. The scale produced is:

G $\overset{+}{\text{A}}$ $\overset{+}{\text{B}}$ d (*deng, dung, dang, ding*)

Rejongs appear in all *gamelan angklung* ensembles, occasionally called *klentengan.*
Lit.: no. 197.

Reketora (Flores). See *Kenite.*

Rekhu (North India). War song; similar to the *tappa.* The text consists of about a dozen couplets.

Remba (East Flores). A fiddle made of half a coconut shell, covered with palmleaf or cardboard. The instrument has one string made of palm fibre. Its name varies: in Larantuka (East Flores) it is called *corra* or *sason(g)*; in Maumere it is called *rebang.* Cf. *Reneka*; *Wu* (Flores).
Lit.: no. 166.

Remel (Turkey). One of the numerous *usul.* Cf. *Raml.*
Lit.: no. 243.

Remo-remo (East New Guinea – Ruro; Papua). Long open-ended vertical bamboo flute with 2-3 holes. A particular technique is required when overblowing and producing the upper octave tones.
Lit.: no. 303.

Renai (East India; Orissa). Simple fiddle with two strings.

Rendang (Java). Long, narrow drum.
Lit.: no. 255.

Reneka (Flores). A Sikka term implying the bridge on the *remba*, across which the single string is strung.
Lit.: no. 166.

Reng (Iran). The instrumental conclusion of the *dastgāh* performed in strict rhythm. Cf. *Dastgāh* (structure).

Reng (Flores). See *Uwe kotang.*

Renggan (Java). Ornament.

Renggong (Sunda District). Colotomic gong pattern; ornament.

Rengin (Japan). An ensemble of singers.

Rengkong (West Java). A bamboo scraper; stick with notches. If there are more than the usual pair of scraper sticks the group is called *saaleutan.* The sticks are used to accompany the *hatong* music. Other names for scraper sticks are *rungkut*; *otot.* In the Solo valley the accompaniment of the *wayang* tales is made by the *engket-engket*, a similar type as the *rengkong.*
Lit.: no. 163.

Renjab (Bali). The modern style in which the tones of figurations in *gamelan* music overlap considerably and thus create a "filled up" sound, much fuller than the ancient sound of *lamba rangkap.* Cf. *Lamba rangkap.*

Rentang (Java). See *Renteng.*

Renteng (*Rentang*) (West Java). The biggest of the single row *bonangs.* It consists of two wings of beating kettles forming a rectangle. The short wing—with the lowest sounding kettles—is called *kachibong* and *indung.* The longer wing is called *renteng*, occasionally also *anak.* Cf. *Bonang.*
Lit.: no. 159.

Reog (East Java). Name of the *ḍogḍog* drum (reference is here made to an East Javanese play [*jatilan*]). Cf. *Ḍogḍog*; *Jedor*; *Reyog.*
Lit.: no. 303.

Reong (Bali). Two small gongs played by two musicians who provide an inter-lacing form of accompaniment, usually based on simple sequences of two intervals.
Lit.: no. 265.

Reong angklung (Bali). In the *gamelan angklung* two *rejongs* are used which produce the required four-note scale material. See *Rejong.*
Lit.: no. 197.

Reon gong (Bali). In the *gamelan gong* two *rejongs*, each with two gongs, are used.
Lit.: no. 197.

Reong kebyar (Bali). As with *reong angklung* and *reon gong* , the *reong kebyar* means the use of 2-6 modern *rejongs* in the *gamelan gong kebyar.* See *Rejong.*
Lit.: no. 197.

Rep (Java). Soft.

Repha (India). One of the ancient 10 basic ways of touching *vīṇā* strings (*dhatu*); striking the string(s) with all fingers close together.
Lit.: no. 292.

Req (*Riqq*) (Arabia; Egypt; Syria). Middle Eastern small frame drum with a circular frame, one skin, and no snare strings.
Lit.: no. 250.

Re rai (Thailand). Bagpipe.
Lit.: no. 255.

Rere (Celebes). Cf. *Rerre.*

Rerre (Central Celebes; Philippines). "Tuning fork idiophone"—see *Buncacan.* Other names of this instrument are: *genggong sakai*, *ore-ore*, *ta-uto*, *druri-dana*, *kakonti*, *pare*, *sase saheng*, *tala lo.*
Lit.: no. 132.

Resik (Java). See *Mleng*; *Pleng.*

Rēva (*Rēwa*) (South India). *Janya rāga* of the 36th *mēḷa* (*Chalanāṭa*).
Tone material:
C D# E A# B c
c B A# E D# C
Lit.: no. 139.

Rēvagupti (South India). *Janya rāga* of the 15th *mēḷa* (*Māyāmāḷavagauḷa*).
Tone material:
C D♭ E G A♭ c
c A♭ G E D♭ C
Lit.: no. 139.

Rēvati (South India). *Janya rāga* of the 2nd *mēḷa* (*Ratnangi*).
Tone material:
C D♭ F G B♭ c
c B♭ G F D♭ C
Lit.: no. 139.

Revith (Ancient Israel). A rattle stick similar to the sistrum of Egypt. The instrument appeared in post-biblical time.

Rewa (North India). Rare *rāga* ascribed to the *Purvi thāta*. It is known in two versions:
Tone material:
(a) C D♭ E G A♭ c
c A♭ G E D♭ C
(b) C D♭ E G A♭ c
c A♭ G (F♯) E D♭ C
Lit.: no. 138.

Reyog (East Java). Folk drama in which trance states of the performers are custom. The same type of drama in Central Java is called *jaran kepang* and in West Java *ebeg*. Cf. *Reog*.

Reyong (Indonesia; Lombok Isl.). A large *bonang*-shaped drum.
Lit.: no. 162.

Reyong (Bali). See *Trompong*.

Rgya-gling (pronounced: *ja-ling*) (Tibet). "Indian pipe." An oboe type with seven finger holes. This instrument is used in pairs. It is related to the *sanayi* south and west of the Himalayas. Its wooden tube topped by a widely flaring copper bell creates penetrating sounds.
Lit.: no. 143.

Rgyud (Tibet). String.

Rgyud-mangs (Tibet). Zither; harp. The Mongolian term is *Yatag*.

Rgyud; Sgrog; Ching-ba; Preng-ba; T'a-gu (Tibet). A string instrument.

Rhab (Sumatra—Toba). *Rebāb* type.

Rheita (Algeria; Morocco). Term for *gaita* when used in French colonial military bands.

Ri (*Re*) (India). Abbreviation for *ṛṣabha*; tone syllable representing the second degree of a scale (e.g., *re* is D if *sa* is C).

Riabuh (India; Manipur). Transverse flute with one finger hole.
Lit.: no. 252.

Riang wulu baba (Flores). See *Baba*; *Go bato*.

Ribāb (North Africa; especially Morocco). Simple form of the *rebāb*.

Richek (Afghanistan; Iran). Small spike fiddle with a rectangular wooden box as body, and a slim neck with two strings.
Lit.: no. 120.

Richik (*Rinchik*) (Bali). Small cymbal (cf. *Gamelan angklung*). Cf. *Cheng-cheng*; *Ke(n)chek*; *Ke(chi)cher*.
Lit.: no. 197.

Ridu (Flores; Ngada). Xylophone with 4-6 loose keys. In the Manggaray this instrument is called *do'u da*. See *Preson*.
Lit.: no. 166.

Rijak (Turkestan). A spike fiddle (*kemānje* type) consisting of a coconut corpus with three resonance holes and without frets. It has two gut and one wire strings.
Lit.: no. 255.

Rijong (Bali). See *Rejong*.

Rikud (Israel-Hebrew). Dance.

Rīṃkari (South India). *Janya rāga* of the 32nd *mēḷa* (*Rāgavardhanī*).
Tone material:
C D♯ F E F G B♭ c
c B♭ G F D♯ C
Lit.: no. 139.

Rimse (Japan). Dance songs.

Rina (*Sua*) (India; Maikal Hills—Gond). The Gond call *rina* a song sung only by women. In olden times the *rina* songs were sung to the Queen of the Gond kingdom.
Lit.: no. 134.

Rinchik (Bali). Small cymbals with a high, gentle silvery tone. They appear in dance music and theatrical performances. See *Setukat.*
Lit.: nos. 163, 197.

Rinchinkan (West Java). Preludes and interludes performed on the *kolenang.* Cf. *Rinchik* (*Setukat*).
Lit.: no. 163.

Rinda (Celebes—Bone). Jew's harp. Among other names of the instrument are: *yanon* (or *saga-saga*) in Thailand; *ka mien* (or *saga-saga*) in Assam; *an-oin* in Malacca; *ego* in Flores.
Lit.: no. 254.

Rindik (Bali). A xylophone used in the *gamelan pejogedan*, a village orchestra consisting of xylophones. The *rindik* has 11 bamboo tubes and has a range similar to that of the *gender.* Cf. *Joged.*
Lit.: no. 197.

Rinḍing (Java). A small jew's harp. There are two types:
1. *Rinding aren*, made of wood.
2. *Rinding wesi*, made of iron.

The latter has a circular shape and its tongue is made of brass or copper.
Lit.: nos. 163, 254.

Ringgit tyang (Java). See *Wayang wong.*

Rinyūgaku (Japan). Music imported from India and Indo-China and used in *tōgaku* performances. See *Gagaku.*
Lit.: no. 185.

Riqq (Egypt). Frame drum (without snare string). Cf. *Req.*
Lit.: no. 190.

Rirandi (West Kenya—Gusii). Gourd horn.
Lit.: no. 299.

Riṣabhapriyā (South India). Occasionally also *Ruṣabhapriyā*). The 62nd *mēḷa*:
C D E F♯ G A♭ B♭ c
The *rāga* with the same name has the same tone material.
Lit.: no. 139.

Riṣe (*Risheh*) (Arabia). The plectrum used in *qānūn* and *'ūd* playing.

Rishabha (India). Tone name. In abbreviated form: *ri* (or *re*). See *Ṛṣabha.* See *Ri.*

Risheh (Arabia). See *Riṣē.*

Rishi (South India). Name of the 7th *chakra* in the system of the 72 *mēḷas*. See *Rāga* (South India).
Lit.: no. 136.

Riti (Senegal; Gambia). Term for a one-stringed spike fiddle made of a calabash. The string is made of a bundle of horsehair. In Guinea the *riti* can be found with four strings. Cf. *Endingidi.*
Lit.: nos. 206, 218.

Rīticandrikā (South India). See *Ratichandrikā.*

Rītigaula (South India). *Janya rāga* of the 20th *mēḷa* (*Naṭabhairavī*).
Tone material:
C E♭ D E♭ F B♭ A♭ F (G) B♭ c
c B♭ A♭ F E♭ F G F E♭ D C
Lit.: no. 139.

Ritsu (*Ritsusen*) (Japan). Mode. "Legal scale." One of the basic scales used in *shōmyō* and *gagaku*. Its material is: *kyū* (usually interpreted as the Western D); *shō*, E; [*ei-shō*, F]; *kaku*, G; *chi*, A; *U*, B; [*ei-u*] c.
Lit.: no. 136.

Ritsu (Japan). Humming, singing with closed mouth. In solemn music this is believed to represent the female principle and the period of autumn and winter. Cf. *Kwaigo-no-ben.*

Ritsu (Japan). Semitone. The term indicates also the 12 semitones of the chromatic scale and refers to the Chinese *lü-lü.*
Lit.: no. 225.

Ritsu-go (Japan). *Kyo-ge.*

Riuteki (Japan). *Ryūteki.*

Riwi-riwi-löchö (Flores; Nias). Bull roarer. See *Jata* (Flores).
Lit.: no. 163.

Rkang-dung (Tibet). See *rKang-dung.*
Lit.: no. 143.

Rkang gling (Tibet). See *rKang-gling.*
Lit.: no. 143.

Rnaom (Kampuchea). Bamboo flute.
Lit.: no. 215.

Rnga (*Rnga*) (Tibet). General term for drum.

Rnga bsangs (Tibet). See *Rnga gsangs.*

Rnga-chung (Tibet). "Small drum." A hand-held drum (*damaru* form). Its body is made either of two human skull bones or wooden cups affixed to each other by their tops. The drumheads are often covered by human skin. Around the waist two narrow strips of thick cloth or leather with little weights at their freely swinging ends rattle against the drumheads when the instrument is twirled to and fro by means of a handle. Cf. *Damaru.*
Lit.: no. 143.

Rnga dbyug (Tibet). Also *rnga lchag*. Curved and slightly flexible drumsticks used for striking the *ch'os-rnga.*
Lit.: no. 143.

Rnga-dpon (Tibet). Chief drummer.

Rnga-gsangs (*Rnga-bsangs*) (Tibet). Strong beat; loud roll on the big drum.

Rnga-lchag (Tibet). See *Rnga dbyug.*

Rnga-lpags (Tibet). Drum skin.

Rnga-pa (Tibet). Drummer.

Rnga-sgra (Tibet). The sound of the (kettle)-drum.

Rnga-shin (Tibet). Wooden body of a drum.

Rnga-shon (Tibet). Drum music.

Rnga-yu (Tibet). Handle of a big drum.

Robāb (Afghanistan). (1) Short lute with (usually) two strings. The Pamir instrument can have six strings. (2) Term for *rabāb*. Cf. *Rebāb*; *Rabōb.*
Lit.: no. 120.

Robāna (Sunda District). See *Rebāna* (*Terbang*).

Robe (Flores). The smallest among the many forms of jew's harp. See *Genggo*; *Ego.*
Lit.: no. 166.

Robēka (*Sason*) (Flores; Maumere). Calabash fiddle with a small round corpus, a long, narrow neck and one or two strings. In Lio (Ende) it is called *mbeka* or *sato.*
Lit.: no. 166.

Roberok (New Guinea). See *Roboro.*

Roboro (New Guinea – Papua). Also *Roberok.* Drum.

Roding (Central Vietnam – Moi). Tube zither with 6, 10, or 12 strings.
Lit.: no. 303.

Roei (Japan). Ancient form of chanted Chinese and Japanese poems. They were popular during the Heian period (794-1192 A.D.) and were used in *gagaku*. See *Gagaku*.
Lit.: no. 185.

Roèl (*Anak*) (Sunda District). See *Indung*.

Rohiṇī (India). Name of the 19th *śruti*. The corresponding note name is *ṣaṭśruti dha* (*kaiśikī ni*), terms used in music theory of the past. Cf. *Śruti*.

Roiza (Burma; Shan State; Kachin). Double reed pipe. The two cylindrical pipes have metal reeds. The melody pipe has eight front finger holes and two rear thumbholes. The thinner drone pipe has no finger holes.
Lit.: no. 252.

Roja (Flores). A women's dance performed for four weeks, each day from sundown to sunrise, in order to protect the village from evil. The proper name is *hama roja*, "stamping-singing." The songs sung to the dance have texts that are said to be in an ancient language understood only by very few persons. Cf. *Hama roja*; *Emunak rua*. A male round dance, the equivalent of the *roja*, is the *hama* (*opak oron*).
Lit.: no. 166.

Rojeh (Java). A thin cymbal without a boss. It is tuned either to *barang* or *nem*. It is used in the *gamelan munggang* and *koḍok ngorek*.
Lit.: no. 163.

Rokeang (Kampuchea). Bell.
Lit.: no. 255.

Rok'on fada (North Nigeria; Niger; Chad; Ghana – Hausa). Ceremonial music (*tambari*; *kakaki*; *farai*; *k'afo*; *ganga*).

Roku-dan (Japan). A well known *koto* piece. The title means "six *dan*" (six variations, sections), a piece based on a leading theme (without any singing). Cf. *Dan*; *Go-dan*; *Shichi-dan*; *Hachi-dan*; *Ku-dan*.
Lit.: no. 185.

Roku gen-kin (Japan). See *Roku-kin*.

Roku-hyōshi (Japan). See *Mu-hyōshi*.

Roku kaké (Japan). See *Kaké*.

Roku-kin (*Roku gen-kin*) (Japan). "The six-stringed zither." Its six silken string pass over two bridges, one placed at the upper, the other at the lower end of the sounding board. The strings are plucked with thumb and first finger of the right hand. Cf. *Ni-genkin*.
Lit.: no. 255.

Rol-cha (West Tibet). Cymbal.

Rol-gsum (Tibet). "The three *rol*," instrumental music: wind instruments, drums, and cymbals.
Lit.: no. 143.

Rol-mo (Tibet). (1) Term for music in general; to perform music; musical instruments. (2) A pair of cymbals with flat rims and wide bosses. Leather or cloth handles are attached to their centers. The upper cymbal strikes the lower one in a vertical motion. Cf. *Sil-snyan*.
Lit.: no. 143.

Rome (Malagasy Republic – Betsileo). Drum with a cylindrical body.
Lit.: no. 251.

Romus (Iran). Modern fiddle with 4-5 strings.
Lit.: no. 255.

Romy (Malagasy Republic). See *Rome*.

Ronda (Flores – Manggaray). A dance. Rows of 6-10 men and women, one dancer behind the other, stamp their feet and sing.
Lit.: no. 166.

Rondro (Malagasy Republic—Tanala). A piece of wood is inserted into a wooden (rice) mortar. The inserted wood is struck with wooden sticks. In the past this instrument was used to create welcoming sounds to greet chieftains. At present it is used as a toy. Cf. *Kakanika-kanika.*
Lit.: no. 251.

Roneat-dec (Kampuchea). Instead of bamboo keys, as the other *roneat* types have, the *roneat dec* has 21 iron keys placed upon a rectangular box. The keys show diatonic tuning and a range of:

Cf. *Mohori*; *Piphat.*
Lit.: nos. 153, 254.

Roneat ek (Kampuchea). A boat-shaped xylophone with 21 bamboo keys. Tuning and range are:

Cf. *Mohori*; *Rang nat*; *Piphat.*
Lit.: no. 49.

Roneat thum (Kampuchea). A boat-shaped xylophone with 17 bamboo keys. It is tuned diatonically and has the following range:

Cf. *Ranat thum*; *Mohori*; *Piphat.*
Lit.: no. 49.

Ronggeng (Java). Female dancers who sing and dance; accompanied by a *gamelan* ensemble. Cf. *Taleḍek.*
Lit.: no. 158.

Ronggeng doger (West Java). A dance of erotic character. It is favored particularly in the Tasik district and is accompanied by a *ketuk tilu.*
Lit.: no. 163.

Ronggeng gunung (West Java). A *gamelan* that plays the accompaniment to the *ronggeng* dance; also to narrative songs about olden times. The *gamelan* consists of three *ketuk*, *kendang*, and *gong.* Cf. *Ketuk tilu.*
Lit.: no. 163.

Rongi (Japan). The dialogue section; the concluding item of the fourth *dan* of the *ha* part of *noh* performances. *Rongi* also indicates the instructional part of Buddhist chant.
Lit.: no. 187.

Rongo (West Africa; Loango). Horn made of an elephant tusk. As the tip is too brittle for being cut, the blowhole is cut a small distance away on the side of the tusk.
Lit.: no. 255.

Rongo (Sudan). Xylophone with 10 keys.

Rong ruyh (Vietnam—Moi). Rattle.

Rong thang (Thailand). Tone name. Cf. *Thang.*

Rōnin (Japan). Samurai without a master and without rank and privileges, having joined the basket-hatted *komosō.*
Lit.: no. 185.

Ronmonea (Kampuchea). Small flat hand drum. Cf. *Mohori.*
Lit.: no. 153.

Roonup (Northeast Thailand; Laos). Finger holes on the *kaen* tubes.
Lit.: no. 203.

Rooria (New Zealand—Maori). Jew's harp.

Roorowera (Solomon Isl.—Malaita). Lullabies; women's songs.
Lit.: no. 318.

Rorañjakan (South India). *Janya rāga* of the 28th *mēḷa* (*Harikāmbhōji*).
Tone material:
C F G A B♭ c
c B♭ A G F C
Lit.: no. 139.

Roria (New Zealand—Maori). See *Rooria.*
Lit.: no. 7.

Rōsai (Japan). The *rosai bushi*, short songs. Their names are taken from their creator, Rosai, a Buddhist priest. The *rosai* reached their greatest popularity in the 17th century. At the present time they are almost forgotten.
Lit.: no. 3.

Rovana (Ancient India). The doubtful name of an obscure fiddle. Allegedly identical with or related to the equally obscure *ravanastron.*
Lit.: no. 254.

Ro-yei (Japan). See *Roei.*
Lit.: no. 225.

Royin(a)-ghum (Iran). Kettledrum with a metal body.
Lit.: no. 255.

Royina-nay (Iran). Metal trumpet.
Lit.: no. 255.

Ṛṣabha (*Rishabha*) (Abbreviated: *ri* or *re*). (1) Sanskrit tone name of the second degree of the heptatonic (diatonic) scale. Cf. *Ṣaḍja* (*Sa*), under the heading of which are listed all tone names. (2) See *Jāti.*

R'shuth (Ancient Israel). The opening part of a sacred hymn. Vocal interpolations are: *k'rovah*; *jozer*; *maaravoth*; *s'liḥah*; *avodah.* Cf. *Siluk.*
Lit.: no. 12.

Rtsing (Tibet). "Rough," a roaring, throaty voice production in sacred chant. This is applied particularly by the *rgyud stod-pa*, the "upper school" of Lhasa.
Lit.: no. 143.

Rtsub-po (Tibet). Musical term for loud, wild singing or playing an instrument.
Lit.: no. 143.

Ru (Malaysia). Tone syllable representing the second note of scales (e.g., *wayang*). See *Chi* (Malaysia) for material of two frequently used scales.

Rūang (Thailand). Instrumental suite; generally a medley of freely linked pieces. The end of the last item, called *lā*, is a stereotyped coda that is used in every *rūang* performance; it is *phlēng reo* and usually has 16 measures played in slow tempo.
Lit.: no. 206.

Ruba (Oceania; Papua—Elema). Bull roarer.
Lit.: no. 311.

Rub'aa (Arabia). Microtones (quartertones). Cf. *Jagā* (*Yagā*), under the heading of which are listed all notes and tone names within the range of two octaves.

Rubāb (North India). See *Rebāb.*

Rubā'i (Iran). See *Dūbeiti.*

Rubembe (Congo). See *Lubembe.*

Ruchiramaṇi (South India). *Janya rāga* of the 62nd *mēḷa* (*Riṣabhapriyā*).
Tone material:
C E F♯ G A♭ B♭ A♭ c
c A♭ G F♯ E D C
Lit.: no. 139.

Ruchiraṅgi (South India). *Janya rāga* of the 36th *mēḷa* (*Chalanāṭa*).
Tone material:
C D♯ F A♯ B c
c B A♯ F D♯ C
Lit.: no. 139.

Rud (Arabia; Iran). (1) Ancient Arabic term for music. (2) Ancient Persian term for lute with a long neck, the forerunner of the *shāhrūd.*

Rūda (Iran). String.
Lit.: no. 255.

Rudieng sulu (*Engsulu*) (Borneo—Sea Dayak). Jew's harp made of brass. If a young man plays this instrument, it means that he seeks a girl's favor and her hand.
Lit.: no. 254.

Rud-jama (Iran). Term for lute.

Rūdra (*Chakra*) (South India). Name of the 11th *chakra* in the system of the 72 *mēḷas*. Cf. *Rāga* (South India).
Lit.: no. 139.

Rudrapriya (South India). *Janya rāga* of the 22nd *mēḷa* (*Kharaharapriyā*).
Tone material:
C D E♭ F G A B♭ c
c B♭ G F E♭ D C
Lit.: no. 139.

Rudra vīṇā (India). This instrument, which appears mainly in the south, has the shape of a lute. The second gourd is small and attached to the top of the tubular (bamboo) neck where it ends in a backward curved animal head. The *rudra vīṇā* has 6-7 wire strings and 2-3 bourdon strings which run along the left side of the fingerboard. The strings are plucked by the player with his fingernails. Cf. *Vīṇā*.
Lit.: no. 254.

Ruganira (Uganda). See *Akakyenkye.*

Ruh (*Ru*) (Malaysia). Tone name. See the list shown under the heading of *Saron*; see also *Chi* (Malaysia). Cf. *Bonang* (Malaysia).

Ruhamo (Congo—Wanande). Large drum that can be beaten only when the chief gives the order.
Lit.: no. 26.

Rujū (*Qaflah*) (Arabia). See *Muwashaḥ*.

Rukinzo (Central Africa; Urundi—Warundi). Royal drum.
Lit.: no. 26.

Rukmāmbari (South India). *Janya rāga* of the 15th *mēḷa* (*Māyāmāḷavagauḷa*).
Tone material:
C D♭ E G B c
c B G E D♭ C
Lit.: no. 139.

Rukmangi (South India). *Janya rāga* of the 8th *mēḷa* (*Hamumattōḍi*).
Tone material:
C D♭ E♭ G B♭ c
c B♭ G E♭ D♭ C
Lit.: no. 139.

Rumana (Thailand). Frame drum with one skin.
Lit.: nos. 184, 255.

Rumwong (Northeast Thailand). Popular entertainment at fairs in which men pay a small fee for being permitted to dance for a while with female members of the group of entertainers.
Lit.: no. 203.

Ru-nenga (South Africa; Transvaal). See *Mu-nenga.*

Rungkut (West Java). See *Rengkong.*

Ruoia (Micronesia; Gilbert Isl.). Group dances.

Rūpācati (South India). See *Rūpāvatī.*

Rūpāciti (South India). See *Rūpāvatī.*

Rūpak (North India). See *Tāla.*

Rūpaka ālāpti (India). See *Ālāpti*; *Khyāl.*

Rūpaka tāla (South India). See *Tāla.*

Rūpamañjari Mallar (North India). A very rare *rāga* subordinated to the *Kafi thāta*. It belongs to the *Mallar* family.
Tone material:
C D E F G (A) B♭ (B) c
c B♭ (A) G F E (E♭) D C; *Vādis*: F, C
Lit.: no. 138.

Rūpāvatī (South India). (1) The 12th *mēḷa*:
C D♭ E♭ F G A♯ B c
(2) As *rāga, Rūpāvatī* can be performed at any time. The tone material is the same as that of the 12th *mēḷa*. Veṅkaṭamakhin (17th century) called this *rāga Rūpaciti*, also *Rūpācati*, *Rūpyanaga*, or *Raupyanaga*.
Lit.: no. 139.

Rura (New Hebrides; Leprosy Isl. Opa). Bamboo flute with three finger holes.
Lit.: no. 255.

Ruṣabhapriyā (South India). See *Riṣabhapriyā*.

Ruṣabhavāhiṇi (South India). See *Rushabhavāhiṇi.*

Rushabhavāhiṇi (South India). *Janya rāga* of the 42nd *mēḷa* (*Raghupriyā*).
Tone material:
C D♭ E♭♭ F♯ G A♯ B c
c B G A♯ F♯ E♭♭ D♭ C
Lit.: no. 139.

Rusuh (West Java; Sunda District). Term for fast tempo. Cf. *Genchlek*; *Wirama*.
Lit.: no. 163.

Ruṣyakētupriya (South India). *Janya rāga* of the 27th *mēḷa* (*Sarasāṅgī*).
Tone material:
C D E F G B c
c B G F E D C
Lit.: no. 139.

Rutu (*Chakra*) (South India). Name of the 6th *chakra* in the system of the 72 *mēḷas*. Cf. *Rāga* (South India).
Lit.: no. 139.

Rutuk (*Tundum*) (Australia). Term for a small *tundum*.
Lit.: no. 190.

Rūyin nāy (Arabia). Reed pipe.
Lit.: no. 76.

Rwa dung (Tibet). Animal horn used in ceremonies of exorcism.
Lit.: no. 190.

Ryo (*Ryosen*) (Japan). "Tube mode." One of the basic scales used in *shōmyō* and *gagaku*. Its material is: *kyū* (usually interpreted as the western note D); *shō*, E; *kaku*, F♯; [*hen-chi*, G♯]; *chi*, A; *U*, B; [*hen kyū*, c♯].
Lit.: no. 136.

Ryo (Japan). (1) See *Awaseru.* (2) Singing with open mouth, which represents the male principle and corresponds with spring and summer. See *Kwaigo-no-ben.* Cf. *Ritsu.*
Lit.: no. 225.

Ryōkaku (Japan). See *Koto* parts.

Ryō-ni-shita (Japan). See *Koto* parts.

Ryong-ko (Korea). A small barrel drum hung from the player's shoulder in such a way that one skin-side faces upward. It is used at festivals and in the accompaniment of *p'ansori.* Cf. *Lung-ku*; *Tai-ko.*
Lit.: no. 179.

Ryo-o (Japan). "King Ryo," a dance of Chinese origin.

Ryū-ha (Japan). A traditional way of teaching: the playing handed down within a school or family.
Lit.: no. 215.

Ryūjishi hayashi (Japan). "Dragon music," a folk melody performed by a *hayashi.*
Lit.: no. 187.

Ryuk-kak (Korea). Six kinds of musical instruments (a related system to the *pa-yin*, the "eight sounds," of China).
Lit.: no. 255.

Ryūkoka (Japan). Term for popular native and imported Westernized music. Cf. *Hayriuta.*
Lit.: no. 185.

Ryuk-ryul (Korea). See *Ryuk-kak.*

Ryūteki (*Ōteki*; *Riūteki*) (Japan). "Dragon flute." A cross flute with 6-7 holes used in *tōgaku.* See *Bugaku*; *Yoko-bue.*
Lit.: no. 225.

S

Sa (India). Solmization syllable, abbreviation of the tone name *ṣaḍja*. *Sa* represents the first degree of scales (e.g., the western note C). The tone syllables representing the heptatonic scale are *sa*, *ri* (*re*), *ga*, *ma*, *pa*, *dha*, *ni*, and do not indicate absolute pitches.
Lit.: no. 136.

Sa (Korea). The second note and symbol of the *kong-chuk-po*. Assuming that *hap* is the western note C, *sa* represents D♭, or D (as required by the mode in use).
Lit.: no. 136.

Sā'āb (East Africa; Somali Republic). Dance. A dance song sung by women only. *Sā'āb* is "an invitation to the dance" and is accompanied by the clapping of hands. The Darod people call the *sā'āb* by the term *batar*.
Lit.: no. 98.

Saaleutan (West Java). See *Rengkong*.

Saam sin kam (China; Canton). Small lute with a round flat body and three strings. The instrument is played with a plectrum.

Ṣaba (Arabia). Tone name. See *Ḥijāz*.

Ṣabā (Arabia). "Doe-love." In contrast to the passionate *'Ushaq*. *Ṣabā*, a typical Arabic *maqām*, is very popular. Two scale forms are distinguished:

(a) $D\ \overset{+}{E\flat}\ F\ G\flat\ A\ B\flat\ c\ d\flat\ \overset{+}{e\flat}\ f$

(b) $D\ E\ \overset{\flat}{F}\ G\ A\ B\flat\ c\sharp\ d$

The *Ṣabā* melody is supposed to start with D, F . . . , and ends with D or F.
Lit.: nos. 64, 121.

Ṣabā (Arabia). Term for semitone.

Ṣabā (Modern Tunisia). *Maqām*.
Tone material:

$\overset{+}{B\flat}\ C\ D\ \overset{+}{E\flat}\ F\ \overset{+}{G\flat}\ A\ B\flat\ c\ d$

Lit.: no. 64.

Ṣabā-Najdī (Middle East). *Maqām*.
Tone material:

$D\ \overset{+}{E\flat}\ F\ \overset{+}{G\flat}\ A\ \overset{+}{B\flat}\ c\ d\ \overset{+}{e\flat}\ f\ \overset{+}{g\flat}\ a$

Lit.: no. 64.

Sabang (Borneo; Upper Sarawak—Bukar Dayak). A large wooden slit-drum.
Lit.: no. 255.

Sabar (Senegal—Wolof). Long drum.
Lit.: no. 255.

Sabas (Central Asia – Dungan; T'ung Kan). Cymbals used to accompany dances.
Lit.: no. 255.

Ṣabā-Zamzamah (Middle East). *Maqām*.
Tone material:

D E♭(+) F G♭ A B♭ c d♭ e f

Lit.: no. 64.

Ṣabbāba (Arabia). "First finger" in *'ud* playing. Indication of pitch.

Ṣabbāba (Arabia). "The young" – a vertical cane flute with six holes in front and one at the back. Cf. *Sobaba* (Madagascar). See also *Shabbaba*.
Lit.: no. 66.

Sabbāba fī majrā al-binṣir (Arabia). See *Aṣab'*.

Sabbāba fī majrā al-wuṣṭā (Arabia). See *Aṣab'*.

Šabbur (Syria). Horn.
Lit.: no. 190.

Sabcha (Ancient Israel). Obscure high-pitched instrument mentioned in the Book of Daniel.
Lit.: no. 309.

Śabda (India). Part of the *bharatan-nāṭyam* that occurs between *jātisvaram* and *varṇam*. *Śabda* literally means "to raise the voice," or "verbal communication"; also the "use of sacred words." Cf. *Nrita*; *Nritta*; *Abhinaya*.

Śabdaghanṭikā (India; Bengal). Metallophone consisting of seven carefully tuned small thin bronze slabs.
Lit.: no. 254.

Sabe (Congo – Bambala). Bow-lute.
Lit.: no. 21.

Sabhā gāna (South India). A piece of music appropriate for a public performance. See *Abhyāsa gāna*.

Sabitum (Sumeria). See *Miritum*.

Sadalik (East Turkestan). Cf. *Sochiba*.

Śadanapriya (South India). *Janya rāga* of the 51st *mēḷa* (*Kāmavardhanī*).
Tone material:

C D♭ E F♯ B c
c B F♯ E D♭ C

Lit.: no. 139.

Saddu (Mesopotamia). Curved horn used for signalling.
Lit.: no. 87.

Sādhāraṇa (India). "Twilight," "in-between." Term used in conjunction with the intonation of *ga* (approximately between natural and flat) in theoretical works.

Sādhāraṇa Ga (India). See *Ṣaṭśruti Ri* (sixth-*śruti Ri*).

Sadhir (*Sadir*) (South India). Old term for classical dance (*bharata nāṭyam*).

Sadiu (Kampuchea). A rarely played zither with one brass string and a half-gourd as corpus. By pressing the corpus against the body of the player the resonance can be altered. The string is beaten with a wooden stick. Cf. *Phin nam tao* (Thailand).
Lit.: no. 264.

Sa'dīya (Arabia). See *Dhikr*.

Ṣaḍja (*Shaḍja*; *Saḍji*) (India). Sanskrit tone name of the first degree of a scale. Its commonly used abbreviation is *sa*. Assuming that *Sa* is interpreted as the western note C, the other degrees of the heptatonic scale and their generally used abbreviations are:

Tone name	Abbreviation	Western equivalent
ṣaḍja (shadja)	*sa*	C
ṛṣabha (rishabha)	*ri (re)*	D
gāndhāra	*ga*	E
madhyama	*ma*	F
pañcama (pañchama)	*pa*	G
dhaivata	*dha*	A
niṣāda (nishāda)	*ni*	B

None of these notes indicate absolute pitches.

The two following terms (*komal*, *tivra*) appear only in North Indian music. *Komal* ("flat") can be used only with the notes *ri*, *ga*, *dha*, and *ni*. *Tivra* ("sharp") is only applicable to the note *ma*. In South India these two terms are not in use. The notes *sa* and *pa* cannot be altered and remain always "natural."
Lit.: no. 136.

Ṣāḍja grāma (Ancient India). Cf. *Ma grāma*.

Ṣāḍjakaiśiki (Ancient India). See *Jāti*.

Ṣāḍjamadhyamā (Ancient India). See *Jāti*.

Ṣāḍjodīcyavatī (Ancient India). See *Jāti*.

Sadr (Near East; Islamic North Africa). See *Shatr*.

Sa-dung (*Sa dueng*) (Thailand). An ivory spike fiddle. Cf. *Cai nhi*; *T'i-ch'in*; *Sa u*; *Sō*; *Sō u*; *Hu ch'in*.
Lit.: no. 254.

Śaḍvidhamārgaṇī (South India). See *Śaḍvidhamārgiṇī*.

Śaḍvidhamārgiṇī (South India). The 46th *mēḷa*:

C D♭ E♭ F♯ G A B♭ c

The *rāga* with the same name uses the identical tone material.
Lit.: no. 139.

Śaḍvidhasvarūpiṇī (South India). *Janya rāga* of the 63rd *mēḷa* (*Latāṅgī*).
Tone material:

C E D E F♯ B c
c B A♭ G F♯ E D C

Lit.: no. 139.

Sa'ed (Egypt). "Arm"—the ebony neck of the *kamānjah*.

Saemon (Japan). See *Saimon*.

Saeng (Burma). A number (usually 21) of *bung* drums placed in a circular framework. The player, seated in its center, can reach each drum without any difficulty. He beats the drums with his hands and fingers.
Lit.: no. 255.

Saeng (*Chap*) (Northeast Thailand). A pair of small cymbals.
Lit.: no. 203.

Saeng (Korea). Also *Saenghwang*. See *Saing*.

Saengjon yesu chae (Korea). Buddhist chant which supposedly establishes a happy rebirth in Nirvana. The chant is performed before death.

Sae-p'iri (Korea). See *Sei-p'iri*.

Sae zuri (Japan). "Chattering," "twittering of birds," unintelligible words a dancer murmurs behind his mask. They are believed to be magic formulas. This happens in the middle of the dance when an incantation was supposed to happen. Then the music stops and the dancer provides his own accompaniment of his murmured words.

Safaai (Turkestan). Sistrum of travelling vendors and beggars.
Lit.: no. 255.

Sa fa fir (Egypt). Pan-flutes of modern Egypt consisting of 24 bamboo pipes.
Lit.: no. 255.

Safare (Arabia). See *Safura*.

Safe (*Sapeh*) (Borneo). Plucked lute type with 2-3 *rotang* strings. The back of the large boat-shaped corpus is open. Cf. *Jimpai* (*Djimpai*); *Kasapi*; *Impai*.
Lit.: no. 157.

Saff (Israel). Dance and musical procession of the Druse marriage ceremonies.
Lit.: no. 14.

Ṣaffāra (Arabia). Small vertical whistle flute.
Lit.: no. 76.

Ṣafīr (Turkey). Metal whistle. See *Ṣafīr-i bulbul.*

Ṣafīr-i-bulbul (Turkey). Obscure "nightingale whistle." According to Lit. no. 81, Ibn Sida (d. 1065) states that the Arabic word was *ṣaffāra*. The instrument is described as a pipe with which a boy whistles at pigeons. The metal used for making the pipe was, according to Al-Fīrūzābādī (d. 1414), copper. Cf. *Sūfaīra.*
Lit.: no. 81.

Safura (*Safure*; *Safare*) (Arabia; Persia). Any type of flute.
Lit.: no. 255.

Sa-gaṇa (South India). See *Ashṭa gaṇas.*

Sagari (Japan). Term used in *koto* playing. It indicates the moving down of the bridge in order to lower the pitch of a string.
Lit.: no. 225.

Sagaru (West Africa; Mali—Dogon). Rattle.
Lit.: no. 303.

Saga-saga (Thailand). See *Yangong.* Long, wooden jew's harp.
Lit.: no. 254.

Sāgāt (*Sağğat*; *Zil*) (Arabia). A tiny cymbal pair. One cymbal is attached by a small loop to the thumb and the other to the middle finger and used in religious ceremonies of dervishes and by dancers in popular performances. The term is also applied to castanets.
Lit.: no. 255.

Sagayan (Philippines). War dance.

Sagembyangan (Java). See *Gembyangan.*

Sage-koto (Japan). A small *koto*, beautifully and richly ornamented, used by the ladies of the Imperical Court. It has nine thin silken strings.
Lit.: no. 225, 250.

Sage-uta (Japan). Short and low range song, a type of *michiyuki*, in the *ha* section of the *noh* play and similar forms.
Lit.: no. 166.

Saghāne (Iran; Turkey). Stick with three jingles (jingle tree). Cf. *Chaghāna.*

Sāgo (Sudan—Agni). *Sansa* with wooden tongues.
Lit.: no. 95.

Sa-grāma (India). The first of the basic scales of Ancient India with *sa* as first note. Its degrees probably were the same as those of modern *toḍi* of South India. (The other two ancient scales were called *Ma-grāma* and *Ga-grāma.*)
Lit.: no. 139.

Sāgu (South India). *Janya rāga* of the 5th *mēḷa* (*Manōrañjanī*).
Tone material:
C E♭♭ G A B c
c B A G E♭♭ C
Lit.: no. 139.

Śahāna (South India). *Janya rāga* of the 28th *mēḷa* (*Harikāmbhōji*).
Tone material:
C D E F G F A B♭ c
c B♭ A G F E F D E D C
(c A B♭ A G F E F D E D C)
Lit.: no. 139.

Sahanāī (North India). An oboe type. See *Sānāyī* and *Mohali* (*Mohorī*). Cf. *Damai-baja.*

Sahavāsiṇi (South India). *Janya rāga* of the 31st *mēḷa* (*Yāgapriyā*).
Tone material:
C D♯ E G B♭♭ c
c B♭♭ G E D♯ C
Lit.: no. 139.

Sah-gāh (*Sigā*; *Sikāh*) (Arabia; Egypt). "The third tone"—tone name. (All tone names are listed within the range of two octaves under the heading of *Jagā* [*Yagā*].) As *maqām* the following scale is used:

+Eb F G A +Bb c d +eb

Lit.: no. 64.

Sahib nahabat (India). "Master drum." Generally a pair of large kettledrums mounted on an elephant.
Lit.: no. 250.

Sāhitya (India). "Association," "connection"; libretto, text.

Śahnāī (*Sahnayi*) (India). See *Sānāyī.*

Šah-nāz (Middle East). *Maqām.*
Tone material:

D Eb F# G A Bb c# d

Lit.: no. 64.

Sahō-no-gaku (Japan). "Music of the left" performed by musicians of *tōgaku.* Cf. *Gagaku.* For "music of the right" see *Koamgaku.*
Lit.: no. 53.

Sahunay (Philippines). A *śahnāy* type with a single reed.

Šāh-war (Middle East). *Maqām.*
Tone material:

F G A Bb C D E F

Lit.: no. 64.

Sai (Thailand). String.

Sa-i (Korea). "Down two." Solmization term referring to the second note below *kung.* For further information, see list of the four basic modes of *ah-ak* shown under the heading of *O-um-yak-po.*
Lit.: no. 136.

Saiba-gaku (*Saibara*) (Japan). Dance with 53 variations of a folk melody, established by Imperial order in the 10th century. It was performed annually at the Imperial Palace and, at rare occasions, can still be heard at the present time.
Lit.: no. 225.

Saibara (Japan). Common term for *saiba-gaku. Saibara* is a folk song, elaborately arranged for *gagaku.* The singer is accompanied by a small instrumental ensemble, often without drums. The instruments are: *shō*, *hichiriki*, *ōteki* (*ryūteki*), *biwa*, *koto* (*gaku-so*). *Saibara* became fashionable during the Heian period (794-1185). Cf. *Gagaku.*
Lit.: no. 136.

Saibari (Japan). Dances and songs to please and honor the Shinto gods.

Saïb-it (Egypt). Ancient long flute open at both ends, without any mouthpiece.
Lit.: no. 255.

Said (Arabia). Neck of the *kemanje.*

Saih (Bali). Series; row; scale; scale-system.
Lit.: no. 197.

Saih angklung (Bali). A four-tone scale; no upper octave range is used:

F G A B, or F# A B c#

Lit.: no. 197.

Saih gambuh (*Suling gambuh*) (Bali). A five-tone scale (derived from *saih* 7 [*saih pitu*]). There are four scales (each with five degrees):

Tembung	beginning	with the	tone	syllable:	*ding*
Selisir	''	''	''	''	*dong*
Baro	''	''	''	''	*deng*
Lebeng	''	''	''	''	*dung*
(*Sunaren*, not in use any more)					*dang*

Lit.: no. 197.

Saih gender wayang (Bali). The *slendro* scale as used in *gender wayang.*
Lit.: no. 197.

Saih lima (Bali). Five-tone scale (*pelog* or *slendro*). The tone syllables are in the traditional order: *ding, dong, deng, dung, dang*, deleting the tones *penyorog* and *pemero*. Cf. *Saih pitu*.
Lit.: no. 197.

Saih nem (Bali). A not frequently used six-tone scale (*pelog*).
Lit.: no. 197.

Saih pitu (Bali). A scale of seven degrees related to the Javanese *pelog*. The pitches vary from one place to the other. Generally it is:
C# D# E F# G# A A# c#
See Lit. no. 197. *Saih 7* (*pitu*) has been described as a mysterious scale used in sacred music. The seven note scale is defined by the tone names: *ding, dong, deng, penyorog* ("inserted"), *dung, dang, pemero* ("false" tone), *ding alit*.
Lit.: no. 197.

Sa il (Korea). "Down one," a solmization term referring to the first note below *kung*. For further information, see list of the four basic *ah-ak* modes shown under the heading of *O-um-yak-po*.
Lit.: no. 136.

Saila (Southeast India; Maikal Hills). Song and dance of the Gond tribe. *Saila*, a cheerful dance, is performed by only by men. Cf. *Rina*.
Lit.: no. 134.

Sailadeśākṣī (South India). See *Deśākṣī* (35th *asampūrṇa mēḷa*).

Saim (Iran). Wire string.

Saimon (Japan). Sacred hymns of the Shinto, Buddhist, and Confucian rituals adjusted into secular forms that later on became popular on the theatrical stage.
Lit.: no. 185.

Saindhavagauḷi (South India). *Janya rāga* of the 7th *mēḷa* (*Senāpāti*).
Tone material:
C D♭ E♭ F G A♭ B♭♭ c
c B♭♭ A♭ F E♭ F D♭ C
Lit.: no. 139.

Saindhavi (*Saindhvi*) (South India). *Janya rāga* of the 22nd *mēḷa* (*Kharaharapriyā*).
Tone material:
(*B♭ A*) *B♭* C D E♭ F G A B♭
(*B♭ A B♭* C D E♭ F G)
B♭ A G F E♭ D C *B♭* (*A B♭* C)
(G F E♭ D C *B♭ A B♭* C)
Lit.: no. 139.

Saindhvi (North India). See *Sindhura*.

Saindhvi (South India). See *Saindhavi*.

Saing (Burma). *Saing* is used as abbreviation of *saing waing ah-pwe*. It is an instrumental ensemble consisting of a vaguely structured group including a *pat waing*, an oboe, flute, a *maung saing*, drums, cymbals, rattles, and bells.

Saing (*Saenghwang*) (Korea). The mouth organ of East Asia. It consists of a wooden bowl into which are fixed with their lower ends 17 bamboo pipes of different lengths. One of the pipes is silent. The *saing* was used in classical and popular music. In the 15th century appeared in Korea a mouth organ with 36 pipes but had little success. Cf. *Cho*; *Sheng* (China); *Shō* (Japan).
Lit.: nos. 137, 179.

Saing hoang (Korea). See *Saing*.

Saingwaing (Thailand). Seventeen small drums placed in a circular framework. See *Saing* (Korea).

Saing waing ah-pwe (Burma). See *Saing*.

Śaivapantuvarālī (South India). See *Pantuvarālī* (45th *asampūrṇa mēḷa*).

Saj' (Old Arabia). Rhymed prose. See *Hija*.
Lit.: no. 76.

Sajāḥ (*Shuḥāj*) (Old Arabia). The tonic (octave: *siyyāḥ*).
Lit.: no. 69.

Sajjat (Arabia). Also *kās*. Syrian equivalent of the Arabian *kāsāt* (*ku'ūs*). Tiny finger cymbals used by dancers.
Lit.: no. 76.

Sajjukāmbhōji (South India). *Janya rāga* of the 28th *mēḷa* (*Harikāmbhōjī*).
Tone material:
C F D C G F A B♭ c
c B♭ G B♭ F E D C
Lit.: no. 139.

Saka (Solomon Isl.). See *Maghiiti.*

Sakadaru (Japan). Wine barrel drum used in folk music.

Sakahogai-no-uta (Japan). Songs of the Drinking Ceremonial.

Sakala (*Nsakala*) (Lower Congo). Vessel rattle.
Lit.: no. 280.

Sakamoriuta (Japan). Drinking songs (one form of *min-yo*).

Sakara (Nigeria; Dahomey). (1) Frame drum with a circular frame made of baked clay. (2) Gourd rattle. Cf. *Sekere.*
Lit.: no. 293.

Sak-ko (Korea). The term was applied to medium-sized barrel drums, each placed in a wooden frame in such a manner that the axis of one barrel had north-south, the other east-west direction. The first of the drums, the *sakko*, was called the "starting drum." The second, only slightly smaller than the first, was the *ung-ko*, the "answering drum."

The start of an *ah-ak* performance involved the following instruments: at the beginning the *sakko* was struck once. This beat was followed by one stroke of the *ung-ko*. The *ung-ko* beat was followed by three beats of the *tchouk* and one beat of the *kunko*. This sequence of three *tchouk* strokes and one of the *kunko* was repeated three times while at the same time the *eu* (*yu*, the "wooden tiger") was scraped three times.
Lit.: nos. 52, 179.

Sa-ku (China; Canton). See *Pang-tzu*; *Sha-ku.*

Sakura (Japan). A variant of the *kumoi koto*-tuning.
Lit.: no. 225.

Sakvā (*Dereng*). Term in Santali language for *śṛṅga* (cow-horn).
Lit.: no. 254.

Sālaga (South India). The 37th *mēḷa*:
C D♭ E𝄫 F♯ G A♭ B𝄫 c
The *rāga* of the same name uses the tone material shown above.
Lit.: no. 139.

Sālaga Bhairavī (South India). *Janya rāga* of the 22nd *mēḷa* (*Kharaharapriyā*).
Tone material:
C D F G A
c B♭ A G F E♭ D C
Lit.: no. 139.

Sālagavēḷāvaḷi (South India). *Janya rāga* of the 47th *mēḷa* (*Suvarṇāṅgī*).
Tone material:
C D♭ E♭ F♯ G B A B c
c B A G F♯ E♭ C
Lit.: no. 139.

Salahan (Java). Suddenly appearing stereotyped phrases (performed, e.g., by a *bedug*), creating a contrast to the regularly moving background of the other instruments of the ensemble. Cf. *Kodok ngorek*; *Ngendelong.*
Lit.: no. 163.

Salah gumun (Java). "Unusual," "extraordinary harmony." A particular manner of beating the *bonang* and *gambang kayu.* Both hands of the player beat two notes, the interval of a fourth apart, and move parallel from one to a second position to and fro. Cf. *Tutukan rangkep.*
Lit.: no. 163.

Salaju (Nepal). Short songs sung in question and answer form. See *Jhamre*.
Lit.: no. 133.

Salaksak (Philippines). Cf. *Itundak*.

Salamani (Turkey). Cane or wooden vertical long flute without a mouthpiece. Both ends are open.
Lit.: no. 255.

Salāmi (India). Slowly beginning dances of the *kathak* performance. The term is derived from the Muslim greeting (*salām*) by raising the hand to the head. Cf. *Kathakaḷi*.

Salang (North India). An obscure *rāga*. It is derived from *rāga Sarang*. Its tone material is only vaguely defined. The notes A and E are avoided entirely, and F is omitted in the ascending line. *Vādis*: C, F.
Lit.: no. 138.

Salangai (South India). Also *Gejjai*. Rattle anklets tied around the ankles of dancers. Cf. *Kinkinī*.
Lit.: no. 260.

Sālaṅganāṭa (South India). See *Sāraṅganāṭa*.

Salāpam (South India). *Janya rāga* of the 14th *mēḷa* (*Vakuḷābharaṇam*).
Tone material:

C E F A♭ B♭ c
c B♭ A♭ F E C

Lit.: no. 139.

Salāsil (Arabia). Castanets; cymbals. Cf. *Silsil*; *Sil-snyan*; *Selslim*; *Zil*; *Sajjat*.
Lit.: no. 255.

Sālava (South India). (1) The 37th *asampūrṇa mēḷa-rāga* without *kaṭapayādi* prefix. (2) The 37th *asampūrṇa mēḷa-rāga* with *kaṭapayādi* prefix was called *Saugandhini*. See *Rāga* (South India).
Lit.: no. 139.

Sālavāṅgam (South India). *Janya rāga* of the 37th *mēḷa* (*Sālaga*).
Tone material:

C D♭ F♯ G A♭ B♭♭ A♭ c
c B♭♭ A♭ G F♯ E♭♭ D♭ C

Lit.: no. 139.

Sālavi (South India). *Janya rāga* of the 37th *mēḷa* (*Sālaga*).
Tone material:

C E♭♭ D♭ E♭♭ F♯ G A♭ B♭♭ A♭ c
c B♭♭ A♭ G F♯ E♭♭ D♭ C

Lit.: no. 139.

Sālavibaṅgāla (South India). *Janya rāga* of the 23rd *mēḷa* (*Gaurīmanōharī*).
Tone material:

C D F G A c
c A G F E♭ D C

Lit.: no. 139.

Salbaq (Middle East; Arabia). Ancient psaltery.

Salbat (North Philippines). Cf. *Topayya*.

Saleju (*Jhamre*) (Nepal). Songs in the form of questions and answers.
Lit.: no. 133.

Salendro (*Surendro*) (Sunda District). Cf. *Slendro*.

Salendro (Java). Or *slendro*. Scales and instruments in the *slendro* system (five approximately equally distant degrees within the octave).
Lit.: no. 255.

Salendro biasa (West Java). "Normal *slendro*"; among the several *slendro* scales, *salendro biasa* can also be called *salendro jawar* or *salendro lempang* (*salendro* straight) or *salendro lanchar* (*salendro* single). These scales have all, more or less, equidistant intervals between the scale degrees. The modern *slendro* form consists approximately of five notes, each distant from the next by ca. 240 cents. Cf. *Slendro*; *Surupan*.
Lit.: no. 163.

Salendro jawar (*Jajawar*) (West Java). See *Salendro biasa.*

Salendro lanchar (West Java). See *Salendro biasa.*

Salendro lempang (West Java). See *Salendro biasa.*

Salet (Malay Peninsula—Plee). Nose flute.
Lit.: no. 313.

Salieng (*Saluang*) (Flores; Menangkabau). See *Salung.*

Saligung (Flores—Timur-Batak). Flute without mouthpiece. The instrument has four finger holes. Cf. *Sordam.*
Lit.: no. 166.

Sa li ne lu (Babylonia). Probably a psaltery.
Lit.: no. 87.

Salka (Arabia). Brass string.
Lit.: no. 255.

Salmak (Iran). Name of one *gusheh* that differs in several small features from the preceding *daramad.*

Śālmali (South India). *Janya rāga* of the 9th *mēḷa* (*Dhēnuka*).
Tone material:
C D♭ E♭ G B c
c B G E♭ D♭ C
Lit.: no. 139.

Salodap (*Salohat*) (Flores—Toba Batak). See *Fu'i dole*; *Taraṭoit.*

Salohat (Flores—Toba Batak). Bamboo flute with central blowhole. Both ends of the tube are open and each can be closed in order to alter the pitch.

Salompret (Java). Trumpet.
Lit.: no. 255.

Saluang (Central Sumatra; Menangkabau). See *Salung.*

Salude (Talaud; Pulau-Pulau Isl.). Bamboo zither with two strings.
Lit.: no. 162.

Salueng (Sumatra; Atjeh). Bamboo flute. Cf. *Nuren*; *Lolowe.* The instrument has various names; some of them are: *hèl-hèl* (Nicobares), *surune ndrawa* (Southern Nias), *bengsi* (Gayo District, Sumatra), *salung* (South Sumatra), *bulo wok* (Borneo), *tulali* (North Celebes), *sawergnil* (Timor, Kai Isl.).
Lit.: no. 166.

Salundi (Java). Ancient *gender* type.
Lit.: no. 163.

Salunding (Borneo). Signalling pipe without fingerholes, used by the Dayak.

Salunding(wesi) (Bali). Name of *gender* with or without resonator tubes.

Salung (Flores; Sumatra). Also *salieng*; *saluang*; *bangsi.* An open flute with four or five finger holes, without mouthpiece. Cf. *Fekor* (*Feko*); *Sunding.*
Lit.: no. 166.

Sam (India). The first beat of rhythmic modes. See *Tāla.*

Sāma (South India). *Janya rāga* of the 28th *mēḷa* (*Harikāmbhōji*).
Tone material:
C D F G A c
c A G F E D C
Lit.: no. 139.

Samā' (Morocco). Vocal music without any instrumental accompaniment. The texts celebrate and praise the Prophet.

Sama graha (South India). A piece of music in which the melody and the *āvarta* of the drummer start simultaneously.

Sama'a (Modern Egypt). Clarinet with six or seven finger holes.

Sa mac (North Vietnam). Name of a scale. See list of scales shown under the heading of *Bac.*

Sama eḍuppu (South India). See *Eḍuppu.*

Sama'ī (Middle East). Cf. *Nauba.*

Sāmakannaḍa (South India). *Janya rāga* of the 17th *mēḷa* (*Sūryakānta*).
Tone material:
C D♭ F E F G A B c
c A G F D♭ C
Lit.: no. 139.

Sāmakurañji (South India). *Janya rāga* of the 12th *mēḷa* (*Rūpāvatī*).
Tone material:
C E♭ A♯ B c
c B A♯ B G F E♭ D♭ C
Lit.: no. 139.

Śāmala (South India). (1) The 55th *asampūrṇa mēḷa-rāga* without *kaṭapayādi* prefix. (2) As rāga with the *kaṭapayādi* prefix (identical with the *mēḷa*). See *Rāga* (South India).
Lit.: no. 139.

Sāmālāpini (South India). *Janya rāga* of the 37th *mēḷa* (*Sālaga*).
Tone material:
C E♭♭ F♯ G B♭♭ c
c B♭♭ G F♯ E♭♭ C
Lit.: no. 139.

Sāman (Vedic India). *Sāmavedic* chant.

Sāmanārāyaṇī (South India). *Janya rāga* of the 13th *mēḷa* (*Gāyakapriya*).
Tone material:
C D♭ F G A♭ B♭♭ c
c G A♭ B♭♭ G F D♭ C
Lit.: no. 139.

Sāmansvarāḷi (South India). *Janya rāga* of the 43rd *mēḷa* (*Gavāmbōdhi*).
Tone material:
C D♭ F♯ G B♭♭ A♭ c
c A♭ G A♭ F♯ E♭ D♭ C
Lit.: no. 139.

Sāmant (South India). *Janya rāga* of the 30th *mēḷa* (*Nāgānandī*).
Tone material:
C D C F E F G A♯ B c
c B A♯ B G F E D C
Lit.: no. 139.

Sāmantagiṅgala (South India). *Janya rāga* of the 32nd *mēḷa* (*Rāgavardhanī*).
Tone material:
C D♯ E F G A♭ B♭ c
c B♭ G A♭ B♭ G F E F D♯ C
Lit.: no. 139.

Sāmantam (South India). (1) The 30th *asampūrṇa-mēḷa-rāga* without *kaṭapayādi* prefix. (2) The 30th *asampūrṇa mēḷa-rāga* with *kaṭapayādi* prefix was called *Nagabharanam.* See *Rāga* (South India).
Lit.: no. 139.

Sāmantamallar (South India). *Janya rāga* of the 17th *mēḷa* (*Sūryakānta*).
Tone material:
C E F G B c
c B G A F E D♭ C
Lit.: no. 139.

Sāmantasālavi (South India). *Janya rāga* of the 21st *mēḷa* (*Kiravāṇi*).
Tone material:
C D E♭ F G A♭ c
c B A♭ G F E♭ D C
Lit.: no. 139.

Sāmantasikhāmani (South India). *Janya rāga* of the 64th *mēḷa* (*Vāchaspati*).
Tone material:
C E F♯ G F♯ A B♭ c
c B♭ A G E C
Lit.: no. 139.

Samantkalyan (North India). A rare *rāga* ascribed to the *Kalyan thāta*. It consists of passages taken from the *rāgas Shuddh-kalyan* and *Hamir*. The tone-material is indistinct on account of the varieties of mixing the material of the two *rāgas*.
Tone material:
C E G B A c
c B A G F♯ A G E G D C
Lit.: no. 138.

Samant-sarang (North India). A *rāga* probably ascribed to the *Kafi thāta*. It consists of a combination of *Bindrabani-sarang* phrases and a characteristic phrase in which the note A appears in the descending line.
Tone material:
C D F G B c
c B♭ A G F D C; *Vādis*: D, G
Lit.: no. 138.

Sāmantvēlāvaḷi (South India). *Janya rāga* of the 44th *mēḷa* (*Bhāvapriya*).
Tone material:
C D♭ E♭ F♯ A♭ G A♭ c
c A♭ B♭ G F♯ E♭ D♭ C
Lit.: no. 139.

Sāmasālavi (South India). *Janya rāga* of the 23rd *mēḷa* (*Gaurīmanōharī*).
Tone material:
C D E♭ F G A c
c B A G F E♭ G C
Lit.: no. 139.

Sāmavarāḷi (South India). *Janya rāga* of the 3rd *mēḷa* (*Gānamūrti*).
Tone material:
C D♭ F G A♭ B c
c B A♭ G F E♭♭ D♭ C (*B* C)
See remark to *Gānamūrti*.
Lit.: no. 139.

Sāmavarāli (South India). (1) The 3rd *asampūrṇa mēḷa-rāga* without *kaṭapayādi* prefix. (2) The 3rd *asampūrṇa mēḷa-rāga* with *kaṭapayādi* prefix was called *Gānasāmavārali*. See *Rāga* (South India).
Lit.: no. 139.

Sāmavedin (Vedic India). A chanter, reciter of the *Sāmaveda*.

Samavēṣiṇi (South India). *Janya rāga* of the 69th *mēḷa* (*Dhātuvardhaṇī*).
Tone material:
C D♯ F♯ A♭ B c
c B A♭ F♯ D♯ C
Lit.: no. 139.

Samba (Nigeria—Yoruba). (1) A small tambourine with a rectangular frame. (2) Frame drum ensemble consisting of the larger *asiko* and two smaller *samba*.
Lit.: no. 293.

Sambasō (Japan). Ancient pieces that accompany traditional *noh* dances (originally dedicatory ceremonial dances meant to purify the shinto shrine at the beginning of the ceremony). At present *sambasō* pieces appear at the beginnings of *kabuki* and *noh* performances, particularly during the month of January.
Lit.: no. 187.

Sam-bun (Japan). Cf. *Kyō-ke*.

Samb-zi (New Guinea). Simple songs sung at festivities.

Sam chuk (Korea). "Three bamboo (tubes)." Bamboo flutes. The largest of the group, the *tai-keum* (*tae-kum*; *chottae*), probably one of the largest flutes in East Asia, has six finger holes and a variable number (usually five) of non-stopped holes at the lower end. The *tai-keum* (*tae-kum*) produces the basic note (B♭) in *ah-ak* performances and assumes the function of a tuning fork.

The next smaller flute is the *chung-keum* (*chung-kum*). It has the same structure as the *tai-keum*.

The smallest flute of the group is the *so-keum* (*so-kum*), again having the same structure as the other two instruments.
Lit.: no. 52.

Śāmbhavi (South India). *Janya rāga* of the 67th *mēḷa* (*Sucharitra*).
Tone material:
C D♯ E F♯ B♭♭ c
c B♭♭ F♯ E D♯ C
Lit.: no. 139.

Sām chan (Thailand). "Third level" ("extended version"). Term used for rhythmical patterns. Cf. *Prop kai*; *Thao.*
Lit.: no. 208.

Sameri (Arabia). Beduin song.

Saṃgīta (*Saṃhitā*; *Sangīta*) (Ancient India). Cf. *Gīta.* Large collection of sacred hymns.
Lit.: no. 292.

Sam-hyon (Korea). Dance music. Three types are distinguished:
1. *Yombul*, the grave, slow moving type.
2. *Taryong*, the cheerful and rhythmically emphasized type.
3. *Kutkori*, the fast, playful type.

Cf. *An-ch'aebi sori.*
Lit.: no. 136.

Samien (*San-hsien*) (China). Long necked lute with three silken strings tuned to 1, 5, 8.

Samisen (Japan). See *Shamisen.*

Samisen-no-fue (*Fuye*) (Japan). Transverse cane flute with seven finger holes.
Lit.: no. 255.

Sam-ji (Korea). Cf. *Tae-kum.*

Saṃkrantanapriya (South India). *Janya rāga* of the 22nd *mēḷa* (*Kharaharapriyā*).
Tone material:
C D E♭ G A c
c A G E♭ D C
Lit.: no. 139.

Sammi (North India). Cf. *Dhris.*

Sampak (Java). The term has the same meaning as *srepegan*; specifically the fastest and most violent form of *srepegan.* See *Sampak galong*; *Karatagan.*
Lit.: no. 163.

Sampak galong (Java—Solo; Jogya). (1) Frequently applied to *srepegan.* (2) The accompaniment of the final battle of the *wayang kulit.* This fight is introduced by the *suluk galong.* Cf. *Sampak*; *Suluk*; *Playon.*
Lit.: no. 163.

Sampho (Kampuchea). Drum with two heads used in the *pin paet.*
Lit.: no. 215.

Sampiang (*Kampiang*) (Borneo). See *Gendang mara.*

Sampiung (West Java). Dance of old men and women before the harvested rice is placed in the hut. The accompaniment is performed by a *kachapi* and a *tarawangsa.*

Sampūrṇa (India). The term indicates that all seven scale notes within the octave are in use and are shown in a regular step-by-step sequence in ascent or descent.
Lit.: no. 138.

Samuius (South Africa—Zulu). Music bow with one wire string.
Lit.: no. 17.

Samurai-odori (*Heko-odori*) (Japan). Popular warrior dance from Kyūshū.
Lit.: no. 185.

Saṃvādī (North India). A note placed usually a fourth or fifth above the *vādī*. At the present time this "consonant" note has lost some of its importance. It served the singer of the past to establish the correct intonation of the notes that appear between the *vādī* and *saṃvādī*. Cf. *Vādī*.

Saṃyōgī (North India). A simple *sarangi* type, the body of which consists of an oblong calabash. Cf. *Sanyōgī*.
Lit.: no. 254.

San (Japan). *Wagon* melody pattern. Cf. *Ji*; *Oru*; *Tsumu*.
Lit.: no. 185.

San (Japan). Also *sen*. Name of the 17th pipe of the *shō*. Cf. *Shō*.
Lit.: no. 225.

San (China—M 5421). Term for "open string." See *chien-tzu*.

Sānāyī (*Śahnāī*; *Śahnāyī*) (North India; Central Asia; Middle East). A popular wooden heterophonic double-reed instrument with a metal bell and seven finger holes. Occasionally two instruments are combined with two closely adjoining mouthpieces which can be blown simultaneously. The sound produced is strong and penetrating. Cf. *Sārnā*; *Zūrnā*; *Sūrnāy*; *Mohali*.
Lit.: no. 250.

Sanchārī (North India). The third section of an elaborate art song (*dhrūpad*). See *Dhrūpad*; occasionally also *khyāl*.
Lit.: no. 138.

Sancho (Korea). See *San-jo*.

Sanda (West Flores). Dance, resembling the *danding*. The *sanda* is performed by men and women mostly indoors. The accompaniment is provided by singing, *sunding*-playing, and *gendang*-beating.
Lit.: no. 166.

Sandanme (Japan). Group of percussion patterns used in *noh* music.
Lit.: no. 187.

Sandau (West Borneo—Belongai Dayak). A bamboo flute with six finger holes.
Lit.: no. 255.

Sandhiprakash-rāga (India). A *rāga* that is to be performed at a time when daylight changes to night, or vice versa (sunset, sunrise). See *Rāga* (*Praharas*).
Lit.: no. 138.

Sandip (New Guinea—Papua). Gong.
Lit.: no. 255.

Sandīpinī (India). Term for the 16th *śruti*. The corresponding note name is *praticatuśśruti dha* (*pratiśuddha ni*). These terms were used in the past in music theory). Cf. *Śruti*.

Sānēyī (India; Bengal). See *Sānāyī*.

Sang (Iran). Little cymbals.
Lit.: no. 77.

Sang (Korea—M 5669). The fourth scale degree and symbol of the *kong chuk-po*. If *hap* is interpreted as the western note C, *sang* represents F. Cf. *Kung-ch'e-p'u* (China).
Lit.: no. 136.

Sang (Korea—M 5673). Solmization term for the second note of the ancient Chinese pentatonic or heptatonic scale.
Lit.: no. 136.

Sang (Korea). Old-fashioned clappers consisting of two wooden slabs.
Lit.: no. 52.

Sang (Turkmeniya). Term for *santir*.

Sanga (*Tanggo*) (South Borneo; Bandjermasin). (1) The fifth note of the *slendro* system of Bandjermasin. (2) The third note of the Javanese (Banyuwangi) *slendro* system. Cf. *Slendro.*

Sanga (Sunda District). The third note of the *slendro* system of the Sunda District. See *Panelu.*
Lit.: no. 163.

Sanga (Java). "Nine." The ninth tone. The number nine is used when the intermediate tones of the scale are added to the basic degrees.

Sanga (*Panelu*) (Indonesia; Cheribon). The third note of the *pelog* system of Cheribon. Cf. *Pelog.*
Lit.: no. 163.

Sangaku (Japan). "Leisurely dance" of Chinese origin. A comedy performed by acrobats and jugglers, light and amusing in contrast to the ponderous and severe *bugaku* performances. The word *sarugaku* ("monkey music") was frequently confused with *sangaku.* Although the two terms had no direct link, they were used indiscriminately. Cf. *San-yüeh* (China).
Lit.: no. 225.

Sangboi (Sierra Leone). Goblet drum.
Lit.: no. 190.

Sange (Japan). See *Kansan.*

Sangen (Japan). Old term for *shamisen*, particularly in *jiuta* (*koto*, *shamisen*, *shakuhachi*) music.
Lit.: no. 185.

San-gen-kin (Japan). A three-stringed (fretless) *koto.* Strings 1 and 3 are tuned to the same pitch and string 2 is tuned a fifth lower. The corpus and the *tsume* have the same shape as those of the *yakumo koto.*
Lit.: no. 225.

Sanggan (*Trachak*; *Angkring*) (Java). The wooden frame upon which the keys of the *gender* rest.
Lit.: no. 163.

Sanghyang (Bali). Ritualistic trance dances accompanied by the *kechak* chorus. There are several of these dances; a few are listed below:

Sanghyang dedari:	two little girls dance as heavenly nymphs.
Sanghyang deling:	two little girls dance as dolls.
Sanghyang kidang:	Boys or men dance as deer.
Sanghyang bōjog:	Boys or men dance as monkeys.
Sanghyang lilipi:	Boys or men dance as serpents.
Sanghyang cheleng:	Boys or men dance as swine.
Sanghyang jaran:	Boys or men dance as riders, sitting on sticks that show carved wooden horse heads.

Cf. *Janger.*
Lit.: nos. 197, 265.

Sanghyang bōjog (Bali). See *Sanghyang.*

Sanghyang cheleng (Bali). See *Sanghyang.*

Sanghyang dedari (Bali). See *Sanghyang.*

Sanghyang deling (Bali). See *Sanghyang.*

Sanghyang jaran (Bali). See *Sanghyang.*

Sanghyang kidang (Bali). See *Sanghyang.*

Sanghyang lilipi (Bali). See *Sanghyang.*

Sang i (Korea). "Up two," solmization term referring to the second note above *kung.* See list of the four basic *ah-ak* modes shown under the heading of *O-um-yak-po.*
Lit.: no. 136.

Sang il (Korea). "Up one," solmization term referring to the first note above *kung.* See list of the four basic *ah-ak* modes shown under the heading of *O-um-yak-po.*
Lit.: no. 136.

Sangini git (Nepal). Dance song performed by women during the *tiz* festival. Nepalese women believe that any girl who does not take part in the *sangini git* will be crippled when reborn.
Lit.: no. 133.

Sangīt(a) (India). General term for music.

Sangju kwongong chae (Korea). Buddhist chant performed for a dead person. The ceremony lasts one day.
Lit.: no. 287.

Sangkah (Bali). Priest's shell horn used in rites to ward off demons and evil.
Lit.: nos. 197, 265.

Sangkultap (Siberia – Vogul). Cf. *Nares-yuh.*
Lit.: no. 250.

Sangna (Kampuchea). Frame drum. Its two drumheads are tuned to the interval of a fourth or fifth. Cf. *Song na* (Thailand).
Lit.: no. 255.

Sang o (Korea). "Up five," solmization term referring to the fifth note above *kung.* See list of the four basic *ah-ak* modes shown under the heading of *O-um-yak-po.*
Lit.: no. 136.

Sangoi (Borneo – Kanowit). Nose flute with three finger holes and one thumbhole.
Lit.: no. 255.

Sangona (Central Celebes). Nose flute with three finger holes. Cf. *Tulali*; *Sangoi.*
Lit.: no. 132.

Sang sa (Korea). "Up four," solmization term referring to the fourth note above *kung.* See the list of the four basic *ah-ak* modes shown under the heading of *O-um-yak-po.*
Lit.: no. 136.

Sang sam (Korea). "Up three," solmization term referring to the third note above *kung.* See the list of the four basic *ah-ak* modes shown under the heading of *O-um-yak-po.*
Lit.: no. 136.

Sang-sngags (Tibet). See *Sngags.*

Sangu (Guinea Coast; Southeast Ghana – Ewe). Term for *sansa.* Cf. *Afosangu*; *Tresangu.*
Lit.: no. 95.

Sangwa (Congo). Rattle.
Lit.: no. 255.

Sanh (Vietnam; Kampuchea). Wooden clappers (generally used in pairs).
Lit.: no. 255.

San-hsien (China – M 5625; 2663). "Three-stringer." A long lute with three silken strings. Its shallow body is covered on top and bottom with snakeskin. The instrument is played with a plectrum, only occasionally with the fingertips. The tunings are: 1, 4, 8, or 1, 2, 6. Cf. *Shamisen*; *Tsebu* (Burma).
Lit.: nos. 209, 250.

Sanj (*Sanǧ*) (Arabia). Cymbal. Cf. *Sanuj*; *Sinj.*
Lit.: no. 255.

Sanje (Inner East Africa). Rattle. *Sansa.*
Lit.: no. 255.

Sanji (Congo). See *Sansa.*

Sanjo (Korea). Also *sancho.* Solo music for the *kaya-(geum)-kum* or the *tai-kum* accompanied by the *chang-ko.* The melody, occasionally derived from Shamanist music of South Korea, consists of a series of improvised variations. Each variation is performed in a different rhythmic mode: *chin-yang-jo*, 3/8, slow tempo; *chung-mori*, moderate 12/4 tempo; *chung-chung-mori*, slightly fast 12/8; *chajin-mori*, fast 12/8; *hwi-mori*, faster 12/8 than *chajin-mori*; *tanmori*, very fast 4/4.
Lit.: no. 277.

Sanjo kayakum (Korea). A composition for the modern *kaya-keum.*

Sanjo tae-kum (Korea). A composition for the *tae-kum.*
Lit.: no. 277.

Sanjū (Japan). Fixed prelude patterns in *shamisen* music.
Lit.: no. 187.

Sanjū (Japan). The top octave five notes in a three-octave system of the *go-on-hakase* notation. Cf. *Shoju*; *Niju*.
Lit.: no. 185.

Sankan gaku (Japan). *Gagaku*, music imported from ancient Korea. See *Gagaku*.

Śaṅkarābharaṇam (South India). (1) Term used for the name of the primary *rāga Dhīraśaṅkarābharaṇam*. (2) *Janya rāga* of the 29th *mēḷa* (*Dhīraśaṅkarābharaṇam*).
Tone material:
C D E F G A B c
c A G F E D C
Lit.: no. 139.

Śaṅkarapriya (South India). *Janya rāga* of the 49th *mēḷa* (*Dhavalāmbarī*).
Tone material:
C D♭ E F♯ B♭♭ c
c B♭♭ F♯ E D♭ C
Lit.: no. 139.

Śaṅkarī (South India). *Janya rāga* of the 29th *mēḷa* (*Dhīraśaṅkarābharaṇam*).
Tone material:
C E G B c
c B G E C
Lit.: no. 139.

Śaṅkha (*Shaṅkha*) (Vedic India). Ancient snail horn. Usually a narrow tube stuck into a large conch shell. In Sanskrit (Yajur Veda) the term is used for *bākura*.
Lit.: no. 250.

Saṅkīrna jāti (South India). See *Tāla*.

Saṅkīrtana (India; Bengal). A passionate type of the *kīrtana*, an ecstatic religious song sung by a chorus accompanied by drums and gongs.

Saṅku (Upper Guinea—Ashanti; Ewe). Harp type. Strings are placed in two layers fastened on fiber rings.
Lit.: no. 255.

Sankyoku (Japan). A *jiuta* ensemble (of three): *koto*, *shamisen*, and either *shakuhachi* or *kokyu*.
Lit.: no. 185.

Śaṅmukhapriyā (South India). The 56th *mēḷa*:
C D E♭ F♯ G A♭ B♭ c
The *rāga* with the same name has the same tone material.
Lit.: no. 139.

San-no-tsuzumi (Japan). A two-headed drum in the shape of an hourglass, imported from Korea. It is played by the leader of the *komagaku* ensemble. Cf. *Tsuzumi*.
Lit.: nos. 215, 225.

Sanomai (Japan). See *Bugaku*.

Sanoo (Northeast Thailand). A Lao term for a musical bow attached to a kite.
Lit.: no. 203.

Sansa (*Sanza*; *Zanza*) (Central and South Africa). This Bantu term designates a simple instrument widely spread across the African continent. It consists of a board or a flat box of wood mostly in rectangular shape that serves as basis. On one side of its top are tied over a small bridge thin, tuned rotan, raphia, or iron tongues in such manner that their ends can vibrate freely when plucked. Cf. *Ambira*; *Bela*; *Bunduma*; *Djimba*; *Ekende*; *Ibeka*; *Kankobele*; *Kasanga*; *Kindanda*; *Kisanji*; *Lulimba*; *Mbira*; *Nsimbi*; *Ompochawa*; *Pokido*; *Tsztze*.
Lit.: no. 255.

San-sagari (Japan). One tuning of the *shamisen* and *kokyū* is done in two fourths: B E A. Cf. *Shamisen*; *Kokyū*.
Lit.: no. 185.

Sanshino (Japan). A small, roughly built *shamisen*.
Lit.: no. 215.

San-shou (China). "Third hand." A musician of the Cantonese theater who plays the cymbals and a spike fiddle.
Lit.: no. 129.

Sānta (India). "Tranquility," "peace." One of the nine emotions (*navarasa*) referred to in music. Cf. *Rasa.*
Lit.: no. 140.

Śantakalyāṇī (South India). *Janya rāga* of the 65th *mēḷa* (*Mechakalyāṇī*). The scale of this *rāga* is identical with that of its primary *rāga* (*mēḷa*) *Mechakalyāṇī.*
Lit.: no. 139.

Śantakalyāṇī (South India). See *Kalyāṇī* (the 65th *asampūrṇa mēḷa*).

Santānamañjari (South India). See *Satyavati* (the 67th *asampūrṇa mēḷa*).

Śantamūrti (*Shantamūrti*) (South India). *Janya rāga* of the 49th *mēḷa* (*Dhavalāmbarī*). The scale of this *rāga* is identical with that of *rāga Śaṅkarapriya* (49th *mēḷa*).
Lit.: no. 139.

Santānamañjari (South India). *Janya rāga* of the 67th *mēḷa* (*Sucharitra*). The scale of this *rāga* is identical with that of its primary *rāga Sucharitra.*
Lit.: no. 139.

Santānika (South India). *Janya rāga* of the 64th *mēḷa* (*Vāchaspati*).
Tone material:

C D E F# Bb c
c Bb F# E D C

Lit.: no. 139.

Śāntasvarūpi (South India). *Janya rāga* of the 16th *mēḷa* (*Chākravāka*).
Tone material:

C E Db F G A Bb c
c Bb A Bb G F Db C

Lit.: no. 139.

Santen (*Srenten*) (Java). See *Rebāb* (Java).

Santir (Iran). A dulcimer. This zither consists of a shallow chestnut box in the form of a symmetrical trapezoid and 18 quadruple brass strings tuned by pegs. The player strikes them with two very light sticks. Cf. *Yang ch'in* ("foreign zither," China).
As there is considerable similarity between the *santir* and the *qanun*, a comparison is indicated:

Santir	*Qanun*
Both sides of the box are oblique.	One side of the box is oblique.
2 wire strings are used for one note.	3 lamb's gut strings are used for one note.
Strings are struck with two small sticks.	Strings are plucked with a small wire plectrum.

Lit.: no. 250.

Santo (Flores; Maumere; Larantuka). Tubular zither with six, seven, or nine strings. Cf. *Kenite*; *Nggo nggri*; *Mapa*; *Gong tondu.*
Lit.: nos. 156, 254.

Santun chengkok (Java—Solo). See *Singgetan.*

Santung (Southeast Celebes). Bamboo tube zither (stick zither). Cf. *Dunde.*
Lit.: nos. 132, 156.

Santun wilet (Java—Jogya). See *Singgetan.*

Santūr (*Santīr*) (Turkey; North India; Iran). Zither known in Iran, but hardly any more in other Arab countries. It has 72 strings arranged in groups of four. There are 18 metal strings, nine of brass and nine of steel. See *Santīr*. The strings are struck with small wooden sticks.
Lit.: no. 250.

Sanūj (Modern Egypt). Finger cymbals. Cf. *Sanj*; *Sinj*; *Sunūj.*

Sanyōgī (*Saṃyōgī*) (North India). Fiddle with four strings and three sympathetic wire strings. The instrument is closely related to the *sarangi.* It is tuned to C *G C* D.
Lit.: no. 254.

San yüeh (China). Music of *po hsi*, the "hundred amusements." In Japan *san yüeh* is called *sangaku*.

Sanza (Africa). See *Sansa*.

Sanzu (Congo – Azande). Board zither with a bark resonator.
Lit.: no. 176.

Sa o (Korea). "Down five," a solmization term referring to the fifth note below *kung*. See the list of the four basic *ah-ak* modes shown under the heading of *O-um-yak-po*.
Lit.: no. 136.

Sao (or *Dich*) (Vietnam). Term for the Chinese *ti*; a transverse bamboo flute with six finger holes and one hole covered with a thin membrane.

Sap (*cheo*) (Vietnam). Name of a scale. See list of scales shown under the heading of *Bac*.

Sapangkon (Java). A complete *gamelan* consisting of two sets of instruments, one tuned in *Pelog*, the other in *Slendro*.
Lit.: no. 163.

Sapeh (*Sapoh*) (Northeast Borneo). Simple lute with an oblong body, a short neck, 2, 3, occasionally also 4, rattan strings (in Southeast Borneo the strings can be made of steel or brass). The instrument is also called *safe*; *djimpai*, in Southeast Borneo; *kachapi*; and in Lonvia, *impai*.

Sapta ghaṇṭikā (India). "Seven bells"; a metallophone consisting of several metal slabs. Later there appeared 14 slabs, occasionally also bells. Also called *sapta svāraba*.
Lit.: no. 254.

Saptaka (India). Seven notes; the octave. Indian theorists distinguish three octaves:

1. *Mandra saptaka*, the lowest octave.
2. *Madhyama saptaka*, the middle octave.
3. *Tara saptaka*, the high octave.

Lit.: no. 136.

Sapta svāraba (India). See *Sapta ghaṇṭikā*.

Saptāsvaktīrani (South India). *Janya rāga* of the 34th *mēḷa* (*Vāgadhīśvarī*).
Tone material:
C D♯ F G A c
c A G F D♯ C
Lit.: no. 139.

Sarad (Bali). See *Rebāb*.

Śārada (South India). Tamil term for *sarōd*.

Śaradabharaṇam (South India). *Janya rāga* of the 34th *mēḷa* (*Vāgadhīśvarī*).
Tone material:
C F E F G F A B♭ c
c B♭ A F G F D♯ C
Lit.: no. 139.

Śaraddyuti (South India). *Janya rāga* of the 25th *mēḷa* (*Mārarañjanī*).
Tone material:
C E D F G A♭ B♭♭ c
(C D E F G A♭ B♭♭ A♭ c)
c B♭♭ A♭ G F E D C
The scale of this *rāga* is very similar to the primary *rāga* (*mēḷa*) *Mārarañjanī*.
Lit.: no. 139.

Sāradhālaṅgi (South India). *Janya rāga* of the 4th *mēḷa* (*Vanaspāti*).
Tone material:
C E♭♭ F A B♭ c
c B♭ A F E♭♭ C
Lit.: no. 139.

Śāradindumukhi (South India). *Janya rāga* of the 64th *mēḷa* (*Vāchaspati*).
Tone material:
C E F♯ G B♭ A B♭ G c
c B♭ A G F♯ E D C
Lit.: no. 139.

Śāradīyā Vīṇā (India). "Autumn *vīṇā*." An unusual name applied to a rare stringed instrument that has no relationship to the *vīṇā*. The

śāradīyā vīṇā (which in Hindi and Marthi usually has the name *sarōd*, in Tamil *śārada*), has the shape of a *sarōd*. It is a fiddle with four gut strings. Only occasionally the player discards the bow and plucks the strings.
Lit.: no. 254.

Saraina (Indonesia; Nias). See *Faritia.*

Sārala-vāmśī (India). A whistle flute with seven finger holes in front and one in the back.
Lit.: no. 255.

Sāramati (*Rati*) (South India). *Janya rāga* of the 20th *mēḷa* (*Naṭabhairavī*).
Tone material:
C D E♭ F G A♭ B♯ c
c B♭ A♭ F E♭ C
Lit.: no. 139

Sarang (*Rāgas*) (North India). Many *rāgas* of this family are subordinated to the *Kafī thāta*, and all represent a group similar to that of the *Mallar rāgas.* Most of the *Sarang* types are to be performed at noon or in the early afternoon. Among the well known *Sarang rāgas* of North India: *Bindrabani Sārang* (the actual *Sarang*); *Madhyamadi Sārang* (*Madhmadi*); *Badhauns Sārang*; *Miyan-ki Sārang*; *Lankadahan Sārang*; *Samant Sārang*; *Nur-Sārang.*

Less clearly defined as a family are the South Indian forms: *Sāraṅga*; *Sāraṅgabharanam*; *Sāraṅgakāpi* (I); *Sāraṅgakāpi* (II); *Sāraṅgalalita*; *Sāraṅgamāruva*; *Sāraṅgnāta.*
Lit.: nos. 138-39.

Sāraṅga (South India). *Janya rāga* of the 64th mēḷa (*Vāchaspatī*).
Tone material:
C D E F♯ G A B♭ c
c B♭ A G F♯ D F D C
In the *vakra* passage in descent the note F♯ is lowered to F.
Lit.: no. 139.

Sāraṅgabharaṇam (South India). *Janay rāga* of the 56th *mēḷa* (*Śaṇmukhapriyā*).
Tone material:
C F♯ G A♭ B♭ A♭ c
c B♭ A♭ G F♯ E♭ C
Lit.: no. 139.

Saraṅgakāpi (I) (South India). *Janya rāga* of the 20th *mēḷa* (*Naṭabhairavī*).
Tone material:
C D G F D C D G B♭ c
c B♭ A♭ G F E♭ D C
See *Saraṅgakāpi* (II).
Lit.: no. 139.

Sāraṅgakāpi (II) (South India). *Janya rāga* of the 20th *mēḷa* (*Naṭabhairavī*).
Tone material:
C D F G B♭ c
c B♭ A♭ G F E♭ D C
See *Sāraṅgakāpi* (I).
Lit.: no. 139.

Sāraṅgalalita (South India). *Janya rāga* of the 3rd *mēḷa* (*Gānamūrti*).
Tone material:
C D♭ E♭♭ F D♭ F G B c
c B A♭ G F D♭ C
Lit.: no. 139.

Sāraṅgamāruva (South India). *Janya rāga* of the 44th *mēḷa* (*Bhāvapriyā*).
Tone material:
C D♭ E♭ F♯ A♭ B♭ c
c B♭ A♭ F♯ G E♭ D♭ C
Lit.: no. 139.

Sāraṅganāṭa (South India). *Janya rāga* of the 15th *mēḷa* (*Māyāmāḷavagaula*).
Tone material:
C D♭ F G A♭ c
c B c A♭ G F E D♭ C
As *rāga*, *Sālanganāṭa*, believed to be the same as *Sāraṅganāṭa*, occasionally shows a different ascending scale:
C D♭ C F G A♭ c A♭ G c
The descent remains unchanged.
Lit.: no. 139.

Sāraṅgī (India). A very popular fiddle, particularly of North Indian and Bengal. It has a wooden corpus which is pulled in at its upper half. The upper part is covered with skin. It has a heavy neck and a large peg box. The *sāraṅgī* has three or four gut strings tuned to c c F C or c c G C (also c G C), and below these top strings 11 (up to 15) thin resonance strings. The latter are tuned in diatonic order according to the scale of the *rāga* performed. The fingering of the gut strings is not executed by the player's fingertips but by his fingernails. The nails eventually turn dark and hard like thick horn. Cf. *Alabusāraṅgī*; *Sarinda.*
Lit.: no. 250.

Sāraṇī (India). (1) Strings that run along the fingerboard (of zithers and lutes). (2) The highest wire string.

Sarasabhāsiṇi (South India). *Janya rāga* of the 34th *mēḷa* (*Vāgadhīśvarī*).
Tone material:
C D♯ E F A c
c A F E D♯ C
Lit.: no. 139.

Sarasāṅgī (South India). (1) The 27th *mēḷa*:
C D E F G A♭ B c
(2) *Rāga Sarasāṅgī* can be performed at any time. Veṅkaṭamakhin (17th century) called this *rāga Saurasena* (*Surasena*) in which the note D is avoided in descent. At the present time the *janya rāga Surasena* employs the note D in ascent and descent.
Lit.: no. 139.

Sarasapriya (South India). *Janya rāga* of the 27th *mēḷa* (*Sarasāṅgī*).
Tone material:
C D E F G A♭ B c
c B G A♭ F E D C
Lit.: no. 139.

Sarasapriya (South India). *Janya rāga* of the 72nd *mēḷa* (*Rasikapriyā*).
Tone material:
C D♯ E F♯ A♯ B c
c B A♯ F♯ E D♯ C
Lit.: no. 139.

Sarasāvāṇi (South India). *Janya rāga* of the 31st *mēḷa* (*Yāgapriyā*).
Tone material:
C D♯ E F A♭ c
c A♭ F E D♯ C
Lit.: no. 139.

Sarashi (Japan). Stereotyped pattern played by the *hayashi* in *kabuki* performances.
Lit.: no. 187.

Sarasīruham (South India). *Janya rāga* of the 44th *mēḷa* (*Bhāvapriyā*).
Tone material:
C D♭ E♭ F♯ A♭ B♭ A♭ c
c B♭ A♭ F♯ E♭ D♭ C
Lit.: no. 139.

Sarasīruhapriya (South India). *Janya rāga* of the 34th *mēḷa* (*Vāgadhīśvarī*).
Tone material:
C D♯ F G A c
c A G F D♯ C
Lit.: no. 139.

Sarasvati (South India). *Janya rāga* of the 64th *mēḷa* (*Vāchaspati*).
Tone material:
C D F♯ G A c
c B♭ A G F♯ D C
Lit.: no. 139.

Sarasvati Manohari (South India). *Janya rāga* of the 28th *mēḷa* (*Harikāmbhōji*).
Tone material:
C D E F A c
c A B♭ G F E D C
Lit.: no. 139.

Sarasvatīraṅgani (South India). *Janya rāga* of the 42nd *mēḷa* (*Raghupriyā*).
Tone material:
C D♭ F♯ G A♯ c
c A♯ F♯ G D♭ C
Lit.: no. 139.

Sarasvati Vīṇā (South India). This instrument, a tube zither, has one large gourd resonator attached to a wide tubular neck with 24 frets. The upper end shows a carved animal head. The instrument has four long metal strings strung along the neck and three shorter metal strings at the side. The strings are plucked with the fingertips of the player. The name of the instrument refers to the goddess of learning.

Sarati (South India). *Janya rāga* of the 66th *mēḷa* (*Chitrāmbarī*).
Tone material:
C D E F♯ G A♯ c
c B G A♯ G F♯ E D C
Lit.: no. 139.

Saravamaṅgala (South India). *Janya rāga* of the 71st *mēḷa* (*Kōsala*).
Tone material:
C D♯ F♯ A B c
c B A F♯ D♯ C
Lit.: no. 139.

Śarāvati (South India). See *Mārarañjanī*.

Śarāvati (South India). (1) The 25th *asampūrṇa mēḷa-rāga* without *kaṭapayādi* prefix. (2) The 25th *asampūrṇa mēḷa-rāga* with *kaṭapayādi* prefix. See *Rāga* (South India).
Lit.: no. 139.

Sarayuda (Java). At times the *gong*, *kenong*, *kempul*, and *ketuk* join the ensemble at the end of a *sendon*; thus the *suluk* part becomes "tamed" or "regulated"—called *sarayuda*.
Lit.: no. 163.

Sarbasnai (Kirgizia). Transverse metal flute with four or five finger holes. It is related to the Iranian *sarbaz-nai* (soldier's *nai*) and the *nai-sarbazi* of the Uzbeks.
Lit.: no. 275.

Sargam (India). Melodies where the singer uses tone syllables (*sa*, *ri*, *ga*, *ma*, etc.) instead of a proper text.

Sargi (India; Bengal). Bow of the *chikara*.

Sarhang (Turkey). See *Nāy*.

Sar hawa (Kurdistan). Freely improvised lute prelude, usually based on folk melodies.
Lit.: no. 229.

Sarinai (Vietnam). Oboe type.

Sarinda (India; Afghanistan). A popular fiddle widely used in North India, Kashmir, and Afghanistan. Its corpus has a remarkable shape: the top of a basically egg-formed shell is pulled together and only the lower part of this pulled-together part is covered with parchment or skin. The upper part that extends to the right and left remains open. Three gut strings are tuned to (e.g.) c c G. The pegs are laterally placed and the fingerboard shows no frets. The heavy bow is strung with horsehair.
Lit.: nos. 250, 254.

Sārmaṇḍal (North India). Marathi name of a board zither plucked with fingertips. The instrument has several names: *kātyāyana vīṇā* or (according to the number of strings) *śatatantrī vīṇā* (zither with a hundred strings). It is also called *svaramaṇḍala* or *surmaṇḍal*. The Tamil term is *churamantalam*. Most common is the Arabic-Hindi name *qānūn* denoting a zither with (21), 22 (or 36) strings, in contrast to the genuine Arabic *qānūn* with (63, 75) 78 strings.
Lit.: no. 254.

Sarnā (India). See *Sānāyī*; *Surnā*.
Lit.: no. 254.

Sarnai (India). Mouth-blown bagpipe chanter. Cf. *Surnā*.

Sarōd (North India). A deeply-waisted long-necked lute. A dialectal form of the term in West Pakistan and Afghanistan is *saroz*. The *sarōd* is popular and is plucked with a plectrum; it is bowed rarely. Usually it has four gut strings tuned to 1-4-5-8; (e.g., C, F, G, c). The first string often appears as a pair in order to stress the low bourdon sound. Below the main strings are strung 10-16 sympathetic wire strings tuned to the tone material of the piece performed. Cf. *Śaradīyā Vīṇā*; *Rabōb*; *Sarrawat*.
Lit.: nos. 250, 254.

Saron (Java; West Java; Bali). A single-octave metallophone consisting of six, seven, or eight slightly curved bronze slabs placed across a wooden trough and struck with a small *tabuh*. There are four one-octave instruments, each with six, seven, or eight slabs, and occasionally appears a multi-octave type. The highest, a discant type, is called by various names: *saron panerus*, *saron selento*, *saron peking*, *saron penitil*, *saron panachah*, *saron selokat*, *saron chente*, *saron titil*, *saron tete lile*. The alto type is called *saron* or *saron barung*. The tenor is called *saron demung*, in West Java *kedemung* and in Indramayu *penurung*. The bass is called *saron slentem* or *salon jengglong*. The multiple-octave instrument is called *gambang gangsa* or *gambang selukat*; in Solo Kraton it is called *chelepita*; when the keys have bosses the name is *pantu*. In West Java, in Indramayu the instrument is called *dempling* or *kedempling*.

Saron (Java). The term *saron* can also be applied to a xylophone: six bamboo slabs are placed on a trough-like box. This xylophone functions as a melody instrument.

Saron (Bali). In Bali is used a *saron* and two *gangsa* (7 keys) tuned an octave apart. One player strike both instruments. There are also two *saron* consisting of wooden blocks with hanging bamboo keys. The *saron menanga* (with seven keys) performs the melody in the same way as the *gangsa*, but each melody note is beaten here twice. The *saron pengulu* with twice four keys is used for performing the figurations with two hammers.

Saron (Malaysia). The medium octave range.

Saron (Malaysia; Johore). A metallophone with seven slabs. There are three types:
1. *Pekang*, the high pitched one.
2. *Saron*, the medium pitched.
3. *Demung*, the low pitched instrument.

The tuning of the three ranges are:

Pekang:	c b♭ a f e c′ b♭′
Saron:	c′ b♭′ a′ f♯′ e′ c♯′
Demung:	c *B*♭ A F♯ E C *B*♭

The tone names are the same in each of the three octave ranges: *chi*, *nem*, *mo*, *lu*, *ruh*, *chi*, *nem*.

Saron barung (Java). See *Saron* (Java). In contrast to the Javanese *saron barung*, the Malayan *saron barung* is identical with the Malayan *saron panerus*.

Saron beusi (Sunda District; West Java). A *saron* with iron keys. Sundanese *beusi* is the Javanese *wesi* (*besi*).
Lit.: no. 163.

Saron chenté (Sunda District). A single-octave *saron*, also called *saron penitil*. See *Saron peking*; *Saron panerus*.

Saron demung (Malaysia). A set of six kettles, tuned to c A G E D C.
Lit.: no. 163.

Saron demung (Java). Single-octave *saron* tuned one octave lower than the *saron barung*. Cf. *Kedemung*.

Saronen (Java). See *Selompret*; *Serunai*.

Saronen (East Java; Madura). Wooden heterophonic double reed instrument with six (seven) finger holes. It has a penetrating sound. Among the various names are: *tetepret*, *tetet*, in Bali and Hindu-Java, also *pereret*, *pleret*, *gem(p)ret*; in the Sunda District *tarompet*. Cf. *Selompret* (Java); *Surnā*.
Lit.: no. 163.

Sarong (West Africa—Mandingo; Sarakole). Harp-lute.
Lit.: no. 255.

Sarong (India—East Bengal; Khassi). Lute with four strings and a vase-shaped corpus.
Lit.: no. 255.

Sarong (Sierra Leone). Harp-lute with six strings, a half-spherical corpus, and a curved neck. The thickest string is made of fiber.
Lit.: no. 255.

Sarong (Assam). Name of the *sārangi*.
Lit.: no. 254.

Saron menanga (Bali). See *Saron* (Bali).
Lit.: no. 265.

Saron panachah (Java; Bali). See *Saron* (Java; Bali).

Saron panerus (Malaysia). See *saron panerus* (Java; Bali). A single-octave *saron*, producing the highest octave range. The instrument is also called *saron peking*, *saron panachah*.
Lit.: no. 163.

Saron pengulu (Bali). A *saron* with twice four keys. The instrument is used for figuration work. See *Saron*.
Lit.: no. 265.

Saron penitil (Sunda District). See *Saron* (Bali; Java).

Saron selento (Java). See *Saron* (Bali; Java).

Saron selokat (Java). See *Saron* (Java; Bali).

Saron slentem (Java). See *Saron* (Java; Bali).

Saron Tete lile (Sunda District). See *Saron* (Java; Bali).

Saron titil (Java). See *Saron tete lile*.

Saron wesi (*besi*). See *Saron beusi*.

Saroz (West Pakistan). See *Sarod*.

Sarpa (India). Twice-curved brass horn.
Lit.: no. 16.

Sarparda (North India). *Rāga* ascribed to the *Bilaval thāta*. *Sarparda* is a morning *rāga* and is believed to be a combination of phrases taken from the *rāgas Alahiya-Bilaval*, *Bihag*, and *Goud*. The tone material is varied as the phrases are used freely.
Tone material (e.g.):
C D E F G A B c
c B (B♭) A G F E D C; *Vādis*: C, G
Lit.: no. 138.

Sarra (Turkey). Oboe type.

Sarrawat (India). A *sārangī* played with a plectrum. Cf. *Sārod(a)*.

Saru (Egypt). An ancient frame drum.
Lit.: no. 255.

Sarugaku (Japan). "Monkey music." Originally a ritual performance inside the temple. Later it became a popular theatrical show. Next to *dengaku* it is the important prototype of the *noh* drama. *Sarugaku* came into existence in the 13th century. It was never sung but only danced and represented comic pantomimes, foolish fun, often reaching the vulgar. After 1420 *sarugaku* employed a chorus that recited the text and gave descriptions of the dances.

The instruments used to accompany the performance, popularly called *noh* dancing, were: *yoko-fue*, *uta-daiko*, *ō-tsuzumi*, and *ko-tsuzumi*. Later the voice parts were written separately and recited without instrumental accompaniment. Cf. *Dengaku*.
Lit.: no. 225.

Sarune (Sumatra—Batak). Also *srune*; *zurna*. A double oboe similar to the Arabic *arghul* with a "male" tube (*laki*), with four or five finger holes (*quayet*), a bamboo reed at the lower end (*tubu*), and a shorter, "female" tube (*puan*) without finger holes used for the bourdon accompaniment. Cf. *Sendiu* (Borneo); *Puwi-puwi*.
Lit.: no. 162.

Saruwaka-komai (Japan). Old style of comic *kabuki*.
Lit.: no. 187.

Sarva rāga mēḷa vīṇā (South India). Cf. *Akhila rāga mēḷa vīṇā*.

Śārvari (South India). *Janya rāga* of the 55th *mēḷa* (*Śyāmalāṅgī*).
Tone material:
C D E♭ F♯ B𝄫 c
c B𝄫 F♯ E♭ D C
Lit.: no. 139.

Sarwad (Arabia). Singing.

Sa sa (Korea). "Down four"; solmization term referring to the fourth note below *kung*. See list of the four basic *ah-ak* modes shown under the heading of *O-um-yak-po*.
Lit.: no. 136.

Sasa (Polynesia; Samoa). Formal dance accompanied by percussion instruments.

Sa sam (Korea). "Down three"; solmization term referring to the third note below *kung*. See list of the four basic *ah-ak* modes shown under the heading of *O-um-yak-po*.
Lit.: no. 136.

Sasando (Timor). Bamboo zither.
Lit.: no. 215.

Śaśankakiraṇi (South India). *Janya rāga* of the 12th *mēḷa* (*Rūpavatī*).
Tone material:
C D♭ E♭ G A♯ c
c A♯ G E♭ D♭ C
Lit.: no. 139.

Sasara (Japan). Rattles, scrapers. Cf. *Bin-sasara*.
Lit.: no. 185.

(Sa)sekaran (Java). See *Sekaran*.

Sasesaheng (Indonesia; Talaud Isl.). Idiophone in the form of a bamboo tuning fork. Cf. *Buncacan*; *Rerre*.
Lit.: no. 167.

Sasgar (Arabia). *Maqām*, of a light, pleasant character, originally called "Son of 'Ajam." The name *Sasgar* is Persian, but the *maqām* is typically Arabic. In Syria it is well known; in Egypt it is almost unknown.
Tone material:
F G A B♭ c d e (or $\overset{+}{\text{e}}$♭ f
Lit.: no. 121.

Sashi (Japan). Highly stylized speech with recitative features in the *noh* drama.
Lit.: no. 187.

Sashi-jō (Japan). See *Noh*; *Yowa*.

Śasiprakāśini (South India). *Janya rāga* of the 16th *mēḷa* (*Chakravāka*).
Tone material:
C D♭ E F G A B♭ c
c B♭ A G E D♭ C
Lit.: no. 139.

Sason (*Corra*) (Flores). See *Remba*.

Sassandu (Timor). Zither made of a bamboo tube with 18 metal strings. Cf. *Susunu*.
Lit.: no. 206.

Ṣaṣṭha (Vedic India). See *Atisvārya*.

Sa tai (Thailand). A refined, highly elegantly polished *rebāb*, richly ornamented with ivory and mother of pearl. Cf. *Tro Khmer*.
Lit.: no. 254.

Satara (North India; Rajasthan). A pair of simple vertical flutes played by one person. The left flute of the pair produces the drone, the right one the melody.

Śat 'Arabān (Middle East). *Maqām.*
Tone material:

G Ab B C D Eb F# G

Ab G (F) Eb D C *B Ab G*

Lit.: no. 64.

Śatatantrī vīṇā (India). "Vina with 100 strings." A board zither with a trapezoid-shaped corpus and 22-36 metal strings. It is known under several names; a few are: *kānūna* (*qānūn*); *svaramandala*; *kātyāyana vīṇā*; *surmaṇḍal*. Cf. *Sārmaṇḍal.*
Lit.: no. 254.

Sa-t'hu-karn (Thailand). Term for sacred music.
Lit.: no. 58.

Sato (Flores—Wolowaru). Bowed lute. See *Robēka.*
Lit.: no. 166.

Sato-kagura (Japan). Shinto festival folk music; the village *kagura* pieces are sung and played. The songs are accompanied by a *hayashi* ensemble. *Sato-kagura* presents dances in front and inside the Shinto shrine. The dances display animal movements and are either comic or symbolically mysterious (devil dances, etc.). Among the dances can be listed: *hyottoko*, the comic bumpkin dance; *okame*, the comic female dance; *nimba*, the dog dance; *shishiodori*, the lion dance.
Lit.: no. 185.

Satong (*Pagan(g)*) (Borneo—Sarawak). Bamboo tube zither with six strings.
Lit.: no. 156.

Śatpadhadhvani (South India). *Janya rāga* of the 70th *mēḷa* (*Nāsikabhūṣaṇī*).
Tone material:

C D# F# G A c

c A G F# D# C

Lit.: no. 139.

Satrud (*Satrughna*) (Thailand). See *Khon.*

Ṣaṭśruti (India). See *Shatśruti.*

Ṣaṭśruti Dha (*Kaiśikī Ni*) (India). The tone name corresponding to *rohiṇī*, the 19th *śruti.* Cf. *Śruti.*

Ṣaṭśruti Ri (*Sādhāraṇa Ga*) (India). The note name corresponding to *rañjanī*, the sixth *śruti.* Cf. *Śruti.*

Satsuma Biwa (Japan). This *biwa* is more graceful than the massive and large instruments of the same family. The *bachi*, having the usual triangular form, is made of thin wood and has an unusually wide striking base. The four (occasionally five) silken strings and the four (occasionally three) frets are the same as those on the other *biwa* types. An interesting feature of *Satsuma-biwa* playing is the use of various trills, vibratos, and similar ornaments which are achieved by the application of the large side of the plectrum.
Lit.: nos. 185, 225.

Satung (South Celebes). Split bamboo zither. Cf. *Kenite* (Flores); *Santo* (Larantuka); *Sesando* or *Pesandon* (Timor; Kupang; Roti).
Lit.: nos. 132, 166.

Satyabhūṣaṇi (South India). *Janya rāga* of the 71st *mēḷa* (*Kōsala*).
Tone material:

C E F# G A B c

c B A G F# E C

Lit.: no. 139.

Satyavatī (South India). *Janya rāga* of the 67th *mēḷa* (*Sucharitra*).
Tone material:

C D# F# G Ab Bbb Ab c

c Bbb Ab G F# E F# D# C

Lit.: no. 139.

Satyavatī (South India). (1) The 67th *asampūrṇa mēḷa-rāga* without *kaṭapayādi* prefix. (2) The 67th *asampūrṇa mēḷa-rāga* with *kaṭapayādi* prefix was called *Santānamañjari.* See *Rāga* (South India).
Lit.: no. 139.

Sa u (Thailand). A large *sa dung* (*sa dueng*) with two strings. Cf. *So*; *So u.*
Lit.: no. 184.

Saugandhinī (South India). See *Sālava* (37th *asampūrṇa mēḷa*).

Śauktika Vīṇā (India). "Mother of pearl lute." The instrument is a *sitar* type, very richly ornamented. Its small corpus ends in an Ibis head. Although *śauktika vīṇā* is a fancy name, the instrument is of no importance in musical practice.
Lit.: no. 250.

Sau-nat (China; Canton). See *So-na.*

Saunay (Philippines—Sulu). Wooden heterophonic double-reed instrument. Cf. *Śāhnāyī* (India). The instrument can also appear in a single reed form.
Lit.: no. 215.

Saun(g) kauk (*Saun gauk*) (Burma). Arched harp consisting of a boat-shaped corpus with a curved neck and 13-14 strings. A smaller type with 5-7 (now nylon) strings has to be mentioned. The tuning of the large harp is:
B♭ E♭ F G B♭ c d f g b♭ c′ d′ f′
Lit.: no. 255.

Saurasena (South India). (1) See *Sarasāṅgī*. (2) See *Janya rāga Surasena* of the 27th *mēḷa.*

Saurāshṭra(m) (*Saurāṣṭram*) (South India). *Janya rāga* of the 15th *mēḷa* (*Māyāmāḷavagauḷa*).
Tone material:
C D♭ E F G A♭ B c
c B A♭ G F E D♭ C
The tone material is identical with that of the prime *rāga* (15th *mēḷa*). Slight differences have been discussed in Lit. no. 139.

Saurāshtra-bhairav (*Saurāshtra-tank*) (North India). *Rāga* ascribed to the *Bhairav thāta*, to be performed in the morning. Performance rules are indistinct.
Tone material (vague), e.g.:
C D♭ E F G (A♭) (A) B c
c B (A) (A♭) G F E D♭ C; *Vādis*: F, C
Lit.: no. 138.

Saurāshtra-tank (North India). See *Saurāshtra-bhairav.*

Sausamsai (Thailand). A fiddle with three strings. An almost obsolete instrument that was favored in the past at the royal court.

Ṣaut (Arabia). "Sound." Originally term for vocal music. Later the term meant "noise," in contrast to *ṭanīn* (musical tone).
Lit.: no. 65.

Ṣaut (Iran; Khorasan; Turkmenia). Piece of music. Cf. *'Amal.*

Sauti (East Africa—Swahili). See *Wimbo, mafuaton. . . .*

Sauti linganifu (Zanzibar). Swahili term for accompaniment.

Sautu (Celebes). Bell made of half a calabash.
Lit.: no. 255.

Sauvīra (South India). *Janya rāga* of the 47th *mēḷa* (*Suvarṇāṅgī*).
Tone material:
C D♭ E♭ D♭ F♯ G A B c
c B G A G F♯ E♭ D♭ C
Lit.: no. 139.

Sauvīra (South India). (1) The 47th *asampūrṇa mēḷa-rāga* without *kaṭapayādi* prefix. (2) The 47th *asampūrṇa mēḷa-rāga* with *kaṭapayādi* prefix. See *Rāga* (South India).
Lit.: no. 139.

Sauvirī (India). The first of the seven *mūrchhanās* derived from the *ma-grāma.*

Savan (India). Religious song for the month *shravan* (August).

Savani (North India). *Rāga* ascribed to the *Bilaval thāta*. The *rāga* has several diverse interpretations (e.g., the late Aladiya Khan of Bombay and his pupils stressed the note B).
Tone material:
C E F G B c
c B A G F G D C; *Vādis*: G, C
Lit.: no. 138.

Savani-bihag (North India). Rare *rāga* ascribed to the *Kalyan thāta*. It is derived from *rāga Savani-kalyan*. The performance rules are indistinct.
Tone material (vague):
C E F G B c
c G F E D C; *Vādis* unclear
Lit.: no. 138.

Savani-kalyan (North India). *A rāga* of recent age, ascribed to the *Kalyan thāta*.
Tone material:
C E F G A c
c B A G E D C; *Vādis*: C, G(B)
Lit.: no. 138.

Savaraṅgi (South India). *Janya rāga* of the 57th *mēḷa* (*Siṃhendramadhyama*).
Tone material:
C D F♯ A♭ B c
c B A♭ F♯ E♭ C D C
Lit.: no. 139.

Sāveri (South India). *Janya rāga* of the 15th *mēḷa* (*Māyāmāḷavagauḷa*).
Tone material:
C D♭ F G A♭ c
c B A♭ G F E D♭ C
Lit.: no. 139.

Sāvitri (South India). *Janya rāga* of the 28th *mēḷa* (*Harikāmbhōji*).
Tone material:
C E F G B♭ c
c B♭ G F E C
Lit.: no. 139.

Saw (Northeast Thailand). (1) General term for bowed lutes; e.g., *saw mai pai* (bamboo fiddle), or *saw bip* (fiddle with a metal can corpus). (2) Traditional singing accompanied by an ensemble of *bee saw*.
Lit.: no. 203.

Sawai git (Nepal). Ballad.
Lit.: no. 133.

Sawangan dara (Java). Little pigeon-tail flutes of several different sizes. These flutes are tied to the flying doves and create a whistling sound.
Lit.: no. 163.

Sawari (Japan). (1) "Rattle." A characteristic sound produced on the *shamisen* and *biwa*. The sound creates a nasal and vibrating effect. (2) The musical climax in puppet shows (*bunraku*).
Lit.: no. 185.

Sawat (Indonesia—Sula Isl.). Goblet-formed drum.
Lit.: no. 162.

Saw bip (Northeast Thailand). "Metal-can fiddle." Generally a kerosene can is used as the corpus. The instrument has two strings.
Lit.: no. 203.

Saw bung mai pai (Northeast Thailand). Bamboo fiddle.

Saw duang (Thailand). A high-pitched fiddle with a cylindrical body and two strings. The hair of the bow is strung between the two strings. The instrument is related to the Chinese *hu-ch'in* and the Thai *sawu*. The *saw duang* is also in use in Vietnam.
Lit.: nos. 51, 203.

Sawergnil (Moluccas; Timor; Kai Isl.). Bamboo flute. See *Nuren*.
Lit.: no. 166.

Šāwīš (Arabia). See *Tabl al-jāwīj* (*shāwīsh*).

Sam Oo (Vietnam). Low-pitched fiddle.
Lit.: no. 51.

Saworo (Nigeria—Yoruba). Leg and ankle bells.

Šawq-i-Afzā (Middle East). *Maqām*.
Tone material:
B♭ C D $\overset{+}{E\flat}$ F G♭ A B♭
Lit.: no. 64.

Šawq-i-'Āwir (Middle East). *Maqām*.
Tone material:
B♭ C D E♭ F G A♭ B♭
Lit.: no. 64.

Šawqi-Dil (Middle East). *Maqām*.
Tone material:
C D $\overset{+}{E\flat}$ $\overset{(\sharp)}{F}$ G A $\overset{+}{B\flat}$ c (c B A♭ G F E♭ D C)
Lit.: no. 64.

Šawqi-Ṭarab (Middle East). *Maqām*.
Tone material:
A B♭ C D $\overset{+}{E\flat}$ F G♭ A B♭ c d♭ e f
Lit.: no. 64.

Saw sam sai (Thailand; Kampuchea). Term for a *rebāb* type with two or three strings.
Lit.: no. 186.

Saw tai (*So tai*) (Thailand). A bowed spike fiddle, beautifully constructed. Its neck is ornamented with inlaid mother of pearl or ivory. The instrument has three silken strings. The Kampuchean term is *tro khmer*. See *Rebāb*.
Lit.: no. 254.

Saw u (*So u*) (Thailand). Fiddle with a body made of half a coconut shell and two strings. In all other respects it is the same as the *saw duang*.

Sawwuri (Arabia). A 5-stringed *tanbūr*.
Lit.: no. 255.

Say pha (Thailand). Narrative song. The performer accompanies himself by clicking four little wooden sticks together.
Lit.: no. 186.

Sāyujyatāyini (South India). *Janya rāga* of the 36th *mēḷa* (*Chalanāṭa*).
Tone material:
C E F G A♯ c
c B A♯ G F E C
Lit.: no. 139.

Saz (Iran; Kurdistan; Turkey). (1) General term for music. (2) A bowed *tanbūr* with a pear-shaped body. It has four wire strings; strings 1, 2, and 4 are made of steel, string 3 is made of brass. The number of strings is variable; occasionally there can be as many as six or seven. The neck has 14-16 frets.
Lit.: no. 254.

Sāz (North India). Bowed spike lute with a round corpus, a long neck, three main gut strings, and 14 thin resonance wire strings. The instrument resembles the *kemānjah*, which now and then was used in musical performances at the court of Hyderabad.
Lit.: no. 254.

Sazagiri (North India). See *Sazgiri*.

Sazanda (Afghanistan). Musician.

Sāzandeh (Kurdistan). Musician. Also *hunarmand*.
Lit.: no. 229.

Sazanza (Japan). Fashionable songs of the 16th century.
Lit.: no. 225.

Sazgiri (North India). Also *Sazagiri*. Rare *rāga* ascribed to the *Marva thāta*.
Tone material:
C D♭ E F F♯ G A♭ A B c
c B A A♭ G F♯ F E D♭ C; *Vādis*: E, B
Lit.: no. 138.

Sāz-i alwāḥ-i fūlad (Middle East). Medieval glockenspiel with iron slabs.
Lit.: no. 76.

Sāz-i kāsāt (*Sāz-i ṭāsāt*) (Middle East; Iran). Ancient earthenware cups used in the same manner as the Indian *jaltarang*.

Sāz-kār (Middle East). *Maqām*.
Tone material:
C D♯ E♭(+) F G A B♭(+) c
Lit.: no. 64.

Sbom-shal (Tibet). See *Sbub-shal.*
Lit.: no. 143.

Sbub-shal (Tibet). "Hollow mouth." Also *sbom-shal* (literally, "heavy mouth"). *Sbub-shal* is a distorted form of *sbug-shal*, or *sbum-zhol*; also *bog*, *bug*. A pair of large brass cymbals with narrow rims and wide bosses.
Lit.: no. 143.

Sbug-zhal (Tibet). See *Sbub-shal*; *Sil-snyan.*

Sbum-zhol (Tibet). See *Sbug-zhal.*

Sbum-zhol (Tibet). See *Sbug shal* (*Sbug-zhal*).

Sco-thom (Kampuchea). Massive, barrel-shaped tam-tam. At festivals two *sco-thom* are played.
Lit.: no. 153.

Sê (*shê*) (China – M 5451). A zither of similar form as the *ch'in.* In the past it had 50 strings; at the present time it has 25 silken strings tuned to:
C D E G A c d e g a c' d' e' g' a' etc.
In contrast to the *ch'in*, the *sê* has no studs but uses moveable bridges. Each group of five bridges is painted in a different color. The *sê* is always played in octaves. By the 4th century the *sê* became obsolete as a solo instrument. Only in modern times did it gain some popularity.
Lit.: no. 136.

Sea (Polynesia). Songs sung and danced by men at the annual Sansa ritual. A group of men, seated on the ground, accompany a few dancers with song and clapping of hands.
Lit.: no. 318.

Sebet (Ancient Egypt). Obsolete flute.

Seblang (Java). Dance of young girls in trances. See *Sanghyang* (Bali).
Lit.: no. 163.

Seb noi (Laos). Instrumental ensemble consisting mainly of fiddles and lutes. Only very occasionally are added a few wind and/or percussion instruments.

Sebsi (Arabia). Double reed.
Lit.: no. 255.

Seburuburu (South Africa – Chwana). A toy bull roarer. Cf. *Sevuruvuru.*
Lit.: no. 151.

Sedasa (*Penggulu*) (Java; Cheribon). (1) "Ten," "tenth tone." The tenth tone of a scale or melody. (2) The second note of the *pelog* system of Cheribon.
Lit.: no. 163.

Sedefli tanbura (Turkey). Very small *tanbura.*
Lit.: no. 255.

Sedeng (*Tengah*) (Java). Middle register.

Sedih (West Java). See *Nalangsa.*

Seekh (Egypt). The iron foot (spike) of the *kamānjah.*

See saw (Laos). Music bow with two strings.
Lit.: no. 255.

See saw duang (Thailand). Cf. *So doran.*
Lit.: no. 255.

See saw oo (Thailand). See *So u.*

Se finjolo (*Segankuru*; *Setinkane*) (South Africa – Chwana). Bowed tube zither.
Lit.: no. 190.

Segah (Iran). See *Dastgāh.*

Šegaṇḍi (South India). Cf. *Jegaṇṭa* (Tamil term).

Segankuru (South Africa). See *Sefinjolo.*

Sege-sege (Sudan—Kanga-Bonu language). Calabash rattle. Cf. *Seke-seke.*
Lit.: no. 95.

Segi (Burma). Large suspended barrel drum.
Lit.: no. 255.

Sego (Flores). Also *gkrego.* A throaty trill performed by the singer.
Lit.: no. 166.

Segolta (Ancient Israel). Notational symbol (∴) used in biblical chant, indicating a strong disjunctive function (the Latin *triangula*).
Lit.: no. 309.

Segwana (South Africa—Chwana). Music bow with resonator. The Thonga call this instrument *tshitendje* (*dende*), the Sotho *sekgapa*, the Sotho of Basutoland *thomo*, the Swazi *ligubu*, the Zulu *ugubu* (*ugumbu*, *gubuolukhulu* or *inkohlisa*), the Xhosa *uhadi.* The Bushman term is *kopo.*
Lit.: no. 151.

Seh (Bali). A signal beaten on the drum to indicate that a change in tempo and in the dance has to occur. *Seh* also refers to the opening beat performed on the leading *gangsa* in modern *kebyar* music.
Lit.: no. 197.

Seḥem (Sudan; Egypt). See *Iba.*

Sehgura (Sierre Leone—Mende). Gourd rattle.
Lit.: no. 190.

Sehtār (Iran). See *Setār.*

Sei (Japan). A brief accented beat performed by the right hand stick on the *kakko.* The stroke is executed by the player in a characteristically circular motion that is referred to as *tomoye.*
Lit.: no. 225.

Seichō (Japan). Traditional, orthodox melody. Cf. *Bushi.*

Sei-in (Japan). "Clear voices." Term used in the theory of singing. See *Kwaigo-no-ben*; *Go-sei*; *Go-ju.* Cf. *Jisei-in.*
Lit.: no. 225.

Sei p'il-lyul (Korea). See *Sei-p'iri*; *P'iri.*

Sei-p'iri (*Sae-p'iri*; *Sei-p'il-lyul*) (Korea). A small sized *hyang-p'iri* with a gentle tone.
Lit.: no. 179.

Seiteki (Japan). Simple cross flute made of bamboo. It has six finger holes and one hole covered with thin paper. The *seiteki* is often used together with the *gekkin*, the *teikin*, and the *keikin.*
Lit.: no. 250.

Sekar ageng (Java). Term in High Javanese for *tembang gede.* Cf. *Tembang.*

Sekaran (Java). The variating, ornamenting of the basic themes in *gamelan* performances.
Lit.: no. 163.

Sekar madya (Java). The High Javanese term for "middle song." The Low Javanese term is *tembang tengahan.*
Lit.: no. 163.

Sekatari (South Africa; Basutoland—Sotho). Bowed tube zither.
Lit.: no. 151.

Sekaten (Java). The *sekaten* week is the time between the sixth and twelfth days of the month of Mulud (excepting Thursday and Friday evenings). At that time a special orchestra, the *gamelan sekati* (ensembles of the native rulers of Solo, Jogya, and Cheribon; in the past also Madura and Banten) perform in memory of the death of Mohammed the Prophet. The *gamelan sekati* is used throughout the days but does not play at night. Cf. *Gamelan munggang.*

Sekawan (Java). See *Papat.*

Sekene (South Africa—Venda). Cf. *Denya.*

Sekere (Nigeria—Yoruba; Dahomey—Nago). Large gourd rattles wound with cowrie shells. The instrument is used only to honor royalty. Cf. *Sakara.*

Seke-seke (Sudan; Nigeria). Cf. *Sege-sege.*
Lit.: nos. 218, 293.

Sekgapa (South Africa—Sotho; Thonga). Music bow. Cf. *Segwana*; *Penda*; *Dende.*
Lit.: no. 151.

Sekgobogobo (*Setsegetsege*) (South Africa; Transvaal—Sotho). Bowed tube zither. Cf. *Tsijolo.*
Lit.: no. 151.

Sekhem (Egypt). Ancient sistrum; its handle has the form of a horseshoe-shaped iron hoop. On top of the handle, embraced by the hoop, is shown the head of Hathor. Within the hoop, on thin metal sticks, small discs rattle when the instrument is shaken. Cf. *Seshest.*
Lit.: no. 100.

Sekkyō-bushi (Japan). *Sekkyo-joruri.*

Sekkyō-jōruri (Japan). *Sekkyō*, an early form of *shamisen* music, was the (narrative) educational medium used by Buddhist monks. It was sung only when it appeared in a stage play of the *jōruri* type. Its forerunner was the *sekkyō-bushi.*

Selento (Java). High-pitched discant *saron.* Cf. *Saron* (alto type); *Demung* (tenor); *Slentem* (bass).

Seli (Nigeria—Yoruba). Two small thin round plates of tin with handles are beaten against each other like cymbals.

Seliko (East Africa; Somali Republic). A dance similar to *deliko* performed generally by women.
Lit.: no. 98.

Selisir (Bali). One of the five pentatonic (or hexatonic) scales used in the *gambuh semar pegulingan* (which is becoming more and more obsolete).
Lit.: nos. 165, 265.

Selisir gong (Bali). Pentatonic scale: C# (*ding*), D (*dong*), E (*deng*), G# (*dung*), A (*dang*).
Lit.: nos. 197, 265.

Selokat (Java). See *Selokkat.*

Selokkat (*Selokat*) (Java). The Jogya name of a *saron* type that produces high-pitched sounds, one octave higher than those of the common *saron* (*saron barung*). The metal slabs of the *selokkat* are thicker than those of other *saron* types. The Jogya name *selokkat* was and is used instead of *saron panerus.*
Lit.: no. 255.

Selompret (*Selompret*; *Sompret*) (Java). Name for an old wooden oboe with conical bore. The instrument has six holes in front and one in the back. It was used to accompany *kuda kepang* dances, whip duels, and *ronggeng* dances where excitement, hypnosis, and frenzied playing have an important role. *Selompret* has various names; a few are mentioned: *saronen* or *serunen* in Madura; *pereret*, *pleret*, *gem(p)ret* in Hindu-Javanese language, *tarompet* in the Sunda Districts; *pereret* in Bali. Cf. *Serunai.*
Lit.: no. 163.

Ṣelṣlē śāma' (Ancient Israel). Hebrew term for clear sounding cymbals.
Lit.: no. 250.

Ṣelṣlē trūa' (Ancient Israel). Hebrew term for harsh, noisy cymbals; related to the Egyptian instruments.

Ṣelṣlīm (Ancient Israel). Talmudic term for *ṣlāṣal*; *ṣelṣlīm*, the Hebrew term for cymbals.
Lit.: no. 250.

Selundeng (*Selunding*) (Bali). General name for the special iron-keyed metallophones of the *gamelan-selundeng.* The large iron keys are suspended over a wooden resonator box. The instrument is rare and sacred and is played at ritual occasions.
Lit.: no. 265.

Šem (Sumeria). See *Shem.*

Semai (Turkey). (1) Specific rhythm and melody. Songs with eight syllables in each textual line. The *semai* deal with simple historical events among the Turkish tribes. (2) *Semai* (*nakish*). Melismatic songs of Turkish origin. Cf. *Kiami-natik.*
Lit.: nos. 34, 243.

Śēmakkalam (*Sōmangalam*) (India). Flat gong struck with one hand. The other hand beats a *thappattai.*
Lit.: no. 260.

Semaku (Timor). See *Bobi.*

Semara (Arabia; Sahara; Nigeria – Hausa; Fulbe; Tuareg). Reed of the *algaīta.* Cf. *Zamr.*

Semar nyampar (Java). A particular manner of striking the *bonang* and *gambang kayu* in limping rhythm that suggests the characteristic step of Semar (the god of love) with his club foot in the following manner. Cf. *Ṭuṭukan rangkep.*
Lit.: no. 163.

Semar Pegulingan (Bali). A softly sounding *gamelan* played during afternoons and evenings for recreational dancing of the members of the court. At present this custom is almost forgotten. In the past four or five modes were used: *tembung* (G# A# B d# e); *selisir* (C# D E G# A); *sunaren* (G A B♭ d e♭ [or e]), *baro* (D E♭ F♭ A B♭), *lebeng* (E F G# B c).
The melody was usually played by the *trompong* or, if the ensemble was small, by one *gender.* Cf. *Saih pitu.*
Lit.: no. 265.

Sembajang (Java).

Sembe (Congo – Basire; Abandya). Small truncated barrel drum.
Lit.: no. 26.

Seme (Japan). Concluding part of the *jōruri.* See also *Chirashi.*

Semer (Ancient Israel). Singing which is applied to the study of the Pentateuch.
Lit.: no. 12.

Semmyo (Japan). Shintō chanting accompanied by percussion instruments.
Lit.: no. 185.

Sempritan (*Sosowitan*) (Java). Piston flute.
Lit.: no. 163.

Sen (Japan). See *San.*

Senāgraṇī (South India). *Janya rāga* of the 7th *mēḷa* (*Senāpati*).
Tone material:
C D♭ E♭ D♭ F E♭ F A♭ B♭♭ c
(c B♭♭) c B♭♭ A♭ G F E♭ D♭ C
Lit.: no. 139.

Senāgraṇī (South India). (1) The 7th *asampūrṇa mēḷa-rāga* without *kaṭapayādi* prefix. (2) The 7th *asampūrṇa mēḷa-rāga* with *kaṭapayādi* prefix. See *Rāga* (South India).
Lit.: no. 139.

Sēnājayanti (South India). *Janya rāga* of the 67th *mēḷa* (*Sucharitra*).
Tone material:
C D# E F# G A♭ B♭♭ c
c A♭ G F# E D# C
Lit.: no. 139.

Senajong (Borneo). Bamboo sticks beaten against each other.
Lit.: no. 162.

Sēnāmani (South India). *Janya rāga* of the 17th *mēḷa* (*Sūryakānta*).
Tone material:
C D♭ E F G A c
c B A G F E D♭ C
Lit.: no. 139.

Sēnāmanoharī (South India). *Janya rāga* of the 47th *mēḷa* (*Suvarṇaṅgī*).
Tone material:
C D♭ E♭ F♯ G A B A c
c B A G F♯ E♭ D♭ E♭ C
Lit.: no. 139.

Senāpāti (*Senāvati*) (South India). (1) The 7th *asampūrṇa mēḷa-rāga*:
C D♭ E♭ F G A♭ B♭♭ c
(2) As *rāga*, to be performed in the morning, it uses the same tone material. Veṅkaṭamakhin (17th century) called this *rāga Senāgraṇī*.
Lit.: no. 139.

Senāvati (South India). See *Senāpati*.

Senayong (Borneo—Land Dayak). Bamboo stamping tubes. See *Pelonchong*.

Sendaren (Java). See *Sundaren*.

Sendari (Java). See *Sundaren*.

Sendhora (North India). See *Sindhura*.

Sendiu (West Borneo—Padang-Dayak). A double clarinet type that consists of two tubes of unequal length. One tube has one, the other five finger holes. A single tongue is cut into the tubes. Cf. *Serunay*; *Serubai*.
Lit.: no. 162.

Senḍon (*Sesenḍon*) (Bali). A prelude in the form of a quiet, more or less improvised song, leading to the *pengawit*, the start of the actual theme of the composition. Cf. *Paṭetan*.
Lit.: no. 197.

Sendon (Java). A short, emotional dirge in *pelog* about Semar, the god of love, and other deities, recited and chanted by the *dalang*. The dirge in *slendro* is called *paṭetan* (or *lagon*). Cf. *Suluk*.
Lit.: no. 163.

Sendratari (Java). "Art," "dance." Dance performance without spoken dialogue. See *Tari*.

Sene ha'u(h) (Timor). Xylophone. Cf. *Katongga kayu*.
Lit.: no. 162.

Sene kaka (*Paking*) (West Timor—Antoni tribe). A split bamboo zither.

Seneng (Java). "Harmony," "untroubled." The feeling created when using a tone material with equidistant intervals between its tones.
Lit.: no. 163.

Šeng (China—M 5742). See *Sheng*.

Senganered (Ethiopia). Name of an obsolete instrument allegedly played when a battle was lost.
Lit.: nos. 147, 255.

Senggol nyimpang (Sunda District). Cf. *Pamanis*.

Sengwelembwe (Congo—Ababua). *Sansa*.
Lit.: no. 21.

Senh (Vietnam). Mouth organ similar to the Chinese *sheng*.

Senj (Iran). Large cymbals.

Senj (written: *Senji*) (Mongolia). "Button hole," "ear," the string holder below the big bridge (*yikhe dewkhe*) of the *khil-khuur*.
Lit.: no. 60.

Sensei (Japan). The venerable teacher.

Sente (South Africa). See *Moroto*; *Motaba*.

Senṭeng (Java). String (cut from the surface of a bamboo tube).
Lit.: no. 163.

Senṭing (Java). See *Rebāb* (Java).

Sentuang (Malaysia; Malacca). Bamboo cross flute with three finger holes.
Lit.: no. 255.

Seperewa (Ghana). Harp-lute with six strings.

Sēphā (Thailand). Recitative-chanting style.
Lit.: no. 208.

Se-p'iri (Korea). A very slim oboe with seven finger holes.

Ser (Ancient Egypt). Frame drum of the 18th dynasty.
Lit.: no. 103.

Serbung (Small Sunda Isl.). Oboe type. (1) See *Bomberdom* (Flores). (2) Cf. *Bumbung* (*Gumbeng*).
Lit.: nos. 162-63.

Serdam (Flores). Open flute without mouthpiece. It has three holes in front and one at the back. Cf. *Fekor*; *Sunding.*
Lit.: no. 166.

Sereng (Java). "Vigorous," "energetic." A passionate feeling when playing *laras nyendari.*
Lit.: no. 163.

Serengwa (Kenya—Nandi). Wooden horn.
Lit.: no. 113.

Serifu (Japan). Recitative (e.g., in *kabuki* performances).
Lit.: no. 187.

Serimba (South Africa). Cf. *Silimba.*

Serimpi (Java). See *Bedaya* (dance).

Sernei (Malay Peninsula). Oboe with a piston tube. This instrument is called *whi* in Thailand; *sempritan*, *sosowitan* in Java; *serompa'ap* in East New Guinea. Cf. *Surnāy.*

Serompa'ap (East New Guinea; New Brittany). Piston flute (or oboe). See *Sempritan* (Java). See *Sernei.*
Lit.: no. 166.

Serompret (Java). See *Selompret.*

Seron (Africa; Republic of Guinea). A harp-lute with 15-19 strings. Cf. *Bolon*; *Kora.*
Lit.: no. 33.

Serubai (*Serunai*; *Sendiu*) (Borneo; Flores). Double clarinet. The instrument has various names. Some of them are: *lebung-lebung*; *basing-basing* of South Celebes; *puwi-puwi*, Celebes; *pelle*; *adan* of South Toraja District.
Lit.: no. 166.

Serunai (*Serubai*) (Malaysia; Sumatra). Richly decorated wooden oboe type, closely related to the *selompret.* Other names of the instrument are: *saronen* (Madura), *srune* (*zurna*) (Atjeh), *sruni* (Java), *pereret* (Bali).

The Malaysian *serunai* (of the *wayang kulit* ensemble) has seven finger holes and one at the back. It produces the notes C D F G A B♭ c d e♭. The various parts of the *serunai* have the following names: *pipit*, the reeds; *mali*, mouthpiece; *caping*, reeds and mouthpiece; *lubang jerit*, the single hole at the back of the tube; *lubang petit*, the finger holes on top of the tube; *batang*, the tube; *copong*, the bell; *kepala copong*, the widely flaring end of the bell.
Lit.: nos. 162, 254.

Serune (Borneo). See *Serunai.*

Serunen (Java). See *Selompret.*

Seruni (Bali). See *Serunai.*

Serutu (West Borneo). Long vertically-blown cane flute with a beak mouthpiece. It has five finger holes grouped into three and two.
Lit.: no. 255.

Sesando (Timor). A tube zither surrounded by a palm leaf resonator with 10-36 copper strings strung in pairs. Cf. *Satung* (Celebes).
Lit.: nos. 156, 162.

Sese (*Zeze*) (Zaire; Kenya; Tanzania). Tube fiddle.
Lit.: no. 218.

Seseg (*Sesegan*) (Java). Accelerando. Cf. *Naek* (Sunda District). The accelerando concerns the speeding up toward the end of a movement in the *gending ageng*. It begins with the first *ketuk* beat after the penultimate *gong* beat and, in the *gending alit*, it appears with the first *ketuk* beat after the *gong* beat before the penultimate one. After the *seseg(an)* follows the *suwuk*, a final rallentando.
Lit.: no. 163.

Sesendon (*sendon*) (Bali). Freely improvised solo playing (*trompong*) in the *gamelan gong*. Two varieties: *selisir*, using the high register, and *tembung*, the lower register.
Lit.: no. 197.

Śeshānanda (South India). *Janya rāga* of the 57th *mēḷa* (*Siṃhendramadhyama*).
Tone material:
C D E♭ F♯ G A♭ c
c B A♭ G F♯ E♭ D C
Lit.: no. 139.

Sesheshet (Ancient Egypt). See *Seshesht*.

Seshesht (Ancient Egypt). A sistrum not found outside of Egypt. See *Sekhem*.

Setār (*Sestar*) (Iran). Lute with a long neck and three strings.

Setinkane (South Africa). See *Sefinjolo*.
Lit.: no. 190.

Setodiko (South Africa—Balubedu). Cross flute.
Lit.: no. 151.

Setolotolo (South Africa—Kapland; Basuto). Music bow played by men only. Cf. *Penda*.
Lit.: no. 151.

Setsegetse (South Africa). See *Sekgobogobo*.

Setukat (*Gembyang*) (West Java). Term for the Javanese *bonang panerus*, the highest-pitched *bonang*. *Setukat* is also called *rinchik*.
Lit.: no. 163.

Setzu (Japan). See *Kyokusetzu*.

Sëu-no-fuye (Japan—Ryukyu Isl.). Pan flutes with 12 pipes.
Lit.: no. 255.

Sevuruvuru (Africa—Basutoland). Cf. *Seburu-buru*; *Luvuvu*.
Lit.: no. 151.

Se wot (West Java). Term for "angry," "furioso."

Seze (Africa—Kenya; Washambala; Congo, Mbanja; Swahili). Stick zither with one or several strings. See also *Dyedye*; *Enzenze*; *Nzenze*; *Zeze*.
Lit.: nos. 21, 176.

Sgeg-mo (Tibet). Dancing girl.

Sgra (Tibet). Sound; voice.

Sgra-dbyangs (Tibet). Musical concord; pleasing tone; harmony.
Lit.: no. 143.

Sgra-snyan (*K'opon*) (Tibet). Fiddle with 3, 4, or 6 strings played by beggars. The top of the neck shows the carved head of a horse or dragon. The *sgra-snyan* (*cha-nem*) is also treated as a long lute. As a fiddle probably of Mongolian

origin, it is played with a bow strung with yak hair (that passes between two pairs of strings). Cf. *Tobshuur* (Mongolia).
Lit.: nos. 62, 190.

Sgrog (Tibet). See *Rgyud.*

Sgrog-ba (Tibet). See *Skyor-ba.*

Sgrung-pa (Tibet). Wandering minstrel.

Shā (South India). One of the mnemonics used in the system of the 72 *mēḷas*. It indicates the sixth *mēḷa* of each of the 12 *chakras.* (All mnemonics have been listed under the heading of *Bhu.*) Cf. *Chakra.*
Lit.: no. 139.

Shaare (Arabia). Oboe type with a conical bore.

Shabaz (Iran; Afghanistan). Bass string.

Shabbāba (Arabia). Vertically-blown cane flute with six front and one thumbhole. See also *Sabbāba.*
Lit.: no. 250.

Shabbai (Israel—Druse). Flute.
Lit.: no. 303.

Bhabdam (South India). Solo dance in which the female performer demonstrates her subtle and elaborate art.

Shabitu (Ancient Mesopotamia; Akkad). See *Sabitum.*

Shabrae duun (Mongolia). Buddhist songs about holy lamas, miracles, famous monasteries, and related religious features.
Lit.: no. 60.

Shachi (East Turkestan). Cf. *Sochiba.*

Shad (Tibet). Mark of punctuation that appears not only in literary works but also in musical notation.
Lit.: no. 143.

Shaḍarāt (Arabia). Staccato tones (in singing).
Lit.: no. 65.

Shaḍava (North India). Hexatonic scale. Cf. *Rāgas.*
Lit.: no. 138.

Shadd (Turkmenistan). Cf. *Shudūd.*

Shadda (Iraq). Frame drum.

Shaḍharat (Arabia). *Shaḍarat.* Cf. *Amālat.*

Shādhilīya (Arabia). See *Dhikr.*

Shaḍja (*Ṣaḍja*) (India). Name of the first note of a scale. Its commonly used abbreviation is *sa.* Cf. *Achyuta Shaḍja.*

Sha'er (Middle East). Poet-composer-singer who performs his songs at marriage processions. Cf. *Saff*; *Ashyk.*

Shāh (Turkey). A modern Turkish *nāy* of medium size. Cf. *Manṣūr*; *Nāy shāh*; *Qīz.*
Lit.: no. 81.

Shahana Kanada (North India). *Rāga* ascribed to the *Kafi thāta.*
Tone material:
C D E♭ F G A B♭(+) c
c B♭ (A) G F E♭ D C; *Vādis*: G, C
Lit.: no. 138.

Shāhīn (Arabia). Ancient wind instrument.

Shahawrāk (Arabia). See *Shawrāk.*

Shahed (Iran). Stressed note (similar to the *vādī* of North India).

Shāhīn (Old Arabia). Fife. See *Tahlīl.*

Shahnāy (*Śanaī*) (North India). Wooden oboe with 7-8 finger holes. Its mouthpiece is generally provided with a lip-supporting circular metal disc. The *shahnāy* is derived from the *sūrnā* (*zūrnā*).
Lit.: no. 255.

Shāhnāz (Iran). Name of one *gusheh* that differs in several small features from the preceding *daramād.*
Lit.: no. 146.

Shāh'nāz (Arabia). (1) Tone name of a note ½ tone higher than *kardān*. (A list of all tone names and notes through two octaves can be seen under the heading of *Jagā* [*Yagā*].) (2) *Maqām* of Persian origin. It is a type of *Ḥijaz-kar.* The name means "diadem of the Shah," and is to be sung in a range in which the note *shāh'nāz* appears. The scale begins with the notes *kardān* (D), *shāh'nāz* (E♭), *jwab sigā* (*F*♯). . . . Cf. *Ḥijaz.*
Lit.: no. 121.

Shah nefir (Iran). Large signal horn in circular form.

Shāhrūd (Persia; Arabia; Egypt). (1) Obsolete arch-lute of ancient Persia known since the 10th century. The instrument is said to have a compass of three octaves. Numbers of strings and tunings are indistinct. (2) Bass string.
Lit.: no. 70.

Shahūkalam (East Turkestan). Cf. *Sochiba.*

Shai-ku (China). See *Sha-ku.*

Shaipūr (Iran). Straight trumpet. Cf. *Karranāy*; *Shofar.*
Lit.: no. 255.

Shā'ir (Old Arabia). Musician-poet-soothsayer.

Shakh (Iran). Shawm.
Lit.: no. 255.

Shākh-i nafīr (Iran). Crooked trumpet. Cf. *Shīsha būrūsī.*
Lit.: no. 81.

Shakhshpakha (Arabia). Rattle.
Lit.: no. 255.

Sha-ku (China—M 5606; M 3479). "Gravel drum." A small drum with a round corpus. Generally it has one skin; only in the North does it appear with two skins. The drum is beaten with thin wooden sticks. The Cantonese name is *sa-ku.* The drum is frequently used in theatrical (puppet) shows. Other names (Mandarin) for *sha-ku* occasionally are: *shai-ku* (M 5624; 3479), "sprinkling drum," and *ti-ku* (M 6222; 3479), "dripping drum."
Lit.: no. 137.

Shakubyōshi (Japan). Clappers. Each consisting of two wooden rectangular slabs. They were used in the imperial court (*gagaku*). The *shakubyoshi* were beaten by the leader of the choir, who used to indicate and maintain tempo, meter, and rhythm. Cf. *Hyōshi*; *Hyōshigi*; *Yotsudake.*
Lit.: no. 185.

Shakū-gyo (Japan). Rattle made of several metal rings attached to the top of a wooden stick.
Lit.: no. 258.

Shakuhachi (Japan). An ancient heavy bamboo flute, blown vertically. The instrument is of Chinese origin and has a pleasant gentle sound, although its size and weight could enable a person to use it as a truncheon in violent quarrels. The instrument has four holes on top and one at the back and a small cut in the rim of the tube where it is touched by the lower lip of the player. The lower end of the tube is slightly bent outward and the inside of the tube lacquered. The instrument can produce the *in-* and *yo-* scales and in recently composed pieces the chromatic scale by applying half-fingering. *Shakuhachi* music can be grouped into three categories:

1. *Honkyoku*: original *shakuhachi* pieces.
2. *Gaikyoku*: solo pieces and other "outside" items played by the *shakuhachi*, *shamisen*, or *koto.*
3. *Shinkyoku*: pieces with melodies that use a wide range; also pieces that imitate Western musical styles.

Cf. *Hitoyogiri.*
Lit.: nos. 185, 273.

Shakujo (Japan). See *Kansan*.

Shakwa (Congo—Wanande). Small drum played to entertain the *mwami* (ruling chief). Lit.: nos. 26, 190.

Shalap (East Turkestan). Cf. *Sochiba*.

Shalishīm (Ancient Israel). A metal percussion instrument, probably a triangle, played by women. Cf. *ṣelṣīm*.
Lit.: no. 255.

Shalshelet (Ancient Israel). Notational symbol (3) used in biblical chant, indicating a weak disjunctive function.
Lit.: no. 309.

Sha-lo (China). "Basin." A large gong that produces a full, booming sound. Cf. *Lo*.
Lit.: no. 250.

Sham (North India). See *Shyam Kalyan*.

Shambar (Arabia). See *Shanbar*.

Shambu kaw (Ethiopia). Bamboo or metal vertical flute with four finger holes.
Lit.: no. 38.

Shamisen (*Samisen*) (Japan). A guitar-shaped instrument. It has an almost rectangular body with rounded edges, a long slim neck, and three silk or nylon strings. An early form of the *shamisen* was the *jamisen* of the Ryukyu Islands. The instrument originated in China (*san-hsien*) and probably came to Japan in the 16th century. Its shape was nearly the same as that of the later *shamisen*. Its neck was shorter and its body was covered with snake skin. The recent *shamisen* is larger, the neck longer, and the body is covered with catskin. The three silken strings are plucked with a plectrum similar to that used by *biwa* players.

The tunings of the instrument are:

hon choshi	*B* E B	Principal tunings
ni-agari	*B* F♯ B	
san sagari	*B* E A	
ichi-sagari	*A* E B	Secondary tunings
roku-sagari	*B* E F♯	

There are various styles of narrative *shamisen* music, some named after their creators: *katarimono, kato-bushi, naniwa-bushi, bungo-bushi, tokiwazu-bushi, gidayu-bushi, utaimono, ko-uta, naga-uta*.
Lit.: no. 185.

Sham-kalyan (North India). *See Shyam-kalyan*.

Shanbar (*Shambar*) (Arabia). An indistinct rhythmical mode. It has some march-like features: dotted eighths followed by the customary sixteenths, one vague triplet of three eighths, and unequal numbers of bars. Cf. *Iqa* (*Iqa'at*).

Shandze (Mongolia). A variant of *tobshuur*; probably of Chinese origin (*san-hsien*). The instrument has a flat, circular body, both sides covered with snakeskin. The three strings are played with a plectrum.
Lit.: no. 61.

Shang (China—M 5669). The name of the fourth (diatonic) degree of the scale expressed by the *kung ch'e-p'u* system. Assuming that *ho* (the basic note) is the western C, *shang* is the note F.
Lit.: no. 136.

Shang (China—M 5673). Solmization syllable and notational symbol indicating the second note of the ancient five and seven tone scales. Cf. *Kung* (China—M 3705), under the heading of which are listed other tone syllables of the two scales.
Lit.: nos. 136-37.

Shang-shou (South China). "Top hand." A musician of the Hong Kong theater who plays the *so-na*, flute, and the *yüeh-ch'in*. Cf. *Erh-shou*; *San-shou*; *Ku-shou*.

Shankara (North India). Serious *rāga* ascribed to the *Bilaval thāta.* It is to be performed at night. Tone material:

C E G A B c

c B A G E (D) C; *Vādis*: E, B

Lit.: no. 138.

Shankara-aran (North India). Obscure *rāga.* Its indistinct tone material can be:

C E G F♯ A G B c

c B G E G D C; *Vādis*: possibly C, G

Lit.: no. 138.

Shankarabharan (North India). Obscure *rāga.* Tone material (vague):

C E G B c

d' c' B G E G E C *B A G*

Lit.: no. 138.

Shankarakaran (North India). Obscure *rāga*; can be ascribed to the *Bilaval thāta.* Tone material:

C E F G A (B) c

c B (B♭) A G F E C

Lit.: no. 138.

Shaṅkarapriya (South India). See *Śaṅkarāpriya.*

Shan kaun-chet (Burma). *Hpa:zi.*

Shankha (*Sankha*) (India). See *Śankha.*

Shannai (Southeast Asia). Cf. *Shenai* (*Śāhnāyī*).

Shantamūrti (South India). See *Śantamūrti.*

Shantu (Nigeria—Hausa). Stamping gourd tube played by women. The Ashanti women call a similar tube *adenkum.*
Lit.: nos. 218, 280.

Shao (China—M 5676a). "Whistle"; the same as *she* (M 5705).
Lit.: no. 137.

Shao-erh (China—M5676; 1759). Clay toy whistle.
Lit.: no. 209.

Shao-hsi (*Hsiao-hsi*) (China). See *Chien-tzu.*
Lit.: no. 136.

Shao-hsiao (China—M 5691; 2619). Panpipes with 10 tubes.

Shap-ro (Tibet). Common dance.

Shaqaf (*shaqef*) (Arabia). Tambourine with jingles.

Shaq-shaq (Arabia; North Africa). Rattle. Cf. *Asakasaka.*
Lit.: no. 95.

Sharada (South India). Tamil term for *sarōd.*
Lit.: no. 190.

Sharadīyā vīṇā (*Śaradīyā vīṇā*) (North India). "Autumn *vīṇā.*" At the present time the instrument is called *sharud* in the Northwest Provinces. It has six strings played with a plectrum and 8-12 sympathetic strings. The neck has no frets.
Lit.: no. 254.

Shari'ī (Middle East). Chanting of the Koran (Quran), recently more elaborately than in the past and shaped into official liturgical performances.

Sharim (Ancient Israel). Male musicians.

Sharot (Ancient Israel). Female musicians. Cf. *Sharim.*

Sharqī (Turkey). "Eastern" *tanbur* with 3-5 strings.
Lit.: no. 81.

Shārūd (Iran). See *Shāhrūd.* Cf. *Sharadīyā Vīṇā.*

Sharwe (Iran). Fars term for *dubeiti.*

Shashkana (Turkey). 17th-century lute with a single string.
Lit.: no. 81.

Shashtaka (North India). Identical with *shadana*. Cf. *Rāga* (North India).
Lit.: no. 138.

Shashtār (Iran; Caucasus; Azerbaijan). "Six-stringer," a small lute with six strings with or without sympathetic strings. Cf. *Chartār*; *Dūtār*; *Panchtār*; *Setār*.

Shasjider duun (Mongolia). Songs performed at banquets and dances, with texts that often transgress traditional decency.
Lit.: no. 60.

Shatatantri vīṇā (*Śatatantrivīṇā*) (India). See *Kanuna*.

Shatr (Islamic North Africa; Middle East). Also *sadr*. A half line; a division of the *abyāt*.

Shatśruti (*Ṣaṭśruti*) (India). (Interval) of six *srutis*.
Lit.: no. 138.

Shauq-afza (Arabia). Obscure *maqām*.
Lit.: no. 121.

Shauktika vīṇā (India). A lute-shaped *sitār* covered with mother-of-pearl.
Lit.: no. 254.

Shawish (Arabia). Cf. *Tabl-al-ǧāwīǧ*.

Shawrāk (*Shahawarāk*) (Arabia). *Maqām* with a Persian name. It uses the scale of *Ḥijaz*, and its songs are always sung very slowly, e.g., in dirges, and usually in the morning. The scale is approximately:

D E♭ F♯ G A B♭ c

Lit.: nos. 64, 121.

Shbih (Iran). Dramatic performances representing the tortures suffered by Shi'ite imams. The performances consist of sung parts, spoken or sung dialogues, preaching, lamenting, and other forms. Another form of *shbih* is the *ta'ziye*.

Sh'e (Tibet). Song; its honorific term is *sung-sh'e*.

She (China – M 8705). "Tongue" used in a *kuan* tube, turning the ancient pitch pipe into a heterophonic reed instrument with nine finger holes in the larger size, eight holes in the smaller.
Lit.: no. 137.

She (China – M 5451). See *Se*. Cf. *Sono-koto*; *Hitsu-no-koto*.

Shegandi (South India). Tamil term for metal percussion disc used in temples.
Lit.: no. 254.

Shekere (Nigeria – Yoruba). Gourd rattle.
Lit.: no. 303.

Shela mulenzhe (South Africa – Venda). "Pour it out." The group song that follows the solo singer-dancer.

Sh'e-ling (Tibet). See *Thre-ling*.

Shem (Mesopotamia – Sumeria). Ancient flute or oboe. Cf. *Sem*.

Shemsha (Arabia). "The Sun." The large resonance hole of the *'ud*.
Lit.: no. 255.

Shemshal (Kurdistan). Noisy oboe type.
Lit.: no. 255.

Shenai (Southeast Asia; Northeast Asia). General term frequently written in various forms: *śāhnāyī*, *saunay*, *serunay*, indicating a popular oboe type.
Lit.: no. 215.

Shendef (Turkey). "Cheerful." Big drum.

Sheneb (Ancient Egypt). Large deep and rough sounding bronze trumpet.
Lit.: no. 100.

Sheng (China—M 5738). The term indicates chief male operatic actors. The old, imposing man with beard is the *lao sheng*, the young man is the *hsiao sheng*, the soldier or fighter the *wu sheng*, the learned man or student the *wen sheng*. Cf. *Tan* (actors who play women's roles; *ching* are the heroes, bandits, and other muscle men; *chou* are the clowns). *Mo* (or *fu-mo*) are modest men, servants, and other figures of lesser importance. *Fu ching* are the lesser types of the *ching*. Cf. *Nah-hsi.*

Sheng (Turkey). Obsolete 18th-century harp type with 24 strings.

Sheng (China—M 5742). A mouth organ symbolizing the *feng-huang*, the mythical bird phoenix. Allegedly it was invented in the third millenium B.C., but the first mention of it was made about 1100 B.C. The body, the wind chest, was first made of gourd, later of wood. Into it were mounted seventeen cane pipes in such a manner as to depict the shape of the tail feathers of the phoenix bird. Each sound-producing pipe has at its lower end a small brass tongue and a vent on its outside which must be stopped by the finger in order to produce a sound. Pipes 2, 5, 6, 7, 8, 10, 11, 12, 13, 14, 15 have vents, while pipes 1, 9, 16, and 17 are silent. The tuning of the instrument can be:

There are several sizes of the instrument. Three popular ones are: *yü* (M 7596), the largest type with 36 pipes; *ta sheng* (big *sheng*) or *cha'o* (M 253) (bird's nest *sheng*) (M 5943, 5742) with 19 pipes; *hsiao ho* (small harmony) (M 2605, 2115), often simply called *ho*, with 13 pipes.

In Confucian ceremonies of the past, six *sheng* were used, three on the east side and three on the west side of the hall. All *sheng* performed unison with the *ti-tzu*. Cf. *Shō* (Japan); *Saing* (Korea).
Lit.: no. 137.

Sheng yen (China—M 5749; 7400). "Cord eyes," the holes that serve for attaching the *pu-yü* (*pang tzu* [M 4912; M 6939] wooden drum) on the supporting posts. Cf. *Pang-tzu* (a).

Sh'e tang-wa (Tibet). (1) To sing. The honoric word is *gü-lu sh'e-pa.* (2) To sing hymns: *gur-ma lem-pa*; its honorific form is *sung-gur sh'e-pa.*
Lit.: no. 143.

Sheung-p'ei ku (China; Canton). See the Mandarin terms *Shuang-p'i ku* and *Pai-p'i ku.*

Shevvali (South India). Name of an ancient mode mentioned in the *Shilappadikaram* (Lit. no. 45).

Shi (Japan). Flute with a rectangular mouthpiece.
Lit.: no. 255.

Shi'ār (Middle East). See *Ši'ār.*

Shibai-shōten (Japan). Popular folk *taiko* pattern used in *kabuki* performances played by flute and *taiko.*
Lit.: no. 187.

Shichi (Japan). The seventh pipe of the *shō.*
Lit.: no. 225.

Shichi-dan (Japan). Seven *dan*; seven variations, sections based on a leading theme.

Shichi-gen-kin (Japan). "The seven-string *kin*," a *koto* tuned to:

G D F E F D E; or: *A E G F♯ G E F♯*
Lit.: no. 225.

Shidai (Japan). The first *dan* of *jo*, the introduction of the *noh* drama. Generally this introduction is called *sō-shidai*, "the priest's entrance."
Lit.: no. 187.

Shidūrghūr (East Turkestan). String instrument.
Lit.: no. 255.

Shigen (Japan). A flat lute similar to the *gekkin* with an octagonal body (like that of the *genkwan*). It has no frets and a vibrating wire is strung inside the body. The *shigen* has four strings tuned like those of the *kokyu*; the upper two strings are unison. The instrument is played without a plectrum.
Lit.: no. 250.

Shi genkin (Japan). See *Shichi genkin.*
Lit.: no. 255.

Shigin (Japan). Chinese poems sung in Japanese style (unaccompanied). During the last century they are accompanied on the *biwa.* Cf. *Tsurugi-mai.*
Lit.: no. 185.

Shigotouta (Japan). A form of *min-yō*. Work songs.

Shih (China—M 5776). The Cantonese manner of notating and naming the second scale degree (*ssu*) of the *kung-ch'e-p'u* system. Cf. *Kung-ch'e-p'u.*
Lit.: no. 136.

Shihābī zūrnā (Turkey). "*Shihāb's* oboe." An instrument similar to the Moroccan (clarinet) form of the *ghaiṭa*.
Lit.: no. 81.

Shih-chih (China). See *Chien-tzu.*

Shih-pu-chi (China—M 5807; 5376; 508). The 10 music ensembles, each with its own instrumental group, singers and dancers, of the T'ang court (618-906). The 10 ensembles represented various imported foreign musical styles (*hu-yüeh*) as well as the imperial banquet music, famous opening and concluding pieces. Cf. *Yen yüeh* (M 7364; 4219a).
Lit.: no. 137.

Shih-pu-chi (China—M 5807; 5376; 508). The 10 orchestras and dance groups, used and controlled by the T'ang court (cf. *Yüeh-fu*). The 10 ensembles can be described as:

1. The imperial banquet music performed in the form of a suite consisting of four movements (*yen-yüeh*) by 31 musicians (who played 28 different instruments) and 20 dancers.
2. The *ching* music—not only Chinese secular, but also foreign music. It was performed by 25 musicians (with 15 instruments).
3. The West Liang music used 18 instruments and four dancers.
4. The Korean (*kao-li*) music used 18 instruments and nine dancers.
5. The Indian (*t'ien-chu*) music employed 12 instrumentalists and five dancers.
6. The Bukhara (*an-kuo*) music used nine instruments and two dancers.
7. The Kutcha (*kuei-tzu*) music used nine instruments and two dancers.
8. The Samarkand (*k'ang-kuo*) was performed by two flutes, two drums, cymbals, and two dancers.
9. The Kashgar (*su-lo*) music was performed by 10 instruments and two dancers.
10. The concluding music of official banquets, the *kao-chang*, used 11 instruments and two dancers. It was the custom that all 10 orchestras performed, one after the other, but it was a rule that never more than 24 musical items could be played at one performance.

Cf. *Ch'i-pu-chi*; *Yen-yüeh.*

Shi-hyōshi (Japan). Four beats (common meter). Cf. *Yo-hyōshi.*
Lit.: no. 225.

Shi-jo (Korea). Song of plain, lyric character, similar to *kagok* pieces. It is accompanied by the *chang-ko*, at times also by *sei-p'iri*, *hae-kum.*
Lit.: no. 215.

Shikafe (Iran). Plectrum; bow.
Lit.: no. 255.

Shika-odori (Japan). "Deer dance." An impressive dramatic Buddhist dance. The dancers wear masks decorated with large plumes. A bamboo flute provides the accompaniment.
Lit.: no. 185.

Shikar (India). See *Tāla.*

Shikari (*Shikari git*) (Nepal). Hunting song.
Lit.: no. 133.

Shikolumbane (South Africa—Thonga). Drum, played together with the *muntshintshi.*
Lit.: no. 151.

Shilaf (North India). See *Zhilaf.*

Shilambu (South India). Ankle rings used by dancers. Cf. *Gejjai.*

Shīlāṅgi (South India). *Janya rāga* of the 65th *mēḷa* (*Mechakalyāṇī*).
Tone material:
C E F# G B c
c B G F# E C
Lit.: no. 139.

Shillalā (Ethiopia). Warrior songs; sung also at festivals and weddings.

Shimai (Japan). *Noh* dances performed separately from the drama. These concert versions are highly popular.
Lit.: no. 185.

Shime daiko (Japan). "Tied drum." See *Uta-daiko.*
Lit.: no. 225.

Shimomu (Japan). The fifth note of the ancient (chromatic) scale. If *ichikotsu*, the first note, is D, *shimomū* is F#. Cf. *Shōmyō.*

Shimomū (Japan). Two modes used by the (Buddhist) Tendai sect. See *Shōmyō.*

Shimpa (Japan). Dramatic plays that came into existence by the end of the 19th century. There were *shimpa* plays, dealing with the Sino-Japanese war and various other modern political subjects, presented in a realistic manner. The *shimpa* were the forerunners of the modern drama (with music).

Shimshāl (Iran; Kurdistan). Vertically-blown flute with six finger holes.

Shin (Japan). "God"; One of the five traditional subjects used in the *noh* drama. The other four subjects are: *nan, nyo, kyo, ki.*

Shina (India; Kashmir). Beak-flute. The two wooden halves of the tube are held together by means of bamboo and iron rings.
Lit.: no. 255.

Shin-gaku (Japan). See *Kwangen-gaku*; *Gagakū.*

Shin gane (Japan). Small *den-sho.*
Lit.: no. 255.

Shinguvo (Congo—Bambole and numerous other tribes). Small slit-drum.
Lit.: no. 21.

Shinkyoku (Japan). Modern pieces for *shakuhachi*; new musical versions of already existing compositions. Cf. *Shakuhachi*; *Gaikyoku*; *Honkyoku.*
Lit.: no. 215.

Shinnai (Japan). Cf. *Bungo-bushi.*

Shinnai-bushi (Japan). Vulgar *shamisen* songs in narrative form, created by Tsuruga Shinnai in 1751. When the government banned the performance of these obscene songs, there appeared in the Yoshiwara, the pleasure district of Tokyo, new and cleaner songs that still can be heard at the present time.
Lit.: no. 225.

Shinobi-sanjū (Japan). *Shamisen* melodic pattern that imitates with its quickly repeated notes the sound of grasshoppers. The pattern is produced together with the sound of temple bells ringing at night.
Lit.: no. 189.

Shino-bue (*Shino-buye*) (Japan). Transverse bamboo or cane flute with seven finger holes. The instrument has a light, gentle tone.
Lit.: no. 255.

Shinsen (Japan). The eleventh of the 12 chromatic tones, usually transcribed with the note c (an octave higher than the Western middle C), if *ichikotsu*, the first note of the scale is D. Cf. *Gagaku.*

Shin-sō (Japan). Cf. *Gaku-sō.*

Shintō music (Japan). See *Kagura.*

Shipalapala (South Africa – Thonga). Side-blown horn. The instrument is made of the horn of the sable antelope. See *Mpalapala*; *Phalaphala*; *Lepapata.*
Lit.: no. 151.

Shi'r (Old Arabia). Verse; song.

Shirabemono (Japan). Pure, instrumental *koto* music.
Lit.: no. 185.

Shirabyōshi (Japan). Female dancers, prostitutes or mistresses of former warriors attached to the imperial court or Shinto shrines perform *mikomai*, sacred and ceremonial dances, to the accompaniment of *imayō* singing. Cf. *Zogei.*
Lit.: no. 187.

Shiragi-gaku (Japan). Court music imported from Silla, one of the medieval kingdoms of ancient Korea (Shiragi is the Japanese name of the Korean Silla). See *Gagaku.*
Lit.: no. 185.

Shiragi koto (Japan). An angular harp with six strings called "Korean *koto*" was used in those sections of court music which had been imported from Korea. Cf. *Kudara koto.*
Lit.: no. 185.

Shiroth (Yemen). Jewish love songs sung by the bridegroom.

Shīsha būrūsī (Turkey). A bottle-shaped bent trumpet similar to the Iranian *shākh-i nafīr.*
Lit.: no. 81.

Shishi odori (Japan). A folk *kagura* dance. One or two men, masked and made up as lions, perform the "lion-dance" during the *o-matsuri.* Cf. *O-matsuri.*
Lit.: no. 185.

Shishya (India). Music student.
Lit.: no. 215.

Shita (Japan). The mouthpiece of the *hichiriki.*
Lit.: no. 225.

Shitakata (Japan). The *hayashi* of *kabuki* music when playing downstairs in the hall and not on the stage. Cf. *Chobo*; *Hayashi-kata.*
Lit.: no. 225.

Shītakiraṇi (South India). *Janya rāga* of the 55th *mēḷa* (*Śyāmalāṅgī*).
Tone material:
C D E♭ F♯ G B♭♭ c
c A♭ B♭♭ A♭ G F♯ E♭ C
Lit.: no. 139.

Shitata (Africa; Malawi). See *Sitata.*

Shite (Japan). The protagonist ("the doer"), the main actor of the *noh* drama. The actor of secondary roles is called *waki.* Cf. *Noh.*
Lit.: no. 187.

Shitloti (South Africa – Thonga). Transverse flute. See *Tshitiringo.*
Lit.: no. 151.

Shiva-bhairav (*Shiv-bhairav*; *Shivmat-bhairav*) (North India). A serious *rāga* to be performed in the morning. It is ascribed to the *Bhairav thāta.*
Tone material:
C D♭ E F G A♭ B c
c B (B♭) A♭ G F E (E♭) D♭ C; *Vādis*: A♭, D♭
Lit.: no. 138.

Shiwaya (South Africa – Thonga). Ocarina type with two finger holes that produces four notes. It is the only globular flute in South Africa.
Lit.: no. 151.

Shixat (North Africa—Berber). Professional female musician entertainers and prostitutes. The male wandering musicians are called *imdyazn.*

Shiz (Arabia). Term for drumsticks and castanets.
Lit.: no. 255.

Shizu-gaki (Japan). One of two brief stereotyped patterns (in rhythm and melody) of the *sō* in *gagaku.* A second pattern is called *haya-gaki.*
Lit.: no. 185.

Škashek (North Africa—Berber). Metal castanets.

Shkewa (Algeria). Bagpipe.
Lit.: no. 15.

Shloka (*Śloka*) (India). The most popular and frequently used epic meter. It appeared in various types of poetry. The meter consisted of four quarters, each containing eight syllables. In the *bharata nāṭyam* the *shlokam* represents the end of the piece.

Shō (Japan). Basically the same in form and structure as the Chinese *sheng* (M 5742). This mouth organ has a lacquered wind box made of cherrywood and a silver mouthpiece. Into the wind box are placed 17 bamboo pipes made of old bamboo. The pipes have small metal reeds which vibrate only if the vents on the low parts of the pipes are closed.

The pipes are arranged in a circular and counterclock direction. The names of the pipes and tones produced are:

1. *hi* b	10. *hachi* E
2. *ho* (*mo*) silent	11. *ichi* B
3. *yotsu* (*kotsu*) A	12. *bi* (*bei*) F#
4. *bo* (*bok*) D	13. *ku* C#
5. *jo* d	14. *otsu* E
6. *kyu* (*gyo*) a	15. *ge* (*gei*) G
7. *shichi* (*hichi*) c	16. *ju* (*jeu*) G#
8. *gon* c#	17. *san* (*sen*) f#
9. *ya* silent	

The *shō* is used predominantly in the *togaku* ensemble. Cf. *Sheng* (China); *Saing* (Korea).
Lit.: nos. 185, 225.

Shō (Japan). Solmization term. It indicates the Chinese *shang* (M 5673) of the ancient five- and seven-tone scales. Cf. *Ryo*; *Ritsu.*
Lit.: no. 136.

Sho'ba (Iran). Old term for *gushe.* It represents small improvised pieces that follow the first *daramad* (*awaz*) of a *dastgāh.*

Shobai (Japan). Introductory section of the *kansan* hymns.

Shobhavari (North India). Obscure *rāga* (even the name is uncertain). It can be ascribed to the *Asavari thāta.* A possible tone material can be.
Tone material:
C D F G A♭ c
c A♭ G F D C (the *vādis* are uncertain)
Lit.: no. 138.

Shofar (*Keren*) (Israel). Hebrew term for goat's or ram's-horn blown at sacred occasions. It has no mouthpiece.
Lit.: no. 255.

Shō-ga (Japan). Solfeggio used in *shō* playing.

Shō-hitsu-no-koto (Japan). A long and richly ornamented *koto* with 25 strings.
Lit.: no. 225.

Shojū (Japan). The lowest pentatonic range of the *go-on-hakase.* Cf. *Niju*; *Sanju.*
Lit.: no. 185.

Shoka (Japan). Sing-song. A system of teaching the basics of music by beating the first two beats of the common meter on one's knee and the other two beats on the floor. *Shoka* represents also a type of solmization syllables; without being distinct, they vaguely indicate the outline of the melody.
Lit.: no. 187.

Shokavāḷi (*Śokavāḷi*) (South India). *Janya rāga* of the 9th *mēḷa* (*Dhēnuka*).
Tone material:

C E♭ F B

(B) A♭ G F D♭ F E♭ C; (A♭ G F D♭ C)

Lit.: no. 139.

Shōko (Japan). A circular or brass gong hung in an ornate frame (representing a cloud or flame patterns) is struck with a stick. It marks the beats together with the *tsuri-daiko*. The *shōko* can be found in large and small sizes and is used in *togaku* and *komagaku* ensembles.
Lit.: no. 225.

Shōku (Japan). The Japanese term for the Chinese *chu* (M 1379).
Lit.: no. 225.

Shōmyō (Japan). General term for recitation, chanting of Buddhist scriptures, sutras, and other texts either in Sanskrit, Chinese, or Japanese.

The Nishi-honga-ji sect used instead of *shōmyō* the Chinese term *bombai* (Brahman chant), a term that also specified the *kansan* category of the Buddhist chant. *Shōmyō* appeared in Japan in the early 9th century. Cf. *Bonsan*; *Kansan*; *Wasan*; *Koshiki*. The tone systems used in *shōmyō* and *gagaku* are almost identical:

Ryo(sen):	e.g., C D E (F♯) G A (B) c
Ritsu(sen):	e.g., C D (E♭) F G (A♭) A c
Chukyoku(sen):	e.g., C (D) E♭ F G (A) B♭ c

Combinations of *ryo* and *ritsu* scales are called *hennon*.

The two important Buddhist sects, Shingon and Tendai, employ the following modes:

The five modes of the Shingon sect are:

ichikotsu:	D E F♯ (G) A B (c♯) d
sōjō:	G A B (c♯) d e (f♯) g
hyōjō:	E (F♯) G A B (c♯) d e
banshiki:	B (c♯) d e f♯ (g♯) a b
ōshiki:	A (B) c d (e) f g a

A group of formulas that are not referring to scales but to more or less specific (Chinese) linguistic tones are: *hyōjō* ("even tone"), the 2nd, 3rd, (or 4th) tones of the scale; *jōshō* ("mounting tone"), the 5th and 6th tones of the scale; *kyoshō* ("parting tone"), 4th-5th or 5th-6th tones; *nisshō* ("entering tone"), a descending glide from one note to the next one below.

The eleven modes of the Tendai sect are:

hyōjō [I]	E F♯ G♯ (A♯) B c♯ (d♯) e
sōjo [I]	G A B (c♯) d e (f♯) g
ōshiki [I]	A B c♯ (d) e f♯ (g♯) a
hyōjō [II]	E F♯ A B d e
shimomu [I]	F♯ G♯ B c♯ e f♯
sōjō [II]	G A c d f g
banshiki	B c♯ e f♯ a b
ichikotsu	D (E) F G A (B) c d
hyōjō [III]	same as Shingon *hyōjō*
shimomu [II]	F♯ (G♯) A B c♯ (d) e f♯
ōshiki [II]	A (B) c d e (f) g a

Lit.: nos. 47, 185.

Shong nong (Thailand). Jew's harp.
Lit.: no. 255.

Shōno-fuye (Japan). A set of 22 pipes (flutes) arranged in raft form. The Chinese prototype is the *p'ai-hsiao*.
Lit.: nos. 225, 255.

Shosa (Japan). Postures; entire dance items in *kabuki* performances.
Lit.: no. 187.

Shōsetsu (Japan). The fourth of the 12 chromatic tones, usually transcribed as F (if *ichikotsu*, the basic tone, is D).
Lit.: no. 185.

Shotang (Siberia—East Yakut). Angular harp with 6-10 metal strings.
Lit.: no. 60.

Shou-ch'iu (China—M 5838; 1221). Iron rattles in the form of small balls.
Lit.: no. 209.

Shou-ku (China—M 5838; 3479). Hand drum used by priests at funerals.
Lit.: no. 209.

Shou-pan (China – M 5838; 4886). Hand rattle (a recent name for *ch'ung-tu*). Cf. *P'ai-pan.* Each of six singers in the Confucian service was in charge of one *shou-pan.* At each word the rattle was struck against the palm of the left hand.

Showqi (Afghanistan). Term applied to both musical amateur or professional.

Shringa (*Śṛṅga*) (India). Cow-horn. Cf. *Raṇa-śṛṅga.*
Lit.: no. 254.

Shrī Rāga (North India). An important *rāga* to be performed at sunset. It is ascribed to the *Purvi thāta.*
Tone material:
C D♭ F♯ G B c
c B A♭ G F♯ E D♭ C; *Vādis*: D♭, G
Lit.: no. 138.

Shrirañjani (North India). *Rāga* ascribed to the *Kafi thāta.*
Tone material:
C E♭ F A B♭ c
c B♭ A F E♭ D C; *Vādis*: F, C
Lit.: no. 138.

Shritank (North India). See *Tanki.*

Shrutī (India). See *Śrutī.*

Shrutī-upanga (*Śrutī-upanga*) (India). See *Nagabaddha.*

Shū (Japan). "To whistle." Term in *koto* playing that indicates that the player performs with his *tsume* a glissando from right to left, usually on the sixth string.

Shu'ab (Central Asia; North India). Branch modes. The term was used by people of the Mogul empire and of the present Turkoman republic. Cf. *Shudud*; *Maqām.*
Lit.: no. 76.

Shu'aobīya (Egypt). Pan pipes. Cf. *Mūsīqāl.*
Lit.: no. 76.

Shuang-ch'in (China – M 5915; 1103). A lute with an octagonal flat body, a long neck, 12 frets, and four strings tuned in pairs in the same way as those of the *yüeh-ch'in.* It is played with a plectrum. At the present time the instrument is rarely used. Cf. *Genkwan.*
Lit.: no. 250.

Shuang-kuan (China – M 5915; 3557). Two small flute or oboe types joined side by side. Cf. *Kuan.*
Lit.: nos. 137, 209.

Shuang-p'i ku (in Cantonese: *Sheung-p'ei ku*) (China). See *Pai-p'i ku.*

Shuang-tan (China). Term used among the *chien-tzu. Cf. Chien-tzu.*

Shu'ar (Arabia; Iran). *Maqām* derived from *maqam Sigā*:
$\overset{+}{E\flat}$ F G A B♭ c d $\overset{+}{e\flat}$
Lit.: no. 121.

Shubal (East Africa; Somali Republic). Dance song, performed by women, only occasionally by men.

Shu-ch'iu (North China). Iron rattle consisting of two hollow globes.
Lit.: no. 209.

Shuddha (North India). Pure; natural. E.g., *shuddha ga* (E natural).

Shuddha-bilaval (North India). *Rāga* ascribed to the *Bilaval thāta.* Often called "morning *Kalyan.*"
Tone material:
C D E F G A B c
c B A G F E D C; *Vādis*: A, E
Lit.: no. 138.

Shuddhamañjari (South India). See *Śuddhamañjari.*

Shuddhamukhari (South India). *Janya rāga* of the 1st *mēḷa* (*Kanakāṅgī*).
Tone material:
C D♭ E♭♭ F G A♭ B♭♭ c
c B♭♭ A♭ (G) F E♭♭ D♭ C *B♭♭* C
Lit.: no. 139.

Shuddha-nath (North India). *Rāga*; only performed by the late Aladiya Khan of Bombay and by his pupils. Otherwise the *rāga* (ascribed to the *Bilaval thāta*) is obscure.
Tone material:
(*B*) C D E F G (A) c
c B♭ A G F (E) D C; *Vādis*: F, C
Lit.: no. 138.

Shuddh-kalyan (North India). *Rāga* ascribed to the *Kalyan thāta*. To be performed at night.
Tone material:
C D E G A c
c B A G (F♯) E D C; *Vādis*: E, A
Lit.: no. 138.

Shuddh Mallār (North India). *Rāga* subordinated to the *Kāfi thāta*. It belongs to the *Mallār* family.
Tone material:
C D G F A c
d c A G F D C; *Vādis*: G, C
Lit.: no. 138.

Shuddh-sarang (North India). *Rāga* ascribed to the *Kafi thāta*. To be performed at noon.
Tone material:
C D F♯ G B c
c (B) B♭ A G E F D C; *Vādis*: D, G
Lit.: no. 138.

Shudūd (singular form: *shadd*) (Turkmenistan; Middle East). A 15th-century term for the 48 modes (cf. *Shu'ab*; *Awāzāt*) derived from the 12 *maqāmāt*. Cf. *Maqām*; *Adwār*.
Lit.: no. 76.

Shughi (Middle East). Islamic hymn praising the Prophet.

Shugs-pa (Tibet). Small pipe (whistle). The player holds the instrument inside his mouth.
Lit.: no. 125.

Shui (China – M 5922). "Water." Term referring to marionettes floating or moved and held up by hydraulic means in Southern puppet shows.
Lit.: no. 129.

Shui-chan (China – M 5922; 149). A set of nine cups filled with different amounts of water and beaten with a stick. Cf. *Jaltarang* (India).
Lit.: no. 209.

Shukla-bilaval (North India). Rare, serious *rāga* ascribed to the *Bilaval thāta*.
Tone material:
C D E F G A (B♭) B c
c B A G F E D C; *Vādis*: F, C
Lit.: no. 138.

Shukti-patta (India). Obscure ancient instrument mentioned in Lit. no. 290.

Shu-ku (China). Frame drum. See *Shou-ku*.
Lit.: no. 209.

Shūlatāriṇi (*Śulatāriṇi*) (South India). *Janya rāga* of the 24th *mēḷa* (*Varuṇapriyā*).
Tone material:
C D E♭ F A♯ c
c A♯ F E♭ D C
Lit.: no. 139.

Shumga (South Africa – East Hottentots). Music bow.
Lit.: no. 255.

Shun (China). A mortar-shaped bell struck with a wooden hammer. The instrument is used at various religious ceremonies.
Lit.: nos. 137, 209.

Shunga (Japan). A simple lute in shape similar to the *kokyū*. It has four strings and five frets placed on a short neck. One of the four strings is much thicker than the rest. The instrument is played by plucking the strings with the fingers.
Lit.: no. 225.

Shu-pan (China). Cf. *Shou-pan* (China – M 5838; 4886).
Lit.: no. 137.

Shūqaifāt (Arabia). Dancer's cymbals.
Lit.: no. 255.

Shūr (Iran). Cf. *Dastgāh.*

Shura-nori (Japan). See *Chu-nori.*

Shuri (Arabia). Tone name. See *Taq ḥiṣār qaba*; *Ḥiṣār.*

Shushira-yantra (India). Sanskrit term for wind instruments.

Shu-ti (China—M 5877; 6217). Vertical flute. See *Ch'ih pa kuan* (China—M 1045, 4845, 3557).

Sh'verim (Ancient Israel). Late biblical term meaning "breaks," performed by the *shofar.* It implies two notes, a small interval apart. The two notes are played in succession, and this feature was repeated in iambic meter.
Lit.: no. 12.

Shyama (North India). See *Shyam-kalyan.*

Shyam-kalyan (*Sham-kalyan*; *Shyama*; *Sham*). Evening *rāga* ascribed to the *Kalyan-thāta.*
Tone material:
C D F♯ G B c
c A B♭ G (F♯) G G E (D) F D C *B* C; *Vādis*: C, F
Lit.: no. 138.

Si (Burma). Drum. The term is also used for a small cymbal or hand bell.
Lit.: nos. 186, 255.

Siang som (Northeast Thailand). The two deleted notes of a basic heptatonic scale in pentatonic music.
Lit.: no. 203.

Siang yao (Northeast Thailand). A manner of chanting sermons by Buddhist monks using the *an nungsü* scale (A C D E G a). Also non-metrical recitation (cf. *Tang yao*). The recitation or chant is richly ornamented despite its somber dignified text.
Lit.: no. 203.

Ši'ār (*Shi'ār*) (Middle East). *Maqām.*
Tone material:
E F♯ G A $\overset{+}{\text{B}\flat}$ c d e f♯ g
Lit.: no. 64.

Siblon (Java). See *Chiblon.*

Sibs (Egypt). A small oboe that performs the melody, while a larger oboe (*aba*) plays the drone note. The term *sibs* indicates also a double clarinet. Cf. *Mizmār*; *Aba.*
Lit.: no. 250.

Si daw (Burma). "Royal drums." A pair of long barrel drums used at ceremonial occasions.

Siddhasēna (South India). *Janya rāga* of the 22nd *mēḷa* (*Kharaharapriyā*).
Tone material:
C E♭ D E♭ F G A c
c B♭ A F G F D E♭ D C
Lit.: no. 139.

Sieng yeuns (Thailand). Basic note of a melody.
Lit.: no. 58.

Sigā (Arabia). Also *Sah-gāh*; *Sikāh.* Tone name of the 6th main note. (A list of all tone names and tones through two octaves can be seen under the heading of *Jagā* [*Yagā*].)

Sigā (*Sikhā*) (Arabia; Iran). *Maqām.* Despite its Persian name ("the third") this *maqām* is very popular among Arabs. *Maqām 'Iraq* is the same as *Sigā*, but is performed a fourth lower. The *Sigā* scale is:
$\overset{+}{\text{E}\flat}$ F G $\overset{+}{\text{A}\flat}$ $\overset{+}{\text{B}\flat}$ c d $\overset{+}{\text{e}\flat}$
The Egyptian *maqām* with the same name uses A♭ (*Ḥiṣar*) instead of A (or $\overset{+}{\text{A}\flat}$ [*Ḥusenī*]). Cf. *Sah-gāh.*

Derivate *maqām*: *Shu'ar*, mentioned in Lit. no. 56; its scale is:
$\overset{+}{\text{E}\flat}$ F G A B♭ c d $\overset{+}{\text{e}\flat}$
Lit.: nos. 56, 121.

Sigeri (Nubia). *Rebāb* type.
Lit.: no. 255.

Sigitot (*Sigittuad*) (Borneo; Sarawak). Spike fiddle with a coconut body and one fiber string. It is played with a small bamboo bow.
Lit.: no. 255.

Sigordang (Sumatra—Batak). Drum; its body is a hollowed tree trunk covered with skin.
Lit.: no. 255.

Sigu mbawa (Nias). Clarinet or oboe types made of bamboo either without or with three or four small finger holes and a large bell consisting of rolled up pandanus or lontara leaves. In Southern Nias the instrument is called *surune ndrawa*. In Sumatra its name is *pupui*, in Timor *mob*, and in Flores *bańsi*.
Lit.: nos. 254-55.

Sigu nihu (Nias). Nose flute made of cane, with four finger holes. The instrument is mostly played by women.
Lit.: no. 255.

Siilili (Kenya—Gisit). Tubular fiddle with three strings. Cf. *Endingidi*.

Si-im-da (Mesopotamia). Sumerian term for horn to be blown at ritual services.
Lit.: no. 87.

Sijem (Java). Gong vertically suspended; it is used in the *gamelan* ensemble.
Lit.: no. 215.

Sijo (Korea). See *Kasa*.

Sikāh (Arabia). See *Sigā*.

Sikāh (*Sikhā*) (Modern Tunisia). *Maqām*.
Tone material:

C D $\overset{+}{\text{E}\flat}$ F G A B♭ c

Cf. *Sah-gāh*.
Lit.: no. 64.

Sikil (Java). See *Rebāb* (Java).

Sikulu (Congo—Kongo). Round drum with two heads. Cf. *Esikulu*.
Lit.: no. 26.

Sikunru (South Celebes). Small clarinet.
Lit.: no. 163.

Sikwi (Congo—Babali). Raft-shaped bamboo zither with 16 strings.
Lit.: no. 220.

Sil (*Sul*) (Korea). A large zither with 25 strings tuned chromatically through two octaves. Each string has its own bridge. The 13th string is not used and its bridge is pushed to the lower end of the board. Cf. *Se* (China). The instrument is played in octaves in the same manner as the *se*.
Lit.: no. 179.

Sil (Ancient Persia). Finger cymbals played in pairs. Cf. *Sinj*; *Zil*; *Sil-sil*; *Ṣelṣlīm*; *Sil-snyau*.
Lit.: no. 78.

Sil (*Sil-sil*) (Tibet). See *Sil-snyan*.

Sila (Congo—Banza; Gobu). Conical drum with two heads. Cf. *Nyi-n'go*.
Lit.: no. 26.

Silambu (*Karchilambu*) (South India). Tubular silver ring-rattles of dancers.
Lit.: no. 260.

Silanga (Tanzania). One of several dances performed by girls.

Sili (Iran). Term for string instrument.
Lit.: no. 255.

Silimba (South Africa). Also *serimba*. A marimba with 12 slabs.
Lit.: no. 255.

Siling (Southern Senegal). Songs sung by two groups of workers in ricefields, or by funeral processions in alternating manner.
Lit.: no. 122.

Silingut (Borneo). Nose flute made of bamboo, with four finger holes.
Lit.: no. 255.

Silir (Java). "Out of tune." In the past occasionally certain tones were not tuned correctly. The unusual *gamelan* sound thus created was called *silir*.
Lit.: no. 163.

Silir (*Gending silir*) (Bali). Short compositions for the *gamelan gong* structured in the form of *gangsaran* pieces.
Lit.: no. 197.

Sil-ma (Tibet). Term for the metallic sound of the cymbals.

iSilongo (South Africa—Zulu). Trumpet.
Lit.: no. 255.

Sil-sil (Tibet). Cymbals. Cf. *Sil*; *Sil-snyan*; *Zil*; *Ṣelṣlīm*; *Salāsil*.
Lit.: nos. 143, 250.

Silsilah (*Khānah*) (Arabia). See *Muwashaḥ*.

Sil-snyan (*Sil-sil*) (Tibet). "Pleasant little ones." The abbot's cymbals. Broad rimmed discs with small bosses. They are struck gently and horizontally by touching and rotating the two rims.
Lit.: no. 143.

Silu (Small Sunda Isl.; East Sumbawa). Oboe type.
Lit.: no. 162.

Siluk (Ancient Israel). Closing song of the main prayers. Cf. *R'shuth*.
Lit.: no. 12.

Sīmantī (South India). *Janya rāga* of the 57th *mēḷa* (*Siṃhendramadhyama*).
Tone material:
C D Eb F# G Ab B c
c G F# Eb D C
Lit.: no. 139.

Sīmantinī (South India). (1) The 57th *asampūrṇa mēḷa-rāga* without *kaṭapayādi* prefix. (2) The 57th *asampūrṇa mēḷa-rāga* with *kaṭapayādi* prefix was called *Sumadyuti*. See *Rāga* (South India).
Lit.: no. 139.

Śīmantinipriya (South India). *Janya rāga* of the 52nd *mēḷa* (*Rāmapriyā*).
Tone material:
C Db E F# A Bb c
c Bb A F# E Db C
Lit.: no. 139.

Simbiṅ (West Africa—Mandingo). Harp with seven strings.
Lit.: no. 255.

Sim(da) (*Si-im*) (Sumeria). Ancient obscure instrument; probably a drum.
Lit.: no. 94.

Siṃhā (India; Bengal). Term for *shringa* (*śṛṅga*).
Lit.: no. 254.

Siṃhamadhyama (South India). *Janya rāga* of the 43rd *mēḷa* (*Gavāmbōdhi*).
Tone material:
C Db Eb F# Bbb c
c Bbb F# Eb Db C
Lit.: no. 139.

Siṃhanādam (South India). *Janya rāga* of the 38th *mēḷa* (*Jalārṇava*).
Tone material:
C Db F# Ab Bb c
c Bb Ab F# Ebb C
Lit.: no. 139.

Siṃhanandana tāla (South India). See *Tāla*.

Siṃhārava (*Sinhārava*) (South India). *Janya rāga* of the 58th *mēḷa* (*Hemāvatī*).
Tone material:
C D F# G Bb c
c Bb G D Eb D C (*Bb* C) (c Bb G F# D Eb D C)
Lit.: no. 139.

Simhārava (South India). (1) The 58th *asampūrṇa mēḷa-rāga* without *kaṭapayādi* prefix. (2) The 58th *asampūrṇa mēḷa-rāga* with *kaṭapayādi* prefix was called *Deśisimhāravam.*
Lit.: no. 139.

Siṃhasvarūpi (South India). *Janya rāga* of the 64th *mēḷa* (*Vāchaspati*).
Tone material:
C E F♯ A B♭ c
c B♭ G F♯ E C
Lit.: no. 139.

Siṃhavāhinī (South India). *Janya rāga* of the 27th *mēḷa* (*Sarasāṅgī*).
Tone material:
C E F G A♭ B c
c B A♭ G F E D C
Lit.: no. 139.

Siṃhela (South India). See *Sinhela.*

Siṃhelabhairavī (South India). *Janya rāga* of the 23rd *mēḷa* (*Gaurīmanōhari*).
Tone material:
C E♭ F G A c
c B A F E♭ D C
Lit.: no. 139.

Siṃhēlakāpi (South India). *Janya rāga* of the 24th *mēḷa* (*Varuṇapriyā*).
Tone material:
C D F G A♯ B c
c B A♯ B G F E♭ C
Lit.: no. 139.

Siṃhēlasāvēri (South India). *Janya rāga* of the 30th *mēḷa* (*Naganandi*).
Tone material:
C F E F G A♯ B c
c B A♯ B G F E C
Lit.: no. 139.

Siṃhelavarāli (South India). *Janya rāga* of the 29th *mēḷa* (*Dhīraśaṅkarābharaṇam*).
Tone material:
C D E F G F A B c
c A G F E F D C
Lit.: no. 139.

Siṃhēlavasantam (South India). *Janya rāga* of the 25th *mēḷa* (*Māraranjanī*).
Tone material:
C D E F G A♭ B♭♭ c
c B♭♭ G F E D C
Lit.: no. 139.

Siṃhendramadhyama (South India). The 57th *mēḷa*:
C D E♭ F♯ G A♭ B c
As *rāga* the same tone material is used.
Lit.: no. 139.

Simsimijah (Arabia; Sinai desert; Egypt). Bedouin lyre with five strings.
Lit.: no. 100.

Simulia kwa utenze (kwa mashairi) (East Africa—Swahili). See *Imba, ghani, lia. . . .*

Sinād (Arabia). Ancient serious song; sung in slow tempo. Cf. *Hazaj.* According to Abu'l Mundhīr Hishām ibn al-Kalbī (d. 819), *sinād* is the "slow refrain with recurrent notes." The singing is classified into three types: *naṣb*, *sinād*, and *hazaj*. *Sinād* is a well developed *naṣb*, a slow and grandiose song type.
Lit.: nos. 73, 76.

Sinawi (Korea). Improvised Shamanist music of Southwest Korea. Cf. *Sanjo.*

Sinden (Java). Singing of men and women when accompanying *bedaya* and *serimpi* dances. According to Lit. no. 163, *sinden* can be described as a solo singing voice with instrumental accompaniment. In Jogya Kraton there are four types of *sinden(an)*:

1. *Sindenan lampah geṇḍing*: the solo voice fits well into the general harmony. Singing occurs intermittently.
2. *Sindenan lampah sekar geṇḍing*: continuous singing with accompaniment of the entire *gamelan.*
3. *Sindenan lampah sekar*: the voice is accompanied by colotomic instruments (*ketuk*, *kenong*, and *gong*). The melody instruments are silent.

4. *Sindenan lampah lagon*: the voice is accompanied by *rebāb*, *gambang*, *gender*, and occasionally also by the *suling*.

A fifth kind is mentioned, the *sindenan lampah jineman*, "soft music," either instrumental or vocal.

Sindenang (Java). See *Sinden.*

Sindenan lampah geṇḍing (Java). See *Sinden.*

Sindenan lampah jineman (Java). See *Sinden.*

Sindenan lampah lagon (Java). See *Sinden.*

Sindenan lampah sekar (Java). See *Sinden.*

Sindenan lampah sekar geṇḍing (Java). See *Sinden.*
Lit.: no. 163.

Sindh (North India). Rare *rāga* with vague performance rules. *Sindh* can be ascribed to the *Kafi thāta.*
Tone material:
C D E F G A (B♭) B c
c B♭ A G F E♭ D C
Lit.: no. 138.

Sindhoda (North India). See *Sindhura.*

Sindhu (South India). *Janya rāga* of the 29th *mēḷa* (*Dhīraśaṅkarābharaṇam*).
Tone material:
C D E D F G c
c B A G B A F G D C
Lit.: no. 139.

Sindhubhairavī (South India). *Janya rāga* of the 10th *mēḷa* (*Naṭakapriya*).
Tone material:
C E♭ F A B♭ c
c B♭ A F E♭ C
Lit.: no. 139.

Sindhuchintāmaṇi (South India). *Janya rāga* of the 9th *mēḷa* (*Dhēnuka*).
Tone material:
C D♭ F E♭ A♭ G A♭ c
c A♭ G F E♭ D♭ C
Lit.: no. 139.

Sindhudhanyāsi (South India). *Janya rāga* of the 20th *mēḷa* (*Naṭabhairavī*).
Tone material:
C E♭ F G A♭ c
c B♭ A♭ F G F E♭ D C
Lit.: no. 139.

Sindhugauri (South India). *Janya rāga* of the 7th *mēḷa* (*Senāpāti*).
Tone material:
C E♭ D♭ E♭ F G c
c A♭ G F E♭ D♭ C
Lit.: no. 139.

Sindhughaṇṭanam (South India). *Janya rāga* of the 37th *mēḷa* (*Sālaga*).
Tone material:
C E♭♭ D♭ E♭♭ F♯ G A♭ c
c A♭ F♯ E♭♭ D♭ C
Lit.: no. 139.

Sindhu Kannaḍa (South India). *Janya rāga* of the 28th *mēḷa* (*Harikāmbhōji*).
Tone material:
C F E F D F G A B♭ A c
c B♭ A G F E D C
Lit.: no. 139.

Sindhukriya (South India). *Janya rāga* of the 11th *mēḷa* (*Kokilapriya*).
Tone material:
C D♭ E♭ F G F A B c
c A G F E♭ D♭ C
Lit.: no. 139.

Sindhu Mandāri (South India). *Janya rāga* of the 29th *mēḷa* (*Dhīraśaṅkarābharaṇam*).
Tone material:
C D E F G c
c B A G E F A G F D C
Lit.: no. 139.

Sindhumāruva (South India). *Janya rāga* of the 54th *mēḷa* (*Viśvambharī*).
Tone material:
C D♭ E F♯ G C
c B A♯ c G F♯ E D♭ C
Lit.: no. 139.

Sindhunāṭakurañji (South India). *Janya rāga* of the 40th *mēḷa* (*Navanītam*).
Tone material:
C D♭ E♭♭ F♯ A B♭ A c
c B♭ A G F♯ E♭♭ D♭ C
Lit.: no. 139.

Sindhura (*Sindura*; *Sendhora*; *Sindhoda*; *Saindhvi*; *Sindhvi*; *Sindhuvi*) (North India). An ancient *rāga* ascribed to the *Kafi thāta*. The *rāga* has two forms of ascent.
Tone material:
(a) C D F G A c
(b) C D F G B c
c B♭ A G F E♭ D C
Lit.: no. 139.

Sindhurāmakriyā (South India). *Janya rāga* of the 15th *mēḷa* (*Māyāmāḷavagauḷa*).
Tone material:
C E F G A♭ B c
c B G A♭ G F E C
Variant of *Sindhurāmakriyā*.
Tone material:
C E F G A♭ B c
c B G A♭ G F♯ E D♭ E C
Lit.: no. 139.

Sindhusālavi (South India). *Janya rāga* of the 19th *mēḷa* (*Jhaṅkāradhvani*).
Tone material:
C F G F B♭♭ A♭ c
c B♭♭ A♭ G F E♭ D C
Lit.: no. 139.

Sindhuvi (North India). See *Sindhura.*

Sindhvi (North India). See *Sindhura.*

Sindura (North India). See *Sindhura.*

Sine keman (Turkey). Fiddle in *rebec* form.
Lit.: no. 255.

Si-ñen (written: *sil-snyan*) (Tibet). See *Sil-snyan.*
Lit.: nos. 143, 305.

Sing (Iran). Large cymbals. Cf. *Śiñj.*
Lit.: nos. 77-78.

Sing (India). A term used for horn; *sing* is derived from the Sanskrit *śṛṅga. Sing* also means cups (as used in the *jaltarang*), in which instances the term is derived from *sinj*, the Sanskrit "to tinkle" or "jingle."

Sing (Laos). Small cymbals. Cf. *Ching* (Thailand).

Siṅga (Former Assam – Garo; India – Prakrit term). Buffalo horn.
Lit.: no. 252.

Siṅgam (South India – Pali term). Term for *śṛṅga.*

Singgetan (Java). Musical fragment. In Jogya it is called *santum wilet*; in Solo *santum chengkok.*
Lit.: no. 163.

Singgul (Indonesia; Sunda District). (1) Term for the Javanese *barang*, the first note of the *slendro* system. The upper octave of this note is called *singgul leutik.* Cf. *Slendro.* (2) *Singgul* (*kuwing, papatet panatup*): the first note of the *pelog* system of the Sunda District. Cf. *Pelog* (tone names).
Lit.: no. 163.

Singgul leutik (Sunda District). See *Singgul.*
Lit.: no. 163.

Singkil (Philippines). (1) Iron ankle rattle. (2) Dance accompanied by gongs and rattling bamboo sticks.
Lit.: no. 215.

Singlatan (Bali). A characteristic manner of drumming in the *pengisep* part of *tabuh 1* (= *tabuh besik* in *tabuh gong*) of the *gamelan gong* music.
Lit.: no. 197.

Sing-sing (New Guinea—Papua). Village festival.
Lit.: no. 215.

Śiṅgum (India). Gujarati term for *śṛṅga.*

Singwe (Congo—Wasongola). Signalling whistle.
Lit.: no. 33.

Sinhārava (South India). See *Siṃhārava.*

Sinhela (*Siṃhela*) (South India). *Janya rāga* of the 18th *mēḷa* (*Hāṭakāmbarī*).
Tone material:
C D♭ E F G A♯ B c
c B A♯ B G F E D♭ C
Lit.: no. 139.

Sinh tien (Vietnam). Clappers consisting of three wooden slabs.
Lit.: no. 297.

Śiñj (India). Rattle, jingle, tinkle. Finger cymbals of the Mohammedans. Cf. *Sing*; *Hsing-erh*; *Sanj*; *Sanūj*; *Sunūj.*
Lit.: no. 78.

Ṣinjān (Old Arabia). Cymbals.
Lit.: no. 70.

Sinkang imilyanga (Congo; Ruanda). Drum.
Lit.: no. 26.

Sinnitu (Ancient Babylon—Akkad). Lute with two strings.
Lit.: no. 87.

Sinom (Java). One of the poetic meters of *tembang machapat*, generally occuring in didactic songs. See *Machapat.*
Lit.: no. 163.

Sinrili (Celebes). Sung heroic poems.
Lit.: no. 162.

Sintīr (Egypt; Syria). Cf. *Santīr.*
Lit.: no. 190.

Sinye (Ghana). Rattles.

Sipa (Burma; former Assam). Long bamboo cross-flute with seven finger holes.
Lit.: no. 252.

Sipahr (Middle East). *Maqām.*
Tone material:
D E♭(+) F G♭ A B♭ c d
Lit.: no. 64.

Sipa na pili (Congo—Bale; Mabali). Board zither without any resonator.
Lit.: no. 176.

Sippi (Congo—Mabali). *Sansa.*
Lit.: no. 21.

Šīr (Sumeria). Song.

Sirah (Bali). See *Kulkul.*

Sirah (Java). "Head." (1) See *Rebāb* (or *Daga*). (2) Top part of a slit-drum.
Lit.: no. 163.

Širbo (Somali Republic). A short dance song; an introduction to a big dance. At the present time it is performed by men and women; originally it was danced by men only.
Lit.: no. 98.

Sirep (Java). A soft gentle beating of various *gamelan* kettles. Cf. *Ngombang.*
Lit.: no. 163.

Siringo (Southeast India; Abujhmar Mts.—Gond). Small brass bells, mostly globular bells in clusters, attached to the back of dancers.
Lit.: no. 135.

Siriri (Kenya). A bowed lyre with six strings.
Lit.: no. 218.

Širnamšub (Sumeria). Song of praise.

Širnamursanga (Sumeria). Hymn to the goddess Inanna.

Sisi (New Ireland; New Mecklenburgh). A set of 10 pan flutes.
Lit.: nos. 115, 255.

Sisindiran bobogohan (West Java). Songs of erotic nature performed with the *ronggeng* dances.
Lit.: no. 163.

Si lo laos (Thailand). Stick zither with two strings.
Lit.: no. 18.

Sissika (Upper Volta—Bisa). Calabash rattle.
Lit.: no. 50.

Śītakiraṇi (South India). See *Shītakiraṇi.*

Sitār (Iran; Afghanistan; North India). "Three stringer." A long lute, now with 4-7 strings and a variable number of thin wire resonance strings. The broad and long neck with 18 frets ends in a small, oval corpus. The strings are plucked with the fingernails. Occasionally a bowed *sitār* can be observed.
Lit.: no. 34.

Sitāra (India). (1) A name used at times for the (Persian) *kemanje-a'jūz* in Hyderabad; occasionally also in Jaipur. (2) (Moorish Spain) in Lit. no. 34 is stated that Ibrāhim ben Haggāg el-lakhmi held his court, where he was surrounded by poets and his *sitāra* (female singers). The term was applied also to the palace orchestra that entertained the ruler and his dignitaries. The orchestra (*sitāra*) was placed behind a richly ornamented curtain.
Lit.: no. 34.

Sitata (*Shitata*) (Malawi). Small *sansa* with seven tongues and a gourd resonator.

Siter (Indonesia). A recent form of the *kachapi.* Instead of the oblong resonance hole, the *siter* has a slit going diagonally across the bottom board. The name is derived from the European word "zither."
Lit.: no. 163.

Sitet (Ethiopia). War drum.
Lit.: no. 102.

Sitlanjani (North Transvaal—Venda). A reed pipe consisting of two pieces of ivory. A piece of buckskin between the ivories forms a vibrating medium. Cf. *Mantsakota.*
Lit.: no. 151.

Sitot (Philippines). Cf. *Itundak.*

Sittawiyya (Egypt). Double clarinet.

Siu-lo (China—Cantonese). See *Wu-lo.*

Siva (Polynesia—Samoa). Dance of standing women (in contrast to seated performers).

Śivadāsi (India). Female temple dancer. See *Dēvadāsi.*

Śivānandi (South India). *Janya rāga* of the 16th *mēḷa* (*Chakravāka*).
Tone material:
C F E F G A B♭
(B♭) A G F E D♭ C *B♭*
Lit.: no. 139.

Siva-ofe (Samoa). Bamboo flute.
Lit.: no. 255.

Śivapriya (South India). *Janya rāga* of the 44th *mēḷa* (*Bhāvapriyā*).
Tone material:
C D♭ E♭ F♯ A♭ B♭ c
c B♭ A♭ F♯ E♭ D♭ C
Lit.: no. 139.

Siwa (New Guinea). Conically-shaped drum.

Siwa (East Africa—Swahili). See *Baragumu.*

Siwa (East Africa). A long simple reed tube.
Lit.: no. 215.

Siwang kakpae chae (*Taeryewang kongmun*) (Korea). Buddhist chant, similar to the *sangju kwongong chae*, but more extended and impressive. Cf. *Sangju kwongong chae.*
Lit.: no. 287.

Siyahi (North India). "Blackness"; the black circular patch of the *tabla* head. Cf. *Tabla.*

Siya-siya (South Celebes). A bamboo stick is beaten with another piece of bamboo. It is believed that this sound drives away evil spirits. Cf. *Lae-lae.*
Lit.: nos. 132, 254.

Siyem (Java). Abbreviation term for *gong siyem.* Cf. *Gong suwukan.*
Lit.: no. 163.

Siyu teki (Japan). Bamboo flute.
Lit.: no. 255.

Siyyāḥ (Old Arabia). Term for octave. Cf. *Sajāḥ.*

Siznik (Kurdistan). Musical instrument.
Lit.: no. 255.

Skad (Tibet). Voice; vocal sound; scream; speech.

Skad-bsang-pa (pronounced: *ge-sang-pa*) (Tibet). Literally, "good voice": an assistant to the *dbu-mdzad-pa* (pronounced: *um-dze-pa*).
Lit.: no. 143.

Skor (*Skor romonea*) (Kampuchea). Goblet drum. Cf. *Thon*; *Darābuka*; *Gedombak.*
Lit.: no. 43.

Skor thom (Kampuchea). A low-pitched barrel drum. Only one of its two heads is beaten with a wooden stick. Cf. *Khong that.*
Lit.: no. 215.

Skrog-pa (*Dkrog-pa*; *Da-ru skrog-pa*) (Tibet). Beating the drum.

Skyor-ba (Tibet). Reciting.

Skyor gdangs (Tibet). "Repeated (recited) chanting." Term for melancholy, sad features in the sacred chant, passages that are performed rhythmically free.
Lit.: no. 143.

Ṣlāṣal (*Ṣelṣlīm*) (Ancient Israel). Cymbals.
Lit.: no. 250.

Slawatan (Java). Songs of praise sung by the *chokekan* and other religious persons. The songs are also called *terbangan* or *jedoran* and, in the Sunda District, *nyalwat.*
Lit.: no. 163.

Slendang (Java). Tube zither.
Lit.: no. 190.

Slendro (Bali). A Javanese term, occasionally used in Bali, for the anhemitonic pentatonic scale of *gender wayang* and similar features. The term refers also to four-tone scales, e.g., the tuning of the *gamelan angklung* and several related deviant forms. Cf. *Saih angklung*; *Saih lima*; *Pelog.*
Lit.: no. 197.

Slendro (*Salendro*; *Surendro*) (Java). One of the two important tonal systems of Java (cf. *Pelog*). *Slendro* is a system with five degrees. The intervals between them are almost equidistant, each having approximately 240 cents.

The *slendro* scale, which in the past consisted of minor thirds and wholetones, now shows various forms from one place to the other. (The cent numbers indicate only one possible form.)

Scale:	♩	♩	♩	♩	♩	♩
		263	223	253	236	225
	nem	*barang*	*gulu*	*dada*	*lima*	*nem*
Tone name in High Javanese:		*(djangga)*		*(tengah)*	*(gangsal)*	

In West Java can be observed two *slendro* scales with the following intervals:

Surupan madenda:
I 360 II 120 III 360 IV 240 V 120 I

Surupan degung:
I 360 II 120 III 240 IV 360 V 120 I

The following list (see pp. 660-61), quoted from Lit. no. 163, p. 102, shows the tone names of the *slendro* system at various locations; the terms are in Javanese and at times in High Javanese. Cf. also *Paṭet.*

Slendro jawar (West Java). See *Salendro biasa* (the normal *slendro* scale).
Lit.: no. 163.

Slenṭem (Java). Low pitched seven-keyed *saron.* See *Selento.*
Lit.: no. 163.

Slenṭem ganḍul (Java; Pasuran). Cf. *Gender slenṭem.*

Slenṭem gantung (Java). Cf. *Gender slenṭem.*

S'liḫah (Ancient Israel). Vocal interpolation to the prayer of repentance. Cf. *R'shuth.*
Lit.: no. 12.

Śnb (Egypt). Hieroglyphic inscription for trumpet (vocalized: *śnobē*).
Lit.: no. 250.

Sngags (Tibet). Incantation of magic formulas, charms, mantras.
Lit.: no. 143.

Sō (Japan). Abbreviated form of *gaku-sō.*

So (Korea). Panpipes (cf. *P'ai hsiao*). The instrument consists of 16 pipes and is used only in the sacrificial music of *ah-ak.* The 16 tubes are placed, side by side in two ways:

1. In the now obsolete *bai-so* where they are arranged from the longest to the shortest.
2. In the *bong-so,* where they are arranged symmetrically showing the long pipes at both ends and the short ones in the middle, imitating the shape of the "phoenix wing."

The chromatic tuning of the pipes resembles that of the stone and bell chimes.
Lit.: no. 52.

Sō (Kampuchea). A fiddle with two strings tuned a fifth apart. The hair of the bow is strung between them. See also *Sa dueng*; *So i*; *So u.*
Lit.: no. 43.

Sobaba (Malagasy Republic). Term for *śab-bāba,* an Arabian end-blown flute with six finger holes in front and one at the back.
Lit.: no. 250.

Sōban (Japan). A roughly sounding pair of gongs used in temples and in the theater (*kabuki*), when crude characters enter the stage.
Lit.: no. 185.

Sobang (Borneo). Also *Ketobung.* Goblet-shaped drum.
Lit.: no. 162.

Sō bang (Laos). A rustic fiddle made of a bamboo tube affixed to a handle.
Lit.: no. 190.

Sober (Java; Madura). Term for the double reed of (e.g.) the *selompret.*
Lit.: no. 163.

Sochiba (East Turkestan). First and basic note of an obscure (6th-7th centuries) *p'i-p'a* scale (cf. Lit. no. 257).

The notes above *sochiba* were *sadalik, badalik, kichi, shachi, shahukalam, shalap, panjam, dzilidzap, hulidzap.* The exact significance of these note-names is indistinct.
Lit.: no. 257.

Soda (Flores). Song; dance tune.
Lit.: no. 166.

Sodina (Malagasy Republic). Flute, originally with three, later with seven finger holes.
Lit.: no. 252.

So do (Kampuchea). Fiddle with one string.
Lit.: no. 43.

So doran (Thailand). Also *Saw duang.* Cf. *See saw* (Laos).

Sō duang (Thailand). Fiddle with two strings and a circular body. The hair of the bow runs between the two strings. Cf. *Hu-ch'in.*

Soe-rap (Korea). Cf. *Tai-pyeng-so.*

Sof pasuq (Ancient Israel). Notational symbol (׃ֽ) used in biblical chant, indicating the end of a sentence (the Latin *punctum*).
Lit.: no. 310.

Ṣofyan (Arabia; Middle East). Rhythmical mode.

Soga (Japan). One of several forerunners of the *noh. Soga* ("fast song") was a form of chanted narrative.

Soga (*Sogha*) (Ghana—Ewe). One of the seven dances for Yeve, the god of thunder. (The names of the other six dances are listed under the heading of *Husago.*)
Lit.: nos. 128, 174.

Soǧaīr (*Sojaī*) (Egypt). See *Kamānjah farkh.*

Sōgaku (Japan). Term for the imported Chinese orchestral music including the accompaniments of *bugaku* and *sangaku* dances. The instruments used are *hichiriki*, *shō*, *taiko*, *kakko*, *shōko.*
Lit.: no. 225.

Sogha (Ghana—Ewe). See *Soga.*

Sogo (Ghana—Ewe). Barrel drum with one head. It is beaten with wooden sticks. The instrument is slightly larger than the *kidi.* Cf. *Kaganu*; *Kidi*; *Atsimevu.*
Lit.: no. 128.

Sogo (Korea). Small drum in fan-shape.

Sogonghu (Korea). "Small harp." Obsolete harp with 13 strings.
Lit.: no. 287.

Soha-Kanada (North India). See *Suha-kanada.*

Sohag (North India). A *rāga* of recent origin. It is rare and can be ascribed to the *Bilaval thāta.*
Tone material:
C (D) E F♯ G A B c
c B (B♭) (A) G F♯ E D C; *Vādis*: E, B
Lit.: no. 138.

Sohani (North India). *Rāga* ascribed to the *Marva thāta.* The views about the performance time vary: generally it is to be four o'clock in the morning. Scale and melodies begin with a descent from the upper *sa.*
Tone material:
c B A F♯ E D♭ C
C D♭ E F♯ A B c; *Vādis*: A, E
Lit.: no. 138.

Sō-hu (China). See *Su-hu.*

Soi (Northeast Thailand). One of the five *kaen* modes. The tones are: *G A* C D E G, one of the two *lum* scales. Also term for the refrain of a folk song.
Lit.: no. 213.

Sō-i (Laos; Kampuchea). Spike fiddle with a cylindrical body, a long slim neck, two strings tuned a fifth apart. Cf. *T'i-ch'in* (China); *Cai-ñi*; *Sō luang* (Thailand).
Lit.: no. 43.

Sojaīr (*Soǧaīr*) (Egypt). See *Kamānjah farkh.*

Sōjō (Japan). The sixth of the ancient Japanese twelve chromatic tones. It can be transcribed as the western note G if *ichikotsu*, the first note, is D. Cf. tuning of the *Sō-no-koto. Gagaku* and *Shōmyō* mode: G A B d e g.
Lit.: no. 185.

Soka (Flores—Lio District). Song, performed by a precentor and chorus.
Lit.: no. 166.

Sokavāḷi (South India). See *Shokavāḷi.*

SLENDRO TONE NAMES

Tones	*Central Java*	*Sunda District*	*Indramayu*	*Jombang Prabalingga*
I	*barang*	*singgul*	*panjang panutup*	*barang*
intermediate tone		*pamiring*		
II	*gulu jongga*	*bem galimer*	*kesekawan*	*tenggok gulu*
intermediate tone		*mangu*		
III	*ḍaḍa tengah*	*panelu*	*panelu*	*ḍaḍa*
intermediate tone		*panangis*		
IV	*lima gangsal*	*kenong*	*pamindo*	*lima*
intermediate tone		*jawil*		
V	*nem*	*barang*	*kesetunggil kesetunggal*	*nem*
intermediate tone		*sorog*		
I′	*barang*	*singgul leutik*		*barang alit*

SLENDRO TONE NAMES—*continued*

Tones	*Banyuwangi Majakerta*	*Madura*	*Bandjermasin*
I	*sorog*	*bheng*	*babon*
intermediate tone			
II	*tangah* *tenggok*	*tenggo'*	*tangeh*
intermediate tone			
III	*sanga*	*lima*	*lima*
intermediate tone			
IV	*lima*	*bharang*	*nam* *bam*
intermediate tone			
V	*nem*	*mettet*	*sanga* *tanggo*
intermediate tone			
I′			

Soke (Gabon Republic). Rattle.

So-keum (*So-kum*) (Korea). Small transverse flute, now obsolete, with six finger holes. Cf. *Sam-chuk*.
Lit.: no. 179.

So keum (*So-kum*) (Korea). A small gong, struck with a wooden mallet. See also *Tai-keum*.
Lit.: no. 179.

Soko (Guinea Republic). Fiddle with a gourd body and one string.
Lit.: no. 33.

So-kong-hu (*Su-kong-hu*) (Korea). Obsolete small harp with 13 silken strings. The Japanese name of this instrument was *kudara koto* (the harp, or zither, from Paikche). Cf. *Kung-hu* (China); *Wa-kong-hu*.
Lit.: no. 179.

Soktok (Korea). Music imported from Central Asia. It appeared also at the Japanese court as *sotoku* (cf. *Koma-gaku*).

Soku (Sudan; also West Africa—Mandingo). Primitive fiddle.
Lit.: no. 95.

So-kum (Korea). See *So-keum*.

Sok-yet (Indonesia; Malacca). Two percussion sticks struck against each other. Cf. *Cai chac* (former Annam).
Lit.: no. 254.

Sōkyoku (Japan). *Koto* music. Cf. *Bungo-bushi*.

So-la (Southwest China). Term used for *so-na*.

So-luang (Thailand). Spike fiddle. Cf. *Sō-i* (Laos); *T'i-ch'in* (China).
Lit.: no. 190.

Som (Tanzania). To read, to recite; song.

Soma (*Soma rāga*) (South India). *Janya rāga* of the 14th *mēḷa* (*Vakuḷābharaṇam*).
Tone material:
C D♭ F G F A♭ B♭ c
c B♭ A♭ F E D♭ C
Lit.: no. 139.

Sōmabhairavī (South India). *Janya rāga* of the 12th *mēḷa* (*Rūpāvatī*).
Tone material:
C D♭ E♭ F G c
c B G A♯ B G F E♭ D♭ C
Lit.: no. 139.

Sōmabhūpāḷam (South India). *Janya rāga* of the 30th *mēḷa* (*Nāgānandī*).
Tone material:
C D F G F A♯ c
c A♯ B G F E D C
Lit.: no. 139.

Sōmadīpakam (South India). *Janya rāga* of the 24th *mēḷa* (*Varuṇapriyā*).
Tone material:
C D G A♯ B c
c B G F E♭ C
Lit.: no. 139.

Sōmaghaṇṭānam (South India). *Janya rāga* of the 40th *mēḷa* (*Navanītam*).
Tone material:
C D♭ E♭♭ F♯ B♭ A B♭ c
c B♭ G A F♯ E♭♭ D♭ C
Lit.: no. 139.

Sōmagiri (South India). *Janya rāga* of the 21st *mēḷa* (*Kiravāṇi*).
Tone material:
C D E♭ F G B c
c B A♭ B F E♭ D C
Lit.: no. 139.

Sōmakiraṇi (South India). *Janya rāga* of the 41st *mēḷa* (*Pāvani*).
Tone material:
C D♭ F♯ G A c
c A G F♯ D♭ C
Lit.: no. 139.

Sōmakriya (South India). *Janya rāga* of the 31st *mēḷa* (*Yāgapriyā*).
Tone material:
C G F D♯ E F A♭ B♭♭ c
c A♭ G F E F D♯ C
Lit.: no. 139.

Sōmamañjari (South India). *Janya rāga* of the 67th *mēḷa* (*Sucharitra*).
Tone material:
C E F♯ G A♭ c
c A♭ G F♯ E C
Lit.: no. 139.

Sōmamukhi (South India). *Janya rāga* of the 27th *mēḷa* (*Sarasāṅgī*).
Tone material:
C E F G A♭ B c
c B A♭ G F E F D C
Lit.: no. 139.

Sōmangalam (South India). See *Śēmekkalam*.
Lit.: no. 260.

Sōmaprabhāvali (South India). *Janya rāga* of the 37th *mēḷa* (*Sālaga*).
Tone material:
C D♭ E♭♭ F♯ G A♭ c
c B♭♭ G F♯ E♭♭ D♭ C
Lit.: no. 139.

Sōmapratāpam (South India). *Janya rāga* of the 26th *mēḷa* (*Chārukeśī*).
Tone material:
C G F A♭ B♭ c
c B♭ A♭ G F E D C
Lit.: no. 139.

Somarāga (South India). See *Soma*.

Sōmataraṅgiṇī (South India). *Janya rāga* of the 17th *mēḷa* (*Sūryakānta*).
Tone material:
C E F G F A B c
c B c A G F E F D♭ C
Lit.: no. 139.

Sombo (Congo – Gombe). Drum.
Lit.: no. 26.

Sombo (Flores). Bamboo clarinet. See *Perere*.
Lit.: no. 166.

Som-pho (Kampuchea). Barrel drum with two skins, placed on a wooden stand.
Lit.: no. 255.

Sompoton (North Borneo – Sabah). Mouth organ with bamboo pipes.
Lit.: no. 215.

Sompret (Java). (1) See *Pepet wuno nio* (Flores). (2) See *Rajori dewangata* (Flores); *Sosowitan*. (3) See *Selompret*.
Lit.: no. 163.

So-na (China – M 5468; M 4609). A formerly popular and noisy oboe type consisting of a wooden tube with a conical bore and a brass or copper bell. The instrument has seven finger holes in front and one in the back. The mouthpiece has a circular metal disc for the player's lips to rest against. The *so-na* is related to the *zurna* of the Middle East, to the *sānāyī* of India, and numerous similar Asian instruments. A *so-na* of small size, frequented in Peking, is called *k'ai-ti*. Cf. *Bishur* (Mongolia); *Chi-na*; *So-la*; *Surna*; *Tai-p'eng-so*.
Lit.: no. 137.

Sonang-gut (Korea). Cf. *Kut*.

Sona-rappa (Japan). Simple trumpet of the candy vendors.
Lit.: no. 255.

Song (Bali). Finger holes (cf. *Suling*).

Sōng chan (Thailand). "Middle version," "second level," term used for rhythmical cymbal patterns. Cf. *Sōng mai*.
Lit.: no. 208.

Songer (New Guinea – Papua). Primitive trumpet.
Lit.: no. 255.

Song gor (Vietnam). See *Hogoi*.

Songgabuwana (Java). Term for *palemahan.* Cf. *Rebāb.*

Songka (Java). Ancient marine shell (trumpet). Lit.: no. 163.

Sōng lang (Vietnam). Clapper made of a small wood-block and a swinging wooden ball. Lit.: no. 297.

Sōng mai (Thailand). "Two beats." Medium tempo in common meter with a gentle accent on the second and a strong accent on the fourth beat.
Lit.: no. 208.

Song na (Thailand). A slim, long barrel or slightly conically-shaped drum with two heads. It is similar to the *tapone*, but slimmer and lighter. The wooden body rests on a wooden stand or can be placed on the lap of the player.

The names and sounds of the right hand beats are: *ting* (long vibrating sound), *tub* (short, dull), *tja* (short), *nang* (long vibrating). The left hand can perform *thoeng* (long vibrating) or *thoe* (short), and both hands playing at the same time perform *phring*. If the *song-na* is used for accompanying songs, it is called *poeng mang*.
Lit.: no. 208.

Songongi (Solomon Isl.). See *Mou hatingaa nge'o.*

Sō-no-koto (Japan). One of the richly ornamented ancient zithers with 13 strings and low bridges imported from China in the 17th century. It became distinguished and fashionable at the imperial court and was used in *bugaku* music. For the tunings of the heavy instrument see *Koto.*

Sonsori (Korea). Form of vocal music. See *Ipch'ang.*
Lit.: no. 287.

Sō-o (Thailand). See *Sō-u.*

Sootsanaen (Northeast Thailand). One of the *kaen* modes using the anhemitonic pentatonic material of the *lum* scale.
Lit.: no. 203.

Sōpāna rīti (South India; Kerala). *Kathakali* style of singing, similar to the manner of chanting prayers.
Lit.: no. 123.

Sora (Java). Loud; forte.

Sora (Korea). Conch shell, a horn with a penetrating sound. See *Na-kag.* Cf. *Hora* (*gai*) (or *jingai*).

Sora geganti (Sunda District). Term for the Javanese *sorogan*, exchange tones used in transposing. The Balinese term is *penyorog.*
Lit.: no. 163.

Sora lelugu (Sunda District). Basic, principal scale tones. Cf. *Naek turuma sora.*
Lit.: no. 163.

Sorath (North India). *Rāga* ascribed to the *Khamaj thāta*. It is to be performed in the evening.
Tone material:
C D F G B c
c B♭ A G F E (E♭) D C; *Vādis*: D, A
Lit.: no. 138.

Sorati (Nepal – Gurung). Also *sorti.* Extensive dance song.
Lit.: no. 133.

Sordam (Indonesia; Toba-Batak). Open flute (with center hole) without mouthpiece. It has 4-5 finger holes. Cf. *Fekor*; *Sunding*; *Saligung.*
Lit.: nos. 162, 166.

Sori (Japan – Tendai sect). "Curve." A *kyoku-setzu*. The feature consists of a rise of 3-4 notes followed by a semitonic downward move, followed again by a gentle upward progress.

Sori (Korea). Song. The singing part of the *p'an-sori*. In this long, one-man "opera" the single performer carries out the dialogue and narration (*aniri*), some acting (*pallim*), and singing (*sori*).

Sori-tekes (*Raket*; *Wayang topeng*) (Java). Masked dance drama. See *Wayang wang*.
Lit.: no. 163.

Sorna (Sikkim—Lepcha). Term for *zurna*.

Sorog (Java; Banyuwangi; Majakerta). The first note of the *slendro* system. Cf. *Slendro*.
Lit.: no. 163.

Sorog (*Pengasih*) (Indonesia; Prabalingga). The first note of the *pelog* system. See *Pelog*.
Lit.: no. 163.

Sorog (Indonesia—Sunda District). Intermediate tone between *barang*, the fifth, and *singgul leutik*, the first note of the upper octave of the *slendro* system. Cf. *Slendro*.
Lit.: no. 163.

Sorog (*Sorog kuwing*) (Indonesia; Sunda District). The seventh note of the *pelog* system. Cf. *Pelog*.
Lit.: no. 163.

Sorog (Java). Sliding; alternating tone. Cf. *Surupan Melog*; *Sorogan*.

Sorogan (Java). Exchange tones (produced by wooden slabs in xylophones and metal keys in metallophones) that enable the performer to modulate from the principal into an auxiliary system. E.g., in *pelog barang* and *bem*, keys are replaced by *barang* keys. The *sorogan* (exchange keys) are kept within the *grobogan*. Cf. *Sora geganti* (Sunda District); *Penyorog* (Bali).
Lit.: no. 163.

Sorog gede (Sunda District). See *Bungur*.
Lit.: no. 163.

Sorog kuwing (Sunda District). Name of the 7th note (*pelog* system) in the Sunda District. Cf. *Sorog*.
Lit.: no. 163.

Sōrokū (Japan). Third degree in rank given to professional musicians. *Sōrokū* is higher in rank than *kengyō*. Cf. *Kotō*; *Genin*; *Gakunin*.
Lit.: no. 225.

Sorti (Nepal). See *Sorati*.

Sōsām saī (Thailand). Spike fiddle with three strings.

Sosanru (*Dunde*) (Celebes—Kagerova). Stick zither. Cf. *Sulepe* (Halmahera); *Tutalo* (Ternate).
Lit.: no. 254.

Sō-shidai (Japan). Cf. *Shidai*.

Sosoangan (West Java). *Soang* = goose. "The pigeon flute"—*sawangan* of Java.
Lit.: no. 163.

Sosowitan (Java; Amboyna). Cf. *Sempritan*; *sernei*.

Sotoku (Japan). Korean entertainment music. The Korean term is *soktok*. *Sotoku* was played at the Japanese court as part of *koma-gaku*.

Sō-u (*sō-o*) (Laos; Thailand). A fiddle with a coconut body, long neck and two strings. The hairs of the bow are strung between the two strings. Cf. *So*; *Tro-u*; *Hu-ch'in*.
Lit.: no. 43.

Sou-lo (China; Canton) (*Su-lo*, Mandarin). See *Wu-lo*.

Sovu (Ghana—Ewe). One of the seven dances for Yeve, the god of thunder. (The names of the other six dances are listed under heading of *Husago*). Cf. *Ahiavui*.
Lit.: no. 128.

Sowito (Flores). Tubular bamboo zither with 2, 5, or 6 strings. Cf. *Gong-tondu.*

Spagane (South Africa – Thonga). Clappers made of wooden slabs, played by male dancers.
Lit.: no. 151.

Sphon (Thailand). *Thapon.*

Sphurita (India). See *Gamak(a).*

Sputalāpiṇī (South India). *Janya rāga* of the 61st *mēḷa* (*Kāntāmaṇi*).
Tone material:
C E F♯ G B♭♭ c
c B♭♭ G F♯ E C
Lit.: no. 139.

Sputalāpiṇī (South India). *Janya rāga* of the 72nd *mēḷa* (*Rasikapriyā*).
Tone material:
C E F♯ G A♯ c
c A♯ G F♯ E C
Lit.: no. 139.

Śr (Ancient Egypt). Term for a drum (hand-drum) with two heads. Cf. *Tbn.*
Lit.: no. 100.

Sralay (Kampuchea). Heavy oboe type with four palm leaf tongues placed in a small brass tube. The tube has six holes. Cf. *Pi-chawa* (Thailand); *Sernai* (Malaysia).
Lit.: no. 254.

Sranḍil (Java; South Surakarta). See *Sranḍul.*

Sranḍul (Java). A popular dance play.

Śravanti (South India). *Janya rāga* of the 5th *mēḷa* (*Manōrañjanī*).
Tone material:
C E♭♭ F A B c
c B A F E♭♭ C
Lit.: no. 139.

Srawing (Java). See *Sumping*; *Rebāb* (Java).

Srenten (Java). See *Santen.*

Srepegan (*Sampak*) (Java). Music that accompanies battle scenes in the *wayang kulit* plays. (Cf. *Karatagan*, in Sundanese). Two types of *srepegan* are distinguished:
1. *Srepegan prang buta chakil*, characterized by the *keprak* rhythm: ♬ | ♪. ♬ ♪.
2. *Srepegan prang buta geḍe*, a fast rhythm: | ♫ ♫ ("big giant").

In both types is used the same melody, but in (1) occurs several times the *ngelik* (sudden move into a higher octave).
Lit.: no. 163.

Srepegan prang buta chakil (Java). Variant of *srepegan* (1).

Srepegan rambangan (Java). A special type of *srepegan* where its melody (solo) is not sung by a group but by a single person (or by two persons: a man and a woman).
Lit.: no. 163.

Śrī (South India). One of the mnemonics used in the system of the 72 *mēḷas*. It indicates the second *mēḷa* of each *chakra* (the other mnemonics can be seen under the heading of *Bhu*). See *Rāga* (South India).
Lit.: no. 139.

Śrī (South India). A variant of *Śrī rāga* (of the 22nd *mēḷa*). The present *Śrī* is a *janya rāga* of the 15th *mēḷa* (*Māyāmāḷavagauḷa*).
Tone material:
C D♭ F G B c d♭′ c
c d♭′ B A♭ G F A♭ E D♭ C
Lit.: no. 139.

Srigak (Java). "Bright," "cheerful." The term is used to describe a *gamelan* in which the intervals *barang-gulu* (in *slendro*) and *penunggul* (*bem*)-*gulu* (in *pelog*) are exceptionally wide (wider than the 240 cents in *slendro* and wider than 140 cents in *pelog*). Cf. *Laras sundari.*
Lit.: no. 163.

Śrīkanti (South India). *Janya rāga* of the 46th *mēḷa* (*Śaḍvidhamārgiṇī*).
Tone material:
C E♭ F♯ G A B♭ c
c B♭ A G F♯ E♭ C
Lit.: no. 139.

Śrīkari (South India). *Janya rāga* of the 52nd *mēḷa* (*Rāmapriyā*).
Tone material:
C D♭ E G A B♭ c
c B♭ A G F♯ E C
Lit.: no. 139.

Śrīkhandalilelpani (South India). *Janya rāga* of the 54th *mēḷa* (*Viśvambharī*).
Tone material:
C D♭ F♯ A♯ B c
c B A♯ F♯ D♭ C
Lit.: no. 139.

Śrīmadhukari (South India). *Janya rāga* of the 50th *mēḷa* (*Nāmanārāyaṇī*). The scale of this *rāga* is identical with that of the primary *rāga* (*mēḷa*) *Nāmanārāyaṇī.*
Lit.: no. 139.

Śrīmālavi (South India). *Janya rāga* of the 6th *mēḷa* (*Tānarūpi*).
Tone material:
C D♭ E♭♭ F G B A♯ B A♯ B c
c G F E♭♭ D♭ C
Lit.: no. 139.

Śrimani (South India). *Janya rāga* of the 2nd *mēḷa* (*Ratnangi*).
Tone material:
C D♭ E♭♭ G A♭ (B♭) c
c B♭ A♭ G E♭♭ D♭ C (*B♭ A♭* C)
Lit.: no. 139.

Śrīmañjula (South India). *Janya rāga* of the 36th *mēḷa* (*Chalanāṭa*).
Tone material:
C D♯ E F G A♯ B c
c B A♯ B G F E D♯ C
Lit.: no. 139.

Śrīmanōhari (South India). *Janya rāga* of the 22nd *mēḷa* (*Kharaharapriyā*).
Tone material:
C E♭ D E♭ F G A c
c A G F E♭ D C
Lit.: no. 139.

Srimpi (*Serimpi*) (Java; Bali). Popular dance performed by four girls.
Lit.: no. 288.

Sring (Armenia). Vertical flute.
Lit.: no. 255.

Śringa (India). See *Śṛṅga.*

Sringāra (India). "Love." One of the nine emotions (*rasas*) expressed in music. Cf. *Navarasa*; *Rasa.*
Lit.: no. 138.

Śringi (South India). Kannarese term for *śṛṅga.*

Śrīrāga (South India). *Janya rāga* of the 22nd *mēḷa* (*Kharaharapriyā*).
Tone material:
C D F G B♭ c
c B♭ G A B♭ G F D E♭ D C
(c B♭ G F D E♭ D C)
Lit.: no. 139.

Śrīrāga (South India). (1) The 22nd *asampūrṇa mēḷa-rāga* without *kaṭapayādi* prefix. (2) The same but with *kaṭapayādi* prefix. See *Rāga* (South India).
Lit.: no. 139.

Śrīrañjaṇi (South India). *Janya rāga* of the 22nd *mēḷa* (*Kharaharapriyā*).
Tone material:
C D E♭ F A B♭ c
c B♭ A F E♭ D C
Lit.: no. 139.

Śṛṅga (*Śringa*) (India). Sanskrit term for cowhorn. The instrument is also made of copper or bronze. A few of the many terms for this instrument are: *siṅgam* in Pālī, *siṅga* in Prakrit, *siṃhā* in Bengali, *sīng* in Hindi, *śiṅgum* in Gujarati, *śringi* in Kannarese.
Lit.: no. 254.

Śṛṅgāriṇī (South India). *Janya rāga* of the 6th *mēḷa* (*Tānarūpi*).
Tone material:
C E♭♭ D♭ G F G c
c B A♯ G F E♭♭ D♭ C
Lit.: no. 139.

Srune (Sumatra—Atjeh). Oboe type. Cf. *Zūrna*; *Sūrnay*; *Sruni*; *Sarune*; *Serunai.*
Lit.: no. 254.

Sruni (Java). Cf. *Srune.*

Sruṅ-pa (Tibet). Minstrels who perform epic songs. Similar to shamans, these minstrel-wizards put themselves into trance and produce various religious and conjuring effects.
Lit.: no. 62.

Śruti (India). Microtonal interval. The term is derived from the Sanskrit root *śru*, "to hear." *Śruti* implies an interval so small that it can be merely recognized by the ear and is not shown in musical notation.

Indian singers and serious performing musicians have paid little attention to the numerous theoretical explanations and calculations in literary works, and refused to determine the exact, fixed microintervals and resulting tones. As the *śrutis* are predominantly created by the mood and the atmosphere of the *rāga* performed, there exist a certain amount of "slightly high" or "slightly low" intonations and intervals. It happens that a serious performer applies at one occasion a certain note a "little high" and, at another occasion, a "little less high," although the same *rāga* and the same mood are presented.

The names of the *śrutis* and their corresponding tone names in theoretical works are:

Śruti name	Tone name
0 *Kṣobhiṇī*	*sa*
1 *Tīvrā*	*pratiśuddha ri*
2 *Kumudvatī*	*śuddha ri*
3 *Mandā*	*praticatuśśruti ri* (*pratiśuddha ga*)
4 *Chhandovatī*	*catuśśruti ri* (*śuddha ga*)
5 *Dayāvatī*	*pratiṣaṭśruti ri* (*pratisādhāraṇa ga*)
6 *Rañjanī*	*ṣaṭśruti ri* (*sādhāraṇa ga*)
7 *Raktikā*	*pratiantara ga*
8 *Raudrī*	*antara ga*
9 *Krodhā*	*pratiśuddha ma*
10 *Vajrikā*	*śuddha ma*
11 *Prasāriṇī*	*pratiantara ma*
12 *Prītiḥ*	*pratikaiśiki ma*
13 *Mārjanī*	*pa*
14 *Kṣitiḥ*	*pratiśuddha dha*
15 *Raktā*	*śuddha dha*
16 *Sandīpinī*	*praticatuśśruti dha* (*pratiśuddha ni*)
17 *Ālāpinī*	*catuśśruti dha* (*śuddha ni*)
18 *Madantī*	*pratiṣaṭśruti dha* (*pratikaiśiki ni*)
19 *Rohiṇī*	*ṣaṭśruti dha* (*kaiśikī ni*)
20 *Ramyā*	*pratikākalī ni*
21 *Ugrā*	*kākalī ni*
22 *Kṣobhiṇī*	*sa*

At the present time all the above mentioned terms are not in use any more except in some theoretical treatises. All that is required now are the name of the seven scale degrees (*sa*, *ri*, *ga*, *ma*, *pa*, *dha*, *ni*) and, in the North *komal* (for flat) and *tivra* (for sharp). The musicians of the South do not use even the two latter terms and expect the performer to know the correct pitches of any *rāga* they perform.

For detailed information see my book Lit. no. 138, pp. 9-10.

Śruti (India). A double reed instrument, conically shaped with a metal bell. With the exception of one, the fingerholes are closed with wax. The instrument serves to produce only one bourdon note.

Śruti nāḍi (South India). The drone pipe of the *alakōja.*

Śrutiprakāśini (South India). *Janya rāga* of the 63rd *mēḷa* (*Latāṅgī*).
Tone material:
C D F♯ A♭ B c
c B A♭ F♯ D C
Lit.: no. 139.

Śrutirañjaṇi (South India). *Janya rāga* of the 61st *mēḷa* (*Kāntāmani*).
Tone material:
C D E F♯ G A♭ B♭♭
B♭♭ A♭ G F♯ E C D C
Lit.: no. 139.

Śruti-upāṅga (South India). Also *bajānā-śruti.* Bagpipe made of goat-leather. Its short mouthpiece resembles the form of a small clarinet. In Telugu, Kannarese, and Malayalam, the instrument is called *titti.* Cf. *Mashak.*
Lit.: no. 254.

Śruti-vīṇā (India). A *sitar* type. It differs from the *sitar* by its 26 frets which allegedly produce the 22 *śrutis.* The instrument, of no consequence, is played with a *mizrab* (wire plectrum).
Lit.: no. 254.

Ssu (China—M 5598). Tone name and notational symbol of the second (main) degree of the *kung-ch'e-p'u* system. Assuming that *ho* (the basic note) represents C, *ssu* would indicate the note D.
Lit.: no. 136.

Ssu-hu (China—M 5598; M 2167). A four-string fiddle of the *hu-ch'in* type (of Peking). The strings are tuned in pairs; the hair of the bow is strung between the two pairs of strings. See *Hu-ch'in.*

Ssu-pu-hsiang (China—M 5598; M 5379; M 2562). See *Ch'in-kang t'ui.*

Stag-dung (Tibet). A pair of vertical pipes made of the thigh bones of a tiger. The pipes are blown in the worship of minor deities and demons and in sorcery rites.
Lit.: no. 305.

Stag-gling (Tibet). High pitched pipe made of a tiger's bone. Cf. *rKang gling*; *rKang-dung.*
Lit.: no. 143.

Stag maḥi ngar skad (Tibet). "The roar of the tigress." A rough, low-pitched, formidable sound chanted by a large group of monks.
Lit.: no. 143.

Stavapriya (*Sthavapriya*) (South India). *Janya rāga* of the 51st *mēḷa* (*Kāmavardhanī*).
Tone material:
C E F♯ G A♭ c
c A♭ G F♯ E C
Lit.: no. 139.

Stavarājarāgan (*Sthavarājarāgam*) (South India). *Janya rāga* of the 46th *mēḷa* (*Śaḍvidhamārgiṇī*).
Tone material:
C D♭ F♯ G A c
c B♭ A F♯ E♭ C
Lit.: no. 139.

Sthavarājam (South India). See *Tivravāhini* (46th *asampūrṇa mēḷa*).

Sthāyi (*Asthāyī*; *Astai*) (North India). The first section of an art song. It is preceded by the rhythmically free *ālāp.* With the beginning of the *sthāyi* the soloist (e.g., the singer) is joined by the drummer and a strict rhythmical structure is established.
Lit.: no. 138.

Stobeong (Borneo—Land Dayak). Jew's harp made of brass.
Lit.: no. 255.

Stoma (Vedic India). Vedic hymn consisting of 5-7 sections:
1. *Prastāva*
2. *Udgītha*
3. *Pratihāra*
4. *Upadrava*
5. *Nidhana*
Lit.: no. 141.

Stotra (Vedic India). Ritual (Vedic) chants sung during the *soma* sacrifice.
Lit.: no. 119.

Śtrī (*Yoṣit*) (India). Old term for "female" *rāgas* (*rāginis*). Now obscure.
Lit.: no. 138.

Stychon (Egypt; Coptic). Also *hink*. Single musical phrase used in responsorial singing.
Lit.: no. 199.

Su (West Africa; Sudan). Drum.
Lit.: no. 95.

Sua (Former Annam). Castanets.
Lit.: no. 255.

Sua (Southeast India). See *Rina*.
Lit.: no. 134.

Suahongi (Solomon Isl.; Bellona Isl.). Dance songs. One or two singers perform one song while the surrounding group sing a different melody. There are seven different songs sung in this way in the course of this long dance epic. Much of the text is ancient and cannot now be understood.
Lit.: no. 246.

Su'aibiya (Arabia). Eight panpipes in raft form, arranged from the longest to the shortest.

Suan-lai (Northeast Thailand). Obscure ancient wind instrument.

Sua-sua (Philippines). "Orange tree dance." Courtship dance.

Šubal (Somali Republic). Dance; usually performed by women. Only rarely danced by men.
Lit.: no. 98.

Śubhakari (South India). *Janya rāga* of the 33rd *mēḷa* (*Gāṅgeyabhushanī*).
Tone material:
C D♯ F G A♭ c
c A♭ G F D♯ C
Lit.: no. 139.

Śubhāli (South India). *Janya rāga* of the 45th *mēḷa* (*Śubhapantuvarālī*).
Tone material:
C D♭ E♭ F♯ A♭ B c
c B A♭ F♯ E♭ D♭ C
Lit.: no. 139.

Śubhapantuvarālī (South India). (1) The 45th *mēḷa*:
C D♭ E♭ F♯ G A♭ B c
(2) As *rāga* the same tone material is shown in the 45th *mēḷa*.

Śubhvāsini (South India). *Janya rāga* of the 65th *mēḷa* (*Mechakalyāṇī*).
Tone material:
C D F♯ A B c
c B A F♯ D C
Lit.: no. 139.

Śubika (South India). *Janya rāga* of the 53rd *mēḷa* (*Gamanaśrama*).
Tone material:
C D♭ F♯ G A c
c A G F♯ D♭ C
Lit.: no. 139.

Sucharitra (South India). (1) The 67th *mēḷa*:
C D♯ E F♯ G A♭ B♭♭ c
(2) As *rāga* the same tone material is used as that of the 67th *mēḷa*.

Śuddha (*Shuddha*) (India). "Natural," "pure," "unaltered." E.g., *śuddha ga* in North India means the third degree of the heptatonic major modus: "natural E," if *sa*, the basic note, is C. In the South where the basic scale (*kanakāṅgī*) is different, *śuddha ga*, also representing the third degree, is E♭♭, if *sa* is C.
Lit.: nos. 136, 138.

Śuddhabaṅgaḷa (South India). *Janya rāga* of the 22nd *mēḷa* (*Kharaharapriyā*).
Tone material:
C D F G A c
c B♭ A F E♭ D C
(occasionally also: c A G F D E♭ D C)
Lit.: no. 139.

Śuddhabhairavī (South India). *Janya rāga* of the 22nd *mēḷa* (*Kharaharapriyā*).
Tone material:
C E♭ F B♭ A c
c B♭ A F E♭ D C
Lit.: no. 139.

Śuddhabhōgi (South India). *Janya rāga* of the 37th *mēḷa* (*Sālaga*).
Tone material:
C D♭ E♭♭ F♯ G B♭♭ A♭ c
c A♭ B♭♭ G F♯ E♭♭ D♭ C
Lit.: no. 139.

Śuddhadēśi (South India). *Janya rāga* of the 20th *mēḷa* (*Naṭabhairavī*).
Tone material:
C D F G A B♭ c (A used in ascent)
c B♭ A♭ G F E♭ D C (A♭ used in descent:
c B♭ A♭ G A♭ F E♭ D C)
Lit.: no. 139.

Śuddha Dha (India). The note name corresponding to *raktā*, the 15th *śruti*. Cf. *Śruti.*

Śuddhadhanyāsi (South India). *Janya rāga* of the 22nd *mēḷa* (*Kharaharapriyā*).
Tone material:
C E♭ F G B♭ G c
c B♭ G F E♭ C
Lit.: no. 139.

Śuddha Ga (India). See *Catuśśruti Ri.*

Śuddhagāndhāri (South India). *Janya rāga* of the 48th *mēḷa* (*Divyamaṇī*).
Tone material:
C D♭ E♭ F♯ B c
c B A♯ B c B G F♯ D♭ C
Lit.: no. 139.

Śuddhagaurīkriya (South India). *Janya rāga* of the 60th *mēḷa* (*Nītimatī*).
Tone material:
C E♭ F♯ G B A♯ B c
c B A♯ G F♯ E♭ C
Lit.: no. 139.

Śuddhaghaṇṭānam (South India). *Janya rāga* of the 34th *mēḷa* (*Vāgadhīśvarī*).
Tone material:
C E F G A c
c B♭ A G F D♯ C
Lit.: no. 139.

Śuddhagīrvaṇi (South India). *Janya rāga* of the 41st *mēḷa* (*Pāvani*).
Tone material:
C D♭ E♭♭ F♯ G A B c
c B G $\overset{+}{F}$ E♭♭ C
In descent the regular note F♯ of this *mēḷa* becomes almost a F-natural.
Lit.: no. 139.

Śuddhajiṅgala (South India). *Janya rāga* of the 33rd *mēḷa* (*Gāṅgeyabhushanī*).
Tone material:
C E F G A♭ B c
c B G F E C
Lit.: no. 139.

Śuddhajyotiṣmati (South India). *Janya rāga* of the 61st *mēḷa* (*Kāntāmani*).
Tone material:
C E F♯ G c
c B♭♭ A♭ G F♯ E D C
Lit.: no. 139.

Śuddhakalānidhi (South India). *Janya rāga* of the 63rd *mēḷa* (*Latāṅgī*).
Tone material:
C E G A♭ B
B A♭ G F♯ E D C
This scale has *niṣādāntya* character.
Lit.: no. 139.

Śuddhakalyāṇi (South India). See *Mohana.*

Śuddhakalyāṇī (*Mōhanakalyāṇī*) (South India). *Janya rāga* of the 65th *mēḷa* (*Mechakalyāṇī*).
Tone material:
C D E G A c
c B A G F♯ E D C
Lit.: no. 139.

Śuddhakāmbhōji (*Śudhakāmbhōji*) (South India). *Janya rāga* of the 14th *mēḷa* (*Vakulābharaṇam*).
Tone material:
C E D♭ F G B♭ c
c B♭ G F E D♭ C
Lit.: no. 139.

Śuddhakannaḍa (South India). *Janya rāga* of the 18th *mēḷa* (*Hāṭakāmbarī*).
Tone material:
C F G A♯ B c
c B G F E C
Lit.: no. 139.

Śuddhakōsala (South India). *Janya rāga* of the 65th *mēḷa* (*Mechakālyāṇī*).
Tone material:
C E F♯ G c
c B A F♯ E D C
Lit.: no. 139.

Śuddhakriya (South India). *Janya rāga* of the 15th *mēḷa* (*Māyāmāḷavagauḷa*).
Tone material:
C D♭ G F G A♭ c
c A♭ G F E D♭ C
Lit.: no. 139.

Śuddhalahari (*Śudhalahari*) (South India). *Janya rāga* of the 64th *mēḷa* (*Vāchaspati*).
Tone material:
C D F♯ A B♭ c
c B♭ A F♯ D C
Lit.: no. 139.

Śuddhalalita (South India). *Janya rāga* of the 17th *mēḷa* (*Sūryakānta*). The material is identical with that of *Lalita*, *janya rāga* of the 17th *mēḷa*.
Lit.: no. 139.

Śuddha Ma (India). The note name corresponds to *vajrikā*, the 10th *śruti*. Cf. *Śruti*. Also if *sa* is assumed to be C, *śuddha ma* stands for the note F.

Śuddha Maddaḷa (India; Kerala). The first rhythmic prelude of the *kathakali* performance.
Lit.: no. 123.

Śuddha Madhya (India). (1) The fourth of the seven ancient *mūrchhanās* derived from the *magrāma*. (2) In North India the note that stands a pure fourth above the basic note (e.g.; F above C); see *Śuddha Ma*.

Śuddhamadhyamam (South India). *Janya rāga* of the 22nd *mēḷa* (*Kharaharapriyā*).
Tone material:
C D F G A B♭ c
c A G A B♭ A G F E♭ D C
Lit.: no. 139.

Śuddhamalahari (South India). *Janya rāga* of the 15th *mēḷa* (*Māyāmāḷavagauḷa*).
Tone material:
C D♭ E G F A♭ c
c A♭ G E D♭ C
Lit.: no. 139.

Śuddha Māḷavi (South India). *Janya rāga* of the 18th *mēḷa* (*Hāṭakāmbarī*).
Tone material:
C E D♭ E F G A♯ B c
c A♯ B G F E D♭ C
Lit.: no. 139.

Śuddhamālavi (South India). (1) The 18th *asampūrṇa mēḷa-rāga* without *kaṭapayādi* prefix. (2) The 18th *asampūrṇa mēḷa-rāga* with *kaṭapayādi* prefix was called in the past *Jayaśuddhamālavi*. See *Rāga* (South India).
Lit.: no. 139.

Śuddhmallār (South India). *Janya rāga* of the 28th *mēḷa* (*Harikāmbhōji*).
Tone material:
C D F G B♭ c
c B♭ A F♯ G B♭ A E F♯ D C
Only in the two indicated passages in descent does the note F become approximately an F♯.
Lit.: no. 139.

Śuddhamañjari (South India). *Janya rāga* of the 4th *mēḷa* (*Vanaspāti*).
Tone material:
C E♭♭ F G F A B♭ c
c B♭ G A F E♭♭ D♭ C
Lit.: no. 139.

Śuddhamanōharī (South India). *Janya rāga* of the 22nd *mēḷa* (*Kharaharapriyā*).
Tone material:
C D E♭ F G A c
c B♭ G F E♭ D C
Lit.: no. 139.

Śuddhamāruva (South India). *Janya rāga* of the 8th *mēḷa* (*Hanumattoḍi*).
Tone material:
C E♭ F G A♭ c
c A♭ G F D♭ E♭ D♭ C
Lit.: no. 139.

Śuddhambhōdi (*Śudhambhodhi*) (South India). *Janya rāga* of the 43rd *mēḷa* (*Gavāmbōdhi*).
Tone material:
C D♭ E♭ F♯ A♭ B♭♭ c
c B♭♭ A♭ F♯ E♭♭ D♭ C
Lit.: no. 139.

Śuddhanāṭa (South India). *Janya rāga* of the 36th *mēḷa* (*Chalanāṭa*).
Tone material:
C E F G B c
c B G F E C
Lit.: no. 139.

Śuddhanavanītam (South India). *Janya rāga* of the 59th *mēḷa* (*Dharmavatī*).
Tone material:
C D E♭ F♯ A B c
c B G F♯ E♭ D C
Lit.: no. 139.

Śuddhanilāmbari (South India). *Janya rāga* of the 35th *mēḷa* (*Śūlinī*).
Tone material:
C F D♯ E F G c
c B G F E C
Lit.: no. 139.

Śuddha rāga (South India). *Janya rāga* of the 57th *mēḷa* (*Siṃhendramadhyama*).
Tone material:
C D E♭ F♯ G B c
c B G F♯ E♭ D C
Lit.: no. 139.

Śuddharasāḷi (South India). *Janya rāga* of the 53rd *mēḷa* (*Gamanaśrama*).
Tone material:
C E F♯ G A c
c A G F♯ E C
Lit.: no. 139.

Śuddharatnabhānu (South India). *Janya rāga* of the 65th *mēḷa* (*Mechakalyāṇī*).
Tone material:
C D E F♯ G c
c B A G F♯ E C
Lit.: no. 139.

Śuddha Ri (India). The note name corresponding to *kumudvatī*, the 2nd *śruti*. At the present time *suddha ri* represents the second degree of the heptatonic scale. Cf. *Śruti*; *Śuddha*.

Śuddhaśaḍjā (Ancient India). The fourth of the seven ancient *mūrchhanās*, derived from the *sa-grāma*.

Śuddhasālavi (South India). *Janya rāga* of the 20th *mēḷa* (*Naṭabhariavī*).
Tone material:
C E♭ F G B♭ c
c B♭ G F D C
Lit.: no. 139.

Śuddhasamant (*Śuddhasīmantī*; *Śuddhasīmantinī*) (South India). *Janya rāga* of the 8th *mēḷa* (*Hanumattōḍi*).
Tone material:
A♭ C D♭ F G A♭
G F E♭ D♭ C
Lit.: no. 139.

Śuddhasāraṅga (South India). *Janya rāga* of the 62nd *mēḷa* (*Riṣabhapriyā*).
Tone material:
C E F♯ G B♭ c
c A♭ G F♯ E D C
Lit.: no. 139.

Śuddhasāveri (South India). *Janya rāga* of the 29th *mēḷa* (*Dhīraśankarābharaṇam*).
Tone material:
C D F G A c (A) c
c A G F D C (*A* C)
Lit.: no. 139.

Śuddhasīmantinī (South India). See *Śuddhasamant.*

Śuddhasiṃhāravam (South India). *Janya rāga* of the 67th *mēḷa* (*Sucharitra*).
Tone material:
C D♯ F♯ E G A♭ B♭♭ c
c A♭ B♭♭ A♭ G F♯ D♯ C
Lit.: no. 139.

Śuddhasvarāvaḷi (South India). *Janya rāga* of the 45th *mēḷa* (*Śubhapantuvarālī*).
Tone material:
C E♭ F♯ G F♯ A♭ B c
c B A♭ F♯ E♭ C
Lit.: no. 139.

Śuddhaśyamala (South India). *Janya rāga* of the 16th *mēḷa* (*Chakravāka*).
Tone material:
C E G A B♭ c
c B♭ A G E C
Lit.: no. 139.

Śuddhataraṅgiṇī (South India). *Janya rāga* of the 28th *mēḷa* (*Harikambhōji*).
Tone material:
C D E F D F G A B♭ A c
c B♭ A G F E D C
Lit.: no. 139.

Śuddhatōḍi (South India). See *Tōḍi* (South India).

Śuddhavarāli (South India). *Janya rāga* of the 28th *mēḷa* (*Harikāmbhōji*).
Tone material:
C D E F A B♭ c
c B♭ A B♭ G F E C
Lit.: no. 139.

Śuddhavasanta (South India). *Janya rāga* of the 29th *mēḷa* (*Dhīraśaṅkarābharaṇam*).
Tone material:
C D E F G B c
c A B G F E D C
Lit.: no. 139.

Śuddhavelāvalī (South India). *Janya rāga* of the 22nd *mēḷa* (*Kharaharapriyā*).
Tone material:
C D F G B♭ c
c B♭ A B♭ G F E♭ D C
Lit.: no. 139.

Śudhakāmbhōji (South India). See *Śuddhakāmbhōji.*

Śudhalahari (South India). See *Suddhalahari.*

Śudhāmbhōdhi (South India). Read *Śuddhāmbhōdhi.*

Sudjikama (South Celebes). A *tjuriga* type.
Lit.: no. 162.

Su-erh-nai (China). Name of the *surnāy.*
Lit.: no. 78.

Sūfaīra (Iran; Arabia). Cf. *Sāfūra*; *Ṣafīr-i bulbul.*
Lit.: no. 109.

Sugagaki (Japan). Stereotyped prelude to *jōruri.*

Suga koto (Japan). Cf. *Wagon.*
Lit.: no. 53.

Sūgātra (South India). *Janya rāga* of the 4th *mēḷa* (*Vanaspāti*).
Tone material:
C F G A B♭ c
c A G F E♭♭ D♭ C
Lit.: no. 139.

Sugh (Armenia). Metrical value in Armenian liturgy. It denotes four metrical units. Cf. *Ket*; *Zoigket*.
Lit.: no. 101.

Sugharai-kanada (North India). *Rāga* ascribed to the *Kafi thāta*. It is to be performed in the late morning.
Tone material:
C D E♭ F G B♭(+) c
c B♭ G F (E♭) D C; *Vādis*: G, C
Lit.: no. 138.

Su-ghosha (India). Sanskrit term for shell trumpet.
Lit.: no. 16.

Sugonghu (Korea). "Standing harp." Obscure harp with 21 strings.
Lit.: no. 287.

Sugs-pa (Tibet). Simple whistle.
Lit.: no. 190.

Sugu (Japan). "Straight sound." A *kyokusetzu*. *Sugu* indicates a brief, trembling vibrato on an important note (Tendai sect).

Su-gu-galli (Mesopotamia). Sumerian term, "the great bull's hide," referring to a giant drum.
Lit.: no. 250.

Sugunabhūṣaṇi (South India). *Janya rāga* of the 22nd *mēḷa* (*Kharaharapriyā*).
Tone material:
C E♭ F G F A B♭ c
c B♭ A G F E♭ F D C
Lit.: no. 139.

Suha-kanada (*Soha-kanada*) (North India). See *Sugharai-kanada*.

Su-hu (*Sō-hu*) (China). Bowed lute with four strings and rear pegs. The flat body has hexagonal shape. Cf. *Erh-hu*; *Dörwen chikhe khuur*; *Hu-ch'in*.
Lit.: no. 209.

Suijo (Japan). The *ryosen* form of *ōshiki*. See *Koto* (tunings).
Lit.: no. 225.

Sujanarañjaṇi (South India). *Janya rāga* of the 63rd *mēḷa* (*Latāṅgī*).
Tone material:
C E D F♯ G A♭ B c
c B A♭ G F♯ E D C
Lit.: no. 139.

Sujaris (South India). *Janya rāga* of the 22nd *mēḷa* (*Kharaharapriyā*).
Tone material:
C D C E♭ D F G B♭ c
c B♭ G F G E♭ F D C
Lit.: no. 139.

Sujaskāvali (South India). *Janya rāga* of the 13th *mēḷa* (*Gāyakapriya*).
Tone material:
C F E F G A♭ B♭♭ c
c A♭ B♭♭ A♭ G F E C
Lit.: no. 139.

Sukadhvani (South India). *Janya rāga* of the 53rd *mēḷa* (*Gamanaśrama*).
Tone material:
C E F♯ G A B c
c B A G F♯ E D* C
*In descent the note *ri* (D) is mostly intoned as D and not as D♭, as now and then stated.
Lit.: no. 139.

Sukasvarāḷi (South India). *Janya rāga* of the 48th *mēḷa* (*Divyamaṇī*).
Tone material:
C D♭ E♭ F♯ G A♯ B c
c G F♯ C D♭ C *B*
Lit.: no. 139.

Suke (Solomon Isl.). "Trumpet" made of two cylindrical tubes placed side by side. One functions as a trumpet; the other, shorter and thinner, serves as a vertically-blown flute.
Lit.: no. 84.

Sukhakari (South India). *Janya rāga* of the 52nd *mēḷa* (*Rāmapriyā*).
Tone material:
C G A B♭ c
c B♭ A F♯ E♭♭* D♭ C
*The note *ga* (E♭♭) in descent is often intoned as low as E♭♭ and not as E.
Lit.: no. 139.

Sukhanīlāmbari (South India). *Janya rāga* of the 40th *mēḷa* (*Navanītam*).
Tone material:
C E♭♭ D♭ E♭♭ F♯ G A c
c B♭ A G F♯ E♭♭ D♭ C
Lit.: no. 139.

Sukhatāyini (South India). *Janya rāga* of the 31st *mēḷa* (*Yāgapriyā*).
Tone material:
C D♯ G A♭ B♭♭ c
c B♭♭ A♭ G D♯ C
Lit.: no. 139.

Śukhavāni (South India). *Janya rāga* of the 13th *mēḷa* (*Gāyakapriya*).
Tone material:
C D♭ E G B♭♭ c
c B♭♭ G E D♭ C
Lit.: no. 139.

Śukhavāni (South India). *Janya rāga* of the 21st *mēḷa* (*Kiravāṇi*).
Tone material:
C D E♭ F A♭ B c
c B A♭ F E♭ D C
Lit.: no. 139.

Su-koa (South Africa—Hottentot). A drum used to accompany dances. The body of the drum is a wooden basin filled with water. The basin is covered with a sheepskin.
Lit.: no. 255.

Su-kong-hu (Korea). See *So-kong-hu*.
Lit.: no. 179.

Suktijapriya (South India). *Janya rāga* of the 46th *mēḷa* (*Śaḍvidhamārgiṇī*).
Tone material:
C E♭ F♯ G A c
c A G F♯ E♭ C
Lit.: no. 139.

Suku (Bali). Notational symbol.
Lit.: no. 197.

Suku (China). Frame drum.
Lit.: no. 258.

Sukui (Japan). Term in *koto* playing. It indicates an upstroke with the thumb.
Lit.: no. 225.

Sukut (Islamic North Africa; Middle East). Pauses, points of rest in musical performances.

Sukutit (Kenya—Nandi). Term referring to foreign drums.
Lit.: no. 255.

Sul (*Sil*) (Korea). Large zither with 25 strings, derived from the Chinese *se*. The *sul* is also called the big *komunko* and is used only in *ah-ak*.
Lit.: nos. 52, 136.

Sula (Congo—Bwaka). Drum in form of two truncated cones joined with the smaller ends. The drum has only one head.
Lit.: no. 26.

Śulatāriṇi (South India). See *Shulatāriṇi*.

Sulepe (North Moluccas—Halmahera). Stick zither with one string. Its body consists of half a coconut shell. See *Sosanru*.
Lit.: nos. 162, 254.

Sulieng nyawa (Sarawak). Flute.
Lit.: no. 166.

Suling (Java; Borneo; Flores; Bali). Bamboo flute (transverse or vertical) with 4-6 finger holes. The instrument appears in various sizes. The *suling* of Bali (usually made in three sizes) has four holes when used in the *gamelan*

angklung, five or six holes in *pelog* and *slendro* systems of Java.
Lit.: no. 166.

Suling banchih (Bali). Flute used in the *arja* play. It accompanies dancers of both sexes.
Lit.: no. 197.

Suling barang (Java). A *suling* with five finger holes.
Lit.: no. 255.

Suling degung (West Java). Long flute with four finger holes used in the *gamelan degung*. Cf. *Surupan degung*.
Lit.: no. 163.

Suling gambuh (Bali). End-blown large bass flute of the *gambuh* ensemble. It has four to six finger holes. Cf. *Suling*.
Lit.: no. 163.

Suling gede (Bali). Large bamboo bass flute.
Lit.: no. 165.

Suling idong (Borneo – Sea Dayak). Nose flute made of bamboo. It has three front finger holes and one at the back.
Lit.: no. 255.

Suling kechil (Southeast Borneo). Small bamboo flute with four finger holes and a beak mouthpiece.
Lit.: no. 255.

Suling nem (Java). A *suling* with five finger holes. Used for the *laras nem* of the *gamelan pelog*. It can be played between 7 p.m. and midnight.
Lit.: no. 255.

Suling nyawa (Borneo – Sea Dayak). Bamboo whistle flute with three or four finger holes. Cf. *Banchi*.
Lit.: no. 255.

Suling parai (Borneo – Dayak). Beak flute made of rice straw. It has four finger holes.
Lit.: no. 255.

Suling rapi (Indonesia; Toradja District). Double flute. One tube has five holes, the other has none. See *Woi doa*.
Lit.: no. 166.

Suling reog (Java). Vertically-blown bamboo flute with three finger holes. The flute provides the accompaniment of the *reog* play.
Lit.: nos. 163, 255.

Suling san (Borneo – Sea Dayak). Transverse bamboo flute with four finger holes and a square mouth hole.
Lit.: no. 255.

Śūlinī (South India). (1) The 35th *mēḷa*:

C D♯ E F G A B c

(2) Veṅkaṭamakhin called the *rāga Śailadēśākṣi*. See Lit. no. 139.

Su-lo (Cantonese: *Sou-lo*) (China). Small gong. See *Wu-lo*.

Su-lo (music) (China). See *Shih-pu-chi*.

Sultāl (North India). See *Tāla*.

Sultane durgi (Egypt; Sudan – Nubia). Large drum, the *tabl turki*.
Lit.: no. 255.

Sulṭānī-'Irāq (Middle East). *Maqām*.
Tone material:

   \+ (♯)   \+   \+
D E♭ (F) G A B♭ c d e♭ f

Lit.: no. 64.

Sulṭānī yak-gāh (Middle East). *Maqām*.
Tone material:

G A B♭ C D E♭ F♯ G

Lit.: no. 64.

Suluk (Java). A collective term for numerous instrumental, orchestral, and vocal formulas, consisting of brief, characteristic melodies that serve to establish the required atmosphere and mood for *wayang* performances. These formulas are grouped into the following categories: *lagon*, *ada-ada*, *suluk plenchung*, *(h)irim-(h)irim* (*irim-irim*), *jenking*, *laras barang miring*, *sendon* (used not only in *wayang* music), *tlutur*, *galong*.

Particularly in Solo the terms *paṭetan* (or *sendon*) represent similar functions as the above mentioned *suluks*.

Ajak-ajakan can be added to the *suluk* group. It represents the accompaniment when *wayang* figures and a *wayang* dancer appear on the stage. (Battle music on the *wayang* stage is called *srepegan* and *sampak*.)
Lit.: no. 163.

Suluk laras barang miring (Java). Short emotional formula consisting of the tones *barang*, *lima*, and *dada* are intoned slightly low, whereby a resemblance with *pelog* is created and therefore an unusual mood. This *suluk* is used in a *wayang* performance when the *rebāb*, *suling* and a singer's voice are heard at the first appearance of Semar, the heroic but somewhat farcical god of love. Semar, the older brother of Batara Guru, the highest god, is always represented by some unusual music.
Lit.: no. 163.

Sumadyuti (South India). See *Sīmantinī* (57th *asampūrṇa mēḷa*).

Sumah (Borneo). See *Gulung-gulung*.

Suma-koto (Japan). See *Ichi-genkin*, the one-string *koto*.
Lit.: no. 225.

Sumanapriyā (South India). *Janya rāga* of the 28th *mēḷa* (*Harikambhoji*).
Tone material:
C D E F E G A G c
c A c G E F D C
Lit.: no. 139.

Sumanisarañjani (South India). *Janya rāga* of the 56th *mēḷa* (*Śaṇmukhapriyā*).
Tone material:
C E♭ F♯ G B♭ c
c B♭ G F♯ E♭ C
Lit.: no. 139.

Sumbang (Java). Term for "abnormal," "out of tune."

Sumbi (West Java). Cf. *Pahul*.

Sumbulaḥ See *Sunbulaḥ* (*Sunbulī*).

Sumiyoshi-odori-uta (Japan). The chant of the priest (when attended by his umbrella bearer) in the temple of Sumiyoshi.
Lit.: no. 225.

Sumle (Cameroon; Congo; Namshi). Iron hand bell.
Lit.: no. 21.

Sumpilan (Java). Cf. *Saron*; *Tawonan*.

Sumping (*Srawing*) (Java). See *Rebāb* (Java).

Sumpotan (Malaysia; Sabah). Mouth organ with eight pipes (one is silent). The instrument is similar to the Chinese *sheng*.

Sumyang (Java; Jogya). Term for the middle range of notes.

Sun (Korea). Small handbell. Cf. *Ton* (Japan).
Lit.: no. 52.

Sunaren (Bali). Hexa- or pentatonic scale used in *gambuh semar pegulingan*.
Tone materials:
G A B♭ d e (e♭); or: F♯ G♯ A c♯ d
Cf. *Semar pegulingan*.
Lit.: no. 197.

Sumbulaḥ (*Zawal*) (Persian: "rose") (Arabia). Tone name of a note ca. a semitone higher than *muḥayer* (*muḥayir*). (A list of all tone names and notes through two octaves can be seen under the heading of *Jagā* [*Yagā*].)

Sundar (Turkey). Obsolete lute. Allegedly it had 10 sympathetic metal strings.
Lit.: no. 81.

Sundarapriya (South India). *Janya rāga* of the 57th *mēḷa* (*Siṃhendramadhyama*).
Tone material:
C D E♭ F♯ G B c
c B G F♯ E♭ C D C
Lit.: no. 139.

Sundaravinōdiṇi (South India). *Janya rāga* of the 65th *mēḷa* (*Mechakalyāṇī*).
Tone material:
C E F# A B c
c B A F# E C
Lit.: no. 139.

Sundaren (Java). A bamboo bow with one string attached to a kite. When kite and bow are in the air, the string vibrates. Other names for *sundaren* are: *sundari*, *sendaren*, *sendari*.
Lit.: no. 163.

Sundari (Java). See *Peteng* (Sunda District); *sundari* serves also as a term for *sitār*.
Lit.: no. 260.

Sunderkauns (North India). Obscure *rāga* ascribed to the *Bhairav thāta*. The tone material is the same as that of *rāga Malkauns* plus the note G.
Lit.: no. 138.

Sunding (Flores – Manggaray). Simple bamboo flute with five finger holes. Other names of the instrument are: *nuren* or *feko* in Larantuka; *klekor* in Riangwulu; *glekor* in Sikka (Maumere); *feko* in Lio (Ende). Cf. *Nuren*.
Lit.: no. 166.

Süng (Northeast Thailand). (1) Lute. Occasionally the term refers to *p'in* (*pin*). (2) Roving groups of minstrels sing, one chorus alternating with another chorus, particularly at Buddhist holidays.

Sung-gur (Tibet). See *Gur-ma*.

Sung-gur sh'e-pa (Tibet). Honorific term for *sh'e tang-wa*.

Sung hsiao (China – M 5559; M 2619). *P'ai-hsiao* type with 16 pipes. *Sung* refers to "odes, hymns" and characterizes the function of the instrument.
Lit.: no. 137.

Sung-sh'e (Tibet). Honorific term for *sh'e* ("song").

Sung shen (China – M 5566; M 5716). "Escorting the spirit back," the last of the six stanzas of the "Hymn in Honor of Confucius." The other stanzas are: *Ying sheng*; *Ch'u hsien*; *Ya hsien*; *Chung hsien*; *Ch'e chuan*. For notation and the entire text see Lit. no. 136, pp. 82-83.

Sung yüeh (China). Hymn music.

Ṣunnūj ṣaghīra (Arabia). Small metal castanets.
Lit.: no. 70.

Ṣunūj (singular: *sinj*) (Old Arabia). Small cup-shaped castanets used by dancers. Cf. *Sājat*.
Lit.: no. 70.

Ṣunūj (Arabia). Plate-shaped cymbals.
Lit.: no. 76.

Suposhiṇi (South India). *Janya rāga* of the 28th *mēḷa* (*Harikāmbhōji*).
Tone material:
C D C F G B♭ A c
c A B♭ G F D F C
Lit.: no. 139.

Supoṣiṇi (South India). See *Suposhiṇi*.

Supradipa(m) (South India). *Janya rāga* of the 17th *mēḷa* (*Sūryakānta*).
Tone material:
C D♭ F G A B c
c B A G F E F D♭ C
Lit.: no. 139.

Supradīpam (South India). (1) The 17th *asampūrṇa mēḷa-rāga* without *kaṭapayādi* prefix. (2) The 17th *asampūrṇa mēḷa-rāga* with *kaṭapayādi* prefix was called *Chhāyavati*. See *Rāga* (South India).
Lit.: no. 139.

Supurga (Turkey). The smallest *nāy* in use.
Lit.: no. 190.

Šuqaifat (Arabia). (1) Clappers, castanets. (2) Little cymbals used by dancers.
Lit.: no. 255.

Sūr (Iran). An oboe (in the Middle East often described as "trumpet") used by dervishes. In North India the *sūr* indicates an oboe that is used to perform the bourdon note to a sung or played melody. Cf. *Śruti.*
Lit.: no. 255.

Ṣūr (Mesopotamia). Horn. Cf. *Sūr* (Iran; North India).

Surabhairavi (South India). *Janya rāga* of the 28th *mēḷa* (*Harikāmbhōji*).
Tone material:
C D G F G A B♭ c
c B♭ A G F C
Lit.: no. 139.

Surabhūṣaṇi (South India). *Janya rāga* of the 4th *mēḷa* (*Vanaspāti*).
Tone material:
C D♭ E♭♭ F G c
c B♭ A B♭ G F D♭ C
Lit.: no. 139.

Surak (Java). Term for high (range).
Lit.: no. 163.

Suramandini (South India). *Janya rāga* of the 29th *mēḷa* (*Dhīraśaṅkarābharaṇam*).
Tone material:
C D E G A B c
c B A G E D C
Lit.: no. 139.

Suramani (South India). *Janya rāga* of the 48th *mēḷa* (*Divyamaṇī*).
Tone material:
C D♭ E♭ F♯ A♯ B c
c B A♯ F♯ E♭ D♭ C
Lit.: no. 139.

Surang (Bali). Name of a notational symbol.
Lit.: no. 197.

Surarañjaṇi (South India). *Janya rāga* of the 36th *mēḷa* (*Chalanāṭa*).
Tone material:
C D♯ E G B c
c B G E D♯ C
Lit.: no. 139.

Surasena (South India). *Janya rāga* of the 27th *mēḷa* (*Sarasāṅgī*).
Tone material:
C D F G A♭ c B c (C D F G A♭ c)
c A♭ G F E D C (c B A♭ G F E D C)
Lit.: no. 139.

Surasena (South India). (1) The 27th *asampūrṇa mēḷa-rāga* without *kaṭapayādi* prefix. (2) The 27th *asampūrṇa mēḷa-rāga* with *kaṭapayādi* prefix was called *Saurasena.* See *Rāga* (South India).
Lit.: no. 138.

Surasindhu (South India). *Janya rāga* of the *15th mēḷa* (*Māyāmāḷavagauḷa*).
Tone material:
C F E F G A♭ B A♭ c
c B A♭ G F D♭ E D♭ C
Lit.: no. 139.

Suraṭavinōdiṇi (South India). *Janya rāga* of the 65th *mēḷa* (*Mechakalyāṇī*).
Tone material:
C E F♯ A B c
c B A G E D C
Lit.: no. 139.

Suraṭi (South India). *Janya rāga* of the 28th *mēḷa* (*Harikāmbhōji*).
Tone material:
C D F G B♭ c
c B♭ A G F E G F D C
Lit.: no. 139.

Suravarāli (South India). *Janya rāga* of the 13th *mēḷa* (*Gāyakapriya*).
Tone material:
C F G A♭ B♭♭ c
c B♭♭ A♭ G F C
Lit.: no. 139.

Surbāhār (*Sur-vāhāra*; *Alāpiṇī-vīṇā*) (India). An instrument of very recent origin. It can be described as a large *kacchapī vīṇā*, plucked, occasionally also bowed. It is of little importance in art music.
Lit.: no. 255.

Surendro (Java). Cf. *Salendro*; *Slendro*.

Surigane (Japan). Small gong used at festive occasions. It is carried on a ribbon by the left hand.
Lit.: no. 185.

Surilit (*Taleot*) (West Java). (1) A small clay ocarina (the Javanese is called *susurilitan*). (2) A whistle used by coachmen. (3) A transverse flute.
Lit.: no. 163.

Suri-zasara (Japan). Scrapers used in folk music.

Surizume (Japan). A term used in *koto* playing; it indicates one of the various glissandi.
Lit.: no. 225.

Surle (Turkey). Term for *zurnā*.
Lit.: no. 250.

Sur Mallār (North India). One of the *rāgas* belonging to the *Mallār* family. *Sur Mallār* is ascribed to the *Kafi thāta*.
Tone material:
C D F G (A) B c
c B♭ (A) G F D C
Lit.: no. 138.

Surmaṇḍal(a) (India). See *Sārmaṇḍal*; *Svaramaṇḍala*.

Sūrnā (*Surnāy*) (Iran; North India). Oboe with a conically-shaped tube. The popular instrument appears in various types and sizes. The term *sūrnāy* can also mean "mouthpiece." Cf. *Sānāyī*; *Zurnā*; *Sūru-nāi* (Mongolia); *Shah-nāy*.
Lit.: no. 254.

Sur-na (or *Harib*) (Tibet). Term for *rgya-glin* when the instrument is used in secular music.
Lit.: no. 143.

Surnāi (*Suru-nāi*) (Kirgizia—Uzbek). Shawm. Cf. *Mizmār*.
Lit.: no. 275.

Surondopi (Flores). See *Keniti*.

Sur-sanga (India). An *esrar* without any resonance strings. It has 4-5 metal strings tuned to F C C G *C*. Cf. *Yantra-kosha*.
Lit.: no. 256.

Sursōta (India). *Tanbura* type which has no bowl and no gourd. It is simply a large tube of bamboo with four *tanbura* strings.

Sur-śriṅgāra (India). Lute with a calabash body, a long neck, two frets, eight wire strings of which seven are sympathetic—only one, at the far right side, is a fingered melody string. The tuning of the instrument is: c c E C *G* C D G.
Lit.: no. 254.

Sur-sum (Tibet). Triangle.
Lit.: no. 143.

Sūrunāi (Iran). Cf. *Sūrnāi*; *Ṣūrnāya*.

Sūru-nāi (Mongolia). Oboe. Cf. *Surnā*.

Surune (Nias Isl.). (1) A nose flute made of cane with square holes. (2) Oboe.
Lit.: nos. 255, 313.

Surune ndrawa (Southern Nias). Cross flute with seven or eight holes. Cf. *Sigu mbawa*; *Nuren*; *Lolowe*.

Surupan (Java). Key. That which is pushed into something. (1) Key-note, tuning tone; tonality; central tone. (2) Tuning. See *Laras*. Basis of a tone system.
Lit.: no. 163.

Surupan ajeng (Java). Scale variety of the *pelog* system.

Surupan cheurik (West Java). See *Surupan madenda.*

Surupan degung (West Java). A second *slendro* scale with irregular intervals between the five degrees.

Surupan jawar (West Java). Scale variety of *slendro.* See *Slendro jawar.*

Surupan lempang (West Java). See *Salendro biasa.*

Surupan madenda (West Java). Term for one of two *slendro* scales with unequal distances between the five degrees. *Surupan madenda* can be called *nyorog malang* or *surupan cheurik* ("weeping" *surupan*), or *nyorog wisaya* ("magic" *nyorog*), or *nyorog rangu-rangu* ("hesitant" *nyorog*). The second *slendro* scale with irregular intervals between the five degrees is *surupan degung. Madenda* is a *slendro* scale with lowered 1st and 3rd scale degrees. *Degung,* also a *slendro* scale (produced by a set of gongs) has lowered 1st, 3rd, and 4th scale degrees.
Lit.: no. 163.

Surupan Malayu (Java). "Malay tone-gender." It has seven (primary) tones and no auxiliary ones. Each of the seven tones can serve as *dasar. Surupan malayu* is probably younger than the other tone-genders (*surupan melog, surupan miring,* and *surupan ajeng*) and is noticeably detached from the other *pelog* types.
Lit.: no. 163.

Surupan Melog (Java). One of the seven-tone scales related to *pelog.* For further information see Lit. no. 163.

Surupan miring (Java). A scale variety related to the *pelog* system. *Miring* denotes "slanting," "lying on one side," "deviating"—the ordinary *gamelan pelog* shows the plain *surupan miring* scale.
Lit.: no. 163.

Survāhara (India). See *Surbahar.*

Sur-vīṇā (India). Lute with a gourd body and 4-6 strings. Although there are some reports that the instrument is bowed (Lit. no. 255), the majority consider the *sur-vīṇā* as a lute, and pluck its strings with a steel plectrum.

Its neck shows the scroll of the European violin. Tuning of four strings: c c G C; tuning of six strings: g d c G E C.
Lit.: nos. 254-55.

Sūryakanta (South India). (1) The 17th *mēḷa*:

C D♭ E F G A B c

(2) *Suryakanta* as *rāga*: Veṅkaṭamakhin (17th century) calls this *rāga Chhāyāvatī* in which the note *pa* (G) is omitted in ascent. Now, in *rāga Sūryakānta* the note G is used in ascent. The tone material is identical with that shown above.
Lit.: no. 139.

Suryakauns (North India). A rare and obscure *rāga* that can be ascribed to the *Bhairav thāta.* Tone material (approximately):

C E F A♭ B♭ c
c B♭ A♭ F E F E C

Lit.: no. 138.

Suryānāi (Old Arabia). An ancient reed pipe. Cf. *Nay.*

Sūryapirai (South India). Frame drum used in Hindu temples. Cf. *Chandrapirai.*
Lit.: no. 260.

Suryuk chae (Korea). Buddhist chant for a drowned person.
Lit.: no. 287.

Susap (Micronesia—Mokil; Pingelap). Bamboo jew's harp.

Sushira (India). Sanskrit term for the category of wind instruments.

Susu (Malaysia). See *Rebāb.*

Susumuck (New Guinea). Drum with one head, placed on a wooden stand.
Lit.: no. 37.

Susunu (*Akadu*) (Malaysia). Bamboo psaltery with a variable number of strings and movable bridges. Cf. *Sassandu* (Moluccas).
Lit.: nos. 219, 255.

Susurilitan (Java). A small ocarina made of terra cotta in the shape of a cockerel or pigeon, usually with two, rarely with three, holes. Cf. *Surilit*; *Taleot*.
Lit.: no. 163.

Sūt (Iran). Also called *nāy labek*. A beak flute with seven finger holes, six in front and one at the back.
Lit.: no. 109.

Sūta (*Māgadha*) (Ancient India). Minstrel; fortune-teller.

Sutari (North India; Punjab). "Camel drum"; a kettledrum.
Lit.: no. 255.

Sutāsāgaram (South India). *Janya rāga* of the 38th *mēḷa* (*Jalārṇava*).
Tone material:
C D♭ E♭♭ F♯ A♭ B♭ c
c B♭ A♭ F♯ E♭♭ D♭ C
Lit.: no. 139.

Suteru (Japan). A *kyokusetzu*. *Suteru* indicates that the voice drops in pitch and volume until it becomes inaudible.

Sutradhara (Ancient India). Sanskrit term. The "thread" (*sutra*)—"bearer" (*dhara*), the narrator who holds the thread of the Buddhist drama. His narration extends to the providing the required atmosphere and background. His counterpart in Indonesia is the *dalang*.

Sūtradhari (South India). *Janya rāga* of the 27th *mēḷa* (*Sarasāṅgī*).
Tone material:
C D F G A♭ c
c A♭ G F D C
Lit.: no. 139.

Sutri nahabat (India). A pair of small copper kettledrums mounted in front of the player on top of a camel back. Cf. *Sāhib nahabat.*
Lit.: no. 254.

Suttae (Korea). Plectrum used in the playing of the *hyon-kum* (*komunko*).

Su-tzu-p'u (China—M 5497; M 6942; M 5386). "Common notation." Despite its name, this notational system never gained much popularity. It is also called "sung notation" and probably experienced various changes during the Yüan period. *Su-tzu-p'u* is related to the *kung-ch'e-p'u*—even the tone names are, more or less, the same in both systems—but it is by far not as distinct and precise as the *kung-ch'e-p'u.*
Lit.: no. 136.

Suvarata (South India). *Janya rāga* of the 13th *mēḷa* (*Gāyakapriya*).
Tone material:
C D♭ E F A♭ c
c A♭ F E D♭ C
Lit.: no. 139.

Suvarṇāmbari (South India). *Janya rāga* of the 50th *mēḷa* (*Nāmanārāyaṇī*).
Tone material:
C D♭ E F♯ B♭ c
c B♭ F♯ E D♭ C
Lit.: no. 139.

Suvarṇāṅgī (South India). (1) The 47th *mēḷa*:
C D♭ E♭ F♯ G A B c
(2) *Rāga Suvarṇāṅgī* has the same tone material as stated above.
Lit.: no. 139.

Suwuk (Java). Rallentando at the end of a piece immediately after the *seseg(an)*. See *Munduk* (*Turun*).
Lit.: no. 163.

Suwukan (Central Java). See *Gong suwukan.*

Su-yüeh (China – M 5497; M 4129a). Secular, common music.

Suz-dal (Arabia). "Burned heart," a sub-*maqām* of *ḥusēnī*:

A B♭ C♯ D $\overset{+}{E}$♭ F G♯ A / A $\overset{+}{B}$♭ c

Cf. *Ḥusēnī* (*maqām*).
Lit.: no. 121.

Sūz-dil-'Ārā (Middle East). "Fire of love," sub-*maqām* derived from *rāst*:

C D $\overset{+}{E}$♭ F G A $\overset{+}{B}$♭ [B] C; or: C D $\overset{+}{E}$♭ F♯ G A B♭ c

The note names are: *rāst*, *dugā*, *sigā*, *ḥijaz*, *nawasā*, *ḥusēnī*, *'ajam* (or *auj*), *kardān*.
Lit.: nos. 64, 121.

Suz-i-dil (Middle East; Modern Egypt). *Maqām*. Cf. *Suz dal.*

Sūz-nāk (Middle East). Cf. *Sūz-dil-'Ārā. Maqām.*
Tone material:

C D E♭ F G A♭ B♭ c

In descent appear:

C $\overset{+}{B}$*♭ A G*

This form of the low descending scale is the cause why the *maqām* is called *delkashe.*

The tone names of *sūz-nāk* are: *rāst*, *dugā*, *sigā*, *jarkā*, *nawā*, *shuri*, *'auj*, *kardān*, *muḥayer*, *sunbula*, etc.
Lit.: nos. 64, 121.

Suzu (Japan). Ancient small bells (jingles, also a tree of bells) used by dancers performing in scarlet ladies' robes in the Shinto temple.
Lit.: nos. 53, 225.

Svādhyāya (Vedic India). Vedic recitation.

Svambhuṣvara (South India). *Janya rāga* of the 29th *mēḷa* (*Dhīraśaṅkarābharaṇam*).
Tone material:

C E G c
c G E C

This *rāga* is of recent origin and allows only limited elaboration.
Lit.: no. 139.

Svara (Ancient India). Term for "interval"; also for "tone" and "note."
Lit.: no. 292.

Svarabat (*Svaragat*) (India). Large lute with six strings, played with a horny plectrum.
Lit.: no. 260.

Svarābharaṇam (South India). *Janya rāga* of the 49th *mēḷa* (*Dhavalāmbarī*).
Tone material:

C E F♯ G A♭ B♭♭ c
c B♭♭ A♭ G F♯ C

Lit.: no. 139.

Svarabhuṣaṇi (South India). *Janya rāga* of the 22nd *mēḷa* (*Kharaharapriyā*).
Tone material:

C E♭ F G A B♭ c
c B♭ A G F D C

Lit.: no. 139.

Svaragat (India). Cf. *Svarabat.*

Svarakalānidhi (South India). *Janya rāga* of the 22nd *mēḷa* (*Kharaharapriyā*).
Tone material:

C F E♭ F G A B♭ c
c B♭ A B♭ G F D E♭ C

Lit.: no. 139.

Svaramaṇḍala (*Surmaṇḍal*) (India). Board zither with (usually) 21 strings. Cf. *Kātyayāna vīṇā*; *Sārmaṇḍal.*

Svara nāḍi (South India). The melody pipe of the *alakōja.*

Svararañjaṇi (South India). *Janya rāga* of the 22nd *mēḷa* (*Kharaharapriyā*).
Tone material:

C D E♭ F B♭ A c
c B♭ G F E♭ F D C

Lit.: no. 139.

Svarasthana (South India). "Places of notes." Terms used by Veṅkaṭamakhin in his *Caturdaṇḍi Prakāśika* (1620) in Sanskrit verses. It lists all 12 (chromatic) notes and spots within the octave:

sa	e.g.	C
śuddha ri		D♭
śuddha ga, or *catuḥśruti ri*, or *pañcśruti ri*		E♭♭ (D)
sādhārana ga, or *ṣaṭśruti ri*		E♭ (D#)
antara ga		E
ma		F
varali or *prati ma*		F#
pa		G
śuddha dha		A♭
śuddha ni, or *catuḥśruti dha*, or *pañcśruti dha*		B♭♭ (A)
kaiśika ni, or *satśruti dha*		B♭ (A#)
kakali ni		B

Lit.: no. 139.

Svarāvali (South India). *Janya rāga* of the 28th *mēḷa* (*Harikāmbhōjī*).
Tone material:
C F E F G B♭ A B♭ c
c B♭ G A F E D C
Lit.: no. 139.

Svaravēdi (South India). *Janya rāga* of the 28th *mēḷa* (*Harikāmbhōjī*).
Tone material:
C F E F G B♭ A B♭ c
c B♭ A B♭ G F E C
Lit.: no. 139.

Svarita (Vedic India). "Resounding tone." In vedic chant this tone stands above the *udātta*. There are various interpretations of the *svarita*. For further information see Lit. no. 141.

Swanga (*Nkwanga*) (Congo). Rattle consisting of two gourds filled with dried seeds and tiny stones.
Lit.: no. 255.

Śyāmala (*Śyāmali*) (South India). *Janya rāga* of the 55th *mēḷa* (*Śyāmalāṅgī*).
Tone material:
C E♭ D E♭ F# G A♭ B♭♭ c
(C E♭ D E♭ F# G A♭ B♭♭ A♭ c)
c B♭♭ A♭ c B♭♭ A♭ G F# E♭ D C
(c B♭♭ A♭ G F# E♭ D C)
Lit.: no. 139.

Śyāmalāṅgī (South India). The 55th *mēḷa*:
C D E♭ F# G A♭ B♭♭ c
The *rāga* with the same name uses the same tone material.
Lit.: no. 139.

Śyāmaḷavarṇi (South India). *Janya rāga* of the 67th *mēḷa* (*Sucharitra*).
Tone material:
C D# E F# G c
c G F# E D# C
Lit.: no. 139.

Śyāmali (South India). See *Śyāmala*.

Śyāmanīlāmbari (South India). *Janya rāga* of the 41st *mēḷa* (*Pāvanī*).
Tone material:
C D♭ E♭♭ F# G A B c
c A B F# E♭♭ D♭ C
Lit.: no. 139.

Sybyzga (Central Asia; Kirgizia). Flute of the Kazakhs; it is identical with the *chōr* (vertical flute).
Lit.: nos. 91, 275.

Szu hsien hsiao t'i-ch'in (China). Modern, colloquial term for the Western violin.

T

Ta (Kurdistan). Term for "string."

Ta (China). See *Chien-tzu.*
Lit.: no. 136.

Ta (India). Basic *tabla* stroke of the right hand. The tip of the second finger strikes the border line between *chanti* and *maidan* with intense force. For further information see Lit. no. 136, p. 227.

Tā (Nepal). Small (single) brass disc.
Lit.: no. 46.

Ta'am (Ancient Israel). The mood, atmosphere of a melody.

Taanga (Polynesia; Tuvalu). Songs about the ancestors.

Ṭaba (Algeria). Term for *maqām*. Cf. *Qōl*; *Habara*; *Naqma.*

Tabaka (Morocco; North Africa; Maghrib). Circular frame drum.
Lit.: no. 255.

Ṭabal (Algeria; Bikra). Big drum. It is played together with the *qeita*. Cf. *Aṭabāl*; *Aṭbāl.*

Tabala (West Africa—Kassonke). Term for the *ṭabl*, a large wooden sacred kettledrum.
Lit.: no. 95.

Tabala (Senegambia—Wolof). These sacred drums are purchased from the neighbors, the Fulbe.

Tabala (India; Bengal). See *Tabla.*

Tabalde (Africa; Sudan). Drum.
Lit.: no. 95.

Tabang-tabang (*Redep*) (Java). Ancient term for frame drum (without jingles) used in Hindu-Javanese literature. Cf. *Terbang.*
Lit.: no. 163.

Tabaq (Sudan—Dongola). Kettledrum with a body made of clay.
Lit.: no. 255.

Ṭabaqa (Arabia). General term for scales.
Lit.: no. 70.

Ṭabbal (Arabia). Kettledrum.
Lit.: no. 109.

Tabbhuan boomboong (Java; Madura). Bamboo stamping drum. Among the many names are: *boku* in Flores, *dal ondel* in Madura, *ding teng-khing* in Besisi, *kendang awi* in West Java, *tekok* in Central Borneo, *took-took* in Mentawai, *toompling* (*boomboong*) in Bali. Lit.: no. 166.

Tabeh-tabehan (Bali). An ancient term for *gamelan* signifying an ensemble of instruments struck (*tabeh*) with sticks and mallets.
Lit.: no. 197.

Tabeuh (Sunda District). See *Gending* (Java and Sunda Districts).

Tabi (Southwest Australia). Aboriginal songs accompanied by a raspy sound.

Ṭabil (Iran). Drum with two heads.
Lit.: no. 255.

Ṭabil Turki (Arabia). Turkish drum.

Tabīr (*Tabīrā*) (Arabia). Drum; kettledrum. Cf. *Kūs.*

Tabir (*Ta'bir*) (Iran). An hourglass-shaped drum. Cf. *Atāmo*; *Gatambore*; *Katamboṅ.*

Ta'bir (Arabia). Congregational singing.
Lit.: no. 234.

Ṭabl (*Tabul*) (Arabia). Term for drum, generally a hand drum with a copper body covered at its open side with skin. Among the many other names are: *atabal, atabule, atama, atukpani, atupani, tabal, tabalde, tabbal, tabla, tabule, tamande, tamatama, tambana, tambari, tubbel, tumbul.*

Tabla (India). This very popular pair of drums is in use all over the northern and central parts of the peninsula. Only in the southernmost parts musicians prefer the ancient *mridanga.* One of the two drums of the *tabla* pair (called *tabla* or *dayan*) has a wooden corpus almost cylindrically-shaped. It has the form of two truncated cones joined with their broad bases. This drum (called *tabla*) has one drumhead. Its tuning is effected by the use of cylindrical small tuning blocks (*addu*) which are placed below braces (*badh*) which stretch the drum skin. By hammering the blocks downward the sound of the drumhead rises, and by hammering them upward the sound goes down. The second drum of the pair is a small kettledrum (called *bayan* or *banya*). It has a small copper kettle and one head which is usually not tuned to a fixed pitch.

The *tabla* (*dayan*) is played with the right hand. It stands next to the *bayan* which, as the name indicates, is played with the left hand. Both drums are placed immediately in front of the player.

The various parts of these drums bear the following names: *girwa* or *puri*, the drumhead; *gajra*, a strip of leather, twisted like a rope, that holds together the tuning straps (*badh*) and the *girwa*; *got*, a thick leather border that covers the rim of the *girwa*; *chanti*, the rim of the drumhead; *maidan*, the "open space" of the drumhead. As already stated, *badh* are the leather tuning straps: *addu*, six or eight small wooden blocks wedged between the corpus and the *badh.* The *addu* serve for tuning the *tabla.* *Indhvi* are the ring-shaped cushions upon which both drums rest.

The *tabla* is tuned invariable to the basic note *sa.* For further details see my book Lit. no. 136.

Ṭabla el-darausha (Arabia). A copper kettledrum used by the dervishes. It is played during the month of Ramadan in order to wake the sleepers at 2 o'clock in the morning to remind them to partake their food. Cf. *Ṭabla el-musaḥer.*
Lit.: no. 255.

Ṭabla el-mesheikh (*El-zehr*) (Arabia; Egypt). A small wooden kettledrum used by beggars.
Lit.: no. 255.

Ṭabla el-musaḥer (Arabia). Baz, a small bronze kettledrum. Cf. *Ṭabla el-darausha.*
Lit.: no. 255.

Ṭabla el-req (Syria; Egypt). See *Req.*

Tablaji (India). *Tabla* player.

Ṭabl albāz (Egypt). Hand drum (kettle form), with a corpus made of copper. It is played only during the month of Ramaḍān.
Lit.: no. 100.

Ṭabla arrakeb (Arabia). A pair of small kettle-drums. The bodies of both drums are made of metal.
Lit.: no. 255.

Ṭabl al-ḥajj (Arabia; Iran). Drum of the pilgrims.

Ṭabl al-jāwīj (*shāwīsh*) (Arabia). A shallow kettledrum played on horseback, struck with one wooden stick.
Lit.: no. 250.

Ṭabl al-kabir (Arabia; Middle East). Great drum. Large kettledrum. Cf. *Kurga.*

Ṭabl al-markab (Arabia). Kettledrum. Identical with the *naqqāra.* Cf. *Qaṣa'a.*
Lit.: no. 250.

Ṭabl al-shāwīsh (Arabia). See *Ṭabl al-jāwīj.*

Ṭablat al-musaḥḥir (*Ṭabla el-musaḥer*) (Turkey). See *Ṭabl-i bāz.*

Tablatarang (India). Instead of cups of the *jaltarang*, the *tablatarang* consists of a variable number of tunable *tablas* placed around the player in a semicircle.

Ṭabl baladī (Turkey; Arabia; North Africa). A flat cylindrical drum; a domestic instrument. The term *ṭabl baladi* is also applied to a small instrumental ensemble consisting of three high-pitched oboes (two *aba* and one *sibs*), a pair of kettledrums (*naqrazān*), and a *ṭabl baladī*, after which the ensemble is named.
Lit.: no. 250.

Ṭabl-i bāz (Turkey). A bird-catcher's drum. The drum is often called *bāz* (type of falcon), or *ṭabl el-musaḥer.* Cf. *Bāz.*
Lit.: no. 81.

Ṭabl khāna (Sudan). The orchestra of the sultan.
Lit.: no. 108.

Ṭabl migrī (Arabia). A shallow kettledrum beaten with leather straps.
Lit.: no. 250.

Ṭabl mukhannath (Arabia). Hourglass-shaped drum. Cf. *Kūbā.*
Lit.: no. 95.

Ṭabl shāmī (Arabia). Kettledrum with a very shallow copper kettle suspended from the neck of the player and struck with two small wooden sticks.
Lit.: no. 250.

Ṭabl turkī (Arabia; Turkey; Middle East). A large, shallow drum carried and played on the back of a donkey.
Lit.: no. 250.

Ṭabn (Ancient Egypt). Tube drum with two heads of the Middle Empire, or a barrel drum of the New Empire.
Lit.: no. 255.

Tabolia (Java). Percussion instrument.
Lit.: no. 255.

Tabolija (Indonesia; Nias). Bamboo tube zither.
Lit.: no. 156.

Tabuan (*Tagbuan*) (Timor; Moluccas – Buru). Tube zither. Cf. *Lakado*; *Be-orla*; *Tatabuan kavan.*
Lit.: no. 156.

Tabuan veteh (Indonesia). See *Tatabuan kavan.*

Tabuh (Bali). A beater; a stroke; the stick or hammer with which the drum or metallophone is struck.
The term is also used for units (ostinato) with fixed numbers of beats. E.g., the *tabuh* in *pegulingan* consists of four *jegog* beats. Each *jegog* beat consists of eight *jublag* beats, and each *jublag* contains eight figuration tones. *Tabuh* also means "gamelan composition."

E.g., *tabuh gong* means *gamelan gong* and *tabuh-tabuhan* means all types of *gamelan* composition, particularly if drums are employed. The sayings "*Tabuhin*! Strike up! Begin playing!" indicate the meaning of this term.
Lit.: no. 265.

Tabuh (Java). (1) Bronze beater of the *slentem*. (2) Wooden beater of the *bonang*. (3) Drum. (4) An ensemble consisting of percussion instruments.
Lit.: no. 163.

Tabuhan Bali (Java). See *Balibalian*.

Tabuhan Reprepan (Java). An orchestra similar to the *gamelan klenengan* but with percussion instruments.
Lit.: no. 163.

Tabuh besik (Bali). An irregular form based on the repetition of a single *palet*. See *Besik*. Cf. *Gending ageng*.
Lit.: no. 197.

Tabuh gari (Bali). Coda in a *gamelan* performance. Cf. *Abhogari* (Bali).
Lit.: no. 197.

Tabuh gong (Bali). Compositions played by the *gamelan gong*.
Lit.: no. 197.

Tabuh keprak (Java). See *Keprak*.

Tabuh kutus (Bali). A form with eight *palets* to the *gongan*. Cf. *Genḍing ageng*; *Tabuh besik*.
Lit.: no. 197.

Tabuh lima (Bali). A form with five *palets* to the *gongan*. Cf. *Genḍing ageng*; *Tabuh besik*.
Lit.: no. 197.

Tabuh nem (Bali). A form with six *palets* to the *gongan*. Cf. *Genḍing ageng*; *Tabuh besik*.
Lit.: no. 197.

Tabuh pat (Bali). A form with four *palets* to the *gongan*. Cf. *Genḍing ageng*; *Tabuh besik*.
Lit.: no. 197.

Tabuh pitu (Bali). A form with seven *palets* to the *gongan*. Cf. *Genḍing ageng*; *Tabuh besik*.
Lit.: no. 197.

Tabuh roh (Bali). A form with two *palets* to the *gongan*. Cf. *Genḍing ageng*; *Tabuh besik*.
Lit.: no. 197.

Tabuh rōhras (Bali). A form with 12 *palets* to the *gongan*. Cf. *Genḍing ageng*.
Lit.: no. 197.

Tabuh-tabuhan (Bali). (1) Term for all types of compositions played by the *gamelan*. (2) An ensemble consisting predominantly of percussion instruments.
Lit.: no. 265.

Tabuh talah (Bali). Introductory music consisting of four or five *palet gongan*, played by the *gamelan gong*.
Lit.: no. 197.

Tabuh telu (Bali). Cf. *Genḍing ageng*; *Tabuh besik*.
Lit.: nos. 197, 265.

Tabule (Senegal; French Guinea; Ivory Coast—Mandingo). Large drum for signalling purposes.
Lit.: no. 255.

Taburana (Indonesia; Nias). See *Tamburu*.

Ta ch'ang (China—M 5943; M 206). Literally, "great brilliance." Name of the music (pantomimes, dances, songs) ascribed to the early emperor Yao.
Lit.: no. 137.

Tachigaku (Japan). Court music performed by standing musicians. Cf. *Gagaku*.
Lit.: no. 185.

Ta ch'in (China). Term for the pianoforte.

Tachi-uta (Japan). Cf. *Kagura*.

Ta ch'ü (China—M 1623; M 5943). Large-scale instrumental pieces.

Tad (North India; Punjab). Large rustic fiddle with four fingered and three sympathetic strings. Cf. *Tid.*
Lit.: no. 254.

Tadabyōshi (Japan). A simple triple meter performed by a *kakko* and *tsuri daiko* and in *gagaku*, but very rarely in *bugaku* dances. The example shown below shows the use of the two drums and drumstrokes:

Lit.: no. 225.

Tadegoto (Japan). Cf. *Kong-hu* (Korea).

Taḍ'if (Arabia). Octave.

Tae (Korea). Big (string). Name of the third (fretted) string of the *hyon-kum* (*komunko*).
Lit.: no. 136.

Tae (Korea). Notational symbol. Cf. *Yul-cha-po.*

Tae-chaeng (*Tae-jaeng*) (Korea). See *Tai-chaing.*

Tae-chuita (Korea). See *Chuita.*

Taegum (Korea). See *Tae-kum.*

Tae-ha-ak (Korea). "Big summer music." One category of *ah-ak* in honor of mountain and river spirits. It represents the music of the Chinese legendary emperor Yü (M 7600). Cf. *Ah-ak.*
Lit.: no. 136.

Tae-ho-ak (Korea). "The great protection music." Music in honor of the female ancestors (one category of *ah-ak*). It represents the music of the Chinese legendary emperor Shen T'ang, the founder of the ancient Shang dynasty (1523-1027 B.C.). Cf. *Ah-ak.*
Lit.: no. 136.

Taejaeng (Korea). See *Tai-chaing.*

Tae-kum (*Tai-keum*; *Tae-gum*; *Chottae*) (Korea). A large transverse bamboo flute of the past. The instrument had six finger holes and, near the lower end, 5, 3, or 1 non-stopped holes. Before the orchestra began to play, the strings and tunable wind instruments were tuned to the lowest note of the *tae-kum* (approximately B♭). The names of the basic pitches of the *tae-kum* were (and are) *il-ji*, *yi-ji*, *sam-ji*, *hoeng-ji*, *u-jo*, *pal-pal jo*, and *mak-mak-jo* (about B♭, C, d♭, e♭, f, g♭, g [a♭]). The production of other semitonic features was done by half-stopping. See *Sam-chuk.*
Lit.: no. 179.

Tae-kwun-ak (Korea). "Big turn music." One type (dance music) of *ah-ak.* It serves to appease and honor the spirits of the four directions.
Lit.: no. 136.

Tae-mu-ak (Korea). "Great Mu [military] music" in honor of the rulers Mun and Mu (in Chinese: Wen and Wu), the founders of the Chou dynasty (1027-256 B.C.). Cf. *Ah-ak.*
Lit.: no. 136.

Taemyon (Korea). Music and dance imported from China representing a whip-swinging man who wears a golden mask. He drives away evil spirits. The musical accompaniment is performed by a flute and a drum (*yao-ku*).
Lit.: no. 52.

Tae-p'yong-so (Korea). Cf. *Tai-pyeng-so.*

Taeryewang kongmun (Korea). Cf. *Siwang kakpae-chae.*

Tae-so-ak (Korea). "Great beauty music." An *ah-ak* type not included in the traditional six categories (cf. *Ah-ak*). *Tae-so-ak* is music in remembrance of the virtues of Emperor Shun. It is also described as music for the four views and five mountains.
Lit.: no. 136.

Ta-gaṇa (South India). See *Ashta gaṇas.*

Taganig (Sumatra). Small *sigordang.*
Lit.: no. 255.

Taganza (Northwest Sahara). Frame drum played by women at wedding feasts.
Lit.: no. 190.

Tagbuan (Timor). See *Tabuan.*
Lit.: no. 254.

Tagerrabt (Tunisia – Gurara). Songs similar to *ahellil* accompanied by one flute, a small two-stringed lute, and several percussion instruments.

Taghbir (Arabia). Cantillation of the Koran.

Tagong (Philippines; Mindanao). Tube zither with six (or fewer) strings. Cf. *Togo*; *Agong.*
Lit.: nos. 156, 220.

Tagonggong (Talaud Isl.). Goblet-shaped drum.
Lit.: no. 157.

T'a-gu (Tibet). See *Rgyud.*

Tahapan sora (Sunda District). See *Wilah* (Java).

Taḥāsin (Arabia). Melismata.

Ṭahēr (*Ṭahir*) (Arabia). An obscure *maqām.* Probably *bayāt* performed in the low octave range (a fourth lower).
Lit.: no. 121.

Ṭāhir (Middle East). *Maqām.*
Tone material:
D E♭(+) F G A B♭(+) c d
Lit.: no. 64.

Tahitahia (Malagasy Republic). A toy clay flute with two finger holes.
Lit.: no. 251.

Tahlīl (and *Talbiyya*) (Old Arabia). Primitive pre-Islamic chanting during pilgrimages and moon worship, accompanied by the *ṭabl* (drum) and *shāhīn* (fife).
Lit.: no. 70.

Tahmīlah (Arabia). Interlude (instrumental).
Lit.: no. 171.

Tah-ryung (Korea). Instrumental ensemble item of programmatic character. The instruments used are flutes, *kayakum*, and *chang-go.*
Lit.: no. 221.

Ta hu-ch'in (China). A large *hu-ch'in* with a pear-shaped body and two silken strings. Cf. *Hu-ch'in.*
Lit.: no. 250.

Tahur (Bismarck Archipelago; New Ireland). Marine shell trumpet.
Lit.: no. 255.

Tai chaing (Korea). Often written *tae-chaeng.* A large *cheng*, an obsolete zither closely related to the Chinese *cheng* and the Japanese *koto.* The instrument has 15 strings and movable bridges. During the Yi dynasty the *tai chaing* was used only in the performance of imported Chinese music.
Lit.: no. 179.

T'ai-ch'ang (China). Name of the ministry of music (*yüeh-fu*) during the Han period (206 B.C. – A.D. 221), and general term for music played at the imperial court (T'ang period A.D. 618-906). Cf. *Fa-ch'ü.* The *t'ai-ch'ang* (of the Han period) employed four orchestras with a total of 829 players which performed at the imperial court. Besides these departments, it

supervised musical matters in the official state examinations. The rules for these examinations remained in use up to A.D. 1904.
Lit.: nos. 55, 227.

Tai-go (*Tai-go*) (Japan). See *Ryong-ko* (Korea).

Tai-keum (*Tae-kum*) (Korea). The big flute with six main holes and five non-stopped holes. Cf. *Sam-chuk*.
Lit.: no. 179.

Tai-keum (*Tae-kum*) (Korea). Also *chottae*. This term indicates not only the big flute (see *Tae-kum*), but also a large gong struck with a mallet covered with deerskin. Cf. *So-keum*.
Lit.: no. 179.

Taiko (*Daiko*) (Japan). One of the three drums of the *noh* ensemble (the other two drums are *ko-tsuzumi* and *o-tsuzumi*). The *taiko* body has a flat barrel form where the diameter of each of the two drumheads is bigger than the height of the drum. The drum rests on a low wooden stand in an oblique manner whereby the upper skin faces the player. The drum is beaten with two thick wooden sticks. The *taiko* is used in *togaku*, *komagaku*, and in *noh* and *kabuki* ensembles.
Lit.: no. 185.

Taikoji (Japan). Main dance item played by the *hayashi*, comparable to *odoriji* in *kabuki*, *mai* of *noh*, *odori* of *joruri*.

Taiko-odori (Japan). Folk dance. Dancers either carry a drum about or dance around the large instrument. See *Odoriji*.
Lit.: no. 185.

Tai-ku (China). Cantonese term for *ta-ku*.

Tai-kum (Korea). See *Tae-kum*.

Taikyoku (Japan). A group of ancient great ballet pantomimes.

Tai-lo (China). Cantonese term for *ta-lo*.

Tainai (Nepal). A small plate of bell metal beaten with a stick.

T'ai-p'ing-hsiao (China—M 2619; M 5303; M 6020). A bamboo whistle flute. It has six front holes and, above them, a hole covered with a delicate membrane which influences the timbre. Its name in Shantung is *hsiao-ti*.
Lit.: no. 250.

Tai-p'yeng-so (*Tae-p'yong-so*) (Korea). "Great flute of peace." A heterophonic double reed instrument with a conical tube ending in a large metal bell. It has seven (6) finger holes on top and one at the back. The instrument is also called *soe-rap* or *hojok* ("Mongolian tube"), or *nallari* when it is used in folk music. The sound produced by this oboe is usually noisy. The instrument, imported from China during the 15th century, became a favorite instrument in military and rural ensembles, and appears also in ceremonial processions and funerals. Cf. *So-na*.
Lit.: nos. 52, 179.

Tairan (Java). Name given to the *terbang* by Arabs who live in Java.
Lit.: no. 163.

Taisen (Japan). A large *kirisen* with a circular body.
Lit.: no. 225.

Taishiki (*Taisiki*) (Japan). *Ryosen* (scale) from the *hyōjō*. Cf. *Sō-no-koto* (tunings).
Lit.: no. 225.

Taishikicho (Japan). *Gagaku* (*ryōsen*) mode. Cf. *Gagaku* (scales).

Tai-tik (China). Cantonese term for "large pipe" (cf. *So-na*). Also called *ti-ta*.
Lit.: no. 129.

T'ai-ts'u (China—M 6020; M 6840). "Great frame." Absolute pitch; the third tone of the spiral of fifths as shown in the *lü-lü*. Traditionally a *yang* ("male") tone, used as basic note in Confucian hymns to be performed

in January. If used as notational symbol only the first syllable (*t'ai*) is used.
Lit.: no. 136.

Tājira (North Africa—Berber). Small bowl-shaped drum.
Lit.: no. 190.

Tajwīd (Iraq). The reading of the Koran.

Tak (Arabia). Half loud; mezzoforte (drumming).

Tak (*tang*) (Java). Drum word. Cf. *Tepak.*
Lit.: no. 163.

Taka (Assam). Bamboo stick (whip) with split end.
Lit.: no. 46.

Takara (Ghana). See *Agbadza.*

Takarrur (Islamic North Africa). Repetition.

Take-bue (*Shino-bue*) (Japan). Bamboo cross-flute with six or seven holes. It is used in folk music and can be blown to the left as well as to the right.
Lit.: no. 185.

Tak-he (Thailand; Kampuchea). A large, massive crocodile-shaped teak wood zither with two gut strings, one brass string, and 11 frets. The instrument rests on small ivory feet. The three strings (tuned to 1, 5, 8) are beaten with a small wooden hammer.

A favorite instrumental trio in Kampuchea combines the *tak-be* with a *tro-u* and the Chinese *yang-ch'in.* Cf. *Mohori*; *Chakay* (*Chakhe*); *Mi-gyaun* (*Megyun*).
Lit.: no. 43.

Takhs (Egypt). Instrumental ensemble consisting of *qanūn*, *nāy*, and one or two other instruments, occasionally Western instruments such as violin, violoncello, flute, clarinet, even string bass and pianoforte.
Lit.: no. 106.

Taki (Solomon Isl.). Strophic songs.
Lit.: no. 246.

Takik (Philippines). (1) A piece of iron struck with a stone. (2) Flirtation dance of the Bontok.

Taki koto (Japan). The favorite zither of the distinguished ladies. It had 13 silken strings strung across movable bridges. The strings were plucked with an ivory plectrum.
Lit.: no. 255.

Takitu (Flores; Manggaray; Ende). (1) Small, one-headed cylindrical drum. (2) A small one-headed goblet-shaped drum. Cf. *Gedang.*
Lit.: no. 166.

Takka (*Dhakka*) (North India). Obscure *rāga.* Probably related to the *rāgas Bhimpalasi* and *Bhairavi.*
Tone material:

C E♭ F G B♭ c
c B♭ A♭ G E♭ D♭ C

Lit.: no. 138.

Takka (South India). *Janya rāga* of the 9th *mēḷa* (*Dhēnuka*).
Tone material:

C E♭ F G F A♭ B c
c B A♭ G F E♭ D♭ C

Lit.: no. 139.

Takol (*Dami*) (Sunda District). See *Keteg.*

Takseem (Arabia). Composition based on improvised variations on a basic, well-known *maqām*. Cf. *Taqsīm.*
Lit.: no. 171.

Taku (China). Large or medium-sized barrel-shaped drum. It rests on a wooden stand of four legs; one drumhead is directed upward. The drum is used in theatrical (and puppet) shows. The Cantonese name of the drum is *tai-ku.*
Lit.: no. 129.

Taku (Japan). See *Thak* (Korea). Also ancient bronze bells.
Lit.: no. 53.

Takuk (Islamic North Africa). Crisp and light drum stroke by touching the rim of the drumhead.

Täkum (Korea). Bamboo flute. Cf. *Tae-kum* (*Tai-keum*).

Tala (India). One of the ancient 10 basic ways of playing the *vīṇā* strings (*dhātu*).
Lit.: no. 292.

Tāla (dialectal: *Tal*) (North India). This Sanskrit term means "clapping of hands" and "rhythm" in all of its additive forms when a fixed number of measures (*vibhāgas*) is repeated throughout the composition. The remarkable characteristic of these groups of measures (*āvartas*) is that the number of beats of the *vibhāgas* may be different from one *vibhāga* to the other.

For instance, the *āvarta* of the ancient *dhamar-tāl* consists of the following four *vibhāgas*:

♩ ♩ ♩ ♩ ♩	♩ ♩	♩ ♩ ♩	♩ ♩ ♩ ♩
X	2	0	3

This *āvarta* (5 + 2 + 3 + 4) appears over and over again. The X and the numbers placed below the beats can be observed in North Indian musical notation and indicate the following: X is called the *sam*, the stressed opening beat of each *āvarta*, performed by special drum beats, generally combined with one of the following notes of the *rāga*: *sa* (the basic note), *vādī*, *samvādī*, occasionally the *vishrantisthan* of the melody. The numbers 2 and 3 merely indicate the place of the *vibhāgas* within the *āvarta*. The number 0, called *khāli* ("open"), is performed in a different manner than the other beats on the drums: the *khāli* sound is muffled, dull, and serves as a warning sign to the soloist, indicating that after a certain fixed numbers of beats the next *āvarta* will begin with the important *sam* where only the above mentioned notes can be performed.

The following list shows the frequently used *tālas* (in the form of single *āvartas*) of North Indian music:

Adachautāl

1 2	3 4	5 6	7 8	9 10	11 12	13 14
X	2	0	3	0	4	0

Brahmtāl

1 2	3 4	5 6	7 8	9 10	11 12	13 14	15 16
X	0	2	3	0	4	5	6

Chautāl

1 2	3 4	5 6	7 8	9 10	11 12
X	0	2	0	3	4

Dādra

1 2 3	4 5 6
X	0

Dhamar-tāl

1 2 3 4 5	6 7	8 9 10	11 12 13 14
X	2	0	0

Dipchandi

1 2 3	4 5 6 7	8 9 10	11 12 13 14
X	2	0	3

Ektāl

1 2	3 4	5 6	7 8	9 10	11 12
X	0	2	0	3	4

Jhampa

1 2	3 4 5	6 7	8 9 10
X	2	0	3

Jhaptāl

1 2	3 4 5	6 7	8 9 10
X	2	0	3

The rhythmical structures of *Jhampa* and *Jhaptal* are the same, but the executions of the drum strokes are different and so are the drum sounds. The same can be observed in *tālas Panjabi* and the popular *Tintal* (or *Trital*). For further information see my book, Lit. no. 136, pp. 191-92.

Rūpak

1 2 3	4 5	6 7	
X	2	3	(no *khāli* beat)

Shikar

1 2 3 4 5 6	7 8 9 10 11 12	13 14 15 16 17
X	0	3 4

(The drumstroke 2 is often not notated)

Sultāl

1 2	3 4	5 6	7 8	9 10
X	0	0	3	0

Tilvada

1 2 3 4	5 6 7 8	9 10 11 12	13 14 15 16
X	2	0	3

Tivra

1 2 3	4 5	6 7	
X	2	3	(no *khāli* beat)

TĀLA
Group of Beats Organized into *Jātis*

Jāti	*Trisra-jāti*	*Chatusra-jāti*	*Khaṇṣa-jāti*	*Misra-jāti*	*Saṅkīrna-jāti*
Eka-tāla(m)	3	4	5	7	9
Rūpaka-tāla	2 + 3	2 + 4	2 + 5	2 + 7	2 + 9
Jhampa-tāla	3 + 1 + 2	4 + 1 + 2	5 + 1 + 2	7 + 1 + 2	9 + 1 + 2
Tripuṭa-tāla	3 + 2 + 2	4 + 2 + 2	5 + 2 + 2	7 + 2 + 2	9 + 2 + 2
Maṭya-tāla	3 + 2 + 3	4 + 2 + 4	5 + 2 + 5	7 + 2 + 7	9 + 2 + 9
Dhruva-tāla	3 + 2 + 3 + 3	4 + 2 + 4 + 4	5 + 2 + 5 + 5	7 + 2 + 7 + 7	9 + 2 + 9 + 9
Āṭa-tāla	3 + 3 + 2 + 2	4 + 4 + 2 + 2	5 + 5 + 2 + 2	7 + 7 + 2 + 2	9 + 9 + 2 + 2

Tintāl
Trital

1 2 3 4	5 6 7 8	9 10 11 12	13 14 15 16
X	2	0	3

Lit.: nos. 136, 138.

Tāla (*Tālam*) (South India). The rhythmical modes of Karnatic (South Indian) music. In contrast to the North, the *tālas* are grouped into five categories in which the northern terms *sam* and *khāli* are not in use. The performing musician has to know when these or similar features occur and in musical notation of the South the signs X, 2, 0, 3 are not shown.

The grouping of beats in each *tāla* is organized into *jātis* and is shown in the list above.

Among irregular *tālas* are: *Chapu tāla* (*Trisra jāti*) 1 + 2; *Chapu tāla* (*Miśra jāti*) 1 + 2 + 2 + 2. *Simhanandana tāla* with 100 units: 8 + 8 + 4 + 8 + 4 + 8 + 2 + 2 + 8 + 8 + 4 + 8 + 4 + 8 + 8 + 4 + 4.
Lit.: no. 136, pp. 193-94.

Tāla (India; South India; Bengal). Gong with a flat surface. Cf. *Jhañjha.*
Lit.: no. 46.

Talāḥin (Old Arabia). Melodic modes.

Talaing (*Mon*) (Burma). Brief songs from Mon-Khmer.

Talalo (Indonesia; Pulau-Pulau Isl.—Banggai; Celebes). Term for *rerre.*
Lit.: no. 167.

Tālam (South India). Tamil term for *tāla* and for small cymbals.

Tālam (South India). *Janya rāga* of the 64th *mēḷa* (*Vāchaspati*).
Tone material:
C E F♯ A B♭ c
c B♭ A F♯ E C
Lit.: no. 139.

Tālamu (South India). *Janya rāga* of the 40th *mēḷa* (*Navanītam*).
Tone material:
C E♭♭ F♯ A B♭ c
c B♭ A F♯ E♭♭ C
Lit.: no. 139.

Tālamu (South India). Telugu term for *tāla.*

Talbiyya (Arabia). See *Tahlīl.*

Taleḍek (Java). Girl dancers. Their dance is accompanied by *gamelan* music. Cf. *Ronggeng.*
Lit.: no. 158.

Talemon (*Chelempung*) (Sumatra). Cf. *Talimpueṅ.*

Talempong (Sumatra—Minangkabau). A small gong ensemble played by women. During the rice harvesting the ensemble is played by men.

Taleng (Bali). Name of a notational symbol.
Lit.: no. 197.

Taleot (West Java; Sumatra). See *Surilit.*

Taletenga (Ghana). Reed pipe.

Talḥin (Old Arabia). Islamic religious cantillation.
Lit.: no. 76.

Tali (Malaysia). See *Rebāb.*

Tālī (India). Rhythmic clapping of hands. Rhythm. Also small bells that beat the meter and rhythm. Cf. *Tāla*; *Jhanjha*; *Mandirā.*
Lit.: no. 250.

Talibeng (Philippines). Bamboo drum.

Ta'līf (Arabia). Theory of composition, music, and prosody.

Ta'līf (Iran). Cf. *Tasnif.*

Talimpueṅ (*Talemon*) (Central Sumatra). One, rarely two, rows of 5-7 simple gongs. The set is not imported from Java but from Singapore. Cf. *Tjelempuṅ*; *Tjalimpueṅ* (related terms used in Sumatra).
Lit.: no. 254.

Talindo (Indonesia; Pulau-Pulau Isl.; Banggai). Stick zither with one string.
Lit.: nos. 156, 162.

Taliya (Sri Lanka). Singhalese term for (1) *tala*; (2) gong.
Lit.: no. 255.

Talīyaka (India). Sanskrit term for cymbal.
Lit.: no. 255.

Tālo (India). Pali term for *tāla.*

Ta-lo (China—M 5943; M 4107). Large gong with a flat surface. It frequently appears in theatrical (puppet) performances. Its Cantonese name is *tai-lo.* Other names are: *kao-pien-lo* (Mandarin); *kau-pin-lo* (Cantonese). Cf. *Lo.*
Lit.: no. 129.

Talot-pote (Thailand). Small drum of South Chinese origin, beaten with the fingers.
Lit.: no. 255.

Ta-lü (China—M 5943; M 4280). Literally, "greatest tube." An absolute pitch; the eighth tone of the circle of fifths as shown in the list of *lü-lü.* Traditionally a *yin* ("female") tone, it was used as basic tone in Confucian hymns performed in the month of December. If used as notational symbol only the first syllable is used (*ta*, M 5943). Cf. *Lü.*
Lit.: no. 136.

Talupak (Philippines). A bamboo tube zither with a large number of strings. The tube is struck against the ground like a stamping stick, and functions also to make holes for planting rice seeds.

Tam (Nilotic Sudan; Congo). Lyre. Cf. *Tohmu*; *Tom*; *Tum.*
Lit.: no. 21.

Tama (Senegal—Wolof). Drum.
Lit.: no. 200.

Tamabue (Japan). An ancient, globular stone ocarina with one hole.
Lit.: no. 53.

Tamak (India—Santali). Cf. *Tarsha.*

Tāmalaki (South India). *Janya rāga* of the 29th *mēḷa* (*Dhīrśaṅkarābharaṇam*).
Tone material:
C F G A B c
c B A G F C
Lit.: no. 139.

Tam am la (Central Vietnam). A group of three gongs used in the *nha nhac*, the "elegant music."
Lit.: no. 297.

Tamande (West Africa – Mandingo). Drum.
Lit.: no. 95.

Tamarugam (South India). Tamil term for *damaru.*

Tāmasarañjani (South India). *Janya rāga* of the 63rd *mēḷa* (*Latāṅgī*).
Tone material:
C D E F♯ G A♭ G c
c A♭ G c B c A♭ G F♯ E D C
Lit.: no. 139.

Tamasha (India). Common term for a cheerful, noisy festivity in which popular songs and lively dances are performed.

Tamasvini (South India). *Janya rāga* of the 4th *mēḷa* (*Vanaspāti*).
Tone material:
C D♭ E♭♭ G A c
c A G E♭♭ D♭ C
Lit.: no. 139.

Tamatama (Sahara; Sudan – Tuareg). Drum.
Lit.: no. 95.

Tamattama (Sri Lanka). Also *tambattam*; pair of kettledrums.
Lit.: no. 46.

Tamba (West Africa – Mandingo). Drum.
Lit.: no. 95.

Tambal (Afghanistan). Tambourin.
Lit.: no. 255.

Tambala (Nepal). See *Jambala.*

Tambana (West Africa – Yalunka). Name of the *tabl*, a drum in hourglass shape.
Lit.: no. 95.

Tambari (North Nigeria – Hausa). Kettledrum.
Cf. *Rok'on fada.*
Lit.: no. 95.

Tambaṭṭam (Sri Lanka). See *Tamattama.* Cf. *Duff*; *Timbutu* (Mesopotamia); *Temettama* (Singhalese).
Lit.: no. 46.

Tambira (Northeast Africa; Somali Republic). Lyra with 6-8 strings.
Lit.: no. 98.

Tambo (Flores; Ngada; Manggaray District). A drum with two heads that resembles the military drum of 18th-century Europe, suitable to produce drum rolls.
Lit.: no. 166.

Tambolo (Celebes – Poso Toradja). Bamboo trumpet.
Lit.: no. 132.

Tambotta (South India). Cf. *Tambaṭṭam.*
Lit.: no. 255.

Tambue (Congo – Luba). Friction drum.
Lit.: no. 17.

Tambur (South India). Malayalam term for drum.
Lit.: no. 255.

Tambūr (Afghanistan). See *Tanbur* (Afghanistan).

Tambūr (*Tanbur*) (South Africa – Grigriqua). A bowed fiddle that imitates in size and shape the European violin.
Lit.: no. 151.

Tambūr (Iran). Term for *tanbūr.*

Tambur (Bali). A gong with a deep rim used for signalling. It is never used in *gamelan* performances.
Lit.: no. 197.

Tambur (Flores). Cf. *Tambo.*

Tambura (India). See *Tanbura.*

Tambūrah (South Sudan). An indigenous lyre.
Lit.: no. 108.

Tamburu (Indonesia; Nias). Goblet-shaped drum. Cf. *Tsjutsju*; *Fodrahi*; *Taburana*.
Lit.: no. 162.

Tam huyēn (Vietnam). See *Dan tam*.

Tamlaga (Mongolia). Shamanistic ritual chant.

Tammānam (South India). Tamil term for *tabla*.

Tammiṭṭam (South India). Malayalam term for *daf*.
Lit.: no. 255.

Tamoji (Japan). Professional musician in charge of *bugaku*, who inherited status and had learned his craft from his ancestors who originally came from Osaka.
Lit.: no. 225.

Tampak dara (Bali). "Dove's footprint," a cross-shaped symbol used in musical notation to denote the *kempli* accent.
Lit.: no. 197.

Tamra (Nepal). A small kettledrum.

Tamukku (South India). Malayalam term for a small cup-shaped drum with a body made of burnt clay. Cf. *Tarshā*.
Lit.: no. 255.

Tan (Vietnam). Buddhist chanting with instrumental accompaniment. Cf. *Tung*.

Tan (Ivory Coast). Song and dance; instrumental music.

Tan (China – M 6037). Stereotyped operatic role. Cf. *Sheng* (China – M 5738); *Hua tan*; *Nan-hsi*.
Lit.: no. 183.

Tan (China). (1) Playing a string instrument. (2) *Hu-ch'in*.

Tān(a) (India). Proper or real *tān*. Variation, melodic figuration. Cf. *Khyāl*.
Lit.: no. 138.

Tānarūpi (South India). (1) The 6th *mēḷa*:
C D♭ E♭♭ F G A♯ B c
(2) As *rāga*, to be performed in the morning, the tone material is that of the *mēḷa*. Veṅkaṭamakhin (17th century) called this *rāga Tanukīrti*.
Lit.: no. 139.

Tanāsuq (Islamic North Africa; Near East). Term for symmetry in music and poetry.

Tanbūr (Afghanistan). Lute with six main strings and 11 sympathetic strings. The number of frets varies (9-15) according to the size of the instrument. There is a remarkable difference between the Afghan *tanbūr* and the North Indian *tanbura*.

Tanbūr (Arabia; Iran). Long lute with a small egg- or pear-shaped corpus and a long neck. It has a variable number of wire strings that run over a large (variable) number of gut frets. The large variety of this instrument (e.g., with eight strings) is called *tanbūr-kabir-turki* ("large Turkish lute"). The Persians do not use the term *tanbūr*, but refer to *tar* ("string"): *dutar*, *setar*, *chartar*, *panchtar*. The word *tanbūr* is used however in *tanbūr-buzurk*, or *tanbūr i gili*.
Lit.: no. 255.

Tanbūra (*Tambura*; *Tampura*) (India). Long-necked lute with four wire strings without any frets. The instrument is used to produce the bourdon drone necessary in Indian art music. The tuning, according to the *rāga* performed, is G c c C; F c c C; B c c C.
Lit.: no. 136.

Tanbūr-al-mīzānī (Near East). "Measured tanbur." A two-stringed *tanbūr*.
Lit.: no. 250.

Tanbūr-baghdadi (Near East). Lute, identical with *tanbūr al mīzānī*.

Tanbūr-bağlama (Turkey; Near East). See *Bağlama*; *Saz*.

Tanbūr-buzurk (Iran). Large *tanbūr.* This lute has a pear-shaped corpus, a long neck, six strings (arranged into 3 + 2 + 1 strings), 19 frets on the neck and six on the body.
Lit.: no. 255.

Tanbūr-i-gili (North Iran). A *tanbūr* used in Gilan on the Caspian Sea.
Lit.: no. 255.

Tanbūr kebīr (*Kabīr*) **tūrkī** (Arabia; Middle East). See *Tanbūr* (Arabia; Iran).
Lit.: no. 190.

Tanbūr küchük (Turkey). Small Turkish *tanbūr* with eight strings.
Lit.: no. 255.

Tanbūr sharqī (Turkey; Middle East). "Eastern *tanbūr.*"

Tan-ch'in (China — M 6047; M 1103). A spike fiddle with a cylindrical bamboo corpus. Similar to the *hu-ch'in*, it has the traditional two silken strings tuned to the interval of a fifth. An iron wire is attached with one end to the lower opening of the bamboo neck. The other end swings freely against the corpus when the instrument is played. The recent Shanghai term for *tan-ch'in* is *ching-hu* (M 1127; M 2167). Cf. *Hu-ch'in*; *Hui-hu.*
Lit.: nos. 209, 250.

Tan-cho (Korea). "Short key"; minor mode.

Tanda (Congo — Bwende). Wooden side-blown trumpet.
Lit.: no. 280.

Tanda ngorot (Bali). Term for a notational symbol denoting a brief glissando or melodic ornament.
Lit.: no. 197.

Tandak (Bali). The singer who describes in his song the events of the *gambuh* theater and the *legong* dance.
Lit.: no. 197.

Taṇḍavam (South India). *Janya rāga* of the 29th *mēḷa* (*Dhīraśaṅkarābharaṇam*).
Tone material:
C E G A B c
c B A G E C
Lit.: no. 139.

Tāṇḍavapriya (South India). *Janya rāga* of the 49th *mēḷa* (*Dhavalāmbarī*).
Tone material:
C D♭ E F♯ G c
c G F♯ E D♭ C
Lit.: no. 139.

Tāṇḍavōllāsini (South India). *Janya rāga* of the 35th *mēḷa* (*Śūlinī*).
Tone material:
C D♯ E G A B c
c B A G E D♯ C
Lit.: no. 139.

Tandilo (Celebes). Bamboo tube zither with two strings.
Lit.: no. 156.

Tandrokaka (Malagasy Republic). Horn.
Lit.: no. 251.

Tang (Java; Sumatra — Mangku; Nagaran). Name of a drum stroke. Cf. *Tak*; *Tepak.*
Lit.: no. 163.

Tangah (South Borneo — Bandjermasin). The second note of the *slendro* system of Bandjermasin. Cf. *Tengah* (Java); *Slendro.*
Lit.: no. 163.

Tang-ak (Korea). Ceremonial court music imported from China. Despite its name, *tang-ak* need not be music dating from the T'ang dynasty. It is festive music that employs the two chimes of bells and stones (*p'yon-chong*, *p'yon-kyeng*) and the mouth organ (*saing*).
Lit.: nos. 136, 179.

Tangala (Lower Congo — Teke). Conical drum made of a hollowed tree trunk. It is used in pairs of unequal sizes and is beaten with wooden sticks.
Lit.: no. 280.

Tangbipa (Korea). See *T'ang p'i-p'a.*

Tang-che (*Glu-len-pa*) (Tibet). To sing.

Tang-chok (*Tang-jok*) (Korea). Small wooden transverse flute with seven holes. Usually it is played together with the bigger (transverse) flute (*tae-kum*) in court music. Originally imported from China and later employed also in serious Korean music. Cf. *Ti* (China); *To buye* (Japan).
Lit.: no. 52.

Tang chuk (Korea). See *Tang chok.*

Tangcup besar (Borneo). See *Gulung-gulung.*

Tangcup-hetjil (Borneo). See *Gulung-gulung.*

Tanggetong (North Sumatra—Toba Batak). Bamboo tube zither. Cf. *Nungneng.*
Lit.: no. 162.

Tanggo (South Borneo). See *Sanga.*

Tangi (Solomon Isl.; Bellona Isl.). Group song in strophic form; lament.
Lit.: no. 246.

Tangin (Japan). Second of the Japanese (chromatic) tones, usually transcribed as D♯ (if *ichikotsu*, the first tone, is D). Cf. *Gagaku.*

Tangishi (Belgian Congo—Tuchiokwe). The master dancer and drummer who instruct the initiates in songs and dances of the circumcision ritual.
Lit.: no. 29.

Tangklit (Sunda District). See *Byang.*

Tangkolnang (North Borneo—Dusun). Bamboo tube zither.
Lit.: no. 162.

T'ang-ku (China—M 6107; M 3479). "Hall drum." Barrel-shaped drum, not of ancient origin and not mentioned in the Classics. It has two skins. It is suspended with rings from a wooden stand and can be found in Buddhist and Taoist temples, but not in Confucian services. It is used in courts of magistrates, in operatic performances, and at various festivities as well as funerals. Cf. *Chen-ku.*
Lit.: no. 137.

Tang-lo (China—M 4107; M 6087). Small, suspended brass gong. It is used by Buddhist and Taoist priests who strike it with a small hammer.
Lit.: no. 209.

T'ang music (China). *T'ang yüeh.* Music of the T'ang period (A.D. 618-907):

Ceremonial Music
- Music in the temple of ancestors
- *Shih-pu-chi* (the 10 orchestras)

Secular Music
- I. *Music of the Two Sections*
  - a) when the performers are standing
  - b) when the performers are seated
- II. *School for Music and Drama*
  - a) The Pearblossom Garden for Men
  - b) The Eternal Spring Garden for Women
- III. *The Two Music Schools*
  - a) "Right" School of Singing
  - b) "Left" School of Instrumental Music and Dancing
- IV. Folk music and dance

Ta ngo (*Mbonda*) (Congo—Ngbandi). Long cylindrical drum played at dances, wrestling games, and when somebody dies. The drums *ta-go* and *to-ngo* are beaten by one single player; one drum is beaten with a stick and the other with the bare hand. Cf. *Bia*; *To-ngo*; also *Kpworo.*
Lit.: no. 26.

Tang-p'il-lyul (Korea). The "*tang-p'iri*"—a bamboo oboe of Chinese origin with seven finger holes, generally played at religious occasions. Cf. *P'iri.*
Lit.: no. 52.

Tang p'i-p'a (Korea). A large lute imported from China. *Tang* does not necessarily refer to the Chinese T'ang period, but to China generally

(while *Hyang* indicates indigenous Korea). The tuning of the four silken strings is, e.g., C F F c. The instrument has 10 (12) frets. A former 5-string *p'i-p'a* became obsolete in Korea during the 15th century.
Lit.: no. 52.

Tang p'i-ri (Korea). See *Tang-p'il-lyul.*

Tang sun (Thailand). Regular rhythm.
Lit.: no. 203.

Tang-tang-tzu (China). See *Tang-tzu.*

Tang tzu (China—M 6087; M 6939). Flat brass gong with turned rim. A temple instrument in Hangchow where it is called *tang-tang-tzu.*
Lit.: no. 209.

Tanguri (Northeast New Guinea). Jew's harp.

Tang yao (Thailand). Free rhythm without any regular beats.
Lit.: no. 203.

Tan Hsiao (China—M 6030; M 2619). Name of *ch'ang ti.*

Ṭanīn (Liberia—Kpelle). Single bell.
Lit.: no. 284.

Tanin (Arabia). Tone.

Tanjidor (Java). A form of brass band with Western instruments (clarinet, trumpet, cornet, euphonium, drum), plus a *kechrek* and gong. The band performs Western marches, polkas, etc., at various festive occasions.

Tanka (Japan). See *Utazawa.*

Tanki (*Shritank*) (North India). *Rāga*, ascribed to the *Purvi thāta*. It is to be performed in the evening.
Tone material:
C D♭ E G A♭ B c
c B A♭ G F♯ E D♭ C; *Vādis*: G, D♭
Lit.: no. 138.

Tan-kuan (China—M 6030; M 3557). Single pipe; vertical flute. Cf. *Kuan.*
Lit.: no. 137.

Taṅkunan (Borneo—Dusun). Tube zither with five strings. See *Ton-ton.*
Lit.: no. 254.

Tanmori (Korea). Cf. *Sanjo.*

Tan nhac (Vietnam). Cf. *Nhac cai cach.*

Tanoo (Thailand). Bow.

Tanpura (India). See *Tanbura.*

Tan-so (Korea). A small, notched, vertically-blown bamboo flute with four finger holes on top and one in the back. Cf. *Tong-so.*
Lit.: nos. 52, 179.

Tan-ta (China). A frequently used small gong. Employed in theatrical and puppet performances.
Lit.: no. 255.

Tan-tabola (*Ta-tabola*) (Celebes—Bolaang). Bamboo tube zither.
Lit.: no. 162.

Tantakar (India). String player. Cf. *Tata.*

Taṅtan (West Africa—Western Mandingo). Tubular drum.
Lit.: no. 255.

Tan-po (Burma). Horn.
Lit.: no. 255.

Tanukīrti (South India). *Janya rāga* of the 6th *mēḷa* (*Tānarūpi*).
Tone material:
C D♭ F G B c
c B A♯ B G F E♭♭ F D♭ C
Lit.: no. 139.

Tanukīrti (South India). (1) The 6th *asampūrṇa mēḷa-rāga* without *kaṭapayādi* prefix. (2) The 6th *asampūrṇa mēḷa-rāga* with *kaṭapayādi* prefix. See *Rāga* (North India).
Lit.: no. 139.

Tanzemono (Japan). A series of conventional *shamisen* pieces consisting of popular music and dances.
Lit.: no. 187.

Tao (*Dao*) (Northeast Thailand). (1) Wind chest of the *kaen*. (2) The leading male performer of the *mawlum plun*.
Lit.: no. 203.

T'ao-ch'i (China). See *Chien-tzu*.
Lit.: no. 136.

T'ao-ku (China—M 6151; M 3479). Small rattle-drum in barrel shape, held by a handle. Two balls suspended on strings attached to the barrel strike the drumheads when the drum is twirled around the handle, like a *damaru*.

Two of these drums were placed on the east and west sides of the Confucian temple and were sounded three times at the end of each verse of the hymn. In ancient ritual music appeared several *t'ao-ku* (up to eight) tied together into a cluster. Cf. *Nei-ko*; *Nei-to*; *Yung-ko*; *Yung-to*; *No-ko; No-to.*
Lit.: nos. 143, 250.

Taouat (Northwest Sahara). Shepherd's cane flute with five finger holes. When played it is held obliquely.
Lit.: no. 190.

Tao-yin (Ancient China—M 6137; M 7429). "Guiding march." Dignified music played after the emperor had arrived (several hours before sunrise) at the first gate of the Confucian temple. When he arrived at the second gate, the emperor left his sedan chair. He was preceded and followed by 11 musicians, 11 ensigns and umbrella bearers, and the *tao-yin* was played. The musicians played the following instruments: two *sheng*, two *ti-tzu*, two *hsiao*, two *yün-lo*, two *tou-kuan* (one player), two drums (one player), and two pairs of wooden clappers (one player). The actual music and its notation can be seen in Lit. no. 136, pp. 89-90.

Tāpa (South India). *Janya rāga* of the 14th *mēḷa* (*Vakulābharaṇam*).
Tone material:
C E G A♭ B♭ c
c B♭ A♭ G E C
Lit.: no. 139.

Tāpasapriya (South India). *Janya rāga* of the 14th *mēḷa* (*Vakulābharaṇam*).
Tone material:
C D♭ E F B♭ c
c B♭ F E D♭ C
Lit.: no. 139.

Tapavasini (South India). *Janya rāga* of the 52nd *mēḷa* (*Rāmapriya*).
Tone material:
C E F♯ G B♭ c
c B♭ A G F♯ E C
Lit.: no. 139.

Taphōn (Thailand). See *Tapone.*
Lit.: no. 255.

Tapil (Iraq; Kurdistan). Clay drum carried on a string suspended from the neck of the player. The drum is beaten with hands and fingers.
Lit.: no. 303.

Tap moṅ (Burma). Gong.
Lit.: no. 255.

Tapone (*Ta:phon*) (Thailand). Large long drum of barrel or slightly conical shape. The corpus is carved from one block of teak wood. The drum rests horizontally on a wooden stand. Of the two drumheads, one is covered with ox or goatskin, the other with calfskin. The skins are held by longitudinal braces and are struck with hands and fingers. The strokes, similar to *mṛdanga* and *tabla* play-techniques, are highly elaborate; each stroke has its own specific name and manner of performance. Cf. *Piphat*; *Song-na.*
Lit.: no. 254.

Tappa (North India). Mohammedan popular song with text in Hindi or Punjabi. Its melody is richly provided with ornaments.

Tappe (India; Punjab). Singing and clapping of hands. Cf. *Tappa.*

Tappeṭa (*Tambattam*) (South India). Telugu term for *daf.*

Tappu (South India). Tamil term for circular frame drum with a cowhide membrance. Cf. *Dappu* (Telugu); *Patha* (Sanskrit).

Taq- (*Tik-*) (Arabia). "High," "more." Prefix to a note name indicating that the sound of the note is slightly higher by a quarter-tone or, better, a microtone. E.g., see *Ḥiṣār* and the slightly higher *Taq-ḥiṣār*. Cf. *Jagā* (*Yagā*), under which heading are listed all note names within the range of two octaves. Cf. *Nam-*.

Taqa (Ethiopia; Egypt). Cf. *Daule.*
Lit.: no. 184.

Taq-ḥijāz (*Taq-ṣaba*; *Tik-ḥijāz*) (Arabia). Note approximately a quarter tone higher than *ḥijāz* (*ṣaba*). (A list of all tone names and notes within two octaves can be seen under the heading of *Jagā* [*Yagā*].)

Taq-ḥiṣār (*Tik-ḥiṣār*; *Tik-qarar-ḥiṣār*) (Arabia). Tone name of a note ca. ¼ tone higher than *ḥiṣār* (*shuri*). (A list of all tone names and notes through two octaves can be seen under the heading of *Jagā* [*Yagā*].)

Taq-ḥiṣār (*Qaba*; *Shuri*; *Tik-qarar-ḥiṣār*) (Arabia). Tone name of a note ca. ¼ tone higher than *ḥiṣār qaba* (*ḍarar-ḥiṣār*). (A list of all tone names and notes through two octaves can be seen under the heading of *Jagā* [*Yagā*].)

Taqil (Arabia). First and second *taqīl*. See *Iqa'at*; *Al thaqīl al-awwal*; *Al thaqīl al-thānī.*

Taq nahaft (*Tik nahaft*) (Arabia; Syria). Tone name for a tone ca. ¼ tone higher than *mahur* (*nahaft*). (A list of all tone names and notes through two octaves can be seen under the heading of *Jagā* [*Yagā*].)

Taq-ṣaba (Arabia). See *Taq-ḥijāz.*

Taq-shāh'nāz (*Tik-shāh-nāz*) (Arabia). Tone name of a note approximately a ca. ¼ tone higher than *shāh-nāz*. (A list of all tone names and notes through two octaves can be seen under the heading of *Jagā* [*Yagā*].)

Taqsīm (*Taqāsīm*; *Takseem*) (Arabia; Islamic North Africa). Improvised, rhythmically free prelude played most frequently on the lute at the beginning of the *nauba* suite. The prelude, similar to the Indian *ālāp*, presents the tone material to be used; it establishes the required mood and prepares player and audience for the performance that is to follow.

The Tunisian term resembling the *taqsīm* is *al-istiftākh*, a prelude performed by the entire instrumental ensemble. Cf. *Muwal.*
Lit.: no. 171.

Taq-zarkala (*Taq-zirkūla*; *Tik-zirgūlah*) (Arabia). Tone name of a note approximately ca. ¼ tone higher than *zarkala* (*zirkula*). (A list of all tone names and notes through two octaves can be seen under the heading of *Jagā* [*Yagā*].)

Taq-zirkula (*Taq-zirgula*) (Arabia). See *Taq-zarkala.*

Tār (Iran; Middle East). "String" (gut string). Long lute with a double resonance corpus, a variable number of strings, and movable frets. The number of strings determines its name: e.g., *dūtar*, two-string lute; *sitār*, three-string lute.
Lit.: no. 255.

Tār (Arabia; Syria; Egypt). Circular frame drum with a goatskin membrane and jingles, without snares. It is played by women.
Lit.: nos. 250, 255.

Ṭār (West Borneo). Frame drum.

Tāra (India). See *Saptaka.*

Ṭarabrab (Iran). Small lute with six strings.
Lit.: no. 78.

Ṭarabrub (Arabia). Tambourin.

Taraf (Iran). Sympathetic string.

Taraffedar (North India). Cf. *Taraf-i tār.*

Taraf-i tār (Iran; North India). *Sitār* with sympathetic strings.
Lit.: no. 254.

Tarai (Borneo – Dayak). Copper plate beaten as a signal instrument. It creates a penetrating sound.
Lit.: no. 255.

Tarai (India). Long, straight trumpet; used in pairs at Śūdra funerals.
Lit.: no. 255.

Ṭarā'iq (Arabia). Popular instrumental piece of the 10th century. Cf. *Rawāsin.*
Lit.: nos. 64, 76.

Ṭarīqa (Arabia). Instrumental prelude. Cf. *Dhikr.*
Lit.: no. 76.

Tari piring (Sumatra). Dance.
Lit.: no. 288.

Taralam (South India). *Janya rāga* of the 27th *mēḷa* (*Sarasāṅgī*).
Tone material:
C D E F A♭ B c
c B A♭ F E D C
Lit.: no. 139.

Tāram (South India). Tamil note name for *ni*, the seventh degree of the heptatonic scale. Cf. *Dravidian music.*

Tarāna (Arabia; Iran). See *Nauba.*

Tarāna (North India). Passages that use as textual material *bol* syllables.

Tarāneh (Iran). A contemporary form of *tasnif*, occasionally using Western harmony and instruments.

Taraṅgiṇī (South India). (1) See *Chārukeshī.* (2) *Janya rāga* of the 26th *mēḷa* (*Chārukeshī*).
Tone material:
C D F E D F G A♭ B♭ A♭ c
c B♭ A♭ G F E D C
Lit.: no. 139.

Taraṅgiṇī (South India). (1) The 26th *asampūrṇa mēḷa-rāga* without *kaṭapayādi* prefix. (2) The 26th *asampūrṇa mēḷa-rāga* with *kaṭapayādi* prefix. See *Rāga* (South India).
Lit.: no. 139.

Taraṇipriya (South India). *Janya rāga* of the 6th *mēḷa* (*Tānarūpi*).
Tone material:
C D♭ E♭♭ A♯ B c
c B A♯ E♭♭ D♭ C
Lit.: no. 139.

Tarannum (Arabia). Cantillations.

Tāra saptaka (India). "The upper octave." Cf. *Saptaka.*

Taratoit (Flores; Toba Batak District). Flute with a central blowhole; it has no finger holes and is played by women.
Lit.: no. 166.

Tāravam (South India). *Janya rāga* of the 15th *mēḷa* (*Māyāmāḷavagauḷa*).
Tone material:
C E F A♭ B C
c B A♭ F E C
Lit.: no. 139.

Tarawaṅgsa (Sunda District). A knee-fiddle with a body that resembles the trough of the *kachapi* (zither). Its neck and head are large and are richly ornamented. The whole instrument seems to be out of proportion. It has two or three strings. Cf. *Cai dan day.*
Lit.: no. 254.

Ṭarḥ (Egypt; Coptic). A manner of responsorial singing without interruption. Cf. *Psali*; *Ṭuruḥat.*

Tari (East Africa; Zanzibar and adjacent mainland – Swahili). See *Kabus'u.*

Tari (Java). Dance. The term appears in *sendratari* (*seni* = art, drama).

Tari asyek (*Tari inai pasir mas*) (Malaysia). Instrumental ensemble. Its instrumentation is the same as that of *makyong.*

Tarija (Morocco). Clay drum with two heads.

Tarik selampit (Malaya). Story teller who performs speaking and singing.

Tari-piring (West Sumatra; Minangkabau). An old harvest dance addressed to the rice goddess. The dancer, who performs at night, holds a plate with a lit candle. The accompaniment is played by a fiddle (*rebana*), a frame drum, and a flute (or clarinet).
Lit.: no. 288.

Ṭarīqa (Arabia; Iran). See *Nauba*; *Dhikr.*

Ta'riya (Islamic North Africa). Cylindrical drums made of clay, played in pairs.
Lit.: no. 34.

Tarjī' (Arabia). Ancient term for a refrain of the song sung by the *dājina.*
Lit.: no. 76.

Tarkīb (Arabia). An ornament performed on the lute when the player produces two notes in the same stroke. The most favored intervals are the octave and the fourth.
Lit.: no. 257.

Tarompet (West Java). "Trumpet." The Javanese *selompret*, a shawm type. The West Javanese instrument has wide wings made of coconut, fitted on the mouthpiece which fit over the lips and cheeks of the player. Cf. *Saronen.*
Lit.: no. 163.

Tarra (Morocco). A Berber drum made of clay or gourd.
Lit.: no. 255.

Ṭarrāb (Arabia). Minstrel.

Tarremut (Bismarck Archipelago). See *Garamut.*

Tarśa (India). See *Tarsha.*

Tarsha (*Tarśa*) (North India). Bengali and Marathi term for a simple clay kettledrum beaten with sticks. Other names are: *tāsā* (Arabia), *tāśah* (Hindi), *ṭamāk* (Santali), *tamukku* (Malayalam). Typical of all these drums is the preponderance of flat, irregularly-shaped clay bowls covered with thin skin. Cf. *Tamukku*; *Nakāra.*
Lit.: no. 250.

Tarumbeta (East Africa – Swahili). Trumpet.

Ṭarumbata (Morocco). Term for the western trumpet. Cf. *Turumpata būrūsī* (Turkey).

Tarumbeta yenye sauti nene sana (East Africa; Zanzibar). Swahili term for trombone.

Taruṇipriya (South India). *Janya rāga* of the 64th *mēḷa* (*Vāchaspati*).
Tone material:
C E D F♯ E G B♭ A c
c B♭ G F♯ D C
Lit.: no. 139.

Tary (Malagasy Republic – Maintirano District). Cylindrical drum.
Lit.: no. 251.

Taryong (Korea). See *Sam-hyon.*

Ṭarz-Jadīd (Middle East). *Maqām.*
Tone material:
B♭ C D E♭ F G A♭ B c
Lit.: no. 64.

Ṭarz-Nwīn (Middle East; Egypt). *Maqam.* Tone material:
C D♭ E♭ F G♭ A B♭ c
Lit.: no. 64.

Tās (*Tāsa*) (Iran). A pair of small, shallow kettledrums.
Lit.: no. 250.

Tāśah (India). See *Tās* (Iran); *Tarśa.*
Lit.: no. 250.

Taṣfīq (Islamic North Africa; Iraq). Hand clapping.

Ta shao (China—M 5943; M 5691). "Great harmony." Name of the court music ascribed to the early emperor Shun (2255-2206 B.C.).
Lit.: no. 137.

Ta sheng (China—M 5943; M 5742). The big *sheng* with 19 pipes. See also *Ch'ao.*

Tasīnfak (Former French Equatorial Africa—Mali). Side-blown horn.

Tasnif (*Ta'līf*) (Iran). The penultimate section for voice and instruments of the *dastgāh* performance. The term originally referred to the concepts of composition, elaboration, the entire song, and textual interpretation. See *Dastgāh* (formal structure). Cf. *Tarāneh.*
Lit.: no. 146.

Taswiyya (Arabia). The manner of tuning the *'ud.*

Tat (Thailand). Curved animal horn used as a signal instrument.
Lit.: no. 17.

Tata (India). General term for string instruments; mentioned in Sanskrit literature and later theoretical works. Cf. *Tantakar.*

Ta-tabola (Celebes). See *Tan-tabola.*

Tatabuan (*Tatabuhan*) (Indonesia; Moluccas). Row of 12 gongs (*bonang*) resting upon a stand with criss-cross bands. Beaten with wooden sticks. Cf. *Kromong*; *Kolintaṅ.*
Lit.: no. 254.

Tatabuhan (Indonesia; Ternate). Bamboo zither.
Lit.: no. 162.

Tatabuhan Kaju (Indonesia; Ambon Isl.). Xylophone with 10-16 keys.
Lit.: no. 162.

Tatabuan kavan (*Tatabuan veteh*; *Tagbuan*) (Indonesia). A "drum-zither"; a five-string zither where the left hand beats the strings and the right drums upon the head of the instrument.
Lit.: no. 254.

Tataganing (*Gondang*) (Sumatra—Toba Batak). A row of wooden, differently tuned barrel drums. Only one of the two heads of each drum is struck.
Lit.: no. 254.

Tataki (Japan). A stereotyped musical pattern appearing as accompaniment of lyrical sections of *samisen* music.
Lit.: no. 187.

Tata kutapa (Ancient India). See *Kutapa.*

Tatalu (Indonesia; Banggai). See *Druri dana.*

Tate (Japan). The leading singer in *nagauta* performances.
Lit.: no. 187.

Tatedi (South Africa—Sotho). Cf. *Moromthwana.*
Lit.: no. 151.

Tate-fushi-mahi (Japan). Rhythmic shield dance.
Lit.: no. 259.

Tatekoto (Japan). Standing *koto.* Term for the obsolete *kugo.*
Lit.: no. 53.

Tattabua (Indonesia; Moluccas; Halmahera). Tube zither. A toy. Cf. *Tatabuan kavan.*
Lit.: no. 254.

Ṭaṭṭari (Ancient India). Sanskrit term for musical instrument.

Tatung (Vietnam – Miao). Xylophone with nine bamboo keys.
Lit.: no. 303.

Taturi (*Turahi*). Curved brass trumpet.

Tau (Northeast New Guinea – Bukaua; Jabim). Shell horn.
Lit.: no. 255.

Tau (New Zealand – Maori). Recitation followed by speech.

Tau baalogha (Solomon Isl. – Bellona Isl.). "Noisy songs." Dance songs. Cf. *Pese hakasa'amoa.*
Lit.: no. 246.

Taueuta (Japan). Cf. *Tauyeuta.*

Taule (New Mecklenburg; New Ireland). Shell horn.
Lit.: no. 255.

Taungua (Solomon Isl.). "To sing serious songs." Cf. *Ose* (Kananga).
Lit.: no. 246.

Taure (Bismarck Archipelago; New Mecklenburg). Shell horn.
Lit.: no. 255.

Ṭāūs (India; Punjab). Term for *tajuś.* Cf. *Mayūrī.*

Ta uto (Celebes; Talaud; Banggai). Term for *buncacan.* Cf. *Rerre.*
Lit.: no. 254.

Tauwi (Bismarck Archipelago; New Mecklenburg). See *Ateba.*

Ta-uye uta (Japan). Songs sung during rice planting and various work-games.
Lit.: no. 225.

Tavalaika (*Menghi*) (South India). Friction drum.
Lit.: no. 17.

Tavil (Sri Lanka; South India). An hourglass-shaped drum. In South India the instrument can also have a cylindrical body.
Lit.: no. 260.

Tawak (Java – Semarang); Borneo – Dayak). Large suspended signalling gong. The hemispherical boss is called *buntut* and the broad and slightly curved rim is called *dada.* In South Borneo it is called *garantoṅ.* Cf. *Busut.*
Lit.: no. 162.

Ta wang (China). See *Kang t'ou.*

Tawāshīh (Islamic North Africa). See *Tawshīh.*

Tawa-tawa (Bali). Small hand-held gong.
Lit.: nos. 197, 265.

Tawaya (Oceania; New Hebrides). Jew's harp made of the bark of a coconut palm tree.
Lit.: no. 184.

Tawi (Bismarck Archipelago). Shell trumpet.
Lit.: no. 255.

Tawonan (*Sumpilan*) (Java). Cf. *Saron.*

Tawshīh (*Tawāshīh*) (Islamic North Africa). Synonym for *muwashah*; one or several sung melodies.
Lit.: no. 171.

Tawṣīl (Arabia). Glissando.

Tawul (New Guinea). Shell trumpet.
Lit.: no. 255.

Tayo (Burma). Fiddle used by blind beggars. It is an imitation of the European violin with three hemp strings.
Lit.: no. 252.

Tayub (Java). "Drinking." Social dancing at a common gathering. Cf. *Ketuk tilu*; *Joged.*

Tayuban (West Java). Dance parties. Cf. *Gamelan tiruan.*

Ta yüeh (China). Cf. *Ya yüeh.*

Tāyuś (*Tāūs*) (India). A bowed "peacock lute," an *esrāra* with four strings and 16 frets. Cf. *Mayūrī*; *Bālasarasvati*; *Mohur.*
Lit.: no. 254.

Taz (East Africa—Swahili). Sing; singsong.

Ta'ziye (Iran). Dramatic religious performance with music and spoken dialogue. See *Shbih.*

Tbel (North Africa—Berber). Large drum with two heads.

Tbn (Ancient Egypt). Tubular drum with two heads. Cf. *Śru.*
Lit.: no. 100.

Tcha pei (Kampuchea—Khmer). Large lute with a heart-shaped, richly decorated body, four strings, and 11-12 frets.
Lit.: no. 43.

Tchi (*Chi*) (Chinese: *Ch'ih*) (Korea). Bamboo or wooden transverse flute with a small, tubular mouthpiece inserted into the mouth hole. The *tchi* has five finger holes and both ends of the tube can be stopped. Into the lower end is cut a cross-shaped opening that can be closed fully or partly. The instrument is tuned chromatically from C to d♯. The 16 notes are produced by stopping, half-stopping, cross-fingering, and using the cross-shaped hole.

The *tchi* was already known in Korea during the 7th century. In recent times it is used in *ah-ak* together with the *hoon* (*hun*). Cf. *Tang chok.*
Lit.: no. 179.

Tchin-ko (Korea). See *Chin-ko.*

Tchouk (*Ch'uk*) (Chinese: *Chu*) (Korea). A rectangular wooden box with a wooden hammer inside. The *tchouk*, called the "starter," is placed to the east of the Confucian orchestra, while the *eu* (Chinese: *yü*) is called the "stopper," which is placed to the west of it.
Lit.: nos. 52, 179.

Tchul-ko (Korea). Cf. *Chol-ko.*

Tchungas (Philippines). Victory dance exalting over the ghosts of killed enemies.

Tchung-ko (*Chung-ko*) (Korea). A medium-sized barrel drum placed upon a wooden stand. The drum is beaten with a wooden mallet. The instrument is mentioned in the 15th century and was used, together with smaller drums, in military dances.
Lit.: nos. 52, 179.

Tebashul (Algeria). Cylindrical drum with two heads and a wooden body.
Lit.: no. 255.

Tebbel (Morocco). Flute.
Lit.: no. 255.

Tebe (Sumba). Jew's harp.
Lit.: no. 162.

Teblun (Sahara; Tuareg). Bowl-shaped drum with one head.
Lit.: no. 255.

Te-chang (Korea). See *Tai-chaing.*
Lit.: nos. 52, 179.

T'e-ch'ing (China—M 1164; M 6165). "Single sounding stone"; also *li-ch'ing*, China (M 1164; M 3902), the "separate *ch'ing*," is a single, L-shaped calcareous stone slab suspended from a wooden frame in the Confucian temple. The large wing of the slab is struck with a mallet in order to sound the correct starting note at the beginning of the verses of the hymn. At the end of the hymn the *t'e-ch'ing* is struck again. Cf. *Thuk kyeng.*
Lit.: nos. 136-37, 184.

T'e-chung (China—M 6165; M 1503). Single large bell. The name is used rarely; instead the terms *yung-chung* and *po-chung* have been and still are in use.
Lit.: no. 137.

Tedang (Indonesia; Alor Isl.). Jew's harp.
Lit.: no. 162.

Tedoc (Kampuchea). Wooden or bamboo cattle bell.
Lit.: nos. 190, 255.

Tedung (Bali). Term for a symbol in musical notation.
Lit.: no. 197.

Teetere (New Zealand—Maori). Trumpet made of a half blade of flax turned into a tube.

Tegoto (Japan). *Koto* interlude played within the *jiuta* cycle.
Lit.: no. 187.

Tegotomono (Japan). Term for *jiuta*, *koto* music; the term can also denote the *kumiuta* and *shirabemono* forms of *koto* music.
Lit.: no. 185.

T'e-hsüan (China). "Prominent chime," a form of *ya-yüeh* performed at plain social occasions for low-ranking officials.

Teiboro (East Guinea—Lake Kutbu area). Musical bow.
Lit.: nos. 84, 190.

Teikin (Japan). A Chinese spike fiddle. Its shape is the same as that of the *keikin*. The *teikin* has only two strings tuned to a fifth. The hair of the bow is strung between the strings.
Lit.: no. 225.

Teikyoku (Japan). *Bombai* chanted in more or less rhythmic manner. Cf. *Jokyoku*; *Yokyoku*; *Shōmyō*.

Tejian Kama (Korea). Ancient small drum.
Lit.: no. 255.

Tek (Turkey). Cf. *Usul.*

Tek (Java). As related in Lit. no. 163, a drum word indicating a stroke with one finger (index or middle) on the large drumhead.
Lit.: no. 163.

Teke (Flores—Nage). Dance and song. The dancers stand close together, stamp the ground with their feet, and perform a rocking motion. The song is led by one singer standing outside the group. The dancers join the leader in the refrain. The performance is believed to waken the dead.
Lit.: no. 166.

Tekep (Bali). The play in a specific mode; to move the fingers when playing the *suling* or *rebāb*. E.g., *tekep selisir* means playing in the *selisir* mode.
Lit.: no. 197.

Teki (Japan). Flute.
Lit.: no. 255.

Tekke (Iran). Piece of music.

Tekkin (Japan). Two rows of metallic slabs (11 and 7) resting upon a wooden resonance box.
Lit.: nos. 254-55.

Tekok (Central Borneo). Cf. *Boku* (Flores).
Lit.: no. 166.

Telali (West Borneo). Term for flute. It can mean a nose-flute with four holes, or a long flute with five holes.
Lit.: no. 255.

Telarli (Borneo—Land Dayak). Beak-flute with two different sets of finger holes: the side opposite the blowhole, the "male" side, has five holes (called *laki*). The side of the blowhole, the "female" side, has two holes (called *puan*).

Tell (Arabia). Brass string.
Lit.: no. 255.

Tellimbilla (*Telumbilla*) (Congo—Kikongo). A wooden trumpet blown from the side.
Lit.: no. 280.

Telu (Java). Slow tempo. Cf. *Wirama siji*; *Karotugel*; *Loro*; *Papat.*
Lit.: no. 163.

Telumbilla (Congo). Cf. *Tellimbilla.*

Tembang (Sunda District). Melodies recited in more or less free rhythm. Two general types are distinguished:
1. *Tembang buhun* (old-fashioned).
2. *Tembang kaäyeanaän* (modern).

Lit.: no. 163.

Tembang (Bali). Poetry; poem; melody; song.
Lit.: no. 197.

Tembang (Java). Melodies in free rhythm. Term for vocal music. Three distinct forms are distinguished:
1. Lyrical sacred epics (High Javanese): *sekar ageng*)
2. Medium type songs (*sekar madya*)
3. Simple songs (*tembang machapat*)

The text obeys rigid rules; there are fixed numbers of syllables per line and formulas concerning the use of vowels of the final syllables in each line.
Lit.: no. 163.

Tembang buhun (Java). "Old fashioned," classical singing, rhythmically free and without any accompaniment. The texts have epic or purely religious character. Three forms are distinguished:
1. *Tembang ranchag*, singing without any ornamentation. The main aim is to present the story with a clearly pronounced text.
2. *Tembang raekan*. In this form it is not the text but the singing that is essential. Performed at night; occasionally the soloist is joined by a chorus.
3. *Beluk*; it follows the *tembang raekan* early morning about 3 a.m. The precentor states line after line and the participants in turn repeat each stated line.

Tembang gedé (High Javanese: *Sekar ageng*) (Java). A song type, the texts of which show ancient sacred and epic Hindu origins. The textual strophes show classical Indian meters.
Lit.: no. 163.

Tembang kaäyeunaän (Java). "Modern," vocal music. There are three kinds:
1. *Lagam kulon*, instrumentally accompanied songs. The instruments are *kachapi, suling*; at the present time appear also guitar and mandoline. Similarly the tuning used were *melog* or *nyorog*, but at the present time Western major and minor scales are favored. People who reject the modern style and prefer the old *tembang buhun*, call the new style *kakawihan* ("imitation singing").
2. *Lagam bandung*, a style similar to *lagam kulon*, is different in ornamentation. The *rebāb* always takes part in *lagam bandung* performances.
3. *Lagam chiawian* (*lagam wetan*), songs mainly in *salendro*, sung in free rhythm.

The accompanying instruments are: *rebāb*, *gambang kayu*, *ketuk*, *kenong*, *kempul*, *goong*, *kendang*, and occasionally a *kendang leutik.* At the present time the *gambang kayu* is replaced by a *kachapi.* The songs are either loudly sung (*lagam kulon*) or gently sung (*lagam bandung*). The melodies are followed by an *alok*, a chorus when all join in the melody.
Lit.: no. 163.

Tembang machapat (Java). Simple, strophic songs. There are different opinions about these songs: they may be of recent age, or they are of very ancient age, perhaps even of pre-Hindu origin. The texts are believed to be pure Javanese; therefore the pre-Hindu theory may be of little value. For textual meters see *Machapat.* See *Tembang.*
Lit.: no. 163.

Tembang raekan (Java). See *Tembang buhun.*

Tembang ranchag (Java). See *Tembang buhun.*

Tembang tengahan (Java). The low Javanese term for the High Javanese *sekar madya*. Cf. *Tembang.*

Tembang terbang (Java). Unison choral singing with *terbang* accompaniment.

Tembong (Flores). See *Laba dera.*

Tembung (Bali). One of the five scales derived from the *saih pitu*.
Lit.: no. 197.

Temeṭṭama (Sri Lanka). Ancient frame drum. Cf. *Ṭimbutu*; *Tambaṭṭam.*
Lit.: no. 190.

Temir-komuz (Central Asia; Kirgizia). Jew's harp usually played by women.
Lit.: nos. 91, 275.

Temmyō (Japan). See *Koto* (parts).

Tempas (West Java). A small *terbang.*

Tempuku (Japan). A small vertical bamboo flute with four finger holes.
Lit.: no. 185.

Temraga (New Hebrides; Torres and Banks Isl.). A scraper played at funerals.
Lit.: no. 84.

Temur (Mongolia). Also *aman-khuur*. An almost obsolete jew's harp. Originally it was used by shamans.
Lit.: nos. 60-61.

Ṭenar jap (East India; Orissa). Cymbals.

Tenbar (Arabia). Drum.
Lit.: no. 255.

Tendor (Southeast India—Hill Maria; Abujhmar mountains; Gond tribes). Jew's harp made of iron in form of a hoop.
Lit.: no. 135.

Tengah (*Tenggok*) (Indonesia; Majakerta). The second note of *slendro* and *pelog* systems as used in Majakerta. Cf. *Slendro*; *Pelog.*

Tengah (Central Java). Another term for *ḍaḍa*, the third note of the *slendro* of Central Java. Cf. *Slendro.*
Lit.: no. 163.

Tengah (*Tangah*) (Java). The middle tone; the middle octave; middle range and octave. Cf. *Seḍeng.*
Lit.: no. 163.

Tengahan (Java). Moderate volume of sound. Poetic meters; see *Machapat.*
Lit.: no. 163.

Teng-dyu (Sikkim—Lepcha). See *K'a-pi.*

Tenggo' (Indonesia; Madura). The second note of *slendro* (in Madura). Cf. *Slendro.*
Lit.: no. 163.

Tenggok (Indonesia; Banyuwangi; Mahkerta). See *Tengah.*

Tenggok (Indonesia; Jombang; Prabalingga). Also *gulu*. The second note of *slendro* (of Jombang and Prabalingga). Cf. *Slendro.*
Lit.: no. 163.

Tengihea (Polynesia; Tongo Isl.). Mourning song.

Teng-teng (Sikkim—Lepcha). Small flat brass plaque usually in the form of a triangular cloud. It is used in ceremonial music and is beaten with a small stick. The plaque has a pleasant high tone.

Teng-teng (Java; Madura). An instrumental ensemble that gets its name from its leading instrument, a small xylophone. Other instruments of the ensemble are: a *kechrek*; a slit-drum; two bamboo idiochords, each with one string; and a *chontang*. Another form of the

teng-teng (ensemble) are: two *sarons* (*teng-teng*), one *gambang*, two *kendang*, one *kencher*, one *gong guchi.* The tuning is *pelog*.
Lit.: no. 163.

Tepak (Java; Jogya). A drum word that indicates a stroke that creates a dull sound called *tak*.
Lit.: no. 163.

Tepan-tepan (Northwest New Guinea; Mac Cluer Gulf). Drum.
Lit.: no. 255.

Tepma (New Guinea). Ritual, round coconut flute. Women are not allowed to see it.
Lit.: no. 312.

Terbana (Bali). Small flat kettledrum. It is played together with flutes as accompaniment of *janger* and *arja* performances.
Lit.: no. 197.

Terbang (Java). Frame drum similar to the *ḍogḍog*. It is never used in the *gamelan*; beggars and itinerant songsters (*chokekan*) like to use it. They use its sound as accompaniment of reciting tales, offering sage counsel, offering virtuous advice, and describing tortures of hell. Today the *terbang* can be found (and called *rebana*) in West Java and the Sunda Archipelago. Cf. *Tembang terbang*; *Macham garongan*; *Kentrung*.
Lit.: no. 163.

Terbang batok (West Java). A tiny *terbang* made of a coconut shell (*batok* = coconut shell). Cf. *Terbang*.

Terbang benjangan (West Java). See *Terbang besar*.

Terbang besar (West Java). The largest *terbang* in West Java. The term is mostly used in the regency of Lebak. Elsewhere the *terbang* is called *gembyung*. In Tasikmalaya this *terbang* is called *terbang benjangan*. Cf. *Terbang*.
Lit.: no. 163.

Terbang gembrung (West Java). A medium-sized *terbang*. Cf. *Pichung lingkup*.

Terbang genjring (West Java). See *Terbang ketimpring*.

Terbang ketimpring (West Java). A flat and small *terbang*; it has two or three small jingling metal discs placed into slits in the side walls. The term appears mainly in the Regency of Lebak. Elsewhere (cf. *Terbang besar*) the *terbang* is called *gembyung* or *terbang genjring*. The latter (also *terbang genjring*) can also indicate an instrumental ensemble with or without a *kendang* that plays accompaniments to songs (often songs with corrupted Arabic words) sung at circumcisions, weddings, and other Mohammedan festivities.
Lit.: no. 163.

Terbang mumuludan (West Java). An instrumental ensemble of five *terbangs* and one *bajidor*. It accompanies religious songs.
Lit.: no. 163.

Terbang salawat (West Java). An orchestra consisting of four *terbangs* and one *kendang*.

Terbangan (Java). See *Slawatan*.

Teruding (Borneo – Dusun). Jew's harp.
Lit.: no. 255.

Terukoothu (South India). Folk theatrical show presenting songs, dances, and prose, all linked with religious events.

Teshaku odori (Ryūkyū; Okinawa). Music and dance at the rice-serving.
Lit.: no. 215.

Teteg (Java). See *Bedug*.

Tetekan (Java). A *kentongan* made of a bamboo tube shaped into a slit-drum.
Lit.: no. 163.

Tete lile (Java; Solo). Term used for *saron panerus*.

Tétèprèt (Java; Banyumas District). The name of *selompret.* Also called *tetet* (in East Java).
Lit.: no. 163.

Tetere (New Zealand—Maori). A wind instrument made of twisted flax blades. Occasionally a beating reed is used. *Tetere* serves as a signal instrument but is also used as a toy. Cf. *Pu tatara*; *Pu kihi.*
Lit.: no. 7.

Tetet (Java). Cf. *Tetepret*; *Gamelan saronen*; *Saronen.*

Tetjer (Java). A set of two gongs.
Lit.: no. 255.

Teuk-chong (Korea). Single bell suspended in an ornamented wooden frame. See the Chinese *T'e-chung.*
Lit.: no. 179.

Teuk-kyeng (Korea). Term for the Chinese *t'e-ch'ing.* A single calcareous stone slab suspended in a wooden frame, placed in the Confucian temple. The stone is tuned to the basic note of the hymn and is struck at the beginning and the end of the hymn.
Lit.: no. 179.

Tevaram (South India). Ancient poetic text sung by two men; it forms part of the *shloka(m)*, the final item of the *bharata nāṭya* performance.

Tewur (Indonesia; Kai Isl.). Shell trumpet. See *Atvur.*
Lit.: no. 156.

T'guthe (South Africa—Hottentots). A fiddle made of one piece of wood; it is a primitive imitation of the Western violin.
Lit.: no. 255.

T'ha (South Africa). Bushman name for *gora.*
Lit.: no. 151.

Tha (Thailand). Right hand drum beat on the *tapone.* The stroke is the same as *theng*, but in *tha*, immediately after the stroke and withdrawing of the hand, hand and fingers of the player move immediately back to the drum in order to dampen the vibrating drumhead.

Thachin-gan (Burma). See *Thachin gyi.*

Thachin-gyi (Burma). Old court songs.

Thae (Korea). See *Yul-cha-po.*
Lit.: no. 136.

Thae-p'yong-so (Korea). See *Tai-pyeng-so* (*T'ai-p'ing-hsiao*) (China).

Thai (Thailand). Term that indicates a simple pentatonic style of music. The five notes are taken from the basic heptatonic scale with equidistant intervals. Cf. *Mon.*

Thak (Korea). Simple bell or jingle often used in martial dances. Cf. *To* (China); *Taku* (Japan).
Lit.: no. 52.

Than-bya tyaw hsit-kyi (or *Pat sabo*) (Burma). See *Chauk-pauk auk-pyan.*

Thandanda (South Africa—Venda). Wooden clappers; carved sticks.
Lit.: no. 151.

Thang (Thailand). Tone name of the first note of the *ranat ek* and *ranat lek* scale (heptatonic, with equidistant intervals between the seven degrees). All tone names are:
1. *Thang* ("sound").
2. *Rong thang* ("second," "low tone").
3. *Oat* ("voice").
4. *Klang* ("middle").
5. *Phong oar* (name of the fifth tone).
6. *Kruert* ("high tone").
7. *Nork* ("outside").

Lit.: no. 58.

Than-gyat (Burma). See *Chauk-pauk auk-pyan.*

Thanh chieng (Vietnam; former Annam). The bent rim of the *chieng* (gong).

Than-hman (Burma). "Correct sound." Tone name, derived from *hne* playing. Below are shown the seven tone names of the *hne*:

1. *Than-hman*, "correct sound," tone name for the tonic, basic note.
2. *Hnapauk*, "second fingerhole" (of the *hne*), seventh degree (counted in descending order).
3. *Thon-bauk*, "third fingerhole" (of the *hne*), sixth degree (counted in descending order).
4. *Lei-bauk*, "fourth fingerhole" (of the *hne*), fifth degree (in descending order).
5. *Nga-bauk*, "fifth fingerhole" (of the *hne*), fourth degree (in descending order).
6. *Chauk-pauk*, "sixth fingerhole" (of the *hne*), third degree (in descending order).
7. *Hkun-nathan-gyi*, "great seventh sound" (of the *hne*), second degree (in descending order).

See *Pat-tala*; *Hsaing-waing*.

Than-hwin (Burma). Also *than-kvin*; *than-lvin*. Bronze cymbal with large boss and flat rim.
Lit.: no. 255.

Than-kvin (*Than-lvin*) (Burma). Cf. *Than-hwin.*

Than la (Vietnam). Cf. *Cai than(h) la.*

Than-lat auk-pyan (Burma). See *Chauk-pauk auk-pyan.*

Than lvin (Burma). Cf. *Than-hwin.*
Lit.: no. 252.

Thanthona (South India; Tanjore). Plucked drum used by beggars. It is similar to the *Yektar* but has two strings.
Lit.: no. 198.

Than-yo (*Hkun-nathan-gyi*) (Burma). See *Chauk-pauk auk-pyan.*

Than-yo chauk-pauk (Burma). Names of *hsaing-waing* modes:

1. *Than-yo chauk-pauk*:	C E F G B
2. *Hkun-nathan-gyi*:	G B C D F
3. *Pat-sabo*:	C D E G A
4. *Nga-bauk*:	F G A C D
5. *Hsit-kye* (or *hnapauk*):	B C D F G
6. *Nga-pauk auk-pyan*:	F A B C D
7. *Lei-bauk auk*:	G A B D E
8. *Than-yo hnapauk*:	B C E F G

Thao (Thailand). A variation form using three tempo renditions: a brief melody performed in a moderate tempo (*song chan*) is followed by an "extended version" in which all notes of the "moderate version" are extended to twice the original duration (*sam chan*). For instance, a quarter note of "moderate version" becomes now a half note in the lower "extended version." This second part is followed by a contracted endpiece in which all notes have only one half the durational values of the original ("moderate") version. This last, fast section is called *chan dio*.
Lit.: no. 208.

Thap (Thailand). Cf. *Thon.*

Thap luc (Former Annam). Cf. *Cai dan thap luc.*

Thapon (*Sphon*) (Thailand). Barrel drum.

Thappattai (South India). Small or medium sized frame drum played with one hand while the other beats a *śēmakkalam.*
Lit.: no. 260.

Thaqāl (Arabia). Solemn, dignified tempo and rhythm.

Thaqīl (Arabia). See *Al-taqīl.*

Thāt (North India). The Hindi (dialectal) term for the Sanskrit *thāṭa.*

Thāṭa (North India). "Parent scale" from which *rāgas* are derived. North Indian music now uses 10 *thāṭas* introduced by Vishnu Nārāyan Bhatkhande (1860-1936). He applied the South Indian system of *Mēḷa (Janaka)-Janya* to North Indian music. The 10 *thāṭas* are:

1. *Kalyan*:	C	D	E	F♯	G	A	B	c
2. *Bilaval*:	C	D	E	F	G	A	B	c
3. *Khamaj*:	C	D	E	F	G	A	B♭	c
4. *Bhairav*:	C	D♭	E	F	G	A♭	B	c
5. *Purvi*:	C	D♭	E	F♯	G	A♭	B	c
6. *Marva*:	C	D♭	E	F♯	G	A	B	c
7. *Kafi*:	C	D	E♭	F	G	A	B♭	c
8. *Asavari*:	C	D	E♭	F	G	A♭	B♭	c
9. *Bhairavi*:	C	D♭	E♭	F	G	A♭	B♭	c
10. *Todi*:	C	D♭	E♭	F♯	G	A♭	B	c

Lit.: no. 138.

Theka (India). Drum phrase. A series of more or less fixed drum strokes represented by *bols* (drum words). Every *tāla* can be expressed by a *theka*. Elaborate *thekas* are called *parands* (variations). For details see Lit. no. 136, pp. 218-63.

Theme (South Africa—Sotho). Cf. *Moromthwana.*
Lit.: no. 151.

Theng (Thailand). A drum beat on the *tapone* performed with the right hand. The beating fingers, held straight, strike the rim of the drumhead and, when withdrawing the hand immediately after the stroke, the head of the drum head is allowed to vibrate freely.
Lit.: no. 208.

Therukootu (South India). Folk theater.

Thevhula (South Africa—Venda). Sacrificial funeral rites for the ruler.

Thimila (South India; Kerala). A long hourglass-shaped drum. It has two heads but the drum is played only on one side with the bare palms. In the past the *thimila* was in use throughout the South. Now it appears only in Kerala in a temple ritual.
Lit.: no. 236.

Thith (Melanesia; New Caledonia). Nose flute.
Lit.: no. 313.

Thod rnga (Tibet). Rattle-drum made of human skull bones in hourglass form. The bones are from persons who died an unnatural death. Cf. *Damaru.*
Lit.: no. 143.

Thoe (Thailand). Term for a short drum beat. See *Song na.*
Lit.: no. 208.

Thoeng (Thailand). See *Thoe.*

Thoet (Thailand). A drum beat on the *tapone* performed by the right hand. The fingers are held straight as in *theng*, but remain on the rim after the stroke and thus prevent the drumhead from vibrating.
Lit.: no. 208.

Tho-ko (Korea). Cf. *To-ko.*

Thomo (*Tuomo*) (South Africa—Basuto). Musical bow with a central calabash. Cf. *Segwana.*
Lit.: no. 151.

Thōṅ (*Thap*) (Thailand). Drum with one head. Its form is that of a large clay goblet, richly ornamented. The *thōṅ* is used in *mahori* and *piphat* ensembles. Cf. *O-tsi.*
Lit.: no. 254.

Thōṅ-bauk (Burma). See *Than-hman.*

Thong (Kampuchea). Richly ornamented drum shaped in the form of a goblet.

Thonk (*Paṭ*) (India). Term for "staccato."

Thon-pauk (Burma). Tone name. See *Pat-tala*; *Hsaing-waing.*

Thoum (Sudan). See *Tom.*

Thrap'pa (Tibet). Dance used in religious entertainment.

Thre-ling (Tibet). Large (transverse) flute. Its honorific term is *sh'e-ling.*

Thro (Burma; Indonesia). String instrument; a *rebāb* type with three silken or horsehair strings.
Lit.: no. 255.

Thuk-chong (Korea). Cf. *T'e-chung* (China). A special clapperless bell suspended within a frame, tuned to the basic note (*huang-chung*; *hwang-chung*). It is struck only at the beginning of a hymn in the temple of palace.
Lit.: no. 52.

Thuk-kyeng (*Teuk-kyeng*; *Thuk-kyong*) (Korea). A L-shaped stone plate made of green jade, marble, or soap stone, suspended in an ornamented wooden frame. It is struck with a hammer made of soft horn at the beginning and end of hymns and verses. Cf. *T'e-ch'ing* (China).
Lit.: no. 52.

Thukūb (Arabia). Finger holes in the *mizmār* and related oboe types.

Thum (*Nyatiti*) (Kenya—Luo). Lyre with 6-8 strings. Cf. *Tom.*
Lit.: no. 157.

Thume lek (Thailand). See *Ranat thong thume.*

Thume mai (Thailand). See *Ranat thume.*

Thumri (India). Hindu love song (its Mohammedan counterpart is the *ghazal*). Its simple melody can often appear in theatrical and dance music. *Thumris* are light and popular, occasionally of religious nature.
Lit.: no. 138.

Thung-so (Korea). See *Tong-so.*

Thungwa (South Africa—Venda). While the *ngoma* of the Venda is used in ceremonies, the *thungwa*, a smaller sized *ngoma*, has less ceremonial character. It has been described as "tenor drum."
Lit.: no. 151.

Thuong trieu nhac (Vietnam). Music of plain assemblies. Court music.

Thupa (Ancient Aramaic; Syria; Israel). See *Tof.*

Thura (Fiji Isl.). Tiba made of bamboo.
Lit.: no. 255.

Thuzo (South Africa—Venda). Leg rattle. Cf. *Mutshakatha.*
Lit.: no. 151.

Tī (*T'i*) (Malaya; Malacca). Tube zither.
Lit.: no. 254.

T'i (China). See *Chien tzu.*

Ti (*Ti-tzu*; *Ti-tse*) (China—M 6217—M 6939). Transverse flute. Its bamboo tube is beautifully lacquered and has six finger holes. A separate hole is covered with a thin skin or paper.
Lit.: nos. 137, 209.

Ṭi (India). See *Din.*

Tia (North India). The three times repeated drum passage of the *mohra.*
Lit.: no. 136.

Tianko (Nigeria—Yoruba). See *Tioko.*

Tiao (China—M 6298). Mode; scale based upon each note of a basic scale. Ancient Chinese music theory mentions scales which begin either with *kung*, *shang*, or *chiao*, *chih*, *yü* called *kung-tiao*, *shang-tiao*, and so forth. Foreign modes were called *wai-tiao.*
Lit.: nos. 93, 209.

T'iao (China—M 6282). See *Chien-tzu.*
Lit.: no. 136.

Tiao-i (China—M 6298; M 2960). Cf. *I* (China).
Lit.: no. 93.

Tiao-tzu (China—M 6298; M 6939). Melody; air.

Tiape (Philippines—Mindanao). Three-string lute.
Lit.: no. 255.

Ti ba (Vietnam). Pear-formed lute with four silken strings. Cf. *P'i-p'a.*

Tibura (Northwest Guinea—Barriai).
Lit.: no. 255.

Tibbu (Ancient Mesopotamia—Akkad). See *Timbutu.*

T'i-ch'in (China—M 6233; M 1103). A fiddle (*erh-hsien*) with a body made of a coconut shell or bamboo section. The instrument has two strings and is frequently used in Shanghai. Cf. *Hu-ch'in*; *Hu-hu*; *Ti-kum* (of Canton).
Lit.: no. 209.

Tid (*Tad*) (North India; Punjab). Fiddle of village musicians. It has four wire strings and three resonance strings strung below the bowed strings. The instrument has a round body which is not covered at its upper half.
Lit.: no. 254.

Tidinit (Mauretania). A lute, occasionally bowed, with a flat body and four strings.
Lit.: no. 190.

Tiḍur (Java). Tambourin.
Lit.: no. 255.

Tiḍuran (Java). Ground zither with one rattan string.
Lit.: no. 163.

T'ieh (China—M 6327). Term for a secondary (stereotyped) role of an operatic actor.
Lit.: no. 183.

T'ieh ma (China). See *Yen-ma.*

T'ieh pan (China—M 6332; M 4885) (*T'ieh P'ai*; China—M 6332; M 4871). An iron slab struck with a short piece of iron, an instrument of blind fortunetellers. Frequently used in Hangchow and Shanghai.
Lit.: no. 209.

T'ieh ti (China). A common, popular iron transverse flute.
Lit.: no. 209.

T'ien (China—M 6362). See *Hsüan.*

T'ien-chu (music) (China). See *Shih-pu-chi.*

Tien-erh (North China). Small gong.
Lit.: no. 209.

Tien-ku (China). Small, flat punctuating drum beaten with two light rods.
Lit.: no. 209.

Tien-tzu (China). A gong of iron or brass suspended in a wooden frame and placed at the gates of temples, official buildings, and monasteries.
Lit.: no. 209.

Tieu (Vietnam). Vertical bamboo or bronze flute with five holes in front and one at the back. Cf. *Hsiao* (China).

Tieu cō (Vietnam). Term for a small drum with two heads.

Tieu nhac (Vietnam). "Small music" (Chinese: *hsiao-yüeh*). Music for the people. Cf. *Nha Nhac.*
Lit.: no. 296.

Tifa (North Moluccas; Halmahera). Goblet-shaped drum.
Lit.: no. 162.

'Tifa-gong (Indonesia; Ceram Isl.). A *tondu* (Flores).

Tifal (*Tival*) (Moluccas). See *Tifa.*
Lit.: no. 254.

Ti-fang hsi (China – M 6198; M 1802; M 2452). Popular musical dramas of the Ming period, subject to numerous, often unexpected, changes by the performers. The *ti-fang hsi* performances are regional and have dialectal features. These operatic styles have numerous names. A few are mentioned below:

1. *I-yang ch'iang* (of I-yang, Kiangsi).
2. *Ch'ing-yang ch'iang* (of Anhwei).
3. *Ch'ing-hsi* (of Hupeh and Szechwan).
4. *Ching-ch'iang* (of Peking).
5. *Kao-ch'iang* (of Kwantung).
6. *Hsiang-chü* (of Hunan).
7. *Kan-chü* (of Kiangsi).
8. *Ch'uan-ch'i* (of Szechwan).
9. *Kun-tiao.*
10. *K'un-ch'ü.*
11. *Pang-tzu ch'iang.*
12. *P'i-huang* (*erh-huang* and *hsi-p'i*).

Lit.: no. 183.

Tigi (*Tī-gū*) (Sumeria). Obscure term. In various translations it is designated as a musical instrument (perhaps a percussion instrument or a vertical flute), or as a special type of hymn. Lit.: no. 94.

Tihal (Lesser Sunda Isl.). Wooden goblet drum. Cf. *O-tsi* (Burma).
Lit.: no. 254.

Tihang (Sunda District). See *Rebāb* (Sunda).

Tihar (*Bibiliku*) (Timor). Small drum in the shape of a goblet.
Lit.: no. 162.

Tik- (Arabia; Iran). See *Taq-*.

Ṭikārā (India). Two pairs of kettledrums. One pair consists of the *dāmāmā* and *ṭikārā*, and the other of *ḍāgarā* and *jhāriḍāp*.
Lit.: no. 254.

Tikel (Java). The outer ridge of the *wideng(an)*. Cf. *Rai.*
Lit.: no. 163.

Tik-ḥijāz (Arabia). Tone name. (All tone names within two octaves are listed under the heading of *Jagā* [*Yagā*].) See also *Taq-ḥijāz.*

Tik-ḥiṣār (Arabia). See *Taq-ḥiṣār.* Cf. *Tik-ḥijāz.*

Tik-jawāb-ḥijāz (Arabia). See *Jwab-taq-ḥijāz* (*ṣaba*). Cf. *Tik-ḥijāz.*

Tiko (Pulau-Pulau Isl.). Bamboo stamping stick.

Ti-ko-tzu (China – M 6198; M 3376; M 6939). "Pigeon on the ground." Humming top made of bamboo. Cf. *K'ung-cheng.*
Lit.: no. 209.

Tik-qarar-ḥiṣār (Arabia). See *Taq-qarār-qaba.* Cf. *Tik-ḥijāz.*

Tik-shāh-nāz (Arabia). See *Taq-shāh'nāz.* Cf. *Tik-ḥijāz.*

Tiktirī (India; Sri Lanka). Sanskrit term for the snake-charmer's double clarinet (see *Binjogi*). Cf. *Pungī* (North India); *Maguḍi* (South India); *Tūmerī* (Sri Lanka); also *Nāsajantra*; *Pāngrā*; *Tuṅbī*; *Tubrī*. Cf. also *Pāmbūnāgasūram*; *Meshek.*
Lit.: no. 254.

Ti-ku (China). See *Sha-ku.*

Ti-kum (China). Cantonese term for *t'i-ch'in.*

Ti-kurikut (Indonesia; Mentawai Isl.). Whizzing box. See *Jata* (Flores).
Lit.: no. 166.

Tik-zirgūlāh (*Tik-zirkulāh*) (Arabia). See *Taq zarkalā.* Cf. *Tik-ḥijāz.*

Tilakaprakāśini (South India). *Janya rāga* of the 6th *mēḷa* (*Tānarūpi*).
Tone material:

C D♭ E♭♭ F G A♯ B c
c B G F E♭♭ D♭ C

Lit.: no. 139.

Tilak-Kamod (North India). Light *rāga* ascribed to the *Khamaj thāta*.
Tone material:
C D F G B c
c B A G (F) E D C; *Vādis*: D, G
Lit.: no. 138.

Tilam (Java). See *Kenḍangan*; *Rebāb* (Java).

Tilang (North India). Light *rāga* ascribed to the *Khamaj thāta.*
Tone material:
C E F G (A) B c
c B♭ (A) G F E (D) C; *Vādis*: E, B
Lit.: no. 138.

Tilik Abero (Ethiopia). Ceremonial heavy kettledrum of the Christian church, carried on a strap placed around the player's neck.
Lit.: no. 102.

Tilingting (West Java). See *Ḍogḍog.*

Tillānā (India). A song having as text an invocation of Rama and other deities. The text is concluded by a series of tone names such as *sa ri ga ma pa*, etc. This song appears as music for the last section of the *bharata nāṭyam* performance.

Tilvada (India). See *Tāla.*

Timbana (Sudan). Term for drum.
Lit.: no. 95.

Timbila (Mozambique – Chopi; Ronga). Xylophone in four sizes (treble-bass) in ensembles.
Lit.: no. 33.

Timbo (Ethiopia). The Galla people use this word for the *massaneqo* and *kerar.*
Lit.: no. 102.

Timbūtu (*Tibbu*; *Tabālu*) (Ancient South Mesopotamia). Frame drum. Cf. *Temettama* (Śri Lanka); *Tambaṭṭam* (South India).

Timiratāriṇi (South India). *Janya rāga* of the 17th *mēḷa* (*Sūryakānta*).
Tone material:
C D♭ F A B c
c B A F D♭ C
Lit.: no. 139.

Timiri (South India). A small *nāgasara.* Cf. *Iḍaibāri.*
Lit.: no. 260.

T'i-mu (China – M 6238; M 4596). "Superscription," subtitles of particular parts of the melody that express inspiring subjects to the creative artist (e.g., "waterfall," "moon reflected in the lake").
Lit.: no. 93.

Tin (Burma; Shan). Lute with three strings. Cf. *Tinse.*
Lit.: no. 252.

Tin (North India). See *Din.*

Tinbuk (*Tutupele*) (New Britain; South New Ireland; Bismarck Archipelago). Xylophone consisting of two slabs.
Lit.: no. 84.

Tindi de kileru (Congo). Ground zither.
Lit.: no. 176.

Tinding (Flores). Bamboo tube zither. Cf. *Bemu nggri-nggo.*
Lit.: no. 156.

Tinebtebak (Philippines). Cf. *Itundak.*

Ting (Thailand). Specific drum beat. See *Song na.* The beat is performed on the *tapone* by the left hand. It is executed in the same manner as *theng.*

Tingkah (*Tingka*) (Sumatra). Cylindrical wooden frame drum with two goatskin heads. It is struck with the knuckles.
Lit.: no. 255.

Ting Ning (Vietnam). Tube zither with eight or more metal strings and two gourd resonators.
Lit.: no. 190.

Tingšak (Mongolia). Clappers.
Lit.: no. 248.

Ting-shags (Tibet). Small, cup-shaped cymbals.
Lit.: no. 143.

Ting-yin (China). See *Chien-tzu* (of Yin).
Lit.: no. 136.

Tinh tau (*Dan tinh*) (Vietnam). Lute with a long neck and a gourd as sound box. The number of strings varies.

Tinki-besar (Borneo). See *Gulung-gulung.*

Tinkie-hetjil (Borneo). See *Gulung-gulung.*

Tinse (Burma; Shan). Lute made of one piece of wood. It has three strings and is played with a plectrum. Cf. *Tin.*
Lit.: no. 252.

Tintal (*Trital*) (North India). Cf. *Tāla.*

Tiṅ thailā (Assam—Naga). Spike fiddle with a gourd body and one string.
Lit.: no. 252.

Tin-tin-sags (Tibet). See *Ting-shags.*

Tioko (*Tianko*) (Nigeria—Yoruba). Vertical flute made of bamboo or ivory with 2-3 finger holes.

Tiparu (Brit. New Guinea; Papua). Bull roarer.
Lit.: no. 311.

Tipcha (Ancient Israel). Notational symbol (֖) used in biblical chant, indicating a weak disjunctive function.
Lit.: no. 309.

Ṭipri (Ancient India). See *Daṇḍa.*

Tirasi (Japan). See *Jiuta.*

Tiraskaraṇi (South India). *Janya rāga* of the 19th *mēḷa* (*Jhaṅkāradhvani*).
Tone material:
C D E♭ A♭ B♭♭ c
c B♭♭ A♭ E♭ D C
Lit.: no. 139.

Tīrghika (South India). *Janya rāga* of the 7th *mēḷa* (*Senāpāti*).
Tone material:
C D♭ E♭ A♭ B♭♭ c
c B♭♭ A♭ E♭ D♭ C
Lit.: no. 139.

Tiripa (India). See *Gamaka.*

Tiruchinnam (South India). Tamil term for a pair of temple trumpets played by one player simultaneously. Both ends of the tubes are held in the player's mouth. The *tiruchinnam* bears also the name *śri churnam.*
Lit.: nos. 26, 250.

Tiryāl (Arabia). Frame drum.
Lit.: no. 109.

Tit (*Tid*) (India). Basic *tabla* stroke for the right hand. The 2nd, 3rd, and 4th fingers jointly strike the center of the *siahi* and, after the stroke, remain on the drumhead. Cf. *Bōl.*
Lit.: no. 136.

Ti-ta (China). See *Tai-tik.*

T'i-t'ang (China—M 6233; M 6110). A small, shallow bowl-shaped gong made of thick brass is carried by a string and is struck with a wooden stick by vendors of candy. It can be heard frequently at funerals and ceremonies in Peking and Shanghai.
Lit.: no. 209.

Titapu (Polynesia; Tubuai Isl.). (1) Musical bow with one or several strings. The player holds one end of the bow in his mouth. (2) Jew's harp (Marquesas Isl.).
Lit.: nos. 84, 190.

Titil (*Peking*) (West Java; Cheribon; Indramayu). Term for the highest sounding *saron.*
Lit.: no. 163.

Titilaras anḍa (Java; Jogjakarta). "Ladder notation" that was used in the palace. It is a notational system consisting of vertical lines (seven for *pelog* and six for *slendro*) crossed by horizontal lines which indicate the *wirama* to a player who already knows melody and tempo to some degree.

Titilaras kepatihan (Java). A notational system more favored than the other forms (*titilaras rante*; *titilaras anda*). The pitches are indicated by abbreviated number-names: *ji* [1] *siji*; *ro* [2] *loro*; *lu* [3] *telu*; *pat* [4] *papat*; *ma* [5] *lima*; *nem* [6] *nem*; *pi* [7] *pitu* or *tu* [7] *pitu*.

Titilaras rante (Java). "Chain notation." A notational system using Arabic numerals and a staff of 13 lines.

Titimotiti (Congo). Ground bow.
Lit.: no. 176.

Titir (*Kentongan*) (Java; Celebes). See *Kulkul.*

Ti-tzu (China—M 6217; M 6939). A popular transverse flute. It appears in various sizes: long, short, a peasant's *ti*, and others. The flute is made of bamboo and has six finger holes and additional holes for ornamental purpose. Next to the mouth hole is one covered by a thin membrane. The instrument is used in the theater, at funerals, weddings, and processions. Cf. *Sei-teki* (Japan).
Lit.: nos. 137, 183.

Titti (South India). Telugu, Kannarese, and Malayalam term for *śruti-upāṅga.*

Tittibadhvani (South India). *Janya rāga* of the 11th *mēḷa* (*Kokilapriya*).
Tone material:

C D♭ E♭ A B c
c B A E♭ D♭ C

Lit.: no. 139.

Tituit (Java). Small slit-stop flute.
Lit.: no. 163.

Tiva (Indonesia; Tanembar; Kai Isl.). A wooden goblet-shaped drum. Other names of the instrument are:

1. *Katambon* (*kasambonan*) (of Borneo).
2. *Fondrahi* (of Nias).
3. *Kralu* (of Celebes).
4. *Tuba* (of Buru and Sula Besi).
5. *Nakotiba* (of Northeast Timor).
6. *Tihal* (of East Timor and Letti).
7. *Tivele* (of Sermata).

Lit.: nos. 156, 254.

Tival (*Tifal*) (Celebes). Cylindrical drum with a palm wood body and a single head. The instrument is used in religious ceremonies. Cf. *O-tsi* (Burma).
Lit.: no. 132.

Tivele (Moluccas; Sermata Isl.). Wooden goblet-shaped drum.
Lit.: no. 254.

Tivolu (Celebes). Small metal bell in the shape of a globule containing little stones. Clusters of these bells are attached to a branch or tied to a string placed around the waists of young dancers.
Lit.: no. 132.

Tīvra (North India). Notational symbol; a small vertical line placed on top on the tone syllable *ma.* At the present time *ma tīvra* indicates the note F♯ (assuming that *sa* is C and *ma* is F). *Tīvra* is notated only in the North, not in the South of India. The term (not the symbol) can also be used occasionally to indicate a "natural" if there had been a "flat" of the same degree preceding. Music theorists of ancient India employed the terms *tīvra*, *tīvratar*, and *tīvratam*, referring to *śrutis. Tīvra*, in the case of *ma*, would mean only one *śruti* higher, *tīvratar* two, and *tīvratam* three *śrutis* higher, a terminology not in use any more. Cf. *ati.*

Tīvra (India). Rhythm. See *Tāla.*

Tīvratar (North India). Cf. *Tīvra.*

Tīvratam (North India). Cf. *Tīvra.*

Tivravahiṇi (South India). *Janya rāga* of the 46th *mēḷa* (*Ṣaḍvidhamārgiṇī*).
Tone material:
C D♭ E♭ F♯ G A G B♭ c
c B♭ A G F♯ E♭ D♭ E♭ F♯ D♭ C
Lit.: no. 139.

Tivravāhini (South India). (1) The 46th *asampūrṇa mēḷa-rāga* without *kaṭapayādi* prefix. (2) The 46th *asampūrṇa mēḷa-rāga* with *kaṭapayādi* prefix was called *Sthavarajam.* See *Rāga* (South India).
Lit.: no. 139.

Tiwa (Indonesia; Moluccas; Kai Isl.). Drum in the shape of a goblet.
Lit.: no. 162.

Tja (Thailand). Term for a specific drum beat. See *Song na.*

Tjalempung (*Chalempung*; *Chelempung*) (Sumatra; Java). Zither with 13 double wire strings. Its corpus, a rhomboid-like box, rests on four feet. The instrument is used in the *gamelan* ensemble.
Lit.: nos. 215, 255.

Tjalimpueṅ (Sumatra). Cf. *Talimpueṅ*; *Chelempung.*

Tjalonarang (*Chalonarang*) (Bali). Dance drama with music provided by the *gamelan bebarongan.*

Tjaluṅ (*Tjalang*; *Chalung*) (Java). A xylophone consisting of 11 to 14 bamboo tube-segments tied together like a rope-ladder. When used the player ties one end of the rope to a tree, the other around his knee.
Lit.: no. 254.

Tjanang (Sumatra). Gong.
Lit.: no. 255.

Tjanang trieng (*Chanang trieng*) (Indonesia; Sumatra). Bamboo zither with three strings.
Lit.: no. 162.

Tjapāra (Korea). See *Chapāra.* The term is used in *saron tjelurin*, the highest pitched *saron* where the plates are substituted by bronze cups. Cf. *Cheluring.*
Lit.: no. 163.

Tjelurin (Java). The term is used in *saron tjelurin*, the highest pitched *saron*, where the plates are substituted by bronze cups. The number of plates or cups is variable; frequently there are seven. Cf. *Cheluring.*
Lit.: no. 163.

Tjeng-tjeng (*Cheng-cheng*) (Bali). Cymbals. Cf. *Kechicher.*

Tjilempung (*Chelempung*) (Java). Zither with 13 double strings.

Tjilempung (Central Sumatra). A row of gongs.
Lit.: no. 159.

Tjing (Korea). Also *gwangmagi* (deep-sounding gong). Cf. *Ching* (Korea).

Tjuriga (*Churiga*) (South Celebes). A knife-shaped iron rattle with small chains attached to it. The sound of the instrument is believed to drive away evil spirits. Cf. *Ana bettjing*; *Kanching.*
Lit.: no. 162.

T'kiah (Ancient Israel). Manner of blowing the *shofar* (*hazozrah*): an energetic push, a long held tone. Cf. *T'ruah.*
Lit.: no. 12.

Tklij (Turkey). Spike fiddle. The instrument is derived from the *kopuz.* After numerous changes it appeared closely related to the Persian *kemenche.*
Lit.: no. 243.

T'koi-t'koi (Africa—Hottentot). Drum with one head and a corpus made of a calabash or wooden block.
Lit.: no. 255.

Tlapakan (Java). See *Pangkon*; *Ganjel.*

Tlutur (Java). A *suluk* that expresses sadness and grief. The tones *dada*, *nem* and *lima*, *barang* (*patet manyura*) are performed flat, a procedure which is believed to create a sad mood.
Lit.: no. 163.

T'na (Burma). Harp with 5-7 strings.

T'o (China). See *Chien-tzu.*
Lit.: no. 136.

To (Nigeria – Jukum). Musical bow with one string struck with a small stick.
Lit.: no. 17.

To (China – M 6431). Simple bell with a metal or wooden tongue and a handle at its apex. Formerly there were four kinds of *to* used in the army. Now the *to* is used by priests for marking time when chanting prayers.
Lit.: no. 1.

T'o (China – M 6462). A wooden slit-drum; a watchman's rattle. Also called *pang.*
Lit.: no. 209.

Toa (Liberia; Guinea). Triangular zither ("*kru* harp").

Toazi (Zanzibar). Swahili term for cymbal.

Tobaha (Ghana). See *Nyayito.*

Tobol (Arab: *Tabl*) (Mauritania). Kettledrum used to accompany songs and dances of religious and civil ceremonies.
Lit.: no. 190.

Tobshuur (Mongolia). Lute type with a trapezoid corpus and two strings. In shape the instrument resembles closely the *khil-khuur*, except that it is plucked and not bowed. In Northwest Mongolia it is very popular with the Oirats. Cf. *Dombra*; *Sgra-snyan* (Tibet).
Lit.: no. 60.

To buni (Ancient Egypt). Harp (term used by Josephus Flavius, 1st century A.D.).
Lit.: no. 250.

To-buye (Japan). Cf. *Tang-chok* (Korea).

Toda (Flores; Nage). Bamboo slit-drum. Four of these and two high cylindrical one-headed drums standing on short legs (*laba toda*) form an ensemble called *todagu.*
Lit.: no. 166.

Todagu (Flores). See *Toda.*

Tōdayam (South India; Kerala). Devotional dance, part of the *kathakali*, performed by two dancers behind a curtain.
Lit.: no. 123.

Tōḍi (North India). Important *thāt-rāga*, supposed to be performed during the late morning. In the past *tōḍi* was described as *rāgini*, the "female" form of *rāga*. At the present time the term *rāgini* has become obscure.
Tone material:

C D♭ E♭ F♯ (G) A♭ B c (with ♭ above D♭ and E♭)

c B A♭ (G) F♯ E♭ D♭ C; *Vādis*: A♭, E♭

The note D♭ is a *vishrantisthan.*
Lit.: no. 138.

Tōḍi (*Janatōḍi*; *Śuddhatōḍi*) (South India). *Janya rāga* of the 8th *mēḷa* (*Hanumattōḍi*).
Tone material:

C D♭ E♭ F A♭ B♭ c

c B♭ A♭ F E♭ D♭ C

Lit.: no. 139.

Tōḍi (South India). (1) The 8th *asampūrṇa mēḷa-rāga* without *kaṭapayādi* prefix. (2) The 8th *asampūrṇa mēḷa-rāga* with *kaṭapayādi* prefix was called *Janatōḍi.* See *Rāga* (South India).
Lit.: no. 139.

Todiane (South Africa). Cf. *Dikomana.*

Tod rnga (*Thod rnga*) (Tibet). Skull drum (cf. Indian *Damaru*).
Lit.: no. 143.

Toduri (Korea). "New piece"; famous music based upon *pohoja* (probably imported from China), elaborated in Korea in form of variations.
Tone material:
C D F G A B♭
Cf. *Po-hu-cha.*
Lit.: no. 136.

Toere (Tahiti). Slim slit-drum.
Lit.: no. 215.

Tof (*toph*) (Ancient Israel). Frame drum, played by women. The Aramaic term was *thupa* (cf. Arabic *Duff*).
Lit.: nos. 12, 255.

Tōgaku (Japan). Court music derived from imported Chinese music ("*t'ang* music") and *rinyugaku* (imported music from India). This music was called "music of the left" because it was performed at the left side of the temple. (The "music of the right" was called *komagaku.*) Cf. *Komagaku*; *Bugaku*; *Gagaku.*

Togha (India). Sanskrit term for cymbals.
Lit.: no. 255.

Togmur (East Bengal). Flute, transversely blown, with seven finger holes.
Lit.: no. 255.

Togo (Philippines; South Mindanao – Bagobo). Tube zither. Cf. *Tagong.*
Lit.: no. 255.

Toheli (India; Bastar State – Muria Gond). A lute type similar to the *sitar.* It has a bamboo neck and a gourd resonator.
Lit.: no. 59.

Tohe-tohe (New Zealand – Maori). "Tonsil"; a free tongue placed inside the tube of the *pukaea.*

Tohila (India; Orissa; Chhota Nagpur). Also *tuila.* Stick zither. See *Bajah.*

Tohmu (Nilotic Sudan; Congo – Mittu). Lyre. Cf. *Tam*; *Tom*; *Tum.*
Lit.: no. 21.

Tohoun (Dahomey). Drum.

Toila (East India; Orissa). Also *dudunga.* Long necked primitive lute with one string.

Tojo charang (West Java). A small *terbang.*
Lit.: no. 163.

Tok (Korea). A long bamboo tube with one end split. The player stamps the ground with the split end. Cf. *Ch'ung-tu* (China).
Lit.: nos. 52, 250.

To Kake (Japan). See *Kake.*

Tokere (Polynesia; Aitutaki). Slit-drum.
Lit.: no. 190.

Tokiwazu (Japan). See *Bungo-bushi.* Cf. *Katarimono.*

To-ko (*Tho-ko*) (Korea). Rattle consisting of two tiny clay drums and jingles, all suspended from a bamboo stick. See *Furi-tsuzumi* (Japan); *T'u-ku* (China).
Lit.: nos. 52, 255.

T'o-ku (China – M 6453; M 3479). Ancient drum mentioned in the *Shih-Ching.* It was used in ritual music. Its head is covered with the skin of a water-lizard, a sacred creature.
Lit.: no. 137.

To-ling (China – M 6431; M 4056). Hand bell with the metal or wooden clapper inside. The handle is attached to the apex.
Lit.: no. 137.

Tologha (Mongolia). Written *tologaj* = "main," main part, the body of a fiddle (*khil-khuur*), usually a wooden box of trapezoid shape. The fiddle of the Torgut tribe has a circular body. The Chinese call this instrument *ta hu-ch'in.*
Lit.: no. 60.

Tolo-tolo (South Africa – Basuto). Musical bow.
Lit.: no. 17.

Tolu bommalu (South India). The Telugu term for the Tamil *nizhalāṭṭam.*

Tom (*Thoum*) (Sudan – Shilluk). A lyre. Cf. *Tom* (Congo).
Lit.: no. 108.

Tom (Congo – Bari). Lyre. Cf. *Tam*; *Tohmu*; *Tum.*
Lit.: no. 17.

Tōmaratārini (South India). *Janya rāga* of the 29th *mēḷa* (*Dhīraśaṅkarābharaṇam*).
Tone material:
C D F G A B c
c B A G F E D C
Lit.: no. 139.

Tomba (West Africa; Sierra Leone – Mandingo). Drum in the form of an hourglass. It is beaten with two sticks.
Lit.: no. 255.

Tombak (*Dombak*) (Iran). Also *zarb.* Drum with a wooden or metal body. The instrument is hand-beaten.

Tombi (South India). Two cane tubes fitted into a bottle-shaped gourd, serving as snake-charmer's instrument. Cf. *Puñji*; *Jinjīvi.*

Tomede (Japan). A unique and peculiar end-piece in *gagaku* music, in which not the entire ensemble but only a few players perform music that gradually becomes thinner in sound and increasingly slower in tempo, until the *biwa* produces three or two slowly played notes and the *gaku-so* ends the piece very softly with one single final note.
Lit.: no. 185.

Tomimoto (Japan). See *Bungo-bushi.*

Tomo (South Africa – Hottentot' Bushmen). Musical bow played with a small bow.
Lit.: no. 18.

Tomoye (Japan). Cf. *Sei.*

Tom-tom (New Guinea). Drum consisting of a bamboo tube with a single membrane.
Lit.: no. 255.

Ton (Japan). Cf. *Sun* (Korea).

Tonbak (*Donbek*) (Iran). Cup-shaped drum with one skin.
Lit.: no. 255.

Toṅbī (*Tūṅbī*) (India). Hindostani term for *tiktirī.*

Tonde (New Guinea). Bull roarer.
Lit.: no. 255.

Tondu (East Flores). A plucked lute (musical bow) with a coconut shell body and one string. Cf. *Koombi-koombi.*
Lit.: no. 166.

Toneri (Japan). Assistants of the *wagon* player who hold the instrument for him in such a position that he can play it while standing upright.
Lit.: no. 185.

Tong (West Africa; Cameroun – Fan). Side-blown trumpet.
Lit.: no. 255.

Tong (Borneo). Jew's harp.
Lit.: no. 255.

Tong (*Kempyang*) (Java). Drum syllable.
Lit.: no. 163.

Tong (*Pen*) (Java; Jogya). See *(Ke)ketek.*

Tong (Sunda District). Also *tengah.* "Middle"; the middle octave register. See *Ḍogḍog* (West Java).
Lit.: no. 163.

Tonga (Samoa). Small wooden drum.
Lit.: no. 255.

Tongali (Philippines – Kalinga). Bamboo nose flute with three finger holes in front and one in the back.

Tong-gong (Java). Cf. *Tong-tong.*

Tongkat krutak (North Borneo). Cf. *Gulung-gulung.*
Lit.: no. 255.

T'ong-ku (China). Small gong. Cf. *T'ung-ku* (China – M 6608; M 3479).
Lit.: no. 209.

Tongkungon (Malaysia; Sabah). Flute.

To ngo (Congo – Ngbandi). Drum. Cf. *Ta ngo.*
Lit.: no. 26.

Tong-pal (Korea). Copper cymbals used in Buddhist ritual and festivities. Cf. *Po* (China); *Batsu* (Japan).

T'ong-skad (Tibet). Songs of working people, usually performed by one or two solo singers and responding chorus.

Tong-so (Korea). Now almost obsolete, a vertical, large flute used in the Confucian temple and at royal banquets where court music of Chinese origin was in high esteem. The instrument had six finger holes, four or five in front, two or one in the back; one of the back holes was covered with a thin paper membrane.

A slightly different *tong-so* has four or five finger holes in front and one in the back. This flute is small and is often called *tan-so.* It still appears at the present time, particularly in folk music.
Lit.: no. 52.

Tong-tieng (South China; North Vietnam – Miao). Gong chime.
Lit.: no. 303.

Tong-tong (Java). Ancient slit drum. Cf. *Tong-gong.*
Lit.: no. 163.

Tonkori (*Ainu Tonkori*) (Japan – Ainu). Zither with five strings.
Lit.: nos. 53, 185.

T'on-skad (Tibet). Working songs.
Lit.: no. 62.

Ton-ton (Borneo – Land Dayaks). Tube zither with three strings. Cf. *Taṅkuṅan.*
Lit.: no. 254.

To'o hakatootonu (Solomon Isl.). See *Mou hatingaa nge'o.*

To'o ki 'angunga (Solomon Isl.). See *Mou hatungaa nge'o.*

Took took (Sumatra; Mentawai Isl.). See *Boku* (Flores). Cf. *Tabhuan bomboong* (Madura).
Lit.: no. 163.

Toompling (*Boomboong*) (Bali). See *Boku* (Flores). Cf. *Tabhuan boomboong* (Madura).

Topayya (Philippines – Kalinga). Instrumental ensemble consisting of six gongs in various sizes. The names of the individual gongs are: *balbal*, *salbat*, *katlo*, *kapat*, *pokpok* (*opop*), *anungos.*

Topeng (Java; West Java; Bali). Classical masked dances performed to celebrate the local ruler. The instrumental ensemble consists of *angklungs* and *ḍogḍogs.* Occasionally also small groups can be observed that consist (beside various other combinations) of *kromong*, three *ketuk*, *rebāb*, blown *gong*, *goong geḍe*, *kenḍang*, and *kenḍang leutik.* The instruments are tuned to *selisir* and, in Bali, the melody is played by a *trompong.*
Lit.: nos. 197, 265.

Toph (Ancient Israel). See *Tof.*

Toragaku (Japan). Old music named after the island Tora (Tonra), the present Saishu (Quelpart). *Toragaku* offered musical accompaniment to dance-plays.
Lit.: no. 53.

Tori (*Akum*) (Southeast India; Abujhmar mountains – Muria Gond). Richly ornamented, side-blown hunting horn made of bronze. Its name is derived from the Sanskrit *turya* (horn).
Lit.: no. 135.

Tori (East Africa; Nilotic Sudan – Bari). A side-blown horn (animal horn).
Lit.: no. 302.

Torimono (Japan). Sacred vocal items of *mi-kagura* (Shinto music), invocations, and *saibari*, songs to honor and please the deities. The *torimono* texts can be Chinese or Japanese poetry.
Lit.: no. 185.

Torine (Japan). Cf. *Netori* (Japan).

Torioi uta (Japan). Songs of wandering minstrels.
Lit.: no. 225.

Tori parra (Southeast India). See *Parrang.*

Torop-jux (Sibiria – East Yakut). Cf. *Shotang.*

Ṭoroṭok (Java). A pair of bamboo clappers.
Lit.: no. 163.

To Rung (Vietnam). Popular xylophone made of a variable number of bamboo slabs.

Tote (Central Borneo – Muara Teive). Panpipes arranged in raft form. In the Sunda District the name for *tote* is *hatong.*
Lit.: no. 166.

Totoro (Congo – Ngombe). Term for *ndundu.*
Lit.: no. 26.

Totogi (Ghana – Ewe). One-headed drum. Cf. *Atsiagbekor.*
Lit.: no. 215.

Tou (pronounced *tu*, "to read") (China – M 6521). Comma. This term and its written form used in musical notation (Sung period) has the same or very similar function as *yün* and *chü.*
Lit.: no. 136.

T'ou-chih-pan (China – M 6489; M 986; M 4885). The "head restrained beat." It indicates the first beat in a measure, the first note of which had been held over (syncopated) from the preceding (e.g., 4th beat). This beat is also called *heh-chih-pan*, "black restrained beat."
Lit.: no. 136.

T'ou-kuan (China – M 6489; M 3557). Oboe type that evolved from Tartar *pi-li.* Cf. *Kuan*; *Tan kuan.*
Lit.: no. 137.

Toung (Vietnam). Jew's harp.

T'ou-pan (China – M 6489; M 4885). See *Cheng-pan.*

Towa (Ivory Coast). A gourd rattle covered with beads.
Lit.: no. 303.

Toyamili (Java). "Running water." A tempo indication; the term refers to a dignified but lively manner of playing in which the sticks (*tabuh*) touch the keys simultaneously. Cf. *Ṭuṭukan rangkep*; *Keter.*
Lit.: no. 163.

Toyavegavāhini (South India). See *Vegavāhini*, the 16th *asampūrṇa mēḷa.*

Trachak (*Angkring*) (Java). "Hoof," "claw." The term indicates the metal pins that hold the keys of the *saron* in place. In Jogya the *trachak* are called *planchak.* Cf. *Sanggan.*
Lit.: no. 163.

Tranh (Vietnam). Board zither with 16 strings.

Tre (Thailand; Kampuchea). Trumpet.
Lit.: no. 255.

Tre ngon (Thailand; Kampuchea). Horn.
Lit.: no. 255.

Tregl-barod (Algeria; Biskra). Dance with guns performed in triple meter.

Tresangu (West Africa; Togo – Ewe). Term for *sansa.* Cf. *Afosangu*; *Sangu.*
Lit.: no. 95.

Tribhinna (India). See *Gamak(a).*

Tridaśarañjani (South India). *Janya rāga* of the 13th *mēḷa* (*Gāyakapriya*).
Tone material:
C Db E Ab Bbb c
c Bbb Ab E Db C
Lit.: no. 139.

Trilōchanapriya (*Trilōcanapriya*) (South India). *Janya rāga* of the 30th *mēḷa* (*Nāgānandī*).
Tone material:
C D E G A# B c
c B A# G F D C
Lit.: no. 139.

Trimūrti (South India). *Janya rāga* of the 56th *mēḷa* (*Śaṇmukhapriyā*).
Tone material:
C D Eb F# Ab Bb c
c Bb Ab F# Eb D C
Lit.: no. 139.

Trimurti (South India). (1) The 56th *asampūrṇa mēḷa-rāga* without *kaṭapayādi* prefix. (2) The 56th *asampūrṇa mēḷa-rāga* with *kaṭapayādi* prefix was called *Chāmaram.* See *Rāga* (South India).
Lit.: no. 139.

Trimūrtipriya (South India). *Janya rāga* of the 9th *mēḷa* (*Dhēnuka*).
Tone material:
C Db Eb Ab B c
c B Ab Eb Db C
Lit.: no. 139.

Tripādaka (South India). *Janya rāga* of the 19th *mēḷa* (*Jhaṅkāradhvani*).
Tone material:
C D F Ab Bbb c
c Bbb Ab F D C
Lit.: no. 139.

T'ri-p'u (Tibet). Bell. Its honorific term is *chha-t'ri.*

Tripuccha (India). See *Gamak(a).*

Tripuṭa tāla (South India). See *Tāla.*

Trisra jāti (South India). See *Tāla.*

Tritāl (North India). See *Tintāl*; *Tāla.*

Tritantrī vīṇā (India). "Three-stringed *vīṇā*" – a rare *vīṇā* in the shape of a *sitar* with three strings.
Lit.: no. 254.

Tritīya (Vedic India). The third-highest note of the *sāmavedic* chant notated as "3."
Lit.: no. 141.

Trivata (India). Melody sung to meaningless syllables.

Triveni (North India). *Rāga* ascribed to the *purvi thāta.* It is to be performed in the evening.
Tone material:
C Db E G B c
c B Ab G E Db C; *Vādis*: Db, G
Lit.: no. 138.

Triyāma (South India). *Janya rāga* of the 18th *mēḷa* (*Hāṭakambarī*).
Tone material:
C Db F A# B c
c B A# F Db C
Lit.: no. 139.

Triyambakapriya (South India). *Janya rāga* of the 3rd *mēḷa* (*Gānamūrti*).
Tone material:

C F D♭ E♭♭ F G c
c B c A♭ G F E♭♭ D♭ C

Lit.: no. 139.

Tro (Kampuchea; Burma). Term for fiddles.
Lit.: no. 190.

Tro-chai (Kampuchea). A bowed lute (*sāraṅgi* type).
Lit.: no. 43.

Tro-duong (Kampuchea). A spike fiddle of Chinese origin, similar to the Annamitic *cai ni.* The body is an ivory cylinder covered on one side with snakeskin. The instrument has two silk strings.
Lit.: no. 153.

Tro-khmer (Kampuchea). A long spike fiddle of the *mohori* ensemble but is used also in the *pip-hat* orchestra. The body is heart-shaped, the neck is made of ivory, and the instrument has three silk strings tuned to d A E. Cf. *Mohori.*
Lit.: nos. 43, 153, 254.

Trompong (Bali). The Balinese term for *bonang.* One (rarely two) horizontally placed rows of kettles; each row consists of five gongs which perform the nuclear melody and appear in the *gamelan gong* and *semar pegulingan.*
Lit.: no. 197.

Trompong barangan (Bali). Set of gongs that performs figurations an octave higher. The figurations appear in the *gong kebyar* ensemble, where four players are required to execute the figurations.
Lit.: no. 265.

Troṅ (Kampuchea). Also *trong.* Goblet drum. Cf. *Cai troṅ.*
Lit.: no. 254.

Tron bat cau (Vietnam). One-headed drum beaten with two sticks. Cf. *Cai bom* (*Cai bōng*).

Troṅ com (Vietnam). "Rice drum" used in *dai nhac.* It is a long barrel drum, very similar in shape to the Indian *mridanga.*

Trōn cai (Vietnam). Small drum with one head.
Lit.: nos. 296-97.

Trōṅ de (Vietnam). Small drum.

Trōṅ nhac (Vietnam). Two frame drums used in ceremonies (in *dai nhac*).
Lit.: no. 296.

Trōng quān (Vietnam). Ground zither often used in folk music.
Lit.: nos. 19, 254.

Tro-u (Kampuchea). Spike fiddle with half a coconut shell as body. The instrument has two strings, and the hair of the bow is strung between the two strings which are tuned a fifth apart. Cf. *Sō-u* (Laos); *Hu-ch'in* (China).
Lit.: no. 254.

T'ruah (Ancient Israel). A manner of blowing the *shofar* (also *hazozrah*). A blaring, warbling, trill-resembling sound. Cf. *T'kiah.*
Lit.: no. 12.

Trung cung chi nhac (Vietnam). Court (palace) music.

Tsa (China—M 6646). Stereotyped role of an operatic actor-singer; the "servant."

Tsa-chü (China—M 6646; M 1593). A musical variety show that became fashionable during the Sung period. The *tsa-chü* were varied in scope, having historical, didactic, supernatural, and farcical subjects, and consisted of a prelude, a low type comedy, followed by poetic episodes filled with singing and dancing, and concluded by a musical endpiece. The instrumental music was dominated by the flute.

The *tsa-chü* of the North reached a peak during the Yüan period (1280-1368) and eventually became the forerunner of the famous Peking opera. Cf. *Hsi Wen.*
Lit.: nos. 182-83.

Tsa-go (Japan). Cf. *Cho-ko* (Korea); *Tsu-ku* (China).

Tšahar-gāh (*Jaharkāh*) (Arabia). See *Chahar-gāh.*

Tšahār-gāh-'Arabī (Middle East). *Maqām.*
Tone material:
F G A B♭ c d e f
Lit.: no. 64.

Tsahār-gāh Turkī (Middle East). *Maqām.*
Tone material:
F G♭(♮) A B♭ c d e♭(+) f
Lit.: no. 64.

Tsakaiamba (Malagasy Republic). Rattle.
Lit.: no. 251.

Tsambi (South Gabon – Lumbu). Bowed lute with five strings.

Tsanasin (*Dsanādsel*) (Ethiopia). Rattles used by priests.
Lit.: no. 102.

Tsaṅ (Burma). Drum.
Lit.: no. 255.

Tsauṅ (Burma; Shan State). A slim, widely curved, and at the lower end boat-shaped, harp with 9-13 silk strings. Cf. *Chank*; *Chaṅga*; *Jank* (Arabic).
Lit.: no. 254.

Tsebu (Burma; Shan State). Lute with a round body covered with snakeskin, a long neck, and three strings tuned to C F c. Cf. *San hsien* (China).
Lit.: no. 252.

Tsele (South Africa – Venda). Cf. *Ndjele.*

Tseng-pan (China – M 6769; M 4885). "Conferring, bestowing beat" – the name of the first beat of a measure in common meter. The beat is also called *heh-pan* (M 2090; M 4885), "black beat."
Lit.: no. 136.

Tse-re (Tibet). Song, tune.

Tshahar-gāh (*Chahār-gāh*) (Modern Egypt). *Maqām.*
Tone material:
F G A B♭ c d e f
Lit.: no. 64.

Tshaiṅ-vaiṅ (*Chaiṅ-vaiṅ*) (Burma). A set of 24 (20) cone-shaped small drums, each tuned to a different note, arranged in a semicircle around the player. The drums are supported by a richly ornamented wooden framework.
Lit.: no. 252.

Tshambar (Tunisia). One of the rhythmical features that occur in the Tunisian *shambar*, a section of the *nawba.*

Tshembe (Congo). See *Nabita.*

Tshig (Tibet). Meaningful textual syllables of the Buddhist chant. Cf. *Tshig lhad.*
Lit.: no. 143.

Tshig lhad (Tibet). Meaningless textual syllables used in the Buddhist chant. For further information see Lit. no. 143.

Tshigwana (South Africa – Venda). Also *tshivhana.* Musical bow. Cf. *Penda.*
Lit.: no. 151.

Tshihoho (*Mfuhlulu*) (South Africa – Bavenda). Small *kwatha*, a side-blown signal instrument.
Lit.: no. 151.

Tshikala (South Africa – Venda). Musical bow. Cf. *Dende.*
Lit.: no. 151.

Tshikasa (Congo). Drum. See *Kikasa.*

Tshikhulu (South Africa – Tshopi). *Mbila* with four (or more) low sounding slabs of no precise pitch. Cf. *Tshilandzana.*
Lit.: no. 151.

Tshikona (South Africa – Venda). National dance.

Tshilandzana (South Africa – Tshopi). Small *mbila* with 10 (recently with 10-14) slabs. Cf. *Dibinde*; *Didole*; *Tshikhulu.*
Lit.: no. 151.

Tshilombe (South Africa – Venda). Dilettante; incompetent musician.

Tshiondo (Congo – Bena Kanioka). War drum.
Lit.: no. 26.

Tshipendani (South Africa; South Rhodesia). Musical bow. Cf. *Penda.*
Lit.: no. 151.

Tshitendje (*Dende*) (South Africa). Cf. *Segwana.*
Lit.: no. 151.

Tshitendole (South Africa – Tshopi). Musical bow played by men. Cf. *Dende.*
Lit.: no. 151.

Tshitiringo (South Africa – Venda). Transverse cane flute with two (four) finger holes. Cf. also Lit. no. 206, where a double transverse flute is mentioned.
Lit.: no. 151.

Tshivhana (South Africa). See *Tshigwana*; *Penda.*

Tshivhilivhi (*Luvuvu*) (South Africa – Venda). Bull roarer.
Lit.: no. 151.

Tshizambi (South Africa – Venda). Cf. *Nxonxoro.*
Lit.: no. 151.

Tsiane (Malagasy Republic – Betsileo). Cylindrical drum.
Lit.: no. 251.

Tsijolo (South Africa – Venda). Bowed tube zither with one metal string. The instrument is played by men only. Cf. *Isikehlekehle*; *Pone*; *Sefinjolo*; *Sekatari*; *Sekgobogobo*; *Udahi.*
Lit.: no. 151.

Tsikaretika (Malagasy Republic). A long bamboo plank struck by a number of persons, each beating it with two sticks. It serves as accompaniment of dances and at funerals. Cf. *Karatsaka*; *Kimbolo*; *Raloba*; *Tsipetrika*; *Volo.*
Lit.: no. 251.

Tsikatray (Malagasy Republic). Rattle.
Lit.: no. 251.

Trikiripika (Malagasy Republic). Rattle.
Lit.: no. 251.

Tsimbi (Congo – Bahuana). Vertically-blown can nose-flute without finger holes.
Lit.: no. 313.

Tsinda (Congo – Mbole; Bosake). Drum. Cf. *Bondundu.*
Lit.: no. 26.

Ts'in-kam (China). Cantonese term; see *Ch'ien-chin.*

Tsin-ku (China). See *Chin-ku.*

Tsipetrika (Malagasy Republic). Also *tanala.* Cf. *Tsikaretika.*
Lit.: no. 251.

Tsipwali (Angola – Luimbe). Drum.
Lit.: no. 26.

Tsitsilo (Congo). See *Kikilo.*

Tsjutjsu (Indonesia; Nias). See *Tamburu.*

Tsnasin (Ethiopia – Galla; Somali). Cf. *Tsanatsel.*

T'sögs-rol (Tibet). A pair of cymbals used by the Um-dze-pa during prayers and meetings. The cymbals are held horizontally and vertically moved against each other gently.
Lit.: no. 143.

Tsou p'i-p'a (China; Giles 11,806). A *p'i-p'a* played on horseback. It has a round body, a long neck, four strings, and 12 frets.
Lit.: no. 209.

Tsu (Japan). A little piece of ivory or bone is inserted into the mouthpiece of the *shakuhachi.*

Tsugai-mai (Japan). See *Bugaku.*

Tsugi-bushi (Japan). See *Nage-bushi.*

Tsuke-gashira (Japan). A *taiko* drum pattern.
Lit.: no. 187.

Tsu-ku (China – M 6824; M 3479). A small barrel drum placed on a wooden stand. Occasionally and erroneously it is called *ying-ku.* In the Confucian service the *tsu-ku* was placed at the west side of the Moon terrace and responded with two beats to each of the three beats of the big *ying-ku* (M 6824; M 3479) (or *po-fu*). In contrast to the *ying-ku*, the body of the *tsu-ku* appears plain and is not ornamented.
Lit.: no. 137.

Tsukushi-gaku (Japan). The term has two related meanings:

1. The old, imported music from China.
2. A style of *koto* music standing between popular and ancient court music.

Cf. *Tsukushi-goto.*
Lit.: no. 185.

Tsukushi-goto (Japan). Old fashioned *koto* music originating partly from Kyushu in the 16th century when the priest Kenjun established a *koto* school that was called Tsukushi after a district in Kyushu. This music was formed into a suite consisting of a series of short songs. Cf. *Kumiuta.*
Lit.: no. 185.

Tsukushi sō (Japan). The old *sō-no-koto*, the forerunner of the present *koto.*
Lit.: no. 53.

Tsula (South Africa – Pedi). Vertical flute made of the leg-bone of an eagle or a wildcat. It is used in rain-making ceremonies and produces a piercing sound.
Lit.: no. 151.

Tsula ya noko (South Africa – Pedi). Panpipes made of the quills of the tail of a porcupine. The quill-tubes are not tuned. The instrument is used by witch doctors in order to prevent epidemic disasters.
Lit.: no. 151.

Tsuma-koto (Japan). A trapezoid-shaped *koto* with 13 strings.
Lit.: no. 225.

Tsume (Japan). Ivory plectrum used for *koto* playing.

Tsumi (Japan). "Pinching." The term refers to *koto* playing when, after a number of tones played with the plectrum, single tones are plucked ("pinched") with the thumb and middle finger. Besides *tsumi* there are a few brief passages which are called *san, ji, oru.*
Lit.: no. 185.

Tsunagi (Japan). The musical transition between a quiet and a lively section in *kumiuta.* Cf. *Kumiuta*; *Nagauta.*

Tsure (Japan). Actors of the *noh* drama who appear beside the *shite* and *waki.*

Tsuri daiko (Japan). Term for the richly ornamented hanging drum of *bugaku.* This barrel drum is suspended from a circular stand. Its upper end represents a golden flame with three balls of fire. The drum is beaten with two wooden sticks. The right side stick is called *obachi* ("male stick") and the left side stick is called *mebachi* ("female stick").
Lit.: no. 250.

Tsuri gane (Japan). Suspended gong.
Lit.: no. 255.

Tsurugi-mai (Japan). Sword dance. Its accompaniment was provided by singing several *shigin.* Recently *biwa* music is used instead.
Lit.: no. 185.

Tsusi (South Africa). Cf. *Motaba.*

Tsuyo (Japan). Cf. *Tsuyogin*; *Noh*; *Yokyoku.*

Tsuyōgin (Japan). The strong martial and powerful style in *noh* music, favored during the Tokugawa period (late 16th century). Cf. *Fushi.*
Lit.: no. 185.

Tsuzumi (Japan). Term for a small, hand-beaten drum in the shape of an hourglass. The drum is either carried on the hip or on the shoulder of the player. The color of the body shows the rank of the player: lilac, the highest; light blue, the next lower; orange, the common rank. Frequently these drums are lacquered and ornamented with gold. The drum is used in *noh* and *kabuki* performances. Cf. *Ō-tsuzumi*; *Oto-tsuzumi*; *San-no-tsuzumi.*
Lit.: nos. 53, 250.

Tsztze (Africa; Central and South). See *Sansa.*

Ttimba (Uganda – Ganda). A small wooden kettledrum, hung on a rope around the player's neck and struck with bare hands. The instrument is considered to be the ruler's drum.
Lit.: no. 302.

Tu (India). See *Di.*

Tuan (China – M 6543). A tune, section of a zither piece.
Lit.: no. 93.

Tuan-hsiao nao-ku (China). Military band of the Han dynasty.

Tub (Thailand). Drum beat on the *tapone* performed by the left hand. It is executed in the same manner as *tha.*

Tuba (Indonesia; Moluccas; Sula Isl.). Goblet drum. Cf. *Tifa*; *O-tsi* (Burma).

Tuba aujota (Moluccas; Sula Isl.). Bamboo tube zither.
Lit.: no. 156.

Tuba kaujota (Moluccas; Sula Isl.). Small drum with two heads, resembling the *marwas.*
Lit.: no. 162.

Tubaile (*Tubbel*) (Arabia). Small kettledrums with bronze kettles.
Lit.: no. 184.

Tubbaile (Arabia). See *Tubaile.*

Tuban iotta (Indonesia; Moluccas; Sula-Besi). Tube zither with 4-6 strings. Cf. *Agong.*
Lit.: no. 254.

Tuba pondi (Moluccas; Sula Isl.). Also *kokondi*; *popondi.* Bamboo tube zither.
Lit.: no. 156.

Tubbel (Sahara; Tuareg). Drum. Cf. *Tubaile.*
Lit.: no. 95.

Tubrī (India). Cf. *Tiktirī*; *Meshek.*

Tubū (Muslim Spain). Term for 24 modes, linked with the four elements.
Lit.: no. 76.

Ṭubūl (Arabia). Drum.

Tuda (East India – Khanda). Name of the *śṛṅga.*
Lit.: no. 255.

Tuddukan (Sumatra; Mentawai Isl). Xylophone with two thick wooden plates and two hollow tree stumps.
Lit.: no. 255.

Tudhrī (Arabia). See *Tudrī.*

Tudra (Southeast India; Gond Tribes – Bastar Muria). Term for *kotor.*
Lit.: no. 135.

Tudrī (*Tudhrī*) (Old Arabia). High trill used by a tavern girl entertainer (*dājina*).

Tudū-kat (*Lelega*) (Indonesia; Mentawai Isl.). Simple xylophone. Cf. *Tjaluṅ*; *Doli-doli.*
Lit.: no. 254.

Tudung(an) (Java). See *Wangsi.*

Tuḍung punḍuk (Java). Name of the *kowangan.*
Lit.: no. 163.

Tuet (Thailand). Drum beat on the *tapone* performed by the left hand. It is executed in the same manner as *thoet.*

Tugal (West Borneo). Cf. *Gulong-gulong* (*Gulung-gulung*).
Lit.: no. 255.

Tüidük (Turkmenistan; Afghanistan). Open ended vertical flute.

Tui-hsiao (China—M 6562; M 2619). Two small clarinet type tubes joined side by side. Cf. *Ch'un kuan*; *Kuan-tzu.*

Tuila (*Tohila*) (India; Chhota Nagpur; Orissa). Stick zither. Cf. *Bajah.*
Lit.: no. 254.

Tujali (Celebes). Cf. *Lolowe; Tulali.*

Tukang gambang (Java). Xylophone player.

Tuk-chong (*Teuk-chong*) (Korea). Single large bell suspended in a richly ornamented frame. Cf. *T'e-chung* (China).
Lit.: no. 52.

Tukang saron. Player of the *saron.*

Tukhra (North India). This term indicates a remarkable short passage (variation) performed only by the drummer. For a few measures he suddenly deviates from the rigidly prescribed drum beats and surprises the audience with his excellent skill. These freely drummed measures may also contain a *tia.*
Lit.: no. 136.

Tukkyong (Korea). A single stone slab (cf. *T'e-ching*) suspended in an ornamented wooden frame.
Lit.: no. 52.

T'u-ku (China—M 6532; M 3479). A drum with a clay body.
Lit.: no. 137.

Tukubaka (Solomon Isl.). See *Ngangibaka.*

Tuku ki ngango (Solomon Isl.). See *Mou hatingaa nge'o.*

Tu-lā koti (Ancient India). See *Nūpura.*

Tulali (Central Celebes). A widely used bamboo flute with four finger holes. Some of its various names are: *bengsi* (North Sumatra), *bulo wok* (Borneo—Kayan), *hel-hel* (Nicobares), *salung*, *bangsi* (South Sumatra), *salu'eng* (Atjeh), *sawergnil* (Kai Isl.), *surune ndrawa* (South Nias). Cf. *Nuren.*
Lit.: no. 132.

Tu-ling (China—M 6512; M 4056). "Single bell." Hangchow term for *ma-ling.*
Lit.: no. 209.

Tultshi (Mongolia). Famous hero-songs.
Lit.: no. 60.

Ṭulum (Northeast Turkey). (1) Bagpipe with two chanter pipes, each provided with five finger holes and a single beating reed. (2) The play-tube of the bagpipe.
Lit.: nos. 15, 243.

Tulumbeta (Central Africa). Kikongo term for trumpet.
Lit.: no. 255.

Ṭulūm dūduyī (Turkey). Bagpipe.
Lit.: no. 81.

Tulumpe (Indonesia; Tonapuh). See *Pare.*

Tulung (Java; Solo). *Gembyakan* performed as a rapid alternation of two beats executed by:

1. four fingers, spread out, beating the large drumhead;
2. the index finger beating the small drumhead.

Lit.: no. 163.

Tum (Nilotic Sudan – Lango; Uganda – Lango; Labwor, Shilluk). Various forms of a plucked string instrument (ground bow; harp with 5-6 strings; lyre). Cf. *Tam*; *Tohmu*; *Tom.*
Lit.: no. 132.

Tum (Arabia). A loud drumbeat.

Tumbaknai (North India; Kashmir). Pot-shaped drum.

Tumbalak (Kurdistan). Cf. *Naqqara*; *Dumbelek.*

Tumbi (Congo – Baholoholo). Goblet drum.
Lit.: no. 26.

Tumbug (Java). "To coincide." A device that connects *pelog* and *slendro gamelan* music on a common note. E.g., *gamelan tumbug nem* indicates that the note *nem* is tuned to the same pitch in *pelog* and *slendro*. Another linking note is *tumbug lima.*
Lit.: no. 158.

Tumbukin (India). Drum.
Lit.: no. 255.

Tumbul (West Central Sahara – Tuareg). Drum.
Lit.: no. 95.

Tumburu vīṇā (India). Name for the *ṭaṅbura* with the usual four metal strings. The fretless lute has the same function as the *ṭaṅbura* that produces bourdon sounds. The name *tumburu* refers also to one of the divine musicians.
Lit.: no. 255.

Tumda (Sikkim – Lepcha). High or low pitched drum.

Tumedak (Java). The low voice range.
Lit.: no. 163.

Tūmerī (Sri Lanka). See *Tiktirī.*
Lit.: no. 184.

Tumoto (New Zealand – Maori). Term for the *kaioraora* songs.

Tuṇ (India). See *Di.*

Tuṅ (Tibet). See *Tung.*

Tunagi (Japan). Also *tsunagi.* See *Jiuta.*

Tuṇava (Ancient India). Sanskrit term for flute.
Lit.: no. 250.

Tūṅbī (India). Cf. *Tiktirī.*

Tunbuk (Iran). Obsolete goblet drum similar to the *darabuka.* See also *Dinbik*; *Donbek.*
Lit.: no. 78.

Ṭunbūr (Pre-Islamic Persia; Arabia). Lute with a long neck, two strings and, at the end of the neck, five frets. These frets indicate a remarkably small compass of unequal microtones.
Lit.: nos. 34, 250.

Tunde (Celebes). Cf. *Sosanru*; *Dunde.* Cf. also the Swahili *Zeze.*

Tundukut (Indonesia; Mentawai Isl.). Xylophone. Cf. *Lelega.*
Lit.: no. 166.

Tundum (*Muk-brogon*; *Rutuk* [*tundum*]) (Australia; Bribbun). Bull roarer.
Lit.: no. 255.

Tung (Vietnam). Buddhist cantillation without instrumental accompaniment. Cf. *Tan.*

T'ung (*Dung*) (Tibet). Horn made of a conch shell mounted with bronze or silver. The instrument produces a clean, deep sound, and is used together with the *sil-sñan.*
Lit.: no. 143.

Tungali (Philippines; Luzon). Nose flute.
Lit.: no. 313.

Tungda (Nepal). Pair of kettledrums.

Tung dyu (Nepal; Sikkim—Lepcha). Jew's harp made of bamboo. Cf. *Binaya*; *machunga.*

Tungga (Korea). The instrumental ensemble that performs on the terrace of the Confucian temple. There are 17 musicians (in the 16th century there were 62). A second ensemble placed in the courtyard below consisted of 15 players (formerly 139) and is called *hon'ga.*
Lit.: no. 52.

Tungge (New Guinea). Jew's harp.

T'ung hsiao (*Feng huang hsiao*) (China—6609.12). A vertically-blown bamboo flute. It has five or six finger holes and one thumbhole. Cf. *Tong-so* (Korea) and the now rare *Dōshō* (Japan). The Cantonese name is *tung-siu.*
Lit.: nos. 137, 209.

T'ung-ku (China—M 6608, 3479). (1) "Rainbow drum." A term for *chin-ku* used in Peking. Two small drums called *t'ung-ku* are attached to each side of the *yin-ku.* (2) A second meaning of *t'ung-ku* indicates a circular brass gong struck with a small wooden hammer (see *Chin-ku*). In Hangchow the gong is called *tang-lo.*
Lit.: no. 137.

T'ung-lo (China). Bronze gong.

T'ung-po (China—M 6623; M 5333). Buddhist bowl (cymbals).
Lit.: no. 78.

Tung siu (China). Cantonese term for *t'ung-hsiao.*

Ṭungṭung (Java). *Gembyakan* beat (in Solo). The same fingers are used as in *tulung*; the only difference is that the two beats on both drumheads are performed simultaneously.
Lit.: no. 163.

Tuni (Sierra Leone—Fula). A tube that can be:
1. a transverse flute with three finger holes;
2. a single reed instrument ending in a large bell.

Cf. *Fuli.*

Tunjung (Java). See *Rebāb* (Java).

Tunshinkidi (Congo—Baluba). Cylindrical drum.
Lit.: no. 26.

Tuntina (India). Cf. *Tuntuṇ.*

Tuṇtuṇ (India). Cf. *Yektar.*

Tuol (Malaysia—Senoi). Small transverse flute with one finger hole.

Tuomo (South Africa—Basuto). See *Thomo*; *Segwana.*

Tuppā (Msopotamia). Aramaic term. See *Tof* (Israel).

Tūra (India). Prakrit term for the Sanskrit *tūrya*, indicating a simple trumpet.
Lit.: no. 254.

Turahī (*Tutārī*) (India). Curved brass trumpet used in religious ceremonies. Cf. *Turaī*; *Tūrya.*

Turaī (India). See *Turahī* or *Bheṛī.*

Turali (Borneo—Dusun). Nose flute with four finger holes, three in front and one in the back.
Lit.: no. 255.

Turam (India—Bastar State). Small kettledrum of the Hill Maria (not Muria) Gond.
Lit.: nos. 59, 134-35, 142.

Tura-zi (South New Guinea). Boat song.

Turburi (India; Bastar State). Small shallow earthenware kettledrum. It is beaten with two small wooden sticks. The instrument is used mainly by the Muria Gond people. Cf. *Kunduri.*
Lit.: no. 59.

Ture angwa (Uganda – Madi). Side-blown horn.
Lit.: no. 302.

Turez-neuin (Arabia). "The new way." *Maqām* derived from *maqām Nahawand* (which uses the same tone material). The notes in ascent are: *rāst, zirkūla, kurdī, jargā, ṣaba, ḥusēnī, 'ajām, kardān, shāhnāz, jawab-sigā* or *sunbula, jawab-jargā, jawab-saba.* In descent occur: *'ajām-'ashirān, shuri,* and *jagā.*
Tone material:
$C\ D\flat\ E\flat\ F\ \overset{+}{G\flat}\ A\ B\flat\ c$
Lit.: no. 121.

Ture-turungale (Uganda). Term for *turi.*
Lit.: no. 190.

Turi (*Ture-turungale*) (Uganda – Madi). Side-blown trumpet made of wood, covered with leather.
Lit.: no. 302.

Tūrī (India; Bengal). Bangali term for *tūrya* (or *bheṛī*). *Turī* is a large trumpet with a shrill, penetrating sound. It was a ceremonial instrument used at the burning of the dead and their widows.
Lit.: no. 254.

Turjupi (East India; Orissa). Cymbals.

Türkü (Turkey). Folk songs with 7, 8, or 11 syllables per line. They are love songs, narratives, and their texts often reflect features of daily life.
Lit.: no. 243.

Turturī (India). See *Tūrya.*

Turu (Liberia – Kpelle). Side-blown wooden or ivory horns.
Lit.: no. 284.

Turu (New Mecklenburg – Kandas). Shell horn.
Lit.: no. 255.

Turubur (*Turuburi*) (Southeast India – Abujhmar Mountains). A small, earthenware or wooden drum of the Hill Maria Gond. The drum has a bowl-shaped body and a skin of untanned cowhide.
Lit.: no. 135.

Turuburi (Southeast India – Abujhmar mountains). See *Turubur.*

Ṭuruḥat (Egypt – Coptic). See *Psali*; *Ṭarḥ.*

Türümpata bürüsī (Turkey). Term for the European trumpet. In Morocco it is called *ṭarunbaṭa.*
Lit.: no. 81.

Turun (Sunda Isl.). See *Mundur.*

Ṭuruq mulūkiyya (Arabia; Persia). Ancient term for the seven modes in music.

Tūrya (India). Sanskrit term for a coiled trumpet. Among the numerous terms used for this instrument are: *bheṛī, turaī, turturī* in Hindostani; *gādar* in Marwari; *tūrī* in Bengali; *bhuri, tuttārā* in Telugu; *tutūri* in Kannarese; *tūryam* in Malayalam; and *pālī, tūra* in Prakrit.
Lit.: no. 254.

Tūryakara (Ancient India). Musicians who play horns and flutes.

Tūryam (South India). Term for *turya* (or *bheri*).

Turz-neuin (Arabia). See *Turez-neuin.*

Tūshiyah (Tunisia). See *Al Tūshiyah.*

Ṭusūt (Arabia). Glass harmonica played with wooden sticks.
Lit.: no. 76.

Tut (Bali). The sound of the open drum (*kenḍang lanang*).
Lit.: no. 197.

Ṭuṭāk (Iran). Whistle flute. Cf. *Qaba duduk.*
Lit.: no. 81.

Tutalo (Moluccas; Ternate Isl.). Stick zither. Cf. *Dunde*; *Sosanru*.
Lit.: no. 254.

Tutārī (India). See *Turahi*; *Turaī*; *Tūrya*.

Tūtik (Kurds; Tatars; Turkmen). Whistle flute. Cf. *Tūtāk*; *Qabā duduk*.
Lit.: no. 255.

Tutila (Lower Congo – Sundi). A conically-shaped two-headed drum. Inside its body is a hard, rattling object that adds to the clattering sound if the drum is beaten. The instrument appears in two sizes: a bigger ("mother") and a smaller ("child"). The *tutila* is often used at funeral ceremonies.
Lit.: no. 280.

Tuttam (South India). Name of the note *ri* in ancient Tamil terminology. Cf. *Dravidian Music*.

Tuttārā (South India). Telugu term for *turya* (*bheri*).

Tutu (Tanganyika – Washambala). Cylindrical drum, always used in pairs, consisting of a large and smaller one.
Lit.: no. 190.

Tutu (North Nias). Cylindrical drum with a wooden body.
Lit.: no. 255.

Tutu (Congo – Kikongo). Small cane flute used as toy by children.
Lit.: no. 190.

Tutugan (Bali). Figurations in certain *trompong* passages in which each tone is repeated.
Lit.: no. 197.

Tutug-tutugan (Bali). A characteristic *ganga* figuration pattern that occurs in the *gamelan gong* of recent times. The pattern employs repeated melody tones.
Lit.: no. 197.

Ṭuṭukan kuna (Java). See *Ṭuṭukan lomba*.

Ṭuṭukan kina (Java). See *Ṭuṭukan lomba*.

Ṭuṭukan lomba (Java). An old-fashioned style of beating the *bonang* and the *gambang kayu* (also called *kuna*, *kina*).
Lit.: no. 163.

Ṭuṭukan rangkep (Java). The "double," "modern" richly ornamented style of beating the *bonang* and *gambang kayu*. The following types are in use: *putut gelut*; *semar nyampar*; *petruk nganḍul*; *salah gumun*. See also *Toyamili*; *Keter*.
Lit.: no. 163.

Tutumedjo (South Africa – Sotho; Venda). Drum with a conically-shaped body. Cf. *Gedzo*; *Murumbu*.
Lit.: no. 151.

Tutung (*Takitu*) (Flores; Manggaray). (1) Small goblet-shaped drum. (2) See *Lotong* (bamboo zither).
Lit.: no. 166.

Tutungulan (West Java). Name of the *bendrong*.
Lit.: no. 163.

Tutupele (New Guinea; New Britain). Also *linbut*. Simple xylophone consisting of two small wooden boards placed across two tree trunks or the legs of a sitting man. See also *Tinbuk*.
Lit.: no. 37.

Tutūri (South India). Kannarese term for *tūrya*.

Tuum (Uganda – Acholi). Side-blown straight, conical trumpet, consisting of two joined wooden tubes covered with leather.
Lit.: no. 190.

Tu-va (Vietnam). Trumpet.
Lit.: no. 255.

Tuwung (Java). Old Hindu-Javanese term for *cheluring*.

Tuzu abe (Congo; Uganda–Lugbwara). Girls scrape the instrument, wooden friction sticks, against a board which covers a hole in the ground, during their dances.
Lit.: no. 190.

Tyamko (Nepal). A pair of unequally sized kettledrums.

Ty be (Vietnam). A pear-shaped lute with four silken strings and 10 bamboo frets. Its tuning is 1, 4, 5, 8. Cf. *Ti ba*; *p'i-p'a*.

Tziltzelim (Ancient Israel). See *Metziltayim*.

Tz'u (China–M 6971). "Verse." Poetic song texts whose irregular lines are made up of sequences of syllables that have a fixed, prearranged pattern of tones (linguistic inflections). This method reaches back to She Yo (5th to 6th century), a celebrated scholar who classified the four tonal inflections of the Chinese language. By the end of the T'ang period (618-906) the *tz'u* showed a fixed pattern of tonal (linguistic) inflections combined with a melody that followed the same pattern. This had become an important feature in Chinese vocal music. See *Ch'ü* (M 1623).
Lit.: no. 243.

Tz'u-fu (China). The first theatrical invocation; praying for happiness in operas puppet dramas and other theatrical plays. Cf. *Chia kuan*; *K'ai-ch'ang*.
Lit.: no. 129.

Tzu-pai (China–M 6960; M 4975). "Self-introduction." A feature in Chinese opera when the actor-singer introduces himself to the audience, either in the form of a recitative or as spoken monologue.
Lit.: no. 136.

U

U (Japan). Tone name indicating the note that appears a major sixth above the basic *kyū*. *U* is the equivalent of the Chinese *yü*. Cf. *Ryo*; *Ritsu* scales.
Lit.: no. 136.

U (Korea). Tone name having the same significance as *U* (Japan) and *yü* (China). Cf. *U* (Japan).
Lit.: no. 136.

U (Vietnam). Tone name. Cf. *Ho*, where all tone names are listed.

Uadaku (Congo). *Sansa* with seven tongues.
Lit.: no. 184.

U amba (South Africa – Venda). "Talking."

U anetsela (South Africa – Venda). "Narrating."

Ub (Sumer). An obscure percussive instrument, probably a frame drum. Cf. *Uppu*.
Lit.: no. 94.

Ubangak (Korea). Term occasionally used for *hyangak* and *tangak*. *Hyangak* means native Korean music, *tangak* means imported Chinese music. Both were performed at the royal court.

Ubar (Australia; Western Arnhem Land). A drum made of a long, hollow tree trunk. The instrument has a secret, mysterious significance.

Ube (Sudan). A drum of various sizes struck by a woman alternately with a stick and her hand.
Lit.: no. 95.

Ubgasha (Uganda; Ruanda). Term for the four finger holes of the *umukuri*.
Lit.: no. 201.

Ubhababa (South Africa). See *Mantshomane*.

Ubhek'indhlela (South Africa – Zulu). Bowed bar zither. Cf. *Tsijolo*.
Lit.: no. 151.

Ubo (Nigeria – Igbo). Term for *sansa* types.

Ubo-agala (Nigeria – Igbo). Bow lute with eight strings.

Ubo-agana (Nigeria). *Sansa* with gourd resonator.

Ubo-akwala (Nigeria). Trough-shaped zither with six strings.

'Ubudhiyya (Iraq). Song. In form, identical with *'atābā.*

Ubuxaka (South Africa—Zulu). A number of wooden sticks tied into a bundle and rattled by women at dances.
Lit.: no. 151.

Uche (Congo; Ituri Forest; Bambute). Drum.
Lit.: no. 255.

Ucheng (Java). See *Penchu.*

Uchi (Japan). "Meanwhile." Term in *koto* playing: the left hand beats the strings below the bridges during a pause in the music. *Uchi* can also be used for several drum patterns.
Lit.: no. 225.

Uchinarashi (Japan). Also *kin.* Bell in form of a metal bowl struck by a stick or hammer at its rim. It was used in Buddhist services.
Lit.: no. 185.

Uchitsuke (*Ukegoe*) (Japan). A *kyokusetzu.* Before the sound of one textual syllable and its musical performance is fully completed, a second syllable and its music is started, all in one breath, thus cutting short the first syllable and creating an uninterrupted progress.

Uchiwa-daiko (Japan). A flat frame drum with one skin. The body ends in a long handle and has the shape of an open fan. The drum is beaten with a thin stick and is used in Buddhist services and by itinerant street musicians.
Lit.: no. 185.

U-cho (*U-jo*) (Korea). One of the four important modes used in *ah-ak.* For all modes see *O-um-yak-po.*
Lit.: no. 136.

U-cho kae-myon-cho (Korea). One of the four important modes used in *ah-ak.* For all modes see *O-um-yak-po.*
Lit.: no. 136.

'Ūd (*Al 'Ud*) (Arabia; Iran; Middle East). "Wood." A short-necked lute of Persian origin, the precursor of the European lute. The instrument had four single (also four pairs of) strings, or three pairs and one speaker string; in North Africa it had (and has) five pairs, in Algeria four and in Egypt seven pairs, played with a plectrum (*zahma*). The medieval lute had frets, the modern instrument has none. The strings were called: *bam* (a Persian term that means "high"; *bam*, however, is the lowest sounding string). The next higher is called *maṭlat*, an Arabic term; the next higher string is *maṭnā*, again an Arabic term; and the highest string is called *zīr*, a Persian term (*zīr awwāl*). In the 9th century a 5th pair was added above *zir* (called either *zir 2* or *zir thani*). In many instances the top string is single. *Zīr* or *zīr thānī* can also be called *had.*

The courses are tuned G A d g c (see *Jagā* [*Yagā*]; *'Ashiran*; *Duga*; *Nawā*; *Kardān*). Cf. *Qasa'a.*
Lit.: nos. 69-70, 255.

Udahi (South Africa—Xhosa). Bowed stick zither. Cf. *Tsijolo.*
Lit.: no. 151.

Udātta (Vedic India). "Raised tone." The recitation tone in *samavedic* chant.
Lit.: no. 141.

Udayaravicandrikā (*Udayaravichandrikā*) (South India). *Janya rāga* of the 22nd *mēḷa* (*Kharaharapriyā*).
Tone material:
C E♭ F G B♭ c
c B♭ G F E♭ C
Lit.: no. 139.

Udayaravichandrikā (South India). *Janya rāga* of the 20th *mēḷa* (*Naṭabhairavī*).
Tone material:
C E♭ F G B♭ c
c B♭ G F E♭ C
Lit.: no. 139.

Uḍekki (Sri Lanka). Drum in the shape of an hourglass.
Lit.: no. 46.

Uḍekkiya (Sri Lanka). See *Uḍekki.*

Udgātṛ (Vedic India). Priest; the leader of the chant.

Udi (Zanzibar; Tanzania). Lute; fiddle. See *Zeze.*

Udongwe (South Africa Mpondo). A globular slitted whistle flute made of dried clay. Into the slit is placed a vibrating blade of grass.
Lit.: no. 151.

Uddukai (South India). Tamil term for *damaru.* The Malayalam term is *udekkiya*, the Telugu term is *udukka* (*uduka*).
Lit.: no. 255.

Udgītha (Vedic India). The second section of a *stoma.* It begins with the humming or chanting the sacred syllable *ōm* performed by the *udgātri* (priest). Cf. *Stoma.*
Lit.: no. 141.

Udgraha (India). See *Ābhōga.*

Udre (Congo – Momvu). Conical drum. Cf. *Kudre.*
Lit.: no. 26.

Udu (Nigeria – Igbo; Edo). Percussion clay pot. Cf. *Idudu egu.*
Lit.: no. 95.

Uḍuka (South India). South Indian term for *dāmaru.* Cf. *Uddukai.*

Uḍukkai (South India). See *Uddukai.* Cf. *Davaṇḍai.*
Lit.: no. 250.

Udupe (South India; Mysore). A drum in goblet shape used in religious ceremonies of the Lingayat sect.

Uffātah (Egypt; Morocco). Vertically-blown flute (held obliquely).

Ufie (*Uhie*) (Nigeria – Igbo). Royal slit-drum.

Ufu-bushi (Okinawa). Serious music of classical nature. "Great song."

Ufu-ufu (North Nias). Pipe used to attract animals.
Lit.: no. 255.

'Ugab (Ancient Israel). Hebrew name for flute or reed pipe. Cf. *Abūb(a).*
Lit.: no. 190.

Ugagweng (New Guinea). Notched flute with two finger holes.
Lit.: no. 258.

Uganga (Nigeria; Cameroun; Bassa). Drum. Cf. *Ganga.*
Lit.: no. 95.

U gaya (South Africa – Venda). To dance solo.

Ugbom-eze (Nigeria – Igbo). Double iron bells.

Ugene (Nigeria – Igbo). Globular clay flute with two finger holes.
Lit.: no. 223.

Ugi (*Uki*) (Japan). Name of a pitch in the *yokyōku* system. Cf. *Yokyōku.*
Lit.: no. 187.

Ugrā (India). Term for the 21st *śruti.* The corresponding note-name is *kākalī-ni.* Cf. *Śruti.*

Ugubhu (*Ugumbu*; *Guguolukhulu*) (South Africa – Zulu). Musical bow with a resonating gourd used for self-accompaniment (singing). Its Swazi name is *ligubhu*, the Xhosa name is *uhadi.* Cf. *Segwana.*
Lit.: no. 151.

Ugun (Solomon Isl.). Shell trumpet.
Lit.: no. 255.

Ugwala (*Unkwindi*) (South Africa—Zulu; Venda). Mouth bow. Name of the *gora.*
Lit.: no. 151.

Ugwali (South Africa—Xhosa; Hottentot). Term for *gora.*
Lit.: no. 151.

Uhadi (South Africa—Xhosa). Musical bow. The term is also applied to Western instruments, e.g., the American pipe organ. Cf. *Ugubhu*; *Segwana.*
Lit.: no. 151.

Uhie (Nigeria). See *Ufie.*

Uhomai (Japan). See *Bugaku.*

Uhō-no-gaku (Japan). Music of the right side. Cf. *Komagaku*; *Gagaku.*

U imba (South Africa). Venda term for singing.

Uimbaji (East Africa-Swahili). See *Kuimba.*

Uin (Caroline Isl.—Ponape). Ceremonial dance.
Lit.: no. 259.

Ujjur karsana (Southeast India; Bastar State—Jhoria Muria Gond). Gotul marriage dance.
Lit.: no. 142.

U-jo (Korea). A basic pitch; a finger hole. Cf. *Tae-kum.*

Ujungam (West Java). Cf. *Main chachih* (Flores).

Ukara (Bali). Notational symbol.
Lit.: no. 197.

Ukegoe (Japan). See *Uchitsuke.*

'Ukēkē (Hawaii). Musical bow with three strings.
Lit.: nos. 37, 278.

Ukkalī (India; Bengal). Also *ukkarī.* Drum.
Lit.: no. 255.

Ukolo (*Ikolo*) (Nigeria—Igbo). Large drum with double slits in the body.

Ukom (Nigeria—Igbo). Small kettledrums placed in a semicircle around the player.

Ukombe (South Africa—Xhosa). Whistle in the form of a double flute. Cf. *Uveve.*
Lit.: no. 151.

Ukuhlabela (South Africa—Nguni). Singing; group recitation.

Ula (Polynesia—Tonga). Dance of standing women.

Uḷai (South India). Tamil note-name for *ma*, the fourth degree of the heptatonic scale.

Ulbura (South Australia). Bull roarer or wooden trumpet of the aboriginals. The performer sings or shouts through the hollow wooden block ("trumpet"). Cf. *Ilpirra.*

Ulem (Java). See *Ombak.*

Ulet (Java). The "weaving together of sounds"; indicating forms of heterophony.
Lit.: no. 163.

Üliger (Mongolia). Epic songs.
Lit.: no. 60.

Ulimba (*Valimba*) (East Africa; Malawi). Large xylophone with gourd resonator.

Ulinganifu wa sauti (East Africa—Swahili). Musical harmony.

'Ulī 'ulī (Hawaii). Rattle. Either it is only one dried gourd, or it consists of three globular calabashes lined up in a row and pierced by a wooden stick. The two outer calabashes contain small rattling particles and the middle one is provided with a thread which, when pulled, causes the two outer globes to turn about and rattle.
Lit.: no. 37.

Ulla (Korea). The counterpart of the Chinese *yün-lo.* Ten circular metal discs suspended in a wooden frame.
Lit.: no. 287.

Ullāsita (India). See *Gamak(a).*

Ulu (Bali). Notational symbol.
Lit.: no. 197.

Ululē (Somali). See *Gobais.*

Ulullul (Kenya—Masai). Name of the drum of a neighboring tribe. The Masai themselves have no musical instrument except a primitive antelope horn.

Ulung (Bali). "To fall." To repeat a musical phrase without any interruption. *Berulung-ulung* means continuous repetition.
Lit.: no. 197.

Uluru (Uganda—Madi). Bamboo trumpet.

Ulur-ulur (Java). Leather or rattan cords which keep the drumheads stretched.
Lit.: no. 163.

Umābharaṇam (South India). *Janya rāga* of the 28th *mēḷa* (*Harikāmbhōji*).
Tone material:
C D E F G A B♭ c
c B♭ G F D E F D C
Lit.: no. 139.

Umakweyana (South Africa—Zulu; Swazi). Musical bow. Its Swazi name is *makhweyane.* Cf. *Dende*; *Imvingo.*
Lit.: no. 151.

Umbaende (South Africa—Bushmen). Bone whistle.
Lit.: no. 151.

Um-dze-pa (Tibet). See *Dbu-mdzad-pa.*

Umerego (Africa; Tanganyika—Watutu). The recitor's hummed prelude to an epic song.
Lit.: no. 29.

Umfece (South Africa—Zulu). Ankle rattles made of cocoons. Cf. *Amafohlwane.*

Umi (Japan). See *Koto* parts.

Umiuta (Japan). Folk songs of sailors and fishermen sung during their work at sea.

Umma (Sumer). Obscure term for musicians who perform laments and praises to the gods.
Lit.: no. 94.

Umpak ngandap (Java). See *Popor kangngisor.*

Umpak ngingil (Java). See *Popor kangduwur.*

Umpan (Japan). Gong with an irregularly-shaped rim.
Lit.: no. 255.

Umqangala (*Umqengele*) (South Africa—Swaziland; Mozambique). Musical bow played by women. Cf. *Lugube.*
Lit.: no. 151.

Umqengele (South Africa). See *Umqangala.*

Umqunge (South Africa—Pedi). Musical bow with the player's mouth used as resonator. Cf. *Umrube*; *Utiyane.*
Lit.: no. 151.

Umrube (South Africa—Xhosa; Zulu). Musical bow. Cf. *Umqunge.*
Lit.: no. 151.

Umtshingi (South Africa—Nguni; Pondo). End-blown flute without finger holes. Cf. *Ixilongo*; *Lekolilo. Umtshingo* is the Zulu term for the Pondo term *umtshingi.* Cf. *Nkongolo.*

Umtshingosi (South Africa—Swaziland). Vertical or cross flute. Cf. *Nkongolo.*

Umudende (Uganda). "Tinkle." Iron clapper.
Lit.: no. 190.

Umuduli (Ruanda). Also *umunahi.* Musical bow.

Umukunto (Congo – Balamba). Goblet drum used for dance music. Cf. *Kituma*.
Lit.: no. 26.

Umukuri (Uganda; Ruanda). Small flute with four finger holes.
Lit.: no. 200.

Umunahi (Central Africa Ruanda). See *Umuduli*.

Umutungu (Congo – Balamba). Calabash drum played by women.
Lit.: no. 26.

Umwere (West Kenya – Kuria). One of the *iribogwe* flutes. The *umwere*, made of a large section of bamboo, is transversely blown and has four finger holes.
Lit.: no. 299.

Umwirongi (Ruanda). Shepherd's and cattleman's bamboo flute with four finger holes.

Unanga (Congo – Warega). Board zither with five or six strings.
Lit.: no. 33.

Unbūb (Arabia). Cylindrical or conical tube used in various oboe types, e.g., *mizmār*.

Undemoū (Congo – Balese). Musical bow, a "changer of illness."
Lit.: no. 176.

Une (Nigeria – Igbo). Musical bow.

Ung (Korea). (1) A notational symbol of the *yul-cha-po* system. (2) A percussion stick. Its ends are beaten with a hammer during religious services.
Lit.: no. 52.

Ungara (New Guinea – Monumbo). Term for the *gerom*.
Lit.: no. 84.

Ung-ko (*Unggo*) (Korea). Drum, identical with the Chinese *ying-ku*. The *ung-ko*, the "answering drum," is slightly smaller than the *sakko*. There are no differences in structure and placing the instrument. Its sound "answers" the sound of the *sakko*.
Lit.: nos. 52, 179.

'Ungu (Solomon Isl.). Introductory songs.
Lit.: no. 246.

Unguoso (Solomon Isl.). Strophic songs sung when men set out to fish sharks.
Lit.: no. 246.

'Unk (Arabia). Term for *Ibrik*.

Unkin (India; Manipur). Jew's harp made of bamboo.
Lit.: no. 252.

Un-kin (Japan). Lute of the *gekkin* type, with four silken double strings and seven frets. It is played with a plectrum.
Lit.: no. 255.

Unkoka (South Africa – Zulu). Musical bow with calabash resonator. Various names of the instrument are: *tshikala* (or *dende*), Venda name; *tshitendole*, Tshopi name; *nkaku* (*nkoka*; *dende*), Thonga name; *sekgapa*, Sotho name; *umakweyana*, Swazi name. Cf. *Isiqwomqwomana*; *Uqwabe*; *Imivingo*; *Inkohlisa*.
Lit.: no. 151.

Unkwindi (South Africa – Zulu). See *Ugwala*.

Un-la (Korea). Gong chimes imported into Korea from China during the 16th century. Cf. *Yün-lo* (China).
Lit.: no. 179.

Unmṛṣṭa (India). One of the ancient 10 basic ways of touching *vīṇā* strings (*dhātu*): a stroke with the index finger of the left hand.
Lit.: no. 292.

Un-mun-ak (Korea). "Cloud-gate music." One type of *ah-ak*; it is music in honor of the spirits of heaven. *Un-mun-ak* represents the music and dances of the legendary Chinese emperor Huang Ti. Cf. *Ah-ak*.
Lit.: no. 136.

'Unnaiz (Arabia). Bagpipe.
Lit.: no. 255.

'Unq (Arabia; Persia). Neck of a string instrument.

Upadrava (Vedic India). The 4th section of a *stoma*. It is sung by the priest alone and is generally formed from the last few syllables of the preceding *pratihāra*.
Lit.: no. 141.

Upāṅga rāga (India). A *rāga* that uses exclusively notes of its parent *rāga*. Cf. *Bhāshāṅga rāga*.

Upatu (Tanzania; Zanzibar—Swahili). Gong or cymbal.

Upopo (Japan—Ainu). Sitting songs.

Uppu (Ancient Mesopotamia; Akkad). See *Ub* (Sumer).
Lit.: no. 94.

Uqwabe (South Africa—Thona). See *Imvingo*; *Inkohlisa*.

Uragoe (Japan). Falsetto singing. The production of these "bad sounds" is not appreciated and approved. The rule is that the voice must never sound higher than *fushō*. Higher sounds than *ōshō* must be avoided. Cf. *Gagaku*.
Lit.: no. 225.

Ura-no-yurushi (Japan). "Rear license." The second diploma issued to the musician who takes the regular course in *koto*, *kokyu*, or *shamisen* playing. Cf. *Omote-no-yurushi*; *Oku-no-yurushi*; *Naka-no-yurushi*.

Uran uran (Java). Song. Singing.

Urar (*Asnimmr*) (Morocco—Berber). Ceremonial songs sung generally by women.

Uraren (Japan). Term used in *koto* playing. It indicates a short sliding across the strings downward, beginning with the last string.
Lit.: no. 225.

U renda (South Africa—Venda). Reciting praise.

Urghan (Middle East). Wind instrument consisting of two parallel pipes, each provided with a single reed. The term is derived from *urghanun* (organum). Cf. *Urghanun*; *Urjan*.
Lit.: nos. 81, 215.

Urghanun burusi (Turkey). Trumpets, horns (17th-century).
Lit.: no. 81.

Urjan (Arabia; Iran). Organ.
Lit.: no. 81.

Urtin duu (Mongolia). Love song, rhythmically vague and drawn out, strophic with refrain. Accompanied by a fiddle. Cf. *Bogino duu*.

Uśāni (*Uśēni*) (South India). See *Husēni* (*Janya rāga* of the 22nd *mēḷa*).
Lit.: no. 139.

'Uša̋yrān (*'Ushayrān*) (Arabia). Name of a scale degree. For information see *Jagā* (*Yagā*), under the heading of which are listed all tone names and notes within the range of two octaves.

'Uśayrān (*'Ushayrān*) (Egypt). See, below, *'Ushayrān*, *maqām* of modern Egypt.

'Uśēni (*Ushēni*) (South India). See *Ḥusēni*.

'Ushāq (Arabia). Tone name; see *Buselik*. Cf. *Jagā* (*Yagā*), under the heading of which are listed all tone names and notes within the range of two octaves.

'Ushāq (Arabia). Literally, "passion." A genuine Arabic *maqām*. Its Iranian equivalent is *Buselik*. The tone material of *'Ushāq* is:

$D\ \overset{+}{E\flat}\ \overset{+}{F\flat}\ G\ A\ B\flat\ c\sharp\ d$

Lit. no. 56 states that *'Ushāq* uses the note c, *Buselik* uses *zirkula* (c♯).
Lit.: no. 121.

'Ushayrān (Arabia). See *'Ashirān*. The *maqām* of modern Egypt has the following tone material:

$A\ \overset{+}{B\flat}\ C\ D\ \overset{+}{E\flat}\ F\ G\ A$

Lit.: no. 64.

'Ushshāq (Arabia). *Maqām*.
Tone material:

$C\ D\ E\ F\ G\ A\ B\flat\ c$

According to Lit. no. 65.

'Ushshāq (Modern Tunisia). *Maqām*.
Tone material:

$C\sharp\ D\ E\ F\ G\ A\flat\ B\ c\ d$

Lit.: no. 64.

'Uššāq-Turkī (Middle East). *Maqām*.
Tone material:

$D\ \overset{+}{E\flat}\ F\ G\ A\ B\flat\ c\ d$

Lit.: no. 64.

Ussul (Turkey). See *Usul*.

Ustād (North India; Afghanistan). Master of music.

Usu-hiki uta (Japan). Songs sung during work or work-games; e.g., "pestle and mortar song" sung by two girls pounding rice or tea.
Lit.: no. 225.

Uṣūl (Turkey; Baghdad). Rhythmical pattern (mode) usually beaten on one or two drums. Musicians distinguish between low sounding beats (*düm*), middle sounding beats (*ka*), and high ones (*tek*).
Lit.: nos. 66, 243.

Usur (Southeast India; Abujhmar mountains; Muria Gond). Transverse flute of the Jhoria Muria Gond, similar or identical to the *hulur* of the Hill Maria Gond.
Lit.: no. 135.

Ut (Turkey). Short-necked lute without frets.
Lit.: no. 243.

Uta (Japan). (1) Stanza; song. (2) Section of narrative music, e.g., *joruri*.

Uta (Equatorial Africa). Musical bow.
Lit.: no. 190.

'Utāb (Old Arabia). See *Dasātīn* (Persia).

Uta-daiko (Japan). "The song drum." Also called *shim-daiko*, the tied drum, and *geza-daiko*, the drum of the Geza theater. The drum is similar to *kaiko* and has the same cylindrical or barrel shape, and is beaten with two wooden sticks which are lifted over the shoulder and then brought down in circular motions. The instrument has two heads and rests on a wooden frame in front of the player.
Lit.: nos. 225, 255.

Utagakari (Japan). Musical transition between the energetic *michiyuki* and the romantic *kudoki*. Cf. *Nagauta*.
Lit.: no. 187.

Utahiko (Japan). Freely recited (chanted) Japanese poems used in the *gagaku* repertory. Cf. *Gagaku*.

Utai (Japan). (1) The vocal part. Singing per se. (2) Unaccompanied songs in the *noh* performance. (3) Textual (verse) sections in the *noh* play. Usually there are lines alternating between seven and five syllables. These 12 syllables are set to music of eight (16) beats. This procedure of combining 7 + 5 syllables with eight (or 16) beats is characteristic of *noh* music. See *Hiranori*. Cf. *Yokyoku*; *Noh*.

Utaimono (Japan). In contrast to the narrative character of *joruri* and the dramatic *gidayu bushi*, the *utaimono* is a set of short lyrical songs for voice and *shamisen*, related to the *ko-uta* style. Cf. *Katarimono*.

Utamai (Japan). The oldest dances and songs of Japan. Cf. *Gagaku.*

Utaratibu (East Africa—Swahili). See *Wimbo, sauti. . . .*

Utari-gunkali (North India). An obscure *rāga* that can be ascribed to the *Bhairavī thāta.* Tone material (vague):

C D♭ *B♭* C D♭ E♭ F G A♭ B♭ C
c A♭ B♭ A♭ G A♭ F E♭ F E♭ D♭ C;
Vādis: indistinct

Lit.: no. 138.

Uta-zaimon (Japan). See *Yamabushi.*

Utete (Zanzibar). Swahili term for shawm; shepherd's flute.
Lit.: no. 255.

Utete (Marquesas Isl.; Samoa). (1) Musical bow; its gut string scraped wtih a small stick. Cf. Lit. no. 17. (2) Small jew's harp (Tonga).
Lit.: no. 84.

Utiyane (South Africa—Swazi). Also *ipiano.* Musical bow. Cf. *Umqunge.*
Lit.: no. 151.

U tshina (South Africa—Venda). To dance.

Uttama (South India). Cf. *Brinda gānam.*

Uttaramandrā (India). The first of the seven ancient *mūrchhanās*, derived from the *sa-grāma.*

Uttarayata (India). The third of the seven ancient *mūrchhanās*, derived from the *sa-grāma.*

Uttari (South India). *Janya rāga* of the 64th *mēḷa* (*Vāchaspati*).
Tone material:

C E F♯ G A B♭ c
c B♭ A F♯ E C *B♭* C

Lit.: no. 139.

Uttu (South India). Oboe type.
Lit.: no. 46.

Utuk-ubruk (*Longser*) (West Java). A *gamelan* that accompanies *wayang purwa*. It consists of two *bonangs*, one *gender*, one *kempul*, one *kencher* (= *kecher*), and one *kendang.*
Lit.: no. 163.

Uvete (Solomon Isl.). Bamboo end-blown flute with three finger holes.
Lit.: no. 255.

Uveve (*Uvuvu*) (South Africa—Zulu). (1) Zulu flute. Cf. *Luveve.* (2) Double whistle flute.
Lit.: no. 151.

Uvumi, kuimba vibaya, kukokoteza sauti (East Africa—Swahili). Singsong.

Uvuru (South Africa—Xhosa). Cf. *Luvuvu.*
Lit.: no. 151.

Uvuvu (South Africa). Se *Uveve.*

Uwajōshi (Japan). An obbligato *shamisen* used in *nagauta* music. It performs an octave higher, embellishing the music played by the leading *shamisen.* Cf. *Kase.*
Lit.: no. 185.

Uwe-kotang (Flores). Bunches of little Chinese pellet bells tied around the shinbones of dancers, together with brass ankle-bands, clapper bells. The pellet bells are called *reng* in the Maumere district. Both, pellet and clapper bells are called *(ng)gorong-gorong* (*wai-wonta*) in the Manggaray district.
Lit.: no. 166.

Uxonxoro (Africa—Bushmen). Musical bow.
Lit.: no. 149.

Uyon-uyon (Java). See *Nguyu-uyu.*

Uzai (South India). The note *ma* (the fourth

scale degree) in ancient Tamil terminology.
Lit.: no. 261.

'Uzal (Arabia). Obscure *maqām*. Allegedly a *Ḥijāz* using the low range (a fourth lower). In the past *'Uzal* was popular.
Lit.: no. 121.

Uzan (Egypt). Lute of Turkish origin.

Uzo (*M'bia*) (Angola—Mbande). Horn made of a hollow branch.

Uzun hava (Turkey). "Long melody." Folk song, rhythmically free, rich with ornaments and repeated single textual lines. The term indicated a song and rarely an instrumental piece. Cf. *Kirik hava.*
Lit.: no. 243.

V

Vāchaspati (South India). The 64th *mēḷa*:
C D E F♯ G A B♭ c
The *rāga* uses the same tone-material.
Lit.: no. 139.

Vādaka (Ancient India). Instrumentalists.

Vādī (*Aṁśa*) (North India). Next to the *sa* (basic note), the most important and stressed note of a *rāga* (see Lit. no. 138, pp. 5-6). This essential note has been the indicator of the correct performance time. If the *vādī* appears in the lower tetrachord of the scale, the performance time of the *rāga* is either the late afternoon, evening, or first part of the night. When the *vādī* stands in the upper tetrachord, the performance time is the late night, the morning, and the early afternoon. This old rule has become increasingly vague. In the *rāgas* of South India the *vādī* and *samvādī* have lost their importance. Cf. *Samvādī*; *Vivādī*; *Anuvādī*.
Lit.: no. 138.

Vādita (*Vādya*; *Kārupravādana*) (Ancient India). Instrumental music.
Lit.: no. 292.

Vādityavinōdini (South India). *Janya rāga* of the 33rd *mēḷa* (*Gāṅgeyabhushanī*).
Tone material:
C D♯ G A♭ B c
c B A♭ G D♯ C
Lit.: no. 139.

Vādya (Ancient India). Also *Kārupravādana.* Sanskrit term for instrumental music. See *Vādita*; *Vāditra.*
Lit.: no. 292.

Vāgadhīśvarī (South India). (1) The 34th *mēḷa*:
C D♯ E F G A B♭ c
(2) As *rāga*: in the old *asampūrṇa* system this *rāga* was called *Bhōgachhāyānāta*. The *rāga* has the same tone material as shown above.
Lit.: no. 139.

Vageshvari (North India). See *Bageshri rāga.*

Vaidika (India). A Brahmin who knows how to chant the Vedic songs and recitations.

Vaiṇaka (Ancient India). Sanskrit term for reed pipe.
Lit.: no. 255.

Vaiśākha (South India). *Janya rāga* of the 54th *mēḷa* (*Viśvambharī*).

Tone material:
C D♭ E F♯ G A♯ B c
c B A♯ B G F♯ E F♯ D♭ C
Lit.: no. 139.

Vaiśākha (South India). (1) The 54th *asampūrṇa mēḷa-rāga* without *kaṭapayādi* prefix. (2) The 54th *asampūrṇa mēḷa-rāga* with *kaṭapayādi* prefix. It was called *Vamśavatī*. Cf. *Rāga* (South India).

Vaj (*Waji*) (Afghanistan). An arched Kafir harp with four or five strings.

Vajrikā (India). Term for the 10th *śruti*. The corresponding note-name is *śuddha ma*. Cf. *Śruti*.
Lit.: no. 138.

Vakamalolo (Fiji Isl.). A *meke* in which the dancers are performing in sitting positions.
Lit.: no. 215.

Vakra (India). "Zig-zag." *Vakra rāgas* (or other melodies) have prescribed zig-zag features in ascending or descending lines.
Lit.: nos. 138-39.

Vakuḷābharaṇam (South India). (1) The 14th *mēḷa*:
C D♭ E F G A♭ B♭ c
(2) As *rāga* performed at any time. Veṅkaṭamakhin called this *rāga Vaṭivasantabhairavī*.
Lit.: no. 139.

Valaji (South India). *Janya rāga* of the 28th *mēḷa* (*Harikāmbhōji*).
Tone material:
C E G A B♭ c
c B♭ A G E C
Lit.: no. 139.

Va-letk-yot (Burma). A split bamboo stick used as a rattle.
Lit.: nos. 252, 254.

Vali (India). See *Gamak(a)*.

Valiha (Malagasy Republic; Ceram; Gorong; Halmahera; West New Guinea). Also *marovany*. A bamboo tube zither with a variable number of strings plucked with the bare fingers.
Lit.: nos. 218, 251.

Valihambalo (Southwest Malagasy Republic). Slit-drum.
Lit.: no. 251.

Vallika (South India). *Janya rāga* of the 4th *mēḷa* (*Vanaspāti*).
Tone material:
C E♭♭ G B♭ c
c B♭ G E♭♭ D♭ C
Lit.: no. 139.

Vaṃśa (Ancient India). Bamboo or reed flute. Cf. *Vansa*.

Vaṃśa-vādaka (Ancient India). Flute player.

Vaṃśavati (South India). See *Vaiśākha* (54th *asampūrṇa mēḷa*).
Lit.: no. 139.

Vāṃśī (*Baṅsi*) (India). Cross flute with 3-4 finger holes. The flute is made of bamboo, cane, or any other wood. It is called by various names. A few are: *bānsrī*; *bānsarī*; *bānsulī*; in South India *piḷḷāṅkulal*; in Sanskrit *muralī*; frequently the Arabic-Persian term *nāy* is used.
Lit.: no. 254.

Vaṃso (South India). Pāli term for the ancient *vāṃśī*.

Van (Vietnam). Instrumental ensemble consisting of four fiddles, each with two strings and differently tuned, and a small drum. The ensemble is used to provide ceremonial music.

Van (Iran; Khorasan). Old angular harp.

Vāṇa (Vedic India). Sanskrit term for sound, music; tube, flute of Yama (*veṇu*). Cf. *Rig Veda* 10,135,7. Often written as *bāna*; synonym with *vīṇā* (*bin*). Cf. ancient Egyptian *Bīn.t*; *Ben*; *Bent*.
Lit.: no. 292.

Vanajamukhi (South India). *Janya rāga* of the 38th *mēḷa* (*Jalārṇava*).
Tone material:
C D♭ E♭♭ F♯ B♭ c
c B♭ F♯ E♭♭ D♭ C
Lit.: no. 139.

Vanaspāti (South India). (1) The 4th *mēḷa*:
C D♭ E♭♭ F G A B♭ c
(2) As *rāga*, it has the same tone material as state above. Veṅkaṭamakhin (17th century) called this *rāga Bhānumatī*.
Lit.: no. 139.

Vandanadhāriṇi (South India). *Janya rāga* of the 65th *mēḷa* (*Mechakalyāṇī*).
Tone material:
C D F♯ G A c
c A G F♯ D C
Lit.: no. 139.

Vaṅgam (South India). *Janya rāga* of the 71st *mēḷa* (*Kosāla*).
Tone material:
C D♯ E F♯ A B c
c B A F♯ E D♯ C
Lit.: no. 139.

Vangiyam (South India). See *Kuzhal.*

Vāṇi (India). Music played by wind instruments; player of wind instruments (*Rig Veda* 31, 8; 3, 30, 10).

Vanshī (India). See *Banshī.*

Vaṅśa (*Vaṃśa*; *Bānsurī*; *Muralī*; *Fillagorī*) (India; Bengal). Reed tube; flute.

Vaṅun lanan (Java). The "male" *bonang* (sounding high).

Vaṅun vadon (Java). The "female" *bonang* (sounding low).

Van vu (Vietnam). The "civilian" dance of the *dai nhac*. Cf. *Vo vu.*

Varāḷi (South India). *Janya rāga* of the 39th *mēḷa* (*Jhālavarāḷi*). The scale of this *rāga* is identical with that of its primary *rāga* (*Jhālavarāḷi*).
Lit.: no. 139.

Varāli (South India). (1) The 39th *asampūrṇa mēḷa-rāga* without *kaṭapayādi* prefix. (2) The 39th *asampūrṇa mēḷa-rāga* with *kaṭapayādi* prefix. It was called *rāga Dhālivarāli.*
Lit.: no. 139.

Varamu (South India). *Janya rāga* of the 22nd *mēḷa* (*Kharaharapriyā*).
Tone material:
C E♭ F A B♭ c
c B♭ A F E♭ C
Lit.: no. 139.

Varata (South India). *Janya rāga* of the 58th *mēḷa* (*Hemāvatī*).
Tone material:
C D F♯ G B♭ c
c B♭ G F♯ D C
Lit.: no. 139.

Varati (*Barari*; *Berari*) (North India). *Rāga* ascribed to the *Marva thāta*. It is to be performed in the evening.
Tone material:
C D♭ E F♯ G A B c
c B A G F♯ E D♭ C; *Vādis*: E, A
Lit.: no. 138.

Varavarṇini (South India). *Janya rāga* of the 3rd *mēḷa* (*Gānamūrti*).
Tone material:
C E♭♭ F G B c
c B G F E♭♭ C
Lit.: no. 139.

Vardhani (South India). *Janya rāga* of the 11th *mēḷa* (*Kokilapriya*).
Tone material:
C E♭ F G F G A B c
c B G A G F E♭ C (*B* C)
Lit.: no. 139.

Vardhani (South India). See *Vivardhani.*

Vāridarañjani (South India). *Janya rāga* of the 72nd *mēḷa* (*Rasikapriyā*).
Tone material:
C D# F# G B c
c B G F# D# C
Lit.: no. 139.

Varja rāga (South India). A *janya rāga* in which one or more notes are deleted in the ascending or descending forms of the scale.

Varṇakariṇa (South India). *Janya rāga* of the 36th *mēḷa* (*Chalanāṭa*).
Tone material:
C D# F G B c
c B G F D# C
Lit.: no. 139.

Varṇam (India). (1) A long and complex piece of music to which the dancer shows her artistry in every possible aspect. The beginning of the *varṇam* appears with text, the second part is provided with *bols* or tone-syllables. The *varṇam* is one of the penultimate items of the *bhāratā nāṭyam* performance. (2) A melody pattern referred to in theoretical works of the past.

Varṇarūpiṇi (South India). *Janya rāga* of the 18th *mēḷa* (*Hātakāmbarī*).
Tone material:
C D♭ E G A# c
c A# G E D♭ C
Lit.: no. 139.

Varudham (South India). *Janya rāga* of the 23rd *mēḷa* (*Gaurīmanōharī*).
Tone material:
C E♭ G A B c
c B A G E♭ C
Lit.: no. 139.

Varuṇapriyā (South India). (1) The 24th *mēḷa*:
C D E♭ F G A# B c
(2) As *rāga*: the same tone material. Veṅkaṭamakhin called it *Vīravasantam*.
Lit.: no. 139.

Varunātmaja (South India). *Janya rāga* of the 39th *mēḷa* (*Jhālavarāḷi*).
Tone material:
C E♭♭ F# A♭ B c
c B A♭ F# E♭♭ C
Lit.: no. 139.

Vasant (*Vasanta*; *Basant*) (North India). Famous *rāga*, ascribed to the *Purvi thāta*. *Vasant* should be performed in spring in a slow, dignified manner. Its melodies should begin with the descending motion, hence the tone-material below is shown in the same manner.
Tone material:
c B A♭ G F# E D♭ C
C (E) F F# A♭ B c; *Vādis*: c, G
Lit.: no. 138.

Vasanta (South India). *Janya rāga* of the 17th *mēḷa* (*Sūryakānta*). This *rāga* has the same features as *Vasanta* of the 15th *mēḷa*. The only difference is that *Vasanta* of the 17th *mēḷa* uses the note A, while *Vasanta* of the 15th *mēḷa* employs A♭.
Lit.: no. 139.

Vasanta (South India). (Not to be mistaken for *Rāgavasant* of the 14th *mēḷa*; also not to be mistaken for *Vasant* of the 17th *mēḷa*.) This *rāga* is a *janya rāga* of the 15th *mēḷa* (*Māyāmāḷavagauḷa*).
Tone material:
C E F A♭ B c
c B A♭ F D♭ C
Lit.: no. 139.

Vasantabhairavi (South India). (1) The 14th *asampūrṇa mēḷa-rāga* without *kaṭapayādi* prefix. (2) The 14th *asampūrṇa mēḷa-rāga* with *kaṭapayādi* prefix. Veṅkaṭamakhin called this *rāga Vāṭivasantabhairavi*. See *Rāga* (South India).
Lit.: no. 139.

Vasantabhupalam (South India). *Janya rāga* of the 2nd *mēḷa* (*Ratnangi*).
Tone material:

C D♭ E♭♭ G A♭ B♭ c
c B♭ A♭ G F A♭ F E♭♭ D♭ C

Lit.: no. 139.

Vasantaghōshi (*Vasantaghōṣi*) (South India). *Janya rāga* of the 29th *mēḷa* (*Dhīraśaṅkarābharaṇam*).
Tone material:

C D G A B c
c B A G D C

Lit.: no. 139.

Vasantagīrvāṇi (South India). *Janya rāga* of the 59th *mēḷa* (*Dharmavatī*).
Tone material:

C D E♭ F♯ G A B c
c A B G F♯ E♭ D C

Lit.: no. 139.

Vasantakannaḍa (South India). *Janya rāga* of the 10th *mēḷa* (*Nāṭakapriya*).
Tone material:

C D♭ E♭ F G B♭ c
(c) A F G E♭ D♭ C *B♭*

Lit.: no. 139.

Vasantamanōharī (South India). *Janya rāga* of the 2nd *mēḷa* (*Ratnangi*).
Tone material:

C D♭ E♭♭ F A♭ B♭ c
c B♭ A♭ F E♭♭ D♭ C

Lit.: no. 139.

Vasantamāruva (South India). *Janya rāga* of the 51st *mēḷa* (*Kāmavardhanī*).
Tone material:

C D♭ E F♯ G A♭ B A♭ c
c A♭ G F♯ E C

Lit.: no. 139.

Vasantanārāyani (South India). *Janya rāga* of the 11th *mēḷa* (*Kokilapriya*).
Tone material:

C D♭ E♭ F G c
c B A G F E♭ D♭ C

Lit.: no. 139.

Vasantamāruva (South India). *Janya rāga* of the 51st *mēḷa* (*Kāmavardhanī*).
Tone material:

C D♭ E F♯ G A♭ B A♭ c
c A♭ G F♯ E C

Lit.: no. 139.

Vasantanārāyani (South India). *Janya rāga* of the 11th *mēḷa* (*Kokilapriya*).
Tone material:

C D♭ E♭ F G c
c B A G F E♭ D♭ C

Lit.: no. 139.

Vasantapriya (South India). *Janya rāga* of the 15th *mēḷa* (*Māyāmāḷavagauḷa*).
Tone material:

C D♭ E F G A♭ G B c
c B G F D♭ C

Lit.: no. 139.

Vasantatāriṇi (South India). *Janya rāga* of the 36th *mēḷa* (*Chalanāṭa*).
Tone material:

C D♯ F G B c
c B G F D♯ C

Lit.: no. 139.

Vasantavarāḷi (South India). *Janya rāga* of the 20th *mēḷa* (*Naṭabhairavī*).
Tone material:

C D F G A♭ B♭
B♭ A♭ G E♭ D C

Lit.: no. 139.

Vasantbahar (North India). *Rāga*. A combination of passages taken from the *rāgas Bahar* and *Vasant*. There are numerous possibilities of combining. For instance:

┌──── *Vasant* ────┐
c B A♭ G F♯ E F♯ E D♭ C

┌──── *Bahar* ────┐
C F G E♭ E♭ F B♭ A A B c

Lit.: no. 139.

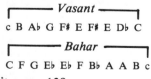

Vasantbhairavī (South India). *Janya rāga* of the 14th *mēḷa* (*Vakuḷābharaṇam*).
Tone material:
C D♭ E F A♭ B♭ c
c B♭ A♭ F G F E D♭ C
Lit.: no. 139.

Vasant-mukhari (North India). *Rāga*. Ascribed to the *Bhairavi thāta*. The *rāga* is to be performed in the morning.
Tone material:
C E F G A♭ B♭ c
c B♭ A♭ G F E D♭ C
Lit.: no. 138.

Vasantmukhāri (South India). *Janya rāga* of the 14th *mēḷa* (*Vakuḷābharaṇam*).
Tone material:
C F E F G A♭ B♭ c
c B♭ A♭ G F E D♭ C
Lit.: no. 139.

Vāsu (or: *Vāsu-chakra*) (South India). Name of the 8th *chakra* in the system of the 72nd *mēḷas*. Cf. *Rāga* (South India).

Vasugarbha (South India). *Janya rāga* of the 56th *mēḷa* (*Śaṇmukhapriyā*).
Tone material:
C D E♭ F♯ B♭ c
c B♭ F♯ E♭ D C
Lit.: no. 139.

Vasukari (South India). *Janya rāga* of the 56th *mēḷa* (*Śaṇmukhapriyā*).
Tone material:
C E♭ F♯ G A♭ B♭ c
c B♭ A♭ F♯ E♭ C (*B♭* C)
Lit.: no. 139.

Vasumati (South India). *Janya rāga* of the 21st *mēḷa* (*Kiravāṇi*).
Tone material:
C D G A♭ B c
c B A♭ G D C
Lit.: no. 139.

Vatāṅan (Java). Elaborately made wooden neck of the *rebāb*.
Lit.: no. 254.

Vaṭivasantabhairavī (South India). See *Vakuḷābharaṇam*. See also *Vasantabhairavī* of the 14th *asampūrṇa mēḷa*.

Vātsalya (India). "Affection toward children." One of the nine emotions (*rasas*) expressed in music. Cf. *Rasa*; *Navarasa*.

Vazang (East Bengal). Large wooden jew's harp.
Lit.: no. 255.

Veda (or: *Veda chakra*) (South India). Name of the 4th *chakra* in the system of the 72 *mēḷas*. Cf. *Rāga* (South India).
Lit.: no. 139.

Vēdaghōshapriya (*Vēdaghōṣapriya*) (South India). *Janya rāga* of the 28th *mēḷa* (*Harikāmbhōji*).
Tone material:
A B♭ C D E F (G)
G F E D C *B♭ A B♭ G*
This *rāga* has *pañchamāntya* character.
Lit.: no. 139.

Vēdandagāmini (South India). *Janya rāga* of the 29th *mēḷa* (*Dhīraśaṅkarābharaṇam*).
Tone material:
C E F G B c
c B G F E C
Lit.: no. 139.

Vēdasvarūpi (South India). *Janya rāga* of the 52nd *mēḷa* (*Rāmapriyā*).
Tone material:
C D♭ E F♯ G A B♭ G c
c B♭ A B♭ G F♯ E C
Lit.: no. 139.

Vēdika (South India). *Janya rāga* of the 44th *mēḷa* (*Bhāvapriyā*).
Tone material:
C D♭ E♭ F♯ B♭ c
c B♭ F♯ E♭ D♭ C
Lit.: no. 139.

Vegavāhini (South India). *Janya rāga* of the 16th *mēḷa* (*Chakravāka*).
Tone material:
C D♭ E F G A B♭ A c
c B♭ A G F E D♭ C
Lit.: no. 139.

Vegavāhini (South India). (1) The 16th *asampūrṇa mēḷa-rāga* without *kaṭapayādi* prefix. (2) The 16th *asampūrṇa mēḷa-rāga* with *kaṭapayādi* prefix was called *Toyavegavāhini.* See *Rāga* (South India).

Veḷāvalī (South India). *Janya rāga* of the 23rd *mēḷa* (*Gaurīmanōharī*).
Tone material:
C D F G A c
c B A G F E♭ D C
Lit.: no. 139.

Velāvali (South India). (1) The 23rd *asampūrṇa mēḷa-rāga* without *kaṭapayādi* prefix. (2) The 23rd *asampūrṇa mēḷa-rāga* with *kaṭapayādi* prefix was called *Gaurīvelāvali.* Cf. *Rāga* (South India).
Lit.: no. 139.

Venava (Sri Lanka). Sinhalese term for fiddle with a coconut (or small cylindrical) body, with two strings—one made of horsehair, the other of flax. The instrument is played with a horsehair bow.
Lit.: no. 254.

Veṇu (Ancient India). Sanskrit term ("cane," "bamboo") for an end-blown, long bamboo flute. The instrument has no finger holes. Cf. *Vāṇa.*
Lit.: nos. 250, 254.

Vibhāga (India). See *Tāla.*

Vibhasa (North India). Also *vibhas. Rāga* ascribed to the *Bhairav thāta.* See *Bibhas.*
Lit.: no. 138.

Vibhāvari (South India). *Janya rāga* of the 6th *mēḷa* (*Tānarūpi*).
Tone material:
C D♭ F G A♯ c
c B G F D♭ C
Lit.: no. 139.

Vichitra vīṇā (*Bichitrabīṇ*) (North India). A *vīṇā* of recent origin. It consists of a broad wooden fingerboard placed upon two polished and ornamented gourds. The instrument has six brass and steel strings and 12 sympathetic wire strings. The *vichitra vīṇā* has no frets and its strings are plucked with a *mizrab* and stopped with a round piece of glass. Cf. *Gotuvādyam*; *Rudra vīṇā.*

Vidhinataka (South India). Religious folk theater.

Vihola (Vietnam). This Portuguese name indicates a bowed lute consisting of a flat wooden box with a rectangular resonance hole in the bottom board. The slightly curved neck has eight frets and supports three copper wire strings.
Lit.: no. 254.

Vihola (Moluccas). Bowed lute with a boat-shaped body. Each of its two strings has on its outside an additional string that produces a bourdon sound. Cf. *Taravangsa*; *Kasapi.*

Vijayābharaṇī (South India). *Janya rāga* of the 64th *mēḷa* (*Vāchaspati*).
Tone material:
C D E F♯ G A B♭ A c
c B♭ A G F♯ E D C
Lit.: no. 139.

Vijayābhīru (South India). *Janya rāga* of the 46th *mēḷa* (*Śaḍvidhamārgiṇī*).
Tone material:
C E♭ D♭ F♯ G B♭ A c
c A G F♯ E♭ D♭ C
Lit.: no. 536.

Vijayabhūshāvaḷi (South India). *Janya rāga* of the 43rd *mēḷa* (*Gavāmbōdhi*).
Tone material:
C D♭ E♭ F♯ G c
c B♭♭ A♭ G F♯ E♭ D♭ C
Lit.: no. 139.

Vijayadīpika (South India). *Janya rāga* of the 61st *mēḷa* (*Kāntāmaṇi*).
Tone material:
C D E F♯ G B♭♭ A♭ c
c A♭ B♭♭ F F♯ E D C
Lit.: no. 139.

Vijayagōtrāri (South India). *Janya rāga* of the 62nd *mēḷa* (*Riṣabhapriyā*).
Tone material:
C D E F♯ G B♭ c
c B♭ A♭ G F♯ E D C
Lit.: no. 139.

Vijayakōsalam (South India). *Janya rāga* of the 66th *mēḷa* (*Chitrāmbarī*).
Tone material:
C D E F♯ G c
c B G F♯ E C
Lit.: no. 139.

Vijayanāgari (South India). *Janya rāga* of the 58th *mēḷa* (*Hemāvatī*).
Tone material:
C D E♭ F♯ G A c
c A G F♯ E♭ D C
Lit.: no. 139.

Vijayanāgari (South India). *Janya rāga* of the 60th *mēḷa* (*Nītimatī*).
Tone material:
C D E♭ F♯ G A♯ c
c A♯ G F♯ E♭ D C
Lit.: no. 139.

Vijayaprata (South India). *Janya rāga* of the 36th *mēḷa* (*Chalanāṭa*).
Tone material:
C D♯ E F A♯ c
c B F E D♯ C
Lit.: no. 139.

Vijayasāmantam (South India). *Janya rāga* of the 58th *mēḷa* (*Hemāvatī*).
Tone material:
C E♭ F♯ G A c
c B♭ A F♯ E♭ D C
Lit.: no. 139.

Vijayasarasvati (South India). *Janya rāga* of the 57th *mēḷa* (*Siṃhendramadhyama*).
Tone material:
C E♭ F♯ G A♭ B c
c B G F♯ E♭ D C
Lit.: no. 139.

Vijayaśrī (South India). *Janya rāga* of the 41st *mēḷa* (*Pāvani*).
Tone material:
C E♭♭ D♭ E♭♭ F♯ G B c
c B G F♯ E♭♭ D♭ C
Lit.: no. 139.

Vijayaśrīkaṇṭhi (South India). *Janya rāga* of the 59th *mēḷa* (*Dharmavatī*).
Tone material:
C E♭ F♯ G c
c B A F♯ E♭ D C
Lit.: no. 139.

Vijayavasanta (South India). *Janya rāga* of the 54th *mēḷa* (*Viśvambharī*).
Tone material:
C F♯ G A♯ B c
c B A♯ G F♯ E C
Lit.: no. 139.

Vikṛta (India). Cf. *Jāti.*

Vilah (Java). A slab of the *saron sentem.*

Vilambit (*Vilamba kāla*) (India). Slow tempo.
Lit.: no. 136.

Vilangwi (Tanganyika—Washambala; Mozambique). Xylophone with 10-15 slabs placed across two banana trunks. The slabs are beaten by two persons with sticks.
Lit.: nos. 130, 255.

Vilap (Nepal). See *Bilap.*

Viḷari (South India). Tamil note name of *dha*, the sixth degree of the heptatonic scale. Also the name of an ancient mode, mentioned in the *Shilappadikaram.*
Lit.: no. 45.

Villupattu (South India). Religious songs accompanied by a musical bow, a rattle, and a percussive clay-pot.
Lit.: no. 46.

Vimali (South India). *Janya rāga* of the 34th *mēḷa* (*Vāgadhīśvarī*).
Tone material:
C D♯ E F G A B♭ A c
c B♭ A G F E C
Lit.: no. 139.

Vimbuza (East and Central Africa; Nyasaland—Wahenge). Dance accompanied by two tall conical drums, each with a single head. Cf. *Mohambu.*
Lit.: no. 155.

Vīn (Iran). Ancient horizontal angular harp with 10-12 strings.

Vin (Armenia). Lute.

Vina (Java). Stick zither.
Lit.: no. 168.

Vīṇā (India). Stick zither. Its history reaches back into the Vedic age. In the past the term *vīṇa* was applied to various stringed instruments. At the present time two types are distinguished:

1. The *bīn*, the *vīṇā* of the North. A bamboo stick rests upon two gourds. On the stick are mounted 16-22 high bridges that produce chromatic sequences. The instrument has seven wire strings, of which four run across the bridges, two on one side of the fingerboard and one on the other. They function as drone strings. The instrument is played with a wire plectrum (*mizrab*).
2. The *rudra vīṇā* of the South. The stick (fingerboard) is integrated with the lower gourd in a manner that a lute-form appears. The fingerboard curves upward and ends in the shape of an animal head. The instrument uses seven wire strings, of which three on one side of the fingerboard create bourdon sounds. The southern *vīṇā* is plucked with the fingertips.

The word *vīṇā* occurs frequently and does not always refer to stick zithers. A few of the terms are: *alapini vīṇā, bharata vīṇā, bichitrabīn, bīn, bipanchī, churamantalam, gōṭuvādyam, kachapī vīṇā, kairāta vīṇā, kāncha vīṇā, kanuna, kshudra katyayaṇa vīṇā, mahānātaka vīṇā, mahātī vīṇā, nāradiya vīṇā, pināka vīṇā, prasarinī vīṇā, ranjanī vīṇā, rudra vīṇā, śāradīyā vīṇā, sarasvati vīṇā, satatantrī vīṇā, śruti vīṇā, tritantri vīṇā, vipanchī vīṇā.*
Lit.: nos. 248, 250.

Vinadhari (South India). *Janya rāga* of the 16th *mēḷa* (*Chakravaka*).
Tone material:
C D♭ E G A B♭ c
c B♭ A G F E D♭ C
Lit.: no. 139.

Vīṇā kunju (India; Malabar Coast). Simple fiddle with one fiber string.
Lit.: no. 260.

Vīṇāvadini (South India). *Janya rāga* of the 28th *mēḷa* (*Harikābhōji*).
Tone material:
C D E G B♭ c
c B♭ G E D C
Lit.: no. 139.

Vinjomba (Africa; Angola). Dance.

Vipañcī vīṇā (India). (1) A lute with nine strings played with a plectrum (*koṇa*). Seven strings produce *śuddha* (normal, natural) notes, the other two accidental (*vikṛta*) notes. (2) A *sitar* type similar to the *kachapi vīṇā.*
Lit.: nos. 254-55.

Vipula (South India). *Janya rāga* of the 32nd *mēḷa* (*Rāgavardhanī*).
Tone material:
C D♯ E G A♭ c
c A♭ G E D♯ C
Lit.: no. 139.

Vira (India). Heroism. One of the nine emotions (*rasas*) expressed in music. Cf. *Navarasa*; *Rasa.*

Vīravasantam (South India). (1) See *Varuṇapriyā.* (2) *Janya rāga* of the 24th *mēḷa* (*Varuṇapriyā*).
Tone material:
C E♭ D F G c
c B A♯ G F E♭ D C
(3) The 24th *asampūrṇa mēḷa-rāga* without *kaṭapayādi* prefix. (4) The 24th *asampūrṇa mēḷa-rāga* with *kaṭapayādi* prefix. See *Rāga* (South India).
Lit.: no. 139.

Vīravikramam (South India). *Janya rāga* of the 4th *mēḷa* (*Vanaspāti*).
Tone material:
C D♭ E♭♭ F G A B♭ c
c B♭ G A F E♭♭ D♭ C
Lit.: no. 139.

Viśārata (South India). See *Vishārata.*

Vishārata (South India). *Janya rāga* of the 3rd *mēḷa* (*Gānamūrti*).
Tone material:
C D♭ F G B c
c B G F E♭♭ C
Lit.: no. 139.

Vishrantisthān (*Visrantisthān*) (North India). A note that has in a *rāga* a function that strongly resembles the importance of a *vādī.* The *vishrantisthān* serves as a stopping place for musical phrases and receives a "stressed note" treatment. Not all *rāgas* have a *vishrantisthān.* See e.g., the note G (*pa*), if *sa* is C, in *rāga Deshkar.*
Lit.: no. 139.

Vishupati (South India). *Janya rāga* of the 52nd *mēḷa* (*Rāmapriyā*).
Tone material:
C D♭ F♯ A B♭ c
c B♭ A F♯ D♭ C
Lit.: no. 139.

Viṣupati (South India). See *Vishupati.*

Viśvambharī (South India). The 54th *mēḷa*:
C D♭ E F♯ G A♯ B c
Also used as *rāga.*
Lit.: no. 139.

Vitapi (South India). *Janya rāga* of the 4th *mēḷa* (*Vanaspāti*).
Tone material:
C D♭ F G A c
c A G F D♭ C
Lit.: no. 139.

Vitika (South India). *Janya rāga* of the 7th *mēḷa* (*Senāpāti*).
Tone material:
C E♭ F G B♭♭ c
c B♭♭ G F E♭ C
Lit.: no. 139.

Vivādī (India). A "wrong" note in a *rāga* that, in some instances, can have ornamental, even characteristic, features. See, for instance, the note *ni komal* (B♭) in *rāga Deshkar. Ni komal* is used only as a very weakly treated starting point of a brief glide down to *dha* (A), the *vādī* of the *rāga.* Although *ni komal* is no regular note of *Deshkar*, the presentation of the *rāga* would be incomplete without its subtle use.
Lit.: no. 138.

Vivardhani (South India). *Janya rāga* of the 29th *mēḷa* (*Dhīraśaṅkarābharaṇam*).
Tone material:
C D F G c
c B A G F E D C
Lit.: no. 139.

Vivardhini (South India). *Janya rāga* of the 28th *mēḷa* (*Harikāmbhōji*).
Tone material:
C D F G c
c B♭ A G F E D C
Lit.: no. 139.

Vivo (Marquesas Isl.; Tahiti). Bamboo nose flute; Jew's harp.
Lit.: no. 7.

Viyanzi (Tanzania – Zaramo). Flutes and drums used for the *mbeta* dance.

Vizugo (Tanganyika – Washambala). Hourglass-shaped wooden double bell or rectangular wooden bell.
Lit.: no. 130.

Voamaintilany (Malagasy Republic – Majunga). Bamboo rattle. Cf. *Doka.*
Lit.: no. 251.

Volo (Malagasy Republic – Farafangana). Percussion beam. Cf. *Tsikaretika.*
Lit.: no. 251.

Võn (Ancient Arabia). Harp with lower chest.
Lit.: no. 76.

Von cõ (South Vietnam). Name of a scale. See list of scales shown under the heading of *Bac.*

Vo vu (Vietnam). Military dance of *dai nhac.* Cf. *Van vu.*

Vṛddha (India). See *Pluta.*
Lit.: no. 136.

Vu (Vietnam). The central boss of the *chieng* (gong).

Vudi-vudi (Congo – Kikongo). Alternate term for *kivudi-vudi.*
Lit.: no. 280.

Vuhudendung (New Hebrides; Pentecost Isl.). Small musical bow held between the teeth of the player and beaten with a small stick.
Lit.: nos. 18, 255.

Vuma (South Africa – Bantu). Literally, "concur," "harmonize." Melody sung by the majority of a choral group.
Lit.: no. 148.

Vul mi myel (Congo; Uganda – Alur). Drum beaten during dances.
Lit.: no. 26.

Vumi (Congo – Kikongo). Globular flute with 2-4 finger holes.
Lit.: no. 280.

Vurum-bumba (West Africa; Congo – Bunda). Also *wurumbumba.* Musical bow.
Lit.: no. 190.

W

Wa (Burma). Wooden clapper.

Wa (Indonesia; Achin). Term for *dermenan.* Cf. *Ra'us woja* (Flores).
Lit.: no. 163.

Wachent (Ethiopia). Oboe type.
Lit.: no. 102.

Wa'di (Ancient Egypt). Also *wadai*; *wadeni.*
Lit.: no. 74.

Wadjh (Arabia). Belly; corpus of lute instruments.

Wadon (Bali). The "female" *kenḍang* drum tuned a whole tone lower than the *lanang.*
Lit.: no. 197.

Wagaku (Japan). *Gagaku* pieces written by Japanese composers. These items were not approved by the Imperial Music Office and were performed outside the palace, in *ō-uta-dokoro* ("big song hall").
Lit.: no. 185.

Wagon (*Yamato goto*) (Japan). Ancient, indigenous six-stringed zither. The strings were made of silk and the bridges were movable. The instrument was used in Shinto music. Cf. *Suga-koto*; *Ya-goto.*
Lit.: nos. 185, 255.

Wagonghu (Korea). "Recumbent harp." Obsolete harp with 13 strings.
Lit.: no. 287.

Wai (China – M 7001). Term for the secondary operatic male actor-singer; e.g., the "elderly male." Cf. *Lao-sheng.*
Lit.: no. 183.

Wai (China). "Outer." The higher-pitched of two fiddle strings. Cf. *Nei.*

Waiata (New Zealand – Maori). Old songs; lamenting, love, funeral, farewell, and similar types that are not shouted but sung.
Lit.: no. 311.

Waiata aroha (New Zealand – Maori). Songs of love (usually not to a person but to the home).
Lit.: no. 228.

Waiata tangi (New Zealand – Maori). Lamentation; consolation songs.
Lit.: no. 228.

Waiata watupaiarehe (New Zealand – Maori). Fairy song.
Lit.: no. 228.

Waiata whaiaipo (New Zealand – Maori). Sweetheart song.
Lit.: no. 195.

Wai wonta (*Ngorong-gorong*) (Flores). See *Ume kotang.*

Wai-tiao (China – M 7001; M 6298). Foreign, barbarian scale. Cf. *Tiao.*
Lit.: no. 93.

Wajh'arḍibār (Middle East). *Maqām.*
Tone material:
$\overset{+}{E\flat}$ F G A B♭ c d e♭
Lit.: no. 64.

Waka (Japan). Short, poetic piece recited in *noh*, following the dance performance.
Lit.: no. 185.

Waki (Japan). The supporting actor who performs secondary roles in the *noh* drama. Cf. *Shite.*
Lit.: no. 185.

Wa-kong-hu (Korea). Obsolete harp with 21 vertically-strung silken strings. Cf. *Kung-hu* (China); *So-kong-hu.*
Lit.: no. 179.

Walé (*Chual*) (Flores). The "answering" chorus; a song performed by precentor and a refrain-singing chorus.
Lit.: no. 166.

Walet-hkok (Burma). Clapper.

Wa let kyong (Burma). A couple of long bamboo slabs, beaten against each other.

Wambi (*Kisumba*) (Congo). Bow-lute. Cf. *Angra okwena.*
Lit.: no. 206.

Wana (Congo – Mandjia). Hand bell.
Lit.: no. 255.

Wanes (Torres strait). Large bull roarer.
Lit.: no. 255.

Wangkis (Sunda District). See *Rebāb* (Sundanese).

Wangsi (Java). Also *bangsi.* Transverse flute of the Middle Javanese period. Also called *wenu, tudung(an).*
Lit.: no. 163.

Wang-tui (China). Instrumental ensemble of the Sung period.
Lit.: no. 227.

Wan-ham (Korea). See *Wul-keum* (*Wul-kum*).

Wani (Flores). See *Waning.*

Wani(ng) (Flores). Large, slender drum with a wooden body, often richly ornamented. It is called *wani* in East Flores, *geda* (*keda*) in Riangwulu (East Flores), *waning* in Maumere, *laba toda* in Nage, and *laba wai* in Ngada. The drum is played with wooden sticks.
Lit.: no. 166.

Wanigushi (Japan). "Mouth of the shark." A gold colored gong hung at the entrances of shrines. When entering, the devotee strikes the gong.
Lit.: no. 225.

Waning (*Wani*) (East Flores). Slender drum with a slightly conical shape. It is also called *genḍing* (*geḍa*; *keḍe*), a heavy bamboo drum with one skin.
Lit.: no. 166.

Wanjing karsana (Southeast India – Muria Gond). *Gotul* song that teaches how to husk rice. Cf. *Gotul pata.*
Lit.: no. 142.

Wan-lo (China). Distorted term for *yün-lo.*

Wann (Arabia). Also *van.* Ancient harp with the resonance corpus at the lower end. (In contrast, *jank* has the resonance corpus above.)

Wang-pi (Tibet). See *Hor-chin.*

Wansamba (Gambia; Ghana; Liberia—Mandingo). Term for *laala* rattle.
Lit.: no. 190.

Wāo (Burma; Southern Shan State—Palaung). Cylindrical reed or bamboo pipe with seven front finger holes and one rear thumbhole. It has a metal free reed.
Lit.: no. 252.

Wa'r (*Wa'ra*) (Ancient Egypt). Term for *wa'yr* (flute).

Wararao (East Africa; Somali Republic). Dance song of men.
Lit.: no. 98.

Warizume (Japan). Term in *koto* playing; a form of *kaki* on the 8th and 7th string is played. When the 7th string has been struck and is vibrating, a "half sharp," a slow moving up by semitone (*yu*), is produced by a glide of the finger. This procedure is executed slowly and appears often in the final phrase of a piece.
Lit.: no. 225.

Warup (Western Torres Strait; North Australia). A large drum in the shape of an hourglass.
Lit.: no. 255.

Wasan (Japan). Buddhist *shōmyō* songs with original Japanese texts. The following *wasan* types can be distinguished:

1. *Wasan* proper, songs that describe and explain the doctrine of the Buddha. They also praise the virtues of the abbot. The texts are in simple Japanese verse form.
2. *Kyoke*, prayers with Japanese text.
3. *Kunka-ka* (*kada* or *ge*), songs with either original Japanese texts or texts of foreign origin translated into Japanese, praising Buddhism.

Lit.: no. 185.

Waṣla (Near East). See *Nauba.*

Watangan (Java). See *Jeneng*; *Rebāb.*

Watar (Arabia). String of the *kemanje.*

Wataribyōshi (Japan). A *hayashi* pattern in *kabuki* music.

Watarimono (Japan). Performing a *gagaku* melody at a different pitch-level, whereby the contour is altered and a new mode becomes apparent.
Lit.: no. 185.

Wawachan (Sunda District). Chants of *tembang buhun.*

Wa-wa erh (China; Shantung). Term for a small brass or copper *sona.* Cf. *K'ai-ti.*
Lit.: no. 209.

Wayang (Java). Term for shadow. Shadows are believed to represent the spirits of ancestors in ancestral worship. The term is used in numerous types of dramatic performances.
Lit.: no. 163.

Wayang chokek (West Java). A dance-play with songs performed by women.

Wayang gambuh (Bali). See *Lampahan.*

Wayang gedok (Java). Shadow play. The musical accompaniment is performed by *gamelan pelog.*
Lit.: no. 163.

Wayang golek (Java). A shadow play with wooden puppets. The older type was called *golek menak*; the younger is called *golek purwa.*
Lit.: no. 163.

Wayang jemblung (Java). A *wayang* type accompanied by the *jemblung.* Its plots are taken from the Amir Hazah cycle. A *dalang* recites and there is no representation on the stage, either by pictures or puppets.
Lit.: no. 163.

Wayang kulit (Java). Shadow play that shows scenes from the Hindu epics *Mahābhārata* or *Rāmāyaṇa*. See *Wayang purwa*. The music is provided by the *gamelan slendro*.
Lit.: no. 163.

Wayang kulit (Bali). Shadow puppet play; theater. The puppets are generally cut from buffalo skin (*kulit* = hide). The performances appear in places where Hinduism is or was prevalent.
Lit.: no. 197.

Wayang kulit (Malaya). The formal structure of these plays show the following standard sequence of items (although subject to variants):

1. *Lagu Bertabuh*, opening item.
2. *Lagu t'o Maha Siku*, music played when Śiva Natarāja or another divinity enters.
3. *Lagu Dewah Panah*, music played when two divine warriors appear.
4. *Lagu Perang*, battle music.
5. *Lagu Dalang*, music played while the *Dalang* narrates and sings about Śri Rāma.
6. *Lagu Hulubalang*, music played when warriors enter and leave.
7. *Lagu Sri Rama Bernagkat Masuk Anjung*, music played when Śri Rāma leaves.
8. *Lagu Blai Blai Berjalan*, music played when any character is travelling.
9. *Lagu Tukar Dalang*, music played when the elder *Dalang* (*Dalang Tua*) performs a ritual.
10. *Lagu Pä' Dogol*, music played for entrance and exit of *Pa'Dogol*.
11. *Lagu Penutup* (*Lagu Mati Geduk*), finale.

Wayang lemah (Bali). A "day-*wayang*" performed during the afternoon.

Wayang orang (Java). See *Wayang wong*.

Wayang parwa (*Wayang purwa*) (Bali). Shadow play which has its plot taken from the *Mahabharata*, which is known in Bali as the *Astadasa parwa* or *Parwa* (18 books).
Lit.: no. 197.

Wayang purwa (Java). See *Wayang parwa*.

Wayang topeng (Java). Drama and mask; shadow play; dance drama. Cf. *Topeng*.
Lit.: no. 163.

Wayang wong (*Wayangorang*; *Ringgit tyang*) (Java; Bali). The modern dance drama with living actors (*wong* = man) without masks. The dialogue is sung and the subjects are taken from the Hindu epics *Mahābhārata* and *Rāmāyana*.
Lit.: no. 163.

Wa'yr (Ancient Egypt). Flute. Cf. *Wa'r*.
Lit.: no. 74.

Waza (Sudan). Ritual music: begging for rain. The ensemble consists of several gourd trumpets (*waza*).

Wazīrlī zūrnā (Turkey). The shawm in the band of the ruler's vizier; e.g., the vizier's shawm of king Solomon (Asaph) was called *aṣafī zūrnā* (or *wazīrlī zūrnā*).
Lit.: no. 81.

Wazn (Arabia). Musical poetic meter.
Lit.: no. 73.

Weda (Paluwe Isl.). See *Ego*.

Wedokan (*Istri*) (Java). Low pitched ("female") gong-kettles of the *bonang*.
Lit.: no. 163.

Wedza (*Wedsa*) (South Africa; South Rhodesia – Mashona). Calabash-music bow.
Lit.: no. 18.

Wei-shun (China – M 5519d; Giles 12,179). An ancient pot-shaped bell of the Chou Dynasty used for ceremonies at the Temple of Ancestors. It is suspended in a wooden frame with the mouth of the bell turned downward. Cf. *Shun*.
Lit.: no. 137.

Wei-yüeh (China – M 7088; M 7499). Reed flute.
Lit.: no. 137.

Wela (Java). Rest, silence; pause of a *kempul* beat. See *Ladrang*.
Lit.: no. 215.

Welen (Liberia—Kpelle). Leg, ankle bells.
Lit.: no. 284.

Weleri (*Goong leutik*) (West Java). See *Katiwul*.
Lit.: no. 163.

Welo (Flores). See *Nuren*; *Feko*.

Wen-sheng (China). See *Sheng* (M 5738); operatic actor-singer.

Wenu (Java). See *Wangsi*.

Were (Nigeria—Yoruba). Rectangular frame drum.

Were-were (*Temraga*) (New Hebrides). Scraper; bull roarer. Cf. *Wer-wer*.

Wer-wer (Java). Also *ower-ower*; *ereg-ereg*. Bull roarer.
Lit.: no. 163.

Weto (Flores; Nage—Boawae). See *Genggo* (*Ego*).

Wezai (Ancient Egypt). Panpipes.
Lit.: no. 109.

Whakaraara paa (New Zealand—Maori). Watching songs.

Whakaeke (New Zealand—Maori). The exact, faultless rhythm and intonation of dance songs performed by a chorus.
Lit.: no. 228.

Whi (Thailand). Wooden vertical flute. Cf. *Sernei*.

Whio (New Zealand). Whistle. See *Porutu*.
Lit.: no. 84.

Wideng(an) (Java). The low part around the boss of a gong. Cf. *Penchu*.
Lit.: no. 163.

Wikongwe (Kenya). See *Kikongwe*.
Lit.: no. 130.

Wilah (*Antawis*) (Java). The interval caused by a single tone-step. The Sunda name is *hambalan*.

Wilet (Java). "Melody." The meandering of a melody. Cf. *Wirama*.
Lit.: no. 163.

Wiletan (*Wilet*) (West Java). Metrical pattern. The entire phrase (*gongan*) is subdivided into two (or multiples of two) *kenongan* (*wiletan*), each containing four beats (*wilet*) of *kempul*, *ketuk* (tuned to *bem* or *barang*), or a 4-beat rest.
Lit.: no. 163.

Wilmurra (North Australia—Algamurra). Bull roarer.
Lit.: no. 255.

Wilwāl (Arabia). The wailing of mourning women.

Wimbo (*ghani*) (Africa—Swahili). Gong.
Wimbo (*au maneno*) *wa kunuizia uchawi* (*uganga*): incantation.
Wimbo chenye mabomba yanayotoa suiti kwa nguvu ya mivukuto, *kinanda*: organ.
Wimbo, *sauti*, *mafuaton ya kupiga ngoma*, *utaratibu*: melody.

Wirama (Java). Tempo; measure; singing in Hindu meters, particularly when performing parts of the *Rāmāyana*: e.g., *wirama wutuh* indicates a complete whole bar (*gongan*). At times *wirama* is incorrectly substituted by *wilet*. Cf. *Wiletan*. Lit. no. 163 presents the following *wirama* terms (from Jogya): *wirama antal* (*wirama kendo*), slow (see *Rangkep*); *wirama kalih*, two (see *Lugu*); *wirama kencheng*, quick; *wirama lomba*, single, unadorned, fast tempo; *wirama loro*, "2"; *wirama lugu*, ordinary, unadorned; *wirama rangkep*, double, folded

in two; *wirama sedeng*, average; *wirama seseg*, narrow, close together; *wirama tanggung* (or *dadi*), right, proper, tempo giusto; *wirama telu*, three (slow tempo); *wirama tikel*, double; *wirama toyamili*, running water.
Tempo indications (from slow to quick): *ngalamba*, *le(n)yepan*, *rangkep*, *lanchar*, *dodoan*, *kering*, *genchlek* (or *rusuh*).

Wirama sari (West Java). "Rhythm—harmony"; skillful dance of recent origin.

Wirama setunggal (Java). See *Wirama siji.*

Wirama siji (Java). Also *wirama setunggal.* Very fast tempo.

Witata (Burma). Name of any drum that is closed at its left side.
Lit.: no. 255.

Wiwitan (Java). See *Bebuka.*

Woi do'a (Flores). Double flute. See identical *Foi kedi.*
Lit.: no. 166.

Woi mere (Flores). See *Foi mere.*

Wo k'ung-hou (China). See *K'ung-hou.*

Wolchōn (Korea). Music imported from Khotan, Central Asia, representing a comic play of drunkards in their struggle for wine.

Woleke (Ghana). See *Agbadza.*

Wol-gum (Korea). See *Wol-kum.*

Woljōn (Korea). See *Wolchōn.*

Wol-kum (Korea). See *Wul-kum.*

Wong-babakan (Java). See *Wong (ba)barang.*

Wong (ba)barang (*Wong babakan*) (Java). Itinerant street musicians of Central Java. They perform mask-plays accompanied by a very simple *gamelan* with iron keys: *gamelan janggrung.*
Lit.: no. 163.

Wong gang (New Guinea). Drum. Cf. *On.*
Lit.: no. 190.

Wong piphat (Thailand). The Khon orchestra (*wong piphat khrerang ha*), a small percussion ensemble. Originally it consisted of five, later of 6-14 instruments: *ranat ek* (xylophone), *khong wong* (set of gongs), *pi* (*sanayi* type), *sphon* (or *thapon*) (*mṛdanga* type), *klong tad* (two big drums), *ching* (a pair of cymbals).
Lit.: no. 207.

Wōn-wōn (*Womo*) (New Guinea). Song performed antiphonally by a leader and a choir.

Woo tip kam (South China). Also *hoi tong baat yam.* Cantonese term for zither with about 16 wire strings strung across two bridges. The body is a wooden box in trapezoidal shape. The player strikes the strings with thin bamboo sticks. Another name of this instrument is *kam.*

Wot (Java). Lower section of the gong-edge where it turns inward.
Lit.: no. 163.

Wreksatama (Java). See *Keṭoprak.*

Wu (China—M 7187). Notational symbol (cf. *Kung-ch'e-p'u*).
Lit.: no. 136.

Wu (West Africa—Ewe). Drum. Cf. *Wuga.*
Lit.: no. 95.

Wu (Flores). A small bow made of a bamboo strip and bamboo fibers. It is used for playing the *remba.*
Lit.: no. 163.

Wugā (Ghana—Ewe). Chief drum. Cf. *Atsiagbekor.* This great and long war drum of

the chiefs is often ornamented with human skulls. Before going into battle the drum is offered food offerings.
Lit.: nos. 215, 255.

Wu-hsien ch'in (Korea). A five-stringed *ch'in* imported from China to Koguryo.

Wu-i (China—M 7180; M 2960). "Not determined." Absolute pitch: the eleventh tone of the spiral of fifths as shown in the *lü-lü.* If used as a notational symbol only the first syllable is used (*wu*). *Wu-i* is traditionally a male (*yang*) tone and is used as the basic note in Confucian hymns performed in September.
Lit.: no. 136.

Wule (Liberia—Kpelle). Song.
Lit.: no. 284.

Wul-keum (Korea). See *Wul-kum.*

Wul-kum (*Wul-keum*; *Wol-kum*; *Wan-ham*) (Korea). A flat lute with a circular body and a long neck. The instrument has four silken strings and 11-14 frets. The tuning of the strings is either 1, 1, 5, 5, or the same as that of the *tang p'i-p'a*, 1, 4, 4, 8. At the present time the *wul-kum* is used rarely. Cf. *Yüeh-ch'in* (China); *Gekkin* (Japan); *Cai dan nuyet* (Vietnam).
Lit.: no. 179.

Wu-lo (China). "Military gong." A small or medium-sized plain gong. It is slightly convex and has a flat center. The *wu-lo* is often used in theatrical performances (puppet drama). Its Cantonese name is *mo-lo*. Several other names in use are: *chia-luan-lo* (Mandarin); *ka-kwun-lo* (Cantonese); *hsiao-lo* (Mandarin); *siu-lo* (Cantonese); *su-lo* (Mandarin); *sou-lo* (Cantonese).
Lit.: no. 129.

Wupu-wupu (Congo—Mambanga). Friction drum.
Lit.: no. 17.

Wurumbumba (Congo—Bunda). Musical bow. Cf. *Vurumbumbum.*
Lit.: no. 255.

Wu-sheng (China—M 7195; M 5738). Stereotyped figure of a principal operatic actor-singer of the *yüan* drama. The term represents the leading part in military plays, the hero who has to be a good acrobat as well as a good actor-singer.

Wuṣtā (Arabia). Second finger (in *'ud* playing).
Lit.: no. 70.

Wuṣtā fi majrāha (Arabia). See *Aṣab'.*

aWuwu (New Guinea). Globular flute made of the shell of a fruit, played by women.
Lit.: no. 255.

X

Xāb (Thailand). Gong.
Lit.: no. 255.

Xalqi (Afghanistan). Turkmen songs.

Xang (Vietnam). Tone name. Cf. *Ho* (where all tone names are listed).

Xe (Vietnam). Tone name. Cf. *Ho* (where all tone names are listed).

Xguthe (South Africa—Hottentot; Bushmen). Simple lute with three or four strings. Cf. *Ramkie*; *Ravekinge*.
Lit.: no. 151.

Xing (Thailand). Little gong.
Lit.: no. 255.

Xin tien (Vietnam). See *Cai xin tien*.

Xu (Vietnam). Cf. *Ho* (where all tone names are listed).

Xunanda (Afghanistan). Singer.

Y

Ya (China—M 7222; cf. M 7214.7) "Tooth"; an ivory plectrum used by zither players. *Ya* indicates also a tubular drum and its strumming sounds.
Lit.: no. 137.

Ya (Japan). The ninth pipe of the *sho* (this pipe is a silent one).
Lit.: no. 225.

Yaba-zi (New Guinea—Marind-anim). Songs sung in festivals.

Ya-cheng (*La-ch'in*) (China—M 3756; M 1103). "Creaking zither." A bowed zither used in North China. It has a wooden body and 10 pairs of silken strings tuned to the anhemitonic pentatonic scale.
Lit.: no. 250.

Yaduga (Central Asia; Mongolia). Cf. *Jatag.*

Yadukulakāmbhōji (*Yarkulakāmbhōji*) (South India). *Janya rāga* of the 28th *mēḷa* (*Harikāmbhōji*).
Tone material:
C D F B A c (C D F E F G A c)
c B♭ A G F E D C
Lit.: no. 139.

Yagā (Arabia). See *Jagā.*

Ya-gaṇa (South India). See *Ashta gaṇas.*

Yāgapriyā (South India). (1) The 31st *mēḷa*:
C D♯ E F G A♭ B♭♭ c
(2) As *rāga*: at present it uses the same material as shown above. Veṅkaṭamakhin (17th century) called this *rāga Kalāvatī* with the following material:
C D♯ E F G A♭ B♭♭ A♭ G A♭ c
c B♭♭ A♭ G F D♯ E F D♯ C
Lit.: no. 139.

Yagibushi (Japan). A *bon-odori-uta*; it is a stylistic category of folk-songs. *Yagibushi* represents drinking- and dancing-songs. The style requires *shamisen* accompaniment, percussion instruments, and clapping of hands.

Yāgiṇi (South India). *Janya rāga* of the 58th *mēḷa* (*Hemāvatī*).
Tone material:
C D F♯ G B♭ c
c B♭ G F♯ D C
Lit.: no. 139.

Ya-goto (Japan). The eight-stringed *koto* developed from the *yamato-goto* (*wagon*).

It has eight double strings strung over two long low bridges.
Lit.: nos. 225, 250.

Ya-gvin (*Ra-gvin*) (Burma). Bronze cymbal with a flat rim and a large boss. Cf. *Ye-gwin.*
Lit.: no. 252.

Ya-hsiao (China—M 7222; M 2619). A *p'ai-hsiao* type with 24 pipes. The word *ya* refers to *ya-yüeh* ("elegant," "refined" music of temple and palace).

Ya-hsien (China—M 7225; M 2699). "The second presentation of offerings," the third of the six stanzas of the Hymn in Honor of Confucius. All six stanzas are: *ying-shen*, *ch'u-hsien*, *ya-hsien*, *chung-hsien*, *ch'e-chuan*, *sung-shen.* For notation and the entire text see Lit. no. 136.

Ya-hyōshi (*hachi-hyoshi*). Eight-beat performance on the *kakko* and *tsuri daiko* in *Bugaku*:

Lit.: no. 225.

Yai (Northeast Thailand; Laos). One of five modes used in *kaen* music, based on anhemitonic pentatonic tone material. Cf. *An nungsü; Lai yai.*
Lit.: no. 203.

Yak (*Yo*) (Korea). A small, vertical notched bamboo flute, one foot long, with three finger holes. It was played in sacrificial ceremonies. Cf. *Ah-ak*; *Yüeh* (*Yo*).
Lit.: nos. 52, 250.

Yak-gāh (Arabia). Tone name. In Persian: "the first" note. (All tone names within the range of two octaves are listed under the heading of *Jagā* [*Yagā*].)

Yak-gāh (*Jagā*; *Yagā*) (Middle East). *Maqām.*
Tone material:

(+) above F♯:
G A B♭ C D E F♯ G

Lit.: no. 64.

Yak-gāh (Modern Egypt). *Maqām.*
Tone material:

+ above B♭ and E♭:
G A B♭ C D E♭ F G

Lit.: no. 64.

Yak natuma (Sri Lanka). Ghost-dance. Exorcistic dance to drive away evil spirits and illness.
Lit.: no. 46.

Yakṣāpriya (South India). See *Yakshāpriya.*

Yakshagāna (South India). Dance and operatic drama in Kannarese supported by important temples. The performers appear in colorful costumes. The *yakshagāna* is becoming gradually obsolete. Cf. *Āṭa* (dance drama).

Yakshāpriya (South India). *Janya rāga* of the 37th *mēḷa* (*Sālaga*).
Tone material:

C D♭ F♯ G A♭ c
c A♭ G F♯ D♭ C

Lit.: no. 139.

Yaktāra (North India; Punjab). Term for *ektar* (*ektara* = "one stringer"). A spike lute with one string. A religious instrument often used by beggars.
Lit.: no. 254.

Ya-ku (China—M 7222; M 3479). Old name of the *hua-ku* (drum) (M 2212; M 3470).
Lit.: no. 209.

Yakumo(n)-koto (Japan). *Koto* with two strings. It is almost the same as the *nigenkin.* The

difference lies only in the body: the corpus of the *nigenkin* is a board, that of the *yakumon* is a flat box.
Lit.: no. 225.

Yamabushi (*Uta-zaimon*) (Japan). Saimon hymns distorted by travelling priests. The *yamabushi* were used to make fun of local events and ridicule love affairs in town. These secularized hymns were sung to the accompaniment of *shamisen* and were called *uta-zaimon.*
Lit.: no. 185.

Yamada-koto (Japan). (1) The *koto* of the present time. It is without inlaid or lacquer ornaments, and the *koto* master stresses the instrument's beauty of the natural wood. The instrument, mainly used by professionals, has the traditional 13 silken strings.
(2) A *koto* school founded by Yamada Kengyo, a *koto* master of the 18th century. This school cultivated and adapted various narrative *shamisen* pieces for the *koto.*
Lit.: nos. 185, 255.

Yaman (North India). See *Kalyan.*

Yaman dunbalayī (Turkey). Kettledrum (*yaman*).
Lit.: no. 81.

Yaman-kalyan (North India). *Rāga* ascribed to the *Kalyan thāta.* Its performance time is uncertain; probably during the first quarter of the night.
Tone material:

C D E F♯ G A B c — characteristic:
c B A G F♯ (F) E D C — (E F♮ E D C)
Vādis: E, B

Lit.: no. 138.

Yamani-bilaval (North India). *Rāga* ascribed to the *Bilaval thāta.* It should be performed in the morning.
Tone material:

C D E F♯ G A B c
c B (B♭) A G (F♯) F E D C; *Vādis*: C, G

Lit.: no. 138.

Yamatobue (*Yamato fuye*) (Japan). "Mountain pass flute." The successor of the *ama-no-toribue.* The *yamatobue* is the indigenous flute of Japan, a transversely-blown bamboo tube with six or seven finger holes. The instrument is wrapped with silk threads and carefully lacquered. Cf. *Kagura bue* (Shinto flute); *Atsuma fuye.*
Lit.: nos. 53, 185, 250.

Yamato koto (Japan). Board zither with six silken strings. See *Wagon.*

Yāmi (South India). *Janya rāga* of the 39th *mēḷa* (*Jhālavarāḷi*).
Tone material:

C D♭ F♯ A♭ B c
c B A♭ F♯ D C

Lit.: no. 139.

Yamilango (Congo—Bateke). Large drum beaten with two sticks. It is played only when there are official festivities held by the chief and his entourage.
Lit.: no. 26.

Yamuna (North India). See *Kalyan.*

Yamunakalyāṇī (South India). *Janya rāga* of the 65th *mēḷa* (*Mechakalyāṇī*).
Tone material:

C D E F♯ G A c (C D E G F♯ G A c)
c A G F♯ G E D C

Lit.: no. 139.

Yang (China). The "male force." In music *yang* was represented by the odd-numbered *lü*:

Lü name	Appropriate time for being basic note in Confucian hymns
wu-i	September
i-tse	July
jui-pin	May
ku-hsi	March
t'ai-ts'u	January
huang-chung	November

See *Yin* ("female force"). See *Lü-lü.*
Lit.: no. 136.

Yang (China). Male gong without boss.

Yang-ch'in (China—M 7252,22). "Foreign zither." An imported zither, probably from Europe. The instrument has a trapezoidal or oval-shaped box as body, two bridges across (or through which) run 14-20 wire strings consisting of 2, 3, or 4-string courses. The players pluck the strings with two bamboo pieces. Cf. *Yang-kum* (Korea).
Lit.: no. 209.

Yang-deb (written: *dbyangs-deb*) (Tibet). Song document; textbook.
Lit.: no. 143.

Yanggum (Korea). See *Yang-kum.*

Yang-keum (Korea). See *Yang-kum.*

Yang'ong (Thailand). Also *Saga-saga.* Long jew's harp made of bamboo.
Lit.: no. 254.

Yang-pan (China). Contemporary operas, "models" that deal with the class struggle and revolutionary matters.

Yangroi (India; East Bengal). Wooden jew's harp.
Lit.: no. 255.

Yang-yig (written: *dbyangs-yig*) (Tibet). Songbook of the Buddhist chant.
Lit.: no. 143.

Yang-zhu (Tibet). Bow of a fiddle.

Yanjung (Korea). See *Hwarang.*

Yan-kin (Japan). Term for the Chinese *yang-ch'in.*
Lit.: no. 225.

Yan-ljin (Tibet). String instrument.
Lit.: no. 125.

Yan-lo (China). Distorted term for *yün-lo* (gong chimes).

Yańon (Thailand). Cf. *Yangong.*

Yantra (India). Sanskrit term for "instrument."

Yao fa (South China). Puppets that are moved by chemical means in Cantonese plays.
Lit.: no. 129.

Yao-ku (China—M 7302; M 3479). "Waist-, loin-drum," a *chien-ku* type. Not to be mistaken for the hourglass-shaped *chang-ku.* Cf. *Hua-ku*; *T'ao-ku.*
Lit.: no. 137.

Ya-pu (China). "Elegant drama." Ming term for the *k'un-ch'ü* (operatic) style). See *Ch'uan-ch'i.* Other, lesser refined styles of the period were called *hua-pu* ("flower drama").

Yarō-kabuki (Japan). In the 17th century women were forbidden to perform on the theatrical stage. Men (*yarō*) in various costumes and make-ups were the only actors allowed.
Lit.: no. 187.

Yaroul (*Orghoul*) (Israel; Druse; Arabia). Double-reed instrument made of bamboo. It can be lengthened or shortened by attachable tubes.
Lit.: no. 157.

Yarukulakāmbhōji (South India). See *Yadukulakāmbhōji.*

Yarut (South New Guinea). Lament (song).

Yasaka (Japan). Cf. *Ichikata.*

Yatag (*Yitag*; *Itag*; *Jataga*) (West and Chakha Mongolia). A formerly popular, now rare, zither with a richly decorated body, 12 open silk strings with high movable bridges, one for each string, similar to the Chinese *cheng.* The strings are plucked with a plectrum (cf. *Khume*, "nail"). The Volga Kalmucks and Kirgizes use only 7-8 brass or gut strings. Cf. *Rgyud-mang* (Tibet).
Lit.: nos. 61, 225.

Yatara byōshi (Japan). Combination of two and three beats in alternation in a *gagaku* dance piece.
Lit.: no. 185.

Ya-ti (China—M 7222; M 6217). Literally, "elegant flute." Operatic Leitmotif that characterizes a fixed situation (or person). The *ya-ti* is common property and is used by many composers in numerous operas. The *ya-ti* are never sung, but invariably appear in the instrumental items, preludes, or interludes of the opera. Cf. *Ch'ü-p'ai.*
Lit.: no. 136.

Yatsu-byōshi (Japan). The eight-beat system of the *noh hayashi* music, to which all phrases, even shorter ones than eight beats, are adapted.
Lit.: no. 185.

Yatughan (Turkestan). A variety of the Chinese *cheng* (M 369). Cf. *Yatag.*

Yavanapuri (North India). See *Jaunpuri.*

Yavanika (India). Curtains at both sides of the theatrical stage indicating the entrance and exit for the actors.

Yayoi koto (Japan). *Koto* type consisting of a long, slim board with four silken strings.

Ya-yüeh (China—M 7222; M 4129a). The "elegant and refined" music, referring to the ancient traditional music representing the pure and noble nature of the music in the Confucian temple and in the imperial palace. The *ah-ak* was the Korean word, and *gagaku* the Japanese word for *ya-yüeh.*
Lit.: no. 136.

Yāzh (South India). Tamil term for an ancient, obscure harp or *vīṇā* with a boat-shaped body and numerous strings. According to Lit. no. 261, it allegedly had 100 strings. Although mentioned in Tamil literature of ancient South India, no trace of this instrument exists. Cf. *Kalam.*

Yeboshi (Japan). Term for the black lacquer cap worn by all musicians of the classical *noh* ensemble. The cap is never removed, not even before persons of the highest rank.
Lit.: no. 225.

Yee-wu (South China). Cantonese term for a fiddle with two strings and coconut or cylindrical bamboo body. The hair of its bow is strung between the two strings.

Ye gwin (Burma). Tuned small cups. Cf. *Ya gvin.*
Lit.: no. 163.

Yektār (India). Dialectal form of *ektār*, a "one-stringer." A beggar's instrument similar to the *anada-lahari* that could be described as a plucked drum. It consists of a vessel open at the top and closed at the bottom and an obliquely rising bamboo stick attached to the vessel. At the upper end of the stick one string is strung from one peg through the center of a membrane inside the vessel. Cf. *Tuṇtuṇ.*
Lit.: no. 254.

Yeli (Equatorial Africa; Cameroun—Babinga). Ritual chant sung by women; the song's magical function is supposed to provide the elephant-hunting men with success.
Lit.: nos. 39, 247.

Yemen (North India). Also *Yaman.* See *Kalyan.*

Yen (China—M 7364). A banquet; festival music of the Sung and T'ang periods.

Yen-ma (*T'ieh-ma*; *Yü-k'o*) (China). Rattle (chime) consisting of small plates of stone, glass, or metal, suspended from the eaves. *Yü-k'o* represents the ancient, literary name of this chime (or rattle).
Lit.: no. 209.

Yen nhac (Vietnam). Banquet music; court music.

Yen-ying-chü (China). Shadow theater of Peking.
Lit.: no. 129.

Yen-hsiao (China; Giles 13, 027; M 2619). *Yen* is a single large flute with five finger holes on top, one below and one at the end of the tube. The instrumet is a *p'ai-hsiao* type.
Lit.: no. 137.

Yen-yüeh (China—M 7364; M 4129a). Recreational, informal, and banquet music performed by the first orchestra of the *shih-pu-chi*. It is a dance suite of four parts. Its melodies used imported Central Asian features (*hu* music). Thus the dignified ancient pentatonic material was often changed by semitones and various ornamentations which found their way into the traditional *ya-yüeh*.
Lit.: no. 137.

Yen-yüeh hsiao (China—M 7364; M 4129a; M 2619). The *p'ai-hsiao* used in banquet music. The instrument had 21 pipes.
Lit.: no. 137.

Yer-ka (Tibet). Bell; group of bells.

Yheku (Assam—Naga). Jew's harp made of bamboo.
Lit.: no. 252.

Yi (China—M 3016). Tone name and notational symbol of the third diatonic degree notated by the *kung-ch'e p'u*. Assuming that *ho* (the basic note) is C, *yi* is E.
Lit.: no. 136.

Yi-fu (South China). Cantonese term for *erh-hu*.

Yi-ji (Korea). Cf. *Tae-kum*.

Yikhe dewkhe (written: *yeke tebke*) (Mongolia—Khalkha). The "big bridge" of the *khil-khuur*. The Khalkha Mongols believe that the bridge, made from a lower human jawbone, will help the prayer to sing with great expression.
Lit.: no. 60.

Yiki-yiki (Australia; North Queensland). Wooden trumpet of the aboriginals.

Yin (China—M 7444). The "female force." In music it is represented by the even-numbered *lü*:

Lü name	Appropriate time for being basic note in Confucian hymns
ying-chung	October
nan-lü	August
lin-chung	June
chung-lü	April
chia-chung	February
ta-lü	December

Cf. *Yang*. See *Lü-lü*.
Lit.: no. 136.

Yin (China). "Female" gong, brass bell with clapper, used by Buddhist priests.
Lit.: no. 255.

Yin (South China). Cantonese term for the two strings on a fiddle. The Mandarin term is *hsien*. The lower pitched string (in Mandarin) is called *nei*, the upper one *wai*.
Lit.: no. 129.

Yin (China). See *Chien-tzu*.
Lit.: no. 136.

Yin-ch'ing (China—M 7418; M 1164) (*Chi* [China—M 481]). A small hemispherical brass bell struck with a metal rod. It is used in Buddhist services. Cf. *Chi*.
Lit.: no. 209.

Ying-chung (China—M 7477; M 1514). "Answering bell." *Lü*. Absolute pitch. The sixth tone of the spiral of fifths as shown in the *lü-lü*. Traditionally *ying-chung* was a *yin* ("female") tone. It was used as basic note in Confucian hymns sung in the month of October. If used as a notational symbol only the first syllable (*ying*) was used.
Lit.: no. 136.

Yin-fu (China—M 7418; M 1922). Musical note.

Ying hsi (China). Shadow puppet theater.

Ying-ku (China—M 7477; M 3479). Drum in the shape of a flour barrel with two heads. The drum is suspended horizontally in a wooden frame and is beaten with two sticks. It is richly ornamented with birds, dragons and flowers. In Confucian worship it is placed on the east side of the Moon Terrace and is struck three times at the end of each verse of the hymn. The large *yin-ku* was also called *chin-ku* (M 1088; M 3479). If its body was plain and not ornamented, it was called *chien-ku* (M 853; M 3479; "established drum"), or *lu-ku* (M 3479; M 4181; "carriage drum") if placed upon a cart. Cf. *Tsu-ku*.
Lit.: nos. 82, 137, 209.

Ying-shen (China—M 7473; M 5716). "Receiving the approaching spirit"—the first of the six stanzas of the Hymn in Honor of Confucius. The other stanzas are: *chu-hsien*, *ya-hsien*, *chung-hsien*, *ch'e-chuan*, *sung-shen*. For notation and the entire text see Lit. no. 136.

Yin-yüeh (China). Music.

Yitag (*Yatag*) (Mongolia). See *Jataga*.

Yi-yang (China). A less important operatic style that was one of the forerunners of the *k'un-ch'ü*.

Yi-yin (China). Cantonese term for the *erh-hsien*.

Yo (China—M 7499). Ancient, vertically-blown bamboo flute, originally with three, later with six holes. Now the *yo* is obsolete and is used only as a wand in the hands of ritual dancers. *Yo* is often pronounced as *yüeh*.
Lit.: nos. 1, 209.

Yo (China—M 4129a). Occasional reading of *yüeh* ("music").

Yo (Congo—Mundang). Xylophone.
Lit.: no. 21.

Yō (Japan). *Yo-sen*, "hand made." Scale derived from the *ritsu* scale and used in folk music:

D (E) G (A) c d

This scale is often combined with the *in* scale.
Variants:

D E G A B d

D E G A c d

D F G A c d (Edo period, 1603-1868)

Cf. *In*.
Lit.: no. 185.

Yo-ch'in (China). A small zither with 13 single or double strings. Cf. *Yo kin* (Japan); *Yüeh-ch'in*.
Lit.: no. 255.

Yodaya (Burma). "Siamese airs." Songs composed in the style of Siamese songs and used in Burmese serious music. The texts of the *yodaya* deal with praise of nature.

Yoga (Java). See *Rebāb*; *Kosok*.

Yōgānandi (South India). *Janya rāga* of the 52nd *mēḷa* (*Rāmapriyā*).
Tone material:

C D♭ E F♯ G A B♭ c

c B♭ A G F♯ E C

Lit.: no. 139.

Yo-hyōshi (Japan). Measure of four beats. Cf. *Ya-hyōshi*.

Yok-chu (Korea). "Power push." A notational symbol for raising the pitch of a zither string by pushing it forward.

Yokeli (West Africa; Ivory Coast Republic). Bull roarer.
Lit.: no. 303.

Yo-kin (Japan). "Chinese *koto*"; small in size, with 13 brass strings that run across high bridges. Cf. *Yo-ch'in*.
Lit.: no. 225.

Yoko bue (Japan). Cross flute, similar to the *yamato bue*, with seven finger holes. Cf. *Ryuteki*.
Lit.: no. 185.

Yokthe pwe (Burma). Instrumental ensemble playing for puppet shows.

Yokyōku (Japan). *Bombai* chanted without strict rhythm; a singing style of *noh* actors and chorus. In contrast to the *kotoba* ("words") type, the *fushi* ("melody") type of *noh* is represented by the following two styles of *yokyōku*:

1. *Yowa* (*yowagin*), the "soft style."
2. *Tsuyō* (*tsuyōgin*), the "strong style."

The *yowa* scale is:

kuri	(approx.)	f′
jō-uki		e′
jō		d′
sashi-jō		c′
chū-uki		b
chū		a
ge-no-chū		e
ge-no-kuzushi		d
ryo		B

The scale of *tsuyo*, the "strong" form, is vague. The degrees *kuri*, *jō*, and *chū* can be represented by the same pitch. The same applied to *ge-no-chū*, *ge*, and *ryo*.
Lit.: nos. 185, 204.

Yombul (Korea). See *Sam-hyen.*

Yongdo (Korea). Four small barrel drums are attached to a wooden pole. When the pole is whirled about, the drums are beaten by small leather strips. Each drum has its own strip. The strips swing with their thickened ends against the drumheads. The *yongdo* is not in use anymore. Formerly it was played in *ah-ak* performances.

Yonggo (Korea). "Dragon drum." A small barrel drum, not in use any more. It was an *ah-ak* instrument.

Yonghar (Turkey). *Tanbur* with three wire strings.
Lit.: no. 255.

Yongsan chae (Korea). Buddhist chant for a dead person. The chant consists of a very long sequence of songs performed during three successive days.
Lit.: no. 287.

Yoraghayi (India; Bengal). A drum in form of a *mridanga* suspended from the neck of the player. The right-side head is the larger one of the two skins and (contrary to the *mridanga*) is beaten with a stick, while the left-hand head is played with the hand.
Lit.: no. 255.

Yō-sen (Japan). See *Yo* ("hard mode").

Yoṣit (India). See *Śtrī.*

Yotsu (*Kotsu*). Name of the third pipe of the *shō*. See *Shō*.
Lit.: no. 225.

Yotsudake (Japan). "Four bamboos." Clappers consisting of four rectangular pieces of bamboo. The player holds in each hand two pieces. The instrument is used in theatrical performances and by beggars. A closely related clapper with two pieces is the *shakubyoshi.* These clappers provide also the music to customary dances on the Ryukyu islands.
Lit.: no. 225.

Yotsudake uta (Japan). A song accompanied by the *yotsudake.*

Young-ko (Korea). A small barrel drum suspended horizontally from a frame. The drums are grouped in form of a wheel. Only the front drum is beaten (cf. *Ney-ko*). The instrument is used in sacrifices to the gods of Earth and Fertility. At the present time it is very rare.
Lit.: no. 179.

Young-to (Korea). Four small barrel drums, one above the other, are pierced by a vertical stick. When the stick is twirled, cords attached to each of the four bodies beat the four drumheads in *damaru*-like manner.
Lit.: no. 136.

Yo-uta (Japan). "Fourth verse." See *Kumi.*

Yowa (*Yowagin*) (Japan). Cf. *Yokyoku*; *Noh.*

Yowagin (Japan). The soft, lyrical manner of the *fushi* (melodious) style in *noh* plays. Cf. *Yokyōku.*
Lit.: no. 185.

Yu (Korea). See *Yul-cha-po.*
Lit.: no. 136.

Yü (China – M 7658). Solmization syllable and notational symbol indicating the note standing a major sixth above *kung* (e.g., A above C) of the ancient five- or seven-tone scales. Cf. *Kung* (M 3705), where the degrees of the scales are listed.
Lit.: nos. 136-37.

Yu (Japan). An ornament used in *koto* playing. A string, e.g., the 9th string (A), is struck briefly. While the string vibrates the stopping finger applies pressure to the bridge and thus raises the pitch of the vibrating string to A♯. This procedure is called *yu.* Before the string ends its vibration, the pressure is released so that the original pitch of the 9th string still becomes audible. This is then followed by striking the 8th string (G♯). Cf. *Ke.*
Lit.: no. 225.

Yü (China – M 7650). This wooden instrument has the form of a tiger resting on a rectangular box. The tiger has on its back 27 (28) "teeth" resembling a saw. At the end of each verse of a Confucian hymn, the attendant strikes the tiger three times on the head with his split bamboo rod, and then moves the rod three times along the teeth-like projections to indicate the end of the verse. Hence, the name "stopper" is applied to the instrument. The *yü* is placed on the west side of the hall which is symbolical for Harvest, Sunset, and Death.
Lit.: no. 250.

Yü (China – M 7596). Term for a *sheng* (M 5742) with 36 reed pipes.

Yua (Ghana). Small wooden flute.

Yubikawa (Japan). Thimble-shaped covers placed on three fingertips of the *ō-tsu-zumi* player. The thimbles, made of papier-mâché, create a sharp, dry effect when they strike the drumhead.

Yuddhagāndharva (Ancient India). Military music.

Yüeh (China – M 7499). A little stick in the form of a small flute held by dancers, instead of a genuine flute. In olden times it was a real flute with three finger holes. Occasionally *yüeh* can still be a flute with six holes, generally called *yo.* Cf. *Yak.*
Lit.: no. 137.

Yüeh (China – M 4129a). General term for music. Also called *Yo.*

Yüeh-ch'in (China – M 7696; M 1103). A flat lute with a circular body that resembles the full moon. Hence it was often called "moon guitar." The instrument has a short neck, 8-10 frets, and four strings either made of silk or of copper wire. The *yüeh-ch'in* was (and is) played either with a plectrum or plucked with the fingers. Cf. *Gekkin* (Japan).
Lit.: nos. 209, 250.

Yüeh-chü (China – M 7704; M 1593a). A pleasant operatic comedy of the Kwantung Province, of comparatively recent origin, with a female cast. The instruments used are *erh-hu, p'i-p'a, sheng,* and one of the flute types.

Yüeh-fu (China – M 4129; M 1928). The imperial ministry of music came into existence during the Han period. Its numerous activities included the supervision of the *ya-yüeh,* sacred and palace, classification of imported music (*hu-yüeh*), and preservation of the many pieces collected by the ministry. Its name meant also the district where the employed musicians and officials were housed, part of the imperial archives, and, of considerable importance, the establishing every few years of the *huang-chung,* the Chinese "Kammerton," and the checking of correct tunings of stone and bell chimes throughout the empire. The *yüeh-fu* had to maintain

the various orchestras for the emperor and one for the empress, and had also its influence in musical education, games (bow and arrows), and the large ballets.
Lit.: nos. 93, 137.

Yüeh-yin (China). Orchestra of the Sung period.
Lit.: nos. 55, 227.

Yuge (Sudan; Uganda—Kakwa; Bongo). Side-blown trumpet.
Lit.: no. 190.

Yü hsiao (China—M 7666; M 2619). *Hsiao* made of jade or marble. It came into use in the Confucian temple during the Yüan dynasty (1260-1368).
Lit.: no. 137.

Yuk (Korea). Tone syllable and symbol for the upper octave of *hap* in the *kong-chuk-po* system.

Yukara (Japan—Ainu). Epic.

Yü-k'o (China). See *Yen ma.*

Yuk-po (Korea). A simple solmization system that came into use during the 15th century. Its symbols employ the Korean Hangul script. The syllables that represent *yuk-po* use various vowels: the dark sounding ones denote lower sounding tones, vowels of brighter sound indicate higher pitched tones. The initial consonants of these syllables indicate the various instruments. E.g., in zither music are used *tǔng, tung, tang, tong, ting*; in *p'iri* music one finds *rǔ, ru, ra, ro, ri.* For further details see my book, Lit. no. 136.

Yuk-tae-kang (Korea). "The six great *kang.*" See *Chung-kan-po.*
Lit.: no. 136.

Yü-ku (China—M 7668; M 3479) (*Yü-t'ung* [China—M 3668; M 6637]). Tubular bamboo drum, painted red and black with a single snakeskin head struck with the fingers. The instrument has a vibrating metal tongue inside its body and is used generally by blind men and fortune tellers.
Lit.: no. 209.

Yukjabaegi (Korea). Song type with numerous variants.
Lit.: no. 215.

Yul-cha-po (Korea). "Principal letter notation." The Korean term for the Chinese *lü* notation. The written symbols are the same as the Chinese, but the names of the tones are differently pronounced.

Korean terms	Western notes e.g.	Chinese *lü*
hwang	C	*huang*
tae	C♯	*ta*
thae (*t'ae*)	D	*t'ai*
hyūp	D♯	*chia*
ko	E	*ku*
chung	F	*chung*
yu	F♯	*jui*
im	G	*lin*
i	G♯	*i*
nam	A	*nan*
mu	A♯	*wu*
ūng	B	*ying*

Lit.: no. 136.

Yün (China—M 7757). One of three signs for pause in notated songs of the Sung dynasty. Cf. *Chü* (M 1541); *Tou* (M 6521).

Yung-chung (China—M 7580; M 1503). The large single bell of the Confucian temple hung in a special bell tower (pagoda) at the east of the temple compound outside the hall. The bell was struck in response to the huge drum (*ku*), which was placed in a pagoda at the west side of the compound outside the hall.
Lit.: no. 137.

Yung-ko (Korea). Drum cluster consisting of eight small barrels which were painted yellow.
Lit.: no. 179.

Yung-to (Korea). Drum group of three small barrels, painted black. Cf. *T'a-ku.*
Lit.: no. 179.

Yün-lo (China). Gong chimes. Ten little gongs are suspended in a wooden frame. All gongs have the same diameter but differ in thickness. They produce the following sounds:

e		e		e
d c B	or:	B c d	or:	d c B
F G A		A G F		A G F
E D C		C D E		E D C

The instrument was played in Buddhist and Confucian services and at the imperial court. The Korean name is *un-la.*
Lit.: nos. 137, 250.

Yūnqār (Turkey). Medieval small lute with three strings.
Lit.: no. 81.

Yun-rye-ak (Korea). Melodies about tranquil spring; peaceful, eternal life; blessings; dignified dances of learned men and warriors.
Lit.: no. 52.

Yǔn-ǔm-pyo (Korea). "Continued sound symbols." The only ekphonetic notation in Korea. The symbols do not indicate specific pitches. They are dashes, hooks, dots, and a few Chinese characters. The symbols are related to the Japanese *heike-biwa* notation. For details see Lit. no. 136.

Yü-pang (China – M 7668; M 4912). A wooden drum carved in the shape of a fish, with a slit along its back and a loose wooden ball inside its body. The instrument is used in temples and monasteries.
Lit.: no. 209.

Yuri (Japan). "To make tremble." A *kyōkusetzu.* A trill-like ornamental feature performed either on the first or fifth note of the scale.
Lit.: no. 85.

Yuri-age (Japan). A *kyōkusetzu* (favored by the Tendai sect). A *yuri* that rises to a higher end-note. Cf. *Ō-yuri.*
Lit.: no. 85.

Yuri-kake-kiru (Japan). "Shake-suspension-cut." A *kyōkusetzu.* As the name conveys, the formula consists of three parts: a *yuri* that begins with a held note, a second part (*kake*) with three held notes linked with brief ornamental features performed in one breath, and a *kiru*, a pause.

Yuri-ori (Japan). A *kyōkusetzu*, a shake that rises in pitch. Cf. *Ō-yuri.*
Lit.: no. 85.

Yü-rük semai (Turkey). A brief concluding *peshref* in a *semai* rhythm. Cf. *Ayin.*

Yü-ti (China). Cf. *Ok-che.*
Lit.: no. 255.

Yü-t'ung (China). See *Yü-ku.*

Yu-yin (China). See *Chien-tzu.* Cf. *Yin.*

Yuyu (North Africa). See *Zagharid.*

Z

Zafan (Ethiopia). Folksong. A soloist sings the verses, the chorus joins with the refrain, and while all sing together the coda, the voices drop out, one by one, until only one single voice is left.
Lit.: no. 257.

Zafat (Yemen). Jewish procession songs. Cf. *Zafat*; *Helleloth.*

Zaghārīd (*Yuyu*) (North Africa). A woman produces a high pitched sound when the birth of an infant is celebrated.

Zago (Japan). Ancient drum, vertically hung. Cf. *Cho-ko.*
Lit.: nos. 52-53.

Zag-sal (Ancient Babylonia—Sumerian). Bow-shaped harp.
Lit.: no. 87.

Zagu (Ethiopia). Vertically-blown flute (similar to the *nāy*). Cf. *Agada.*
Lit.: no. 102.

Zaguf (Kashmir; Turkestan). See *Agada.*

Zahirok (Iran; Baluchistan). Song sung while traveling (or working).

Zahma (Arabia). Quill plectrum used when playing lutes.

Zā'ida (Arabia). Fiorituras; ornaments in music.

Zajal (Egypt; Islamic North Africa and Middle East). Sung poetry; strophic song: an alternation between the soloist and choir. The poetry used has popular character. Cf. *Nawba* (Eastern type).

Zakhma (Arabia). Club-sized wooden sticks used by dervishes for beating the *qudūm.*

Zakkal (Ancient Mesopotamia—Akkadian). Harp, vertically strung.
Lit.: no. 87.

Zalzal (Ancient Israel). Metal rattle.

Zāmar (Akkad). To sing.

Zāmar (Morocco—Berber). Two cane pipes with single reeds tied together and placed into big cow-horn bells. Each pipe has six finger holes. Cf. *Zamr*; *Zummare.*

Zamataba (Gabon). A one-string harp.

Zambi (South Africa—Thonga). See *Nxonxoru*; *Tshizambe*.
Lit.: no. 151.

Zami (Sumeria). Obscure string instrument; probably a harp or lyra. The term may also indicate praise-songs or hymns.
Lit.: no. 94.

Zāmir (Iran; Arabia). Musician.

Zammāra (Iraq). A popular double-reed pipe. Cf. *Zāmar*.
Lit.: no. 78.

Zamr (Arabia). Single (or double) reed pipe with seven finger holes. An 8th hole is at the back. See *Qabā zūrnā* (Egypt).
Lit.: nos. 34, 250.

Zamr (Islamic North Africa). A double clarinet type. Cf. *Zummarāh*.

Zamr al-sughayyir (Egypt). See *Jūrā zūrnā*.

Zamr el-kebir (Arabia). A large *zamr*.

Zamr el-soghair (Arabia). A small *zamr*.

Zamr mujwiz (Jordan). Double clarinet type.

Zamr siyāh nāy (Arabia). "Black *nay*." Cf. *Nāy siyāh*.
Lit.: no. 190.

Zamzam (Ancient Mesopotamia). Obscure instrument in the cult of the dead and in praise of the king.
Lit.: no. 94.

Zamzamma (India). *Gamak*; fast vibrato.

Zanbaq (Arabia). Ancient cane flute of Persian origin.

Zang (Afghanistan). Small bell.
Lit.: no. 255.

Zangak (Armenia). Also *zanakik*. Small bells.
Lit.: no. 109.

Zange (Japan). Buddhist prayer and confession.

Zangora (Equatorial Africa—Nzakara). Xylophone.
Lit.: no. 33.

Zangs-dung (Tibet). Very large copper horns, played in pairs. Cf. *Rag-dung*; *Dbang-dung*.
Lit.: no. 143.

Zangskar (India; Kashmir). Cross flute. Cf. *Murali*.

Zangūla (Iran; Afghanistan). Bell; jingle (in tambourine frame).
Lit.: no. 255.

Zangūlah (Middle East). *Maqām*.
Tone material:

C D♭ E F G A B♭(+) c

Lit.: no. 64.

Zanza (Africa; Congo). See *Sansa*. Cf. also *Abuboyo*; *Afonsangu*; *Akadongo k'abaluru*; *Ambira*; *Bamboli*; *Biti*; *Chisanchi*; *Deze*; *Dimba*; *Diti*; *Ekende*; *Geliti*; *Ibeka*; *Ikimbe*; *Insimbi*; *Isanzi*; *Jimba*; *Kabarome*; *Kalumba*; *Kankobele*; *Kansambi*; *Kasanga*; *Kasayi*; *Kibanda*; *Kibiti*; *Kimbanda*; *Kinditi kia nsi*; *Kisachi*; *Kisanchi*; *Kisansi*; *Likembe*; *Lukembi*; *Lukeme*; *Lusukia*; *Marimba*; *Maringa*; *Mbichi*; *Mbila*; *Mbira*; *Mbobila*; *Modeku*; *Molo*; *Muzumbi*; *Ngala*; *Nsansi*; *Nsimbi*; *Nzangwa*; *Ompochawa*; *Pokido*; *Sago*; *Sengwelembwe*; *Sippi*; *Tresangu*; *Uadaku*; *Zeze*; *Zimba*.
Lit.: nos. 190, 255.

Zao (Vietnam). See *Bao*.

Zaouzaya (Northwest Mauritania). A shepherd's bark flute with four front finger holes.

Zaqef qatan (Ancient Israel). Notational symbol

(⁚) used in biblical chant, indicating a strong disjunctive attitude.
Lit.: no. 309.

Zaqufl (Ethiopia). Wind instrument, similar to the *nāy*.

Zarb (Iran). Cf. *Tombak*.

Zār (Egypt; Sudan). (1) Song of exorcism. (2) Gentle consoling music performed by a singer, or by two or three flutes and drums in the dim light of a perfumed room where women gather in order to find peace and comfort.

Zara (Upper Volta—Bisa). Ankle rattles, clusters of small rattles.
Lit.: no. 50.

Ẓarb (*Dombek*) (Iran). Single-headed goblet-shaped drum.

Zarbasnāy (Turkestan). Transverse *nāy* made of brass or copper.
Lit.: no. 255.

Zarbi (Iran). Rhythmic, measured.

Zare (Upper Volta; North Rhodesia—Bisa). Ankle rattle.
Lit.: no. 50.

Zarkala (*Zirkula*; *Zir gūlah*) (Arabia). Tone name of a note one half tone higher than *rast*. (A list of all tone names and notes through two octaves can be seen under the heading of *Jagā* [*Yagā*].)

Zarqa (Ancient Israel). Notational symbol (~) used in biblical chant, indicating a weak disjunctive function.
Lit.: no. 309.

Zarr (Egypt). See *Zar*.

Zashiki-sadame (Japan). The proper way of body posture when singing *jōruri*; it is required to sit in a dignified manner and show no distortion of the face.
Lit.: no. 225.

Zat pwe (Burma). Instrumental ensemble performing secular music. Cf. *Yokthe pwe*.
Lit.: no. 185.

Zauj (Arabia). Couplet.

Zawā'id (Old Arabia). Ornaments used within a melody: trills and turns.
Lit.: no. 81.

Zawal (Arabia). See *Sunbula*.

Zawaq (Algiers—Biskra). Shepherd's wooden flute with five finger holes.
Lit.: no. 20.

Zāwīl (Middle East). *Maqām*.
Tone material:

C D E♭(+) F G A(♭) B c

Lit.: no. 64.

Zawk-i-Ṭarab (Middle East). *Maqām*.
Tone material:

D E♭ F G A♭ B c d e♭ f♯ g a

Lit.: no. 64.

Zedzilava (Malagasy Republic). Musical bow.
Lit.: no. 18.

Zejel (Arabia). See *Zajal*.

Zekr (Algeria—Biskra). Song without accompaniment.

Zelzele šama (Ancient Israel). Brightly sounding cymbals.
Lit.: no. 255.

Zelzele therua (Ancient Israel). Noisy cymbals.
Lit.: no. 255.

Zēmā (Ethiopia). Term for the modi: *ge'ez*; *'ezl*; and *araray*. These modi were used in sacred chant.

Zemmārē (Ethiopia). Liturgical (Coptic) eucharistic canticles.

Zeng (Iran). Finger-cymbals (tiny bells, clappers) used by dancers.
Lit.: no. 248.

Zenk (Kurdistan). Bell.
Lit.: no. 109.

Zen-nga (Ladakh). Morning and evening music. Both employ drums. Also *zim-nga.*

Zenze (Congo—Luba). Stick zither. Cf. *Nzenze.*
Lit.: no. 176.

Zeybek (Turkey). Popular dance music in the fixed rhythm of 9/8, each measure divided into 2/8+2/8+2/8+3/8, named after the mountain people who live near Izmir. The *zeybek* is performed in slow tempo.
Lit.: no. 32.

Zeze (East Africa—Swahili). (1) Board zither. Cf. also *Zanza*; *Sansa.* (2) Fiddle with one string.
Lit.: no. 215.

Zeze (Congo; Uganda). Barrel drum.
Lit.: no. 176.

Zhai (Afghanistan). Gut string.
Lit.: no. 255.

Zehdü (North Assam—Hrusso). *Dhol* type; barrel drum with two heads, of which one is beaten with the hand.
Lit.: no. 46.

Zhezhilava (Malagasy Republic). Musical bow.
Lit.: no. 255.

Zhih (Iran; Kurdistan). Gut string.

Zhilaf (*Zilaf*; *Shilaf*) (North India). *Rāga* allegedly of Persian origin. Two types exist:

1. *Rāga* ascribed to the *Bhairav thāta*, to be performed in the morning.

   Tone material:

   C E F G A♭c (*Jaunpuri* and *Bhairav* material)

   c A♭ G F E C; *Vādis*: A♭, C (if *Jaunpuri* and *Bhairav* are used)

2. *Rāga* ascribed to the *Asavari thāta*, consisting of elements taken from the *rāgas Jaunpuri*, *Khat*, or *Jaunpuri* and *Bhairav*.

The combination of the two elements does not permit presenting a distinct tone material. The following tone material is one of several possibilities:

C D♭ E F G B c

c B♭ A♭ G F E D♭ C; *Vādis*: A♭, E♭

Lit.: no. 138.

Zichirei (Japan). Rattle with three small bells. Cf. *Kajirei.*
Lit.: no. 190.

Ziker (Sudan). Sufi ritual group dance "remembering God." The dance is accompanied by percussion instruments. Cf. *Dhikr.*

Zil (Turkey; Kurdistan). Small finger bells; or, medium-sized copper cymbals. Cf. *Sil*; *Çegane.*
Lit.: no. 229.

Zilaf (North India). See *Zhilaf.*

Zilli def (Turkey). Frame drum with pairs of *zil* (jingles) inserted into openings cut into the frame.

Zillī māshā (Turkey). Cf. *Chaghāna.*

Zimare (Iran; Kurdistan). See *Duzele.*

Zimba (Congo—Babunda). *Sansa.*
Lit.: no. 33.

Zīr (Arabia). Term of Persian origin for the highest string of the *'ud.* Although it produces the highest pitch, *zīr* means "down, below." See *'Ud.*

Zīr (Arabia). Cf. *Zīr thānī.*

Zīrāfkand (Arabia). *Maqām.*
Tone material:

C E♭♭ E♭ F A♭♭ A♭ B♭♭ c♭ c

Lit.: no. 65.

Zīr awwāl (*Zīr*) (Arabia). The fourth-highest string of the *'ud.* See *Zir.* Cf. *Zīr thānī.*

Zirgūlah (Arabia). See *Zarkala. Maqām.*
Tone material:

D E F♯ G A $\overset{+}{\text{B}\flat}$ $\overset{(\sharp)}{\text{c}}$ d

Lit.: no. 64.

Zirkūla (Arabia). See *Zarkala.*

Zīr thānī (Arabia). Also "*zīr 2.*" The top string (the fifth) of the *'ud*, tuned a fourth higher than the *zīr* (*awwāl*) string. Cf. *'Ud.*

Zitengulo (North Rhodesia – Ila; Tonga). Improvised songs sung when a person dies and is buried.
Lit.: no. 99.

Ziyabilo (North Rhodesia – Ila; Tonga). Song.
Lit.: no. 99.

Zlöö (Ivory Coast). Songs of praise.

Zogaku (Japan). Also *zokugaku.* All music that is not *gagaku.*

Zōgei (Japan). "Mixed arts." Songs and dances that can be performed at the imperial court. E.g., *shirabyōshi* was danced by professional female performers to the singing of *imayō.*
Lit.: no. 53.

Zoigket (Armenia). Metrical value in Armenian liturgy. *Zoigket* denotes two metrical units. Cf. *Ket*; *Sugh.*
Lit.: no. 101.

Zokugaku (Japan). *Shamisen* music often described as music of the common people. It was scorned by the literate society but remained of interest. Cf. *Zogaku.*

Zoku sō (Japan). A *sō-no koto* derived from the *tsukushi sō*. At the present time it is called *koto.*
Lit.: no. 53.

Zokyoku (Japan). Light, popular music.

Zomari (Africa – Swahili). See *Anjomara.*

Zong-ak (Korea). "Pure music." A special type of former solemn palace music of Buddhist origin. Since Confucianism forced Buddhism from the palace, *zong-ak* was accepted in the Buddhist temples.
Lit.: no. 145.

Zon-so (Liberia – Kpelle). Leg rattles.
Lit.: no. 284.

Zorna (Iran; Kurdistan). See *Zūrnā.*

Zoso-kee (Liberia – Kpelle). Basket rattle.
Lit.: no. 284.

Zuglum (Philippines; South Mindanao). An imported plucked string instrument with a slim corpus and two fiber strings, one of which runs over seven frets.
Lit.: no. 255.

Zukra (Tripoli; Tunisia). Also *zuqqāra.* A mouth-blown bagpipe with two parallel chanters. Each has five finger holes.
Lit.: no. 250.

Zulami (Arabia). Double shawm of the 14th century. One tube had six holes; the other had none. Cf. *Nāy zunami.*
Lit.: no. 255.

Zumari (Kenya). Double-reed instrument with a wide bell.

Zummārah (Arabia; Turkey; Kenya). A double clarinet consisting of two cane tubes tied together side by side. Both tubes are provided with beating reeds and each tube has four fingerholes. The instrument has an unusually noisy sound. Cf. *Mashura*; *Zāmar*; *Arghul.*
Lit.: nos. 243, 250.

Zummārah arbawija (Arabia). A *zummārah* with four finger holes in each of the two tubes.
Lit.: nos. 250, 255.

Zummārah bi-soạn (Arabia). Crude bagpipe. Rarely found in Ėgypt.
Lit.: no. 255.

Zummārah khamsauia (Arabia). A *zummārah* with five finger holes in each of the two tubes.
Lit.: no. 255.

Zummārah sabauia (Arabia). A *zummārah* with five finger holes in the left closed tube and two in the right open tube.
Lit.: no. 255.

Zummārah sattawija (Arabia). A *zummārah* with six finger holes in each of the two pipes.
Lit.: no. 255.

Zuqqara (*Zukra*) (Arabia). Bagpipe.
Lit.: no. 255.

Zuqra (Tripoli; Tunisia). Oboe type. Cf. *Mizmār.*

Zurna (Turkey). Shawm with eight finger holes.

Zūrnā (North Africa – Berber). Oboe type. In Algeria and Lybia it is called *ghaiṭa.*

Zūrnā (Near East; Arabia; Iran; Turkey; Caucasus). Shawm in the form of a cone-shaped bowling pin with a flaring bell. The mouthpiece has two small reeds. The instrument has seven front finger holes and one thumbhole in the rear. It is widely in use. Some of its names are: *sānāyī*, *srnai*, *sernei*, *serunai*, *srune*, *sur-na*, *surnāy.*
Lit.: no. 255.

Zurr (Mongolia; Kalmuck). A vertical flute with three finger holes related to the Bashkir *kura* and the Kirghiz *cho'or.*
Lit.: no. 60.

Zuzu (Congo – Balese). Ground bow.
Lit.: no. 176.

Zwilombe (South Africa – Venda). See *Tshilombe.*

Literature

1. Aalst, J. A. van. *Chinese Music.* Shanghai, 1884, 1933, 1939.

2. Aarflot, Olav. *Kinsisk Musikk.* Oslo, 1948.

3. Adriansz, Willem. "Rōsai." *Ethnomusicology* 13/1 (1969): 101-23.

4. Agrawala, V. K. *Traditions and Trends in Indian Music.* Meerut, 1966.

5. Alender, I. S. *Musical Instruments of China* [in Russian]. Moscow, 1958.

6. Al Faruqi, Lois Ibsen. "Muwashshaḥ: A Vocal Form in Islamic Culture." *Ethnomusicology* 19/1 (1975): 1-29.

Al-Khulay. *See* El-Kholay, no. **56.**

7. Anderssen, Johannes Carl. *Maori Music.* New Plymouth, New Zealand, 1934.

8. Andersson, Otto. *The Bowed Harp.* London: W. Reeves, 1930.

9. Angul, Hammerich. *Das musikhistorische Museum zu Kopenhagen: Beschreibender Katalog.* Copenhagen, 1911.

10. Ankermann, Bernhard. "Afrikanische Musikinstrumente." *Ethnologisches Notizblatt* 3 (Berlin, 1901).

11. Arndt, P. P. *Mythologie, Religion und Magie im Sikagebiet (östl. Mittelflores).* Ende-Flores, 1932.

12. Avenary, Hanoch. "Jüdische Music: Geschichte der jüdischen Musik." *Die Musik in Geschichte und Gegenwart* 7 (1958), cols. 225-61.

13. Ayyangar, Raghunathaswami Rangaramanuja. *History of South Indian (Carnatic) Music. . . .* Madras, 1972.

14. Bahat-Ratzon, Noemi. "Le Saff-procession dansée dans les cérémonies du mariage druze." *Orbis musicae* 3/5 (Tel Aviv, 1975-76).

Literature

15. Baines, Anthony. *Woodwind Instruments and Their History.* London: Faber and Faber, 1957.

16. Bake, Arnold. "Indische Musik." *Die Musik in Geschichte und Gegenwart* 6 (1957), cols. 1150-85.

17. Balfour, Henry. "The Friction Drum." *Journal of the Royal Anthropological Institute* 37 (London, 1907): 67-92.

18. ———. *The Natural History of the Musical Bow.* Oxford: Clarendon Press, 1899.

19. ———. "Report on a Collection of Musical Instruments from the Siamese Malay States and Peak." In *Fasciculi Malayensis, Anthropology,* pt. IIa. Liverpool, 1904.

20. Bartók, Béla. "Die Volksmusik der Araber von Biskra und Umgebung." *Zeitschrift für Musikwissenschaft* 2 (1919-20): 489-522.

21. Baumann, H. "Die materielle Kultur der Azande und Mangbetu." *Bässler Archiv* 2 (Berlin, 1927).

22. Berliner, Paul. "The Poetic Song Texts Accompanying the *Mbira Dzavadzimu.*" *Ethnomusicology* 20/3 (1976): 451-82.

23. *Bharatanāṭyaśāstra.* English transl. by Manomohan Ghosh. Calcutta, 1951 and 1961.

24. Bischoff, Friedrich, and Walter Kaufmann. "Die Melodie der Gesänge des Bulgan Schamanen." *Zentralasiatische Studien* 10 (Wiesbaden, 1976): 311-25.

25. Bodrogi, Tibor. *Yabim Drums in the Biro Collection.* Budapest: Orszaros Nepraszi Muzeum, 1950.

26. Boone, Olga. "Les Tambours du Congo Belge et du Ruanda-Urundi." *Annales du Musée du Congo Belge.* Tervueren, 1951.

27. ———. "Les Xylophones du Congo Belge." *Annales du Musée du Congo Belge.* Tervueren, 1936.

28. Brandel, Rose. "Africa." In Willi Apel, *Harvard Dictionary of Music.* 2nd ed. Cambridge, Mass.: Belknap Press of Harvard University Press, 1969.

29. ———. *The Music of Central Africa.* The Hague: Nijhoff, 1961.

30. Brunet, Jacques. Notes to recording *Balinese Theater and Dance Music,* ed. Alain Danielou. UNESCO Collection: Musical Source. Philips 6586 013. Berlin/Venice, 1970.

31. Buchner, Alexandr. *Musikinstrumente im Wandel der Zeit.* Prague, 1951. English transl. by Bořek Vančura as *Musical Instruments: An Illustrated History.* New York: Crown, 1973.

32. Bulut, Tarik. Notes to recording *Folk and Traditional Music of Turkey,* ed. Harold Courlander. New York: Ethnic Folkways P 404, 1953.

33. Chauvet, Stephen. *Musique nègre.* Paris: Société d'Éditions Géographiques, Maritimes et Coloniales, 1929.

34. Chottin, Alexis, and Hans Hickmann. "Arabische Musik." *Musik in Geschichte und Gegenwart* 1 (1949-51), cols. 577-601.

35 . Clements, Ernest. *Introduction to the Study of Indian Music.* London: Longmans, Green, 1913.

36. Codrington, Robert Henry. *The Melanesiens,* vol. 7. Oxford: Clarendon Press, 1891.

37. Collaer, Paul. "Ozeanien." *Musikgeschichte in Bildern* 1/1. Leipzig, 1965.

38. Courlander, Harold. "Notes from an Abyssinian Diary." *Musical Quarterly* 30/3 (July 1944): 345-55.

39. ————. Notes to recording *Music of Equatorial Africa.* New York: Ethnic Folkways FE 4402, 1950, 1964.

40. Crossley-Holland, Peter. "Tibetan Music." *Grove's Dictionary of Music and Musicians,* 5th ed. (1954).

41. Crossley-Holland, Peter, and Laurence Picken. "Chinese Music." *Grove's Dictionary of Music and Musicians,* 5th ed. (1954).

42. Danielou, Alain, gen. ed. *The Music of Viet-Nam,* with notes by Tran-Van-Khe and Nguyen-Huu-Ba. UNESCO Collection, 22. Kassel, 1971?

43. ————. *La Musique du Cambodge et du Laos.* Pondichery: Institut Français d'Indologie, 1957.

44. ————, gen. ed. Notes to recording *Sung Poetry of the Middle East.* UNESCO Collection: Musical Source. Philips 6586 013, n.d.

45. ————, transl. *Shilappadikaram* [The Ankle Bracelet], by Prince Ilango Adigal. New York, 1965.

46. ————. "Südasien, die indische Musik und ihre Traditionen." *Musikgeschichte in Bildern* 1/4. Leipzig, 1978.

47. Demiéville, P. "Bombai." In *Hōbōgirin.* Tokyo, 1930.

d'Erlanger, Rodolphe. *See* Erlanger, Rodolphe d', no. **64.**

48. Deval, K. B. *Theory of Indian Music as Expounded by Somanatha.* Poona, 1916.

49. Duriyanga, Phra Chen. *Thai Music.* Bangkok, 1948, 1953, 1956.

50. Duvelle, Charles. Notes to recording *Musique Bisa de Haute-Volta* (formerly *OCORA* SOR 10). Haute Volta: Academie Charles Cros, 1962.

51. Duy, Pham. Notes to recording *Music of Viet-Nam.* New York: Ethnic Folkways FE 4352, 1965.

52. Eckardt, Andreas. *Koreanische Music.* Mitteilungen der deutschen Gesellschaft Natur- und Völkerkunde Ostasiens, 24B. Tokyo, 1930.

53. Eckardt, Hans. "Japanische Musik." *Die Musik in Geschichte und Gegenwart* 6 (1957), cols. 1720-53.

54. ————. *Das Kokönchomonshu des Tachibana Narisue als musikgeschichtliche Quelle.* Wiesbaden: D. Harrassowitz, 1956.

Literature

55. Eckardt, Hans, and Kenneth Robinson. "Chinesische Musik." *Die Musik in Geschichte und Gegenwart* 2 (1952), cols. 1195-1216.

56. El-Kholay, Muhamed Kamel (Muhammad Kamil Al-Khula'i). *Musiqa esh-Sharqije.* (*La Musique orientale,* par M. Kamel El-Kholay.) Cairo, 1904?

57. Elkin, A. P. Notes to recording *Tribal Music of Australia.* New York: Ethnic Folkways FE 4439, 1953.

58. Ellis, Alexander J. "Über die Tonleitern verschiedener Völker." *Sammelbände für vergleichende Musikwissenschaft* 1 (Munich, 1922): 1-76. (Transl. of *On the Musical Scales of Various Nations* [London: Society of Arts, 1885].)

59. Elwin, Verrier. *The Murias and Their Gotul.* Bombay: Oxford University Press, 1947.

60. Emsheimer, Ernst. "Mongolen." *Die Musik in Geschichte und Gegenwart* 9 (1952), cols. 460-65.

61. ————. "Preliminary Remarks on Mongolian Music and Instruments." In *The Music of the Mongols* 1 (VIII Ethnography 4). Stockholm, 1943.

62. ————. "Tibet." *Die Musik in Geschichte und Gegenwart* 13 (1966), cols. 385-90.

63. ————. "Über das Vorkommen und die Anwendungsart der Maultrommel in Sibirien und Zentral-Asien." *Ethnos* 6 (Stockholm, 1941): 109-27.

64. Erlanger, Rodolphe d'. *La Musique arabe.* 5 vols. Paris: P. Geuthner, 1930-49.

65. Farmer, Henry George. "Arabian Music." *Grove's Dictionary of Music and Musicians,* 5th ed. (1954).

66. ————. "Bagdad." *Die Musik in Geschichte und Gegenwart* 1 (1949-51), cols. 1079-83.

67. ————. "Byzantine Musical Instruments in the Ninth Century." *Journal of the Royal Asiatic Society* (London, 1925), 299-304.

68. ————. "Egyptian Music." *Grove's Dictionary of Music and Musicians,* 5th ed. (1954).

69. ————. *Historical Facts for the Arabian Musical Influences.* Hildesheim: G. Olms, 1970.

70. ————. *A History of Arabian Music to the XVIIIth Century.* London: Luzac, 1929.

71. ————. *The Minstrelsy of the Arabian Nights.* Bearsden, Scotland: author, 1945.

72. ————. "Mizmar." *Encyclopedia of Islam,* ed. M. Th. Houtama, A. J. Wensinck, E. Levi-Provencal, H. A. R. Gibb, and W. Heffening, vol. 3, pt. 1. London, 1936.

73. ————, transl. and ed. *Music, the Priceless Jewel.* From the *Kitab al-'iqd al-farid of Ibn 'Abd Rabbihi.* Bearsden, Scotland: author, 1942.

74. ————. "The Music of Ancient Egypt." *The New Oxford History of Music,* vol. 1, ed. Egon Wellesz. London, 1957.

75. ————. "Music of Ancient Mesopotamia." *The New Oxford History of Music,* vol. 1, ed. Egon Wellesz. London, 1957.

76. ———. "The Music of Islam." *The New Oxford History of Music,* vol. 1, ed. Egon Wellesz. London, 1957.

77. ———. "Persische Musik." *Die Musik in Geschichte und Gegenwart* 10 (1962), cols. 1093-1102.

78. ———. *Studies in Oriental Musical Instruments,* 2nd ser. Glasgow: Civic Press, 1939.

79. ———. "Sufi and Darwish Music." *Grove's Dictionary of Music and Musicians,* 5th ed. (1954).

80. ———. "Syrian Music." *Grove's Dictionary of Music and Musicians,* 5th ed. (1954).

81. ———, transl. and ed. *Turkish Instruments of Music in the Seventeenth Century as Described in the Siyāḥat Nāma of Ewliyā Chelebī.* Glasgow: Civic Press, 1937.

82. Fernald, H. E. "Ancient Chinese Musical Instruments. *Museum Journal* 17/4 (Philadelphia: University of Pennsylvania, 1926).

83. Fischer, Erich. "Beiträge zur Erforschung der chinesischen Musik." *Sammelbände der internationalen Musikgesellschaft* 12 (1910-11): 153-206.

84. Fischer, Hans. *Schallgeräte in Ozeanien.* Baden-Baden, 1958.

85. Flygare, G. W. "Buddhist Intonation." In *Occasional Papers of the Kansai Asiatic Society.* Kyoto, June 1958.

86. Fox-Strangways, Arthur Henry. *The Music of Hindostan.* Oxford: Clarendon Press, 1914.

87. Galpin, Francis W. "Babylonian Music." *Grove's Dictionary of Music and Musicians,* 5th ed. (1954).

88. Geldner, Karl Friedrich, transl. *Der Rig Veda,* vol. 3. London, Leipzig, 1951.

89. Gerson-Kiwi, Edith. "Musique." In *Dictionnaire de la Bible.* Paris, 1950, 1957.

90. Gibson, H. E. "Music and Musical Instruments of Shang." *Journal of the North China Branch of the Royal Asiatic Society* 68 (Shanghai, 1937): 8-18.

91. Golos, George S. "Kirghiz Instruments and Instrumental Music." *Ethnomusicology* 5/1 (1961): 42-48.

92. Gosvami, Oma. *The Story of Indian Music: Its Growth and Synthesis.* Bombay: Asia Publising House, 1957, 1961.

93. Gulik, Robert Hans van. *The Lore of the Chinese Lute.* Tokyo: Sophia University, 1940.

94. Hartmann, Henrike. *Die Musik der sumerischen Kultur.* Dissertation, Frankfurt a.M., 1960.

95. Hause, Helen E. "Terms for Musical Instruments in the Sudanic Languages." Supplement no. 7 to the *Journal of the American Oriental Society* 68/1 (New Haven, Conn., 1948): 1-70.

96. Heinitz, Wilhelm. "Ein Materialbeitrag zur Kenntnis der arabischen Musik." *Zeitschrift für Musikwissenschaft* 4 (1922): 193-98.

97. ————. "Probleme der afrikanischen Trommelsprache." *Beiträge zur Kolonialforschung* 4 (1943).

98. ————. "Über die Musik der Somali." *Zeitschrift für Musikwissenschaft* 2 (1919-20): 257-63.

99. Hickman, Hans. "Afrikanische Musik." *Die Musik in Geschichte und Gegenwart* 1 (1949-51), cols. 123-31.

100. ————. "Ägyptische Musik." *Die Musik in Geschichte und Gegenwart* 1 (1949-51), cols. 92-105.

101. ————. "Armenische Musik." *Die Musik in Geschichte und Gegenwart* 1 (1949-51), cols. 653-55.

102. ————. "Äthiopische Musik." *Die Musik in Geschichte und Gegenwart* 1 (1949-51), cols. 105-12.

103. ————. *Catalogue général des antiquités égyptiennes au Musée du Caire.* Cairo, 1949.

104. ————. "Cymbales et crotales dans l'Egypte ancienne." *Annales du Service des Antiquités de l'Egypte* 49 (Cairo, 1950).

105. ————. "Flöteninstrumente: Flötencharakter und -formen; Alterum: Orient und Antike." *Die Musik in Geschichte und Gegenwart,* 4 (1956), cols. 319-30.

106. ————. "Music and Musical Education in Egypt." *Hinrichsen's Musical Year Book,* no. 6. London, 1950.

107. ————. "Rassel." *Die Musik in Geschichte und Gegenwart* 11 (1963), cols. 9-12.

108. ————. "Sudan." *Die Musik in Geschichte und Gegenwart* 12 (1963), cols. 1667-69.

109. ————. *Terminologie arabe des instruments de musique.* Cairo, 1947.

110. Hickmann, Hans, and Alexis Chottin. "Arabische Musik." *Die Musik in Geschichte und Gegenwart* 1 (1949-51), cols. 577-601.

111. Hilke, H. "Die Ingessana in Dar-Fung." *Zeitschrift für Ethnologie* 84/2 (1959): 212-37.

112. Hill, Clifford Alden, and Sviataslav Podstavsky. "The Interfacing of Language and Music in Hause Praise-Singing." *Ethnomusicology* 20/3 (1976): 535-40.

113. Hollis, Alfred Claude. *The Nandi.* Oxford: Clarendon Press, 1909.

114. Hood, Mantle. *The Nuclear Theme as a Determinant of Patet in Javanese Music.* Groningen: J. B. Wolters, 1954.

115. Hornbostel, Erich M. von. "Notiz über die Musik der Bewohner von Süd- Neu-Mecklenburg." *Sammelbände für vergleichende Musikwissenschaft* 1 (Munich, 1922): 349-58.

116. ————. "Völkerkunde im Lichte verleichender Musikwissenschaft." *Bässler Archiv* 7 (1932).

117. Hornbostel, Erich M. von, and Otto Abraham. "Studien über das Tonsystem und die Musik der Japaner." *Sammelbände der internationalen Musikgesellschaft* 4 (1903): 302-60. Reprinted in *Sammelbände der internationalen Musikgesellschaft* 1 (1922).

Literature

118. Hornbostel, Erich M. von, and Curt Sachs. "Classification of Musical Instruments," transl. Anthony Baines and Klaus P. Wachsmann. *Galpin Society Journal* 14 (1961): 3-29.

119. Howard, Wayne. *Samavedic Chant.* New Haven: Yale University Press, 1977.

120. Husmann, Heinrich. "Afghanistan." *Musik in Geschichte und Gegenwart* 1 (1951), cols. 121-23.

121. Idelssohn, Abraham Z. "The Various Scale Modes of the Arabian Musical System." *Quarterly Magazine of the International Music Society* (Leipzig, 1913). See also "Die Maquamem der arabischen Musik," *Sammelbände der internationalen Musikgesellschaft* 15 (1913-14): 1-63.

122. Irvine, Judith T., and J. David Sapir. "Musical Style and Social Change among the Kujamaat Diola." *Ethnomusicology* 20/1 (1976): 67-86.

123. Iyer, K. Bharata. *Kathakali.* London, 1955.

124. Jargy, Simon. "Iraq." Notes to recording *Ud classique Arabe par Munir Bashir.* Paris: O.R.T.E., 1971.

125. Jäschke, Heinrich August. *A Tibetan-English Dictionary.* 1881; reprint, New York: Frederick Ungar, 1965.

126. Jenks, Albert Ernest. *The Bontoc Igorot.* Manila: Bureau of Public Printing, 1905.

127. Jensen, Adolf Ellegaro. *Im Lande des Cada.* Stuttgart: Strecker und Schröder, 1936.

128. Jones, Arthur Morris. *Studies in African Music.* London: Oxford University Press, 1959, 1961.

129. Kagan, Alan L. "Cantonese Puppet Theater." Ph.D. dissertation, Indiana University, 1978.

130. Karasek, A. "Beiträge zur Kenntnis der Waschambara." *Bässler Archiv* 7 (Leipzig, Berlin, 1918-22).

131. Kataoka, Gidô. "Shōmyō." *Die Musik in Geschichte und Gegenwart* 12 (1965), cols. 643-49.

132. Kaudern, W. *Musical Instruments in Celebes.* Gothenborg, 1927.

133. Kaufmann, Walter. "Folksongs of Nepal." *Ethnomusicology* 6/2 (1962): 93-114.

134. ————. "Folk Songs of the Gond and Baiga." *Musical Quarterly* 27/3 (July 1941): 280-88.

135. ————. "The Musical Instruments of the Hill Maria, Jhoria Muria and Bastar Muria Gond Tribes." *Ethnomusicology* 5/1 (1961): 1-9.

136. ————. *Musical Notations of the Orient.* Bloomington, Indiana University Press, 1967.

137. ————. *Musical References in the Chinese Classics.* Detroit Monographs in Musicology, 5. Detroit: Information Coordinators, 1976.

138. ————. *The Ragas of North India.* Bloomington: Indiana University Press, 1968.

139. ————. *The Ragas of South India.* Bloomington: Indiana University Press, 1976.

140. ————. "Rasa, Rāga-Māla, and Performance Times in North Indian Rāgas." *Ethnomusicology* 9/3 (1960): 272-91.

141. ————. "Some Reflections on the Notations of the Vedic Chant." *Essays in Musicology: A Birthday Offering to Willi Apel.* Bloomington: Indiana University Press, 1968.

142. ————· "The Songs of the Hill Maria, Jhoria Muria and Bastar Muria Gond Tribes." *Ethnomusicology* 4/3 (1960): 115-28.

143. ————. *Tibetan Buddhist Chant.* Bloomington: Indiana University Press, 1975.

144. Kebede, Ashenafi. "The Bowl-Lyre of Northeast Africa. *Krar:* The Devil's Instrument." *Ethnomusicology* 21/3 (1977): 379-96.

145. Keh, C. S. "Die koreanische Musik." *Sammlung musikwissenschaftlicher Abhandlungen* 17 (Strasbourg, 1935).

146. Khatschi-Khatschi. "Der Dastgāh." *Kölner Beiträge zur Musikforschung* 19 (Regensburg, 1962).

147. Kiesewetter, Raphael Georg. *Die Musik der Araber.* Leipzig: Breitkopf und Härtel, 1842.

148. Kirby, Percival Robinson. "Bantu." *Musik in Geschichte und Gegenwart* 1 (1949-51), cols. 1219-29.

149. ————. "Buschmann- und Hottentottenmusik." *Die Musik in Geschichte und Gegenwart* 2 (1952), cols. 501-11.

150. ————. *Dictionary of Musical Terms Used by the Native Races of South Africa.* Johannesburg, 1953.

151. ————. *The Musical Instruments of the Native Races of South Africa.* London, 1934; reprint, Johannesburg: Witwatersrand University Press, 1953, 1968.

152. ————· The Musical Practices of the l'Auni and Khomani Bushmen." *Bantu Studies* 10 (Johannesburg, 1936): 373-431.

153. Knosp, Gaston. "Über annamitische Musik." *Sammelbände der internationalen Musikgesellschaft* 8 (1906-07): 137-66.

154. Krishnaswamy, S. *Musical Instruments of India.* Faridabad, Boston, n.d.

155. Kubik, Gerhard. "The Phenomena of Inherent Rhythms in East and Central African Instrumental Music." *African Music* 3/1 (1962): 33-42.

156. Kunst, Jaap. *Een en ander over de muziek en den dans op de Kei-eilanden.* Amsterdam: Royal Tropical Institute, 1945.

157. ————. *Ethnomusicology.* 3rd ed. The Hague: Nijhoff, 1959.

158. ————. "Gamelan." *Die Musik in Geschichte und Gegenwart* 4 (1955), cols. 1351-54.

159. ————. "Gong." *Die Music in Geschichte und Gegenwart* 5 (1956), cols. 517-22.

160. ————. "Hindu-Javanische Musik." *Die Musik in Geschichte und Gegenwart* 6 (1957), cols. 451-53.

161. ————. *A History of Arabian Music.* London, 1929.

162. ————. "Indonesische Musik." *Die Musik in Geschichte und Gegenwart* 6 (1957), cols. 1185-99.

163. ————. *Music in Java: Its History, Its Theory and Its Technique.* The Hague: Nijhoff, 1949.

164. ————. "Music in Nias," transl. Emile van Loo. *Internationales Archiv für Ethnographie* 38 (Leiden, 1940).

165. ————. *The Music of Bali and Its Emotional Appeal.* Britain, Holland, 1949.

166. ————. *Musik in Flores.* Leiden: E. J. Brill, 1942.

167. ————. *Muziek en dans in de Buitengewesten.* Amsterdam, 1946.

168. ————. "The Origin of the Kemanak." *Bijdragen tot de taal-, land- en Volkenkunde van Nederlandsch-Indie,* pt. 116. The Hague, 1960.

169. ————. *A Study on Papuan Music.* Weltevreden: Kolff, 1931.

170. ————. "Sudanese Music." *Art and Letters: India and Pakistan,* new series, 22/2 (1949).

171. Laade, Wolfgang. Notes to recording *Tunisia,* vol. 1. New York: Ethnic Folkways FW 8861, 1962.

172. Lachmann, Robert. *Musik des Orients.* Breslau: F. Hirt, 1929.

173. Lachmann, Robert, and Mahmud El-Hefni. *Ja'qūb Ibn Isḥāq Al-Kindī, "Risāla fī ḥubr tā'līf al-alḥan."* Leipzig: Kobla, 1931.

174. Ladzekpo, Seth. Notes to recording *Music of the Ewe of Ghana.* New York: Asch AHM 4222, 1969.

175. Lane, Edward W. *Manners and Customs of the Modern Egyptians.* London: J. M. Dent, 1908.

176. Laurenty, J. S. *Les Chordophones du Congo Belge et du Ruanda-Urundi.* Tervueren: Musée Royal de l'Afrique Centrale, 1960.

177. Lawrence, Peter. "The Ngaing of the Rai Coast." In *Cultures of the Pacific,* ed. T. G. Harding and B. J. Wallace. New York: Free Press, 1970.

178. Lee, Byong Won. "Structural Formulae of Melodies in the Two Sacred Buddhist Chant Styles of Korea." *Korean Studies* 1 (Hawaii, 1977): 111-96.

179. Lee, Hye-ku. *A History of Korean Music.* Seoul, n.d.

180. Levis, J. H. *The Foundations of Chinese Musical Art.* Peiping, 1936.

181. Lindblom, G. "Die Stosstrommel insbesondere in Afrika." *Ethnos* 10 (Stockholm, 1945): 17-38.

182. Liu, Wu-chi. *An Introduction to Chinese Literature.* Bloomington: Indiana University Press, 1966.

183. Mackerras, Colin P. *Rise of the Peking Opera.* Oxford, 1972.

184. Mahillon, Victor. *Catalogue descriptif et analytique de Musée Instrumental du Conservatoire Royal de Bruxelles.* 5 vols. Brussels, 1893-1922.

185. Malm, William P. *Japanese Music and Musical Instruments.* Rutland, Vt., and Tokyo: C. E. Tuttle Co., 1959.

186. ————. *Music Cultures of the Pacific, the Near East and Asia.* Englewood Cliffs, N.J.: Prentice-Hall, 1967.

187. ————. *Nagauta: The Heart of Kabuki Music.* Rutland and Tokyo: C. E. Tuttle Co., 1963.

188. *Manyoshu.* Ed. and published by Nippon Gakujutsu Shinkokai. Tokyo, 1940.

189. Marcel-Dubois, Claudif. *Les Instruments de musique de l'Inde ancienne.* Paris: Presses Universitaires de France, 1941, 1946.

190. Marcuse, Sibyl. *Musical Instruments: A Comprehensive Dictionary.* New York: Norton, 1975.

191. Massoudieh, Mohammed Taghi. "Die Musikforschung in Iran." *Acta Musicologica* 48 (1976): 12-20.

192. Matthews, Robert Henry. *Matthews' Chinese-English Dictionary.* Cambridge, Mass.: Harvard University Press, 1960.

193. Maung Than Mying. Introduction and notes to recording *Burmese and Traditional Music,* ed. Harold Courlander. New York: Ethnic Folkways P 436, 1953.

194. McLean, Mevyn. "Song Loss and Social Context Among the New Zealand *Maori.*" *Ethnomusicology* 9 (1965): 296-304.

195. ————. "Song Types of the New Zealand Maori." *Studies in Music* 3 (University of Western Australia Press, 1969): 53-69.

196. McPhee, Colin. "The Balinese Wayang Koelit and Its Music." *Djawa* 16 (Jogjakarta, 1936).

197. ————. *Music in Bali.* New Haven: Yale University Press, 1966.

198. Meerwarth, Aleksandr Mikhailovich. *A Guide to the Collection of Musical Instruments . . . of the Indian Museum, Calcutta.* Calcutta, 1917.

199. Ménard, Renée. "Koptische Musik." *Die Musik in Geschichte und Gegenwart* 7 (1958), cols. 1619-27.

200. Merriam, Alan P. Notes to recording *Africa South of the Sahara.* New York: Ethnic Folkways FE 503, 1957.

201. ————. "The Ethnographic Experience: Drum-Making Among the Bala (Basongye)." *Ethnomusicology* 13/1 (1969): 74-100.

202. Meshākah, Mikhāil. "A Treatise on Arab Music," transl. by Rev. Eli Smith of Beirut. *J.A.O.S.* 1/3 (New Haven, 1847).

203. Miller, Terry. "Kaen Playing and Mawlum Singing in Northeast Thailand." Ph.D. dissertation, Indiana University, 1977.

204. Minagawa, Tatsuo. "Japanese *Noh* Music." *Journal of the American Musicological Society* 10/3 (Fall 1957): 181-200.

205. Monier-Williams, Monier. *Sanskrit-English Dictionary.* Oxford: Clarendon Press, 1960.

206. Montandon, George. *La Généologie des instruments de musique.* Archives suisses d'Anthropologie generale, 3/1. Geneva, 1919.

207. Montrisart, Chaturang. "That Classical Dance." *Journal of the Music Academy Madras* 32 (1961).

208. Morton, David. *The Traditional Music of Thailand.* Berkeley: University of California Press, 1976.

209. Moule, G. E. "A List of the Musical and Other Sound-Producing Instruments of the Chinese." *Journal of the North China Branch of the Royal Asiatic Society* 39 (London, 1908).

210. ————. "Notes on the Ting-chi, or Half Yearly Sacrifice to Confucius." *Journal of the North China Branch of the Royal Asiatic Society* 33 (Shanghai, 1901): 130-56.

211. Muhammed, Darwish. "Safa'a il-auqat fi'alm al-na'amat." Referred to by Abraham Z. Idelssohn, "The Various Scale Modes," no. **121**, above.

212. Murasaki, Shikibu. *The Tale of Genji,* transl. Arthur Waley. New York, 1935.

213. Murdock, George Peter. *Our Primitive Contemporaries.* New York: Macmillan, 1934.

214. ————. *Outline of World Cultures.* New Haven: Human Relations Area Files, 1963.

215. Music Educators National Conference. "Music in World Cultures." *Music Educators Journal* 59/2 (1972): 22-139.

216. Naidu, Venkata Narayanaswami, Srinivasulu Naidu, Venkata Rangayya Pantulu. *Tāṇḍava Lakṣaṇam.* Madras, 1936.

217. Nasaruddin, Mohamed Ghouse. "Dance and Music of the Desa Performing Arts of Malaya." Ph.D. dissertation, Indiana University, 1979.

Nāṭyaśāstra. See Bharatanāṭyaśāstra, no. **23**.

Nijenhuis. See Te Nijenhuis, no. **292**.

218. Nketia, J. H. Kwabena. *The Music of Africa.* New York: Norton, 1974.

219. Norlind, Tobias. "Beitraege zur chinesischen Instrumentengeschichte." *Svensk tidskrift før Musikforskning* 15 (1933).

220. ————. *Systematik der Saiteninstrumente.* Stockholm, 1936.

221. Ochojski, Paul M. Notes to recording *Korea.* New York: Ethnic Folkways FE 4325, 1965.

222. Oost, P. Joseph van. "La musique chez les Mongols des Urdus." *Anthropos* 10-11 (1915-16): 358-96.

223. Ortiz, Fernando. *Los instrumentos de la música afrocubana.* Havana: Direccion de Cultura del Ministerio de Education, 1952-55.

Literature

224. Panum, Hortense. *The Stringed Instruments of the Middle Ages.* Rev. English ed. by Jeffrey Pulver. London: W. Reeves, 1939.

225. Piggott, Sir Francis. *The Music and Musical Instruments of Japan.* London: B. T. Batsford, 1909.

226. Piggott, Sir Francis, and A. H. Fox-Strangways. "Japanese Music." *Grove's Dictionary of Music and Musicians,* 5th ed. (1954).

227. Pischner, Hans. *Musik in China.* Berlin: Henschen Verlag, 1955.

228. Platt, Peter. "Ozeanine: Neusseeland (Maori)." *Die Musik in Geschichte und Gegenwart* 10 (1962), cols. 527-33.

229. Poche, Christian. Notes for recording *Kurdish Music.* Musical Sources. Philips 6586 019, n.d.

230. Popley, Herbert Arthur. *The Music of India.* London: Association Press, 1921, 1950.

231. Prajnananda (Swami). *A History of Indian Music.* Calcutta: Ramakrishna Vedanta Math, 1963.

232. Premakumar. *The Language of Kathakali.* Allahabad, Karachi, 1948.

233. Pugh-Kitingan, Jacqueline. "Huli Language and Instrumental Performance." *Ethnomusicology* 21/2 (1977): 205-32.

234. Qureshi, Regula. "Ethnomusicological Research Among Canadian Communities of Arab and East Indian Origin." *Ethnomusicology* 16 (1972): 381-96.

235. Raghavan, V. *The Number of Rasas.* Madras: Adyar Library, 1940.

236. Rajagopalan, L. S. "The Mizhavu." *Journal of the Music Academy, Madras* 45 (Madras, 1974).

237. ———. "Thimila." *Journal of the Music Academy, Madras* 42 (Madras, 1971).

238. Ramachandran, N. S. *The Ragas of Karnatic Music.* Madras: University of Madras, 1938.

239. Rāmāmātya. *Svaramēḷakalānidhi.* Ed. and transl. into English by M. S. Ramaswami Aiyar. Annamalia, Aknamala University, 1932.

240. Ranade, Ganesh Haris. *Hindusthani Music.* Sangli, 1938.

241. Rattray, Robert Sutherland. *Ashanti.* Oxford: Clarendon Press, 1923, 1955.

242. Reinhard, Kurt. *Chinesische Musik.* Eisenach, Kassel: E. Roth, 1956.

243. ———. "Türkische Musik." *Die Musik in Geschichte und Gegenwart* 13 (1966), cols. 953-68.

244. Ribeiro, Julian. *Music in Ancient Arabia and Spain.* Stanford: Stanford University Press, 1929.

245. Robertson, E. D. Notes for recording *Temiar Dream Songs from Malaya.* New York: Ethnic Folkways P 460, 1955.

246. Rossen, Jane Mink. "Ethnomusicological Field Work on Bellona Island." *Orbis musicae* 3/5 (Tel-Aviv, 1975-76).

247. Rouget, Gilbert. Notes for recording *Music of Equatorial Africa.* New York: Ethnic Folkways FE 4402, 1950.

248. Sachs, Curt. *Geist und Werden der Musikinstrumente.* Berlin: G. Reimer, 1929.

249. ———. *Handbuch der Musikinstrumentenkunde.* Leipzig: Breitkopf und Härtel, 1920.

250. ———. *The History of Musical Instruments.* New York: Norton, 1940.

251. ———. *Les Instruments de musique de Madagascar.* Paris: Institut d'Ethnologie, 1938.

252. ———. *Die Musikinstrumente Birmas und Assams.* Munich: G. Franzsches, 1917.

253. ———. *Die Musikinstrumente des alten Ägyptens.* Berlin: K. Curtius, 1921.

254. ———. *Die Musikinstrumente Indiens und Indonesiens.* Berlin: G. Reimer, 1915, 1923.

255. ———. *Reallexikon der Musikinstrumente.* Berlin: T. Bard, 1913.

256. ———. *Rhythm and Tempo.* New York: Norton, 1953.

257. ———. *The Rise of Music in the Ancient World.* New York: Norton, 1943.

258. ———. *Sammlung alter Musikinstrumente bei der Staatlichen Hochschule für Musik, Berlin.* Berlin: J. Bard, 1922.

259. ———. *World History of the Dance.* New York: Norton, 1937.

260. Sambamoorthy, P. *Catalogue of the Musical Instruments Exhibited in the Government Museum, Madras.* Madras, 1931.

261. ———. *Dictionary of South Indian Music and Musicians.* 3 vols. Madras: Indian Publishing House, 1952-71.

262. ———. *South Indian Music.* 6 vols. Madras: Indian Publishing House, 1955-69.

263. Śārṅgadeva. *Saṅgītaratnākara.* Ed. S. Subrahmnya Sastrī. 4 vols. Madras: Adyar Library, 1943-44.

264. Saunders, E. Dale. *Mudra.* New York: Routledge & Kegan Paul, 1960.

265. Schlager, Ernst. "Bali." *Die Musik in Geschichte und Gegenwart* 1 (1949-51), cols. 1109-15.

266. Schmidt, P. Joseph. "Neue Beiträge zur Ethnologie der Nor-Papua." *Anthropos* 28 (1933): 321-54.

267. Schlosser, Julius von. *Die Sammlung alter Musikinstrumente.* Vienna: A. Schroll & Co., 1920.

268. Schneider, Marius. "Australien und Austronesien." *Die Musik in Geschichte und Gegenwart* 1 (1949-51), cols. 869-78.

269. ———. "Gesänge aus Uganda: Ein Beitrag zur musikalischen Formbildung in Wechselgesang." *Archiv für Musikforschung* 2 (1937): 185-243.

270. ———. "Tonysteme: Außereuropäische." *Die Musik in Geschichte und Gegenwart* 13 (1966), cols. 547-58.

271. ———. "Zur Trommelsprache der Duala." *Anthropos* 47 (1952).

272. Seetha, S. "Lavani, the Marathi Folk Musical Form." *Bulletin of the Institute of Traditional Cultures, Madras,* July-Dec. 1976.

273. Sekai, Ongaku Zenshu. *Gesammelte Werke der Weltmusik.* Ed. Kanda Hosui and others. 118 vols. Tokyo, Shunju-sha, 1930. Vols. 17, 18, 22, 25, 27, 43, 48 contain transcriptions of Japanese music.

Shilappadikaram, by Prince Ilango Adigal. *See* no. **45**.

274. Simon, R. "Zur Chronologie der indischen Musikliterature." *Zeitschrift für Indologie und Iranistik* (1923).

275. Slobin, Mark. *Kirgiz Instrumental Music.* New York: Society for Asian Music, 1969.

276. ———. *Music in the Culture of Northern Afghanistan.* Tucson: University of Arizona Press, 1967.

277. Smith, Barbara. Notes to recording *Music from Korea,* vol. 1: *The Kayakeum.* Honolulu: East-West Recording, 1965.

278. ———. "Ozeanien: Allgemeines." *Die Musik in Geschichte und Gegenwart* 10 (1962), cols. 520-28.

279. Smith, Edna. "Musical Training in Tribal West Africa." *African Music* 3/1 (1962): 6-10.

280. Soederberg, Bertil. *Les Instruments de musique du Bas-Congo et dans les regions avoisinantes.* Stockholm, 1956.

281. Stauder, Wilhelm. *Die Leiern und Harfen der Sumerer.* Frankfurt, 1957.

282. ———. "Sumerisch-babylonische Musik." *Die Musik in Geschichte und Gegenwart* 12 (1965), cols. 1737-52.

283. Steinmann, A. "Über anthropomorphe Schlitztrommeln in Indonesien." *Anthropos* 23 (1938).

284. Stone, Ruth M. "Communication and Interaction Processes in Music Events Among the Kpelle of Liberia." Ph.D. dissertation, Indiana University, 1979.

285. Stumpf, Carl. "Tonsystem und Musik der Siamesen." *Sammelbände für vergleichende Musikwissenschaft* 1 (1922): 127-77.

286. Sur, Donald. "Korea." In Willi Apel, *Harvard Dictionary of Music,* 2nd. ed. Cambridge, 1969.

287. *Survey of Korean Arts: Traditional Music* (various authors). Seoul: National Academy of Arts, 1973.

288. Suwanto, Raden. Notes to recording *Music of Indonesia.* New York: Ethnic Folkways FE 4406, 1949.

289. Syon, Kyon, ed. *Ak-hak-koe-pom* (1493). Facsimile ed. Keijo, Japan: Koten-Kanko-Kai, 1933.

290. Tagore, Sourindro Mohun. *Short Notices of Hindu Musical Instruments.* Calcutta, 1877.

291. Tanabe, Hisao. *Japanese Music.* Tokyo: Kokusai Bunka Shinkokal, 1936, 1937.

292. Te Nijenhuis, E. *Dattilam: A Compendium of Ancient Indian Music.* Leiden, 1970.

293. Thieme, Darius L. "A Descriptive Catalogue of Yoruba Musical Instruments." Ph.D. dissertation, Catholic University of America, 1969.

294. Thornton, Philip. *The Voice of Atlas.* London: A. Maciehose & Co., 1936.

295. Toyotaka, Komiya. *Japanese Music and Drama in the Meiji Era.* Tokyo, 1956.

296. Tran-Van-Khe. *La Musique vietnamienne traditionelle.* Paris: Presses Universitaires de France, 1962.

297. ——————. Notes to recording *South Viet Nam Entertainment Music.* UNESCO Collection: Musical Sources. Philips 6586 028, n.d.

298. Tschopik, Harry, Jr. Foreword to recording *Maori Songs,* with introduction and commentary by Ulric Williams. New York: Ethnic Folkways FE 4433, 1952.

299. Varnum, John P. Notes to recording *Music of Kuria and the Gusia of Western Kenya.* New York: Ethnic Folkways FE 4223, 1972.

300. Vatter, Ernst. *Ata Kiwan.* Leipzig: Bibliographisches Institut, 1932.

301. *La Vie du Sahaa.* Exhibition Catalogue, Musée de l'Homme. Paris, 1960.

302. Wachsmann, Klaus P. Chapter on musical instruments. In Margaret Trowell and K. P. Wachsmann, *Tribal Crafts of Uganda.* London, 1953.

303. ——————, ed. *International Catalogue of Published Records of Folk Music.* London: International Folk Music Council, 1960.

304. ——————. "Ostafrika." *Die Musik in Geschichte und Gegenwart* 10 (1962), cols. 436-48.

305. Waddell, L. A. *Lamaism.* Reprint, Cambridge, 1939.

306. Waley, A. *The Nō Plays of Japan.* New York, 1920.

307. Wegner, Max. *Die Musikinstrumente des alten Orients.* Münster: Aschendorff, 1950.

308. Wehr, Hans. *A Dictionary of Modern Arabic,* ed. Milton Cowan. Ithaca: Cornell University Press, 1961.

309. Werner, Eric. "Jewish Music." *Grove's Dictionary of Music and Musicians,* 5th ed. (1954).

310. Wiant, Bliss. *The Music of China.* Hong Kong, 1965.

311. Williams, F. E. *Bull-Roarers in the Papuan Gulf.* Port Moresby, 1936.

312. Wirz, Paul. *A Description of Musical Instruments from Central North-Eastern New Guinea.* Amsterdam: Royal Tropical Institute, 1952.

313. Wolf, Siegfried. *Zum Problem der Nasenflöte.* Leipzig, 1941.

314. Wöss, Margareta. "No, das japanische Gesamtkunstwerk." *Österreichische Musikzeitschrift* 10 (1955).

315. Youngerman, Suzanne. "Maori Dancing Since the Eighteenth Century." *Ethnomusicology* 18/1 (1974): 75-100.

316. Yupho, Dhanit. *Thai Musical Instruments.* Ed. and transl. David Morton. Bangkok, 1960.

317. Zamfir, C., and I. Zlotea. *Metodá da Cobza.* Bucharest, 1955, 1956.

318. Zemp, Hugo. "'Are'are Classification of Musical Types and Instruments." *Ethnomusicology* 22/1 (1978): 37-68.

319. ———. Notes to recording *Musique polynésienne d'Ontong Java (Iles Salomon).* Collection Musée de l'Homme, ed. Gilbert Rouget. Vogue LD 785, 1971.

320. Zonis, Ella. *Classical Persian Music.* Cambridge, Mass.: Harvard University Press, 1973.

321. ———. "Persia." In Willi Apel, *Harvard Dictionary of Music,* 2nd ed. Cambridge, 1969.